The History of Chinese Legal Civilization

Jinfan Zhang

The History of Chinese Legal Civilization

Ancient China—From About 21st Century B.C. to 1840 A.D.

Volume 2

Jinfan Zhang
China University of Political Science and Law
Beijing, China

Chief Translator: Lixin Zhang
Other Translators: Ruiying Liu
China University of Political Science and Law, Beijing, China

Xing Li
China University of Political Science and Law, Beijing, China

Yue Wang
China University of Political Science and Law, Beijing, China

Xiaoqi Ou
China University of Political Science and Law, Beijing, China

Chen Yan
China University of Political Science and Law, Beijing, China

Qichen Liao
China University of Political Science and Law, Beijing, China

Sponsored by Chinese Fund for the Humanities and Social Sciences (本书获中华社会科学基金中华外译项目资助)

ISBN 978-981-10-1027-9   ISBN 978-981-10-1029-3   (eBook)
https://doi.org/10.1007/978-981-10-1029-3

© Springer Nature Singapore Pte Ltd. 2020

This work is subject to copyright. All rights are reserved by the Publisher, whether the whole or part of the material is concerned, specifically the rights of translation, reprinting, reuse of illustrations, recitation, broadcasting, reproduction on microfilms or in any other physical way, and transmission or information storage and retrieval, electronic adaptation, computer software, or by similar or dissimilar methodology now known or hereafter developed.

The use of general descriptive names, registered names, trademarks, service marks, etc. in this publication does not imply, even in the absence of a specific statement, that such names are exempt from the relevant protective laws and regulations and therefore free for general use.

The publisher, the authors, and the editors are safe to assume that the advice and information in this book are believed to be true and accurate at the date of publication. Neither the publisher nor the authors or the editors give a warranty, expressed or implied, with respect to the material contained herein or for any errors or omissions that may have been made. The publisher remains neutral with regard to jurisdictional claims in published maps and institutional affiliations.

This Springer imprint is published by the registered company Springer Nature Singapore Pte Ltd.
The registered company address is: 152 Beach Road, #21-01/04 Gateway East, Singapore 189721, Singapore

Introduction

The Origin and Main Features of Chinese Legal Civilization

Early in the era of "Huang Di" (Yellow Emperor, a legendary ruler) as was recorded in historical documents, Chinese legal civilization dawned on the land of China. It was recorded that after defeating and exterminating the whole clan of San Miao, "Huang Di" (Yellow Emperor) adopted its criminal penalty, inheriting, and passing on the "Five Cruel Penalties" created by Chi You, the leader of San Miao, which ushered in the prelude of Chinese legal history. In Xia Dynasty, around the twenty-first century B.C., a relatively stable and united country came into being, and "Xia Xing" (The Penal Code of Xia), also called "Yu Xing" (The Penal Code of Yu) containing over 3000 articles based on the "Five Cruel Penalties" was developed. During the more than 4000 years of development since Xia Dynasty, Chinese legal civilization was passed down from generation to generation without interruption, and its continuity, systematicness, and integrity were unrivalled among the ancient civilizations. Moreover, the people in the Han, Tang, Song, and Ming dynasties had exerted such a great influence on the neighboring countries with their advanced legal civilization that it had made it possible for Chinese law to stand proudly in the family of legal systems in the world.

The economic pattern of agrarianism, the political system of despotism, the social structure of family-centered patriarchy, the stable blood and geographical relationships, the unified and multi-ethnic national composition and the Confucianism-dominated ideology in ancient China have constituted a unique national condition which has further determined the main feature of Chinese legal civilization.

Introducing "Li" (Rites) Into Law and Integrating "Li" (Rites) with Law

"Li" (rites) originated from the religious ceremonies at the last stage of clan society. Because it not only fitted in with the national conditions of the ancient society which was dominated by patriarchal ethics but also performed the function of governance in accordance with social customs and exercised the power of spiritual deterrent, after entering the class society, "Li" (rites) was transformed by the rulers into a code of conduct which had reflected the hierarchical order and become an effective means of government. As a social phenomenon, "Li" (rites) had not only originated early, but also run throughout the whole ancient society, influenced every field of social life and adjusted the behavioral relations between individuals, between man and society, and between man and the state. The mutual penetration and integration of "Li" (rites) and "Fa" (law) constitutes the main feature of Chinese legal civilization.

Because the major function of "Li" (rites) was to "distinguish the noble from the humble, the superior from the inferior," and to establish a patriarchal and hierarchical order of "Zun Zun" (showing respect to nobility represented by the emperor), "Qin Qin" (showing respect to relatives represented by parents), "Zhang Zhang" (showing respect to the seniors) and "Nan Nv You Bie" (giving different treatments to males and females), it was accepted and guaranteed by the state. Thus, a systematic project to integrate "Li" (rites) with "Fa" (law) under the guidance of Confucianism was conducted. If it could be regarded as the beginning of the combination of "Li" (rites) and "Fa" (law) for the Confucian scholars in Han Dynasty to introduce "Li" (rites) into law through interpreting, annotating and making reference to Confucian classics when hearing cases, an inseparable relationship of "Ben" (the essence) and "Yong" (application) between "Li" (rites) and "Fa" (law) had formed in Tang Dynasty. Just as was recorded in *Tang Lv Shu Yi* (*The Comments on Tang Code*), "'De' (virtue) and 'Li' (rites) are the essence of administration while punishment is only a supplementary method, just as day and night are mutually interdependent to be a whole day and spring and autumn are mutually interdependent to be a whole year." The principle of "Gang Chang" (the Chinese ethical tradition) in "Li" (rites) had guided the enactment of "Fa" (law), meanwhile, the codes of "Li" (rites) were constantly legalized, codified, and finally became the mandatory rules for the regulation of people's conducts as well as the criteria for people to tell the right from the wrong.

The hierarchy of "Li" (rites) was consistent with the privilege of "Fa" (law), which was mutually complementary to achieve a lasting political stability of a country: to take "Li" (rites) as the guidance and "Fa" (law) as the criterion; to gain popular support by applying "Li" (rites) prudently and to distinguish the good from the evil by enforcing "Fa" (law) explicitly; to use "Li" (rites) to overstate the benevolent governance and to use "Fa" (law) to demonstrate the equity of administration; to execute "Fa" (law) with the guidance of "Li" (rites) to reduce the opposition in its enforcement, and to reinforce "Li" (rites) with "Fa" (law) to endow "Li" (rites) with more powerful authority; to introduce "Li" (rites) into

"Fa" (law) to make "Fa" (law) more moralized, so that not only the evil could be punished but also "Fa" (law) could be greatly promoted; to attach "Fa" (law) to "Li" (rites) to make morality legalized, so that "Fa" (law) could be resorted to when the principles of "Li" (rites) were violated. All this have proved that the operation of state apparatus could be promoted effectively by the integration of "Li" (rites) and "Fa" (law), which is of great significance in maintaining social stability. For this reason, "Li Zhu Xing Fu" (employing rites as the primary means, punishment as the supplement) and their integration in practice had always been an established policy in every feudal dynasty. Therefore, the combination of "Li" (rites) and "Fa" (law) and the unification of family and legal obligation embodied therein had exerted a great and extensive influence ever since.

"Yi Ren Wei Ben" (People-Oriented) and "Ming De Shen Fa" (Promoting Virtue and Being Prudent in the Enforcement of Punishment)

Humanism is the philosophical foundation of ancient Chinese legal civilization. Early at the beginning of Western Zhou Dynasty, the rulers learned from the downfall of the Shang Dynasty the importance of "Min Xin" (popular support) and "Min Qing" (the condition of the people) in ruling the country, so put forward the immortal theory that "man should not take water as a mirror but the people"[1] and connected worshiping "Tian" (Heaven) with protection of the people. The pre-Qin Confucian scholars had not only developed the theory of humanism and Confucius' theory that "the benevolent love the others," but also affirmed the status, value, and dignity of human beings and emphasized that "Ren" (benevolence) should be regarded as a basic principle in dealing with interpersonal relationships. Later, Confucius' theory of benevolence was further developed by Meng Zi (Mencius), who had put forward the theory of benevolent governance by attaching great importance to the people and advocated that "the people are the most important, next comes the country, so the ruler is the least important."[2]

The Confucian humanism is reflected in law in the following aspects: (1) emphasizing "De Zhu Xing Fu" (employing moral teaching as the primary means, punishment as the supplement) and stressing education; (2) helping and caring about the old, the young, women and the disabled; and (3) attaching importance to people's lives by implementing the reviewing system for death penalty.

Therefore, the legalization of humanism has been passed down and developed from generation to generation, which is another important feature of Chinese legal civilization.

---

[1] "Jiu Gao" (Announcement to Ban Alcohol) in *Shang Shu* (*The Book of Historical Document*).
[2] "Jin Xin" (With all One's Heart) (Part 2) in *Meng Zi* (*Mencius*).

Following "Tian Li" (Heavenly Principles) and Enforcing Laws According to Specific Circumstances

Dong Zhongshu, a Confucian scholar in Han Dynasty, based on the interaction between "Tian" (Heaven) and man, not only proposed that "'San Gang' (three cardinal guides) of 'Wang Dao' (the benevolent government) relied on 'Tian' (heaven)", but also even ethicized "Tian" (Heaven) itself. The Confucian scholars in Song Dynasty took a further step and even regarded "San Gang" (three cardinal guides, namely, ruler as the guide of subjects, father as the guide of son, and husband the guide of wife) as "Tian Li" (heavenly principles), so "Tian Li" (heavenly principles) was embodied as the national law, which had given "Guo Fa" (national law) a sense of irresistible mystery. Thus, enforcing law in accordance with "Min Qing" (the condition of the people) had harmonized both "Guo Fa" (national law) and "Ren Qing" (human feeling), which had not only given "Guo Fa" (national law) a touch of ethics, but also made it possible for "Guo Fa" (national law) to gain public support besides guaranteeing the state power, so that when "Guo Fa" (national law) was enforced, it would be more effective. That was exactly the starting point and the end-result of the unification of "Tian Li" (heavenly principles), "Guo Fa" (national law), and "Ren Qing" (human feeling). The harmony and mutual complementation of the three elements had constituted the essential connotation of ancient Chinese legal civilization, which was not accidental, but was determined by the ancient Chinese patriarchal social structure, the long-lasting cultural accumulation, the national mindset, and the political and legal consciousness.

The harmony of "Tian Li" (heavenly principles), "Guo Fa" (national law), and "Ren Qing" (human feeling), the integration of "Tian Li" (heavenly principles) and "Ren Qing" (human feeling), the combination of ethics and law, and the unification of family and legal obligation, etc. had exerted a great influence not only on the development of ancient Chinese law but also on the law of other countries in the cultural circle of Confucianism in the east, such as ancient Korea, Japan and Vietnam.

The Family-Oriented Principle and the Ethical Legal System

In ancient Chinese law, the family-oriented social structure was protected and patriarchal system was affirmed, which not only was the foundation of the stability of the country, but also a necessary condition for the existence and development of feudal natural economy. Therefore, patriarchy was also introduced into the administrative and legal areas and it was often preached that the emperor was "Tian Zi" (the son of Heaven), the parent of the people and the embodiment of national patriarchy. In addition, the local officials of "Zhou" (subprefecture) and "Xian" (county) were also called parenting magistrates to strengthen imperial and administrative power.

The core in ethical legislation was the legalization of family obligation and the differentiation of punishments for the same crimes committed by people of different classes. As for the family rules employed to regulate the domestic relations, they were in a subordinate position in feudal legal system; but they were important supplementary parts to state law. All the behaviors against the national law would be forbidden by family rules, so the family members who disobeyed family rules would naturally not be tolerated by the national law. Therefore, such family rules supported by state law had a great regulating function, which was unique in ancient China.

Because of family orientation, the law of "Zu Zhu" (killing of the whole clan of a criminal) was made and the emphasis on ethics and kinship had led to more severe punishment for the infringement of the rights of kinsmen. The long-standing patriarchal system had laid a solid foundation for the family-oriented and ethical legal system. In addition, The Confucian doctrines of "Li Xue" (Neo-Confucianism: a Confucian school of idealist philosophy of the Song and Ming Dynasties) had provided the theoretical basis for the ethical legal system of family-orientation, and the despotic political system had in turn asserted a special claim to the patriarchal system. Thus, the legal relationship of rights and obligations expressed by the identification of the family, the nation, and "Fu Zhi" (mourning apparel system) was unique to Chinese legal civilization.

Pursuing No Litigation and Settling Conflicts by Mediation

Under the despotic rule of monarchs in ancient China, the primary task of the law was to safeguard the public power, i.e., the right of ruling by the state, thus the criminal law, which was used primarily for the punishment of the violation of state interests, was especially emphasized. However, the awareness of private rights was relatively weak, and property disputes among individuals were regarded as trivial matters, therefore there had lacked necessary legal mediation in this respect. As a result, civil law was sporadic and not systematic.

Moreover, the value of individual persons was determined by their ranking in ethical order and social status, and there was no extensive development of contractual relations or any movement for the freedom of individuals. As for the lawsuits for private rights, the rulers regarded them as no more than trivial disputes and paid little attention. In practice, what those officials pursued was to reduce or even to eliminate litigation, because it would be regarded as the evidence of their good reputation and their achievements in officialdom.

It had been the goal of administration since Confucius "to make sure that there were no litigations."[3] Thus, it not only became the value orientation of officials "to eliminate litigation," it also exerted an extensive influence on the public. This was

---

[3]"Yan Yuan" (Yan Yuan, one of Confucius' disciples) in *Lun Yu* (*The Analects*).

not incidental because it resulted from the profound sediment of traditional Chinese culture in which the members of the society were closely related because of the blood relationship of living together of the whole family, the geographical relationship of being neighbors from generation to generation, the national psychology of pursuing harmony and the economic structure of agricultural society in particular, so it was regarded as the guideline to live in harmony without conflict. Even when there were disputes, they were expected to be mediated by the patriarchs and their neighbors, so the civil mediation system in ancient China had reached to a very advanced degree, which was unique in the ancient world. As mediation was based on "Li" (rites), customs and "Fa" (law), its popularity not only promoted the development of legal culture featured by the combination of "Li" (rites) and "Fa" (law), but also reduced people's burden of litigation, and ultimately facilitated the formation of the general mood of society. However, the mediation system with the cooperation in and out of court had also resulted in the negative consequence that the public had little notion of the rights of litigation.

The World Position of Chinese Legal Civilization

In the history of world legal system, ancient Chinese legal system not only had an earlier origin, it also was in the vanguard of development for a long time. *Yun Meng Qin Jian* (*Amounts of Bamboo Writing Slips in Qin Dynasty Excavated in Yunmeng*) which was unearthed has proved that "everything had certain rules to regulate" even in the state of Qin around the fourth century B.C. Therefore, compared with the early feudal laws of the western countries, *Qin Lv* (*Qin Code*) was made over 1000 years earlier than *Lex Salics,* which was made in the Frankish Kingdom. In contents, it was no match for *Yun Meng Qin Jian* (*Amounts of Bamboo Writing Slips in Qin Dynasty Excavated in Yunmeng*) because it was still a customary law.

As a model of Chinese feudal codes, *Tang Lv* (*Tang Code*) in particular, was applied for reference as the parent law by the neighboring countries and regions for a long time. Taking Japan as an example, *Jin Jiang Ling* (*The Ōmi Code*) enacted in the reign of Emperor Tenji and *Tian Wu Lv Ling* (*The Temmu Decree*) enacted in the reign of Emperor Temmu were both modeled on the "Ling" (decree) during the reign of Zhenguan in the Tang Dynasty. *Taihō Lv Ling* (*Taihō Code*), which had an epoch-making significance in Japanese legal history, had copied *Tang Lv Shu Yi* (*The Comments on Tang Code*) both in terms of the titles of chapters and contents, with just some deletion and combination made. For instance, "Yi Qin" (the Diligence: including military and civil officials who have displayed great diligence in their work through thorough occupation of public affairs) and "Yi Bin" (the Guests of the State: to treat the descendants of previous dynasties as guests of the state who could enjoy a legal privilege) in "Ba Yi" (The Eight Deliberations) were omitted and "Ba Yi" (The Eight Deliberations) was reduced to "Liu Yi" (Six Deliberations), so was *Yanglao Lv* (*Yoro Code*) which was made after *Taihō Lv Ling* (*Taihō Code*). Doctor Kuwabara Jitsuzoh, a Japanese scholar of legal history, had pointed out that "all the codes of the imperial society from the Nara Age to the Heian Age were based on *Tang Lv* (*Tang Code*) both in form and contents."[4] Doctor Hozumi Nobushige also said that *Xing Lv Gang Ling* (*The Programme for the New Code*) issued in December of the 3rd year of Meiji (1870) "was based on the codes of Tang, Ming and Qing dynasties in China."[5]

Besides Japan, Korea also drew reference from *Tang Lv* (*Tang Code*) during its 447 years of ruling. It was stated in "Xing Fa Zhi" (The Record of the Criminal Law) in volume eighty-four of *Gao Li Shi* (*The History of Korea*) that "almost all the systems of Korea were made by following those of the Tang Dynasty. As for the criminal law, those from *Tang Lv* (*Tang Code*) were also adopted and applied in accordance with the actual conditions of Korea."

Tang Lv (*Tang Code*) also had a great influence on the feudal codes of Vietnam. *Xing Shu* (*The Criminal Book*) enacted in the reign of the Emperor Li Taizun and *Guo Chao Xing Lv* (*The National Criminal Codes*) enacted during the reign of Chen Taizun were both adopted from *Tang Lv* (*Tang Code*). It was noted in *Xing Lv Zhi* (*The Record of Criminal Code*) in volume thirty-three of *Li Chao Xian Zhang Lei Zhi* (*The Record of Laws and Regulations of the Past Dynasties*) written by a Vietnamese scholar named Pan Hui in the nineteenth century that "according to the criminal laws of Li and Chen…when laws were made at the time, the laws of Tang and Song dynasties were also followed with the leniency and severeness of the punishment deliberated on."[6]

To the time of Ming Dynasty, *Ming Lv* (*Ming Code*) became another Chinese law that had had an important influence on Southeast Asian countries besides *Tang Lv* (*Tang Code*). In *Xing Dian* (*The Criminal Code*) and *Xing Fa Da Quan* (*Encyclopedia of Criminal Laws*) in *Jing Guo Da Dian* (*Gyeongguk Daejeon* or *Complete Code of Law*), *Da Dian Xu Lu* (*A Extended Record to the Great Code*) and *Xu Da Dian* (*A Sequel to the Great Code*) which were enacted in the reign of Li Guicheng, the founder of Korea, the key provisions in the *Ming Lv* (*Ming Code*) were all adopted. Moreover, many other laws were all directly influenced by *Ming Lv* (*Ming Code*), such as *Jia Long Huang Yue Lv Li* (*The Laws and Precedents of Jialong*) made in the reign of Nguyễn Phúc Ánh, Emperor Gao of Vietnam, *Qin Ding Da Na Nan Hui Shi Li* (*The Vietnamese Codes and Laws Made by Imperial Order*) made in the reign of Nguyễn Phúc Tuyền, Emperor Xianzu of Vietnam, *Xin Lv Gang Ling*

---

[4]Kuwabara Jitsuzoh (Japan), *Zhong Guo Fa Zhi Shi Lun Cong* (*The Review on Chinese Legal History*), p. 213, quoted from Yang Honglie's *Zhong Guo Fa Lv Dui Dong Ya Zhu Guo Zhi Ying Xiang* (*The Influence of Chinese Law on the East Asian Countries*), China University of Political Science and Law Press, 1999, p. 4.

[5]Hozumi Nobushige (Japan), *Ri Ben Xin Min Fa* (*The New Civil Law of Japan*), quoted from Yang Honglie's *Zhong Guo Fa Lv Dui Dong Ya Zhu Guo Zhi Ying Xiang* (*The Influence of Chinese Law on the East Asian Countries*), China University of Political Science and Law Press, 1999, p. 274.

[6]Quoted from Yang Honglie, *Zhong Guo Fa Lv Dui Dong Ya Zhu Guo Zhi Ying Xiang* (*The Influence of Chinese Law on the East Asian Countries*), China University of Political Science and Law Press, 1999, p. 420.

(*The Guiding Principles of New Law*), and *Gai Ding Lv Li* (*The Revised Laws and Precedents*) made in Japanese Meiji period.

As the laws of the neighboring countries were attached to the Chinese legal system for a long time, and more importantly, because Chinese law not only had its own uniqueness but also its progressiveness in legal culture, it is universally acknowledged in the world as one of the most important legal systems, namely, the Chinese legal system.

To sum up, the ancient Chinese legal civilization has had an important position in the history of world legal civilization, which has manifested the great contribution made by Chinese nation to the development of world legal system.

Contents

8	**The Legal Civilization of Northern and Southern Song Dynasties Fostered by Commercial Economy**		**649**
	8.1	The National Policy and Characteristics of the Legislation of the Early Song Dynasty	651
		8.1.1 The National Policy of Strengthening the Centralization of Authority	651
		8.1.2 The Characteristics of the Legislation	653
	8.2	The Administrative Law for Strengthening the Centralization of Authority	662
		8.2.1 The System Reform for Strengthening the Centralization of Authority	664
		8.2.2 The Enrichment of the Official Administrative Law	671
	8.3	Criminal Law Aiming to Maintain the Centralization of Authority	699
		8.3.1 "Dao Zei Zhong Fa" (Severe Punishment for Robbery and Theft)	700
		8.3.2 The Changes of the Penal System Shown by "She Zhang Fa"	712
	8.4	Civil Law Adapting to the Development of Commodity Economy	716
		8.4.1 The Expansion of Household Registration and the Changes of People's Identities	717
		8.4.2 New Development of Property Rights	723
		8.4.3 The New Achievements of the Law of Obligation	730
		8.4.4 Marriage and Inheritance for the Improvement of Women's Social Status	739
	8.5	The Economic and Financial Law Made with the Spirit of Reform	748
		8.5.1 Agricultural, Industrial, and Commercial Legislation	748

	8.5.2	The Financial Legislation	760
8.6		The Judicial System of "Ju Yan Fen Si" (The Separation of Interrogation and Conviction)	772
	8.6.1	The Change of Judicial System	772
	8.6.2	Perfection of the Judicial Proceedings of Civil Procedure	775
	8.6.3	The Creation of the System of "Ju Yan Fen Si" (The Separation of Interrogation and Conviction)	780
8.7		The Historical Role of the Legal System and the Achievement of "Lv Xue" (The Study of Statutory Laws) in the Southern and Northern Song Dynasties	788
8.8		The Legal Systems of Liao, Western Xia, and Jin Dynasties Compared with That of the Song Dynasty	792
	8.8.1	The Legal System of the Liao Dynasty	793
	8.8.2	The Legal System of Western Xia Dynasty	799
	8.8.3	The Legal System of the Jin Dynasty	813

9 The Legal System of "Zu Shu Bian Tong" in the Yuan Dynasty 833

9.1		The Legislative Achievements of "Fu Hui Han Fa" (Sticking to and Integrating the Laws of the Han Nationality)	835
9.2		The Administrative Legislation and Management System with National Characteristics	846
	9.2.1	The Administrative Law of "Zu Shu Bian Tong"	846
	9.2.2	The Management System with Its Distinctive Features	848
	9.2.3	The Official Administration Law Focused on Supervision	855
9.3		Criminal Law Made by Combining Reference to the Old Systems of the Tang and Song Dynasties and Innovation	868
	9.3.1	Executing Penalties According to "Fu Zhi" (Mourning Apparel System)	869
	9.3.2	Changing "Shi E" (The Ten Abominations) to "Zhu E" (Various Abominations)	870
	9.3.3	The Penalty System and the Principle of Making Criminal Law with National Characteristics	873
9.4		The Civil Law with National Differences	880
	9.4.1	Classifying the People According to Their Ethnic Identities	880
	9.4.2	The Characteristics of the Times of the Protection of Property Rights	882
	9.4.3	The Making of Debt Contract	887
	9.4.4	Marriage and Inheritance Law with the Integration of the Laws of Mongolian and Han Nationalities	893
9.5		The Trial System with Diverse Jurisdiction	900
	9.5.1	The Diversified Judicial Organization System	900

		9.5.2	Concurrency of Regional Jurisdiction and Ethnic and Religious Jurisdiction	902
		9.5.3	Mediation Extensively Practiced in Civil Trials	904

10 The Legal System of the Ming Dynasty: The Final Form of Chinese Legal Civilization 909

- 10.1 Legislative Ideology and Achievements of the Ming Dynasty .. 911
  - 10.1.1 Zhu Yuanzhang's Legislative Ideology in the Early Ming Dynasty 911
  - 10.1.2 The Making of *Da Ming Lv* (*The Great Ming Code*), the Amendment of *Wen Xing Tiao Li* (*The Ordinance for Inquisition*), and the Issuing of *Ming Hui Dian* (*The Collected Statutes of Ming Dynasty*) 924
- 10.2 The Administrative Legislation for the Strengthening of Absolutism 946
  - 10.2.1 The Major Changes of the Central Administrative System 947
  - 10.2.2 The Law on the State Officials to Maintain the Operation of Bureaucracy 958
  - 10.2.3 The Change of the Supervisory System and Enriching of Supervision Law 968
- 10.3 Criminal Law Reflecting the Thoughts of Ruling the Country with Severe Penalties 977
  - 10.3.1 The Ideology of "Bringing Order Out of the Troubled Times by Enforcing Severe Penalties" and Its Influence on the Legislation of Criminal Law 978
  - 10.3.2 The Penal System Focusing on the Punishment of Treacherous People and the Applicable Principles of Criminal Law 995
- 10.4 Further Development of Civil Law 1001
  - 10.4.1 "Ren Hu Fen Bian" (Separation of Registered and Actual Residence) and the Subjects of Civil Rights 1002
  - 10.4.2 The Usufruct of Estate Rights and the Expansion of Guarantee 1005
  - 10.4.3 The New Development of the Law of Obligation 1011
  - 10.4.4 Marriage and Inheritance Law Adapted from That of the Tang and Song Dynasties 1016
- 10.5 Economic Legislation Adapting to the Economic Development 1022
  - 10.5.1 The Agricultural Legislation Encouraging Land Reclamation 1023
  - 10.5.2 The Government-Run Handicraft Industry with the Promotion of the System of "Jiang Ji" (The Craftsman Household Registration) 1026

		10.5.3	The Strengthening of "Jin Que Zhi Du" (The System of State Monopoly for Some Important Goods) in Commerce	1029
		10.5.4	The Making of the Laws on Metallic and Paper Money	1035
	10.6	The Change of Jurisdiction and the Joint Trial System		1038
		10.6.1	The Change of the Administration of "San Fa Si" (Three Judicial Departments)	1039
		10.6.2	The Judicial Procedures Emphasizing Judicial Jurisdiction	1046
		10.6.3	The Newly Created "Hui Shen Zhi Du" (The Joint Trial System)	1049
	10.7	The Achievement of "Lv Xue" (The Study of Statutory Laws) and the World Position of *Da Ming Lv* (*The Great Ming Code*)		1057
		10.7.1	The Achievement of "Lv Xue" (The Study of Statutory Laws)	1057
		10.7.2	The World Position of *Da Ming Lv* (*The Great Ming Code*)	1062
11	**The Legal System of the Qing Dynasty: The Final Form of Chinese Legal Civilization**			**1071**
	11.1	The Foundation of the Legal System Before Entering Shanhaiguan		1072
		11.1.1	The Transition from Jurchen Customary Law to Statute Law	1073
		11.1.2	Initiation of the Legal System of "Can Han Zhuo Jin"	1077
		11.1.3	Characteristics of the Legal System in the Early Period	1088
	11.2	The Complete Implementation of the Legislative Principle of "Can Han Zhuo Jin"		1097
		11.2.1	*Da Qing Lv Li* (*The Laws and Precedents of Great Qing*): The Main Achievements of "Can Han Zhuo Jin"	1098
		11.2.2	*Da Qing Hui Dian* (*The Collected Statutes of Great Qing*) and the Making of Departmental Regulations	1107
		11.2.3	The National Legislation Made according to *Li Fan Yuan Ze Li* (*The Regulation for the Bureau of National Minority Affairs*)	1114
	11.3	The Legalization of the Administrative System and the System of Official Management		1129
		11.3.1	The Change of Administrative System	1129
		11.3.2	The Legalization of Official Management	1156

11.4	The Criminal Law Made to Strengthen the Autocratic Ruling		1166
	11.4.1	The Main Crimes in *Da Qing Xing Lv* (*The Criminal Law of Great Qing*)	1166
	11.4.2	The Penalty System and the Principle for the Application of Criminal Law	1182
11.5	Codification of Civil Law		1189
	11.5.1	Social Structure and Identity	1190
	11.5.2	The Further Enrichment of Property Rights	1205
	11.5.3	The Perfection of "Zhai Fa" (Law of Obligation)	1224
	11.5.4	Marriage, Family, and Inheritance Mixed with the Custom of the Jurchen Nationality	1235
11.6	Enriching of the System of Economic Law		1251
	11.6.1	The New Development of Tax Legislation	1251
	11.6.2	The Industrial and Commercial Legislation of Secluding the Country from the Outside World	1253
	11.6.3	The Legislation Ensuring Water Transportation	1259
11.7	The More Complete Judicial System		1261
	11.7.1	Reform of the Judicial System	1261
	11.7.2	The More Specific Criminal and Civil Litigation	1269
	11.7.3	The Criminal Trial and "Hui Shen Zhi Du" (The Joint Trial System)	1276
	11.7.4	The Civil Trial with the a Combination of Judgment and Mediation	1291
11.8	The New Achievement of "Lv Xue" (The Study of Statutory Laws) and Its Impact on Legislation and the Judiciary		1301

Contents for Volume 1

1. **The Origin of Chinese Legal Civilization: The Legal Systems of the Xia and Shang Dynasties** 1
   - 1.1 The Earliest Dawn of Chinese Legal Civilization: The Legal System of the Xia Dynasty 1
     - 1.1.1 The Disintegration of Clan Society and the Emergence of Legal System 2
     - 1.1.2 The Pathway for China to Move Towards Legal Civilization 7
     - 1.1.3 From the Primitive Customs to the Law in Class Society 10
     - 1.1.4 The State Structure and Legal System of Xia Dynasty 19
   - 1.2 The Legal System of Shang Dynasty Under the Ruling of Theocracy 28
     - 1.2.1 The Unity of Kingship Rights, Family Authority and Theocracy 28
     - 1.2.2 The Extension of the Scope of the State Management and Division of the Duties of Officials 31
     - 1.2.3 The More Enriched Contents of Legislation 33
     - 1.2.4 The Judicial System Under the Influence of Theocratic Law 43

2. **The Early Developed Form of the Chinese Legal Civilization: The Legal System of Western Zhou Dynasty** 45
   - 2.1 Setting Up the Administrative Management System Protected by Dukes and Princes and Dominated by Royal Families 46
   - 2.2 Implementing the Comprehensive Strategy of Ruling by "Li" (Rites), "Yue" (Music), "Zheng" (Government) and "Xing" (Punishment) 52

	2.3	Establishing the Guiding Principle of "Jing Tian Bao Ming" (Respecting Heaven and Protecting the People) and "Ming De Shen Fa" (Promoting Virtue and Being Prudent in the Enforcement of Punishment).......................... 59
	2.4	The Legal Contents of *Lv Xing* (*The Penal Code of Lv*) and *Jiu Xing* (*The Code Nine Penalties*).................. 62
		2.4.1 The Administrative Laws in Inscriptions and Documentary Records........................... 66
		2.4.2 The Criminal Law: Emphasizing Public Rights and Being Cautious with Patriarchal Clan System....... 69
		2.4.3 The Civil Law Beginning to Take Shape............. 84
	2.5	The Judicial Activities with the Initial Differentiation of Criminal and Civil Litigation........................ 99
3	The Legal System of the Spring and Autumn and Warring States Period Featured by Social Transformation and Legal Reform..... 113	
	3.1	The Reform Adaptable to Social Transformation............. 114
	3.2	The Collapse of the System of "Shi Qing" (Inheritance of Noble Titles) and the Formation of Bureaucratic System..... 119
	3.3	Confucianism and Legalism in "Bai Jia Zheng Ming" (The Contention of a Hundred Schools of Thought)........... 124
	3.4	The Legal Reform Adaptable to Social Transformation......... 144
		3.4.1 The Issuing of the Statute Laws in the Vassal States and the Legislative Activities in the Spring and Autumn Period............................ 144
		3.4.2 Legislations in Each State in the Warring States Period and *Fa Jing* (*Canon of Laws*) Written by Li Kui..................................... 149
4	The Legal System of Qin Dynasty with "Laws Made in Every Field"... 157	
	4.1	The Legal System of Qin Dynasty Recorded in *Yun Meng Qin Jian* (*Amounts of Bamboo Writing Slips in Qin Dynasty Excavated in Yunmeng*)............................... 158
		4.1.1 The Nature of *Qin Lv* (*Qin Code*) Recorded in *Yun Meng Qin Jian* (*Amounts of Bamboo Writing Slips in Qin Dynasty Excavated in Yunmeng*).......... 158
		4.1.2 The Main Contents of *Qin Lv* (*Qin Code*) in *Qin Jian*................................... 162
		4.1.3 The Judicial System Stressing the Responsibility of Officials.................................. 225
	4.2	The Legal System of Qin Dynasty After Its Unification........ 231
		4.2.1 The State System Reflecting Despotism and the Centralization of State Power..................... 232

| | | 4.2.2 | "Ming Fa Du" (Make Law Known to the People) and "Ding Lv Ling" (Making Laws and Decrees) | 237 |

5 The Confucianization of the Legal Systems in Western and Eastern Han Dynasties 249
    5.1 The Establishment of Western Han Dynasty and the Change of the Legislative Policy 250
    5.2 The Legislative Activities and the Forms of Law 266
    5.3 The Enriching and Development of Administrative Law 276
        5.3.1 The Establishment of the Operation Mechanism of State Institutions Headed by the Emperor 276
        5.3.2 The Strengthening of Official Management 283
    5.4 The Criminal Law in Documents and *Han Jian* (*The Bamboo Slip of Han Dynasty*) 298
        5.4.1 The Main Accusation in the Laws of Han Dynasty 299
        5.4.2 The Penalty System Reform of Abolishing Corporal Punishment 320
        5.4.3 The Criminal Principle Under the Influence of Confucianism 334
    5.5 The Development of Civil Legal Relationship and Civil Legislation 343
        5.5.1 Identity and Civil Rights 343
        5.5.2 The Ownership and Legal Protection 345
        5.5.3 The Legal Adjustment and Protection of Debt 347
        5.5.4 Marriage, Family and Inheritance 351
    5.6 The Economic Laws of "Zhong Nong Yi Shang" (Encouraging Agriculture and Restraining Commerce) 355
    5.7 The Judicial System Under the Influence of Confucianism 360
        5.7.1 The Judicial System 361
        5.7.2 The Litigation and Jurisdiction 363
        5.7.3 Trial 364
    5.8 The Rising of the Private Law Annotation 376

6 The Legal Systems of Wei, Jin, Southern and Northern Dynasty: The Legislative Progress and Cultural Amalgamation 381
    6.1 The Legislative Achievements in Wei, Jin, Southern and Northern Dynasty 382
        6.1.1 The Legislative Achievement of "San Guo" (Three Kingdoms) Represented by *Wei Lv* (*Wei Code*) 385
        6.1.2 The Legislative Achievements of Western and Eastern Jin and Southern Dynasty Represented by *Jin Lv* (*Jin Code*) 393
        6.1.3 The Legislative Achievements in Northern Dynasty Represented by *Bei Wei Lv* (*Bei Wei Code*) and *Bei Qi Lv* (*Bei Qi Code*) 403

6.2	The Basic Contents of the Laws in Different Dynasties........	418
	6.2.1 The Strengthening of the Tendency of the Codification of Administrative Law...........................	418
	6.2.2 The Tendency of Applying Severe Punishments and the Drafting of "Zhong Zui Shi Tiao" (Ten Felonies).................................	436
	6.2.3 The Civil Law Under the Privileged System of "Shi Zu" (the Gentry).........................	454
6.3	Inheriting the Judicial System of Han Dynasty.............	466

7 The Legal Systems of Sui and Tang Dynasties: The Finalization of the Forms of Chinese Legal Civilization.................... 471

7.1 The Legal System of Sui Dynasty Made by Adopting the Strong Points of the Laws of Southern and Northern Dynasties... 471

    7.1.1 Legislation in the Early Period of Sui Dynasty and the Historical Role of *Kai Huang Lv* (*The Code Made in the Year of Kai Huang*)................... 472

    7.1.2 The Management System and the System of "Kai Ke Qu Shi" (To Recruit Talents Through Imperial Examination) in Sui Dynasty....................... 479

    7.1.3 The Establishment of the Basic Framework of Feudal Criminal Law.......................... 482

    7.1.4 The Civil and Economic Laws Centered on "Jun Tian Zhi" (The System of Land Equalization) and "Zu Yong Diao Fa" (Law on Farmland Rent, Handicraft Tax, and Corvée)...................... 487

    7.1.5 The Judicial System of the Centralized Government...... 489

7.2 The Legal System of Tang Dynasty Symbolizing the Establishment of Chinese Legal System................ 495

    7.2.1 The Legislative Ideology Drawn from the Lessons of the Extinction of Sui Dynasty................... 496

    7.2.2 The Legislative Activities and the Major Legislative Achievements................................. 509

    7.2.3 The Organic Law of the Administrative Organs and the Official Administration Law................. 518

    7.2.4 The Finalized Criminal Law....................... 550

    7.2.5 The More Complicated Civil Law................... 567

    7.2.6 The Strengthening of the Legal Adjustment of Economic Relationships....................... 600

    7.2.7 The Judicial System Tending To Be Perfect............ 609

    7.2.8 The Characteristics of *Tang Lv* (*Tang Code*) and Its World Position.......................... 627

7.3 The Legal Systems of "Wu Dai Shi Guo" (Five Dynasties and Ten Kingdoms)..................................... 642

Chapter 8
The Legal Civilization of Northern and Southern Song Dynasties Fostered by Commercial Economy

(960 A.D.–1279 A.D.)

In the history of Chinese legal civilization, the period of Northern and Southern Song dynasties is an era when remarkable achievements had been made since the Tang Dynasty.

At the beginning of the Song Dynasty, because the policies of "Bu Li Tian Zhi" (establishing no land system) and "Bu Yi Jian Bing" (having no prohibition on the annexation of land) were taken, the circulation of land ownership was improved unprecedentedly and the number of landlords with medium-sized and small-sized farms were dramatically increased. Additionally, the tenants were no longer the private property of their masters and became registered households of the state under the land tenancy system, which had generally stimulated people's enthusiasm for production and promoted the recovery and development of agriculture. In turn, agricultural development also provided a material foundation for the development of handicraft industry and commerce. So during the Song Dynasty, China became a well-known trading country in the world.

The prosperity of the social economy also fostered the development of science and technology. So great achievements were made in the fields of papermaking, gunpowder making, movable-type printing, compass, astronomy, medicine, and mathematics. Academic thoughts were also encouraged in the relatively relaxed political atmosphere, so many schools of thoughts appeared, such as the academic thoughts of "Cheng Zhu Li Xue" (neo-Confucianism: a Confucian school of idealist philosophy of Cheng Hao, Cheng Yi, and Zhu Xi), which was depictive of the philosophical theories of Song scholars and the school of mercantilism represented by Chen Liang and Ye Shi. Hence, under the great commercial impact, the traditional view of stressing "Yi" (justice) and neglecting "Li" (benefit) was changed into stressing both of them.

At the beginning of the Song Dynasty, in order to prevent the reoccurrence of great chaos caused by the separatist regimes of "Fan Zhen" (local regimes) in the period of "Wu Dai Shi Guo"; to strictly control the military, political, and financial powers of the local government; and to strengthen the centralization of authority, great weight was given to the construction of a legal system and "Fa Zhi" (the ruling of law) was strongly advocated. Therefore, law was regarded as "the principle of governing a state and the discipline for ruling a country."[1] "Only after the legal system is established is it possible to provide a guidance for the handling of other affairs and for ruling the country successfully."[2] Chen Liang once made a comparison of the legal systems of the Han, Tang, and Song dynasties, and he said, "In Han Dynasty, people are stressed; in Tang Dynasty, both people and law are stressed; at present, law is stressed."[3]

Since much weight was given to "Fa Zhi" (the ruling of law) in the Song Dynasty, the officials, whether in the central or local government, all paid much attention to the study of law so that reading law books became a general mood of the society even within the circle of "Shi Da Fu" (literati and officials). From the records of the legal judgment of the Southern and Northern dynasties remaining till date, it can be seen that those judicial officials were not only expert at law but also at making judgments by taking the consideration of "Fa" (law), "Li" (reason) and "Qing" (human relationships). In order to properly implement the principles of "Yuan Fa Duan Zui" (making judgments in accordance with the law), the system of "Ju Yu Fen Si" (separating interrogation from adjudication) was also established in Song Dynasty.

Moreover, great achievements were made in the construction of the legal system of the Northern and Southern Song dynasties. For example, *Song Xing Tong (The Penal Code of Song Dynasty)* and *Qing Yuan Tiao Fa Shi Lei (The Legal Provisions and Cases Made in the Year of Qingyuan)* were enacted. These laws not only reflected the characteristics of the times but also enriched civil and economic legislation, strengthened administrative legislation for the centralization of authority, and reformed the legal system. With respect to "Lv Xue" (the study of statutory laws), the practice of making comments on legal provisions, which had been carried out since the Han, Wei, and Jin dynasties, was inherited. Analysis of legal cases was also emphasized, and the legal experiences of the previous dynasties were summarized. Therefore, many works about "Lv Xue" (the study of statutory laws), such as *Zhe Yu Gui Qian (Collections of Lawsuits)* and *Tang Yin Bi Shi (Collection of Criminal Cases)*, were written. It is worth mentioning that *Xi Yuan Ji Lu (Collection of Unjust Cases Rectified)*, which was compiled by Song Ci, was a comprehensive summary of forensic medicine in ancient China, and it was the earliest work about forensic medicine not only in China but also in the world. This book had been translated and published in ancient Korea, Japan, France, Britain, Germany, and Holland since the Ming Dynasty, so it not only showed the great achievement of the

---

[1] "Xuan Ju" (Election) in *Song Hui Yao Ji Gao (Collected Essays of the Historical Records of Song Dynasty)*, Chapter 11, Vo. 13.
[2] *Xu Zi Zhi Tong Jian Chang Bian (Sequel to the Full-length Book of History as a Mirror)*, Vol. 143, in September of the 3rd year of Qingli.
[3] Chen Liang (Song Dynasty), "Ren Fa" (Relying on Laws) in *Chen Liang Ji (Collected Works of Chen Liang)*, Vol. 11.

legal civilization of the Song Dynasty but also the great contribution that the Chinese made to the world legal culture.

The ruling of the Southern and Northern dynasties coexisted with the ruling of the Liao, Xi Xia, and Jin dynasties, which had made it possible for the Chinese culture of the central plains to spread to more extensive regions and to be exchanged with many other nationalities. The existing legal codes of the Liao, Xi Xia, and Jin dynasties reflected not only the imprints of the exchanging of different legal culture but also the rapid improvement in the legal civilization of small minorities and their contribution to the enrichment and development of the Chinese legal system.

8.1 The National Policy and Characteristics of the Legislation of the Early Song Dynasty

8.1.1 *The National Policy of Strengthening the Centralization of Authority*

The Song Dynasty was a unified feudal regime set up after the great disintegration of "Wu Dai Shi Guo" (Five Dynasties and Ten Kingdoms) and the hundreds of years of feudal separatist ruling of "Fan Zhen" (local regimes). In the early period of the Song Dynasty, in view of the disaster and threat that the feudal separatist ruling of "Fan Zhen" (local regimes) had brought to Chinese ethnic groups and the central government, the basic national policy of consolidating the unified country was adopted by the rulers to build a strong system for the centralization of authority and to prevent "the local powers from usurping the power because the monarchical power was too weak."[4]

Since the local power was weakened under the blow of Huang Chao's uprising, it was possible for the policy of taking back the military and financial powers of local generals taken by Emperor Song Taizu after the unification of the whole country to be carried out nationwide. Even though the national power of the Northern and Southern Song dynasties was not as strong as that of the Han and Tang dynasties, the autocratic power of centralization was even stronger so that no public separate regimes were ever established since then. In the Song Dynasty, a man named Ye Shi once made a historical comment on this situation:

> In view of the malpractice of Tang Dynasty and "Wu Dai" (the Five Dynasties), the power of "Fan Zhen" (local regimes) was taken back by the imperial court and then controlled by the emperor. As a result, the trifle matters such as the registering of soldiers, the collection of tax, and the appointment of the heads of local places were all decided by the emperor himself. In order to avoid the malpractice and to bring the advantages of the government into a full play, the ruling class depended more on law instead of the officials and more on government staff

---

[4]*Xu Zi Zhi Tong Jian Chang Bian* (*Sequel to the Full-length Book of History as a Mirror*), Vol. 2, in July of the 2nd year of Jianlong.

instead of officials with higher ranks. So they tried every way to prevent their power from being weakened and the systems which were different from those of ancient times were adopted. As a result, the government power was greatly strengthened. But even so, was it the proper way? On the contrary, there lacked talents in the country and the national power became weak both at home and abroad. Although the country was big, yet it was on guard against of the people, which was caused by the abuse of the law.[5]

During the early period of the Song Dynasty, the rulers paid more attention to ruling the country and controlling the society by law. Emperor Taizu once said, "Before forbidding others to do bad deeds, the emperor himself should abide by the law first."[6] Emperor Taizong had also repeatedly told his officials that "the law codes are very useful administrative principles. So if officials are ignorant about the law, they will make mistakes whenever they do things; if they can read law books carefully, their legal knowledge will be surely enriched."[7] Emperor Renzong regarded "Fa Zhi" (the ruling of law) as the first condition of ruling the country, and he said that "if the legal system is established, there will be principles for handling all affairs, so it will definitely become easier to rule the country."[8] Influenced by the abovementioned theories of showing respect to and stressing the law, most of the emperors in the Song Dynasty showed "prudence in hearing the cases" and "showed care for the prisoners." Additionally, they took active measures to encourage legislative activities and to strengthen the construction of a legal system. In the 3rd year of Jianlong (962 A.D.), Zhang Zimu, a law expert, suggested that *Latter Zhou Xing Tong (The General Penal Code of Latter Zhou Dynasty)* should be abolished. Later on, "Gong Bu Shang Shu" (the minister of the department of works), called Dou Yi in "Da Li Si" (The Bureau of Judicial Review), presented a memorial to the emperor and suggested that *"Zhou Xing Tong (The Penal Code of Zhou Dynasty)* should be revised because its provisions are too complicated and misleading."[9] Then Emperor Taizu assigned Dou Yi to be responsible for the amendment. In August of the 4th year of Jianlong (963 A.D.), *Song Jian Long Xiang Ding Xing Tong (The Detailed General Penal Code of Jianlong Period of Song Dynasty)* (hereinafter referred to as *Song Xing Tong: The Penal Code of Song Dynasty)* was created by the people, among them Dou Yi, Su Xiao, Xi Yu, Zhang Xirang, Feng Shuxiang, and so on; printed through woodblock printing; and enacted in China. So it was in the Song Dynasty that a national basic code was issued and enacted in such way in Chinese legal history.

---

[5]Ye Shi (Song Dynasty), "Xin Shu" (New Writings) in *Shui Xin Bie Ji (Other Collected Works of Shui Xin)*, Vol. 14.

[6]"Gai Qie Dao Zang Ji Qian Zhao" (The Imperial Edict on Changing the Calculating Methods of Stolen Goods by Thieves) in "Xing Fa" (The Criminal Law) (Part 1) in *Song Da Zhao Ling Ji (Collected Grand Edicts and Decrees of the Song Dynasty)*, Vol. 200.

[7]Li You (Song Dynasty), "Bing Xing" (The Military Law) in *Song Chao Shi Shi (The Anecdotes of Song Dynasty)*, Vol. 16.

[8]*Xu Zi Zhi Tong Jian Chang Bian (Sequel to the Full-length Book of History as a Mirror)*, Vol. 2, in September of the 3rd year of Qingli.

[9]"Zhao Ling" (Imperial Edicts) in *Yu Hai (The Jade Ocean)*, Vol. 6.

Song Xing Tong (*The Penal Code of Song Dynasty*) was made on the basis of *Da Zhong Xing Lv Tong Lei* (*Catalogue of the Penal Law in the Period of Dazhong*), which was made during the reign of Emperor Xuanzong in the Tang Dynasty; *Tong Guang Xing Lv Tong Lei* (*The Catalogue of the Penal Code of Tonggang*), which was made in Later Tang Dynasty; and *Xian De Xing Lv Tong Lei* (*The Catalogue of the Penal Code of Xiande*), which was made in Later Zhou Dynasty. In its drafting, both "Lv" (criminal law) and "Chi" (instruction) were equally stressed, while "Ling" (decree), "Ge" (injunction), and "Shi" (standard) were coedited, which was a great change of the style of compilation since Qin, Han, and Tang dynasties. *Song Xing Tong* (*The Penal Code of Song Dynasty*) consisted of thirty volumes, twelve chapters, and five hundred and two articles. As to the titles of the chapters, those of *Tang Lv* (*Tang Code*) were followed, but each chapter was subdivided into categories, so the twelve chapters were further divided into two hundred and thirteen categories. The selected penal norms generally applied in "Chi" (instruction), "Ling" (decree), "Ge" (injunction), "Shi" (standard), and the memorials "approved by the emperor," which were submitted by Dou Yi, Su Xiao, etc. from the 2nd year of Kaiyuan to the 3rd year of Jianlong in the Tang Dynasty, were attached to the appendix of the legal text.

8.1.2 The Characteristics of the Legislation

After *Song Xing Tong* (*The Penal Code of Song Dynasty*) was issued, although it was discussed and debated on several times, namely, in the 4th year of Qiande during the reign of Emperor Taizu (966 A.D.), in the 4th year of Xi'ning during the reign of Emperor Shenzong (1071 A.D.), in the 1st year of Shaosheng during the reign of Emperor Zhezong (1094 A.D.), and in the 1st year of Shaoxing during the reign of Emperor Gaozong (1131 A.D.), only a few changes were made therein. So it can be said that *Song Xing Tong* (*The Penal Code of Song Dynasty*), made during the Song Dynasty, was still the most comprehensive legal code of the times. However, social development and newly emerged legal relationship were beyond the scope of its adjustment, so pertinent adjustments were regularly carried out by means of "Chi" (instruction) and "Ling" (decree) issued by the emperors. With the increase in the number of "Chi" (instruction), its legal effect became greater than that of statute law; therefore, in judicial practice, it had played an important role in "measuring the punishment of crimes,"[10] which was a reflection of the consolidated power of the autocratic centralization system in legislation.

The so-called "Chi" (instruction) refers to the imperial edicts issued by the emperors for a particular person or matter at a particular time. Because "Chi" (instruction) was flexible and could be used to supplement and amend the laws, it

---

[10]"Xing Fa Zhi" (The Record of the Criminal Law) (Part 1) in *Song Shi* (*The History of Song Dynasty*).

was widely used by the rulers. Gradually, its scope of adjustment was extended, so that it covered almost all the basic activities of the nation, as was described that apart from the imperial court, "'Chi' (instruction) is issued for each 'Si' (bureau), 'Lu' (ancient administrative region), 'Zhou' (subprefecture) and 'Xian' (county)."[11] In the 1st year of Xianping during the reign of Emperor Zhenzong (998 A.D.), the number of "Chi" (instruction) had reached to 18,555.

In order to collect and sort out the large number of scattered "Chi" (instruction), to delete duplicate and contradictory parts, and to issue "Chi" (instruction) through certain procedures so that it could be changed to specific legal provisions to obtain universal efficacy and stability, the compilation of "Chi" (instruction) had been carried out ever since the early Song Dynasty. During the reign of Emperor Taizu of the Song Dynasty, *Jian Long Bian Chi (The Collection of Instructions Made in Jianlong Period)*, which was made up of one hundred and six articles, was issued together with *Song Xing Tong (The Penal Code of Song Dynasty)*. After the reign of Emperor Taizong, more "Chi" (instruction) was successively issued, such as *Tai Ping Xing Guo Bian Chi (The Collection of Instructions Made in Taiping Xingguo)*, consisting of fifteen volumes; *Chun Hua Bian Chi (The Collection of Instructions Made in Chunhua Period)*, consisting of thirty volumes; *Xian Ping Bian Chi (The Collection of Instructions Made in Xianping Period)*, consisting of twelve volumes; *Da Zhong Xiang Fu Bian Chi (The Collection of Instructions Made in Da Zhong Xiang Fu)*, consisting of thirty volumes; *Tian Sheng Bian Chi (The Collection of Instructions Made in Tiansheng Period)*, consisting of twelve volumes; *Qing Li Bian Chi (The Collection of Instructions Made in Qingli Period)*, consisting of twenty volumes; and *Jia You Bian Chi (The Compilation of Instructions Made in Jiayou Period)*, consisting of thirty volumes. During the reign of Emperor Shenzong, *Yuan Feng Bian Chi Ling Ge Shi (The Collection of Instructions, Decrees, Injunctions and Standards Made in Yuanfeng Period)* was issued and enacted extensively. Based on rough statistics, during the two hundred and ninety years from the 4th year of Jianlong during the reign of Emperor Taizu (963 A.D.) to the 2nd year of Baoyou during the reign of Emperor Lizong in the South Song (1284 A.D.), more than two hundred and forty codes were successively amended, among which the newly compiled "Chi" (instruction), "Ling" (decree), "Ge" (injunction), and "Shi" (standard) occupied more than 80%. In this case, the compilation of "Chi" (instruction) was the most important and frequently carried out legislative activities during the Song Dynasty.

Among those codified *Bian Chi (The Collection of Instructions)*, some were applicable to the whole country, some were applicable to the different organs of the central government, and some were specifically applicable to "Si" (bureau), "Lu" (ancient administrative region), "Zhou" (subprefecture), and "Xian" (county). The changes in the legal system during the Song Dynasty could be seen from the compiled of "Chi" (instruction) in different periods. It was recorded in "Xing Fa

---

[11]"Xing Fa Zhi" (The Record of the Criminal Law) (Part 1) in *Song Shi (The History of Song Dynasty)*.

Zhi" (The Record of the Criminal Law) in *Song Shi* (*The History of Song Dynasty*) that "the legal system of Song Dynasty which was set up on the basis of 'Lv' (criminal law), 'Ling' (decree), 'Ge' (injunction) and 'Shi' (standard) of Tang Dynasty needed to be revised according to concrete circumstances, so there appeared the compilation of 'Chi,'" which was consistent with historical realities. Because the compilation of "Chi" (instruction) was a regular legislative activity, it was and most important characteristic of legislation in the Song Dynasty.

"Da Li Si" (The Bureau of Judicial Review) was in charge of the codification of *Bian Chi* (*The Collection of Instructions*) in the early period of the Song Dynasty, but during the reign of Emperor Renzong, "Xiang Ding Bian Chi Suo" (the office of the compilation of instructions) was especially set up to be in charge of such affair. But *Bian Chi* (*The Collection of Instructions*), made in the Song Dynasty, was unfortunately lost.

It can be inferred from what was mentioned above that "Lv" (criminal law) was the statute law of the country and the backbone of the legal system, so it was characterized by stability, comprehensiveness, and authority; "Chi" (instruction) consisted of imperial edicts that were temporarily issued to specific people in specific situations, so it had the greatest legal effect. In the earlier stage of the Northern Song Dynasty, "Lv" (criminal law) and "Chi" (instruction) were implemented in parallel; however, after the political reform of Emperor Shenzong, "Chi" (instruction) was gradually employed as a supplementary regulation to "Lv." Emperor Shenzong once explicitly declared that "if 'Lv' (criminal law) cannot be appropriately applied to deal with all matters, or if no accurate provisions can be found in 'Lv' (criminal law), then 'Chi' (instruction) should be applied."[12] What he said had shown the value of "Chi" (instruction) and its function as supplementary to law. In order to amend and modify the current law, "in the early years of Xi'ning, a bureau for revising 'Chi' was set up, and the people who had once complained about the inappropriateness of the law were ordered to gather together to hold collective discussions and to undertake the revision work."[13] In judicial practice, it was a statutory requirement to settle cases in accordance with the "Lv," and only when there were no provisions in "Lv" could "Chi" (instruction), "Ling" (decree), "Ge" (injunction), and "Shi" (standard) be applied. Just like what was recorded in "Zhi Guan Zhi" (The Record of State Officials) in *Song Shi* (*The History of Song Dynasty*), "cases must be settled in accordance with law; if the law is not applicable, the cases should be settled in accordance with 'Chi' (instruction), 'Ling' (decree), 'Ge' (injunction) and 'Shi' (standard)." However, in fact, "Chi" (instruction) was often used as the most fundamental legal source so that "Chi" (instruction), "Ling" (decree), "Ge" (injunction), and "Shi" (standard) were often directly employed by Emperor Shenzong without mentioning "Lv" (criminal law). In "Xing Fa Zhi" (The Record of the

---

[12]"Xing Fa Zhi" (The Record of the Criminal Law) (Part 1) in *Song Shi* (*The History of Song Dynasty*).

[13]"Xing Fa Zhi" (The Record of the Criminal Law) (Part 1) in *Song Shi* (*The History of Song Dynasty*).

Criminal Law) in *Song Shi* (*The History of Song Dynasty*), the following words were also recorded: "'Lv' (criminal law) existed beyond 'Chi' (instruction)," which actually did not mean that the central position of "Lv" (criminal law) was changed in the legal system; instead, it merely emphasized the value of "Chi" (instruction).

By implementing "Lv" (criminal law) and "Chi" (instruction) simultaneously, the stability of law was maintained, the scope of adjustment was expanded, and the flexibility of the law was brought into full play. The targets that "Chi" (instruction), "Ling" (decree), "Ge" (injunction), and "Shi" (standard) adjusted in the Song Dynasty were slightly different from those of the Tang Dynasty. For example, "a provision to ban what has happened is referred to as 'Chi'; a provision to ban what has not happened is referred to as 'Ling'; a provision to warn people is referred to as 'Ge'; and a provision for people to observe is referred to as 'Shi.'"[14] Clearly, all of these four kinds of "code of the law" had their corresponding targets and functions to be adjusted. But during the reign of Emperor Mingzong, "Chi" (instruction), as a supplement to "Lv" (criminal law), actually took the place of "Lv" (criminal law) or even overrode "Lv" (criminal law), so that the power of legislation was abused by the emperor himself. It was recorded in "Xing Fa Zhi" (The Record of the Criminal Law) in *Song Shi* (*The History of Song Dynasty*) that "every time when Emperor Huizong wrote imperial edicts in person, he had willfully changed the old law; ... when Cai Jing was 'Zai Xiang' (the prime minister), he had bent the law for his own personal gains, so he even presented memorials to the emperor to require that imperial edicts be applied beyond the law." So if people did not obey those imperial edicts, they would be punished for the "crime of violating the system." Moreover, those four forms of laws were easy to be applied by judicial officials for their own benefit. As a result, the original legislative procedure ceased to exist, making it difficult to maintain legal order.

Apart from making a compilation of "Chi" (instruction), "Li" (precedent) was also drafted. The so-called "Li" (precedent) originated from "Bi" (analogy) and "Li" (precedent) (both were legal forms) made in the Han and Tang dynasties. According to its targets of adjustment, "Li" (precedent) was divided into "Duan Li" (legal precedents) and "Shi Li" (precedents). "Duan Li" (legal precedents) were used as the precedent regulation for punishing crimes and measuring penalties. Because it was easy to be cited in application, "Chi" (instruction) gradually developed from being merely an initial temporary provision containing individual precedent cases to being a common system. In order to make "Li" (precedent) a law with universal legal effect, its compilation was started in the time of Qingli, and the fruit of the compilation was included in *Qing Li Bian Chi* (*The Collection of Instructions Made in Qingli Period*). During the reign of Emperor Shenzong, *Xi Ning Fa Si Duan Li* (*The Legal Precedents of Xi'ning Legal Bureau*) and *Yuan Feng Duan Li* (*The Legal Precedents Made in Yuanfeng Period*) were made; during the reign of Emperor Zhezong, *Yuan Fu Xing Ming Duan Li* (*The Legal Precedents on the*

---

[14]"Xing Fa Zhi" (The Record of the Criminal Law) (Part 1) in *Song Shi* (*The History of Song Dynasty*).

8.1 The National Policy and Characteristics of the Legislation of the Early Song... 657

Names of Offences Made in Yuanfu Period) was made; and during the reign of Emperor Huizong, *Chong Ning Duan Li* (*The Legal Precedents Made in Chongning Period*) was made. In the periods of Emperor Gaozong, Emperor Xiaozong, and Emperor Ningzong in the Southern Song Dynasty, *Shao Xing Xing Ming Yi Nan Duan Li* (*The Legal Precedents on Difficult Offence Names Made in Shaoxing Period*), *Qian Dao Xin Bian Te Zhi Duan Li* (*The Legal Precedents on Specially Newly-Compiled Imperial Edicts Made in Qiandao Period*), and *Kai Xi Xing Ming Duan Li* (*Legal Precedents on Offence Names of Kaixi*) were made. The seven legal precedents mentioned above were not only important forms of law but also the most important legislative achievements of the Song Dynasty. Although there was not as many "Li" (precedent) as there was "Chi" (instruction), it had its own continuity, so its position in the judiciary gradually strengthened. In a word, the prevalence of the compilation of "Li" (precedent) was another characteristic of the legislation in Song Dynasty.

On the other hand, "Shi Li" (precedents), also referred to as "Zhi Hui" (commanding), included, among others, "Nei Pi Zhi Hui" (internal commanding), which was especially issued by the emperor, and instructions for subordinate offices issued by the bureaus of "Shang Shu Sheng" (The Department of Secretary). "Zhi Hui" (commanding) was also applied as established precedents, but in the Northern Song Dynasty, it was not compiled separately. With the change of historical conditions in the Southern Song Dynasty, it became more and more popular to hear cases according to "Zhi Hui" (commanding), so it gradually became a new form of law after it was compiled and edited. For example, in the 21st year of Shaoxing (1151 A. D.), *Yan Fa Xu Jiang Zhi Hui* (*Commanding for the Legal Amendment of Salt Law*), consisting of one hundred and thirty volumes, and *Cha Fa Xu Jiang Zhi Hui* (*Commanding for the Legal Amendment of the Law of Tea*), consisting of eighty eight volumes, were drafted.

As to the application of "Li" (precedent), according to principles of the early period of Northern Song Dynasty, "if there are no provisions in law, 'Li' (precedent) should be applied."[15] However, just like what Liu Yizheng had commented on the result of the application of "Li," "although there are laws and decrees, the officials could still find loopholes to do things for their personal gains. Now everything is decided by what is recorded in the precedent cases, how can it possibly prevent those officials from deceiving people?"[16] In the Southern Song Dynasty, "although there are laws and decrees, cases are heard by the officials according to 'Li' (precedent). However, if some provisions can be found in law but cannot be found in 'Li' (precedent), the settlement of cases might often be delayed."[17] Especially under

---

[15]"Xing Fa Zhi" (The Record of the Criminal Law) (Part 1) in *Song Shi* (*The History of Song Dynasty*).

[16]"Xing Fa Zhi" (The Record of the Criminal Law) (Part 1) in *Song Shi* (*The History of Song Dynasty*).

[17]"Xing Fa Zhi" (The Record of the Criminal Law) (Part 1) in *Song Shi* (*The History of Song Dynasty*).

the guidance of the principle that "'Zhi Hui' (commanding) should be naturally regarded as the established precedent"[18] and "'Xu Jiang Zhi Hui' (the emperor's commanding for the legal amendment of law) should be naturally regarded as the complement of 'Chi' (instruction),"[19] the scope of application of "Li" (precedent) became more extensive. As a result, "much weight was given to 'Li' (precedent)," and officials even "refused to settle cases without 'Li' (precedent)."[20] Emperor Xiaozong tried to rectify the malpractice by limiting the scope of application of "Li" (precedent) and "Zhi Hui" (commanding), so he ordered that if judicial officials wanted to change the provisions of law, "they should first be approved by the emperor himself,"[21] but it was of very little effect.

No doubt, the improvement of the legal status of "Lv" (criminal law) and the establishment of legislative procedure in the Song dynasty had exerted great influence on the Ming and Qing dynasties.

In the 3rd year of Chunxi during the reign of Emperor Xiaozong in the Southern Song Dynasty (1175 A.D.), *Chun Xi Chi Ling Ge Shi* (*The Collection of Instructions, Decrees, Injunctions and Standards Made Chun Xi Period*) was issued. Soon Emperor Xiaozong realized that the mixed compilation of "Chi" (instruction), "Ling" (decree), "Ge" (injunction), and "Shi" (standard) had made "the law book loosely organized. What is more, it is not easy for the officials to read the whole contents, but it has made it convenient for some of them to play favouritism and commit irregularities"[22]; therefore, he decided to compile a code in the form of "Shi" (standard), by which the stylistic rules and layout formed in the compilation of laws were changed. Later on, *Chun Xi Tiao Fa Shi Lei* (*The Legal Provisions and Cases Made in Year of Chunxi*) was successfully compiled, which consisted of four hundred and twenty volumes, thirty three categories, and four hundred and twenty subcategories. According to the record of "Lv Ling" (Legal Orders) (Part Two) in "Zhao Ling" (Imperial Edicts) in *Yu Hai* (*The Jade Ocean*), on the 5th of January of the 6th year of Chunxi (1178 A.D.), Zhao Xiong presented a memorial to the emperor and suggested that "'Shi Da Fu' (literati and officials) do not have any knowledge of laws, so some officials will have chances to make fool of them about the legal provisions. If today the provisions can be categorized and included into different law books with all of the provisions on similar subjects included in one book, it will be easier to be applied, so that those officials will not have any chance to obtain their own benefits by bending the law." Then imperial orders were issued to

---

[18]Zhu Bian (Song dynasty), *Qu Wei Jiu Wen* (*The Old Anecdotes of Qu Wei*), Vol. 2.

[19]Chen Zhensun (Song Dynasty), *Zhi Zhai Shu Lu Jie Ti* (*An Annotated Bibliography of the Private Collections of Zhizhai*), Vol. 7.

[20]Ye Shi (Song Dynasty), "Shang Xiao Zong Huang Di Zha Zi" (An Official Letter Presented to Emperor Xiaozong) in *Shui Xin Xian Sheng Wen Ji* (*The Collected Works of Mr. Shui Xin*), Chapter 1, Vol. 1.

[21]"Xing Fa Zhi" (The Record of the Criminal Law) (Part 1) in *Song Shi* (*The History of Song Dynasty*).

[22]"Xing Fa Zhi" (The Record of the Criminal Law) (Part 1) in *Song Shi* (*The History of Song Dynasty*).

"Chi Ju" (the ancient government office in charge of drafting legal regulations) to order them to have "Chi" (instruction), "Ling" (decree), "Ge" (injunction), Shi" (standard), and "Shen Ming" (statement) collected, categorized, and compiled in one book following the style of *Li Bu Qi Si Tiao Fa Zong Lei* (*The Catalogue of Law for the Seven Bureaus of the Department of Personnel*). Finally, on May 28th of the 7th year of Chunxi, the code (with 420 volumes), consisting of thirty three general categories and four hundred and twenty subcategories, was completed. Then it was titled *Tiao Fa Shi Lei* (*Legal Provisions and Cases*) and issued by the emperor on March 1st of the 8th year of Chunxi.

During the reign of Emperor Ningzong, *Qing Yuan Tiao Fa Shi Lei* (*The Legal Provisions and Cases Made in the Year of Qingyuan*) was compiled and presented to the emperor by Xie Shenfu and others, so it was published and enacted in July of the 3rd year of Jiatai (1203 A.D.). According to the record of *Yu Hai* (*The Jade Ocean*), there were more than one hundred and forty volumes in *Qing Yuan Tiao Fa Shi Lei* (*The Legal Provisions and Cases Made in the Year of Qingyuan*), but now only sixteen categories and forty eight volumes remained. In the 11th year of Lizong Chunyou (1251 A.D.), based on *Qing Yuan Tiao Fa Shi Lei* (*The Legal Provisions and Cases Made in the Year of Qingyuan*) and *Chun You Chi Ling Ge Shi* (*The Collection of Instructions, Decrees, Injunctions and Standards Made in the Year of Chunyou*), *Chun You Tiao Fa Shi Lei* (*Legal Provisions and Cases Made in Year of Chun You*) were drafted, which consisted of four hundred and thirty volumes. This compilation was the last major legislative activity of the Song Dynasty. Since then, "the cases were all settled according to the code, so no revision was conducted any more."[23]

Tiao Fa Shi Lei (*The Legal Provisions and Cases*) refers to a law book compiled by collecting "Chi" (instruction), "Ling" (decree), "Ge" (injunction), "Shi" (standard), "Shen Ming," (statement), etc. together according to different catalogues and classifications for the purpose of easy application. The compilation of *Tiao Fa Shi Lei* (*The Legal Provisions and Cases*) was another innovation in the style of codification in the Song Dynasty, which had provided a blueprint for the formation of the codes of the Yuan Dynasty. So it was the third feature of the legislation in Song Dynasty.

The land policy of free land annexation in the Song Dynasty had not only promoted land trade but also fostered the development of the whole commodity economy and changed the traditional view of stressing "Yi" (justice) and neglecting "Li" (benefit). Li Gou in the Northern Song Dynasty pointed out for the first time that "human beings are benefit-oriented, why don't people talk about it? ... Desire is the nature of human beings, why don't people talk about it?"[24] In the Southern Song Dynasty, "Shi Gong Xue Pai" (utilitarian school), which advocated utilitarianism,

---

[23]"Xing Fa Zhi" (The Record of the Criminal Law) (Part 1) in *Song Shi* (*The History of Song Dynasty*).
[24]Li Gou (Song Dynasty), "Yuan Wen" (The Original Text) in *Li Gou Ji* (*Collected Works of Li Gou*).

began to spring up, and Chen Liang, one of the representatives of this school, stated that "when one achieves success, he achieves virtue; so success just means rationality."[25] Ye Shi and Chen Qiqing also criticized the theory and the policy of "Zhong Nong Yi Mo" (encouraging agriculture and restraining commerce). Ye Shi said, "The four kinds of people get what they need by exchanges and then it is possible for the county to become prosperous and the people moralized. Therefore, the theory of 'Yi Mo Hou Ben' (emphasizing agriculture and neglecting commerce) is wrong."[26] Zheng Zhidao also said that "in old times, people were classified into four groups, namely, 'Shi' (scholars), 'Nong' (peasant), 'Gong' (artisan), 'Shang' (businessmen). If scholars study hard, they can achieve official titles; if peasants work hard in fields, they can get good harvests; if craftsmen work hard on handicrafts, they can get clothing and food; if businessmen work hard in business, they can accumulate wealth and goods. So these four groups of people are just doing their own work."[27]

Due to the impact of a commodity economy, not only "Shi Da Fu" (literati and officials) showed the tendency to betray the traditional ideology, but also the supreme monarch himself had advocated for wealth and profits. Emperor Shenzong of the Song dynasty once issued a decree and stated that "for the administrative affairs, the management of monetary matters are the most urgent,"[28] so "if any officials working in or out of the imperial court know the business of managing monetary matters, please present memorials to me to make detailed reports on the matter."[29]

The change from stressing "Yi" (justice) and neglecting "Li" (benefit) to stressing both "Yi" (justice) and "Li" (benefit) was caused by the developing commodity economy and was also the reason for the further development of such economy. Under such circumstances, the legal norms employed to adjust civil relationships were further enriched and developed. In *Song Xing Tong* (*The Penal Code of Song Dynasty*), more provisions were made for adjusting civil relationships than those in *Tang Lv Shu Yi* (*The Comments on Tang Code*). For example, in "Hu Hun Lv" (Statues on Marriage, Tax and Household Registration) in *Song Xing Tong* (*The Penal Code of Song Dynasty*), the categories "Hu Jue Zi Chan" (no male heirs to succeed the household property), "Si Shang Qian Wu" (money and goods for the dead and injured), "Dian Mai Zhi Dang Lun Jing Wu Ye" (the property mortgaged or

---

[25]Chen Liang (Song Dynasty), "Zhi Chen Tong Fu Shu" (A Letter to Chen Tongfu) in *Chen Liang Ji* (*Collected Works of Chen Liang*), Vol. 29.

[26]Ye Shi (Song Dynasty), "Ping Zhun Shu" (On Fair Trade) in "Shi Ji" (The Records of the Grand Historian) (Part 1) in *Xi Xue Ji Yan* (*Notes of Learning*), Vol. 19.

[27]Chen Qiqing (Song Dynasty), "Zhong Ben Ye" (Emphasis of the Essence) in "Yu Su Qi Pian" (Seven Writings of Yu Su) in *Jia Ding Chi Cheng Zhi* (*Records on Chicheng in Jiading*), Vol. 37.

[28]"Shi Huo Zhi" (The Records of National Finance and Economy) in *Song Shi* (*The History of Song Dynasty*) (Book 2), Vol. 8.

[29]"Yan Cai Li Ke Cai Lu Shi Shi Zhe Zhen Shang Zhao" (Decrees on Rewards for Those Whose Suggestions of Monetary Matter Management Have Been Accepted) in "Cai Li" (Money and Profits) (Part 2) in *Song Da Zhao Ling Ji* (*Collected Grand Edicts and Decrees of Song Dynasty*), Vol. 184.

sold through discussion and bargain), and "Hun Tian Ru Wu" (The Matters of Marriage and Land) were added, which were not included in the codes of previous dynasties. In *Song Xing Tong* (*The Penal Code of Song Dynasty*), detailed and elaborate regulations were also stipulated on the inheritance of the property of households without male heirs, the handling of the money and goods for the dead and injured, the punishment of the young and the inferior of the households for their mortgaging the fields and houses or the pawning of the property without authorization, the time limit for the legal proceedings of marriage and land litigation, the standards for pawning the property, and the principles of handling lost property.

Additionally, a series of civil laws were made, such as *Hu Jue Tiao Guan* (*Regulations on Households with no Male Heirs*), *Yi Zhu Cai Chan Tiao Fa* (*Regulations on Will and Property*), *Yuan Feng Shi Bo Fa Fa Ze* (*Rules for Shipping in Yuanfeng*), *Hu Jue Tian Chi* (*Imperial Decrees on Households with no Male Heirs*), and *Hu Hun Chi* (*Imperial Instructions on Household and Marriage*). The government did not consider disputes over land among the people as "trivial matters" any more; instead, it was stressed that "the civil affairs are the most important thing in administration,"[30] which could be proved by the judgments on civil cases recorded in *Ming Gong Shu Pan Qing Ming Ji* (*Collections of Enlightened Judgments*).

The rich contents of civil law in the Song Dynasty had reflected both the needs of social life and the importance attached to the protection of private ownership. Many economic laws were also made to solve financial problems, so it was the fourth feature of the legislation in Song Dynasty.

In summary, the three hundred years of legislative activities in the Northern and Southern Song dynasties were imprinted with the characteristics of the times, and in many aspects the achievements of the Song Dynasty were greater than those of the Sui and Tang dynasties. In the Song Dynasty, legislative technology was also obviously improved and historical experiences that could be used for reference were accumulated. For example, during the reign of Emperor Shenzong, in the process of drafting special laws, much attention was paid to extensive discussions before they were used in trials. For example, "Mian Yi Fa" (the law on the exemption of compulsory service) issued in "Xi Feng Reform" was made after several discussions were held in the imperial court. Then it was tried out in "Zhou" (subprefecture) and "Xian" (county) and was "publicized to the public for a month." After "being approved by citizens, its real effect was then tested."[31] So it was not until the whole procedure was performed that it was made into a new law and implemented countrywide, which had fully shown their serious attitude toward legislation. This was also an important measure taken to ensure that the newly made law can meet the real needs of the society. Although the measure was not completely carried out, the

---

[30]Li Xinchuan (Song Dynasty), *Jian Yan Yi Lai Xi Nian Yao Lu* (*An Annual Record of the Most Important Events since the Reign of Jianyan*), Vol. 159, in April in the 19th year of Shaoxing.

[31]"Shi Huo Zhi" (The Records of National Finance and Economy) in *Song Shi* (*The History of Song Dynasty*) (Book 1), Vol. 5.

procedure for making it was still what was worth learning from among the legislative activities during the Song dynasty.

In the Song Dynasty, because there were a variety of legal forms and old and new laws were simultaneously implemented, there was great confusion in terms of law enforcement. This was taken advantage of by judicial officials, who made use of laws to obtain personal gains at their whim. Xia Song during the Song Dynasty opined that "the provisions in 'Lv' (criminal law), 'Ling' (decree), 'Ge' (injunction), 'Shi' (standard) and the articles in *Song Xing Tong* (*The Penal Code of Song Dynasty*) and *Bian Chi* (*The Collection of Instructions*) were not only all mixed up, but also contradictory to each other. Moreover, the wicked officials often engaged in malpractices for selfish ends, so they were guilty for passing unjust judgments in red ink."[32]

8.2 The Administrative Law for Strengthening the Centralization of Authority

In accordance with the basic national policy of strengthening the autocratic centralization system, a huge bureaucratic organization was set up in the Song Dynasty, and the administrative system was started to be reformed. In order to confirm the new administrative system and to maintain the mutual relationship and effective operation of the state organs, many administrative laws were made and normalized. Apart from the comprehensive administrative laws in the twenty two categories of "Zhi Zhi Lv" (Statutes on the State Office System) included in *Song Xing Tong* (*The Penal Code of Song Dynasty*), corresponding administrative laws and regulations were also made on the organization and management of administrative institutions, the selection of officials through "Ke Ju" (the imperial examination), the assessment of officials, officials' ranks and salaries, supervisory affairs, etc. Especially in *Qing Yuan Tiao Fa Shi Lei* (*The Legal Provisions and Cases Made in the Year of Qingyuan*), which was compiled and revised by Xie Shenfu in the Southern Song Dynasty, "Chi" (instruction), "Ling" (decree), "Ge" (injunction), and "Shi" (standard) were collected, and the illustrations attached to imperial decrees, issued for sixty years from the early years of the Southern Song Dynasty to the years of Qingyuan, were added. Besides, a two-volume appendix titled *Kai Xi Chong Xiu Shang Shu Li Bu Shi Lang You Xuan Ge* (*The Revised Injunction for the Election of Ministers and Deputy Ministers of the Department of Personnel in Kaixi Period*), which was a part of *Kai Xi Chong Xiu Qi Si Fa* (*The Newly Revised Law for Seven Bureaus in Kaixi Period*), enacted in March of the 2nd year of Kaixi (1206 A.D.), was included. Therefore, a large number of materials on administrative law were included in *Qing Yuan Tiao Fa Shi Lei* (*The Legal Provisions and Cases Made in the*

---

[32]Huang Wei, Yang Shiqi (Ming Dynasty), "Fa Ling" (Decree) in *Li Dai Ming Chen Zou Yi* (*Memorials Submitted to the Emperor by the Famous Officials in Different Dynasties*), Vol. 210.

8.2 The Administrative Law for Strengthening the Centralization of Authority

Year of Qingyuan). So from the two categories of *Qing Yuan Tiao Fa Shi Lei* (*The Legal Provisions and Cases Made in the Year of Qingyuan*), namely, "Zhi Zhi" (Statutes on the State Office System) and "Wen Shu" (Official Documents), it can be seen that this law did cover a large scope of subject matter.

For example, in the category of "Zhi Zhi" (Statutes on the State Office System), the following contents are included: the duties of officials, presenting oneself before the emperor, presenting memorials to the emperor, the appeals of the ministers, imperial inspectors delaying time, appointing and removing officials from their offices, the examinations for selecting officials, the assessment of officials, filling out official forms, official missions, taking official posts, imperial selection of officials, staying at home and waiting for appointment, prison, inspection tour made by inspectors, inspectors' informing against others, the inspection tours of "Xun Wei" (an official just below the magistrate of county), inspecting pickets, discussing and commenting on public affairs, determining the scales of architecture, revealing information in transmission, officials' relatives being suspected for committing crimes, exchanging official positions, dismissing and appointing officials in local governments, being dismissed from office and being exempted from compulsory service, leaving official positions without authorization, and welcoming and bidding farewell. Additionally, provisions on the following were made: officials committing crimes together with their colleagues, dispatching and borrowing objects in one's supervisory area, courier stations, entering offices without permission, current officials moving houses, being picked up and seen off by official staff, asking other official staff for help, officials being on duty, dispatching and borrowing boats, sending for doctors to look after parents, asking for leave, retirement, laying down one's life for the country, bounties bestowed by a monarch or an official, bestowing and conferring official titles upon the descendants of the meritorious, promoting and demoting through assessments, petitioning to send awards to others, rewarding, promoting dismissed officials, the death of officials, etc.

In the category of official documents, the following were included: imperial edicts and instructions, amnesty, official documents, authorizing and dispatching documents, filing documents, records of receiving and delivering documents, printing documents through woodblock printing, destruction and loss of official documents, pawning or selling documents, owning forbidden books privately, etc.

In the Song Dynasty, although collections of administrative laws were not made in the form of code, unlike *Tang Liu Dian* (*The Six Statutes of Tang Dynasty*), to a certain extent, *Qing Yuan Tiao Fa Shi Lei* (*The Legal Provisions and Cases Made in the Year of Qingyuan*) could be referred to as a compilation of administrative law. Apart from *Qing Yuan Tiao Fa Shi Lei* (*The Legal Provisions and Cases Made in the Year of Qingyuan*), the codes that are retained up to present include *Li Bu Qi Si Fa* (*Law for Seven Bureaus of the Department of Personnel*) and *Jing Ding Li Bu Tiao Li* (*Regulations for the Department of Personnel in Jingding Period*).

8.2.1 The System Reform for Strengthening the Centralization of Authority

In order to strengthen the centralized authority, in the Song Dynasty, both central and local administrative systems were extensively reformed and adjusted. In the Song Dynasty, the system of "San Sheng" (the three departments), which was carried out in the Tang Dynasty, was followed, but it was separated from the system of "Zai Xiang" (the prime minister):

> "Zhong Shu Ling" (head of the secretariat), "Shi Zhong" (assistant officers) and "Shang Shu Ling" (ancient official equivalent to prime minister) do not participate in the affairs of imperial court; "Shi Lang" (vice minister) and "Ji Shi" (an official title) are not responsible for the affairs of "San Sheng" (the three departments); "Jian Yi" (the Advisory Consultant) is not responsible of admonition "Qi Ju" (the Life Consultant) is not responsible for keeping records; "Zhong Shu Chang Que She Ren" (the official in charge of drafting imperial edicts), "Men Xia Han Chu Tang Si" (the Super Attendant) and "Si Jian" (advisor) and "Zheng Yan" (official in charge of offering advice) are not responsible for offering advice without the approval of special imperial edicts.[33]

The supreme administrative institution was "Zhong Shu Men Xia" (the supreme state organization), but it was different from that in the Tang Dynasty because it was not joined with the institution of "Zai Xiang" (the prime minister) but was an administrative institution independent from "San Sheng" (the three departments). Its chief was referred to as "Zhong Shu Men Xia Ping Zhang Shi," who performed the job of "Zai Xiang" (the prime minister). Usually there were two to three members in the institution, and the size of the institution was not fixed. "Can Zhi Zheng Shi" (deputy prime minister) was the deputy "Zai Xiang" (the prime minister). "Zhong Shu Men Xia" (the supreme state organization) had the rights to issue orders to subordinate agencies, and the subordinate agencies had the responsibility of reporting directly to "Zhong Shu Men Xia" (the supreme state organization), which was described as "assisting the emperor, governing the officials, dealing with the daily affairs and taking charge of the routines in every aspect."[34] But military power was shared by "Shu Mi Yuan" (Privy Council), financial power was divided between the "San Si Shi" (Inspectors of the Three Departments), and all the affairs, minor or major, should be reported to the emperor to be handled according to imperial edicts. Thus, the power of "Zai Xiang" (the prime minister) was weaker than before. Emperor Taizong even appointed seven "Zai Xiang" (prime ministers) at the same time so that there was no chance for any of them to grab all the power for themselves. Additionally, Emperor Taizong, in setting up "Chai Qian Yuan" (the bureau of missions), "Shen Xing Yuan" (The Case Review Court), "Li Jian Si" (official in charge of supervising the counties and towns), "Shen Guan

---

[33]"Xing Fa Zhi" (The Record of the Criminal Law) (Part 1) in *Song Shi* (*The History of Song Dynasty*).

[34]"Xing Fa Zhi" (The Record of the Criminal Law) (Part 1) in *Song Shi* (*The History of Song Dynasty*).

8.2 The Administrative Law for Strengthening the Centralization of Authority

Yuan" (a bureau responsible for investigating officials after they had committed crimes), and "Kao Ke Yuan" (the bureau of assessment), further weakened the power of "Zai Xiang" (the prime minister) in handling national affairs. The rights of "Zai Xiang" (the prime minister) to use "Zha Zi" (official letters) to give instructions to his subordinates was also restricted by the order issued in July of the 2nd year of Taizong (996 A.D.). It was ordered that "from today forward, all the important affairs must be reported to the emperor for decision; if 'Zha Zi' needs to be used, it should also be reported to the emperor at once"[35]; otherwise, the subordinate offices had the right to seal "Zha Zi" (official letters) and present them to the emperor by themselves. The weakened power of "Zai Xiang" (the prime minister) in the Song Dynasty showed the strengthening of imperial power.

In the early period of the Song Dynasty, the change of the administrative management system had no doubt strengthened the centralization of power, but at the same time, it led to many problems, such as the overlapping of institutions, the fragmentary allocation of duties, the redundancy of officials, and lower administrative efficiency. Therefore, in the 5th year of Yuanfeng during the reign of Emperor Shenzong (1082 A.D.), a major administrative institution reform was carried out based on *Tang Liu Dian* (*The Six Statutes of Tang Dynasty*); consequently, the system of "San Sheng Liu Bu" (Three Departments and Six Ministries) was adopted. Under the reform, "Zai Xiang" (the prime minister) began to take charge of "San Sheng" (the three departments) and was given more power, which was referred to as "authorizing power to 'Zhong Shu Sheng' (the supreme organization in charge of the state affairs)."[36] This reform launched by Emperor Shenzong was carried out after the centralized authority was consolidated, so it was helpful to be aware of the political conflicts to authorize "Zai Xiang" (the prime minister) some real power. In the Song Dynasty, different titles were given to "Zai Xiang" (the prime minister), but during the reign of Emperor Xiaozong in the Southern Song Dynasty, the title of "Zai Xiang" (the prime minister) was finally settled, and it was called "Zuo Cheng Xiang" (the chief prime minister) and "You Cheng Xiang" (the deputy prime minister). The deputy "Zai Xiang" (prime minister) was called "Can Zhi Zheng Shi" (deputy prime minister).

In order to command a large army with millions of soldiers and to deal with the problems caused by domestic trouble and foreign aggression, "Shu Mi Yuan" (Privy Council) was established as the highest military administrative institution following the old systems of "Wu Dai" (the Five Dynasties), which was "responsible for the confidential military work, defense, border garrison and military orders. Besides, it was also responsible for carrying out confidential missions to help to handle the state affairs, to manage the duties of guards, to recruit soldiers to safeguard the palace, to

---

[35]*Xu Zi Zhi Tong Jian Chang Bian* (*Sequel to the Full-length Book of History as a Mirror*), Vol. 40, in July of the 2nd year of Zhidao.

[36]"Guan Zhi" (The State Official System) in *Yu Hai* (*The Jade Ocean*), Vol. 121.

examine and evaluate official's performance, to appoint and promote officials, to open up wasteland in border areas, and to give rewards and enforce punishments."[37]

The head of "Shu Mi Yuan" (Privy Council) was referred to as "Shu Mi Shi" and had the same rank as "Zai Xiang" (the prime minister), so the head of "Shu Mi Yuan" and "Zai Xiang" (the prime minister) were referred to as "Er Fu" (the two governmental offices) in the Song Dynasty, through which "orders were issued" by the imperial court.[38] By setting up "Shu Mi Yuan" (Privy Council), the imperial court not only strengthened the management of military forces but also further centralized military power so that the army was firmly controlled by the emperor, which had become an important link in strengthening the centralization of authority. In the reform, it was suggested that "Shu Mi Yuan" (Privy Council) be abolished, but the suggestion was rejected by Emperor Shenzong. He said, "It is forbidden by my ancestors to allow a particular department to control the military power, so instead they appointed particular ministers to take the charge to check and balance the power, so why should I abolish it?"[39] However, even though it was convenient for the emperor to control "Er Fu" (the two governmental offices) to maintain a balance between them, it was difficult for them to cooperate with each other when dealing with political affairs. When "Shu Mi Shi" (the director of Privy Council) "went to the emperor to report the state affairs, 'Zhong Shu' (the Prime Minister) would do the same thing, but they did not know what the other might have said, so they became suspicious of each other." Consequently, "'Zhong Shu' (the Prime Minister) wanted to launch an attack, but 'Shu Mi Shi' (the director of Privy Council) just wanted to defend. How can orders be issued uniformly?"[40] In order to resolve the conflict, in war time, "Zai Xiang" (the prime minister) often held the concurrent post of "Shu Mi Shi" (the director of Privy Council). After Emperor Lizong's reign in the Southern Song Dynasty, the political problems became more serious, so it became a custom for "Zai Xiang" (the prime minister) to hold the concurrent post of "Shu Mi Shi" (the director of Privy Council). Even though "Shu Mi Yuan" (Privy Council) and "Zhong Shu Men Xia" (the supreme state organization) were called "Er Fu" (the two government offices), the position of the former was slightly lower, so the rank of its chief official was equal to deputy "Zai Xiang" (the prime minister).

In order to solve the financial problems, "San Si" (The Three Departments), namely, "Yan Tie Si" (The Department of Salt and Iron), "Du Zhi Si" (The Department of Finance), and "Hu Bu Si" (The Department of Revenue), was set up as the supreme financial institution responsible for tax collection, expenditure of and income from money and grain, and household registration over the country. Although the position of "San Si" (The Three Departments) was slightly lower than

---

[37]"Xing Fa Zhi" (The Record of the Criminal Law) (Part 2) in *Song Shi* (*The History of Song Dynasty*).

[38]"Tang Han Zhuan" (The Biography of Tanghan) in *Song Shi* (*The History of Song Dynasty*).

[39]"Xing Fa Zhi" (The Record of the Criminal Law) (Part 2) in *Song Shi* (*The History of Song Dynasty*).

[40]Wang Mingqing (Song Dynasty), *Hui Zhu Hou Lu* (*The Notes by Wang Mingqing*), Vol. 1.

that of "Er Fu" (the two government offices), since finance played a special role for the subsistence of the country, the power of the ministers of "San Si" (The Three Departments) became so great that they were called "Ji Xiang" (the prime minister responsible for finance).

Since "She Guan Yuan" (a bureau responsible for investigating officials after they had committed crimes) was set up outside of "Li Bu" (The Department of Personnel) and "Shen Xing Yuan" (The Case Review Court) was set up outside of "Xing Bu" (The Department of Punishment), the power of "Liu Bu" (The Six Departments) was obviously weakened.

In view of the functions of the local administration system, great changes were made to stop separatism and to consolidate the power of the central government. Generally speaking, local power was weakened, and the central government had a much stricter control over local power.

In the early period of the Song Dynasty, two levels of local administrative organization, namely "Zhou" (subprefecture) and "Xian" (county), were set up. In order to prevent local officials from forming cliques and grabbing central power, the position of magistrate in "Zhou" (subprefecture) and "Xian" (county) was held by the local officials or the magistrates were appointed by the imperial court. Especially, during the reign of Emperor Taizu, the military power of "Jie Du Shi" (military governor) and the financial and the administrative power of "Zhou" (subprefecture) and "Xian" were all taken back by the central government, and the system of "Fan Zhen" (local regime), which was in charge of the administration of outlying prefectures, was abolished. Consequently, "Jie Du Shi" (the military governor) accepted the empty titles of generals, ministers, and meritorious royal relatives and thus "was strictly controlled by the government with no chances of resistance."[41] This was the most important method that the emperors used in the Southern and Northern dynasties to successfully centralize the power.

In order to strengthen control over the local governments, the system of the Tang Dynasty was followed, so "Jian Cha Qu" (supervisory areas) was established above "Dao" (the administration district below the province), while "Lu" (ancient administrative region) was set up above "Zhou" (subprefecture), the highest level of local administration. Under "Lu" (ancient administrative region), "Jing Lue An Fu Shi" (ancient official, head of 'Lu', responsible for military affairs) was set up, which was responsible for military affairs. "Zhuan Yun Shi" (official in charge of transportation) (named "Cao Si" in the Southern Song Dynasty) was set up to be in charge of collecting taxes from one or several supervisory areas. Except for the necessary appropriation expenditure, all tax collected by "Zhou" (subprefecture) should be transferred to the central government by "Zhuan Yun Shi" (official in charge of transportation). Later on, "Zhuan Yun Shi" (official in charge of transportation) was granted more power to take charge of the affairs of defense, public security, money, grain, and supervision. Therefore, they became the chief officials above "Fu"

---

[41]"Chen Liang Zhuan" (The Biography of Chen Liang) in "Ru Lin Zhuan" (The Biography of the Confucian Scholars) in *Song Shi* (*The History of Song Dynasty*) (Book 6).

(ancient administrative district between province and county) and "Zhou" (subprefecture). Moreover, "Ti Dian Xing Yu" (judicial commission, which was named "Xian Si" in the Southern Song Dynasty) was set up to take charge of justice, and "Ti Ju Chang Ping Shi" (official in charge of relief and water conservancy) was set up to take charge of the relief work in disaster areas or the iron and salt business. The four institutions mentioned were not attached to each other, but they supervised each other and were only responsible to the emperor.

"Fu" (ancient administrative district between province and county), "Zhou" (subprefecture), "Jun" (shire), and "Jian" (ancient supervisory office) were at the same administrative level, and they were very important organizations for local government and tax collection. However, the position of "Fu" (ancient administrative district between province and county) was higher than that of "Zhou" (subprefecture), which were later also raised to the level of "Fu" (ancient administrative district between province and county) because the emperor used to be the head of "Zhou" (subprefecture) before he ascended the throne. "Jun" (shire) was a military region in the Tang Dynasty, but it became an administrative region after "Wu Dai" (the Five Dynasties); "Jian" (ancient supervisory office) was set up in mining areas and was not responsible for civil affairs. At this level of administration, "Zhou" (subprefecture) was the main administrative organization, while there were only a small number of "Fu" (ancient administrative district between province and county), "Jun" (shire), and "Jian" (ancient supervisory office). Moreover, "Jun" (shire) and "Jian" (ancient supervisory office) had no rights of jurisdiction over "Xian" (county), and the heads of "Fu" (ancient administrative district between province and county), "Zhou" (subprefecture), "Jun" (shire), and "Jian" (ancient supervisory office) were called "Zhi Fu," "Zhi Zhou," "Zhi Jun," and "Zhi Jian," respectively, who were appointed by the emperor to prevent powerful military officers in the local areas from defying orders of the imperial government. In the early years of Emperor Taizong, the heads of "Zhou" (subprefecture) and "Jun" (shire) along the northwest borders were all civil officials. Since the imperial court was afraid that "Zhi Zhou" (subprefectural magistrates) would become too powerful and would act as counterweights to the central government, two Chinese characters, namely, "Quan Zhi" (temporarily acting as), were added to official titles, such as "Quan Zhi Zhou Shi" (temporary head of subprefecture), to show that "if the official do not deserve their titles," "they can not stay in their positions for long." Then it was clearly stipulated that "the magistrates of the local areas should be changed every three years" and that the officials are not allowed to take posts in their hometown to prevent the officials from setting up separatist regimes. Additionally, in all "Fu" (ancient administrative district between province and county) and "Zhou" (subprefecture), the post of "Tong Pan" (official in charge of agriculture, water conservancy, and litigation under subprefecture) was set up to be in charge of "reporting the affairs to the emperor" by sharing the powers of "Zhi Fu" (magistrate of a prefecture) and "Zhi Zhou" (subprefectural magistrates). "Tong Pan" (official in charge of agriculture, water conservancy, and litigation under subprefecture), who functioned as the supervisor, was responsible for financial as well as other affairs in "Zhou" (subprefecture). Besides, all orders issued by "Zhou" (subprefecture) were invalid if they were not signed by "Tong Pan," who was in charge of reporting the affairs of "Zhou" (subprefecture) to the emperor at any time, so it appears that they became the spies of the emperor in the local places; therefore, they were referred to as "monitors of subprefectures." Nevertheless, although it seemed that "Tong Pan" (official in charge of agriculture, water conservancy, and litigation under subprefecture) had great power, they gradually became the deputy governors of "Zhou" (subprefecture) with the consolidation of the system of centralization of authority.

"Zhi Xian" (magistrate of a county) was the head of "Xian" (county). At the time of "Wu Dai" (the Five Dynasties), military officers (namely, "Zhen Jiang" or general of defense) were often appointed and sent to "Xian" (county) by "Jie Du Shi" (military governor) to take charge of local affairs, but this situation was changed. However, the position of "Xian Wei" (commandant of county) was restored to be in charge of the catching and arrest of thieves and other judicial affairs. If there were cases of theft, it was the responsibility of "Xian Wei" (commandant of county) to have the thieves arrested.

Below the level of "Xian" (county), basic level organizations such as "Du Bao" (grassroots organization consisting of five hundred households), "Da Bao" (grassroots organization consisting of fifty households), "Bao" (grassroots organization consisting of ten households), etc. were established

In summary, the change of local administrative system was described by Fan Zuyu:

> The power of the heads of "Xiang" (townships) and "Zhen Jiang" (general of defense) was taken back and given to "Xian" (county); the power of "Xian" (county) was taken back and given to "Zhou" (subprefecture); the power of "Zhou" (subprefecture) was taken back and given to "Jian Si" (official with right of supervising counties and towns); the power of "Jian Si" was taken back and given to the imperial court.[42]

After the later period of the Tang Dynasty, the separatists in "Fan Zhen" (local regimes) who had "once dominated several 'Zhou' (subprefecture) and who had acted as a counterweight to the imperial court by relying on their military forces"[43] were almost wiped out. As a result, the central government had a tighter control over the local government.

The characteristics of the administrative system of the Song Dynasty are as follows.

Firstly, the central and local administrative system was changed to strengthen the authority of the central government, so that the power of the local government was seriously weakened and it was unable to act in emergency cases.

Secondly, "the official titles were separated from their responsibilities," and "the names of offices was separated from their functions," which had caused the

---

[42] Fan Zuyu (Song Dynasty), "Zhuan Dui Tiao Shang Si Shi Zhuang" (Four Reports to the Emperor on the State Affairs) in *Fan Tai Shi Ji* (*Collected Works of Fan Taishi*), Vol. 22.

[43] Wen Tianxiang (Ming Dynasty), "Ji Wei Shang Huang Di Shu"(A Memorial to the Emperor in the Year of Ji Wei) in *Wen Shan Xian Sheng Quan Ji* (*Complete Works of Mr. Wen Shan*), Vol. 3.

overlapping of and confusion among government institutions. Consequently, although the officials had official ranks and salaries, they had no real power because their official titles were just nominal. For example, "Dian Ge Xue Shi" (scholar of imperial court) was an honorary title granted to renowned senior officials, and only the officials with the title of "Chai Qian" (being dispatched) had the real power to take charge of the responsibilities, which led to the situation where "Shang Shu" (the minister) was sent to handle the affairs that were put in the charge of "Zhi Zhou" (subprefectural magistrates). The purpose of setting up the system was to prevent officials from usurping their power, but it had caused so much confusion in the official system that "about eighty or ninety percent of the officials of 'Pu She' (the supervisor of other officials), 'Shang Shu' (the minister), 'Cheng' (councilor), 'Lang' (vice minister), 'Yuan Wai' (deputy head of a subministry department or an honorary title) were not clear about their responsibilities."[44] During the reign of Emperor Zhenzong, it was suggested by some officials that the number of redundant staff should be cut down, so it turned out that there were totally more than 195,000 redundant officials. In the Southern Song Dynasty, "compared with the previous periods, the amount of land of 'Zhou' (subprefecture) and 'Xian' (county) was greatly reduced, but the land which the officials owned was almost five times more than that before."[45]

Thirdly, high salaries were paid to officials. During the reign of Emperor Taizu, "the military power of his generals were deprived of by the means of 'Bei Jiu' (cups of wine or peaceful methods)"; he gave them plenty of gold, silver, farmland, and beautiful houses in exchange for their military power. Later on, in order to give full play to the function of the bureaucratic institution, meet the needs of the officials, and strengthen the ruling of the autocratic monarchy, the high salary system was carried out by the imperial court. According to the system, the officials' salary included the following: official salary (maximum was 400,000 *qian*), grain subsidy (maximum was 100 *dan* per month), post subsidy, administrative expenses, rewarded farmland (maximum was 40 *qing*), expenses for tea, allowance for business trips, allowance for food, allowance for coal, etc. In addition, the officials were given money to pay for the employment of servants and their clothes and food supply. The senior officials could employ one hundred servants, and the expenses for the food of each servant was thirty *wen*; as to the expenses for the clothing of the servants, each *pi* of silk was one *guan*, each *pi* of cotton cloth was three hundre and fifty *wen* (a monetary unit, one *wen* is 1/1000th *guan* of money), and each *liang* of cotton was forty *wen*. Clearly, after becoming an official, his clothes, food, and other necessities would be provided on time by the imperial court. During the time when Fan Zhongyan was "Can Zhi Zheng Shi" (deputy prime minister), the reward that the

---

[44]"Zhi Guan Zhi" (The Record of State Officials) in *Song Shi* (*The History of Song Dynasty*) (Book 1).

[45]Song Qi (Song Dynasty),"Shang San Rong San Fei Shu" (A Memorial to the Emperor about Three Redundant and Unnecessary Charges) in *Jing Wen Ji* (*The Collected Works of Jing Wen*), Vol. 26.

emperor gave to him was one thousand *mu* of good farmland in the suburb of Suzhou. So the case is that "the emperor was always worried that the rewards given to his officials were not enough, while the common people's wealth was all plundered with nothing left."[46] However, the generous salaries offered to those officials had not eliminated the corruption and greediness of those bureaucrats.

8.2.2 The Enrichment of the Official Administrative Law

8.2.2.1 The Selection, Assessment, Grading, and Retirement of Officials

In the Song Dynasty, in order to strengthen the management of the large groups of officials, their selection, appointment, transfer, assessment, reward, and punishment were all standardized and regulated by law. In the Song Dynasty, even though there were many channels for selecting officials, undoubtedly the most important one was the system of "Ke Ju" (the imperial examination). In the early period of the Song Dynasty, "Ke Ju" (the imperial examination) was held once a year, while during the reign of Emperor Shenzong, "it was held once every three years," so it had become a custom since then. With the development of a feudal economy, the number of landlords with medium-sized and small-sized farms greatly increased, so they were required to take part in government administration by way of "Ke Ju" (the imperial examination); moreover, in order to consolidate the foundation for the centralization of authority, the emperor needed to enlist the services of the gifted "Shi Da Fu" (literati and officials) and to control their ideology, as was described in the saying that "in the holy dynasty (Song Dynasty), the door of 'Ke Ju' (the imperial examination) is widely open, so everyone hopes to sit and pass the examination instead of giving themselves up or fooling around together with the thieves and evil people.".[47]

At the beginning, the contents of "Ke Ju" (the imperial examination) focused on poetry and prose and sometimes on Confucian classics and argumentation. During the reign of Emperor Renzong, Ou Yangxiu and Fan Zhongyan suggested that the subjects of the examination should be political discourses so that the candidates of "Ke Ju" (the imperial examination) could pay more attention to the proper ways of administering. Since then, the discourses on politics became the major subjects of the examination. It should be especially pointed out that because Emperor Taizong had encouraged "the students of Confucian classics to read and be familiar with law and the judicial officials to read and be familiar with the Confucian classics,"[48] "Ming Fa Ke" (the subject of law) was introduced, so law became an important

---

[46]Zhao Yi (Qing Dynasty), "Song Zhi Lu Zhi Hou" (The High Official Salaries of the Song Dynasty) in *Er Shi Er Shi Zha Ji* (*Reading Notes of the Twenty-Two Official Histories*), Vol. 25.

[47]Wang Yong (Song Dynasty), *Yan Yi Yi Mou Lu* (*Well-Planned for Posterity*), Vol. 1.

[48]"Xuan Ju Kao" (An Examination of Election) (Part 5) in *Wen Xian Tong Kao* (*A General Textual Research of the Documents*), Vol. 32.

subject of "Ke Ju" (the imperial examination). When reform was carried out by Emperor Shenzong, "Ming Fa Ke" (the subject of law) became very popular, so the candidates would be enrolled only if "they can master the basic principles of 'Lv' (criminal law), 'Ling' (decree), 'Xing Tong' (penal code and law), and 'Da Yi' (cardinal principles of righteousness), or if they can settle the lawsuits according to law."[49] Indeed, the examination subjects in "Ke Ju" (the imperial examination) had played a guiding role, as was once said by a famous minister named Peng Ruli in the period of Emperor Shenzong: "The scholars do not have legal knowledge, but after the law is taken as a subject of the examination by Your Majesty, everyone is talking about the law."[50]

As to the methods of examination, three methods were used by the imperial court, namely, "Hu Ming" (concealing the name of the examinee on the test paper), "Teng Lu" (transcribing the test paper by others), and "Hui Bi Zhi Du" (the avoidance system) (the directors and other officials of the examination authority must recuse themselves from marking their relatives' examination papers) in order to avoid fraudulent practices in the examination. The methods of "Ke Ju" (the imperial examination) used in the Song Dynasty were followed by the later dynasties.

In order to make it easier for rulers to control "Ke Ju" (the imperial examination), "Dian Shi" (the final imperial examination) was further institutionalized, and the emperor himself would preside over the final imperial examination to select talents every three years. In view of the malpractice where "Zuo Zhu" (the official in charge of the civil examination) and "Men Sheng" (examinee) often formed different political groups to attack each other during the Tang Dynasty, an imperial edict was issued, which ordered that "it is forbidden for the selected candidates to express their gratitude to the masters privately"[51] because the examinees could only be the "Men Sheng" (examinee) of the emperor. Moreover, they were forbidden to refer to the chief officials responsible for the examination as "great teachers" or "respected teachers," and they were also forbidden to call themselves "Men Sheng" (examinee).

Because the family background and social status of the candidates were not made a criteria for taking "Ke Ju" (the imperial examination), even Buddhist monks and Taoist priests and people of other schools of thoughts could all take the imperial examination, so the sources of enlisting talents were broadened and the democratic color of the imperial examination was added. Accordingly, the number of enrolled students and selected officials was increased. Take "Jin Shi Ke" (the most difficult exam in the imperial examination: usually Confucian classics and poetry would be examined) as an example: in the Tang Dynasty, there were no more than twenty or thirty people who passed "Ke Ju" (the imperial examination) for "Jin Shi" (those

---

[49]"Xuan Ju Kao" (An Examination of Election) (Part 4) in *Wen Xian Tong Kao* (*A General Textual Research of the Documents*), Vol. 31.

[50]"Feng Su" (The Customs and Habits) (Part 2) in *Li Dai Ming Chen Zou Yi* (*Memorials Submitted to the Emperor by the Famous Officials in Different Dynasties*), Vol. 116.

[51]Zeng Gong (Song Dynasty), "Gong Ju" (The Civil Examination) in "Ben Chao Zheng Yao Ce" (Important Political Policy of the Dynasty) in *Yuan Feng Lei Gao* (*The Collected Works of the Reign of Yuanfeng*), Vol. 49.

who passed the imperial examination at the national level in ancient China) at a time, but in the Song Dynasty, there were three classes for "Jin Shi" (those who passed the imperial examination at the national level in ancient China): the first was "Ji Di," the second was "Ci Jin Shi Chu Shen," and the third was "Ci Tong Jin Shi Chu Shen." Usually, the total number of enrollment of "Jin Shi" (those who passed the imperial examination at the national level in ancient China) was about two to three hundred, and sometimes it could reach to five to six hundred. In the Tang Dynasty, after enrollment, "Jin Shi" (those who passed the imperial examination at the national level in ancient China) would be qualified to be appointed as officials, so they were appointed to official positions only after they had passed the examination held by "Li Bu" (The Department of Personnel). However, in the Song Dynasty, as long as the candidates had passed the imperial examination, they could immediately be appointed officials by taking off their civilian clothes and putting on their official robes. Those who were at the top of the enrollment list could be appointed as "Zhu Shou Pan Guan" (an enrolled assistant to the chief local official), "Zhi Xian" (magistrate of a county), "Mu Zhi" (the subordinates of local officials), etc. During the early period of the Song Dynasty, many talented people, such as Wang Sizong, Lv Mengzheng, Su Yijian, Liang Hao, Cheng Su, Sun He, Sun Yue, Chen Yaozi, Wang Zeng, Li Di, Liang Gu, and Zhang Shide were selected through "Ke Ju" (the imperial examination), which showed that the reform of the imperial examination system had played a positive role in the Song Dynasty.

In order to create conditions for "Ke Ju" (the imperial examination) to cultivate reserve forces for the bureaucratic groups, in the Song Dynasty, schools that were subordinate to "Guo Zi Jian" (the highest educational body in ancient China) were set up in the capital and in "Lu" (ancient administrative region), "Zhou" (subprefecture), and "Xian" (county). "Guo Zi Sheng" refers to the descendants of the officials of "Qi Pin" (the seventh rank) or the ranks above it in the capital; "Tai Xue Sheng" refers to the descendants of the officials of "Qi Pin" (the seventh rank) or the ranks lower to it and the talented people. In the 2nd year of Yuanfeng (1079 A. D.), *Xue Ling (The Order on Education)* was issued, in which the number of students, the methods and time for the temporary and formal examination, the sources of the tuition fees, and so on were stipulated. In addition, it was forbidden for the teachers in "Zhou" (subprefecture) to have other jobs. If the school houses of "Zhou" (subprefecture) and "Xian" (county) were occupied for no reason, the violators would be punished by "Zhang" (flogging with heavy sticks) for one hundred strokes; "if those subordinates refused to move away from the school houses, they would be punished for the same offence."[52]

In addition to "Ke Ju" (the imperial examination) and "Chang Ke" (ordinary examination), there were also other channels for selecting officials, such as "Zhi Ju" (an examination subject temporarily set up) and "Jian Ju" (recommendation).

---

[52]"House and Courier Station" quoted from "Za Chi" (Miscellaneous Instructions) in "Zhi Zhi Men" (The Category of Official System) (Part 7) in *Qing Yuan Tiao Fa Shi Lei (The Legal Provisions and Cases Made in the Year of Qingyuan)*, Vol. 10.

According to "Xuan Ju Zhi" (The Record of Election) in *Song Shi* (*The History of Song Dynasty*), "'Chang Ke' (ordinary examination) is not set up in 'Zhi Ju' (an examination subject set up temporarily), so in order to select the great talents in the country, the emperor often sets the theme of the examination by himself."

In the early period of the Song Dynasty, senior department and provincial officials could recommend their subordinate officials in the capital or the chief officials of "Zhou" (subprefecture) and "Xian" (county) to be officials in the imperial court. "Zai Xiang" (the prime minister) and "Yu Shi" (the censor) could also recommend officials in the imperial court to be "Zhuan Yun Shi" (official in charge of transportation). In order to prevent officials from stooping to flattery and making false recommendation, the responsibilities of the officials who wanted to make recommendation were strictly regulated. If a referee had committed a crime, the referrer should be punished together with him. In the 1st year of Xi'ning, in view of the malpractice existing in the recommendation of officials, an imperial edict was issued to have the system abolished, so the task of selecting officials was granted to "Xuan Guan Yuan" (The Bureau of Official Selection) under "Li Bu" (The Department of Personnel). In the 1st year of Yuanyou during the reign of Emperor Zhezong (1086 A.D.), the recommendation system was restored and "Shi Ke Jian Ju Qu Shi Fa" (Ten Subjects for Recommending Officials) was issued.[53] The details are as follows.

First, if one is righteous, pure, and strong-willed, he can be recommended to "Shi Biao Ke" (the subject of "Shi Biao" or a model for others) (without considering whether he has an official title).

Second, if one has good moral integrity, he can be recommended to "Xian Na Ke" (the subject of "Na Xian" or an adviser) (he should have an official title).

Third, if one is extremely intelligent and courageous, he can be recommended to "Jiang Shuai Ke" (the subject of "Jiang Shuai" or a military general) (he should have a civil or military official title).

Fourth, if one is just and wise, he can be recommended to "Jian Si Ke" (the subject of "Jian Si" or an inspector) (he should have an official title of "Zhi Zhou" or a title higher).

Fifth, if one is proficient in Confucian classics, he can be recommended to "Jiang Du Ke" (the subject of "Jiang Du" or a teacher teaching Confucian classics) (without considering whether he has an official title);

Sixth, if one is knowledgeable, he can be recommended to "Gu Wen Ke" (the subject of "Gu Wen" or a consultant) (without considering whether he has an official title).

Seventh, if one's style of writing is elegant and graceful, he can be recommended to "Zhu Shu Ke" (the subject of "Zhu Shu" or a writer) (without considering whether he has an official title).

---

[53]"Shi Ke" (Ten Subjects) quoted from "Jian Ju Ge" (The Injunction for Recommendation) in "Xuan Ju Men" (The Category of Election) (Part 1) in *Qing Yuan Tiao Fa Shi Lei* (*The Legal Provisions and Cases Made in the Year of Qingyuan*), Vol. 14.

8.2 The Administrative Law for Strengthening the Centralization of Authority

Eighth, if one is just and competent to handle lawsuits, he can be recommended to "Gong De Shi Ke" (the subject of "Gong De Shi" or a member of the judiciary) (he should have an official title).

Ninth, if one is skillful in managing monetary matters, he can be recommended "Gong Si Ju Bian Ke" (the subject of "Gong Si Ju Bian" or public and private convenience) (he should have an official title).

Tenth, if one is familiar with law, he can be recommended to "Yan Ke" (the subject of "Yan" or case trial) (he should have an official title).

"Shi Ke Jian Ju Qu Shi Fa" (Ten Subjects for Recommending Officials) was only applied for eight months. Although it was implemented again during the reign of Emperor Gaozong, it was no match for "Ke Ju" (the imperial examination).

In the Song Dynasty, as to the system for selection of officials, two methods of obtaining official titles were distained by the people: one was "En Yin" (the appointment of the descendants of those who had made great contribution to the state); the other was "Mai Guan Yu Jue" (selling official ranks and titles). According to the law of "En Yin," the descendants of the aristocratic bureaucrats could directly become officials "according to the status of their elders in their family," and an official could even bring benefit to dozens of his descendants at a time. The wealthy families could also spend money buying official titles. Consequently, "the people who were not very wealthy could also become officials. If one had small but valuable goods which were worth hundreds of thousands of *qian*, he could sell them in three different places and earn more than 1000 strings of copper coins, so he can become an official by buying an official title. Thus, almost every one could easily become an official by putting on official robes. Actually there were so many such people in every 'Zhou' (subprefecture) and 'Xian' (county)."[54]

In the Southern Song Dynasty, "Mai Guan Yu Jue" (selling official ranks and titles) became a very important source of financial revenue for the state.

As to the selection of officials, in the early period, it was managed by both "Zhong Shu Sheng" (the supreme organization in charge of state affairs) and "Shen Guan Yuan" (a bureau responsible for investigating officials after they had committed crimes). After the reform during the reign of Emperor Shenzong, "Li Bu" (The Department of Personnel) was put in charge of the selection of civilian officials, and "Bing Bu" (The Department of Defense) was made in charge of the selection of military officials.

It needs to be pointed out that the avoidance system of the Song Dynasty was further perfected on the basis of those of Sui and Tang dynasties. For example, "Xiang Guan Hui Bi," namely, the head of "Zhou" (subprefecture) and "Xian" (county) should not take up a post in "Xian" (county) or in "Dao" (the administration district below the province) where he was born or in the places where he had lived or where he had real estate. For another example, the princple of "Qin Xian Hui Bi" was established, the father and son or brothers or relatives should withdraw themselves

---

[54]"Zhi Guan" (State Officials) in *Song Hui Yao Ji Gao* (*Collected Essays of the Historical Records of Song Dynasty*) (Book 39), Vol. 55.

from handling cases together and the officials should withdraw themselves from their subordinate officials when they were taking their posts in the neighboring two government offices. If local officials had family relationship, they should withdraw themselves from working together. In order to implement "Qin Xian Hui Bi," the measure of "Bi Qin Yi Ren" was carried out, wherein two officials with the same official ranks should be exchanged if one of them needed to avoid working with his relatives. The purpose of the establishment of the avoidance system was to prevent officials from obtaining benefits for their relatives or friends by bending the law. Therefore, this system had its reasonableness.

In order to strengthen the power of the state through centralization of authority, great importance was attached to the management of officials in accordance with law, so a unique system for their assessment was formed.

During the early period of the Song Dynasty, the system of the Tang Dynasty was adopted. According to stipulations, officials working in or out of the imperial court should be assessed once every year, and in one term of office, the officials should be assessed three times. Especially, specific regulations were made for the terms of the promotion of judicial officials, and strict rules for the assessment of officials and the conditions of avoidance were also formed. It was recorded that "the court of penal law is a place where judgment is made and penal cases are reviewed . . . and one term of office for officials is three years."[55] So "officials' work should be assessed at the end of each year. The officials with no achievements should be demoted or dismissed, while the officials with achievements should be promoted and rewarded."[56] Moreover, "the officials with close relationship or ties of kinship should withdraw themselves and avoid working together."[57]

During the reign of Emperor Taizong, the legal criteria for assessment and the officials who needed to be assessed in "Zhou" (subprefecture) and "Xian" (county) were provided in detail:

> If the chief officials of "Zhou" (subprefecture) and "Xian" (county) have made achievements in governing the place and winning the respect and adoration of the people, or if they are honest and upright, or wise and fair-minded when handling local affairs, or have successfully settled people's grievance in trying cases, or have the storehouses filled with grain or have made the society safer by reducing the number of bandits and thieves, they shall be reported to the central government by the office of 'Zhuan Yun Si' (Office of Transportation) in the district where they work in. Moreover, if they can still deal with the daily problems when

---

[55]"Yu shi Tai, Liu Nei Quan, Nan Cao Xing Bu Da Li Si Bing San Zhou Nian Wei Man Zhao" (Imperial Edict about the Officials of "Yu Shi Tai", Personnel Appraisal Agency of "Li Bu" and "Da Li Si" Reporting to Emperor Every three Years) in "Guan Zhi" (The State Official System) (Part 1) in *Song Da Zhao Ling Ji* (*Collected Grand Edicts and Decrees of the Song Dynasty*), Vol. 160.

[56]"Zhi San Si Tui Guan Zhao" (The Imperial Edict on Judges of Three Departments) in "Guan Zhi" (The State Official System) (Part 1) in *Song Da Zhao Ling Ji* (*Collected Grand Edicts and Decrees of the Song Dynasty*), Vol. 160.

[57]"Qin Xian" (Avoid Working with Relatives) quoted from "Zhi Zhi Ling" (Decrees on the Official System) in "Zhi Zhi Men" (The Category of Official System) (Part 5) in *Qing Yuan Tiao Fa Shi Lei* (*The Legal Provisions and Cases Made in the Year of Qingyuan*), Vol. 8.

they are in courier stations or on their way to present themselves before the emperor, they should be highly praised and rewarded. Nevertheless, if the chief officials are extremely corrupt and always delay the hearing of cases, or often violate the rules, or their supervisory areas are in disorder because of the increase of bandits and thieves, their bad deeds will also be notified and criticized."[58]

"The officials with high score in assessment are recommended to be in the top rank; the officials with moderate score are recommended to be in the middle rank; the officials who deal with daily affairs slowly with disorder in their supervisor areas are recommended to be in the low rank. So the officials are assessed at the end of year."[59] During the reign of Emperor Zhenzong, it was specified in "Zhou Xian San Ke Fa" (Three Assessment Methods for the Officials of "Zhou" and "Xian") that "the officials who are honest, diligent, upright, and who can show care for the common people are recommended to be in the top rank; the officials who are diligent but who do not have a reputation of honesty, or who are upright but who do not have a reputation of good governor are recommended to be in the middle rank; the officials who are timid, corrupt and wretched are recommended to be in the low rank."[60]

In the 1st year of Xi'ning during the reign of Emperor Shenzong (1068 A.D.), the law on the assessment of officials, titled *Shou Ling Si Shan Si Zui* (*The Principles of Four Good and Four Best Behaviors for Chief Officials*) was enacted. "Si Shan" (the four excellent moral standards) and "Si Zui" (the four best behaviors) refer to the principles carried in the Tang Dynasty. "Si Shan" (the four excellent moral standards) included "'De Yi' (virtue and righteousness), 'Qing Sheng' (honesty and prudence), 'Gong Ping' (impartiality), 'Qin Ge' (diligence and hard working)," while "Si Zui" (the four best behaviors) included "trying legal cases fairly without interfering with tax collection; distributing corvee averagely without being troubled by theft; persuading people to pay tax with a good management of farming and sericulture; relieving the hungry and the poor with the construction of water conservancy; increasing the number of household registration with renovation of registration books."[61] In *Qing Yuan Tiao Fa Shi Lei* (*The Legal Provisions and Cases Made in the Year of Qingyuan*), "Si Zui" (the four best behaviors) was further detailed: "the best behaviors for 'Sheng Chi' (the increase of population)" meant that "the number of household registration have increased, the newly-born babies and the old people have been registered accurately without mistakes"; "the best behaviors for 'Zhi Shi' (government affairs)" meant that "there are no grievances in the judgment of cases and there is no disturbance in urging people to pay tax"; "the best behaviors for 'Quan Ke' (the encouragement of tax payment)" meant that "the people are encouraged to work on farming and sericulture, the wasteland is opened, the animals are fed, and water conservancy is constructed"; "the best behaviors for 'Yang Zang' (caring for the old and arranging the funerals)" meant that "bandits are eliminated,

---

[58]"Xuan Ju Zhi" (The Record of Election) in *Song Shi* (*The History of Song Dynasty*) (Book 6).
[59]"Xuan Ju Zhi" (The Record of Election) in *Song Shi* (*The History of Song Dynasty*) (Book 6).
[60]"Xuan Ju Zhi" (The Record of Election) in *Song Shi* (*The History of Song Dynasty*) (Book 6).
[61]"Xuan Ju Zhi" (The Record of Election) in *Song Shi* (*The History of Song Dynasty*) (Book 6).

people are guaranteed safety, the poor are relieved and prevented from becoming refugees."[62]

As to the assessment of the supervisors of "Lu" (ancient administrative region), "Jian" (ancient supervisory office), and "Si" (bureau), during the reign of Emperor Shenzong, "Qi Shi" (Seven Matters) was made, which included the following: to encourage farming and sericulture and to open wasteland, to make offerings to refugees and to increase the number of households, to promote what is beneficial and abolish what is harmful, to punish wickedness and to fairly settle legal cases, to avoid making wrongful conviction, to punish bandits and thieves, and to recommend talents.[63]

On the basis of "Qi Shi" (Seven Matters), Emperor Gaozong of the Southern Song Dynasty issued "Ba Shi" (Eight Matters) for the assessment of "Jian Si" (official in charge of supervising the counties and towns) and "Ling Shou" (governor): whether the recommendation of officials was appropriate, whether farming and sericulture were encouraged, whether the wasteland in their supervisory areas were opened, whether the household registration in their supervisory areas was increased, whether they had promoted what was beneficial and abolished what was harmful, whether they had made wrongful conviction, whether they had redressed unjust cases, whether the number of bandits and thieves was reduced.[64]

The officials were assessed according to their achievements and accomplishments, and their rewards and punishment were given according to the results of the assessment, as was described by Su Xun: "Where there are officials, there are assessments for them; where there are assessments, there are rewards or punishments for them."[65] Therefore, if one was found deceitful and dishonest in the assessment, he would be severely punished.

As for the punishment of dishonest chief officials of "Zhou" (subprefecture) and "Xian" (county), it was clearly provided in the article of "Kao Ke" (The Official Examination) in "Zhi Zhi Chi" (Imperial Instruction on the Official System) in *Qing Yuan Tiao Fa Shi Lei* (*The Legal Provisions and Cases Made in the Year of Qingyuan*). The concrete stipulations are as follows:

> For the assessment of "Jian Si" (official with right of supervising counties and towns), if they have concealed what ought to be reported, or if they have added or deleted randomly what ought to be reported, those in charge shall be punished by "Tu" (imprisonment) for two years.

---

[62]"Kao Ke" (The Official Examination)in "Kao Ke Ge" (Injunction on Official Assessment) in "Zhi Zhi Men". (The Category of Official System) (Part 2) in *Qing Yuan Tiao Fa Shi Lei* (*The Legal Provisions and Cases Made in the Year of Qingyuan*), Vol. 5.

[63]"Zhi Guan" (State Official) in *Song Hui Yao Ji Gao* (*Collected Essays of the Historical Records of Song Dynasty*) (Book 20), Vol. 10.

[64]"Kao Ke" (The Official Examination) in "Kao Ke Shi" (Forms of Official Assessment) in "Zhi Zhi Men" (The Category of Official System) (Part 2) in *Qing Yuan Tiao Fa Shi Lei* (*The Legal Provisions and Cases Made in the Year of Qingyuan*), Vol. 5.

[65]Su Xun (Song Dynasty), "Shang Huang Di Shu" (A Memorial to the Emperor) in *Jia You Ji* (*Anthology in the Reign of Jiayou*), Vol. 9.

8.2 The Administrative Law for Strengthening the Centralization of Authority

In the assessment of "Zhi Zhou" (subprefectural magistrates) and "Xian Ling" (county magistrate), if there is falsification, or if the examinees are evaluated as "excellent" or "poor" by practicing fraud, the supervisor will be punished by "Tu" (imprisonment) for two years; if the examinees are evaluated as "Shang" (excellent), his punishment shall be reduced by two levels; if the examinees are evaluated as "Zhong Xia" (below the average), his punishment shall be reduced by one more level; if one supervisor is instigated by an official to give an false assessment, both the supervisor and the official will be punished for the violation of law; if senior officials are involved in the false assessment mentioned above, they shall be punished the same; if the officials who are recommended by others have violated law, those in charge shall be punished by "Zhang" (flogging with heavy sticks) for one hundred strokes and the relevant officials in charge shall be punished three levels lighter.

In the annual assessment of "Jian Si" (official with right of supervising counties and towns), if the supervisors make unfair or false reports about the achievements of officials to the imperial court, or they have drawn false conclusions or taken a wait-and-see attitude toward the powerful ones who have asked them to give false assessment, they should be punished for the violation of law and their penalties should by increased by one level.

In the Song Dynasty, the method for the assessment of officials was also improved, which was reflected by the use of "Li Zhi" (assessment record) and the application of the method of "Mo Kan" (assessment). "Mo Kan" refers to the assessment of "Ji Lu Guan" (official who is paid a salary but who has no responsibilities when it comes to the affairs of his department unless he is summoned by the emperor and whose promotion is determined by his qualification and records of service) who were promoted or demoted by officials or government offices assigned by the imperial court or the assessment of officials who were chosen to serve in the government offices of the capital. "Li Zhi" (assessment record) refers to the documents for the assessment of officials, which were written by the chief officials of each department. In the 2nd year of Duangong during the reign of Emperor Taizong (989 A.D.), "Shen Guan Yuan" (a bureau responsible for investigating officials after they had committed crimes) was established for the assessment of capital officials and "Kao Ke Yuan" (the bureau of assessment) was established for the assessment of subordinate officials of "Zhou" (subprefecture) and "Xian" (county). It was recorded in history books that "in the early days, the emperor worried that it was difficult to distinguish the honest officials from the dishonest, so he ordered to establish 'Mo Kan Yuan' to evaluate the performance of the officials. Later on 'Shen Guan Yuan' (a bureau responsible for investigating officials after they had committed crimes) was responsible for the assessment of the performance of the officials in the capital. The subordinates and the chief officials of 'Zhou' (subprefecture) and 'Xian' (county) were assessed by other bureaus."[66] So it was from the 4th year of Xianping during the reign of Emperor Zhenzong (1001 A.D.) that "Mo Kan" (assessment) was implemented to evaluate the performance of the officials of the capital. According to "Xuan Ju Zhi" (The Record of Election) in *Song Shi* (*The History of Song Dynasty*), in the 4th year of Xianping during the reign of Emperor Zhenzong, the emperor "ordered 'Shen Guan Yuan' (a bureau responsible for investigating officials after

---

[66]Shang Lu (Ming Dynasty), *Tong Jian Gang Mu Xu Bian* (*Sequel to the Outlines and Details of the History as a Mirror*), Vol. 2.

they had committed crimes) to evaluate the performance of the senior and junior officials in the capital by answering questions so as to decide their promotion or demotion. Thus, the practice of 'Mo Kan' (assessment) was started for the officials in the capital." The assessment of the subordinate officials in the capital and the chief officials of 'Zhou' (subprefecture) and 'Xian' (county) was started in the 7th year of Xiangfu during the reign of Dazhong (1014 A.D.) According to the record in "Xuan Ju Zhi" (The Record of Election) in *Song Hui Yao Ji Gao* (*Collected Essays of the Historical Records of Song Dynasty*), "the officials of 'Zhong Shu Men Xia' (the supreme state organization) said that 'the officials in 'Zhou' (subprefecture) and 'Xian' (county) should be recommended by the civil and military officials at the end of the year. Now it is decided that one official should be recommended by the guarantee of five other officials. If the recommended official has committed any crimes, those referrers shall also be punished for the same offence. The office of 'Liu Nei Quan' (responsible for the assessment of officials) should be responsible for the assessment of those officials. So his suggestion is approved by the emperor." In the 3rd year of Qingling during the reign of Emperor Renzong (1043 A.D.), the law on the system of "Bao Ren" (recommending someone for a post with personal guarantee) in the assessment was made by the emperor's advisor, Fan Zhongyan, and it was declared that "the officials in the imperial court including 'Lang Zhong' (head of a subministry department) and 'Shao Qing' (the vice president) should be promoted with the guarantee of five 'Qing Wang Guan' (the senior officials above third rank)."[67] As to the laws on the system of "Bao Ren" (recommending someone for a post with personal guarantee) in the recommendation, much importance was attached to the time, qualification, and records of the service, but the merits and accomplishments of officials were often neglected. During the reign of Qingli, Zhang Fangping, who was a scholar of "Han Lin Yuan" (The Hanlin Academy), suggested that "the officials should be promoted according to their merits and achievements in the assessment; or must be appointed and recommended according to imperial orders; if an official has made no achievements or he is recommended without following imperial orders, he should be promoted according to his years of service. Besides, those officials should be recommended by honest and knowledgeable officials with good reputation. According to this method, the officials in power are responsible for recommending 'Qing Wang Guan' (the senior officials above third rank), who then are responsible for recommending 'Qin Min Guan' (the most basic local officials). If there are vacant posts, the officials should be jointly recommended by several subordinates, This has fully shown the emperor's intention of recruiting talents and loving his subjects."[68]

Another regulation was made during the reign of Emperor Yuanfeng, according to which civil officials should be assessed for the first time after they had served in the government for three to four years according to their official ranks, and military

---

[67]"Xuan Ju Zhi" (The Record of Election) in *Song Shi* (*The History of Song Dynasty*) (Book 6).
[68]"Xuan Ju Zhi" (The Record of Election) in *Song Shi* (*The History of Song Dynasty*) (Book 6).

8.2 The Administrative Law for Strengthening the Centralization of Authority

officials should be assessed for the first time after they had served in the government for five years.

In order to ensure the implementation of the system of "Mo Kan" (assessment), the following was stipulated during the Song Dynasty:

> If the officials who are informed to be assessed or who are the candidates to be promoted have lost the relevant documents such as "Lu Bai" (the imperial decrees written on the blank paper), "Gao Chi" (certificates of appointment), "Xuan Li" (official documents), "Yin Zhi" (forms or other certificates), or have failed to be assessed, they shall be punished by "Zhang" (flogging with heavy sticks) for one hundred strokes; if their chief officials have failed to report the cases to "Li Bu Shang Shu" (the minister of the department of personnel), they should be punished by the same penalty.[69]

Even though the regulation on "Mo Kan" (assessment) was detailed and elaborate in the Song Dynasty, once they entered the official circles, as a matter of routine, civil officials would be promoted to positions one rank higher every three years and military officials would be promoted every five years as long as they had made no serious mistakes during that period, no matter what their achievements and accomplishments were. Therefore, "as a matter of routine, after serving two terms of office, the chief officials of 'Xian' (county) will be promoted to 'Tong Pan' (official in charge of agriculture, water conservancy and litigation under prefecture and subprefecture); after serving two terms of office of 'Tong Pan', they will be promoted to 'Zhi Zhou' (subprefectural magistrates)." So consequently, "the virtuous and the stupid are granted the same official ranks, while the honest and the dishonest are given the same treatment."[70] Therefore, during their time of service in government offices, officials usually worked not to make achievements but to avoid making mistakes. For this reason, although laws for the assessment of the performance of officials were made, most of them merely became scraps of paper. In the end, "the old, sick, vulnerable, incapable, evil and avaricious people ... were all holding posts in 'Zhou' (subprefecture) and 'Xian' (county) without being dismissed ... so that 80 to 90 percent of 'Zhou' (subprefecture) and 'Xian' (county) were misruled."[71] After moving to the south of China, the power was usurped by the wicked "Zai Xiang" (the prime minister) so that national power began to decline. Consequently, the law on the assessment of officials became just a scrap of paper.

In the early period of the Song Dynasty, the system of "Jiu Pin" (the ninth rank), which was implemented in the Tang Dynasty, was followed, and one principal and one accessory official were appointed for every rank, so there were totally eighteen levels. Moreover, "San Guan" (ancient honorary official title), which was divided

---

[69]"Mo Kan Sheng Gai" (Assessment of Promotion and Demotion of Officials) quoted from "Shang Ling" (Orders of Rewards) in "Zhi Zhi Men" (The Category of Official System) (Part 10) in *Qing Yuan Tiao Fa Shi Lei* (*The Legal Provisions and Cases Made in the Year of Qingyuan*), Vol. 13.

[70]Fan Zhongyan (Song Dynasty), "Tian Sheng Wu Nian Shang Zhi Zheng Shu" (An Official Memorial to the Emperor in the 5th year of Tiansheng) in *Fan Wen Zheng Gong Ji* (*Collected Works of Fan Zhongyan*), Vol. 8.

[71]*Xu Zi Zhi Tong Jian Chang Bian* (*Sequel to the Full-length Book of History as a Mirror*), Vol. 141, in May of the 3rd year of Qingli.

into twenty nine ranks, was also established following that of Tang Dynasty. During the time when reform was carried out by Emperor Shenzong, the law on official ranks was amended, so honorary official titles were either abolished or replaced by "Ji Lu Guan" (official who is paid a salary but who has no responsibilities when it comes to the affairs of his department unless he is summoned by the emperor and whose promotion is determined by his qualification and records of service); this way, official ranks in the early period of the Song Dynasty were simplified.

The officials' salaries were paid according to official ranks. In the early period of the Song Dynasty, the rulers believed that "it is useless to persuade officials to be honest and upright with low salaries, so it is better to pay high salary to fewer officials than pay low salary to the redundant officials."[72] Therefore, imperial decrees were issued successively on "increasing the salaries of officials" and "reducing the number of officials" and "government staff." However, these decrees were not implemented in practice, but more money was collected from the common people. The officials' salary included money, maize, and cloth, and it was increased or decreased according to the income of public revenues. With the development of a feudal merchandise–money relationship, before the reform was carried out in the period of Yuanfeng, government-paid maize was discounted to cash. Thus, it was a great development in the salary system to pay salary to officials with cash during the Song Dynasty. During the reform, which was carried out by Emperor Shenzong in the period of Yuanfeng, in addition to the salary paid in the form of cash, other supplies distributed by the government were also discounted to money, to be paid to the officials monthly. In the period of Emperor Huizong, it was popular for officials to hold more than one post concurrently to earn more salaries, such that one official could even earn salaries from more than ten offices. Evidently, redundant personnel not only caused low administrative efficiency but also increased the financial burden of the government; therefore, a retirement system for officials was enforced by the imperial court.

According to law, officials should retire upon reaching seventy years old, but many of them were unwilling to retire because they wanted to continue to receive salaries from the government. During the reign of Emperor Renzong, Bao Zheng suggested that if civil and military officials who were seventy years old were unwilling to retire, they would be "impeached by 'Yu Shi Ti' (The Censorate)"[73] so that a compulsory retirement system could be implemented. Wang Anshi also pointed out that "senior officials shall retire at seventy years old, because it is written

---

[72]"Sheng Xi Chuan Zhou Xian Guan Zeng Feng Zhao" (Imperial Decree on the Increase of the Salaries of Officials in 'Zhou' (subprefecture) and 'Xian' (county) of Xichuan Area) in "Guan Zhi" (The State Official System) (Part 1) in *Song Da Zhao Ling Ji* (*Collected Grand Edicts and Decrees of the Song Dynasty*), Vol. 160.

[73]"Zhi Guan Zhi" (The Record of State Officials) in *Song Shi (The History of Song Dynasty)* (Book 10).

in the Confucian classics, and now it has become a law."[74] However, in reality, the law on the retirement of officials was not strictly implemented. As to the treatment of retired officials, if they were meritorious, they would be paid their full salaries or more. During the reign of Emperor Taizu, when Wang Yanchao retired, he was paid the same salary as that of a senior general according to an imperial edict, and when Shangguan Zheng retired, he was also paid his full salary. After the reign of Emperor Taizu, retired officials were paid full salaries or half of their salaries. In order to encourage all officials to retire on time, "when it is the time for civil or military officials to retire, they will be promoted to the positions one rank higher or their sons or grandsons will be given special privileges."[75] In other words, official titles would be conferred upon their descendants.

Because officials who were seventy years old were unwilling to retire but more people were selected to be officials through "Ke Ju" (the imperial examination), it was prevalent to sell official ranks. As a result, the number of the bureaucratic team surged greatly, which led to a situation where "there are more officials but fewer official positions." In order to change this situation, more honorary official titles were granted, so that there were more officials who earned salaries but were fewer officials who were actually taking charge of particular affairs. Consequently, the officials just "spent more days idling at home than handling affairs."[76] Most of them just became a large group of candidates waiting to fill the vacancy of the current official positions. In order to prevent idle officials from colluding with the local forces to interfere with political affairs, it was provided in law that the officials whose term of office had expired and who were awaiting for new appointment should not live in the place where he had been working. So "if the term of office of the local government officials has expired for fewer than three years, but if they still live in the place where they used to be the officials, they should be punished by 'Tu' (imprisonment) for one year."[77] Even if there was a vacancy for "Zhi Zhou" (subprefectural magistrates) or "Tong Pan" (official in charge of agriculture, water conservancy, and litigation under subprefecture) or "Xian Ling" (county magistrate), it should not be filled by "the officials who are waiting for the new appointment."[78] If an idle official had lived in a place for seven years or longer, the place where he lived

---

[74]Wang Anshi (Song Dynasty), "Sun Li Tai Zi Zhong Yun Zhi Shi Zhi" (The Imperial Edict about the Retirement of Sun Li's Prince) in "Wai Zhi" (Imperial Mandate) in *Wang Lin Chuan Ji (Collections of Wang Linchuan)*, Vol. 53.

[75]"Zhi Guan" (State Official) in *Song Hui Yao Ji Gao (Collected Essays of the Historical Records of Song Dynasty)* (Section 28) (Chapter 77).

[76]*Xu Zi Zhi Tong Jian Chang Bian (Sequel to the Full-length Book of History as a Mirror)*, Vol. 386, in August of the 1st year of Yuanyou.

[77]"Waiting for the Vacancies of Official Positions" quoted from "Zhi Zhi Chi" (Imperial Instruction on the Official System) in "Zhi Zhi Men" (The Category of Official System) (Part 4) in *Qing Yuan Tiao Fa Shi Lei (The Legal Provisions and Cases Made in the Year of Qingyuan)*, Vol. 7.

[78]"Substituting for the Absent Official" quoted from "Zhi Zhi Chi" (Imperial Instruction on the Official System) in "Zhi Zhi Men" (The Category of Official System) (Part 3) in *Qing Yuan Tiao Fa Shi Lei (The Legal Provisions and Cases Made in the Year of Qingyuan)*, Vol. 6.

would be regarded as his hometown, so the principle of "Hui Bi Bei Guan" (the official should not take up a post in his hometown or in the places where he had lived or where he had real estate) would be applied, so "he should not be granted an official title in the place."[79] Moreover, the officials whose "farmland and property ranked the third class or higher" "should not held official posts in their hometown,"[80] In the Song Dynasty, although some restrictions were imposed upon the idle officials, it was impossible to effectively prevent those officials from colluding with the influential forces and despotic gentry to "interfere with the government affairs of 'Zhou' (subprefecture) and 'Xian' (county)." As a result, the officials and "influential families" usually ganged up to exploit the common people. In the Song Dynasty, on the one hand, restrictions were imposed upon the idle officials to prevent them from interfering with political affairs; on the other hand, the economic interests of those idle officials were guaranteed by receiving special treatment. For example, when the government was selling government-owned land, "it was forbidden for the magistrates and officials of 'Zhou' (subprefecture) and 'Xian' (county) to buy the land," but "it did not include the officials waiting to fill the vacancy of official positions,"[81] which had actually encouraged the idling officials to annex more land. Because idle officials increased greatly, in the middle of the Southern Song Dynasty, the number of idle officials were even many times more than that of the incumbent officials. In order to be appointed or promoted as early as possible after the assessment, the officials spent much time visiting and bribing the senior officials, which had further accelerated the deterioration of official management.

In conclusion, although the administrative regulations of the Song Dynasty were elaborate, because the laws and instructions were diversified and complicated and there were no established legal systems, it was difficult for them to be implemented. Therefore, the government was full of redundant officials, which had become a heavy burden to the nation, as was pointed out by Ouyang Xiu: "The main reason for the decline of the country and for the troubles in the public and private field is that there are too many redundant officials."[82]

---

[79]Li Xinchuan (Song Dynasty), *Jian Yan Yi Lai Xi Nian Yao Lu* (*An Annual Record of the Most Important Events since the Reign of Jianyan*), Vol. 175, in April in the 19th year of Shaoxing.

[80]"Zhi Guan" (State Official) in *Song Hui Yao Ji Gao* (*Collected Essays of the Historical Records of Song Dynasty*) (Book 50), Vol. 61.

[81]"Shi Huo" (National Finance and Economy) in *Song Hui Yao Ji Gao* (*Collected Essays of the Historical Records of Song Dynasty*) (Boo 23), Vol. 5.

[82]Ouyang Xiu (Song Dynasty), "Zai Lun An Cha Guan Li Zhuang" (A Memorial about Further Discussion of Supervisory Officials) in "Zou Yi" (Memorials to the Emperor) (Part 10) in *Ou Yang Xiu Ji* (*Collections of Ouyang Xiu*), Vol. 106.

8.2.2.2 The Development of the Supervisory System and the Supervision Law

In the Song Dynasty, "Yu Shi Tai" (The Censorate) was set up by following the system of the Tang Dynasty, which had functioned as the highest supervisory institution in charge of "inspecting the misbehaviors of the officials and rectifying and strengthening the disciplines."[83] Although "Yu Shi Da Fu" (Grand Censor) was the chief official in "Yu Shi Tai" (The Censorate), he was not responsible for handling actual affairs, and the official who handled particular affairs was named "Yu Shi Zhong Cheng" (Grand Censor). Under "Yu Shi Tai" (The Censorate), there were many subsidiary organs, such as "Tai Yuan," "Dian Yuan," and "Cha Yuan." "Shi Yu Shi" (subordinate to Grand Censor) and "Dian Zhong Shi Yu Shi" (the attendant censor in the palace) were responsible for giving advice and discussing government affairs. "Jian Cha Yu Shi" (the supervisory censor) was in charge of inspecting the affairs of "Liu Cao" (the six departments) and hundreds of other government offices, so it was referred to as "Liu Cha" (censor of six departments), but sometimes it was also in charge of giving advice to the emperor. Thus, "Jian Cha Yu Shi" (the supervisory censor) was "responsible for both conducting supervision and giving advice."[84]

In addition to "Yu Shi Tai" (The Censorate), "Jian Yuan" (Bureau for Imperial Expostulation), which was mainly responsible for giving advice to the emperor during the Tang Dynasty, was set up as an independent office in the Song Dynasty. The bureau consisted of "Zuo You Jian Yi Da Fu" (the chief and deputy officials in charge of conducting discussions on national matters), "Si Jian" (advisor), and "Zheng Yan" (official in charge of offering advice). "If the orders which are issued or the affairs which are handled are found to be inappropriate or unreasonable, the important ones should be discussed in the imperial court, and the less important ones should be written, sealed and presented to the emperor." So "the malpractice of the imperial court, the misconduct of the ministers and other officials and the malfeasance of the 'San Sheng' (The Three Departments) and other bureaus are all supervised and rectified."[85] "Jian Guan" (supervisor) also had the right of "Feng Wen Yan Shi" (impeaching officials according to rumors). Obviously, "Jian Yuan" (Bureau for Imperial Expostulation) was an independent organization, but it had responsibilities similar to that of "Yu Shi Tai" (The Censorate), so "Yu Shi Tai" (The Censorate) and "Jian Yuan" (Bureau for Imperial Expostulation) coexisted. The purpose for doing so was not only to weaken the power of "Jian Guan" (supervisor) but also to expand their supervisory power over other officials. Lv Hui, who was then "Shi Yu Shi" (subordinate of Grand Censor), clearly expressed his opinion in a

---

[83]"Zhi Guan Zhi" (The Record of State Officials) in *Song Shi* (*The History of Song Dynasty*) (Book 4).

[84]"Guan Zhi" (The State Official System) in *Yu Hai* (*The Jade Ocean*), Vol. 121.

[85]"Zhi Guan Zhi" (The Record of State Officials) in *Song Shi* (*The History of Song Dynasty*) (Book 1).

memorial to the emperor: "'Yu Shi Tai' (The Censorate) and 'Jian Yuan' (Bureau for Imperial Expostulation) are like the ears and eyes of Your Majesty, so they are established to prevent the officials from concealing the truth from Your Majesty and to help Your Majesty to make wise decisions."[86]

As for the supervisory system of the Song Dynasty, the power of "Yu Shi" (the censor) was expanded to expostulate with the emperor and to carry out administrative supervision. According to the system, "all corrupt officials, from those in imperial court to 'Zhou' (subprefecture) and 'Xian' (county), from 'Zai Xiang' (the prime minister) to all other officials shall be impeached."[87] During the reign of Emperor Shenzong, "Yu Shi" (the censor) named Tang Tong once impeached Wang Anshi, who was then "Zai Xiang" (the prime minister), before the emperor. In addition, "Yu Shi Tai" (The Censorate) was responsible for the regular checking and recording of the work of incumbent civil and military officials, as well as the assessment of "Jian Si" (official in charge of supervising the counties and towns) and "Jun Shou" (governor). If local officials arrived in the capital after their terms of office had expired or if capital officials needed to be promoted or moved to local governments, they all should go through the evaluation process of "Tai Can," "Tai Xie," and "Tai Ci" (all important ceremonial systems of seeing the emperor and expressing their thanks in court in the middle and late Tang Dynasty). "For the old and sick, or incompetent and corrupt officials ... or those were incapable of serving in the government, they will be impeached by 'Yu Shi' (the censor)."[88]

Since "Yu Shi" (the censor) had great power, its appointment was decided by the emperor himself. The right of "Zai Xiang" (the prime minister) to appoint and recommend "Yu Shi" (the censor) during the Tang Dynasty was abolished in the Song Dynasty, so the officials recommended by "Zai Xiang" (the prime minister) or the relatives or friends of "Zai Xiang" (the prime minister) were not allowed to be appointed as "Yu Shi" (the censor) in order to guarantee his supervision of the central office. Besides, officials who had not completed two terms of office should not be appointed as "Yu Shi" (the censor) to ensure that he has enough practical experience in administering and that the power of supervision is properly exercised.

Under the regulation of "Feng Wen Tan Ren" (impeaching officials according to rumors), it was allowed for "Yu Shi" (the censor) to handle cases without necessarily showing any evidence. Even if the impeachment conducted by "Yu Shi" (the censor) was not appropriate, he would not be punished. Moreover, "Yu Shi" (the censor) was ordered to present memorials to the emperor monthly, which was referred to as "monthly work," so if "Yu Shi" (the censor) did not present any memorials within one hundred days after taking office, he would be dismissed and transferred to an office outside the capital or be imposed with a fine and ordered to pay "Ru Tai Qian"

---

[86]"Lv Hui Zhuan" (The Biography of Lv Hui) in *Song Shi* (*The History of Song Dynasty*).

[87]*Xu Zi Zhi Tong Jian Chang Bian* (*Sequel to the Full-length Book of History as a Mirror*), Vol. 371, in March of the 1st year of Yuanyou.

[88]"Zhi Guan" (State Official) in *Song Hui Yao Ji Gao* (*Collected Essays of the Historical Records of Song Dynasty*) (Book 9), Vol. 55.

(compensation for the insult of the Censorate). Therefore, the regulation of "Feng Wen Tan Ren" (impeaching officials according to rumors) had reflected the emperor's state of mind of guarding against his ministers, as well as his heavy reliance on the office that had acted as his eyes and ears. Eventually, it had encouraged abuse in the exercise of the impeaching power by "Yu Shi Tai" (The Censorate).

Even though "Yu Shi Tai" (The Censorate) and "Jian Yuan" (Bureau for Imperial Expostulation) were two independent offices, their duties overlapped. Hence, "Jian Guan" (supervisor) "could also perform the duties of supervision" and "Tai Guan" (the official in censorate) also had the responsibility to expostulate. In the 2nd year of Yuanfeng during the reign of Emperor Shenzong (1079 A.D.), the emperor "issued an imperial edict and ordered that three of the six censors to be responsible for conducting supervision and three of them for conducting expostulation." In the 8th year (1085 A.D.), another imperial edict was issued to order the supervisory officials to conduct expostulation.[89] The purpose of the combination of "Yu Shi Tai" (The Censorate) and "Jian Yuan" (Bureau for Imperial Expostulation) was to make the two offices fully perform the function of supervision in order to maintain the feudal bureaucratic administration.

In the Song Dynasty, the supervisory systems of "Jian Si" (official in charge of supervising the counties and towns) and "Tong Pan" (official in charge of agriculture, water conservancy, and litigation under subprefecture) were established in local governments, and the supervisory executives were sent by the emperor to the local governments of "Lu" (ancient administrative region) to take charge of the four institutions that were in charge of military, administrative, financial, and penal affairs. The supervisory executives in the four institutions were independent from each other and were only held responsible to the emperor. "Tong Pan" (official in charge of agriculture, water conservancy, and litigation under subprefecture) was the supervisor of "Zhou" (subprefecture), and he was in charge of the supervision of "Zhi Zhou" (subprefectural magistrates) and the subordinate officials. Emperor Renzong had explicitly pointed out that "'Tong Pan' (official in charge of agriculture, water conservancy and litigation under prefecture and subprefecture) is established in 'Zhou' (subprefecture) so that they can jointly handle the affairs with 'Zhi Zhou' (subprefectural magistrates) in the jurisdiction. So if a 'Zhi Zhou' (subprefectural magistrates) has ever committed a crime, it should be reported to me in memorial by 'Tong Pan' (official in charge of agriculture, water conservancy and litigation under prefecture and subprefecture)."[90]

So a supervisory network which covered almost every aspect of the administration was established by the supervisory system consisting of supervisory executives and "Tong Pan" (official in charge of agriculture, water conservancy and litigation under subprefecture).

---

[89]"Guan Zhi" (The State Official System) in *Yu Hai* (*The Jade Ocean*), Vol. 121.

[90]Sun Fengji (Song Dynasty), "Tong Pan Jun Zhou" (Tong Pan in Military Strategic Places) in *Zhi Guan Fen Ji* (*Separate Records for the State Offices*), Vol. 41.

To sum up, the expansion of the supervisory organs and their power in Song Dynasty had accelerated the centralization of the authority. Because the great supervisory power of "Yu Shi" (the censor) was subordinate to imperial power, the rise and fall of his status depended on how much the emperor trusted him. In order to avoid abuse of supervisory power by Yu Shi" (the censor), mutual supervision between the supervisory and other organizations was conducted. For example, "Shang Shu Sheng" (The Department of Secretary) had the power of "impeaching 'Yu Shi' (the censor) for his misconducts."[91] Also, "Jian Si" (official in charge of supervising the counties and towns) in each "Lu" (ancient administrative region) could conduct mutual supervision and impeachment. If they failed to do so, they would be punished for their misconduct. No doubt, the law of mutual supervision had strengthened the supervisory mechanism, so it was a very important development in the supervisory system of the Song Dynasty.

In addition, in order to prevent "Yu Shi" (the censor) from misusing the power of "Feng Wen Tan Ren" (impeaching officials according to rumors) and to prevent them from disclosing their past misconduct to show their personal resentment against some officials, in the 1st year of Huangyou during the reign of Emperor Renzong (1049 A.D.), an imperial edict was issued: "From today forward, if what 'Yu Shi' (the censor) has heard has nothing to do with the gains and losses of the imperial court or the benefits and suffering of the people, "Feng Wen Tan Ren" (impeaching officials according to rumors) is prohibited, so anyone who violates this edict shall be punished."[92]

With the expansion of the supervisory organs and the improvement of the supervisory system, the supervisory legislation was also further enriched and developed.

The main form of supervision law in the Song Dynasty included "Zhao" (decree), "Chi" (instruction), "Ling" (decree), and "Ge" (injunction), etc., which fully reflected that laws were made according to imperial orders. The main contents and characteristics of "Zhao" (decree), "Chi" (instruction), "Ling" (decree), and "Ge" (injunction) are summarized as follows.

Firstly, as to the supervision law of the Song Dynasty, the legal tradition of the Han and Tang dynasties was inherited and the characteristics of the time were highlighted, which was mainly expressed in the fact that the autocratic imperial power and centralization of authority were maintained. For example, it was declared clearly that the supervisors, who were the legal subjects for the exercise of supervisory power, were just like the emperor's eyes and ears. On October 16th of the 5th year of Chongning (1106 A.D.), *Jie Yue Jian Si Ti Liang Gong Shi Huai Jian Yu Bi Shou Zhao (The Handwritten Manuscript of Imperial Edict on Admonishment of Supervisory Executives for Their Misconducts in Official Business)* was issued, and

---

[91]"Zhi Guan Zhi" (The Record of State Officials) in *Song Shi (The History of Song Dynasty)* (Book 1).

[92]*Xu Zi Zhi Tong Jian Chang Bian (Sequel to the Full-length Book of History as a Mirror)*, Vol. 166, in January of the 1st year of Huangyou.

it was stated that "the supervisory executives have been sent to different 'Lu' (ancient administrative region) to serve as the eyes and ears of the Emperor."[93] On December 21st of the 1st year of Zhenghe (1111 A.D.), it was also stated in the imperial edict of *Jie Chi Tai Guan Yan Shi Yu Bi Shou Zhao* (*The Handwriting Manuscripts of Imperial Edict on Reprimanding the Officials of the Censorate and the Bureau of Expostulation*) that "'Tai Jian' (central surveillance agency) is like my eyes and ears, so in ancient times, they are endowed by sages with great responsibilities to expostulate with the monarchs and to impeach the evil officials without doing anything wrong to the righteous men. That is why the wise emperors are be able to let things take their own course, to solicit opinions from all sides, to give the proper awards and penalties, to recruit all the talents, to manage the officials properly, to make all officials follow the correct path and to deal with the state affairs just by sitting on their thrones gracefully and solemnly."[94]

Meanwhile, in *Xun Chi Bai Si Zhao* (*The Imperial Edict on Admonishing the Officials of Various Bureaus*), it was clearly stated that "'Yu Shi' (the censor) is like my eyes and ears and it is your responsibility to uphold the principle of 'Yu Shi Tai' (The Censorate) and to eliminate the wicked officials. If you do nothing just out of fear, or if you impeach others by violating law, you should be severely punished."[95] Just because the supervisors were like the emperor's eyes and ears does not mean they can do anything; if "they do things out of personal grudges or show favor to someone, or handle the affairs dishonestly and unreasonably"[96] or deceived the emperor or took bribes by bending the law, they would be severely punished.

Secondly, the responsibilities and punitive measures of "Jian Si" (official in charge of supervising the counties and towns) and "An Cha Guan" (head of judicial commission) were provided in detail. The following regulations are described in detail in "Zhi Zhi Ling" (Decrees on the Official System) in *Qing Yuan Tiao Fa Shi Lei* (*The Legal Provisions and Cases Made in the Year of Qingyuan*):

> The supervisory executives shall make an inspection tour to "Zhou" (subprefecture) and "Xian" (county) in the first and the latter half of the year respectively to redress the mishandled cases and grievance, to investigate the gains and losses, to recommend the officials who abide by the law and who follow the principles of "Li" (rites), to impeach the evil and corrupt officials and to present memorials to the emperor.
>
> The supervisory executives shall get familiar with the supervisory places in "Zhou" (subprefecture) and "Xian" (county) and shall arrange officials to make inspection tours. All the places should be inspected before the end of the year. The inspection of all prisons should be carried out in January of the next year for every two years, and the places that have been

---

[93]"Jie Chi" (Exhortations and Instructions) (Part 7) in *Song Da Zhao Ling Ji* (*Collected Grand Edicts and Decrees of the Song Dynasty*), Vol. 196.

[94]"Jie Chi" (Exhortations and Instructions) (Part 8) in *Song Da Zhao Ling Ji* (*Collected Grand Edicts and Decrees of the Song Dynasty*), Vol. 197.

[95]"Jie Chi" (Exhortations and Instructions) (Part 8) in *Song Da Zhao Ling Ji* (*Collected Grand Edicts and Decrees of the Song Dynasty*), Vol. 197.

[96]"Jie Chi" (Exhortations and Instructions) (Part 8) in *Song Da Zhao Ling Ji* (*Collected Grand Edicts and Decrees of the Song Dynasty*), Vol. 196.

inspected and the days of inspection should all be reported to "Shang Shu Sheng" (The Department of Secretary).

Wherever the supervisory executives arrive when they are making inspection tours, they are allowed to be entertained with wine and meals, but they are not allowed to receive money. The supervisory executives should conduct mutual supervision.

When the supervisory executives make inspection tours, they are allowed to meet the guests, but they are not allowed to pay them a visit.

Wherever the supervisory executives arrive when they are making inspection tours, what they should do is only to inspect the doubtful legal cases and to check the official documents. If there are no illegal affairs or cases of negligence, the supervisory executives should not order the prisoners to make confessions. If there are no official business to deal with, the supervisory executives should not live in one place for more than three days.

The supervisory executives are allowed to command the subordinate officials in "Lu' (ancient administrative region) or "Zhou" (subprefecture) to make inspection tours, which shall be regarded as part of the inspection work assigned to the officials according to the plan of the year.

The supervisory executives shall check the prisoners in "Zhou" (subprefecture) and "Xian" (county) in person every quarter of the year. If there are any unjust cases, they should report them to the emperor after their grievances are redressed.

The supervisory executives shall send officials to the places under their administration each year to supervise and urge that the cases be settled as soon as possible. The inspection of the places shall start from the last ten days of May and shall finish before July 15th after the place is inspected. The places that have been inspected and the days of inspection should all be reported to "Shang Shu Sheng" (The Department of Secretary).

If the cases dealt with by "Zhou" (subprefecture) or "Si Li Yuan" (office of justice) involve the criminals or officials with official titles or mandated women who are punishable by "Tu" (imprisonment) or above, they are allowed to be tried by the supervisory executives, even though the supervisory departments are not responsible for the cases. If there are doubtful points in the cases or the accused claim they are wronged, or the cases that are mishandled in someone's favor need to be transferred to other departments, official documents should be sent to the departments where the cases ought to be dealt with and orders shall be issued to the officials of the departments to deal with the cases. If those officials do not obey what the official documents have instructed, or even if they obey the instructions but they do not deal with cases properly, they should be reported to the emperor.

When the supervisory executives inspect the prisons in "Zho'" (subprefecture) and "Xian" (county) every year, if the prisoners are found to be held in detention beyond legally prescribed time limits or they have grievances, the names and ranks of the officials responsible for the cases shall be recorded in the impeachment and reported to the emperor.

Every year the punishment of those who have killed or abandoned their own children or grandchildren shall be posted up on the wall in "Zhou" (subprefecture) and "Xian" (county) or rural regions to make it known to the public, and the supervisory executives shall frequently supervise and urge to redress the cases.

When the routing inspectors and "Xian Wei" (commandant of county) are in the government office, they should inspect the training work of the soldiers in person. Besides, the training activities should be documented which should be frequently checked by the supervisory executives.

Wherever the supervisory executives arrive when they are making inspection tours, they should inspect the training of archers once a year; if they fail to do so, they should send other officials to do the inspection.

For the soldiers of garrison forces who are sent on a mission, but who came back to the military camp without authorization, if the soldiers are under the pretext of illness to stay in the camp or to avoid the compulsory service with the connivance of some officials, or if the later investigation of the case is not conducted thoroughly or mishandled, the officials

8.2 The Administrative Law for Strengthening the Centralization of Authority

responsible for the case shall be impeached by the supervisory executives on a inspection tour after the case is discovered.

If the deputy generals and the officers responsible for military training cannot deal with the military affairs properly, or if they violate the rules or settle cases unfairly, they should be punished by the chief officials of "Zhou" (subprefecture) and "Xian" (county), and then their cases should be reported to "Jing Lue An Fu Shi" (ancient official, head of "Lu", responsible for military affairs) and "Qian Xia Si" (the title of military official who is responsible for the military affairs of one prefecture or district); if they are impeached, their power shall be transferred to other generals and the cases shall be inspected by the supervisory executives when they are making inspection tours.

The military supplies distributed to the generals of the troops should be examined once a year by the officials of "Zhuan Yun Si" (Office of Transportation) and "Ti Dian Xing Yu Si" (judicial commission).

The Imperial Guards recruited in each "Zhou" (subprefecture) shall be inspected by the officials of "Zhuan Yun Si" (Office of Transportation). If anyone violates the law, the cases should be heard by the officials of "Ti Dian Xing Yu Si" (judicial commission) according to instruction.

When delivering the documents of the officials of "Zhuan Yun Si" (Office of Transportation) or supervisory executives to the subordinate departments, the documents should be sealed before delivering and should not be delivered by staff in other offices. Particular people in the place where the supervisory executives will go to inspect should be chosen to receive and deliver the documents.

In the places where the supervisory executives are conducting investigation, the abilities of the incumbent officials must be reported. The reports must be written by "Zhi Zhou" (subprefectural magistrates) and "Tong Pan" (official in charge of agriculture, water conservancy and litigation under subprefecture) and be sent to "Shang Shu Sheng" (The Department of Secretary). The reports about the abilities of the military officers must be sent to "Shu Mi Yuan" (Privy Council).

At the end of every year, the supervisory executives and "An Cha Guan" (head of judicial commission) shall report the names of corrupt officials to "Shang Shu Sheng" (The Department of Secretary).

The supervisory executives shall report the indecisive, incompetent and unaccomplished chief officials of "Xian" (county) to "Shang Shu Sheng" (The Department of Secretary) in the first and latter half of the year respectively.

If one subordinate department is reported to have neglected the implementation of law, the supervisory executives shall notify the subordinate supervisory department in detail by sending an official document and then shall command subordinate supervisory executives to have the law implemented, even though it is not their responsibility. If the official of the office is old and sick and unable to take the responsibility, the supervisory executives shall report it to the emperor, even though the official is not a member of the department. The supervisory executives should also hear the legal cases that ought to be heard in their department. It is not until a case has been accepted by the department responsible for the case that it is allowed for other departments to have the case settled.

If one official is reported to have committed a crime, or if the crime is serious, the case shall be inspected by "An Cha Guan" (head of judicial commission) in person and his subordinates who are honest and able and who have no relationship with the accused should be sent to investigate whether the accusation is true, and then the case should be reported to the emperor after it has been settled. The officials who are appointed to investigate the case shall conduct thorough investigation of the matter according to law, and they are not allowed to ask others to make accusations personally by posting a notice. If the official punishable for the crime of "Zuo Zang" (embezzlement) has left his post, or if he has been accused for his crime, he shall be punished by the inspector.

If there is no supervisor in the governmental office, "Fa Yun" (the official responsible for transport) and the supervisory executives shall take the responsibility of reporting the wrongdoings and injustice to the emperor. And mutual supervision shall be conducted by "Fa Yun" (the official responsible for transport), the supervisory executives, and the subordinate officials of "Jing Lue An Fu Shi" (ancient official, head of "Lu", responsible for military affairs); reports shall be made by the bureaus where they are working if they have done something illegally.

If department officials have committed crimes, their cases should be handled by the supervisory executives and the chief officials of "Lu" (ancient administrative region) according to law. Besides, their salaries should be suspended and mutual supervision should be conducted by the supervisory executives.[97]

The regulations in "Zhi Zhi Chi" (Imperial Instruction on the Official System) in *Qing Yuan Tiao Fa Shi Lei* (*The Legal Provisions and Cases Made in the Year of Qingyuan*) are listed as follows:

If the supervisory executives cannot inspect all the supervisory areas on their inspection tours, they shall be punished by "Zhang" (flogging with heavy sticks) for one hundred strokes; if they have inspected the supervisory areas but failed to make reports, their punishment shall be reduced by two levels.

If the supervisory executives have discovered that the military officials or archers have crossed the boundary lines by making up various excuses, the violators shall be punished by "Zhang" (flogging with heavy sticks) for one hundred strokes.

If there are porters who are available, but the supervisory executives still hire others at the expense of the government, they shall be punished by "Tu" (imprisonment) for two years.

When a supervisory executive is inspecting "Zhou" (subprefecture) and "Xian" (county) as a matter of annual routine, if he is entrusted with very important task but he fails to to so due to illness or other reasons, however if he is still given wine, food or presents, he shall be punished for illegally receiving presents according to law.

If the supervisory executives are in charge of inspecting, supervising and urging the settlement of cases but instead assign those tasks to other subordinate officials without permission, they shall be punished by "Tu" (imprisonment) for two years.

When the officials of "Zhuan Yun" (Office of Transportation) or the supervisory executives are making inspection tours, if the accompanying subordinates receive presents by violating the regulation, they shall be punished for "Shou Suo Jian Lin" (illegally accepting the people's money and property in one's supervisory area).

When the supervisory executives are making inspection tours, if the accompanying officials or soldiers ask for presents from the places where they inspect, they are to be accused.

If the officials of "Zhou" (subprefecture) and "Xian" (county) escape the inspection of the supervisory executives, they should be punished by "Zhang" (flogging with heavy sticks)

---

[97] According to *Ming Li Chi* (*Instruction on Statues and Terms*), "Jian Si" (official in charge of supervising the counties and towns) refers to the officials of "Zhuan Yun"(Office of Transportation), "Ti Dian" (Office of Judiciary), "Xing Yu" (Office of Prison), "Ti Ju Chang Ping Si" (office in charge of relief and water conservancy); "An Cha Guan"(head of judicial commission) refers to the officials with ranks higher than "Tong Pan" (official in charge of agriculture, water conservancy and litigation under subprefecture) in supervisory departments or the "Zhi Zhou" (subprefectural magistrates)and "Tong Pan" who are responsible for all the affairs of their departments." See the articles of "Jian Si Xun Li" (The Inspection Tours of Supervisory Executives) and "Jian Si Zhi Tong An Ju" (The Inspections and Reports of the Supervisory Executives and Deputy Chief Executive) in "Zhi Zhi Men" (The Category of Official System) (Part 4) in *Qing Yuan Tiao Fa Shi Lei* (*The Legal Provisions and Cases Made in the Year of Qingyuan*), Vol. 7.

for one hundred strokes; if they hinder the work of the supervisory executives or try every method to curry favor with them, they should be ordered to be stopped and never be appointed officials again, and their penalties shall be aggravated by one level.

If "Jian Si" (official with right of supervising counties and towns) know that some departments have delayed carrying out the law, they should write official letters to instruct other subordinate supervisory officials to handle the cases, though it is not the responsibility of the supervisory executives. If, after giving the instruction, the subordinate officials do not investigate the cases and fulfill the responsibility or if the subordinate officials apply very lenient punitive measures or if "Jian Si" (official with right of supervising counties and towns) conceal the truth to the emperor, the penalty of the supervisory executive shall be one level lighter than that for the subordinate supervisory officials; if "Jian Si" (official with right of supervising counties and towns) has neglected his responsibility, but other supervisory executives fail to have him redressed, the supervisory executives shall be punished one level lighter than that for the violators; if "Jian Si" (official with right of supervising counties and towns) harbors and conceals an official who has committed the crime of "Zuo Zang" (embezzlement), both of them shall be punished.

If there are illegal acts in other government departments, they should be reported by the supervisory executives, "Zhi Zhou" (subprefectural magistrates) and "Tong Pan" (official in charge of agriculture, water conservancy and litigation under prefecture and subprefecture) to the emperor and relevant punitive measures should be taken.

In inspecting the various government departments, the supervisory executives should report the criminal acts of the officials to the emperor according to facts. Moreover, the supervisory executives should not exchange information with each other. If the department officials have been accused and reported to the emperor, or if they are proved to be innocent by evidence, they can be pardoned.[98]

More detailed regulations are recorded in "Jiu Ku Chi" (Imperial Instructions on Stables) and "Za Chi" (Collection of Imperial Instructions on Miscellaneous Affairs) in *Qing Yuan Tiao Fa Shi Lei* (*The Legal Provisions and Cases Made in the Year of Qingyuan*):

> When making inspection tours, if the official staff accompanying "Fa Yun" (the officials responsible for transport) and the supervisory executives are given the tickets of courier stations (by which the official staff can use the carriages and horses of the courier stations freely) against the law, the official staff and the officials who give the tickets shall be punished by "Tu" (imprisonment) for two years.
>
> If "Fa Yun" (the officials responsible for transport) and the supervisory executives sell the alcoholic drink given to them as presents, they shall be punished by "Zhang" (flogging with heavy sticks) for one hundred strokes.
>
> If the soldiers have escaped when they are sent on a military mission without taking their families, the officials ought to record the registration and report the cases to the superior officials; if they fail to do so even if they have been urged by prestigious people, both the officials and the soldiers shall be punished by "Tu" (imprisonment) for two years. If "Fa Yun" (the officials responsible for transport) and the supervisory executives fail to settle the cases, they shall be punished for the same crime as those who have been convicted.
>
> When the supervisory executives (and the subordinate officials) are making inspection tours, boats should be provided along the rivers. If the soldiers and horses which are

---

[98]"Jian Si Xun Li" (The Inspection Tours of Supervisory Executives) and "Jian Si Zhi Tong An Ju" (The Inspections and Reports of the Supervisory Executives and Deputy Chief Executive) in "Zhi Zhi Men" (The Category of Official System) (Part 4) in *Qing Yuan Tiao Fa Shi Lei* (*The Legal Provisions and Cases Made in the Year of Qingyuan*), Vol. 7.

employed are not used in inspection tours, or if excessive number of solders and horses are used in the inspection, or if the soldiers and horses are still dispatched even if the supervisory executives have completed the mission and returned to the supervisory department, the officials responsible shall be punished by "Zhang" (flogging with heavy sticks) for one hundred strokes.[99]

Thirdly, administrative efficiency was increased by conducting administrative inspections to check whether the delivery of official documents were delayed in the offices at all levels or whether there were malpractices in performing their duties. In December of the 5th year of Yuanfeng (1082 A.D.), an imperial edict was issued by Emperor Shenzong, and it was ordered that "'Yu Shi Tai' (The Censorate) should send one 'Yu Shi' (the censor) to 'San Sheng' (The Three Departments) in autumn and winter to check whether the official documents are delayed. Besides, 'Yu Shi' (the censor) should not interfere with other matters in 'San Sheng' (The Three Departments)."[100] In the 6th year of Yuanfeng, another imperial edict was issued by the emperor to "Yu Shi Tai" (The Censorate): "Every half a year 'Yu Shi' (the censor) should be sent by turns to examine whether the official documents of 'San Sheng' (The Three Departments) are delayed and whether there are mistakes. If no such arrangement is made, each department of 'San Sheng' (The Three Departments) should send one official to examine the affairs of their own department. Besides, the work of each province should be inspected by the officials of 'Yu Shi Tai' (The Censorate)."[101] The work of local government offices should be examined each year or each season or should be examined by the supervisory executives when they make regular inspection tours.

Fourthly, as to the supervisory work of local governments, the focus was judicial and economic supervision. In December of the 7th year of Dazhongxiangfu during the reign of Emperor Zhenzong (1014 A.D.), "an imperial edict was issued by the emperor and it was ordered that official inspection should be conducted by 'Zhuan Yun Shi' (official in charge of transportation) and 'Ti Dian Xing Yu' (judicial commission) in Chuanxia, Guangnan and Fujian, if any officials are found to be corrupted, or to have violated the law, or have tortured the prisoners cruelly, they should be reported to the emperor."[102] In April of the 9th year of Dazhongxiangfu (1016 A.D.), another edict was issued by Emperor Zhenzong, and it was ordered that "if the convicts punishable by 'Da Bi' (capital punishment) in 'Lu' (ancient administrative region) in 'San Jing' (the three cities in ancient China) are imprisoned or dead for unreasonable reasons, 'Jiu Cha Ti Dian Xing Yu' (the officials of picket of

---

[99]"Jian Si Xun Li" (The Inspection Tours of Supervisory Executives) in "Zhi Zhi Men" (The Category of Official System) (Part 4) in *Qing Yuan Tiao Fa Shi Lei* (*The Legal Provisions and Cases Made in the Year of Qingyuan*), Vol. 7.

[100]"Zhi Guan" (State Official) in *Song Hui Yao Ji Gao* (*Collected Essays of the Historical Records of Song Dynasty*) (Book 11), Vol. 17.

[101]"Zhi Guan" (State Official) in *Song Hui Yao Ji Gao* (*Collected Essays of the Historical Records of Song Dynasty*) (Book 11) Vol. 17.

[102]*Xu Zi Zhi Tong Jian Chang Bian* (*Sequel to the Full-length Book of History as a Mirror*), Vol. 83, in December of the 7th year of Dazhongxiangfu.

judicial commission) should be appointed to have the cases investigated."[103] In March of the 7th year of Qingli during the reign of Emperor Renzong (1047 A.D.), it was ordered that "whenever conducting inspections in 'Zhou' (subprefecture) and 'Xian' (county), 'Zhuan Yun Shi' (official in charge of transportation) and 'Ti Xing Shi' (judicial official) should interrogate the prisoners first in prison. If a prisoner dies during the imprisonment, the condition should be checked and reported to the two above departments; if doubtful points are found in the cases or if the dead prisoner has been found to have bruises of torture on his body, the files of the case should be checked and the case should be investigated by special officials according to law."[104]

In November of the 3rd year of Xi'ning during the reign of Emperor Shenzong (1070 A.D.), an imperial edict was issued, and the supervisory executives were ordered to conduct an investigation of the judgments that were already made. If mishandled cases are discovered, they should be redressed and memorials about the cases should be submitted to the emperor afterward.[105]

In addition, in "Duan Yu Ling" (Decrees on Trials and Punishments) in *Qing Yuan Tiao Fa Shi Lei* (*The Legal Provisions and Cases Made in the Year of Qingyuan*), the following regulations are provided concerning the supervisory power of supervisory executives:

When an impeachment is conducted by the supervisory executives, it should be recorded and presented to "Xing Bu" (The Department of Punishment) and "Shang Shu Sheng" (The Department of Secretary) within thirty days. If the impeachment of any other officials is conducted without investigation or with personal grudges, which has caused the dismissal of those officials who are proved to be innocent afterwards, it must be reported to the emperor.[106]

If the supervisory executives want to hear the cases of the accused, they should ask the help of the yamen runners in the government of "Zhou" (subprefecture) and "Xian" (county) where they stay. If the places where they stay are not "Zhou" (subprefecture) and "Xian" (county), they should hire some other men nearby, who should be sent back after the work is finished. If the subordinate officials hear cases without the help of yamen runners, they can also ask or employ some other people to help them. When "An Cha Guan" (head of judicial commission) is making inspection tours, they should not imprison the accused in rooms or hold them in custody with chains.[107]

---

[103] *Xu Zi Zhi Tong Jian Chang Bian* (*Sequel to the Full-length Book of History as a Mirror*), Vol. 83, in April of the 9th year of Dazhongxiangfu.

[104] "Xing Fa" (The Criminal Law) in *Song Hui Yao Ji Gao* (*Collected Essays of the Historical Records of Song Dynasty*) (Book 55) Vol. 6.

[105] "Xing Fa" (The Criminal Law) in *Song Hui Yao Ji Gao* (*Collected Essays of the Historical Records of Song Dynasty*) (Book 25) Vol. 4.

[106] "Jian Si Zhi Tong An Ju" (The Inspections and Reports of the Supervisory Executives and Deputy Chief Executive) in "Zhi Zhi Men" (The Category of Official System) (Part 4) in *Qing Yuan Tiao Fa Shi Lei* (*The Legal Provisions and Cases Made in the Year of Qingyuan*), Vol. 7.

[107] "Jian Si Xun Li" (The Inspection Tours of Supervisory Executives) in "Zhi Zhi Men" (The Category of Official System) (Part 4) in *Qing Yuan Tiao Fa Shi Lei* (*The Legal Provisions and Cases Made in the Year of Qingyuan*), Vol. 7.

Clearly, for the misconducts of the local judicial officials, they should be dealt with by the heads of the judicial offices themselves according to law, referred to as "An Zhi," or they should be reported to the emperor and be decided by him, which is referred to as "An He Yi Wen," or they should be frequently dealt with by "Shang Shu Sheng" (The Department of Secretary) through administrative litigation.

Additionally, the national policy of regarding agriculture as the foundation of the country was maintained through economic supervision. For example, it was stipulated in "Kao Ke Ling" (Edicts of Assessments) in *Qing Yuan Tiao Fa Shi Lei* (*The Legal Provisions and Cases Made in the Year of Qingyuan*) that "the supervisory executives shall conduct the supervision of their supervisory places in spring and autumn every year to encourage peasants to farm after they receive the hand-written manuscript of imperial edict. When they are making inspection tours, the supervisory executives should check the work of the chief officials of 'Zhou' (subprefecture) and 'Xian' (county) to see if they are diligent when they are supervising and encouraging agriculture production. For the annual assessment of the chief officials of 'Zhou' (subprefecture) and 'Xian' (county), their performance should be evaluated, their scores (excellent or poor) should be given (if they are replaced before the end of year, their achievements should be assessed by the successors), recommendations should be made and memorials should be reported to the emperor before the end of January in the next year. [One 'Zhi Zhou' (subprefectural magistrates) should be recommended by each 'Zhou' (subprefecture); two 'Xian Ling' (county magistrate) should be recommended if there are more than fifty 'Xian' (county) in the area; one 'Xian Ling' (county magistrate) should be recommended by each county if there are fewer than fifty 'Xian' (county) in the area, or the position should be filled until there is a vacancy]. When it is the time for an official to be dismissed from his office, his position should be filled by the officials who are in the list of recommendation (this regulation is also applicable to the situation where one official is replaced)."[108]

Moreover, according to "Nong Sang Men" (The Category of Farming and Sericulture) in *Qing Yuan Tiao Fa Shi Lei* (*The Legal Provisions and Cases Made in the Year of Qingyuan*), "if the officials have disturbed the peasants in their tour of supervising and encouraging agriculture production, they shall be punished by 'Tu' (imprisonment) for two years. (If the officials indulge their staff in doing the same things, they shall receive the same punishment as their staff)." "When the chief officials are sent to the rural areas to inspect farming (on February of the 15th every year), they should not be accompanied by additional staff and should not go for a stroll by taking the advantage of inspection. Besides, girls should be not invited to sing and dance to entertain the invited guests."[109] During flood, drought, and other

---

[108]"Jian Si Xun Li" (The Inspection Tours of Supervisory Executives)in "Zhi Zhi Men" (The Category of Official System) (Part 4) in *Qing Yuan Tiao Fa Shi Lei* (*The Legal Provisions and Cases Made in the Year of Qingyuan*), Vol. 7.

[109]"Quan Nong Sang" (Inspection of Farming and Sericulture) quoted from "Zhi Zhi Chi" (Imperial Instruction on the Official System) and "Zhi Zhi Ling" (Decrees on the Official System) in "Nong Sang Men" (The Category of Farming and Sericulture)in *Qing Yuan Tiao Fa Shi Lei* (*The Legal Provisions and Cases Made in the Year of Qingyuan*), Vol. 49.

disasters, "if what the supervising executives and other officials report in the memorials is not true or is just partially true, they shall be punished for the violation of law."[110]

Due to its special historical background, the tax revenue was also strictly supervised by the imperial government of the Song Dynasty because it was very important for the maintenance of national activities. It was stipulated in "Fu Yi Men" (The Category of Tax and Corvee Service) in *Qing Yuan Tiao Fa Shi Lei* (*The Legal Provisions and Cases Made in the Year of Qingyuan*) that "it is allowed to pay households tax by using other stuff, but the median value of the stuff discounted should be estimated by 'Zhuan Yun Si' (Office of Transportation) in the first ten days of the month for the payment of the tax. Those who violate the regulations shall be impeached and reported to the emperor by 'Ti Dian Xing Yu' (judicial commission)." "If the tax is diverted for other usage without reporting to the emperor, or if the reports is made to the emperor but before it is approved by the emperor, the tax has been diverted for other usage, those involved shall be punished by 'Tu' (imprisonment) for two years."[111] "If the common people engage in land transaction, they should pay tax according to official contracts"; "if anyone in 'Zhou' (subprefecture) and 'Xian' (county) violates the regulation, he should be severely punished."[112]

Fifth, the supervisors' legal responsibilities were strictly stipulated; at the same time, severe punitive measures were also provided in detail in the supervision law. If the supervisors failed to inspect what they ought to inspect or they behaved like tyrants or they took bribes by bending the law, they would either be dismissed from their offices or be punished by "Zhang" (flogging with heavy sticks) for one hundred strokes or by "Tu" (imprisonment) for two years or by "Liu" (exile) to a distance of 2000 *li* or be prohibited from becoming officials again.

According to *Jie Yue Jian Si Ti Liang Gong Shi Huai Jian Yu Bi Shou Zhao* (*The Handwritten Manuscript of Imperial Edict on Admonishment of Supervisory Executives for Their Misconducts in Official Business*), issued in the 5th year of Chongning (1106 A.D.), "the supervisory executives, who are acting as the emperor's ears and eyes, are responsible for the the daily affairs of 'Lu' (ancient administrative region). If 'Jin Jiang Zhi Hui' (Military Commanders) and 'Ti Liang Gong Shi' (title of military officials who were responsible for transferring military

---

[110]"Shang Shu Zou Shi" (Presentation of Memorials) quoted from "Zhi Zhi Chi" (Imperial Instruction on the Official System) in "Zhi Zhi Men" (The Category of Official System) (Part 1) in *Qing Yuan Tiao Fa Shi Lei* (*The Legal Provisions and Cases Made in the Year of Qingyuan*), Vol. 4.

[111]"Zhi Yi Zhe Bian" (Paying Tax by Using Other Things and Evading the Tax) quoted from "Fu Yi Ling" (Decrees on Tax and Corvée) in "Hu Hun Chi" (Imperial Instruction on Households and Marriage) in "Fu Yi Men" (The Category of Tax and Corvee Service) (Part 2) in *Qing Yuan Tiao Fa Shi Lei* (*The Legal Provisions and Cases Made in the Year of Qingyuan*), Vol. 48.

[112]"Ke Fu" (Compulsory Tax and Corvee) quoted from "Sui Chi Sheng Ming" (The Statement of the Imperial Instructions) in "Fu Yi Men" (The Category of Tax and Corvee Service) (Part 4) in *Qing Yuan Tiao Fa Shi Lei* (*The Legal Provisions and Cases Made in the Year of Qingyuan*), Vol. 48.

orders, reporting the results of battles and enemy actions and conducting surveillance of military officials) who have take a wait-and-see attitude to avoid their responsibilities, or colluded with fellow officials to deceive the emperor, or concealed and sheltered the wrongdoings, or behaved in a brash way to mess up the truth, … or mishandled the penal cases of imperial court still do things out of personal grudges or show favor to someone or handle affairs dishonestly or unreasonably, they shall not only be dismissed from their posts according to imperial order, but also be punished by 'Liu' (exile) to a distance of 2,000 *li* and shall never be appointed as officials again no matter what crimes they have committed or how the cases are redressed or how they have been dismissed from office or punished. This order must be made known to all people of 'Lu' (ancient administrative region)."[113]

In order to have a basis for their prosecution and to prevent them from abusing their power for personal gains, the law on mutual supervision was especially made for the supervisory executives, which was the most typical among the supervisory laws and regulations in the Song Dynasty. The specific regulations are as follows:

> If there are no supervisors but there are illegal acts or law breakers in the governmental offices, "Fa Yun" (the official responsible for transport) and the supervisory executives shall take the responsibility of reporting the wrongdoings and injustice to the emperor. Moreover, mutual supervision shall be conducted between "Fa Yun" (the official responsible for transport) and the supervisory executives. The subordinate officials of "Jing Lue An Fu Shi" (ancient official, head of "Lu", responsible for military affairs), "Fa Yun" (the official responsible for transport) and the supervisory executives shall be mutually supervised and shall report their wrongdoings to the government.
>
> If department officials have committed crimes, their cases should be handled by "Jian Si" (official with right of supervising counties and towns) and "Jun Shou" (governor) according to the law, and their salaries should be suspended. Mutual supervision should be conducted by the different bureaus.
>
> As to disaster relief, different bureaus have different responsibilities: "An Fu Si" (Office of Placation) is responsible for settlement; "Zhuan Yun Si" (Office of Transportation) is responsible for evaluating the impact of disaster, dispensing charity to the refugees and tax collection; "Chang Ping Si" (office in charge of relief and water conservancy) is responsible for the sale of grain and the loan business; "Ti Dian Xing Yu Si" (judicial commission) is responsible for supervising the malpractice and misconducts. If there is violation of law, it is allowed for the various bureaus to conduct mutual impeachment and to make reports to "Shang Shu Sheng" (The Department of Secretary).
>
> If "Jian Si" (official with right of supervising counties and towns) know that some departments have delayed carrying out the law, they should write official letters to instruct other subordinate supervisory officials to handle the cases, though it is not the responsibility of "Jian Si" (official with right of supervising counties and towns). If, after giving the instruction, the subordinate officials do not investigate the cases and fulfill the responsibility or if the subordinate officials apply very lenient punitive measures or if "Jian Si" (official with right of supervising counties and towns) conceal the truth to the emperor, the penalty of the supervisory executive shall be one level lighter than that for the subordinate supervisory officials; if one supervisory executive has neglected his responsibility, but other supervisory executives fail to have him redressed, "Jian Si" (official with right of supervising counties and towns) shall be punished one level lighter than that for the violators; if "Jian Si" (official

---

[113]"Jie Chi" (Exhortations and Instructions) (Part 7) in *Song Da Zhao Ling Ji* (*Collected Grand Edicts and Decrees of the Song Dynasty*), Vol. 196.

with right of supervising counties and towns) harbors and conceals an official who has committed the crime of "Zuo Zang" (embezzlement), both of them shall be punished.[114]

The mutual supervision of the supervisory officials was one of the governing tactics used by the emperors of the Song Dynasty to control the ministers—an embodiment of the theory of "Yi Lun Xiang Jiao" (ministers having different opinions restraining each other) in the supervisory system. According to the article of Renchen in July of the 3rd year of Xi'ning (1070 A.D.) in volume two hundred and thirteen of *Xu Zi Zhi Tong Jian Chang Pian* (*Sequel to the Full-Length Book of History as a Mirror*), "after Emperor Zhenzong appointed Kouzhun as the minister, someone asked the emperor why he did so. He answered: 'the ministers with different opinions may restrain each other so that they dare not commit rash acts.'" In this sense, the so-called "Yi Lun Xiang Jiao" refers to a situation where the ministers who had different political opinions and different responsibilities may expose, denounce, monitor, and restrain each other, which had shown the emperors' intention to "make proper preparations and arrangements for the hidden dangers that need to be prevented."[115]

In conclusion, the supervisory system of the Song Dynasty is famous for the comprehensive contents of its supervision law, so it became a good example in administrative legislation and was institutionally guaranteed. However, under the feudal autocratic system, the supervisory system failed to play its due role even though a strict supervisory network had been established. This was because the monarch was beyond the constraints of the supervision law, as he was both the motive power of formulating all the supervision laws and regulations and the core of the supervisory network. Just for this reason, the supervision and punishment of the officials were always changed according to the emperors' will, which had shown the limitation of the supervision of the feudal supervisory laws and regulations.

8.3 Criminal Law Aiming to Maintain the Centralization of Authority

During the period of the Northern and Southern Song dynasties, criminal law mainly included *Song Xing Tong* (*The Penal Code of Song Dynasty*) and other several special criminal laws and a large number of imperial commands and collections of regulations. The initial purpose of making criminal law was to punish the felonies of

---

[114]"Jian Si Zhi Tong An Ju" (The Inspections and Reports of The Supervisory Executives and Deputy Chief Executive) quoted from "Zhi Zhi Ling" (Decrees on the Official System) and "Zhi Zhi Chi" (Imperial Instruction on the Official System) in "Zhi Zhi Men" (The Category of Official System) (Part 4) in *Qing Yuan Tiao Fa Shi Lei* (*The Legal Provisions and Cases Made in the Year of Qingyuan*), Vol. 7.

[115]*Xu Zi Zhi Tong Jian Chang Bian* (*Sequel to the Full-length Book of History as a Mirror*), Vol. 17, in October of the 9th year of Kaibao.

"Shi E" (The Ten Abominations). Moreover, harsh punishments were imposed upon bandits and thieves to maintain the rule over the country. The law on the punishment of bandits and thieves was changed: the lenient punishment was gradually changed to severe ones, and the policy of crime prevention was changed to that of imposition of severe penalty. Further changes in the law on criminal punishment were made: the mitigated penalty of "Zhang" (flogging with heavy sticks) was changed to partial restoration of corporal punishments. Such development had shown the intensification of social conflicts and the corruption of bureaucratic politics in Song Dynasty.

8.3.1 "Dao Zei Zhong Fa" (Severe Punishment for Robbery and Theft)

The crime of "Shi E" (The Ten Abominations) included in the legal codes of Sui and Tang dynasties was still the focus of punishment in the criminal law of the Northern and Southern Song dynasties. In the Northern and Southern Song dynasties, the offenders of "Mou Fan" (plotting rebellion or plotting to endanger the country), "Mou Da Ni" (great sedition), and "Mou Pan" (treason) were punished by "Yao Zhan" (cutting at the waist), "Qi Shi" (exposing the executed body publicly at markets), and even "Ling Chi" (the punishment of dismemberment and lingering death). In cases of unlawful possession of weapons and "concealing the criminals without reporting," the offenders should be punished by "Zhan" (beheading). In order to prevent people from meeting secretly to plot rebellion in the name of religion, "the acts such as preaching heresies, gathering at night and leaving in the day, killing people and offering their bodies as sacrifices to gods are all forbidden in the law, so the people's behaviors are all strictly supervised."[116] During the period of Tianxi in the reign of Emperor Zhenzong, the crimes of "fraudulently calling up evil spirits and cursing," "writing evil doctrines into books," and "practicing witchcraft" were all included in the same category of "Shi E" (The Ten Abominations).[117] During the reign of Emperor Huizong, the officials of "Zhou" (subprefecture) and "Xian" (county) were required to take preventive measures to guard against wickedness and witchcraft, so if they had neglected their supervisory duties, they would be punished.

The scope of punishment for the violation of "Zhi" (imperial decree) was expanded in the Song Dynasty in order to maintain the emperor's dignity. It was recorded in "Shu Ling" (Imperial Writs) in volume nine of *Tang Liu Dian* (*The Six Statutes of Tang Dynasty*) that "the imperial edicts are issued for seven purposes: ...

---

[116]"Xing Fa Zhi" (The Record of the Criminal Law) (Part 1) in *Song Shi* (*The History of Song Dynasty*).

[117]"Xing Fa Zhi" (The Record of the Criminal Law) (Part 1) in *Song Shi* (*The History of Song Dynasty*).

8.3 Criminal Law Aiming to Maintain the Centralization of Authority

the second one is called 'Zhi Shu' (imperial decrees), namely, to grant great rewards, to offer great official titles, to carry out political reforms and to pardon the war captives; the third one is called 'Wei Lao Zhi Shu' (imperial decrees for showing comfort), namely, to express the emperor's appreciation for the services rendered, to praise the talents and to encourage the diligent." Clearly, the violation of "Zhi" (imperial decree) referred to the crime of violating imperial edicts, which were issued as laws. In the Song Dynasty, the scope of punishment for the violation of "Zhi" (imperial decree) was expanded. So if "Zhi" (imperial decree) was intentionally violated, the offenders would be punished by "Tu" (imprisonment) for two years; if "Zhi" (imperial decree) was violated by negligence, the offenders would be punished lighter than that of the intentional one for the crime of involuntary violation. The expanded scope of punishment can be seen from the following imperial edict issued by Emperor Renzong in October of the 1st year of Tiansheng:

> If a warden recruits the common people to do things by posting up notices without reporting to his senior officials, he should be punished for violating "Zhi" (imperial decree); but if the person whom he has recruited is found guilty of some crime, he should be punished for his dereliction of duty.[118]

In November, another edict was issued by the emperor, and it was stipulated that "from today forward, if any sorcerer, in the name of evil spirits, stops supplying food, clothes and medicine to a patient or isolates the patient from his relatives or intends to murder the patient, he and the conspirators shall be punished according to the article of laying curses upon people; if the sorcerer has no grudges against the patient, he should be punished for violating the regulation by negligence; if the sorcerer instigates the respectable people to preach witchcraft as followers, he should be punished for violation of 'Zhi' (imperial decree)."[119]

Additionally, the penalties for counterfeiting official documents and seals became much severer, and those involved should be punished by "exiling to places at a distance of 3,000 *li*, which was the maximum penalty, but now it is changed into 'Jiao' (hanging)"; in the past, the crime of counterfeiting official seals "is not punished by death penalty, even if the criminal is a recidivist, but now the violator shall be punished by 'Jiao' (hanging)."[120]

"Dao Zei Zhong Fa" (Severe Punishment on Robbing and Theft) was a very important criminal principle in Song Dynasty. Since "Dao Zei Zhong Fa" (Severe Punishment on Robbing and Theft) had brought great suffering to the people in the period of "Wu Dai" (the Five Dynasties), when drafting *Song Xing Tong* (*The Penal Code of Song Dynasty*) in the 3rd year of Jianlong, Emperor Taizu suggested that

---

[118] "Kui Song" (Giving Presents) in "Pang Zhao Fa" (Decrees for the Reference of Enforcement) in "Zhi Zhi Chi" (Imperial Instruction on the Official System) in *Qing Yuan Tiao Fa Shi Lei* (*The Legal Provisions and Cases Made in the Year of Qingyuan*), Vol. 9.

[119] *Jian Yan Yi Lai Xi Nian Yao Lu* (*An Annual Record of the Most Important Events since the Reign of Jianyan*), Vol. 175, in October of 26th year of Shaoxing.

[120] "Xing Fa Zhi" (The Record of the Criminal Law) (Part 3) in *Song Shi* (*The History of Song Dynasty*).

"simple measures must be taken in governing the state and compassion must be shown to the people."[121] Therefore, relatively more lenient penalties were executed in the Song Dynasty than in the period of "Wu Dai" (the Five Dynasties). For the cases of theft, if the value of the stolen property accounted to five *guan* (a monetary unit, one *guan* is a string of 1000 coins) of money, the thief would be sentenced to death; if the value of the stolen property was less than five *guan*, the thief would be punished by "Chi" (flogging with light sticks) for twenty strokes with penal servitude for three years. For the cases of robbery, if the value of the robbed property accounted to three *guan*, the robber should be sentenced to death; if the value of the property was less than three *guan*, the robber should be punished by "Chi" (flogging with light sticks) for twenty strokes with penal servitude for three years. But compared with the penalties in *Tang Lv* (*Tang Code*), these penalties were still much severer. Taking the crime of robbery as an example, it was provided in "Zei Dao Lv" (Statutes on Stealing and Robbery) in *Tang Lv Shu Yi* (*The Comments on Tang Code*) that "if injury is caused in robbery, the convicts shall be punished by 'Jiao' (hanging); if death is caused, the convicts shall be punished by 'Zhan' (beheading)"; "for the case of robbery, if the criminal carries a stick when he is committing robbery, but if he does not rob any property from the victim, the criminal shall be punished by 'Liu' (exile) to a distance of 3,000 *li*." However, according to the imperial edict issued on the 7th of July in the 5th year of Xiande in Zhou state, which was recorded in "Zei Dao Lv" (Statutes on Stealing and Robbery) in *Song Xing Tong* (*The Penal Code of Song Dynasty*), all bandits would be "sentenced to death" without caring whether they carried sticks or whether they had stolen any goods. "If the person who plots robbery does not share the illegally obtained property but participates in the robbery, or if he does not participate in the robbery but shares the property, he shall be punished the same as those who have participated in the robbery"; "if the person who conspires to plot the robbery participates in the robbery but does not share the illegally obtained property, or he does not participate in the robbery but shares the property, he will be punished by 'Liu' (exile) one level lighter than those who participate in the robbery." So it was clear that although the rulers in the Song Dynasty advocated that "simple measures must be taken in governing the state and compassion must be shown to the people," the criminal acts that had brought harm to social security and state interests would still be punished by harsh penalties.

The penalties became severer in the Song Dynasty just because the conflicts between classes turned out to be much sharper. Especially, the great peasant uprising led by Wang Xiaobo and Li Shun had made the rulers greatly shocked and panic-stricken. In order to suppress the uprising, an edict was issued by Emperor Taizong, and it was stated that "if those gangsters dare to continue to put up a stiff resistance without surrendering themselves, they should all be killed immediately without

---

[121]"Xing Fa Zhi" (The Record of the Criminal Law) (Part 3) in *Song Shi* (*The History of Song Dynasty*).

pardoning." As a result, "countless people were killed or drown to death."[122] During the reign of Emperor Taizong, "severe penalties were even enforced upon the people who cut the bark of mulberries or cudrania tricuspidata." So even the starving people who ate the bark of mulberries or *Cudrania tricuspidata* because of hunger would be punished according to the amount of the bark that they had cut off. If the bark of the trees that was cut off amounted to forty two *chi*, it would be one *gong*; if it was three *gong*, the violator should be sentenced to death penalty.[123] Just as what was written in "Xing Fa Zhi" (The Record of the Criminal Law) in *Song Shi* (*The History of Song Dynasty*): "The wicked and evil-minded people were severely punished by Emperor Taizu and Emperor Taizong." In view of the domestic strife and foreign aggression, it was clearly stated by Emperor Taizong that "foreign aggression is just the trivial affair of the border regions, so they can be prevented, but only the wickedness and evilness are difficult to be dealt with. So it is fearful because it may cause domestic strife."[124] During the reign of Emperor Renzong, "a period of justice" and "a time ruled by benevolent monarchs" were boasted; however, though the law of "Qiang Dao" (robbery) was revised, the penalties were still much severer than those in *Tang Lv* (*Tang Code*). For example, the robbers should be punished by "Tu" (imprisonment) for two years even though they did not carry sticks with them when they were committing the crime; if the convicts carried sticks with them but did not share the illegally obtained property, they would be punished by "Liu" (exile) to a distance of 3000 *li*; if the convicts carried sticks with them during the robbery, shared the illegally obtained property, and injured the victim, they would be sentenced to death. So every year, the offenders who were punished by death penalty were "one hundred times more than those in Tang Dynasty."[125]

After the middle of the reign of Emperor Renzong, the burden of peasants became much heavier because of the large scale of land annexation and frequent aggression of other countries. Consequently, "the bandits and thieves ran amok everywhere,"[126] so "it was difficult to deal with the situation in the towns and villages."[127] In order to suppress the bandits and thieves, in the 7th year of Jiayou during the reign of Emperor Renzong (1062 A.D.), a punitive measure called "Wo Cang Zhong Fa" (severe punishment for harboring criminals) was taken as a supplement to the

---

[122]Li You (Song Dynasty), "Xiao Ping" (Suppression of Usurpers) in *Song Chao Shi Shi* (*The Anecdotes of Song Dynasty*), Vol. 17.

[123]"Xing Fa Zhi" (The Record of the Criminal Law) (Part 1) in *Song Shi* (*The History of Song Dynasty*).

[124]*Xu Zi Zhi Tong Jian Chang Bian* (*Sequel to the Full-length Book of History as a Mirror*), Vol. 32, in August of the 2nd year of Chunhua.

[125]"Xing Fa Zhi" (The Record of the Criminal Law) (Part 1) in *Song Shi* (*The History of Song Dynasty*).

[126]*Xu Zi Zhi Tong Jian Chang Bian* (*Sequel to the Full-length Book of History as a Mirror*), Vol. 143, in September of the 3rd year of Qingli.

[127]Bao Zheng, "Qing Su Chu Jing Dong Dao Zei" (A Plea for the Elimination of Bandits and Thieves from Jingdong soon) in *Li Dai Ming Chen Zou Yi* (*Memorials Submitted to the Emperor by the Famous Officials in Different Dynasties*), Vol. 317.

common law to impose severe punishment upon the people who harbored criminals. The so-called "Wo Cang Zhong Fa" (severe punishment for harboring criminals) refers to a collection of imperial edicts about "the punishment of the crime of harboring bandits and thieves"[128] in the counties around the capital, which were adopted as special criminal laws applicable to specific regions. The making of the special criminal law was a great change in the history of Chinese criminal law, which had exerted a great influence on the development of the feudal criminal law of the dynasties after the Song Dynasty. So the penalties for "Qiang Dao" (robbery) were also used to punish the people who harbored criminals; at the same time, the counties around the capital were classified as the areas where "heavy penalties should be applied," which meant that within the area, any offender who had committed the crime of "Qiang Dao" (robbery) would be severely punished to strengthen the public security of the area.

When Emperor Yingzong succeeded to the throne, the tradition of "Dao Zei Zhong Fa" (Severe Punishment on Robbing and Theft) was also continued. In the 3rd year of Zhiping (1066 A.D.), an imperial edict was issued: "In the counties of Changheng, Kaocheng, Dongming in Kaifeng Fu (Kaifeng prefecture), and in the counties of the subprefectures of Cao, Pu, Chan and Hua, the evil people always gang together to rob people of their property and to kill the constable who are sent to catch the criminals, so severe punitive measures need to be taken to suppress those criminals immediately."[129] In those places mentioned above, "if an accused has committed robbery or if he is punishable by death penalty, his family property shall be confiscated and be awarded to the informers. Moreover, his children shall be exiled to a place 1,000 *li* away to serve in the army. Even if an amnesty is offered by the emperor ... they will still be exiled to the island of Shamen; if the accused is punishable by 'Tu' (imprisonment), he shall be sent to the military prison in the isolated place of Guangnan with his face tattooed, and half of his family property shall be confiscated and be awarded to the informers. Moreover, his children shall be exiled to a place 500 *li* away to serve in the army. Even if an amnesty is offered by the emperor, they will not allowed to be pardoned to return home."[130] As for the harsh penalties that were enforced during the reign of Emperor Yingzong, not only were the retroactive forces of law emphasized, but the relatives of the offenders were also implicated with their family property confiscated. So the bandits and thieves were actually punished for the crime of "Fan Ni" (treachery). Just as what Fan Zuyu had said, "In the areas where severe penalties are executed, all people are criminals. If one person commits crime, his wife and children will all be implicated with his family property confiscated, so the penalties enforced upon him is the same as those

---

[128]*Xu Zi Zhi Tong Jian Chang Bian* (*Sequel to the Full-length Book of History as a Mirror*), Vol. 344, in March of the 7th year of Yuanfeng.

[129]"Bing" (Military) in *Song Hui Yao Ji Gao* (*Collected Essays of the Historical Records of Song Dynasty*) (Book 28), Vol. 11.

[130]"Bing" (Military) in *Song Hui Yao Ji Gao* (*Collected Essays of the Historical Records of Song Dynasty*) (Book 26), Vol. 11.

8.3 Criminal Law Aiming to Maintain the Centralization of Authority

for 'Fan Ni' (treachery) ... so the areas are different from other places because harsher penalties are specially applied."[131]

In the 4th year of Xi'ning during the reign of Emperor Shenzong (1071 A.D.), "Dao Zei Zhong Fa" (Severe Punishment on Robbing and Theft) was revised, so the areas where severe penalties were applied were expanded to more than ten districts, including the western and eastern areas of Huannan; Fujian; the western and eastern areas of Hebei; the western and eastern areas of Jingdong, Shannxi, Yongxing, and Jingji; etc. According to "Xing Fa Zhi" (The Record of the Criminal Law) in *Song Shi (The History of Song Dynasty)*, "till the time of Yuanfeng, in the districts of Hebei, Jingdong, Huainan and Fujian, severe penalties were also enforced. Consequently, severe penalties were also enforced in more and more 'Jun' (shire) and 'Xian' (county) nationwide." Meanwhile, the concept of "Zhong Fa Zhi Ren" (offenders punishable by severe punishment) and the relevant penalties were also put forward. It was recorded in history books that "the law was amended in the period of Yuanfeng ... though some of the places were not included in the areas where severe punishments were enforced, the bandits and thieves there were all harshly punished."[132] The so-called "Zhong Fa Zhi Ren" (offenders punishable by severe punishment) mainly referred to the rebellious peasants who took part in the armed uprising and rebellion against the ruling class. The penalties enforced upon the offenders punishable by severe punishment were not differentiated by regions, so once they were arrested, they would be punished by death penalty with their family property confiscated, to be awarded to the informers, and their wives exiled to places 1000 *li* away without being pardoned or permitted to go back home even though amnesties were offered. If bandits and thieves "have killed government officials or killed altogether three people, or burned one hundred houses, or rampaged through 'Zhou' (subprefecture) and 'Xian' (county) or robbed the boats in rivers, even though the places where they stay are not included in the areas where severe penalties are enforced, they should still be severely punished."[133] So it was required that local officials in the places where severe penalties were enforced must punish the bandits and thieves "with firm hands and strong determination. Moreover, they should show hatred to the evildoers as if they were their personal enemies and regard the struggle of fighting against crimes as their own responsibilities."[134]

In the reign of Emperor Zhezong, the places where severe penalties were enforced had covered 71% of the twenty four districts of the country. Moreover, "Zei Dao Lv" (Statutes on Stealing and Robbery) in *Song Xing Tong (The Penal Code of Song Dynasty)* was replaced by "Ze Dao Zhong Fa" (Severe Punishment for Robbing and

---

[131] *Xu Zi Zhi Tong Jian Chang Bian (Sequel to the Full-length Book of History as a Mirror)*, Vol. 478, in October of the 7th year of Yuanyou.

[132] *Xu Zi Zhi Tong Jian Chang Bian (Sequel to the Full-length Book of History as a Mirror)*, Vol. 344, in March of the 7th year of Yuanfeng.

[133] *Xu Zi Zhi Tong Jian Chang Bian (Sequel to the Full-length Book of History as a Mirror)*, Vol. 344, in March of the 7th year of Yuanfeng.

[134] *Xu Zi Zhi Tong Jian Chang Bian (Sequel to the Full-length Book of History as a Mirror)*, Vol. 468, in November of the 6th year of Yuanyou.

Theft), so the penalties were even severer than those enforced during the reign of Emperor Shenzong. For example, "in the places where severe penalties were applied, if the bandits had cruelly robbed more than five people, they should be severely punished. After the period of Shaosheng (during the reign of Zhezong), the offenders of banditry and theft were all severely punished without considering how many people they had robbed."[135] As to the crime of criminal harboring, those involved would be punished by "Liu" (exile) to a distance of 500 *li* after being punished by "Zhang" (flogging with heavy sticks) during the reign of Emperor Shenzong, but during the reign of Emperor Zhezong, those involved should be punished by "Si" (death penalty).

The process for the implementation of "Ze Dao Zhong Fa" (Severe Punishment for Robbing and Theft) mentioned above had reflected that when social crisis deepened, the rulers mainly relied on severe penalties and strict laws. During the reign of Emperor Shenzong, Wen Yanbo said: "In Tang Dynasty and in the period of 'Wu Dai' (the Five Dynasties), strict laws were executed to resolve the problems of the time. Therefore, beyond the law, the punishment of 'Tu' (imprisonment) and 'Liu' (exile) were changed to 'Si' (death penalty). So although it is helpful to keep the country peaceful for hundreds of years to enforce lenient penalties, yet harsh penalties are inherited and applied. What is worse, some are even harsher than those in the old laws."[136] In fact, it was impossible to prevent the crimes caused by the domestic policy of encouraging land annexation and the foreign policy of exchanging peace with money and the strengthening of the centralization of authority only by enforcing severe penalties. During the reign of Emperor Renzong, a wise scholar named Liu Chang opined that "the lack of food and clothes is the root of banditry and theft; the unequal distribution of tax is the root of banditry and theft; the neglect of moralization is also the root of banditry and theft," so "if much attention is only attached to the elimination of banditry and theft without attaching to the problem of food and clothes, it is like trying to stop the flow of water by blocking the water sources; if much attention is only attached to the elimination of banditry and theft without attaching to the moralization of bandits and thieves, it is like trying to save some alcohol containers from fire after the fire begin to burn."[137] During the reign of Emperor Zhezong, Fan Zuyu also said that since the period of Xi'ning, the military inspectors of "Zhou" (subprefecture) "have specially imposed severe penalties upon banditry and theft ... now there are places where severe penalties are executed and

---

[135]"Xing Fa Zhi" (The Record of the Criminal Law) (Part 1) in *Song Shi* (*The History of Song Dynasty*).

[136]"Xing Fa Zhi" (The Record of the Criminal Law) (Part 3) in *Song Shi* (*The History of Song Dynasty*).

[137]Liu Chang (Han Dynasty), "Huan Dao Lun" (On Bandits and Theft) in *Gong Shi Ji* (*The Work of Mr. Gongshi*), Vol. 40.

8.3 Criminal Law Aiming to Maintain the Centralization of Authority

there are also particular people who are severely punished ... However, within the two decades after the implementation of severe penalties, what we hear is not the elimination of the crimes of banditry and theft, but the increase instead."[138] Su Xun also pointed out that the application of severe penalties had made people risk danger in desperation. He said:

> The common people are treated as if they were bandits and thieves, so they are punished by the penalties which are used to punish the bandits and thieves. The people are suppressed and disciplined by severe penalties so that they are already shaking with terror and holding their breath in fear, which has forced the people to make up their mind to become bandits and thieves without caring much about that they are the ones in the families whom their parents, wives and children merely depend on. This is the very reason that has led to the social turmoil.[139]

No doubt, such suggestions on solving the root problems were helpful to "stop the flow of water by blocking the water sources"; however, they did not attract the emperor's attention, and had only become a legacy for the later emperors.

During the reign of Emperor Xiaozong in the Southern Song Dynasty, the punishment of "Si" (death penalty) was not applied to bandits and thieves; instead, the word "bandit" was tattooed on their faces to show humiliation and so they can be easily controlled. However, if a person had committed banditry or theft twice, even if he was merely an accessory to the crime, he would be punished by death penalty.

In addition to "Dao Zei Zhong Fa" (Severe Punishment on Robbing and Theft), the severe penalties imposed on corruption also reflected the features of times. In view of the fact that many officials often took bribes by bending the law and had set up separatist regimes by exercising local power since the period of "Wu Dai" (the Five Dynasties), which had endangered the government of Later Zhou Dynasty, severe penalties were enforced to punish corrupt officials, encourage officials to abide by the law, and enforce the law after the unified regime of the Song Dynasty was established. During the reign of emperors Taizu and Taizong, corrupt officials were not allowed to be pardoned even though amnesties were offered, so they were either punished by "Qi Shi" (exposing the executed body publicly at markets) or by "Zhang" (flogging with heavy sticks) in the imperial court or by "Liu" (exile) to Shamen Island with their faces tattooed. During the reign of Emperor Taizu, "an official named Guo Yi who were responsible for the official documents in the Prefecture of Daming was punished by 'Qi Shi' (exposing the executed body publicly at markets)"; "the officials in Caihe such as Wang Xun and so on were punished by 'Zhe' (to open and split, breaking apart the criminal's body) because they had mixed sand into the military grain"; "a general named Shi Yanzuo was punished by 'Zhan' (beheading) and 'Qi Shi' (exposing the executed body publicly at markets) for obtaining illegal property in collusion with the officials in his

---

[138] Fan Zuyu (Song Dynasty), "Zhuan Dui Tiao Shang Si Shi Zhuang" (Four Reports to the Emperor on the State Affairs) in *Fan Tai Shi Ji* (*Collected Works of Fan Taishi*), Vol. 22.

[139] Su Xun (Song Dynasty), "Zhang Yizhou Hua Xiang Ji" (The Portrait of Zhang Yizhou) in *Jia You Ji* (*Anthology in the Reign of Jiayou*), Vol. 15.

supervisory area."[140] The application of the principles of "Yi" (deliberation: cases involving eight privileged groups were not to be tried directly by judicial organs but to be reported to and decided by the emperor; thus, the accused would usually be pardoned or remitted), "Qing" (petition: cases involving officials above the 5th rank shall be reported to and decided by the emperor, the punishment other than death penalty would be remitted by one degree), "Jian" (mitigation: except for death penalty, other punishments on officials above the 7th rank and their families could be remitted by one degree), "Shu" (atonement), or "Guan Dang" (giving up one's official position for the atonement of a crime) was limited in order to severely punish the crime of "Tan Zang Wang Fa" (taking bribes by bending the law) by officials. During the reign of Emperor Taizong, an imperial edict was issued, and it was stipulated that the officials who had committed the crime of "Zuo Zang" (embezzlement) should never be appointed officials again even though they were pardoned by amnesties and that this should be made a permanent regulation in law. The severe penalties employed in these particular periods were helpful for rectifying the problems, disciplining the officials, and preventing corruption, but it ended up with nothing definite after the early period when the emperor tried to persuade the ministers to hand over their military power: "You can select good farmland and houses, you can prepare the estate that can be kept forever for your descendants, and you can buy more singsong and dancing girls, drink every day and enjoy the happiness to in your lives."[141] Later on, in order to strengthen the centralization of authority and to win the support of the ministers, "the emperor was always worried that the rewards given to his officials were not enough, while the common people's wealth was all plundered with nothing left."[142] For these reasons, it was impossible to punish those corrupt officials by sticking to strict punitive measures.

From the reign of Emperor Zhenzong, the punishment for corrupt officials became more lenient, and the penalty of "Zhan" (beheading) and "Qi Shi" (exposing the executed body publicly at markets) for the crime of "Zuo Zang" (embezzlement) was almost abolished. During the reign of Emperor Yingzong, even if more than 180,000 *dan* of rice in Fuguo Granary in the capital was damaged, the officials responsible for the granary was just punished by "being dismissed from his office." Especially, during the reign of Emperor Huizong, because Caijing and Tong Guan were given important positions, the country was plagued by widespread corruption, so that the management of officials became out of hand. Consequently, "only one tenth of the officials were honest but nine tenths of the officials were corrupted."[143]

---

[140]Zhao Yi (Qing Dynasty), "Song Chu Yan Cheng Zang Li" (Severe Punishments for the Corrupt Officials of Song Dynasty) in *Er Shi Er Shi Zha Ji* (*Reading Notes of the Twenty-Two Official Histories*), Vol. 24.

[141]*Xu Zi Zhi Tong Jian Chang Bian* (*Sequel to the Full-length Book of History as a Mirror*), Vol. 2, in July of the 2nd year of Jianlong.

[142]Zhao Yi (Qing Dynasty), "Song Zhi Lu Zhi Hou" (The High Official Salaries of the Song Dynasty) in *Er Shi Er Shi Zha Ji* (*Reading Notes of the Twenty-Two Official Histories*), Vol. 25.

[143]Li Xin (Ming Dynasty), "Shang Huang Di Wan Yan Shu" (A 10,000-Word Memorial to the Emperor) in *Kua Ao Ji* (*Collected Works of Kua Ao*), Vol. 19.

In the later period of the Song Dynasty, "it was even impossible to conduct serious investigation of the wrongdoings of the corrupt officials."[144] Originally it was stipulated that the officials who had committed the crime of "Zuo Zang" (embezzlement) should never be appointed officials again even though they were pardoned by amnesties, but now this regulation was wantonly trampled.

In the stipulations about the punishment for the crime of "Zuo Zang" (embezzlement) in the Northern and Southern Song dynasties, it is easy to find that in the early period of the Song Dynasty relevant stipulations were more lenient compared with the ones in *Tang Lv* (*Tang Code*). According to what was provided in "Jian Zhu Shou Cai Wang Fa" (Chief Officials Taking Bribes by Bending the Law in Their Supervisory Areas) in *Tang Lv Shu Yi* (*The Comments on Tang Code*), if a chief official had taken bribes by bending the law in his supervisory area or if he had accepted fifteen *pi* of cotton cloth, he would be punished by "Jiao" (hanging); if the official had merely taken bribes without bending the law or if he had accepted thirty *pi* of cotton cloth, he would be punished by "Liu" (exile) with penal servitude; if the officials whose monthly salaries were less one *dan* of grain had accepted twenty *pi* of cotton cloth, he would be punished by "Jiao" (hanging); if the official had merely taken bribes without bending the law or if he had accepted forty *pi* of cotton cloth, he would be punished by "Liu" (exile) with penal servitude. It was specified in the provision of "Shou Suo Jian Lin Cai Wu" (illegally accepting people's money and property in one's supervisory area) that if an official received property amounting to fifty *pi* of cotton cloth from their supervisory areas, he would be exiled to a place 2000 *li* away; if they demanded for the property by force, they would be punished for bending the law; if a chief supervisor stole what was entrusted to his care, his punishment would be two levels severer than that for theft; if the property he had stolen amounted to thirty *pi* of cotton cloth, he would be punished by "Jiao" (hanging). Although the stipulations in *Song Xing Tong* (*The Penal Code of Song Dynasty*) were the same as those in *Tang Lv* (*Tang Code*), they were amended in "Chi" (instruction), which was attached to it. For example, in the law for the punishment of the crime of "Zuo Zang" (embezzlement), if the property taken amounted to fifteen *pi* of cotton cloth, those involved would be punished by "Jiao" (hanging), but in the attached "Chi" (instruction), the estimated value was changed to twenty *pi*. For cases where the law had been bent, the estimated value for the crime of "Zuo Zang" (embezzlement) committed by the officials with no salaries was changed from twenty *pi* of cotton cloth to twenty five *pi*; however, for cases where the law had not been bent, the estimated value for the crime of "Zuo Zang" (embezzlement) committed by the officials with no salaries, which was punishable by "Liu" (exile) with penal servitude, was changed from forty *pi* of cotton cloth to more than fifty *pi*, and the cases should be reported to the emperor for his decision. Compared with *Song Xing Tong* (*The Penal Code of Song Dynasty*), the penalties in

---

[144]Zhao Yi (Qing Dynasty), "Song Chu Yan Cheng Zang Li" (Severe Punishments for the Corrupt Officials of Song Dynasty) in *Er Shi Er Shi Zha Ji* (*Reading Notes of the Twenty-Two Official Histories*), Vol. 24.

Qing Yuan Tiao Fa Shi Lei (*The Legal Provisions and Cases Made in the Year of Qingyuan*) were more lenient. For example, in the provision of "Kui Song" (Giving Presents) in "Zei Dao Chi" (Imperial Instruction on Stealing and Robbery) in "Zhi Zhi Men" (The Category of Official System), it was provided that "if the chief officials steal what are entrusted to their care, or steal the property under their supervision, they (who are not exempted) shall be exiled to 'Zhou' (subprefecture) where they were born; if the value of the stolen property amounts to thirty five *pi* of cotton cloth, they shall be punished by 'Jiao' (hanging)." According to the stipulation in "Zhi Zhi Chi" (Imperial Instruction on the Official System), "if the illegal property which the chief officials receive or demand amounts to one hundred *pi* of cotton cloth by force, or if they are the appointed officials by the imperial court, their punishment shall be decided by the emperor, and the other officials shall be exiled to the cities where they were born." In the provision of "Li Shang" (Rewards) in "Zhi Zhi Men" (The Category of Official System), "Zhi Zhi Chi" (Imperial Instruction on the Official System) was quoted, in which it was stipulated that "the officials who have received property amounting to fifty *pi* of cotton cloth without bending the law shall be exiled to the cities where they were born." It was written in the provision of "Cang Ku Shou Qi" (Chief Officials of Warehouses Receiving Illegal Property) in "Zhi Zhi Chi" (Imperial Instruction on the Official System) in "Ku Wu Men" (The Category of Warehouse Affairs) that "as for the chief officials responsible for supervision ... if they receive or demand for one hundred *pi* of cotton by force, they shall be exiled to the places where they were born."

Moreover, due to the strengthening of autocracy, the legislative and judicial power of the emperor was also greatly expanded in the Song Dynasty, so officials who committed the crime of "Zuo Zang" (embezzlement) were often exempted from punishment by the emperor according to the extralegal forms of lenient punishment. During the reign of Emperor Zhenzong, the punishment for corrupt officials was changed from "Zhan" (beheading) and "Qi Shi" (exposing the executed body publicly at markets) to being exiled to the remote islands with the punishment of "Zhang" (flogging with heavy sticks). But during the reign of Emperor Renzong, "even the punishment of 'Liu' (exile) and 'Zhang' (flogging with heavy sticks) were seldom executed."[145] During the reign of Emperor Shenzong, the punitive measures of "Qing" (to tattoo on the face) and "Zhang" (flogging with heavy sticks) were abolished; during the reign of Emperor Huizong, whether they were officials appointed by the imperial court or ordinary official staff, if they had committed the crime of "Zuo Zang" (embezzlement), they would all be punished by the disciplinary sanction of "being dismissed from office." Especially, "the junior corrupt officials

---

[145]Zhao Yi (Qing Dynasty), "Song Chu Yan Cheng Zang Li" (Severe Punishments for the Corrupt Officials of Song Dynasty) in *Er Shi Er Shi Zha Ji* (*Reading Notes of the Twenty-Two Official Histories*), Vol. 24.

8.3 Criminal Law Aiming to Maintain the Centralization of Authority

were severely punished with the exception of the senior ones,"[146] which had further contributed to the corruption of officials.

It was recorded in *Hui Zhu Lu Hou Lu* (*The Notes by Wang Mingqing*), written by Wang Mingqing, that there was even a convention in the Song Dynasty that discussed that "the ministers should not be punished by death penalty":

> The laws are lenient in our dynasty. So if the ministers have committed crimes, different penalties should be enforced, but death penalty should not be inflicted presumptuously. It is said that an edict is made and hidden by Emperor Taizu in the Imperial Ancestral Temple, and he has promised not to impose death penalty upon the ministers and "Yan Guan" (official responsible for giving advice to the emperor); otherwise, the offenders would be punished. It has shown the sincerity of the emperor, which is incomparable by the previous dynasties.

Emperor Zhezhong also said, "The convicted ministers are exempted from death penalty to achieve the unfulfilled aspiration of our ancestors."[147] In the late Ming and early Qing dynasties, Wang Fuzhi wrote in his book *Song Lun* (*On Song Dynasty*): "During the reign of Emperor Taizu, an edict was issued to his descendants and he promised that 'Shi Da Fu' (literati and officials) would not be punished by death penalty. So from then on, no civil officials had been sentenced to death until the end of Song Dynasty." Therefore, the promise of imposing no death penalties upon the ministers was made in the early period of the Song Dynasty in order to unify the ruling class, to win the support of the ministers, and to consolidate the power of the autocratic centralization. Then during the period of the Northern and Southern Song dynasties, ministers who had committed crimes were either punished by death penalty or pardoned because it was helpful to mediate the disputes between the parties within the ruling class. For example, during the reign of Emperor Taizong, after "Bing Bu Shang Shu" (the minister of the department of defense) named Lu Duoxun as having colluded with the King of Qin and committing serious crimes against the state, he was only punished by being removed from office and exiled to Yazhou. During the reign of Emperor Zhenzong, "Zai Xiang" (the prime minister) named King Wei as having colluded with an eunuch named Lei Yungong and deceiving the emperor, but he was only demoted and exiled to Yazhou after Emperor Renzong ascended the throne. During the reign of Emperor Gaozong in the Southern Song Dynasty, "the punitive measures (applied to officials) were always lenient. So although many officials had committed serious crimes, none of them had ever been sentenced to death penalty."[148] As a result, lenient punishments had led to "rampant

---

[146] Wang Fuzhi (Ming Dynasty), *Du Tong Jian Lun* (*Comments on Reading the History as a Mirror*), Vol. 28.

[147] "Xing Fa Zhi" (The Record of the Criminal Law) (Part 2) in *Song Shi* (*The History of Song Dynasty*).

[148] "Xing Fa Zhi" (The Record of the Criminal Law) (Part 2) in *Song Shi* (*The History of Song Dynasty*).

crimes everywhere,"[149] which not only undermined the management of officials and weakened the authority of the law but also led to the perishing of the Song Dynasty.

8.3.2 The Changes of the Penal System Shown by "She Zhang Fa"

As for punishments during the Song Dynasty, those in the Tang Dynasty were followed, which were divided into five kinds, namely, "Chi" (flogging with light sticks), "Zhang" (flogging with heavy sticks), "Tu" (imprisonment), "Liu" (exile), and "Si" (death penalty). As to the punishment of death penalty, in addition to "Jiao" (hanging) and "Zhan" (beheading), the punishment of "Ling Chi" (the punishment of dismemberment and lingering death), which was implemented in the period of "Wu Dai" (the Five Dynasties), was also adopted during the reign of Emperor Renzong in order to punish the people in the Jinghu area because they had offered the bodies of people as sacrifices to spirits and had "spread offensive and unruly words."[150] Till the time of Emperor Shenzong, the punishment of "Ling Chi" (the punishment of dismemberment and lingering death) was used to crack down on felonies like "Fan Ni" (treachery), which was harmful to the ruling of the country. During the whole period of the Northern Song Dynasty, the punishment of "Ling Chi" (the punishment of dismemberment and lingering death) was only mentioned in imperial edicts, while in the period of the Southern Song Dynasty, it was written in statutory criminal law, together with the punishment of "Jiao" (hanging) and "Zhan" (beheading). The so-called punishment of "Ling Chi" (the punishment of dismemberment and lingering death) "is the most severe punishment because the bodies of the convicts are dismembered before their necks are cut."[151] "Ling Chi" (the punishment of dismemberment and lingering death) was explicitly described in the book *Du Lv Pei Xi* (*A Handbook of Law*), written by a famous legal expert of the Qing Dynasty: "the bodies of the convicts were cut apart piece by piece with no slices of muscles left before their genital organs were finally cut off. As to the female convicts, their female genitalia and stomachs were cut open before their viscera were taken out. Besides, their bodies were also dismembered and minced."[152] Shen Jiaben of the Qing Dynasty wrote in his textual research that "the original meaning of 'Ling

---

[149]Xu Ji (Song Dynasty), "Ce Wen" (Questions and Answers on Politics) in *Jie Xiao Xian Sheng Wen Ji* (*The Collected Works of Mr. Jie Xiao*), Vol. 29.

[150]"Xing Fa Zhi" (The Record of the Criminal Law) (Part 2) in *Song Shi* (*The History of Song Dynasty*).

[151]"Xing Fa Zhi" (The Record of the Criminal Law) (Part 3) in *Song Shi* (*The History of Song Dynasty*).

[152]Wang Mingde (Qing Dynasty), "Ling Chi" (The Punishment of Dismemberment and the Lingering Death) in *Du Lv Pei Xi* (*A Handbook of Law*) (Book 2), Vol. 4.

Chi' referred to a range of rolling hills, but now it refers to killing the convicts by the lingering death."[153]

Moreover, the punishments such as "Yao Zhan" (cutting at the waist), "Xiao Shou" (the penalty of hanging the head of the criminal on top of a pole for public display), "Yi Zu" (implicating the nine generations of a family), "Zhang Sha" (beating convicts to death with a heavy stick), etc. were also restored in the Song Dynasty. The illegal abuse of penalties showed that the rulers of the Song Dynasty tried hard to intimidate the large number of "bandits" by employing harsh penalties, which was in fact a great regression of the feudal penal system. So the practice of writing extralegal brutal corporal punishment into law in the Yuan, Ming, and Qing dynasties could be traced back to the Song Dynasty. Indeed, the legalization of brutal punishments was not only against the trend of historic development but also against the rulers' ideology of advocating and stressing the law in the Song Dynasty. During the Song Dynasty, "Shi Da Fu" (literati and officials) continued to present memorials to the emperors appealing for the abolishment of extralegal cruel punishment, but the situation was not changed, which was caused directly by the increasingly strengthened feudal autocratic system and growing isolation.

Additionally, the wide application of the auxiliary penalties and the revival of the corporal punishment also demonstrated changes in the penalty system of the Song Dynasty. The main auxiliary punishment included "Ci Pei" (being exiled with the face tattooed). In the early period of the Song Dynasty, "Ci Pei Zhi Fa" (law on the exile of the criminal with his face tattooed) was made by Emperor Taizu, who boasted of "his benevolence to the people." The punishment was a substitute punishment for those who were exempted from the death penalty, which combined the punishment of "Jue Zhang" (beating the criminal's back, legs, and buttocks with heavy sticks), "Liu Pei" (life exile), and "Ci Mian" (tattooing the face of a criminal). However, due to sharp social conflict and the trend of "employing severe punishment," criminals who had committed serious crimes or who should have been punished by "Liu" (exile) would also be punished by "Zhang" (flogging with heavy sticks) and "Qing" (to tattoo on the face). After the reign of Emperor Tazong, the punishment of "Ci Pei" (being exiled with the face tattooed) gradually became a common punitive measure. And in the collection of imperial edicts issued during the reign of Emperor Zhenzong, forty six crimes were punishable by "Ci Pei" (being exiled with the face tattooed), but the number reached to one hundred and seventy in the collection of imperial edicts issued in the years of Qingli during the reign of Emperor Renzong. In the years of Xi'ning during the reign of Emperor Shenzong, crimes punishable by "Ci Pei" (being exiled with the face tattooed) even reached to more than two hundred. In the years of Chunxi during the reign of Emperor Xiaozong, even more five hundred and seventy kinds of crimes were punishable by "Ci Pei" (being exiled with the face tattooed), so that "there were so many

---

[153] Shen Jiaben (Song Dynasty), "Ling Chi" (The Punishment of Dismemberment and the Lingering Death) in "Xing Fa Fen Kao" (Separate Textual Research on Penal Law) (Part 2) in *Li Dai Xing Fa Kao* (*A Textual Research of the Criminal Laws in the Past Dynasties*).

criminals who were punished by 'Ci Pei' (being exiled with the face tattooed) that the tattooed criminals could be seen everywhere."[154] Since the punishment of "Liu" (exile), which was prevalent in the period of "Wu Dai" (the Five Dynasties), was adopted in the Song Dynasty, criminals who were punished by "Ci Pei" (being exiled with the face tattooed) were also exiled to the northwest border areas and registered in military troops; therefore, they were referred to as "Pei Li" (exiled slaves), who often served as laborers in troops. If amnesties were offered by the emperor, those who had committed relatively minor crimes would be allowed to go back home, but those who had committed relatively serious crimes would never be allowed to do so. The word "Ci" in the punishment of "Ci Pei" (being exiled with the face tattooed) referred to one of the corporal punishments in ancient times, which was also called "Qing Xing" (punishment of tattooing on the face). The implementation of "Ci Pei" (being exiled with the face tattooed) in the Song Dynasty was severely criticized by the people in the later periods. For example, in the Ming Dynasty, Qiu Jun stated in *Da Xue Yan Yi Bu* (*Supplement to the Deductive Meaning of the Great Learning*): "The punishment of 'Ci Pei' (being exiled with the face tattooed) which was inherited from the period of 'Wu Dai' (the Five Dynasties) was implemented by the Song Dynasty. A criminal punishable by this punishment was exiled with his face tattooed and his back flogged, which meant that, altogether three penalties were enforced upon the person who had committed only one crime." The punishment of "Ci Pei" (being exiled with the face tattooed) was widely used in the Song Dynasty. Some bureaucrats and "Shi Da Fu" (literati and officials) even suggested restoring the corporal punishment due to the stress of peasant uprising. For example, Zeng Bu, Han Jiang, etc. once strongly suggested having the corporal punishment restored comprehensively. The scholars of "Li Xue" (neo-Confucianism: a Confucian school of idealist philosophy of the Song and Ming dynasties), namely, Zhang Zai and Zhu Xi, even advocated that corporal punishments were "made by the previous monarchs to prevent wickedness," so they were "benevolent measures."[155]

The implementation of "She Zhang Fa" (replacing the punishment of "Chi" (flogging with light sticks), "Zhang" (flogging with heavy sticks), "Tu" (imprisonment), and "Liu" (exile) with the punishment of beating the criminal's back, legs, and buttocks with heavy sticks) had typically reflected changes in the punishment system of the Song Dynasty. After the unification of the country, "She Zhang Fa" (replacing the punishment of "Chi" (flogging with light sticks), "Zhang" (flogging with heavy sticks), "Tu" (imprisonment), and "Liu" (exile) with the punishment of beating the criminal's back, legs, and buttocks with heavy sticks) was made by Emperor Taizu to get rid of "the brutal punishment of 'Wu Xing' (Five Penalties)" and to carry out the policy of lenient and benevolent ruling. According to this

---

[154]"Xing Fa Zhi" (The Record of the Criminal Law) (Part 3) in *Song Shi* (*The History of Song Dynasty*).
[155]Zhu Xi (Song Dynasty), "Da Zhang Jing Fu" (The Answers to Zhang Jingfu's Questions) in *Zhu Wen Gong Wen Ji* (*Collected Works of Zhu Xi*), Vol. 25.

8.3 Criminal Law Aiming to Maintain the Centralization of Authority

punitive measure, "the criminals punishable by 'Liu' (exile) would be exempted from being sent to places far away; the criminals punishable by 'Chi' (flogging with light sticks) and 'Zhang' (flogging with heavy sticks) would be exempted from serving as laborers and the strokes of flogging for the criminals punishable by 'Chi'(flogging with light sticks) would be reduced."[156] With the implementation of *Song Xing Tong* (*The Penal Code of Song Dynasty*) in the 4th year of Jianlong (963 A.D.), "She Zhang Fa" (replacing the punishment of "Chi" (flogging with light sticks), "Zhang" (flogging with heavy sticks), "Tu" (imprisonment), and "Liu" (exile) with the punishment of beating the criminal's back, legs, and buttocks with heavy sticks) was officially written into the article of "Wu Xing" (Five Penalties) in "Ming Li Lv" (Statutes and Terms), which showed one of changes in the penal system of the Song Dynasty. "Li Bu Shang Shu" (the minister of the department of personnel) named Zhang Zhao, who was ordered by the emperor to make "She Zhang Fa," presented a memorial to the emperor to make a detailed report of the scope of application, the function, and the contents of "She Zhang Fa." The following is what was written in the memorial:

> Regarding Your Majesty's edict asking us to make detailed regulations to replace the punishment of "Tu" (imprisonment), "Liu" (exile), "Chi" (flogging with light sticks) and "Zhang" (flogging with heavy sticks) [except the punishment of "Mian" (exemption), "Dang" (redeeming one's official position for the atonement for a crime) and "Shu" (redemption) that should be reported to Your Majesty for Your Majesty's decision] with the punishment of flogging according to the levels of the punishment written in the law book, we humbly reply that the system of "Wu Xing" (Five Penalties) has been carried out for ages, though changes have been made in different dynasties, the leniency and the severity of the penalties remain unchanged. By abiding by Your Majesty's wise opinions, we have made new punitive measures for officials to avoid inappropriate application of the punishment when they are dealing with cases. We hope Your Majesty would order the relevant department to have them implemented. The following are the four levels of the punishment of "Liu" (exile): the punishment of "Liu" (exile) with one level severer is replaced by the punishment of flogging for twenty strokes with three years of labor service; the punishment of "Liu" (exile) to a distance of 3,000 *li* is replaced by the punishment of flogging for twenty strokes with one year of labor service; the punishment of "Liu" (exile) to a distance of 2,500 *li* is replaced by the punishment of flogging for eighteen strokes with one year of labor service; the punishment of "Liu" (exile) to a distance of 2,000 *li* is replaced by the punishment of flogging for seventeen strokes with one year of labor service. The following are the five levels of the punishment of "Tu" (imprisonment): "Tu" (imprisonment) for three years is replaced by the punishment of flogging for twenty strokes; "Tu" (imprisonment) for two and a half years is replaced by the punishment of flogging for eighteen strokes; "Tu" (imprisonment) for two years is replaced by the punishment of flogging for seventeen strokes; "Tu" (imprisonment) for one and a half years is replaced by the punishment of flogging for fifteen strokes; "Tu" (imprisonment) for one year is replaced by the punishment of flogging for thirteen strokes. The following are the five levels of the punishment of "Zhang" (flogging with heavy sticks): the punishment of "Zhang" (flogging with heavy sticks) for one hundred strokes is reduced to twenty strokes; the punishment of "Zhang" (flogging with heavy sticks) for ninety strokes is reduced to eighteen strokes; the punishment of "Zhang" (flogging with heavy sticks) for eighty strokes is reduced to seventeen strokes;

---

[156]"Xing Kao" (A Textual Research of the Criminal Penalties) (Part 7) in *Wen Xian Tong Kao* (*A General Textual Research of the Documents*), Vol. 32.

the punishment of "Zhang" (flogging with heavy sticks) for seventy strokes is reduced to fifteen strokes; the punishment of "Zhang" (flogging with heavy sticks) for sixty strokes is reduced to thirteen strokes. The following are the five levels of the punishment of "Chi" (flogging with light sticks): the punishment of "Chi" (flogging with light sticks) for fifty strokes is reduced to ten strokes; the punishment of "Chi' (flogging with light sticks) for forty to fifty strokes is reduced to eight strokes; the punishment of "Chi" (flogging with light sticks) for ten to twenty strokes is reduced to seven strokes. Besides, the size of the sticks used in flogging is set according to the old regulation in *Yu Guan Ling* (*Order of Warden*). The ordinary sticks officially used should be three *chi* and five *cun* in length and the large end should be two *cun* in width and the small end should be nine *fen* in width. The small sticks should be four *chi* and five *cun* and the big and small end should be six *fen* and five *fen* in width respectively. The ordinary stick is used in the cases of "Tu" (imprisonment), "Liu" (exile), "Chi" (flogging with light sticks) and "Zhang" (flogging with heavy sticks). In the cases of "Liu" (exile), the convicts should serve labor service for one year after being flogged; in the cases of "Liu" (exile) with labor service, the convicts should serve labor service for three years after being flogged; in the cases of "Tu" (imprisonment), the convicts are exempted from labor service after being flogged; in the cases of "Tu" (imprisonment) and "Liu" (exile), the convicts should be flogged on the back; in the cases of "Chi" (flogging with light sticks) and "Zhang" (flogging with heavy sticks), the convicts should be beaten on their backs and buttocks. Moreover, the size of the sticks used in inquisition is set according to the old regulations as well.[157]

"She Zhang Fa" (replacing the punishment of "Chi" (flogging with light sticks), "Zhang" (flogging with heavy sticks), "Tu" (imprisonment), and "Liu" (exile) with the punishment of beating the criminal's back, legs, and buttocks with heavy sticks) had made the regulation on the replacement of "Zhang" (flogging with heavy sticks) more complete. In the reign of Emperor Huzong, though some minor changes were made, it remained unchanged on the whole. When "She Zhang Fa" (replacing the punishment of "Chi" (flogging with light sticks), "Zhang" (flogging with heavy sticks), "Tu" (imprisonment), and "Liu" (exile) with the punishment of beating the criminal's back, legs, and buttocks with heavy sticks) was initially implemented, it was not applied to the cases of "Si Xing" (death penalties) in order to crack down on the serious crimes, but later it was combined with "Ci Pei Fa" (law on the exile of the criminal with his face tattooed), so it took the place of "Si Xing" (death penalties) gradually.

8.4 Civil Law Adapting to the Development of Commodity Economy

The development of a commodity economy during the Northern and Southern Song dynasties not only increased the complexity of civil legal relationship but also greatly enriched the contents of civil law, so it became a landmark in the history of Chinese civil law.

---

[157]"Qian De Yuan Nian San Yue Gui You" (Gui You in March of the 1st Year of Qiande) in *Chang Bian* (*The Complete Records*), Vol. 4.

8.4.1 The Expansion of Household Registration and the Changes of People's Identities

According to the principle of "collecting tax according to products and material resources," registered permanent residents in the country were divided into "Zhu Hu" (households having real estate) and "Ke Hu" (households having no real estate but renting other people's farmland) in the Song Dynasty, and the previous manor system was replaced by the tenancy system. The tenants were also registered as "Ke Hu" (households having no real estate but renting other people's farmland) and became the permanent residents of the state, so they were not the personal property of the landlords any more, though they did not have estates, it was a great breakthrough of their personal identities and legal positions. Due to different living areas, registered residents were further divided into "Xiang Cun Hu" (rural residents) and "Fang Lang Hu" (urban residents). "Zhu Hu" (households having real estate) was divided into different levels according to "whether they had paid hundreds of *guan* for tax, or they had several *qing* of farmland, or they had large amount of property, or they had rent out the farmland."[158] Since tax was paid according to the levels of the registered residents, registration was updated every three years in order to record the household changes in time. Both "Zhu Hu" (households having real estate) and "Ke Hu" (households having no real estate but renting other people's farmland) had the qualifications of civil subjects. The people who were regarded as "Jian Min" (rabbles or people of lower social status) or who did not have independent personalities in the Tang Dynasty, such as employed workers, laborers, and maidservants, became "Qi Min" or registered residents of the imperial government, and they were able to participate in civil activities as subjects of civil rights. Because "Ke Hu" (households having no real estate but renting other people's farmland) and "Dian Ke" (tenant) had their own rights, which were required for the subjects of civil rights, their personal security was guaranteed.

As for people's capacities, it was stipulated in "Hu Hun Lv" (Statutes on Marriage, Tax and Household Registration) in *Song Xing Tong* (*The Penal Code of Song Dynasty*) that "male and female under three years old were called 'Huang' (ignorant youth), under fifteen years old were called 'Xiao' (youth), under twenty years old were called 'Zhong' (middler); above twenty one years old were called 'Ding' (adult), above sixty years old were called 'Lao' (elder)..."[159] From what is mentioned above, we can see that the age limit for "Ding" (adult) in the Song Dynasty was twenty one, so people at that age started to have full capacities. It was stipulated that "those who are below ten and above eighty years old and those who are 'Du Ji' (the incapacitated)" were limited in disposing capacities; if "they

---

[158] *Xu Zi Zhi Tong Jian Chang Bian* (*Sequel to the Full-length Book of History as a Mirror*), Vol. 376, in April of the 1st year of Yuanyou.

[159] "Tuo Lou Zeng Jian Hu Kou Men" (The Category of Missing, Increasing and Decreasing the Household in Registration) in "Hu Hun Lv" (Statutes on Marriage, Tax and Household Registration) in *Song Xing Tong* (*The Penal Code of Song Dynasty*), Vol. 12.

have committed the crime of 'Fan Ni' (treachery) or murder which were punishable by 'Si' (death penalty), their cases shall be reported to the emperor for final decision; if they have committed the crime of 'Dao' (theft) which has caused injury, their penalties can be redeemed; if they have committed other crimes other than the ones mentioned above, they shall be exempted from punishment." Moreover, "the people who are above ninety or under seven years old" belonged to those without disposing capacities, so "though they have committed the crimes punishable by 'Si' (death penalty), they shall be exempted from punishment."[160]

In order to prevent the households from evading tax and corvee by reducing their resident levels through "establishing separate household registers and dividing the family property," it was forbidden in law for the residents to establish separate households. According to the rule made in the 1st year of Kaibao during the reign of Emperor Taizu, if the paternal parents or parents were still alive, it was forbidden for the sons or grandsons to establish separate household registers or to divide the family property. In August of the next year, the chief officials of the counties of Sichuan and Shannxi where there were many cases of registration of separated households and family property division were informed that "if a person is discovered to have established a separate household register and divided the family property when his parents are still alive, he shall be sentenced to death penalty."[161] Although such acts were exempted from the punishment of "Si" (death penalty) during the reign of Emperor Taizong, it was still "punishable according to the law."[162] So the separation of households was illegal unless some procedures were performed after the parties concerned had applied to the government. Because household registration was the basis for tax collection and the criterion for the assessment of the achievements of officials, "the county officials who could increase the registered population by attracting more residents could apply for promotion and salary increase."[163] Consequently, some of the officials were promoted and rewarded by taking advantage of the occasion to increase registered households through fraud and deception, which had led to the situation where there were more registered households but fewer "Ding" (adult) in reality. Additionally, because "Ding" (adult) was often cruelly exploited by the local government, "some families would rather have their sons abandoned, or sold as servants, or sent to temples to be Taoists or Buddhists."[164]

---

[160]"Lao You Ji Ji Fu Ren Fan Zui Men" (The Category of the Offences Committed by the Elder, the Young, the Incapacitated, and Women) in "Ming Li Lv" (Statues and Terms) in *Song Xing Tong (The Penal Code of Song Dynasty)*, Vol. 4.

[161]*Xu Zi Zhi Tong Jian Chang Bian (Sequel to the Full-length Book of History as a Mirror)*, Vol. 10, in August of the 2nd year of Kaibao.

[162]*Xu Zi Zhi Tong Jian Chang Bian (Sequel to the Full-length Book of History as a Mirror)*, Vol. 24, in November of the 8th year of Taiping Xingguo.

[163]"Hu Kou Kao" (An Examination of the Registered Permanent Residence) (Part Two) in *Wen Xian Tong Kao (A General Textual Research of the Documents)*, Vol. 11.

[164]*Xu Zi Zhi Tong Jian Chang Bian (Sequel to the Full-length Book of History as a Mirror)*, Vol. 24, in June of the 4th year of Dazhongxiangfu.

8.4 Civil Law Adapting to the Development of Commodity Economy

Although the bureaucrats and landlords had a dominating position among civil right subjects, their economic position and political privilege were different from those of the powerful and influential families and the gentry in the old times. Especially, because of the rapid development of the commodity economy, few of the distinguished ministers, generals, or "Zai Xiang" (the prime minister) could even maintain their wealth and honor for "as long as three generations."[165]

The social status of the businessmen was obviously changed since they were referred to as "the people who can bring wealth to the country"[166]; they were registered as "Fang Lang Hu" (urban residents) and became permanent residents of cities and towns. So they were not registered as "Shi Ji" (the household registration of merchants) any more and became common people with their legal rights and interests protected. Therefore, accordingly, those "who have extorted money and goods from them or bought on credit and owed them money" should be punished.[167] Moreover, the businessmen also had the right to become government officials by taking the examination of "Ke Ju" (the imperial examination), which showed that their social status was also improved.

In the Song Dynasty, the traditional regulation between "Shi" (senior officials) and "Shu" (the common people) or "Liang" (the decent people) and "Jian" (people of a lower social status than common people) were followed. For example, in *Song Xing Tong* (*The Penal Code of Song Dynasty*), almost all provisions of *Tang Lv* (*Tang Code*) were inherited, according to which "Bu Qu" (the private army), "Nu Bi" (slave girls and maidservants), and "Guan Hu" (criminals and their relatives who became servants of officials) were included in "Jian Min" (rabbles or people of lower social status). Moreover, an edict was also issued by Emperor Renzong to "prohibit the wealthy and influential families from marring the women of their own clans."[168] However, in reality, "officials are appointed without considering their family background, people get married without considering whether they are influential or wealthy,"[169] and "friends are made without considering whether they are common people or officials."[170] Especially, because the economic exploitation of tenants was not as cruel as before, the tenants were free to move to other places if their renting contracts had expired. In the 5th year of Tiansheng (1027 A.D.), an edict was issued by Emperor Renzong, and it was ordered that the restriction on the migration of tenants should be abolished in the areas of Jianghuai, Liangzhe, Jinghu, Fujian, and

---

[165]Lv Hao (Song Dynasty), "Shang Qiu Xian Zong Qing Shu" (Letters to Emperor Xianzong) in *Yun Xi Gao* (*Manuscript of Yun Xi*).

[166]*Xu Zi Zhi Tong Jian Chang Bian* (*Sequel to the Full-length Book of History as a Mirror*), Vol. 10, in April of the 8th year of Xi'ning.

[167]Li Yuanbi (Song Dynasty), "Shu Shi Mai Pai" (Buying Cards at Book Markets) in *Zuo Yi Zi Zhen* (*Self-Admonition of Zuo Yi*), Vol. 8.

[168]"Ren Zong Ben Ji" (The Record of Emperor Renzong) (Part 1) in *Song Shi* (*The History of Song Dynasty*).

[169]"Shi Zu Lue" (Brief Introduction of the Clan) in *Tong Zhi* (*The General Records*), Vol. 25.

[170]Lv Dejon (Song Dynasty), "Guo Shi Xiang Gui" (Advice about the Misconduct) in *Lv Shi Xiang Yue* (*The Village Pact of Mr. Lv*).

Guangnan: "From today forward, the tenants can move to other places without the permission of their landlords, so they can consult with their landlords on their migration after they have paid their rent. The landlords and the tenants should deal with the issue properly, but before the tenants move to other places they should inform their landlords."[171] If their landlords had "stopped their moving unreasonably, the cases should be heard by the local county government,"[172] which was obviously a very important expression of the expansion of personal freedom of tenants. According to another relevant provision in law, tenants should not take joint liabilities for the illegal acts of their landlords.

Additionally, tenants had the right to pay or return the rent according to the contract; if they "were forced to farm the land," the tenants were allowed to file lawsuits. However, if the tenants owed rent or defaulted on the payment of their rent, the landlords were allowed to "file lawsuit to the government" to "ask the officials to deal with the cases." Su Shi once pointed out that "the tenants are the people whom the landlords depend on. So if all the tenants leave where they live because of hunger, the land of the landlords will be left uncultivated."[173] If there were disputes between landlords and tenants, the law would always be in favor of the landlords. For example, "if a tenant beats his landlord, his penalty shall be one level severer than that for a common person; nevertheless, if a landlord beats his tenants or if the crime is not as serious as the one punishable by 'Zhang' (flogging with heavy sticks), he shall not be punished; if the crime is more serious than the one punishable by 'Tu' (imprisonment), the penalty he receives should be one level lighter than that for the common person."[174] In the years of Yuanyou during the reign of Emperor Zhezong, it was stipulated that if a landlord had beaten his tenants to death, the penalty he received should be one level lighter than that for a common person before he was exiled to a neighboring "Zhou" (subprefecture). However, during the period of Shaoxing in the Southern Song Dynasty, the place of exile in this provision was changed to "Zhou" (subprefecture) where the person lived.

During the Southern Song Dynasty, due to the political situation, the precarious imperial government depended more on the support of the landlord class. Therefore, the policy of cruel economic exploitation on tenants was adopted again so that in some areas, "the tenants were again tied to farmland" and the wives of tenants were even forbidden to marry again after their husbands died. In the 1st year of Shaoxi during the reign of Emperor Guangzong (1190 A.D.), it was forbidden for tenants to

---

[171]"Shi Huo" (National Finance and Economy) in *Song Hui Yao Ji Gao* (*Collected Essays of the Historical Records of Song Dynasty*) (Book 24), Vol. 1.

[172]"Shi Huo" (National Finance and Economy) in *Song Hui Yao Ji Gao* (*Collected Essays of the Historical Records of Song Dynasty*) (Book 24), Vol. 1.

[173]Su Shi (Song Dynasty), "Qi Jiang Sun Ruo Mi Dai Yu Ren Hu Ling Zhen Ji Dian Ke Zhuang" (A Memorial about Asking for Loaning Rice and Giving Relief to the Tenants) in "Zou Yi Ji" (A Collection of Memorials) in *Su Wen Zhong Gong Quan Ji* (*The Complete Works of Su Shi*), Vol. 14.

[174]*Xu Zi Zhi Tong Jian Chang Bian* (*Sequel to the Full-length Book of History as a Mirror*), Vol. 445, in July of the 5th year of Yuanyou.

sue their landlords according to law, but the landlords were permitted to torture their tenants in their own way. In *Yuan Dian Zhang* (*The Collection of Statutes of Yuan Dynasty*), there is the following record: "Before the perishing of the Song Dynasty, the landlords could willfully kill their tenants because they had regarded the tenants just as worthless."[175]

In the Song Dynasty, an unprecedented development was made in the handcraft industry that had acted as the basis for commodity exchange, including mining and metallurgy, shipbuilding, spinning and weaving, porcelain making, and papermaking. Moreover, the recruitment and employment system was extensively established in both private-owned and state-owned handicraft industries, so the employed workers not only gained their own freedom but also got rid of the master–slave relationship and formed a relatively equal relationship with the employers. The employed handicraft workers also obtained their qualifications as civil rights subject and began to participate in civil activities actively.

The change of the social status of "Nu Bi" (slave girls and maidservants) had most clearly reflected the change in social relationship. Although they were once regarded as "animal products," they had changed from being objects of property ownership to being subjects of civil rights. During the Northern and Southern Song dynasties, it was very rare to see the fact that some families had served as servants for generations or had become official servants because of their crimes. The reason for people working as "laborers" and "the maidservants" in the houses of bureaucrats and wealthy people was that they had no other means of livelihood because of wars; consequently, they became servants after being introduced by "Ya Ren" (middleman), so that a master-and-servant relationship was formed with the owners of the houses only within the period of the validity of the contract. According to law, it was forbidden to employ servants or to make someone "Nu Bi" (slave girls and maidservants) by force. If the offenders had abducted and sold women as "Nu Bi" (slave girls and maidservants) by violating the law, they would be harshly punished and the women would be freed.

The relationship between "the laborers" and "maidservants" and the owners of the house was that of employment. So "Nu Bi" (slave girls and maidservants) was one of the parties of the contract but no longer the private property of the house owners. Therefore, the personal rights of "Nu Bi" (slave girls and maidservants) were protected by law, and they not only had the independent right of personality but also the rights to decide whether they would stay or leave. Besides, the owners were specifically forbidden to punish or kill "Nu Bi" (slave girls and maidservants) privately. So the terms and expressions "Guan Hu" (criminals and their relatives who became servants of officials), "Za Hu" (families registered as workers), and "Liang Ren" (the decent people) and the discriminatory remarks of regarding "'Nu Bi' (the slave girls and maidservants) and 'Jian Ren' (rabbles or people of lower social status) as animal products," which were specially used in *Song Xing Tong*

---

[175]"Xing Bu" (The Department of Punishment) (Part 4) in *Yuan Dian Zhang* (*Statutes of Yuan Dynasty*), Vol. 42.

(*The Penal Code of Song Dynasty*), were "clearly abolished in law"[176] or were criticized as "regulations which should be abolished."[177]

However, it was impossible for the new social relationship that was formed on the basis of the development of a commodity economy to transcend the feudal hierarchical system. For example, it was stipulated in *Song Xing Tong* (*The Penal Code of Song Dynasty*) that if a landlord "chooses the daughter of 'Liang Ren' (the decent people) to be the wife of his slave, he shall be punished by 'Tu' (imprisonment) for one year; the penalty that 'Liang Ren' (the decent people) receives shall be one level lighter, and the marriage shall be dissolved; if the slave of the landlord marries a daughter of 'Liang Ren' (the decent people), the penalty which the slave receives shall be the same; if the landlord knows the circumstance, he shall be punished by 'Zhang' (flogging with heavy sticks) for one hundred strokes; if he registers the daughter of 'Liang Ren' (the decent people) as a maidservant in household registration, he shall be punished by 'Liu' (exile) to a distance of 3,000 *li*; if a man recklessly mistakes a maidservant for 'Liang Ren' (the decent people) and marries her, he shall be punished by 'Tu' (imprisonment) for two years (if a maidservant falsely claims she is of common family, she shall receive the same penalty) with their identities rectified after the punishment."[178] As another example, "if a 'Bu Qu' (the private army) or a 'Nu Bi' (the slave girls and maidservants) files a lawsuit against his or her master, or if it is not a case of 'Mou Fan' (plotting rebellion or plotting to endanger the country), 'Mou Da Ni' (great sedition) and 'Mou Pan' (treason), 'Bu Qu' (the private army) or 'Nu Bi' (the slave girls and maidservants) shall be punished by 'Jiao' (hanging); …if 'Nu Bi' (the slave girls and maidservants) appeals to be a 'Liang Ren' (the decent people) and also falsely claims that she is forced to be a 'Jian Min' (rabbles or people of lower social status), she shall be punished by 'Tu' (imprisonment) for three years."[179] These stipulations are not mere formalities because they could be proved by what was recorded in *Huang You Fa* (*The Law of Huangyou*): "Those who plunder people and force them to be 'Nu Bi' (the slave girls and maidservants) shall be punished by 'Jiao' (hanging)."[180]

---

[176]Fei Gun (Song Dynasty), "Guan Hu Za Hu" (Official Servants and Miscellaneous Households) in *Liang Xi Man Zhi* (*Notes of Liang Xi*), Vol. 9.

[177]Zhao Yanwei (Song Dynasty), *Yun Lu Man Chao* (*Notes Written at the Cloud-Covered Foothill*), Vol. 4.

[178]"Zhu Yu Nu Qu Liang Ren Men" (The Category of the Landlord Choosing Wives for his Slaves from the Common Families) in "Hu Hun Lv" (Statutes on Marriage, Tax and Household Registration) in *Song Xing Tong* (*The Penal Code of Song Dynasty*), Vol. 14.

[179]"Nu Bi Gao Zu Men" (The Category of Maidservants Filing Lawsuits against their Masters) in "Hu Hun Lv" (Statutes on Marriage, Tax and Household Registration) in *Song Xing Tong* (*The Penal Code of Song Dynasty*), Vol. 24.

[180]"Shi Huo" (National Finance and Economy) in *Song Hui Yao Ji Gao* (*Collected Essays of the Historical Records of Song Dynasty*) (Book 69), Vol. 69.

8.4.2 New Development of Property Rights

During the Northern and Southern Song dynasties, further progress was made in the areas of "Suo You Quan" (ownership), "Dian Quan" (pawn rights), "Yong Dian Quan" (rights of permanent rent), "Xiang Lin Quan" (right of adjacent), the right of joint ownership (of clan property), copyright, etc. so that a complete system of property rights was established.

"Suo You Quan" (ownership) was the most important part of property rights. In the Song Dynasty, "Suo You Quan" (ownership) was divided into estate ownership (proprietor rights) and property ownership (owner rights). For the ownership of real estate, the core was the ownership of farmland. The farmland that had no owners or that was left uncultivated or that was abandoned by the owners who had fled away or that was left by owners who had no heirs was all confiscated by the government to become "Guan Tian" (state-owned land). With the implementation of the policy of "having no restriction on land annexation" and because of the relationship between commodities and currency, the system of state-owned land ownership gradually declined but the system of privately owned land ownership was developed rapidly instead. Consequently, in the Northern and Southern Song dynasties, "Guan Tian" (state-owned land) tended to be privatized, so did the official rent. Thus, the private ownership of land had occupied a dominant position and it had become one of the major features of the ownership relationship, on the basis of which, the system of the private farmland ownership of landlords and land tenancy system were developed extensively.

Private real estate ownership derived mainly from the acquisition of farmland, trade, inheritance, and reward granted by the emperor. Take the farmland as an example; in the early period of the Song Dynasty, ownership of newly cultivated land was legally recognized in order to promote agricultural production and to encourage people to open up wasteland. After ascending the throne, Emperor Taizu issued an edict and ordered that "the chief officials of the local government should tell the people that if they can plant mulberry and date trees and open up wasteland, they shall be exempted from paying the original rent."[181] During the reign of Emperor Taizong, in view of the change of ownership of land, which had been caused by wars since the time of "Wu Dai" (the Five Dynasties), and disputes over farmland, a policy was adopted in which it was provided that "the land which has been cultivated belongs to 'Yong Ye Tian' (family farmland)."[182] During the early period of the Southern Song Dynasty, it was also specified in law that if tenants had cultivated the land "for five years, or if no one has claimed for the owner of the

---

[181]"Shi Huo" (National Finance and Economy) in *Song Shi* (*The History of Song Dynasty*) (Book 1), Vol. 1.

[182]"Shi Huo" (National Finance and Economy) in *Song Shi* (*The History of Song Dynasty*) (Book 1), Vol. 1.

land, the land should can be granted to the tenant as 'Yong Ye Tian' (family farmland)."[183]

In the early period of the Northern Song Dynasty, in order to legally recognize private ownership of land, "Hong Qi" (contract in red color), a kind of certificate of property ownership of land that was officially accepted by the government, was issued. So it needed not only the signing of contracts but also the acknowledgement of the government to transfer property ownership, which was proved by the following record: "the official approval of the government departments are needed before the business transaction,"[184] and in the transaction, contract tax was considered a very important condition. It was ordered in the imperial edict issued in the 2nd year of Kaibao during the reign of Emperor Taizu (969 A.D.) that "in the transaction of land mortgage, contract tax should be paid to the government before the contract is stamped officially. Moreover, the tax should be paid within two months after the contract is signed."[185] Additionally, since contracts with official stamps were used as important evidence in solving disputes over land, it was ruled that "any disputes over land shall be solved by the government according to the contract,"[186] and "the disputes over land shall be solved by the government according to the contract."[187] In addition, "any cases which involve land disputes are to be settled according to contract,"[188] and "the lawsuits over the land property shall be settled according to the relevant evidence, whether the land is officially or privately owned."[189] Based on this stipulation, an elaborate contract tax system was established. According to the stipulation in *Song Xing Tong (The Penal Code of Song Dynasty)*, "if official documents are forged or if words in official documents are added or deleted randomly, the offenders shall be punished by 'Zhang' (flogging with heavy sticks)

---

[183]"Shi Huo" (National Finance and Economy) in *Song Shi* (*The History of Song Dynasty*) (Book 1), Vol. 4.

[184]"Shou Ji Cai Wu Zhe Fei Yong" (The Category of Paying the Fees by the Property in Deposit), quoted from "Za Ling" (Miscellaneous Orders) in "Za Lv" (Miscellaneous Laws) in *Song Xing Tong* (*The Penal Code of Song Dynasty*), Vol. 24.

[185]"Zheng Que Kao" (An Examination of National Commodity Tax and Government Monopoly) (Part 6) in *Wen Xian Tong Kao* (*A General Textual Research of the Documents*), Vol. 19.

[186]"Wu Ye Chui Jin Mai Ren Gu Zuo Jiao Jia" (The Seller of the Real Estate Intentionally Making Matters Complicated) in "Hu Hun Men" (The Category of Households and Marriage) in *Ming Gong Shu Pan Qing Ming Ji* (*Collections of Enlightened Judgments*), Vol. 5.

[187]"Wang Zhi Zhi Zhu Shi Zheng Di" (Wang Zhizhi in Dispute with Zhu Shi over Land) in "Hu Hun Men" (The Category of Households and Marriage) in *Ming Gong Shu Pan Qing Ming Ji* (*Collections of Enlightened Judgments*), Vol. 6.

[188]"Wei Zuo Fen Mu Qu Shu" (Redeeming by Fabricating Tombs) in "Hu Hun Men" (The Category of Households and Marriage) in *Ming Gong Shu Pan Qing Ming Ji* (*Collections of Enlightened Judgments*), Vol. 9.

[189]"Guo Er Shi Nian Ye Zhu Si Zhe Bu De Shou Li" (No Accepting of the Cases after the Owner Having been Dead for twenty years) in "Hu Hun Men" (The Category of Households and Marriage) in *Ming Gong Shu Pan Qing Ming Ji* (*Collections of Enlightened Judgments*), Vol. 9.

for one hundred strokes."[190] If a person had lost his contract, he should ask his neighbors to testify about the contract and should reapply to the government within two months. Many people had lost their contracts in the period of the Southern Song Dynasty because of wars, so an order was issued on the 3rd of the 4th leap month of the 2nd year of Shaoxing (1132 A. D.):

> A man whose contract has lost due to the war is allowed to have a certificate of household registration in his own county according to his statement after he asks their neighbors to testify about the facts. If his neighbors refuse to testify or the chief county official refuses to give a certificate of household registration, he is allowed to present his appeals and complaints to a higher level department and the relevant people shall be punished harshly. Besides, the neighbors and the owners should show their own evidence respectively.[191]

In order to protect ownership of real estate, except by virtue of legal dealings, tenancy, pawn, and mortgage, it was forbidden for any stolen property to be sold or pawned. "If a person sells the illegally obtained land, he shall be punished by 'Zhang' (flogging with heavy sticks) for one hundred strokes; if the circumstances of the crime are serious, he shall be punished for the crime of robbery; if 'Ya Bao' (intermediary agent) knows the circumstances without reporting it to the government, he shall be punished the same."[192] If the buyers knew the circumstances but still bought the land, the money he paid should be confiscated by the government. For example, "if a person pawns and sells his own land twice, he shall be punished by 'Zhang' (flogging with heavy sticks) for one hundred strokes; if 'Ya Bao' (intermediary agent) knows the circumstances without reporting it to the government, he shall be punished the same."[193] If the young or the inferior of a family "mortgage and pawn the family property without permission or conceal the truth from the superior or the elderly of the family, or counterfeit the signatures of the elderly, the young and 'Ya Bao' (intermediary agent) shall all be severely punished, and the money and the property shall be returned to the owners respectively."[194] Till the Southern Song Dynasty, if a young of a family pawned their farmland without permission, the money he earned would be confiscated and the land would be returned to the owner. Moreover, the superior or the elderly would be given a 5-year-long prescribed period to file a lawsuit against the young: "The elder person

---

[190]"Wei Zao Bao Yin Fu Jie" (Counterfeiting Seals, Almanacs, and so on) in "Zha Wei Lv" (Statutes on Fraud and Forgery) in *Song Xing Tong (The Penal Code of Song Dynasty)*, Vol. 25.

[191]"Shi Huo" (National Finance and Economy) in *Song Hui Yao Ji Gao (Collected Essays of the Historical Records of Song Dynasty)* (Book 70), Vol. 139.

[192]"Cong Xiong Dao Mai Yi Si Di Tian Ye" (A Man Illegally Selling His Dead Brothers' Land) in "Hu Hun Men" (The Category of Households and Marriage) in *Ming Gong Shu Pan Qing Ming Ji (Collections of Enlightened Judgments)*, Vol. 5.

[193]"Chong Die" (Pawning and Selling a Piece of Land Twice) in "Hu Hun Men" (The Category of Households and Marriage) in *Ming Gong Shu Pan Qing Ming Ji (Collections of Enlightened Judgments)*, Vol. 9.

[194]"Dian Mai Zhi Dang Lun Jing Wu Ye Men" (The Category of Mortgaging or Selling the Property By Bargaining) in "Hu Hun Lv" (Statutes on Marriage, Tax and Household Registration) in *Ming Gong Shu Pan Qing Ming Ji (Collections of Enlightened Judgments)*, Vol. 13.

has a 5-year-long prescribed period for filing a lawsuit against the young who mortgages and sells the family land without permission."[195] It needs to be pointed out that if the superior or the elderly illegally sold the property of the inferior or the young, it was also allowed for the latter to "appeal to the government get them back with no limitation of time"[196] to show equal protection of ownership. Since the system of "Tun Tian" (wasteland opened up by garrison troops or peasants) and "Ying Tian" (wasteland cultivated by peasants employed by the government) was set up by the government, it had been forbidden to encroach upon peasants' farmland by taking advantage of the situation. If a peasant's farmland was occupied, he could file a lawsuit and appeal for the return of his land in accordance with law.

As for the obtaining of ownership of personal property, except for buying and selling, inheritance, and bestowal, other important ways included discovering hidden property, picking up lost property, salvaging floating objects, occupying derelicts, ownership of products and interests, etc. Taking salvaging floating objects as an example, according to "Di Nei De Su Cang Wu" (Discovering the Hidden Objects in Someone's Own Land) quoted from "Za Ling" (Miscellaneous Orders) in "Zai Lv" (Miscellaneous Laws) in *Song Xing Tong* (*The Penal Code of Song Dynasty*), "in the cases where pieces of wood or bamboo are drifted away by flood, if a person collects them, puts them on the banks of a river, posts a notice beside them and then reports the affair to the government, he shall be rewarded after the owner claims the objects. If he collects the drifting objects from a river, he shall be rewarded two fifth of the objects; if he collects the drifting objects from water in other places, he shall be rewarded one fifth of the objects; if the drifting objects are not claimed by anyone within thirty days, they shall be granted to the person who collects them." In *Qing Yuan Tiao Fa Shi Lei* (*The Legal Provisions and Cases Made in the Year of Qingyuan*), drifting objects were further divided into public and private objects. Moreover, the reward for the person who had collected the objects was also increased. If the drifting objects were not claimed by anyone, all of them should be granted to the person who had collected them.

Infringement upon the ownership of personal property should require compensation according to law. If a person intentionally disturbed or infringed upon one's property ownership, besides penal punishment, he should also pay economic compensation to the victim. Other acts such as destroying, abandoning, or losing government-owned or privately owned objects or government-owned or privately owned animals; damaging or embezzling government-owned or privately owned crops; and cutting down public forests and killing or injuring government-owned or privately owned livestock should also be punished by paying compensation or being

---

[195]"Shu Zhi Zheng Zai Pan" (The Retrial of the Lawsuits Filed by the Uncle and the Nephew) in "Hu Hun Men" (The Category of Households and Marriage) in *Ming Gong Shu Pan Qing Ming Ji (Collections of Enlightened Judgments)*, Vol. 9.

[196]"Bei You Wei Suo Sheng Fu Mai Ye" (The Humble and the Young Selling the Property of their Biological Father) in "Hu Hun Men" (The Category of Households and Marriage) in *Ming Gong Shu Pan Qing Ming Ji (Collections of Enlightened Judgments)*, Vol. 9.

sentenced according to law. So property ownership was strictly protected by making elaborate provisions on compensation for damages.

Meanwhile, pawning was a common practice that was also legalized and systematized in the Song Dynasty.

Pawning was considered different from selling. In the sale of property, after the owner had sold his property, he could not have it back by redemption, so in this sense, it was considered a "dead" sale. Pawning, on the other hand, was considered "alive," which meant that the owner of the object could get it back by paying the redemption price within a time limit. Therefore, the price of a pawned object was much lower than that of the object that was sold in market. Most of the people who pawned farmland were land-holding peasants; in other words, through the pawning system, the landlords could not only gain the profits of the land by paying a very low price but also legally obtain ownership of the land if the peasants were not able to afford the redemption price. In this case, the law showed partiality for the persons who had the pawn rights. According to *Song Xing Tong* (*The Penal Code of Song Dynasty*), it was allowed for the person who "has a contract which is proved to be genuine" to pay the redemption price; "if a person has no contract, or if it is hard to determine whether the contract he holds is genuine or false, he is not permitted to pay the redemption,"[197] which had made it convenient for the people who had the pawn rights to obtain ownership of houses or land that had been pawned. It was recorded in *Ming Gong Shu Pan Qing Ming Ji* (*Collections of Enlightened Judgments*) that in order to "appropriate the property of an ordinary person," when he wanted to redeem the property he had pawned, "the wealthy man might try every means to refuse the redemption on various excuses such as the contract having been lost or the head of his family being not at home, so that the matter was delayed for months. When the ordinary person sued the wealthy person, the latter would ask the judge to delay the settlement of the cases by every means. Then the case was delayed to be heard without time limitation or sometimes was even rejected. So several months later when the time limit of redemption had expired, it was impossible for the ordinary person to redeem his property any more. ... This was the exact reason why the wealthy and powerful people had large pieces of land, while the poor had nothing at all."[198]

In order to legalize the establishment of "Dian Quan" (pawn rights), certain legal formalities and procedures should be performed.

Firstly, a pawn contract should be made. It was recorded in history books that "the farmland should be pawned according to contracts"[199]; so "according to the law, the

---

[197]"Dian Mai Zhi Dang Lun Jing Wu Ye Men" (The Category of Mortgaging or Selling the Property By Bargaining) in "Hu Hun Lv" (Statutes on Marriage, Tax and Household Registration) in *Ming Gong Shu Pan Qing Ming Ji* (*Collections of Enlightened Judgments*), Vol. 12.

[198]"Dian Zhu Qian Yan Ru Wu" (The Person with Pawning Rights Delaying Receiving the Redemption) in "Hu Hun Men" (The Category of Households and Marriage) in *Ming Gong Shu Pan Qing Ming Ji* (*Collections of Enlightened Judgments*), Vol. 9.

[199]Chen Xiang (Song Dynasty), "Jiao Yi Bu Ping Chao" (Doing Business without Paying Money) in *Zhou Xian Ti Gong* (A *Guide to Subprefecture and county*), Vol. 2.

land and houses should be pawned according to contracts. The owner of the land or houses and the pawnbroker should have a copy of the contract respectively, which is commonly used and which is known by everyone in the world"[200]; "if one pawns off his house or land, he should not only have the certificate of the property with the official stamps, but also the contracts of pawning as well. Besides, the owner of the land or houses and the pawnbroker should have a copy of the contract respectively, so that the redemption should be paid according to the contract which they have signed."[201] After signing the contract, procedures such as stamping by the government, paying tax, and transferring ownership should all be performed before legalization of the pawn rights.

Secondly, "the relatives" and "the close neighbors" had preemptive pawn rights. According to the provisions of "Hu Hun Lv" (Statutes on Marriage, Tax and Household Registration) in *Song Xing Tong* (*The Penal Code of Song Dynasty*), if one had pawned his property, "he should first ask his relatives if they would like to buy; if they refuse, he should ask his close neighbors; if his close neighbors refuse, he then can ask the other people"; if "the price his relatives offer is not acceptable, he can ask other people who would like to pay higher prices."[202]

Thirdly, in a pawn contract, the number of *qing* and *mu* of the land, the specific arrangement, and the names of the guarantors should be written. So "in the contract, if the number of '*qing*' and '*mu*' of the land, the specific arrangement, the location of the close neighbors, the tax and corvee, the names of the property owners, the neighbors, 'Ya Bao' (intermediary agent) and the person who writes the contract are not written, the relevant people should be punished for the crime of pawning off the land and houses illegally."[203]

The prescription period should also be included in the contract; usually the prescription period was thirty years, so "thirty years later, ... redemption is not allowed."[204]

Fourthly, the disposition right of the head of family was protected. In the pawning of the property, the head of family and the buyer "should sign the contract in their presence." If the head of family could not come back from a far away place or because of war, "it should be reported to the officials of 'Zhou' (subprefecture) and

---

[200]"Dian Mai Yuan Wu Ji Wu Qi Ju Nan Yi Qu Shu" (No Redeeming for the Pawned Houses without Showing the Contracts) in "Hu Hun Men" (The Category of Households and Marriage) in *Ming Gong Shu Pan Qing Ming Ji* (*Collections of Enlightened Judgments*), Vol. 5.

[201]"Shi Huo" (National Finance and Economy) in *Song Hui Yao Ji Gao* (*Collected Essays of the Historical Records of Song Dynasty*) (Book 61), Vol. 64.

[202]"Dian Mai Zhi Dang Lun Jing Wu Ye Men" (The Category of Mortgaging or Selling the Property By Bargaining) in "Hu Hun Lv" (Statutes on Marriage, Tax and Household Registration) in *Ming Gong Shu Pan Qing Ming Ji* (*Collections of Enlightened Judgments*), Vol. 13.

[203]"Shi Huo" (National Finance and Economy) in *Song Hui Yao Ji Gao* (*Collected Essays of the Historical Records of Song Dynasty*) (Book 61), Vol. 65-66.

[204]"Dian Mai Zhi Dang Lun Jing Wu Ye Men" (The Category of Mortgaging or Selling the Property By Bargaining) in "Hu Hun Lv" (Statutes on Marriage, Tax and Household Registration) in *Ming Gong Shu Pan Qing Ming Ji* (*Collections of Enlightened Judgments*), Vol. 13.

8.4 Civil Law Adapting to the Development of Commodity Economy

'Xian' (county) for their approval before the transaction is conducted."[205] If the young or the inferior of a family pawned the family property without permission or counterfeited the signatures of the elderly, they shall all be harshly punished.

In order to protect the interests of the people who had "Dian Quan" (pawn rights), "it is forbidden for one object to be pawned twice." If there were cases in which one object was pawned twice, the owner of the object, "Ya Bao" (intermediary agent), the neighbors, and the people who had signed their names on the contract "should be punished for the crime of robbery according to the profits each person has earned,"[206] and the money should be returned to the person who had "Dian Quan" (pawn rights). If the owner of the object was not able to pay the money back, "Ya Bao" (intermediary agent) and the neighbors who had signed their names on the contract should jointly pay back the money and the pawned object should be returned to its first owner. In the Southern Song Dynasty, the punishment for repeated pawning of the same object was much severer: "As to the cases of pawning, if one pawns his farmland or house twice, he shall be punished by 'Zhang' (flogging with heavy sticks) for one hundred strokes; if 'Ya Bao' (intermediary agent) knows the circumstances, he shall be punished the same."[207] The redemption right of the person who pawned the objects was also protected. In the early period of the Song Dynasty, it was stipulated that "if the person whose contract of pawning is examined to be obviously genuine, he is allowed to pay redemption to get the objects back, no matter how old he is."[208] In the Southern Song Dynasty, if the person who had pawned the property wanted to pay for the redemption price to get the property back before the expiration of the time limit, "he is allowed to to so." If "the person who has 'Dian Quan' (pawn rights) deliberately delays the time to keep the property, he shall be punished by 'Zhang' (flogging with heavy sticks) for one hundred strokes" and "shall be ordered to return the property back to its owner immediately after taking the ransom."[209] However, the property owner could only pay the ransom at the time agreed upon in the contract. If the property was not redeemed after the redemption period had expired, the person who had "Dian Quan" (pawn rights) could not obtain ownership of the pawned land or houses, but he could pawn the land

---

[205]"Dian Mai Zhi Dang Lun Jing Wu Ye Men" (The Category of Mortgaging or Selling the Property By Bargaining) in "Hu Hun Lv" (Statutes on Marriage, Tax and Household Registration) in *Ming Gong Shu Pan Qing Ming Ji* (*Collections of Enlightened Judgments*), Vol. 13.

[206]"Dian Mai Zhi Dang Lun Jing Wu Ye Men" (The Category of Mortgaging or Selling the Property By Bargaining) in "Hu Hun Lv" (Statutes on Marriage, Tax and Household Registration) in *Ming Gong Shu Pan Qing Ming Ji* (*Collections of Enlightened Judgments*), Vol. 13.

[207]"Chong Die" (Pawning and Selling a Piece of Land Twice) in "Hu Hun Men" (The Category of Households and Marriage) in *Ming Gong Shu Pan Qing Ming Ji* (*Collections of Enlightened Judgments*), Vol. 9.

[208]"Dian Mai Zhi Dang Lun Jing Wu Ye Men" (The Category of Mortgaging or Selling the Property By Bargaining) in "Hu Hun Lv" (Statutes on Marriage, Tax and Household Registration) in *Ming Gong Shu Pan Qing Ming Ji* (*Collections of Enlightened Judgments*), Vol. 13.

[209]"Dian Zhu Qian Yan Ru Wu" (The Person with Pawning Rights Delaying Receiving the Redemption) in "Hu Hun Men" (The Category of Households and Marriage) in *Ming Gong Shu Pan Qing Ming Ji* (*Collections of Enlightened Judgments*), Vol. 9.

or houses off to other people. In addition, the change of prescription period of "Dian Quan" (pawn rights) was also stipulated. If the contents of the land or real estate contract was confusing or the pawnbroker and the property owner were already dead after the land or house had been pawned for twenty years, redemption of the land or houses could not be allowed, which proved that the rate of increase of pawned land and houses in the Southern Song Dynasty was faster than that in the Northern Song Dynasty. However, if the contents of the contract were clear and both the pawnbroker and property owner were alive, the person who had pawned the property had the right to redeem the property without time limit.

Since the law on pawn rights in the Northern and Southern dynasties was elaborate and clear, it was praised for being "as splendid and glorious as the sun and the stars."[210]

In the Song Dynasty, "Dian" (pawn) and "Zhi" (pledge) were not clearly differentiated. "Zhi" (pledge) referred to the rights that the borrowers had when they pledged objects to moneylenders to borrow money, so the pledged objects were forbidden to be sold without authorization. According to *Song Xing Tong (The Penal Code of Song Dynasty)*, "it is forbidden for the person who receives the pledged objects to sell them unless with the presence the owner."[211] If the property owner or the object owner did not redeem the property or object before the time limit, the pawnbroker could sell the property or the object after reporting to the chief officials of market and use the proceeds of the sale to pay off the debt. After the debts were paid off, the extra money should be given to the property or object owner.

8.4.3 The New Achievements of the Law of Obligation

During the period of the Northern and Southern Song dynasties, the commodity economy was highly developed, the contents of the law of obligation were greatly enriched, and the system of the law of obligation was complete and perfect, so the law of obligation had taken a leading role in the world. In the Northern and Southern Song dynasties, the most common debts included those incurred through legal acts, such as signing of contracts; infringement acts; illegal profit making; and voluntary service.

Due to the complicated property relationship between individuals and between officials and civilians, the civil right–obligation relationship between creditors and debtors was required to be regulated by contracts, which in turn led to the increase of debts incurred by contracts. On the other hand, extensive acceptance of contracts

---

[210]"Kai Gai Qi Shu Zhan Ju Bu Ken Huan Shu" (Refusing to Return the Pawned Property by Changing the Content of the Contract) in "Hu Hun Men" (The Category of Households and Marriage) in *Ming Gong Shu Pan Qing Ming Ji (Collections of Enlightened Judgments)*, Vol. 9.

[211]"Shou Ji Cai Wu Zhe Fei Yong" (The Category of Paying the Fees by the Property in Deposit) in "Za Lv" (Miscellaneous Laws) in *Song Xing Tong (The Penal Code of Song Dynasty)*, Vol. 26.

8.4 Civil Law Adapting to the Development of Commodity Economy

also increased the forms of contracts were also increased due to their extensive application, so that many kinds of contracts, such as sales contract, mortgage contract, loan contract, employment contract, lease contract, etc. were all made. Because contract paper was officially printed and issued, the form of contracts was unified and standardized, which not only effectively prevented the counterfeiting of contracts but also reduced disputes. Additionally, the contract tax and contract mortgage were systematized.

The subject matter of the contract, the price and method of calculation, the prescription period, etc. were also elaborately stipulated.

It was stressed that when making contracts, the contract should be signed with the "consensus" agreement of the two parties without being "signed by force." If the contract "was signed without the consensus of one party" or if "one party was compelled to signed the contract," the offenders "should be severely punished." Moreover, contracts became legal only after they were signed by "Ya Bao" (intermediary agent) and the people who wrote the contracts and only after contract tax was collected and recorded by the government.

It needs to be noted that as a result of the rapid development of the commodity economy, the contract system was also affected by market competition, so that an advanced form of contract—a competing contract—was made during the Northern and Southern Song dynasties, including competing contracts signed in the renting and selling of "Guan Tian" (state-owned land) and competing contracts signed in the transferring of the right of management of government-owned industry and commerce. These competing contracts were similar to the bidding law and auction law in the later period.

Debts incurred by infringement acts refers to those debts incurred due to the negligent or intentional illegal acts of a person, which brought about the infringement upon the property and personal rights of others, which had led to the formation of a credit–debt relationship between actors and aggrieved parties for the compensation of damages. Because the nature and degree of infringement acts were different, the actors were punished differently so that they were made to pay "compensation" or be sentenced to different penalties beyond the "compensation". In order to protect private ownership of real estate, in the case of infringement upon one's ownership of land, it was allowed for the person with ownership to file lawsuits against the wrongdoer at any time "without the restriction of time limit" and to present his appeals to high-level government organizations through "Yue Su" (overstepping indictment). Even when the private land of ordinary people was occupied by the government, it was allowed for them to present their complaints to courts of higher level or the imperial court to ask for the return of their land.

As to infringement of personal property, usually the owner of the original object should be compensated or the compensation should be made according to the object's discounted price; those who could not afford the compensation should be prosecuted for their criminal action.

As to acts of personal infringement, criminal sanctions were be given. "Bao Gu System" (the system whereby an offender was ordered by law to help the victim recover within a prescribed period, and the punishment for the crime committed by the offender was determined according to the means of injury and the degree of recovery) was also practiced. However, as a result of the commodity economy, the actors were required to make economic compensation to the aggrieved parties (including in homicide cases). If reconciliation was made privately by the parties by accepting money, those involved would be punished for the crime of robbery.

If the abovementioned infringement acts had caused damages because of force majeure or unartificial factors or the prescription period for the compensation of damages had expired, the payment of damages should be exempted.

Debts incurred through illegally made profits refers to a credit–debt relationship formed by causing damages to others while bringing profits to oneself without legal basis. For example, if "an official has lent the things of government to others by mistake and failed to have them back," the person who received the objects (the beneficiary) had made profits illegally. Therefore, he should return the original object or pay compensation according to the value of the object.[212]

The debts incurred by voluntary service referred to the practical acts of self-management or service which people provided in order to prevent the interests of other people from being damaged, so that a creditor-debtor relationship between the manager and other person was formed although there were no statutory or agreed obligations. During the period of the Northern and Southern Song dynasties, many landowners fled away because of wars, and their land was then cultivated by other people. When the landowners came back, they needed to pay the cost of production to the people who had cultivated the land for them. Such debts incurred by voluntary service were common and typical in the Song Dynasty.

Under the debt guaranty system, there were two kinds of guaranty: credibility guaranty and property guaranty. With regard to the former, the methods of "three guarantors for one obligation," "guarantors assuming debts," "joint liability of guarantors for one obligation," etc. were adopted. For example, it was provided in "Li Qian" (Debts) in "Cai Yong Men" (The Category of Finance) in *Qing Yuan Tiao Fa Shi Lei* (*The Legal Provisions and Cases Made in the Year of Qingyuan*), quoted from *Guan Shi Ling* (*Order on Border Market*), that "if a debtor defaults on the debt, the case shall be dealt with by the government; if the debtor flees away, the debt shall be assumed by the guarantors." As for the latter, "Wu Bao" (guaranty of mortgaged property) and "Qian Bao" (guaranty of money) were included. During the Northern and Southern Song dynasties, mortgage was guaranteed by real estate, but ownership over the mortgaged real estate would not be transferred. Moreover, "Zhi Quan" (pledge rights) was guaranteed by the personal property, and ownership of the pledged personal property would be transferred to the creditor. Therefore, before the time limit for the debtor's performance of his obligation that was provided in the contract expired, it was forbidden for the creditor to occupy the mortgaged property; nevertheless, he was allowed to occupy the pledged personal property. If the debtor defaulted after the time limit expired, it was allowed for the creditor to deal with the

---

[212]"Li Qian" (Debts), quoted from "Li Qian Ling" (Decrees for Debts) in "Cai Yong Men" (The Citatory of Finance) (Part 3) in *Qing Yuan Tiao Fa Shi Lei* (*The Legal Provisions and Cases Made in the Year of Qingyuan*), Vol. 32.

mortgaged property, but its value should be fairly estimated. And after the debts were paid off, the extra money should be given to the debtor. The following stipulation was recorded in *Qing Yuan Tiao Fa Shi Lei* (*The Legal Provisions and Cases Made in the Year of Qingyuan*):

> Those who cannot afford to pay for the tax are allowed to pay by using objects, but it should be recorded; if the objects are not redeemed within one year, they will be confiscated by the government; if a person does not have enough money or objects to pay for the tax, it shall be paid by the relevant people.[213]

Clearly, this stipulation was similar to mortgage and lien in modern civil law, and the so-called "Qian Bao" (guaranty of money) refers to the deposit paid for the guaranty of a debt.

In the transaction of personal property, the regulations for the guaranty of the product defect in *Tang Lv* (*Tang Code*) was adopted. However, in the transaction of personal property and human trafficking, there were disputes involving the demands of the third party. So the liabilities to the guarantee of the third party's demands were generally regulated in the sale contracts in order to protect the ownership of the buyer.

During the Northern and Southern Song dynasties, elaborate stipulations were made concerning the performance of obligation, failure in the performance of obligation, and the discharge of debts. So the obligor, the number and quality of the subject matter, as well as the time limit for the performance of obligation were all clearly provided in *Song Xing Tong* (*The Penal Code of Song Dynasty*): "The person who receives the pledged objects is not allowed to sell them to others except to the owner himself"[214]; "if the government had paid money to the mortgagers in advance, then the time limit, the number and the weight should be recorded"[215]; "the number of the mortgages and the time for payment should be regulated"[216]; and "the spoiled and shoddy articles will be confiscated by the government, while the small articles shall be returned to the owners."[217] "One day ... refers to the time period from morning to night. ... and one year consists of three hundred and sixty days"; "leap months are counted by days; but one year does not refer to the leap year. The time period of one year should start from the first month."[218]

---

[213]"Shang Shui" (Commercial Tax), quoted from "Chang Wu Ling" (Orders Issued by Chang Wu Agency) in "Ku Wu Men" (The Category of Warehouse Affairs) (Part 1) in *Qing Yuan Tiao Fa Shi Lei* (*The Legal Provisions and Cases Made in the Year of Qingyuan*), Vol. 36.

[214]"Shou Ji Cai Wu Zhe Fei Yong" (The Category of Paying the Fees by the Property in Deposit) in "Za Lv" (Miscellaneous Laws) in *Song Xing Tong* (*The Penal Code of Song Dynasty*), Vol. 26.

[215]"Shi Huo Zhi" (The Records of National Finance and Economy) (Chapter 8) in *Song Shi* (*The History of Song Dynasty*) (Chapter One) (Book 2).

[216]"Chai Ke Fu Yi Bu Jun Ping Ji Shan Fu Lian Jia Yi Men" (The Category of Unfair and Illegal Tax Collection) in "Hu Hun Lv" (Statutes on Marriage, Tax and Household Registration) in *Song Xing Tong* (*The Penal Code of Song Dynasty*), Vol. 13.

[217]"Jiao Dou Cheng Bu Ping" (Rectifying Inaccurate "Dou" and Scale) in "Za Lv" (Miscellaneous Laws) in *Song Xing Tong* (*The Penal Code of Song Dynasty*), Vol. 26.

[218]"Za Tiao" (Miscellaneous Rules) in "Ming Li Lv" (Statues and Terms) in *Song Xing Tong* (*The Penal Code of Song Dynasty*), Vol. 6.

With regard to default of payment after the expiration of time, the regulations in *Tang Lv* (*Tang Code*) were adopted, and those involved would be punished according to the number of subject matter and days delayed. Moreover, compensation should be made compulsorily:

> If the debt is one *pi* of cotton cloth or more, the offender shall be punished by "Chi" (flogging with light sticks) for twenty strokes for a delay of twenty days and his penalty shall be increased by one level for each delay of twenty days with the maximum penalty of "Chi" (flogging with light sticks) for sixty strokes; if the debt is thirty *pi* of cotton cloth, his punishment shall be increased by two levels; if the debt is one hundred *pi*, his punishment shall be increased by three levels and the compensation for the loss should be made.
>
> If a person seized the property of the debtor to pay for the debt and the value of the seized property had exceeded that prescribed in the contract without reporting to the official, he shall be punished for "Zuo Zang" (embezzlement).
>
> As to the cases of public or private debts, if a person has defaulted by violating the contract, his property should be seized by the creditor, but the cases shall all be reported to and judged by officials; if the cases are not reported, or if the value of the property seized by the creditor by force, such as "Nu Bi" (the slave girls and maidservants) and animal products, has exceeded the value prescribed in the contract, the creditor shall be punishable for the offence of "Zuo Zang" (embezzlement).[219]

The following regulation, which was stipulated in "Za Ling" (Miscellaneous Orders) in the later period of the Tang Dynasty, was specially included in *Song Xing Tong* (*The Penal Code of Song Dynasty*): "The cases involving mortgages on the public or private property with contracts signed between individuals will not be accepted by the the government offices ... those who have lost their family fortune are permitted to offer compulsory service by working as laborers for the compensation of debts, so the males of the debtors' families are permitted to make the compensation by working as laborers ..."[220]

However, it can be seen from the social reality of the Song Dynasty that the sanctions imposed upon the debtors who could not perform the obligation were economic, so the compensation made by the guarantors also mainly included economic liabilities but not personal coercive measures. But if someone had compelled other people to offer compulsory service as a payment for debts, he should take criminal responsibility. For example, an edict was issued by Emperor Taizong in the 2nd year of Zhidao (996 A.D.), and it was stipulated that "in the areas of Jiangzhe and Fujian, the men and women who are compelled to offer compulsory service as a compensation for the debts shall return home, and anyone who wants to harbor them shall be punished."[221] This edict was written into law later on. In view

---

[219]"Shou Ji Cai Wu Zhe Fei Yong" (The Category of Paying the Fees by the Property in Deposit), quoted from "Za Ling" (Miscellaneous Orders) in "Za Lv" (Miscellaneous Laws) in *Song Xing Tong* (*The Penal Code of Song Dynasty*), Vol. 26.

[220]"Shou Ji Cai Wu Zhe Fei Yong" (The Category of Paying the Fees by the Property in Deposit), quoted from "Za Ling" (Miscellaneous Orders) in "Za Lv" (Miscellaneous Laws) in *Song Xing Tong* (*The Penal Code of Song Dynasty*), Vol. 26.

[221]"Tai Zong Ji" (The Record of Emperor Taizong) in *Song Shi* (*The History of Song Dynasty*) (Book 2).

8.4 Civil Law Adapting to the Development of Commodity Economy

of the fact that the businessmen had compelled men and women in the families of the debtor to offer compulsory service as payment for their debts, on the 6th of April in the 2nd year of Longxing during the reign of Emperor Xiaozong in the Southern Song Dynasty, Huang Zushun in Zhitan "Zhou" (subprefecture) presented a memorial to the emperor and stated that "in Hunan, if a person owns a businessman a small sum of money for buying salt, then the businessman even dares to force the men and women of this person's family to be 'Nu Bi' (the slave girls and maidservants). Thus, I appeal to Your Majesty to punish them by the penalty of 'Tu' (imprisonment)." Later on, a law was made by "Xing Bu" (The Department of Punishment), in which it was provided that "if a person owns a businessman a small sum of money for buying salt, but if the businessman compels the men and women of the debtor to be 'Nu Bi' (the slave girls and maidservants), the businessman should be punished according to what is stipulated in the article: 'If a person compels the debtor to offer compulsory service as a compensation, he should be punished by 'Zhang' (flogging with heavy sticks) for one hundred strokes with his money confisticated.'" This regulation was approved by Emperor Xiaozong.[222]

In order to get economic compensation from debtors who defaulted on their debts, the most important thing was to file a lawsuit in court to be settled compulsorily by the government, which was referred to as "Jian Huan," "Jian Na," or "Jian Li." Besides, the payment should be suspended until the debtors could afford to perform the obligation, which showed that stricter measures had been taken by the government to deal with so-called trivial cases. This was one of the most distinctive characteristics of times during the Song Dynasty.

As for the elimination of debt, except for the payment of debt by the debtor, there were other ways, which are discussed in the following.

If a debtor or a guarantor did not have the ability to pay back the money or the debtor or the guarantor had died before the obligation was performed, he should be acquitted of the debt after a certain period of time. It was written in the edict issued in November of the 2nd year of Shaoxi during the reign of Emperor Guangzong that "if the family property of the debtor is estimated insufficient to pay off the debts, but the prison guards and 'Ya Bao' (intermediary agent) still kept asking him to pay the debt, the debtors should be acquitted of the debts. So this regulation is not to be violated by anyone."[223] In *Ming Gong Shu Pan Qing Ming Ji* (*Collections of Enlightened Judgments*), the judgment that Hu Shibi made in the case of Li Wusan's default on his debt was based on legal facts, so it was stated that:

> This department has sent his brother to the country under escort to enforce his payment of the debt. Now months have passed but he has not paid one penny; however, he has been moaning with hunger and cold and there are not many days ahead of him. Even though he owes debts, it is impossible to force him to pay the debts off, let alone that his case of default is not true. According to law, if someone defaults on debts, the government should make him

---

[222] "Shi Huo" (National Finance and Economy) in *Song Hui Yao* (*Collections of Historical Records in Song Dynasty*) (Book 15), Vol. 27.

[223] "Shi Huo" (National Finance and Economy) in *Song Hui Yao Ji Gao* (*Collected Essays of the Historical Records of Song Dynasty*) (Book 30), Vol. 31.

pay off the debts and the maximum penalty for him is "Zhang" (flogging with heavy sticks) for one hundred strokes without keeping him in custody. Today, considering that he has suffered so dreadfully, it is not suitable to keep him in custody. So is it proper to punish him by "Zhang" (flogging with heavy sticks)? Therefore, he is exempted from the compulsory payment of debt. Moreover, he should be given one *dou* of rice for relief.[224]

It was also provided in *Qing Yuan Tiao Fa Shi Lei* (*The Legal Provisions and Cases Made in the Year of Qingyuan*) that "if a person has already died and has no fraudulent conducts, he is acquitted of the debt; if a person has fraudulent conducts, but he has already died and has left no property, he is allowed to be discharged of his debt."[225]

If it was beyond the prescription period and there was no contract as evidence, the debtor–creditor relationship would naturally terminated. According to an edict issued in the 3rd year of Jianlong during the reign of Emperor Taizong's (962 A.D.), "in the cases where it is beyond the prescription period of pawn and mortgage with no contracts signed or it is hard to distinguish the true and false contracts thirty years later, the pawned or mortgaged objects are not allowed to be redeemed."[226] Later on, influenced by the commodity economy, the circulation of goods became quicker so that the prescription period for paying back debts was shortened from twenty to ten years. For example, it was regulated in the Southern Song Dynasty that "in the cases of disputes over land or houses, if the contents of a contract were confusing or the buyer or the owner died twenty years later, the case would not be accepted by the government."[227] In cases of land or house mortgage, "if the person died ten or twenty years later after he had mortgaged the land or the house, the case would not be accepted by the government."[228] If the debtor were unable to perform the obligation because of war or some other factors, the period of war or other events should not to be included in the prescription period: "If the debtors were detained in some places for some reason, the period of detaining should not be included in the

---

[224]"Qian Fu Ren Shi Wu Cong Chu He Mian Jian Li" (Exempting Debtors Unable to Pay off Debts from Compulsory Payment) in "Hu Hun Men" (The Category of Households and Marriage) in *Ming Gong Shu Pan Qing Ming Ji* (*Collections of Enlightened Judgments*), Vol. 9.

[225]"Li Qian" (Debts), quoted from "Li Qian Ling" (Decrees for Debts) in "Cai Yong Men" (The Citatory of Finance) (Part 3) in *Qing Yuan Tiao Fa Shi Lei* (*The Legal Provisions and Cases Made in the Year of Qingyuan*), Vol. 32.

[226]"Dian Mai Zhi Dang Lun Jing Wu Ye Men" (The Category of Mortgaging or Selling the Property By Bargaining) in "Hu Hun Lv" (Statutes on Marriage, Tax and Household Registration) in *Ming Gong Shu Pan Qing Ming Ji* (*Collections of Enlightened Judgments*), Vol. 13.

[227]"Wang Jiu Su Wang Si Zhan Qu Tian Chan" (Wang Jiu Suing Wang Si Occupying his Land) in "Hu Hun Men" (The Category of Households and Marriage) in *Ming Gong Shu Pan Qing Ming Ji* (*Collections of Enlightened Judgments*), Vol. 4.

[228]"Cao Si Song Xu Deyu Deng Zheng Tian Shi" (A Dispute over Land among Xu Guoyu and Other People Reported by the Office in Charge of Water Transportation) in "Hu Hun Men" (The Category of Households and Marriage) in *Ming Gong Shu Pan Qing Ming Ji* (*Collections of Enlightened Judgments*), Vol. 4.

prescription period."²²⁹ It was also stipulated in *Qing Yuan Tiao Fa Shi Lei* (*The Legal Provisions and Cases Made in the Year of Qingyuan*) that "if it is beyond the prescription period, everyone who was involved in the case should make a statement; if the settlement of the case is obstructed or delayed, those involved shall be punished severely according to law."²³⁰ Although the shortening of the prescription period for filing a lawsuit was helpful for the people who had practically cultivated the land to obtain ownership over it, it also made it convenient for the landlords to annex the land of land-holding peasants by acquiring their land in the form of mortgage.

Debts were also discharged because of amnesties offered by the government or according to government orders. During the Northern and Southern dynasties, the emperors often issued imperial edicts to relieve the debtors of their debts. For example, when Emperor Guangzong succeeded the throne, he announced in an imperial edict that "all the debts, no matter how long they have been borrowed, should be eliminated."²³¹ If there were natural disasters, sometimes the government also ordered to eliminate official or private debts in order to maintain social order.

Among the contracts, the contract of "She Mai" is especially needed to be mentioned. "She Mai" means loaning on credit, and the date of payment would be agreed upon before the money is paid back. According to *Song Hui Yao* (*Collections of Historical Records in Song Dynasty*), in June of the 1st year of Qianxing (1022 A. D.), an edict was issued by Emperor Zhenzong making the law of "She Mai":

> If a buyer wants to buy a large quantity of goods on credit, he should collect the objects and property he has in accordance with the value of the goods, and he should have three or five guarantors to make a contract. Besides, the date of returning the money should be written in the contract. If he breaches the contract ... or if the joint guarantors have no property but have fraudulently claimed that they have objects and property, or if the guarantors have conspired with the owner of the shop and "Ya Bao" (intermediary agent) to deceive the passengers about the quality of the goods without making a bargain, they should be severely punished.²³²

In July of the 11th year of Chunxi during the reign of Emperor Xiaozong (1184 A. D.), another edict was issued: "From today forward, if a person wants to buy tea on credit, or if he has parents and elder brothers, they should all jointly sign their names

---

²²⁹"Dian Mai Zhi Dang Lun Jing Wu Ye Men" (The Category of Mortgaging or Selling the Property By Bargaining) in "Hu Hun Lv" (Statutes on Marriage, Tax and Household Registration) in *Ming Gong Shu Pan Qing Ming Ji* (*Collections of Enlightened Judgments*), Vol. 13.

²³⁰"Li Shang" (Rewards), quoted from "Sui Chi Sheng Ming" (The Statement of the Imperial Instructions) in "Zhi Zhi Men" (The Category of Official System) (Part 10) in *Qing Yuan Tiao Fa Shi Lei* (*The Legal Provisions and Cases Made in the Year of Qingyuan*), Vol. 13.

²³¹Hong Mai (Song Dynasty), "She Fang Zhai Fu" (Discharging of Debts) in *Rong Zhai San Bi* (*Essays Written in Rongzhai*), Vol. 9. The Statement of the Imperial Instructions.

²³²"Shi Huo" (National Finance and Economy) in *Song Hui Yao Ji Gao* (*Collected Essays of the Historical Records of Song Dynasty*) (Book 5), Vol. 23.

on the contract."[233] So it is clear that when selling goods on credit during the Song Dynasty, people must mortgage their property by means of contract. For the people who mortgaged their property, their parents and elder brothers must be joint guarantors and must sign their names in the contracts. If the buyer did not have guarantors, they needed to write a pledge with information on the amount of money they should pay back; if the buyers were "deceived about the goods," the lawsuit would not be accepted by the government to protect the rights of the sellers who sold products on credit.

Partnership contracts began to be used to deal with agricultural production as a result of the development of the tenancy system. An imperial edict was issued in the 7th year of Taiping Xingguo during the reign of Emperor Taizong (983 A.D.):

... One family has seeds, another family has a man and the other has a cow. Then they are given a piece of wasteland, so more people are gathered and the contract for borrowing seeds and employment of laborers are signed. At harvest time, the crop production is distributed according to the proportion prescribed in the contract, so no lawsuit is filed to the government.[234]

However, partnership contracts were mainly used within the business circle to solve the problem of insufficient funds, and they were commonly referred to as "joint funds for business" or "joint property," but risks were also shared by the partners involved. This was one of the most important reasons for the continuous expansion of the scale of the commodity economy in the Northern and Southern Song dynasties.

The partnership was also reflected in the transportation, sale of goods, contracting and management of overseas trade. In partnership contracts, the parties involved should take joint or various liabilities, so they not only "raised money jointly" but also shared losses jointly. In the 3rd year of Tianxi during the reign of Emperor Zhenzong (1019 A.D.), Wang Cen in Zhiying Tianfu pointed out that "five families jointly bought a winery, so every year they should pay 30,000 *min* (a monetary unit, one *min* is about 1,000 *wen*) for tax. They were in debt for a long time, so two families had gone bankrupt and the other three had been accused."[235] As to the distribution of benefits, they should be "distributed fairly" according to the funds of each party after deducting money for tax and for the salaries of the operators.

Apart from the main forms of contracts mentioned above, other forms of contracts, such as intermediary contract, commission contract, and work contract, were also relatively developed.

---

[233]"Shi Huo" (National Finance and Economy) in *Song Hui Yao Ji Gao* (*Collected Essays of the Historical Records of Song Dynasty*) (Book 26), Vol. 31.

[234]"Shi Huo" (National Finance and Economy) in *Song Hui Yao Ji Gao* (*Collected Essays of the Historical Records of Song Dynasty*) (Book 126), Vol. 63.

[235]*Xu Zi Zhi Tong Jian Chang Bian* (*Sequel to the Full-length Book of History as a Mirror*), Vol. 94, in November of the 3rd year of Tianxi.

8.4.4 Marriage and Inheritance for the Improvement of Women's Social Status

As far as marriage legislation in the Song Dynasty is concerned, it was basically similar to the regulations in *Tang Lv* (*Tang Code*) in terms of the parents' or the elders' right of deciding marriage, the important elements in the establishment of a marriage relationship, the legal age for marriage, the marriage taboo, the dissolution of the marriage, etc. But the historical background of the advanced commodity economy of the Song Dynasty was surely reflected in marriage relationships. For example, with the improvement of the status of "Nu Bi" (slave girls and maidservants), marriage between officials and "Nu Bi" (slave girls and maidservants) was no longer forbidden by the government. However, it was forbidden for "Nu Bi" (slave girls and maidservants) to contract marriage with their master's relatives who live together with them. These show that the conventional rule of prohibiting marriages between "Liang" (the common people) and "Jian" (people of a lower social status than common people) was changed somehow. As another example, although it was forbidden in *Song Xing Tong* (*The Penal Code of Song Dynasty*) for husbands to marry off their wives or concubines to others privately, it was actually allowed for the poor, who suffered from hunger and cold, to pawn and rent out their wives. Many such cases were recorded in *Qing Ming Ji* (*The Collections of the Enlightened Judgments*). In general, according to the divorce law of the Song Dynasty, marriage relationship could be canceled by "He Li" (peaceful dissolution of marriage); if so, the relevant party would not hold liability. As national conflict became much sharper in the Song Dynasty, in the northwest frontier regions where national relations were complicated, marriage between the Han people and domesticated minority nationalities was prohibited. In August of the 1st year of Zhidao during the reign of Emperor Taizong (995 A.D.), an imperial edict was issued, according to which "the marriages between the people in the northwest frontier regions and the small minorities are prohibited."[236] In March of the 1st year of Yuanyou during the reign of Emperor Zhezong (1086 A.D.), it was declared by "Hu Bu" (The Department of Revenue) that "as for the small minorities that have paid allegiance to us, they are allowed to get married except those in Sanlu and the surrounding areas (where people are forbidden to get married); the people that have paid allegiance to us in Yongzhou and Youjiang are allowed to marry people in Shengdi (the place where marshal palace locates) and Xitong (ethnic areas in southwest China),"[237] which shows that the prohibition of marriage among the minorities in the frontier regions was always emphasized because it was linked to national security. The provisions were only a little leniently enforced compared with the previous ones.

---

[236]"Tai Zong Ben Ji" (The Biography of Emperor Taizong) in *Song Shi* (*The History of Song Dynasty*) (Book 2).

[237]*Xu Zi Zhi Tong Jian Chang Bian* (*Sequel to the Full-length Book of History as a Mirror*), Vol. 373, in March of the 1st year of Yuanyou.

As far as divorce was concerned, it should be noted that women's initiative in divorce was extended, which was obviously a progress compared with the laws of the previous dynasty. For example, "according to law, if the man and the woman had already got married, but the man was exiled to other places, it was allowed for the wife to divorce if she hoped to"[238]; if the wife was raped by her husband's relatives, even if it was an attempted one, the wife was also allowed to divorce if she hoped to."[239] As seen from literary documents, there were various reasons for women to divorce their husbands during the Song Dynasty. So it not only showed that the traditional concept of "being loyal to the husband for all one's life" had been challenged but also that women's social status at that time was greatly improved.

What was relevant to this was that if the woman whose husband had died (or who had divorced) had remarried, she would receive the compassion of society as well as the protection of law. As was stated in the imperial edict issued in the 7th year of Dazhongxiangfu during the reign of Emperor Zhenzong (1014 A.D.): "From now on, if the husband died "but the wife could not provide for herself, she is allowed to marry another man."[240] Moreover, according to the order issued in the 5th year of Yuanyou during the reign of Emperor Zhezong (1090 A.D.), "if women who live with their parents or whose husbands are dead cannot provide for themselves because of poverty, they can remarry according to marriage law after one hundred days after their husbands has died,"[241] but they "shall not own the former husbands' property,"[242] which meant that "once divorced, it is no longer legal to inherit the former husbands' property."[243]

Furthermore, divorce was allowed if the bridegroom did not get married with no reason three years after the engagement. But the bride should "personally report her remarriage to the government, and the betrothal presents and the dowry should be

---

[238]"Yi Cheng Hun Er Fu Li Xiang Bian Guan Zhe Ting Li" (The Wife Being Allowed To Divorce if the Husband Exiled) in "Hu Hun Men" (The Category of Households and Marriage) in *Ming Gong Shu Pan Qing Ming Ji (Collections of Enlightened Judgments)*, Vol. 9.

[239]"Zhu Se Fan Jian" (Various Crimes of Adultery), quoted from "Hu Ling" (Decrees on Household) in "Za Men" (The Miscellaneous Category) in *Qing Yuan Tiao Fa Shi Lei (The Legal Provisions and Cases Made in the Year of Qingyuan)*, Vol. 80.

[240]*Xu Zi Zhi Tong Jian Chang Bian (Sequel to the Full-length Book of History as a Mirror)*, Vol. 82, in January of the 7th year of Dazhongxiangfu.

[241]Su Shi (Song Dynasty), "Qi Gai Ju Sang Hun Qu Tiao Zhuang" (A Memorial about Asking for the Change of the Articles about Mourning and Marriage) in "Dong Po Zou Yi" (Dongpo's Memorials to the Emperor) in *Su Wen Zhong Gong Quan Ji (The Complete Works of Su Shi)*, Vol. 13.

[242]"Yi Jia Qi Yu Ju Qian Fu Wu Ye" (The Married Wife Wanting to Occupy the House Property of Her Ex-Husband) in "Hu Hun Men" (The Category of Households and Marriage) in *Ming Gong Shu Pan Qing Ming Ji (Collections of Enlightened Judgments)*, Vol. 9.

[243]"Jian Jiao Li You Cai Chan" (An Inspection of the Property of the Orphaned Children) in "Hu Hun Men" (The Category of Households and Marriage) in *Ming Gong Shu Pan Qing Ming Ji (Collections of Enlightened Judgments)*, Vol. 8.

returned to the other party."²⁴⁴ If the husband was away from home without returning for three years or did not make contact for six years, the remarriage or divorce of the wife was also allowed; if the younger brothers or sisters of the widow's husband would be helpless once the widow got remarried or if their younger child needed to be supported or the husband's property needed to be taken care of, the widow could marry another man in her ex-husband's home, which was called "Jie Jiao Fu." This new form of remarriage for the widows which was very popular in Song Dynasty had shown its great impact on the traditional "Li Jiao" (feudal ethical code) and the achievement for "women's emancipation"

As to the remarriage of widows, the concept of "Shi Da Fu" (literati and officials) was also greatly changed in the Song Dynasty. For example, famous statesman and poet Wang Anshi had strongly urged his daughter-in-law to remarry; the master of "Li Xue" (neo-Confucianism: a Confucian school of idealist philosophy of the Song and Ming dynasties), Cheng Yi, also persuaded his niece and his nephew's wife to remarry; even the two empresses of Emperor Zhenzong and Renzong remarried. Nevertheless, the doctrines of "Cheng Zhu Li Xue" (Neo-Confucianism: a Confucian school of idealist philosophy of Cheng Hao, Cheng Yi, and Zhu Xi) in the Song Dynasty still influenced marriage and family legislation. For example, if a widow failed to preserve her chastity after her husband's death, "the belongings of her ex-husband, such as 'Bu Qu' (the private army), 'Nu Bi' (the slave girls and maidservants), land and houses are not to be at her disposal."²⁴⁵ In *Ming Gong Shu Pan Qing Ming Ji* (*Collections of Enlightened Judgments*), there were many court verdicts, such as "a woman shall not serve two husbands" and "a couple shall stay together all their lives," which were regarded as behaviors of "being educated and propriety-minded."

According to law, the status of the wife in the family was not equal to that of her husband, namely, "although the wife is neither the servant nor the child, her status is the same as that of a close relative, a servant or a child."²⁴⁶ Therefore, the personal rights of the wife at home were controlled by her husband. If the couple committed the same crime, they would be dealt with differently. Nevertheless, if the husband died, the wife would have all the rights belonging to the patriarch. For example, in trade and business, it would be considered illegal to conduct a transaction without negotiating with the woman householder or without the signature of the widowed mother; otherwise, it would be punishable.

---

²⁴⁴"Zhu Ding Hun Wu Gu San Nian Bu Cheng Hun Zhe Ting Li" (Allowing two Persons Having not Been Married after three years of Engagement to Divorce) in "Hu Hun Men" (The Category of Households and Marriage) in *Ming Gong Shu Pan Qing Ming Ji* (*Collections of Enlightened Judgments*), Vol. 9.

²⁴⁵"Bei You Si Yong Cai Men" (The Category of Misappropriating the Property by the Humble and the Young) in "Hu Hun Lv" (Statutes on Marriage, Tax and Household Registration) in *Song Xing Tong* (*The Penal Code of Song Dynasty*), Vol. 12.

²⁴⁶"Gao Zhou Qin Yi Xia Men" (The Category of Suing Relatives below Close Relatives) in "Dou Song Lv" (Statutes on Litigation) in *Song Xing Tong* (*The Penal Code of Song Dynasty*), Vol. 24.

Inheritance law in the Song Dynasty, though based on that of the Tang Dynasty, had included more articles, so it became more standardized and detailed and reached a relatively more perfect level. In the inheritance law of the Song Dynasty, the inheritance of "Zong Tiao" (the succession to the headship) and property inheritance were started to be separated. For the inheritance of "Zong Tiao" (the succession to the headship), "Di Zhang Zi" (the eldest son born of the legal wife) was considered the first heir; if there was no "Di Zhang Zi" (the eldest son born of the legal wife), "Shu Zi" (the son born of a concubine) would succeed. Families with no descendants may pass on the family line by finding a junior of the clan to be the successor or authorizing a close elder relative to find an inheritor for them if their father and mother both died. A person adopted from a different family could also be a legitimate heir, according to "Qin Zi Sun Fa" (law of biological male descendants). It was explained in *Ming Gong Shu Pan Qing Ming Ji* (*Collections of Enlightened Judgments*) that "the families without descendants must adopt a son of their own family line, but it is forbidded to adopt a son from a different clan. So there might be no descendants of the same clan who can be chosen as the heir, or even though there are descendants, they are reluctant to be heirs, or even they themselves are willing to do so, but their two families are at odds with the each other. If the succession of family line is conducted compulsorily, there will be no gratitude among them, then what is the use of doing that? So this is why it is allowed for an adopted person with a different surname to be the heir according to law."[247] But the adopted child shall be no more than three years old, and once the adoption is completed, the child will be treated as their own. So "if an abandoned child who is under the age of three is adopted, even if his surname is different, he should be regarded as their own child in the family."[248]

As to the inheritance of property, the provision of "Ying Fen" (Dividing of Property) in *Hu Ling* (*The Decree of Household*), which was carried out in the Tang Dynasty, was basically followed: "As for the land, houses and property, the brothers of the owner should share out equally"; "if a brother of the owner dies, the dead brother's son will be the candidate of the succession; if the brothers of the owner all die, his brothers' sons may share his belongings equally."[249] But some amendments were made to a certain extent.

Firstly, detailed provisions were made about the distribution of women's inheritance. For instance, an unmarried girl, a married woman who returned to her family

---

[247]"Shuang Li Mu Ming Zhi Zi Yu Tong Zong Zi" (Adopting the Children with Same and Different Surnames as Heirs) in "Hu Hun Men" (The Category of Households and Marriage) in *Ming Gong Shu Pan Qing Ming Ji* (*Collections of Enlightened Judgments*), Vol. 7.

[248]"Yi You Yang Zi Bu Dang Qiu Li" (No Allowing to Appoint New Heirs if Having Adopted Sons) in "Hu Hun Men" (The Category of Households and Marriage) in *Ming Gong Shu Pan Qing Ming Ji* (*Collections of Enlightened Judgments*), Vol. 7.

[249]"Bei You Si Yong Cai Men" (The Category of Misappropriating the Property by the Humble and the Young) in "Hu Hun Lv" (Statutes on Marriage, Tax and Household Registration) in *Song Xing Tong* (*The Penal Code of Song Dynasty*), Vol. 12.

of birth, a married woman, and a widow were differentiated by law, and the inheritance that they were supposed to enjoy was also specified.

An unmarried girl who had brothers had no right of inheritance, and she could only have half of her unmarried brother's betrothal gifts as her dowry. "The father's sisters who are unmarried can get half of the man's betrothal presents."[250] Only when there were no male descendants in the family could the unmarried girl inherit all the family's property, and the right of inheritance of an adopted daughter was the same as that of the real daughters.

As for a married woman who returned to her own family, her right of inheritance was the same as that of the family's unmarried girl in the early Song Dynasty. According to *Song Xing Tong* (*The Penal Code of Song Dynasty*), "if a married woman is divorced by her husband, or if the husband dies with no sons left and she has got no share of the property of her husband's family, but if she returns to her family where there are no descendants, she will enjoy the right of inheritance as an unmarried girl."[251] But from the period after the reign of Emperor Zhezong to the South Song Dynasty, where there were no male descendants, a married woman who returned home could only share half of the household property as was shared by an unmarried girl.

As to a married woman, if there were no male descendants or an unmarried girl in her family, she could have one third of the inheritance, and the other parts would be confiscated by the government. "If there is no married woman in the family, then the married aunt, elder sister, younger sister and niece each can get one share of the inheritance."[252]

As far as the right of inheritance of the widow is concerned, if her husband died with no sons left and she did not remarry, she could get her husband's inheritance. However, if she decided to remarry, she would not be allowed to take away her husband's property. In the South Song Dynasty, some changes were made in the law, and it was stipulated that "if a widow has no male descendants nor any relatives living with her to share the inheritance, but if she has married a 'Jie Jiao Fu' (a husband who marries into and lives in the woman's dead husband's family, who has no right of inheritance), she can inherit part of her ex-husband's property which should be no more than 5,000 *guan* if it is registered by the officials; if the woman is willing to return to the current husband's family or she has died, then her right of inheritance should be handled according to *Jue Hu Fa* (*Law for Families*

---

[250]"Bei You Si Yong Cai Men" (The Category of Misappropriating the Property by the Humble and the Young) in "Hu Hun Lv" (Statutes on Marriage, Tax and Household Registration) in *Song Xing Tong* (*The Penal Code of Song Dynasty*), Vol. 12.

[251]"Hu Jue Zi Chan Men" (The Category of the Property of the Families without Descendants) in "Hu Hun Lv" (Statutes on Marriage, Tax and Household Registration) in *Song Xing Tong* (*The Penal Code of Song Dynasty*), Vol. 12.

[252]Quoted from "Tian Sheng Hu Jue Tiao Guan" (Regulations about Families Without Descendants Issued in the Years of Tianheng) in "Shi Huo" (National Finance and Economy) in *Song Hui Yao Ji Gao* (*Collected Essays of the Historical Records of Song Dynasty*) (Book 58), Vol. 61.

Without Offspring)."²⁵³ However, if the widow remarried or lived and died in the family of the current husband, the property of her ex-husband would be confiscated.

Secondly, the rights of inheritance of "Yi Fu Zi" (posthumous child), "Bie Zhai Zi" (illegitimate child), "Yi Zi" (adopted son), and "Zhui Xu" (a son-in-law who lives in the home of his parents-in-law) were provided in detail by law.

The right of "Yi Fu Zi" (posthumous child) was equal to that of "Qin Zi" (parent child). The law of the Song Dynasty was quoted in the judgment of "Nv Xu Bu Ying Zhong Fen Qi Jia Cai Chan" (No Sharing of the Property of His Wife's Family by the Son-in-Law) in *Ming Gong Shu Pan Qing Ming Ji* (*Collections of Enlightened Judgments*), and it was stated that "according to law, if the parents are dead, the daughters can get half of the property inherited by the son, and 'Yi Fu Zi' (posthumous boy) can also get the same amount as a male heir. So the property of 'Zhou Bing' (his father) will be divided into three parts, among which two parts belong to 'Yi Fu Zi' (posthumous boy) and one part belongs to Xi Yiniang (his mother)."

An illegitimate child was called "Bie Zhai Zi," and some special provisions for the rights of inheritance of "Bie Zhai Zi" (illegitimate children) were included in *Song Xing Tong* (*The Penal Code of Song Dynasty*): "So the judgment made on the 24th of May of the 6th year of Tianbao in Tang Dynasty is approved ... If a man has illegitimate daughters or sons with a concubine (who is not formerly ranked in the household register) outside the family, all relationship among them will be cut off. Even if they file a lawsuit, it is not to be accepted by the government and the accuser will be driven away."²⁵⁴ This showed that for "Bie Zhai Zi" (illegitimate child) who had been ranked in the household register, his lawsuit would be accepted and heard; otherwise, the lawsuit would be rejected. Generally speaking, the regulations of the Southern Song Dynasty were more lenient compared with those of the Northern Song Dynasty, which provided that "for 'Bie Zhai Zi' (illegitimate child) whose father has died and who has no proof of his identity, his lawsuit will not be accepted."²⁵⁵ This showed that the lawsuit would not be accepted if the father of the child was dead or the child could not prove his parentage. Nevertheless, provided that he could prove his genetic connection with his father, his identity would be officially recognized, and he would be given certain rights of inheritance whether the child had been ranked in the household register or whether he had lived with his father.

Because women were free to remarry in the Song Dynasty, "the remarried women would rather take the child of her ex-husband to her current husband's home than

---

²⁵³"Fu Wang Er You Yang Zi Bu De Wei Zhi Hu Jue" (Forbidding the Families with Adopted Children to be Categorized as those without Descendants after the Death of the Husband) in "Hu Hun Men" (The Category of Households and Marriage) in *Ming Gong Shu Pan Qing Ming Ji* (*Collections of Enlightened Judgments*), Vol. 8.

²⁵⁴"Bei You Si Yong Cai Men" (The Category of Misappropriating the Property by the Humble and the Young) in "Hu Hun Lv" (Statutes on Marriage, Tax and Household Registration) in *Song Xing Tong* (*The Penal Code of Song Dynasty*), Vol. 12.

²⁵⁵"Wu Zheng Ju" (With No Evidence) in "Hu Hun Men" (The Category of Households and Marriage) in *Ming Gong Shu Pan Qing Ming Ji* (*Collections of Enlightened Judgments*), Vol. 8.

8.4 Civil Law Adapting to the Development of Commodity Economy

bear new babies for the current husband." The son of the ex-husband was called "Yi Zi" (adopted son),[256] who was not allowed to adopt his stepfather's surname. So after his stepfather died, he should return to his own clan. Besides, an adopted son had no rights of inheritance, but he could possess some of his mother's own property.

"Zhui Xu" (a son-in-law who lives in the home of his parents-in-law) generally refers to a man who was willing to marry into and to live at the home of his parents-in-law because of poverty. In consequence, "Zhui Xu" had no social status or rights at home; however, he had the right to share the property of his wife's family, so it was only under exceptional circumstances that he could acquire some of their property. For example, if the son-in-law was in charge of the property of his wife's family and was engaged in business, "after the wife's family members all died, he could get three tenths of the profit which he earned."[257]

Lastly, the regulation on the inheritance of families without descendants was made to protect private property. Families with no descendants were divided into "Li Ji" (to adopt a male of the next generation from the same branch of family or same clan as one's heir) and "Ming Ji" (to authorize a close elder relative to adopt an inheritor for them if the couple both died). According to the record of "Zhi Hui Chun Xi" (General Chun Xi) in *Ming Gong Shu Pan Qing Ming Ji (Collections of Enlightened Judgments)*, "'Li Ji' (to adopt a male of next generation from the same branch of family or same clan as one's heir) is used if the husband has died but the wife is still alive, or if they have no child of their own, so the decision of adopting a junior as the successor shall be made by the wife. 'Ming Ji' (to authorize a close elder relative to adopt an inheritor for them if the couple both die) is used if both of the couple have died or if they have no child of their own, so the decision of adopting a junior as the successor shall be made by a close elder relative."[258] To a certain extent, "the way of adopting a junior as a successor is equivalent to choosing a son as a successor of his father's property, which means that the property should be totally granted to the inheritor."[259] According to *Hu Ling (The Decree of Household)*, "if the adopted junior dies afterwards, another inheritor may be chosen by a close elder relative. As to the family property, the inheritor may get one fourth of it if

---

[256]"Yi Zi Bao Bing Qin Zi Cai Wu" (Adopted Child Possessing the Property of Parent-Child) in "Hu Hun Men" (The Category of Households and Marriage) in *Ming Gong Shu Pan Qing Ming Ji (Collections of Enlightened Judgments)*, Vol. 7.

[257]"Li Ji You Ju Bu Wei Jue Hu" (Forbidding the Families with the Evidence of Adopted Heirs to be Categorized as those without Descendants) in "Hu Hun Men" (The Category of Households and Marriage) in *Ming Gong Shu Pan Qing Ming Ji (Collections of Enlightened Judgments)*, Vol. 7.

[258]"Ming Ji Yu Li Ji Bu Tong" ["Ming Ji" (to authorize a close elder relative to adopt an inheritor for them if the couple both die) Being Different from "Li Ji" (to adopt a junior of the clan as the successor)] in "Hu Hun Men" (The Category of Households and Marriage) in *Ming Gong Shu Pan Qing Ming Ji (Collections of Enlightened Judgments)*, Vol. 7.

[259]"Ming Ji Yu Li Ji Bu Tong" ["Ming Ji" (to authorize a close elder relative to adopt an inheritor for them if the couple both die) Being Different from "Li Ji" (to adopt a junior of the clan as the successor)] in "Hu Hun Men" (The Category of Households and Marriage) in *Ming Gong Shu Pan Qing Ming Ji (Collections of Enlightened Judgments)*, Vol. 7.

there are unmarried girls in the family; if there are also married women who return to the family, the inheritor may get one fifth of the property; if there are unmarried girls or married women who returned home in the family, the property will be divided into four parts, and the amount that each of them may get will be decided according to *Jue Hu Fa* (*Law for Families Without Offspring*); if there are only married women who returned home, in addition to the parts given to the adopted child according to *Jue Hu Fa* (*Law for Families Without Offspring*), half of the property left is given to the females, and the remainder shall be confiscated by the government; if there are only married women remaining in the family, then the property will be divided into three parts, among which two parts shall be equally distributed to the married women, and the rest will be confiscated by the government; if there are no unmarried girls, nor married women who returned home nor married women in the family, one third of the property will be given to the adopted child."[260] But whether by "Ming Ji" (to authorize a close elder relative to adopt an inheritor for them if the couple both died) or "Li Ji" (to adopt a male of the next generation from the same branch of family or same clan as one's heir), adoption should be conducted seriously. According to law, they should have similar "Zhao Mu" (the patriarchal system of arranged order and order of generation in the temple or cemetery), which means that they should have similar status in the family hierarchy. Moreover, the son of one family who was adopted by an heirless family could not be adopted by another family as an inheritor to prevent him from illegally inheriting the properties of the two families. Once a person of "Zhao Mu" (the patriarchal system of arranged order and order of generation in the temple or cemetery) was decided to be "Si Zi" (adopted son), he would not allowed to be repatriated with no reason. According to *Ming Gong Shu Pan Qing Ming Ji* (*Collections of Enlightened Judgments*), "if a family has no male descendants, it is allowed to adopt a child with status in the family hierarchy similar to 'Zhao Mu' (the patriarchal system of arranged order and order of generation in the temple or cemetery) as the son or grandson."[261] "As for the adopted child, when the foster father or foster grandfather dies, he is not to be repatriated by the foster grandmother or foster mother with no reason,"[262] unless "he has wasted the family fortune, or has failed to wait upon the old, or has made obvious

---

[260]"Chu Fen Gu Yi Cai Chan" (Disposing the Property of Orphans) in "Hu Hun Men" (The Category of Households and Marriage) in *Ming Gong Shu Pan Qing Ming Ji* (*Collections of Enlightened Judgments*), Vol. 8.

[261]"Yi Li Zhao Mu Xiang Dang Ren Er Tong Zong Wang Su" (People Recklessly Accusing the Relatives of the Same Clan) in "Hu Hun Men" (The Category of Households and Marriage) in *Ming Gong Shu Pan Qing Ming Ji* (*Collections of Enlightened Judgments*), Vol. 8.

[262]"Fu Zai Li Yi Xing Fu Wang Wu Yi Huan Zhi Tiao" (The Article about Forbidding the Adopted Child to Return to his Parents after the Death of the Foster Father) in "Hu Hun Men" (The Category of Households and Marriage) in *Ming Gong Shu Pan Qing Ming Ji* (*Collections of Enlightened Judgments*), Vol. 8.

mistakes. So he will be sent back after being approved and verified by the officials and the close senior relatives."[263]

On the basis of "Yi Zhu Chu Fen" (dealing with inheritance according to wills) in the Tang Dynasty, some progress was also made in testamentary succession in the Song Dynasty. "If the will of the dead is proved true, then it should be proceeded as is told to."[264] So testamentary succession was regarded not only as a measure that "all wise men have taken to deal with the disputes after death"[265] but also as an important evidence in judicial judgment; therefore, age of testamentary capacity was stipulated for testators. According to the records in *Ming Gong Shu Pan Qing Ming Ji (Collections of Enlightened Judgments)*, "because the testator is only seven years old and his will may not be real, it seems hard to be accepted."[266] There were two kinds of wills in the Song Dynasty, namely, nuncupative will and written will, with the former having a relatively lesser probative force. Besides, a written will should be made "by the testators with the evidence of the government"[267] and "shall be sealed by the officials."[268] "So any will without official seal is only regarded as the private document of the dead,"[269] which would not be recognized by the official government. Disputes over the property that was distributed according to a will should be filed to the government within three years. In *Ming Gong Shu Pan Qing Ming Ji (Collections of Enlightened Judgments)*, it was recorded that lawsuits involving an unfair will filed beyond the prescription period (five years or ten years) were not accepted by the government.

In conclusion, the development of commodity economy of Song Dynasty had provided the material basis for the development of civil legislation, so that the laws like the property law, the law of obligations and the marriage and inheritance law had

---

[263]"Chu Ji Zi Bu Xiao Le Ling Gui Zong" (The Unworthy Adopted Child Being Compelled to Return to His Own Clan) in "Hu Hun Men" (The Category of Households and Marriage) in *Ming Gong Shu Pan Qing Ming Ji (Collections of Enlightened Judgments)*, Vol. 8.

[264]"Shi Huo" (National Finance and Economy) in *Song Hui Yao Ji Gao (Collected Essays of the Historical Records of Song Dynasty)* (Book 58), Vol. 61.

[265]Yuan Cai, "Yi Zhu Gong Ping Wei Hou Huan" (Avoiding Future Trouble by Making a Fair Will) in *Yuan Shi Shi Fan (Mr. Yuan: A Model of the People)*, Vol. 1.

[266]"Xian Li Yi Zi Si Jiang Lai Ben Zong You Zhao Mu Xiang Dang Ren Shuang Li" (Appointing Double Heirs by Adopting an Heir First and the Adopting a Relative's Son of the Same Family in the Future) in "Hu Hun Men" (The Category of Households and Marriage) in *Ming Gong Shu Pan Qing Ming Ji (Collections of Enlightened Judgments)*, Vol. 8.

[267]"Xian Li Yi Ding Bu Dang Yi Nie Zi Yi Zhi" (Replacing the Formerly Adopted Unworthy Heir by the Son Born of Concubines) in "Hu Hun Men" (The Category of Households and Marriage) in *Ming Gong Shu Pan Qing Ming Ji (Collections of Enlightened Judgments)*, Vol. 7.

[268]"Fu Zi Ju Wang Li Sun Wei Hou" (The Grandson Being Chosen as the Heir after the Death of the Father and Son) in "Hu Hun Men" (The Category of Households and Marriage) in *Ming Gong Shu Pan Qing Ming Ji (Collections of Enlightened Judgments)*, Vol. 8.

[269]"Seng Gui Su Cheng Fen" (The Inheritance by Monks after their Resuming Secular Life) in "Hu Hun Men" (The Category of Households and Marriage) in *Ming Gong Shu Pan Qing Ming Ji (Collections of Enlightened Judgments)*, Vol. 8.

reached a very advanced level and it had become a new chapter in the history of Chinese civil law.

8.5 The Economic and Financial Law Made with the Spirit of Reform

In the process of commercialization of agricultural products in the Song Dynasty, the production of cotton, silk, sugar, and other agricultural products increased rapidly, which had further provided a broad market of raw materials for the development of the handicraft industry. Moreover, achievements were made at different levels in shipbuilding, porcelain making, spinning, manufacture of weaponry, printing, mining, and metallurgy. Besides, the quality, manufacturing techniques, and scales of the products had all exceeded those of the Tang Dynasty, and household handicraft workshops were built all over the rural areas. So with the development of agriculture and the handicraft industry, trade prospered, cities sprang up, commercial houses emerged, and overseas trades dramatically expanded, all of which had promoted the development of the economic laws of the Song Dynasty.

Moreover, in order to get through the financial crisis of overexpenditure and to get rid of the difficult situation, financial legislation was strengthened by the Southern and Northern Song governments in order to intensify the collection, appliance, management, and supervision of capital by means of law.

8.5.1 Agricultural, Industrial, and Commercial Legislation

In early Song Dynasty, the policy of non-implementation of a land system and noncontroling of land annexation was carried out in order to adapt to the dramatic change in land relationship happening since the middle of the Tang Dynasty, which had rapidly given private land ownership a dominant position. Consequently, public land such as "Tun Tian" (wasteland opened up by garrison troops or peasants), "Ying Tian" (wasteland that could not be cultivated by peasants employed by the government), "Guan Zhuang" (official land), "Zhi Tian" (professional farmland, which was granted as part of official salary according to official rank in ancient China), "Xue Tian" (school farm), "Jian Mu Di" (horse pasture), etc. occupied only 4.3% of the national land.[270] Because of this circumstance, the main task of agricultural legislation was to protect private land ownership, to consolidate land relationship, and to promote agricultural development. Since early Song Dynasty, "Shu Qian Yin Qi" (a law in the Song Dynasty that required real estate sellers to pay

---

[270]Qi Xia, *Song Dai Jing Ji Shi* (*The Economic History of Song Dynasty*) (Book 1), Shanghai People's Publishing House, 1987, p. 340.

tax to the local government at a set time) had always been the legal basis for acquiring land property. Furthermore, private land transactions were not intervened in by the government, and all kinds of criminal sanctions were taken to prevent others to infringe upon legal land relationship.

In view of the large amount of wasteland caused by war after the period of "Wu Dai" (the Five Dynasties), the policy of reclaiming wasteland was actively carried out by the imperial court in order to increase revenue and to help the refugees settle down. The settlers' rights of freeholding of newly cultivated land were affirmed by law, and the total area of reclaimed land was made as the criterion for assessing the achievements of local government officials. So it was not until the South Song Dynasty that the policy of changing reclaimed wasteland into permanent private land was continued to be implemented by the government.

During the reign of Emperor Shenzong, the land policy of non-implementation of land system and noncontroling of land annexation had led to very serious consequences, such as false records of land and real estate, unfair tax, and overburden of debt for peasants of the middle and lower classes. In August of the 5th year of Xi'ning (1072 AD), *Fang Tian Jun Shui Fa* (*Square Land Tax System*) was issued, in which it was stipulated that land should be measured by county magistrates in September of every year, and the land should be divided into five degrees according to the land shape and the condition of the soil, with 1000 *bu* in the four directions of east, west, south, and north as one *fang*. After the measurement, the land tax would be estimated once again and it for forbidden to exceed the quota of the tax. So if land transaction was carried out, the amount of land should be decided according to newly measured land. In consequence, a large amount of land and estate that was left out before was discovered again due to the implementation of *Fang Tian Jun Shui Fa* (*Square Land Tax System*). The so-called "Zi Hu" (unregistered farmer), who had previously sought refuge in rich people's homes, became "Bian Hu Qi Min" (registered farmer) again; hence, the national revenue was increased. But with the failure of reform and the opposition of the landlords, *Fang Tian Jun Shui Fa* (*Square Land Tax System*) was finally abolished. In the Southern Song Dynasty, "Jing Jie Fa" (Law for Dividing the Land) was made and implemented to measure land and to set up the standard for tax collection, but it had no effect in the end.

In order to strengthen the management of irrigation and water conservancy, in September of the 2nd year of Xi'ning (1069 AD), *Nong Tian Li Hai Tiao Yue* (*The Treaty of Irrigation and Water Conservancy*) was issued by "Tiao Li Si" (the department in charge of making regulations), and it was the best representation of the law on irrigation and water conservancy. The main goal of this treaty was to "reclaim the waste field, to construct the water conservancy projects, to build dams,"[271] and to develop agricultural production. The main contents are as follows:

> For all water engineering that needed to to be repaired or built, the expenses of labor and materials should be paid by the local residents according to family ranks, and those who

---

[271] "Shi Huo" (National Finance and Economy) in *Song Hui Yao Ji Gao* (*Collected Essays of the Historical Records of Song Dynasty*) (Book 28), Vol. 1.

intentionally refused to donate building materials would be severely punished. If the project was huge and financial resources of the people were insufficient, the officials should lend them money, and the wealthy people in "Xian" (county) should "lead money to the poor and earn interests according to law. Moreover, the officials should press for the payment of debt by making records"[272]. The individuals who rendered great service to the project by investment would be rewarded according to their contribution or be employed according to their merits.

No doubt, the provisions of *Nong Tian Li Hai Tiao Yue* (*The Treaty of Irrigation and Water Conservancy*) had aroused people's enthusiasm in all walks of life, so it was beneficial to the construction of an irrigation system and the development of agricultural production.

As to the regulation of handicraft industry, it was characterized by the guarantee of the strictly centralized management system. All the handicraft industries which were closely related to the national economy and the people's livelihood or which were tremendously profitable, such as the handicraft production of metals like copper, iron, gold, and silver, were mainly operated and supervised by "Jian" (ancient supervisory office) and "Ye" (official in charge of smelting) which were established by the state. Although private workshops were allowed to do business, they must get permission from the government; otherwise, they would be punished for the crime of robbery. During the years of Zhenghe, *Cha Ma Fa* (*Laws on Tea-Horse Trading*) was enacted by the government, and it was provided that "melting furnaces and iron for smelting should not only be provided by the government, but also operated by the people employed by government."[273] But in fact, those who had furnaces were all rich people, so the workers not only suffered from cruel economic exploitation but also became dependent on the furnace owners. In the Northern Song Dynasty, some households that mainly engaged in spinning and weaving appeared in some areas, so they were called "Ji Hu" (the households specializing in the manual silk industry or cotton industry). In the 2nd year of Mingdao, it was stipulated that only two thirds of the damask produced by "Ji Hu" (the households specializing in the manual silk industry or cotton industry) could be sold, and the rest would be bought by the government, which had no doubt caused its fast development.[274]

As to project construction, in Song Dynasty, *Tang Lv* (*Tang Code*) was followed, so illegal construction was prohibited. For all illegal construction "that have been carried out without being reported and approved by the government," "the person in charge will be punished one level lighter than that for the crime of 'Zuo Zang' (embezzlement)." If illegal construction is carried out with more than ten workers

---

[272]"Shi Huo" (National Finance and Economy) in *Song Hui Yao Ji Gao* (*Collected Essays of the Historical Records of Song Dynasty*) (Book 28), Vol. 1.

[273]"Zheng Que Kao" (An Examination of National Commodity Tax and Government Monopoly) (Part 5) in *Wen Xian Tong Kao* (*A General Textual Research of the Documents*), Vol. 18.

[274]"Shi Huo" (National Finance and Economy) in *Song Hui Yao Ji Gao* (*Collected Essays of the Historical Records of Song Dynasty*) (Book 23), Vol. 64.

hired, the person in charge will be punished for the crime of 'Zuo Zang' (embezzlement)."[275]

In order to make the quality of handicraft products reach a statutory standard and to guarantee the inheritance of artistry, it was required that technical training should be conducted in various ways by the craftsmen within a stipulated time so that the artistry could be passed down from father to son or passed down to other members of the family or passed down through a system of apprenticeship. Besides, it was required that certain procedures should be followed in the manufacture of some products, and samples should be made by state officials with the names of producers and production time inscribed on the products in order to clarify the responsibilities and to decide the legal responsibility. So the gradual replacement of servitude system by recruitment system in the management of industrial production had met the needs of the development of productivity and promoted the development of handicraft production.

The commercial prosperity of the Song Dynasty had brought about the expansion of the market and promoted the development of market management regulations, which was not only reflected in *Song Xing Tong* (*The Penal Code of Song Dynasty*) and the relative laws and orders but also in the specialized law of market management, namely, *Shi Yi Fa* (*Trading Law*), which was formulated and promulgated during the political reform of Wang Anshi in March of the 5th year of Xi'ning (1072 A.D.). *Shi Yi Fa* (*Trading Law*) consisted of totally twelve provisions and sub-provisions, and its main content was to establish "Shi Yi Wu" (market management bureau) in the capital area of Kaifeng as a specialized institution to regulate price. So 1,000,000 *guan* of funds was appropriated to "Shi Yi Wu" (market management bureau) by the imperial government so as to stabilize the price by buying and selling goods according to market conditions. Besides, "Shi Yi Wu" (market management bureau) also provided loans to merchants who borrowed money with their real estate mortgaged, for which an annual interest of two *fen* would be charged. Moreover, an annual interest of two *fen* would also be charged for the goods that merchants bought on credit, which would be paid after half or one year. Because abundant funds were raised by "Shi Yi Wu" (market management bureau), it was possible to buy the unsalable goods timely or to sell goods to merchants on credit so as to stabilize prices and to control the market.

Before the establishment of "Shi Yi Wu" (market management bureau), relevant affairs such as stabilizing prices, selling and purchasing of goods, and providing loans to small and medium businessmen were all manipulated by big businessmen. So the implementation of *Shi Yi Fa* (*Trading Law*) had made it possible for the imperial court to take the huge profits away from those big businessmen, which had greatly contributed to the stabilization of the market economy, the strengthening of the centralized management of the country, and the increasing of the quotient tax

---

[275]"Xing Zao Liao Qing Men" (The Category of Making Building Materials) in "Shan Xing Lv" (Statutes on Sending Troops without Authorization) in *Song Xing Tong* (*The Penal Code of Song Dynasty*), Vol. 16.

revenue. Therefore, after the implementation of *Shi Yi Fa* (*Trading Law*) in the capital area of Kaifeng, it was put into practice nationwide in succession.

The law on weights and measures and price control was an essential part of the laws of market management, so the relevant regulations in *Guan Shi Ling* (*Order on Border Market*) and *Tang Lv Shu Yi* (*Comments on Tang Code*) were continued to be implemented.

In the Song Dynasty, although "Shi Fang Zhi" (the system of strict separation of residential and trading areas and the strict control of the time and place of trading by laws), which was established in the Tang dynasty, was abolished and the trade of businessmen was not restricted by space and time, monopoly law, which embodied the traditional policy of "restraining commerce," covered a much wider range, including daily necessities such as salt, tea, alcohol, vitriol, aromatic drug, iron, coal, vinegar, and other things so as to provide a sufficient supply to the state. Among these things, salt and tea were the most important, so the relevant legislation was stricter and detailed.

Because profit made from selling salt was a major source of fiscal revenue in the Song Dynasty, according to the statistics of the later years of Tianxi during the reign of Emperor Zhenzong, salt profit accounted for 13.2% of the national fiscal revenue. In the later years of Shaoxing in the Southern Song Dynasty, the ratio even reached to 54.5%[276] of the national income. Therefore, transactions of salt were monopolized by the state. During the reign of Emperor Renzong, in order to get rid of public disturbances in the transportation and selling of salt and to ensure the salt profit of the state, "Guan Que Fa" (Law on Official Monopoly) was replaced by "Tong Shang Fa" (Trade Law), by which the overall the production of salt was controlled by the government. As to the transportation and sale of salt, it consisted of official transportation and sale, as well as commercial transportation and sale. Official transportation and sale was exclusively in the charge of "Shi Yi Wu" (market management bureau). As to commercial transportation and sale, after the businessmen obtained "Yan Yin" (certificates for transporting taxed salts) under the control of government, they could have exclusive sale or sale on a commission basis, but smuggling was forbidden. "Those who have smuggled one *liang* of salt shall be punished by 'Chi' (flogging with light sticks) for forty strokes; those who have smuggled two *jin* of salt shall be punished two levels severer; those who have smuggled twenty *jin* of salt shall be punished by 'Tu' (imprisonment) for one year. For every twenty *jin* of salt, the punishment will be one level severer, and those who have smuggled two hundred *jin* of salt shall be exiled in the town."[277]

In early Song Dynasty, in order to severely punish the private manufacturing of salt, in the 2nd year of Jianlong (961 A.D.) an imperial edict was issued, and it was ordered that "anyone who manufactures three *jin* of salt without permission shall be

---

[276]Qi Xia, *Song Dai Jing Ji Shi* (*The Economic History of Song Dynasty*) (Book 2), Shanghai People's Publishing House, 1987, p. 855.

[277]"Shi Huo" (National Finance and Economy) in *Song Hui Yao Ji Gao* (*Collected Essays of the Historical Records of Song Dynasty*) (Book 19), Vol. 26.

put to death; anyone who transports ten *jin* of salt to the forbidden area shall also be put to death,"[278] Afterward, lenient policy was carried out, but severe punishment was restored during the reign of Emperor Renzong. In the Southern Song Dynasty, "not only the huge expenditure of the imperial court fully depended on the profits made in tea and salt transaction,"[279] but the "military spending also mostly depended on salt tax,"[280] so those who committed the crime of illegal smuggling of salt "are often punished severely beyond the legal provisions."[281] Especially, the people who smuggled salt illegally or stole salt with weapons would inevitably be put to death.

In addition to the legislation on preventing illegal salt transactions, special officials were also appointed to supervise the manufacture of salt, to search for smugglers, and to reward informers, which had provided important precedents for the salt law made in the Ming and Qing dynasties.

Cha Fa (Regulations of Tea) was roughly equivalent to the regulation on salt. There were official tea gardens, as well as private "Yuan Hu" (tea planters). Private tea planters borrowed "Ben Qian" (capital) from the government and paid 20% interest. The tea they produced was all sold to the government and then was sold exclusively by "Chang Wu" (salt and iron monopoly management organizations). Moreover, six "Que Huo Wu" (monopoly tax commissions) were set up to be in charge of the business. If anyone had hidden tea without turning it over to the government or had smuggled tea, the tea would be confiscated and the violator would be punished according to the value of the products; those who smuggled private tea with weapons would all be put to death once they were arrested.[282] If the official in charge had smuggled tea that was worth 500 *qian*, he would be exiled to a distance of 2000 *li*; if the smuggled tea was worth 1500 *qian*, he would be put to death.[283]

Apart from official selling, the commercial sellers must go to "Que Huo Wu" (monopoly tax commissions) in Dongjing (now Kaifeng City) to pay for tea tax to get a tea selling license and then go to the appointed places of "Que Huo Wu" (monopoly tax commissions) to get the tea for selling. So in the Song Dynasty, *Cha Fa (Regulations of Tea)* was revised many times so as to include "Yuan Hu" (tea planters) and tea merchants in the track of state monopoly to be cruelly exploited. During the reign of Emperor Zhezong, "You Si Jian" (deputy advisor) Su Che

---

[278]"Shi Huo" (National Finance and Economy) in *Song Hui Yao Ji Gao (Collected Essays of the Historical Records of Song Dynasty)* (Book 18), Vol. 23.

[279]"Shi Huo" (National Finance and Economy) in *Song Hui Yao Ji Gao (Collected Essays of the Historical Records of Song Dynasty)* (Book 3), Vol. 26.

[280]"Shi Huo" (National Finance and Economy) in *Song Hui Yao Ji Gao (Collected Essays of the Historical Records of Song Dynasty)* (Book 7), Vol. 26.

[281]"Shi Huo" (National Finance and Economy) in *Song Hui Yao Ji Gao (Collected Essays of the Historical Records of Song Dynasty)* (Book 5), Vol. 26.

[282]*Xu Zi Zhi Tong Jian Chang Bian (Sequel to the Full-length Book of History as a Mirror)*, Vol. 5, in August of the 2nd year of Qiande.

[283]*Xu Zi Zhi Tong Jian Chang Bian (Sequel to the Full-length Book of History as a Mirror)*, Vol. 5, in August of the 2nd year of Qiande.

submitted a memorial to the emperor and stated that "since the state monopoly on tea, severe penalties are enforced to punish the illegal sale, smuggling is prohibited, the grade of tea is strictly regulated, less money is paid to buy more goods, lower price is fixed for the tea by years, thus the price was reduced by half compared with that of the previous year."[284] "Shi Yu Shi" (subordinate of "Yu Shi Zhong Cheng" or Grand Censor) Liu Zhi also stated that "although in name what the official has done is to stabilize the price for 'Yuan Hu' (tea planters), while in fact it is just like extortion. . . . If they want to cut down tea plants, they will ban tea business; if they want to plant more tea plants, they will raise the tea price. So it is said by the local people that the land does not produce tea but disasters."[285]

In the Southern Song Dynasty, except for some provinces, *Cha Yin Fa* (*Law on Tea License*) was extensively implemented. *Cha Yin Fa* (*Law on Tea License*) consisted of "Chang Yin" (tea license for long distance) and "Duan Yin" (tea license for short distance). So official transportation and sale was changed to private sale by the civilians. But a contract had to be signed with the relatives who often acted as guarantors. According to an imperial edict issued in the 11th year of Chunxi (1148 A.D.), "from now on, tea shall be sold on credit to purchasers, if he has parents or brothers, they shall sign contracts together."[286]

In addition, "Cha Ma Si" (the office in charge of tea-horse trading) was also set up to be in charge of transporting tea to minority regions in exchange of horses in the Sichuan area. But private sale and smuggling were strictly prohibited, so the offenders would be punished according to military law.

The expansion of the scope of monopoly and the strengthening of legal regulation in the Song Dynasty were a reflection of the enhancing of absolutism in the economic field, which was contradictory to the free development of the commodity economy. But because the income from monopolized selling was the main sources of state revenue, in the years of Yuanfeng during the reign of Emperor Shenzong, the income from tea, salt, alcohol, vitriol, etc. had reached to over 26,570,000 *guan* of money. Therefore, although "Jin Que Zhi Du" (the system of state monopoly for some important goods) was against market competition and had also curbed the momentum of the development of the commodity economy, it was essential to maintain the ruling of the state.

In the Song Dynasty, great achievements were made in foreign trade, which was unprecedented in the history of Chinese feudal society. Especially, overseas trade was extended to Europe, Asia, and Africa, which had made China the contemporary famous trade power in world. This was not accidental. Firstly, the development of commodity economy had provided the material basis for the overseas trade.

---

[284]Su Zhe (Song Dynasty), "Lun Shu Cha Wu Hai Zhuang" (On the Five Kinds of Harm Done to Teaplanting in Sichuan Area) in *Luan Cheng Ji* (*The Anthology of Luancheng*), Vol. 36.

[285]"Shi Huo Zhi" (Records of National Finance and Economy) in *Song Shi* (*The History of Song Dynasty*) (Book 2), Vol. 6.

[286]"Shi Huo" (National Finance and Economy) in *Song Hui Yao Ji Gao* (*Collected Essays of the Historical Records of Song Dynasty*) (Book 26), Vol. 31.

8.5 The Economic and Financial Law Made with the Spirit of Reform

Secondly, overseas trade had alleviated the financial problems faced by the imperial court. Thirdly, there were no political factors in carrying out the policy of banning overseas trade. Fourthly, since the years of Emperor Taizong, the guiding ideology of "attracting foreign people to conduct commercial intercourse and to increase the wealth" was established,[287] so people were sent to countries near the South China Sea by the government to solicit businessmen. After the reign of Taizong, even more positive measures were taken by emperors Zhenzong, Renzong, Shenzong, Gaozong, and Xiaozong to attract and reward overseas businessmen, which had guaranteed the continuous progress of overseas trade.

As to the ways of doing overseas trade, one was by means of official trade, called "Chao Gong" (paying tribute to the court) and "Hui Ci" (awards in return). All goods belonging to this category were free of tax. The second way was trade among the people. In order to strengthen the management of overseas trade, "Shi Bo Si" (the office in charge of the management of foreign trade) was set up in the major ports of Guangzhou, Hangzhou, Mingzhou, Quanzhou, Mizhou, Xiuzhou, Wenzhou, and Jiangyin to supervise ship businessmen, to levy customs duties, and to purchase goods.

So corresponding legal adjustments were inevitably needed for the development of overseas trade. In the Song Dynasty, regulations about Sino–foreign trade, as well as long-standing trade legislation in *Tang Lv Shu Yi* (*Comments on Tang Code*), such as "the form of trade," "the market management," "the prohibiting of private trade," etc. were all inherited. It was recorded in *Song Shi* (*The History of Song Dynasty*) that "the law of overseas trade was put into practice since there were trade contacts between China and Nanyue (in present-day Vietnam) ... In the Northern Wei Dynasty, trading posts were built in southern frontier; in Sui and Tang dynasties, trading posts were built in northeast. Besides, decrees were issued during the reign of Kaiyuan and legal provisions were carried out in all areas.... During the early Song Dynasty, the systems of the Zhou Dynasty were followed."[288] The form of overseas trade and the number of foreign businessmen in the Song Dynasty were incomparable to those in the Tang Dynasty; therefore, in the *Song Xing Tong* (*The Penal Code of Song Dynasty*), a provision about "the money of the wounded and deceased businessmen and the people in 'Zhu Fan' (ethnic minorities on the frontier) and 'Bo Si Fu' (the middle east)" was especially added so as to protect the rights of ownership of property of foreign businessmen and their relatives. In addition, decrees were successively issued by the government as complementary forms of law on foreign trade. Emperor Xiaozong once clearly pointed that "since no trade

---

[287]"Zhi Guan" (State Officials) in *Song Hui Yao Ji Gao* (*Collected Essays of the Historical Records of Song Dynasty*) (Book 24), Vol. 44.

[288]"Shi Huo Zhi" (Records of National Finance and Economy) in *Song Shi* (*History of Song Dynasty*) (Book 8), Vol. 2.

regulations are made in the four 'Jun' (shire) in Hainan, the imperial instructions shall be obeyed by the local people."[289]

The representative foreign trade regulation of the Song Dynasty was *Shi Bo Tiao Fa* (*Laws on Overseas Trade*), and its main contents are as follows.

Setting up agencies for foreign trade management: overseas trade regulatory authorities such as "Shi Bo Si" (the office in charge of the management of foreign trade), "Shi Yi Si" (bureau for trade), "Bo Yi Wu" (a state-run trading firm), "Ya Hang" (broker house), "Hai Guan" (customs), "Yang Hang" (foreign firm), and other agencies were set up, among which "Shi Bo Si" (the office in charge of the management of foreign trade) was the most important agency, and its main duty was to receive merchants and those who paid tribute to the emperor at home and abroad, to levy tax, to manage merchandise trade, and to associate with foreign guests.

Deciding on the basic standard of taxation: since the Tang Dynasty, the standard of taxation levied on foreign traders had been about "one tenth" or "two tenths." In the Song Dynasty, it was stipulated that "from now on, for the four kinds of products of borneol, agilawood, clove, and amomum cardamomum that the businessmen of small minorities trade, the tax shall be levied at the rate of 10% as before,"[290] and "the tax rate of the goods shall be no more than 20%."[291] Moreover, it was forbidden for the goods to be stealthily traded without paying tax; otherwise, the offender would be punished. But if accidents happened to the merchant ship or goods were damaged, the tax could be reduced or exempted. "If the cargo ship encountered gale, after it arrived at the ports, they should report to those in charge immediately and went to "Shi Bo Si" (the office in charge of the management of foreign trade) to ask for tax exemption."[292] If anyone had evaded tax intentionally or refused to pay tax, he would be punished according to law. As "Que Mai Zhi" (monopolized selling) was imposed on foreign goods in the Song Dynasty, all imported monopolized commodities such as ivory and jewels would be purchased by the government.

For foreign goods, only after "Gong Ping" (official testimonial papers) was obtained could they be sold in other places. The valid contract that was accepted and signed by officials and merchants, namely, the system of "Gong Ping," was also carried out in overseas trade. During the years of Xi'ning, an order was issued by Emperor Shenzong, according to which "businessmen in overseas trade shall show the official testimonial paper in their sale of goods."[293] During the reign of Emperor

---

[289]"Fan Yi" (Ethnic Minorities) in *Song Hui Yao Ji Gao* (*Collected Essays of the Historical Records of Song Dynasty*) (Book 84), Vol. 4.

[290]"Zhi Guan" (State Officials) in *Song Hui Yao Ji Gao* (*Collected Essays of the Historical Records of Song Dynasty*) (Book 26), Vol. 44.

[291]"Shi Huo Zhi" (Records of National Finance and Economy) in *Song Shi* (*History of Song Dynasty*) (Book 2), Vol. 8.

[292]"Shi Huo Zhi" (Records of National Finance and Economy) in *Song Shi* (*History of Song Dynasty*) (Book 2), Vol. 8.

[293]Su Shi (Song Dynasty), "Qi Jin Shang Lv Guo Wai Guo Zhuang" (A Memorial about Prohibiting Merchants to Go Abroad) in "Dong Po Zou Yi" (Dongpo's Memorials to the Emperor) in *Su Wen Zhong Gong Quan Ji* (*The Complete Works of Su Shi*), Vol. 8.

8.5 The Economic and Financial Law Made with the Spirit of Reform

Huizong, in view of the increased number of business activities between foreign businessmen and the people, an imperial edict was issued, and it was stipulated that although "the commercial intercourse is allowed," "'Gong Ping' (official testimonial papers) should be issued by "Shi Bo Si" (the office in charge of the management of foreign trade) after "examining the facts"[294] to insure the sale of the shipped goods.

Forbidding human trafficking and the manufacturing of weapons and military supplies: according to the law of the Song Dynasty, if merchants or freighters engaged in human trafficking, the "merchants, freighter owners, merchant heads in charge of transportation, the proprietress as well as the captains of the ship will be punished by 'Zhang' (flogging with heavy sticks) for one hundred strokes respectively with the goods confiscated, and the whistleblower will be rewarded half of the value of the confiscated goods"[295]; "those who manufacture or sell weapons and their leaders shall be sentenced to two years of imprisonment" with "the weapons confiscated"; if a person voluntarily surrendered himself, he shall be punished "one level lighter."[296]

Protecting the legal rights of foreign merchants: for all foreign businessmen in China, as long as they receive "Yan Fu" (certificate) or other official documents issued by "Shi Bo Si" (the office in charge of the management of foreign trade), their legal rights would be protected in China, including their rights of settlement and marriage. During the years of Xi'ning, there were a large number of "foreign trade caravans who settle with their wives and children in Guangzhou."[297] Gu Yanwu once made a textual research and noted that "'Shi Bo' (overseas trade) had been set up in Guangzhou since Tang Dynasty. Afterwards the businessmen often registered for permanent residence, which had continued till Song Dynasty. With exotic goods and strange accents, they mostly settle and build towns with stones along the seashore to bring up their descendants there."[298] Moreover, foreign businessmen were allowed to intermarry with the local officials, and the Arabian businessmen were allowed to build churches, appoint bishops in "Fan Fang" (the habitation of foreign traders), make pilgrimage, and do religious service in accordance with the Muslim custom. It was especially forbidden to detinue the goods of foreign traders; otherwise, the offenders would be punished. As to the goods that had been taxed, if they were not sold outside the state, they should not be taxed again. The remaining goods that had already been taxed and those that had been sold out "shall not be

---

[294]"Zhi Guan" (State Officials) in *Song Hui Yao Ji Gao* (*Collected Essays of the Historical Records of Song Dynasty*) (Book 8), Vol. 44.

[295]"Shi Bo" (Overseas Trade) in *Xu Wen Xian Tong Kao* (*A Sequel of the General Textual Research of the Documents*), Vol. 26.

[296]"Xing Fan Jun Xu" (The Provision of Trafficking Military Supplies) in "Que Jin Men" (The Category of Monopoly) (Part 2) in *Qing Yuan Tiao Fa Shi Lei* (*The Legal Provisions and Cases Made in the Year of Qingyuan*), Vol. 29.

[297]"Xing Fa" (Criminal Law) in *Song Hui Yao Ji Gao* (*Collected Essays of the Historical Records of Song Dynasty*) (Book 21), Vol. 2.

[298]Gu Yanwu (Ming Dynasty), *Tian Xia Jun Guo Li Bing Shu* (*On the Advantages and Disadvantages of All the Provinces and Counties in China*), Vol. 10.

detained; ... otherwise, 'Yue Su' (overstepping indictment) is allowed, and the offenders shall be sentenced according to the value of the booty."[299]

In addition, the methods for the disposal of the property of foreign traders who died in China were also provided. For example, "if the dead businessman has parents, legal wife and sons, or full brothers, unmarried sisters, unmarried daughters, nephew or followers, they are free to receive and deposit the property." If his parents, wife, and children were not with him, "a tombstone shall be installed with detailed records" in order to "look for his relatives in his native place." On the condition that "his relatives cannot be found," according to *Hu Jue Fa* (*Law of Heirless Household*), "all his belongings shall be confiscated, and the information of the dead should be recorded in detail."[300] In dealing with foreign-related disputes, "Hua Wai Ren Xiang Fan Tiao" (The Provision of Foreigners Offending Each Other) in *Tang Lv* (*Tang Code*) was followed in *Song Xing Tong* (*The Penal Code of Song Dynasty*), according to which "for foreigners, if they offend their fellow countryman, the punishment will be enforced in accord with their own law; if they offend people of other nationalities, they shall be punished according to this law."[301] This showed that for foreign-related disputes, the principle of regionalism and the principle of nationality were applied in combination. When Wang Dayou was the magistrate of Quanzhou, he expressed his disagreement at the story that "when foreign businessmen have disputes with the native people, as long as no mayhem is committed, ox can be used as the compensation." He said, "How can it happen that we apply foreign laws to deal with disputes in China. Since we are in China, we should apply Chinese laws."[302] When Wang Huanzhi was the magistrate of Guangzhou, "a foreign trade caravan killed a slave. So the violator was punished by 'Chi' (flogging with light sticks) by 'Shi Bo Shi' (the official in charge of the management of foreign trade) according to the previous cases. It was forbidden for him to be exempted from punishment, which was in accordance with the law."[303]

Forbidding officials to engage in overseas trade without permission, punishment of officials in charge of foreign trade for their delinquency: according to the law of the Song Dynasty, businessmen who wanted to trade overseas needed to apply for a series of formalities, such as business approval and license, to show state monopoly on overseas trade. In order to prevent unfair competition, influential officials were forbidden to engage in overseas trade privately, not to mention the officials in charge

---

[299]"Zhi Guan" (State Officials) in *Song Hui Yao Ji Gao* (*Collected Essays of the Historical Records of Song Dynasty*) (Book 34), Vol. 44.

[300]"Si Shang Qian Wu Men" (The Section about the Money and Goods for the Dead and Injured) in "Hu Hun Lv" (Statutes on Marriage, Tax and Household Registration) in *Song Xing Tong* (*The Penal Code of Song Dynasty*), Vol. 12.

[301]"Hua Wai Ren Xiang Fan Tiao" (The Provision of Foreigners Offending Each Other) in "Ming Li Lv" (*Statutes and Terms*) in *Song Xing Tong* (*The Penal Code of Song Dynasty*), Vol. 6.

[302]"Wang Da You Zhuan" (The Biography of Wang Dayou) in *Song Shi* (*The History of Song Dynasty*).

[303]"Wang Huan Zhi Zhuan" (The Biography of Wang Huanzhi) in *Song Shi* (*The History of Song Dynasty*).

8.5 The Economic and Financial Law Made with the Spirit of Reform

of overseas trade forcibly plundering the shipped goods by abusing their power. All "those who have traded with foreign businessmen privately shall be punished if the volume of trade reach to one hundred *qian* of money. If the trade value is over 15 *guan* of money, those involved would be exiled to islands with the their faces tattooed."[304] If officials in "Shi Bo Si" (the office in charge of the management of foreign trade) and local "Zhi Zhou" (subprefectural magistrates) and "Tong Pan" (official in charge of agriculture under prefecture) had embezzled the shipped goods in the name of "He Mai" (bought on a large scale various things), they would be punished by "Liu" (exile). Moreover, it was especially forbidden for "Shi Bo Si" (the office in charge of the management of foreign trade), "Hai Guan Jian Du" (Superintendent of Customs), "Zhi Fu" (magistrate of a prefecture), "Du Fu" (the viceroys and procurators), and "Hai Fang Xun Bu Si" (superintendent of police on coast defense) to collude with profiteering merchants; to commit illegalities for personal gains; to purchase, steal, and transport contraband, drugs, crude opium, etc. illegally; or "to send people overseas to trade on precious things owned by individuals without permission" or else the offender would "be severely punished."[305] In the 6th year of Zhenghe (116 A.D.), when traders in "Da Shi Guo" (Arab Empire) offered objects as tribute, Cai Mengxiu, who was in charge of the trade affairs of Guangdong, detained the goods and forcibly took aromatic drugs away without payment. The foreign traders appealed to the local government, so Emperor Huizong ordered the case to be handled by "Ti Xing Si" (judicial office); consequently, he was sentenced to two years of imprisonment for the crime of stealing.[306]

In conclusion, in Song the Dynasty, overseas trade was encouraged and protected, which had played a positive role in stimulating the development of the social economy. For instance, in the 12th year of Jiading (1219 A.D.), it was ordered to prohibit the exchange of silver, copper, and iron with foreign countries, but it was allowed to exchange spun silk, silk cloth, etc. with foreign countries, which had greatly promoted silk production. The law that was made to attract foreign businessmen and to expand and regulate Sino-foreign trade is a spectacular achievement in Chinese ancient legal history.

---

[304]"Shi Huo Zhi" (The Record of National Finance and Economy) in *Song Shi* (*The History of Song Dynasty*) (Book 8), Vol. 2.
[305]"Zhi Guan" (State Officials) in *Song Hui Yao Ji Gao* (*Collected Essays of the Historical Records of Song Dynasty*) (Book 3), Vol. 44.
[306]"Da Shi Guo Zhuan" [Historical Events of Da Shi Guo (Arab Empire)] in *Song Shi* (*The History of Song Dynasty*).

8.5.2 The Financial Legislation

8.5.2.1 Qian Fa (The Regulation on Metallic Money)

No doubt, the development of the commodity economy inevitably led to the development of monetary relationship. In the North Song Dynasty, the currency was mainly made of copper and iron. Kaifeng Fu (Kaifeng prefecture) and the other twelve regions exclusively used copper cash, Shanxi and Hedong used both copper cash and iron cash, and the Chuanshu region (present-day Sichuan province) exclusively used iron cash. It was forbidden for copper to outflow to the regions of "Fan Jie" (a region inhabited by the aborigines of Taiwan) or to the regions south of Yangtze River and beyond the Great Wall without permission (or "Lan Chu" (to cross the border without authorization)); otherwise, the offenders would be punished. If the officials of frontier regions had neglected their supervisory duty, if it was less than five *guan* of money, they would be punished; if it was over five *guan* of money, they would be punished by death penalty. In the years of Shaoxing during the reign of Emperor Gaozong in the South Song Dynasty, the decree for the "crime of taking copper cash out of boundaries" was issued, and it was provided that those who traded with foreign businessmen with copper cash would be sentenced to two years of imprisonment and exiled to places thousands of miles away. Meanwhile, the circulation of coins that were not legally standardized, namely the so-called low-purity underweight coins, was strictly prohibited. As to nongovernmental coinage, the initiator and the ringleader should be punished by "Jiao" (hanging); "Lin Bao" (neighbor) should be sentenced to one year of imprisonment; "Li Zheng" (head of "Li": the basic resident organization in ancient China), "Fang Zheng" (chief official of neighborhood), and "Cun Zheng" (chief official in village) would be punished by "Zhang" (flogging with heavy sticks) for sixty strokes.

With the development of the merchandise-money economy, the earliest paper currency in the world, i.e., "Jiao Zi, the credit money acting as a means of payment," was created. "Jiao Zi," as a currency, originated from Sichuan. Because iron money was heavy, was of little value, and was inconvenient to carry, it could not meet the needs of commercial activities; some wealthy traders raised funds to issue paper currency, called "Jiao Zi", which could be exchanged at anytime and which could circulate at a fixed period. Moreover, every three years, a new edition of currency was issued to replace the old ones. In the 1st year of Tiansheng during the reign of Emperor Renzing (1023 A.D.), in view of the fact that the nongovernmental "Jiao Zi" (paper currency) often caused disputes over credit issues, the government-run "Jiao Zi Wu" (the institution in charge of the circulation of banknotes in the Song Dynasty) was formally set up at Yizhou to prevent the private manufacturing of paper money and to establish the legal status of paper currency. As to the circulation of "Jiao Zi" (paper currency), fixed time limit, legalized issuing quota, face value, circulation domain, and the exchange ratio to copper cash were established. Moreover, a certain amount of reserve fund was needed, and those who forged "Jiao Zi" (paper currency) should be punished according to law. During the years of Xi'ning, because of the increase of monetary circulation, "Jiao Zi" (paper currency) devalued 75%. In the time of Emperor Huizong, he attempted to issue more paper money to solve the financial difficulties, which thus damaged the credibility of "Jiao Zi" (paper currency).

In the Southern Song Dynasty, the mining industry gradually declined, while foreign trade had led to the outflow of copper cash; consequently, paper money replaced copper cash and became the main means of payment. There were two kinds of paper money in the Southern Song Dynasty: "Chuan Xia Jiao Zi" (paper money used in the areas of Sichuan and the Three Gorges) and "Hui Zi," which circulated in certain areas. In order to maintain the credit of paper money and to meet the needs of the rapid development of commodity exchanges, it was stipulated that "as for the mortgage of land and houses, horses and cattle, and vessels and vehicles, etc. among the civilians, 'Hui Zi' should be used."[307] In the meantime, "the price of paper money is fixed to control the local despots."[308] If one had used the forged "Hui Zi," "he will be put to death."[309]

The issuing of paper money in the Southern and Northern Song dynasties not only met the needs of the development of a commodity monetary relationship but also made up for the fiscal deficit. However, when the reign of Emperor Lizong came, "Liao Zhi Ju" (Bureau of Paper Money Printing) was set up to print more paper money, which thus led to serious inflation, as was described in the saying that "the people had just looked upon it as dirt." This finally led to the collapse of the social economy.[310]

Additionally, there were also bills of exchange called "Zheng Qian" or "Bian Qian" and checks called "Tie Zi" and "Yan Chao," which are like the securities used today.

8.5.2.2 Financial Law

Increase in financial requirement and the dependence of the country on revenue had made the fiscal legislation far exceed that of the previous dynasties.

In early Song Dynasty, the financial crisis was not yet so serious; "...till the reign of Emperor Zhenzong, heaven worshipping ceremonies are often held to pray for good events at home; while overseas, there are many issues like keeping good relationships and maintaining border peace. So, there are more and more discussions

---

[307]"Shi Huo Zhi" (The Record of National Finance and Economy) in *Song Shi* (*The History of Song Dynasty*) (Book 3), Vol. 2.
[308]"Shi Huo Zhi" (The Record of National Finance and Economy) in *Song Shi* (*The History of Song Dynasty*) (Book 4), Vol. 2.
[309]"Xiao Zong Ben Ji" (The Biography of Emperor Xiaozong) in *Song Shi* (*The History of Song Dynasty*), Vol. 3.
[310]Li Zengbo (Song Dynasty), "Jiu Shu Chu Mi Zou" (A Secret Memorial about Saving the Silk Processing Industry in Sichuan Area) in *Ke Zhai Xu Gao* (*Sequel of Essays Written in Kezhai*) (Book 2), Vol. 3.

about the national finance and economy of the state."[311] After years of peaceful development, financial deficit occurred frequently during the reign of Emperor Renzong. In the time of Emperor Shenzong, financial deficit had become an urgent problem. Therefore, Emperor Shenzong gave priority to financial management in his political reform. Wang Anshi, the initiator of the reform, said "What can unite all people together is money; what can manage the money is law; what can protect the law is government officials. So if the officials are not competent, it is impossible to protect the law; if the law is not perfect, it is impossible to manage the wealth."[312] The financial reform launched by Wang Anshi had brought about the increase of the national revenue, so financial balance improved. However, when Emperor Ranzong gave up the new reform, the country was again trapped in financial difficulties. According to "Shi Huo Zhi" (The Record of National Finance and Economy) in *Song Shi* (*The History of Song Dynasty*), "since the years of Chongning, although there are many population, national treasury is becoming deficient." In the time of the Southern Song Dynasty, "the national treasury has become empty, while the expenditure is kept increasing; the sources have been exhausted, while the wasting never ends."[313] So in that period, the national finance was on the verge of collapsing.

The national revenue was mainly used to pay salaries, military expenditure, sacrificial expenses, and the cost for the maintenance of social order and peace; as was recorded in "Guo Yong Kao" (The Investigation of State Revenue and Expenditure) in *Wen Xian Tong Kao* (*A General Textual Research of the Documents*), "maybe the deficit of national finance is caused by military expenditure, sacrificial expense, salary for the redundant officials and awards granted by the emperor at the sacrificial ceremonies." Long before the reform of Yuan Feng, "San Si Shi" (Inspectors of the Three Departments) was set up by the imperial court to manage state finance, while "Zhuan Yun Shi" (official in charge of transportation) was set up to be in charge of the local finance; at the same time, "San Si Shi" (Inspectors of the Three Departments) was set up to be in charge of national affairs, while "Zhuan Yun Shi" (official in charge of transportation) was set up in charge of foreign affairs. Through this system, financial management was guaranteed from the local to the central level. After the reform of Yuan Feng, "San Si" (The Three Departments) was replaced by "Hu Bu" (The Department of Revenue), with its original power held by the emperor, "Zai Xiang" (the prime minister), and "Hu Bu" (The Department of Revenue) respectively. In the Southern Song Dynasty, in order to get over the financial crisis, the centralized system of administration was strengthened to encourage the local government to increase its income. The imperial government controlled the local financial expenditure through annual, quarterly, and monthly economic supervision

---

[311]"Shi Huo Zhi" (The Record of National Finance and Economy) in *Song Shi* (*The History of Song Dynasty*) (Book 1), Vol. 1.

[312]Wang Anshi (Song Dynasty), "Du Zhi Fu Shi Ting Bi Ti Ming Ji" (Inscribing the Name on the Parlor Wall by the Vice Minister of the Department of Finance) in *Lin Chuan Xian Sheng Wen Ji* (*Collected Works of Wang Anshi*), Vol. 82.

[313]"Li Cai" (Financial Management) in *Li Dai Ming Chen* Zou Yi (*Memorials Submitted to the Emperor by the Famous Officials in Different Dynasties*), Vol. 273.

8.5 The Economic and Financial Law Made with the Spirit of Reform   763

in order to prevent the local government from illegally misappropriating the funds. But although consequently financial power was taken back by the central government, the local government of "Zhou" (subprefecture) and "Jun" (shire) became so poorer and weaker that it was difficult to be dealt with.

It was difficult to meet the needs of strengthening financial management by the enforcement of few financial laws and regulations in *Song Xing Tong* (*The Penal Code of Song Dynasty*). Therefore, administrative laws and regulations were issued by the government in the form of "Chi Ling" (imperial decree) to control financial expenditure, so that even sacrificial expenses were strictly controlled. According to "Shi Huo Zhi" (The Record of National Finance and Economy) in *Song Shi* (*The History of Song Dynasty*), "regulations were also made for the budget of annual spending as well as the budget for the sacrificial expenses." During the reign of Emperor Shenzong, in order to reinforce the management of "Shang Ji" (local officials regularly write the budget revenue and the increase of registration, land, and treasury on a wooden board and report to higher authorities), even the account books were institutionalized, so the violators were punished.

The main financial legislation in the Song Dynasty is as follows:

8.5.2.2.1 (1) Tax Law: The Tax Law of the Song Dynasty Mainly Consisted of Land and Commercial Tax

With respect to land tax, "Liang Shui Fa" (two-tax law) of the Tang Dynasty was followed, and it was called "the regular tax." It was stipulated that "in view of the difference of transportation and the time span of the growth of the crops, the deadline for paying tax can be prolonged."[314] Although the rate of regular tax was fixed, the additional tax that was collected in various names was often several times more than the regular tax. Tax collectors were responsible for auditing the tax, as well as supervising and urging people to pay off the land tax before the deadline. According to the imperial edict issued in the 4th year of Jianlong (963 A.D.), "when it is time to pay tax, people should be informed to pay tax at the designated warehouse. If it is not audited before the first deadline, or if the taxpayer still cannot pay off the tax before the deadline, auditing should be made by the householder, the other family members or the county magistrate and his assistant."[315] As auditing was a necessary procedure before informing and urging people to pay tax, the tasks of informing and urging must be taken before the deadline, so "officials should be sent by 'Zhou' (subprefecture) which is in charge of tax payment to 'Xian' (county) to notify the taxpayers. If the officials have been sent by 'Xian' (county) to collect tax without

---

[314]"Tian Fu" (Land Tax) (Part 4) in *Wen Xian Tong Kao* (*A General Textual Research of the Documents*), Vol. 4.

[315]"Shi Huo" (National Finance and Economy) in *Song Hui Yao Ji Gao* (*Collected Essays of the Historical Records of Song Dynasty*) (Book 1), Vol. 47.

auditing or without conducting auditing before the deadline, they shall be punished by 'Zhang' (flogging with heavy sticks) for one hundred strokes."[316]

In order to insure the full payment of spring and autumn tax, in *Song Xing Tong* (*The Penal Code of Song Dynasty*), a series of penalties was stipulated for "those who fail to pay tax beyond the time limit." In the Southern Song Dynasty, with the worsening of the financial situation, legislation on the punishment of tax delinquency was more detailed and comprehensive: "Those who default on tax shall be punished by 'Chi' (flogging with light sticks) for forty strokes; those who default every year or who refuse to pay tax with violent resistance shall all be punished by 'Zhang' (flogging with heavy sticks) for sixty strokes; . . . those from the families of government officials shall be punished by 'Zhang' (flogging with heavy sticks) for one hundred strokes".[317] "If a taxpayer flees to some other place, or does not return when the tax is due, his household items shall be sold or confiscated by the government."[318] Moreover, the local county officials, copyists, householders, assistants of county magistrates, and chief magistrates of "Zhou" (subprefecture) would be punished differently according to the amount of delinquency. To avoid the evading of tax, a responsibility system of joint guarantee was also established, and informers were rewarded.

Apart from the importance of land tax, the importance of commercial tax to national expenditure was also gradually known by the people. In *Meng Xi Bi Tan* (*Dream Pool Essays*), it was recorded that "at present, the national expenditure has not been reduced, so there should be no evasion of tax. Since it cannot be collected from mountains, rivers as well as merchants, it must be collected from peasants. However, since it is already a heavy burden to peasants, why should it not be collected from merchants?"[319] So early in the Song Dynasty, "Shui Chang" (a designated site for tax collection) and "Shui Wu" (taxation affairs) were set up in "Zhou" (subprefecture) and "Xian" (county) to collect commercial tax with the authorization of "Hu Bu" (The Department of Revenue). If "Shui Wu (taxation affairs) was set up by the tax collectors without being applied or approved by "Shang Shu" (the minister) in "Hu Bu" (The Department of Revenue) or "even though they are permitted, they do not collect tax as is ordered to, the tax collectors and the applicants should be punished by 'Zhang' (flogging with heavy sticks) for one

---

[316]"Ju Cui Zu Shui" (Urging People to Pay Tax), quoted from "Hu Hun Chi" (Imperial Instructions on Household and Marriage) in "Fu Yi Men" (The Category of Tax and Corvée) in *Qing Yuan Tiao Fa Shi Lei* (*The Legal Provisions and Cases Made in the Year of Qingyuan*), Vol. 47.

[317]"Wei Qian Zu Shui" (Defaulting on Tax) in "Hu Hun Chi" (Imperial Instructions on Household and Marriage) in "Fu Yi Men" (The Category of Tax and Corvée) in *Qing Yuan Tiao Fa Shi Lei* (*The Legal Provisions and Cases Made in the Year of Qingyuan*), Vol. 47.

[318]"Ge Mian Zu Shui" (Tax Exemption) in "Hu Hun Chi" (Imperial Instructions on Household and Marriage) in "Fu Yi Men" (The Category of Tax and Corvée) in *Qing Yuan Tiao Fa Shi Lei* (*The Legal Provisions and Cases Made in the Year of Qingyuan*), Vol. 47.

[319]Shen Kuo (Song Dynasty), "Guan Zheng" (Civil Affairs) (Part 2) in "Qing Li Zhong Lu" (The Year of Qingli) in *Meng Xi Bi Tan* (*Dream Pool Essays*), Vol. 12.

hundred strokes."[320] But "Shui Chang" (a designated site for tax collection) and "Shui Wu" (taxation affairs) "were built almost everywhere," even "at remote villages," despite the repeated prohibition. In some places, "posts were illegally established to collect tax openly."[321]

To strengthen the control of commercial tax, local tax supervisors were dispatched by the imperial court. In the 3rd year of Yongxi (986 A.D.), an order was issued, which provided that "the supervisor shall be the envoy of the imperial court, and the post will be held by the government officials in the capital by turns at the regular interval of three years."[322] Thereafter, it became a rule for tax supervisors to be dispatched by "Li Bu" (The Department of Personnel) to be in charge of affairs such as examining goods, collecting tax, and so on.

During the reign of Emperor Taizu, *Shang Shui Ze Li* (*The Regulations of Commercial Tax*) was once issued to adjust the commercial tax, as was described in the record that "at the founding of the country, *Shang Shui Ze Li* (*The Regulations of Commercial Tax*) was issued for the first time, which was followed then by the later dynasties."[323] "All taxable things in 'Zhou' (subprefecture) and 'Xian' (county) should be recorded according to the rule with the names of taxable things recorded and posted outside the door of the office."[324] It was thus clear that at the initial stage, in *Shang Shui Ze Li* (*The Regulations of Commercial Tax*), only the names of taxable things and the tax rate of 20% of "Zhu Shui" (tax levied according to the amount of goods) and 30% of "Guo Shui" (a kind of commercial tax paid when traders transport goods) were roughly listed without mentioning the amount of tax for each kind of goods. On the 17th of September of the 5th year of Chongning (1106 A.D.), an imperial edict was issued to "Hu Bu" (The Department of Revenue):

> From today on, the dispatched officials shall carefully conduct a national survey of the amount of tax and the names of taxable goods in the past five years, make detailed rules by referring to the items of the taxation and the amount of tax, then released them to each "Lu" (ancient administrative region) to be carried out. So it should be amended every ten years and obeyed forever.[325]

Since then, the contents of *Shang Shui Ze Li* (*The Regulations of Commercial Tax*) were expanded; it not only included some newly revised tax items but also

---

[320]"Shang Shui" (Commercial Tax) in "Jiu Ku Chi" (Imperial Instructions on Stables) in "Ku Wu Men" (The Category of Warehouse Affairs) in *Qing Yuan Tiao Fa Shi Lei* (*The Legal Provisions and Cases Made in the Year of Qingyuan*), Vol. 36.

[321]"Shi Huo" (National Finance and Economy) in *Song Hui Yao Ji Gao* (*Collected Essays of the Historical Records of Song Dynasty*) (Book 24), Vol. 18.

[322]"Zheng Que Kao" (An Examination of National Commodity Tax and Government Monopoly) (Part 1) in *Wen Xian Tong Kao* (*A General Textual Research of the Documents*), Vol. 14.

[323]"Zheng Que Kao" (An Examination of National Commodity Tax and Government Monopoly) (Part 1) in *Wen Xian Tong Kao* (*A General Textual Research of the Documents*), Vol. 14.

[324]"Shi Huo" (National Finance and Economy) in *Song Hui Yao Ji Gao* (*Collected Essays of the Historical Records of Song Dynasty*) (Book 43), Vol. 17.

[325]"Shi Huo" (National Finance and Economy) in *Song Hui Yao Ji Gao* (*Collected Essays of the Historical Records of Song Dynasty*) (Book 28), Vol. 17.

specified the rate of various goods and the time limit for its revision. According to the stipulation, legal revision should be conducted every ten years. In the Southern Song Dynasty, price fluctuation had affected the stability of tax, so *Shang Shui Ze Li* (*The Regulations of Commercial Tax*) was revised every half a year so that the tax could be adjusted according to the price of commodities.

As "Zhu Shui" (tax levied according to the amount of goods) was levied on salt merchants while "Guo Shui (a kind of commercial tax paid when traders transport goods) was levied on other businessmen," with the former paying 10% for every 1000 *qian* and the latter 20% for every 1000 *qian*, commercial tax had become an essential source of income for national finance. So in order to guarantee commercial tax, those who evade tax would be punished. According to *Qing Yuan Tiao Fa Shi Lei* (*The Legal Provisions and Cases Made in the Year of Qingyuan*), "if tax is evaded for the things taxable, or if there are fraud and deception in tax payment, the taxpayers will be punished for the crime of false declaration; if the person in charge has been transferred to other units, it is forbidden for him to be examined again. So even if there are mistakes, it should not be regarded as false declaration."[326] Generally, tax evaders would be punished by "Chi" (flogging with light sticks) for forty strokes. However, if the tax reached to ten *guan* of money, he would be punished by "Zhang" (flogging with heavy sticks) for eighty strokes. Moreover, he had to pay the overdue tax with one third of the taxable goods confiscated by the government.

There were also some goods included in monopolized commodities in the Song Dynasty that were managed and sold by businessmen under the direct control of the government, so there were also problems of tax collection on the monopolized goods. For example, an imperial edict was once issued by Emperor Zhenzong to "San Si" (the three departments), and it was ordered that "tea, salt and alcohol tax should be collected to pay annual national expenditure, but land tax should not be increased so as to reduce the burden of the people."[327] Some tea peasants often used low-quality tea to make up for the quota that they could not fulfill, so special legislation was made by the government to prevent such illegal acts.

8.5.2.2.2 (2) Shang Gong Qian Wu Fa (Law on Paying Tribute of Money and Goods to the Central Government)

The law originated from "Shang Gong," the system of paying tribute of money and goods to the imperial court directly, which was created after "An Shi Zhi Luan" (the Rebellion of An Lushan and Shi Siming) in the Tang Dynasty. In the Song Dynasty,

---

[326]"Shang Shui" (Commercial Tax) in "Chang Wu Ling" (Orders Issued by Chang Wu Agency) in "Ku Wu Men" (The Category of Warehouse Affairs) in *Qing Yuan Tiao Fa Shi Lei* (*The Legal Provisions and Cases Made in the Year of Qingyuan*), Vol. 36.

[327]"Shi Huo Zhi" (The Record of National Finance and Economy) in *Song Shi* (*The History of Song Dynasty*) (Book 1), Vol. 2.

8.5 The Economic and Financial Law Made with the Spirit of Reform

a series of legal provisions that could strengthen the centralization of authority were formulated. For example, an order was issued in the 3rd year of Jianlong (962 A.D.), which declared that "from now on, the annual tax, the profits made from the monopolized goods and the money which should be handed over to the central government by the government of 'Zhou' (subprefecture) shall all be transported to the capital by official vessels and vehicles."[328] In the 3rd year of Qiande (965 A.D.), another order was issued, and it was stipulated that "all the gold and silk, other than the expenditures of each 'Zhou' (subprefecture), shall be presented to the imperial court with no private possession."[329] In the 3rd year of Xi'ning (1070 A.D.), a new "Ge" (injunction) was made about delivering money and goods to the imperial court, with the legal time and specific amount especially stipulated. According to *Qing Yuan Tiao Fa Shi Lei* (*The Legal Provisions and Cases Made in the Year of Qingyuan*), in the Southern Song Dynasty, more detailed laws were made about paying tribute, with the time limit, amount, and quality comprehensively stipulated. As to the time of delivering goods and money, during the years of Yuanfeng, it was decided that the tribute should be paid by "Zhou" (subprefecture) and "Xian" (county) at the end of the year, which was changed to twice a year during the reign of Chongning and twice or three times a year in the Southern Song Dynasty. If the deadline was exceeded, the officials in charge would be punished by "Zhang" (flogging with heavy sticks) for eighty to one hundred strokes.

In the new "Ge" (injunction) issued in the years of Xi'ning, the amount of money and goods were also specified. So except the spring and autumn tax, more than ten kinds of tax were combined together to be included in the tribute to be paid to the imperial court, which was called "Wu E Shang Gong." The amount of "Wu E Shang Gong" was increased greatly, so those who could not meet the quota would be punished. In the 1st year of Xuanhe, twenty two "Cao Chen" (official in charge of water transport of grain to the capital) was demoted because of their failure to deliver sufficient amount of money and goods. After the capital was moved to the south, "the expenditures of imperial court and the army all depended on the tribute goods and money in addition to the tea and salt tax," so "the delaying of paying tribute is not allowed."[330] Moreover, there were also strict requirements for the quality of the tribute goods and money with even every *wen* of money carefully counted. If the "purity or weight of the tribute money is not up to the standard, or if the officials have embezzled the money, the relevant officials shall compensate one hundred *wen* of money for each *wen* which is lost or which is unqualified." As to the tribute grain, it was provided that "in each 'Zhou' (subprefecture), 'Tong Pan' (official in charge of agriculture under prefecture) shall be entrusted to collect what is the best quality

---

[328]"Shi Huo Zhi" (The Record of National Finance and Economy) in *Song Shi* (*The History of Song Dynasty*) (Book 3), Vol. 1.

[329]"Guo Yong Kao" (The Investigation of State Revenue and Expenditure) (Part 1) in *Wen Xian Tong Kao* (*A General Textual Research of the Documents*), Vol. 23.

[330]Li Xinchuan (Song Dynasty), *Jian Yan Yi Lai Xi Nian Yao Lu* (*An Annual Record of the Most Important Events since the Reign of Jianyan*), Vol. 93, in September of the 5th year of Shaoxing.

beyond boundaries and to arrange the concrete affairs of shipment."[331] In addition, the tribute goods should not be embezzled or retained for personal use or else "the violator should be punished according to specific laws."[332]

8.5.2.2.3 (3) Laws on Account Management

In order to strengthen financial management, more than forty kinds of standard account formats were affirmed by the government. Moreover, the relevant laws on account, such as the compilation, recording, submission, and reviewing of account, were also formulated. So accordingly, the violators would be punished by "Zhang" (flogging with heavy sticks). After the government was moved to the south, many orders were issued to "Jian Si" (official in charge of supervising the counties and towns) of each "Lu" (ancient administrative region), and it was stated that "the population, land, money and goods in 'Zhou' (subprefecture) and 'Xian' (county) shall be carefully recorded by the inspection officials of each department according to law."[333] And it was further stated that "as to the tax accounts of each 'Zhou' (subprefecture) and 'Xian' (county), samples should be supplied by 'Zhuan Yun Si' (Office of Transportation) so that careful records can be made. If the handwriting is illegible and scrawled, the writer shall be punished by 'Zhang' (flogging with heavy sticks) for one hundred strokes, and be be removed from his office and never be appointed again. Moreover, his recording must be corrected within one day. If the official have dereliction of duty, he shall be punished by 'Zhang' (flogging with heavy sticks) for eighty strokes; anyone who makes false reporting shall also be punished according to this law."[334]

The purpose of unifying the account was to make it more convenient to conduct the checking of "Shang Ji" (local officials regularly write the budget revenue and the increase of registration, land, and treasury on a wooden board and report to higher authorities). The system of annual report of "Shang Ji," which had been implemented since the Qin and Han dynasties, was changed to monthly, quarterly, and yearly report. In *Qing Yuan Tiao Fa Shi Lei* (*The Legal Provisions and Cases Made in the Year of Qingyuan*), the range of application of every kind of account, the method of submission, and the time limit for submission were all stipulated in detail. For example, "the spring and autumn tax shall be collected from the 1st of January and from the 1st of April respectively, both of which should be completed within

---

[331]"Shang Gong" (Paying Tribute of Money and Goods to the Imperial Court), quoted from "Cang Ku Ling" (Decrees on Warehouses) in "Cai Yong Men" (The Category of Finance) in *Qing Yuan Tiao Fa Shi Lei* (*The Legal Provisions and Cases Made in the Year of Qingyuan*), Vol. 30.

[332]"Shi Huo" (National Finance and Economy) in *Song Hui Yao Ji Gao* (*Collected Essays of the Historical Records of Song Dynasty*) (Book 38), Vol. 35.

[333]"Shi Huo" (National Finance and Economy) in *Song Hui Yao Ji Gao* (*Collected Essays of the Historical Records of Song Dynasty*) (Book 15), Vol. 11.

[334]"Shi Huo" (National Finance and Economy) in *Song Hui Yao Ji Gao* (*Collected Essays of the Historical Records of Song Dynasty*) (Book 18), Vol. 11.

8.5 The Economic and Financial Law Made with the Spirit of Reform   769

forty five days by each 'Zhou' (subprefecture). Thereafter, the collection of the two kinds of tax shall be submitted to 'Zhuan Yun Si' (Office of Transportation) before the deadline"[335]; "the tribute goods and money should be sent to 'Mo Kan Si' (ancient office in charge of inspection) and 'Shen Ji Yuan' (ancient office in charge of auditing) in the middle of May of the next year, and the two administrative offices shall complete their inspection within five days respectively and then submit to 'Zhuan Yun Si' (Office of Transportation) for reviewing. Moreover, the tribute goods shall be submitted to 'Hu Bu Shang Shu' (the minister of the department of revenue) at the end of March"[336]; "'Chang Wu' (salt and iron monopoly management organizations) of the warehouses of each 'Zhou' (subprefecture) shall submit the account and hand over the tax collected in the past two months to 'Ti Dian Xing Yu Si' (judicial commission) for registration one month before the New Year. At the end of each year, the registered report shall be submitted to the account office of 'Shang Shu' (the minister) in 'Hu Bu Zhang Si' (the accounts department of the department of revenue)."[337] As to the reviewing of "Shang Ji" (local officials regularly write the budget revenue and the increase of registration, land, and treasury on a wooden board and report to higher authorities), before the reform of Yuan Feng, it was first handled by "San Si" (The Three Departments) and then was reported to the emperor, but after the reform, it was handled by "Zhuan Yun Si" (Office of Transportation) and "Hu Bu" (The Department of Revenue).

8.5.2.2.4 (4) Laws on Financial Supervision

As financial management was the primary task of the country, both financial administration law and financial supervision law were made. If the financial laws and regulations were violated by the officials and the civilians, administrative or criminal sanctions would be enforced.

In the early Song Dynasty, financial administration and auditing were combined with an internal auditing system, so they were in the charge of "Du Mo Kan Si" (ancient office in charge of internal auditing), which was affiliated to "San Si" (The Three Departments). However, there was a major disadvantage for this system. According to historical records, "the cases about the old accounts are in the charge of 'San Si' (The Three Departments), so from the middle of Zhizhong to early Xi'ning, the accounts that have not been checked within the four years have reached

---

[335]"Shui Zu Zhang" (Rent and Tax Account) in "Fu Yi Ling" (Decrees on Tax and Corvée) in "Fu Yi Men" (The Category of Tax and Corvée) in *Qing Yuan Tiao Fa Shi Lei* (*The Legal Provisions and Cases Made in the Year of Qingyuan*), Vol. 48.

[336]"Shang Gong" (Paying Tribute of Money and Goods to the Imperial Court) in "Cang Ku Ling" (Decrees on Warehouses) in "Cai Yong Men" (The Category of Finance) in *Qing Yuan Tiao Fa Shi Lei* (*The Legal Provisions and Cases Made in the Year of Qingyuan*), Vol. 30.

[337]"Chang Wu" (Administration of Monopoly) in "Cang Ku Ling" (Decrees on Warehouses) in "Ku Wu Men" (The Category of Warehouse Affairs) in *Qing Yuan Tiao Fa Shi Lei* (*The Legal Provisions and Cases Made in the Year of Qingyuan*), Vol. 30.

to over 120,000, which has led to the great losses of money, silk and army provisions."[338] After the reform during the years of Yuanfeng, financial administration and auditing were separated and an external auditing system was formed, so "Bi Bu" (ancient government office in charge of prison and penalty) was made solely in charge of central auditing supervision. Moreover, "Zhuan Yun Shi" (official in charge of transportation) was sent by the imperial court to local places "to exclusively manage the account auditing"[339]; "Tong Pan" (official in charge of agriculture, water conservancy, and litigation under subprefecture) was responsible for the supervision and inspection of institutions such as "Fu" (ancient administrative district between province and county), "Shi" (city), "Jun" (shire), "Jian" (ancient supervisory office); "Xian Ling" (county magistrate) was concurrently responsible for the financial auditing and supervision of "Xian" (county). In the Southern Song Dynasty, "Shen Ji Yuan" (The Court of Auditors) was set up in the main military bases to reinforce the auditing and supervision of army provisions.

As is seen from above, a multilevel financial supervision system was formed from local to central government in the Song Dynasty, which was not done in the previous dynasties and which had fully shown that finance was the lifeblood of the Song Dynasty.

To cope with the extensive establishment of financial supervision institutions, financial supervision law was also made by the government.

Firstly, the joint liability of supervisory officials was defined. If "Zhu Si" (director) in charge of supervision was found to have practiced fraud in tax collection, "on the basis of the amount of the losses, he would be punished for the crime of robbery. If 'Zhu Si' (director) is in the know, he shall be punished the same; if he does not know, he shall be punished four levels lighter than that for the violator."[340] "Those who have made mistakes in tax accounts shall be punished by 'Zhang' (flogging with heavy sticks) for eighty strokes and his assistant shall be punished two levels lighter."[341]

Secondly, the time limit for the submission of accounts for auditing was stipulated. According to *Qing Yuan Tiao Fa Shi Lei* (*The Legal Provisions and Cases Made in the Year of Qingyuan*), "the spring tax shall be collected from the 1st of January; the autumn tax, the 1st of April and both should be completed within forty five days. Thereafter, the collection of the two kinds of tax shall be submitted to

---

[338]"Zhi Guan Zhi" (The Record of State Officials) in *Song Shi* (*The History of Song Dynasty*) (Book 3).

[339]"Shi Huo" (National Finance and Economy) in *Song Hui Yao Ji Gao* (*Collected Essays of the Historical Records of Song Dynasty*), Vol. 11.

[340]"Shu Ke Shui Dou Liu Shi Wu Men" (Tax Evasion) in "Jiu Ku Lv" (Statutes on Stables) in *Song Xing Tong* (*The Penal Code of Song Dynasty*), Vol. 15.

[341]"Bu Zhang Qi Bi" (Fraud in Accounting) in "Hu Hun Chi" (Imperial Instructions on Household and Marriage) in "Fu Yi Men" (The Category of Tax and Corvée) in *Qing Yuan Tiao Fa Shi Lei* (*The Legal Provisions and Cases Made in the Year of Qingyuan*), Vol. 48.

'Zhuan Yun Si' (Office of Transportation) before the deadline."[342] "If the accounts were delayed and were not sent to 'Mo Kan Si' (ancient office in charge of inspection) for auditing in time with no reason, for one day delayed, the offender shall be punished by 'Zhang' (flogging with heavy sticks) for sixty stokes; for three days, the punishment shall be one level severer."[343]

Finally, the legal norms for budget and final accounts were established. It was recorded in "Shi Huo Zhi" (The Records of National Finance and Economy) in *Song Shi* (*The History of Song Dynasty*) that "the annual expenditure as well as the great sacrificial expenses were all regulated in the established law," so it can be seen that although there was already the practice of budget, there were no such names. The final account was also referred to as "Zhang Zhuang" (the state of account), which was made according to legal procedures based on the result of the implementation of the budget and which was the main content of "Shang Ji" (local officials regularly write the budget revenue and the increase of registration, land, and treasury on a wooden board and report to higher authorities). On the basis of budget and final accounts *Kuai Ji Lu* (*The Accounting Record*) was compiled in the Northern and Southern Song dynasties. Moreover, six volumes of *Jing De Kuai Ji Lu* (*The Jingde Accounting Record*) and thirty volumes of *Xiang Fu Kuai Ji Lu* (*The Xiangfu Accounting Record*) and other records could also be found in history books.

All in all, gradually the financial legislation in Song Dynasty was specialized, and it had become a relatively independent category in the legal system. The purpose of financial legislation was to accumulate as much wealth as possible by centralizing financial power in the central government, so it played a very important role in the Song Dynasty over a certain period, but it had failed to and actually it was impossible to eliminate the growing financial and political crisis. With the expansion of bureaucractic and military organization, and the export of currency to sue for peace abroad, the financial situation tended to become worse. After the years of Qingli during the reign of Emperor Renzong, it was impossible to make ends meet every year with a deficit of over three million *min*. In the 2nd year of Zhiping during the reign of Emperor Yingzong (1065 A.D.), the deficit had reached to 15.7 million *min*.[344] "So the annual revenue was only enough for one month of expenditure with two thirds spent by the army and the left ones wasted by the redundant officials."[345] Emperor Shenzong "had always worried about the deficit, so he even discussed its

---

[342]"Shui Zu Zhang" (Rent and Tax Account) in "Fu Yi Ling" (Decrees on Tax and Corvée) in "Fu Yi Men" (The Category of Tax and Corvée) in *Qing Yuan Tiao Fa Shi Lei* (*The Legal Provisions and Cases Made in the Year of Qingyuan*), Vol. 48.

[343]"Dian Mo Yin Xian" (Checking what was Concealed) in "Jiu Ku Chi" (Imperial Instructions on Stables) in "Cai Yong Men" (The Category of Finance) in *Qing Yuan Tiao Fa Shi Lei* (*The Legal Provisions and Cases Made in the Year of Qingyuan*), Vol. 32.

[344]"Guo Yong Kao" (The Investigation of State Revenue and Expenditure) in *Wen Xian Tong Kao* (*A General Textual Research of the Documents*), Vol. 24.

[345]"Shi Huo Zhi" (The Record of National Finance and Economy) in *Song Shi* (*The History of Song Dynasty*) (Part 1) (Book 2).

causes with his courtiers every day."[346] He once sighed with sadness and said that "it is the redundant troops that had exhausted the national revenue."[347] In order to increase fiscal revenue, the rulers of the Song Dynasty laid more importance on financial legislation. Emperor Gaozong once said that "since state finance is deficient, the measures must be taken to reduce expenditures."[348] That was why financial management had become the core of the political reform initiated by Wang Anshi. During the reign of Emperor Huizong, the currency law was frequently changed by the officials Cai Jing and Tong Guan to share the profits made by the salt and tea merchants in order to increase and supplement the state tax revenue. It was recorded in history books that during the years of Chongning and Zhenghe (1102 A.D.–1117 A.D.), "Xun Huan Fa" (circulation law) was made by Cai Jing, so "only two years after the new law was implemented, the revenue had reached to 40,000,000 guan."[349] Therefore, it was only because of the special significance of financial management that it was possible for "San Si" (The Three Departments) to occupy a prominent position in state organizations.

8.6 The Judicial System of "Ju Yan Fen Si" (The Separation of Interrogation and Conviction)

8.6.1 The Change of Judicial System

The judicial system of the early Song Dynasty was patterned after the system of the Tang Dynasty. But the function and power of "Fu An" (reviewing) of "Xing Bu" (The Department of Punishment) was strengthened, and it was used as one of the most important measures to concentrate judicial power to the central government. During the reign of Emperor Taizu, it was explicitly ordered that the major cases must be reported to "Xing Bu" (The Department of Punishment) for complete reviewing. "Da Li Si" (The Bureau of Judicial Review) was only in charge of "hearing the cases but was not in charge of making judgments."[350] In August of the 2nd year of Chunhua during the reign of Emperor Taizong, apart from "Da Li Si" (The Bureau of Judicial Review) and "Xing Bu" (The Department of Punishment), "Shen Xing Yuan" (The Case Review Court), which consisted of six officials,

---

[346]"Shi Huo Zhi" (The Record of National Finance and Economy) in *Song Shi* (*The History of Song Dynasty*) (Part 1) (Book 2).

[347]"Bing Zhi" (The Record of Army) in *Song Shi* (*The History of Song Dynasty*) (Book 10).

[348]*Jian Nian Yi Lai Xi Nian Yao Lu* (*An Annual Record of the Most Important Events since the Jianyan Reign*), Vol. 95, in November of the 5thyear of Shaoxing.

[349]"Shi Huo Zhi" (The Record of National Finance and Economy) in *Song Shi* (*The History of Song Dynasty*) (Part 4) (Book 2).

[350]"Zhi Guan Zhi" (The Record of State Officials) in *Song Shi* (*The History of Song Dynasty*) (Book 5).

8.6 The Judicial System of "Ju Yan Fen Si" (The Separation of Interrogation and...

including "Zhi Yuan" (ancient official in charge of military and political affairs) and "Xiang Yi Guan" (ancient official in charge of reviewing cases), was established inside the palace in order to strengthen the emperor's control over judicial power. All cases that were reviewed by "Xing Bu" (The Department of Punishment) should be reported to "Shen Xing Yuan" (The Case Review Court) for a detailed discussion and then submitted to the emperor for approval. So "Shen Xing Yuan" (The Case Review Court) was directly under the control of the emperor rather than "Zai Xiang" (the prime minister). During the reign of Emperor Zhenzong, it was newly ordered that the cases that were to be submitted to the emperor by "Shen Xing Yuan" (The Case Review Court) should first be sent to "Zhong Shu Sheng" (the supreme organization in charge of state affairs) for discussion and then be submitted to the emperor for approval. Furthermore, the major cases, namely, the cases of "Zhao Yu," which needed to be approved by the central government, should be heard by "Zhi Kan Yuan" (The Provisional Superior Court). The establishment of "Shen Xing Yuan" (The Case Review Court) restricted the power of "Da Li Si" (The Bureau of Judicial Review) and "Xing Bu" (The Department of Punishment), so no chief official was appointed in "Da Li Si" (The Bureau of Judicial Review) and the post was concurrently held by other officials. At the time when reform was carried out by Yuanfeng during the reign of Emperor Shenzong, due to the overlapping of government organs, "Shen Xing Yuan" (The Case Review Court) was abolished, and the original power of "Da Li Si" (The Bureau of Judicial Review) and "Xing Bu" (The Department of Punishment) were restored. Since then, one "Da Li Si Qing" (equivalent to president of the Supreme Court) and two "Shao Qing" (the vice president) were appointed as the head and deputy officials.

As for "Yu Shi Tai" (The Censorate), it had supervisory authority over the judiciary. Apart from its function of supervision, it was also in charge of hearing major cases. Its jurisdiction mainly included criminal cases involving "Ming Guan" (appointed official) or "Si Fa Guan" (judicial officials), as well as major and serious cases that were difficult for local officials to handle. All officials who were accused of misconduct or negligence should be investigated by "Yu Shi Tai" (The Censorate) first before they were reported to and tried by "Da Li Si" (The Bureau of Judicial Review). "Yu Shi Tai" (The Censorate) was also entitled to dispatch "Yu Shi" (censor) to participate in the hearing of major cases as an exercise of its power of judicial supervision.

If members of royal families violated the law in the capital, the cases should be heard by "Da Zong Zheng Si" (in charge of the conviction of members of royal families); if it is outside the capital, the cases should be heard by "Wai Zong Zheng Si" (in charge of the conviction of members of royal families outside the capital). Punishment above "Tu" (imprisonment) should be decided by the emperor himself.

There were also specific judicial organs in charge of military offenses, such as "Shu Mi Yuan" (Privy Council), "Dian Qian Si" (the Palace Command), "Shi Wei Ma Bu Jun Si" (Imperial Body Guards), "Jing Lue An Fu Si" (ancient office responsible for military affairs of a place), "Zong Guan Si" (Office of General Administration), "Du Jian" (Supervisor), and "Jian Ya" (officer in charge of military forces).

As for the local judicial organs, "Ti Dian Kai Feng Fu Jie Zhu Xian Zhen Gong Shi" (local magistrate of Kaifeng) was set up in the capital and the suburbs to take charge of the prisons in the counties and towns within the area, which was called "Ti Dian Jing Ji Xing Yu" in the Southern Song Dynasty. "Ti Dian Xing Yu Gong Shi" (judicial commissioner), which was called "Ti Xing" for short, was set up in each "Lu" (ancient administrative region), and the government office was called "Xian Si." "Ti Xing" was mainly in charge of reviewing and investigating the judgments made by affiliated towns and counties and the prison accounts that were reported every ten days. If there were any doubtful cases, "he will be asked to go at once to have a inspection."[351] "Ti Xing" often made inspection tours around each "Zhou" (subprefecture) and "Xian" (county), and "wherever he goes, he shall interrogate the prisoners and check official documents. If it was discovered that the criminal suspects were imprisoned for a long time without being sentenced, or the thieves had escaped without being caught, 'Ti Xing' should report what he learned to the central government and impose punishments upon the officials."[352] It is thus clear that "Ti Xing" was a government organization that was put in charge of supervising the judicial work of "Zhou" (subprefecture) and "Xian" (county) to strengthen judicial activities. So "Xun An Shi" (official assigned to supervise the local officials) in the later period was merely derived from "Ti Xing."

In "Zhou" (subprefecture), "Si Kou Yuan" (judiciary organ in charge of civil and criminal cases) (later changed to "Si Li Yuan") was set up, and the commanding official was called "Si Kou Can Jun" (head of "Si Kou Yuan") (later called "Si Li Can Jun"), who "takes charge of lawsuits and interrogation ... without holding other positions."[353] In order to strengthen its control over local judicial power and to supervise the activities of local judicial officials, it was ordered that in every "Zhou" (subprefecture), prison accounts should be reported in every ten days, and false information was not allowed to be provided.

"Tui Kan Yuan" (local adjudication organ), which was set up by "Jian Si" (official in charge of supervising the counties and towns), "Zhou" (subprefecture), and "Jun" (military) near the place where the cases occurred, was the local temporary judicial organ in charge of major and doubtful cases and cases of cassation in local places.

In the Song Dynasty, judicial officials were appointed by the imperial court, and the candidates were mainly Confucian intellectuals, so the situation where judicial affairs had always been controlled by local military officers such as "Ma Bu Yuan" (military court) and "Ya Xiao" (junior military official) since the period of "Wu Dai" (the Five Dynasties) was changed. Judicial officials had to pass the examinations

---

[351]"Xing Fa Zhi" (The Record of the Criminal Law) in *Song Shi* (*The History of Song Dynasty*) (Book 1).

[352]"Zhi Guan Zhi" (The Record of State Officials) in *Song Shi* (*The History of Song Dynasty*) (Book 7).

[353]"Zhi Guan Zhi" (The Record of State Officials) in *Song Shi* (*The History of Song Dynasty*) (Book 7).

about "Lv Yi" (interpretation of laws and decrees) and "An Li" (cases). So only those who had passed the examination could be appointed as officials, and the outstanding ones could even be recommended to "Da Li Si" (The Bureau of Judicial Review). As "Ming Fa Ke" (the subject of law) was set up in "Ke Ju" (the imperial examination) to encourage scholars to study law, the current officials were also required to take the examinations regularly. "When the officials such as 'Zhi Zhou' (subprefectural magistrates), 'Tong Pan' (official in charge of agriculture, water conservancy and litigation under prefecture and subprefecture), 'Mu Zhi' (the subordinates of local officials) and the officials in 'Zhou' (subprefecture) and 'Xian' (county) returned to the capital after the expiration of the term of office, they would be examined orally about legal knowledge. If they could not answer the questions, they would be punished according to the specific circumstances."[354] In Southern Song Dynasty, "even 'Jin Shi' (those who passed the imperial examination at the national level in ancient China) who is recommended to be an legal official must take the examination of law."[355] So in a short time, "people nationwide vie with each other to study laws and decrees,"[356] which not only set up the general mood of society for studying law but also fostered the development of jurisprudence.

8.6.2 Perfection of the Judicial Proceedings of Civil Procedure

With respect to the method of, restriction on, and procedure for prosecution, those of the Tang Dynasty were mainly followed in the Northern and Southern Song dynasties. As to the method of prosecution, first, private prosecution could be initiated by the victim himself; second, the prosecution could be initiated by the victim's relatives or other insiders of the feudal government; third, the criminal could voluntarily surrender himself. In early Song Dynasty, the age limit for the complainant was below eighty and above ten years old, but no age limit for the serious cases involving "Mou Fan" (plotting rebellion or plotting to endanger the country) was specified. In the 4th year of Qiande (966 A.D.), the upper age limit of the complainant was seventy years old. Moreover, it was forbidden for the seriously ill people or pregnant women to prosecute. In the Southern Song Dynasty, it was stipulated that the lawsuits filed by "married and widowed women who have no descendants in the name of 'Fu Nv' (adult women) are not to be accepted."[357] To avoid false

---

[354]"Xuan Ju" (Election) in *Song Hui Yao Ji Gao* (*Collected Essays of the Historical Records of Song Dynasty*) (Book 11), Vol. 13.
[355]"Xuan Ju Zhi" (The Record of Election) in *Song Shi* (*The History of Song Dynasty*) (Book 3).
[356]"Xuan Ju Kao" (An Examination of Election) (Part 11) in *Wen Xian Tong Kao* (*A General Textual Research of the Documents*), Vol. 38.
[357]Huang Zhen (Song Dynasty), "Ci Song Yue Shu" (Regulations on Litigation) in "Gong Yi" (Official Documents) in *Huang Shi Ri Chao* (*Essays by Huang Zhen*), Vol. 78.

accusation, if "irrelevant accusation is made, the complainant shall be punished by 'Jue Zhang' (beating the criminal's back, legs and buttocks with the heavy stick) and 'Jia Hao' (cangue: a large wooden collar worn by petty criminals as a punishment) for ten days."[358] If it was a serious case of homicide, it should be prosecuted by the relatives of the deceased.

The status of the complainant had an important effect on the priority for the acceptance of cases. In light of the social/occupational structure of the Song Dynasty, people's social status was divided into five classes, namely, "Shi" (scholars), "Nong" (peasant), "Gong" (artisan), "Shang" (businessmen), and "Za" (the miscellaneous). Therefore, the order for the acceptance of cases was, firstly, "Shi" (scholars), then "Nong" (peasant), "Gong" (artisan), "Shang" (businessmen), and, finally, "Za Ren" (necromancer, dawdler, servant, etc.).

The written form of complaint followed that of the Later Zhou Dynasty, and the complaint could be written by the complainant himself or by others. If the litigant was illiterate, he could also use a blank sheet as his complaint. With the increase of litigation activities, the requirement for the complaint became more and more strict, and the complaint should be written in a standard format at "Shu Pu" (book store), which was registered in the feudal government office. Moreover, it could be submitted only after it was "guaranteed" by another person, and it could be accepted by the government only after it was checked and considered qualified by "Kai Chai Si" (subordinate office of "San Si," in charge of emperor's decrees and memorial to the throne). The requirements for the complaint was explained in detail by Huang Zhen in *Ci Su Yue Shu* (*Regulations on Litigation*): "Those which are not written in 'Shu Pu' (book store) shall not be accepted; those without guarantees shall not be accepted; those with more than two hundred characters shall not be accepted, and those concerning two things shall not be accepted."[359]

Because of the commodity economy, in the Song Dynasty, it was not only allowed but also encouraged to protect individual rights by law. "Deng Wen Gu Yuan" (petitioning agency) and "Deng Wen Jian Yuan" (agency accepting the complaints of citizens) were established to accept the lawsuits filed. In October of the 4th year of Chunhua (993 A.D.), a person named Mu Hui, who lived near the capital city, complained that his servant had lost a piglet by "Wo Deng Wen Gu" (beat the drum and deliver the complaints, it is one of the important direct complaints in ancient China). So an edict was issued by Emperor Taizong to grant him 1000 *qian* of money for compensation. The emperor said to "Zai Xiang" (the prime minister): "It seems funny that such a petty thing still needs my decision. But if we deal with state affairs with this attitude, there will be no injustices among the

---

[358]"Xing Fa" (Criminal Law) in *Song Hui Yao Ji Gao* (*Collected Essays of the Historical Records of Song Dynasty*) (Book 12), Vol. 3.

[359]Huang Zhen (Song Dynasty), "Ci Song Yue Shu" (Regulations on Litigation) in "Gong Yi" (Official Documents) in *Huang Shi Ri Chao* (*Essays by Huang Zhen*), Vol. 78.

people."³⁶⁰ When the renowned, upright, and honest official Bao Zheng was the magistrate in Kaifeng Fu (Kaifeng prefecture), some reforms were carried out: in the past, litigants were not allowed to enter the court gate, so they had to hand in the complaints to the officials at the court gate, but now the front door was widely open for litigants to present their complaints.

What is worth mentioning is that the method that the officials used to impeach others is not only commonly used but also very effective. In the Song Dynasty, the supervisory function was taken seriously, so the central government encouraged "Tai Jian" (central surveillance agency) to impeach officials and to initiate administrative litigation. Therefore, envoys were regularly dispatched to inspect the impeaching work around the country. Meanwhile, a system of "Jian Si" (official in charge of supervising the counties and towns) was also established to supervise and impeach each other to prevent criminal activities. If the local officials concealed the civil criminals, they should be reported by the officials in the know to the government or else they would be punished. Several provisions were stipulated in "Xing Bu Ge Chi" (injunction and instruction of the department of punishment), according to which "if there are evil-doers (those who hurt or murder grandparents, parents, and other relatives) among the folks, the magistrate of 'Zhou' (subprefecture) and 'Xian' (county) shall be demoted according to the specific circumstances of the case; if the magistrate conceals the case, he would be convicted by 'Lu Shi Can Jun' (the local supervisor) and reported to the emperor."³⁶¹

During the Northern and Southern Song dynasties, the development of private land ownership and the expansion of the scope of civil right subjects had brought about a lot of civil disputes, which had caught the attention of the government, so a system of civil procedure and a judicatory system that were more explicit and substantial than those of the Tang Dynasty were established.

The complaint must be the direct interested party of the case, so according to law, those who were not the direct interested party were not allowed to file lawsuits. As to the lawsuits filed by a senior, the diseased or the disabled, and women, their relatives could act on behalf of them. For civil disputes among relatives, they could sue each other, so there were a lot of lawsuits involving an inferior family member suing a superior one for unfair allocation of inheritance among the existing case records of the Song Dynasty. This kind of litigation relation was uncommon in the Han, Qing, Ming, and Tang dynasties, which was not only the result of the development of private ownership but also that of the new ideology of "Yi" (justice) and "Li" (benefit).

As for civil procedure, "Xian" (county) was the first level of trial and "Zhou" (subprefecture) the second. "According to law, if the trial conducted in 'Xian'

---

[360] *Xu Zi Zhi Tong Jian Chang Bian* (*Sequel to the Full-length Book of History as a Mirror*), Vol. 34, on the day of Ding Chou in October of the 4th year of Chunhua.

[361] Sima Guang (Song Dynasty), "Min You Fan E Ni Qi Bu Ling Zhang Guan Zi He Zhuang" (A Memorial to the Emperor about Freeing Officials from Exposing their own Faults for the Felonies Committed by the Civilians) in *Wen Guo Wen Zheng Gong Wen Ji* (*The Collected Works of Sima Guang*), Vol. 28.

(county) is unfair, it can be tried again in 'Zhou' (subprefecture)." So the case could even be appealed to "Lu" (ancient administrative region), then all the way to the imperial court by "Wo Deng Wen Gu" (beat the drum and deliver the complaints, it is one of the important direct complaints in ancient China). This showed that great importance was attached by the government to the petty things related to land and field among the people, which was a noticeable feature of the civil procedure law in Song Dynasty.[362]

The prosecution of civil procedure needed to be initiated within a certain period of time. According to *Za Ling* (*Miscellaneous Orders*) in the Tang Dynasty, "the lawsuits about 'Tian Zhai' (land and houses), 'Hun Yin' (marriage) and 'Zhai Fu' (debts) will only be accepted in the period from the 1st of October to the 30th of March, except for the cases involving previous criminal records and the crime of forcible seizure." In *Song Xing Tong* (*The Penal Code of Song Dynasty*), a supplementary provision that was more operable was made: "All lawsuits about 'Tian Zhai' (land and houses), 'Hun Yin' (marriage), 'Zhai Fu' (debts) (original note: debts that are legally permitted) that were filed after the 1st of October and before the 30th of January shall be accepted, and the cases shall be settled before the 30th of March; or else the official shall inform the emperor of the reasons for the delay of the punishment. If the cases are about the crime of forcible seizure and the like, but if they have nothing to do with peasants, then the case can be heard at any time without being restricted by the aforementioned time limit."[363]

Furthermore, for all civil procedures that had exceeded the prescription period, they should not be heard anymore. "For the appeal of land and houses with unclear title deeds, if twenty years have passed or if the house owner or landowner have died, the case shall not be accepted,"[364] "As to the land and houses for sale, if after three years the prosecutor complains of the offset of profit and debts, the case shall not be accepted"[365]; "if it has been three years since the land or house has been mortgaged, while the prosecutor complains of failing to consult the neighbor, which he should have done, the case shall not be accepted"[366]; "If the prosecutor complains of the unfairness three years after the division of property, and ten years after the deceased

---

[362]"Xing Fa" (Criminal Law) in *Song Hui Yao Ji Gao* (*Collected Essays of the Historical Records of Song Dynasty*) (Book 32), Vol. 28.

[363]"Hun Tian Ru Wu Men" (The Category of Marriage and Land) in "Hu Hun Lv" (Statutes on Marriage, Tax and Household Registration) in *Song Xing Tong* (*The Penal Code of Song Dynasty*), Vol. 13.

[364]"Wu Su, Wu Rong, Wu Hui Hu Zheng Tian Chan" (A Dispute over Land among Wu Su, Wu Rong and Wu Hui) in "Hu Hun Men" (The Category of Households and Marriage) in *Ming Gong Shu Pan Qing Ming Ji* (*Collections of Enlightened Judgments*), Vol. 4.

[365]"You Cheng Song You Hong Fu Di Dang Tian Chan" (You Cheng Suing You Hong's Father for Pawning Land) in "Hu Hun Men" (The Category of Households and Marriage) in *Ming Gong Shu Pan Qing Ming Ji* (*Collections of Enlightened Judgments*), Vol. 4.

[366]"You Qin You Lin Zai San Nian Nei Zhe Fang Ke Shou Shu" (Allowing Those with Relatives and Neighbors to Redeem within three years) in "Hu Hun Men" (The Category of Households and Marriage) in *Ming Gong Shu Pan Qing Ming Ji* (*Collections of Enlightened Judgments*), Vol. 9.

has made the will, the case shall not be accepted."[367] "As is prescribed by law, after the death of parents and grandparents, if the mortgage of the common land and houses of the family is arbitrarily conducted by some rightful heir, who has appropriated the profit to himself, the other heirs should be entitled to reclaim the original property and require the seller to return the property to the vendee. If ten years have passed, other rightful heirs should not claim for the return of property but should turn to the illegal seller for compensation. If it has been ten years since the mortgage is conducted and the seller has been dead; or if it has been twenty years since the mortgage is conducted, the relevant liabilities shall be exempted, so neither part shall file a lawsuit."[368] "Only when the property of one's junior is stolen and sold by the elder is he allowed to file a lawsuit despite the time limit."[369]

As for "Yue Su" (overstepping indictment), although the provision that was stipulated in *Tang Lv (Tang Code)* was followed, and it was stated that "the prosecutor who has filed lawsuit by 'Yue Su' (overstepping indictment) and the officials who has accepted it shall be punished by 'Chi' (flogging with light sticks) for forty strokes respectively," the penalty was mitigated according to the imperial decrees issued. Especially after the reign of Emperor Huizong, in order to maintain a stable social order, it was allowed for people to sue the local officials for their illegal exploitation by "Yue Su" (overstepping indictment). According to the imperial edict issued on the 11th of December of the 3rd year of Zhenghe (1113 A.D.), for the supervision officials who "do not enforce punishment according to law, or who enforce severer punishment than he should or have caused injuries," "it is allowed to appeal to 'Shang Shu Sheng' (The Department of Secretary) by 'Yue Su' (overstepping indictment)."[370] In the Southern Song Dynasty, in order to maintain a stable social order and to gain the support of the people, all people in Sichuan and Shaanxi were permitted to "file lawsuits through 'Xuan Fu Chu Zhi Si' (local administrative organization)".[371] Additionally, in order to guarantee the regular circulation of commodity and to increase the revenue income of the state, if officials in charge of taxation had encroached upon the legal interests of the merchants and if it was "ignored by 'Shui Wu Si' (tax department), the victims were allowed to file

---

[367]"Zhi Yu Chu Ji Shu Zheng Ye" (A Dispute over Property between Nephew and Uncle Adopted by Others) in "Hu Hun Men" (The Category of Households and Marriage) in *Ming Gong Shu Pan Qing Ming Ji (Collections of Enlightened Judgments)*, Vol. 5.

[368]"Cao Si Song Xu De Yu Deng Zheng Tian Shi" (A Dispute over Land among Xu Guoyu and Other People Reported by the Office in Charge of Water Transportation) in "Hu Hun Men" (The Category of Households and Marriage) in *Ming Gong Shu Pan Qing Ming Ji (Collections of Enlightened Judgments)*, Vol. 4.

[369]"Bei You Wei Suo Sheng Fu Mai Ye" (The Humble and the Young Selling the Property of their Biological Father) in "Hu Hun Men" (The Category of Households and Marriage) in *Ming Gong Shu Pan Qing Ming Ji (Collections of Enlightened Judgments)*, Vol. 9.

[370]"Zhi Zhang Bu Ru Fa Jue Fa Guo Duo Xu Yue Su Yu Bi" (Overstepping Indictment Allowed for those being Flogged Illegally) in "Xing Fa" (Criminal Law) (Part 2) in *Song Da Zhao Ling Ji (Collected Records about Imperial Edicts and Orders of Song Dynasty)*, Vol. 202.

[371]"Xing Fa" (Criminal Law) in *Song Hui Yao Ji Gao (Collected Essays of the Historical Records of Song Dynasty)* (Section 5) (Chapter 3).

lawsuits to 'Shang Shu Sheng' (The Department of Secretary) by 'Yue Su' (overstepping indictment), and 'Cao Chen' (official in charge of water transport of grain to the capital) shall be severely punished according to the relevant regulation".[372]

In early Song Dynasty, strict laws were made to severely punish those who lodged false accusation. But in the later period, the law of "Wu Gao Fan Zuo" (Punishments for Those Lodging Wrong Accusations) was abolished, which had led to a lot of false accusation.

8.6.3 The Creation of the System of "Ju Yan Fen Si" (The Separation of Interrogation and Conviction)

The rulers of the Song Dynasty stressed not only the selection of judicial officials but also the system construction. The trial jurisdiction of the Song Dynasty was more explicit than that of the Tang Dynasty, so accordingly all crimes punishable by or below the punishment of "Zhang" (flogging with heavy sticks) were under the jurisdiction of "Xian" (county), namely, "the minor crimes punishable by or below the punishment of 'Zhang' (flogging with heavy sticks) are to be decided by 'Xian' (county)."[373] But for the major cases punishable by or above the punishment "Tu" (imprisonment), the suspects and relevant files should be sent to "Zhou" (subprefecture). Before the reform of Yuanfeng, "Zhou" (subprefecture) was granted the power to hear and settle cases punishable by or above the penalty of "Tu" (imprisonment) or even up to death penalty; after the reform, the cases of capital punishment needed to be reviewed by the officials in charge of prisons at the level of "Lu" (ancient administrative region). To avoid misuse of punishment, it was provided that "Pan Guan" (an assistant to the chief local official) or "Tui Guan" (official in charge of criminal penalty), who were affiliated to "Zhou" (subprefecture) and "Can Jun" (assistant to a ranking official or general in ancient China), should hold joint liability for the judgment made in the name of "Zhi Zhou" (subprefectural magistrates). As to the major cases involving death penalty, "if minor crimes are punished severely, or major crimes are punished leniently, or if there are doubtful points in the case, or the criminals are pitiful," the case should be submitted to the imperial court and be prudently settled by "Da Li Si" (The Bureau of Judicial Review). If "Zhi Zhou" (subprefectural magistrates) failed to submit to the imperial court a case that should be submitted or if he had submitted to the imperial court

---

[372]"Shang Shui" (Commercial Tax), quoted from "Sui Chi Sheng Ming" (The Statement of the Imperial Instructions) in "Ku Wu Men" (The Category of Warehouse Affairs) (Part 1) in *Qing Yuan Tiao Fa Shi Lei* (*The Legal Provisions and Cases Made in the Year of Qingyuan*), Vol. 36.

[373]"Duan Zui Yin Lv Ling Ge Shi Men Shu Yi" (The Commentary on the Category of Making Judgments according to Laws, Decrees, Injunctions and Standards) in "Yu Guan Ling" (The Order of Warden) in "Duan Yu Lv" (Statutes on Trials and Punishments) in *Song Xing Tong* (*The Penal Code of Song Dynasty*), Vol. 30.

8.6 The Judicial System of "Ju Yan Fen Si" (The Separation of Interrogation and...

cases that should not be submitted, he would be severely punished. But according to law, it was forbidden for officials to pass the buck, and it also was forbidden for them to take the liberty to submit the case to the emperor without trial. But the procedure of submitting memorials to the emperor was "only to require the emperor to aggravate the punishment for the major cases which were punished leniently instead of mitigating the punishment for the minor cases which were punished severely,"[374] which was very common because it was determined by the nature of the feudal system of submitting memorials to the emperor.

Before the reform of Yuanfeng, the cases punishable by the penalty below "Zhang" (flogging with heavy sticks) could be settled after being reviewed by "Xing Bu" (the Department of Punishment), while the major cases should be sent to and reviewed by "Shen Xing Yuan" (The Case Review Court). However, after the reform, "all cases must be settled by 'Da Li Si' (The Bureau of Judicial Review), reviewed by 'Xing Bu' (The Department of Punishment), then submitted to 'Zhong Shu' (the prime minister) and finally decided by the emperor."[375] Sometimes the emperor would gather "Han Lin Xue Shi" (member of the Imperial Academy); "Zhong Shu She Ren" (the official in charge of drafting imperial edicts in "Zhong Shu Sheng"), who was responsible for drafting imperial edicts; "Tong Ping Zhang Shi" (the prime minster); "Can Zhi Zheng Shi" (deputy prime minister); "Yu Shi" (the censor); "Jian Guan" (supervisor); etc. to discuss the cases together, which was called "Za Yi" (miscellaneous discussions), then judgment was made.

According to the criminal law of the Song Dynasty, "all crimes shall be settled where it has been committed."[376] If a case was committed in two places, "the suspect should be transferred to and investigated in the places where the crime was committed in sequence, and then be judged concurrently."[377] Because criminal proceedings and the judicial procedure were so complicated that "some cases may take one or two years to be settled," sometimes "the criminals may have died in the prison, or many of those who are implicated in the cases may have already been ill or dead when lenient treatment is finally approved."[378]

---

[374]"Zun Shou Fa Zhong Qing Qing Shang Qing Fa Yu Bi Shou Zhao" (An Imperial Edict about Abiding by the Law on Enforcing Severe Punishment for Minor Crimes) in "Xing Fa" (Criminal Law) (Part 2) in *Song Da Zhao Ling Ji* (*Collected Records about Imperial Edicts and Orders of Song Dynasty*), Vol. 202.

[375]"Xing Fa Zhi" (The Record of the Criminal Law) in *Song Shi* (*The History of Song Dynasty*) (Book 3).

[376]"Jue Qian" (Trials and Punishments) in "Duan Yu Ling" (Decrees on Trials and Punishments) in "Xing Yu Men" (The Category of Punishment) (Part 3) in *Qing Yuan Tiao Fa Shi Lei* (*The Legal Provisions and Cases Made in the Year of Qingyuan*), Vol. 30.

[377]"Bu He Kao Xun Zhe Qu Zhong Zheng Wei Ding Men" (The Category of Using Collecting Evidence in the Settlement of Cases Unsuitable for Interrogation under Torture) in "Duan Yu Lv" (Statutes on Trials and Punishments) in *Song Xing Tong* (*The Penal Code of Song Dynasty*), Vol. 29.

[378]"Xing Fa Zhi" (The Record of the Criminal Law) in *Song Shi* (*The History of Song Dynasty*) (Book 3).

The rulers of the Song Dynasty not only emphasized that the officials should have a good mastery of law but also stressed that the law should be fairly enforced, so the requirements for judicial officials were very explicit and strict. In December of the 8th year of Tianbao, it was ordered by Taizu that "'Tui Zhuang' (regulation) should be re-examined by 'You Si' (official) in detail and the new edition with thirty three articles in total should be issued to the public."[379] Although "Tui Zhuang" (regulation) was long lost, it was no doubt that the contents were related to the duties of judicial officials. During the reign of Emperor Huizong, it was stipulated that the officials in charge of "Zhou" (subprefecture) and "Xian" (county) should not entrust their assistants to try the cases and they should do so by themselves; or else they would be sentenced to two years of imprisonment. So since then it had become a convention for officials to interrogate the criminals by themselves. Especially the system of "Ju Yan Fen Si" (The Separation of Interrogation and Conviction) was created. The word "Ju" referred to trying the cases, while "Yan" referred to choosing the suitable legal articles. So special officials were appointed to take charge of the two offices respectively, while neither of them was allowed to do the other's job and no one was allowed to overstep the rule. So accordingly, "'Yu Si' (the prison department) is in charge of trying the cases, while 'Fa Si' (the judicial department) is in charge of making judgments, and both offices are established to be in charge of their own duties to prevent evil doing."[380] "Ju Yan Fen Si" (The Separation of Interrogation and Conviction) was established in order to avoid unfair verdicts caused by the improper application of a complicated law, but at the same time, it had promoted the progress of making judgments according to law. So the practice of "Ju Yan Fen Si" (The Separation of Interrogation and Conviction) not only improved the quality of judicial judgments but also avoided improper application of the law and prevented officials from gaining private benefits by taking advantage of their power. Therefore, the system was continued to be implemented without change till the end of the Song Dynasty.

To prevent judicial officials from making unfair sentences by playing favoritism, the laws and regulations of the Tang Dynasty were followed in the Song Dynasty, so "Hui Bi Zhi Du" (the avoidance system) was strictly enforced. In cases where the judge was a relative of the defendant or they had taken the same imperial examination, he should withdraw from the hearing of the cases. Additionally, if the former judge of the trial was a relative of the latter, avoidance was also needed. It was also stipulated during the reign of Emperor Shenzong that the officials of "Da Li Si" (The Bureau of Judicial Review) were "forbidden to go outside the capital to visit or meet guests"[381] to prevent them from accepting bribes by bending the law.

---

[379]*Xu Zi Zhi Tong Jian Chang Bian* (*Sequel to the Full-length Book of History as a Mirror*), Vol. 16, in December of the 8th year of Kaibao.

[380]"Shen Xing" (Prudent Punishment) in *Li Dai Ming Chen Zou Yi* (*Memorials Submitted to the Emperor by the Famous Officials in Different Dynasties*), Vol. 217.

[381]*Xu Zi Zhi Tong Jian Chang Bian* (*Sequel to the Full-length Book of History as a Mirror*), Vol. 296, in February of the 2nd year of Yuanfeng.

During the interrogation, it was usually forbidden to ask about anything irrelevant to the cases; otherwise, the judges "shall be prosecuted." But the cases involving theft and homicide were exceptions. As testimony was the main evidence in settling the cases, it was legal to extort confessions by torture. According to *Song Xing Tong* (*The Penal Code of Song Dynasty*), when hearing a case, it was required that the cases should be investigated repeatedly. If there were any doubtful points or if the defendant refused to plead guilty, it was advisable to extract confession by torture. But the torture employed during interrogations in the Song Dynasty was far brutal than that in the Tang Dynasty because apart from the widely used so-called lawful instruments of torture, such as "Chi" (flogging with light sticks), "Zhang" (flogging with heavy sticks), etc., other punishments, such as "Jia Bang" (clamp rod), "Nao Gu" (head iron hoop), and "Chao Gun" (leg vise), were also applied so as to "extort confession, to urge the payment of the fine and to close the case in time."[382]

Apart from the testimony of the accused, witness testimony and physical evidence were also stressed. For example, it was provided that people like "Lao" (elder), "You" (young), and "Fei Ji" (the disabled) were excepted tortured, so their conviction would be based purely on witness testimonies. In order to strictly carry out the testimony system, according to law, those who belonged to "Xiang Rong Yin" (prohibiting indictment or testifying against each other between relatives) and those who belonged to "Lao" (elder), "You" (young), and "Fei Ji" (the disabled) were forbidden to testify, and they would be punished if they gave false testimony. The importance of physical evidence was fully reflected in *Song Xing Tong* (*The Penal Code of Song Dynasty*). For example, "for the cases where the bribes are discovered or there are no doubtful points," even if the suspect does not admit his guilt, he will still be convicted based on evidence. The bribes discovered, which is mentioned here, are clearly physical evidence.[383] If the person with relevant interests was ill, injured or dead, he should be examined in order to obtain physical evidence; "if the feigned illness, injury or death had resulted in false examination, the person with related interests shall be punished one level lighter according to the specific circumstances; if the illness, death or injury are real but they are failed to be accordingly examined, the person in charge shall be convicted for the crime of 'Ru Zui' (to intentionally sentence an innocent person guilty or a misdemeanor felony)."[384] Famous medicolegal works such as *He Yan Ge Mu* (*Tables of Verification*), *He Yan Zheng Bei Ren Xing Tu* (*Pictures of Human Figures to be Verified*), and *Xi Yuan Ji Lu* (*Collection of Unjust Cases Rectified*) and books on settling lawsuits such as *Tang Yin Bi Shi* (*Collection of Criminal Cases*) and *Zhe Yu Gui Jian*

---

[382]"Xing Fa Zhi" (The Record of the Criminal Law) in *Song Shi* (*The History of Song Dynasty*) (Book 2).

[383]"Bu He Kao Xun Zhe Qu Zhong Zheng Wei Ding Men" (The Category of Using Collecting Evidence in the Settlement of Cases Unsuitable for Interrogation under Torture) in "Duan Yu Lv" (Statutes on Trials and Punishments) in *Song Xing Tong* (*The Penal Code of Song Dynasty*), Vol. 29.

[384]Song Ci (Song Dynasty), "Tiao Ling" (The Laws and Decrees) in *Xi Yuan Ji Lu* (*Collection of Unjust Cases Rectified*), Vol. 1.

(*Collections of Lawsuits*) were published successively, due to the emphasis on inquisition and the summary of experience in judicial adjudication.

After judgment, criminals were required to write a written confession marked with their signature, which would be used as basis for their judgment. "The confession, which is required to be written by the criminal, shall be reviewed by prison inspectors. If the criminal is unable to write, the custodial official shall write for him; ... the official shall show the confession to the criminal and tell him the meaning of the characters on it, but the criminals who can write shall write by themselves."[385] Confessions of the criminals should be checked by other officials, which was called "Lu Wen," and only after that could sentences be made. For the major cases, "Ju Lu" (joint checking) should be held together by "Zhi Zhou" (subprefectural magistrates), "Tong Pan" (official in charge of agriculture, water conservancy, and litigation under subprefecture), and "Mu Zhi Guan" (the subordinates of local officials). If the officials in charge failed to refute and rectify the inappropriate judgments in time, they would be punished; if the criminal retracted his testimony during the checking, the case should be tried again.

The formal judgment of the case should be read to the criminal. If there were no doubtful points, the judgment could be enforced. Criminals at that time were permitted to appeal to higher judicial offices, but "Yue Su" (overstepping indictment) was forbidden, and they should appeal step by step by following the procedure. The appeal period was one to three years, but anyone who "tries to reverse the verdict" would be punished severely. A peer review of the appeal should be firstly conducted by different departments, which was called "Bie Tui"; if a further appeal was lodged, the case should be reviewed by the higher judicial offices, which was called "Yi Tui"; if the appeal was lodged to the imperial court, the case would be heard by the officials appointed by the emperor, but the judge in the first instance would not be allowed to participate in the retrial.

To improve the efficiency of the judicial office, the time limit for adjudication was explicitly provided. For all cases to be judged by "Da Li Si" (The Bureau of Judicial Review), the settlement of major cases should not exceed twenty five days; less important cases, twenty days; minor cases, ten days. For the retrial before "Shen Xing Yuan" (The Case Review Court), the settlement of major cases should not exceed fifteen days; less important cases, ten days; minor cases, five days. For the so-called major, less important, or minor cases, there were also specific provisions: the case involving over twenty *min* of money was classified as a major case; over ten *min*, a less important case; less than ten *min*, a minor case. But despite the time limit, the delaying of settlement and the waste of time and energy were unavoidable in judicial practice.

The judicial power of the emperor was consolidated in the Song Dynasty, which was manifested not only in their control of important judicial activities through

---

[385]Xie Weixin (Song Dynasty), "Kuan Bian" (Argument about the Provisions of Law) in "Xing Fa Men" (The Category of Criminal Law)in *Shi Lei Bei Yao* (*Collections of Materials for Analogy*), Vol. 23. (additional collection).

"Shen Xing Yuan" (The Case Review Court), though it was abolished in the reform of Emperor Shenzong, but also in their control of the activities of central judicial organizations by the reviewing conducted by "Men Xia Sheng" (the organization in charge of examining the imperial edicts in ancient China), the deliberation conducted by "Zhong Shu Sheng" (the supreme organization in charge of state affairs), and the joint review conducted by the administrators. Moreover, for the lawsuits filed in the capital, the judgment would also be supervised by the emperor at regular intervals. For example, "Emperor Taizong usually presided at the trial of lawsuits and made judgments in person. If there were doubtful cases in capital prisons, he would often decide by himself."[386] In the 5th year of Chongning (1107 A.D.), an imperial edict was issued by Emperor Huizong, in which he openly argued in favor of the arbitrary action of the imperial power to influence public opinion, and he said that "those who are expert at deciding people's life and death are kings, so it is the emperor who has the rights to make decisions." Thereafter, on the 6th year of Chongning (1108 A.D.), another imperial decree was issued, which stated that "for all cases settled by the emperor, it is forbidden for the litigants to appeal to 'Shang Shu Sheng' (The Department of Secretary); otherwise both the officials and the litigants shall be punished for disobeying the emperor."[387] To ensure the control of judicial power, the emperor also demanded that in the circumstances that "minor crimes are punished severely, or major crimes are punished leniently," if there were no explicit provisions, they should be submitted to the emperor for decision. In addition, the system of "Yu Shi" (the censor) was also controlled by the emperor, so extensive judicial supervision was conducted.

Like criminal trials, civil trials should be handled by the officials of "Zhou" (subprefecture) and "Xian" (county) in person, and avoidance was needed if it was necessary. During the trial, the litigants and witnesses must appear in court, or compulsory measures should be taken by the officials to bring the litigants to the trial, which was called "Ji Shou." For civil trials, evidence played a very important role in making a thorough investigation of the cases. Civil evidence included documentary evidence, physical evidence, witness testimony, statement of the parties, expert conclusion, records of inspection, and so on. Documentary evidence was the most common evidence in civil trials, which included deeds, certificates, "Zhen Ji Bu" (the original account), writ, testament, betrothal invitation, genealogy, etc. In addition to physical evidence, litigants' statements and witness testimony were also commonly used as basis for conviction in civil trials. The authenticity of the evidence would be verified by government officials or by on-site surveys.

In general, torture was forbidden, and the judicial principle of "Qin Shu Xiang Rong Yin" (concealment of crimes among relatives or refusing to testify among relatives in court) was not applicable in civil trials. Some civil cases were collected in

---

[386]"Xing Fa Zhi" (The Record of the Criminal Law) in *Song Shi* (*The History of Song Dynasty*) (Book 2).

[387]"Xing Fa Zhi" (The Record of the Criminal Law) in *Song Shi* (*The History of Song Dynasty*) (Book 2).

Ming Gong Shu Pan Qing Ming Ji (*Collections of Enlightened Judgments*), from which we can see that one litigant's brother and grandmother had appeared in court as witnesses.

Further progress was also made in civil mediation. Official mediation was divided into direct official mediation and civil mediation conducted according to orders. Civil mediation was mainly conducted by neighbors and relatives. Civil mediation was relatively popular because it was favorable not only to settling civil disputes timely but also to avoiding the escalation of conflicts, reducing the number of lawsuits, and preventing officials from doing evil deeds.

In order to avoid influencing production due to the delay of civil trials, time limit was especially specified for civil trial settlement. In the 2nd year of Qiandao during the reign of Emperor Xiaozong, it was stipulated that if a civil litigation in "Zhou" (subprefecture) and "Xian" (county) was not settled within half a year, an appeal was permitted to be lodged. "If the settlement of civil litigation is delayed for a long time by the officials of 'Zhou' (subprefecture) and 'Xian' (county), it should be handled according to the law: if the officials of 'Xian' (county) cannot make judgment, it should be handled by the officials of 'Zhou' (subprefecture); if the officials of 'Zhou' (subprefecture) still cannot make judgment, it should be handled by 'Jian Si' (official with right of supervising counties and towns). So from now on, the cases that cannot be settled after over half a year in 'Zhou' (subprefecture) and 'Xian' (county) shall all be heard by 'Jian Si' (official with right of supervising counties and towns)."[388] It was then stipulated in the years of Qingyuan during the reign of Emperor Ningzong that "the accepted lawsuits shall be settled on that very day. If the facts need to be verified, the case shall be settled within five days; the case in 'Zhou' (subprefecture) and 'Jun' (shire) shall be settled within ten days, and the case monitored by 'Jian Si' (official with right of supervising counties and towns) shall be settled within half a month; however, there will be exceptions if there is a good reason for the overdue case; or else, 'Yue Su' (overstepping indictment) is allowed."[389] According to *Yue Shu Bang* (*Lists of Constraints*), issued by Zhu Xi, when he was a magistrate in Tanzhou, for the civil actions sued through "Xian" (county), "time limit is scheduled, so from today on, for the cases of theft unsolved in 'Xian' (county), they should be settled within a month; the cases of fighting that have caused injuries, or the cases involving 'Lian Bao' (if someone in the neighborhood has committed crimes, the neighbors should report to the government, or they will be punished for being related with the offender) and 'Bao Gu' (the system whereby an offender was ordered by law to help the victim recover within a prescribed period, and the punishment for the crime committed by the offender was determined according to

---

[388]"Xing Fa" (Criminal Law) in *Song Hui Yao Ji Gao* (*Collected Essays of the Historical Records of Song Dynasty*) (Book 32), Vol. 3.

[389]"Xing Fa" (Criminal Law) in *Song Hui Yao Ji Gao* (*Collected Essays of the Historical Records of Song Dynasty*) (Book 40), Vol. 3.

8.6 The Judicial System of "Ju Yan Fen Si" (The Separation of Interrogation and...

the means of injury and the degree of recovery), fifty days; the cases of marriage and land, two months."[390]

The principle of "Ju Yan Fen Si" (The Separation of Interrogation and Conviction), which was implemented in the Song Dynasty, was also applicable in civil actions. Laws relevant to the case should be checked by the prosecuting attorney so that the judicial officials could make judgment. But because of the lack of civil legal provisions, there were also instances where judgments were made according to the doctrine of "Li" (rites) or social customs, which were flexibly handled by the judicial officials.

After judgment, it was required that "Duan You" (reasons for settlement) should be sent to the parties concerned to explain the causes of the case, the claim of the litigants, the facts of and the reason for the dispute, the acknowledged facts and applicable laws, and so on. If not satisfied with the judgment, a litigant could appeal to "Zhou" (subprefecture), "Fu" (ancient administrative district between province and county), "Jun" (army), and "Jian" (ancient supervisory office) for the settlement of the case by the judicial officials of "Zhou" (subprefecture); if the litigant was still not satisfied, he could appeal to "Jian Si" (official in charge of supervising the counties and towns), who could transfer the case to the authorized official of the neighboring "Zhou" (subprefecture) for adjudication; if still not satisfied, the litigant could appeal to "Hu Bu" (The Department of Revenue), the institution for the final judgment of civil actions. "If the affair is in the charge of the department, or if it can not be settled by 'Jian Si' (official with right of supervising counties and towns) of 'Jun' (shire) and 'Xian' (county), then the lawsuit should be accepted by the department."[391] All the appellate cases on "land and bond," "the division of family property and separation of families," "the mortgage of estate," "the time limit of civil actions in agricultural production," the affairs of "Hu Jue" (No Male Heirs), "claims for the descendants," etc. were all heard by the government offices affiliated to "Hu Bu" (The Department of Revenue) or reviewed by the local "Jian Si" (official in charge of supervising the counties and towns) of "Zhou" (subprefecture) and "Xian" (county). To avoid delaying of settlement, in October of the 6th year of Jiading during the reign of Emperor Ningzong (1214 A.D.), special measures were taken by "Hu Bu" (The Department of Revenue) to inspect and press for the settlement of unresolved cases in local places.

Song Dynasty was famous for the intensification of the centralized autocracy. The prosperity of the commodity economy and scientific development had made the traditional culture enter a period of fastigium. Not only essayists, poets, and "Ci Ren" (ci poets) came forth in large numbers, but many thinkers and philosophers, such as Cheng Yi, Cheng Hao, Zhu Xi, Zhang Zai, etc., also emerged. Mr. Chen Yinque once pointed out that "the culture of Chinese nation had witnessed thousands

---

[390]Zhu Xi (Song Dynasty), "Yue Shu Bang" (Lists of Constraints) in *Zhu Wen Gong Wen Ji (Collected Works of Zhu Xi)*, Vol. 100.

[391]"Zhi Guan Zhi" (The Record of State Officials) in *Song Shi (The History of Song Dynasty)* (Book 3).

of years of development, so it reached its peak in Song Dynasty."[392] The same was true with legal culture. For example, the number of criminal law books recorded in "Yi Wen Zhi" (Books and Records) in *Song Shi* (*The History of Song Dynasty*) had reached to 221 kinds and 7955 volumes, while in the Tang Dynasty, which was the flourishing age of feudal rule of law, the number of criminal law books documented in history books was only "61 kinds and 1004 volumes."[393] So brilliant achievements were made in legal culture in spite of the poverty and weakness of the Song Dynasty.

8.7 The Historical Role of the Legal System and the Achievement of "Lv Xue" (The Study of Statutory Laws) in the Southern and Northern Song Dynasties

Based on the historical background of the Song Dynasty, legislation was not constrained by old laws and the judicature was not confined to old rules; instead, pragmatic thinking and reform were advocated. So in terms of legislation, there was a tendency to specialize; with respect to the judicature, a series of new systems were established; as to "Lv Xue" (the study of statutory laws), great achievements were made and many imperishable works of law were written. Therefore, it can be said that the period of the Southern and Northern Song dynasties was one of the eras when greatest achievements were made in the legal system after the Tang Dynasty. In fact, some provisions even surpassed those of the Tang Dynasty, which were also unattainable during the Ming and Qing dynasties. The legal system of the Song Dynasty not only enriched the Chinese legal system but also highlighted the rationale and wisdom of the traditional legal system of our country. So it had played an important role in Chinese legal civilization.

Early in the Song Dynasty, in order to strengthen the centralization of authority and to promote economic development, legal systems were extensively established and various laws were strictly implemented, which had helped to maintain a stable ruling order. However, with the reinforcement of absolutism, the national statutory law was more and more impacted by provisional legislation such as "Chi" (instruction) and "Li" (precedent), as was described in the statement that "the provisional legislation challenged the statutory law, so changes were made everywhere randomly."[394] Consequently, the original supplementary legal measures became

---

[392]Chen Yinque, *Chen Yin Que Xian Sheng Wen Ji* (*The Collected Works of Mr. Chen Yinque*), Vol. 2, Shanghai Classics Publishing House, 1989, p. 245.

[393]"Jing Ji Kao" (A Textual Research of Classic Works) (Part 28) in *Wen Xian Tong Kao* (*A General Textual Research of the Documents*), Vol. 210.

[394]"Xing Fa Zhi" (The Record of the Criminal Law) in *Song Shi* (*The History of Song Dynasty*) (Book 1).

malpractices instead, which had resulted in redundant legal forms and complicated contents, as was described in the record that "matters, whether big or small, whether in or out of the court; crimes, whether minor or serious, can all be dealt with by the laws which are already ready made."[395] Not only that, but in the later period of the Northern Song Dynasty, it was exceedingly common for a law to repealed by a statement of the emperor. It was recorded in "Xing Fa Zhi" (The Record of the Criminal Law) in *Song Shi* (*The History of Song Dynasty*) that "some imperial edicts were usually randomly issued by Emperor Huizong to have the original rules changed ...When Cai Jing was in charge the administration of the country, out of his own benefit, he even requested the emperor to issue imperial edicts so that he could act beyond law." The emperor's continuous expansion of legislative power had made a great impact upon the established legislative procedure and it had destroyed the legal system which was established with difficulty. In the end, the law had lost its authority over the people know their outlines. What was especially serious was that the legislators delayed the issuing of the decrees because they could not be implemented; the laws were violated because they could not be carried out. In the end, law had lost its authority and stability. As a result, the people felt perplexed because of the inconstancy of law and the country was entrapped in poverty and weakness.

It needs to be pointed out that the relatively loose political environment and the encouragement of studying laws and regulations had made legal thoughts more active, and some noted lawbooks were written successively. For example, in *Xing Tong Fu* (*Discussions of Criminal Provisions*), written by Fu Lin, who was "Lv Xue Bo Shi" (Scholar of Law) at the time, was very influential because in the book, *Xing Tong* (*criminal law*), which was issued in 963 A.D., was adapted and compiled into a lawbook in the form of rhymes. The book was footnoted by the author himself, so it was very easy to understand and remember. Even in the Jin and Yuan dynasties, *Xing Tong Fu* (*Discussions of Criminal Provisions*) was still annotated, so there were as many as ten types of annotations. During the reign of Emperor Renzong, Sun Shi, who was "Zhi Jiang" (assistant lecturer) of "Guo Zi Jian" (the highest educational body in feudal China), was appointed to write *Lv Wen Yin Yi* (*Pronunciation and Meaning of Law*) and *Lv Ling Shi Yi* (*Interpretation of Law and Order*), which showed that great attention was paid to the study of law in "Guo Zi Jian" (the highest educational body in feudal China) at the time.

In the Song Dynasty, it is not only the judicature that was stressed, but the analysis of cases and the summary of experiences were also paid attention to, so two books, *Zhe Yu Gui Jian* (*Collections of Lawsuits*) and *Tang Yin Bi Shi* (*Collection of Criminal Cases*), were written. *Zhe Yu Gui Jian* (*Collections of Lawsuits*), written by Zheng Ke, was the first collection of cases about adjudication and judicial examination in history, with analysis, comments, and summaries added. The book expressed the author's idea of "Shang De Huan Xing" (stressing moral education

---

[395]Gu Yanwu (Ming Dynasty), "Fa Zhi" (Legal System) (quoted from what Ye Shiyu said in Song Dynasty) in *Ri Zhi Lu* (*The Record of Daily Reading*), Vol. 8.

while mitigating criminal punishments), "Ming Shen Yong Xing" (being prudent in the infliction of punishment), and "Yan Fang Wang Lan" (avoiding perverting the law to suit private interests). Meanwhile, it also expressed the author's bitter resentment to some cruel and fatuous officials for their "inflexible administration of justice and over-rigorous law enforcement," so the book became a very important reference material for studying Chinese ancient judicature. Based on *Zhe Yu Gui Jian* (*Collections of Lawsuits*), *Tang Yin Bi Shi* (*Collection of Criminal Cases*) was written by Gui Wanrong, with "totally one hundred and forty four articles, all of which were about the analysis of doubtful cases since time immemorial." In this work, experiences and lessons relating to judicial adjudication in the past dynasties were comprehensively summarized, including law enforcement, judgment of cases, calculation of penalty, examination of the judicature, and so on. The book was praised by Emperor Lizong and was translated into Japanese and published abroad at a very early time, so it was widely distributed. There were also valuable historical law materials about judicial cases in *Ming Gong Shu Pan Qing Ming Ji* (*Collections of Enlightened Judgments*).

A remarkable breakthrough was achieved in medical jurisprudence due to the scientific and technological progress of the Song Dynasty. For example, *Xi Yuan Ji Lu* (*Collection of Unjust Cases Rectified*) was written, wherein Song Ci made reference to cases about forensic autopsy examination recorded in the works of predecessors and combined them with his own experience. *Xi Yuan Ji Lu* (*Collection of Unjust Cases Rectified*), which consisted of five volumes and fifty three sections,[396] was a comprehensive summary of Chinese ancient medical jurisprudence. The book was not only the earliest and most complete medical jurisprudence monograph in China but also the first one in the world. So once the book was published, it was ordered to be issued nationwide, which had made it one of the compulsory reading materials for officials who were in charge of handling homicide cases in the Southern Song Dynasty. That was why the book was regarded as "Jin Ke Yu Lv" (the golden law and precious rule) and the standard for later generations.

Xi Yuan Ji Lu (*Collection of Unjust Cases Rectified*) was first translated into Korean by Korean envoys in the Ming Dynasty. After that, the book was translated and published successively by Japan, France, Britain, Germany, and Holland, which had fully shown the outstanding contribution of the Chinese nation to world legal civilization.

Since Song Dynasty was set up soon after Tang Dynasty was overthrown, the chapter heading and contents of *Song Xing Tong* (*The Penal Code of Song Dynasty*) mostly followed those of *Tang Lv Shu Yi* (*Comments on Tang Code*). So the space of legal interpretation was limited, so that the legal interpretation was mainly focused upon the compilation and analysis of cases to provide supplements to judicature. Especially, the publishing of *Xi Yuan Ji Lu* (*Collection of Unjust Cases Rectified*) was a remarkable achievement in the new study of "Lv Xue" (the study of statutory

---

[396]"Fa Jia Lei" (The Category of Legalist) in "Zi Bu" (The Section of Zi) in *Si Ku Quan Shu Zong Mu* (*General Catalogue of Complete Library in the Four Branches of Literature*).

8.7 The Historical Role of the Legal System and the Achievement of "Lv Xue" (The... 791

laws). The change of official law annotation in Tang Dynasty to private law annotation in Song Dynasty was related to the comparatively loose political environment, but what was more important, it was related to the pressing internal and external troublesome situation, because the government had already had no time or capability to deal with the problem.

Additionally, the scholars of "Li Xue" (neo-Confucianism: a Confucian school of idealist philosophy of the Song and Ming dynasties), the reformers, and the utilitarian school of the Song Dynasty also debated heatedly on the purpose of legislation, the reform, the leniency and severity of decrees, the restoration of corporal punishment, and so on, which had no doubt promoted the development of legal thoughts and culture. Moreover, criminal law books recorded in "Yi Wen Zhi" (Books and Records) in *Song Shi* (*The History of Song Dynasty*) reached to two hundred and twenty kinds, which was four times more than that in "Yi Wen Zhi" (Books and Records) in *Xin Tang Shu* (*The New Book of Tang Dynasty*).

The scholars of "Li Xue" (neo-Confucianism: a Confucian school of idealist philosophy of the Song and Ming dynasties) represented by Cheng Hao, Cheng Yi, and Zhu Xi in the Song Dynasty, further advocated the principles of "San Gang" (three cardinal guides) and "Wu Chang" (five constant virtues) and regarded them as the manifestation of "Tian Li" (heavenly principles). They claimed that "Zhang" (unrestrained), to be specific, equaled to "San Gang" (three cardinal guides) and "Ji" (restrained) equaled to "Wu Chang" (five constant virtues). So the reason for the prevalence of this principle was that it existed everywhere and was suitable for all.[397] To uphold the principle of "Cun Tian Li" (retaining the heavenly principles), it was necessary to obey the rule of "Mie Ren Yu" (subduing human desires), "if 'Tian Li' (heavenly principles) exists, the human desire must be eliminated; 'Tian Li' (heavenly principles) and 'Ren Yu' (human desires) can not co-exist."[398] To curb and punish crimes induced by "Ren Yu" (human desires), the scholars of "Li Xue" (neo-Confucianism: a Confucian school of idealist philosophy of the Song and Ming dynasties) advocated that complicated and strict laws and brutal punishments should be enforced. Zhu Xi once advised the emperor to "enforce strict laws" and "to punish one severely to serve as a warning to others...so to make no one dare to commit the crime ever again."[399]

---

[397]Zhu Xi (Song Dynasty), "Zhu Zi" (The Scholars of Various Schools) (Part 3) in *Zhu Zi Quan Shu* (*The Complete Works of Zhu Xi*), Vol. 60.

[398]Li Jingde (Song Dynasty), "Li Xing" (Doing One's Best) in *Zhu Zi Yu Lei* (*Collection of Zhu Xi's Quotations*), Vol. 13.

[399]Li Jingde (Song Dynasty), "Lun Zhi Dao" (On Governance) in *Zhu Zi Yu Lei* (*Collection of Zhu Xi's Quotations*), Vol. 180.

8.8 The Legal Systems of Liao, Western Xia, and Jin Dynasties Compared with That of the Song Dynasty

China has been a unified multiethnic country since ancient times. In addition to the Han nationality, the minority nationalities have all made positive contribution to the creation of Chinese legal civilization. The formation of the legal system of "Hua Xia" (an ancient name for China), tracing to its source, was developed from Miao nationality with "Xing" (punishment) as the prototype. The period from remote antiquity to the pre-Qin times was the beginning of the national amalgamation and unification of the Chinese nation. With "Hua Xia" (an ancient name for China) nationality as the main branch, it had integrated with the tribes called Dongyi, Nanman, Xirong, and Beidi, as well as with other tribes in history, and finally formed a national community of a considerable size. It was because of the success of the national amalgamation that the unified powerful and prosperous feudal empire of the Qin and Han dynasties were founded. In this process the early integration of legal wisdom of all nationalities was initiated. The period of the Wei, Jin, and Southern and Northern dynasties is another important time of national amalgamation and integration of legal culture. It is the persistent creation of legal systems and exchanges of legal culture of all Chinese nationalities that has made it possible for the Chinese legal system to become mature and to be finalized in the Sui and Tang dynasties.

After the Tang Dynasty, China stepped into the later period of feudal society, during which the Liao, Western Xia, Jin, Yuan, and Later Jin regimes were established successively by Qidan, Dangxiang, Jurchen, Mongol, and Man nationalities. Some of these regimes were confined to the border areas, some had expanded to southern China, while some were unified national regimes. On the one hand, they continued to absorb the advanced legal culture of the Han nationality to improve the legal civilization of their own; on the other hand, as they abandoned the backward tradition in their customary law, they paid great attention to the preservation of their inherent national spirit and strove to integrate it with the trend of the times. During this period of national amalgamation, which was carried on with a much longer time span and a wider range, remarkable achievements were made by the national minorities in the building of a legal system, such as the administrative law of the Yuan Dynasty and the national legislation of the Later Jin Dynasty, so rich legislative and judicial experiences were accumulated, which has become an important chapter in the history of the legal system of Chinese minority nationalities and has greatly enriched the Chinese legal system.

Since the establishment of the Northern Song Dynasty, they had pursued the basic state policy of strengthening the centralized autocracy at home and compromising by ceding territories and paying indemnities to the Liao and Jin regimes humiliatingly in exchange for their peaceful coexistence abroad. For example, in the 1st year of Jingde (1004 A.D.), after Song and Liao reached a peace agreement and formed the Chanyuan Alliance, Song promised to give 300,000 of silver and silk to Liao every year to seek temporary peace.

During the confrontation between the Song and Liao dynasties, Western Xia regime was established by a branch of the Qiang nationality in the area around Ningxia, Gansu, and Shanbei (north of Shaanxi Province), and it often invaded the northwestern part of the Song Dynasty; therefore, the same policy of giving silver and silk to Western Xia was taken in exchange for temporary peace.

In 1115 A.D., the Jin Dynasty was established by the Jurchen nationality in Heilong River Valley in the Northeast. In the 3rd year of Tianhui during the reign of Emperor Taizong (1125 A.D.), the Jin Dynasty defeated the Liao Dynasty, then it headed south, occupied Kaifeng, the capital of Song Dynasty in 1126 A.D., and captured the emperor and many other ministers, so the Northern Song Dynasty perished in the end. The imperial clansmen and the civil and military officials of the Song Dynasty who escaped southbound in panic made Lin'an the capital in 1138 A.D., which was called South Song Dynasty in history. Emperor Gaozong of the South Song Dynasty followed in the steps of the rulers of the Northern Song Dynasty and indulged themselves in enjoyment and momentary ease. They were satisfied with the remaining half of the country with no intention of recovering the lost territory, so that the two regimes of Song and Jin dynasties coexisted for a long time.

8.8.1 *The Legal System of the Liao Dynasty*

In 916 A.D., Yelv Abaoji from the Qidan (Khitan) nationality in the north proclaimed himself emperor, ascended the throne with the reign title of Shence, founded the military-feudal Liao Dynasty, and ruled all of the nationalities in the north. The production and residence patterns of the Qidan (Khitan) nationality and Han nationality were different, with the former engaged in "fishing and hunting for food and living on horses" and the latter engaged in "tilling the land for food, and living inside the city walls," so the policy of "dividing and ruling" was adopted by the rulers of the Liao Dynasty: "Khitans are treated in accordance with the national system of Qidan (Khitan) nationality, while the people of Han nationality are treated in accordance with the system of Han nationality." So the native customary law was applied to the people of Qidan. For minor crimes, "judgments are made according to the situation of the crimes"; for serious crimes, "judgments are made according to the temporarily made legislations"[400]; "for the people of Han nationality, judgments are made according to the laws and decrees in *Tang Lv (Tang Code)*." With respect to the organization of political power, "Bei Mian Guan" (official in the north) was set up to rule the Khitans, while "Nan Mian Guan" (official in the south) was set up to rule the Han people, with both positions held only by the nobility of the Qidan (Khitan) nationality. During the reign of Emperor Shizong, the regime's political organization was established by mainly following that of the Tang Dynasty and then was gradually improved.

---

[400]"Xing Fa Zhi" (The Record of the Criminal Law) in *Liao Shi (The History of Liao Dynasty)*.

In the case of legislative activities, in the 6th year of Shence (921 A.D.), an imperial edict was issued by Taizu (the first founder of the dynasty) Yelv Abaoji of the Liao Dynasty, and it was ordered that "laws should be made by the ministers to strengthen the administration of Qidan (Khitan) and other nationalities,"[401] which had lifted the curtain of the legal construction of the Liao Dynasty. In the same year, *Jue Yu Fa* (*Law on Settling Lawsuits*), the first statute law of the Liao Dynasty, was drafted by Yelv Tulvbu according to an imperial edict.[402]

As for the guiding principle of the legislation in the early Liao Dynasty, the law of the Han Dynasty was adopted; at the same time, "its national convention was also taken into consideration."[403] During the reign of Emperor Taizong, the Bohai regime was overthrown. According to an edict, "Bohai people shall be punished in accord with the laws of Han people,"[404] so the scope of application of the laws of the Han nationality was obviously expanded.

In the reign of Emperor Shengzong, as far as the Qidan (Khitan) nationality is concerned, the transformation from slavery to feudal system was basically completed, which had made it possible to carry out economic and political reforms. Emperor Shengzong himself had paid much attention to the study of the culture of the Han nationality since his childhood. In order to carry out legal reform, he first ordered to have *Han Lv* (*Han Code*) translated and applied as the basis for the reformation of the legal system. Meanwhile, he ordered the ministers inside and outside the capital to point out the problems in the existing law and put the focus of the reform on the solution to the problems, like "implementing different legal systems for the minorities and Han people" and implementing the same national laws without exception. He once stated that "the affairs related to Han nationality shall all be handled in accordance with the laws of Southern Dynasty, which shall not be violated by anyone."[405] Till then, the national policy of Liao Dynasty which was featured by stressing minority groups and neglecting Han nationality was gradually changed. In the 7th year of Taiping (1027 A.D.), *Tiao Zhi* (*Regulations*) was enacted, in which it was stipulated that the same law should be applied to both Khitan and Han people if they had committed same crimes; if Khitans had committed the crime of "Shi E" (The Ten Abominations), they "shall also be punished according to law," which not only showed the influence of the advanced legal culture of the central plain but also reflected the process of the feudalization of law in the Liao Dynasty.

In the 5th year of Chongxi (1036 A.D.), *Chong Xi Xin Ding Tiao Zhi* (*Chong Xi Newly Enacted Regulations*), which consisted of five hundred and forty seven

---

[401]"Xing Fa Zhi" (The Record of the Criminal Law) in *Liao Shi* (*The History of Liao Dynasty*).

[402]"Ye Lv Duo Zhe Fu Di Yelv Tu lv Bu Zhuan" (The Biography of Yelv Tulvbu, Yelv Duozhe's Brother) in *Liao Shi* (*The History of Liao Dynasty*).

[403]"Han Zhi Gu Zhuan" (The Biography of Han Zhigu) in *Liao Shi* (*The History of Liao Dynasty*).

[404]"Xing Fa Zhi" (The Record of the Criminal Law) in *Liao Shi* (*The History of Liao Dynasty*).

[405]"Sheng Zong Ji" (The Record of Emperor Shengzong) in *Qi Dan Guo Zhi* (*The Record of Qidan*).

articles, was made by Emperor Xingzong following the legal system of the Tang Dynasty. The law was the basic code of the Liao Dynasty, in which the four forms of punishment, i.e. "Si" (death penalty), "Liu" (exile), "Tu" (imprisonment), and "Zhang" (flogging with heavy sticks) were established. "Ba Yi" (The Eight Deliberations) and "Ba Zong" (eight indulgence) were also included in the law to protect the interests of the aristocrats and bureaucrats. As it were, from then on, although some characteristics of the slavery law were still preserved in the law of the Liao Dynasty, yet as far as its basic nature was concerned, it was a feudal law. According to historical records, "laws were made by (Yelv) Shucheng, and it was forbidden for the officials to act in collusion with each other to play tricks,"[406] which had fully shown its status in the legislative history of the Liao Dynasty.

In the 6th year of Qingning during the reign of Emperor Daozong (1060 A.D.), *Qing Ning Tiao Zhi* (*Qing Ning Regulation*) was enacted. In the 6th year of Xianyong, *Xian Yong Chong Xiu Tiao Zhi* (*Newly Revised Regulations in the Reign of Xian Yong*), which consisted of seven hundred and eighty nine articles, was issued on the basis of *Chong Xi Tiao Zhi* (*Chong Xi Regulation*) because it was believed that although "Khitan and Han people differ in customs, the same national law shall be implemented."[407] So all the laws and decrees of the Han people were included in the law and were generally applied to both the Khitan and Han people, by which the laws of the north and south tended to be unified. *Xian Yong Chong Xiu Tiao Zhi* (*Newly Revised Regulations in the Reign of Xian Yong*) was the most comprehensive code of the Liao Dynasty, which was made on the basis of the summary of legislative experiences of the previous dynasties. Afterward, the law was amended many times, so there were as many as 1400 articles in the law, which had led to the situation where "the decrees are so complicated that it is not only difficult for the officials to fully understand them, but also difficult for the common people to know what to do to, so they were involved in more criminal acts. Besides it also provided the officials with more opportunities to collude with each other in malpractices."[408] Therefore, in the 5th year of Da'an (1089 A.D.), an imperial edict was issued by Emperor Daozong to "restore the old law," namely, to continue to apply *Chong Xi Tiao Zhi* (*Chong Xi Regulation*).

All the codes that were made in the Liao Dynasty were lost. So based on the records in *Liao Shi* (*The History of Liao Dynasty*), it can be seen that its legal form is mainly "Zhi Tiao" (article) and "Tiao Zhi" (regulation), supplemented by "Lv" (criminal law), "Ling" (decree), "Li" (precedent), etc., which to a certain extent reflected the rapid progress of legal civilization, and it even exerted great influence on *Yuan Dian Zhang* (*Statutes of Yuan Dynasty*) and *Lv Li* (*Laws and Precedents*) in the Ming and Qing dynasties. Additionally, based on the criminal punishments and relevant events, one can see the historical development from "implementing

---

[406] "Ye Lv Shu Cheng Zhuan" (The Biography of Yelv Shucheng) in *Liao Shi* (*The History of Liao Dynasty*).

[407] "Xing Fa Zhi" (The Record of the Criminal Law) in *Liao Shi* (*The History of Liao Dynasty*).

[408] "Xing Fa Zhi" (The Record of the Criminal Law) in *Liao Shi* (*The History of Liao Dynasty*).

different legal systems for the minorities and Han people" to "implementing the same national laws without exception."

The basic constitution of the legal system in the Liao Dynasty is the written criminal law, which is not only the most important achievement of the Liao Dynasty but also a reflection of what is generally occurring at the initial stage of development of legal civilization. Around the founding of the state, there were only two felonies, i.e., "Mou Pan" (plotting rebellion or plotting to endanger the country) and "Dao Qie" (theft). With the expansion of territory, the development of the economy and politics and the complication of inter-class relationship, various criminal acts increased. The main crimes recorded in *Shi Li* (*Cases*) are as follows:

Taking bribes by officials, injustice in executing law, loose defense, delaying in going to official posts, leakage of the palace secrets, false accusation, and so on.

Retreating in battles, failing to prepare for war, making mistakes in dispatching troops, taking in spies, unlawfully owning weapons and so on.

Illegal levying of tax, arbitrary assigning of corvee, smuggling salt, illegal trading with foreign countries and so on. According to the law of Liao Dynasty, it was forbidden to trade with other countries in copper cash, iron, books, sheep and horses without authorization; or else the violators should be severely punished. Moreover, the person who carried ten *guan* of money out of Nanjing (now Beijing) would be executed.

Mob fighting, murder, human trafficking, document forgery, raping and so on. Especially in the 12th year of Tonghe (994 A.D.), an imperial edict was issued by Emperor Shengzong, in which it was stipulated that "the Khitans who have committed the crime of 'Shi E' (The Ten Abominations) shall be punished according to the criminal law of the Han nationality".[409] So "Shi E" (The Ten Abominations) which were recorded in the criminal laws of Sui and Tang dynasties were completely adopted in Liao Dynasty, which had reflected the function of law in the maintenance of the monarchical and patriarchal power.

The applicable principles of the criminal law had fully reflected the feature of the criminal law of the Liao Dynasty, as well as the progress which they have made on the basis of national amalgamation and social development. Because different legal systems were applied to small minorities and the Han nationality and small minorities were regarded as superior to the Han nationality, different punishments were enforced for the same crime in early Liao Dynasty. After the reform carried out by emperors Shengzong and Daozong, the system of applying different criminal laws to different nationalities was basically changed. Su Zhe, who once had served as an envoy to Liao dynasty to take an on-the-spot investigation, had submitted a memorial to the emperor after returning to Song dynasty: "It has been a long time that in the northern regime Khitans are leniently treated, while the Han people are maltreated. We have visited the dukes and marquises, and it shows that this problem only exists in the cases involving the quarrelling and fighting of the ordinary people. As to the influential or the rich Han families, there are no such problems."[410] Therefore, it is because of the reduction of national contradiction that has promoted the social development and progress of legal civilization.

---

[409]"Sheng Zong Ji" (The Record of Emperor Shengzong) in *Liao Shi* (*The History of Liao Dynasty*) (Book 4).

[410]Su Zhe (Song Dynasty), *Luan Cheng Ji* (*The Anthology of Luancheng*), Vol. 43.

As another example, before the reign of Emperor Shengzong, slaveholders were not only allowed to enslave or punish slaves but to kill them randomly. In the 20th year of Tonghe (1006 A.D.), an imperial edict was issued by Emperor Shengzong, and it was stipulated that "where slaves or 'Nu Bi' (slave girls and maidservants) deserve to to be punished by death penalty, they shall all be handled by 'You Si' (official), and it is forbidden for their owners to kill them without authorization."[411] Meanwhile, slaveholders were allowed to enforce other punishments on slaves. So the policy of allowing the masters to randomly kill their slaves and "Nu Bi" (the slave girls and maidservants) was changed and they were forbidden to do so anymore without authorization, which had fully reflected that a new relationship was established in the development from slavery to feudal society. It was stipulated previously in the laws of Tang and Song dynasties that "slaves and 'Nu Bi' (the slave girls and maidservants) are equivalent to livestock", but this law was different, because it had reflected that the fundamental rights of slaves and "Nu Bi" (the slave girls and maidservants), such as the personal rights and the rights to make a living were completely protected.

As for the penalty system, before the founding of the Liao Dynasty, those who committed felonies in Qidan (Khitan) tribes were usually punished by death penalty, "Ji Mo" (the cancelation of a household registration), confiscation of the property, and serving as slaves. According to the unwritten law of "Ji Mo" (the cancelation of a household registration) of the Qidan (Khitan) nationality, criminals who were punished by "Ji Mo" (the cancelation of a household registration) should serve as household slaves of royal families and aristocrats without personal freedom.

Furthermore, some unique punishments were included, such as "Tou Ya" (cliff jumping), wherein a rebellious aristocrat should jump off a cliff to die; "Sheng Cuo" (bury alive), which is a severe punishment on rebels; "She Gui Jian," wherein criminals who committed a capital crime should be shot dead by arrow blizzard or be hit by wooden sword. During the reign of Emperor Taizong, if a minister had committed a crime that was not punishable by death penalty, he would be hit on the back with a wooden sword (which had a flat side and a ridgy side) or be hit with an iron bud (forge wrought iron into iron bud with a three-*chi*-length willow shank). The thieves and smugglers would be flogged for five to seven strokes or be hit by sandbags. Under the brutal ruling of Emperor Muzong, sandbags with wooden handles were made with animal skins and half a liter of sand, so criminals would be beaten with it for fewer than five hundred strokes. For those who refused to admit the crimes that they had committed, they would be punished by "Bian Luo," that is, "Bian" (whipping) and "Luo" (put hot iron on the flesh), and those who should be punished by "Luo" (put hot iron on the flesh) for thirty times would be punished by "Bian" (whipping) for three hundred strokes; those who should be punished by "Luo" (put hot iron on the flesh) for fifty times would be punished by "Bian" (whipping) for five hundred strokes.

It is worth mentioning that during the reign of Emperor Shengzong, "Xing Ming" (law), which was used in the feudal codes of the Han nationality, began to be adopted

---

[411] "Xing Fa Zhi" (The Record of the Criminal Law) in *Liao Shi* (*The History of Liao Dynasty*).

officially. In *Chong Xi Xin Ding Tiao Zhi* (*Chong Xi Newly Enacted Regulations*), which was enacted during the reign of Emperor Xingzong, "Xing Ming" (law) was classified into four categories, i.e., "Si" (death penalty), "Liu" (exile), "Zhang" (flogging with heavy sticks), and "Tu" (imprisonment). "Si" (death penalty) included "Jiao" (hanging), "Zhan" (beheading), "Ling Chi" (the punishment of dismemberment and lingering death), and "Zu Zhu" (killing of the whole clan of a criminal); "Liu" (exile) included being exiled to a border town or to an outbound remote place, with the additional punishment of "Qing" (to tattoo on the face); "Zhang" (flogging with heavy sticks) included the punishment of beating with a sandbag, wooden sword, iron bud, etc.; "Tu" (imprisonment) included life imprisonment, five years' imprisonment, one-and-a-half years of imprisonment, etc. Late in the Liao Dynasty, Emperor Tianzuo restored "Tou Ya" (cliff jumping) and other death penalties because of the numerous peasant uprisings. In brief, the punishment of the Liao Dynasty was cruel and cumbersome, just as was recorded in "Xing Fa Zhi" (The Record of the Criminal Law) in *Liao Shi* (*The History of Liao Dynasty*): "there are many punishments which are rarely used and which are without fixed patterns, so it is hard to record all of them."

As for the judicial system, "Jue Yu Guan" (official in charge of lawsuit settlement), the elder who dealt with tribal affairs before the founding of the country, was endowed with certain judicial power. During the reign of Taizu, *Jue Yu Fa* (*Law on Lawsuits Settlement*) was enacted and full-time judicial officials called "Yi Li Bi" were appointed. Moreover, "Yi Li Bi Yuan" (court) was established by Emperor Taizong, and many other subordinate officials were appointed to be in charge of the judiciary. Meanwhile, "Bing Xing Fang" (criminal office), which was in charge of the judiciary, was also set up in "Bei Shu Mi Yuan" (North Privy Council) and "Nan Shu Mi Yuan" (South Privy Council), which were in charge of the military and political affairs of the Khitan and Han people, respectively. The head of "Shu Mi Yuan" (Privy Council) could also settle the cases by himself. If an aristocrat had violated the law, the case should be heard by the local government official first, then be sent to "Bei Shu Mi Yuan" (North Privy Council) and "Nan Shu Mi Yuan" (South Privy Council) for reviewing, and finally be submitted to the imperial court for final decision. In the 12th year of Tonghe during the reign of Emperor Shengzong (994 A. D.), judicial offices and procuratorial organs such as "Da Li Si" (The Bureau of Judicial Review), "Xing Bu" (The Department of Punishment), "Yu Shi Tai" (The Censorate), and so on were set up. To overcome the malpractice of enforcing different punishments on the Khitan and Han people for the same crime, in the 6th year of Taiping (1026 A.D.), an imperial edict was issued: "From now on, if the aristocrats are prosecuted, whether minor or serious crimes, the cases shall be heard by the local government offices, and then be sent to "Bei Shu Mi Yuan" (North Privy Council) and "Nan Shu Mi Yuan" (South Privy Council) for reviewing."[412] So Han officials had the rights to hear cases of Khitans and to pass sentences according to law. During the reign of Emperor Xingzong, a memorial was submitted to the

---

[412]"Xing Fa Zhi" (The Record of the Criminal Law) in *Liao Shi* (*The History of Liao Dynasty*).

emperor by the uncle of the emperor, named Yelv Chongyuan: "Many unjust sentences are made because Han officials are forbidden to interrogate prisoners. So I propose that 'Jing Xun Shi' (inspector) of Qidan (Khitan) nationality should be established in 'Wu Jing' (five cities in ancient China, including Shangjing, Dongjing, Zhongjing, Nanjing and Xijing) respectively."[413] Thereafter, if Khitans had violated the law, they should be dealt with by "Jing Xun Shi" (inspector) of "Wu Jing." But the post of "Jing Xun Shi" (inspector) and their subordinates were still mostly held by Han officials, and "the cases involving the four nationalities (Qidan, Han, Bohai and Xi) shall all be settled according to the laws of Han nationality."[414] In summary, the rulers of the Liao Dynasty had made a positive contribution to the elimination of the national misunderstanding in legislation and judicature in the country, so the historical experience that they provided is well worth our attention.

In the areas lived by the Han people, it was still the officials of "Zhou" (subprefecture) and "Xian" (county) who were in charge of the judicial affairs concurrently.

To make direct appeal easier, "Zhong Yuan" (Bell Court) was established during the reign of Taizu, by which people could toll the bell to lodge a complaint, on the basis of which "Deng Wen Gu Yuan" (petitioning agency) and "Gui Yuan" (ancient government office in charge of complaints and appeal) were set up during the reign of Emperor Shengzong. If a person had no one to complain about his injustice, he was allowed to sue in "Yu Shi Tai" (The Censorate), where his complaints would be reviewed by officials. Moreover, officials were sent by Emperor Shengzong to various regions to handle the backlog of cases, and some of the major ones would be settled according to the emperor's own will. Even if the aristocrats and bureaucrats had broken the law, they could still enjoy legal privileges stipulated in "Ba Yi (The Eight Deliberations), "Ba Zong" (eight indulgence), as well as the laws about "Shu Zui" (atonement). For example, if the senior officials had broken the law when on duty or if people over seventy years old or below fifteen years old had committed crimes, they could atone for their crimes by paying ransom money.

Based on all this, so the legal system of the Liao Dynasty had exerted an important influence on the newly emerged Jin Dynasty.

8.8.2 The Legal System of Western Xia Dynasty

Western Xia Dynasty was a regime founded mainly by the Dangxiang nationality. From the Later Tang Dynasty to the Northern Song Dynasty, Dangxiang people with the surname of Tuoba had governed the five "Zhou" (subprefecture) in the northern

---

[413]"Ye Lv Chong Yuan Zhuan" (The Biography of Yelv Chongyuan) in "Ni Chen Zhuan" (The Biography of Traitors) (Part 1) in *Liao Shi* (*The History of Liao Dynasty*).

[414]Yu Jing (Song Dynasty), "Qi Dan Guan Yi" (Official Etiquette of Qidan) in *Wu Xi Ji* (*The Anthology of Wuxi*), Vol. 18.

territories as "Jie Du Shi" (military governor) of the Central Plain Dynasty. So they gradually strengthened the power and became a local authority that separated itself from the other districts. In the process of cultural exchange with the Han nationality, the political, legal, and military systems of the Song Dynasty were basically followed in the Western Xia Dynasty.

In October of the 1st year of Baoyuan (1038 A.D.) in the Song Dynasty, the chieftain of the Dangxiang nationality named Li Yuanhao ascended the throne and founded Da Xia Dynasty, mainly consisting of the Dangxiang nationality, which was called Xi Xia Dynasty in history. So it coexisted with the Southern Song and Jin dynasties and lasted for one hundred and ninety years. It was finally conquered by the Yuan Dynasty.

The administrative system of the Western Xia Dynasty was set up by imitating that of the Northern Song Dynasty, so the central administrative organs such as "Zhong Shu Sheng" (the supreme organization in charge of state affairs), "Shu Mi Yuan" (Privy Council), "San Si" (the three departments), "Yu Shi Tai" (The Censorate), "Nong Yong Si" (ancient office in charge of agriculture), "Qun Mu Si" (ancient office in charge of animal husbandry), "Guan Ji Si" (the department of official statistics), "Shou Na Si" (ancient office in charge of taxation), "Mo Kan Si" (ancient office in charge of inspection), "Fei Long Yuan" (ancient office in charge of imperial horse breeding), "Wen Si Yuan" (ancient office in charge of manufacture), "Fan Xue" (ancient office in charge of minority studies), "Han Xue" (ancient office in charge of Han nationality studies) were all established. "Fan Xue" and "Han Xue" were the educational institutions that teach the royal family and cultivate bureaucrats. "Shang Shu Sheng" (The Department of Secretary) was established as the highest administrative organ.

As for the local administrative system of the Western Xia Dynasty, a two-level system, namely, the system of "Zhou" (subprefecture) and "Xian" (county), was established. Local official positions, including "Zhou Zhu" (governor), "Tong Pan" (official in charge of agriculture under prefecture), "Zheng Ting" (supervisor), "Du An" (police), etc., were appointed by the central government. "Jun" (prefecture) and "Fu" (ancient administrative district between province and county) were established in political centers and important military forts.

For the appointment of government officials in the Western Xia Dynasty, there was no distinction between the Dangxiang and Han people. As was recorded in "Xia Guo Zhuan" (The Historical Records of State of Western Xia) in *Song Shi* (*The History of Song Dynasty*), "the official posts below 'Zhong Shu Ling' (head of the secretariat), 'Zai Xing' (the prime minister), 'Shu Shi' (the Military Affairs Commissioner), 'Da Fu' (senior officials in ancient China), 'Shi Zhong' (assistant officers) and 'Tai Wei' (the minister of defense) can be held by both minorities and the Han people." But military official posts were mostly held by the Dangxiang people.

As to the legal system, there was no written law in the early Dangxiang clan society, as was described in the records that "military spirits were encouraged, and there were no decrees about tax and corvée." So common law had played a very important role for the adjustment of the society. With the establishment of the state of Western Xia, the legal system also reached a new level of development.

After the founding of the state, its first emperor, Li Yuanhao, deeply influenced by Confucian culture, once studied the works of *Han Lv* (*Han Code*). So far, although no laws that were enacted at the beginning of the Western Xia Dynasty have been discovered, in the light of the existing volumes of codes written in the middle and later period of the Western Xia Dynasty, we can infer that the legal system was already well established at the beginning of the Western Xia Dynasty.

Many official documents of the Western Xia Dynasty were discovered in the early twentieth century, such as the military code, *Zhen Guan Zhi Jing Tong* (*Codes in Zhenguan Period*), issued in the years of Zhenguan during the reign of Emperor Chongzong; *Tian Sheng Gai Jiu Xin Ding Lv Ling* (*New Laws and Orders of Tiansheng Period*), issued in the years of Tiansheng during the reign of Emperor Renzong; *Xin Fa* (*New Law*) issued in the 5th year of Guangding during the reign of Emperor Shenzong (1215 A.D.); and so on, among which the most representative one was *Tian Sheng Gai Jiu Xin Ding Lv Ling* (*New Laws and Orders of Tiansheng Period*).

Tiansheng was the reign title of Emperor Renzong of the Western Xia Dynasty, and it was a time of great prosperity in history. The systematic character and completeness of *Tian Sheng Gai Jiu Xin Ding Lv Ling* (*New Laws and Orders of Tiansheng Period*) showed that it was the product of a prosperous and flourishing age. The title "Xin Jiu Gai Ding" (a revised one) undoubtedly means that it is a revision of the original statutes and orders.

In *Tian Sheng Gai Jiu Xin Ding Lv Ling* (*New Laws and Orders of Tiansheng Period*), which altogether consisted of 20 volumes, 150 categories, and 1460 articles, the layout and compilation style of "Yi Xing Wei Zhu" (priority is given to penalties) and "Zhu Fa He Ti" (the integration of various laws) were adopted. Except for some missing articles in several volumes, the rest was left intact. The main contents of each volume are as follows: volume one, "Shi E" (The Ten Abominations); volume two, "Ba Yi" (The Eight Deliberations) and the penalty reduction for the old, the young, and the seriously sick people; volume three, 'Dao Qie' (theft) and 'Bu Dao' (arresting), pawn, and loan; volume four, frontier patroling and defending against foreign invasion; volume five, weapons; volume six, inspection of military status and dispatching of military expedition; volume seven, surrender and defection of the small minorities; volume eight, arson, fighting against each other, rape, and marriage; volume nine, administration of justice, prison, and litigation; volume ten, official ranks, appointment, and transferring; volume eleven, intercourse of envoys, monks, and temples and distribution of property; volume twelve, safeguarding of the palace and keeping secret; volume thirteen, snitching and courier; volume fourteen, manslaughter, accidental injury, and fighting; volume fifteen, reclaiming wasteland, trenching, bridge repairing, tribute of grain, and paying tax; volume sixteen, land rent and lease; volume seventeen, granary supply and weights and measures; volume eighteen, salt affairs and trade tax; volume nineteen, livestock rearing; volume twenty, crime and punishment.

In "Song Lv Biao" (On Law) in *Tian Sheng Gai Jiu Xin Ding Lv Ling* (*New Laws and Orders of Tiansheng Period*), the tenet of the law revision was stated:

> The all-mighty emperor would like to follow the great achievements of our ancestors and to act in accordance with the ancient morality. In order to fully show the outstanding ability of our deceased emperors, I, as well as other officials have had discussions together and made a comparison of the old and new statutes and decrees. If there are doubtful points, we have adopted the commonly used ones by following the public opinion. So there are twenty volumes in total. According to the imperial order, the work is entitled *Tian Sheng Gai Jiu Xin Ding Lv Ling* (*New Laws and Orders of Tiansheng Period*). The work is delicate and well designed, so it is dedicated to His Majesty. According to the imperial instruction, the new statutes and decrees shall be issued nationwide to be carried out.

In the five categories in volume ten of *Tian Sheng Gai Jiu Xin Ding Lv Ling* (*New Laws and Orders of Tiansheng Period*), the official ranks and names of government organizations of the Western Xia Dynasty were listed in detail. The government organs consisted of five "Si" (office), namely, "Shang" (first rank), "Ci" (second rank), "Zhong" (secondary), "Xia" (low rank), and "Mo" (the lowest rank), and various numbers of subordinate offices were established in each "Si" (office). For example, the "Si" (office) of "Shang" (first rank) included "Zhong Shu" (the prime minister) and "Shu Mi" (the Military Affairs Commissioner); the "Si" (office) of "Ci" (second rank) included seventeen subordinate offices in total, namely, "Dian Qian Si" (the Palace Command), "Yu Shi" (the censor), "Zhong Xing Fu" (the capital of Xi Xia), "San Si" (the three departments), "Seng Zhong Gong De Si" (office of Buddhist affairs), "Chu Jia Gong De Si" (office of Taoist affairs), and others; the "Si" (office) of "Zhong" (secondary) included twenty six offices, such as "Da Heng Li Yuan" (the office in charge of calendar compilation), "Du Zhuan Yun Si" (Office of Transportation), "Chen Gao Si" (office of judicial affairs), "Du Mo Kan Si" (ancient office in charge of inspection), "Shen Xing Si" (office of criminal affairs), etc.; the "Si" (office) of "Xia" (low rank) and "Mo" (the lowest rank) also included dozens of other central and local organs. There were five organs that were not included in the five levels of "Si" (office), e.g., "Mi Shu Jian" (the official in charge of the national collection and compilation work) and "Fan Han Da Xue Yuan" (Academy of Minority and Han Nationality). In *Tian Sheng Gai Jiu Xin Ding Lv Ling* (*New Laws and Orders of Tiansheng Period*), the official position and the relevant number of officials in each office were also stipulated, and some were similar to the contents in "Zhi Guan Zhi" (Record of State Officials) in the officially written history books. Moreover, the number of official positions, such as "Zheng" (director), "Fu" (deputy), "Tong," "Pan" (both ancient official titles), and "Cheng Zhi" (advisor of the emperor), was explicitly stipulated. For example, there were six principal official positions in "Zhong Shu" (the supreme organization in charge of state affairs), including four "Zhong Shu" (the prime minister), one "Fu Zhong Shu" (deputy prime minister), and one "Tong Zhong Shu" (the prime minister). In addition, eight principal officials and eight "Cheng Zhi" (advisor of the emperor) were appointed in "Zhong Xing Fu" (the capital of Xi Xia) and "Dian Qian Si" (the Palace Command); four principal officials and four "Cheng Zhi" (advisor of the emperor) were appointed in "Xuan Hui Yuan" (an institution in charge of palace affairs in ancient China), "Huang Cheng Si" (spy agency), and "Gui Xia Si" (judicial office). Furthermore, specialized provisions were also made, in which the specification and weight of seals of each office were stipulated in detail. The seals were divided into four types: pure gold, pure silver, silver-clad copper, and copper. So from the crown prince to "Zhong Shu" (the prime minister), "Shu Mi" (the Military Affairs Commissioner), and junior officials, the weight of seals was reduced respectively, i.e., from one hundred *liang* to nine *liang* of silver in variety.

Apart from the bureaucratic organizations, in *Tian Sheng Gai Jiu Xin Ding Lv Ling* (*New Laws and Orders of Tiansheng Period*), the following are also stipulated in detail: the transferring of officials "after three years of service regardless of their ranks"; the provisions on the punishment of "the officials like 'Cheng Zhi' (advisor of the emperor), 'Xi Pan' (judge), 'Du An' (police), 'An Tou' (judicial official), etc. who did not go to or delayed in taking their appointed posts"; and provisions on the punishment of "those who deliver false imperial decrees or pretend to be officials." In "Shi Lai Wang Men" (the category of intercourse of envoys), it was also stipulated that "when officials of our country serve as envoys abroad, they are forbidden to bring more goods or people with them without permission; otherwise, they shall be sentenced to one year's imprisonment after they arrived in foreign countries with the goods or people."

In conclusion, provisions about the duties of officials in *Tian Sheng Gai Jiu Xin Ding Lv Ling* (*New Laws and Orders of Tiansheng Period*) were as detailed as those in the criminal laws of the Tang and Song dynasties, which is praiseworthy for a dynasty founded by minorities living in border regions.

Although *Tian Sheng Gai Jiu Xin Ding Lv Ling* (*New Laws and Orders of Tiansheng Period*) (*Tian Sheng Lv Ling* for short) was mainly about criminal punishment, it was in fact a comprehensive code with the integration of many laws, among which there were also contents of civil and economic laws, although they were relatively incomplete. In "Zhu Di Men" (the category of land tenancy), private land was allowed to be sold, but it was forbidden to buy "adjacent land" by force; otherwise, "the common people shall be punished by 'Zhang' (flogging with heavy sticks) for thirteen strokes, while the officials shall be imposed with a fine of a horse with the bribery confiscated," which showed that individual rights of land ownership were recognized by law and "Di Ce" (land license) was regarded as evidence of land ownership. Additionally, it was forbidden to "expand one's own land by occupying others' and to illegally steal the crops from the neighboring land." Those who had illegally occupied others' land would be punished one level lighter than that for robbery, according to the size of the area and the price of the land, and those who had stolen crops from a neighboring land would be punished for the crime of robbery according to an estimated price.

Existing title deeds for houses in the Western Xia Dynasty show that landholders had the right to sell their own land. The title deed is as follows:

In the 22nd year of Tiansheng in Western Xia Dynasty (1170 A.D.), the title deed of selling the house by a widow Yehe Shibao and her children (translated from the language of Western Xia):

In the 22nd year of Tiansheng, the drafter, widow Yehe Zhibaoyin, is to sell her stretch of waste land that is used to keep the animals, along with three huts and two trees to the woman named Yehe willingly. The agreed price is two grown-up camels, one two-humped camel, one Xinbu camel and four camels in total. Hereafter, no one shall bother about this land, or else Baoyin shall take full responsibility. If anyone goes back on her decision, she shall be found guilty in accordance with the decrees. Anyone who refuses to obey shall have thirty *hu* of wheat confiscated, and both parties shall carry out the deed once it is signed. It is located near "Si Tang" (hall) covering an area of twenty two *mu*. It borders Yehe Huigusheng on the north, Yehe Xie on the east and south, and Liangweimingshan Mountain to the west.

The drafter of the deed: Yehe Zhibaoyin
The son of the drafter who discussed together: Moluo Gezhang
The son of the drafter who discussed together: Moluo Koubian
Witness: Yehe Sheng ☐ (signature)
Liang Gouren (signature)☐ He Yisheng (signature)

If "someone is incapable of tilling the land and abandons it, after three years..., if anyone is willing to cultivate it, he shall ask for permission from 'Zhuan Yun Si' (Office of Transportation) ... and after registration, he is allowed to till the land"; that is, he would obtain ownership.

According to "Shou Na Zu Men (The Category of Rent Collection) in *Tian Sheng Lv Ling* (*New Laws and Orders of Tiansheng Period*), the rent was mainly paid with cereals and rice every December, but the amount should be registered by "Zhuan Yun Si" (Office of Transportation).

As for the civil juristic acts of sale and pawn, the interests of the first purchaser and pawner were protected by law. For example, "for houses, farmland, people, objects, etc., if the two buyers all want to buy, their order of priority should be taken into consideration; the first buyer shall get the staff and the money of the late-comers shall be returned." "If someone has pawned houses or land to another person, or has not redeemed them, the property shall not be sold to others. But if the pawnee sells them illegally, he shall be imposed with a fine of a horse if he is an official; or he shall be punished by 'Chi' (flogging with light sticks) for thirteen strokes if he is a common people. If the pawnee gives both the principal and the interest to the pawner, he is allowed to sell the staff."

Apart from real estate, the sharing of jointly owned personal property and livestock should be permitted by the heads of the household. If "the sons and grandsons, brothers, wife, or daughters-in-law share them at will without asking for permission, they shall be punished according to the amount they have actually shared with no compensation."

In *Tian Sheng Gai Jiu Xin Ding Lv Ling* (*New Laws and Orders of Tiansheng Period*), "Cui Suo Zhai Li Men" (The Category of Pressing for Payment of Debt) was also especially included. "So the people in the country were permitted to lend government or private money. For one *min*, the interest should be less than five *qian*; for one *hu*, the interest should be less than one *hu*." If the borrower did not return the borrowed money when it was due, the lender would have the right to reclaim the payment or he could sue. Whether official or common people, the act of default should be punished. "For the loans less than ten *min* of money, the officials shall be imposed with a fine of five *min*, while the common people shall be punished by 'Chi' (flogging with light sticks) for thirteen strokes. For the loans more than ten *min*, the officials shall be imposed with a fine of a horse, while the common people shall be punished by 'Chi' (flogging with light sticks) for thirteen strokes." It was also allowed to pay the debt by working as laborers, and "the number of days and measuring method of labor cost for men and women are the same as those for the compensation of the crime of robbery." The existing "deed for cereal lending" in the Western Xia Dynasty is as follows:

> In the 1st year of Guangding (1211 A.D.) is Western Xia Dynasty, the cereal lending deed of Yehe Xiaogoushan (translated from the language of Western Xia):
> On the 26th of April of the 1st year of Guangding, the drafter Yehe Xiaogoushan borrows three *dan* of cereals from Yi'e'a Jin'gangmao, the capital plus interest being four *dan* and five *dou*, in exchange for a black she-ass, a Quanchi camel, a donkey foal and so on. Liang Yuebao, his wife Nan Gongshan and others are guarantors. The deed is due on the 1st of August of the same year. If the pawner fails to return the cereals, he is willing to give up his pawned livestock.
> Deed drafter: Xiaogoushan
> Guarantor: Liang Yuebao
> Guarantor: Wife, Nan Gongshan
> Guarantor: □ Lifuchengsheng
> Guarantor: Kang Maosheng
> Notary: EElayuequan
> Moluoxitie
> □□□ (signature)
> Ba □(signature)

In "Dang Pu Men" (The Category of Pawnshop), the relationship of the rights and responsibilities of "the possessor and the shopkeeper" was provided. If the pawner failed to redeem the pawnage when it was due, the pawnee shall not be allowed to sell them off at will. But if the pawnee sold the pawnage illegally, for the worth of over ten *min* of money, the pawnee would be punished by one year's imprisonment.

Among the existing deeds of the Western Xia Dynasty, wheat deed was also found, and the content is as follows:

> In the 11th year of Tianqing in Western Xia Dynasty, the wheat deed of Wunvlangsu:
> On the 3rd of May of the 11th year of Tianqing, the deed drafter Wunvlangsu pawns a fur coat in exchange for five *dou* of barley at an interest rate of 3% and five *dou* of wheat at an interest rate of 4%. The total amount of principal and interest is one *dan* three *dou* five *sheng*. The pawn is due on the 1st of August. If the pawner does not redeem her coat on time, the pawnee can sell it at will.
> Deed drafter: Wunvlangsu (signature)
> Witness: Ejing□□(signature)

As to marriage, it was stipulated in "Wei Hun Men" (The Category of Marriage) in *Tian Sheng Gai Jiu Xin Ding Lv Ling* (*New Laws and Orders of Tiansheng Period*) that the conditions for marriage included the dictates of parents, the promise of matchmakers, and the age limit of the bride (usually above thirteen years old). In addition, the value of dowry was especially emphasized. If the family of the bridegroom was unable to afford the dowry, the bridegroom could serve as a free laborer in the family of the bride for three years; if the two parties were willing to get married, they would be permitted to do so after three years of service. Moreover, different requirements for the varieties and quantity of dowry were stipulated in different statutes. The dowry that "Zai Xiang" (the prime minister), princes, and dignitaries prepared "shall be no more than three hundred categories," and camels, horses, clothes, decoration, gold and animal skin, etc. should be no more than one hundred and fifty categories. The dowry that the bureaucrats below princes prepared "shall be not more than two hundred categories," and camels, horses, clothes, decoration, gold and animal skin, etc. should be no more than one hundred categories. For the common people, the dowry should be limited to "one hundred categories," and other things should be no more than twenty categories. The dowry of the family of the bride, such as "Gai Zhang" (cloth, silk, and velvet hung up to shelter from the outside), was also stipulated according to their social status.

According to the custom of marriage of the Dangxiang nationality, the system of polygamy was adopted. But except for titles, there was no difference between the legal wife and concubines. According to law, the first woman whom a man married was regarded as the legal wife, while the later ones were the concubines.

In the aspect of marriage taboos, the laws of the Tang Dynasty were generally followed. Those who married people with the same surnames would be sentenced to three years of imprisonment, which was relatively severer than *Tang Lv* (*Tang Code*) because the punishment in *Tang Lv* (*Tang Code*) was two years of imprisonment.

For divorce, the article of "Qi Chu" (seven reasons to repudiate the wife: "being unfilial to parents-in-law," "failing to bear a male offspring," "being lascivious," "being jealous," "having severe illness," "gossiping," and "committing theft") was basically followed, but there was no punishment for the wife's leaving her husband without permission. According to *Tang Lv* (*Tang Code*), wives or concubines who deserted their husbands should be sentenced to two years of imprisonment, and the remarried ones under this condition should be punished two levels severer. Because there were many wars in Western Xia Dynasty, if the husband became a captive or if they had children, they were allowed to divorce after ten years; if they had no children, they were allowed to divorce after five years. For those unmarried, the engagement would become invalid after three years.

As for the economic legislation of the Western Xia Dynasty, the traditional system of "Jin Que Zhi Du" (the system of state monopoly for some important goods) was adopted. Moreover, the prohibition against alcoholic drinks was especially stressed. According to law, "it is forbidden to make wine privately; or else the violator would be punished by 'Chi' (flogging with light sticks) for thirteen strokes for less than one *min* of wine, and the accessories would be punished by 'Chi' (flogging with light sticks) for ten strokes . . . If over twenty *min* of wine, the violator will be punished by life imprisonment and the accessories will be punished by twelve years of imprisonment; if the purchasers know of the illegal trade, he shall be punished one level lighter than that for the accessories; if the purchasers are innocent, he shall be exempted from punishment." Moreover, the informers would be awarded. As for salt trading, there was no explicit prohibition, but it was stipulated that it was forbidden for salt dealers "to evade tax. . ., those violators will be punished for the crime of robbery."

Meanwhile, the law on market management was mainly about the conversion of old and new regulations on weights and measures and the confirmation and endorsement of relevant standards. Provisions on the taxation of transactions involving commodity goods, as well as tax evasion, were also stipulated in detail.

In "Ta Guo Mai Mai Men" (The Category of Overseas Trade) in *Tian Sheng Gai Jiu Xin Ding Lv Ling* (*New Laws and Orders of Tiansheng Period*), the legal norm for overseas trade was also stipulated. The people who did business abroad should "have the official and private goods separately sold without mixing them up." "If a person secretly replaced the high quality official goods with the low quality private goods, he shall be sentenced to two years of imprisonment." Moreover, the amount of official goods should be recorded and registered before the sale, and the money earned in the sale and the amount, quality, and variety of the official goods should be examined and registered. If any losses were caused to the government due to the replacement, "the violator shall be punished for the crime of robbery based on the profit made in the illegal trade"; if the person had illegally raised the price at will, "he shall be punished for the crime of 'Zuo Zang' (embezzlement)." Because of the close trade relationship with Song and Jin dynasties, relatively detailed laws were made on overseas trade in Western Xia dynasty.

With the progress of the society and after adoption of the legal civilization of Han nationality, "He Duan Guan" (judge) was begun to be appointed to adjudicate the disputes in the Western Xia Dynasty after the Dangxiang people migrated inland. So it was recorded by Zeng Gong in *Long Ping Ji* (*Collections of Long Ping*) that "eloquent people were appointed by 'Fan Zu' (the small minorities) as 'He Duan Guan' (judge) to hear the cases. For homicides, thousands of ransom money should be paid." Moreover, judicial offices such as "Chen Gao Si" (Office of Prosecution) and "Shen Xing Si" (Office of Criminal Affairs), as well as criminal procedure and the statutory duties of judiciaries, were recorded in *Tian Sheng Gai Jiu Xin Ding Lv Ling* (*New Laws and Orders of Tiansheng Period*) and *Fan Han He Shi Zhang Zhong Zhu* (*Collections of Current Laws of Minority and Han Nationality*), compiled by Gulemaocai in the Western Xia Dynasty. For example, it was stipulated in "Zhu Si Pan Zui Men" (The Category of Making Convictions by Each Department) that "the cases shall be settled by the relevant departments within a certain period of time. For death penalty and life imprisonment, etc. the time limit is forty days; for penal servitude, the time limit is twenty days, and for other minor or major official business, the time limit is ten days. If a case has not been settled by the officials in time, 'Du An' (police), 'An Tou' (judicial official), 'Si Li' (clerk), and the other people involved shall be punished by 'Chi' (flogging with light sticks) for thirteen strokes, and officials shall be imposed with a fine of a horse. However, if the two parties concerned are both absent, the afore-mentioned time limit shall not be applied."

The cases that had already been settled should be reviewed by "Bian Jing Ci Shi" (prefectural governor in the frontier), "Jian Jun Si" (supervisor), and "Jing Lue Cha Jian" (inspector) in each season and should be carefully checked in accordance with law. "If there is any fault, it should be reviewed once again; if not, it should be put on the record and submitted for notification; if officials of each department have not reported the cases in each season or the officials of 'Zhong Shu' (the Prime Minister) and 'Shu Mi Ju' (Privy Council) have not checked it carefully, they shall all be punished for dereliction of duty."

"Inquisition by repeated torture" was allowed to be applied to get the testimony, and an official who had caused the death of the suspects by using torture legally were considered innocent, but if death was caused by illegally applying the punishment of "Zhang" (flogging with heavy sticks) or beyond the statutory times, the official should be sentenced to two years of imprisonment. If a case had not yet been finally settled, "'Yue Su' (overstepping indictment) is forbidden"; otherwise, "the officials who accept the case will be imposed with a fine of one horse and the common people shall be punished by 'Chi' (flogging with light sticks) for thirteen strokes." The judiciaries who took bribes by bending the law should be dismissed or punished.

In the existing *Gua Zhou Shen Pan Dang An Can Juan* (*The Remnant Volumes of the Judgment Files of Guazhou*) issued in the 2nd year of Tiancilishengguoqing (reign title), documentary records about the settlement of disputes over livestock and money among the folks in Guazhou, which occurred from February to June of that year, were recorded, which had clearly reflected the real situation of the civil actions during the Western Xia Dynasty. So undoubtedly, it was the result of the influence of the advanced system of civil litigation in the Song Dynasty.

In "Xing Yu Zhang Men" (The Category of Prison and Punishment) in *Tian Sheng Gai Jiu Xin Ding Lv Ling* (*New Laws and Orders of Tiansheng Period*), the rules for the prison management system were also specified. For example, "Du Jian" (supervisor) and "Xiao Jian" (junior supervisor) were appointed to supervise the prisoners. If the prisoners who were ill had not received any treatment or if any prisoner had died of shortage of food and clothes, the officials in charge should be punished accordingly; if the prisoners had committed suicide because of negligence of the prison guards, "the petty guards shall be imposed with a fine of one horse."

Tian Sheng Gai Jiu Xin Ding Lv Ling (*New Laws and Orders of Tiansheng Period*) was a code that integrated the legal cultures of Han and Qiang nationalities. Both in text structure and legal contents, not only the laws of the Tang and Song Dynasties were followed, but their own native common laws were also integrated, so it was one of the most outstanding features of the code. A detailed explanation is as follows: *Ming Li Lv* (*Statutes and Terms*) was abolished; "Shi E" (The Ten Abominations) was divided into "Shi Men" ((ten categories," namely, "Mou Ni Men" (or "Mou Fan": plotting rebellion or plotting to endanger the country in *Tang Code*), "Shi Xiao De Li Men" (or "Mou Da Ni": great sedition in *Tang Code*), "Bei Pan Men" (or "Mou Pan": treason in *Tang Code*), "E Du Men" (or "E Ni": abusing or murdering the elders in *Tang Code*), "Wei Bu Dao Men" (or "Bu Dao": depravity in *Tang Code*), "Da Bu Gong Men" (or "Da Bu Jing": being greatly irreverent in *Tang Code*), "Bu Xiao Shun Men" (or "Bu Xiao": being unfilial in *Tang Code*), "Bu Mu Men" (or "Bu Mu": inharmonious in *Tang Code*), "Shi Yi Men" (or "Bu Yi": injustice in *Tang Code*), "Nei Luan Men" (or "Nei Luan": committing incest in *Tang Code*)). Moreover, the ten categories of felonies and the relevant thirty nine articles in "Shi E" (The Ten Abominations) were collected together. As for its contents, ethical crimes were comparatively reduced, i.e., the provisions in "Bu

Mu Men" (or "Bu Mu": inharmonious in *Tang Code*) and "Nei Luan Men" (or "Nei Luan": committing incest in *Tang Code*) were reduced, compared with *Tang Lv* (*Tang Code*), but many specific regulations were added in "Wei Bu Dao Men" (or "Bu Dao": depravity in *Tang Code*), which had shown that although in the Western Xia Dynasty emphasis was laid on the absorption of Han culture, and especially in the reign of Emperor Renzong, Confucianism also witnessed progress by leaps and bounds, yet the old tradition of the nomadic people had impeded the complete absorption of the ethical law. Moreover, during the time when customary law was in dominance in the Western Xia Dynasty, criminal law was both savage and brutal. After accepting the penalty systems of the Tang and Song dynasties, although the country was rapidly moving toward legal civilization, because of intense internal national conflict and class contradiction, the punishment for the crime of endangering the ruling of the imperial court and the privileges of the aristocracy was aggravated. For example, it was stipulated in "Mou Ni Men" (or "Mou Fan": plotting rebellion or plotting to endanger the country in *Tang Code*) that as for those who would "attempt to kill the officials, or to damage the throne, whether with accomplices or by himself, as long as the evidence is clear and the plan has been carried out, both the principal and the accessary criminal shall be decapitated with swords with their family members punished by 'Lian Zuo' (being punished for being related to somebody who committed an offence)." "For those who have committed the crime of 'Mou Ni' (plotting rebellion or plotting to endanger the country), if they have deluded people by words or by force, even if they have failed, the initiators and the accomplices shall all be decapitated with swords with their parents, wives, children, etc. punished by 'Lian Zuo' (being punished for being related to somebody who committed an offence). Moreover, they shall be punished by living in remote places, or being sent to garrison the frontier, or serving in the army for their whole lives." Even if the drunken or crazy people had said anything about rebellion, they would be considered as plotting rebellion, so they would be punished for the crime of 'Mou Ni' (plotting rebellion or plotting to endanger the country) after they were reported to the government. In "Bei Pan Men" (treason), for those who had already defected, "the initiators shall be decapitated with swords, with the accomplices sentenced to life imprisonment, or banished to different places to garrison the frontier, or sentenced to thirteen years of penal servitude." Moreover, the wives and children should also be punished by "Lian Zuo" (being punished for being related to somebody who committed an offense) and be sent to the countryside to serve penal servitude.

In "Wei Bu Dao Men" (depravity), detailed regulations were made for the punishment of the crimes of intentional injury and homicide that were committed among the common people or committed against officials by common people or committed against common people by officials or committed between officials. For those who would "kill people by means of incantation or religious rites," the initiator would be punished according to "the law of intentional homicide."

In *Tian Sheng Gai Jiu Xin Ding Lv Ling* (*New Laws and Orders of Tiansheng Period*), the crime of "Dao Zei" (theft) was divided into nine categories, in which all provisions related to "Dao Zei" (theft) were collected; this was different from the arrangement in the Tang and Song dynasties. The nine categories included "Dao Qin Men" (stealing from relatives), "Za Dao Men" (miscellaneous theft), "Qun Dao Men" (gang robbery), "Chong Dao Men" (repeated theft), "Dao Pei Chang Fan Huan Men" (the thief compensating the damages), "Zi Gao Chang Huan Jie Zui Jian Ban Yi He Men" (the discussion on reducing the punishment for voluntary surrenders by half), "Zhui Gan Bu Ju Gao Dao Shang Men" (rewarding those who search, arrest, and inform against the thieves), "Sou Dao Zong Ji Men" (arresting the thieves), and "Wen Dao Men" (interrogating the thieves). In view of special national conditions, some provisions that were not included in *Tang Lv (Tang Code)* were included in the laws of the Western Xia government. According to *Tang Lv (Tang Code)*, the domestic animals which were stolen by thieves were also regarded as the common property which was the same as other things, but in the social economic life of Dangxiang nationality in Western Xia Dynasty, animal husbandry still occupied a very important position, therefore, domestic animals were discriminated from other property in respect of the object stolen by thieves, so such crimes were punished differently. Moreover, the articles of "livestock" was put in the first chapter of the law to show its importance. For example, if it was proved to be true that a person stealthily took away the meat of dead animals belonging to others, "the official shall be imposed with a fine of one horse, while the common people shall be punished by 'Chi' (flogging with light sticks) for thirteen strokes" with the stolen skin and meat returned to the owner. If the skin had been used and the meat had been eaten, they should be compensated according to the law on theft. As to acts of stealing others' forage or loosely kept domestic animals or damaging others' pasture, the criminal involved should be punished for the crime of robbery.

"Qun Dao Men" (the category of gang robbery) was also mentioned in *Dao Zei Lv (Statutes on Robbing and Theft)*: "if over five people have conspired to or participate in the theft, regardless of the amount, the action shall be regarded as 'Qun Dao' (gang robbery)." The earliest record of "Qun Dao" (gang robbery) could be found in *Qin Jian (The Bamboo Writing Slips in Qin Dynasty)*, and the inclusion of the regulation in *Tian Sheng Gai Jiu Xin Ding Lv Ling (New Laws and Orders of Tiansheng Period)* had shown that a much severer punishment was enforced upon the crime of "Qun Dao" (gang robbery) which involved over ten accomplices, and that all criminals, whether principals or accessories, officials or the common people, should be killed, with their wives punished by "Lian Zuo" (being punished for being related to somebody who committed an offence); it would not be regarded as the crime of "Qun Dao" (gang robbery) if five people had plotted to carry out the plan, but one or two of them did not participate in the crime, the criminals should be punished for the crime of robbery or larceny. The initiator would be punished by "Jiao" (hanging), and the accessories would be sentenced to twelve years of imprisonment.

It was stipulated in "Dao Hui Fo Shen Di Mu Men" (the category of stealing and destroying Buddha and god statues and tombs) that for the acts of destroying Buddha, Taoist and "Tianzun" statues, the temples of Confucius, and so on, the initiator would be sentenced to six years of imprisonment and the accessories to three years. If monks or Taoist priests participated in theft, their punishment would be doubled. In the provision of "Dao Hui Tian Zun Fo Xiang" (destroying the statues of Buddha and supreme gods) in *Tang Lv* (*Tang Code*), the punishment for the destruction of the statues of Buddha and supreme gods was only included, but not for the destruction of the statues of Confucius. But in *Tian Sheng Lv Ling* (*New Laws and Orders of Tiansheng Period*), the punishment for the destruction of Confucius statues was added, which had reflected the feature of the times, because Confucianism was greatly respected during the reign of Emperor Renzong in the Western Xia Dynasty. Emperor Renzong once announced that Confucius should be honored as Emperor Wenxuan, so temples for sacrifices were ordered to be set up in "Zhou" (subprefecture) and "Xian" (county) nationwide. Moreover, laws were made to enforce punishment for the destruction of Confucius statues.

The principle of enforcing severe punishment on recidivists in *Tang Lv* (*Tang Code*) was also reflected in *Tian Sheng Gai Jiu Xin Ding Lv Ling* (*New Laws and Orders of Tiansheng Period*). But because the penalty of "Liu" (exile) was not included in the legal system of the Western Xia Dynasty, in "Chong Dao Men" (repeated theft), those who "are convicted for their previous acts of theft, or who have completed their short-term forced labor service, or who have been exempted from the punishment of long-term imprisonment and forced labor but who have committed the crime of theft again, shall all be punished for their newly committed crimes. If a person has committed the crime of theft once again before he completes his service of short-term forced labor, except for death penalty, comparison should be made between the unfinished short-term imprisonment and the punishment of the new crimes, and the criminal shall be punished according to the more serious crimes he has committed in view of the concrete circumstances. For a person who has committed a minor crime, a severer punishment shall be enforced; for a similar crime, the punishment shall be one level severer. Usually, the punishment on recidivists includes life imprisonment and a long-term imprisonment; ...If a person has been sentenced to life imprisonment, but he commits theft again which is punishable by one month of penal servitude, the criminal shall be punished by 'Jiao' (hanging) without regarding whether the crime is serious or not."

As to the offense of rape, it was divided into four categories according to regulations in the eighth volume of *Tian Sheng* Gai *Jiu Xin Ding Lv Ling* (*New Laws and Orders of Tiansheng Period*): "Duo Qi Men" (the category of forcibly taking a married woman as wife), "Qin Ling Qi Men" (the category of offending and insulting a married woman), "Wei Shi Cang Qi Men" (the category of seducing a married woman by power and influence), and "Xing Fei Li Men" (the category of indecent assaulting).

To a certain extent, these four categories fully reflected the characteristics of the legislation of the Western Xia Dynasty. For example, according to the category of "Duo Qi Men" (the category of forcibly taking a married woman as wife), if the man and the woman had an unlawful sexual relationship, both of them would be sentenced to three years of imprisonment, while in *Tang Lv* (*Tang Code*), the punishment was only one-and-a-half years of imprisonment; if a person had seduced and spirited away the wife of other people for over three months or if a person was bribed to keep it a secret, he would be sentenced to three years of imprisonment; if the wife was forcibly taken away, which was reported to the local government by the husband himself, the case should be accepted by "Ya Men" (the government offices) for the "crime of 'Duo Qi Men' (the category of forcibly taking a married woman as wife)." Before the husband filed a lawsuit, mediation should be conducted for the two parties according to law. According to "Qin Ling Qi Men" (the category of offending and insulting a married woman), which was a result of the influence of a hierarchical ideology, the punishment for those who offended a superior was much severer than that for those who offended an inferior, which was similar to those in *Tang Lv* (*Tang Code*). As to the punishment of carnal abuse of underage girls, the criminal would be sentenced to six years of imprisonment, if no injury was caused, or else the criminal would be sentenced to eight years of imprisonment; if the carnal abuse resulted in death, the criminal should be punished by "Jiao" (hanging). It was provided in "Xing Fei Li Men" (the category of indecent assaulting) that adultery between the relatives of "Xiao Gong" (the person wearing the mourning apparel of soft sackcloth in the fourth mourning degree) belonged to indecent assaulting, which was similar to the crime of "Nei Luan" (committing incest), which was committed between family members in *Tang Lv* (*Tang Code*). The difference was that "Nei Luan" (committing incest) in *Tang Lv* (*Tang Code*) referred to having illegal sexual intercourse with the relatives above "Xiao Gong" (the person wearing the mourning apparel of soft sackcloth in the fourth mourning degree), while in law of the Western Xia Dynasty, if a person had an illegal sexual relationship with the relatives "who are in the period of five months of wearing the mourning apparel" (including "Xiao Gong"), he would be considered having committed the crime of indecent assaulting.

Although the penalty system of the Western Xia Dynasty originated from the Tang and Song dynasties, some changes were made. For example, the principal penalty was divided into three kinds, namely, "Zhang" (flogging with heavy sticks), "Tu" (imprisonment), and "Si" (death penalty). The strokes of flogging varied from seven to twenty; the term of imprisonment varied from three months to twelve years and all the way to life imprisonment; the death penalty was divided into "Jiao" (hanging) and decapitation with swords. Moreover, the penalty for officials could be reduced according to their official ranks, including the punishment of imposing "the fine of horses" and "the fine of money" and the punishment of "the demotion or dismissal from their official positions in the government or in the army." Apart from principal penalties, accessory penalties such as "Qing" (to tattoo on the face) and the wearing of iron cangues were also set up. The punishment of "Qing" (to tattoo on the face) was applied to the crimes of "Shi E" (The Ten Abominations), "Dao Qie" (theft), violation of military orders, "Chi Jin" (acts forbidden by edicts), and the crimes which were punishable by long-term imprisonment in "Za Zui" (miscellaneous offenses). So four characters should be tattooed on the back of the hands of a criminal who was sentenced to one to four years of imprisonment, six characters should be tattooed on the back of the ears of a criminal who was sentenced to five to six years of imprisonment, eight characters should be tattooed on the face of a criminal who was sentenced to eight to ten years of imprisonment, ten characters should be tattooed on the face of a criminal who was sentenced to twelve years to life imprisonment. However, those with official ranks would not be tattooed, and the punishment of wearing iron cangue was applied to herdsmen, peasants, boatmen, carters, and servants who were sentenced to "Tu" (imprisonment). Prisoners with short-term punishment should wear an iron cangue that was three *jin*, and prisoners with long-term punishment should wear an iron cangue which was five *jin*.

As for the penalty reduction for "Ba Yi" (The Eight Deliberations), the officials could redeem their penalties with their official ranks; in addition the penalty reduction for "Lao" (elder), "You" (young), "Fei Ji" (the disabled) and "Du Ji" (the incapacitated) was also stipulated, which were by and large the same as those in *Song Lv* (*Song Code*) with just a few changes. For example, the range of "Yi Qin" (the cases that involved "Huang Qin": the relatives of the emperor) in "Ba Yi" (The Eight Deliberations) was expanded, with the kinsmen and in-laws of the emperor and relatives of the empress included. The provisions about penalty reduction by redeeming with official ranks were further specified, and comparison was made with those punishments on "Shu Ren" (the common people) who had committed the same crimes. The provision about the exemption of punishment for "Lao" (elder), "You" (young), "Fei Ji" (the disabled), and "Du Ji" (the incapacitated) was much strictly carried out. According to *Tang Lv* (*Tang Code*), if a person was still young when he committed a crime and had already become a grown-up when he was arrested, he would be judged according to the laws for juveniles; however, he should be judged according to the laws for adults of the Western Xia Dynasty.

Finally, *Tian Sheng Gai Jiu Xin Ding Lv Ling* (*New Laws and Orders of Tiansheng Period*) is the first code in Chinese history that is written in the languages of minority nationalities, which is made up of totally 200,000 words with the exclusion of annotations and cases, so it is the most detailed ancient law existing today.

8.8.3 The Legal System of the Jin Dynasty

The Jin Dynasty, founded in the Aumer Basin in Heilongjiang River valley in 1115 A.D., is a regime mainly consisting of the Jurchen nationality. The history of the Jurchen nationality can be traced back to early Western Zhou Dynasty. Through the long period of time of "Wu Dai" (the Five Dynasties), i.e., Han, Wei, Jin, Sui, and Tang dynasties, the Jurchen nationality had been living, multiplying, and developing despite the changes of their names. Till the eleventh century A.D., other tribes were absorbed into the Mohe nationality and finally formed the Jurchen nationality. Rising gradually from the Black Mountain and the White River, the nationality developed from a dependent state of the Liao Dynasty to a rebellious independent state. In 1115 A.D., the Jin Dynasty was founded, and Huining was made its capital; at the same time, Aguda, the chief of the Wanyan tribe, proclaimed himself emperor and was called Emperor Taizu of Jin.

Before the establishment of the dynasty, the Jurchen nationality was long ruled by customary and common law. As customary and common law were fit for the economic level, the cultural quality, and the psychological state of the Jurchen tribes at the time, it had a great binding force. But obviously it was contradictory to the increasingly developing private ownership and class polarization, so in the early eleventh century, in order to reform the old customs of the Jurchen nationality and to establish an order to maintain the ruling of the nobility, "Tiao Jiao" (rule) was made by the chief Shilu (Emperor Zhaozu) of the Wanyan tribe to "restrain" and "control" the various tribes. But most of the tribes were dissatisfied with the newly made rules, so that "Emperor Zhaozu's uncles and the tribe members even wanted to bury the emperor alive."[415] In view of the fact that "'Tiao Jiao' (rules) was rejected, and the tribal members still stuck to the old customs," Emperor Zhaozu had to implement the newly made rules by violence, which was described as "pacifying those who obey the rules and punishing those who disobey them."[416] But "Tiao Jiao" (rule), which was implemented by Emperor Zhaozu in the reformation of the old customs, had not gone beyond the scope of unwritten common law, which had a strong color of theocratic law. For example, it was recorded in "Xie Li Hu Zhuan" (Biography of Xie Lihu) in *Jin Shi* (*The History of Jin Dynasty*) that "traditionally, if someone is killed, a sorcerer will be requested to curse the killer: tying a knife on the top of the stick, entering the house of the killer with other people, and chanting the curse…, then the sorcerer will scratch the ground with the knife, plunder the animal products and other belongings of the killer and go back. Once cursed, the financial situation of killer's family will decline."

In the middle of the eleventh century, Emperor Jingzu Wugunai was granted the title of "military governor of Sheng Jurchen tribe" by the Liao Dynasty, after which "the status of the monarch-subject relationship of different tribes began to be established."[417] At the end of the eleventh century, Emperor Muzong, named Yingge, unified the Jurchen tribes, as was described in the record that "all the people of the forty seven tribes have submitted themselves to his ruling." So accordingly, the decrees of the Wanyan tribe became the only authoritative ones for the whole tribal federation, according to which "all administrations are conducted"; "hereafter, all orders are unified and obeyed by the public without being doubted."[418]

In the early days of the new country, the first emperor, Wanyan Aguda, in order to pacify the nobles who had achieved notable merits in the founding of the state and to stabilize the existing ruling order, declared in his enthronement: "I will not change the old customs, though I am now the emperor."[419] So the state government, which was mainly made up of the monarch's close relatives or trusted followers, was adopted, which was called "Bo Ji Lie" (the supreme organization to decide national affairs). Anban Bojilie, the chief executive who took charge of state affairs, was the legal heir to the throne of the Jin Dynasty, and Guolunhulu Bojilie, who was the

---

[415]"Shi Ji" (The World Record) in *Jin Shi* (*The History of Jin Dynasty*).
[416]"Shi Ji" (The World Record) in *Jin Shi* (*The History of Jin Dynasty*).
[417]"Ye He Zhuan" (The Biography of Ye He) in *Jin Shi* (*The History of Jin Dynasty*).
[418]"Shi Ji" (The World Record) in *Jin Shi* (*The History of Jin Dynasty*).
[419]"Wan Yan Sa Gai Zhuan" (The Biography of Wanyan Sagai) in *Jin Shi* (*The History of Jin Dynasty*).

military commander-in-chief, also shared in the decision-making. As to the common law, it still played the role of adjustment, as was noted in "Xing Zhi" (The Record of Punishment) in *Jin Shi* (*The History of Jin Dynasty*): "In early Jin Dynasty, the legal system was simple and there was no distinction between the noble and the humble and the high and the low, and the leniency and severity. The minor crimes were punished by whipping with willow twigs, while the murderers and robbers were put to death by hitting on the head. Besides, about four tenths of their property would be confiscated by the government and the rest given to the victims as compensation with their family penalized as "Nu Bi" (slave girls and maidservants). It was permitted if the relatives of the criminals requested to atone for their crimes with horses, cattle and sundries. In addition, felonies were also allowed to be redeemed, but for fear that he was indistinguishable from the common people, his nose or ear was often cut off."

From what is mentioned above, we can see the development of the legal systems of the Jurchen nationality before entering central plains. Thereafter, the rulers of the Jin Dynasty had actively absorbed the progressive legal culture of the Han nationality, on the basis of which splendid achievements were made in the rapid development of the legal system.

Early in his accession to the throne, Emperor Taizong Wanyan Cheng followed the deceased Taizu's teaching of "abiding by the old systems"; meanwhile, he actively supported the military action against the Song Dynasty. In the 3rd year of Tianhui (1125 A.D.), the troops of the Liao Dynasty was defeated, so he continued his attack on the Song Dynasty southward. In the 4th year of Tianhui (1126 A.D.), Bianjing, the capital of the North Song Dynasty, was occupied, and Emperor Huizong and his son Qinzong were captured. So the North Song Dynasty was finally overthrown, and the Jurchen people entered the central plains in the end. With the expansion of territory and in the face of the great number of Han people who lived under the influence of advanced mode of production and culture, it was impossible to continue to maintain the new ruling order with traditional common law, so they had no choice but to adopt the laws and regulations of the Liao and Song dynasties. It was recorded in "Xing Zhi" (The Record of Punishment) in *Jin Shi* (*The History of Jin Dynasty*) that "although Emperor Taizong followed the ancestors' teaching of ruling the country in accordance with the old systems, to a certain extent, the laws of Liao and Song dynasties were also adopted," which had ushered in a new stage of development of the legal system in the Jin Dynasty. During the reign of Emperor Taizong, the old laws of previous dynasties were adopted and new instructions were issued to make up for the deficiency of common law. Although the ministers had repeatedly suggested that "laws of long lasting should be made according to the new circumstances,"[420] no measures were taken to make statute codes during that period.

During the reign of Emperor Xizong Wanyan Tan, the ruling area of the country was expanded to the Yellow River basin. Thus, through continuous reform, the state

---

[420]"Wan Yan Sa Gai Zhuan" (The Biography of Wanyan Sagai) in *Jin Shi* (*The History of Jin Dynasty*).

system became increasingly complete. In order to eliminate the confusion caused by the coexistence of the old laws of the Tang and Song dynasties and the common law of the Jurchen nationality, after occupying Henan in the 3rd year of Tianjuan (1140 A.D.), "an imperial edict was issued and it was stipulated that all punishments should be enforced according to law."[421] Besides, it was further confirmed that the laws of the Tang and Song dynasties should be continuously applied in the areas inhabited by the Han people. Early in the years of Huangtong, "it was ordered that laws should be made by the ministers by referring to the systems and laws of Sui, Tang, Liao and Song dynasties. Consequently, the law entitled *Huang Tong Zhi* (*Huang Tong System*) was issued and carried out both home and abroad."[422] *Huang Tong Zhi* (*Huang Tong System*), which was the first code of written law of the Jin Dynasty, contained over 1000 articles, and it was known in history as *Huang Tong Xin Zhi* (*Huang Tong New System*). Moreover, according to "Xi Zong Ji Nian Si" (The Fourth Annals of Emperor Xizong) (Volume twelve) in *Da Jin Guo Zhi* (*The Records of Great Jin Dynasty*), "up to the autumn of July of the 5th year of Huangtong, ... over 1000 articles were newly issued, most of which were made by following those of Song Dynasty with some of them created independently..." It is thus clear that although the main contents of the laws of the Song dynasty were followed, still some new laws were made according to the old systems of the Jurchen nationality. For instance, "as to a person who beats his wife to death, if he does not use a knife, he should exempted from punishment." In addition, "the term of imprisonment varies from one to five years, and the punishment of 'Zhang' (flogging with heavy sticks) varies from one hundred and twenty to two hundred stokes"; "where a monk or a nun commits adultery, or someone commits robbery, he shall be put to death without regarding whether he has stolen anything." All these mentioned above were not included in the laws of the Tang and Song dynasties.

In the 9th year of Huangtong (1149 A.D.), after Wanyan Liang, King of Hailing, came to power, "some of the old rules were changed." During the years of Zhenglong, the unbalanced *Xu Jiang Zhi Shu* (*Amendments to Law*), which was made arbitrarily, was enacted concurrently with *Huang Tong Zhi* (*Huang Tong System*). Consequently, "the right and wrong were confused" and "the officials often did not know what to do, which had in the end led to serious corruption."[423]

After his enthronement, Emperor Shizong Wanyan Yong tried to change the chaotic situation caused by the inconsistency of laws and orders. At the time, the ruling of the Jin Dynasty was already consolidated, which had provided the objective condition for the reform of legal systems. Besides, Emperor Shizong, who was known as "Xiao Yao and Shun" (Yao and Shun the junior) in history, also attached much importance to legislation, and he once even stated that "the law is a very important instrument to guarantee equality."[424] With his support, great achievements

---

[421]"Xing Zhi" (The Record of Punishment) in *Jin Shi* (*History of Jin Dynasty*).
[422]"Xing Zhi" (The Record of Punishment) in *Jin Shi* (*The History of Jin Dynasty*).
[423]"Yi La Zao Zhuan" (The Biography of Yila Zao) in *Jin Shi* (*The History of Jin Dynasty*).
[424]"Xing Zhi" (The Record of Punishment) in *Jin Shi* (*History of Jin Dynasty*).

were made in the reform of the legal system of the Jin Dynasty. In the 17th year of Dading (1177 A.D.), a special legislative organ was established, and Yila Zao, who was "Da Li Qing" (the president of the supreme court of justice) at the time, was ordered to conduct a systematic revision to *Huang Tong Zhi* (*Huang Tong System*) and *Zheng Long Zhi* (*Zheng Long System*), which were made during the reign of emperors Huangtong and Zhenglong, respectively, as well as *Jun Qian Quan Yi Tiao Li* (*The Jun Qian Contemporary Regulations*) and *Xu Xing Tiao Li* (*Amendment Regulation*), which were made in the early years of Dading. In the compilation, the principle of "deleting what is repetitious and rectifying what was wrong according to the order of priority" was applied. Where "there are omissions in the system, provisions shall be added to make up for them; where there are omissions and doubtful points in the system and law, or where there are doubtful points which can not be decided, revisions were made according to imperial edict." If the laws that were adopted in the existing legislation or that were issued in the early years of Dading, such as *Jun Qian Quan Yi Tiao Li* (*The Jun Qian Contemporary Regulations*), were still feasible, they should be included in the statute made. So it took about five years to complete *Da Ding Chong Xiu Zhi Tiao* (*Da Ding Newly Revised Laws*). The law consisted of 12 volumes and 1190 articles, and it had been the most important legislative activity in the Jin Dynasty since its founding. As "the laws of central plains were extensively implemented,"[425] since the years of Dading, even more laws of Han nationality had been adopted in this code.

The reign of Emperor Zhangzong Wanyan Jing was the most flourishing period of the Jin Dynasty, during which social economy was rapidly developed, politics was stable, and national integration was greatly promoted. Moreover, the culture of the Han nationality, which was centered around Confucianism, was generally accepted by the Jurchen people. For example, Zhangzong was an emperor who actively supported the Chinesization of the nation. As for the legal system, the seventy years of experience since the founding of the country was summarized, and more laws of the Tang and Song dynasties were adopted after weighing the pros and cons of the integration of the laws of Han and "Fan" (minority nationality), which began the legal civilization of the Jin Dynasty.

At the beginning of his enthronement, Emperor Zhangzong, in view of the fact that "'Li' (rites), 'Yue' (music), 'Zheng' (government) and 'Xing' (punishment) were in disorder because of the application of the old systems of Liao and Song dynasties"[426] and that "'Zhi' (imperial decree) and 'Lv' (criminal law) were mixed up," in the 1st year of Mingchang (1190 A.D.), "Xiang Ding Suo" (office of inspecting and checking) was set up to conduct an examination of the laws and decrees. In the 3rd year of Mingchang (1192 A.D.), *Ming Chang Lv Yi* (*Ming Chang Code*) was drafted by "Xiang Ding Suo" (office of inspecting and checking) "on the basis of the current systems and laws according to the actual conditions by referring

---

[425]Liu Qi (Song Dynasty), *Gui Qian Zhi* (*The Record of Returning to Seclusion*), Vol. 12.

[426]"Wan Yan Shou Zhen Zhuan" (The Biography of Wanyan Shouzhen) in *Jin Shi* (*The History of Jin Dynasty*).

to the penal codes of previous dynasties which were applicable in today to make up for the deficiency and by explaining the provisions with the annotations of penalty system."[427] *Ming Chang Lv Yi* (*Ming Chang Code*) was compiled on the basis of the law codes of previous dynasties by taking the annotations of *Song Xing Tong* (*The Penal Code of Song* Dynasty) as the official interpretation. Therefore, it was basically a Hanized law code both in spirit and content. Moreover, matters such as "Que Huo" (monopolized commodities), "Bian Bu" (border regions), and "Quan Yi" (adapting to circumstances), etc. were included in *Chi Tiao* (*The Legal Provisions*) or *Tai He Chi Tiao* (*The Legal Provisions of Tai He*).

After *Ming Chang Lv Yi* (*Ming Chang Code*) and *Tai He Chi Tiao* (*The Legal Provisions of Tai He*) were enacted, because they were considered imperfect, new laws were ordered to be drafted. So the laws and decrees were revised once again under the leadership of Yan Gongzhen, who believed that "Jin people have always regarded legalists as their ancestors." In December of the 1st year of Taihe, a new law consisting of twelve chapters was made. Generally speaking, its table of contents was the same as that of *Tang Lv* (*Tang Code*), so it was commented in "Xing Zhi" (The Record of Punishment) in *Jin Shi* (*The History of Jin Dynasty*) that "it is actually just the republication of *Tang Lv* (*Tang Code*)." At the end of the provision of the new law, "notes were added to give further explanations and answers." The law was titled *Tai He Lv Yi* (*Tai He Code*), which consisted of thirty volumes and five hundred and sixty three articles.

Besides *Tai He Lv Yi* (*Tai He Code*), many other laws were also formulated, including *Lv Ling* (*Laws and Orders*), consisting of twenty volumes; *Xin Ding Chi Tiao* (*The Newly Made Legal Provisions*), consisting of thirty volumes; *Liu Bu Ge Shi* (*The Injunction and Standard of Six Departments*), consisting of thirty volumes, which were collectively referred to as *Tai He Lv Ling Chi Tiao Ge Shi* (*Laws, Orders, Legal Provisions, Injunctions and Standards in Tai He Period*) and which was enacted in May of the 2nd year of Taihe (1202 A.D.).

Tai He Lv Ling Chi Tiao Ge Shi (*Laws, Orders, Legal Provisions, Injunctions and Standards in Tai He Period*) was the most complete law code of the Jin Dynasty, and it was also the epitome of legislation since emperors Xizong and Shizong, which had marked the achievement of feudalization and Hanization of the legal systems in the Jin Dynasty. With the decline of the country, large-scale law revision activities were not carried out any more, so *Tai He Lv Ling Chi Tiao Ge Shi* (*Laws, Orders, Legal Provisions, Injunctions and Standards in Tai He Period*) was continuously applied all the way to the collapse of the Jin Dynasty.

Tai He Lv Ling Chi Tiao Ge Shi (*Laws, Orders, Legal Provisions, Injunctions and Standards in Tai He Period*) and *Liu Bu Ge Shi* (*The Injunction and Standard of Six Departments*), which were enacted during the reign of Emperor Zhangzong, were basically administrative legislation. There were also some articles of administrative laws in *Xin Ding Chi Tiao* (*The Newly Made Legal Provisions*). To a certain extent,

---

[427]"Xing Zhi" (The Record of Punishment) in *Jin Shi* (*The History of Jin Dynasty*).

Yuan Dian Zhang (*Statutes of Yuan Dynasty*), which was well known, was made on the basis of the administrative laws of the Jin Dynasty.

In the 4th year of Tianhui (1126 A.D.) during the reign of Emperor Taizong, "the official system was set up, and the government organizations such as 'Si' (office), 'Fu' (ancient administrative district between province and county) and 'Si' (bureau) under 'Shang Shu Sheng' (The Department of Secretary) were established."[428] After Emperor Xizong ascended the throne, "Zhong Shu Sheng" (the supreme organization in charge of state affairs), "Men Xia Sheng" (the organization in charge of examining imperial edicts in ancient China), and "Shang Shu Sheng" (The Department of Secretary) were established following the systems of the Song dynasty. "Shang Shu Sheng" (The Department of Secretary) was known as "Zheng Fu" (government), and there were with six affiliated departments under it, which were in charge of administrative affairs; "Shu Mi Yuan" (Privy Council) was in charge of military and political affairs, and "Yu Shi Tai" (The Censorate) was in control of supervision. In the 5th year of Tianhui (1137 A.D.), an imperial edict was issued by Emperor Xizong to establish "Xing Tai Shang Shu Sheng" (a local administrative department) in Bianjing as an agency of "Shang Shu Sheng" (The Department of Secretary). Thenceforth, in some important regions, "Xing Tai Shang Shu Sheng" (a local administrative department) was successively set up to exercise power on behalf of the central government. "Xing Tai Shang Shu Sheng" was abbreviated as "Xing Tai" or "Xing Sheng." In order to avoid conflicts over civil and military affairs between "Shu Mi Yuan" (Privy Council) and "Zhong Shu Sheng" (the supreme organization in charge of state affairs), "Zai Zhi" (the prime minister and the head of Privy Council) in "Shang Shu Sheng" (The Department of Secretary) was usually appointed to hold a concurrent post to be in charge of "Shu Mi Yuan" (Privy Council). In April of the 1st year of Tianxing (1232 A.D.), it was ordered by Emperor Aizong Wanyan Shouxu that "'Shu Mi Yuan'(Privy Council) should be combined with 'Shang Shu Sheng' and be headed by 'Zai Xiang' (the prime minister)."[429]

As to local government organizations, "Lu" (ancient administrative region), "Zhou" (subprefecture), "Fu" (ancient administrative district between province and county), and "Xian" (county) were set up following the systems of the Song Dynasty. As to the grassroots organizations, "Fang" (neighborhood) was set up in cities, and "She" (community) was set up in township. But in some areas inhabited by the Jurchen people and in some other places, the traditional "Meng An Mou Ke" (the military and social units) was still preserved. According to "Bing Zhi " (The Record of Army) in *Jin Shi* (*The History of Jin Dynasty*), "'Meng An' referred to 'Qian Fu Zhang' (title of senior military officer)" and "'Mou Ke' referred to 'Bai Fu Zhang' (title of military officer, lower than 'Qian Fu Zhang')," which was a traditional method of the organization of troops. After Emperor Xizong, though

---

[428]"Han Qi Xian Zhuan" (The Biography of Han Qixian) in *Jin Shi* (*The History of Jin Dynasty*).
[429]"Bai Hua Zhuan" (The Biography of Bai Hua) in *Jin Shi* (*The History of Jin Dynasty*).

the titles were preserved, the nature of the organization had already been changed, so it had become a mixture of military and local administrative organizations.

The important official positions in the government of the Jin Dynasty were mainly held by imperial clansmen, bigwigs, and the superior officials of "Meng An Mou Ke" (the military and social units), while the lower-level official positions were mostly held by the people of Han nationality. Since the reign of Emperor Taizong, in order to adapt to the expansion of the administrative regions, the system of "Ke Ju" (the imperial examination) was adopted in the selection of officials, which had attracted a large number of scholars who want to hold official posts in "Zhou" (subprefecture) and "Xian" (county). The examination of "Ke Ju" (the imperial examination) was held every three years, with its contents mainly centered on "Jing Yi" (Confucian classics argumentation) and "Ci Fu" (poems and prose). Discourses on politics, laws, and decrees were also included. During the reign of Emperor Zhangzong, "Zhi Ju Hong Ci Ke" (the emperor himself made an examination) was established, and during the reign of Emperor Shizong, "Nv Zhen Ce Lun Jin Shi Ke" (examinations on the current Jurchen political problems and suggestions to the court) was established, in which the Jurchen people were exclusively enrolled. The examinees could also directly take "Hui Shi" (the metropolitan examination) and "Dian Shi" (the final imperial examination) on the Confucian classics of the Jurchen edition. The establishment of "Ce Lun Jin Shi Ke" not only promoted the learning of Confucian classics by the Jurchen people but also improved their cultural quality, reinforced ethnic cultural integration, and provided a model for the Yuan and Qing dynasties.

Although there was no ethnic restriction for the qualification to take the examination, there were still requirements for personal identity. Those who were with lower social status such as "Jian Min" (rabbles or people of lower social status) and "Fang Liang Ren" (uninhibited people), those who committed the crimes of "Shi E" (The Ten Abominations) and "Jian Dao" (rape and theft), and those who belonged to "Ding You Ren" (those in mourning period for the death of their parents) were all forbidden to take the exam. The admission rate of the imperial examination was not fixed, and those who became "Jin Shi" (those who passed the imperial examination at the national level in ancient China) should be appointed as "Wen San Guan" (ancient honorary title for civil officials), who could be appointed as "Zhi Shi Guan" (in charge of specific government affairs) after they passed the recruitment examination.

In order to select capable persons, imperial edicts were issued repeatedly by emperors Shizong and Zhangzong, and it was stipulated that loyal and honest officials should be recommended by officials above "Qi Pin" (the seventh rank); many talented people were selected through this, so the team of bureaucracy grew. As for special appointments, it was exclusively restricted to imperial clansmen, noblemen, and descendants of Confucius.

In conclusion, as for the official appointment in the Jin Dynasty, although priority was given to the system of "Ke Ju" (the imperial examination), different measures were taken for different nationalities with different social status, which was described as "appointing and dismissing officials by following the laws of both

8.8 The Legal Systems of Liao, Western Xia, and Jin Dynasties Compared with That of... 821

Tang and Song dynasties."[430] So not only was the social basis of the regime enlarged, but the relevant laws were also enriched with the implementation of laws such as *Gong Ju Cheng Shi Tiao Li Ge Fa* (*Laws and Regulations on Civil Examinations for Government Officials*), *Yin Xu Fa* (*Law on Appointing Different Ranks of Officials According to the Contribution of the Previous Generation*), etc.

As for the assessment of officials, the relevant laws of the Tang and Song dynasties were basically followed, and officials were promoted, demoted, rewarded, or punished according to the assessment result. What should be mentioned is the requirements for and the regulations on a clean and honest government. For example, if a county magistrate had practiced fraud as to the debt of the tribesmen "for over three days, he shall be demoted one rank lower or be removed from his office"[431]; "if he accepts presents on his birthday, "even if he was a 'Zai Zhi' (the prime minister and the head of Privy Council) or 'Shu Mi' (the Military Affairs Commissioner), he shall be removed from his office."[432] Meanwhile, attention was paid to giving full play to the supervising function of the supervisory organs. Emperor Zhangzong had once warned his "Jian Guan" (supervisor): "'Jian Guan' (supervisor) is not established just for showing off, but for checking the actual effects, so I hope it is helpful. You are all selected by the royal court to give advice, so you shall state outright without telling lies if it concerns national interests as well as the goodness and evilness of the officials."[433]

Because of the chaotic condition caused by war and the complicated class and national relationship, criminal penalties were aggravated. According to historical records, "although the articles of law are revised in accordance with those of the former dynasties, the laws of Jin Dynasty are so strict that generally speaking more severe punishments are adopted."[434] For example, the rebels and thieves who threatened the rule of the Jin Dynasty were all put to death by "Ling Chi" (the punishment of dismemberment and lingering death). Moreover, the local officials' responsibility of arresting thieves were strictly provided, and the violators would be punished by "Zhang" (flogging with heavy sticks) for one hundred strokes. Meanwhile, "the system of reporting the cases of theft and robbery to the government was established," and those who failed to do so would be punished by "Zhang" (flogging with heavy sticks) for one hundred strokes.

A thief would be sentenced to at least three years of imprisonment if he had stolen others' property, and if the property stolen was worth more than ten *guan*, he would be punished by five years of imprisonment; if it was over thirty *guan*, he would be

---

[430] "Xuan Ju Zhi" (The Record of Election) in *Jin Shi* (*The History of Jin Dynasty*) (Book 3).
[431] "Shi Zong Ji" (The Biography of Emperor Shizong) in *Jin Shi* (*The History of Jin Dynasty*), Vol. 2.
[432] "Shi Zong Ji" (The Biography of Emperor Shizong) in *Jin Shi* (*The History of Jin Dynasty*), Vol. 1.
[433] "Zhang Zong Ji" (The Biography of Emperor Zhangzong) in *Jin Shi* (*The History of Jin Dynasty*) (Book 2).
[434] "Ku Li Zhuan" (The Biographies of Brutal Officials) in *Jin Shi* (*The History of Jin Dynasty*).

punished by life imprisonment and "Ci Mian" (tattooing the face of a criminal). "As for the robbers, they shall all be put to death whether they have gotten the property or not."

With the development of imperial autocracy, behaviors like "Fan Gong Jin" (violating the prohibitions for palaces), "Fan Hui" (violating a taboo), and "Mo Shi Huang Quan" (ignoring imperial authority) were all listed as crimes, and the offenders would be punished by "Zhang" (flogging with heavy sticks) for one hundred and twenty strokes or be put to death.

In order to improve the management of bureaucracy and to strengthen the ruling of the state, a series of specific regulations was issued to fight against corruption, such as *Zhi Guan Fan Zui Tong Zhi Xiang Jiu Cha Fa* (*The Law of the Mutual Supervision of the Crimes Committed by Colleagues*), *Jun Qian Shou Cai Fa* (*The Law of Accepting Money by Military Officers*), and *Jun Qian Chai Fa Shou Zang Fa* (*The Law of Accepting Bribery by Military Officers*). Many officials, from princes to commanding officers or officials of "Lu" (ancient administrative region), "Fu" (ancient administrative district between province and county), "Zhou" (subprefecture), and "Xian" (county), were demoted or were deprived of their ranks of nobility or were removed from their positions or were put to death.

Furthermore, officials who had gambled or were involved in fortune telling or drunk alcohol illegally should be punished by law.

To guarantee the victory in war, military laws such as *Chu Zheng Jun Tao Wang Fa* (*The Law of Army Deserters*), *Qin Bu Tao Jun Shang Ge Ji Ju Ting Ren Zui* (*On the Rewarding of Arresting Army Deserters and the Crime of Hotel Keeper*), etc. were enacted. Those who "advance and retreat without permission, or who have lost the opportunities in the war and lost the battles shall all be beheaded"; "those who are not well prepared for the attacks of the enemy, or retreat in the battle, or do not pursue the retreating enemy, shall all be beheaded according to law."[435] Moreover, those who abandoned the cities in the enemy attacks would also be put to death.

The penalty system of the Jin Dynasty was established by reference to that of the Tang and Song dynasties, and it was divided into three categories, i.e., "Si" (death penalty), "Tu" (imprisonment), and "Zhang" (flogging with heavy sticks). As for the punishment of "Si" (death penalty), apart from "Zhan" (beheading) and "Jiao" (hanging), many other punishments were enforced, such as "Zu Zhu" (killing of the whole clan of a criminal), "Ling Chi" (the punishment of dismemberment and lingering death), "Zhe" (to open and split, breaking apart the criminal's body), and "Hai" (killing and then chopping the body to flinders). As for "Tu Xing" (penal servitude), it was divided into seven classes from one to five years. In reference to the penalty system of the Liao Dynasty, the punishment of life imprisonment was enforced: if a thief had stolen property worth over thirty *guan* of money, he would be sentenced to life imprisonment. A supplementary punishment of "Jue Zhang" (beating the criminal's back, legs, and buttocks with heavy sticks) was also enforced on a criminal who was sentenced to "Tu Xing" (penal servitude): "a criminal who is

---

[435]"Feng Bi Zhuan" (The Biography of Feng Bi) in *Jin Shi* (*The History of Jin Dynasty*).

sentenced to fewer than two years of imprisonment will be punished by 'Zhang' (flogging with heavy sticks) for sixty strokes; over two years, he will be punished by 'Zhang' (flogging with heavy sticks) for seventy strokes; and a woman criminal will be punished by 'Zhang' (flogging with heavy sticks) for fifty strokes, all of which are included in *Chi Tiao* (*The Legal Provisions*)."[436] The strokes of the punishment of "Zhang" ranged from twenty to two hundred. Since the punishment of "Liu" (exile), which had been applied since the Sui and Tang dynasties, "is not applicable today"[437]; it was replaced by a four-year imprisonment with a supplementary punishment of "Zhang" (flogging with heavy sticks). Moreover, the punishments from "Zhang" (flogging with heavy sticks) to "Si" (death penalty) could all be atoned for with copper money. As far back as the time of Jurchen tribal society, it was acceptable to atone for crimes with horses and cattle. So during the reign of Emperor Zhangzong, the system of the Tang Dynasty was followed, and it was stipulated that one could atone for his crime with copper money, but the amount was twice as much as that which was provided in the laws of Tang dynasty. In the later period of the Jin Dynasty, the copper money used in the atonement for crimes could be converted into silver money because it "is not only helpful to criminal punishment but also beneficial to the government officials."[438]

As for the principles of criminal law of the Jin Dynasty, what is worth mentioning is the restriction on the scope of application of "Ba Yi" (The Eight Deliberations). The kinsmen of the emperor who were not within those wear mourning apparel were all excluded from "Yi Qin" (the cases that involved "Huang Qin": relatives of the emperor). In addition, "Yi Xian" (the morally worthy: including worthy men or superior men whose speech and conduct were greatly virtuous and may be taken as a model for the country) was only limited to those who had committed public crimes, while in practice the punishment for some minor crimes, which should be punished leniently, was often not mitigated.

Emperor Xizong once remarked that "people shall be treated equally according to the national legislation regardless of their social ranks. How can it be that different punishment is enforced because the offender is my kinsman."[439] Emperor Shizong also stated that "the law is a very important instrument to guarantee equality." In criticizing "Shang Shu Sheng" (The Department of Secretary) for remitting the punishment for the crimes committed by the relatives of empresses in reference to "Ba Yi" (The Eight Deliberations), Emperor Shizong pointed out that "if the punishment for the royal relatives are reduced, they will be rampant and unbridled .... twenty years ago, my kinsman, 'Jie Du Shi' (military governor) Wulindachaowuchang committed a crime punishable by death, but I did not forgive him; if I have done it today, it may create a precedent of unfair judgment for the

---

[436]"Xing Zhi" (The Record of Punishment) in *Jin Shi* (*The History of Jin Dynasty*).

[437]"Xing Zhi" (The Record of Punishment) in *Jin Shi* (*The History of Jin Dynasty*).

[438]"Shi Huo Zhi" (The Record of National Finance and Economy) in *Jin Shi* (*The History of Song Dynasty*) (Book 3).

[439]"Ye He Zhuan" (The Biography of Ye He) in *Jin Shi* (*The History of Jin Dynasty*).

future generations."[440] He was also against the principle of "Yi Xian" (the morally worthy: including worthy men or superior men whose speech and conduct were greatly virtuous and may be taken as a model for the country), and he said that "if someone has rendered a great service for the country, it is advisable to appraise his exploit. As for 'Yi Xian', since he is virtuous, how should he violate the law?"[441] According to historical records, Emperor Shizong "had never bent the law for the benefit of his relatives or acquaintance,"[442] which was no doubt related to the comparatively weaker consciousness of privilege of the Jurchen rulers, but more importantly, it was so done to prevent "Wai Qi" (relatives of an emperor on the side of his mother or wife) from having too much power and to guard against their violation of law.

As for the application of criminal law, it also showed the characteristics of national oppression. For example, if a Jurchen hurt a person of Han or Qidan (Khitan) nationality, he would not be considered guilty, but if a person of Han nationality had slightly offended a Jurchen, he would be executed, which had led to the situation where Hans and Khitans were often wounded and killed by Jurchens on the excuse of minor offenses or that their family property was confiscated with no reason.

According to the law of household registration in the Jin Dynasty, "male and female under two years old are recorded as 'Huang' (ignorant youth); under fifteen, 'Xiao' (youth); at sixteen, 'Zhong' (middler); at seventeen, 'Ding' (adult); at sixty, 'Lao' (elder). The females whose husbands died were recorded as 'Gua Qi Qie' (widow), while those who were 'Fei Ji' (the disabled) and 'Du Ji' (the incapacitated) were not regarded as 'Ding' (adult)."[443] It was thus obvious that in the Jin Dynasty, people acquired the capacity to act once they reached seventeen years old. In the law of household registration of the Jin Dynasty, people were classified into "Ben Hu" (native household) (or "Meng An Mou Ke" (the military and social units)), "Han Hu" (Han household), "Qidan Hu" (Khitan household), and "Za Hu" (miscellaneous household) according to nationality, among which "Ben Hu" (native household) had the highest social status, followed by "Qidan Hu" (Khitan household) (they both fell into the category of common people), and all were included in "Liang Min" (the decent people) in registration. Furthermore, "Jian Hu" (those who became slaves of officials because of committing crimes) and "Guan Hu" (criminals and their relatives who became servants of officials) belonged to "Jian Min" (rabbles or people of lower social status), among whom "Nu Bi" (slave girls and maidservants), who had the lowest status, had no household registration, so they could only depend on their masters. "Nu Bi" (slave girls and maidservants) were mostly the common people

---

[440]"Xing Zhi" (The Record of Punishment) in Jin *Shi* (*The History of Jin Dynasty*).

[441]"Shi Zong Ji" (The Biography of Emperor Shizong) in *Jin Shi* (*History of Jin Dynasty*), Vol. 2.

[442]"Shi Zong Ji" (The Biography of Emperor Shizong) in *Jin Shi* (*The History of Jin Dynasty*), Vol. 2.

[443]"Shi Huo Zhi" (The Record of National Finance and Economy) in *Jin Shi* (*The History of Jin Dynasty*) (Book 1).

who were captured during wars or who were punished because they "could not afford to pay the fine." According to the legal system of the Jin Dynasty, there was extremely strict differentiation between "Liang Min" (the decent people) and "Jian Min" (rabbles or people of lower social status), so that it was a crime to treat "Liang Min" (the decent people) as slaves. But if "Nu Bi" (slave girls and maidservants) had rendered military exploit or if they had become "Nu Bi" (slave girls and maidservants) just because of a natural disaster or epidemic disease, they could become "Liang Min" (the decent people) by paying ransom money.

In terms of ownership, "Guan Tian" (state-owned land), which was owned by the state through martial spoliation, occupied a large portion of the national land. Moreover, the land of the peasants was repeatedly plundered by the government through land measurement, which further made many people destitute and homeless.

As for the "Guan Tian" (state-owned land) that the Jurchens possessed, they only had the right of usage and usufructuary right but had no right of disposal. With the strengthening of the influence of the feudal mode of production, a feudal tenancy relationship also developed rapidly among the Jurchens. Many "Ben Hu" (native household) and soldiers who went to war had leased their land to peasants of the Han nationality to collect rent. Although it was prohibited, it was impossible to prevent the growing trend of the feudal tenancy system. Therefore, in September of the 4th year of Taihe (1204 A.D.), *Tun Tian Hu Zi Zhong Ji Zu Dian Fa* (*The Law on Farmers Tilling Their Own Farmland and Land Leasing*)[444] was issued by Emperor Zhangzong, so the reality of feudalization of land ownership of the Jurchen people was accepted.

Most of the land in north China, Shaanxi, and other places was owned by landlords and the landholding peasants of the Han nationality, so they had to pay tax to the state. In addition, "the sale or mortgage of land was not prohibited."[445]

As for the law of obligation, the fruit of the Song Dynasty was inherited, according to which contracts have to be made in land transaction, as well as in debit and credit. However, the existing bills are mainly about land sale. To take "Xiu Wu Xian Ma Yong Fu Zi Mai Di Qi" (The Land Sale Lease by the Sons and Father in Xiuwu County), signed in the 28th of Dading (1188 A.D.), as an example[446]:

> The land seller, the deceased taxpayer Ma Yu, his son Ma Yong and younger son Ma He of Mafang Village, Qixian Township, Xiuwu County, make a contract to sell two *mu* three *li* of land to Wang Taihe and Wang Chongde, the disciples of Quanzhen Sect as permanently owned land to build their temple. The agreed price is sixteen *guan* of money. The contract takes effect the moment it is completed. The details are listed as follows:

---

[444]"Zhang Zong Ji" (The Biography of Emperor Zhangzong) in *Jin Shi* (*The History of Jin Dynasty*) (Book 4).

[445]"Shi Huo Zhi" (The Record of National Finance and Economy) in *Jin Shi* (*The History of Jin Dynasty*) (Book 2).

[446]Zhang Chuan Xi, *Zhong Guo Li Dai Qi Yue Hui Bian Kao Shi* (*A Textual Research and Interpretation of the Collected Contracts of the Past Dynasties of China*) (Book 1), Peking University Press, 1995, p. 530.

The bamboo land in the south of the village is to be sold: twenty six *bu* five *fen* to the east, twenty six *bu* five *fen* to the west, sixteen *bu* to the south and ten *bu* to the north. Along with the land in the east: twenty six *bu* to the east, eighteen point five *bu* to the west and ten *bu* to the south, but to the north there is no land. There is a river in the east. The buyer and the seller agree that all the tax, materials and money within the area shall be checked according to law and shall be in the possession of Ma Yu's family. Moreover, they are in charge of the payment of the tax. The bamboos and trees within the area are not included in the sale.

When it rains, ox carts are allowed to pass through.

The area is to be sold to the disciples of Quanzhen Sect as permanently owned land. There are no such inside stories as things related to bribes or debts. And the date of the drafting of the contract is added to guarantee the deal, with no default of payment existed. For fear that people do not believe it, this article is written out as an evidence.

The December of the 28th year of Dading

The contractor the seller, Ma Yong (Signature)

The co-contractor Ma He (Signature)

The follower of the middleman, Wang Shoumiao (Signature)

The contract drafter, Wang Ying of the village (Signature)

The sum including the contract tax and the agency fee, sixteen *guan* of money, on the 23rd.

In this land sale lease, the four boundaries of the land were clearly demarcated, the property right was explicitly stipulated, as was described that "there are no obstacles." Moreover, the transference of property right was completed the moment "the dealing is conducted." In addition to Ma Yong, who was one of the concerned parties, the contractors also included the "co-contractor," that is, a person of his own clan, the "middleman," and the "contract drafter." As is seen above, the main elements of a sale contract are already complete.

As to the guarantee of a debt contract, usually a person was used as a hostage; if the redemption was unrealized at maturity, the party involved would become a "Nu Bi" (slave girls and maidservants), which was so widespread in the Jin Dynasty that it had even caused social instability. Therefore, an imperial edict was issued by Emperor Taizong in the 9th year of Tianhui (1118 A.D.), and it was stipulated that "the property shall be redeemed by the government."[447] In November of the 3rd year of Dading (1163 A.D.), Emperor Shizong stated even more clearly in the imperial edict that "in Zhongdu, Pingzhou, and the famine-stricken areas or the areas plundered by Khitans, when someone's wife is mortgaged, she shall be redeemed by the government."[448] Therefore, it was characteristic of the law of obligation in the Jin Dynasty for officials to redeem the "Nu Bi" (slave girls and maidservants) who were mortgaged. On the one hand, the validity of loan contracts was acknowledged to protect the interests of creditors; on the other hand, redemption was conducted with public funds to ease the sharp social contradiction.

The system of marriage and inheritance of the Jin Dynasty was influenced by the patriarchal etiquette of the Han nationality, and some of the traditional national customs were reformed during the process of the great national integration, but its

---

[447]"Tai Zong Ji" (The Biography of Emperor Taizong) in *Jin Shi* (*The History of Jin Dynasty*).

[448]"Shi Zong Ji" (The Biography of Emperor Shizong) in *Jin Shi* (*The History of Jin Dynasty*), Vol. 1.

distinctive characteristics were still retained. After entering the central plains, for the purpose of consolidating its power, the Jurchen people who moved to North China, Shaanxi, and some other places were allowed to intermarry with the Han people and the Khitans. According to "Bing Zhi." (The Record of Army) in *Jin Shi (The History of Jin Dynasty)*, "the whole China is ruled by Jin rulers, so considering that the population of our own clan is not large enough. . ., we allow our people to intermarry with Qidan (Khitan) and Han people for national solidarity." So the policy was taken by the rulers of the Jin dynasty as a way to obtain "a long-term benefit," so that even the imperial concubines of Jin emperors were mostly women of Han nationality.

Marriage between persons of the same surnames was not prohibited according to the old customs of the Jurchen people, but since the reign of Emperor Taizu, they were reformed in accordance with the marriage system of the Han nationality. So "anyone who marries a person with the same surname shall be divorced and be punished by 'Zhang' (flogging with heavy sticks)"[449]; however, according to law, marriage between "Liang Ren" (the decent people) and "Jian Min" (rabbles or people of lower social status) was not strictly forbidden. In April of the 10th year of Tianhui (1132 A.D.), the emperor stated in the imperial edict that "if a 'Liang Ren' (the decent people) marries a slave, provided that she knows of his social status, she shall be regarded as a legal wife."[450] In the 2nd year of Taihe (1202 A.D.), Emperor Zhangzong reasserted that "if a slave marries the daughter of a 'Liang Ren' (the decent people), the marriage shall be recognized as lawful. . ., and the children of the slave will be regarded as 'Liang Ren' (the decent people)."[451] But the intermarriage between "Nu Bi" (slave girls and maidservants) in Jurchen families and "Liang Ren" (the decent people) should be first approved by the head of the household, "then the marriage shall be permitted after getting the registered documents of the close clan relatives and the elders of the neighborhood."[452] But marriage between cousins was not forbidden by law.

The system of polygamy was carried out for emperors, nobles, and bureaucrats of the Jin Dynasty. For the common people, monogamy was basically carried out; however, they were allowed to take concubines. The legal status of husband and wife was unequal compared with that in the system of the Han nationality. For example, "the person who beats his wife to death without using weapons shall not be punished."[453] Although the decree that "it is guilty for one to beat his innocent wife to death" was enacted during the reign of Emperor Shizong,[454] in fact it had little constraining force legally.

---

[449]"Tai Zu Ji" (The Biography of Emperor Taizu) in *Jin Shi (The History of Jin Dynasty)*.

[450]"Tai Zong Ji" (The Biography of Emperor Taizong) in *Jin Shi (The History of Jin Dynasty)*.

[451]"Xing Zhi" (The Record of Punishment) in *Jin Shi (The History of Jin Dynasty)* (Book 1).

[452]"Shi Huo Zhi" (The Record of National Finance and Economy) in *Jin Shi (The History of Song Dynasty)* (Book 1).

[453]Hong Hao (Song Dynasty), *Song Mo Ji Wen (The Sketches in Jin Dynasty)*.

[454]"Shi Zong Ji" (The Biography of Emperor Shizong) in *Jin Shi (The History of Jin Dynasty)*, Vol. 2.

In terms of the inheritance system, generally, the laws of the Song Dynasty were adopted in the inheritance of status and property. According to *Shi Xi Meng An Mou Ke Qian Shou Ge* (*The Instruction of the Hereditary System of Meng An Mou Ke*), the successor should be "Di Zi" (the son born of the legal wife) who is over twenty five years old, and "inheritance is allowed only after the successor has read the Confucian classics and the history written in Jurchen language first."[455] As to the amount of inheritance of property for women, it was smaller compared with that during the Tang and Song dynasties, which had reflected a decline in women's social status as a whole.

In the field of economic law, first, the law of "Que Jin" (Monopoly) was perfected. In accordance with the system of the Jin dynasty, salt, alcohol, yeast, tea, vinegar, incense, cinnabar, tin, and iron all belonged to the materials of "Que Jin" (Monopoly). In addition, salt smuggling was especially strictly punished, so even if the Jurchens who were with special privileges were involved in salt smuggling, they would get the same punishment as the common people.

In order to control trade and business, "Shi Ling Si" (Market Management Office) was set up, and *Shang Shui Fa* (*Commercial Tax Law*) was enacted in the 20th year of Dading (1180 A.D.), according to which the tax rate of goods was usually set between three percent and four percent.

In the Jin Dynasty, a series of laws was made about the issuance, circulation, and management of currency, such as Chao *Fa* (*Law on Currency*) and *Qian Fa* (*Law on Money*), according to the financial legislation of the Song Dynasty. Besides, rich experience was accumulated in controlling the amount of banknotes in circulation; in raising the credit of banknotes with the support of the state; in prohibiting counterfeiting, buying, and selling of banknotes; in regulating the main materials used in minting coin money, etc. But under the joint attack of the South Song and Yuan dynasties, the national power of the Jin Dynasty became increasingly weaker, and problems of financial inflation and disorder could not be solved through strict financial legislation.

The judicial system of the Jin Dynasty was patterned after the judicial systems of the Tang and Song dynasties and was established after the reform carried out by Emperor Xizong; the central judicial organs consisted of "Xing Bu" (The Department of Punishment), "Da Li Si" (The Bureau of Judicial Review), and "Yu Shi Tai" (The Censorate). "Yu Shi Tai" (The Censorate) was subdivided into "Deng Wen Gu Yuan" (petitioning agency) and "Deng Wen Jian Yuan" (agency accepting the complaints of citizens). Official positions in the central judicial organs were held by the Jurchen, Han, and Khitan people. Moreover, officials were appointed in charge of language translation to avoid misunderstanding caused by the use of different languages by different nationalities. Da Xing, the prince of Yuan, was once praised by the emperor because "he can deal with the cases involving Jurchen people in Jurchen language, he deal with the cases involving Han people in

---

[455]"Shi Zong Ji" (The Biography of Emperor Shizong) in *Jin Shi* (*The History of Jin Dynasty*), Vol. 3.

Chinese," and "he can deal with things impartially and enforce punishment appropriately."[456]

As for the local judicial organs, those of the Tang and Song dynasties were adopted. So judicial work was conducted by the administrators of "Lu" (ancient administrative region), "Fu" (ancient administrative district between province and county), "Zhou" (subprefecture), and "Xian" (county). During the reign of Emperor Zhangzong, at the level of "Lu" (ancient administrative region), "Ti Xing Si" (judicial office) was set up to be in charge of judicatory inspection. Later, its name was changed to "An Cha Shi Si," which was highly stressed by the emperor. In the areas inhabited by Jurchen and other ethnic minorities, judicial affairs were taken charge of by officials of "Meng An Mou Ke" (the military and social units), as well as other officials such as "Tu Li" (judicial official).

As for the prosecution of cases, there were three ways: mutual impeaching by officials themselves, lodging a complaint by the parties concerned and their relatives, and voluntary surrender by the criminal himself. What is worth mentioning is that the principle of "Qin Shu Xiang Rong Yin" (concealment of crimes among relatives or refusing to testify among relatives in court) was not included in the Jin code, and relatives were allowed to lodge accusations against each other. So accordingly, it was allowed for the inferior and the young to accuse the superior and the elder and the servants to accuse their masters, which was obviously prohibited by the feudal code of the Han nationality. But if the accusation was false, the detractors would be punished.

Officials in "Zhou" (subprefecture) and "Xian" (county) had the power to flog criminals to death, and they were "allowed to hear all lawsuits by themselves,"[457] which led to a situation where several posts were often concurrently held by officials and judicial decisions were made arbitrarily. In order to change it, *Zhou Xian Guan Ting Song Tiao Yue* (*Treaty of Hearing Litigations for Subprefecture and County Magistrates*) was enacted by Emperor Zhangzong, in which it was provided that "the violators shall be impeached by 'An Cha Si' (The Judicial Commission)."[458] But only a temporary effect was achieved by this method, and it did not, and as a matter of fact it was also impossible to, eliminate the local judicial disorder of the late Jin Dynasty.

As inquisition by torture was frequently misused, even Emperor Shizong had lamented with a sigh: "Under cruel torture, the officials can get anything that he wants, so 'Jian Dian' (commander of imperial guards) has never bother to show any compassion to the prisoners."[459]

---

[456]"Shi Zong Ji" (The Biography of Emperor Shizong) in *Jin Shi* (*The History of Jin Dynasty*), Vol. 3.
[457]Li Shi (Ming Dynasty), "Jin Zhi" (The Record of Jin Dynasty) in *Li Dai Xiao Shi* (*A Brief History of the Past Dynasties*), Vol. 62.
[458]"Xing Zhi" (The Record of Punishment) in *Jin Shi* (*The History of Jin Dynasty*).
[459]"Yi La Dao Zhuan" (The Biography of Yila Dao) in *Jin Shi* (*The History of Jin Dynasty*).

As is shown above, during the reign of Emperor Xizong, Shizong and Zhangzong in Jin Dynasty the legal system was fully implemented, which was not only closely related with the social and economic progress, but also with the attention paid by these emperors to the feudal legal system and with their active promotion of Hanization of their own culture.

After the Jurchens settled in central plains, there was an intense collision between their traditional legal ideology and the orthodox feudal legal ideology of "Hua Xia" (an ancient name for China). During the process, the two cultures gradually interpenetrated and integrated because of the affinity and the transformative nature of the progressive and old legal culture, and because of the need to maintain the ruling of the extensive regions of Han nationality, so that the orthodox Confucian legal ideology finally became the guiding theory and theoretical basis of the legislation of Jin Dynasty. Emperor Xizong, who was very familiar with Confucian classics because had learned from Confucian scholars of the central plains was "just like a young prince of Han nationality"; moreover, his successor, Emperor Shizong, had even taken loyalty and filial piety as the criterion of regulating the relationship between monarchs and officials and rectifying the malpractice of society, which had further legalized and standardized the ethic morality centered around loyalty and filial piety.

During the reign of Emperor Zhangzong, "the society is prosperous, the country is peaceful, and people enjoyed a fairly happy life. At the same time, under the rule Emperor Zhangzong, 'Li' (rites) and 'Yue' (music) were rectified, the criminal law was revised and the bureaucratic system was established, so that the regulations and codes which were made had become the models for others to follow."[460] It was because the supreme rulers of the Jin Dynasty had actively participated in the promotion of Hanization that the legal ideology of the Jurchen people was gradually changed, which had provided an extensive mass basis and ideological foundation for the application of the laws of the Tang and Song dynasties.

The contents and basic form of the laws in the Jin Dynasty were similar to those in the Tang and Song dynasties; even the relationship among the various legal forms were basically the same, except for some minor differences. For example, with regard to the application of "Zhi" (imperial decree) and "Lv" (criminal law), Emperor Shizong once said: "Where there are no formal articles in 'Zhi' (imperial decree), 'Lv' (criminal law) shall be used."[461] During the reign of Emperor Zhangzong, it was stipulated that "the loopholes in the legal system should be supplemented by 'Lv' (criminal law)."[462] Therefore, this showed that "Zhi" (imperial decree) was more flexible and pertinent; more importantly, it showed that the provisions of "Lv" (criminal law), which was mostly made up of legal provisions

---

[460]"Zhang Zong Ji" (The Biography of Emperor Zhangzong) in *Jin Shi* (*History of Jin Dynasty*) (Book 1).

[461]"Xing Zhi" (The Record of Punishment) in *Jin Shi* (*History of Jin Dynasty*).

[462]"Xing Zhi" (The Record of Punishment) in *Jin Shi* (*History of Jin Dynasty*).

8.8 The Legal Systems of Liao, Western Xia, and Jin Dynasties Compared with That of...

from the Tang and Song dynasties, were no match to "Zhi" (imperial decree) in terms of their authority and feasibility.

The legal system of the Jin Dynasty was complete and systematic compared with that of the Liao Dynasty; at the same time, it also proved that although it was based on the laws of the Tang and Song dynasties, there were further developments made. As was stated in "Wen Yi Lie Zhuan Xu" (The Preface of Collected Biographies of Literature and Art) in *Jin Shi* (*The History of Jin Dynasty*) that "although there are no differences between Jin Dynasty and Liao Dynasty since they had all conquered the world by military forces, still it was incomparable by Liao Dynasty for its achievements made in legal codes by civil rather than the military means, which had made it ranked among the great dynasties like Tang and Song dynasties." In early Yuan Dynasty, Yuanhao Wen also thought that "because laws and regulations which were comparable to those of Han and Tang dynasties had been made in Jin Dynasty after its foundation,"[463] it had exerted a direct influence on Yuan and Latter Jin Dynasty. Before the founding of the Yuan Dynasty, *Tai He Lv Ling Chi Tiao Ge Shi* (*Laws, Orders, Legal Provisions, Injunctions and Standards in Tai He Period*) was often used by Mongolian rulers to make judgments, and it was not until the 8th year of Zhiyuan (1271 A.D.) that it was ordered by Kublai Khan that *"Tai He Lv Ling Chi Tiao Ge Shi* (*Laws, Orders, Legal Provisions, Injunctions and Standards in Tai He Period*), which was made Jin Dynasty should abandoned."[464] Moreover, the ruler of the Later Jin Dynasty, Nurhaci, also gained great experience from the legal system of the Jin Dynasty in reforming the old Jurchen custom and building the new legal system. So even on his death bed, Nurhaci told the chieftain of "Ba Qi Gu Shan" (a name of the military and political organization unit in "Ba Qi") "to strictly abide by law, to reward the merit and punish the offense impartially by following his example (Emperor Zhangzong of Jin Dynasty)."[465]

However, during the ruling of the Jin Dynasty, the country was constantly in chaos because of war. There was also fierce power struggle inside the ruling circles, which turned statute law into a mere formality. After the reign of Emperor Zhangzong, the national power of the Jin Dynasty gradually declined, politics was corrupted, and the legal system was destroyed, which led to its final destruction by the Mongolian Yuan Dynasty.

---

[463]"Yuan Hao Wen Zhuan" (The Biography of Yuanhao Wen) in *Jin Shi* (*The History of Jin Dynasty*).
[464]"Shi Zu Ji" (The Record of Emperor Shizu) in *Yuan Shi* (*The History of Yuan Dynasty*) (Book 4).
[465]*Man Zhou Shi Lu* (*The Record of Manchu*), Vol. 8.

Chapter 9
The Legal System of "Zu Shu Bian Tong" in the Yuan Dynasty

(1279 A.D.–1368 A.D.)

In the early thirteenth century A.D., Genghis Khan, the great leader of Mongolians, unified the various nomadic Mongolian tribes and founded the Mongolian Empire, so he was proclaimed as the Great Khan of the entire Mongolia.

After the founding of the Mongolian Empire, in order to consolidate his rule, Genghis Khan undertook necessary military, administrative, and legal constructions and formed military administrative organizations comprised of army units of 10 households, 100 households, 1000 households, and 10,000 households, with all the Mongolian tribes of herdsmen organized into these groups. "Qian Hu Zhang" (the chief of one thousand households) and "Wan Hu Zhang" (the chief of ten thousand households) were appointed directly by the Khan himself. At the same time, "Ling Hu Fen Feng Zhi Du" (the System of Household Enfeoffment) was also established by Genghis Khan, according to which Genghis Khan's sons, relatives, and meritorious officials of merit were granted a different number of household enfeoffment. In order to expand the power of Khan, Genghis Khan increased the number of imperial guards ("Qie Xue" (Kheshigs, that is, imperial guards)) under his direct control to 10,000. In addition, he appointed "Duan Shi Guan" (judicial officials) to be in charge of the recording of "Zha Sa" (the Yasa or customary law) and used it as the basis for dealing with civil and criminal litigation. The state of Mongolia was basically established with the formation of the systems mentioned above.

With the consolidation of the foundation of the state and because of the greed of "dividing the land and sharing the wealth," the Mongolian ruling group, led by Genghis Khan families, soon wiped out the Western Xia Dynasty by virtue of a strong military force. In 1234 A.D., the Mongols, allied with the Southern Song

---

Translator's note: "Zu Shu Bian Tong" (following old conventions and systems of ancestors and making changes by adopting the established systems of Han nationality in accordance with special circumstances).

Dynasty, wiped out the Jin Dynasty, and then launched a military campaign against the Southern Song Dynasty. In 1264 A.D., the Mongols occupied most part of the central plains, so the ruling center was moved south from "Shang Du" (Upper Capital, near Dolonnur in Mongolia today) to "Zhong Du" (Middle Capital, Yan Jing, now Beijing). In 1271 A.D., Kublai Khan, Emperor Shizu of the Yuan Dynasty, founded the Yuan Dynasty with the support of some Han landlords. And in the following year, he changed "Zhong Du" (Middle Capital) to "Da Du" (Great Capital). In 1279 A.D., the Mongols finally overthrew the Southern Song Dynasty, so the Yuan Dynasty completed its rule of the whole country, as a result of which the long-term separation and confrontation was ended. So Yuan Dynasty was the first unified regime in Chinese history which was established by the ethnic minorities represented by Mongolian nationality.

The rulers of the Yuan Dynasty, on the one hand, actively carried out the construction of political power and a legal system by referring to the old systems of the Tang and Song dynasties and, on the other hand, established the legal system of the Yuan Dynasty by following some of the ruling methods and customary law of the Mongolian Empire.

The socio-economic and class structure under the rule of the Yuan Dynasty was relatively complex, but the feudal relationship of production occupied a dominant position, and the main class conflict was still that between the landlord and the peasant class.

It should be pointed out that although the Yuan Dynasty was established by a minority regime centered by the Mongolian nationality, under the historical situation of the later period of the feudal society, certain achievements were still made in the social economy by overcoming difficulties and setbacks, on the basis of which cultural development was further promoted.

In the ruling of the country, the policy of "Chong Wen Shi" (stressing cultural and educational affairs) and "Yong Ru Chen" (recruiting Confucian officials) was advocated by Yelv Chucai, a famous politician and thinker at the early period of the Yuan Dynasty. With his active encouragement, during the reign of Emperor Taizu, Confucian scholar Yao Shu was appointed to hold a very important official position, and in the time of Emperor Taizong, more Confucian scholars were recruited. Yelv Chucai even petitioned the emperor to grant the hereditary title of "Yan Sheng Gong" (Duke Yansheng) to Kong Yuankai, the descendant of the 51st generation of Confucius. He was also given "Lin Miao Di" (the Confucian forest, temple, and mansion) as a present. At the same time, under the leadership of Yelv Chucai, the ministers and their descendants were organized to interpret the Confucian classics and to study the doctrines of the previous sages. He said: "'San Gang Wu Chang' (three cardinal guides and five constant virtues) is the 'Ming Jiao' (feudal cardinal guides) of the previous sages, which have been followed by all rulers of the country ever since, so they are like the sun and the stars in the sky."[1]

---

[1]"Ye Lv Chu Cai Deng Zhuan" (The Biography of Yelv Chucai and Others) in *Yuan Shi* (*The History of Yuan Dynasty*).

With the emergence of Confucianism, "Cheng Zhu Li Xue" (neo-Confucianism: a Confucian school of idealist philosophy of Cheng Hao, Cheng Yi and Zhu Xi) was regarded as the official doctrine, and great achievements were also made in historiography. For example, books like *Meng Gu Mi Shi* (*The Secret History of Mongolia*), *Wen Xian Tong Kao* (*A General Textual Research of the Documents*), and *Yuan Jing Shi Da Dian* (*Great Code of Yuan Dynasty*) and the official histories of the Liao, Jin, and Song dynasties written in this period all had great historical value. As for drama, literature, and art, brilliant achievements were also made; in the field of natural science, the astronomy of the Yuan Dynasty had reached the development of astronomy in Yuan Dynasty had reached its peak in ancient China. Especially, large-scale cultural exchange and integration were carried out with Asian, African, and European countries in the Yuan Dynasty, which were unmatched by those of the prosperous ages of Tang and Song dynasties, all of which had provided an important condition for the rapid development of legal civilization in Yuan Dynasty.

Although "Fa Zhi" (the ruling of law) was not advocated in the Yuan Dynasty, legislative institutions that were rich in national features and characteristics of the times were established based on the advanced legal culture of the Han nationality guided by Emperor Shizu's policy of "Zu Shu Bian Tong" (following old conventions and systems of ancestors and making changes by adopting the established systems of the Han nationality in accordance with special circumstances). Thus, it still occupies a very important position in the history of Chinese legal civilization.

9.1 The Legislative Achievements of "Fu Hui Han Fa" (Sticking to and Integrating the Laws of the Han Nationality)

Prior to the unification of China, a simple statute law called "Da Zha Sa" (the Great Yasa or customary law) had been started to be established in the Yuan Dynasty. At the time of founding the state, Genghis Khan ordered Guo Baoyu to be in charge of making laws, so *Tiao Hua Wu Zhang* (*The Five Regulations of Mongolian Empire*) was promulgated, which was the earliest statute law of the Mongolian Empire. In judicial practice, it was allowed to settle lawsuits by referring to *Jin Lv* (*Jin Code*), as was described in the saying that "the disputes and lawsuits were settled by the officials of various departments according to *Jin Lv* (*Jin Code*)."[2] As for the methods of criminal punishment, those who had committed felonies were put to death, and the other criminals were tried and punished by "Chi" (flogging with light sticks) according to concrete circumstances. In May of the 6th year of Ogadai Khan (1234), a meeting was held together with other kings and ministers, and *Tiao Ling* (*The Laws and Decrees*) was issued. According to this law, as far as state affairs

---

[2]"Xing Fa Zhi" (The Record of Criminal Law) (Part1) in *Yuan Shi* (*The History of Yuan Dynasty*).

were concerned, if any officials had talked about what they should not discuss, the offenders would be punished by "Chi" (flogging with light sticks), "Zhang" (flogging with heavy sticks), and "Si Xing" (death penalty), and any officials "who have failed to abide by this law shall be removed from his position."[3] But generally speaking, customary law was still in a dominant position.

Out of the need to rule the whole country, proposals like "Zun Yong Han Fa" (abiding by the laws of the Han nationality) and "Fu Hui Han Fa" (sticking to and integrating the laws of the Han nationality), which were put forward by the bureaucrats of the Han nationality, were adopted by Emperor Shizu. Emperor Shizu actively participated in the compilation of the statute laws of the Yuan Dynasty, which was done by taking into account "the existing law of the state," namely, the customary laws of the Mongolian Empire, and "adopting the law codes of Tang and Song dynasties" and referring to "the old legal systems of Liao and Jin dynasties" in order to regulate the social relationship that newly emerged in the Yuan Dynasty after the unification of China. Thus, it was not accidental that "Fu Hui Han Fa" (sticking to and integrating the laws of the Han nationality) was used by Emperor Shizu as a legislative guideline. In order to rule the entire China, Mongolian nobles, who fell behind the Han nationality in economy, culture, and state administration, had to refer and adapt the advanced method of ruling and legal culture of the Han nationality. Therefore, "Fu Hui Han Fa" (sticking to and integrating the laws of the Han nationality) was not only their only choice but also a wise choice. The so-called "Fu Hui Han Fa" (sticking to and integrating the laws of the Han nationality) meant to selectively adopt the laws of the Han nationality and retain some of the original systems and traditional customs of the Mongolian nationality, such as "following the fundamental laws of former emperors and adopting the established systems of the previous dynasties," so that "Zu Shu" (following old conventions and systems of ancestors) and "Bian Tong" (making changes by adopting the established systems of the Han nationality in accordance with special circumstances) could be well integrated to form the legal system of the Yuan Dynasty.

Thus, through "Fu Hui Han Fa" (sticking to and integrating laws of the Han nationality), not only the privileged positions of the Mongolian nobles were maintained, but the actual need to rule the whole country was also stressed, so that the Mongolian culture and Han culture were both absorbed and integrated at different degrees in the area of either legislation or the judiciary. "Fu Hui Han Fa" (sticking to and integrating with the laws of Han nationality), which was carried out in order to promote the existing feudal, economic and political relationships, had made it possible to establish a complete set of legal system and order, to stabilize the social production and life in a short time and to play an active and historical role in helping the rulers of Yuan Dynasty to establish a regime nationwide. However, although the rulers of Yuan Dynasty had advocated "Zu Shu Bian Tong" (following old conventions and systems of ancestors and making changes by adopting the established systems of Han nationality in accordance with special circumstances)

---

[3]"Tai Zong Ji" (The Record of Emperor Taizong) in *Yuan Shi* (*The History of Yuan Dynasty*).

and absorbed the basic spirit and content of the laws of Tang and Song dynasties, yet because of the intrinsic conservatism of the rulers, their acceptance of the advanced legal culture of Han nationality were limited either in the depth and breadth, so that strong characteristics of Mongolian customary law and "Hui Hui Fa" (the law of the Hui people or the Moslem law) were reflected in the legislation of the Yuan Dynasty. As to the degree of Hanization of the legal system, it was not as well accomplished in the Yuan Dynasty as it was in the Northern Wei Dynasty, nor had it reached the level of Emperor Shizong and Emperor Zhangzhong in Jin Dynasty; however, the historical position and value of the legal system of the Yuan dynasty could not be denied just on that account.

In the 8th year of Zhiyuan during the reign of Emperor Zhiyuan (1271), an imperial edict was issued by Emperor Shizu, and it was stipulated that "*Tai He Lv* (*Tai He Code*) of Jin Dynasty is forbidden to be used."[4] In the 10th year of Zhiyuan during the reign of Emperor Zhiyuan (1273), *Xing Ge* (*The New Injunctions*) was formulated by Emperor Shizu with the help of the bureaucrats of the Han nationality, such as Shi Tianxiang and Yao Shu. It was stated that the punishments used in the Song Dynasty, such as "Bian Bei" (whipping the back), "Qing Mian" (to tattoo on the face), and so on, were abolished. That was why it was later known as the era of "lenient laws" and "light punishments." In the 27th year of Zhiyuan during the reign of Emperor Zhiyuan (1290), He Rongzu, "Can Zhi Zheng Shi" (deputy prime minister) of "Zhong Shu Sheng" (the supreme organization in charge of state affairs), "had written a law code which was later called *Zhi Yuan Xin Ge* (*The New Injunctions in the Reign of Zhiyuan*). The law included ten affairs, such as 'Gong Gui' (public regulations), 'Zhi Min' (ruling the people), 'Yu Dao' (guarding against theft), 'Li Cai' (financial management) and so on. Then another order was issued and it was stipulated that the law should be printed and promulgated so that it could be abided by all people." In the following year, *Zhi Yuan Xin Ge* (*The New Injunctions in the Reign of Zhiyuan*) was formally issued, which was not only the first code issued after China was unified by the Yuan Dynasty but also the basic law of the Yuan Dynasty that featured "Zhu Fa He Ti" (the integration of various laws). So generally speaking, "*Zhi Yuan Xin Ge* (*The New Injunctions in the Reign of Zhiyuan*) was compiled on the basis of the various 'Shi Li' (precedents) which were implemented at a certain time, without referring to the old laws by 'Bi Fu' (legal analogy)." "Ge" (injunction), which first emerged as a legal form in the Tang Dynasty, was a separate supplementary law and was second only to "Lv" (criminal law) among the several legal forms. But in the Yuan Dynasty, "Ge" (injunction) had become one of the most important legal forms, so it was no longer a supplementary law.

The full text of *Zhi Yuan Xin Ge* (*The New Injunctions in the Reign of Zhiyuan*) was lost, and only ninety six articles were retained in *Tong Zhi Tiao Ge* (*The General Legal Provisions and Injunctions*) and *Yuan Dian Zhang* (*The Collection of Statutes of Yuan Dynasty*). Moreover, through *Li Xue Zhi Nan* (*A Guide to Bureaucratics*),

---

[4]"Shi Zu Ji" (The Record of Emperor Shizu) (Part 4) in *Yuan Shi* (*The History of Yuan Dynasty*).

written by Xu Yuanrui in the Yuan Dynasty, we can have a glimpse of the basic contents of "ten affairs" in *Zhi Yuan Xin Ge* (*The New Injunctions in the Reign of Zhiyuan*): "'Gong Gui' (public regulations) refers to the laws and regulations which officials should always abide by; 'Xuan Ge' (criteria for selecting talents) refers to the standards for selecting and evaluating talents; 'Zhi Min' (ruling the people) refers to providing the common people with the necessities of life and settling lawsuits fairly; 'Li Cai' (financial management) refers to managing money and grain and stabilizing prices; 'Fu Yi' (tax and corvee) refers to collecting land tax and allocating corvee services equally; 'Ke Cheng' (tax) refers to regulating tax, such as salt and liquor tax; 'Cang Ku' (warehouse) refers to being prudent in handing out, collecting or receiving goods according to the law; 'Zao Zuo' (construction and manufacture) refers to project supervision and determining the use of materials; 'Fang Dao' (guarding against theft) refers to preventing and eliminating cheating and theft; 'Cha Yu' (hearing criminal lawsuits) refers to interrogating prisoners."[5]

As a "general outline of law," it was impossible for *Zhi Yuan Xin Ge* (*The New Injunctions in the Reign of Zhiyuan*) to meet the actual needs of judicial practice; therefore, in March of the 3rd year of Dade during the reign of Emperor Chengzong (1299), He Rongzu was ordered to have "new laws and decrees formulated." In February of the following year, another imperial order was issued: "'Lv Ling' (the laws and decrees) are very good forms of laws, so they should be made as early as possible." According to the order, *Da De Lv Ling* (*The Laws and Decrees of Dade*), consisting of about 380 articles, was completed by He Rongzu[6] but was criticized by senior officials because it was "full of errors,"[7] so it was not issued in the end. During the reign of Emperor Renzong, "'Ge' (injunction), 'Li' (precedent) and 'Tiao Hua' (rule) which was relevant to disciplines were collected into a book" titled *Feng Xian Hong Gang* (*The Fundamental Rules and Guiding Principles for Disciplines*), This was a very important feudal supervision law for official management and administration.

In the 3rd year of Zhizhi during the reign of Emperor Yingzong (1323), on the basis of *Zhi Yuan Xin Ge* (*The New Injunctions in the Reign of Zhiyuan*) and *Feng Xian Hong Gang* (*The Fundamental Rules and Guiding Principles for Disciplines*), *Da Yuan Tong Zhi* (*General Regulations of the Great Yuan Dynasty*) was made by Wanyan Nadan and Cao Boqi, which was a collection of all of the "Tiao Ge" (legal provisions and injunctions), "Zhao Ling" (imperial edicts), and "Duan Li" (legal precedents) of the previous dynasties that had existed since Emperor Shizu. *Da Yuan Tong Zhi* (*General Regulations of the Great Yuan Dynasty*) consisted of twenty chapters, including "Ming Li" (The Categories of Penalties and General Principles), "Wei Jin" (Palace Guards), "Zhi Zhi" (State Office System), "Ji Ling" (Decrees on Sacrifices), "Xue Gui" (Regulations for Learning), "Jun Lv" (Military Law), "Hu Hun" (Marriage, Tax and Household Registration), "Shi Huo" (National Finance and Economy), "Da E" (Abominations), "Jian Fei" (Committing Fornication), "Dao

---

[5]Xu Yuanrui (Yuan Dynasty), *Li Xue Zhi Nan* (*A Guide to Bureaucratics*).

[6]"Cheng Zong Ji" (The Record of Emperor Chengzong) in *Yuan Shi* (*The History of Yuan Dynasty*).

[7]"He Rong Zu Zhuan" (The Biography of He Rongzu) in *Yuan Shi* (*The History of Yuan Dynasty*).

Zei" (Stealing and Robbery), "Zha Wei" (Fraud and Forgery), "Su Song" (Litigation), "Dou Ou" (Fighting), "Sha Shang" (Killing and Injuring), "Jin Ling" (Prohibitions), "Za Fan" (Miscellaneous Crimes), "Bu Wang" (Arresting), "Xu Xing" (Penalty Reduction), and "Ping Fan" (Rehabilitation). Altogether it contained 2529 articles, including 1151 articles of "Tiao Ge" (legal provisions and injunctions), 717 articles of "Duan Li" (legal precedents), 94 articles of "Zhao Zhi" (imperial edicts), and 577 articles of "Ling" (decree). It was recorded in "Xing Fa Zhi" (The Record of Criminal Law) in *Yuan Shi* (*The History of Yuan Dynasty*) that "in Emperor Yingzong's era, 'Zai Zhi' (the prime minister and the head of Privy Council) and Confucian officials were ordered to complete the book with addition and deletion by referring to the previous codes." So the law was titled *Da Yuan Tong Zhi* (*General Regulations of the Great Yuan Dynasty*), which was divided into categories: "Zhao Zhi" (imperial edicts), "Tiao Ge" (legal provisions and injunctions), and "Duan Li" (legal precedents). "Zhao Zhi" (imperial edicts) consisted of 94 articles; "Tiao Ge" (legal provisions and injunctions) consisted of 1151 articles, and "Duan Li" (legal precedents) consisted of 717 articles, so the law was roughly a collection of the legal systems and "Shi Li" (precedents) made since Emperor Shizu. The so-called "Tiao Ge" (legal provisions and injunctions) referred to government orders made by the emperors or issued by the central authorities to the subordinate organs, which was a mixture of "Ling" (decree), "Ge" (injunction), and "Shi" (standard) of the Tang Dynasty. The so-called "Duan Li" (legal precedents) referred to "the established practices for judicial judgment" and "the common practices," some of which were "'Shi Li' (precedents) for judicial judgments," namely, "the legislations made for a particular case, and a precedent formulated after the settlement of each case." The so-called "Zhao Zhi" (imperial edicts) referred to "orders for judicial officials issued by the Emperor without following 'Ge' (injunction) and 'Li' (precedent)."

In *Da Yuan Tong Zhi* (*General Regulations of the Great Yuan Dynasty*), the main contents of "Wu Xing" (Five Penalties), "Shi E" (The Ten Abominations), "Ba Yi" (The Eight Deliberations), and other regulations and the laws of the Tang and Song dynasties were adopted. As was described in "Xian Dian Zong Xu" (General Preface to Constitution) in *Jing Shi Da Dian* (*Great Code of Yuan Dynasty*), "'Ming Li' (categories of penalties and general principles) referred to the ancient laws and classics of the previous dynasties, including 'Wu Xing' (Five Penalties), 'Wu Fu' (relatives within the five degrees of mourning), 'Shi E' (The Ten Abominations) and 'Ba Yi' (The Eight Deliberations). Although politics changed and laws were amended, yet the names of these ancient laws remained unchanged." So some of them "were still applied secretly, though not openly, and some of them were continued to be applied in practice, although abolished nominally."[8] At the same time, as needed for the ruling of the Yuan Dynasty, new provisions that were not

---

[8]Wu Cheng (Yuan Dynasty), "Da Yuan Tong Zhi Tiao Li Gang Mu Hou Xu" (The Epilogue to the Outlines of General Regulations of the Great Yuan Dynasty) in *Cao Lu Wu Wen Zheng Gong Quan Ji* (*Complete Works of the Revered Mr. Wu Wenzheng*). Vol. 19.

included in the laws of the Tang and Song dynasties were also added. Thus, *Da Yuan Tong Zhi* (*General Regulations of the Great Yuan Dynasty*) was a representative code of law of the Yuan Dynasty, which was applied for the longest time, with its main contents retained in "Xing Fa Zhi" (The Record of Criminal Law) in *Yuan Shi* (*The History of Yuan Dynasty*).

After the promulgation of *Da Yuan Tong Zhi* (*General Regulations of the Great Yuan Dynasty*), the compilation of *Da Yuan Sheng Zheng Guo Chao Dian Zhang* (or *Yuan Dian Zhang* (*The Collection of Statutes of Yuan Dynasty*) for short) was also completed. The law consisted of 60 volumes, 10 categories, and 373 sections, including "Zhao Ling" (Imperial Edicts), "Sheng Zheng" (Imperial Administration), "Chao Gang" (The Rules of Imperial State), "Tai Gang" (The Principles of Imperial Court), "Li Bu" (The Department of Personnel), "Hu Bu" (The Department of Revenue), "Li Bu" (The Department of Rites), "Bing Bu" (The Department of Defense), "Xing Bu" (The Department of Punishment), and "Gong Bu" (The Department of Works). In addition, under each entry, a number of "Tiao Ge" (legal provisions and injunctions) were added. *Yuan Dian Zhang* (*The Collection of Statutes of Yuan Dynasty*), which was compiled by the local government, was a collection of "Tiao Ge" (legal provisions and injunctions), "Zhao Ling" (imperial edicts), and "Duan Li" (legal precedents), which were relevant to the various aspects of social life, such as society, economy, politics, military, and law and which had been in effect for more than fifty years since the reign of Emperor Shizu of the Yuan Dynasty. Among the categories, "Xing Bu" (The Department of Punishment) was the largest, with a total of nineteen chapters. To a certain extent, *Yuan Dian Zhang* (*The Collection of Statutes of Yuan Dynasty*) fully reflected the development and change of the legal systems of the Yuan Dynasty, so it was one of the most important materials for research on the history of the Yuan Dynasty. According to the book catalogues in *Si Ku Quan Shu* (*Complete Library in the Four Branches of Literature*), a new collection of laws was contained in *Yuan Dian Zhang* (*The Collection of Statutes of Yuan Dynasty*), in which events that occurred in the 3rd year of Zhizhi during the reign of Emperor Yingzong were continued to be recorded. Yet some of the historical facts recorded in *Yuan Dian Zhang* (*The Collection of Statutes of Yuan Dynasty*) were not recorded in the history of the Yuan Dynasty.

At the end of the Yuan Dynasty, in the 2nd year of Zhishun (1331) during the reign of Shundi, *Jing Shi Da Dian* (*Great Code of Yuan Dynasty*) was completed, which consisted of ten chapters, namely, "Di Hao" (Imperial Titles), "Di Xun" (Imperial Orders), "Di Zhi" (Imperial Systems), "Di Xi" (Imperial Lineage), "Zhi Dian" (Codes on Governance), "Fu Dian" (Codes on Tax), "Li Dian" (Codes on Rites), "Zheng Dian" (Codes on Political Affairs), "Xian Dian" (Codes on Punishment), and "Gong Dian" (Codes on Works), with a total of 880 volumes. *Jing Shi Da Dian* (*Great Code of Yuan Dynasty*) was a collection of "Lv" (criminal law), "Ling" (decree), and "Shi" (standard), which style and layout was patterned according to *Yuan Dian Zhang* (*The Collection of Statutes of Yuan Dynasty*). As to its contents, they were mostly the same as those of *Yuan Dian Zhang* (*The Collection of Statutes of Yuan Dynasty*) and *Da Yuan Tong Zhi* (*General Regulations of the Great Yuan Dynasty*); among its chapters, "Xian Dian" (Codes on Punishment) was made the basis of "Xing Fa Zhi" (The Record of Criminal Law), which was included in *Yuan Shi* (*The History of Yuan Dynasty*). But unfortunately, the original book was lost, and only a small part could be found in the existing pages of *Yong Le Da Dian* (*The Great Canon of Yongle*).

In the 6th year of Zhizheng (1346), *Zhi Zheng Tiao Ge* (*Legal Provisions and Injunctions in the Period of Zhizheng*) was made on the basis of *Da Yuan Tong Zhi* (*General Regulations of the Great Yuan Dynasty*). The number of its original volumes was unknown, and now there are only 23 volumes that are included in *Yong Le Da Dian* (*The Great Canon of Yongle*), with a total of 2909 articles and 27 sections, including "Ji Si" (Sacrifice), "Hu Ling" (Decrees on Household), "Xue Ling" (The Order on Education), "Xuan Ju" (Election), "Cang Ku" (Warehouse), "Bu Wang" (Arresting), "Fu Yi" (Tax and Corvee), "Yu Guan" (Warden), and so on. Because many "Zhao Zhi" (imperial edicts) and "Tiao Ge" (legal provisions and injunctions) were successively enacted in the more than twenty years following the promulgation of *Da Yuan Tong Zhi* (*General Regulations of the Great Yuan Dynasty*), it was inconvenient for people to make reference to the previous contents, but it had made it easier for the crafty officials to play with literary skills by bending the law. Hence, it was necessary "to make laws and regulations by adopting the legal systems of previous dynasties so that the civilians may know what they should avoid doing and the officials may know what they should abide by."[9]

As seen from the whole Yuan Dynasty, the reign of Emperor Yingzong was a period in which legislation was carried out actively and great achievements were made. As a product of the new policy of Emperor Yingzong, *Da Yuan Tong Zhi* (*General Regulations of the Great Yuan Dynasty*) was the only complete and systematic written law in the Yuan Dynasty. So its promulgation had marked a major shift from the Mongolian customary law to the written law of the Han nationality in Yuan Dynasty. *Da Yuan Tong Zhi* (*General Regulations of the Great Yuan Dynasty*) was already very similar to the laws of the Tang and Song dynasties in both form and content. Since *Zhi Yuan Xin Ge* (*The New Injunctions in the Reign of Zhiyuan*) was issued by Emperor Shizu in the 28th year of Zhiyuan (1651), no amendments had been made to the legal system over a long period of time. So the promulgation of *Da Yuan Tong Zhi* (*General Regulations of the Great Yuan Dynasty*) had changed the chaotic situation where "there were judicial precedents to refer to, but there were no laws to abide by" in judicial practice. The law was applied nationwide for more than forty years.

Yuan Dian Zhang (*The Collection of Statutes of Yuan Dynasty*), as another legislative achievement during the reign of Emperor Yingzong, was very creative in style and layout. It was a complete collection of laws, in which the central and local administration system and the judicial and supervisory systems were recorded. Moreover, it reflected the further separation of civil litigation and criminal litigation, as well as the strengthening of judicial supervision. Therefore, it can be said that it

---

[9]"Xing Kao" (A Textual Research of the Criminal Penalties) in *Xu Wen Xian Tong Kao* (*A Sequel of the General Textual Research of the Documents*), Vol. 135.

had inherited the legacy of *Tang Liu Dian* (*The Six Statutes of Tang Dynasty*) in the past dynasties and had taken the lead in the compilation of "Hui Dian" (the collected statutes) in the later Ming and Qing dynasties.

The legal system of the Yuan Dynasty, as a unified legal system that was established during the rule of the whole country by the ethnic minorities in the late feudal society, had played an active role in restoring and developing agricultural production, increasing population and households, and promoting exchanges between different ethnic groups. Moreover, it had made an outstanding contribution to administrative supervision, civil litigation, and forensic science, so it was considered as a model by the later generations.

Legislation in the Yuan Dynasty has the following attributes: firstly, "Tiao Ge" (legal provisions and injunctions) and "Duan Li" (legal precedents) became the main forms of law. "Tiao Ge" (legal provisions and injunctions), which originated from "Xing Chi" (imperial instructions) of the Song Dynasty, was great in number and was easy and flexible to be used. "Duan Li" (legal precedents), in the meantime, was also the basic component of some codes. For example, in *Zhi Zheng Tiao Ge* (*Legal Provisions and Injunctions in the Period of Zhizheng*), as many as 1050 "Duan Li" (legal precedents) were included. So it had shown the guiding ideology of the rulers of the Yuan Dynasty, which was reflected in legislation: "With the change of times, some of the outdated laws should be discarded and some of the suitable ones should be adopted according to the current situations."[10] Since in some "Duan Li" (legal precedents) traces of the Mongolian customary law were obviously seen, there existed a kind of pluralistic structure in the legal system, which was characteristic of the period of the Yuan Dynasty and which was different from the legal systems of the Tang and Song dynasties. But the widespread application of "Duan Li" (legal precedents) also brought about the malpractice where "there were judicial precedents to refer to, but there were no laws to abide by." Secondly, "Sheng Zhi" (imperial edicts) became the most flexible and applicable form of legislation; it was also endowed with supreme legal force because it was not only based on the supreme authority of the traditional power of Khan in the Mongolian empire but was also influenced by the feudal absolutism of the Tang and Song dynasties, which was eloquently expressed by the existing "Sheng Zhi Bei" (imperial edict tablet) of the Yuan Dynasty. "Sheng Zhi Bei" (imperial edict tablet) covered various aspects, such as official appointment, temple maintenance, spy prevention, property protection, tax payment, and relief of corvee services. Some "Sheng Zhi" (imperial edicts) were just the emperor's admonitions on legal cases, which seemed to have exerted some influence on the making of *Da Gao* (*The Great Imperial Mandate*) in the Ming Dynasty. Since individual will was often placed above the law by the Yuan emperors or the law was replaced by their own will, national legislation lacked sufficient binding force. When summarizing the lessons of the downfall of the Yuan Dynasty, it was stated in "Xing Fa Zhi" (The Record of Criminal Law) in *Yuan Shi* (*The*

---

[10]"Cheng Zong Ji" (The Record of Emperor Chengzong) in *Yuan Shi* (*The History of Yuan Dynasty*).

9.1 The Legislative Achievements of "Fu Hui Han Fa" (Sticking to and Integrating...

History of Yuan Dynasty) that "the main reason for the downfall of the Yuan Dynasty is that things are often decided arbitrarily or according to personal will rather than law." Thirdly, ethnic inequalities in the law were openly affirmed in the form of legislation in order to maintain the privileges of the Mongolian nationality and to confirm the administrative management system of oppressing the other nationalities and the judicial practice of enforcing different punishment for the same crime. Fourth, the principle of "ruling the ethnic groups according to their own customs" was implemented. So all the legal norms of all ethnic groups were almost included in the code; particularly, the traditional Mongolian customary law concerning administrative and military systems, marriage, religion, punishment, justice, and so on were all retained. Fifthly, the legal privileges of Buddhism and Taoism were confirmed and protected, and a judicial system wherein religious and secular powers coexisted was formed, which at the same time provided convenience for monks and priests to interfere with state affairs. Sixthly, because political, military, and religious organs were concurrently in charge of judicial affairs, the judicial system was "without checks and balances," which resulted in various drawbacks, such as decentralization of judicial power and arbitrary judgment of cases.

In the Yuan Dynasty, no codes of law like *Tai He Lv* (*Tai He Code*), which were made in the Jin Dynasty and which could be handed down for generations, were made, nor was there a unified and systematic legal form, but the legal civilization of the Han, Qidan (Khitan), and Jurchen ethnic groups were collected, and innovations were made in order to inherit the legal civilization.

As the founder of the Yuan Dynasty, Genghis Khan, in order to achieve the strategic goal of establishing a unified empire, put forward the policy of "integrating the laws of various states and ruling the ethnic groups according to their own customs,"[11] which had served as a guidance to and had exerted a far-reaching influence on the national policy, legislation, management supervision, religion, and so on in the Yuan Dynasty.

After Emperor Shizu Kublai Khan occupied the central plains, he recruited a great number of Confucian scholars from the Han nationality as his advisors. Under their influence, Emperor Shizu changed from "Ge Cong Ben Su" (ruling the ethnic groups according to their own customs) to "Fu Hui Han Fa" (sticking to and integrating the laws of the Han nationality). In the 2nd year of Zhiyuan (1265), Confucian scholar Xu Heng stated in his memorial to the emperor that "a study of the previous dynasties has shown that of all the rulers of northern nomadic empires who have taken over the central plains, only those who have implemented the laws of Han nationality could last long," so "it has to take at least thirty years to change from the customs of northern nomadic tribes to the laws of Han nationality."[12] *Zhi Yuan Xin Ge* (*The New Injunctions in the Reign of Zhiyuan*), which was issued in the 28th year

---

[11]"Xing Bu" (The Department of Punishment) (Part 19) in *Yuan Dian Zhang* (*The Collection of Statutes of Yuan Dynasty*), Vol. 57.

[12]Su Tianjue (Yuan Dynasty), *Yuan Wen Lei* (*A Collection of Essays of Yuan Dynasty*), Vol. 13.

of Zhiyuan (1291), was a great legislative achievement made by combining "the old systems of the empire" and "the laws of Han nationality."

Wu Cheng, a scholar in the late Yuan Dynasty, proved in *Da Yuan Tong Zhi Tiao Li Gang Mu Hou Xu* (*The Postscript to the Outlines of General Regulations of the Great Yuan Dynasty*) that *Da Yuan Tong Zhi* (*General Regulations of the Great Yuan Dynasty*) was also a law made by integrating "the old systems of the empire" and "the laws of the Han nationality." He said: "The ancient laws have been abolished, but this law is newly made in the imperial Yuan Dynasty on the basis of the ancient laws, so even though different words are used, their meanings are generally the same, so as a result, the ancient laws are still used secretly, but not openly, namely, they are only abolished nominally, but in fact are continued to be applied."[13]

In addition to the laws of the Han nationality, *Tai He Lv* (*Tai He Code*) of the Jin Dynasty was adopted at the beginning of the Yuan Dynasty. Though it was prohibited in the 8th year of Zhiyuan (1271), *Jin Lv* (*Jin Code*) was undoubtedly still used for reference in both legislative and judicial practices until *Zhi Yuan Xin Ge* (*The New Injunctions in the Reign of Zhiyuan*) was issued in the 28th year of Zhiyuan (1291).

Furthermore, some achievements were also made in the private legal writings of "Lv Xue" (the study of statutory laws) in the Yuan Dynasty. For example, annotations were made to *Xing Tong Fu* (*Discussions of Criminal Provisions*) by Fu Lin of the Song Dynasty in order to help officials to hear and settle cases. According to the annotated versions in the Yuan Dynasty, four versions were collected in Shen Jiaben's *Zhen Bi Lou Cong Shu* (*Series of Collections of Books of Zhen Bi Lou*): *Xing Tong Fu Jie* (*Explanation of the Discussions of Criminal Provisions*), *Cu Jie Xing Tong Fu* (*A Brief Explanation of the Discussions of Criminal Provisions*), *Bie Ben Xing Tong Fu Jie* (*Another Explanation of the Discussions of Criminal Provisions*), and *Xing Tong Fu Shu* (*Comments on the Discussions of Criminal Provisions*). Of the four versions, *Xing Tong Fu Shu* (*Comments on the Discussions of Criminal Provisions*), written by Shen Zhongwei during the reign of Emperor Shundi, was the most famous. In the book, *Xing Tong Fu* (*Discussions of Criminal Provisions*) was explained sentence by sentence by Fu Lin, and two categories of contents, namely, "Zhi Jie" (direct interpretation) and "Tong Li" (the general rules), were provided after the explanation of each sentence, with the former one providing explanatory notes by referring to *Tang Lv Shu Yi* (*The Comments on Tang Code*) and the latter one taking "Tiao Li" (legal provisions and injunctions) or verdicts of the Yuan Dynasty as evidence. The "Tiao Li" (legal provisions and injunctions) cited were, for the most part, difficult to be found in *Da Yuan Tong Zhi* (*General Regulations of the Great Yuan Dynasty*) and *Yuan Dian Zhang* (*The Collection of Statutes of Yuan Dynasty*), so it had provided rare materials for the study of the laws

---

[13] Wu Cheng (Yuan Dynasty), "Da Yuan Tong Zhi Tiao Li Gang Mu Hou Xu" (The Epilogue to the Outlines of General Regulations of the Great Yuan Dynasty) in *Cao Lu Wu Wen Zheng Gong Quan Ji* (*Complete Works of the Revered Mr. Wu Wenzheng*), Vol. 19.

of Yuan Dynasty. In addition, annotated versions such as *Xing Tong Fu Shi Yi* (*Interpretation of the Discussions of Criminal Provisions*) and *Xing Tong Fu Zhu* (*Notes on the Discussions of Criminal Provisions*) were also found in other works.

In the Yuan Dynasty, the books on officials' political education, such as *Li Xue Zhi Nan* (*A Guide to Bureaucratics*) by Xu Yuanrui, *Za Zhu* (*Miscellaneous Writings*) by Hu Diyu, and *Wei Zheng Zhong Gao* (*Advice for the Governance of the State*) by Zhang Yanghao were also very popular. Of the three books, *Li Xue Zhi Nan* (*A Guide to Bureaucratics*) was the most famous. The author stated in the preface of the book: "I once heard that those who are capable of governing the state always give priority to governance, and to achieve the goal of governance, they must have a good knowledge of the law, because only in this way can they deal with the criminal trials successively. So if criminal punishments are fair and just, they will be obeyed by the people willingly."

Private legal works often focused on the application of the law, and this tradition could be traced back to the Han and Tang dynasties. What was different was that great importance was attached to officialdom by the people in the Yuan Dynasty, but the officials were mostly the Mongolians who were not familiar with official administration. Therefore, in the private legal works of that time, stress was laid on both providing guidance for "how to be officials" and how to apply the law. For example, "Li Shi Ding Lv Zhi Tu" (The Plan for Learning Law from Judicial Officials) and "Wei Zheng Jiu Yao" (Nine Key Elements for Officials) were both included in *Li Xue Zhi Nan* (*A Guide to Bureaucratics*).

It should also be noted that further achievements were made in forensic medicine in the Yuan Dynasty on the basis of the research in the Song Dynasty.

In "Zhu Dao" (Various Thefts) (Part 2) in "Xing Bu" (The Department of Punishment) (Part 5) in *Yuan Dian Zhang* (*The Collection of Statutes of Yuan Dynasty*), examination of the corpse was listed as a separate category, in which the "rules of autopsy" and the requirements for witnesses were explained in detail. *Da Yuan Yan Shi Ji* (*Autopsy Records of the Great Yuan Dynasty*) was made up of four parts: part one was about autopsy laws and regulations, with sixteen formal laws, nineteen subsidiary "Tiao Ge" (legal provisions and injunctions), and "Tong Li" (the general rules); part two was about "the rules of autopsy" on regulating autopsy officials; part three was about "the rules of accounts for autopsy," namely, the format of autopsy reports and the contents covered in the report. It was stipulated that "if the affairs have not been settled, or the principal and accessory offenders have not been identified," the role of principal offenders or accomplices should not be decided hastily; part four was about "the methods of autopsy," which was annexed with two drawings.[14] *Da Yuan Yan Shi Ji* (*Autopsy Records of the Great Yuan Dynasty*) was a summary of the accumulated experiences relating to autopsy in judicial practice, so it represented the level of Chinese forensic science at that time.

---

[14]"Xian Dian" (Codes on Punishments) in "Jing Shi Da Dian" (Great Code of Yuan Dynasty) in *Yong Le Da Dian* (*The Great Canon of Yongle*) (Continued), Vol. 914. Vol.

In addition, some works similar to Song Ci's *Xi Yuan Ji Lu* (*Collection of Unjust Cases Rectified*) were also written, but unfortunately most of them were lost. The only works that have been passed down to present is *Wu Yuan Lu* (*The Record of Fairly Settled Cases*), written by Wang Yu from Dongou, which was completed in "the period of the changing of the reign title by Emperor Zhida." Although most part of it was based on the materials of *Xi Yuan Ji Lu* (*Collection of Unjust Cases Rectified*), it was more accurate and comprehensive because many comments and remarks were added in the book. The book had been translated and published in Korea and Japan. In the 17th year of Jiajing in the Qing Dynasty (1811), *Xi Yuan Ji Lu* (*Collection of Unjust Cases Rectified*), *Wu Yuan Lu* (*The Record of Fairly Settled Cases*), and *Ping Yuan Lu* (*The Record of Redressing the Unjsut Cases*) were collected together and published by Wu Zi from Quanjiao in the late Ming Dynasty, which was titled *Song Yuan Jian Yan San Lu* (*Three Records of Autopsy in Song and Yuan Dynasties*).

9.2 The Administrative Legislation and Management System with National Characteristics

9.2.1 The Administrative Law of "Zu Shu Bian Tong"

The Yuan Dynasty was a regime ruled mostly by Mongolians, who were backward in both economy and culture, so after the reunification of the whole country, its urgent task was to establish a centralized authority, to conduct effective national administration, and to give full play to the role of bureaucratic institutions at all levels; therefore, great importance had been attached to the making of administrative laws by its rulers ever since the founding of the Yuan Dynasty. *Zhi Yuan Xin Ge* (*The New Injunctions in the Reign of Zhiyuan*) was the first code issued after China was unified by the Yuan Dynasty; although the original text was lost, it can be seen from its existing scattered articles that it was in nature a code of administrative regulation that all officials should follow. According to "Shi Zu Ji" (The Record of Emperor Shizu) in *Yuan Shi* (*The History of Yuan Dynasty*), "a book with ten affairs, such as 'Gong Gui' (public regulations), 'Zhi Min' (ruling the people), 'Yu Dao' (guarding against theft), 'Li Cai' (financial management) and so on was compiled by He Rongzu. The book was entitled *Zhi Yuan Xin Ge* (*The New Injunctions in the Reign of Zhiyuan*) and was ordered to be printed and published so that all officials could abide by it." Among the twenty chapters of *Da Yuan Tong Zhi* (*General Regulations of the Great Yuan Dynasty*) that were representative of the legislation in Yuan Dynasty, "Zhi Zhi" (State Office System), "Jì Lìng" (Decrees on Sacrifices), "Xue Gui" (Regulations for Learning), and "Shi Huo" (National Finance and Economy) all belonged to administrative law. Especially, *Yuan Dian Zhang* (*The Collection of Statutes of Yuan Dynasty*), which was categorized according to "Liu Bu" (The Six Departments), namely, "Li Bu" (The Department of Personnel), "Hu

Bu" (The Department of Revenue), "Li Bu" (The Department of Rites), "Bing Bu" (The Department of Defense), "Xing Bu" (The Department of Punishment), and "Gong Bu" (The Department of Works), was a collection of administrative decrees and regulations that had comprehensively reflected the regulations and institutions of the Yuan Dynasty.

In addition, from a number of rules and regulations that were made for administrative public affairs, we can see the overall adjustment of administrative laws and the important role that it played in maintaining the normal functioning of state organs. For example, in view of the fact that government affairs were sluggishly handled by the central and local state organs and that official businesses were delayed by the officials' neglect of their duties, in the 8th year of Zhiyuan (1271), "Xing Yi Gong Shi Cheng Xian" (The Time Limits for Signing and Issuing Official Documents) was issued by Emperor Shizu following the regulations of the Song Dynasty, and it was provided that "in future, for all the government offices inside and outside capital..., the trivial matters shall be settled within seven days; the less important matters, fifteen days and the important matters, twenty days. If 'Ling Shi' (official responsible for clerical affairs) are slow in handling official business, they shall be punished."[15] In the 28th year of Zhiyuan (1291), it was further stipulated in *Zhi Yuan Xin Ge* (*The New Injunctions in the Reign of Zhiyuan*) that "all documents accepted by government offices" had to be handled by "Yin Bi" (get printed) or "Fu Jue" (get delivered) within the day. If it was an "urgent matter, it should be delivered immediately upon arrival."[16] As for "the trivial matters," they should be settled within five days; the less important matters (those needed to be checked and reviewed), seven days; and the important matters (those needed to be calculated in book accounts or consulted), ten days. Moreover, "The offenders shall be punished at any time according to whether the matters were important or not and the time of delaying."[17]

In order to urge and encourage government offices to complete their official business by complying with the time limits, an official business warning system was established. It was stipulated in the 8th year of Zhiyuan (1271) that "as for the official business of all government offices in the capital," the first warning should be issued on the 10th day, and the second after five more days. As for the official business "which was reported from other parts of the country to the capital," if the distance was less than 500 *li*, the first warning should be issued on the 15th day and the second after ten more days; if the distance was over 500 *li*, the first warning should be issued on the 30th day and the second after twenty more days, and the time limit could be extended accordingly; if the distance was over 3000 *li*, the first

---

[15] "Li Bu" (The Department of Personnel) (Part 7) in *Yuan Dian Zhang* (*The Collection of Statutes of Yuan Dynasty*), Vol. 13.

[16] Huang Shijian, "Gong Gui" (Public Regulations) in "Zhi Yuan Xin Ge" (The New Injunctions in the Reign of Zhiyuan) in *Yuan Dai Fa Lu Zi Liao Ji Cun* (*A Collection of Legal Materials in Yuan Dynasty*), Zhejiang Ancient Books Publishing House, 1988.

[17] "Li Bu" (The Department of Personnel) (Part 7) in *Yuan Dian Zhang* (*The Collection of Statutes of Yuan Dynasty*), Vol. 13.

warning should be issued on the 70th day and the second after sixty more days. According to the usual practice, those who failed to report after three warnings would be considered to have defied their superior officials, so they "should be sentenced and punished expediently by the relevant department according to the concrete circumstances, and the officials outside the capital should be reported to and punished by the provincial government."[18]

For matters within their duties, it was forbidden for subordinate government offices to pass the buck, and only "when appropriate reports have been worked out accordingly are they allowed to report to the superiors"; otherwise, they should be impeached and punished by the supervisory officials. But if the matters "ought to be reported" to the superior offices, "they must be settled in accordance with law," and "those who refuse to to so" "shall be investigated and punished according to the concrete circumstances."[19]

9.2.2 The Management System with Its Distinctive Features

As for the administrative law of Yuan Dynasty, it was the core content to establish the administrative management system with national characteristics. Since the founding of the Yuan Dynasty, the experience of Han nationality in ruling the feudal states was adopted by the Mongolian nobility, by which the primitive tradition of the army being commanded by "Wan Hu Zhang" (the chief of ten thousand households) and legal administration being controlled by "Duan Shi Guan" (judicial officials) was gradually changed, so the administrative management system with national characteristics was finally established.

The supreme ruler of the Yuan Dynasty was called Great Khan, and he was formally elected by "Ku Lie Er Ta" (the conference of tribal leaders) in the period of the Mongolian Empire, so the remnants of clan democracy were retained. After the succession of throne by Emperor Shizu in 1260, in order to establish the supreme authority of the emperor, "Ku Lie Er Ta" (the conference of tribal leaders) was abolished, and instead the hereditary system was adopted. Under the emperor, "Zhong Shu Sheng" was the supreme state administrative organ, as was described in the following: "'Zhong Shu Sheng' (the supreme organization in charge of the state affairs) is the foundation of politics and it is in charge of all political and military affairs."[20] The main purpose for replacing the long-standing system of "San Sheng" (the three departments) with the system of "Zhong Shu Sheng" (the supreme

---

[18]"Li Bu" (The Department of Personnel) (Part 7) in *Yuan Dian Zhang* (*The Collection of Statutes of Yuan Dynasty*), Vol. 13.

[19]"Li Bu" (The Department of Personnel) (Part 7) in *Yuan Dian Zhang* (*The Collection of Statutes of Yuan Dynasty*), Vol. 13.

[20]"Tai Gang" (The Principles of Imperial Court) (Part 2) in *Yuan Dian Zhang* (*The Collection of Statutes of Yuan Dynasty*), Vol. 6.

organization in charge of state affairs) was to improve the efficiency of the administration of the state and to reduce the conflict between different organs of authority.

After Emperor Shizu, the official position "Zhong Shu Ling" (head of the secretariat), which served as the head of "Zhong Shu Sheng" (the supreme organization in charge of state affairs) and whose function was to take charge of important military and political affairs, was seldom set up in order to prevent it from monopolizing power. Even if it was set up, it was usually held concurrently by the prince. Under "Zhong Shu Ling" (head of the secretariat), official positions such as "Zuo You Cheng Xiang" (the chief and deputy prime minister), "Ping Zhang Zheng Shi" (the head of the provincial secretariat), "Zuo You Cheng" (the left and right vice prime minister) and "Can Zhi Zheng Shi" (deputy prime minister) were established. Since "Zhong Shu Ling" (head of the secretariat) was concurrently held by the prince who was not on duty in the office by himself, "Zuo You Cheng Xiang" (the chief and deputy prime minister) and "Zuo You Cheng" (the left and right vice prime minister) were in charge of the actual responsibilities of governmental affairs, they were collectively referred to as "Zai Zhi" (the prime minister), and their meeting place was called "Zheng Shi Tang" (The Chamber of Meeting), which was not only helpful to the centralized processing of the governmental affairs, but also to the balancing of the administration power of the central officials. Under "Zhong Shu Sheng" (the supreme organization in charge of state affairs), the following six departments were established: "Li Bu" (The Department of Personnel), "Hu Bu" (The Department of Revenue), "Li Bu" (The Department of Rites), "Bing Bu" (The Department of Defense), "Xing Bu" (The Department of Punishment), and "Gong Bu" (The Department of Works), which were in charge of the various state affairs. As for the subordinate state administrative organs of "Liu Bu" (The Six Departments), such as "Yuan" (institution), "Si" (bureau), "Jian" (ancient supervisory office), and "Fu" (ancient administrative district between province and county), those in the Tang Dynasty were basically followed, except for a slight change in the number of administrative organs. But the chief leaders of all the government bodies must be selected from the Mongolians to highlight the powerful status of the Mongolian nobility.

Out of the need to strengthen the autocratic centralization of state power, it was emphasized in the Yuan Dynasty that "if high-ranking officials are assigned to 'Zhou' (subprefecture) and 'Jun' (shire) outside the capital to fill a position, they must show the official documents of 'Zhong Shu Sheng' (the supreme organization in charge of the state affairs)," and those "who report to the Emperor directly rather than through 'Zhong Shu Sheng' (the supreme organization in charge of the state affairs), or have reported to the Emperor but failed to deliver imperial edicts to the government offices through 'Zhong Shu Sheng' (the supreme organization in charge of the state affairs) shall be punished for violating 'Zhi' (emperor's order)."[21]

In the Yuan Dynasty, the system of the Song Dynasty was followed, so "Shu Mi Yuan" (Privy Council) continued to be in charge of military affairs, and as usual, the

---

[21]"Xing Fa Zhi" (The Record of Criminal Law) in *Yuan Shi* (*The History of Yuan Dynasty*).

prince concurrently held the position of "Shu Mi Shi" (the director of Privy Council). Under "Shu Mi Shi" (the director of Privy Council), official positions such as "Shu Mi Fu Shi" (the deputy director of Privy Council), "Tong Zhi Yuan Shi" (deputy director of the Privy Council), and so on were set up. But "Shu Mi Yuan" (Privy Council) and "Zhong Shu Sheng" (the supreme organization in charge of state affairs) were no longer "the two parallel government departments" because the legal status of "Shu Mi Yuan" (Privy Council) was lower than that of "Zhong Shu Sheng" (the supreme organization in charge of state affairs). Since "Shu Mi Yuan" (Privy Council) was in charge of national military affairs, as well as military maneuver, only the Mongolian nobles were qualified to serve as its chief officers. With regard to military secrets, such as military deployment, registration of armymen, and military maneuver, they were discussed secretly only by two or three senior officials who were close to the emperor, as was described in the saying that "even among the courtiers of 'Shu Mi Yuan' (Privy Council), who were specially in charge of the army, only one or two senior officers knew the military secrets. Therefore, people had no knowledge of the approximate number of troops in the one hundred years of history of Yuan Dynasty."[22] Although officials from the Han nationality could serve in "Shu Mi Yuan" (Privy Council), they were not allowed to intervene in military secrets. The strict control of military power by the supreme rulers had reflected the important role of military forces in maintaining the Mongolian rule in the Yuan Dynasty and in strengthening the centralization of state power.

At the beginning of the Yuan Dynasty, out of the need for a military expedition, "Xing Shu Mi Yuan" (Provincial Privy Council) was set up in Sichuan, Jianghuai, and other places by following the old system of the Jin Dynasty. After Emperor Shizu's unification of China, most of "Xing Shu Mi Yuan" (Provincial Privy Councils) were abolished, with only those in Sichuan and Lingbei retained. At the end of the Yuan Dynasty, in order to suppress the people's uprising against the Yuan Dynasty, which broke out in various places, more "Xing Shu Mi Yuan" (Provincial Privy Councils) were successively set up to contain the uprising expediently.

The newly established institutions in the central government included "Meng Gu Han Lin Yuan" (The Mongolian Hanlin Academy), which was in charge of the drafting of the emperor's "Zhao Zhi" (imperial edicts); "Tong Zheng Yuan" (The Bureau of Transmission), which was in charge of postal stations; "Jiang Zuo Yuan" (The Bureau of Craftwork), which was in charge of craftsmen; "Ji Xian Yuan" (The Bureau for the Assembly of Virtuous Persons), which was in charge of school affairs; and "Xuan Zheng Yuan" (The Bureau of Buddhist and Tibetan Affairs), which was in charge of religious and ethnic affairs. Since Lamaism was held in high esteem and religious policies were carried out by the rulers of the Yuan Dynasty, "Xuan Zheng Yuan" (The Bureau of Buddhist and Tibetan Affairs), which was in charge of religious affairs, had played an important role. It was endowed with great power and was concurrently in charge of local Tibetan affairs. The official

---

[22]"Bing Zhi" (The Record of Army) in *Yuan Shi* (*The History of Yuan Dynasty*).

9.2 The Administrative Legislation and Management System with National...

candidates for "Xuan Zheng Yuan" (The Bureau of Buddhist and Tibetan Affairs) were selected from both monks and laymen, so it can be seen that monks and priests were given a high social status in the country and had an important influence on the politics of the Yuan Dynasty. In addition, many organs that were in charge of handicraft and financial management were also set up, but they overlapped with each other in terms of their functions and power, which had led to certain disorder in the system.

As to the local agencies, generally the old systems of the Song and Jin dynasties were followed. In the early days of development, they were divided into three levels, namely, "Lu" (ancient administrative region), "Fu" (ancient administrative district between province and county) or ("Zhou" (subprefecture)), and "Xian" (county). From the reign of Emperor Taizu, all the residents of the conquered cities were massacred by the Yuan troops if they had resisted, so to the time when local authorities were pacified, great changes had taken place. During this process, for the consolidation of the Mongolian regime, Minister Yelv Chucai, who was an official with political vision, opposed the traditional barbaric policy and suggested that chief officials be appointed in "Zhou" (subprefectures) and "Jun" (shire). After Emperor Taizong ascended the throne, Yelv Chucai proposed once again that the senior officials be appointed in "Zhou" (subprefectures) and "Jun" (shire) so as to rule the military and civilians separately. He said: "In all 'Zhou' (subprefectures) and 'Jun' (shire), the local governor should exclusively take charge of civil affairs, while 'Wan Hu Zhang' (the chief of ten thousand households) should be totally responsible for the military administration. The tax which they are in charge of should not be embezzled by the influential officials."[23] Since Yelv Chucai was highly respected by Emperors Taizu and Taizong, and he had even served as "Zhong Shu Ling" (head of the secretariat), his proposals were very helpful for the rulers of the Yuan dynasty in adopting the local systems of the Song and Jin dynasties.

As for the local system, besides imitating the old systems of the Song and Jin dynasties, "Xing Zhong Shu Sheng" (the provincial supreme organization in charge of daily affairs) was set up as a temporary agency to strengthen local control. Since the establishment of "Xing Zhong Shu Sheng" (the provincial supreme organization in charge of daily affairs) was helpful to the strengthening of the feudal centralized system, soon "Xing Sheng" (province) was set up to act as the permanent administrative region; finally, four levels of political power were formed, namely, "Xing Sheng" (province), "Lu" (ancient administrative region), "Fu" (ancient administrative district between province and county) or ("Zhou" (subprefecture)), and "Xian" (county). The establishment of "Xing Zhong Shu Sheng" (the provincial supreme organization in charge of daily affairs) was a significant change in the local administrative bodies of the Yuan Dynasty. At that time, apart from Hebei, Henan, Shandong, Shanxi, and some other areas (called "Fu Li": the central region) that were directly governed by "Zhong Shu Sheng" (the supreme organization in charge

---

[23]"Ye Lv Chu Cai Deng Zhuan" (The Biography of Yelv Chucai and Others) in *Yuan Shi* (*The History of Yuan Dynasty*).

of state affairs) and the Tibetan region, which was directly governed by "Xuan Zheng Yuan" (The Bureau of Buddhist and Tibetan Affairs), the other part of the Yuan Empire was divided into eleven "Xing Sheng" (provinces), four of which were especially set up to deal with ethnic affairs in the border areas.

The official position of "Cheng Xiang" (the prime minister) was set up in "Xing Zhong Shu Sheng" (the provincial supreme organization in charge of daily affairs), which was usually held by the Mongolian princes and noblemen. "Cheng Xiang" (the prime minister) had great power and "was in charge of all the important military and political affairs,"[24] so even officials with the same ranks should kneel down to him when making reports. Under "Cheng Xiang" (the prime minister), official positions such as "Ping Zhang Zheng Shi" (the head of the provincial secretariat), "Zuo You Cheng" (the left and right vice prime minister), and "Can Zhi Zheng Shi" (deputy prime minister) were set up. So "Xing Sheng Zhi" (the system of province) in the Yuan Dynasty had a significant impact on the construction of the provincial government in the Ming and Qing dynasties. "Xing Zhong Shu Sheng" (the provincial supreme organization in charge of daily affairs), "Xing Shu Mi Yuan" (Provincial Privy Council), and "Xing Yu Shi Tai" (The Provincial Censorate) were three important organizations in charge of local political, military, and supervisory affairs, respectively, on behalf of the central government of the Yuan Dynasty, which showed that great importance was attached by the Yuan rulers to the control of local governments by central authority. This was because the implementation of the policy of national oppression had caused sharp social contradictions during the Yuan Dynasty that it was necessary to establish local agencies with great power to deal with urgent incidents promptly.

Below "Xing Sheng" (province), usually four levels of political divisions, namely, "Lu" (ancient administrative region), "Fu" (ancient administrative district between province and county), "Zhou" (subprefecture), and "Xian" (county) were set up in "Fu Li" (the central region), but in remote areas, there were usually only three levels of political divisions, namely, "Lu" (ancient administrative region), "Zhou" (subprefecture) (or "Fu" (ancient administrative district between province and county)), and "Xian" (county). In "Lu" (ancient administrative region), "Zong Guan Fu" (The General Governor's Office) was set up, with "Zong Guan" (The General Governor) as the chief official; in "Fu" (ancient administrative district between province and county) (also called "San Fu"), "Zhi Fu" (magistrate of a prefecture) (or "Fu Yin" (the chief official of prefecture)) was set up; in "Zhou" (subprefecture), "Zhou Yin" (governor of a subprefecture) (called "Zhi Zhou" (subprefectural magistrates) in a small subprefecture) was set up; in "Xian" (county), "Xian Yin" (governor of a county) was set up. But in all local government offices at the level of "Lu" (ancient administrative region) or below, whether it was "Zong Guan Fu" (The General Governor's Office) and "San Fu" ("Jing Zhao," "You Fu Feng," "Zuo Feng Yi") or "Zhou" (subprefecture) and "Xian" (county), usually "Da

---

[24]"Bai Guan Zhi" (The Record of the Officials of all Ranks) in *Yuan Shi* (*The History of Yuan Dynasty*).

Lu Hua Chi" (judicial official) was appointed. "Da Lu Hua Chi" (judicial official) was a Mongolian official who held the real power and who was in charge of all local affairs. So although he was of the same rank with that of the chief officials in local governments, he had greater power. In fact, he was not only the supervisor of the local administrative officials but also the supreme leader in charge of local government affairs.

In addition, between "Xing Sheng" (province) and "Lu" (ancient administrative region), two kinds of "Dao" (the administration district below the province) were set up: one was "Xuan Wei Shi Si" (the government office in remote areas), which was set up in border areas inhabited by minorities to handle military and civil affairs; the other one was "Su Zheng Lian Fang Shi Si" (the government supervising office), which was set up all over the country to handle supervisory affairs (first named "Ti Xing An Cha Si" (the governmental office in charge of the administration of justice)). "Su Zheng Lian Fang Shi Si" (the government supervising office) was under the leadership of the central "Yu Shi Tai" (The Censorate) and "Xing Yu Shi Tai" (The Provincial Censorate) in Jiangnan and Shanxi, so it was in fact a local supervisory organ.

In order to further control the inhabitants of the country, below "Xian" (county), grassroots organizations such as "Cun She" (village community) and "Li Jia" (social organizations at the grassroots level) were set up. "She" (community) was formed in every fifty households, and the landlords and venerable persons of the Han nationality in the countryside were selected as "She Zhang" (head of the community) to be responsible for governing civilians, handling civil litigation, levying tax, allocating corvee service, and promoting moral education. But above "She Zhang" (head of the community), a Mongolian "Ti Dian Guan" (official in charge) was appointed to be responsible for supervision. Especially, a Mongolian troop or "Tan Ma Chi Jun" (an elite army in the Yuan Dynasty) was dispatched to be stationed in communities to carry out military rule on the pretense of forming a community with the civilians.

Under "Cun She" (village community) was "Li Jia" (social organizations at the grassroots level). Every twenty households formed a "Jia" (administrative division consisting of twenty households). "Jia Zhu" (the head of the "Jia") was usually held by the Mongolians or the Semu (the nationalities in the western or northwestern regions), who had unparalleled authority over the residents, with all their food, clothing, and other items entirely supplied by the residents. The local government system was characterized by military suppression and national oppression.

At the beginning of Yuan Dynasty, the hereditary system was used as to the appointment of local officials of "Zhou" (subprefecture) and "Xian" (county) were. However, with the suggestion of some officials from Han nationality such as Lian Xixian, the hereditary system of local officials was abolished by Emperor Shizu, which had greatly weakened the power of Mongolian nobility in appointing officials within their jurisdiction and strengthened the rule of the centralized government.

It should be noted that since the Yuan Dynasty, China had begun to exercise administrative jurisdiction over Tibet. Early in the year 1253, Emperor Xianzong of the Mongolian Empire once sent troops to Tibet; as a result, the four hundred years of chaos that had lasted since the late Tang Dynasty was ended and Tibet was unified in the end. Since then, Tibet had been integrated within the territory of China and became an inalienable part of the Chinese territory. In the era of Emperor Shizu, the theocratic system was reformed in Tibet, and it was continued to be implemented there for hundreds of years. "Xuan Zheng Yuan" (The Bureau of Buddhist and Tibetan Affairs) was responsible for the management of Tibetan affairs, and a "Xuan Wei Shi" (the official in charge of military and civil affairs in remote areas) was stationed in Tibet and was responsible for collecting tax and tributes, carrying out household survey, evaluating local officials, as well as other affairs. Postal and military stations were also set up in Tibet in order to strengthen its ties with the inland areas.

To sum up, the administrative bodies of Yuan Dynasty are redundant and the systems are in great disorder, but it cannot be denied that creativity is shown in the process of making adjustment according to changing circumstances and different customs.

The system for selecting officials in the Yuan Dynasty was formed in the era of Emperor Shizu. According to "Bai Guan Zhi Xu" (The Preface to the Record of the Officials of All Ranks) in *Yuan Shi* (*The History of Yuan Dynasty*), after Kublai Khan ascended the throne, he "established the royal court rituals, built cities, and then ordered Liu Bingzhong and Xu Heng to appoint officials inside and outside the capital by drawing on the historical experience." Since ethnic principles were emphasized in the selection of officials, the positions of chief officials in the central or local governments were, as usual, held by the Mongolian nobles. As for the appointment of deputy senior officials, priority was given to the Semu (the nationalities in the western or northwestern regions), while the Han people could only serve as lower or subordinate officials. In the entire period of the Yuan Dynasty, Shi Tianze and He Weiyi were the only two persons of Han nationality who had served as "Cheng Xiang" (the prime minister), but they had eventually become Mongolian nobles completely. Sometimes the Han people served as "Fu Cheng Xiang" (vice prime minister), but they were not allowed to get involved in confidential affairs. For example, Han Yuanshan was "Zuo Cheng" (left vice prime minister) and Han Yong was "Can Zhi Zheng Shi" (deputy prime minister), but when "Cheng Xiang" (the prime minister) Tuotuo made reports in the inner court, "they were ordered to withdraw because the report involved military secrets and because Han Yuanshan and Han Yong were Han people."[25] In "Shu Mi Yuan" (Privy Council), the Han people were forbidden to serve as chief officials, and there were no more than four people from the Semu (the nationalities in the western or northwestern regions) nationality who had been appointed as "Shu Mi Shi" (the director of Privy Council) in the Yuan Dynasty. With respect to the important military affairs such as the registration of armymen, "the Han people were not allowed to even know their

---

[25]"Han Yuan Shan Zhuan" (The Biography of Han Yuanshan) in *Yuan Shi* (*The History of Yuan Dynasty*).

numbers."[26] In addition to exercising military power, the Mongolian nobles also controlled taxation because it was regarded as the financial lifeline of the country, while in the Yuan Dynasty, Lu Shirong, who had wantonly extorted the hard-won possessions of all ethnic groups, was the only Han official who had ever controlled the tax collection in the Yuan Dynasty.

9.2.3 The Official Administration Law Focused on Supervision

At the beginning of the Yuan Dynasty, Yelv Chucai proposed recruiting a large number of famous Confucian scholars as officials through the examination of "Ke Ju" (the imperial examination); he also suggested allowing scholars who were captured in the war as slaves to take the examination with their owners. If the slave masters had concealed or forbidden the slaves to take the examination, they would be put to death. As a result, among the 4030 candidates who were selected, the free slaves accounted for about one quarter. But racial inequality still existed even in the examination of "Ke Ju" (the imperial examination) in Yuan Dynasty. According to the system, three hundred people who were selected by "Xiang Shi" (the provincial examination) were allowed to go to the capital to take "Hui Shi" (the metropolitan examination), and one hundred people would be selected from them to take "Dian Shi" (the final imperial examination). Twenty-five people from the Mongolians, Semu (the nationalities in the western or northwestern regions), Hans, and Southerners were selected to take "Jing Shi" (imperial examination in capital city). The examinees in "Xiang Shi" (the provincial examination), "Hui Shi" (the metropolitan examination), and "Dian Shi" (the final imperial examination) were divided into two groups: one group consisting of Mongolians and Semu (the nationalities in the western or northwestern regions) and the other group consisting of Hans and Southerners. For the two groups, not only was the examination paper different, but the examination results were also posted on different name rolls. The examination results for the Mongolians and Semu (the nationalities in the western or northwestern regions) were posted on the right roll (according to the Mongolian system, the right side was superior), while the examination results for the Han people and Southerners were posted on the left roll. As to their appointment after passing the examination, there was also a disparity in terms of superiority and inferiority. Generally speaking, the Mongolians were superior to the Semu (the nationalities in the western or northwestern regions), while the Semu (the nationalities in the western or northwestern regions) were superior to the Han people and Southerners.

In addition to selecting officials by "Ke Ju" (the imperial examination), officials with educational background may also be appointed after they graduate, and they were classified as follows: "Guo Zi Jian" (the highest educational body in ancient

---

[26]"Bing Zhi" (The Record of Army) in *Yuan Shi* (*The History of Yuan Dynasty*).

China), "Meng Gu Zi Xue" (The School of Mongolian Lexicology), "Hui Hui Guo Xue" (School of Hui Studies), "Yi Xue" (Medical School), "Yin Yang Xue" (School of Yin Yang Theory) and so on. Besides, the officials were also selected from through recommendation in the names of "Yi Yi" (hermits), "Mao YI" (persons of extraordinary talents, abilities and virtues), "Qiu Yan" (request for advice), "Jin Shu" (offering proposals to the Emperor), "Tong Zi" (the qualification test for imperial examination), etc. The noble families or families of meritorious officials enjoyed the privileges of "Yin Xi" (children inherit their ancestor's positions). With political corruption in the Yuan Dynasty, the methods of selecting officials became more diversified, so that "the constable who was in charge of arresting thieves were promoted for their achievements, farmers were appointed as officials because of their good harvest. Besides, even craftsmen had the qualification to be appointed as officials and sometimes the slaves were also appointed as petty officials. Kings and princes were bestowed with 'Tou Xia' (households belonging to kings, meritorious officials, and so on, who were conferred on them as conquered people) to recommend people to be officials and ethnic groups in remote and bordering areas were granted the hereditary positions of local magistrates."[27] Since career in government office was considered complex and sophisticated, even though a series of regulations was made for the selection of officials, such as "Sui Chao" (court officials), "Wai Ren" (appointments in other places than the capital), "Sheng Xuan" (official selected by the department of personnel), "Bu Xuan" (official selected by the various departments of central government), "Wen Guan" (civil officials), "Wu Guan" (military officers), "Kao Shu" (examinations), and "Zi Ge" (qualifications), "in fact few people knew the tricks of the system of selecting officials: some of them were promoted by randomly making reference to precedents, or by 'Jie Zi' (taking advantage of others' psychology), or by their achievements; some of them were demoted, some of them had practiced favoritism by violating law, some of them had benefited themselves at the expense of public interests."[28]

As for the performance evaluation of officials in the Yuan Dynasty, an evaluation system was established and legal regulations were made. As far as the evaluation system for officials was concerned, "Zhong Shu Sheng" (the supreme organization in charge of state affairs) was charged with the assessment of officials in the capital, while "Li Bu" (The Department of Personnel) was held responsible for the assessment of local officials, as was described in the saying that "'Li Bu' (The Department of Personnel) ... was in charge of the rules and regulations for the evaluation of the performance of all officials."[29] Since the system of the Jin Dynasty was followed in the Yuan Dynasty, both "Guan" (officials) and "Li" (petty officials) were recruited, and "'Yi Shi' (petty officials in charge of translation), 'Ling Shi' (official responsible for clerical affairs), 'Tong Shi' (petty officials in charge of presenting memorials and

---

[27]"Xuan Ju Zhi" (The Record of Election) in *Yuan Shi* (*The History of Yuan Dynasty*).

[28]"Xuan Ju Zhi" (The Record of Election) in *Yuan Shi* (*The History of Yuan Dynasty*).

[29]"Bai Guan Zhi" (The Record of the Officials of all Ranks) in *Yuan Shi* (*The History of Yuan Dynasty*).

other matters) and 'Shi Jin' (petty officials in charge of official promotion) in 'Zhong Shu Sheng' (the supreme organization in charge of the state affairs), 'Yu Shi Tai'(The Censorate) and 'Liu Bu' (The Six Departments) all were listed as government personnel."[30] Moreover, great importance was attached to "Li" (petty officials), who were familiar with administrative affairs and who were in charge of handling specific daily work, for example, "Chuan Shi" (petty officials in charge of financial matters), "Ling Shi" (official responsible for clerical affairs), "Shu Xie" (petty officials in charge of transcription), "Quan Xie" (petty officials in charge of interpretation and recording), "Shu Li" (scribes), "Dian Li" (petty officials in charge of documents, archives, and other government documents), and so on. Whether the officials were recruited through "Ke Ju" (the imperial examination) or were appointed after they graduated from school or were appointed by "Yin Xi" (children inherit their ancestor's positions) or by recommendation, they usually should serve first as "Li" (petty officials) and would then be promoted to official positions after taking the official qualification examination. Therefore, the official examination was divided into two categories, namely, "Zhi Guan" (state officials) and "Li Yuan" (petty officials). The full term of office was thirty months for the officials within the capital, three years for the local officials, and two years for "Qian Gu Dian Shou" (chief officials in charge of tax). The officials within the capital were promoted one rank after passing the first examination, while the local officials were promoted to higher ranks after the first examination, with one rank higher after the second examination or two ranks higher after the third examination. During the reign of Emperor Shizu, the full term of office for "Li Yuan" (petty officials) was ninety months, but during the reign of Emperor Chengzong, it was provided that for "Li Yuan" (petty officials) within the capital, the term of office for the first examination was thirty months and for the third examination ninety months, while the full term of office for "Li Yuan" (petty officials) outside the capital was one hundred and twenty months. If they passed the official examination when their full term of office expired, "Li Yuan" (petty officials) would be offered official posts below "Liu Pin" (the sixth rank).

As far as the examination of law was concerned, "Wu Shi San Deng Kao Ke Sheng Dian Fa" (The Rules About the Official Examination Involving Five Matters and Three Levels) was made during the reign of Emperor Shizu, and the so-called five matters referred to "Hu Kou Zeng" (the increase of households), "Tian Ye Pi" (the opening up of wasteland), "Su Song Jian" (the decrease of litigation), "Dao Zei Xi" (the eliminating of thieves and robbers) and "Fu Yi Ping" (the equal allocation of tax and corvee service). "The officials who have met the five requirements mentioned above are regarded as top quality candidates..., while the officials who have met three requirements are regarded as qualified candidates..., the officials who have failed to meet the five requirements will be demoted or removed from their

---

[30]"Xuan Ju Zhi" (The Record of Election) in *Jin Shi* (*The History of Jin Dynasty*).

office."³¹ In the 22nd year of Zhiyuan (1285), an imperial edict was issued by Emperor Shizu, and it was stipulated that "the civil officials should be responsible for the five matters ... At the end of each year, they will be examined and the officials who have met the five requirements or have made outstanding achievements in the central and local government offices within their terms of office are regarded as qualified. After the first examination, titles shall be conferred upon the wives of qualified officials; after the second examination, the sons of qualified officials shall be given the right of 'Yin Xu' (to be granted different ranks of officials according to the contribution of the previous generation), and after the third examination, titles shall be conferred upon the parents and grandparents of qualified officials; those officials whose performance is not qualified for the grant of a title shall be promoted according to their abilities; those officials who have made special achievements in their official career shall be given a special promotion."³² If civil officials had taken bribe by violating the law, they would be forbidden to hold their posts again; if they had taken bribe without violating the law, they would be removed from office and would not to be appointed until three years later; if they had committed the same crime again, it would be forbidden for them to hold their posts again. In the 4th year of Zhida (1310), it was declared by Emperor Wuzong that "those officials who are honest, prudent, fair and diligent, or who have made prominent achievements in their political career, or who have met the five requirements shall be promoted specially through recommendation by 'Jian Cha Yu Shi' (the supervisory censor) and 'Su Zheng Lian Fang Si' (the government supervising office). While those officials who have sought personal gains at the expanse of the public interests, or who have taken bribery and failed to meet the five requirements shall be found guilty according to law, once the accusation prove to be true."³³ In order to ensure the quality of the official examination, "Yu Shi Tai" (The Censorate) was put in charge of checking and inspection. In the 11th year of Dade during the reign of Emperor Chengzong (1307), an imperial edict was issued wherein it was stipulated that "supervision and investigation shall be carried out strictly by 'Jian Cha Yu Shi' (the supervisory censor) and 'Lian Fang Si' (the government supervising office) with the final results of the official examination and the name list of the best and worst officials presented to the higher level authority at the end of the year, according to which the officials shall be demoted or promoted."³⁴

Because the supervising officials were powerful and influential, special provisions were made for their examination. Moreover, at the end of their term of office,

---

³¹Sun Chengze (Ming Dynasty), "Wu Shi Kao Shou Ling" (Evaluating the Magistrates in 5 Aspects) in *Yuan Chao Dian Gu Bian Nian Kao* (*The Chronicles of Classic Allusions of Yuan Dynasty*) in *Si Ku Quan Shu* (*Complete Library in the Four Branches of Literature*).

³²"Bai Guan Zhi" (The Record of the Officials of all Ranks) (Part 4) in *Xin Yuan Shi* (*The New History of Yuan Dynasty*).

³³"Xing Bu" (The Department of Punishment) (Part 8) in *Yuan Dian Zhang* (*The Collection of Statutes of Yuan Dynasty*), Vol. 46.

³⁴"Sheng Zheng" (Imperial Administration) (Part 1) in *Yuan Dian Zhang* (*The Collection of Statutes of Yuan Dynasty*), Vol. 2.

their work would be assessed by "Su Zheng Lian Fang Si" (the government supervising office), and they would be considered "qualified" if "'Dao' (the administration district below the province) which they are in charge of is prosperous and peaceful, or if the civilians have no grievances"; however, they would be considered "unqualified" if they "are rigid and critical of trivial things, or it they often make trouble, or they do not know the important principles or fail to find out the truth through investigation, or their acts have led to people's great discontent and grievances." "Yu Shi Tai" (The Censorate) was in charge of the assessment of supervising officials, and the assessment results "would be presented to 'Zhong Shu Sheng' (the supreme organization in charge of the state affairs) to decide whether they should be promoted or demoted."[35]

If the supervising officials at all levels could "carry out the supervisory work whole heartedly, or manage the country according to law, or get the respect of the subordinate officials or bring peace and prosperity to 'Dao' (the administration district below the province)," they would "be considered as 'qualified'"; however, they would be considered "unqualified" if they "have not dealt with the important matters with due diligence, or are rigid and critical of trivial things, or do not know the important principles." "Xing Yu Shi Tai" (The Provincial Censorate) regularly conducted their assessment to decide whether they should be promoted or demoted.[36]

Although rules were made for the assessment of officials in Yuan Dynasty, it was difficult to put them into practice due to political chaos. Especially, "the petty officials and secretaries often obtained personal gains by taking advantage of their power and playing with literary skills."[37]

In the 22nd year of Zhiyuan during the reign of Emperor Shizu (1285), an official salary system was implemented, and monthly salary was begun to be paid to the officials in silver, which was replaced later by cash money. The monthly salary for "Cheng Xiang" (the prime minister) was one hundred and forty *guan* of money and fifteen *dan* of rice, and the monthly salary for officials below "Cheng Xiang" (the prime minister) was reduced according to their official ranks. As for the officials outside the capital, they were also granted two to sixteen *qing* of "Zhi Tian" (professional farmland, which was given as official salary according to official rank in ancient China).

As regards the retirement of officials, during the reign of Emperor Taizu, Wang Pan, who was then "Tai Chang Shao Qing" (the deputy head of Tai Chang Temple in charge of imperial ceremonies and sacrifices), once pointed out that "according to the employment system of previous dynasties, people started their official career at twenty and retired from office at seventy, so it might give them a sense of shame to

---

[35]"Tai Gang" (The Principles of Imperial Court) (Part 2) in *Yuan Dian Zhang* (*The Collection of Statutes of Yuan Dynasty*), Vol. 6.

[36]"Tai Gang" (The Principles of Imperial Court) (Part 2) in *Yuan Dian Zhang* (*The Collection of Statutes of Yuan Dynasty*), Vol. 6.

[37]"Xuan Ju Zhi" (The Record of Election) in *Yuan Shi* (*The History of Yuan Dynasty*).

provide them with financial help and to show them compassion for their senility. Nowadays, since there is no age limit for officials, it is impossible for the officials who are old and sick to be removed from office. Consequently, the officials themselves do not have a sense of shame, nor does the imperial court consider it wrong, which really should be stopped."[38] Finally, his advice was accepted by Emperor Shizu, so seventy years old was taken as the age for official retirement, but actually the system was not strictly implemented. When Mongolian and Semu officials (the nationalities in the western or northwestern regions) retired, they both were promoted one rank as special treatment. However, senior assistants and ministers in "Han Lin Yuan" (The Hanlin Academy) and "Ji Xian Yuan" (the Bureau for the Assembly of Virtuous Persons), who offered consultation to the court, were not allowed to retire at the age of seventy.

Among the administrative laws of the Yuan Dynasty, those that best reflected the characteristics of the times were the laws for the supervision of officials. After the establishment of a unified regime, in order to get rid of the long-standing old, indolent, and slack practices and customs of the Mongolian people and to supervise the administrative activities of the officials of the Han and other ethnic minority groups, great importance was attached to the functioning of the supervisory organs. Emperor Shizu once clearly explained the relationship between "Zhong Shu Sheng" (the supreme organization in charge of state affairs), "Shu Mi Yuan" (Privy Council), and "Yu Shi Tai" (The Censorate), as well as the reason for his emphasis on "Yu Shi Tai" (The Censorate): "Emperor Shizu once said that 'Zhong Shu Sheng' (the supreme organization in charge of the state affairs) is my left hand, 'Shu Mi Yuan' (Privy Council) is my right hand, and 'Yu Shi Tai' (The Censorate) is in charge of giving medical treatment to my two hands. So his idea of stressing the function of 'Yu Shi Tai' (The Censorate) has been followed invariably by the successive generations."[39] Since great importance was attached by the emperors to the supervisory organs, their status was improved significantly. The central supervisory departments, namely, "Yu Shi Tai" (The Censorate) and "Zhong Shu Sheng" (the supreme organization in charge of state affairs), were independent of each other and were given equal status. The official rank of "Yu Shi Da Fu" (Grand Censor) was raised from "Cong Er Pin" (the accessary second rank) to "Cong Yi Pin" (the accessary first rank). Moreover, the supervisory authority of "Yu Shi Tai" (The Censorate) was reinforced, so that it was all within the jurisdiction of "Yu Shi Tai" (The Censorate) to rectify administrative violations and malpractices, to prevent illicit manufacturing, to correct miscarriage of justice, to inspect officials' performance of their duties, to punish civil and military officials for their gross negligence and serious violation of regulations, etc. It was recorded in "Zhi Zhi" (State Office System) in "Xing Fa Zhi" (The Record of Criminal Law) in *Yuan Shi* (*The History of Yuan Dynasty*) that "the officials of 'Yu Shi Tai' (The Censorate) were in charge of

---

[38]"Wang Pan Zhuan" (The Biography of Wang Pan) in *Yuan Shi* (*The History of Yuan Dynasty*).
[39]Ye Ziqi (Ming Dynasty), "Za Lun Pian" (Miscellaneous Essays) in *Cao Mu Zi* (*Collection of Notes and Stories by Ye Ziqi*), Vol. 3.

9.2 The Administrative Legislation and Management System with National...

rectifying the official regulation, managing the official assessment, arranging sacrifices in the court, inspecting 'Xing Ren' (official in charge of delivering imperial orders and conferring titles of nobility) on diplomatic mission, presenting and transmitting memorials about military and political affairs, and transferring and conveying the people's complaints and injustice. Besides, they were also in charge of the following affairs: 'Xing Ming' (Law), 'Fu Yi' (Tax and Corvee), 'Quan Xuan' (selection of officials by evaluating their qualifications), 'Kuai Ji' (financial matters), 'Diao Du' (dispatching), 'Ying Shan' (preparing meals), 'Ju Kan' (interrogation), 'Shen Yan' (trial and conviction), 'Gou Ji' (examination and checking), as well as the punishment of the corruption of officials, the prohibition of random enforcement of laws, the arrangement of the helpless and homeless people and forceful annexation."

In order to regulate the activities of supervisory organs, a series of supervisory laws and regulations was established in the Yuan Dynasty. In the 5th year of Zhiyuan during the reign of Emperor Shizu (1268), under the leadership of "Shi Yu Shi" (subordinate of Grand Censor), Gao Ming, "thirty six articles of 'Tai Gang' (the principles of imperial court) were formulated," which was also called *Xian Tai Ge Li (The Rules and Regulations for the Censorate)*. In the 6th year of Zhiyuan (1269), *Cha Si Ti Cha Tiao Li (The Supervisory Regulations of the Investigation Offices)* was issued to provide the specific duties of supervising officials in each "Dao" (the administration district below the province); in the 14th year of Zhiyuan (1277), *Xing Tai Ti Cha Tiao Li (The Supervisory Regulations of the Provincial Censorate)* was issued to provide the specific duties of "Xing Yu Shi Tai" (The Provincial Censorate). Later, many other laws were made; for example, *Jin Zhi Cha Si Tiao Li (The Regulations for the Administration of Investigation Offices)* was issued in the 21st year of Zhiyuan (1284), *Cha Si He Cha Shi Li (Matters for the Supervision of Investigation Offices)* in the 25th year of Zhiyuan (1289), and *Lian Fang Si He Xing Tiao Li (The Regulations for the Investigation Offices)* in the 29th year of Zhiyuan (1292). The supervisory laws and regulations were gradually perfected with the efforts of Emperor Shizu, so that "they were followed invariably by the successive generations" after him. Therefore, it can be said that *Feng Xian Hong Gang (The Fundamental Rules and Guiding Principles for Disciplines)*, made during the reign of Emperor Renzong, was a complete collection of laws for administrative supervision.

In *Xian Tai Ge Li (The Rules and Regulations for the Censorate)*, the jurisdiction of "Yu Shi Tai" (The Censorate) was clearly specified. So "Yu Shi Tai" (The Censorate) was granted the power to impeach all central and local officials in "Zhong Shu Sheng" (the supreme organization in charge of state affairs), "Shu Mi Yuan" (Privy Council), "Zhi Guo Yong Shi Si" (government office in charge of finance), and other offices for their criminal acts and violations of law, to rectify the folk customs, to sort out official documents in all government offices, to supervise sacrificial affairs and diplomatic missions, and to look into matters concerning old and sick officials and their assessment. Honest, competent, fair, and upright officials would be reported to the emperor; mean, incompetent, and despicable officials would be investigated and punished. As to the transfer and promotion of officials, they would be transferred or promoted at the end of their term of office. If they were transferred and promoted without following "Tiao Ge" (legal provisions and injunctions) or if they were promoted without permission from the government, they should be checked, investigated, and punished by "Yu Shi Tai" (The Censorate). In addition, "if the officials had bought things with "He Mai" (bought various things on a large scale) without following the actual market price by taking the advantage of their power, or misappropriated official money, or embezzled part of what should be distributed, or embezzled public property illegally or transferred and borrowed public property, or begged for money and goods, or failed to hand in all tax to government offices by keeping the extra amount," they would all be investigated and punished by "Yu Shi Tai" (The Censorate). Moreover, if the supervision officials had caused abnormal deaths and injuries to the imprisoned or revealed information in arresting and trying serious offenders and checking official documents or were entrusted with the case by the litigants at his private residence, they would also be investigated and punished. Meanwhile, the judicial supervisory power of "Yu Shi Tai" (The Censorate) was clearly defined: "Litigants shall first complain to the government office concerned. If they have grievances, the civilian households should appeal to 'Zuo You Bu' (government offices in Yuan Dynasty) of 'Zhong Shu Sheng' (the supreme organization in charge of the state affairs), the military households to 'Shu Mi Yuan' (Privy Council), and business households to 'Zhi Guo Yong Shi Si' (government office in charge of finance). If the trial and judgment are not handled appropriately, the officials should be reported and impeached by 'Yu Shi Tai' (The Censorate)"; "if the officials in the government offices have committed crimes ... supervision and investigation should be conducted by 'Yu Shi Tai' (The Censorate)"; "if people are wrongfully imprisoned or interrogated by torture, or if there are cases which should not accepted and heard in the first place in government offices, supervision and investigation should be conducted by 'Yu Shi Tai' (The Censorate) according to the real situation. If there are really injustice, the reason for its occurrence shall be reported immediately and a document shall be issued to the government offices where the case has been accepted and tried, so that the unjust cases can be settled and rectified as soon as possible. If the government officials who have accepted and heard the case have broken the law, investigations shall be conducted," and "those officials who have caused abnormal deaths and injuries to the imprisoned shall be investigated by 'Yu Shi Tai' (The Censorate) according to the real situation."

In addition, "Yu Shi Tai" (The Censorate) had the right to investigate on and deal with the following matters: slack supervision of private transactions of certain goods, obstruction and violation of the rules of paper currency, failure to report disasters, decrease of population, neglect of farming and sericulture, reduction and damage of the granaries, officials' drinking excessively in tea houses, failure to report disputes at borders, failure to defend border cities, and so on.

It was also specifically stipulated in *Xian Tai Ge Li* (*The Rules and Regulations for the Censorate*) that "if officials have failed to fulfill the responsibility which they should, they should be investigated, supervised and punished by 'Yu Shi Tai' (The Censorate)"; by this, the scope of supervision, investigation, and impeaching of "Yu

Shi Tai" (The Censorate) was so greatly expanded that the provisions could be interpreted arbitrarily to some extent.

In the local supervisory regulation of *Xing Tai Ti Cha Tiao Li* (*The Supervisory Regulations of the Provincial Censorate*), the scope of the function and power of "Xing Zhong Shu Sheng" (the provincial supreme organization in charge of daily affairs) was specified. Accordingly, it had the following rights: impeaching officials in "Xing Zhong Shu Sheng" (the provincial supreme organization in charge of daily affairs), "Xuan Wei Si" (the government office in remote areas), and the government offices below them for their treacherous and evil acts or for their illegal obtaining of official documents without permission; conducting investigations on officials for their acts of bribery or embezzling, transferring, and borrowing government money; conducting investigations on officials who were responsible for monitoring the implementation of government decrees but who had delayed their supervisory work or who had carried out their supervisory work but did not report their illegal and criminal acts to the relevant authorities, which had led to the failure of implementation of government decrees; conducting investigations on officials for their criminal acts of misusing punishment, levying tax and allocating corvee services unfairly, reducing the registration of households, decreasing and damaging granaries, collecting property and allocating corvee services without authorization, manufacturing illegally, refusing to pay money in "He Mai" (bought on a large scale various things), and so on; conducting investigations on officials for their failure to report warning at borders, their failure to execute commands strictly, their failure to wear their clothes and armors properly, their failure to report military victories truthfully, their failure to hear a case justly, their failure to sentence and to convict criminals properly when handling criminal cases and lawsuits, their intentionally exonerating the guilty or implicating the innocent by taking other people's money; and all other irrational and unfair acts. In the meantime, if officials nationwide could, through good governance, reduce the cases in litigation, stabilize the political situation, make people live in peace, wipe out thieves, and make people in local places live peacefully, they would be recommended to the court for promotion; however, if the officials were greedy and tyrannical or if they did not know the principles of running a country or if they had undermined official business and brought harm to the common people or if they were incompetent due to senility and failing health, they would all be investigated and punished. Finally, a special provision was made in *Xing Tai Ti Cha Tiao Li* (*The Supervisory Regulations of the Provincial Censorate*): "If there is anything that can bring benefit and eliminate harm, or anything that needs to be changed because it is inconvenient to the people, it shall all be reported to 'Yu Shi Tai' (The Censorate) and 'Zhong Shu Sheng' (the supreme organization in charge of the state affairs) and then memorials shall be submitted to the Emperor. If the officials have not fulfilled the responsibilities which they should, they should be investigated by 'Xing Yu Shi Tai' (The Provincial Censorate) and punished by 'Bi Fu' (legal analogy). Besides, the problems should be handled by referring to the existing law and measures should be taken immediately." Thus, it can be seen that the local procuratorial power of "Xing Yu Shi Tai" (The Provincial Censorate) was very extensive.

In *Cha Si Ti Cha Tiao Li* (*The Supervisory Regulations of the Investigation Offices*) issued in the 6th year of Zhiyuan (1269), the statutory supervisory responsibility of "Bei Yu" (military officer in charge of border defense) in the frontier regions was emphasized: firstly, it was forbidden for the banned goods to be traded privately at borders, and precautions should be taken to prevent spies to sneak across the borders. Moreover, if officials in border regions were sluggish in defense and the enforcement of prohibition, they should be investigated and punished; if the guards at strategic passes, ferries, and forts had deliberately caused trouble and obstructed the travelers, they should be investigated and punished. Secondly, the specific requirements for litigation and trial were provided: litigants should complain first to the government office in charge and then file a lawsuit from bottom up; if the trial and judgment were mishandled, the litigants could go and complain to "Ti Xing An Cha Si" (the governmental office in charge of the administration of justice); if litigants had filed a lawsuit by "Yue Su" (overstepping indictment) or had lodged a false charge, they should be punished in accordance with imperial edicts and decrees; whenever criminals were tried in the capital or in "Fu" (ancient administrative district between province and county), "Zhou" (subprefecture), and "Xian" (county), they should be tried by "Gong Zuo Yuan Wen" (a way of hearing cases in the Yuan Dynasty wherein several senior officers and chief officials try a case collectively) rather than tried by the petty officials assigned. Finally, the rights of "Ti Xing An Cha Si" (the governmental office in charge of the administration of justice) in recommending officials, as well as the contents of official assessment, were clarified: "if there are people who are virtuous, capable and qualified for the political career in 'Lu' (ancient administrative region), 'Zhou' (subprefecture), and 'Xian' (county), they shall be reported and recommended to 'Ti Xing An Cha Si' (the governmental office in charge of the administration of justice) to be investigated, then reports should be made to 'Zhong Shu Sheng' (the supreme organization in charge of the state affairs) by 'Yu Shi Tai' (The Censorate)." The officials of "Ti Xing An Cha Si" (the governmental office in charge of the administration of justice) should be evaluated and assessed by "Yu Shi Tai" (The Censorate), and those who had brought about prosperity and peace to "Dao" (the administration district below the province) or who knew the principles of ruling the country or who were able to find out the truth through investigations so that local civilians had no grievances should be considered qualified; however, those who were rigid and critical of trivial things or did not know important principles or had failed to find out the truth through investigations so that civilians had a lot of grievances should be considered unqualified. Based on their actual performance, their assessment results should be presented to "Zhong Shu Sheng" (the supreme organization in charge of state affairs) for final decision.

Judicial supervision was one of the most important functions and powers of the supervision officials mentioned above, and it was stipulated in "Xing Fa Zhi" (The Record of Criminal Law) in *Yuan Shi* (*The History of Yuan Dynasty*) that "when important cases involving murder are heard and judged by 'Da Zong Zheng Fu' (a central judicial organ of Yuan Dynasty), official documents and files should be written in Chinese characters, and they should be transferred to 'Yu Shi Tai' (The

Censorate), and then be reviewed by 'Jian Cha Yu Shi' (the supervisory censor)"; "as for the inquisition of prisoners, apart from major cases entrusted by the imperial court, it shall not be conducted at night; otherwise, it should be investigated by 'Lian Fang Si' (the government supervising office)"; "even if found guilty of treason, all prisoners convicted of a felony shall be examined and reviewed by 'Yu Shi Tai' (The Censorate) first, and then be executed in market place; all the prisoners inside and outside the capital shall be examined and reviewed by the senior officials of each 'Lu' (ancient administrative region), or 'Jian Cha Yu Shi' (the supervisory censor) and 'Lian Fang Si' (the government supervising office) immediately, so that the persons with minor offences be released and the persons with felonies be punished. If the prisoners have grievances, their unjust cases should be reviewed and rectified."

Since the emperor was always very suspicious of his subordinate officials under the autocratic system, he particularly relied on "Jian Cha Yu Shi" (the supervisory censor) and "Su Zheng Lian Fang Shi" (the government supervising official). "Jian Cha Yu Shi" (the supervisory censor), who was subordinate to "Cha Yuan" (a government office under the Censorate) of "Yu Shi Tai" (The Censorate), acted as the eyes and ears of the emperor, so he was specialized in making reports to the emperor, as was described in the saying that "if there are any law breakers in the government offices within the capital, they should be impeached by 'Jian Cha Yu Shi' (the supervisory censor)." As for "Su Zheng Lian Fang Shi" (the government supervising official), who was subordinate to "Xing Yu Shi Tai" (The Provincial Censorate), he was stationed permanently in the supervision area of each "Dao" (the administration district below the province) to supervise the local officials, as was described in the saying that "they have the rights to inspect 'Xing Ren' (official in charge of delivering imperial orders and conferring titles of nobility) on diplomatic missions ... and transferring and conveying the people's complaints and injustice".[40] With respect to officials' dereliction of their duties and other acts, such as "bribery, fraud, tax evasion, and other crimes stipulated in the criminal law," "the total number of violators and the circumstances of the crimes" should be reported by "Su Zheng Lian Fang Shi" (the government supervising official) to the imperial court.[41]

In order to prevent "Lian Fang Shi" (the government supervising official) from abusing power and undermining the rule of law, "Xing Yu Shi Tai" (The Provincial Censorate) was set up in Jiangnan and Shanxi by "Yu Shi Tai" (The Censorate) to strengthen its leadership over "Su Zheng Lian Fang Shi" (the government supervising official). According to "Zhi Zhi" (State Office System) in "Xing Fa Zhi" (The Record of Criminal Law) in *Yuan Shi* (*The History of Yuan Dynasty*), "the officials of 'Xing Yu Shi Tai' (The Provincial Censorate) are mainly in charge of conducting investigations on the various military and civilian officials who have committed crimes in 'Xing Sheng' (province), 'Xuan Wei Si' (the government office in remote areas) and the government offices below them, conducting investigations on the poor

---

[40]"Xing Fa Zhi" (The Record of Criminal Law) (Part 1) in *Yuan Shi* (*The History of Yuan Dynasty*).
[41]"Xing Fa Zhi" (The Record of Criminal Law) (Part 1) in *Yuan Shi* (*The History of Yuan Dynasty*).

people who are homeless and unemployed and conducting investigations on the powerful and tyrannical people who have seized the interests of the common people and the judicial officials who are unqualified for their work. Moreover, the rest of their responsibilities also include those which were stipulated in the regulations of 'Yu Shi Tai' (The Censorate)." At the same time, rules and regulations were also made for the evaluation of "Su Zheng Lian Fang Shi" (the government supervising official). Officials who could promptly report the "grievances" within their respective jurisdiction to "Yu Shi Tai" (The Censorate) should be "recorded" to be used as evidence for their future promotion. However, if "inappropriate impeachment has been made," they should be held responsible for the "misconduct" and "shall be punished."

So the formation of the system of the central and local supervisory organs, the elevation of their status, and the making of supervisory regulations were all inseparable from the special historical condition of the ruling of Yuan Dynasty. The Yuan regime was ruled by Mongolian nobles, so they had to depend on the landlords and bureaucrats of the Han nationality to achieve their goal of controlling the whole country, but at the same time, they also worried that the officials of the Han nationality could raise their own social status by making use of their power, which was harmful to the ruling of Mongolian nobles. Therefore, the policy of making use of and guarding against the officials of the Han nationality was taken, so activities of local officials of the Han nationality were closely monitored by the Yuan rulers through supervisory organs, which was precisely the reason why the position of "Yu Shi Da Fu" (Grand Censor) "is held by the people with Mongolian surnames (Mongolian nobles)."[42] In the 6th year of Zhizheng during the reign of Emperor Shundi (1346), He Weiyi, the official from the Han nationality, was appointed "Yu Shi Da Fu" (Grand Censor) by the emperor, so he was especially granted a Mongolian surname, called Taiping. But the ordinary officials of the Han nationality were even ineligible to serve as clerks of local supervisory organs. In addition, Mongolian and Semu nobles (the nationalities in the western or northwestern regions) and bureaucrats lacked the experience and ability to manage a huge unified country; even Emperor Shizu also admitted that "it is impossible for the incumbent and incompetent officials to administer government affairs efficiently"[43]; therefore, the proposal of strengthening the supervisory organs, which was put forward by officials from the Han nationality, was adopted in order to better the management of officials, to improve administrative efficiency, and to give a full play to the role of state organs through supervisory organizations because they believed that "only by making laws and principles can the country be well governed."

Due to the extensive functions and powers of supervisory organs in the Yuan Dynasty, importance was attached to the selection of the officials of "Yu Shi Tai" (The Censorate); therefore, "the promotion of officials is often decided by the

---

[42]"Tai Ping Zhuan" (The Biography of Taiping) in *Yuan Shi* (*The History of Yuan Dynasty*).

[43]"Zhang Xiong Zhuan" (The Biography of Zhang Xiong) in *Yuan Shi* (*The History of Yuan Dynasty*).

Emperor himself, and those who are selected must be honest, upright and loyal to the country so that they can be sincere and magnanimous in the governance of the state." If the supervisory officials had broken the law or neglected their duties, they should be punished more severely. According to "Zhi Zhi" (State Office System) in "Xing Fa Zhi" (The Record of Criminal Law) in *Yuan Shi* (*The History of Yuan Dynasty*), "as for the supervision officials, they should be recommended for promotion according to their excellent performance in the official evaluation and impeached according to the evidence of their crimes. If promotion and impeachment are conducted inappropriately, they shall be punished." Moreover, "if the supervision officials have committed the crime of bribery, they shall be punished more severely; even if they have not broken the law, they shall be removed from their offices." In *Yuan Dian Zhang* (*The Collection of Statutes of Yuan Dynasty*), there were also the following provisions: "it is forbidden for 'Yu Shi Tai' (The Censorate), 'An Cha Si' (The Judicial Commission), and 'Jian Cha Yu Shi' (the supervisory censor) ... to correct others' mistakes until they have straightened out their own wrong thoughts, words and deeds, so it is forbidden for them to inform against others by taking bribes; if they have committed crimes in the future, they shall be punished one level severer than other officials, even if an amnesty is offered by the Emperor, they shall not be pardoned..."

As to the local supervising officials, in August of the 21st year of Zhiyuan (1355), *Jin Zhi Cha Si Tiao Li* (*The Regulations for the Administration of Investigation Offices*) was particularly made to keep them under control. For example, "of the officials inside and outside the capital who have committed bribery, those who have committed minor offences shall be punished by 'Zhang' (flogging with heavy sticks) and those who have committed serious offences shall be put to death; if 'Yan Guan'(official responsible for giving advice to the emperor) has failed to report the cases of bribery, they shall be punished for the same crime as 'Zuo Zang' (embezzlement)"[44]; "it is forbidden for the local supervision officers to accept others' gifts on account of birthday, holiday, and farewell and welcome parties, and those violators shall be convicted of bribery; it is forbidden for 'Xun An' (inspector) to marry the local women, and those violators shall be punished according to the law; it is forbidden for the local supervision officials to visit their relatives and accept the property offered as gifts in local places where their offices locate or in the places where they are going to inspect, and those violators shall be shall be punished for the crime of bribery."[45]

---

[44]"Xing Zhi" (Criminal System) (Book 2) in "Xing" (Criminal Law) (Book 2) in *Xu Tong Dian* (*Xu Tong Code*), Vol. 180.

[45]"Tai Gang" (The Principles of Imperial Court) (Part 2) in *Yuan Dian Zhang* (*The Collection of Statutes of Yuan Dynasty*), Vol. 6.

9.3 Criminal Law Made by Combining Reference to the Old Systems of the Tang and Song Dynasties and Innovation

Before Emperor Shizu ascended the throne, the penalty system was in disorder and laws were often made to deal with specific matters. For example, in order to ensure the occupation of the plundered people in the battlefield, "Cang Wang Fa" (the law against the concealment of fugitives) was implemented, and it was stipulated that "whoever shelters and gives food to fugitives shall be put to death; whether it is in the city or in the countryside, if the member of one family violates the law, the other families in the neighbourhood shall be punished by 'Lian Zuo' (being punished for being related to somebody who committed an offence)."[46] "Cang Wang Fa" (the law against the concealment of fugitives) developed from "Zha Sa" (the Yasa or customary law), which was made during the reign of Genghis Khan. According to "Zha Sa" (the Yasa or customary law), "whoever finds a runaway slave or captive but does not return him to his owner shall be put to death," and "whoever gives food or clothing to a captive without the permission of his owner shall also be put to death."[47]

After Emperor Shizu ascended the throne, *Tai He Lv* (*Tai He Code*), which was made in the Jin Dynasty, and the Mongolian customary law were implemented, but the chaotic state of the criminal law was not changed, so Liu Bingzhong and Yao Shu, the officials from the Han nationality, once made a suggestion to Emperor Shizu: "Now officials of all ranks are self-conceited. Besides, they have abused their power for their own gains and decided whether to put a person to death or not out of their own wills," so it was very necessary to "make a law according to the ancient ones by taking the current situations into consideration so that no officials dare to misconduct beyond their own duties."[48] In addition, "laws should be made; trials and criminal penalties should be investigated; the power of deciding people's life and death should be taken back by the imperial court, by which the dukes and princes can be prevented from exclusively grabbing all power to themselves, the people guilty of felonies will not get away from punishments, the people guilty of minor offences will be exempted from death penalty, and injustice will be rectified."[49] Their suggestions were accepted by Emperor Shizu, so at end of the 8th year of Zhiyuan (1271), *Tai He Lv* (*Tai He Code*), which was made in the Jin Dynasty was ordered to be abolished and the legal culture of the Han nationality was extensively absorbed. Generally speaking, the criminal law of the Yuan Dynasty was mainly made up of

---

[46]Su Tianjue (Yuan Dynasty), *Yuan Wen Lei* (*A Collection of Essays of Yuan Dynasty*), Vol. 57, quoted from *Ye Lv Chu Cai Shen Dao Bei* (*The Tablet on the Pathway to the Tomb of Yelv Chucai*) by Song Zizhen.

[47]Riasanovsky (Russia), *Mongolian Customary Laws*.

[48]"Liu Bing Zhong Zhuan" (The Biography of Liu Bingzhong) in *Yuan Shi* (*The History of Yuan Dynasty*).

[49]"Yao Shu Zhuan" (The Biography of Yao Shu) in *Yuan Shi* (*The History of Yuan Dynasty*).

"Tiao Ge" (legal provisions and injunctions) and "Duan Li" (legal precedents), so when the famous *Da Yuan Tong Zhi (General Regulations of the Great Yuan Dynasty)* was formulated, it still contained 717 articles of "Duan Li" (legal precedents). Although the criminal law of the Yuan Dynasty was different from those of the Tang and Song dynasties in both form and name, to some extent, their basic spirit was followed. Famous scholar Wu Cheng in the late period of the Yuan Dynasty had commented: "*Da Yuan Tong Zhi (General Regulations of the Great Yuan Dynasty)* is issued nationwide. Although the ancient laws have been abolished, yet this law is newly made in the imperial Yuan Dynasty on the basis of the ancient laws, so even though different words are used, their meanings are generally the same. Consequently, the ancient laws are still used secretly, but not openly; that is to say, they are only abolished nominally, but in fact are continued to be applied. Why so? Because 'Zhi Zhao' (imperial orders) and 'Tiao Ge' (legal provisions and injunctions) are similar to 'Chi' (instruction), 'Ling' (decree), 'Ge' (injunction) and 'Shi' (standard) and the contents of 'Duan Li' (legal precedents) … are compiled by following the orders of the categories of ancient laws. Since the new law is made in the imitation of the ancient laws, it is impossible for people to violate the law even if they want to. Isn't it that the ancient laws are still applied secretly, though not openly, namely, they are only abolished nominally but in fact continued to be applied?"[50] When Emperor Wenzong read "Xian Dian" (Codes on Punishments) in *Jing Shi Da Dian (Great Code of Yuan Dynasty)*, he said to his courtiers: "Isn't it *Tang Lv (Tang Code)*?"[51] Thus, we can see the inherent relationship between the criminal law of the Yuan Dynasty and those of the Tang and Song dynasties.

9.3.1 Executing Penalties According to "Fu Zhi" (Mourning Apparel System)

Under the influence of the legal culture of the Tang and Song dynasties, criminal penalties in the Yuan Dynasty were also executed according to "Wu Fu" (relatives within the five degrees of mourning) and the Confucian ethical code of "San Gang Wu Chang" (three cardinal guides and five constant virtues). Early at the beginning of the Yuan Dynasty, when *Da De Dian Zhang (Collection of Laws of Dade)* was drafted, "Sang Fu Tu" (The Diagram of Mourning Apparel) was included in it. So "Sang Fu Tu" (The Diagram of Mourning Apparel) was also included in the ritual system of "Li Bu" (The Department of Rites) in *Yuan Dian Zhang (The Collection of Statutes of Yuan Dynasty)*. In particular, the special provisions of "Wu Fu" (relatives within the five degrees of mourning) were included in *Da Yuan Tong Zhi (General*

---

[50]Wu Cheng (Yuan Dynasty), "Da Yuan Tong Zhi Tiao Li Gang Mu Hou Xu" (The Epilogue to Outlines of General Regulations of the Great Yuan Dynasty) in *Cao Lu Wu Wen Zheng Gong Quan Ji (Complete Works of the Revered Mr. Wu Wenzheng)*, Vol. 19.

[51]"Jie Xi Si Zhuan" (The Biography of Jie Xisi) in *Yuan Shi (The History of Yuan Dynasty)*.

Regulations of the Great Yuan Dynasty), as was stated in "Xian Dian Zong Xu" (General Preface to Constitution) in *Jing Shi Da Dian* (*Great Code of Yuan Dynasty*) that "during the reign of Emperor Zhizhi, *Da Yuan Tong Zhi* (*General Regulations of the Great Yuan Dynasty*) was compiled and 'Wu Fu' (relatives within the five degrees of mourning) was included in the law."[52] "Wu Fu" (relatives within the five degrees of mourning) was an important label for the differentiation of the patriarchal hierarchy of superiority and inferiority, as well as the relationship between relatives, so it was not only a ritual system but also a legal system. In the criminal law of the Yuan Dynasty, "Wu Fu" (relatives within the five degrees of mourning) was listed in the first chapter of a special article, which showed that the rulers of the Yuan Dynasty had taken a positive attitude toward absorbing the orthodox legal culture. Moreover, it had provided a precedent for the Ming and Qing dynasties to list "Wu Fu" (relatives within the five degrees of mourning) in the first chapter of the law. In addition, in the criminal law of the Yuan Dynasty, usually a much severer punishment was enforced for offenses against ethics. For example, "if a son kills his parents, even if he dies of hunger or disease in prison, his corpse shall still be dismembered and exposed publicly"; "if a son rapes his father's concubine in the mourning period of his parents, he shall be punished by 'Zhang' (flogging with heavy sticks) for ninety seven strokes and the woman shall return to her parents' home."[53] However, it was provided in the laws of the Tang and Song dynasties that if a person's parents and grandparents were still alive, it was forbidden for him to live separately and to divide the property of the family, while in the criminal law of the Yuan Dynasty, this was not explicitly prohibited, and in *Yuan Dian Zhang* (*The Collection of Statutes of Yuan Dynasty*), there was even a record of a case about sons and grandsons living separately and having the family property divided with the permission of the parents.

9.3.2 Changing "Shi E" (The Ten Abominations) to "Zhu E" (Various Abominations)

As far as the criminal law of the Yuan Dynasty was concerned, although the old legal systems of the Tang and Song dynasties were followed, some innovations were also made out of the reality of ruling. For example, "Shi E" (The Ten Abominations) was changed to "Zhu E" (various abominations). "Shi E" (The Ten Abominations) was the most serious offense in the laws of the Tang and Song dynasties, and in the Yuan Dynasty, the basic contents of "Shi E" (The Ten Abominations) were followed, but the name of "Shi E" (The Ten Abominations) was changed to "Zhu E" (various abominations). Of these crimes, preventing "Mou Fan" (plotting rebellion or plotting

---

[52] Su Tianjue (Yuan Dynasty), "Xian Dian Zong Xu" (A General Preface to Constitution) in *Yuan Wen Lei* (*A Collection of Essays of Yuan Dynasty*), Vol. 42.

[53] "Xing Fa Zhi" (The Record of Criminal Law) (Part 3) in *Yuan Shi* (*The History of Yuan Dynasty*).

to endanger the country), a crime endangering the regime, was the focus of suppression activities, and it was stipulated that "those who attempt to endanger the country shall be put to death; for those who discuss treachery with no reason, the advocator shall be put to death, while the followers shall be punished by 'Liu' (exile); those who plot a rebellion secretly shall be put to death; if the householder as well as the two neighbors know about the crime but do not report to the government, they shall be convicted of the same crime; if there are already signs of rebellion, the principal offender and the accomplices shall all be put to death by 'Ling Chi' (the punishment of dismemberment and the lingering death) and the accessories shall be put to death; those who know about the crime but do not report ... shall be punished by 'Liu' (exile) to a remote place with their family property confiscated as well, and those relevant shall be punished by 'Lian Zuo' (being punished for being related to somebody who committed an offence) for the same crime; the traitors who have rebelled against the imperial court but wo refuse to surrender themselves shall be put to death; for those who mislead the masses with wild rumours or who gang together to make insurrection against the Emperor, the principal offender and accomplices shall all be put to death with their family property confiscated." So it can be seen that the crime of "Mou Fan" (plotting rebellion or plotting to endanger the country) was harshly punished, and many people had been implicated for the crime.

In order to prevent the Han people from gathering together to jeopardize the ruling of the Yuan Dynasty by using force, the Han people were prohibited from hunting with bows and arrows in groups of more than twenty people, and later on, all the Han people were prohibited from hunting regardless of their number. In the areas south of Yangtze River where anti-Yuan struggles were very fierce, curfews were imposed over a long period of time, and people were forbidden to walk on the streets or to light up oil lamps and candles in the house or to close the doors from dusk till dawn. Moreover, civil activities such as ordinary martial arts training, "public gathering to offer sacrifices to gods and pray for blessings," "offering sacrifices to gods to repay their blessings," "setting up markets for public gathering for buying and selling" in holidays, etc. were all strictly prohibited without exception.

In order to take strict precautionary measures against possible anti-Yuan armed insurrection, the crime of illicit possession and manufacturing of weapons was specially provided in the criminal law of the Yuan Dynasty. According to *Da Yuan Tong Zhi (General Regulations of the Great Yuan Dynasty)*, the possession of guns, knives, crossbows, bows and arrows, armor, as well as the tools that could be used as weapons, such as iron rulers, "Tie Gu Duo" (a weapon in ancient China whose name literally means iron flower bud), iron rods containing blades, and so on, constituted the crime of illicit possession of weapons. In the 23rd year of Zhiyuan during the reign of Emperor Shizu (1287), a "Chi Ling" (imperial decree) was issued by Emperor Shizu on the basis of the legal provision that "all Han people are prohibited from holding weapons," and it was ordered that "any Han people who hold iron rulers, 'Shou Wo' (a stick that can be used as weapon in ancient China) and iron rods with blades shall be punished by the local authorities." Moreover, civilians who illegally possessed more than ten sets of bows and arrows (a set consisting of a bow and thirty arrows) or illegally held ten weapons would be sentenced to death;

those who illegally possessed a complete set of armor would also be sentenced to death, and those who did not hold a complete set of armor would be punished according to how many pieces of armor they possessed. With the intensification of class struggle, even the archers and armymen from the Han nationality who were employed to capture thieves and robbers were not allowed to hold weapons during ordinary times, and only when they were sent to battles would they be given weapons; however, they would be "taken back and stored in arsenals" when the war was over. Furthermore, iron tools, which could be used as weapons, were exclusively sold by the government; if civilians illegally manufactured weapons, they would be convicted of the same crime as those who illegally held weapons, so they would all be sentenced to death. Iron craftsmen who could make ironware were supervised strictly by the government to prevent them from making weapons, but the Mongols and Semu (the nationalities in the western or northwestern regions) were not forbidden to do so. So it can be seen that the prohibition of illicit possession and manufacturing of weapons was mainly directed against the Han people.

Not only illicit possession and manufacturing of weapons were prohibited, but even illicit ownership and breeding of horses were also prohibited. If anyone had violated the law, all his property should be confiscated. Over the few decades from the reign of Emperor Shizu to that of Emperor Shundi, even more than 700,000 civilian horses were confiscated.

In addition, in order to maintain the imperial power and to safeguard the personal safety of the emperor, "whoever offends the rulers by making random and offensive remarks shall be put to death with their family property confiscated" and "whoever slanders the rulers maliciously by writing 'Ci Qu' (a genre of poetic verse in ancient China) shall be put to death." For the monks and Taoist priests with legal privileges, if they had forged scriptures to offend the rulers and confuse the masses, "the principal offender shall be punished by 'Zhan' (beheading) and the accessories shall be punished respectively according to the circumstances." So It can be seen from above that the punishment for the crime of offending the rulers was already expanded to the ideological and cultural fields.

If anyone had found fault in the emperor's carriages or any official had criticized the imperial decrees, they should also be found guilty of offending the rulers, so all of them would be punished according to law, except when special amnesty was offered by the emperor. Even in the case of amnesty, officials who had criticized imperial decrees would still be removed from their offices without being appointed as officials any more. As for "those who have stolen the imperial wares of the Emperor, they shall all be put to death regardless of the principal or the accessory offenders, and those who know about the fact but still buy them at lower prices shall be punished one level lighter than the statutory punishment."

Those who masterminded the forgery of "Fu Bao" (an ancient coin) or made them illegally by accepting other people's money should all be sentenced to death, and those who were involved in the forgery of "Zhi Chi" (imperial instruction) would be punished the same way as those involved in the forgery of "Fu Bao" (an ancient coin). In addition, those who changed "Zhi Shu" (imperial orders) randomly by adding or deleting of words and those who forged the characters of official seals of government offices by violating "Zhi Chi" (imperial instruction) would all be sentenced to death; those "Shi Guan" (official who worked around the emperor) who delivered false orders of the emperor would be punished by "Zhang" (flogging with heavy sticks) for one hundred and seven strokes and be removed from their offices without being appointed as officials again. Moreover, the chief conspirators, makers, and accomplices in the forgery of paper currency would all be sentenced to death; even if their parents were already old and there were no other young men in their family, their requests for penalty reduction would not be accepted, and also their family property would be confiscated. If two neighbors knew about the crime but did not report it, they would be punished by "Zhang" (flogging with heavy sticks) for seventy seven strokes; if "Fang Zheng" (chief official of townships), "Zhu Zhou" (the head of a grassroots organization in the countryside in ancient China), and "She Zhang" (head of the community) had neglected their supervisory duties, they and the soldiers on patrol would all be punished by "Chi" (flogging with light sticks) for forty seven strokes. And "Bu Dao Guan" (officers responsible for catching thieves) and garrison patrol officers would be punished by "Chi" (flogging with light sticks) for thirty seven strokes.

Those who entered the hall of the imperial palace with knives without permission would be punished by "Zhang" (flogging with heavy sticks) for eighty seven strokes and would be punished by "Liu" (exile) to remote places; those who entered the imperial palace without permission to steal gold and jade jewelry and other treasures would be put to death; of those who entered the imperial gardens illegally to hunt animals belonging to the government, the principal offender would be punished by "Zhang" (flogging with heavy sticks) for eighty strokes and "Tu" (imprisonment) for two years, and the accessories would be punished one level lighter than the statutory punishment and would be punished by "Ci Zi" (to make humiliating tattoo on one's body, especially on one's face) at the same time.

9.3.3 The Penalty System and the Principle of Making Criminal Law with National Characteristics

As for the penalty system of the Yuan Dynasty, the system of "Wu Xing" (Five Penalties), namely, "Chi" (flogging with light sticks), "Zhang" (flogging with heavy sticks), "Tu" (imprisonment), "Liu" (exile), and "Si" (death penalty), was continued to be applied, but the strokes of the punishment of "Chi" (flogging with light sticks) and "Zhang" (flogging with heavy sticks) were based on the number seven. So there were six levels of "Chi" (flogging with light sticks), namely, seven strokes, seventeen strokes, twenty seven strokes, thirty seven strokes, forty seven strokes, and fifty seven strokes, and five levels of "Zhang" (flogging with heavy sticks), namely, sixty seven strokes, seventy seven strokes, eighty seven strokes, ninety seven strokes, and one hundred and seven strokes. The reason why the base number was reduced from ten to seven in Yuan Dynasty was that Emperor Shizu decided to do a good deed because he had stated that "'Tian' (Heaven) has spared him once, 'Di' (Earth) has spared him once, so I have spared him once."

In addition, there were five levels of the punishment of "Tu" (imprisonment), namely, one year, one-and-a-half years, two years, two-and-a-half years, and three years. The strokes of "Zhang" (flogging with heavy sticks) ranged from sixty seven to one hundred and sevenstrokes. As for the punishment of "Liu" (exile), there were only three places of destinations—Liaoyang, Huguang, and Yibei without any differences of the distance of *li*. According to "Xian Dian Zong Xu" (General Preface to Constitution) in *Jing Shi Da Dian* (*Great Code of Yuan Dynasty*), "the Southerners are exiled to the North, while the Northerners are exiled to the South, which is generally the case for the punishment of 'Liu' (exile)." According to "Xing Fa Zhi" (The Record of Criminal Law) in *Yuan Shi* (*The History of Yuan Dynasty*), the punishment of "Si" (death penalty) was classified into two categories, namely, "Zhan" (beheading) and "Ling Chi" (the punishment of dismemberment and lingering death). It was mentioned in "Xian Dian Zong Xu" (General Preface to Constitution) in *Jing Shi Da Dian* (*Great Code of Yuan Dynasty*) that "for the death penalty, there is only one punishment of 'Zhan' (beheading) without that of 'Jiao' (hanging) … Below the punishment of 'Zhan' (beheading), the punishment of 'Zhang' (flogging with heavy sticks) for one hundred and seven strokes and the punishment of 'Ji Liu' (being exiled to a remote place after the registration and confiscation of the criminals' property) are established," but the punishment of "Ling Chi" (the punishment of dismemberment and lingering death) was not mentioned. According to *Da Yuan Tong Zhi* (*General Regulations of the Great Yuan Dynasty*), which was preserved in the block-printed edition of *Shi Ling Guang Ji* (*Detailed Records of Anecdotes*), made during the reign of Zhishun, the punishment of "Si" (death penalty) was classified into "'Jiao' (hanging) and 'Zhan'(beheading)." Besides, "two levels of death penalties were recorded, namely, 'Jiao' (hanging) and 'Zhan' (beheading)," in criminal law, which was quoted in the general rules of *Xing Tong Fu Shu* (*Comments on the Discussions of Criminal Provisions*). So it can be seen that "Si Xing" (death penalties) is usually divided into "Jiao" (hanging) and "Zhan" (beheading).

The punishment of "Ling Chi" (the punishment of dismemberment and lingering death) was mainly applied for the crime of "Da Ni" (great sedition) and "Da E" (great abominations) (including "Bu Xiao" (being unfilial)). As for the principal offenders and the accomplices, they would be punished by "Ling Chi" (the punishment of dismemberment and lingering death) without exception. Later, the accessories of "Mou Fan" (plotting rebellion or plotting to endanger the country) and those who concealed the crime without making reports were all punished by "Ling Chi" (the punishment of dismemberment and lingering death). If children and grandchildren killed their grandparents and parents or if an adulteress killed her husband by herself in consultation with the adulterer, they would also be punished by "Ling Chi" (the punishment of dismemberment and lingering death). If the criminal who had killed their parents had died before the execution, their corpses would still be dismembered and exposed publicly.

Although various provisions mentioned above were made on criminal punishment in the Yuan Dynasty, they were redundant and arbitrary in practice. At the same time, lynching was also legally conducted.

In addition, the redeeming system was also implemented. It was stipulated that "the officials are allowed to redeem their crimes by paying ransom if their crimes are not serious; they are also allowed to do so if they have violated the ban on going out at night. Besides, anyone who is older than seventy or younger than fifteen years old may redeem his crime by paying ransom if he can not bear the punishment of 'Zhang' (flogging with heavy sticks), and anyone who is 'Du Ji' (the incapacitated) may also redeem his crime by paying ransom money."[54]

9.3.3.1 Dividing and Ruling According to Ethnic Standards

If the Mongolians had committed crimes, it was not allowed for them to be tortured for a confession and except for the crime of death penalty, it was forbidden for them to be imprisoned or be taken into custody. If the Han people had committed theft, the offenders would be tattooed on the left arm for the first time, on the right arm for the second time, and on the neck for the third time; if the Han people had committed robbery, the offenders would be tattooed on the neck for the first time. However, if the Mongolians had committed theft or robbery, they would not "be subjected to the punishment of 'Ci Zi' (to make humiliating tattoo on one's body, especially one's face)"; if they were so punished, the officials concerned would be punished by "Zhang" (flogging with heavy sticks) or being removed from their office. In *Meng Gu Shi* (*The Mongolian History*), written by Dohsson, what Emperor Taizong had once said was quoted: "According to the law of Genghis Khan, it will be punished by imposing a fine of forty 'Ba Li Shi' (the monetary unit of Mongolia in Genghis Khan's era) in gold to kill a Muslim, while if a people of Han nationality was killed, the compensation was only equal to the money paid for a donkey." In addition, if there were disputes between the Mongolians and the Han people, according to criminal law, the two parties would be punished in accordance with the principle of overt inequality. For example, if the Mongolians beat the Han people, it was forbidden for the Han people to fight back, so they could only "complain to officials"; if the Mongolians killed the Han people in a quarrel or while intoxicated, they would be punished at most by serving in the army or by paying for "Shao Mai Yin" (the money spent on the funeral and burial of the dead). But under the same circumstances, if the Han people beat the Mongolians and Semu (the nationalities in the western or northwestern regions) to death, apart from paying for "Shao Mai Yin" (the money spent on the funeral and burial of the dead), they would also be sentenced to death penalty. Thus, it can be seen that different punishments were implemented for the same crime committed by different ethnic groups. But the northern Han landlords who had surrendered to the Mongolians earlier were given special

---

[54]"Xing Fa Zhi" (The Record of Criminal Law) (Part 1) in *Yuan Shi* (*The History of Yuan Dynasty*).

treatment. For example, the laws of illicit possession of bows and arrows were not applicable to them, and Emperor Shizu once said to Wang Weihe, the Han official: "You are not the same as other Han people, so you are not prohibited from owning bows and arrows."[55]

9.3.3.2 Strict Implementation of Different Punishments for the Same Crime Between Masters and Slaves and Between Monks and the Common People

According to the laws of the Yuan Dynasty, it was legitimate to keep "Nu Bi" (the slave girls and maidservants), so it was very easy for the Mongolians and Semu (the nationalities in the western or northwestern regions) to take the prisoners as "Nu Bi" (the slave girls and maidservants), as was described in the saying that "the Mongolians ... keep those people whom they have captured in the battlefield at home as slaves."[56] For example, the aristocratic bureaucrat Ariq Qaya had forcibly seized 3000 households of captives as domestic slaves. In addition, some people became slaves just because all of their property had been confiscated for their crimes, some because they were in debt, and some because they were born of slave parents. So all these people had become the sources of slave supply. Since it was legitimate to keep slaves at home, there were often "hundreds and thousands of, and tens of thousands of slaves at most" in the Mongolian and Han aristocratic and bureaucratic families. It was recorded in the book *Chuo Geng Lu* (*The Record of the Suspending of Farming*), written by Tao Zongyi in the Yuan Dynasty, that "(in Yuan Dynasty) male slaves are called 'Nu' (slaves), female slaves are called 'Bi' (slave girls), and the collective name for slaves and slave girls is 'Qu Kou' (a general term for slaves and slave girls)." There were so many slaves that they "even accounted for nearly half of the population of the country." But generally, it was forbidden for the Han people and the Southerners to take the Mongolians or Semu (the nationalities in the western or northwestern regions) as slaves. Moreover, through "Kuo Tian" (measuring the land to check on tax evasion), "Kuo Ma" (recruiting civilian horses), and "Kuo Hu" (registering households), many farmers were forced to give up their farmland and were reduced to serfs of the state or the nobles.

The measurement of penalty and conviction were completely different according to the different identities of the master and the slave. At the beginning of the founding of the country, "since the legal system was not established, if slaves committed crimes, they could be killed by the slave masters without authorization."[57] After the founding of the country, although local authorities were responsible for the trial of the criminal cases of slaves, slave masters could still kill the innocent "Nu Bi" (the slave girls and maidservants) at will, for which they would

---

[55]"Shi Zu Ji" (The Record of Emperor Shizu) in *Yuan Shi* (*The History of Yuan Dynasty*).
[56]"Xing Fa Zhi" (The Record of Criminal Law) (Part 2) in *Yuan Shi* (*The History of Yuan Dynasty*).
[57]"Bu Lu Hai Ya Zhuan" (The Biography of Buluhaiya) in *Yuan Shi* (*The History of Yuan Dynasty*).

only be punished by "Zhang" (flogging with heavy sticks) for eighty seven strokes. If the slave masters killed slaves while they were drunk, the punishment could also be reduced, but if the slave masters killed slaves because the slaves had disobeyed them or had beaten or scolded them, they would not be found guilty. But if the slaves had killed or wounded the slave masters or even sued the slave masters under whatever circumstances, even for manslaughter, they would be sentenced to death without exception; if the slaves had abused the slave masters, they would be punished by "Zhang" (flogging with heavy sticks) for one hundred and seven strokes, as well as two years of "Ju Yi" (penal servitude). "After they have finished their term of 'Ju Yi' (penal servitude), they would return to their former slave owners' houses" and continue to be slaves. It was also confirmed in law that the slave masters had the right to privately enforce various brutal punishments, such as "Ci Mian" (tattooing the face of a criminal), "Tie Jia" (wearing the iron cangue), "Ding Tou" (nailing the head), and "Yi Bi" (cutting off the nose). If the slave masters had raped the female slaves or the wives of slaves, they would not be punished any way, but if the slaves had raped the wives and daughters of their slave masters, they would certainly be punished by "Si Xing" (death penalties). In short, the person of slaves was completely ignored, and their lives were without guarantee; they were merely regarded as talking animals, and their price was just the same as donkeys.

Since religious policy was vigorously promoted by the rulers of the Yuan Dynasty, religious consciousness also penetrated into criminal law. If monks and Taoist priests had committed ordinary crimes, they were not subjected to the punishment of common law; if the "common people had assaulted the monks who were from the western regions, their hands would be cut off; if they had insulted the monks who were from the western regions with abusive words, their tongues would be cut off." So the judicial organs had only the right to deal with the felonies committed by monks and Taoist priests, such as "Jian Dao" (rape and theft), "Zha Wei" (fraud and forgery), "Sha Shang" (killing and injuring), "Ren Ming" (homicide), etc.; in general, "if monks, Taoist priests and Confucian scholars have disputes among themselves, they are not interfered in by the local authorities."[58] In the 2nd year of Zhida (1309), Gong Ke and other monks had a dispute over the occupation of a road with a concubine of Heerbala, a king of a vassal, and they dragged her out of the vehicle and beat her. For this case, "an imperial edict was even issued by the emperor to have these monks exempted from punishment," from which we can clearly see the privileges of the monks and Taoist priests, as well as the characteristics of the penal law of the Yuan Dynasty.

---

[58]"Xing Fa Zhi" (The Record of Criminal Law) (Part 1) in *Yuan Shi* (*The History of Yuan Dynasty*).

9.3.3.3 Aggravating Punishment for the Crime of "Zei Dao" (Stealing and Robbery)

Besides feudal exploitation, there also existed the oppression of slavery in the Yuan Dynasty. So people lived in great poverty, and there were many thieves and robbers around. Consequently, the principle of aggravating punishment for the crime of "Zei Dao" (stealing and robbery), which had been implemented since the period of "Wu Dai" (the Five Dynasties), was followed in the Yuan Dynasty. In *Tang Lv* (*Tang Code*), the following rules are stipulated:

> "As far as the punishment for robbery is concerned, if the offenders have failed to get any property in the robbery, they shall be punished by 'Tu' (imprisonment) for two years; if they have robbed one *chi*, they shall be punished by 'Tu' (imprisonment) for three years, with the punishment aggravated by one level for every two *pi*; if they have robbed ten *pi* or have wounded people, they shall be punished by 'Jiao' (hanging); if they have killed people, they shall be punished by 'Zhan' (beheading); if they have robbed people with rods, but if they have failed to get any property in robbery, they shall be punished by 'Liu' (exile) for 3000 *li*; if they have robbed five *pi*, they shall be punished by 'Jiao' (hanging); if they have wounded people, they shall by punished by 'Zhan' (beheading)." "As far as the punishment for theft is concerned, if the offenders have failed to get any property, they shall be punished by 'Chi' (flogging with light sticks) for fifty strokes; if they have stolen one *chi*, they shall be punished by 'Chi' (flogging with light sticks) for sixty strokes, with the punishment aggravated by one level for every one *pi*; if they have stolen five *pi*, they shall be punished by 'Tu' (imprisonment) for one year, with the punishment aggravated by one level for every five *pi*; if they have stolen fifty *pi*, they shall be punished by 'Yi Liu' (exile with labor service) additionally."

However, it was provided in an imperial decree issued by Zhiyuan that "all the robbers shall be put to death; those who steal cattle and horses shall be punished by 'Yi' (to cut down the nose); those who steal donkeys and mules shall be punished by 'Qing E' (tattooing on the forehead) and the offenders for the second time shall be punished by 'Yi' (to cut down the nose); those who steal sheep and pigs shall be punished by 'Mo Xiang' (tattooing on the neck); the offenders for the second time shall be punished by 'Qing' (to tattoo on the face); the offenders for the third time shall be punished by 'Yi' (to cut down the nose), but if they commit the crime again after they have been punished by 'Yi' (to cut down the nose), they shall be put to death."[59] So it can be seen that corporal punishments are extensively restored in the Yuan Dynasty in order to prevent theft and robbery. Moreover, the robbers are all put to death without exception.

9.3.3.4 More Lenient Punishment for Officials Committing the Crime of "Zuo Zang" (Embezzlement)

Detailed provisions were made on the classification and penalties for the crime of "Zuo Zang" (embezzlement) in the penal system of the Yuan Dynasty, and charges

---

[59]"Shun Di Ji" (The Record of Emperor Shun) in *Yuan Shi* (*The History of Yuan Dynasty*).

such as "Qu Shou" (accepting property), "Qin Dao" (embezzlement by theft), "Qin Zhan" (embezzlement), "Hui Qian" (receiving commission), "Guo Qian" (getting profits from taking bribes on behalf of others), "Shou Zang" (taking bribes for the first time), and "Zang Fa" (confiscation of money and property illicitly obtained) and the characteristics of such crimes were all provided in detail. During the reign of Emperor Chengzong, great importance was attached to official administration, and it was emphasized that "if the administrative officials are not self-disciplined by themselves, how can they control the other people?" Therefore, an imperial edict was issued:

> In future, those officials who accept property by bending the law shall never be appointed as officials again in addition to being convicted of bribery according to the regulations; those who accept property without bending the law shall be suspended from their office for three years before they can be appointed as officials again; but if they commit the crime again, they shall never be appointed as officials any more for all their lives.[60]

But generally speaking, the officials who were guilty of "Zuo Zang" (embezzlement) were given fairly lenient punishment. For example, those who accepted property by taking the advantage of their government posts and bending the law should be removed from their office and would not be appointed as officials anymore; those who accepted property without bending the law should be suspended from their office for three years, but if they committed the crime again, they should not be appointed as officials anymore; those who did not have official salary should be sentenced to one level lighter than the statutory punishment; those who accepted one to ten *guan* of money by bending the law would be punished by "Chi" (flogging with light sticks) for forty seven strokes; those who accepted ten to twenty *guan* of money by bending the law would be punished by "Chi" (flogging with light sticks) for fifty seven strokes; those who accepted twenty to fifty *guan* of money by bending the law would be punished by "Zhang" (flogging with heavy sticks) for seventy seven strokes; those who accepted more than one hundred *guan* of money by bending the law would be punished by "Zhang" (flogging with heavy sticks) for one hundred and seven strokes; those who accepted one to twenty *guan* of money without bending the law would be punished by "Chi" (flogging with light sticks) for forty seven strokes; those who accepted twenty to fifty *guan* of money without bending the law would be punished by "Chi" (flogging with light sticks) for fifty seven strokes; those who accepted fifty to one hudred *guan* of money without bending the law would be punished by "Zhang" (flogging with heavy sticks) for sixty seven strokes; those who accepted one hundred to one hudred and fifty *guan* of money without bending the law would be punished by "Zhang" (flogging with heavy sticks) for seventy seven strokes; those who accepted two hundred to three hundrd *guan* of money without bending the law would be punished by "Zhang" (flogging with heavy sticks) for ninety seven strokes; those who accepted more than three hundred *guan* of money without bending the law would be punished by "Zhang"

---

[60]"Li Bu" (The Department of Personnel) (Part 5) in *Yuan Dian Zhang (The Collection of Statutes of Yuan Dynasty)*, Vol. 11.

(flogging with heavy sticks) for one hundred and seven strokes and by being removed from their office without being appointed as officials again. For the officials who accepted property but who confessed their crimes and surrendered themselves, those who confessed completely and honestly would be exempted from punishment, but those who did not confess completely and honestly would be found guilty of bribery only on the basis of the bribes they had concealed. The officials who had sought bribes by threatening the criminal would be punished by "Chi" (flogging with light sticks) for twenty seven strokes even if they had not obtained any property, those who had accepted money to entrust officials with matters on behalf of others would be convicted according to the crime of "Zuo Zang" (embezzlement), and those who had illegally occupied state-owned land would be punished by "Wang Fa" (taking bribes by bending the law). Even if the officials who were guilty of "Zuo Zang" (embezzlement) died, their families would still be ordered to hand in the bribes.

9.4 The Civil Law with National Differences

During the reign of Yuan Dynasty, the feudal economy of the central plain region was greatly impacted by the backward nomadic economy, so that the commodity economy, which was highly developed in the Song Dynasty, was severely damaged, and there was even a recession. Generally speaking, the civil legal relationships compatible with the commodity economy also remained stagnant, which had seriously restrained the momentum of the development of civil law in the Song Dynasty. But the development of civil law was also promoted by the economic and marital intercourses between different ethnic groups, such as the implementation of the system of "Qi Wei" (the identification documents issued by the government) and the establishment of the time limit for the near relatives and neighbors of the pawner to buy the property preferentially. Especially, in marriage legislation, the original ethnic customs were retained and the influence of the concept of the feudal "Li Jiao" (feudal ethical code) was stubbornly rejected, so it possessed distinctive characteristics by itself.

9.4.1 Classifying the People According to Their Ethnic Identities

Before the Mongols entered the central plains, they still lived in slavery society, so it was not until after they entered the central plains that they began their process of feudalization under the influence of the advanced mode of production of the Han nationality, so that considerable remnants of slavery were inevitably retained. Thus, there existed a huge slave class composed of house slaves, military slaves, temple slaves, "Bo Lan Xi" (captured slaves in official custody), and so on in the social constitution. These slaves, who were called "Nu" (slaves), "Nu Bi" (the slave girls and maidservants), and "Qu Kou" (a general term for slaves and slave girls) in the law of the Yuan Dynasty, could be freely traded, transferred, or even killed by their owners, so they were the objects of ownership who did not enjoy any legal civil rights and "are regarded the same as money and goods."

With the recovery of the social economy, the feudal tenancy system gradually occupied a dominant position; the identity of tenants was equivalent to that of serfs, so landlords could enslave not only the tenants themselves but also their families. Especially in certain areas south of Yangtze River, the children of tenants were also legal slaves of the landlords.

In order to strengthen the dominant position of the Mongolian nobles, in the Yuan Dynasty, the population of the country was compulsively divided into four classes according to ethnic standards, namely, the Mongols, the Semu (the nationalities in the western or northwestern regions), the Han people (the northern Han people, the Khitans, Jurchens, and Koreans were collectively called the Han people), and the Southerners (the southern Han people and other ethnic groups). Among them, the Mongols had the highest social status, while the Han people, especially the Southerners, had the lowest social status. By this classification, the Mongolian nobles attempted to undermine the unity of all ethnic groups and to institutionalize ethnic oppression so as to maintain the dominant position of the Mongolian nobles. The four classes that were classified according to ethnic standards were of a political nature, so it also affected the equal exercise of the civil rights of these four classes. In addition, in the privately compiled historical records of the Yuan Dynasty, there was also the so-called classification of the social structure, consisting of ten classes: Class 1: "Guan" (officials), Class 2: "Li" (petty officials), Class 3: "Seng" (monks), Class 4: "Dao" (Taoist priests), Class 5: "Yi" (medical men), Class 6: "Gong" (engineers and technicians), Class 7: "Jiang" (craftsmen and artisans), Class 8: "Chang" (prostitutes), Class 9: "Ru" (intellectuals), and Class 10: "Gai" (beggars), but there was no accurate and solid evidence for this classification. For example, in November of the 25th year of Zhiyuan (1288), an imperial edict was declared in "Wu Xi Mian Xiu Cai Za Fan Chai Yi Zhao Bei" (An Edict Monument in Wuxi About Exempting the Intellectuals from Miscellaneous Corvee Services) in the name of the emperor:

> In future, if the registered intellectuals do business, they shall pay commercial tax; if they engage in farming, they shall pay land tax, but they shall be exempted from other miscellaneous corvee services. They should be relieved from these duties by the local authorities, and it is forbidden for them to be molested unreasonably in the Confucian temple school by the officials. Please do according to this decree.

It can be seen from this edict that the registered intellectuals could not only do business, but they were also protected by the local government and were exempted from corvee servitude.

9.4.2 The Characteristics of the Times of the Protection of Property Rights

According to the civil law of the Yuan Dynasty, property included personal property and real estate property. Although the old laws of the Tang and Song dynasties were followed in the Yuan Dynasty in terms of the legal protection of property ownership, land ownership of the temple estates was given special protection since religion was advocated by the rulers of the Yuan Dynasty. For example, in the 2nd year of Zhongtong (1261), it was explicitly expressed in the imperial monument of Baoyan Temple in Linxian county that "it is forbidden for anyone to seize the land, the water and soil, the bamboo gardens, the gardens with water-mills, the pawnshops, the bathhouses, the shops, the places for rental quarters, and the places for making vinegar and liquor which are owned by the temples by force."[61] The so-called "Xiu Shi Li Qi" means that "nobody is allowed to bully and humiliate people by taking the advantage of one's or somebody else's power." As another example, according to the inscription records of Wanshou Palace in Chongyang (a famous Taoist temple in Xi'an, Shanxi province) in the 5th year of Zhiyuan (1268), "no corvee tax is to be collected on the water and soil, the bamboo and reed fields, the water-mills, the landscape gardens, the pawnshops, the bathhouses, the inns, and the places of making vinegar, etc. which are owned by the Taoist temples."[62] In the 30th year of Zhiyuan (1293), it was also instructed in the imperial monument of Bolin Temple in Zhaozhou county, Hebei province, that "nobody is allowed to seize by force the water and soil, the landscape gardens, the grinding mills, the shops and the bathhouses of the temple, and the temple is exempted from grain tax."[63] There were a lot more similar inscriptions of imperial edicts that were taken in order to protect the economy of the temples in the Yuan Dynasty, but they are not going to be cited here due to their huge number.

The old laws of the Tang and Song dynasties were also followed in the Yuan Dynasty in terms of acquisition of property ownership. What is more, clear and specific provisions were made on the ownership of buried objects. According to "Za Ling" (Miscellaneous Orders) in *Tong Zhi Tiao Ge* (*The General Legal Provisions and Injunctions*), in April of the 11th year of Zhiyuan (1274), Wang Bailu, who lived on Xijing road, and some others had discovered some buried objects in the land of He Er, so the local authorities proposed that the people who discovered the buried objects share them equally with the owner of the land. The case was approved by "Zhong Shu Sheng" (the supreme organization in charge of state affairs) and was established as a usual practice:

---

[61]Cai Meibiao, *Yuan Dai Bai Hua Bei Ji Lu* (*A Collection of Monuments with Vernacular Inscriptions in Yuan Dynasty*), Science Press, 1955.

[62]Cai Meibiao, *Yuan Dai Bai Hua Bei Ji Lu* (*A Collection of Monuments with Vernacular Inscriptions in Yuan Dynasty*).

[63]Cai Meibiao, *Yuan Dai Bai Hua Bei Ji Lu* (*A Collection of Monuments with Vernacular Inscriptions in Yuan Dynasty*).

9.4 The Civil Law with National Differences

In future, if people discover buried objects in public land, half of what they have discovered shall be confiscated by the government, and the other half shall be given to the people who have discovered the objects; if people dig and discover the buried objects in other people's land, they shall share these objects equally with the owner of the land according to the case mentioned above; if people discover the buried objects in leased public and private land or houses, it should be handled according to the same regulation as was applied to the owner of the land; if people have discovered ancient artifacts, treasures, and fantastic objects, they shall report to the government and present them to the imperial court immediately, and they shall be paid for these objects at a roughly estimated price; if people have faked or concealed the buried objects, all these objects shall be recovered and confiscated, moreover, they shall also be convicted of crimes.

In addition, according to *Da Yuan Tong Zhi* (*General Regulations of the Great Yuan Dynasty*), "for the buried objects which people have discovered, if they are discovered in other people's land, they shall be shared equally with the owner of the land; if they are discovered in public land, half of these objects shall be handed over to the authorities; if they are discovered in the land of tenants, it should be handled according to the same regulation as was applied to the owner of the land." According to the provision in *Tang Lv* (*Tang Code*), "if they have concealed the buried objects and do not give them to the owner of the land, they shall be punished three levels lighter than that for the crime of 'Zuo Zang' (embezzlement) according to the part payable to the owner of the land," but this provision was deleted in *Da Yuan Tong Zhi* (*General Regulations of the Great Yuan Dynasty*).

The characteristics of the social economy and the class structure of the Yuan Dynasty also endowed the protection of ownership with the characteristics of the times. For example, in May of the 2nd year of Zhongtong during the reign of Emperor Shizu (1261), it was announced in the decree that nobody was allowed to slaughter horses and cattle; if anyone had violated the law, he "shall be punished by 'Zhang' (flogging with heavy sticks) for one hundred strokes; if the two neighbors know about the crime and do not make report to the government, they shall be punished one level lighter than the statutory punishment; if the officials have neglected their supervisory duties, they shall also be punished one level lighter than the statutory punishment".[64] Moreover, if horses and cattle died in civilians' homes, the civilians should apply to the officials for the identification of the causes of death to avoid being suspected of violation of law. Thus, the special lawsuit of "Shen Si Niu Ma" (lawsuits about the death of cattle and horses) was introduced in the Yuan Dynasty.

For another example, "Qu Kou" (a general term for slaves and slave girls) and "Qian Wu" (money and goods) could be freely disposed of by their owners because they were both regarded as the property. Nevertheless, because the missing of livestock and escaping of "Qu Kou" (a general term for slaves and slave girls) had seriously damaged the interests of the owners, the legal provisions were made about the rights of official custody and claim. In August of the 5th year of Zhongtong during the reign of Emperor Shizu (1264), it was provided in the imperial edict that

---

[64]"Xing Bu" (The Department of Punishment) (Part 19) in *Yuan Dian Zhang* (*The Collection of Statutes of Yuan Dynasty*), Vol. 57.

"all 'Bo Lan Xi' (captured slaves in official custody), livestock, etc. which are captured in the country shall be in the charge of the officials of 'Lu' (ancient administrative region), and 'Fu' (ancient administrative district between province and county). ... Within ten days, they shall be claimed by the owners, and after that, they shall be kept as 'Bo Lan Xi' (captured slaves in official custody)."[65] After they were claimed by the owners, the document called "Ben Zhu Shi Ren" (Claimed by the Owner) should be drawn up as an official proof of ownership. Those who privately kept "Bo Lan Xi" (captured slaves in official custody), livestock, and other things should "send them to the local authorities within three days. If they conceal the captured goods, or do not send them to the local authorities within the time limit," they would be punished, while "those who have reported the offences to the government shall be awarded accordingly."[66]

In the Yuan Dynasty, the system of "Dian Quan" (pawn rights) of the Song Dynasty was generally followed, under which the pawn applicable to real estate was called "Dian Zhi" (mortgage) or "Zhi Dian," while the pawn applicable to the human body was called "Dian Gu" (hiring out by mortgage). The establishment of "Dian Quan" (pawn rights) was preconditioned by the conclusion of "Dian Qi" (the pawn contract), which already had fixed forms. Here is an example of a format of contract for the purchase of land on mortgage:

> ××× (name) in ××× "Du" (ancient administrative region) in ××× "Li" (a basic resident organization consisting of five neighborhoods).
>
> ××× (name) has several sections of "Wan Tian" (farmland for late-autumn crops) which is owned by himself, totaling ××× *mu* ××× *bu*, whose output value is ××× *guan*. One section is situated at ××× (place name) in ××× "Du" (ancient administrative region). It is from ××× in the east, to ××× in the west, from ××× in the south, to ××× in the north. The land is farmed by ××× (name), handing in ××× *dan* of rice every winter. Now that we are short of money and corvee services are heavy, I am willing to have ×× (name) as the broker, and make a contract to completely sell (or sell on mortgage) the section of land within the above mentioned four boundaries to ××× (name) in ××× "Li" (a basic resident organization consisting of five neighborhoods). The three parties have negotiated and decided that the current price is ××× *guan* in "Zhong Tong Chao" (the paper money made in the year of Zhongtong), and should be paid all in cash. The seller is not forced to sell the land to pay the debts. The payment is made completely when all the necessary documents involved in the contract have been delivered. The land to be sold (or sold on mortgage) is the real estate of our own, that is, the deal is done openly without concealing anything from families and without violating the law. If any such things happen, ××× (name) is willing to take the responsibility for it and will repay the debts with other property without implicating the person who buys (or buys on mortgage) the land. After the contract is concluded, the land owner shall pay the tax in the local authorities for property management, and then the property permanently belongs to the owner. In order to prevent the children and grandchildren from seizing or redeeming the land in the future, all "Zhu Qi" (contract with an official seal) of the real estate documents of the previous deals shall be handed over, and be signed and marked in the local authorities. The tax should be paid for the money

---

[65]"Xing Bu" (The Department of Punishment) (Part 28) in *Yuan Dian Zhang* (*The Collection of Statutes of Yuan Dynasty*), Vol. 56.

[66]"Xing Bu" (The Department of Punishment) (Part 28) in *Yuan Dian Zhang* (*The Collection of Statutes of Yuan Dynasty*), Vol. 56.

9.4 The Civil Law with National Differences

earned in the dealing under the name of the owner ××× as tax to be paid. The above contract is concluded together by both sides and they shall act accordingly. So the above contract has been signed.

Day: ×× Month: ××× Year: ××× the Seller: ××× Contract: ×××
"Zhi Qi" (friend): ×××
"Ya Ren" (middleman): ×××
Witness: ×××

Here is a contract format for the sale of a house on mortgage:

××× (name) in ××× "Du" (ancient administrative region) in ××× "Jia" (administrative division consisting of twenty households).

××× (name) has a house which is owned by himself, totaling ××× rooms ××× *jia* (measure word, the space between two pillars). The house is situated at ××× (place name) in ××× "Du" (ancient administrative region). It is from ××× in the east, to ××× in the west, from ××× in the south, to ××× in the north. The house is inhabited by ××× (name). Now that because of poverty, it is difficult for the owner to earn his livelihood, the owner is willing to have ××× (name) as the broker, and completely sell (or sell on mortgage) the house and land within the above mentioned four boundaries to ××× (name) in ××× "Li" (a basic resident organization consisting of five neighborhoods). The three parties have negotiated and decided that the current price is ××× *guan* in "Zhong Tong Chao" (the paper money made in the year of Zhongtong), and should be paid all in cash. The seller is not forced to sell the land to pay the debts. The payment is to be made completely when all the necessary documents involved in the contract have been delivered. The house to be sold (or sold on mortgage) is the real estate of the owner himself, that is, the deal is done openly without concealing anything from families and without violating the law. If any such things happen, ××× (name) is willing to take the responsibility for it without implicating the person who buys (or buys on mortgage) the land. After the contract is concluded, the house owner shall pay the tax in the local authorities for property management, and then the property permanently belongs to the owner. In order to prevent the children and grandchildren from seizing or redeeming the house in the future, all "Zhu Qi" (contract with an official seal) of the previous deals shall be handed over, and be signed and marked in the local authorities. The above contract is concluded together by both sides and they shall act accordingly. So the above contract has been signed.

Day: ××× Month: ××× Year: ××× the Seller: ××× Contract: ×××
"Zhi Qi" (friend): ×××
"Ya Ren" (middleman): ×××
Witness: ×××[67]

According to "Dian Qi" (the pawn contract), the pawnee not only possessed the pawn and enjoyed the legal right to use and make profit from the pawn but also had the obligation to keep the pawn. However, it was not allowed for the pawner to pawn the same property twice. The pawner should have the right to redeem the property even when the pawn time expired, and it was not allowed for the pawnee to refuse the pawner's right to redeem the pawn.

In the contract of buying and selling on mortgage, parents had the right of discretion. According to *Da Yuan Tong Zhi* (*General Regulations of the Great*

---

[67]The above two contract formats are quoted from Zhang Chuanxi, *Zhong Guo Li Dai Qi Yue Hui Bian Kao Shi* (*A Textual Research and Interpretation of the Collected Contracts of the Past Dynasties in China*) (Book 1), Peking University Press, 1995.

Yuan Dynasty), "in the pawn business of land and houses, certificates will be issued and account books will be created by the government office based on the elders' signatures and marks"; otherwise, the contract is considered invalid. At the same time, legal restraints were clearly specified in the regulation. For example, "if the pawnee is unwilling to make a deal, he shall sign a waiver within ten days, and those who do not return the pawn after the time limit shall be punished by 'Chi' (flogging with light sticks) for seventeen strokes; if the pawnee is willing to make a deal, both sides shall negotiate a price and sign the contract within fifteen days; those who do not pay the money after the time limit shall be punished by 'Chi' (flogging with light sticks) for twenty seven strokes, then the deal can be conducted."[68] Since people were brutally exploited in the Jiangsu and Zhejiang regions, areas south of Yangtze River, during the Yuan Dynasty, such that there occurred situations where one's wife was used as a pawning object, which was tacitly approved by law, it was declared that "after the wife of the pawner was sold into the house of the pawnee, she could legally become the wife or concubine of the pawnee."[69]

The pawn or mortgage of personal property should be conducted in "Jie Dian Ku" (pawn shop), and it was also necessary to issue "Jie Tie" (the pawn contract) so that the pawnshop could make a profit accordingly. According to the law of the Yuan Dynasty, "it is forbidden to mortgage outside the pawnshop, or to mortgage without a contract or to charge interest illegally."[70] The pawnshop was responsible for keeping the pawn, and compensation should be paid if the pawn was damaged or lost. The pawnshop could dispose of the property of the pawner to repay the debt only after a certain period of time, and if there was a surplus, it should be given to the pawner. In the 7th year of Dade (1303), Xiong Rui in Longxing "Lu" (ancient administrative region) in Jiangxi province sued Chengde Pawnshop for refusing to allow him to redeem the pawn, but the pawnshop argued that "since a year has passed, the pawn period has expired, so the pawn has been taken off the shelf." In order to solve the dispute, the local authorities referred to the legal precedent of "Zhong Shu Sheng" (the supreme organization in charge of state affairs), which was made in the 2nd year of Yuanzhen (1296), and it was stipulated that "in future, when a pawnshop provides pawn loans, it is allowed to take the pawn off the shelf only after the pawner has not redeemed the pawn in two years." After the deliberations of "Li Bu" (The Department of Rites), it was believed that "the various objects are pawned to make profit, but because the legal provisions are different, many disputes and lawsuits have been caused"; therefore, it was stipulated uniformly that "if the pawn has not been redeemed within two years, it shall be taken off the shelf according to the legal provision for the trading of gold and silver," so that it was approved by "Zhong Shu Sheng" (the supreme organization in charge of state

---

[68]"Xing Fa Zhi" (The Record of Criminal Law) (Part 3) in *Yuan Shi* (*The History of Yuan Dynasty*).

[69]"Xing Bu" (The Department of Punishment) (Part 19) in *Yuan Dian Zhang* (*The Collection of Statutes of Yuan Dynasty*), Vol. 57.

[70]"Xing Fa Zhi" (The Record of Criminal Law) (Part 4) in *Yuan Shi* (*The History of Yuan Dynasty*).

9.4 The Civil Law with National Differences 887

affairs) "to be carried out nationwide as a permanent legal provision."[71] In *Da Yuan Tong Zhi* (*General Regulations of the Great Yuan Dynasty*), enacted in the 3rd year of Zhizhi (1323), the pawn redemption period was extended to three years, and it was provided that "if the property is pawned, ... if it has not been redeemed in three years, the pawned property can be sold by the pawnshop. If the pawnage is lost by the pawnshop, double compensation shall be paid by the pawnshop on the day of redemption according to the price of the original pawned property. Although there is the income of interest, it can not be used to offset the losses."

9.4.3 The Making of Debt Contract

In Yuan Dynasty, it was fairly common that debt problems often arose in contractual relationships. Moreover, the types of contract increased greatly and the contract formats tended to be formalized. For example, the written contract was divided into "Qi Shi" (the pattern of contract), "Yue Shi" (the pattern of agreement), "Pi Shi" (the pattern of note), and "Bang Shi" (the pattern of notice). "Qi Shi" (the pattern of contract) was used for sale, mortgage, and employment; "Yue Shi" (the pattern of agreement) for lease; "Pi Shi" (the pattern of the note) for loan; and "Bang Shi" (the pattern of notice) for the special sale of an individual.

"Mai Mai Qi Yue" (sale contract): as for the sale of land and houses, the system of the Song Dynasty was followed, according to which the right of disposition of land and houses of the seniors and superiors was confirmed and the preemptive rights of the seller's near relatives and neighbors and the pawnees were guaranteed. "When military families and other various households sell their land or houses on mortgage, the certificate should be issued and the account book should be created according to the elders' signatures and marks. Besides, the seller shall also inquire whether their near relatives, neighbors or pawnees are willing to buy the land or houses first."[72] But the time period for the preemptive right was strictly regulated in the law of the Yuan Dynasty so that the sale of the land or houses could be conducted smoothly. If the near relatives, the neighbors, or the pawnees "are unwilling to make a deal, they shall sign a waiver within ten days; those who do not sign a waiver after the time limit shall be punished by 'Chi' (flogging with light sticks) for seventeen strokes; those who are willing to make a deal shall offer a price within fifteen days and a contract shall be signed according to the law; those who do not pay after the time limit shall be punished by 'Chi' (flogging with light sticks) for twenty seven strokes,

---

[71]"Hu Bu" (The Department of Revenue) (Part 13) in *Yuan Dian Zhang* (*The Collection of Statutes of Yuan Dynasty*), Vol. 27.

[72]"Hu Bu" (The Department of Revenue) (Part 5) in *Yuan Dian Zhang* (*The Collection of Statutes of Yuan Dynasty*), Vol. 19.

then the deal can be conducted."[73] However, "if the relatives, neighbors, or pawnee have intentionally impeded the dealing by extorting signatures, contracts, money and goods, they will be punished by 'Chi' (flogging with light sticks) for twenty seven strokes,"[74] "and the relatives, neighbors, or pawnees who are in the places one hundred *li* away should not be inquired."[75] So it was a new provision in the law of the Yuan Dynasty to restrict the time of the preemptive rights of the relatives, neighbors, and pawnees.

In land sale, the system of "Qi Wei" (the identification documents issued by the government) was implemented; namely, the tax receipt should be stuck at the end of the contract after payment of the tax and after the property rights were transferred in order to prevent evasion of national tax in the transfer of land ownership. The contract paper and tax voucher which were confirmed by "Ban Yin Kan He" (credentials for verification sealed by the government) issued by the government were not only important documents to verify the legality of the contract, but also very important evidence in the verification of litigation. In *Tong Zhi Tiao Ge (The General Legal Provisions and Injunctions)*, it was recorded that "in May of the 10th year of Dade ... in the future mortgage transaction, in addition to vouchers issued according to law, two contract paper shall be completed and signed by both parties of the deal, and then tax should be paid to the relevant authorities. Besides, the original copy of the deed should be kept by the pawnee and the contract should be kept by the owner, so that the owner can have the pawn redeemed even after many years to avoid disputes and lawsuits. By the way, relevant reports should be made by 'Du' (ancient administrative region) and 'Sheng' (province)."[76] The system of "Qi Wei" (the identification documents issued by the government), which was implemented in the Yuan Dynasty, had a direct influence on the Ming and Qing dynasties. So it was stipulated in *Ming Lv (Ming Code)* that "in the mortgage of land or houses, the seller shall get tax certificate to complete the transferring of the property rights;... those who do not do so shall be punished by 'Chi' (flogging with light sticks) for ten to forty strokes for one to five *mu* of land." On the other hand, it was stipulated in *Hu Bu Ze Li (The Regulation of the Department of Revenue)*, which was issued in the Qing Dynasty, that both parties of the deal should "go to the local authorities in 'Zhou' (subprefecture) and 'Xian' (county)" to check the registration book and to "deal with the transferring of the property rights." Moreover, according to "Zheng Que Kao" (An Examination of National Commodity Tax and Government Monopoly) (Part 6) in *Qing Chao Wen Xian Tong Kao (A General Textual Research of the Documents of Qing Dynasty)* (Vol. 31), "if the contract paper is with official seal but without 'Qi Wei' (the identification documents issued by government)," it would be considered illegal. The contract paper signed after paying tax was called "Hong Qi"

---

[73]"Hu Bu" (The Department of Revenue) (Part 5) in *Yuan Dian Zhang (The Collection of Statutes of Yuan Dynasty)*, Vol. 19.

[74]"Xing Fa Zhi" (The Record of Criminal Law) in *Yuan Shi (The History of Yuan Dynasty)*.

[75]"Xing Fa Zhi" (The Record of Criminal Law) in *Yuan Shi (The History of Yuan Dynasty)*.

[76]*Tong Zhi Tiao Ge (The General Legal Provisions and Injunctions)*, Vol. 16.

(contract with an official seal) and it was with a sense of notary meaning, whereas the contract paper signed without paying the tax was called "Bai Qi" (contract without an official seal), which had lesser effectivity than "Hong Qi" (contract with an official seal) a sense of notary. The following are some examples of "Hong Qi" (contract with an official seal) and "Bai Qi" (contract without an official seal):

"Hong Qi" (contract with an official seal) for the Sale of Mountain Land by Feng Ziyong and others in Huizhou in the 2nd Year of Yuantong (1334):

> Feng Ziyong and his brother Feng Ziliang in Zaicheng, for want of money to pay household expenses, are willing to sell the hill at ××× (place name) in Babao in Shixidu, which is completely an ancestral estate. The tax for No. 2180 hill is evaluated at one *qiao* (unit of money) and the tax for No. 90 hill is evaluated at three *qiao* (unit of money) by "Diao Zi" (land registration). The hill is located in the areas from Wanxin in the east, to Changling in the west, from the land of Shuangwukou in the south, to Wutouao in the north. Today the hill within the above mentioned four boundaries is to be sold completely according to the contract signed with Xie Nengjing in Xidu for his use. The negotiated current price is four *qian* of silver, without including the management expenses before the deal is made. The payment of the money and the necessary documents of the deal are to be all delivered to each other with no delay. So Xie Nengjing has the right to enter the hill to cultivate the land from now on. Besides, there are no previous deals for the hill, that is, no families have made any duplicate transaction with the outsiders. If anything like this happens, the seller will take the responsibility for it without involving the buyer. After the sale of the hill, neither party can go back on the deal, and the party who goes back on the deal shall voluntarily pay a fine of one *qian* of silver to the other party with this paper still used as the contract paper. Lest there should be no guarantee in the future, this contract paper is completed as proof.
>
> April 2nd of the 2nd year of Yuantong
> Contractor: Feng Ziyong (Signature)
> And his brother: Feng Ziliang (Signature)
> Contract dictator: Feng Zongyi (Signature)

"Bai Qi" (contract without an official seal) for the Sale of Wasteland by Wang Bizhao in Longyuan in the 2nd Year of Yuanzhen (1296):

> Wang Bizhao in Longyuan now has an ancestral estate, a piece of wasteland at "Mingtanzhaozhoubang" (place name) in Yibao in Bendu. The tax for No. 514 land is evaluated at 4.25 *fen*, and half of the tax should be paid. Today the wasteland is to be sold to Wang Ming for his use according to contract. The negotiated current price is one *liang* of "Wen Yin" (silver of best quality) by the three parties on the same day, and all the payment is to be completed when the deal is done. The payment of the money and the necessary document of the deal are to be delivered to each other with no delay. Moreover, there are no previous or duplicate transactions for the wasteland, and if anything like this happens, the seller will take the responsibility for it without involving the buyer. All the grain tax will be calculated and paid according to the contract, so there will be not any additional tax payment. Lest there should be no guarantee in the future, this contract paper is completed as proof.
>
> March 30th of the 2nd year of Yuanzhen.
> Contractor: Wang Bizhao (Signature)
> In his own writing without "Ya Ren" (middleman).[77]

---

[77]The above two contract formats are quoted from Zhang Chuanxi, *Zhong Guo Li Dai Qi Yue Hui Bian Kao Shi* (*A Textual Research and Interpretation of the Collected Contracts of the Past Dynasties in China*) (Book 1).

The main contents of the abovementioned sale and purchase contracts include the boundaries of the property: the object of transfer, the price, the middleman, and especially the seller's guarantee of transferring property rights, which are all important components of sale and purchase contracts.

Thus, contracts are needed for the sale or mortgage of land. Documents should also be prepared for the exchange or withdrawal of land. For example, the document for the exchange of land between Hu Dingqing and Zheng Guifu in Huizhou in the 10th year of Zhizheng (1350) is as follows:

> Hu Dingqing in Shierdu (name of place) has a piece of "Xia Di" (summer-crop farmland), which is situated at Huangjingwukou (name of place) in Sibao in Shiwudu, with "Lai Zi" (land registration) NO. 944. This land borders the mountain land with "Lai Zi" (land registration) NO. 942 and the land with "Lai Zi" (land registration) NO. 914 in Shiwudu, which Hu Dingqing's uncle Zheng Shijing has bought from Wang Yuan'e. ... Now since stone foundation has not been built up, Hu Dingqing has negotiated an agreement through his relative Zheng Guifu to exchange a piece of "Xia Di" (summer-crop farmland) with "Lai Zi" (land registration) NO. 944, which borders Zheng Shijing's land, with a piece of Zheng Shijing's mountain land beyond the newly built stone embankment at Huangjingwukou (name of place), with land price [?],[78] with the stone embankment opposite as the border. The land within the newly built stone embankment at Huangjingwukou (name of place) belongs to Zheng Shijing, while the piece of mountain land beyond the newly built embankment at Huangjingwukou (name of place) belongs to Hu Dingqing; the piece of "Xia Di" (summer-crop farmland) with "Lai Zi" (land registration) NO. 944 above the buried stone belongs to Zheng Shijing, while the land below belongs to Hu Dingqing. After the two families exchange the land today, according to the agreement, they are willing to exchange the land and may not go back on the deal in the future. If any party goes back on the deal, the party is willing to be imposed with a fine of eleven *guan* of money in "Zhong Tong Chao" (the paper money made in the year of Zhongtong) according to this document. Lest there should be no guarantee in the future, this exchange document is completed as proof.
> January 15th of the 10th year of Zhizheng.
> Hu Dingqing
> The person in charge of the exchange: Zheng Guifu

For the bulk sale of personal property such as horses and cattle, contracts should also be made by following an established style. For example, the contract format for the sale of cattle is as follows:

> ××× (name) in ××× "Li" (a basic resident organization consisting of five neighborhoods) in ××× "Xiang" (townships)
> ××× (name) has a head of cattle of ××× horn in ××× colour, which is ××× years old now. Now that life is poor and difficult, the owner is willing to have ××× (name) as the broker, to sell the above mentioned cattle to ××× (name). The three parties have negotiated the price of ××× *guan*. The payment of the money is to be completed with no delay when all the necessary documents involved in the contract have been delivered. The cattle to be sold is raised in the owner's cattle stable, that is, the cattle is not stolen and sold. If there is anything false, ××× (name) is willing to take the responsibility for it without involving the buyer. Lest there should be no guarantee in the future, this document is completed as proof. So the above contract has been made.

---

[78](Translator's note: the question mark is in the original text).

Day: ×× Month: ××× Year: ×××
The Seller: ×××
"Ya Ren" (middleman): ×××

Among the various contracts of the Yuan Dynasty, the loan contract is the most basic form. According to Xu Yuanrui's interpretation in "Qian Liang Zao Zuo" (Money and Grain Manufacturing) in *Li Xue Zhi Nan (A Guide to Bureaucratics)*, "it is called 'Jie' (lending) to lend property to others, and it is called 'Dai' (borrowing) to borrow property from others." For the loan contract, apart from the signatures of the lender and borrower, those of the middleman and witnesses should also be included. As far as the interest rate on private debt was concerned, the rule that the profit made by the creditor should not exceed the principal was usually followed. So it was provided in *Da Yuan Tong Zhi (General Regulations of the Great Yuan Dynasty)* that "as for borrowing money, even for a long time, the rule that the interest made by the creditor should not exceed the principal should be followed. If anyone tries to earn interest from others by changing the interest rate of the contract or increasing the original interest, or by taking others' cattle, horses or other property by force, or by capturing others' children as 'Nu Bi' (the slave girls and maidservants), they all shall be severely punished, and the extra interest income which they have received should be returned and their principal and interest income should be confiscated." In *Yuan Dian Zhang (The Collection of Statutes of Yuan Dynasty)*, the following provisions are stipulated:

> "It is forbidden for the borrowers to be charged excessively by money lenders", and "those who have charged the borrowers extra interest shall have their principal and interest income confiscated". "As to the borrowing or lending of money, the monthly interest for one *liang* of money is three *fen*, even if the money is borrowed for a long time, the rule that the profit made by the creditor should not exceed the principal should be followed ... So it is forbidden for the debtors to be imprisoned privately by the lender, or their families or livestock to be taken away forcefully".

No doubt, these strict regulations had shown from another aspect the seriousness of the exploitation of usury in Yuan Dynasty.

In order to prevent officials from extorting civilians, the old system of the Tang and Song dynasties was followed in the Yuan Dynasty, and officials were strictly forbidden to borrow money from civilians and were especially forbidden to borrow goods from government warehouses; offenders would be punished for the crime of robbery, and compensation should be paid at the same time. In addition, "the inferior and young were forbidden to borrow money privately;... otherwise, the lender, borrower, 'Ya Bao' (intermediary agent) and guarantee shall all be punished without pardoning."

As for the payment of debt, generally speaking, it was forbidden by law for the creditor to demand the payment of debt by commandeering the debtor's families or livestock, but it was allowed by law for the debtor to offset the debt by selling out his labor. For example, it was stipulated in *Zhi Yuan Za Ling (The Miscellaneous Orders in the Reign of Zhiyuan)* that "those who are too poor to pay the debt can hire out their wives and children to offset their debts."[79] Due to social unrest and cruel exploitation in the Yuan Dynasty, it was very difficult for debtors to repay their debts as scheduled, so it was fairly common for the government officials to come forward to force the debtors to perform their obligations.

It should be noted that although usury exploitation was prohibited by law, yet the law often lacked the due binding force in practice. The Mongolian nobles, officials, and the Hui people usually lent money and then collected interest much higher than the statutory rates. Moreover, they often forced the debtors to offset their debts by selling their labor, as was described in the saying that "... the debt is doubled for the first year, and then the debt and interest are further doubled for the second year, which is called 'Yang Gao Li' (the interest of the lamb, a kind of usury in Yuan Dynasty), so the vicious circle never stops, which has often led to family disintegration. So some debtors even has to pay debts by mortgaging their wives and children, but it is still impossible for them to pay off their debts in the end."[80]

In the Yuan Dynasty, civil employment relationship prevailed. Usually, the employed were page boys and porters; sometimes women were even employed as concubines. In order to protect the interests of employers and employees by contracts and to achieve "He Gu" (employing at rational prices),[81] corresponding "Qi Shi" (the pattern of contract) was established according to different objects of employment. Take the following personal employment as an example:

×××(name) in ×××"Li" (a basic resident organization consisting of five neighborhoods) in ×××"Xiang" (townships).

×××(name) has a son named ×××, aged ×××. Now the annual harvest is poor, and it is difficult to provide for the family, so ×××(name) is willing to have ××× as the guarantee, to hire out the above mentioned son as a page boy to ×××(name) in ××× "Li" (a basic resident organization consisting of five neighborhoods) for three years. The three parties have negotiated the price of ××× *guan* of money each year. So ××× *guan* of the money shall be paid in advance, with all the rest paid on the date of the settlement of the debt. After ×××(name) is employed, he shall take care to serve the employer and follow his order, and it is not allowed for him to defy the employer, to disobey his order, to behave rudely, to steal the property or other various items from the employer's household together with outsiders, or to leave without permission. If anything like this happens, ×××(name) will take the responsibilities for the compensation of the losses. If anything unfortunate happens to the son in the employer's household in the future, it is completely his own fate, and ×××(name) shall not blame anybody for it. Lest there should be no guarantee in the future, this document is completed as proof. So the above contract has been made.

Day: ××× Month: ××× Year: ×××

---

[79]Huang Shijian, *Yuan Dai Fa Lu Zi Liao Ji Cun* (*A Collection of Legal Materials in Yuan Dynasty*), Zhejiang Ancient Books Publishing House, 1988, p. 40.

[80]Su Tianjue(Yuan Dynasty), "Ye Lv Chu Cai Shen Dao Bei" (*The Tablet on the Pathway to the Tomb of Yelv Chucai*) by Song Zizhen in *Yuan Wen Lei* (*A Collection of Essays of Yuan Dynasty*), Vol. 57.

[81]"He Gu" (Being Employed with Appropriate Payment) is explained as the following: "'He' refers to being agreeable to both parties, 'Gu' referring to employing and being employed" in *Li Xue Zhi Nan* (*A Guide to Bureaucratics*) by Xu Yuanrui (Yuan).

The Father: ××× (name)
Guarantee: ××× (name)[82]

Among the personal employment contracts, in addition to the contracts on selling labor by waiting on others, there were some contracts on people who were hired out as concubines.

Apart from personal employment, there was also the employment of porters, who were usually employed by government officials. According to the different characteristics of water and land transportation, different "Qi Shi" (the pattern of contract) was used, for example:

> Porter ××× (name) in ××× "Li" (a basic resident organization consisting of five neighborhoods), ××× "Xian" (county), ××× "Zhou" (subprefecture).
>
> ××× (name) and other porters today have ××× (name), "Hang Lao" (the head of the trade) in ××× "Li" (a basic resident organization consisting of five neighborhoods) and ××× "Xiang" (townships) as the guarantee, and is hired to transport ××× *dan* of luggage owned by the official ××× (name) in ××× department to ××× (name of the destination). The three parties have negotiated the price of ××× *guan* of money. So ××× *guan* of money for food shall be paid in advance, with all the rest borrowed on the way whenever necessary and cleared off on the settlement date. After ××× (name) and other porters receive the luggage, they shall take care of the luggage on the road carefully. Besides, the luggage must be safely transported without being damaged or delayed, and it is forbidden to extort wine and food on the road without authorization. If anything unexpected happens in future, "Hang Lao" (the head of the trade) is willing to pay back the above mentioned goods and to hire other porters to take over the task and transport the luggage to the consignee. Lest there should be no guarantee in the future, this document is completed as proof. So the above contract has been made.
>
> Day: ××× Month: ××× Year: ×××
> The Porter: ××× (name)
> "Hang Lao" (the head of the trade): ××× (name)

In the above "Qi Shi" (the pattern of contract) for the employment of porters, the most important terms included: "leave without permission", "damaged", and "Hang Lao" (the head of the trade) "is willing to pay back", etc. by which the employees were strictly restricted to "take care of the luggage".

9.4.4 Marriage and Inheritance Law with the Integration of the Laws of Mongolian and Han Nationalities

Before the reunification of China by the Yuan Dynasty, the basic lifestyle in the country was nomadic, so marriage relationships were relatively casual and there were no legal restrictions. After the reunification of China, although influenced by the feudal ideology of "Li Jiao" (feudal ethical code) and "Lun Chang" (feudal order of importance), some original Mongolian traditions were still retained. So as early as

---

[82]Zhang Chuanxi, *Zhong Guo Li Dai Qi Yue Hui Bian Kao Shi* (*A Textual Research and Interpretation of the Collected Contracts of the Past Dynasties of China*) (Book 1).

the era of Emperor Taizu, it was recorded that "after Emperor Genghis Khan was born, he conquered all the countries from sunrise to sunset, and ruled them according to their own customs."[83] In terms of marriage, in the Yuan Dynasty, different ethnic groups were allowed to act in accordance with their own customs and habits without being unified. In the 8th year of Zhiyuan (1271), it was stated that "if people of different nationalities get married with those of their own races, their own customs and laws should be followed." For example, if a person from the Han nationality "has a wife but marries another woman," it was not acceptable by law, so the two parties should be sentenced to be divorced. But according to the Mongolian customary law of "Zha Sa" (the Yasa or customary law), polygamy was allowed, so "Mongols are not subject to this restriction" and could follow their own customs.[84] In addition, for Mongols, the policy of "Fu Xiong Di Hun" (a kind of marriage custom, that is, marriages with the father's concubine and brother's wife) was implemented, that is, the son could take in the father's concubine or the younger brother could take in the elder brother' s wife or the elder brother could take in the younger brother's wife. But for the people of Han nationality, if the nephew took in the aunt, they would be found guilty of adultery and be sentenced to be divorced; if the son took in the father's concubine in the mourning period of his parents, they each would be punished by "Zhang" (flogging with heavy sticks) for one hundred and seven strokes and be sentenced to be divorced; if the elder brother took in the younger brother's wife, the male would be punished by "Zhang" (flogging with heavy sticks) for one hundred and seven strokes and the female ninety seven strokes, and then they would be sentenced to be divorced. But if the younger brother took in the dead brother's wife, it was permitted by law because it belonged to the category of marriage of relatives allowed by law. This law developed from the Mongolian customary law, and it was applicable to the Han people.

Marriages had to be concluded with marriage certificates, and the contents of the marriage certificates were clearly defined:

> The ambiguous and misleading words may not be used in marriage certificates, instead the bride-price and gifts must be recorded in detail. Moreover, the certificate must be signed by the bridegroom and his matchmaker respectively. In the reply of the bride's family, the number of the betrothal presents received must also be specified and signed by the bride and the matchmaker respectively. In addition, the characters of "He Tong" (contract) must be written obviously on the back of the marriage certificates of both parties, and the marriage certificates should be kept by the two parties respectively. If there are obscure words in the marriage certificate or there are not the signatures of the parties concerned or there are not the characters of "He Tong" (contract), the marriage certificates shall be considered invalid when a dispute or lawsuit is filed to the government office.[85]

---

[83]"Xing Bu" (The Department of Punishment) (Part 19) in *Yuan Dian Zhang* (*The Collection of Statutes of Yuan Dynasty*), Vol. 57.

[84]"Hun Yin Li Zhi" (The Marriage Ritual System) in "Hu Ling" (Decrees on Household) (Part 2) in *Tong Zhi Tiao Ge* (*The General Legal Provisions and Injunctions*), Vol. 3.

[85]"Hu Bu" (The Department of Revenue) (Part 4) in *Yuan Dian Zhang* (*The Collection of Statutes of Yuan Dynasty*), Vol. 18.

9.4 The Civil Law with National Differences

In addition, private agreement was also a form of marriage contract with legal effect. It was recorded in "Xing Fa Zhi" (The Record of Criminal Law) in *Yuan Shi* (*The History of Yuan Dynasty*) that "if a woman has already promised to marry, or agreed to the bridegroom's marriage proposal, or reached a private agreement, or accepted the bride-price, but if she has broken the promise of marriage, she shall be punished by 'Chi' (flogging with light sticks) for thirty seven strokes."

Different bride prices were also clearly specified in the laws of the Yuan Dynasty according to family status: "The bride-price for rich households includes one *liang* of gold, five *liang* of silver, six 'Biao Li' (unit of measure, or sets of clothes) of color satin dress material, and forty *pi* of miscellaneous silk; the bride-price for average households includes five *qian* of gold, four *liang* of silver, four 'Biao Li' (unit of measure, or sets of clothes) of color satin dress material, and thirty *pi* of miscellaneous silk; the bride-price for poor households includes three *liang* of silver, two 'Biao Li' of color satin dress material, and fifteen *pi* of miscellaneous silk."[86] At the same time, it was forbidden by the law of the Yuan Dynasty to take advantage of the marriage relationship to achieve financial gains. If a husband made his wife or concubine marry again because of his avarice or because he had accepted money, he would be punished. If the bride had brought with her property as dowry, an agreement should be made to show the transfer of property rights. For example, in the 6th year of Zhizheng (1346), Wu Lanyou in Xiuning county signed the following agreement on the dowry to marry off his daughter:

> Wu Lanyou in Chunyi "Li" (a basic resident organization consisting of five neighborhoods) in Xiuning "Xian" (county) is marrying off his daughter Yiniang into the family of Xiang Jiefu in Shiyi "Du" (ancient administrative region) in Qimen "Xian" (county). Now he has one *qiu* (unit of area) of "Zhong Tian" (average land), which is situated at Shuizhen "Ting" (township) to be registered for commercial use. The land stretches from Shoutian in the east, to Zhangjiatian in the west, from Zhangjiatian in the south, to Lijiatian in the north. The original rent for the field is twenty one *cheng* (unit of weight, one *cheng* is about 7.5 kilogram). Now a piece of land worth sixteen *cheng* of rent shall be given to Yiniang as laundry expenses. For the rest of land which is worth five *cheng* of rent, Xiang Jiefu is willing to trade for the land at Huantanwutangku (name of a place) in Liubao in Yidu in Xiuning "Xian" (county), which is bought from Yang Zhihyun and which is worth five *cheng* of rent. So both parties shall rent and manage the land respectively with the grain tax paid accordingly. In addition, there were other two pieces of mountain land which were originally bought from Wu Rongfu and which situated at Xiawunankenger (name of a place). So there are totally four pieces of land. The land is bought legally in accordance with the original land sale contracts, and shall be given to his daughter Yiniang to buy jewelry. All the original land sale contracts shall be delivered to the buyer with this agreement, so that the descendants will not have any disputes in future. After all the above mentioned land is given to the bride today, Yiniang's husband Xiang Jiefu has the right to report to the government office to pay tax, to grow seedlings, to harvest crops voluntarily, and to own the property permanently. Since the land situated at Shuizhen "Ting" (township) has the same land deed with other property, it has not been handed over to the buyer. If he needs the land deed in future, the parents of the bride shall hand over the deed, and testify for the buyer if needed. If the descendants have disputes over the land, it is allowed for Xiang

---

[86]"Hu Bu" (The Department of Revenue) (Part 4) in *Yuan Dian Zhang* (*The Collection of Statutes of Yuan Dynasty*), Vol. 18.

Jiefu to file lawsuits to the government office according to the deed so that the disputes can be settled. Lest there should be no guarantee in the future, this document is completed as proof.
October 15th of the 6th year of Zhizheng.
Father: Wu Lanyou (Signature)
Contract dictator: Wu Tangsun (Signature)[87]

As for the restrictions on marriage, the old laws of the Tang and Song dynasties were basically followed. For example, it was forbidden for people with the same surnames to get married. According to the provision of "Tong Xing Bu De Wei Hun" (No Marriages for the People with the Same Surnames) in "Hun Yin" (Marriage) in "Hu Bu" (The Department of Revenue) in *Yuan Dian Zhang* (*The Collection of Statutes of Yuan Dynasty*), a memorial submitted by "Shang Shu Sheng" (The Department of Secretary) was approved by the emperor in October of the 25th year of Zhiyuan (1288): "the couples with the same surnames who have got married before the specified time shall not be sentenced to be divorced, but after the specified time ... shall be prohibited from getting married." During the reign of Zhiyuan, Chen Liang in Zhangzhou "Lu" (ancient administrative region) and Youxi "Xian" (county) sued his neighbor Cai Fu for marrying Cai Da's daughter Cai Guangniang, because she had the same surname as him. After the investigation of Zhejiang province, it was discovered that Cai Guangniang was adopted and had been brought up by the Cao family since the 28th year of Zhiyuan (1290), so their marriage did belong to the case of marriage of the same surnames; thus, she was allowed to reunite with her husband.[88]

Moreover, it was also forbidden for "Liang Ren" (the decent people) to get married with "Jian Min" (rabbles or people of lower social status). According to the provision of "Qu Kou Jia Qu" (The Marriages of Slaves and Slave girls) in "Hun Yin" (Marriage) in "Hu Bu" (The Department of Revenue) (Part 4) in *Yuan Dian Zhang* (*The Collection of Statutes of Yuan Dynasty*), "it is forbidden for 'Qu Kou' (a general term for slaves and slave girls) to get married with 'Liang Ren' (the decent people)." But according to the provision of "Liang Jian Wei Hun" (The Marriages of the Decent People with Rabbles) in "Hu Ling" (Decrees on Household) in *Tong Zhi Tiao Ge* (*The General Legal Provisions and Injunctions*) (Vol. 3), "in July of the 14th year of Zhiyuan, it is decided after deliberation by 'Hu Bu' (The Department of Revenue) in 'Zhong Shu Sheng' (the supreme organization in charge of the state affairs) that if 'Qu Kou' (a general term for slaves and slave girls) marry 'Liang Ren' (the decent people), it is allowed for their sons to be registered as 'Liang Ren' (the decent people) and live together with their father. So after 'Qu Kou' (a general term for slaves and slave girls) has died, the sons may apply for a new household residence and serve as male servant, and the sons of military 'Qu Kou' (a general term for slaves and slave girls) shall be regarded as 'Tie Hu' (Mercenary) of 'Liang

---

[87] Zhang Chuanxi, *Zhong Guo Li Dai Qi Yue Hui Bian Kao Shi* (*A Textual Research and Interpretation of the Collected Contracts of the Past Dynasties of China*) (Book 1).

[88] "Hu Bu" (The Department of Revenue) (Part 4) in *Yuan Dian Zhang* (*The Collection of Statutes of Yuan Dynasty*), Vol. 18.

9.4 The Civil Law with National Differences

Ren' (the decent people)." Thus, it can be seen that after the 14th year of Zhiyuan (1277), the prohibition of "Liang Jian Wei Hun" (The Marriages of the Decent People with Rabbles) was not strictly enforced. According to the Mongolian customary law, if slaves married their owners, they could become "Liang Ren" (the decent people) under certain conditions; therefore, the prohibition of marriages between "Liang Ren" (the decent people) and "Jian Min" (rabbles or people of lower social status) in the Yuan Dynasty was not as strict as that of the Tang and Song dynasties.

Incest marriages and marriages with married women and concubines were prohibited among the Han people. "Among the Han people and the southerners, the sons are prohibited from marrying their father's concubines after their father has died, and the younger brothers are prohibited from marrying their elder brothers' wives after their elder brothers have died." For those who had married women intentionally, "the matchmakers and the parties of the marriage shall all be punished, with the money confiscated and the women concerned sentenced to return to their parents' homes."[89] As for the dissolution of marriage, in *Yuan Dian Zhang (The Collection of Statutes of Yuan Dynasty)*, the provisions of "Qi Chu" (seven reasons to repudiate the wife: "being unfilial to parents-in-law," "failing to bear a male offspring," "being lascivious," "being jealous," "having severe illness," "gossiping," and "committing theft") and "Yi Jue" (a system of forced divorce because of fighting, scolding, killing, and raping of the relatives of both parties) were made. But in the most important code, *Da Yuan Tong Zhi (General Regulations of the Great Yuan Dynasty)*, no such provisions were made, which showed that Mongols had a stiff resistance to the feudal ethics of the Han nationality concerning marriage relationship. But according to law, if the couples' relationship was bad, they were allowed to divorce freely, as was described in the saying that "if the couples are on bad terms with each other ... or if they are willing to divorce by an agreement, they shall be allowed to do so without being punished. If a husband writes 'Xiu Shu' (a letter by husband to wife announcing divorce) to get the divorce certificate in the government office, it is allowed for the wife to remarry."[90] After a man and a woman were engaged, if the man "has not married the woman for no reason within five years, the woman is allowed to remarry."[91] In addition, if the fiancé "has committed theft or has been sentenced to 'Liu' (exile) to a remote place, the fiancée is allowed to remarry by law,"[92] which was reasonable because it was in line with human nature. Meanwhile, it was also a negation of the feudal doctrine that "women should be faithful to their husbands all their lives." Besides, those who committed bigamy were forced to divorce by law, and "if those who have had wives and concubines take in other wives or concubines, they shall be punished by 'Chi' (flogging with light

---

[89] "Xing Fa Zhi" (The Record of Criminal Law) (Part 2) in *Yuan Shi (The History of Yuan Dynasty)*.
[90] "Hu Hun" (Marriage, Tax and Household Registration) in *Da Yuan Tong Zhi (General Regulations of the Great Yuan Dynasty)*.
[91] "Xing Fa Zhi" (The Record of Criminal Law) (Part 2) in *Yuan Shi (The History of Yuan Dynasty)*.
[92] "Xing Fa Zhi" (The Record of Criminal Law) (Part 2) in *Yuan Shi (The History of Yuan Dynasty)*.

sticks) for forty seven strokes and be sentenced to be divorced."[93] If the current officials took prostitutes as their wives, they would not only be dismissed and be sentenced to be divorced but would also be punished by 'Zhang' (flogging with heavy sticks) for fifty seven strokes.

As to inheritance, the Mongols and Semu (the nationalities in the western or northwestern regions) followed their own basic customary laws. According to Mongolian customary law, the father's property should be inherited by the youngest son, but later, due to the influence of the laws of the Han nationality, the system of "Zhu Zi Jun Fen Zhi" (the property being shared equally by all sons) was implemented, but their actual shares varied. According to the regulation, "of all the people who have the right to share the land, estate and property, each of the sons born by his wife shall share four-tenths, each of the sons born by his concubines three-tenths, and each of the illegitimate sons and the sons of favorite slave girls one-tenth."[94]

For the daughters and widows in the families of "Hu Jue" (No Male Heirs), they all had the right of inheritance or the right of conditional inheritance. For example, the unmarried daughters enjoyed full inheritance rights, but the married daughters enjoyed partial inheritance rights. Moreover, the widows could enjoy full inheritance rights only under the circumstances that she had no sons, no daughters or any nephews.

For "Guo Fang Zi" (brother's son adopted as one's heir), he enjoyed full inheritance rights, but if the uncles had their own sons after the adoption, "Guo Fang Zi" (brother's son adopted as one's heir) could share the property with other natural sons equally. For example, in the 2nd year of Tianli (1329), an adoption contract was drafted by Xie Hesun in Huizhou for adopting a son. The contents are clearly specified as follows:

> □□□[95] Xie Hesun's father Xie Shengsi has two sons, the eldest son Xie Xuansun and the second son Xie Hesun. Now the eldest son Xuansun has four sons, and Hesun had a son named Zhusun, who unfortunately died young. Today Hesun intends to have his elder brother's second son Zuosun adopted, so tells their mother. According to their mother's decision, Hesun has adopted his elder brother Xuansun's second son Zuosun to be the heir and to enshrine temple incense. If Hesun has his own son in the future, his son shall share all his property equally with Zuosun, whether the life is easy or difficult. The adoptive relationship shall start with the signing of adoption contract today. After Zuosun is adopted, the two families may not regret over the matter; if either family does, they shall be imposed with a fine of fifty *ding* (unit of measure for gold and silver) in "Zhong Tong Chao" (the paper money made in the year of Zhongtong), and the contract documents shall continue to be used. Lest there should be no guarantee in the future, this document is completed as proof.
> May 10th of the 2nd year of Tianli.
> Xie Hesun (Signature)

---

[93]"Xing Fa Zhi" (The Record of Criminal Law) (Part 2) in *Yuan Shi* (*The History of Yuan Dynasty*).

[94]"Qin Shu Fen Cai" (Relatives Sharing the Property) in "Hu Ling" (Decrees on Household) (Part 3) in *Tong Zhi Tiao Ge* (*The General Legal Provisions and Injunctions*), Vol. 4.

[95](Translator's note: the words in original text are missing).

9.4 The Civil Law with National Differences

Xie Ali (Signature)[96]

For the distribution of ancestral household property, household division contracts should be made to avoid disputes. For example, in the 10th year of Zhizheng (1350), Wu Deren and others in Huizhou concluded a household division contract as follows:

> Wu Deren and his brother Wu Haining shared with the woman named Ting Mei a piece of ancestral residential land, which is divided into two parts: a larger one for the communal property of Ting Mei and a smaller one for the communal property for Deren brothers □. □Ting Mei's share of the property has been sold to Ting Chun, Ting Wu, and Deren brothers. Now after the negotiation by the both parties, Deren is willing to □□□ with Ting Chun and Ting Wu for their convenience to manage their estate, and Deren brothers to manage their estate of the larger part. The upper section of the larger part is connected with our family's residential land for tenants and domestic servants, so a boundary tablet is to be erected across the house and a stone is to be buried to mark the boundary. On the boundary between the two families, there will be a common road, which is three *chi* wide, including two *chi* from Ting Chun and Ting Wu, and one *chi* from Deren brothers. The land stretches from the hill to the ditch outward. □ The road will be occupied and blocked by both parties. All the property which the Ting family has bought from Ting Mei will be a share of household property for Deren brothers. After the conclusion of the contract today, both parties shall manage their estates in accordance with the contract. So they shall be allowed to change their residence, build their houses freely, and manage their estate according to the contract permanently. Thus, the erected tablet will be taken as the boundary, and the land covers all the rest of the land beyond the ditch to the building lot of Ting Song. Lest there should be no guarantee in the future, three copies of this document are completed and each party keeps one as proof.
> February 16th of the 10th year of Zhizheng.
> Wu Deren (Signature)
> Contract witness: Wu Shouqing (Signature)[97]

If brothers belonged respectively to civilian and military households, they could still adopt each other's sons to continue the family line, but they had to change the household registration of their adopted sons. In a case, the elder brother of a person named Zhen so and so in Pingyan "Lu" (ancient administrative region) was a household of "Chong Jun" (to be forced to join the army). When he got old and did not have children, he wanted to adopt his brother's son to serve as "Tie Hu" (Mercenary) and be part of the supplement forces of the regular army. The case was settled after deliberations by "Zhong Shu Sheng" (the supreme organization in charge of state affairs), and it was ruled that his nephew should be removed from the civilian household registry, inherit his uncle's ancient profession, and undertake the corvee service of "Tie Hu" (Mercenary). Subsequently, this ruling became a fixed precedent: "In future, if the people in the families of civilian households are

---

[96] Zhang Chuanxi, *Zhong Guo Li Dai Qi Yue Hui Bian Kao Shi* (*A Textual Research and Interpretation of the Collected Contracts of the Past Dynasties of China*) (Book 1).
[97] Zhang Chuanxi, *Zhong Guo Li Dai Qi Yue Hui Bian Kao Shi* (*A Textual Research and Interpretation of the Collected Contracts of the Past Dynasties of China*) (Book 1).

childless, but they have nephews in the military households to continue the family line, the adoption shall be handled fully in accordance with to the above case."[98]

9.5 The Trial System with Diverse Jurisdiction

9.5.1 The Diversified Judicial Organization System

During the rule of the Yuan Dynasty, judicial power was diversified, but as far as the judicial system was concerned, certain achievements were still made. Early in the era of the Mongolia Empire, there were neither fixed judicial organs nor the so-called litigation procedures. After the reunification of China, "Xing Bu" (The Department of Punishment) and "Yu Shi Tai" (The Censorate) were begun to be established in the Yuan Dynasty following those of the Song Dynasty, and "Da Zong Zheng Fu" (a central judicial organ of the Yuan Dynasty) was also established on the basis of "Zha Lu Wu Chi" (judicial officials) of Mongolia. "Da Zong Zheng Fu" (a central judicial organ of the Yuan Dynasty) was not only the agency for the administration of the affairs of the Mongolian nobles but also the central judicial organ with independent jurisdiction. In "Da Zong Zheng Fu" (a central judicial organ of the Yuan Dynasty), "the princes of Mongolia act as its head," and the official position of Mongolian "Duan Shi Guan" (judicial officials) was established, who was responsible for handling cases involving the Mongolian nobles, as well as lawsuits involving the Mongols and Semu (the nationalities in the western or northwestern regions) near the capital area, as was described in the saying that if the Mongols had committed crimes, "the Mongolian judicial officials shall be chosen to hear the case and to execute the punishment of 'Zhang' (flogging with heavy sticks)."[99] Although both the chief officials of the "Da Zong Zheng Fu" (a central judicial organ of Yuan Dynasty) and "Yu Shi Tai" (The Censorate) were "officials of 'Cong Yi Pin' (the accessary first rank)", the chief official of "Da Zong Zheng Fu" (a central judicial organ of the Yuan Dynasty) was not subject to the supervision of "Yu Shi Tai" (The Censorate).

Since emphasis was laid on religion, and particularly Lamaism was advocated in the Yuan Dynasty, the Grand Lama was exalted by the emperor as "Di Shi" (teacher of the emperor, an honorary title for the first monk in the Yuan Dynasty) and "Guo Shi" (teacher of the state, an honorary title for eminent monks in Yuan Dynasty). The average monks also had great power, as well as distinguished social status, so they enjoyed not only the legal privilege to be exempt from corvee services but also certain judicial privileges, so that "Xuan Zheng Yuan" (The Bureau of Buddhist and

---

[98]"Hu Jue Cai Chan" (No Male Heirs to Succeed the Property) in "Hu Ling" (Decrees on Household) (Part 2) in *Tong Zhi Tiao Ge* (*The General Legal Provisions and Injunctions*), Vol. 3.

[99]"Hu Jue Cai Chan" (No Male Heirs to Succeed the Property) in "Hu Ling" (Decrees on Household) (Part 2) in *Tong Zhi Tiao Ge* (*The General Legal Provisions and Injunctions*), Vol. 3.

9.5 The Trial System with Diverse Jurisdiction

Tibetan Affairs), which was in charge of religious affairs, became the highest religious judicial organ and was responsible for handling major cases and disputes among monks or those between monks and laymen. During the reign of Emperor Chengzong, in order to control the jurisdiction of "Xuan Zheng Yuan" (The Bureau of Buddhist and Tibetan Affairs), an edict was issued: "From now on, if Buddhist officials and monks commit crimes, the prisoners shall be tried by 'Yu Shi Tai' (The Censorate) together with the central and local organs of 'Xuan Zheng Yuan' (The Bureau of Buddhist and Tibetan Affairs). If the officials of 'Xuan Zheng Yuan' (The Bureau of Buddhist and Tibetan Affairs) act unfairly out of personal considerations by bending the law, they shall be punished by 'Yu Shi Tai' (The Censorate)."[100] In addition to "Xuan Zheng Yuan" (The Bureau of Buddhist and Tibetan Affairs), abbots of temples also had certain rights of interrogation. Except for crimes such as theft, fraud, forgery, assault, and homicide that were committed by monks, which should be tried by judicial organs, disputes and lawsuits between monks themselves should be tried and settled by the abbots of the temples.

In addition, "Zhong Zheng Yuan" (a government office in charge of the empress' financial revenue, construction, supply, and so on), which was in charge of the daily affairs of the court, was concurrently responsible for the trial of cases involving court officials. Cases related to Taoism, on the other hand, were tried by "Dao Jiao Suo" (Taoist Institution); "Shu Mi Yuan" (Privy Council), which was in charge of military affairs, was concurrently responsible for major military cases and cases involving military officers with or above the rank of "Xiao Wei" (official post in the army just below the general). These judicial organs were administered separately and were independent of each other, but whenever a public prosecution was held, they had to make an appointment to have the cases heard jointly with other organs concerned, so that it often led to chaos, particularly in the transfer of official documents, and delay in the settlement of cases, which had seriously affected the unitary exercise of judicial power and the efficiency of the trial.

As for the local judicial organs, they were divided into "Xing Sheng" (province), "Lu" (ancient administrative region), "Fu" (ancient administrative district between province and county) or "Zhou" (subprefecture), and "Xian" (county). "Xing Sheng" (province) was a local supreme government and judicial organ. "Su Zheng Lian Fang Shi Si" (the government supervising office) was set up to be in charge of the judicial administrative supervision of each "Lu" (ancient administrative region), and "Tui Guan" (official in charge of criminal penalty) was set up in each "Lu" (ancient administrative region) to be in charge of litigation. The chief officials of "Fu" (ancient administrative district between province and county), "Zhou" (subprefecture), and "Xian" (county) were concurrently in charge of local judicial administration, and the post of "Da Lu Hua Chi" (judicial official), which was usually held by Mongols, was also set up in "Lu" (ancient administrative region), "Fu" (ancient administrative district between province and county), "Zhou"

---

[100]"Cheng Zong Ji" (The Record of Emperor Chengzong) (Part 3) in *Yuan Shi* (*The History of Yuan Dynasty*).

(subprefecture), and "Xian" (county). "Da Lu Hua Chi" (judicial official) also had the right to directly interrogate prisoners, and his power overrode that of the local chief officials. Therefore, local judicial power was actually controlled by the Mongolian officials. If there were major disputes between the armymen and civilians or between monks and laymen, "joint hearing" should be held by the local chief officials together with Mongolian and religious officials.

The heads of the grassroots organizations "Xiang" (townships) and "Li" (a basic resident organization consisting of five neighborhoods), called "She Zhang" (head of the community), was in charge of recording the misbehaviors of those who were disobedient to their parents or who were ferocious toward other people and posting these records with large font on their doors. These posters were not allowed to be removed from their doors until they had corrected their mistakes; if they did not do so within a year, they would be punished by serving as laborers in "She" (community), which, however, was not a grassroots judicial organ.

9.5.2 Concurrency of Regional Jurisdiction and Ethnic and Religious Jurisdiction

Although the judicial system was in disorder during the Yuan Dynasty, some progress had been made in the litigation and trial system. So "litigation" was already listed as a special section in the codes, which had reflected the trend of separation between procedural law and substantive law. At the same time, different procedures were also provided for civil and criminal lawsuits. For example, generally it was not allowed for parties in a civil case to be taken into custody, and when military officers were sent on a mission of patrol inspection, they were not allowed to accept civil complaints. Moreover, "Tui Guan" (official in charge of criminal penalty) was especially appointed to be in charge of criminal penalty. If lawsuits involved different household registers and nationalities or disputes arose between monks and laymen, they should be jointly heard by immediate superior officials, which was referred to as "Yue Hui" (joint hearing). The system was usually applied to both civil and the minor criminal cases.

As to the private prosecution, the stipulations of Tang and Song dynasties were followed and it was provided that "the date should be clearly notified, the evidence of the crime should be clearly stated, and the doubtful points should be avoided".[101] Besides, it was strictly forbidden for slaves to accuse their masters, which had reflected the characteristics of the times under the rule of Yuan Dynasty. At the same time, under the influence of the culture of Han dynasty, it was forbidden for sons to accuse their fathers or wives to accuse their husbands, which had shown the integration of the Mongolian and Han culture.

---

[101]"Xing Fa Zhi" (The Record of Criminal Law) (Part 4) in *Yuan Shi* (*The History of Yuan Dynasty*).

9.5 The Trial System with Diverse Jurisdiction

Although litigants were allowed to appeal to higher authorities level by level, "Yue Su" (overstepping indictment) was prohibited, and it was provided that "the crimes which are punishable by 'Zhang' (flogging with heavy sticks) for fewer than fifty seven strokes shall be settled by 'Si' (bureau) and 'Xian' (county); the crimes punishable by 'Zhang' (flogging with heavy sticks) for fewer than eighty seven strokes shall be settled by 'San Fu' (prefecture), 'Zhou' (subprefecture), and 'Jun' (shire); the crimes punishable by 'Zhang' (flogging with heavy sticks) for fewer than one hundred and seven stokes shall be settled by 'Xuan Wei Si' (the government office in remote areas) and 'Zong Guan Fu' (The General Governor's Office)."[102] In Yuan Dynasty, the system of "Deng Wen Gu" (Deng Wen Drum, one of the most important ways of direct appeal in ancient China) was also set up so that people could complain their injustice by beating the drum. In addition, "Cheng Yu Su" (complaining directly to the Emperor), which was the equivalent of "Yao Che Su" (the parties intercept the emperor on the way to file a lawsuit directly to the emperor himself) in the Tang Dynasty, was set up. But this kind of complaint could only be accepted if the cases remained unsettled after they had been tried by all levels of the judicial organs of "Zhou" (subprefecture) and "Xian" (county) and other central government offices such as "Sheng" (province), "Bu" (department), "Tai" (bureau), and "Yuan" (institution); they should be punished if they had made up the stories.

In addition to regional jurisdiction, special jurisdiction was also exercised according to different nationalities, identities, and religion. For example, "if Mongolian officials have committed any crime, the Mongolian judicial officials shall be chosen to hear the case, so is the exercise of the punishment of 'Zhang' (flogging with heavy sticks)"; "if 'Si Qie Xue' (Kheshigs, or imperial guards), or the princes and sons-in-law of the Emperor, or the Mongols and Semu (the nationalities in the western or northwestern regions) have committed the crime of 'Jian Dao' (rape and theft) and 'Zha Wei' (fraud and forgery), they shall be punished by 'Da Zong Zheng Fu' (a central judicial organ of Yuan Dynasty)"[103]; "if the Mongols and the Semu (the nationalities in the western or northwestern regions) who are in the army station of 'Si Qie Xue' (Kheshigs, or imperial guards), or the Han people who are within the jurisdiction of 'Shang Du' (Upper Capital) and 'Da Du' (Great Capital) have disputes with each other, the cases shall be tried by 'Da Zong Zheng Fu' (a central judicial organ of Yuan Dynasty), while the lawsuits involving the Han, Mongols and Semu (the nationalities in the western or northwestern regions) in 'Lu' (ancient administrative region), 'Fu' (ancient administrative district between province and county), 'Shi' (city), 'Jun' (shire), 'Jian' (ancient supervisory office), 'Zhou' (subprefecture), and 'Xian' (county) shall all be handled by 'Xing Bu'(The

---

[102]"Xing Bu" (The Department of Punishment) (Part 1) in *Yuan Dian Zhang* (*The Collection of Statutes of Yuan Dynasty*), Vol. 39.

[103]"Xing Fa Zhi" (The Record of Criminal Law) (Part 1) in *Yuan Shi* (*The History of Yuan Dynasty*).

Department of Punishment)."[104] The lawsuits of the Hui people should first be heard by the masters of "Ha De" (the Hui nationality) according to "Hui Hui Fa" (the law of the Hui people or the Moslem law). In the 1st year of Huangqing during the reign of Emperor Renzong (1312), an imperial edict was issued: "The masters of 'Ha De' (the Hui nationality) are only in charge of chanting the scriptures and they are not allowed to interfere with the major or minor cases involving Hui people, such as "Xing Ming" (law), "Hu Hun" (marriage, tax and household registration) and "Qian Liang" (money and grain). All these cases shall be heard by the government offices in accordance with the law."[105]

As for "the cases of 'Dou Song' (litigation), 'Hun Tian' (marriages and land), 'Liang Fu' (grain tax), 'Qian Zhai' (debts), 'Cai Chan' (property), 'Zong Cong Ji Jue' (adoption of heirs among clanmen), and the injustice in 'Ke Cha' (one of the items of taxation in Yuan Dynasty) which occurred among the military men and their households, they should be heard by military officers specially appointed. "If there were disputes among monks, the cases should generally be handled jointly by the abbots of temples and the chief officials in charge." "The major crimes, such as 'Jian Dao' (rape and theft), 'Zha Wei' (Fraud and Forgery), injury and murder shall all be heard by government officials, but the other disputes among monks, whatever they are, shall all be settled by the chief monks in charge of the temples."[106] If there were "disputes among monks, Taoists and Confucianists, they shall be heard jointly by the the heads of the three sects without being interfered by the government offices."[107] Since special jurisdiction was often linked to special courts and laws, it not only impeded the unitary implementation of national laws but also made it more convenient for officials to seek private gains by bending the law and being lenient to criminals. It was recorded in "Xing Fa Zhi" (The Record of Criminal Law) in *Yuan Shi* (*The History of Yuan Dynasty*) that the monks in the west regions are "unscrupulously indulgent to prisoners" so that they have "committed all kinds of crimes."

9.5.3 Mediation Extensively Practiced in Civil Trials

According to the laws of the Yuan Dynasty, "Gu Chu Ru Ren Zui" (to deliberately increase or reduce the punishment when making sentences) was prohibited in hearing cases. If the crime was committed intentionally, those involved should be

---

[104]"Bai Guan Zhi" (The Record of the Officials of all Ranks) (Part 3) in *Yuan Shi* (*The History of Yuan Dynasty*).

[105]"Xing Bu" (The Department of Punishment) (Part 18) in *Yuan Dian Zhang* (*The Collection of Statutes of Yuan Dynasty*), Vol. 53.

[106]"Xing Bu" (The Department of Punishment) (Part 18) in *Yuan Dian Zhang* (*The Collection of Statutes of Yuan Dynasty*), Vol. 53.

[107]"Xing Fa Zhi" (The Record of Criminal Law) (Part 1) in *Yuan Shi* (*The History of Yuan Dynasty*).

9.5 The Trial System with Diverse Jurisdiction

punished for full crimes or be punished one level lighter than the statutory punishment for the person whom they had misjudged; if the crime was committed unintentionally, those involved should be punished three to five levels lighter than the statutory punishment. "As for the crimes punishable by death penalty, they must be heard carefully before the execution." However, these regulations were not seriously implemented in practice because not only the emperor's imperial decrees, which had the highest judicial authority in decisions concerning the life and death of a person, should be considered, but even the empress' orders should also be carefully observed.

In the trial, the cases which were settled should be completely implemented, and there were many examples on the application of judicial precedents in existing records of the Yuan Dynasty. For example, "Qian Hu" (official in charge of 1000 families) Wang Jizu was accused of getting married before his father's funeral, then a case that was settled in the 26th year of Zhiyuan (1289) was discovered by "Li Bu" (The Department of Rites): "Before his brother's funeral was completed, Wang Tang'er and his sister-in-law He Zhenzhen got married on the night of 'Ting Sang' (keeping a corpse in a temporary shelter before burial), which had seriously violated social customs"; thus, it was suggested that "they should be sentenced to be divorced." According to this judicial precedent, it was ruled by "Li Bu" (The Department of Rites) that "Wang Jizu gets married during the time of 'Ting Sang' (keeping a corpse in a temporary shelter before burial) without showing any sorrow for his father, which has obviously violated 'Gang Chang' (the Chinese ethical tradition) and corrupted social morality, and constituted the most serious crime," so "they shall be sentenced to to be divorced" with Wang Jizu removed from his position of "Qian Hu" (official in charge of 1000 families).[108]

Since oral confession was the most important basis for settling cases, it was legitimate to extort confession by torture. But if "the criminals who have committed minor crimes are flogged to death illegally," "the relevant judicial officials shall be punished."[109] In fact, what "Xing Li" (petty officials in charge of carrying out punishment) were concerned about was just the amount of bribes accepted, and they cared not about any injustice to the cases so that the criminals were often wantonly tortured by them during inquisition.

Some new regulations were also made on the acquisition of documentary evidence and autopsy. For example, judicial officials were not only forbidden to confiscate people's family property without permission but also forbidden to "file lawsuits by taking excerpts from the private letters of the criminals" or "making sentences by fabricating or distorting facts."[110] In *Yuan Dian Zhang* (*The Collection*

---

[108]"Xing Bu" (The Department of Punishment) (Part 18) in *Yuan Dian Zhang* (*The Collection of Statutes of Yuan Dynasty*), Vol. 53.

[109]"Xing Fa Zhi" (The Record of Criminal Law) (Part 1) in *Yuan Shi* (*The History of Yuan Dynasty*).

[110]"Xing Fa Zhi" (The Record of Criminal Law) (Part 4) in *Yuan Shi* (*The History of Yuan Dynasty*).

of Statutes of Yuan Dynasty), "Zhu Sha Jian Yan Tiao" (A List of Items for Checking and Inspecting the Killed) was included; at the same time, autopsy measures, which should be conducted on the same day, were also provided.

Although the regulations on avoidance and appeal and the prohibition of night interrogation were included in the criminal law of the Yuan Dynasty, they were not carried out in practice. In most cases, people were imprisoned randomly, and many innocent people were implicated illegally and treated brutally without investigating the actual situations. In his famous book *Dou E Yuan (Snow in Midsummer)*, Guan Hanqing, a famous dramatist in the Yuan Dynasty, stated through the dialogues of the characters in his play: "The officials have no intention to try cases according to law, while the common people have no way to speak up their injustices"; although "'Ya Men' (the government offices) has opened to the south since ancient times, there are unjust cases everywhere," which was exactly a portrayal of the judicial darkness that existed during the Yuan Dynasty.

In view of the fact that judicial injustice was the most important cause for social turbulence, the rulers of the Yuan Dynasty paid great attention to rehabilitating the miscarriages of justice. In the history of the Chinese legal system, it was in the Yuan Dynasty that the provision of "Ping Fan" (rehabilitating miscarriages of justice) was included for the first time in criminal law, and it was provided that officials who had made achievements in correcting miscarriages of justice should be rewarded. It was stated in "Xing Fa Zhi" (The Record of Criminal Law) in *Yuan Shi (The History of Yuan Dynasty)* that "those who have rehabilitated more than one serious cases shall also be promoted one rank and be transferred to a higher position; those who have rehabilitated more than one miscarriage of justice shall be promoted by 'Jian Yi Zi' (the system of promoting officials by reducing time qualification); those petty officials who have rehabilitated the miscarriages of justice in 'Lu' (ancient administrative region), 'Fu' (ancient administrative district between province and county) and 'Cao' (department) shall be promoted to hold positions in 'Dao' (the administration district below the province), 'Xuan Wei Si' (the government office in remote areas) and 'Bu' (department)."

It is noteworthy that with the obvious increase of economic exchanges between the various ethnic groups, a large number of civil disputes occurred, and "of the numerous civil lawsuits, the cases of 'Hun Tian' (marriages and land) occupy the largest proportion."[111] In order to solve the increasing civil disputes, new achievements were made in the civil litigation system.

According to the provision in "Wu Xian Fa" (a law on time limit for service, a judicial system in the Song Dynasty), "the cases involving 'Hun Yin' (marriage), 'Liang Jian' (the decent and the rabbles), 'Jia Cai' (family property), and 'Tian Zhai' (land and houses) should be accepted on March 1st and settled in October 1st;" this provision was followed in the Yuan Dynasty. Moreover, the scope of civil procedure agent system was expanded. According to "Xing Fa Zhi" (The Record of Criminal

---

[111]"Xing Bu" (The Department of Punishment) (Part 15) in *Yuan Dian Zhang (The Collection of Statutes of Yuan Dynasty)*, Vol. 53.

9.5 The Trial System with Diverse Jurisdiction

Law) in *Yuan Shi (The History of Yuan Dynasty)*, "if the retired and acting officials have to engage in lawsuits with civilians, their family members are allowed to serve as their agents in the trial, but the cases should not be interfered with by the officials in charge." In addition, "Lao" (elder), "Fei Ji" (the disabled), and "Du Ji" (the incapacitated) were allowed to let their relatives live together with them to serve as their agents in lawsuits. As for women, if "there are no men in the family, or if they have no other choices, so they have to file lawsuits to government offices, it is allowed for their clan relatives to serve as their agents in lawsuits. If their accusations are true, their cases shall be settled according to the law, but if their accusations are false, the women shall be found guilty, but the agents shall not be implicated..."; "if the women live in widowhood, or if they are helpless, or if although they have sons, it is impossible for them to file lawsuits for various reasons, they shall not be subjected to this regulation." So it is undoubtedly a historical progress to extend the civil procedure agent system to the ordinary people in the Yuan Dynasty, as is commented by Xu Chaoyang in modern times: "It generally starts from Yuan Dynasty to allow the ordinary people to appoint agents in litigation."[112]

Mediation was extensively used in civil proceedings. According to *Zhi Yuan Xin Ge (The New Injunctions in the Reign of Zhiyuan)*, "as for the disputes and complaints of 'Hun Yin' (marriage), 'Jia Cai' (family property), 'Tian Zhai' (land and houses), and 'Zhai Fu' (debts), if no serious offences were involved, they shall be mediated by 'She Zhang' (head of the community) through persuasion to avoid the delaying of farmwork and to reduce the lawsuits of government office."[113] The mediation methods included civil mediation and judicial mediation. In civil mediation, "She Zhang" (head of the community) was responsible for "settling the civil disputes between neighbors by persuasion," and the mediation results were legally binding on the parties concerned. Generally speaking, it was forbidden for the parties in litigation to file the lawsuit again for the same facts and reasons. According to the records in *Yuan Dian Zhang (The Collection of Statutes of Yuan Dynasty)*, "If lawsuits concern such matters as 'Hun Yin' (marriage), 'Jia Cai' (family property), 'Tian Zhai' (land and houses), and 'Zhai Fu' (debts), etc. without violating the law, it is forbidden for the government offices in charge to randomly accept and retry the cases again once the lawsuits are withdrawn; otherwise the cases shall be investigated by 'Lian Fang Si' (the government supervising office), so the relevant officials shall be punished." "In future, as to the lawsuits concerning 'Hun Yin' (marriage), 'Jia Cai' (family property), 'Tian Zhai' (land and houses), and 'Zhai Fu' (debts), if the plaintiffs and defendants are willing to withdraw the lawsuits and settle the disputes peacefully, they should be allowed to do so. But if they file the lawsuit again later, or if it is found out after investigation that there are no other illegal acts, it should not be accepted by the government office in charge"; "in future, as to the

---

[112] Xu Chaoyang, *Zhong Guo Su Song Fa Su Yuan (Tracing the Source of China's Procedural Law)*, The Commercial Press, 1973, p. 60.

[113] "Tian Ling" (Decrees on Farmland) in *Tong Zhi Tiao Ge (The General Legal Provisions and Injunctions)*, Vol. 16.

lawsuits concerning such matters as 'Hun Yin' (marriage), 'Jia Cai' (family property), 'Tian Zhai' (land and houses), and 'Zhai Fu' (debts), if the parties concerned are willing to withdraw the lawsuits, or if after careful examination it is found out that the lawsuits involve no other illegal acts, they should be allowed to do so. But it is forbidden for them to file the lawsuits again randomly; otherwise, the offenders shall be punished by law."

No doubt, the extensive practice of mediation was inseparable from the social and historical condition at the time because "the cases of 'Hun Tian' (marriages and land) occupy the largest proportion among the numerous civil lawsuits." Thus, the rulers sought to ease the social tension through mediation so as to reduce the pressure imposed by judicial organs. Zhang Yanghao, who was a contemporary of the Yuan Dynasty, said: "As far as the lawsuits between kinship relatives are concerned, they shall be handled slowly rather than urgently, leniently rather than harshly, because it can help the parties concerned understand their own mistakes to deal with the lawsuits slowly, while it may help breed evilness to deal with the lawsuits harshly. But what is indeed appropriate is that the judicial officials should go to 'Li' (a basic resident organization consisting of five neighborhoods) where the parties live to give them guidance." Certainly, the mediation system in the Yuan Dynasty had exerted a significant influence on the Ming and Qing dynasties.

To sum up, the legal system of Yuan Dynasty was featured by the predomination of Mongols in the late feudal society with Mongols as the main body, which not only reflected its ethnic characteristics, but also the characteristics of the times. Thus, it had made a certain contribution to the development of Chinese legal civilization.

During the ruling of the Yuan Dynasty, due to serious land annexation, heavy tax, and corvee service, as well as wars and natural disasters, a large number of "Bian Hu Qi Min" (ordinary people incorporated into the household registry) who were "original inhabitants in the countryside" were forced to leave their hometown and became refugees. Although on the one hand many measures were taken to relieve the sufferings of the refugees, on the other hand tough sanctions were imposed by the rulers of the Yuan Dynasty; eventually, the problems remained unsolved. Finally, the local disturbance had led to a nationwide anti-Yuan uprising, which had resulted in the perishing of the Yuan Dynasty and the reestablishment of a feudal dynasty with the Han nationality as the main body, namely, the Ming Dynasty.

Chapter 10
The Legal System of the Ming Dynasty: The Final Form of Chinese Legal Civilization

(1368 A.D.–1644 A.D.)

The Ming Dynasty is an important dynasty in the late feudal society of China. During its two hundred and seventy six years of ruling, both economy and culture had reached a new height. After the middle of the Ming Dynasty, with the emergence of the sprout of capitalist production in the handicraft industry and agriculture in Jiangsu and Zhejiang areas, achievements were made in culture, science and technology, which was not only significant in summing up the experience, but also very creative. The making of *Yong Le Da Dian* (*The Great Canon of Yongle*) shocked the whole world at that time, and it has been the world's greatest encyclopedia so far. Moreover, books like *Ben Cao Gang Mu* (*Compendium of Materia Medica*), *Nong Zheng Quan Shu* (*Comprehensive Treatise on Agricultural Administration*), *Tian Gong Kai Wu* (*Heavenly Creations*), and other works were all the epitome of traditional technology. In education, government-operated schools were set up at all levels from the central government to the local "Xian" (county) and "She" (community), and education in private academy was also booming. Especially, Western science and culture began to be introduced into China, which had broadened the vision of the Chinese people.

The legal system of Ming Dynasty which was formed under the historical background mentioned above had played an important role in inheriting the laws of Tang and Song dynasties and initiating the establishment of the legal system of Qing Dynasty. The expansion of the scale of legislative adjustment, the enrichment of the contents, and the improvement of the legislative technique had all contributed to the formation of the new legal system. At the same time, to meet the needs of a unified judicial power, a judicial system reform was carried out, which had stimulated the upsurge of private legal annotation and led to the emergence of great masters of "Lv Xue" (the study of statutory laws), such as Wang Kentang and Lei Menglin. So "Lv Xue" (the study of statutory laws) in the Ming Dynasty was an important symbol of the new stage of development of the Chinese legal civilization.

Although *Da Ming Lv* (*The Great Ming Code*) did not have as widespread an influence as *Tang Lv* (*Tang Code*) had, it still had a far-reaching impact on Japan and especially on Korea. During the Edo period in Japan, the books about *Ming Lv* (*Ming Code*) were once in great demand for reference. After the founding of the Chosun Dynasty, in his imperial edict on ascending the throne, Emperor Taejo Lee Chenggui clearly stated: "From now on, all public and private criminals must be tried by the judicial officials outside the capital according to *Da Ming Lv* (*The Great Ming Code*)."[1] In *Chao Xian Jing Guo Da Dian* (*Gyeongguk Daejeon* or *Complete Code of Law*), it was also recorded that "in order to help to rule the state, the matters such as the trial, judgment and imprisonment of criminals should be handled according to *Da Ming Lv* (*The Great Ming Code*)." "For fear that the laws might be broken by the ignorant people, Emperor Taejo then ordered 'You Si' (officials) to have *Da Ming Lv* (*The Great Ming Code*) translated into local dialects so that it could be easily understood by the public. Besides, it was required that the law should be applied in all convictions, which had fully shown that Emperor Taejo had paid great attention to people's lives by following the norms of other emperors."[2] In February of the 4th year of Emperor Taejo (1371), *Da Ming Lv* (*The Great Ming Code*) was translated and published in the name of *Da Ming Lv Zhi Jie* (*A Literary Interpretation of the Great Ming Code*), from which we can see the historical value of Chinese legal civilization represented by *Da Ming Lv* (*The Great Ming Code*).

The dramatic strengthening of the autocratic system of the Ming Dynasty was directly related to the rise and fall of its legal system. So the making of *Da Ming Gao* (*Imperial Mandates of Great Ming Dynasty*) in the early Ming Dynasty was itself the product of the highly developed monarchical power, while the judicial intervention of eunuchs and "Jin Yi Wei" (secret service of the Ming Dynasty) was a representation of the totalitarian political corruption in the judicial administration. What was once illegal turned to be legal, so the ruling crisis in the Ming Dynasty was naturally inevitable. In his book *Ming Yi Dai Fang Lu* (*Waiting for Dawn*), Huang Zongxi, a thinker of "Zhe Dong Xue Pai" (the School of Eastern Zhejiang), had sharply criticized the autocratic system because it had led not only to "the downfall of the state" but also the "disgrace of the intellectuals." So he called out with a loud cry that "the law of one family" should be replaced by "the law of the world." Huang Zongxi's thought showed the spirit of democracy, so it was of some enlightening significance.

---

[1] "Tai Zu" (Emperor Taizu) in *Chao Xian Wang Chao Shi Lu* (*The Record of Chosun Dynasty*), Vol. 1.

[2] Zheng Daochuan (Korea), 'Xian Dian Zong Xu' (A General Preface to Constitution) in *Chao Xian Jing Guo Dian* (*Gyeongguk Daejeon* or *Complete Code of Law*) in *San Feng Ji* (*Collections of Sanfeng*), Vol. 7.

10.1 Legislative Ideology and Achievements of the Ming Dynasty

10.1.1 Zhu Yuanzhang's Legislative Ideology in the Early Ming Dynasty

Zhu Yuanzhang, who was born into a poor peasant family, gradually became a general with a large number of troops; meanwhile, he also became one of the important leaders of "Hong Jin Jun" (the Red Turban Army) in the peasant uprising at the end of the Yuan Dynasty. In order to consolidate the newly occupied territories and to seize the national political power, he paid great attention to the construction of both political power and the legal system in the occupied territory. In the 15th year of Zhizheng (1355), within the territory under his jurisdiction, he changed "Tai Ping Lu" to "Tai Ping Fu," "Guang De Lu" to "Guang Xing Fu," and "Ji Qing Lu" to "Ying Tian Fu" ("Lu" and "Fu": both ancient administrative regions) and set up official positions in "Fu" (ancient administrative district between province and county), "Zhou" (subprefectures), and "Xian" (county). In the following year, Zhu Yuanzhang called himself "Wu Guo Gong" (The Duke of Wu), and later he renamed himself "Wu Wang" (The King of Wu). Then he established "Zhong Shu Sheng" (the supreme organization in charge of state affairs) and began to set up the official positions of "Zuo You Cheng Xiang" (the chief and deputy prime minister), to be in charge of administrative management; "Zuo You Du Du" (the chief and deputy military viceroys and procurators), to be in charge of military affairs; and "Yu Shi Da Fu" (Grand Censor), to be in charge of supervision. Moreover, he also established "Xing Zhong Shu Sheng" (the provincial supreme organization in charge of daily affairs) and "Xing Du Du Fu" (provincial offices of military affairs), to be in charge of local military affairs, so the organizational structure of the future Ming regime was basically established.

In 1367, Zhu Yuanzhang occupied Wuchang. At the time of ascending the throne of "Wu Wang" (The King of Wu), he proposed that "at the beginning of the founding of the state, the first priority is to rectify the disciplines."[3] So the drafting of *Lv Ling* (*The Laws and Decrees*) was put on the agenda, and Li Shanchang and other officials were ordered to make and issue *Da Ming Lv Ling* (*The Laws and Decrees of Ming Dynasty*) for enforcement. According to the records of "Xing Fa Zhi" (The Record of Criminal Law) in *Ming Shi* (*The History of Ming Dynasty*), "after Emperor Taizu of Ming Dynasty conquered Wuchang, he soon started to discuss about drafting laws and decrees with his ministers. In October of the 1st year of Wu, he appointed 'Zuo Cheng Xiang' (the chief prime minister) Li Shanchang as 'Zong Cai Guan' (chief executive officer) to be in charge of making 'Lv Ling' (the laws and decrees), at the same time, he also appointed other twenty people as 'Yi Lv Guan' (legal officials)

---

[3]"Kai Guo Gui Mo" (The Plan for the Founding of the State) in *Ming Shi Ji Shi Ben Mo* (*The Ins and Outs of the Records in the History of Ming Dynasty*), Vol. 14.

including 'Can Zhi Zheng Shi' (deputy prime minister) Yang Xian and Fu Huan, 'Yu Shi Zhong Cheng' (Grand Censor) Liu Ji, 'Han Lin Xue Shi' (member of the imperial academy) Tao An and so on. ... In December, the law was completed."

Since it not only met the requirement of the people but also was beneficial to the development of society to fight against the tyranny of the Yuan Dynasty and to reconstruct a unified state with the landlords of the Han nationality as the main body and since Zhu Yuanzhang had accumulated greater strength in the anti-Yuan struggle, he eventually won the final victory. In the first month of the lunar calendar in 1368, Zhu Yuanzhang ascended the throne in Nanjing as the emperor, took "Da Ming" (Great Ming) as the title of the country and "Hong Wu" (vastly martial) as the title of his reigning, and reestablished a feudal autocratic dynasty whose national power was far stronger than that of the Song Dynasty.

In the early Ming Dynasty, the political situation was very complex: externally, the remaining forces of the Yuan Dynasty were posing a serious threat to the new regime; internally, some powerful landlords took an uncooperative attitude toward the new regime, and the dark official management resulted from political corruption in the late Yuan Dynasty, which continued to have a corrosive effect on the newly established Ming regime. Moreover, after the baptism of the peasant uprising in the late Yuan Dynasty, great changes had taken place in the relationship of the balance of class forces. Under such a historical background, in order to consolidate the new regime, to protect national defense, to rectify social order, and to develop economy, a strong centralized regime had to be established, so absolutism was highly developed in the Ming Dynasty.

The rulers of the Ming Dynasty, represented by Zhu Yuanzhang, paid great attention to summarizing the historical experience of the previous dynasties, particularly the historical experience of the Song Dynasty, in strengthening the centralized power and the legal system and regarded law not only as "a tool to guard against the common people but also a technique to govern the state."[4] They emphasized that only by the establishment of the legal system was it possible to "ensure social stability and to maintain the harmony of different classes," so "it is the most urgent matter at the beginning of the founding of the state."[5] Therefore, after the unification of the whole country, Liu Weiqian, Hu Weiyong, and other officials were ordered to make *Da Ming Lv* (*The Great Ming Code*) in time so as to establish the basis of the legal system of the Ming Dynasty.

Although Zhu Yuanzhang, Emperor Taizu of the Ming Dynasty, was born into a poor peasant family, he paid great attention to drawing the historical lessons of the feudal rulers. Moreover, he had witnessed the peasant uprising, which was caused by political corruption and the violation of laws and disciplines at the end of the Yuan Dynasty, so he was fully aware of the importance of reestablishing the feudal ruling

---

[4]"Shou Fa" (Abiding by the Law) in *Ming Tai Zu Bao Xun* (*The Imperial Decrees of Emperor Taizu of Ming Dynasty*), Vol. 3.

[5]"Jing Guo" (Governing the State) in *Ming Tai Zu Bao Xun* (*The Imperial Decrees of Emperor Taizu of Ming Dynasty*), Vol. 1.

10.1 Legislative Ideology and Achievements of the Ming Dynasty

order and legal system. He said that "the rulers of Yuan Dynasty were fatuous and arbitrary so that they had failed to have laws and disciplines established. In addition, state affairs were neglected by the emperors, while power was grabbed by the officials arbitrarily, so the emperors' right to enforce punishment was usurped by the evil officials. As a result, the law was ineffective and people were divided in their opinions, which had resulted in the upheaval and the ultimate fall of the country."[6] He stressed that "it is by law that the world can be governed by the imperial court."[7]

In the late Yuan Dynasty, "there were so many redundant 'Tiao Ge' (legal provisions and injunctions) that they were often made use of by the officials to commit illegal acts such as exonerating the guilty or implicating the innocent, which had brought about great harm to the society."[8] So in order to avoid the malpractice, to make it easier for people to understand law, and to make it more convenient for officials to implement the law, early in October of the 1st year of Wu (1367), Li Shanchang and other officials were ordered to make *Lv Ling* (*The Laws and Decrees*). Then Zhu Yuanzhang told them:

> It is important to make the laws concise, appropriate, and easy for people to understand, because if regulations are redundant, or if one case is settled according to different rules, it may lead to inappropriate punishments. Moreover, it is more convenient for judicial officials to take the opportunity to commit crimes, which is not the intention of the law. As the saying goes, if the size of fishing net mesh is too small, there will be no big fish left in the water, so if regulations are redundant, no one will be exempted from the punishment in the country. Therefore, some provisions and penalties should be carefully studied and made by referring to the previous laws. So please present them to me, and I shall deliberate and make comments on them by myself.[9]

When *Da Ming Ling* (*The Decrees of Great Ming Dynasty*) was issued in the 1st year of the Hongwu (1368), he once again pointed out: "... Ancient 'Lv Ling' (The Laws and Decrees) are very simple, but the laws of later generations gradually become complicated and redundant. What is worse, even the meaning of some of the provisions are difficult to be understood, so how can we make people understand the meaning of laws so that they will not be violated? Since it is difficult for people to understand the laws, then it is possible for the treacherous officials to make false charges against them. I am very worried about this. Therefore, the *Lv Ling* (*The Laws and Decrees*) which is to be made today should be simplified by deleting the unnecessary parts, so that they are normalized with the ideas directly stated. I hope that they can be understood easily by all people without being violated."[10]

In order to "make it easier for people to understand and obey the law," in the 30th year of Hongwu (1397), *Da Gao* (*The Great Imperial Mandates*) was "deliberately

---

[6] *Ming Tai Zu Bao Xun* (*The Imperial Decrees of Emperor Taizu of Ming Dynasty*), Vol. 14.

[7] *Ming Tai Zu Bao Xun* (*The Imperial Decrees of Emperor Taizu of Ming Dynasty*), Vol. 116.

[8] *Ming Tai Zu Bao Xun* (*The Imperial Decrees of Emperor Taizu of Ming Dynasty*), Vol. 27.

[9] "Xing Fa Zhi" (The Record of Criminal Law) (Part 1) in *Ming Shi* (*The History of Ming Dynasty*).

[10] Qiu Jun (Ming Dynasty), "Ding Lv Ling Zhi Zhi" (Establishing the System of the Laws and Decrees) (Part 2) in *Da Xue Yan Yi Bu* (*Supplementation to the Explanations of the Great Learning*), Vol. 130.

formulated to tell people the way of pursuing good fortune and avoiding disaster."[11] In order to avoid the misunderstanding caused by redundant regulations, to avoid the situation that one case was settled according to different rules and to avoid the ambiguity that might be exploited by the evil officials to seek private gains, the "redundant and complicated regulations which may be made use of by the treacherous officials to exonerate the guilty or implicate the innocent are completely deleted."[12] *Da Ming Lv Ling* (*The Laws and Decrees of Ming Dynasty*), which consisted of "totally 145 articles of 'Ling' (decree) and 285 articles of 'Lv' (criminal law) was issued in December of the 1st year of Wu."[13] *Da Ming Lv Ling* (*The Laws and Decrees of Ming Dynasty*) was more concise and much easier to be understood than the laws of the Tang and Song dynasties. After the founding of the unified Ming Dynasty, *Da Ming Lv Ling* (*The Laws and Decrees of Ming Dynasty*) was amended several times, and much attention was also attached to the implementation of the idea of simplicity and appropriateness, as was stated in "Xing Fa Zhi" (The Record of Criminal Law) in *Ming Shi* (*The History of Ming Dynasty*) that "it is probable that *Ming Lv* (*Ming Code*) is much simpler than *Tang Lv* (*Tang Code*)."

Based on his understanding that "if the size of fishing net mesh is too small, there will be no big fish left in the water, so if regulations are redundant, no one will be exempted from the punishment in the country," Zhu Yuanzhang's ideal goal of legal system construction was to have those evildoers punished eventually, which had shown the open-mindedness of a statesman who had experienced the peasant uprising in the late Yuan Dynasty.

However, under the historical condition that various contradictions continued to be intensified in the late feudal society, it was difficult to carry out his thoughts of "Fa Gui Jian Dang" (it is of priority for the laws to be concise and appropriate) in the long term. After the middle of the Ming Dynasty, in order to prevent treacherous officials from committing crimes by taking advantage of legal loopholes, many regulations were made, so that there were even two or three regulations for one matter. In the legal system of the Ming Dynasty, "'Lv' (criminal law) refers to the established laws which are applied for generations, while 'Li' (precedent) refers to the temporary imperial decrees,"[14] but the problem that "Lv" (criminal law) was often broken for the citing of "Li" (precedent) while "Li" (precedent) often ran counter to "Lv" (criminal law) was getting worse. What was more, "Chang" (the short form for three secret agencies "Dong Chang," "Xi Chang," and "Nei Chang") and "Wei" (the short form for "Jin Yi Wei" (secret service of the Ming Dynasty)) were rampant, which not only undermined the original intention of ruling the state by law but also initiated the tyrannical ruling of the Ming Dynasty, which was unprecedented in history.

---

[11] "Xing Fa Zhi" (The Record of Criminal Law) (Part 1) in *Ming Shi* (*The History of Ming Dynasty*).
[12] "Xing Fa Zhi" (The Record of Criminal Law) (Part 1) in *Ming Shi* (*The History of Ming Dynasty*).
[13] "Xing Fa Zhi" (The Record of Criminal Law) (Part 1) in *Ming Shi* (*The History of Ming Dynasty*).
[14] "Xing Fa Zhi" (The Record of Criminal Law) (Part 1) in *Ming Shi* (*The History of Ming Dynasty*).

10.1 Legislative Ideology and Achievements of the Ming Dynasty

In order to maintain the stability of the legal system, it was forbidden for the established laws to be changed randomly. In the 25th year of Hongwu (1392), it was proposed by "Xing Bu" (The Department of Punishment) that "if the provisions of 'Lv' (criminal law) are different from 'Li' (precedent), it is advisable to have 'Lv' (criminal law) amended," but it was immediately "declined by Zhu Yuanzhang on the ground that 'Li' (precedent) is only the measure for expediency, so the established 'Lv' (criminal law) must not be changed."[15] When *Da Ming Lv* (*The Great Ming Code*) was completed in the 30th year of Hongwu (1397), an order was particularly issued: "My descendants shall all abide by the law, and if any amendments are discussed to be made by the ministers, they shall all be found guilty of changing the ancestral system."[16] It showed that utmost importance was attached by Zhu Yuanzhang to the maintenance of the stability of the law. So it was precisely because of this that *Da Ming Lv* (*The Great Ming Code*) "has been inherited by generations and nobody dares to make slight changes."[17] However, laws should be changed with society and times because the stability of the law was only relative, which was shown clearly by the repeated amendment of *Wen Xing Tiao Li* (*The Ordinance for Inquisition*), which had been used as the supplementary law after the mid-Ming Dynasty.

In addition to "Fa Gui Jian Dang" (it is of priority for the laws to be concise and appropriate), which was put forward to maintain the stability of law, Zhu Yuanzhang also attached great importance to "Ming Xing Bi Jiao" (integrating punishment with moral teachings) and "Yi Li Dao Min" (guiding people with rites). The principle of "Ming Xing Bi Jiao" (integrating punishment with moral teachings) was not only a Chinese traditional legal thought of long-standing but also Zhu Yuanzhang's theoretical basis for the rule of law. In *Da Gao* (*The Great Imperial Mandates*), which was revised during his reign, the importance of "Ming Xing Bi Jiao" (integrating punishment with moral teachings) was repeatedly stressed. In the principle of "Ming Xing Bi Jiao" (integrating punishment with moral teachings), "Ming Xing" (making people understand criminal law) was especially emphasized, and "Xing" (punishment) was used to make up for the deficiencies of moral teaching. In order to achieve "Ming Xing" (making people understand criminal law), not only legislation was stressed; special attention was also paid to making officials and civilians understand the law, to improving the legal institutions, and to preventing crimes by the publicity of law. Early in December of the 1st year of Wu (1367), when *Da Ming Ling* (*The Decrees of Great Ming Dynasty*) was issued, for fear that the law might not be understood by the common people, Zhu Yuanzhang "ordered 'Da Li Qing' (the president of the supreme court of justice) Zhou Zhen to sort out all the matters among the people from the existing 'Lv Ling' (the laws and decrees), including 'Li Yue' (rites and music), 'Zhi Du' (system), 'Qian Liang' (money and grain), and 'Xuan Fa' (selection) and to have them classified and compiled into a book with interpretations

---

[15]"Xing Fa Zhi" (The Record of Criminal Law) (Part 1) in *Ming Shi* (*The History of Ming Dynasty*).
[16]"Xing Fa Zhi" (The Record of Criminal Law) (Part 1) in *Ming Shi* (*The History of Ming Dynasty*).
[17]"Xing Fa Zhi" (The Record of Criminal Law) (Part 1) in *Ming Shi* (*The History of Ming Dynasty*).

provided. The book, known as *Lv Ling Zhi Jie* (*A Literal Interpretation of the Laws and Decrees*), was later issued to all 'Jun' (shire) and 'Xian' (county). After Emperor Taizu read it, he said happily: 'So fewer offences will be committed by my people ever since.'"[18] Similar records can also be found in *Ming Tong Ji* (*The Records of the History of Ming Dynasty*):

> In November of the 1st year of Wu, it is ordered that "Lv Ling" (the laws and decrees) be formulated by "Zhong Shu Sheng" (the supreme organization in charge of the state affairs) in detail. Since Tang and Song dynasties, cases had been heard according to the established laws in all dynasties except Yuan Dynasty, during which the old systems were abolished and "Tiao Ge" (legal provisions and injunctions) was adopted, which had made it easier for officials to be involved in fraud and embezzlement. Soon after Wuchang was conquered, Zhu Yuanzhang had begun to discuss the making of law. So "Tai Jian" (official in charge of supervision, advice and suggestion) was set up and "An Cha Si" (The Judicial Commission) in each "Dao" (the administration district below the province) were sent on inspection tours in "Jun" (shire) and "Xian" (county). Besides, he also wanted to make laws to be abided by the officials inside and outside the capital.

In February of the 5th year of Hongwu (1372), in view of the fact that "the criminal laws are often violated by the common people because of their ignorance," Zhu Yuanzhang particularly "ordered 'Shen Ming Pavilion' (a court built by Zhu Yuanzhang) be set up in every 'Li' (a basic resident organization consisting of five neighborhoods), 'She' (community), 'Fu' (ancient administrative district between province and county), 'Zhou' (subprefecture), 'Xian' (county) and 'Xiang' (townships). Whenever people in the area committed crimes, their wrong doings were recorded and posted on the pavilion so that people could be disciplined." In August of the 15th year of Hongwu (1382), with respect to the malpractice existing in the implementation of "Shen Ming Pavilion" (a court built by Zhu Yuanzhang), an instruction was again given to "Li Bu" (The Department of Rites):

> The names of criminals should be posted on "Shen Ming Pavilion" (a court built by Zhu Yuanzhang) in "Jun" (shire) and "Xian" (county) nationwide in order to make their crimes known to public to encourage the good and punish the evil. But now only "Za Fan" (miscellaneous crimes) and minor crimes are generally recorded by the officials so that the errors made accidentally by law-abiding people have become their lifelong burdens. So even if they want to correct their errors and make a fresh start, they have no ways of doing so. Therefore, you should discuss the issue in detail.

Accordingly, a proposal was put forward by "Li Bu" (The Department of Rites): "From now on, those who have committed the crime of 'Shi E' (The Ten Abominations), 'Jian Dao' (rape and theft), 'Zha Wei' (fraud and forgery), 'Gan Fan Ming Yi' (violating the accepted social ethics and moral principles), 'You Shang Feng Su' (violating the social customs) and 'Zei' (banditry), and those who have been sentenced to 'Tu' (imprisonment) should be recorded on the pavilion, while the other minor crimes and the public and private misdeeds which are not harmful to the socially accepted ethics should be removed so that the law-abiding people can turn

---

[18]"Xing Fa Zhi" (The Record of Criminal Law) (Part 1) in *Ming Shi* (*The History of Ming Dynasty*).

over a new leaf ... 'Zhi Yue Ke' (approved by the emperor)."[19] Since "Shen Ming Pavilion" (a court built by Zhu Yuanzhang) was a system set up at the grassroots level to carry out the principle of "Ming Xing Bi Jiao" (integrating punishment with moral teachings), it was provided in "Za Fan" (miscellaneous crimes) in "Xing Lv" (The Penal Code) in *Da Ming Lv* (*The Great Ming Code*) that "those who tear down the building of 'Shen Ming Pavilion' (a court built by Zhu Yuanzhang) and destroy the boards shall be punished by 'Zhang' (flogging with heavy sticks) for one hundred strokes and 'Liu' (exile) for 3000 *li*." Apart from "Shen Ming Pavilion" (a court built by Zhu Yuanzhang), other ritual systems, such as "Jing Shan Ting" (a pavilion where the behaviors of well and evildoers should be put down so as to show reward and punishment), "Xiang Yin Jiu Li" (community wine-drinking ceremonies, a kind of drinking and eating etiquette), "Ji Li" (offering sacrifice to devils), "Ji She Ji" (ceremonies held to show respect to the gods of earth and grain), etc.,[20] were also established to achieve the goal of "Ming Xing Bi Jiao" (integrating punishment with moral teachings).

The four chapters in *Da Gao* (*The Great Imperial Mandates*), written by Zhu Yuanzhang himself from the 18th year to 20th year of Hongwu (1385–1387), can best reflect the thoughts of "Ming Xing Bi Jiao" (integrating punishment with moral teachings), and it was mainly a collection of the official and civilian criminal cases, the harsh orders issued beyond the law, and the exhortations about pursuing good fortune and avoiding disaster. In order to extensively publicize the contents of *Da Gao* (*The Great Imperial Mandates*) and to deter the common people, it was required that "each household should have one copy of it," and "it should be read carefully by all the people to take as a warning."[21] In the 31st year of Hongwu (1398), the three chapters of *Da Gao* (*The Great Imperial Mandates*) were even introduced to schools and were used as texts of "Guo Zi Jian" (the highest educational body in ancient China) and the contents of the examination of "Ke Ju" (the imperial examination). Besides, in villages, *Da Gao* (*The Great Imperial Mandates*) was also taught by teachers in private schools. At every village festival, *Da Gao* (*The Great Imperial Mandates*) was explained by especially assigned people at public gatherings. "In the whole country, more than 193,400 teachers and students who had lectured and studied *Da Gao* (*The Great Imperial Mandates*) were selected and invited to the imperial court to be awarded money and then sent back home."[22] In the 30th year of Hongwu (1397), when *Da Ming Lv Gao* (*The Imperial Codes and Mandates of Ming Dynasty*) was completed, Zhu Yuanzhang went to Meridian Gate to meet all the ministers by himself to tell them the purpose of drafting the law: "The law is in the

---

[19]Shen Jiaben (Qing Dynasty), "Shen Ming Pavilion" (a court built by Zhu Yuanzhang) in *Lv Ling* (*The Laws and Decrees*) (Part 9) in *Li Dai Xing Fa Kao*(*A Textual Research of the Criminal Laws in the Past Dynasties*).

[20]Luo Dongyang, *Ming Tai Zu Li Fa Zhi Zhi Yan Jiu* (*A Study on the Rule of Rites and Law in the Reign of Emperor Taizu of Ming Dynasty*), Higher Education Press, 1998, p. 102.

[21]"Ban Xing Da Gao" (Promulgating Great Mandates) in *Yu Zhi Da Gao* (*The Great Imperial Mandates*).

[22]*Ming Tai Zu Shi Lu* (*The Record of Emperor Taizu of Ming Dynasty*), Vol. 253.

hands of officials but they are unknown to all the common people, so I ordered the judicial officials to select important provisions from *Da Gao* (*The Great Imperial Mandates*) and attached them to the code ... to be issued nationwide, so that all the people can know what they should comply with."[23] In feudal times, on the one hand, laws were interpreted to a certain extent by the rulers to the common people so that they could abide by it; on the other hand, they deliberately made people legally blind so that those who had secretly stored the penal code of the state were often severely punished.

Zhu Yuanzhang emphasized "Ming Xing Bi Jiao" (integrating punishment with moral teachings); at the same time, he also paid great attention to "Yi Li Ding Lv" (making laws according to rites) and "Yi Li Dao Min" (guiding people with rites). He believed that "Li" (rites) and "Fa" (law) were both "Guo Zhi Ji Gang" (the discipline and law of the state), and "'Li' (rites) is the preventive measure of the state",[24] while "'Xing' (penalty) is what the Emperor has adopted to guard against the people,"[25] so they were both interconnected. In the 1st year of Hongwu (1368), when *Da Ming Lv* (*The Great Ming Code*) was begun to be made and enforced in the whole country, Zhu Yuanzhang once "ordered four Confucian officials to teach twenty articles of *Tang Lv* (*Tang Code*) to the judicial officials every day,"[26] which had reflected his emphasis on the integration of "Li" (rites) and "Fa" (law). Among the feudal codes, *Tang Lv* (*Tang Code*) was a model of the integration of "Li" (rites) and "Fa" (law), which had reflected the strategy of managing state affairs and safeguarding national security, which had been constantly improved since the Han Dynasty, just as what was said in "Tang Lv Shu Yi Xu" (Preface to the Comments on Tang Code): "'De' (virtue) and 'Li' (rites) are the essence of 'Zheng Jiao' (political instruction); while 'Xing Fa' (criminal punishment) is its application, so they are inseparable, just like dawn and dusk which are an inseparable part of a day, and spring and autumn which are an inseparable part of a year."

Because the function of "Li" (rites) was to promote feudal moral cultivation and to constrain the common people spiritually to make them obey the rule of the state, it could play a role that could not be played by legal deterrent, of which Zhu Yuanzhang had a deep understanding when summing up historical experiences. He said: "'Li' (rites) and 'Yue' (music) are like the delicious food for ruling the state, while 'Xing' (punishment) and 'Zheng' (government) are like the medicine to get rid of the malpractices."[27] So only by "changing the people by cultivating their virtues"[28] and "governing them by strict laws, regulations and harsh punishments"[29] could long-term stability be maintained. Therefore, it was exactly under the guidance

---

[23]"Xing Fa Zhi" (The Record of Criminal Law) (Part 1) in *Ming Shi* (*The History of Ming Dynasty*).

[24]*Ming Tai Zu Shi Lu* (*The Record of Emperor Taizu of Ming Dynasty*), Vol. 80.

[25]*Ming Tai Zu Shi Lu* (*The Record of Emperor Taizu of Ming Dynasty*), Vol. 167.

[26]"Xing Fa Zhi" (The Record of Criminal Law) (Part 1) in *Ming Shi* (*The History of Ming Dynasty*).

[27]*Ming Tai Zu Shi Lu* (*The Record of Emperor Taizu of Ming Dynasty*), Vol. 162.

[28]*Ming Tai Zu Shi Lu* (*The Record of Emperor Taizu of Ming Dynasty*), Vol. 131.

[29]*Ming Tai Zu Shi Lu* (*The Record of Emperor Taizu of Ming Dynasty*), Vol. 220.

of "Yi Li Ding Lv" (making laws according to rites) and "Yi Li Dao Min" (guiding people with rites) that in February of the 7th year of Hongwu (1374), "Xing Bu Shang Shu" (the minister of the department of punishment) Liu Weiqian and "Han Lin Xue Shi" (member of the Imperial Academy) Song Lian, who were appointed to undertake the task of making *Da Ming Lv* (*The Great Ming Code*), gave a special explanation in "Jin Ming Lv Biao" (memorial to the emperor about the presentation of *Ming Code*): "The table of contents is compiled completely in accordance with *Tang Lv* (*Tang Code*)..., consisting of totally 606 articles and 30 volumes. So some are added or deleted, while others are retained by following the old system to achieve appropriateness in enforcement."[30] In the 22ndyear of Hongwu (1389), with respect to the revised *Ming Lv* (*Ming Code*), Zhu Yuanzhang said to his "Tai Sun" (a title for the emperor's grandson adopted as the heir to the throne):

> "The reason why 'Er Xing Tu' (the chart of two punishments) is listed first in the book and 'Ba Li Tu' [the chart of eight 'Li' (rites)] is listed next is that 'Li' (rites) should be emphasized".... So his "Tai Sun" requested that more than five articles be revised, which is approved by Emperor Taizu. Then his "Tai Sun" once again requested: "Since the purpose of 'Ming Xing' (making people understand the criminal law) is for 'Bi Jiao' (to make up for the deficiencies in moral teaching), wherever 'Wu Lun' (five cardinal relationships in ancient China between ruler and subject, father and son, husband and wife, between brothers and between friends) is concerned, it is proper to uphold 'Qing' (human relationships) by bending the law." Thus, an order is issued by Emperor Taizu to have seventy three articles revised.[31]

Although it was impossible to find the specifically revised provisions in the history books, undoubtedly the principle of laying stress on "Li" (rites) and "Bi Jiao" (making up for the deficiencies in moral teaching) was carried out.

In the 30th year of Hongwu (1397), when *Da Ming Lv* (*The Great Ming Code*) was completed, Zhu Yuanzhang once went to Meridian Gate and said to all his ministers: "I have followed the examples of ancient people in governing the state, so I guide people by expounding 'Li' (rites), and constrain the evil and ferocious by formulating 'Fa' (law),"[32] which was in fact a summary of Zhu Yuanzhang's thirty years of experience of governing the state. The so-called "guiding people by expounding 'Li' (rites)" meant guiding people by using traditional "Li" (rites) so that they could have a full understanding of "Li" (rites) to avoid the execution of "Xing" (penalty) and to reduce crimes; the so-called "constraining the evil and ferocious by formulating 'Fa' (law)" meant punishing "the evil and ferocious" people who had posed a serious threat to the ruling of the state by formulating "Fa" (law) so that they would show fear to "Fa" (law) and refrain themselves from committing crimes. This was Zhu Yuanzhang's summary of the integration of "Li" (rites) and "Fa" (law) under the new historical conditions.

---

[30] "Xing Fa Zhi" (The Record of Criminal Law) (Part 1) in *Ming Shi* (*The History of Ming Dynasty*).

[31] "Xing Fa Zhi" (The Record of Criminal Law) (Part 1) in *Ming Shi* (*The History of Ming Dynasty*).

[32] "Yu Zhi Da Ming Lv Xu" (The Preface to Imperial Great Ming Code) in *Da Ming Lv* (*The Great Ming Code*).

Since "Lun Li" (ethics) and "Qin Qing" (affection between family members) are the core content of "Li" (rites), the legal provisions in *Da Ming Lv* (*The Great Ming Code*) had mainly reflected the integration of "Li" (rites) and "Xing" (punishment), such as enforcing different punishments for the same crimes committed by the superior and the inferior and the noble and the humble: "'Cun Liu Yang Qin' (the criminal can be pardoned in order to take care of their parents if their parents are old and have nobody to depend on)," "Qin Shu Xiang Wei Rong Yin" (concealment of crimes among relatives or refusing to testify among relatives in court), "prohibiting 'Nu Bi' (the slave girls and maidservants) from informing against their masters," "prohibiting younger brothers from informing against elder brothers, wives against their husbands, and 'Nu Bi' (the slave girls and maidservants) against their masters," and so on. Moreover, in judicial practice, "wherever 'Wu Lun' (five cardinal relationships in ancient China between ruler and subject, father and son, husband and wife, between brothers and between friends) is concerned, it is proper to uphold 'Qing' (human relationships) by bending the law." When handling cases involving ethics, Zhu Yuanzhang himself once had bent the law for the benefit of his favorites to show his belief in "guiding people by expounding 'Li' (rites)." For example, "a father was falsely accused and arrested, so his son filed a lawsuit to 'Xing Bu'(The Department of Punishment), but he was convicted of 'Yue Su' (overstepping indictment) by the judicial officials. Emperor Taizu said: 'The son filed a lawsuit about his father's grievances out of the most pure human emotion, so he shall not be convicted of crime." Another example: "a son broke law, and the father offered a bribe to ask for the exoneration his son, so he was convicted by 'Yu Shi' (the censor). Emperor Taizu said: 'The son is sentenced to death, and the father has tried to save him, which is only out of human emotion. So only the son shall be punished, and the father shall be pardoned.'"[33] A third example: "a father in Shanyang was convicted of crime and should be punished by 'Zhang' (flogging with heavy sticks), but the son instead begged to be punished by 'Zhang' (flogging with heavy sticks) for his father. The Emperor said: 'I shall bend the law for the dutiful son', in the end the father was specifically released."[34] So "Qu Fa Yuan Qing" (bending the law according to the concrete situations) was an embodiment of "Ming Xing Bi Jiao" (integrating punishment with moral teachings) and "Li Fa Xiang Zuo" (mutual promotion of rites and law) in judicial practice, and it had indeed played a guiding role, but this principle was only applied to common cases, which were of little harm to the state and society. Due to the different historical situations in the Tang and Ming dynasties, the punishment for certain crimes was also different. As far as the violation of "Li" (rites), customs, and moral teachings was concerned, the punishment was more lenient in *Ming Lv* (*Ming Code*) than in *Tang Lv* (*Tang Code*); however, with respect to the serious crimes of endangering the rule of the state, the

---

[33]"Xing Fa Zhi" (The Record of Criminal Law) (Part 1) in *Ming Shi* (*The History of Ming Dynasty*).
[34]"Kai Guo Gui Mo" (The Plan for the Founding of the State) in *Ming Shi Ji Shi Ben Mo* (*The Ins and Outs of the Records in the History of Ming Dynasty*), Vol. 14.

punishment was much severer in *Ming Lv* (*Ming Code*) than in *Tang Lv* (*Tang Code*).

In the early Ming Dynasty, "the bad habits of Yuan Dynasty were still followed by people, and favoritism was practiced at the expenses of the public interest, so that crimes increased considerably,"[35] which had led to a situation where "the bodies of offenders newly punished by 'Qi Shi' (exposing the executed body publicly at markets) had not been moved away, yet the criminals punishable by 'Da Bi' (capital punishment) were already sent under guard."[36] Especially, the inherent feudal order was destroyed by the peasant uprising of "Hong Jin Jun" (The Red Turban Army), which was naturally considered "the troubled times" by Zhu Yuanzhang, who himself had changed from a leader of "Hong Jin Jun" (the Red Turban Army) to the feudal emperor. Therefore, in order to solve these problems, Zhu Yuanzhang declared that "since I am governing the state in troubled times, severe punishments must be enforced."[37] It was recorded in "Xing Fa Zhi" (The Record of Criminal Law) in *Ming Shi* (*The History of Ming Dynasty*) that "at the beginning, Emperor Taizu thought that the punishments in the late Yuan Dynasty were arbitrary and lenient, so harsh laws were used in punishing the crimes." After Emperor Jianwen ascended the throne, he stated when he gave instructions to the judicial officials: "*Da Ming Lv* (*The Great Ming Code*) is made by my grandfather himself, and when he asks me to read it carefully, I find out that the punishments are much severer than those of previous dynasties. This is probably because the criminal law which is applied to govern the state in troubled times is different from that which is commonly applied for all generations."[38] The ideology of "enforcing severe punishments in troubled times" was the inheritance of the principle of enforcing different punishments according to different circumstances, which was made in the early Zhou Dynasty to carry out the policy of "prudent punishment." No doubt, it had a far-reaching influence on the later generations.

Generally speaking, the principle of governing the state by applying harsh laws was mainly manifested in the following aspects: the scope of the punishment for crimes like "Fan Pan" (plotting rebellion) and "Da Ni" (great sedition) was expanded; the measurements for the crime of "Zei Dao" (stealing and robbery) and other crimes involving "treasury, money, grain and other matters" were aggravated; the officials who were involved in "Tan Zang Wang Fa" (taking bribes by bending the law) or dereliction of duty were harshly punished so as to "rectify the discipline and law" and to eliminate the long-standing malpractice caused by political corruption in the late Yuan Dynasty. It was stated in "Xun Li Zhuan Xu" (The Preface to Xun Li Zhuan) in *Ming Shi* (*The History of Ming Dynasty*) that "in late Yuan Dynasty, the official administration was arbitrary and indulgent, and the people lived in destitution, so the corrupt officials were severely punished and harsh

---

[35] "Xing Fa Zhi" (The Record of Criminal Law) (Part 1) in *Ming Shi* (*The History of Ming Dynasty*).

[36] "Xu" (The Preface) in *Yu Zhi Da Gao* (*The Great Imperial Mandates*).

[37] "Xing Fa Zhi" (The Record of Criminal Law) (Part 1) in *Ming Shi* (*The History of Ming Dynasty*).

[38] "Xing Fa Zhi" (The Record of Criminal Law) (Part 1) in *Ming Shi* (*The History of Ming Dynasty*).

laws were made by Taizu of Ming Dynasty." Therefore, the measures of enforcing severe punishments on corrupt officials, which were taken in the early Ming Dynasty, were concentratedly reflected in *Da Gao* (*The Great Imperial Mandates*), which was made by Zhu Yuanzhang himself.

Zhu Yuanzhang, who was born into a poor family, knew very well that the disturbance and harmfulness that were brought about by the corrupt officials were important reasons for the rebellion of the common people. So he once warned his ministers:

> When I was a civilian, I often saw that many officials in "Zhou" (subprefecture) and "Xian" (county) were indifferent to the suffering of the people and were often greedy and lustful instead. In addition, they had indulged themselves in drinking, neglected their duties, and turned a blind eye to all people's suffering, so I really felt very angry deep in my heart. Now that the harsh laws have been made, whenever I discover that officials have taken bribery and bullied my people, I will have them severely punished.

Therefore, *Da Gao* (*The Great Imperial Mandates*), made by Zhu Yuanzhang himself, was mostly about the punishment of corrupt officials.[39] Since most of the harsh decrees in *Da Gao* (*The Great Imperial Mandates*) were made extralegally and they were the extralegal laws made according to "imperial orders," to some extent they had tightened the net of justice. Consequently, the measurement of penalty in *Da Gao* (*The Great Imperial Mandates*) was also generally much severer than that in *Da Ming Lv* (*The Great Ming Code*). In the three chapters of *Da Gao* (*The Great Imperial Mandates*), various cruel punishments were listed, such as "Mo Mian" (tattooing the offenders on the face or forehead with indelible ink), "Wen Shen" (tattooing), "Tiao Jin Qu Zhi" (picking off tendons and cutting off fingers), "Duo Zhi" (cutting off one or more fingers), "Duan Shou" (cutting off one or both hands), "Yue Zu" (amputating one or both feet), "Yan Ge Wei Nu" (castration to be slaves), "Zhan Zhi Jia Ling" (cutting off toes and wearing a cangue), "Chang Jia Hao Ling" (being punished by wearing "Jia Hao" (cangue: a large wooden collar worn by petty criminals as a punishment)), "Jia Xiang You Li" (being paraded by wearing a cangue), "Zuo Jiao" (with one's feet tied up), and so on. It was stated in "Xing Fa Zhi" (The Record of Criminal Law) in *Ming Shi* (*The History of Ming Dynasty*) that "there were hundreds of thousands of criminals punishable by 'Ling Chi' (the punishment of dismemberment and the lingering death), 'Xiao Shi' (the penalty of hanging the head of the criminal on top of a piece of wood) and 'Zu Zhu' (when a man commits a crime, the whole clan are implicated) according to the three chapters of *Da Gao* (*The Great Imperial Mandates*). Moreover, there were millions of criminals punishable by 'Qi Shi' (exposing the executed body publicly at markets) or other lighter penalties." However, most of these cruel penalties were not included in *Ming Lv* (*Ming Code*), which showed that the emperor had tried to deter "the evil and lawless people" by enforcing punishments arbitrarily. In addition to the cases recorded in *Da Gao* (*The Great Imperial Mandates*), Zhu Yuanzhang had made use of many other cases to kill people wantonly, such as "Kong Yin An" (a case

---

[39] *Ming Tai Zu Shi Lu* (*The Record of Emperor Taizu of Ming Dynasty*), Vol. 39.

involving officials settling account in the Department of Revenue with blank account books in 1367), the bribery case of Guo Huan, and other long-standing cases harmful to the people.

But it should be noted that the fundamental object of Zhu Yuanzhang in managing officials using harsh laws was to rule the people, which was a concrete practice of the legalist ideology of "wise rulers administering their officials, rather than their people." For this reason, although it was only two years and one month from the making of the first version of *Da Gao* (*The Great Imperial Mandates*) to the issuing of *Da Gao Wu Chen* (*The Great Imperial Mandates to Military Officials*), the proportion of articles and cases against corrupt officials was reduced, while the proportion against scoundrels was increased. Especially in the 30th year of Hongwu (1397), in the original thirty six articles about "Zhen Fan Si Zui" (felonies punishable by death penalty) and "Za Fan Si Zui" (minor crimes punishable by death penalty) in *Da Gao* (*The Great Imperial Mandates*), which were incorporated into *Lv Gao* (*The Imperial Laws and Mandates*), the focus of attack not only included corrupt officials but also "vagrants," "hermits," and "idle people."

The measure of managing officials using harsh laws taken in the early Ming Dynasty was helpful not only to the consolidation of official administration but also to the adjustment of class relationships and to the strengthening of the central power. However, severe punishments were only effective momentarily, and it was impossible to get rid of the crimes fundamentally. So Shen Jiaben in the Qing Dynasty had commented that "Taizu of Ming Dynasty found out that after the laws and disciplines of Yuan Dynasty were abolished, many people benefited themselves at the expense of public interests by practicing favoritism, so severe laws were applied so that the social customs could be changed. The strict decrees in *Da Gao* (*The Great Imperial Mandates*) were mostly issued extralegally. In the preface, he wrote: 'The bodies of offenders newly punished by 'Qi Shi' (exposing the executed body publicly at markets) had not been moved away, yet the criminals punishable by 'Da Bi' (capital punishment) were already sent under guard'; however, the social customs had not been changed, why the severe punishments had not achieved any effect?"[40] Zhu Yuanzhang himself also felt the limitation of severe punishments. He once said: "I want to eliminate the corrupt officials who take bribery; however, some officials are killed for taking bribery at the sunrise, and then some other officials commit the same crimes at the sunset."[41] When he returned to his hometown after retirement, Liu Ji, who once advocated the application of severe laws, suggested to Zhu Yuanzhang: "Since the state authority has been established, much lenient punishment should be applied in the ruling of the state." On his deathbed, he spoke his last words: "The urgent task at present is to cultivate virtue and reduce

---

[40]Shen Jiaben (Qing Dynasty), "Ming Da Gao Jun Ling Kao" (An Examination of the Harsh Laws in the Great Imperial Mandates of Ming Dynasty) in *Li Dai Xing Fa Kao*(*A Textual Research of the Criminal Laws in the Past Dynasties*).

[41]Liu Chen, *Guo Chu Shi Ji* (*A Chronicle of Events at the Beginning of Ming Dynasty*).

punishment. Pray to the heaven for everlasting."[42] Liu Ji's last words were very influential to Zhu Yuanzhang, so in the 28th year of Hongwu (1395), he went in person to Fengtian Gate and said to all his ministers:

> For more than forty years since I rose in revolt, I have had a profound view of what is true and false. So in order to punish the treacherous people and the scoundrels, sometimes extra judicial punishment has been adopted. But since extra judicial punishments are not statutory laws, it is forbidden for my descendants to issue "Lv" (criminal law) and *Da Gao* (*The Great Imperial Mandates*) any more, so the severe penalties like "Qing Ci" (tattooing), "Fei" (to amputate the feet), "Yi" (to cut down the nose), and "Yan Ge" (castration) should be abolished. If officials dare to request for the application of the punishments mentioned above, they shall be severely punished.[43]

In the 30th year of Hongwu (1397), he once again declared in *Da Ming Lv Xu* (*The Preface to Imperial Great Ming Code*): "No criminals shall be tattooed any more except those and their families who have plotted rebellion. Besides, they should be tattooed according to law." Although Zhu Yuanzhang had repeatedly said that "it is a temporary and expedient measure to apply harsh laws in troubled times," its harmfulness was unpredictable. Take "Ting Zhang" (being flogged in imperial court) for example; Zhu Yuanzhang once gave an order to beat "Gong Bu Shang Shu" (the minister of the department of works) Xia Xiang to death, so the custom of "Dian Bi Xing Zhang" [the Emperor's executing of "Zhang" (flogging with heavy sticks) at court] was started since then. After that, "Ting Zhang" (being flogged in imperial court) unexpectedly became a conventional punishment. During the reign of Wuzong, because of others' admonition of a southward inspection tour, one hundred and forty six ministers were flogged in imperial court by Emperor Wuzong, and eleven of them were beaten to death. During the reign of Shizong, because of the incident of "Da Li" (the behavorial principles between ruler and subject), one hundred and thirty four ministers were flogged in imperial court, and sixteen of them were beaten to death.

10.1.2 The Making of Da Ming Lv (The Great Ming Code), the Amendment of Wen Xing Tiao Li (The Ordinance for Inquisition), and the Issuing of Ming Hui Dian (The Collected Statutes of Ming Dynasty)

10.1.2.1 The Making of *Da Ming Lv* (*The Great Ming Code*)

Da Ming Lv (*The Great Ming Code*) began to be drafted in the 1st year of Wu (1367), and it took thirty years to be completed. It was recorded in "Xing Fa Zhi" (The Record of Criminal Law) in *Ming Shi* (*The History of Ming Dynasty*) that "at the time

---

[42]"Liu Ji Zhuan" (The Biography of Liu Ji) in *Ming Shi* (*The History of Ming Dynasty*).

[43]"Tai Zu Ji" (The Record of Emperor Taizu) (Part 3) in *Ming Shi* (*The History of Ming Dynasty*).

of Taizu, *Lv Ling* (*The Laws and Decrees*) was first drafted in the 1st year of Wu (the Dynasty of Wu), amended in the 6th year of Hongwu, further improved in the 22nd year, and issued nationwide in the 30th year. After years of painstaking efforts, the law of Yuan Dynasty was finally made by Emperor Taizu, so thereafter all the cases inside and outside the capital were heard in accordance with the law issued in the 30th year of Hongwu." However, its real legislative process was much more complicated than what was outlined in "Xing Fa Zhi" (The Record of Criminal Law). For example, in the 6th year of Hongwu (1373), *Da Ming Lv* (*The Great Ming Code*) was made by Liu Weilian and Song Lian on the basis of *Da Ming Lv Ling* (*The Laws and Decrees of Ming Dynasty*) and was issued nationwide in the 1st year of Wu (the Dynasty of Wu). In the 9th year of Hongwu (1376), because "there is still some inappropriateness" in the law, Zhu Yuanzhang ordered "Cheng Xiang" (the prime minister) Hu Weiyong, "Yu Shi Da Fu" (Grand Censor) Wang Guangyang, and other officials to "have detailed discussions and to have thirteen articles of the law revised." In the 22nd year of Hongwu (1389), in view of the fact that both the organization of "Zhong Shu Sheng" (the supreme organization in charge of state affairs) and the official position of "Zai Xiang" (the prime minister) were abolished in the 13th year of Hongwu (1380) and the power of "Zhong Shu Sheng" (the supreme organization in charge of state affairs) was thus divided into "Liu Bu" (The Six Departments), namely, "Li Bu" (The Department of Personnel), "Hu Bu" (The Department of Revenue), "Li Bu" (The Department of Rites), "Bing Bu" (The Department of Defense), "Xing Bu" (The Department of Punishment), and "Gong Bu" (The Department of Works), a suggestion was put forward by "Xing Bu" (The Department of Punishment): "In recent years, various and inconsistent amendments have been made in 'Tiao Li' (regulation), which has often led to the unjust settlement of cases. So 'Tiao Li' (regulation) should be revised, categorized and issued home and abroad so that people can understand what they should comply with." As to the law amendment made in the 22nd year, it was not simply made by the officials of "Han Lin Yuan" (The Hanlin Academy) and "Xing Bu" (The Department of Punishment) by "randomly choosing the new regulations issued in recent years and incorporating them into the law according to different categories," but it was made with great innovation. For example, "Ming Li Lv" (Statutes and Terms) was placed in the first part of the book with the rest of the laws subdivided into six categories according to the system of "Liu Bu" (The Six Departments), namely, "Li" (Personnel), "Hu" (Revenue), "Li" (Rites), "Bing" (Defense), "Xing" (Punishment), and "Gong" (Works), with a total of 30 volumes and 460 articles. Therefore, the structure of the code, which had been used for 800 years since the Sui and Tang dynasties, was changed. In the 30th year of Hongwu (1397), *Qin Ding Lv Gao* (*The Imperial Laws and Mandates Made by Imperial Order*), consisting of a total of 147 articles, was compiled by Zhu Yuanzhang to provide supplementary provisions for the crimes of death penalty (including "Zhen Fan Si Zui" (felonies punishable by death penalty) and "Za Fan Si Zui" (minor crimes punishable by death penalty)) in *Da Ming Lv* (*The Great Ming Code*). *Lv Gao* (*The Imperial Laws and Mandates*) was attached to the 460 articles of *Ming Lv* (*Ming Code*), so generally the newly made law was called *Da Ming Lv* (*The Great Ming Code*). Till then, after thirty years of hard work, the codification of *Da Ming Lv* (*The Great Ming Code*) was finally completed. Thus, "it was immediately promulgated home and abroad to make all the people in the world know what they should comply with."[44]

Qin Ding Lv Gao (*The Imperial Laws and Mandates Made by Imperial Order*) was made in order to punish corrupt officials, "vagrants," and "idle people" and to suppress speeches that were against the ruling of the imperial court, so many provisions, such as "Dai Xing Si Tan (official on probation continuing to be involved in corruption), "Yi Fu" (habitual loafer), "Guan Li Xia Xiang" (official going to the countryside), "Huan Zhong Da Fu Bu Wei Jun Yong" (scholar officials in the country without providing service to the emperor), "Zu Dang Xiang Min Chu E" (preventing villagers from eliminating gangsters illegally), and so on were added to the law. The punishments in *Lv Gao* (*The Imperial Laws and Mandates*) were much severer than those in the law, so "it is obvious that the penalties are inappropriately enforced." But it was not until the middle of the Ming Dynasty that *Lv Gao* (*The Imperial Laws and Mandates*) was finally abolished.

The table of contents of *Da Ming Lv* (*The Great Ming Code*) is as follows: one volume of *Ming Li Lv* (*Statutes and Terms*), including "Wu Xing" (Five Penalties), "Shi E" (The Ten Abominations), and "Ba Yi" (The Eight Deliberations); two volumes of *Li Lv* (*Statutes on Personnel*), including "Zhi Zhi" (State Office System) and "Gong Shi" (Formula); seven volumes of *Hu Lv* (*Statutes on Households*), including "Hu Yi" (Household Corvee), "Tian Zhai" (Land and Houses), "Hun Yin" (Marriage), "Cang Ku" (Warehouse), "Ke Cheng" (Tax), "Qian Zhai" (Debts), and "Shi Chan" (Markets); two volumes of *Li Lv* (*Statutes on Rites*), including "Ji Si" (Sacrifice) and "Yi Zhi" (Ceremonial Regulations); five volumes of *Bing Lv* (*Statutes on Military Affairs*), including "Gong Wei" (Palace Guards), "Jun Zheng" (Military Administration), "Guan Jin" (Strategic Pass and Ferry), "Jiu Mu" (Farming and Husbandry), and "You Yi" (Postal Service and Courier Station); eleven volumes of *Xing Lv* (*The Penal Code*), including "Dao Zei" (Theft), "Ren Ming" (Homicide), "Dou Ou" (Fighting), "Ma Li" (Assaulting), "Su Song" (Litigation), "Shou Zang" (Accepting Booty), "Zha Wei" (Fraud and Forgery), "Fan Jian" (Adultery), "Za Fan" (Miscellaneous Crimes), "Bu Wang" (Arresting), and "Duan Yu" (Trials and Punishments); and two volumes of *Gong Lv* (*Statutes on Handicraft Industry*), including "Ying Zao" (Construction), and "He Fang" (Flood Prevention). As to the legislative process of *Da Ming Lv* (*The Great Ming Code*), it took more than thirty years from its drafting to its final promulgation, which showed that the rulers of the Ming Dynasty represented by Zhu Yuanzhang had taken an active and prudent attitude toward legislation. In "Jin Da Ming Lv Biao" (Memorial to the Emperor About the Presentation of Ming Code), it was stated by Liu Weiqian and other officials that "whenever one chapter is completed, it is then copied and presented to the Emperor to be posted on the walls of west corridor of the palace, so the Emperor often reviewed and commented on it with brush and ink by himself … With emperor's careful consideration, the law which is used as the criterion for future

---

[44]"Xing Fa Zhi" (The Record of Criminal Law) (Part 1) in *Ming Shi* (*The History of Ming Dynasty*).

generations is finally completed after taking 'Tian Li' (heavenly principles) and 'Ren Qing' (human feelings) into consideration."

After repeated revision, a new structure was created in *Da Ming Lv* (*The Great Ming Code*), which indicated that not only the basic spirit and contents of *Tang Lv* (*Tang Code*) were absorbed, but also the experience of legal construction since the Tang Dynasty, especially the experience of the thirty years of early Ming Dynasty, was also integrated in *Da Ming Lv* (*The Great Ming Code*); therefore, it was an important feudal code in which achievements had been made in both form and content under the new historical conditions. Besides, its regulations were much simpler than those of *Tang Lv* (*Tang Code*), and its legislative spirit was much stricter than that of *Song Lv* (*Song Code*). As "a statutory law" that "had been passed down from generation to generation," *Da Ming Lv* (*The Great Ming Code*), which consisted of 460 articles, had never been changed till the end of the Ming Dynasty. On the one hand, it reflected that the norms specified in *Da Ming Lv* (*The Great Ming Code*) had played its due role of adjustment with the supplement of "Li" (precedent); on the other hand, it was also inseparable from Zhu Yuanzhang's insistence on the stability of law and the severe punishments that were enforced upon the arbitrary changing of *Lv Ling* (*The Laws and Decrees*). After each great social upheaval in ancient China, the farsighted rulers of the new dynasty always devoted themselves to legislative work and to the subsistence of the stability of law in order to consolidate the unity, to rectify law and discipline, to establish legal authority, and to maintain the stability of social order. In order to ensure the prudent amendment of law, strict procedures were once stipulated in *Tang Lv* (*Tang Code*): "Of all 'Lv' (criminal law), 'Ling' (decree) and 'Shi' (standard), those which are inappropriate for enforcement shall be submitted to 'Shang Shu Sheng' (The Department of Secretary) for discussion and approval first, and then they shall be reported to the Emperor; anyone who has changed them arbitrarily in enforcement without asking for discussion and approval shall be sentenced to 'Tu' (imprisonment) for two years."[45] In *Ming Lv* (*Ming Code*), similar provisions were also made; however, it was only the subjective desire of rulers to keep the law unchanged because it was the irresistible objective law to change with the times. Therefore, the leniency and severity of punishment should be decided according to the social situations at that time. Although Zhu Yuanzhang emphasized that it was forbidden for his descendants to change the established laws and the ancestral legal system, it was in fact impossible for him to prevent his descendants from supplementing and revising the laws with the amendments of "Li" (precedent), which had finally led to various malpractices. For example, "'Li' (precedent) was generated from 'Lv' (criminal law), and more 'Li' (precedent) was generated from 'Li' (precedent), which had led to more malpractices." Moreover, "more cases were arbitrarily judged by corrupt officials without following the law,"[46] all of which had not been expected by Zhu Yuanzhang.

---

[45] *Zhi Zhi Lv* (*Statutes on State Office System*) in *Tang Lv Shu Yi* (*The Comments on Tang Code*), Vol. 11.

[46] "Xing Fa Zhi" (The Record of Criminal Law) (Part 1) in *Ming Shi* (*The History of Ming Dynasty*).

Prior to the drafting of *Da Ming Lv* (*The Great Ming Code*), *Da Ming Ling* (*The Decrees of Great Ming Dynasty*), which was much simpler and easier, was made, as was described in the saying that "at the beginning of the founding of the state, before *Da Ming Lv* (*The Great Ming Code*) was formulated, *Ling* (decree) was first made and issued in the country."[47] *Da Ming Ling* (*The Decrees of Great Ming Dynasty*) was made according to the category of "Liu Ke" (the six offices), by which a system of *Liu Ling* (*The Decrees*) was formed, namely, *Li Ling* (*The Decrees of Personnel*), *Hu Ling* (*The Decrees of Household*), *Li Ling* (*The Decrees of Rites*), *Bing Ling* (*The Decrees of Defence*), *Xing Ling* (*The Decrees on Penalty*), and *Gong Ling* (*The Decrees of Works*), with a total of one hundred and forty one articles. "'*Li Ling*' (*The Decrees of Personnel*) consisted of eighteen articles, including 'Xuan Yong' (Selecting Officials) and 'Xuan Shi' (Appointment); *Hu Ling* (*The Decrees of Household*) consisted of of twenty four articles, including 'Lou Kou Tuo Hu' (omitting to register households or household members) and 'Jie Na Guan Wu' (transmitting government goods); *Li Ling* (*The Decrees on Rites*) consisted of seventeen articles, including 'Chao He Ban Ci' (Order of Classes in Imperial Audiences or Congratulatory Ceremonies) and 'Feng Zeng' (titles and objects bestowed by the Emperor); *Bing Ling* (*The Decrees of Defence*) consisted of ten articles, including 'E She Zhi Hou Ren' (setting up the position of surveillance official) and 'Zhi Gei Fen Li' (proportion of payment); *Xing Ling* (*The Decrees of Penalty*) consisted of seventy articles, including 'Wu Xing' (Five Penalties) and 'Li Zhang Fan Zang Qian Xi' (leader of a neighborhood being exiled for taking bribery); *Gong Ling* (*The Decrees of Works*) consisted of two articles, including 'Zao Zuo Jun Qi' (manufacturing of weapons) and 'Zhi Zao Duan Pi' (weaving satin cloth)."[48] In addition, according to the record of *Xu Wen Xian Tong Kao* (*A Sequel of the General Textual Research of the Documents*), "there were altogether one hundred and forty five articles of *Ling* (decree): twenty articles of *Li Ling* (*The Decrees of Personnel*), twenty four articles of *Hu Ling* (*The Decrees of Household*), seventeen articles of *Li Ling* (*The Decrees of Rites*), eleven articles of *Bing Ling* (*The Decrees of Defence*), seventy one articles of *Xing Ling* (*The Decrees on Penalty*), and two articles of *Gong Ling* (*The Decrees of Works*)," which were four articles more than those of *Da Ming Lv* (*The Great Ming Code*) compiled in the 38th year of Wangli (1405).

Da Ming Ling (*The Decrees of Great Ming Dynasty*), which consisted of more than one hundred and forty articles, was concise in content, and it was the legal form that was made to make it easier to conduct timely adjustment to the relationship involving "Liu Ke" (the six offices) at the beginning of the Ming Dynasty. Qiu Jun believed that "this imperial decree is probably similar both to 'Yue Fa San Zhang' (three-point covenant) which Emperor Gaozu of Han Dynasty issued after entering

---

[47]"Wei Ling" (Disobeying the Order) in "Za Fan" (Miscellaneous Crimes) in *Xing Lv* (*The Penal Code*) in *Da Ming Lv Ji Jie Fu Li* (*Great Ming Code with Collected Commentaries and Appended Sub-statutes*), Vol. 26.

[48]"Wei Ling" (Disobeying the Order) in "Za Fan" (Miscellaneous Crimes) in *Xing Lv* (*The Penal Code*) in *Da Ming Lv Ji Jie Fu Li* (*Great Ming Code with Collected Commentaries and Appended Sub-statutes*), Vol. 26.

the Central Shaanxi Plain and to 'Yue Fa Shi Er Tiao' (twelve-article covenant) which Emperor Gaozu of Tang Dynasty issued after entering the capital."[49] In fact, "Yue Fa San Zhang" (three-point covenant), made in the Han Dynasty, and "Yue Fa Shi Er Tiao" (twelve-article covenant), made in Tang Dynasty, were both incomparable to *Da Ming Lv* (*The Great Ming Code*) in terms of its nature and function, which could be proved by the imperial edict that Zhu Yuanzhang had issued for the enactment of *Lv Ling* (*The Laws and Decrees*) on January the 18th of the 1st year of Hongwu (1368). He said: "'Lv Ling'(The Laws and Decrees) are the measures to govern the state: 'Ling' (decree) stresses instructing people before they commit crimes, while 'Lv' (criminal law) stresses governing people after they commit crimes."[50] So it can be seen that "Ling" (decree) was in parallel with "Lv" (criminal law) and that it was the actual basic law to govern the state, so it was a stable legal form. In "Xing Fa Zhi" (The Record of Criminal Law) in *Ming Shi* (*The History of Ming Dynasty*), the relationship between "Ling" (decree) and "Lv" (criminal law) is explained as follows: "The 'Ling' (decree) enacted in the 1st year of Hongwu referred to those which were not contained in the law but which could be cited as evidence by the judicial officials. But they had to be submitted to the Emperor for approval before being carried out by the judicial officials." It can be seen that judicial officials were extremely cautious in citing "Ling" (decree) as evidence, and it was not until they were approved by the emperor that it was allowed for them to be used in the settlement of the cases.

In *Da Ming Lv* (*The Great Ming Code*), which was made on the basis of the thirty years' experience of legal construction and issued in the 30th year of Hongwu (1397), the relevant provisions of *Da Ming Ling* (*The Decrees of Great Ming Dynasty*), such as "Gong Shi Zi Jue Gai Zheng" (conscientiously rectifying the wrongs in handling public affairs) in *Li Ling* (*The Decrees of Personnel*), "He Gu He Mai" (patronizing and buying on friendly terms) in *Hu Ling* (*The Decrees of Household*), were adopted, which had shown the important value of *Da Ming Ling* (*The Decrees of Great Ming Dynasty*) in law enforcement. Even in *Wen Xing Tiao Li* (*The Ordinance for Inquisition*), which was enacted during the reign of Jiajing in the middle of the Ming Dynasty, there still contained the provision that "property shall be divided according to *Da Ming Ling* (*The Decrees of Great Ming Dynasty*)."

---

[49]Qiu Jun (Ming Dynasty), "Ding Lv Ling Zhi Zhi" (Establishing the System of the Laws and Decrees) (Part 2) in *Da Xue Yan Yi Bu* (*Supplementation to the Explanations of the Great Learning*), Vol. 130.

[50]Quoted from Huai Xiaofeng, *Da Ming Lv Dian Jiao Ben Fu Lu* (*An Appendix to the Punctuated and Proofread Edition of the Great Ming Code*), Liaoning Publishing House, 1990, p. 229.

10.1.2.2 The Making of *Ming Da Gao* (*The Great Imperial Mandates of Ming Dynasty*)

Ming Da Gao (*The Great Imperial Mandates of Ming Dynasty*) was a special legal form that had the greatest legal effect and that was made without going through the general legislative procedures. Meanwhile, it was also an important supplement to the penal codes in *Da Ming Lv* (*The Great Ming Code*).

Da Gao (*The Great Imperial Mandates*) was made because "there are many people in the country who do not follow moral teachings."[51] "Although the punishment is severe, the offenders still just do whatever they want,"[52] so that "the bodies of offenders newly punished by 'Qi Shi' (exposing the executed body publicly at markets) had not been moved away, yet the criminals punishable by 'Da Bi' (capital punishment) were already sent under guard."[53] Therefore, the rulers of the Ming Dynasty tried to moralize "the evil persons" through admonition[54]; at the same time, it was supplemented with harsh punishments and severe laws so as to "warn the obstinate, ignorant and evil people." Consequently, altogether a total of 236 articles were made by Emperor Taizu, including *Yu Zhi Da Gao* (*The Great Imperial Mandates*), which consisted of 74 articles; *Yu Zhi Da Gao Xu Bian* (*The Sequel of the Great Imperial Mandates*), which consisted of 87 articles; *Yu Zhi Da Gao San Bian* (*The Third Edition of the Great Imperial Mandates*), which consisted of 43 articles; and *Da Gao Wu Chen* (*The Great Imperial Mandates to Military Officials*), which consisted of 32 articles. In the four volumes of *Da Gao* (*The Great Imperial Mandates*), 156 criminal cases involving officials and civilians during the period from the 18th year to the 20th year of Hongwu were collected, so that "the good can be regarded as examples to follow, while the evil can serve as warnings." Moreover, some admonitions were elaborately prepared according to "Gang Chang Ming Jiao" (feudal cardinal guides and constant virtues) to guide people "to seek good fortune and avoid disaster." In addition, some severe punishments and strict decrees that could not be found in *Da Ming Lv* (*The Great Ming Code*) were also added.

The preface of *Yu Zhi Da Gao San Bian* (*The Third Edition of the Great Imperial Mandates*) not only reflected Emperor Taizu's bewildered and helpless state of mind in the face of the worsening situation but also explained the reason for the making and successive issuing of *Da Gao* (*The Great Imperial Mandates*). He said:

> Since I am not so gifted nor of great virtue, and I have taken all the measures to control the situation but in vain. The first volume of *Da Gao* (*The Great Imperial Mandates*) was enacted in November of the 18th year of Hongwu (1385) to notify my subjects.... However,

---

[51]"Hou Xu" (The Epilogue) in *Yu Zhi Da Gao Xu Bian* (*The Sequel of the Great Imperial Mandates*).

[52]"Hou Xu" (The Epilogue) in *Yu Zhi Da Gao Xu Bian* (*The Sequel of the Great Imperial Mandates*).

[53]"Xu" (The Preface) in *Yu Zhi Da Gao* (*The Great Imperial Mandates*).

[54]"Xu" (The Preface) in *Yu Zhi Da Gao* (*The Great Imperial Mandates*).

some unemployed, treacherous and lawless people ... still commit crimes frequently, which has not only forced the government to apply brutal punishments, but also brought about great destruction to their families ... I could not bear to see the result, so the sequel of *Da Gao* (*The Great Imperial Mandates*) is issued again to warn the ignorant and lawless people so that they can correct their errors. ... However, since then, the moral teachings have not been followed by the treacherous and lawless people, so for the third time, *Da Gao* (*The Great Imperial Mandates*) is enacted to have them instructed.

In the epilogue to *Da Gao San Bian* (*The Third Edition of the Great Imperial Mandates*), Liu Sanwu also said:

Considering that since ancient times, there have been no customs that can not be changed and there have been no people who can not be reformed by persuasion, so during the intervals of his important work, the criminal cases of officials and civilians are categorized and collected into *Er Gao* (*The Second Great Imperial Mandates*) by the Emperor. So the law is enacted in the country to let people know what should be encouraged and what should be punished ... However, some evil people still indulge in the bad customs ... are treacherous and fraudulent to the others, which is unusual ... For fear that the examples of these evil acts be followed by the officials and civilians in the country, which may lead to their own punishment and execution, despite his important work, the Emperor manages to have *Da Gao* (*The Great Imperial Mandates*) drafted once again to make people understand that it is forbidden for them to cheat others with those tricks and deceits, because it can only lead to their own tragedy.

Ming Da Gao (*The Great Imperial Mandates of Ming Dynasty*), which was named after *Da Gao* (*The Great Imperial Mandate*) according to the classic literature of *Shang Shu* (*The Book of Historical Document*), was made to admonish the people, as was stated in the saying that "'Da Dao' (way, or the great universal truth) is explained so as to admonish the people in the country."[55] It was precisely because of this that in the last article of *Yu Zhi Da Gao* (*The Great Imperial Mandates*), the emperor declared that "the reason for the implementation of *Da Gao* (*The Great Imperial Mandates*) is to show clearly the good fortunes and disasters. Therefore, whether it be officials, civilians, or people of other nationalities, one copy should be owned by each household. If they have committed crimes punishable by 'Chi' (flogging with light sticks), 'Zhang' (flogging with heavy sticks), 'Tu' (imprisonment) and 'Liu' (exile), they each shall be sentenced to one level lighter than that of the statutory punishment; but for those offenders without a copy in the household, they shall each be sentenced to one level heavier than that of the statutory punishment. Thus, it should be read carefully by all the people as a warning." In the last article of *Da Gao Xu Bian* (*The Sequel of the Great Imperial Mandates*) and *Da Gao San Bian* (*The Third Edition of the Great Imperial Mandates*), the emperor once again stressed that "of the laws I have compiled, one is *Da Gao* (*The Great Imperial Mandates*) and the other one is *Da Gao Xu Bian* (*The Sequel of the Great Imperial Mandates*), which are both 'Ben' (the essence) of the high and the low and the most valuable treasures of the people, so they are issued nationwide so that each household can have one copy. Those who are bold enough to show disrespect without having one are not the subjects under my rule, so they shall be deported to remote

---

[55] *Shang Shu Kong Shi Zhuan* (*The Book of Historical Document by Kong Anguo*).

areas and never be allowed to return." "There are altogether three volumes in *Da Gao* (*The Great Imperial Mandates*), and at least one copy should be kept by each household of all my subjects. Besides, they should be recited by the family members to take as a admonishment. Those who do not comply with it shall be deported to remote areas." It can be seen from what is mentioned above that the so-called admonition from *Da Gao* (*The Great Imperial Mandates*) and the practice of "Xiao Min Yi Fa" (making people understand the law) advocated by Emperor Taizu were both backed up by severe punishment.

In addition to the admonishment, *Da Gao* (*The Great Imperial Mandates)* also "warned and disciplined the ignorant and lawless people" through severe punishments, strict laws, and the criminal cases of officials and civilians, which could function as "Bi Fu" (legal analogy). Therefore, it was made in order to enforce punishment upon corrupt officials and treacherous and lawless people. For example, it was stipulated in "Xiang Min Chu Huan" (Eliminating Perils by Villagers) in *Yu Zhi Da Gao·*(*The Great Imperial Mandates·*) that it was allowed for the virtuous and upright heroic people in the city and countryside to arrest corrupt officials and treacherous and lawless civilians in "Sheng" (province), "Fu" (ancient administrative district between province and county), "Zhou" (subprefecture), and "Xian" (county) and take them to the capital. "Whoever dares to prevent and intercept them shall be sentenced to 'Xiao Ling' (hanging someone's head on the city gate)."[56] Later, it was further provided in *Da Gao San Bian* (*The Third Edition of the Great Imperial Mandates*) that "if actions are taken by civilians to arrest the officials who have brought suffering to people;... if anyone dares to stop them, he will be punished by 'Zu Zhu' (killing of the whole clan of a criminal)."[57] As another example, in order to intimidate and punish the literary and Confucian scholars who did not cooperate with the rulers of the Ming Dynasty, the severe law of *Huan Zhong Shi Fu Bu Wei Jun Yong* (*Literati and Officials Nationwide Without Serving the Emperor*) was enacted, and the offenders should all be punished by "Zu Zhu" (killing of the whole clan of a criminal).[58] Compared with *Da Ming Lv* (*The Great Ming Code*), different punishments were obviously enforced for the same crime in *Da Gao* (*The Great Imperial Mandates*). According to *Ming Lv* (*Ming Code*), those officials who concealed or failed to report official documents in each "Ya Men" (the government offices) should be punished by "Zhang" (flogging with heavy sticks) for eighty strokes, and the officials who violated the time limits in collecting grain tax should be punished by "Zhang" (flogging with heavy sticks) for one hundred strokes, but in accordance with *Da Gao* (*The Great Imperial Mandates*), such offenders should be punished by "Ling Chi" (the punishment of dismemberment

---

[56]"Xiang Min Chu Huan" (Eliminating Perils by Villagers) in *Yu Zhi Da Gao* (*The Great Imperial Mandates*).

[57]"Min Na Hai Min Gai Li" (Civilians Arresting Harmful Officials) in *Yu Zhi Da Gao San Bian* (*The Third Edition of the Great Imperial Mandates*).

[58]"Su Zhou Ren Cai" (Talents in Suzhou) in *Yu Zhi Da Gao San Bian* (*The Third Edition of the Great Imperial Mandates*).

and lingering death). As for the punishments for the malpractices of "delaying transmitting official documents," "failing to carry out the matters that ought to be carried out deliberately," failing to seriously implement the laws on "Guan Fang" (official documents, litigations, and seals), and "Kan He" (a letter of introduction), and so on, they were all much severer in *Da Gao* (*The Great Imperial Mandates*) than those in *Da Ming Lv* (*The Great Ming Code*). Therefore, the enactment of *Da Gao* (*The Great Imperial Mandates*) not only strengthened the imperial power but also deterred the officials and civilians, so it had played a positive role in consolidating the regime of the early Ming Dynasty.

Since *Da Gao* (*The Great Imperial Mandates*) was the actual imperial law rather than ordinary legislation labeled with imperial names, it was more authoritative and legally effective. Except for the part of admonition, in general, corresponding criteria for penalties were set up in each part of *Da Gao* (*The Great Imperial Mandates*), so it was a criminal legal norm in a true sense. It was precisely because of this that Emperor Taizu ordered the judicial officials to "make judgments by reference to *Da Gao* (*The Great Imperial Mandates*)" and "to enforce punishment on the criminals by reference to the prohibitions in *Da Gao* (*The Great Imperial Mandates*)."[59] In March of the 26th year of Hongwu (1393), *Zhu Si Zhi Zhang* (*The Duties of Each Bureau*) was enacted, and it was stipulated that "if officials in the department are convicted of crimes punishable by 'Chong Jun' (to be forced to join the army), they shall be tried and convicted in accordance with *Lv* (*The Criminal Law*) and *Da Gao* (*The Great Imperial Mandates*)."[60] In addition, according to *Da Ming Hui Dian* (*The Collected Statutes of Ming Dynasty*), "in the 28th year of Hongwu, the Emperor agreed that 'judicial officials shall comply with those provisions included in *Lv* (*The Criminal Law*) and *Da Gao* (*The Great Imperial Mandates*).'"[61] Moreover, in practice, there were many cases in which criminals were convicted and sentenced according to *Da Gao* (*The Great Imperial Mandates*), so it was an effective law at the time, "which should not only be forever abided by imperial court, but also be complied with by all judicial officials."[62]

Not only that, in order to give *Da Gao* (*The Great Imperial Mandates*) a normal legal form, since the 26th year of Hongwu (1393), the articles of *Da Gao* (*The Great Imperial Mandates*) were continually incorporated into the established laws of the state by Emperor Taizu. For example, its five articles were included in *Chong Jun Tiao Li* (*The Regulations on Military Exile*), enacted in the 26th year of Hongwu (1393); its twenty eight articles were included in the regulation of *Zhen Fan Za Fan*

---

[59]"Xu" (The Preface) in *Yu Zhi Da Gao San Bian* (*The Third Edition of the Great Imperial Mandates*).
[60]"Si Men Ke" (Office of Penalty Affairs) in "Xing Bu Zhi Zhang" (The Duties of the Department of Punishment) in *Zhu Si Zhi Zhang* (*The Duties of Each Bureau*) (Book 6).
[61]"Chao Zha" (The System of Checking and Registration) in *Wan Li Da Ming Hui Dian* (*The Collected Statutes of Ming Dynasty Made in in the reign of Wanli*), Vol. 178.
[62]Qiu Jun (Ming Dynasty), "Ding Lv Ling Zhi Zhi" (Establishing the System of the Laws and Decrees) (Part 2) in *Da Xue Yan Yi Bu* (*Supplementation to the Explanations of the Great Learning*), Vol. 130.

Si Zui (Felonies and Minor Crimes Punishable by Death Penalty), enacted in the same year; its twenty two articles were included in *Qiu Hou Chu Jue (Late Autumn Executions)* and *Gong Yi Zhong Shen (Life Penal Servitude)*, enacted in the 30th year of Hongwu (1397). Especially, its thirty six articles were included in *Qin Ding Lv Gao (The Imperial Laws and Mandates Made by Imperial Order)* in May of the 30th year of Hongwu (1397). Thereafter, the original *Da Gao (The Great Imperial Mandates)* was seldom applied, as was recorded in "Xing Fa Zhi" (The Record of Criminal Law) in *Ming Shi (The History of Ming Dynasty)*: "After the enactment of *Qin Ding Lv Gao (The Imperial Laws and Mandates Made by Imperial Order)*, the severe laws in *Da Gao (The Great Imperial Mandates)* were not applied any more." In the 31st year of Hongwu (1398), Emperor Jianwen ascended the throne. In view of the fact that extrajudicial punishments were harmful to "the appropriateness of 'Qing' (human relationships) and 'Fa' (law)," he declared in his imperial edict: "In future, when officials and civilians have committed crimes punishable by 'Wu Xing' (Five Penalties), they shall be judged by the judicial officials completely in accordance with *Da Ming Lv (The Great Ming Code)*, with no need of strictly following the former legal provisions (Wu Shen Wen)."[63] The term "Wu Shen Wen" (with no need of strictly following the legal provisions) mentioned above implicitly meant the complete abolition of the four volumes of *Da Gao (The Great Imperial Mandates)*. However, after replacing Emperor Jianwen, in order to stabilize the regime that he usurped, Emperor Chengzu not only restored the practical effect of the thirty six articles of the original *Da Ming Lv Gao (The Imperial Laws and Mandates of Ming Dynasty)* but also repeatedly issued "Chi Ling" (imperial decree) to "order the people nationwide to recite *Da Gao (The Great Imperial Mandates)*. So at the time of 'Xiang Yin' (community wine-drinking ceremonies), *Da Gao (The Great Imperial Mandates)* would often be explained by some people as was in the past."[64] Moreover, "the virtuous and upright people were often selected to read and explain *Da Gao (The Great Imperial Mandates)* and *Lv Ling (The Laws and Decrees)*."[65] It was not until April of the 19th year of Yongle (1421) after Emperor Chengzu's ruling was consolidated and the influence of Emperor Jianwen was already eliminated long before that it was announced that "in future, when the prisoners are tried by judicial officials, they shall be convicted and sentenced totally in accordance with *Da Ming Lv (The Great Ming Code)*, with no need of following the previous legal provisions, 'Bang Wen' (announcements) and 'Tiao Li' (regulation) randomly."[66] During the reign of emperors Renzong and Xuanzong, the four chapters of *Da Gao (The Great Imperial Mandates)* and the thirty six articles of *Lv Gao (The Imperial Laws and Mandates)* were all abolished. Huo Tao who lived at the times of Emperor Jiajing said that "during the reign of Emperor Hongwu, all 'Sheng Yuan' (also called 'Xiu Cai': those who passed the imperial examination at lower level in ancient

---

[63] Jiang Qing (Ming Dynasty), *Jiang Shi Mi Shi (The Secret History of Mr. Jiang)*, Vol. 1.
[64] *Ming Tai Zong Shi Lu (The Record of Emperor Taizong of Ming Dynasty)* (Book 2), Vol. 10.
[65] *Ming Tai Zong Shi Lu (The Record of Emperor Taizong of Ming Dynasty)*, Vol. 39.
[66] *Ming Tai Zong Shi Lu (The Record of Emperor Taizong of Ming Dynasty)*, Vol. 236.

China) nationwide were ordered by the Emperor to read *Gao (Imperial Mandates)*, *Lv (Criminal Law)* and *Jiao Min Bang Wen (A Public Notice to People)*, and the children of common people were also ordered to read the three chapters of *Da Gao (The Great Imperial Mandates)*; but today few students and scholars know anything about *Gao (Imperial Mandates)* and *Lv (Criminal Law)* anymore," so "it was gradually abolished after the reign of Zhengde and Xuantong, and there is nothing left in the recent years."[67]

It was of historical inevitability for the termination of the actual effects of four chapters of *Ming Da Gao (The Great Imperial Mandates of Ming Dynasty)* because although it could only achieve a temporary effect to govern the state and people with severe punishment, it was impossible to reach the ideal state of "Min Mian Er Wu Chi" (The people just want to avoid being punished for their crimes, but they have lost their sense of shame). Moreover, it was harmful to the uniform application of the law and the stability of the country because the articles of *Da Gao (The Great Imperial Mandates)* were in conflict with those of *Da Ming Lv (The Great Ming Code)*. Therefore, during the reigning of emperors Jianwen, Renzong, Xuanzong, and Yingzong, it was declared that "in future, when prisoners are tried, the cases should be judged by the judicial officials completely in accordance with *Da Ming Lv (The Great Ming Code)* with no need of strictly following the former legal provisions; otherwise the offenders shall be punished by law,"[68] all of which were indeed the right thing to do to reform the established law after taking into consideration the concrete times and situation.

10.1.2.3 The Revision of *Wen Xing Tiao Li (The Ordinance for Inquisition)*

After Emperor Xiaozong, the revision of *Wen Xing Tiao Li (Regulations on Trials and Punishments)*, which was successively carried out during the reign of the three emperors, was the major legislative achievement in the middle and late Ming Dynasty; meanwhile, it was also an inevitable result of the social development of the legal system. After the completion of *Da Ming Lv (The Great Ming Code)* in the 30th year of Hongwu (1397), Emperor Taizu Zhu Yuanzhang believed that the law was almost perfect because it was made on the basis of thirty years of experience, so before he died, he especially instructed on his deathbed: "Not even one single word of the established law can be changed,"[69] "so that even if the ministers only want to have a slight change of the law, they shall be punished for the crime of changing the ancestral system."[70] However, the continuously changing and developing social life

---

[67] *Ming Tai Zong Shi Lu (The Record of Emperor Taizong of Ming Dynasty)*, Vol. 83.

[68] Fu Fengxiang (Qing Dynasty), *Huang Ming Zhao Ling (The Imperial Edicts of Ming Dynasty)*, Vol. 7 to 10.

[69] "Xu" (The Preface) in *Huang Ming Zu Xun (The Ancestral Instructions of Ming Dynasty)*.

[70] "Xing Fa Zhi" (The Record of Criminal Law) (Part 1) in *Ming Shi (The History of Ming Dynasty)*.

was bound to be in conflict with the code, which had ever remained unchanged. Therefore, the tradition of hearing cases according to "Chi" (instruction) in the Song Dynasty was followed by the rulers of the Ming Dynasty. According to this tradition, the cases were presented and reported to the Emperor by the ministers and then "was set up as 'Shi Li' (precedents) by the Emperor after considering the gains and losses"[71] to be applied in judicial practices to make up for the insufficiency of legal provisions. For example, *Liu Tu Zui Tiao Li* (*Regulations on the Crimes Punishable by Exile*) was enacted during the reign of Emperor Yongle, and *Gui Zhou Tu Ren Duan Zui Li* (*Regulations on the Judgment of Guizhou Natives*) was enacted during the reign of Emperor Xuande. But in the early Ming Dynasty, on the one hand, judicial officials were allowed to hear the cases by citing "Li" (precedent) to prevent treacherous offenders from escaping punishment; on the other hand, the emperor worried that the breaking of "Fa" (law) by the application of "Li" (precedent) would cause disorder in the legal system. Therefore, in the 22nd year during the reign of Emperor Hongwu (1389), Zhu Yuanzhang once ordered that "the additional regulations be incorporated into law according to different categories." At the time of Emperor Chengzu, it was also forbidden to hear cases by "randomly making reference to 'Bang Wen' (announcements) and 'Tiao Li' (regulation)." In the 1st year of Chenghua (1465), considering that it became rampant to break "Fa" (law) by making reference to "Li" (precedent), Emperor Xianzong "also ordered the judicial officials to hear cases completely in accordance with formal laws with all 'Tiao Li' (regulation) abolished."[72] However, it was impossible for the law that was made seventy years before to be effectively adjusted to adapt to the rapid changes of social relationship. So even Emperor Xianzong, who once ordered to "have all 'Tiao Li' (regulation) abolished" in the 18th year of Chenghua (1482), had to agree to the application of *Xie Zha De Cai Zui Li* (*Regulations on the Crimes of Financial Fraud*). Thereafter, it was more difficult to stop the application of "Li" (precedent). Since "Li" (precedent) was made according to individual cases, it inevitably led to the redundancy of "Tiao Li" (regulation), which had made it difficult for them to be applied uniformly. Because "in some cases, there are even three to four 'Li' (precedent) for one matter, or in some other cases, 'Li' (precedent) was changed frequently according to new situations,"[73] the ministers of Emperor Xianzong proposed that a unified *Wen Xing Tiao Li* (*The Ordinance for Inquisition*) be formulated. But restrained by the old system, the suggestion was only approved by Emperor Xianzong without being implemented.

When Emperor Xiaozong ascended the throne, it was almost one hundred years since *Da Ming Lv* (*The Great Ming Code*) was promulgated, so the contradiction between "Fa" (law) and "Li" (precedent) became even more conspicuous. In May of the 5th year of Hongzhi (1492), a memorial was submitted by "Hong Lu Shao Qing" (the deputy executive of the bureau in charge of state ceremonial) Li Sui to undertake

---

[71] *Ming Dian Hui* (*A Collection of Decrees and Regulations of Ming Dynasty*), Vol. 180.
[72] "Xing Fa Zhi" (The Record of Criminal Law) (Part 1) in *Ming Shi* (*The History of Ming Dynasty*).
[73] *Huang Ming Tiao Fa Shi Lei Zuan* (*Annals of the Legal Cases in Ming Dynasty*) (Book 3), p. 372.

10.1 Legislative Ideology and Achievements of the Ming Dynasty

the revision of *Wen Xing Tiao Li* (*The Ordinance for Inquisition*), so "Xing Bu Shang Shu" (the minister of the department of punishment) Peng Shao had made some comments by taking advantage of this opportunity:

> What is recorded in criminal law is quite limited, but the circumstances for the crimes which are committed in the world are limitless, so some of the minor crimes are punished severely, while some of the serious crimes are punished leniently, which are all decided by the Emperor. Then they are set up as "Shi Li" (precedents) by the Emperor after taking the gains and losses into consideration, and are applied mainly by judicial officials in the capital, but seldom applied by judicial officials outside the capital. Thus, the punishments enforced according to "Shi Li" (precedents) outside the capital are often inappropriate. Therefore, it is advisable that subordinate officials should be selected to collect all "Shi Li" (precedents) which have been approved by the Emperor and include them in different categories. Then they should be discussed by officials to be uniformly applied both inside and outside the capital concurrently with *Da Ming Lv* (*The Great Ming Code*), so that "Shi Li" (precedents) can be fully established and the circumstances of crimes can be completely included.[74]

Finally, the amendment of *Wen Xing Tiao Li* (*The Ordinance for Inquisition*) was approved by Emperor Xiaozong, so in December of the 11th year of Hongzhi (1498), an imperial edict was issued: "Since there are too many 'Tiao Li' (regulation), it is difficult for judicial officials to apply by them in the trial of prisoners. For those practicable, they should first be examined by 'San Fa Si' (Three Judicial Departments) thoroughly, and then be presented article by article to the Emperor for final decision. As to the remaining redundant and unworkable 'Tiao Li' (regulation), they shall be abolished completely."[75] In February of the 13th year of the Hongzhi (1500), according to the order of the emperor, "Xing Bu Shang Shu" (the minister of the department of punishment) Bai Ang presented *Wen Xing Tiao Li* (*The Ordinance for Inquisition*), which consisted of 279 articles, to the emperor "to require that it be established as a formal law to be applied nationwide."[76] On March the 2nd, *Wen Xing Tiao Li* (*The Ordinance for Inquisition*), which was commonly called *Hong Zhi Wen Xing Tiao Li* (*The Ordinance for Inquisition Made in the Reign of Emperor Hongzhi*), was finally issued.

Hong Zhi Wen Xing Tiao Li (*The Ordinance for Inquisition Made in the Reign of Emperor Hongzhi*) was made on the basis of major revisions of *Da Ming Lv* (*The Great Ming Code*). Except that much severer punishment was executed for the crime of dereliction of duty, punishments for ordinary crimes were generally replaced by more lenient ones. At the same time, the scope of application of "Shu Xing" (atonement) was also expanded. For example, "all the military and civilian servants of different nationalities, 'She Yu' (armymen without military status and the officials of lower ranks in 'Qi'), and men of ability and power, as well as civil and military officials, 'Jian Sheng' (the students in 'Guo Zi Jian': the highest educational body in ancient China), 'Sheng Yuan' (also called 'Xiu Cai': those who passed the imperial examination at lower level in ancient China), 'Guan Dai Guan' (an official of higher

---

[74] *Ming Dian Hui* (*A Collection of Decrees and Regulations of Ming Dynasty*), Vol. 180.
[75] *Ming Xiao Zong Shi Lu* (*The Record of Emperor Xiaozong of Ming Dynasty*), Vol. 145.
[76] *Ming Xiao Zong Shi Lu* (*The Record of Emperor Xiaozong of Ming Dynasty*), Vol. 159.

ranking), 'Zhi Yin' (an official in charge of an official seal), 'Cheng Chai' (clerical officials), 'Yin Yang Sheng' (a man practising astrology, divination, and so on), 'Yi Sheng' (a medical man), 'Lao Ren' (the elder), and 'She Ren' (an official responsible for writing imperial edicts) can all atone for their crimes punishable by 'Chi'(flogging with light sticks), 'Zhang'(flogging with heavy sticks), 'Liu'(exile) and 'Za Fan Si Zui' (minor crimes punishable by death penalty) by working as labours to transport charcoal, ash, and bricks or by paying tax or by handing in rice,"[77] which had reflected from one aspect the characteristics of the times, which were featured by relative stability of the social order. But in order to strengthen the control of government-run mining patent to increase tax, the sale of official and private "Yin Yan" (official salt taxed according to *yin* (unit of weight)) and illegal mining of minerals were prohibited, and the offenders would be sentenced to "Chong Jun" (to be forced to join the army) or "Zhan Shou" (beheading) according to the concrete circumstances. In addition, many regulations were made in order to restrict the power of "Zong Fan" (royal families and vassal) because they had shown a strong tendency toward separatism: "It is forbidden for 'Wang Fu' (royal palace) to meet with foreigners without authorization and to bring humiliation to local authorities ... All affairs in 'Wang Fu' (royal palace), such as distributing money and grain shall not be carried out until they are reported to and approved by the Emperor...,"[78] and none of the princes were allowed to go out of the city with no reason. For the descendants of those whose ancestors had been entitled to the privilege of "Ba Yi" (The Eight Deliberations) but whose titles of nobility were later removed, if they had committed crimes, they could be "directly questioned and punished by the judicial officials."[79]

Hong Zhi Wen Xing Tiao Li (*The Ordinance for Inquisition Made in the Reign of Emperor Hongzhi*) was much more concise, better organized, and in good order with those unnecessary parts deleted. So to a considerable extent, the malpractice of replacing "Fa" (law) with "Li" (precedent) and breaking "Fa" (law) with the application of "Li" (precedent) was rectified, so it became an important legislation that was "supplementary to law." Just as what was said by Yang Lian, who was "Ji Shi Zhong" (the senior assistant of the emperor and the supervisor of officials) at the time: "*Wen Xing Tiao Li* (*The Ordinance for Inquisition*) is made according to Emperor Taizu's point of view that 'simplicity is the core of legislation', so the current lengthy and redundant regulations were completely abolished, so that 'Li' (precedent) can make up for the inefficiency of 'Fa' (law) without confusing its real intention and can be followed by the judicial officials."[80] So *Hong Zhi Wen Xing*

---

[77] *Hong Zhi Wen Xing Tiao Li* (*The Ordinance for Inquisition Made in the Reign of Emperor Hongzhi*) (The first provision of the separate edition).

[78] *Hong Zhi Wen Xing Tiao Li* (*The Ordinance for Inquisition Made in the Reign of Emperor Hongzhi*) (The No. 99 and No. 102 provision of the separate edition).

[79] *Hong Zhi Wen Xing Tiao Li* (*The Ordinance for Inquisition Made in the Reign of Emperor Hongzhi*) (The No. 8 provision of separate edition).

[80] "Xing" (Punishment) (Part 1) in *Ming Hui Yao* (*Collections of Historical Records in Ming Dynasty*), Vol. 64.

Tiao Li (*The Ordinance for Inquisition Made in the Reign of Emperor Hongzhi*) was a summary of the one hundred years of legislative experience of criminal law, and it had played a founding role in the making of *Wen Xing Tiao Li* (*The Ordinance for Inquisition*) during the reign of emperors Jiajing and Wanli.

After the reign of Hongzhi, decades of years passed from the reign of Emperor Zhengde to that of Emperor Jiajing, so it was inevitable that the enforcement of previous statutes became inappropriate again. Although new policies were carried out by Emperor Shizong at the beginning of his reign, he took a negative attitude toward the making of new regulations. In the 7th year of Jiajing (1528), an imperial edict was issued: "All work of the judicial organization of the government inside and outside the capital should be undertaken in accordance with *Da Ming Lv* (*The Great Ming Code*) and 'Tiao Li' (regulation) which were enacted in the 13th year of Hongzhi, so there is no need to make any new regulations."[81] Not until October of the 29th year of Jiajing (1550), when dramatic changes had taken place in social, economical, and political relationships, did Emperor Shizong have to issue another imperial edict to order "Xing Bu Shang Shu" (the minister of the department of punishment) Gu Yingxiang to be in charge of the amendment of *Wen Xing Tiao Li* (*The Ordinance for Inquisition*). So it was required that "the regulation should be followed by all judicial offices inside and outside the capital. In future, if any judicial officials dare to intentionally sentence an innocent person guilty or a misdemeanor felony by making reference to regulations arbitrarily, they shall be severely punished".[82]

Jia Jing Wen Xing Tiao Li (*The Ordinance for Inquisition Made in the Reign of Emperor Jiajing*) altogether consisted of 385 provisions, including the original 376 provisions and the 9 provisions that were made in the 34th year of Jiajing (1555). *Jia Jing Wen Xing Tiao Li* (*The Ordinance for Inquisition Made in the Reign of Emperor Jiajing*) was based on *Hong Zhi Wen Xing Tiao Li* (*The Ordinance for Inquisition Made in the Reign of Emperor Hongzhi*), with fewer provisions deleted and more added, which had fully reflected the legal requirements of the changing social relationship. Since the Ming Dynasty began to decline after the reign of Emperor Hongzhi, class contradiction became increasingly sharper, and power struggle within the ruling group became particularly fiercer, all of which had added some new features to *Jia Jing Wen Xing Tiao Li* (*The Ordinance for Inquisition Made in the Reign of Emperor Jiajing*).

First, because the refugees who "escaped to the mountain valleys" had posed a threat to social stability, their punishment was aggravated. It was stipulated that "if the military and civilian in border areas flee to the remote villages inhabited by ethnic minorities to avoid corvee services, they shall be punished by 'Chong Jun' (to be forced to join the army) 'Bian Yuan' (outlying areas) all their lives if they are proved guilty through investigation and inquisition. If 'Li Zhang' (head of 'Li': the basic resident organization in ancient China), 'Zong Xiao Qi' (junior military officer) in

---

[81]*Ming Shi Zong Shi Lu* (*The Record of Emperor Shizong of Ming Dynasty*), Vol. 94.

[82]*Ming Shi Zong Shi Lu* (*The Record of Emperor Shizong of Ming Dynasty*), Vol. 368.

charge and the neighbors know of the matter but do not inform against these people, they shall be punished respectively."[83]

Second, those who traded illegally with ethnic minorities in the border areas were severely punished. "Those who smuggle tea privately to the border areas to trade with ethnic minorities, or sell tea privately to ethnic minorities in the central plains on their way home after paying tribute to the court, regardless of the amount of *jin*, shall be banished to 'Yan Zhang' (jungles), together with 'Xie Jia' (broker) and 'Ya Bao' (intermediary agent) in the know."[84] "Those who buy the goods of ethnic minorities before they have reported to or been inspected by the government offices after the tribute ships arrive, or those who help to buy the illegal goods for ethnic minorities shall be punished by 'Chong Jun' (to be forced to join the army) in the border areas."[85]

Third, the influence of "Zong Fan" (royal families and vassal) were continued to be weakened, and the power of the centralized authority was strengthened. So it was stipulated that "if 'Wang Fu' (royal palace) accepts grains illegally, or gets involved in matters such as land disputes and lawsuits concerning the army and civilians, their cases shall be heard and judged impartially by all judicial government offices, and it is forbidden for 'Zhang Shi Si' (government office in full charge of affairs involving a prince's mansion) to accept complaints and lawsuits wantonly, or to delay the settlement of cases in charge."[86] If anyone had extorted "Jie Hu" (tax officials who collect and distribute tax) or plundered property by cheating or harassed the postal offices "by making use of the power of influential officials" or "the fame of families of 'Jin Shi' (attendants of the emperor)," he should be reported to the imperial court and be punished or be banished to border areas.[87]

The making and implementation of *Jia Jing Wen Xing Tiao Li* (*The Ordinance for Inquisition Made in the Reign of Emperor Jiajing*) strengthened the status of "common law," "which had been been enacted as supplementary ones," and the revisions made in *Hong Zhi Wen Xing Tiao Li* (*The Ordinance for Inquisition Made in the Reign of Emperor Hongzhi*) were also clearly targeted, so it had played an important role in judicial practice.

After Emperor Shenzong ascended the throne, in view of the fact that there was still ambiguity in terms of the measurement of sentences in *Wen Xing Tiao Li* (*The*

---

[83]"Tao Bi Chai Yi Tiao Li" (Regulations on Evading Corvée Service) in *Jia Jing Wen Xing Tiao Li* (*The Ordinance for Inquisition Made in the Reign of Emperor Jiajing*).

[84]"Si Cha Tiao Li" (Regulations on Illegal Sale of Tea) in *Jia Jing Wen Xing Tiao Li* (*The Ordinance for Inquisition Made in the Reign of Emperor Jiajing*).

[85]"Si Chu Wai Jing Ji Wei Jin Xia Hai" (Going abroad and Sea Illegally) in *Jia Jing Wen Xing Tiao Li* (*The Ordinance for Inquisition Made in the Reign of Emperor Jiajing*).

[86]"Ying Yi Zhe Zhi Fu Zu You Fan" (Crimes Committed by the Parents or Paternal Grandparents of those with the Privilege of Eight Deliberations) in *Jia Jing Wen Xing Tiao Li* (*The Ordinance for Inquisition Made in the Reign of Emperor Jiajing*).

[87]"Shou Zhi Liu Nan Tiao Li" (Regulations on Deliberately Interfering in the Collection and Distribution of Government Goods) in *Jia Jing Wen Xing Tiao Li* (*The Ordinance for Inquisition Made in the Reign of Emperor Jiajing*).

10.1 Legislative Ideology and Achievements of the Ming Dynasty 941

Ordinance for Inquisition), which was implemented during the reign of emperors Hongzhi and Jiajing, *Wen Xing Tiao Li* (*The Ordinance for Inquisition*) was further amended by court officials from the perspective of standardization. After ten years of hard work, *Wan Li Wen Xing Tiao Li* (*The Ordinance for Inquisition Made in the Reign of Emperor Wanli*), which was described as "elaborate and appropriate," was issued according to an imperial decree on April 11th of the 13th year of Wanli (1585).

Wan Li Wen Xing Tiao Li (*The Ordinance for Inquisition Made in the Reign of Emperor Wanli*), which consisted of three hundred and eighty two provisions in total, was issued thirty five years after the enactment of *Jia Jing Wen Xing Tiao Li* (*The Ordinance for Inquisition Made in the Reign of Emperor Jiajing*). The law was made seriously with a specific purpose, just as what "Xing Bu Shang Shu" (the minister of the department of punishment) Shu Hua pointed out in *Chong Xiu Wen Xing Tiao Li Ti Gao* (*The Revised Draft of The Ordinance for Inquisition*): in order to "make 'Li' (precedent) to make up for 'Lv' (criminal law)" and to "set up 'Li' (precedent) in accordance with 'Lv' (criminal law)," it was necessary to make "'Li' (precedent) more durable, practicable, and easy to understand, to get rid of the malpractice of the over-lenient and over-severe enforcement of 'Fa' (law), and to keep balance between 'Qing' (human relationships) and 'Fa' (law)." According to this tenet of the amendment, further normalization of the measurement of penalty and sentence had become the main characteristics and achievements of *Wan Li Wen Xing Tiao Li* (*The Ordinance for Inquisition Made in the Reign of Emperor Wanli*). For example, it was stipulated in both *Hong Zhi Wen Xing Tiao Li* (*The Ordinance for Inquisition Made in the Reign of Emperor Hongzhi*) and *Jia Jing Wen Xing Tiao Li* (*The Ordinance for Inquisition Made in the Reign of Emperor Jiajing*) that "it is regarded as 'Za Fan Si Zui' (minor crimes punishable by death penalty) to steal property from the palace treasury, which can be redeemed by 'Shu Xing' (atonement), but it is still regarded as 'Zhen Fan Si Zui' (felonies punishable by death penalty) to steal clothing or personal objects from 'Cheng Yu' (horse carriage of the Emperor), which shall be judged in accordance with the law." But in *Wan Li Wen Xing Tiao Li* (*The Ordinance for Inquisition Made in the Reign of Emperor Wanli*), the provision was changed, and it was stipulated that "as for the crime of stealing property from the palace treasury, if the property is clothing or personal objects stolen from a 'Cheng Yu' (horse carriage of an emperor), the offence is still regarded as 'Zhen Fan Si Zui' (felonies punishable by death penalty); but for the rest of property, if 'Jian Shou' (supervisors or custodians) steals thirty *liang* of silver, or the objects such as money or silks worth more than thirty *liang* of silver; or 'Chang Ren' (ordinary persons) steals sixty *liang* of silver, or the objects such as money or silks worth more than sixty *liang* of silver, the offenders shall all be banished to 'Bian Wei' (border guarding post) for life exile. 'Nei Fan' (eunuch criminals) shall be banished to 'Jing Jun' (an army of eunuchs) after the Emperor's approval." For the provision of "Lue You" (abducting women and children) and "Lue Mai" (robbing and trafficking) of "Liang Ren" (the decent people) in *Wen Xing Tiao Li* (*The Ordinance for Inquisition*) made in the years of Hongzhi and Jiajing, the original provision that second and third offenders should both be banished as before was changed in *Wan Li Wen Xing Tiao Li* (*The Ordinance for Inquisition Made in the Reign of Emperor Wanli*), and it was stipulated that "the offenders for the second time shall be punished by wearing 'Jia Hao' (cangue: a large wooden collar worn by petty criminals as a punishment) of one hundred *jin* for a month, and then be banished as before; while the offenders for the third time shall all be banished to 'Ji Bian' (extreme remote areas) for life exile, regardless of the offences committed before or after the revision of the law" to show the corresponding difference between crime and punishment.

In face of the intensification of class resistance, in order to ensure the revenue income of the state, which was necessary for the operation of the state, the articles of "Yan Shou Cheng Chi" (taking strict precaution to defend the cities) and "Yan Cheng Fan Si Yan" (enforcing severe punishment on illegal salt trading) were added in *Wan Li Wen Xing Tiao Li* (*The Ordinance for Inquisition Made in the Reign of Emperor Wanli*): "Of all 'Fu' (ancient administrative district between province and county), 'Zhou' (subprefecture) and 'Xian' (county) in the border and coastal areas as well as in the central regions, whether 'Wei Suo' (border guarding posts) is located in the same or in a different city, if the defenders fail to defend the city tenaciously, or abandon the city without permission and flee away under the attack of barbarians, thieves and robbers, or if the defenders do not build military facilities to defend the city so that the city is captured, looted and burned, the officials in charge of 'Wei Suo' (border guarding posts) and the 'Bu Dao Guan' (officers responsible for catching thieves) shall all be punished by 'Zhan' (beheading) according to the legal provision that border-defense military officers shall be punished by 'Zhan' (beheading) for losing the city." With respect to illegal transactions of salt, countermeasures were already adopted in *Jia Jing Wen Xing Tiao Li* (*The Ordinance for Inquisition Made in the Reign of Emperor Jiajing*) to have offenders severely punished. "If a violent mob of illegal salt traders have gathered more than ten persons ... to resist the government troops, or if they have killed or wounded three or more than three people or led to their death [or 'Ming' (lives)], they shall all be punished by 'Zhan' (beheading) according to the legal provision that the robbers who have obtained property by robbery shall be punished by 'Zhan' (beheading)." In *Wan Li Wen Xing Tiao Li* (*The Ordinance for Inquisition Made in the Reign of Emperor Wanli*), the word "Ming" (lives) was changed to "Ren" (people), which meant that as long as they killed or wounded three or more than three people, even if it did not result in death, they would be punished by "Zhan" (beheading) anyway. So it can be seen that although it is a change of only one word, it has implied a much stricter punishment for the crime. As another example, if a gang of fewer than ten people had resisted arrest or had wounded people or had caused harm resulting in the death of two people, the principal and accessory offenders "shall all be punished according to the legal provision that when criminals are arrested by the government officials, if the gangs gather to seize the criminals by force on the way, the principal and accessory offenders shall be punished by 'Zhan' (beheading) and 'Jiao' (hanging) respectively." However, it was stipulated clearly in *Wan Li Wen Xing Tiao Li* (*The Ordinance for Inquisition Made in the Reign of Emperor Wanli*) that the principal offender "shall be punished by 'Zhan' (beheading) according to law without necessarily referring to other established legal provisions or submitting them to the Emperor for approval; while only the accessories should be punished by 'Jiao' (hanging) according to the legal provision that it should be punished by 'Jiao' (hanging) for the gang of people who take the criminals away by force on the way and make people wounded." This change also reflected the legislative intent of cracking down on the principal offenders.

After the promulgation of *Wan Li Wen Xing Tiao Li* (*The Ordinance for Inquisition Made in the Reign of Emperor Wanli*), *Ming Lv* (*Ming Code*) and "Li" (precedent) were combined together and published according to the stylistic rules and layout of "using 'Lv' (criminal law) as the main body and 'Li' (precedent) as the annotation."

To sum up, the revision of *Wen Xing Tiao Li* (*The Ordinance for Inquisition*), which was carried out during the three periods of the reigning of emperors Hongzhi, Jiajing, and Wanli, was another important legislative activity in the mid and late Ming Dynasty, which was not only an adaption and improvement of the forms of "Chi" (instruction) and "Li" (precedent) in the Tang and Song dynasties but also an embodiment of the achievements of "Lv Xue" (the study of statutory laws) in the Ming Dynasty. So the historical value lay not only in its breaking through the shackles of the doctrine of "no changing of the established laws handed down from their forefathers" in light of the development of social life but also in its normalization and unifying of criminal regulations and in the changing of "Yi Li Po Lv" ((breaking 'Lv' (criminal law) with the application of 'Li' (precedent)) to "Yi Li Bu Lv" (supplementing 'Lv' (criminal law) with the application of 'Li' (precedent)), which had no doubt played a positive role not only in the uniform application of *Ming Lv* (*Ming Code*) but also in the improvement of the accuracy and efficiency of judicial judgment. It was precisely because of this that in the 18th year of Kangxi (1679), apart from *Da Qing Lv Ji Jie Fu Li* (*Great Qing Code with Collected Commentaries and Appended Sub-statutes*), *Wen Xing Tiao Li* (*The Ordinance for Inquisition*) was ordered to be made by Emperor Kangxi, which had fully shown the historical influence of the amendment of *Wen Xing Tiao Li* (*The Ordinance for Inquisition*) by the three emperors of the Ming Dynasty.

Although the legal system of the Ming Dynasty was established during the reign of Emperor Hongwu, legal relationship was based on social relationship, so it was impossible for the laws made temporarily in one dynasty to be applied in all dynasties. Therefore, although harsh penalties were applied by Zhu Yuanzhang to ensure that the statutory laws handed down from the forefathers remained unchanged, it was impossible for him to stop the progress of social life. Thus, it was historically inevitable to create *Wen Xing Tiao Li* (*The Ordinance for Inquisition*). Although there were various arguments in the course of making *Wen Xing Tiao Li* (*The Ordinance for Inquisition*), it eventually was completed in response to the proper time and conditions. So its formulation also reflected the improvement in legislative techniques in the mid and late Ming Dynasty.

10.1.2.4 The Making of *Ming Hui Dian* (*The Collected Statutes of Ming Dynasty*)

In the early Ming Dynasty, in light of the lessons drawn from the downfall of the Yuan Dynasty and the decline of national power, which were caused by the corruption of officials in the late Yuan Dynasty, after the founding of the state, management of officials was vigorously rectified and severe punishments were extensively adopted to have officials of all ranks controlled and punished by Emperor Taizu. At the same time, preparation was also actively made for the formulation of administrative laws in order to have the duty, power, and responsibility of officials regulated and the administrative efficiency improved. Especially after the abolition of "Zhong Shu Sheng" (the supreme organization in charge of state affairs) in the 13th year of Hongwu (1380), significant changes were made in the administrative system, so it was needed to be confirmed in the form of law to adjust the increasingly complex administrative relations. However, since at that time efforts were made mainly on the revision of *Da Ming Lv* (*The Great Ming Code*), it was not the right time to make administrative laws, so only a few relevant provisions, such as the provision on preventing officials from monopolizing the power, the provision on requiring officials to be conscientious and responsible, and the provision on the assessment of officials, were added to *Da Ming Lv* (*The Great Ming Code*). At the same time, *Zhu Si Zhi Zhang* (*The Duties of Each Bureau*) was enacted, which had provided an initial framework for the compilation of *Da Ming Hui Dian* (*The Collected Statutes of Ming Dynasty*).

Thereafter, in the 4th year of Jianwen (1402), *Gong Chen Si Zui Jian Lu Li* (*The Regulations on Official Salary Reduction for the Punishment of the Meritorious Statesman Guilty of Capital Offences*) was issued, and during the reign of emperors Hongzhi and Jiajing, *Wang Fu Jin Li Liu Tiao* (*Six Prohibitory Regulations for the Royal Palace*) and *Zong Fan Jun Zheng Tiao Li* (*The Regulations for the Military Administration of Vassals*) were issued, although all of them were just offprint administrative regulations. During the reign of Yingzong, in view of the fact that "the decrees and regulations in the past dynasties are all scattered, overlapped and messy" and it was difficult for officials to make reference, the amendment of *Hui Dian* (*The Collected Statutes*) was started. In the 10th year of Hongzhi during the reign of Emperor Xiaozong (1497), a special imperial edict was issued to Confucian ministers by Emperor Xiaozong, and it was ordered that "on the basis of the books about official duties of each department in 'Zhong Mi' (the place for a collection of books and cultural relics in the Court) and by making reference to books concerning 'You Si' (officials), all materials concerning 'Li Du' (the law and rites) shall be collected and edited according to the order of different offices, with subordinates headed by different officials and with all the affairs concerned allocated to different official posts. So the law is called *Da Ming Hui Dian* (*The Collected Statutes of Ming Dynasty*)." In the 15th year of Hongzhi (1502), the law, which consisted of one hundred and eighty volumes in total, was finally completed. Therefore, "it is specially ordered to be published and issued home and abroad by the Emperor so

10.1 Legislative Ideology and Achievements of the Ming Dynasty

that it shall be observed by the future generations from now on. . . . All the measures concerning the imperial court and the people, whether big or small, should all be well-founded, justifiable and appropriate."[88] But *Hong Zhi Hui Dian* (*The Collected Statutes of Hongzhi*) was not issued for enforcement.

During the reign of Emperor Wuzong, after "being carefully studied by 'Nei Ge' (The Cabinet) with some omission supplemented and shortcomings corrected by referring to other books," it was formally issued nationwide, which was commonly known as *Zheng De Hui Dian* (*The Collected Statutes of Zhengde*). In "Yu Zhi Ming Hui Dian Xu" (The Preface to the Collected Statutes of Ming Dynasty), Emperor Wuzong pointed out that "this is a matter concerning the survival of our country and the successful government of the state and education of the people. . ., therefore, I ordered it be published so that it can be followed by both officials in the government and the people nationwide, be used as the basis by archaeologists, and be followed as rules by those who want to make contribution and achievements. So it is only after its publication that everything else can fall into its proper place, the state can be successfully governed, the public can be generally educated, and 'Fa Zhi' (the ruling of law) can last forever."[89] On April 10 of the 6th year of Zhengde (1511), Emperor Wuzong stated in *Chi Yu Nei Ge* (*The Imperial Instruction to the Cabinet*) that "since its implementation, the malpractices have been eliminated, so it should be passed down to future generations to fulfill my wish to rule the state by following the examples of my ancestors."[90]

In the 8th year of Jiajing during the reign of Emperor Shizong (1529), the compilation of the law was continued by Emperor Shizong, which was commonly known as *Jia Jing Xu Zuan Hui Dian* (*A Sequel to the Collected Statutes of Jiajing*). On April 6 in the same year, Emperor Shizong stated in *Chi Yu Nei Ge* (*The Imperial Instruction to the Cabinet*): "I hope that this 'Tong Dian' (the general code) which is made in this generation will not only be abided by all official departments, but also be used as the basis by the future generations . . . to let all the countrymen know what they should do."[91]

In the 4th year of Wanli during the reign of Emperor Shenzong (1576), *Hui Dian* (*The Collected Statutes*) was revised, and it was completed in the 15th year of Wanli (1587), which was commonly known as *Wan Li Chong Xiu Hui Dian* (*The Collected Statutes Revised in the Reign of Wanli*). Emperor Shenzong stressed in *Yu Zhi Chong Xiu Da Ming Hui Dian Xu* (*The Preface to the Revision of the Collected Statutes of Ming Dynasty*) that "the ministers and officials of all ranks inside and outside the capital must follow the existing laws and regulations when performing their duties,

---

[88]"Yu Zhi Da Ming Hui Dian Xu" (The Preface to the Collected Statutes of Ming Dynasty) in *Da Ming Hui Dian* (*The Collected Statutes of Ming Dynasty*) (during the reign of Hongzhi).

[89]"Yu Zhi Da Ming Hui Dian Xu" (The Preface to the Collected Statutes of Ming Dynasty) in *Da Ming Hui Dian* (*The Collected Statutes of Ming Dynasty*) (during the reign of Zhengde).

[90]*Ming Xiao Zong Shi Lu* (*The Record of Emperor Xiaozong of Ming Dynasty*), Vol. 123.

[91]"Huang Di Chi Yu Nei Ge" (The Emperor's Imperial Instruction to the Cabinet) (Part 2) in *Da Ming Hui Dian* (*The Collected Statutes of Ming Dynasty*).

because only by ruling in this way can the state be as solid as metal and stone, and only by carrying out such laws and regulation can mutual trust be as true as the four seasons ... so that the descendants of all generations can live in peace and happiness, which will last forever."

As is shown in the above records, *Hui Dian* (*The Collected Statutes*), which had rich contents and detailed accounts, was drafted according to the officially compiled "Lv" (criminal law), "Ling" (decree), "Li" (rites), "Shi" (standard), "Xian Gang" (laws and disciplines), and "Dang An Ji Ce" (files and books) of the government offices in the Ming Dynasty. So it was the fundamental principle and law in which all "the laws and decrees of the previous dynasties and the established regulatory documents of the whole dynasty" were collected.[92] Therefore, it was taken seriously by the supreme rulers. In the compilation of *Da Ming Hui Dian* (*The Collected Statutes of Ming Dynasty*), the stylistic rules and layout of *Tang Liu Dian* (*The Six Statutes of Tang Dynasty*) were mainly followed, the official system of "Liu Bu" (The Six Departments) was taken as the key link, and the duties and "Shi Li" (precedents) of the administrative organs were stated respectively according to the order of "Zong Ren Fu" (The Imperial Clan Court), "Liu Bu" (The Six Departments), "Du Cha Yuan" (The Court of Censors), "Liu Ke" (the six offices), "Si" (bureau), "Fu" (ancient administrative district between province and county), "Jian" (ancient supervisory office), and "Si" (office). But it was different from *Tang Liu Dian* (*The Six Statutes of Tang Dynasty*) in that it was not only a collection of administrative laws but also a collection of important laws with the feature of administrative codes, which all countrymen should abide by. As an important legislative achievement in the Ming Dynasty, it had provided a priori experience for the making of "Wu Chao Hui Dian" (the collected statutes made during the reign of the five emperors) in the Qing Dynasty.

10.2 The Administrative Legislation for the Strengthening of Absolutism

The making of *Ming Hui Dian* (*The Collected Statutes of Ming Dynasty*) not only provided a great support to the administrative legal system of the Ming Dynasty but also showed the trend of codification of administrative law, so it had marked a new achievement in the legislation of the late feudal society and became the fundamental law for the regulation of the national activities of the Ming Dynasty.

---

[92]"Yu Zhi Chong Xiu Da Ming Hui Dian Xu" (The Preface to the Revision of the Collected Statutes of Ming Dynasty) in *Da Ming Hui Dian* (*The Collected Statutes of Ming Dynasty*).

10.2.1 The Major Changes of the Central Administrative System

In the early Ming Dynasty, by following the old system of "Yi Sheng Zhi" (One Department System) of the Song and Yuan dynasties, "Zhong Shu Sheng" (the supreme organization in charge of state affairs) was set up to exercise control over "Liu Bu" (The Six Departments) and was in full charge of the national administration. In addition, "Du Du Fu" (Offices of Military Affairs) was set up to exercise control over all military affairs inside and outside the capital, and "Yu Shi Tai" (The Censorate) was set up to be in charge of supervision, which were collectively called "San Da Fu" (The Three Great Departments). Moreover, "Xing Zhong Shu Sheng" (the provincial supreme organization in charge of daily affairs) was set up in local regions as the supreme local administrative body to be in charge of the local political, military, and judicial affairs. Below "Xing Sheng" (province), "Fu" (ancient administrative district between province and county), "Zhou" (subprefecture), "Xian" (county), and other local governments were also set up. "Xing Du Du Fu" (provincial offices of military affairs) was set up to act as the supreme local military organ. In the fierce military struggle, in order to win the war and to cope with the rapidly changing situation, it was necessary to give local political and military chief officials the power to independently deal with various affairs; therefore, in addition to "Zhong Shu Sheng" (the supreme organization in charge of state affairs) and "Du Du Fu" (Offices of Military Affairs), which were given central political and military power, the chief officials of "Xing Sheng" (province) and "Xing Du Du Fu" (provincial offices of military affairs) were also given relatively great power. After the unified political power of the Ming Dynasty was stabilized, this relationship of power allocation was already in a condition that needed change; therefore, Zhu Yuanzhang, Emperor Taizu of the Ming Dynasty, immediately began to concentrate on eliminating the power of the prime minister, which had endangered the imperial power, and to solve the sharp contradiction of separation of power between the central and local governments to strengthen the centralized power so that "the Emperor can get the supreme position, have the most authoritive power, and act arbitrarily in granting rewards and enforcing punishments."[93]

In the early Ming Dynasty, "Cheng Xiang" (the prime minister) not only had the right to participate in the decision-making of important national affairs but also had the right to issue orders and to directly control "Liu Bu" (The Six Departments) and other departments, so he became the most important person below the emperor. "Cheng Xiang" (the prime minister) was the emperor's assistance, but to a certain extent, he had balanced the exercise of imperial power. Therefore, Zhu Yuanzhang longed to have the system of "Cheng Xiang" (the prime minister) abolished. He firstly began to make public opinion and said that "'Cheng Xiang' (the prime minister) in the previous dynasties are mostly good at grabbing all the power," so

---

[93] *Ming Tai Zu Shi Lu* (*The Record of Emperor Taizu of Ming Dynasty*), Vol. 129.

he attributed the downfall of the Qin, Han, Tang, Song, and Yuan dynasties completely to "the prime minister's usurping power and interfering with politics."[94] Then he took all possible measures to weaken the authority of "Cheng Xiang" (the prime minister). In June of the 10th year of Hongwu (1377), an order was issued in which it was stipulated that "if subjects of the country want to give advice to and discuss political affairs with the Emperor, their opinions shall be submitted directly to the Emperor in sealed memorials,"[95] and "the major or minor government affairs shall all be handled by the royal prince first, and then be reported to the Emperor."[96] In July, "Tong Zheng Shi Si" (The Transmission Office), which was made up of one "Tong Zheng Shi" (The Transmission Officer), one "Zuo Tong Zheng" (The Chief Transmission Officer), and one "You Tong Zheng" (The Deputy Transmission Officer), was set up. The office was in charge of "delivering Emperor's orders, reporting the views of his subjects and ensuring the transmission of official documents."[97] So all the memorials of the ministers inside and outside the capital had to be submitted to the emperor via "Tong Zheng Shi Si" (The Transmission Office), by which the right of "Cheng Xiang" (the prime minister) to gain access to memorials was deprived. Besides, the emperor's orders were also passed on to the relevant organs and officials through "Tong Zheng Shi Si" (The Transmission Office). So if people wanted to put forward their opinion or to complain about their grievances or to report wrongful acts to the emperor, they could seal their memorials and submit them directly to the emperor via "Tong Zheng Shi Si" (The Transmission Office). In the spring of the 11th year of Hongwu (1378), because "Cheng Xiang" (the prime minister) Hu Weiyong "had controlled the overall administrative power of 'Zhong Shu Sheng' (the supreme organization in charge of the state affairs) ... acted wantonly and manipulated his power for personal gains,"[98] an order was issued to "forbid 'Liu Bu' (The Six Departments) to make reports to 'Zhong Shu Sheng' (the supreme organization in charge of the state affairs) when presenting their memorials to the Emperor,"[99] by which "Cheng Xiang" (the prime minister) was deprived of his power to control "Liu Bu" (The Six Departments). In the 13th year of Hongwu (1380), more than 15,000 "Hu Dang" (supporters of Hu Weiyong) and meritorious officials were killed in the name of suppressing the rebellion of "Zuo Cheng Xiang" (the chief prime minister) Hu Weiyong; meanwhile, "Zhong Shu Sheng" (the supreme organization in charge of state affairs) was repealed by seizing this opportunity, and the official position of "Cheng Xiang" (the prime minister) was also abolished; consequently, "Cheng Xiang" (the prime minister) was removed

---

[94]"Hu Lan Zhi Yu" (Cases of Hu Weiyong and Lan Yu) in *Ming Shi Ji Shi Ben Mo* (*The Ins and Outs of the Records in the History of Ming Dynasty*), Vol. 13.

[95]*Ming Tai Zu Shi Lu* (*The Record of Emperor Taizu of Ming Dynasty*), Vol. 113.

[96]*Ming Tai Zu Shi Lu* (*The Record of Emperor Taizu of Ming Dynasty*), Vol. 113.

[97]"Tong Zheng Shi Si" (The Transmission Office) in *Da Ming Hui Dian* (*The Collected Statutes of Ming Dynasty*), Vol. 212.

[98]*Ming Tai Zu Shi Lu* (*The Record of Emperor Taizu of Ming Dynasty*), Vol. 129.

[99]*Ming Hui Yao* (*Collections of Historical Records in Ming Dynasty*), Vol. 9.

10.2 The Administrative Legislation for the Strengthening of Absolutism   949

from his office, with his power completely controlled by the emperor himself. So the system of "Cheng Xiang" (the prime minister), which had lasted for more than 1000 years, and the system of "San Sheng" (the three departments), which had lasted for more than 700 years in Chinese history, finally came to an end, and the conflict between the imperial power and "Xiang Quan" (the power of prime minister), which had long existed since the establishment of the imperial system in the Qin Dynasty, finally ended up with the emperor being victorious.

After the abolition of "Zhong Shu Sheng" (the supreme organization in charge of state affairs), the power and status of "Liu Bu" (The Six Departments) ("Liu Bu" (The Six Departments), namely, "Li Bu" (The Department of Personnel), "Hu Bu" (The Department of Revenue), "Li Bu" (The Department of Rites), "Bing Bu" (The Department of Defense), "Xing Bu" (The Department of Punishment), and "Gong Bu" (The Department of Works)), were greatly increased, so they became the highest central administrative organs that were directly responsible to the emperor in handling state affairs. Among "Liu Bu" (The Six Departments), "Li Bu" (The Department of Personnel) was in charge of the selection, appointment, and assessment of civil and military officials; "Hu Bu" (The Department of Revenue) was in charge of the population, land tax, and finance of the whole country; "Li Bu" (The Department of Rites) was in charge of imperial examination, etiquette, and sacrifices; "Bing Bu" (The Department of Defense) was in charge of the selection and appointment of military officials and military maneuvers and training; "Xing Bu" (The Department of Punishment) was in charge of criminal punishments; and "Gong Bu" (The Department of Works) was in charge of construction, manufacturing, and water conservancy. The jurisdiction of "Hu Bu" (The Department of Revenue) and "Xing Bu" (The Department of Punishment) was divided according to region, and each of them had jurisdiction over thirteen subordinate "Si" (bureau), which had never been the case in the previous dynasties. Henceforth, the organizational system of the central organs consisting of "Liu Bu" (The Six Departments) and twenty four "Si" (bureau), which had existed since the Sui and Tang, dynasties was ended. In each of "Liu Bu" (The Six Departments), there was one "Shang Shu" (the minister) and two "Shi Lang" (vice minister). And "Shang Shu" (the minister) of "Liu Bu" (The Six Departments) was at the same time the statutory member of "Jiu Qing" (the nine high-rank officials in ancient times), so he could participate in the research and discussion of important policies and the settlement of significant cases nationwide. So each department of "Liu Bu" (The Six Departments) just focused one of the tasks, as was described in the saying that "it is forbidden for the power and authority to be concentrated exclusively in one department," and "Shang Shu" (the minister) was only directly responsible to the emperor to carry out the emperor's orders, it had not only reduced the threat to imperial power, but also ensured the exercise of the emperor's dictatorial power. Therefore, ten years after this system was implemented, an imperial edict was issued by Emperor Taizu to have it affirmed institutionally: "'Cheng Xiang' (the prime minister) is removed from his office and 'Fu' (ancient administrative district between province and county), 'Bu' (department), 'Yuan' (institution), and 'Si' (bureau) have been set up to handle the various government affairs respectively. Besides, relevant laws have been made in detail. Therefore, it is forbidden to set up the system of 'Cheng Xiang' (the prime minister) by the future Emperors; if any official dares to submit memorials to the Emperor to ask for the establishment of the system of 'Cheng Xiang' (the prime minister), he will be punished by death penalty."[100]

The major reform of the central administrative system in the Ming Dynasty was a further development of the autocratic centralization system that existed since the Tang and Song dynasties, as was described in the saying that "whether home or abroad, the memorials are all submitted to the Emperor for approval. As for the decision of important affairs and settlement of doubtful cases, it is required that the officials should only report to the Emperor in person to ask for imperial edicts."[101] However, since "everything is decided by the Emperor himself without allowing others to interfere" and "numerous affairs have been handled every day, how is it possible for him to handle everything perfectly?"[102] So Emperor Taizu deeply felt that "it is necessary to ask assistant ministers to help him if a monarch wants to rule the state effectively."[103] Therefore, in the 15th year of Hongwu (1382), Emperor Taizu began to choose officials from "Han Lin Yuan" (The Hanlin Academy) and other agencies of "Wen Han" (official documents and correspondence) by following the system of the Song Dynasty, to appoint them as the emperor's advisers and to grant them the title of "Dian Ge Da Xue Shi" (Palace Grand Secretary) to be in charge of drafting imperial edicts without "allowing them to settle the state affairs."[104] During the reign of Emperor Chengzu, literary attendant officials such as "Shi Du" (reading attendant), "Bian Xiu" (official in charge of the edition and drafting of documents), and "Jian Tao" (official in charge of compiling state history) in "Han Lin Yuan" (The Hanlin Academy) were ordered to participate in discussing confidential affairs in "Wen Yuan Ge" (Pavilion of the Imperial Library), so they were officially known as "Nei Ge" (The Cabinet). "Since then, 'Nei Ge' (The Cabinet) began to participate in dealing with the confidential affairs."[105] But generally speaking, the official rank of "Nei Ge Da Xue Shi" (cabinet grand secretary) was only "Wu Pin" (the fifth rank), and they only did things as they were commanded, so "Nei Ge" (The Cabinet) was only equivalent to an institution of secretariat. During the reign of Emperor Xuanzong, in order to help the ministers in "Nei Ge" (The Cabinet) to exercise their powers and to improve their efficiency, some ministers of "Liu Bu" (The Six Departments) were included in "Nei Ge" (The Cabinet) to hold concurrent posts as "Da Xue Shi" (grand secretary). For example, "Bing Bu Shang

---

[100]"Zhi Guan Zhi" (The Record of State Officials) (Part 1) in *Ming Shi* (*The History of Ming Dynasty*).

[101]Liao Daonan (Ming Dynasty), *Dian Ge Ci Lin Ji* (*The Record of Officials in the Hanlin Academy*).

[102]"Qiu Yan" (Requiring for Advice) in *Ming Tai Zu Bao Xun* (*The Imperial Decrees of Emperor Taizu of Ming Dynasty*), Vol. 3.

[103]*Ming Tai Zu Shi Lu* (*The Record of Emperor Taizu of Ming Dynasty*), Vol. 133.

[104]*Ming Jing Shi Wen Bian* (*The Collected Essays of the Statecraft of Ming Dynasty*), Vol. 293.

[105]"Xie Jin Zhuan" (The Biography of Xie Jin) in *Ming Shi* (*The History of Ming Dynasty*).

10.2 The Administrative Legislation for the Strengthening of Absolutism

Shu" (the minister of the department of defense) Yang Shiqi, "Gong Bu Shang Shu" (the minister of the department of works) Yang Rong, and "Li Bu Shang Shu" (the minister of the department of rites) Yang Pu all joined "Nei Ge" (The Cabinet) and held concurrent posts as "Nei Ge Da Xue Shi" (cabinet grand secretary). Later on, it became an established system, and the functions and powers of "Nei Ge" (The Cabinet) gradually became more and more important. Especially, in the early years of Emperor Yingzong, since the Emperor was very young and since most of "Da Xue Shi" (grand secretary) were the senior statesmen of previous periods, "Nei Ge Da Xue Shi" (cabinet grand secretary) became so power that "he even completely controlled 'Liu Bu' (The Six Departments) and his instructions were followed by everyone."[106] During the reign of Emperor Shizong, "Da Xue Shi" (grand secretary) Xia Yan and Yan Song successively held power, so their power was as great as that of "Cheng Xiang" (the prime minister). To a certain extent, their "official ranks are higher than those of the officials of 'Liu Bu' (The Six Departments),"[107] so that "even the ministers of 'Liu Cao' (the six departments) had submitted themselves to their command,"[108] "and they are obviously 'Zai Xiang' (the prime minister) in a real sense."[109] But since Emperor Taizu had made it a rule to forbid his descendants to set up the system of "Cheng Xiang" (the prime minister), "Nei Ge Da Xue Shi" (cabinet grand secretary) was only called "Fu Chen" (assistant minister) and "Shou Xi Da Xue Shi" (the chief grand secretary) was only called "Yuan Fu" (the first assistant minister) or "Shou Fu" (the primary assistant minister). Although "Nei Ge Da Xue Shi" (cabinet grand secretary) did not have the title of "Cheng Xiang" (the prime minister), due to their responsibility of "Piao Ni Pi Da (drafting replies to the memorials submitted by officials for the emperor's reference), they could play politics more conveniently as compared with "Cheng Xiang" (the prime minister) because "Cheng Xiang" (the prime minister) did not directly participate in drafting imperial edicts. From the perspective of the state system, "Da Xue Shi" (grand secretary) was not the supreme executive official, and he did not have a direct leadership relationship with "Liu Bu" (The Six Departments). Moreover, in the Ming Dynasty, among "Shou Fu" (the primary assistant minister), only Yan Song and Zhang Juzheng had the real power; the others only had to rely on the emperor or even the eunuchs, which could be proved by the fact that the right of "Nei Ge Shou Fu" (the primary assistant minister of the cabinet) to draft replies to memorials was restricted by the system of "Huan Guan Pi Hong" (eunuchs giving instructions or comments on memorials submitted to the emperor in red). So "Nei Ge" (The Cabinet) only had the right to draft imperial edicts according to the emperor's

---

[106]"Zhi Guan Zhi" (The Record of State Officials) (Part 1) in *Ming Shi* (*The History of Ming Dynasty*).

[107]"Zhi Guan Zhi" (The Record of State Officials) (Part 1) in *Ming Shi* (*The History of Ming Dynasty*).

[108]"Yan Hai Wo Luan" (The Invasion of Coastal Areas by Japanese Pirates) in *Ming Shi Ji Shi Ben Mo* (*The Ins and Outs of the Records in the History of Ming Dynasty*), Vol. 55.

[109]"Zhi Guan Zhi" (The Record of State Officials) (Part 1) in *Ming Shi* (*The History of Ming Dynasty*).

decrees; they had no right to participate in the decision on state affairs. The establishment of "Nei Ge" (The Cabinet), which was in charge of "receiving orders from the emperor and issuing them to 'Liu Bu' (The Six Departments),"[110] was the result of the high development of a centralized monarchy.

According to the system of the Ming Dynasty, eunuchs in "Si Li Jian" (in charge of the inner eunuch and intrauterine affairs within the court) were in charge of assisting the emperor in answering the officials' memorials in the imperial court. At the beginning, they were only in charge of "submitting the memorials and documents, and giving instructions or comments on officials' memorials in red ('Pi Zhu') according to 'Ge Piao' (drafting replies to memorials on behalf of the emperor on a note pasted on the margin of a page by the cabinet)."[111] But gradually they became actual representatives of "Xiang Quan" (the power of minister), and their words were like the laws of the court. It was recorded in "Zhi Guan Zhi" (The Record of State Officials) in *Ming Shi* (*The History of Ming Dynasty*) that "the cabinet's work of 'Ni Piao' (drafting replies to the memorials submitted by officials for emperor's reference) was subjected to the eunuchs' power of 'Huan Guan Pi Hong' (eunuchs giving instructions or comments on memorials submitted to the emperor in red), so to a certain extent, 'Xiang Quan' (the power of minister) was actually usurped by the eunuchs, who had really controlled the laws and disciplines of the court, and the promotion and demotion of 'Xian Shi' (able and virtuous persons) and 'Da Fu' (senior official in feudal China)." During the reign of Emperor Wuzong, eunuch Liu Jin, who was in charge of "Si Li Jian" (in charge of the inner eunuch and intrauterine affairs within the court), was considered very powerful and influential, so every time "Shou Fu Da Xue Shi" (the chief grand secretary) drafted a reply, he had to "go to Liu Jin's office first to ask for instructions before writing."[112] On the ground that "Si Li Jian" (in charge of the inner eunuch and intrauterine affairs within the court) had played politics through "Pi Hong" (giving instructions or comments on officials' memorials in red), Huang Zongxi, a thinker of the late Ming Dynasty, had criticized the abolishment of "Cheng Xiang" (the prime minister) and the establishment of "Nei Ge" (The Cabinet) in the Ming Dynasty. He said:

> The failure to govern the state perfectly in Ming Dynasty started from the Emperor's abolishment of "Cheng Xiang" (the prime minister) ... Maybe some people say that when they go to "Nei Ge" (The Cabinet) to deal with official affairs, they find that "Zai Xiang" (the prime minister) is only abolished in name, but the position is still retained in reality. My answer is: it is not the case. The people go to "Nei Ge" (The Cabinet) for "Pi Da" (writing replies or comments on memorials submitted to the emperor), just like people who are in charge of official documents and correspondence in the offices of senior officials, so their task is easy; moreover, the purpose of "Pi Da" (writing replies or comments on memorials

---

[110] "Feng Yuan Biao Zhuan" (The Biography of Feng Yuanbiao) in *Ming Shi* (*The History of Ming Dynasty*).

[111] "Zhi Guan Zhi" (The Record of State Officials) (Part 3) in *Ming Shi* (*The History of Ming Dynasty*).

[112] "Liu Jin Yong Shi" (Liu Jin in Power) in *Ming Shi Ji Shi Ben Mo* (*The Ins and Outs of the Records in the History of Ming Dynasty*), Vol. 43.

10.2 The Administrative Legislation for the Strengthening of Absolutism

submitted to the emperor) is to get instructions from the emperor first and then to draft the replies, how can it be said that they act as a real "Zai Xiang" (the prime minister)! I believe that eunuchs today are the people who really act as "Zai Xiang" (the prime minister). ... The power of deciding people's lives and death has been taken from prime ministers and given to the eunuchs ... So the reason why eunuchs have acted as "Zai Xiang" (the prime minister) is that "Cheng Xiang" (the prime minister) has been abolished.[113]

Eunuchs were supposed to be the Emperor's attendants, but they gradually monopolized the power and interfered in political affairs because of their frequent association with the Emperor and because of the Emperor's suspicion of "Wai Guan" (the officials from outside the court). Overall, the eunuchs' interference in political affairs during the Ming Dynasty was more serious than that in the Han and Tang dynasties, which had precisely reflected the decadence of the authoritarian system.

As to the local administrative system, before the establishment of the unified national regime, "Xing Zhong Shu Sheng" (the provincial supreme organization in charge of daily affairs) was established as the supreme local administrative organ and was in full charge of the military, administrative, civil, financial, and judicial affairs within its jurisdiction, but after the unification of the regime, the organization became a barrier to the strengthening of the centralized authority. So in the 9th year of Hongwu (1376), an order was issued to abolish the system of "Xing Zhong Shu Sheng" (the provincial supreme organization in charge of daily affairs); consequently, senior local officials such as "Ping Zhang Zheng Shi" (the head of the provincial secretariat), "Zuo You Cheng" (the left and right vice prime minister), and so on were dismissed. Moreover, by following the system of the Song Dynasty, "Cheng Xuan Bu Zheng Shi Si" (The Provincial Administrative Commission), "Du Zhi Hui Shi Si" (The Provincial Military Commission), and "Ti Xing An Cha Shi Si" (The Provincial Judicial Commission) were established, which jointly formed the provincial government organs in charge of administrative, military, and judicial affairs, respectively. In the early Ming Dynasty, there were thirteen "Cheng Xuan Bu Zheng Shi Si" (The Provincial Administrative Commissions) across the country, which were in full charge of administrative, civil, taxation and other affairs, with "Zuo You Bu Zheng Shi" (chief and deputy local administrative officials) as the supreme local administrative officials. "Du Zhi Hui Shi Si" (The Provincial Military Commission) was responsible for military affairs; it also had jurisdiction over "Wei Suo" (border guarding posts) in local provinces, with "Du Zhi Hui Shi" (the chief military general) as the supreme local military officer. "An Cha Shi Si" (The Provincial Judicial Commission) was responsible for criminal punishment and the supervision of the provinces, with "An Cha Shi" (head of judicial commission) as the supreme local judicial official. After the middle of the Ming Dynasty, since "Xun Fu" (procurators) were assigned to many places, "An Cha Shi" (head of judicial commission) gradually became the subordinate official of "Xun Fu" (procurators).

---

[113]Huang Zongxi (Ming Dynasty), "Zhi Xiang" (The Appointment of Prime Minister) in *Ming Yi Dai Fang Lu* (*Waiting for Dawn*).

So the establishment of "San Si" (The Three Departments) in local places gradually specialized the function of local authorities and improved their work efficiency; moreover, since the three departments were of equal status, were independent of each other, and were all under the direct leadership of the emperor, they not only decentralized the power of the chief officials in each province but also strengthened the mutual balance of the three organs so that it was much easier for them to be controlled by the emperor.

Below "Sheng" (province), the two levels of the local government of "Fu" (ancient administrative district between province and county) and "Xian" (county) were established, but the local organ of "Lu" (ancient administrative region), which was established in the Song and Yuan dynasties, was abolished. "Fu" (ancient administrative district between province and county) was headed by "Zhi Fu" (magistrate of a prefecture), while in the capital it was headed by "Fu Yin" (the chief official of prefecture). Although there were no differences between "Zong Guan Fu" (The General Governor's Office) and "San Fu" ("Jing Zhao," "You Fu Feng," "Zuo Feng Yi") as far as "Fu" (ancient administrative district between province and county) in the Ming Dynasty was concerned, there were differences of "Zhi Li Zhou" (subprefectures directly under the jurisdiction of the Provincial Administrative Commission) and "San Zhou" (subprefectures directly under the jurisdiction of prefectures) as far as "Zhou" (subprefecture) was concerned, with "Zhi Li Zhou" (subprefectures directly under the jurisdiction of the Provincial Administrative Commission) directly under the leadership of "Bu Zheng Shi Si" (Provincial Administrative Commissions), which was roughly equivalent to "Fu" (ancient administrative district between province and county) in status, and with "San Zhou" (subprefectures directly under the jurisdiction of prefectures) directly under the leadership of "Fu" (ancient administrative district between province and county), which was roughly equivalent to "Xian" (county) in status. The governors of "Zhou" (subprefecture) were known as "Zhi Zhou" (subprefectural magistrates), and below "Fu" (ancient administrative district between province and county), a number of subordinate "Xian" (counties), headed by "Zhi Xian" (the magistrate of a county), were established.

In order to strengthen the central government's control of and supervision over the local government, the supervisory region of "Dao" (the administration district below the province) was set up between "Sheng" (provinces) and "Fu" (ancient administrative district between province and county). One "Sheng" (province) was divided into a number of "Dao" (the administration district below the province), and one "Dao" (the administration district below the province) had jurisdiction over a number of "Fu" (ancient administrative district between province and county). As far as "Dao" (the administration district below the province) was concerned, there were the differences of "Shou" (the officials in charge of civil affairs sent by "Bu Zheng Si") and "Xun" (the officials in charge of criminal affairs sent by "An Cha Si"): the local office that was in charge of the taxation of "Dao" (the administration district below the province) was called "Fen Shou Dao" (the local administrative commission), which was controlled by "Zuo You Can Zheng" (senior officers under "Bu Zheng Shi") and "Can Yi" (junior officers of "Bu Zheng Shi Si"), who were the assistant officers of "Bu Zheng Shi Si" (Provincial Administrative Commissions), while the local office that was in charge of the judicial affairs of "Dao" (the administration district below the province) and that was respectively supervising the officials of "Fu" (ancient administrative district between province and county) was called "Fen Xun Dao" (the local judicial commission), which was controlled by "Fu Shi" (deputy commissioner) and "Qian Shi" (junior officers of "An Cha Shi Si"), who were assistant officers of "An Cha Shi Si" (The Provincial Judicial Commission). In addition, some "Dao Yuan" (local chief administrator), who had no fixed jurisdiction positions but who were assigned some specific duties, were also appointed as was needed, such as "Du Liang Dao" (the official in charge of grain transportation) and "Ti Xue Dao" (the official in charge of educational affairs). But "Dao" (the administration district below the province) was not regarded as a level of government.

In the early Ming Dynasty, by following the example of "Ci Shi Zhi Du" (the local supervisory system) of the Han Dynasty, large supervisory regions were established according to provincial units, and "Jian Cha Yu Shi" (the supervisory censor), who was called "Xun An Mou Chu Jian Cha Yu Shi" (censors inspecting certain regions), was sent to these areas to conduct inspection. In the years of Yongle during the reign of Emperor Chengzu, "Xun Fu Zhi Du" (the system of procurators) was established on its basis. "Xun Fu" (procurators) was a temporarily appointed official at the beginning, but it gradually became a permanent official post after Emperor Xuanzong. In order to facilitate the exercise of supervisory powers, "Xun Fu" (procurators) was concurrently granted the titles of "Fu Du Yu Shi" (the deputy of the court of censors) or "Jian Du Yu Shi" (assistant of the court of censors), "Bing Bu Shi Lang" (vice director of the department of defense), "Ti Du Jun Wu" (highest local military official), "Zan Li Jun Wu" (associate local military official), and so on. But they were not entitled to deal with important military issues or problems involving several provinces. Therefore, in the years of Jingtai during the reign of Emperor Daizong, "Zong Du Zhi Du" (the system of viceroy) was created. "Zong Du" (viceroy) was in command of the military and supervisory powers of several provinces or some large provinces and was granted the title of "Bing Bu Shang Shu" (the minister of the department of defense) or "Bing Bu Shi Lang" (vice director of the department of defense) or "Du Yu Shi" (the head of the court of censors). "Zong Du" (viceroy) and "Xun Fu" (procurators) had higher status and authority than "Bu Zheng Shi" (provincial administrative commissioners), but till the end of the Ming Dynasty, they were not the supreme administrative officials at the provincial level.

In addition, by following the systems of the Song Dynasty, "Xun Jian Si" (inspection commission) was set up in all major cities and towns across the country "to be specifically in charge of examining the spies travelling to and fro, trafficking illegal salt trade and arresting the army deserters, the escaped prisoners, and the strange looking and suspicious people without a travel passes."[114] After Emperor Xiaozong, "Bu Dao Tong Pan" (official in charge of catching thieves in the Ming

---

[114]"Bing Bu" (The Department of Defense) (Part 7) in *Da Ming Hui Dian* (*The Collected Statutes of Ming Dynasty*), Vol. 129.

Dynasty), "Bu Dao Zhou Pan" (assistant official in charge of catching thieves in the Ming Dynasty), "Bu Dao Zhu Bu" (assistant in charge of documents in the Ming Dynasty), and other police agencies were set up in local places, which had demonstrated the deepening and strengthening of the autocratic ruling.

As to the grassroots organization, "Fang" (neighborhood) was established in cities, "Xiang" (townships) was established near the cities, and "Li" (a basic resident organization consisting of five neighborhoods) was established in the countryside. Every one hundred and ten households made up one "Li" (a basic resident organization consisting of five neighborhoods), which was headed by a "Li Zhang" (head of "Li": the basic resident organization in ancient China); below the "Li" (a basic resident organization consisting of five neighborhoods) was "Jia" (administrative division consisting of twenty households), which was headed by a "Jia Zhang" (the head of "Jia"), who was responsible for the local civil, educational, taxation, litigation, and other affairs. "Li Zhang" (head of "Li": the basic resident organization in ancient China) had played a very important role in implementing government policies and maintaining the grassroots social order, as was described in the saying that "it is beneficial to civil affairs of the common people and is helpful to the government offices in the settlement of lawsuits."[115]

In summary, the reform of the local administrative system of the Ming Dynasty was carried out under the guidance of the policy of strengthening the autocratic monarchy, which was manifested mainly in the abolition of "Xing Sheng Zhi" (the system of province) and the overlapping establishment of local supervisory regions. By reform, not only was the independent powers owned by "Xing Sheng" (province) in the Yuan Dynasty eliminated, but the tendency of weakening of the power of the local organs in the Song Dynasty was also avoided. The rulers of the Ming Dynasty knew very well that officials in charge of governing the common people were of vital importance to the state; therefore, they paid more attention to the administration of local officials. In the 17th year of Hongwu (1384), the regulations on "Ba Shi" (Eight Matters) for "Fu" (ancient administrative district between province and county), "Zhou" (subprefecture), and "Xian" (county) were issued in the country for people to comply with perpetually. It was emphasized in the regulation that officials at all levels must fulfill their duties, improve efficiency, and conduct supervision over their subordinates. For the government of "Fu" (ancient administrative district between province and county), "Zhou" (subprefecture), and "Xian" (county), particular attention was paid to the duties of "Xian Guan" (county magistrates) who were heads of the basic administrative units. Thus, *Dao Ren Xu Zhi San Shi Yi Tiao* (*Thirty One Instructions for Newly Appointed Officials*) was once issued to "Xian Guan" (county magistrates), and it was stipulated that the newly appointed "Xian Guan" (county magistrates) should first learn about matters such as criminal punishment, household registration, land and grain, justice, finance, and others; second, they should know "how many families in the county have been punished for the crimes

---

[115]Gu Yanwu (Ming Dynasty), "Xiang Ting Zhi Zhi" (Official in the Township Public House) in *Ri Zhi Lu* (*The Record of Daily Reading*), Vol. 8.

10.2 The Administrative Legislation for the Strengthening of Absolutism

committed," "how many officials in the county have been removed from the office and stayed at home, and how many of them have been sentenced to death because they have committed crimes or violated the law while serving for the imperial court"[116] so that they could better grasp the political situation of residents in the county, strengthen the surveillance system, and prevent behaviors that might endanger the state. For the officials of "Fu" (ancient administrative district between province and county), "Zhou" (subprefecture), and "Xian" (county), if there were "incorruptible, honest and upright officials, imperial orders should be delivered by 'Xing Ren' (official in charge of delivering imperial orders and conferring titles of nobility) to have them promoted and rewarded."[117] During the reign of Emperor Hongwu, the local people were even allowed to recommend "Xian Guan" (county magistrate) by themselves. For example, "Zhang Zhen was an assistant of 'Xian Guan' (county magistrates) in Shanghai, but the local people required that he should be appointed 'Xian Guan' (county magistrates) because he had shown solicitude for the local people in a proper way ... so 'Li Bu' (The Department of Personnel) ... was put in a difficulty situation. The Emperor said that this was what the local people had hoped, so their will should be followed, consequently the requirement was approved." "Yang Gong, a 'Dian Shi' (subordinate official in charge of catching criminals and prisons under county magistrate) in Jiaohe, won the popular support of the local people, so when 'Zhi Xian' (the magistrate of a county) Lin Jun was transferred to another place, 'Fu Lao' (the prestigious old people in charge of public affairs in ancient China) of the county presented a memorial to the Emperor and asked Yang Gong to take Lin Jun's place because of his honesty and diligence, but it was rejected by 'Li Bu Shang Shu' (the minister of the department of personnel) Wang Zhi on the ground that Yang Gong was a minor official. The Emperor said: 'Since he is recommended by the local people, their will should be understood and followed. So if restricted by qualifications, the ways of appointment would surely become narrow. I hope that you can understand my intention'. Finally, Yang Gong was assigned to the post and he had proved himself by his competence."[118] Although the above regulations of "Fu" (ancient administrative district between province and county), "Zhou" (subprefecture), and "Xian" (county) and the instructions for the newly appointed "Xian Guan" (county magistrate) had no doubt reflected the intention to suppress local forces, its main focus was to encourage local officials to carry out their administration more effectively.

In the early Ming Dynasty, in order to consolidate the ruling of the Zhu family, the system of granting titles of king to the king's sons and giving them the power to defend "Fan Guo" (vassal states) was implemented. The kings with conferred titles enjoyed great political and economic privileges. After the occurrence of "Hu Lan Zhi

---

[116]"Li Bu" (The Department of Personnel) (Part 8) in *Da Ming Hui Dian* (*The Collected Statutes of Ming Dynasty*), Vol. 9.

[117]"Zhi Guan Zhi" (The Record of State Officials) (Part 4) in *Ming Shi* (*The History of Ming Dynasty*).

[118]*Gu Jin Tu Shu Ji Cheng* (*A Complete Collection of Ancient and Modern Books*), Vol. 689.

Yu" (Cases of Hu Weiyong and Lan Yu), they were also granted military power and were sent to guard the border areas as princes to decide on military affairs all by themselves. The inland major cities were also guarded by the princes because it was believed that it was only the descendants of the Zhu family who could provide the most reliable protection. However, after the occurrence of "Jing Nan Zhi Bian" (Jing Nan Rebellion) (the 4th son of Emperor Taizu rebelled against his nephew), in which "Yan Wang" (The Prince of Yan) Zhu Di seized the throne, the reliability of royal blood relationship was destroyed by the open power struggle. After Emperor Chengzu ascended the throne, except for their economic privileges, the military and political powers of the kings were deprived and strict precautions were taken against them.

10.2.2 The Law on the State Officials to Maintain the Operation of Bureaucracy

Although the autocratic imperial power of the Ming Dynasty was highly intensified, it did not mean that the Emperor ruled the state individually; rather, it meant that the operation of the whole bureaucracy was maintained with the emperor as the axis. Without the unified bureaucracy throughout the country, it would be difficult for the emperor to exercise supreme authority.

In the early Ming Dynasty, Emperor Taizu managed state affairs all by himself, and he once said: "I have handled everything conscientiously." According to the records of *Chun Ming Meng Yu Lu* (*The Record of the Capital Areas in Ming Dynasty*), within eight days from September 14 to 21 of the 17th year during the reign of Emperor Hongwu (1384), 1160 memorials and 3291 cases were sent to the imperial court, and the numerous and jumbled official documents were difficult for any individual to deal with, so they had to be handled with the help of the ministers. Emperor Taizu and Emperor Chengzu held court personally three times a day, and they also "summoned ministers to the palace to decide on various government affairs now and then."[119] Emperor Yingzong only held court in the morning, but at the time of Emperor Xiaozong, in order to timely discuss official business with the ministers, he resumed holding court in the afternoon. "Yu Shi" (the censor) Jiang Wan had once commented on that and suggested that "it is better to discuss important national affairs rather than make replies to all the ordinary memorials and trivial matters at the court held in the afternoon."[120] But after Emperor Xiaozong, few emperors went to courts any more, let alone go to court for three times a day. Emperor Wuzong "held court only three to five days each month, and for each time no more than two things

---

[119]"Liu Qiu Zhuan" (The Biography of Liu Qiu) in *Ming Shi* (*The History of Ming Dynasty*).
[120]"Jiang Wan Zhuan" (The Biography of Jiang Wan) in *Ming Shi* (*The History of Ming Dynasty*).

10.2 The Administrative Legislation for the Strengthening of Absolutism

would be reported to him"[121]; Emperor Shizong "had not even held court by himself for more than twenty years"[122]; Emperor Shenzong "had not held court by himself for thirty years,"[123] which once again showed the decadence of the feudal authoritarian system. However, even so, the state machine was still running, which was inseparable from the division of bureaucratic responsibilities assigned to different posts and their proper coordination, so that the more intensive the absolutism was, the more redundant the bureaucracy became. Although the policy of reducing redundant officials was implemented in both the periods of the reigning of Emperor Renzong and Emperor Xuanzong, because they thought that it was better to reduce officials than to make matters simplified, it was impossible for them to stop the trend of the expansion of state organs. During the reign of Emperor Jiajng, "Ji Shi Zhong" (the senior assistant of the emperor and the supervisor of officials) Liu Tiqian said: "Today there are two most harmful things, namely, redundant officials and unnecessary expenses. According to the official system of previous dynasties, there were 7,500 officials in Han Dynasty, 18,000 in Tang Dynasty, and 34,000 in Song Dynasty. However, at present, since the 5th year of the reign of Emperor Chenghua, the number of military officers has exceeded more than 80,000, and civil officials more than 100,000 ... The number of officials keeps increasing day by day and year by year, so it is even impossible to be calculated completely."[124] During the reign of Emperor Tianqi, Xie Xuelong, "Ji Shi Zhong" (the senior assistant of the emperor and the supervisor of officials) of "Xing Ke" (the department of punishment), gave the following statistics on the increase of officials: "At the beginning of the founding of the state, there were more than 5,400 civil officials and more than 28,000 military officers; during the reign of Emperor Shenzong, the number of civil officials reached to more than 16,000 and military officers more than 82,000. Now I do not know how many times the number of officials has increased."[125]

In the Ming Dynasty, "there are about four ways to select officials: 'Xue Xiao' (school), 'Ke Mu' (the examination of different subjects), 'Jian Ju' (recommendation), and 'Quan Xuan' (selection of officials by evaluating their qualifications). 'Xue Xiao' (school) was intended to have them educated, 'Ke Mu' (the examination of different subjects) was intended to have the candidates for officials examined, 'Jian Ju' (recommendation) was intended to have officials recruited from outside, and 'Quan Xuan' (selection of officials by evaluating their qualifications) was intended to assign officials to different posts across the country so that all the talents

---

[121]"Wang Yuan Zheng Zhuan" (The Biography of Wang Yuanzheng) in *Ming Shi* (*The History of Ming Dynasty*).

[122]"Shi Zong Chong Dao Jiao" (Emperor Shizong Advocating Taoism) in *Ming Shi Ji Shi Ben Mo* (*The Ins and Outs of the Records in the History of Ming Dynasty*), Vol. 52.

[123]"He Zong Yan Zhuan" (The Biography of He Zongyan) in *Ming Shi* (*The History of Ming Dynasty*).

[124]"Liu Ti Qian Zhuan" (The Biography of Liu Tiqian) in *Ming Shi* (*The History of Ming Dynasty*).

[125]"Xie Xue Long Zhuan" (The Biography of Xie Xuelong) in *Ming Shi* (*The History of Ming Dynasty*).

of the country can be gathered."[126] But in the Ming Dynasty, "Ke Ju" (the imperial examination) was the basic way of selecting officials. According to "Xuan Ju Zhi" (The Record of Election) in *Ming Shi* (*The History of Ming Dynasty*): "as for the system of Ming Dynasty, 'Ke Ju' (the imperial examination) was very prevalent, by which the ministers in power were all selected. Moreover, talents were also recruited by schools to take the examination of 'Ke Ju' (the imperial examination). So officials selected from schools were only second to those selected from 'Ke Ju' (the imperial examination), and other officials were also selected from miscellaneous backgrounds. However, 'Jin Shi' (those who passed the imperial examination at the national level in ancient China), 'Ju Gong' ('Ju Ren'(those who passed the imperial examination at the provincial level in ancient China) and "Gong Shi" (a successful candidate in the imperial examination at the metropolitan level)), and the people from miscellaneous backgrounds could be recruited simultaneously. Although some of them were more relied on, yet none of them would be neglected." Early in the 3rd year of Hongwu (1370), an imperial edict was issued by Emperor Taizu to start selecting officials through "Ke Ju" (the imperial examination): "Since August of this year, 'Ke Ju' (the imperial examination) has been specially established in order to study Confucian classics, to cultivate good conduct, and to learn the knowledge of both modern and ancient times. I shall examine the successful candidates of 'Ke Ju' (the imperial examination) in the court by myself and assign them to different posts according to their learning and their ranking."[127] In the 6th year of Hongwu (1373), because "the candidates were mainly tested on language and diction, after they were recruited, it was difficult for many of them to handle the matters properly in practice,"[128] "Ke Ju" (the imperial examination) was once canceled. But in the 15th year of Hongwu (1382), "'Ke Ju' (the imperial examination) was resumed in order to select more officials, and it was decided that it should be held every three years."[129] Generally speaking, "Ke Ju" (the imperial examination) in the Ming Dynasty included "Xiang Shi" (the provincial examination), "Hui Shi" (the metropolitan examination), and "Dian Shi" (the final imperial examination). "Xiang Shi" (the provincial examination) was held in the years of "Zi," "Mao," "Wu," and "You" (terrestrial branch used in combination with the Heavenly Stems to designate years, months, days, and hours in ancient China; here it means every four years), while "Hui Shi" (the metropolitan examination) was held in the years of "Chou," "Chen," "Wei," and "Xu" (terrestrial branch used in combination with the Heavenly Stems to designate years, months, days, and hours in ancient China; here it means every four years). A successful candidate in "Xiang Shi" (the provincial examination) was called "Ju Ren" (those who passed the imperial examination at the provincial level

---

[126]"Xuan Ju Zhi" (The Record of Election) (Part 1) in *Ming Shi* (*The History of Ming Dynasty*).

[127]"Kai Guo Gui Mo" (The Plan for the Founding of the State) in *Ming Shi Ji Shi Ben Mo* (*The Ins and Outs of the Records in the History of Ming Dynasty*), Vol. 14.

[128]"Kai Guo Gui Mo" (The Plan for the Founding of the State) in *Ming Shi Ji Shi Ben Mo* (*The Ins and Outs of the Records in the History of Ming Dynasty*), Vol. 14.

[129]"Tai Zu Ji" (The Record of Emperor Taizu) (Part 3) in *Ming Shi* (*The History of Ming Dynasty*).

in ancient China), and a successful candidate in "Hui Shi" (the metropolitan examination) was qualified for "Dian Shi" (the final imperial examination). After "Dian Shi" (the final imperial examination), the candidates were divided into "San Jia" (the top-three levels): "Yi Jia" (first level) included three candidates who were given the title of "Jin Shi Ji Di" (a successful candidate who ranked among the top three in the palace exam), "Er Jia" (second level) included several candidates who were given the title of "Jin Shi Chu Shen" (a successful candidate who ranked among the second in the palace exam), and "San Jia" (third level) included a number of candidates who were given the title of "Tong Jin Shi Chu Shen" (a successful candidate who ranked among the third in the palace exam). In the 7th year of Yongle (1409), an imperial edict was issued wherein it was stipulated that important state officials such as "Yu Shi" (the censor) should be selected through "Ke Ju" (the imperial examination) because it was regarded as a formal way of selecting officials. From then on, more importance was attached to official appointment through "Ke Ju" (the imperial examination).

As for the contents of "Ke Ju" (the imperial examination), Liu Ji's opinion was accepted by Emperor Taizu: subjects like *Si Shu* (*The Four Books* (*The Great Learning, The Doctrine of the Mean, The Confucian Analects, and The Works of Mencius*)) and *Wu Jing* (*The Five Classics* (*The Book of Songs, The Book of History, The Book of Changes, The Book of Rites and The Spring and Autumn Annals*)) should be made the topics of the examination; the examinees were only allowed to put forward their ideas in the examination on behalf of the sage and persons of virtue according to the interpretation of Confucian classics by "Cheng Zhu Li Xue" (neo-Confucianism: a Confucian school of idealist philosophy of Cheng Hao, Cheng Yi, and Zhu Xi), and they were not allowed to express their own opinions. During the reign of Emperor Xianzong, the form of "Ba Gu" (a stereotyped imperial examination) was created, in which the examinees were required to write paragraphs of "Dui Ou" (a rhetoric device) in the form of articles and to fill their writing with fancy and polished phrases, so the method was completely out of touch with the reality of social life. Besides, it confined the scholars' thinking more strictly than did the method used in selecting scholars according to their poems and essays during the reign of Emperor Taizong in the Tang Dynasty, which had shown that absolutism in culture and ideology was further strengthened to produce a large number of tamed tools to serve for the autocratic system. Gu Yanwu had once pointed out poignantly: "I think that 'Ba Gu' (a stereotyped imperial examination) is more harmful than 'Fen Shu' (burning books), because more talents are ruined than in 'Xian Yang Zhi Jiao' (the burying alive of scholars in the suburbs of Xianyang), in which more than four hundred and sixty Confucian scholars are buried alive."[130] Since selecting officials through "Ba Gu" (a stereotyped imperial examination) was a very clever method of maintaining the feudal rule and confining the scholars' thoughts, although it was attacked by many people, it still continued to be used for hundreds of years with the

---

[130]Gu Yanwu (Ming Dynasty), "Ni Ti" (Preparing Topics) in *Ri Zhi Lu* (*The Record of Daily Reading*), Vol. 16.

support of the government, and it was not until the late Qing Dynasty that it was abolished.

Apart from "Ke Ju" (the imperial examination), there were other ways of appointing officials, such as "Jian Ju" (recommendation) and "Juan Na" (donating food or money to buy an official position). "Jian Ju" (recommendation) was mainly implemented during the reign of Emperor Taizu. Early in the 6th year of the reign of Emperor Hongwu (1373), Emperor Taizu "summoned the talented people of the country to the capital, and appointed them as 'Shou Ling' (prefects or magistrates)."[131] He also "asked 'You Si' (official) to recommend the talented people primarily on the basis of their moral conduct and their on the basis of their talent for writing."[132] In the 12th year of Hongwu (1376), "the learned and experienced people in the country were summoned to the capital by the officials courteously,"[133] and in the 13th year of Hongwu (1377), "an imperial edict was issued to order official to recommend the people who were clever, upright, filial and hard working, or who were gifted and morally integrated, or who were proficient in literature and arts of necromancy, astrology, medicine, etc."[134]; in the 14th year of Hongwu (1378), "another imperial edict was issued to ask the officials to recommend the knowledgeable and experienced people and to send them to capital courteously"[135]; in the 15th year of Hongwu (1379), "Ke Ju" (the imperial examination) was restored, but "Jian Ju" (recommendation) was retained; in the 19th year of Hongwu (1380), "an imperial edict was issued to ask people to recommend those who were knowledgeable about Confucian classics, or morally integrated in conduct, or experienced, or familiar with current affairs to be officials. Those over sixty years old were appointed as imperial consultants in 'Han Lin Yuan' (The Hanlin Academy); those under sixty years old were appointed in 'Liu Bu' (The Six Departments), 'Bu Zheng Shi Si' (The Provincial Administrative Commission) and 'An Cha Shi Si' (The Provincial Judicial Commission),"[136] but if an official was recommended improperly, the referrer should be punished by "Lian Zuo" (being punished for being related to somebody who committed an offense). Moreover, Emperor Renzong "ordered officials home and abroad to recommend talented people, but at the same time, the law of 'Ju Zhu Lian Zuo Fa' (the law on the punishment of recommending personnel when the recommended officials were found guilty) was strictly enforced."[137] During the reign of Emperor Hongwu, the talented people were "unconventionally recruited" by "Chao Qian" (the skip-level promotion) and "Te Zhuo" (special promotion). For example, Zhang Wan from Poyang took and passed the palace examination as

---

[131]"Kai Guo Gui Mo" (The Plan for the Founding of the State) in *Ming Shi Ji Shi Ben Mo* (*The Ins and Outs of the Records in the History of Ming Dynasty*), Vol. 14.

[132]"Xuan Ju Zhi" (The Record of Election) (Part 3) in *Ming Shi* (*The History of Ming Dynasty*).

[133]"Tai Zu Ji" (The Record of Emperor Taizu) (Part 2) in *Ming Shi* (*The History of Ming Dynasty*).

[134]"Tai Zu Ji" (The Record of Emperor Taizu) (Part 2) in *Ming Shi* (*The History of Ming Dynasty*).

[135]"Tai Zu Ji" (The Record of Emperor Taizu) (Part 2) in *Ming Shi* (*The History of Ming Dynasty*).

[136]"Tai Zu Ji" (The Record of Emperor Taizu) (Part 3) in *Ming Shi* (*The History of Ming Dynasty*).

[137]"Ren Zong Ji" (The Record of Emperor Renzong) in *Ming Shi* (*The History of Ming Dynasty*).

10.2 The Administrative Legislation for the Strengthening of Absolutism

"Gong Shi" (a successful candidate in the imperial examination at the metropolitan level) and was granted the official title of "Ji Shi Zhong" (the senior assistant of the emperor and the supervisor of officials). "One day, the Emperor asked him about the financial revenue income of the state and the number of registered households, he answered the questions correctly. The Emperor felt very happy, so immediately promoted him to the post of 'Zuo Shi Lang' (left vice minister)."[138] Huang Fu, who was an imperial college student and held the post of "Jin Wu Qian Wei" (one of the imperial guards), had submitted a memorial to the Emperor on important state plans, and "Emperor Taizu was amazed by him, so specially promoted him to 'You Shi Lang' (right vice minister) in 'Gong Bu' (The Department of Works)."[139]

During the reign of Emperor Jingtai, since there was not enough grass to feed the horses in the Xuanda area, "Juan Na" (donating food or money to buy an official position) was applied by the emperor in appointing officials, and those who donated 1500 *shu* (unit of weight) of grass would be selected as the candidate. During the reign of Emperor Chenghua, a system of appointing officials by donating grain was once established, but it was criticized by "Ji Shi Zhong" (the senior assistant of the emperor and the supervisor of officials) Wang Rui and other officials. In the 19th year of Chenghua (1483), Wang Rui pointed out: "Today, 'Xing Men' (the access to official career) is wide open, and it is like doing business in the market to sell ranks and titles ... so that the servants, the humble people, the businessmen and the children can all be promoted."[140] "Yu Shi" (the censor) Zhang Shi and others also exposed: "Recently, the low and humble people with inferior social status all wishfully hope to become senior officials, and the people of humble origins have all held the official position of 'Qing Yao' (senior official above the fifth rank). Some civil officials do not know a single word, and some military officers have never shot a single arrow ... In a day, dozens of people can get official positions, and in a department, hundreds of people can receive official salaries. So there has never been such a government decree since ancient times."[141] In the Ming Dynasty, people not only could get official positions by "Juan Na" (donating food or money to buy an official position) but also could enter "Guo Zi Jian" (the highest educational body in ancient China) by donating grain and money, which had led to the redundancy of officials and the corruption of officials.

In order to centralize the power over personnel in the central government, the system of "Ting Tui" (recommendation by the court) and "Bu Tui" (recommendation by the six departments) were implemented by the rulers of the Ming Dynasty. Officials like "Da Xue Shi" (grand secretary), "Li Bu Shang Shu" (the minister of the department of personnel), and "Shi Lang" (vice minister) in various departments, as well as "Zong Du" (viceroy) and "Xun Fu" (procurators), were all appointed through

---

[138]"Zhang Wan Zhuan" (The Biography of Zhang Wan) in *Ming Shi* (*The History of Ming Dynasty*).
[139]"Huang Fu Zhuan" (The Biography of Huang Fu) in *Ming Shi* (*The History of Ming Dynasty*).
[140]"Wang Rui Zhuan" (The Biography of Wang Rui) in *Ming Shi* (*The History of Ming Dynasty*).
[141]"Wang Rui Zhuan" (The Biography of Wang Rui) in *Ming Shi* (*The History of Ming Dynasty*).

"Ting Tui" (recommendation by the court), while officials below "Tai Chang Si Qing" (the head of "Tai Chang Si" in charge of imperial ceremonies and sacrifices) were usually appointed through "Bu Tui" (recommendation by the six departments). In the Ming Dynasty, when officials were appointed, their qualifications were often stressed, as was described in the saying that "the officials who are in charge of selecting officials should not make random comments on whether the candidates are virtuous or not, instead the candidates should be evaluated according to their qualifications."[142] Ye Xianggao in the Ming Dynasty had once commented on the change from stressing talents to stressing qualifications in selecting officials:

> From the reign of Emperor Hongwu to the reign of Emperor Yongle, the country was roughly in its early years, so all people had put to use what they were skilled in regardless where they came from. This is because at that time attention was paid only to people's talents rather than their qualifications. During the reign of Emperor Xuande, Zhengtong, Chenghua and Hongzhi, great achievements were made in culture and education, so people's social ranks and class were already well established. Those high level and trusted officials of royal families were mostly cultivated and courteous people who were selected through "Zhi Ke" (a special examination system, under which officials were recommended by ministers and then examined by the Emperor); those who had noble ambitions and special talents were also selected through other ways occasionally, and they had not met with opposition from the senior officials of the imperial courts. This is because at that time people were judged according to their qualifications rather then other qualities. Since the reign of Emperor Jiajing and Longqing, more and more importance was attached to "Zhi Ke" (a special examination system, where officials were selected through recommendation by ministers and examination held by the Emperor), so nine out of ten senior officials had been selected from "Ke Ju" (the imperial examination). Even if a person was of great ability and had extraordinary talents, he would mostly be restricted by his qualifications so he had no opportunity to show his ability and talents. This is because stricter qualifications were stipulated for officials, which had brought damage to the talented people ... Therefore, the country did not suffer from the lack of talented people, but rather from the restrictions on the talented people.[143]

In the Ming Dynasty, "Hui Bi Zhi Du" (the avoidance system) was carried out in appointing officials, which mainly included "Qin Zu Hui Bi" (kinship avoidance), "Ji Guan Hui Bi" (native place avoidance), and "Zhi Wu Hui Bi" (duty avoidance). With respect to "Zhi Wu Hui Bi" (duty avoidance), a decree was issued in the 1st year of Hongwu (1368): "Of all fathers, elder brothers and uncles who are senior officials in 'Liang Jing' (Beijing and Nanjing), those whose younger brothers, sons and nephews are 'Ke Dao Guan' [the officials in 'Ke' and 'Dao' (both government offices including the deaconry and the supervisory censor] shall be transferred to other posts of the same ranks." It was stipulated in another decree that "of the officials who are with supervisor-subordinate relationships in the government offices inside and outside the capital, if they have the relationship of father and son, brothers, and uncles and nephews, those with lower official ranks shall be transferred

---

[142]"Zhou Xu Zhuan" (The Biography of Zhou Xu) in *Ming Shi* (*The History of Ming Dynasty*).

[143]Ye Xianggao (Ming Dynasty), "San Tu Bing Yong Yi" (Proposal of Selecting Officials by Using Three Ways Simultaneously) in *Cang Xia Cao* (*Collected Poems and Essays by Ye Xianggao*), Vol. 2.

10.2 The Administrative Legislation for the Strengthening of Absolutism

to other posts for avoidance, which is approved by the Emperor in the 5th year of Wanli, so accordingly, the persons in lower positions shall be transferred to other posts according to the official ranking."[144] With respect to "Ji Guan Hui Bi" (native place avoidance), during the reign of Emperor Hongwu, the law on the rotation of officials in south and north was made to show admonishment. "Zhi Wu Hui Bi" (duty avoidance) included the avoidance of officials of "Hu Bu" (The Department of Revenue) and officials in other government offices such as supervision, imperial examination, and the judiciary, as well as officials within "Wu Fu" (the five government offices in ancient China). For example, it was stipulated that people in Zhejiang, Jiangxi, and Susong were not allowed to be officials in "Hu Bu" (The Department of Revenue), which was obviously a precautionary measure. In addition, it was forbidden for officials in "Wang Fu" (royal palace) "to be transferred to other places in all their lives."[145]

The gradual improvement of "Hui Bi Zhi Du" (the avoidance system) reflected the new development of the official administration in the Ming Dynasty.

As for "Kao Ke" (The Official Examination), it was divided into two categories: "Jing Cha" (the general assessment of officials in the capital) and "Wai Cha" (the general assessment of officials outside the capital). "Jing Cha" (the general assessment of officials in the capital) referred to the evaluation of the performance of officials in the capital. Accordingly, "the officials over 'Si Pin' (the fourth rank) made a personal statement first, so they were assessed by the Emperor himself, while the officials below 'Wu Pin' (the fifth rank) were assessed respectively according to 'Zhi Shi' (retirement), 'Jiang Diao' (demotion or transferring) and 'Xian Zhu Wei Min' (removed from office and living as civilians). Finally an official register was prepared and was presented to the Emperor for approval."[146] "Jing Cha" (the general assessment of officials in the capital) was held every six years, which referred to the evaluation of the performance of the officials outside the capital. "Accordingly, the officials in 'Zhou' (subprefecture) and 'Xian' (county) were assessed monthly with the evaluation results reported to 'Fu' (ancient administrative district between province and county), and the senior and junior officials in 'Fu' (ancient administrative district between province and county) were assessed annually with the evaluation results reported to 'Bu Zheng Si' (the government office in charge of civil affairs at the provincial level). In the third year, a general investigation on the real performance of the subordinate officials was carried out by 'Xun Fu' (procurators) and 'Ti Xing An Cha Shi' (the governmental official in charge of the administration of justice), and a complete report of the investigation results would be prepared and the unqualified officials would be punished according to 'Ba Fa' (eight

---

[144]"Li Bu" (The Department of Personnel) (Part 4) in *Da Ming Hui Dian* (*The Collected Statutes of Ming Dynasty*), Vol. 5.

[145]Shen Defu (Ming Dynasty), "Fan Guo Sui Feng Guan" (The Appointments of Officials in Vassal States) in *Wan Li Ye Huo Bian* (*A Privately Compiled History of the Reign of Wanli*), Vol. 4.

[146]"Xuan Ju Zhi" (The Record of Election) (Part 3) in *Ming Shi* (*The History of Ming Dynasty*).

standards)."[147] The so-called "Ba Fa" (eight standards) referred to the eight standards for evaluating officials: first, "Tan" (corruption); second, "Ku" (mercilessness); third, "Fu Zao" (fickleness); fourth, "Bu Ji" (lack of ability); fifth, "Lao" (old); sixth, "Bing" (illness); seventh, "Pi" (fatigue), and eighth, "Bu Jin" (imprudence). Whether the they were officials inside or outside the capital, they were firstly assessed three years after they took office; secondly, after six years; and, finally, after nine years. The completion of evaluation in each period was called "Kao Man" (the complete evaluation), and the results of the complete evaluation were divided into three levels, namely, "Shang" (excellent), "Zhong" (average), and "Xia" (poor). Accordingly, the officials' performance was divided into competent, average, and incompetent, according to which the officials were demoted or promoted. "Kao Ke" (The Official Examination) was conducted by "Li Bu" (The Department of Personnel), and "Li Bu Shang Shu" (the minister of the department of personnel) "was in charge of issuing government decrees which were relevant to the selection, appointment, awarding, and assessment of officials in the country to examine and select talents."[148] The subordinate "Kao Gong Si" (Bureau of Performance Evaluation) "was responsible for evaluating and inspecting the officials inside and outside the capital and supervising the affairs such as surveillance and recommendation."[149]

The evaluation system of the Ming Dynasty was very strict, but at the same time, relevant rules and regulations were also made, as was described in the saying that "the evaluation system of Ming Dynasty, which was established by following the examples of Tang Yao and Yu Shun in the remote ancient times, and by drawing on the experience of previous dynasties, was the most perfect."[150] Moreover, it was strictly implemented in the early Ming Dynasty. For example, in the 18th year of Hongwu (1385), "Li Bu" (The Department of Personnel) reported to the emperor that of all the 4117 government officials in "Bu Zheng Si" (the government office in charge of civil affairs at the provincial level), "Ti Xing An Cha Shi Si" (The Provincial Judicial Commission), "Fu" (ancient administrative district between province and county), "Zhou" (subprefecture), and "Xian" (county) across the country, those who were competent amounted to one tenth, those who were average amounted to seven tenths, those who were incompetent amounted to one tenth, and those who were corrupt, bad, and incompetent amounted to one tenth. The competent officials were promoted, the average ones resumed their posts, the incompetent ones were demoted, the corrupt ones were turned over to government offices to be punished by law, and the stupid ones were removed from office. If the results of evaluation were inappropriate, the relevant officials could defend for themselves; but

---

[147]"Xuan Ju Zhi" (The Record of Election) (Part 3) in *Ming Shi* (*The History of Ming Dynasty*).

[148]"Zhi Guan Zhi" (The Record of State Officials) (Part 1) in *Ming Shi* (*The History of Ming Dynasty*).

[149]"Li Bu" (The Department of Personnel) (Part 6) in *Da Ming Hui Dian* (*The Collected Statutes of Ming Dynasty*), Vol. 12.

[150]Sun Chengze (Ming Dynasty), "Kao Ke" (The Official Examination) in *Chun Ming Meng Yu Lu* (*The Record of the Capital Areas in Ming Dynasty*), Vol. 34.

10.2 The Administrative Legislation for the Strengthening of Absolutism

the authorities in charge would also be punished if their assessment was false. Moreover, those officials who were particularly outstanding in their performance could be exempted from the assessment. During the reign of Emperor Hongwu, since Zhang Dan, "Bu Zheng Si" (the government office in charge of civil affairs at the provincial level) of Yunnan, "was the best in his performance in the country, so he was exempted from the assessment according to the Emperor order which was specially issued to 'Li Bu' (The Department of Personnel)."[151] Li Zongxin was "Zhi Fu" (magistrate of a prefecture) of Baoning, and "a special edict was issued by the Emperor, and it was stated that Li Zongxin was a capable official, so he was exempted from the assessment."[152] The official who was removed from his office in "Jing Cha" (the general assessment of officials in the capital) could still resume his post, but the official who was removed from his office in "Da Ji" (the general examination of officials every three years) would no longer be appointed.

After the middle of the Ming Dynasty, many problems and malpractices existed in the assessment of officials, so it had become a mere formality. During the reign of Emperor Shenzong, the system was criticized by "Zuo Fu Du Yu Shi" (the left deputy of the court of censors) Shi Qiushun: "For example, when the final assessment of 'Jing Guan' (the official in the capital) was completed, all officials in Henan 'Dao' (the administration district below the province) were considered as competent; as for 'Gei You' (career records given by the former superior government office) for the officials outside the capital, they were all generally recommended to remain in office by 'Xun Fu' (procurators) and 'Ti Xing An Cha Shi' (the governmental official in charge of the administration of justice). So the regulations which were applied in examining and evaluating officials were just used as a method for officials to make deals with each other. Although they dared to practise favoritism, yet they did not dare to deal with the problems according to law, so that the evil officials were not punished nor the good ones rewarded or encouraged, which was one of the long-standing drawbacks of official assessment."[153]

The salaries of officials in the Ming Dynasty were paid in rice, banknotes, cloth, salt, and so on according to nine ranks and eighteen levels. In history, the Ming Dynasty was well known for its low salaries; for example, after the middle of the Ming Dynasty, rice was expensive and banknotes were cheap, so if banknotes were converted into rice, the salary for a "Zhi Xian" (the magistrate of a county) of "Qi Pin" (the seventh rank) was less than two *liang* of silver. As a result of low salaries for officials, it became a social occurrence at that time for high-ranking officials to become rich by corruption and the minor officials to get rid of poverty by engaging in malpractices. In feudal times, official corruption was determined by the nature of the regime itself, but low salary might be one of the reasons.

As for the retirement of officials, according to an imperial edict issued in the 1st year of Hongwu (1368), officials should retire at seventy to improve the efficiency of

---

[151] "Zhang Dan Zhuan" (The Biography of Zhang Dan) in *Ming Shi* (*The History of Ming Dynasty*).
[152] *Gu Jin Tu Shu Ji Cheng* (*A Complete Collection of Ancient and Modern Books*), Vol. 599.
[153] "Qiu Shun Zhuan" (The Biography of Qiu Shun) in *Ming Shi* (*The History of Ming Dynasty*).

national administration. In the 13th year of Hongwu (1380), the rule was changed, and it was stipulated that "the civil and military officials aged over sixty are allowed to retire, and at the same time, 'Gao Chi' (certificates of appointment) should be granted to them."[154] In the 4th year of Hongzhi during the reign of Emperor Xiaozong (1491), it was also stipulated that "of the officials who retire from old age and illness, those aged over fifty five shall retire in official ceremonial dresses; those aged below fifty five shall be removed from office and stay at home; ... those aged over sixty five shall not be recruited any more."[155] Moreover, officials retired not simply of old age. For example, officials who needed to go back home to care for their parents were also allowed to retire, which was called "Gui Yang" (going back home to care for parents). As for "the officials who could not hold office due to old age and illness," they should be forced to retire any time. As for retirement of officials, they were granted land or salary or both. Some retired officials were even granted servants. For example, in the early period of Chenghua, when "Hu Bu Shang Shu" (the minister of the department of revenue) Yang Ding retired, he was granted two *dan* of rice every month, and four servants each year. Moreover, it was forbidden for the retired officials to remain in the capital and in the place where they had worked in order to prevent the retired officials from colluding with the incumbent officials inside and outside of the capital. In order to encourage officials to return home after retirement, they were allowed to be transported home using official vehicles and were received by government offices on the way home.

10.2.3 The Change of the Supervisory System and Enriching of Supervision Law

To meet the need of strengthening the autocratic monarchy, the supervisory organ, which had acted as the disciplinary department and the "eyes and ears of the Emperor," was further improved, both in status and in function and power. Emperor Taizu once pointed out that "three important 'Fu' (government office) have been established by the state: 'Zhong Shu Sheng' (the supreme organization in charge of the state affairs) is in full charge of government affairs, 'Du Du Fu' (Offices of Military Affairs) is in full charge of military affairs, and 'Yu Shi Tai' (The Censorate) is in full charge of inspection, on which the disciplines and laws of the imperial court completely depended; so the supervisory responsibilities of 'Yu Shi Tai' (The Censorate) were especially important."[156]

---

[154]"Tai Zu Ji" (The Record of Emperor Taizu) (Part 2) in *Ming Shi* (*The History of Ming Dynasty*).

[155]"Li Bu" (The Department of Personnel) (Part 7) in *Da Ming Hui Dian* (*The Collected Statutes of Ming Dynasty*), Vol. 13.

[156]"Zhi Guan Zhi" (The Record of State Officials) (Part 2) in *Ming Shi* (*The History of Ming Dynasty*).

10.2 The Administrative Legislation for the Strengthening of Absolutism

In the early Ming Dynasty, as far as the supervisory organs were concerned, the old systems of the Tang and Song dynasties were followed, so "Yu Shi Tai" (The Censorate) was established in the central government. In the 15th year of Hongwu (1382), the supervisory organ was expanded, and "Yu Shi Tai" (The Censorate) was changed to "Du Cha Yuan" (The Court of Censors), which was also called "Feng Xian Ya Men" (the government office in charge of disciplines and laws)[157] and which was put in charge of "impeaching the various government offices, rectifying the unjust sentences, and investigating and inspecting the officials in 'Dao' (the administration district below the province) ... As to the serious cases and felonies ... they would be settled fairly by 'Xing Bu' (The Department of Punishment) and 'Da Li Si' (The Bureau of Judicial Review)."[158] "Du Cha Yuan" (The Court of Censors) was headed by "Zuo You Du Yu Shi" (the chief and deputy of the court of censors), with "Zuo You Fu Du Yu Shi" (the left and right deputy of the court of censors) and "Zuo You Qian Du Yu Shi" (the chief and deputy assistant of the court of censors) as their subordinates. In the 10th year of Emperor Xuande (1435), according to the provincial system at that time, an additional thirteen "Dao" (administration districts below the province) were established, with one hundred and ten "Jian Cha Yu Shi" (supervisory censors) appointed, who were respectively in charge of capital and local supervision. In order to "investigate and rectify the malpractices of officials inside and outside the capital," "Jian Cha Yu Shi" (the supervisory censor) was often sent to make inspection tours of the local authorities. Besides, "Xun An Yu Shi" (the inspecting censor) was in charge of investigating local officials to see whether they had ruthlessly persecuted the common people or whether they were disloyal to the emperor or whether they were in line with the requirements of imperial decrees; therefore, they were granted great power. Moreover, "'Xun An Yu Shi' (the inspecting censor) was also in charge of inspecting and supervising 'Fan Fu Da Cheng' (ministers in remote regions) as well as the officials in 'Fu' (ancient administrative district between province and county), 'Zhou' (subprefecture) and 'Xian' (county). Those corrupt officials would be impeached, the important matters would be reported to the Emperor for final decision, while the minor matters would be handled immediately by them without authorization."[159] So they had played an important role in maintaining the legal system and in rectifying the system of managing officials. It was stated in "Xun Li Zhuan" (The Biography of Excellent Officials) in *Ming Shi* (*The History of Ming Dynasty*) that "'Shou Ling' (prefects or magistrates) was in fear of the laws," so "the official management remained honest and upright for more than one hundred years." In the middle of the Ming Dynasty, He Qiyuan especially pointed out: "No dynasties have ever paid

---

[157]"Du Cha Yuan" (The Court of Censors) (Part 1) in *Da Ming Hui Dian* (*The Collected Statutes of Ming Dynasty*), Vol. 290.
[158]"Zhi Guan Zhi" (The Record of State Officials) (Part 2) in *Ming Shi* (*The History of Ming Dynasty*).
[159]"Zhi Guan Zhi" (The Record of State Officials) (Part 2) in *Ming Shi* (*The History of Ming Dynasty*).

more attention to supervision than our times."[160] Even Emperor Shizong believed that "it all depends on 'Xun An Yu Shi' (the inspecting censor) whether the common people live a happy life, or whether the official management is good or not."[161] Since "Xun An Yu Shi" (the inspecting censor) often made inspection tours on behalf of the emperor, their status was equal to that of provincial governors, so even "Zhi Fu" (magistrate of a prefecture) and "Zhi Xian" (the magistrate of a county) would have the ritual of prostration ceremony when visiting them. However, their great power also made it convenient for them to obtain personal gains by abusing their power. Early in the era of Emperor Chengzu, minister Liang Tingdong submitted a memorial to the emperor and stated that "Xun An Yu Shi" (the inspecting censor) claimed to interrogate, examine, investigate, and punish corrupt officials, but wherever they went, they would be bribed by the officials with 20,000 to 30,000 *liang* of silver. Thus, if one more "Xun An Yu Shi" (the inspecting censor) was appointed in the country, the burden of paying one million *liang* of silver would be passed on to the people. After the middle of the Ming Dynasty, it became more rampant for "Xun An Yu Shi" (inspecting censors) to abuse their power.

When "Du Yu Shi" (the head of the court of censors) made inspection tours, they were often especially ordered by the emperor to be in charge of other affairs concurrently; those who were concurrently in charge of administrative and civil affairs were called "Xun Fu" (procurators), those who were concurrently in charge of military affairs were called "'Ti Du' (military commander)," and those who were concurrently in charge of administrative, financial, and military affairs were called "Zong Du" (viceroy). At first, "Zong Du" (viceroy) and "Xun Fu" (procurators) were only temporary official positions, then during the reign of Emperor Jiajing, in order to strengthen the suppression home and resist foreign aggressions abroad, they became permanent positions in the inland or border areas. "Zong Du" (viceroy) and "Xun Fu" (procurators) were far more powerful than "Xun An Yu Shi" (the inspecting censor), and they had the right to "take actions according to the concrete circumstances." But "Xun Fu" (procurators) and "Ti Xing An Cha Shi" (the governmental official in charge of the administration of justice) both had supervisory power, so in the middle of the Ming Dynasty, the struggle between "Xun Fu" (procurators) and "Ti Xing An Cha Shi" (the governmental official in charge of the administration of justice) became increasingly more intense due to their overlapping power.

In addition to supervisory power, "Du Cha Yuan" (The Court of Censors) was also endowed with judicial power over major cases, military supervisory power to dispatch "Yu Shi" (the censor) in wartime, and the power to inspect specific matters. However, generally, the official rank of "Yu Shi" (the censor) was only "Zheng Qi Pin" (the principal seventh rank), but they were very powerful just because they were dispatched by the emperor himself to act as his eyes and ears. Since the activities of

---

[160] Wang Qi (Ming Dynasty), "Zhi Guan Kao" (An Examination of State Officials) in *Xu Wen Xian Tong Kao* (*A Sequel of the General Textual Research of the Documents*), Vol. 89.

[161] *Ming Shi Zong Shi Lu* (*The Record of Emperor Shizong of Ming Dynasty*), Vol. 248.

"Yu Shi" (the censor) were necessary to maintain the normal operation of the country, their selection was very strict. As usual, they must be "Jin Shi" (those who passed the imperial examination at the national level in ancient China) or "Ju Ren" (those who passed the imperial examination at the provincial level in ancient China). Emperor Chengzu had once said to the officials of "Li Bu" (The Department of Personnel): "'Yu Shi' (censors) are the eyes and ears of the imperial court, so it is appropriate to recruit officials who are not only knowledgeable, but also familiar with the principles of governing the state."[162] Moreover, they also needed to be selected through examination, and they had to be employed on probation before they were formally appointed. If "Yu Shi" (the censor) had committed crimes, their punishment would be three times severer than those for the common people; if they had committed bribery, they would be given a much severer punishment; if they had conducted investigation of the cases but failed to report them within the prescribed time limit, they would be interrogated and punished by law. In the era of Emperor Xuanzong, Shao Qi was in charge of the work of "Du Cha Yuan" (The Court of Censors), so "he was ordered to have an investigation of 'Yu Shi' (censors), finally, more than twenty of them were demoted or removed from office due to their incompetence."[163]

In addition to the system of "Du Cha Yuan" (The Court of Censors), the organization of "Liu Ke" (the six offices), which was given independent supervisory power, was established. In the 15th year of Hongwu (1382), "Zhong Shu Sheng" (the supreme organization in charge of state affairs) was abolished. So after the status of "Liu Bu" (The Six Departments) was raised, in order to supervise their activities, the original "Jian Guan" (supervisor) was abolished, and its power was given to "Ji Shi Zhong" (the senior assistant of the emperor and the supervisor of officials). Meanwhile, the system of independent supervisory organs of "Liu Ke Ji Shi Zhong" (the supervisor of the six offices) was created. The so-called "Liu Ke" (the six offices) included "Li Ke" (the office of personnel), "Hu Ke" (the office of revenue), "Li Ke" (the office of rites), "Bing Ke" (the office of defense), "Xing Ke" (the office of punishment), and "Gong Ke" (the office of works), and in each office there was one "Ji Shi Zhong" (the senior assistant of the emperor and the supervisor of officials), one "Zuo Du Ji Shi Zhong" (the chief supervisor), and one "You Du Ji Shi Zhong" (the deputy supervisor), who were mainly in charge of supervising the officials in "Liu Bu" (The Six Departments), as was described in the records that "they were in charge of attending upon the Emperor, putting forward advice, rectifying the Emperor's behaviors, taking supplementary measures and supervising the officials of 'Liu Bu' (The Six Departments)."[164] All matters that were reported to the emperor

---

[162]"Zhi Guan" (State Official) (Part 5) in *Ming Hui Yao* (*Collections of Historical Records in Ming Dynasty*), Vol. 33.

[163]Huang Yu (Ming Dynasty), "Du Tang Xian Zhao" (Forshadow for the Headquarter) in *Shuang Huai Sui Chao* (*Historical Notes by Huang Yu*), Vol. 4.

[164]"Zhi Guan Zhi" (The Record of State Officials) (Part 3) in *Ming Shi* (*The History of Ming Dynasty*).

by "Liu Bu" (The Six Departments) should first be reviewed by "Ji Shi Zhong" (the senior assistant of the emperor and the supervisor of officials), and the matters could be rejected when considered inappropriate. The matters that "Liu Bu" (The Six Departments) carried out according to imperial orders should also be registered at the office of "Ji Shi Zhong" (the senior assistant of the emperor and the supervisor of officials) to make it more convenient to check their implementation. The establishment of "Liu Ke Ji Shi Zhong" (the supervisor of the six offices) had a restrictive function on "Liu Bu" (The Six Departments), whose status and authority were already greatly strengthened. At the same time, it had also shared the supervisory power of "Du Cha Yuan" (The Court of Censors). Although there was a certain division of work between "Du Cha Yuan" (The Court of Censors) and "Liu Ke Ji Shi Zhong" (the supervisor of the six offices), the division was not absolute because they could impeach and inform against each other to make it easier for the emperor to control them. In the exercise of power, "Ji Shi Zhong" (the senior assistant of the emperor and the supervisor of officials) often drew wrong conclusions by mistaking trivial things for major ones with false analogy, which had led to a lot of miscarriages of justice. So although overlapping supervisory organs were set up in the Ming Dynasty, honesty and uprightness in the management of officials had not been maintained because of the nature of the feudal supervision system.

"Tong Zheng Shi Si" (The Transmission Office), established in the 10th year of Hongwu (1377), had a specific function of remonstration. Emperor Taizu once made a clear statement on the necessity of establishing "Tong Zheng Shi Si" (The Transmission Office), and he further explained its function:

> Government affairs are like water, so they are expected to flow smoothly, that is why the government officials are called "Tong Zheng" (efficient administration), because the minister in charge is required to carry out the decrees and to supervise other officials so that all government orders can be transmitted everywhere unimpeded. Therefore, the officials who are in charge of submitting memorials to the emperor shall speak frankly; the officials who are in charge of rectifying the malpractices shall not curry favour with any officials in their evil deeds; the officials who are in charge of giving detailed accounts shall not conceal any facts, and the officials who are in charge of recommending people to the Emperor shall not obstruct.[165]

According to *Da Ming Hui Dian* (*The Collected Statutes of Ming Dynasty*), "Tong Zheng Shi Si" (The Transmission Office) had the following function and power: "to convey the Emperor's orders, to report the opinions of his subjects, to ensure the transmission of official documents in government offices, to submit all memorials nationwide to the emperor, to pass on people's advice and suggestions to the emperor, and to give a full account of the matters such as complaint, military information, natural disaster and extraordinary natural phenomenon."[166] But after

---

[165]"Zhi Guan Zhi" (The Record of State Officials) (Part 2) in *Ming Shi* (*The History of Ming Dynasty*).

[166]"Tong Zheng Shi Si" (The Transmission Office) in *Da Ming Hui Dian* (*The Collected Statutes of Ming Dynasty*), Vol. 212.

10.2 The Administrative Legislation for the Strengthening of Absolutism

the middle of the Ming Dynasty, eunuchs were in charge of delivering imperial orders and passing on messages, so "Tong Zheng Shi Si" (The Transmission Office) existed only in name, and it was eventually abolished during the reign of Emperor Shenzong.

"Ti Xing An Cha Shi Si" (The Provincial Judicial Commission) was the local supervisory organ, which was also called "Xing Zai Du Cha Yuan" (The Provincial Court of Censors) or "Wai Tai" (The Outside Censorates). They were "in charge of the punishment, the impeachment and other affairs in the province. Moreover, they were also in charge of rectifying the malpractices of officials, punishing evil and ferocious persons, settling lawsuits, and redressing the miscarriages of justice so as to uphold the discipline and to rectify official management."[167] "Ti Xing An Cha Shi" (the governmental official in charge of the administration of justice) was put in charge of the following duties: "to tour around the country, to patrol around and inspect social customs, to transmit the imperial decrees, to investigate the suffering of the common people, and to promote and demote officials according to their performance"; they were given great power to act independently, so they were often called "the guardian of the guiding principle of the country."[168] After the middle of the Ming Dynasty, eunuchs usurped the power; local supervisory activities were under the jurisdiction of eunuchs, and government officials were under the supervision of domestic servants of the emperor, which indicated that there were nothing left for "Gang Ji" (social order and law), "Li" (rites) and "Fa" (law).

In the Ming Dynasty, not only a system of supervisory organ was established from the central to the local government, but a more comprehensive supervision law was also formulated so as to confirm the power and function of the supervisory organs and the procedures for their activities to ensure the exercise of supervisory rights. In the 26th year of Hongwu (1393), on the basis of the implementation of the policy of managing officials with harsh punishment, supervisory laws and regulations were formulated successively, among which *Xian Gang Zong Li* (*The General Legal Regulations*) was a representative. In *Xian Gang Zong Li* (*The General Legal Regulations*), only several separate provisions were included, so in the 4th year of Zhengtong (1439), they were amended and expanded into a large-scale fundamental supervision law consisting of fifteen sections altogether, including "Xian Gang Zong Li" (the general legal regulations), "Du Fu Jian Zhi" (the appointment of viceroys and procurators), "Ge Dao Fen Li" (the separate jurisdiction of each "Dao" (the administration district below the province)), "Jiu He Guan Xie" (rectifying and impeaching the malpractices of officials), "Kao Fu Bai Guan" (inspecting and examination of officials), "Ji Que Xuan Yong" (selection of officials to fill an urgent vacancy), "Zou Qing Dian Chai" (reporting to the emperor for the appointment of officials), "Chu Xun Shi Yi" (matters involving the tours of inspection), "Zhao Shua

---

[167]"Zhi Guan Zhi" (The Record of State Officials) (Part 4) in *Ming Shi* (*The History of Ming Dynasty*).
[168]Sun Chengze (Ming Dynasty), "Du Cha Yuan" (The Court of Censors) in *Chun Ming Meng Yu Lu* (*The Record of the Capital Areas in Ming Dynasty*), Vol. 48.

Wen Juan" (checking official documents), "Hui Dao Kao Cha" (inspecting officials in "Dao" (the administration district below the province)), "Wen Ni Xing Ming" (interrogation and conviction of criminals), "Zhui Wen Gong Shi" (inquiring about official business), "Shen Lu Zui Qiu" (trying criminals), "Jian Li Jiu Yi" (supervising and rectifying rites and ceremonies), and "Fu An Tong Li" (the general rules for imperial inspectors and the provincial surveillance commissioners).

In the 26th year of Hongwu (1393), *Jiu He Guan Xie Gui Ding* (*Provisions for Rectifying and Impeaching the Malpractices of Officials*) was also formulated, in which the four provisions of "Du Cha Yuan" (The Court of Censors) were stipulated in detail for the punishment of civil and military officials for their malpractices:

> Of all the civil and military officials, those who prove to be treacherous villains, who gang up to be engaged in evil doings, who tyrannically abuse their powers or bring disorder to the political affairs of the imperial court so that imperial benevolence can not be transmitted to the common people and natural disasters and extraordinary natural phenomena may occur repeatedly shall all be reported to the Emperor and be impeached, regardless of their power and wealth, as long as the above mentioned malpractices are proved to be true.
>
> Of all the officials of all ranks, those who are incompetent, or who are of low quality, or who are inefficient in government administration but who are wantonly greedy without abiding the law, shall all be immediately impeached and punished.
>
> Of all the officials outside the capital, those who disturb and harass the kind and honest people, who break law by taking bribery so that fields are left uncultivated, and the common people suffer, shall all be reported to the Emperor for inquisition after it has proved to be true.
>
> Of all the officials committing academic misconducts, those who present a written statement to the Emperor to ask to be selected and appointed by changing the established law, or those who are of low talent and morality but who come forward to recommend themselves, shall all be immediately impeached and punished to guard against officials' pursuit of fame and fortune.[169]

In the same year, other laws were also made, including *Tong Zheng Shi Si Dian Zhang* (*The Statutes of the Transmission Office*) (General Rules), which consisted of five articles and eleven provisions; "Shi Li" (precedents), which consisted of six articles; the general rules of *Liu Ke Ji Shi Zhong* (the supervisor of the six offices), which consisted of thirty six articles; and "Shi Li" (precedents) for other departments; which consisted of one hundred and thirty seven articles. In the general rules, the scope of duties was stipulated, and in "Shi Li" (precedents), the working rules were listed in detail. In addition, in *Ze Ren Tiao Li* (*Regulations on Responsibilities*), which was enacted during the reign of Emperor Hongwu, the responsibilities of government offices at all levels, from "Li Jia" (social organizations at the grassroots level) to "Xian" (county), "Zhou" (subprefecture), "Fu" (ancient administrative district between province and county), and "Bu Zheng Si" (the government office in charge of civil affairs at the provincial level), were stipulated, which were all the legal bases for "Xun An Yu Shi" (the inspecting censor) to supervise the local

---

[169]"Du Cha Yuan" (The Court of Censors) (Part 1) in *Da Ming Hui Dian* (*The Collected Statutes of Ming Dynasty*), Vol. 290.

10.2 The Administrative Legislation for the Strengthening of Absolutism

officials. If they had colluded with each other to indulge in corrupt practices, they would be investigated and punished with no exception.

In the 26th year of Hongwu (1393), *Chu Xun Shi Yi (Matters Concerning the Tours of Inspection)* was also made especially for "Jian Cha Yu Shi" (the supervisory censor) who were sent to conduct inspection tours. The law consisted of twenty seven articles, which covered a wide range of supervisory matters, such as tax and corvee, the registration of households, litigation, farmland, road, military supply, schools, courier stations, weights and measures, etc. But it mainly focused on the regulation of "Jian Cha Yu Shi" (the supervisory censor). For example, "after 'Jian Cha Yu Shi' (the supervisory censor) arrive at their inspection areas, they shall first interrogate the prisoners and check case files; if they still have spare time, they shall first go to the sacrificial altars to check whether the sacrificial utensils and houses are complete or in good condition. Then they shall visit and give relief to the old and orphan and inquire whether they have been distributed food and clothing. Besides, they shall go around to inspect the warehouses to check whether there are deficits for land tax; to encourage school education and to examine students to see whether they have achieved good results. In this process, as long as it is discovered that there are fraud and deception, those involved shall be immediately investigated and punished in accordance with the law." For the accepted lawsuits involving officials, if the officials belonged to local "Xian" (county), the cases should be heard by "Fu" (ancient administrative district between province and county); if the officials belonged to "Fu" (ancient administrative district between province and county), the cases should be heard by "Bu Zheng Si" (the government office in charge of civil affairs at the provincial level); if the officials belonged to "Bu Zheng Si" (the government office in charge of civil affairs at the provincial level), the cases should be heard by "An Cha Si" (The Judicial Commission). "If the lawsuits involved the officials of 'An Cha Si' (The Judicial Commission), or the complaints are about the wrongful convictions and the other malpractices conducted by the officials of government office, it is forbidden for 'Jian Cha Yu Shi' (the supervisory censor) to entrust the cases to other government offices, and the cases should be heard by themselves in person,"[170] from which we can see the great power of "Jian Cha Yu Shi" (the supervisory censor).

In addition, *Xun Fu Liu Cha (Six Inspection Tasks for Procurators)* was made, which included "Qing Li Zhi" (rectifying official management), "Cheng Dao Zei" (enforcing punishment on thieves and robbers), "Su Bian Zheng" (rectifying the administration in border areas), "Xu Zai Li" (offering relief to people in poverty-stricken areas), "Jin Qi Lao" (showing respect to the aged people), and "Bian Ren Min" (making people's life more convenient). Meanwhile, *Xun Fu Qi Cha (Seven Inspection Tasks for Procurators)* was also made, which included "Xue Yuan Yu" (redressing the miscarriages of justice), "Qing Jun Yi" (rectifying military affairs), "Zheng Guan Feng" (rectifying officials' working style), "He Guan Jian"

---

[170]"Du Cha Yuan" (The Court of Censors) (Part 2) in *Da Ming Hui Dian (The Collected Statutes of Ming Dynasty)*, Vol. 210.

(impeaching the evil officials), "Qing Shu Li" (strengthening the management of subordinate officials), "Zheng Fa Ji" (rectifying the law and discipline), and "Su Dao Fei" (eliminating thieves and robbers). Whether six tasks or seven tasks, the focus was on rectifying the system for managing officials, which was the general strategy for ruling the state in the early Ming Dynasty; "Xun Fu" (procurators) and "Xun An" (inspector) were both responsible for this special mission.

Due to the high position and great power of the supervision officials, restrictive laws and regulations were also made for them, such as *Jian Guan Zun Shou Liu Kuan* (*Six Provisions for Supervisory Officials*), *Jian Ji Jiu Kuan* (*Nine Supervisory Disciplines*), and *Man Ri Zao Bao Ce Shi* (*The Format for the Reports Made on Man Ri* (one of the 12th day of the zodiac)). It was stipulated that supervision officials should not "cling to the habitual ways and muddle along, nor to neglect their duties"; "they should not against the common interests of the public for their personal gains"; they should be "careful and prudent" in trying cases and "upright, serious, impartial, hard-working, cautious and discreet" in their conducts; wherever they go, they should "conform to reason and abide by law"; they should "take precautions against gossiping"; they should not "entrust official business" to local officials; they should recommend the virtuous people immediately if they got to know them, arrest the evil people immediately if they saw them, correct mistakes immediately if they found them; report the advantages and disadvantages immediately if they have discovered them. Besides, promotion and demotion should be made according to evidence.[171]

To sum up, the foundation for the supervision law of the Ming Dynasty was laid down during the reign of Emperor Taizu, which was inseparable from Zhu Yuanzhang's ideology of strict official management. With repeated revisions made during the reign of emperors Chengzu, Renzong, and Xuanzong till the 4th year of Zhengtong (1439), *Xian Gang Tiao Li* (*Legal Regulations*) had reached a "very perfect" degree with "regulations listed separately according to categories."[172] When *Da Ming Hui Dian* (*The Collected Statutes of Ming Dynasty*) was compiled during the reign of Emperor Xiaozong, the duties and "Shi Li" (precedents) of the supervisory organs were included first, but in *Wan Li Chong Xiu Hui Dian* (*The Collected Statutes Revised in the Reign of Wanli*), as many as five regulations concerning supervision and remonstration were already included. Among the feudal supervision laws, the one made in the Ming Dynasty was relatively more comprehensive, which was the inheritance and development of the supervision laws of the Han, Tang, Song, and Yuan dynasties; meanwhile, it had also provided an important historical source for the supervisory legislation in the Qing Dynasty. Since laws were made for supervisory organs and rules were made for the supervisory officials, it had played the role of rectifying the malpractice of officials. For example, in the 9th year of Hongwu (1376), "Yu Shi Da Fu" (Grand Censor) Wang Guangyang and Chen Ning

---

[171]"Du Cha Yuan" (The Court of Censors) (Part 2) in *Da Ming Hui Dian* (*The Collected Statutes of Ming Dynasty*), Vol. 210.

[172]"Du Cha Yuan" (The Court of Censors) (Part 1) in *Da Ming Hui Dian* (*The Collected Statutes of Ming Dynasty*), Vol. 290.

informed against the malpractice of "Cheng Xiang" (the prime minister) Li Shanchang, so both Li Shanchang and his son were removed from their offices and were punished; in the 14th year of Yongle (1416), "Yu Shi" (the censor) Liu Guan made a report to the emperor and said that Gu Wangsui was incompetent and brutal, so Gu Wangsui was removed from his office; in the 19th year of Chenghua (1483), "Yu Shi" (the censor) Xu Yong and other officials informed against eunuch Wang Zhi for his crimes, so Wang Zhi was removed from his office. However, since Emperor Wuzong, constant power struggle occurred among the supervisory officials, eunuchs, and powerful ministers, so some supervisory officials were even flogged to death or were forced to retire because they had reported the evildoing of eunuch Liu Jin to the emperor, which had fully shown the great power of eunuchs. It is worth mentioning that in the 35th year of Jiajing (1556), "Yu Shi" (the censor) Zou Yinglong had submitted a memorial about the evildoing of Yan Song and his son to the emperor, which was finally approved, so that the father and son of the Yan family were severely punished. Gu Yanwu spoke highly of the supervisory officials in the Ming Dynasty in his book *Ri Zhi Lu* (*The Record of Daily Reading*), and he thought that although the state was troubled by domestic turmoil and foreign aggression and treacherous ministers and powerful eunuchs had acted outrageously and ferociously since the mid-Ming Dynasty, there was still no sign of the collapse of the Ming dynasty. One of the reasons was that the supervisory system was still playing an important role at the time.[173]

10.3 Criminal Law Reflecting the Thoughts of Ruling the Country with Severe Penalties

In the Ming Dynasty, which was in the late period of feudal society, class contradiction was extremely sharp and complicated. Therefore, in the process of carrying out the extremely autocratic ruling, there appeared extralegal crimes and penalties. As far as the enforcement of the criminal law was concerned, in most cases, the punishment for those who seriously jeopardized the country and society was particularly severe. Emperor Zhu Yuanzhang once said: "Since Yuan Dynasty perished because of its mitigated penalties, severe ones must be applied to rule China effectively."[174]

---

[173]Gu Yanwu (Ming Dynasty), *Ri Zhi Lu* (*The Record of Daily Reading*), Vol. 9.
[174]Liu Ji (Ming Dynasty), "Huang Di Shou Shu" (The Emperor's Calligraph) in *Cheng Yi Bo Wen Ji* (*The Collections of Cheng Yibo*), Vol. 1.

10.3.1 The Ideology of "Bringing Order Out of the Troubled Times by Enforcing Severe Penalties"[175] and Its Influence on the Legislation of Criminal Law

10.3.1.1 Expanding the Scope of Punishment for Those Involved in the Crime of "Fan Ni" (Treachery)

In accordance with *Ming Lv* (*Ming Code*), "Mou Fan" (plotting rebellion or plotting to endanger the country) and "Mou Da Ni" (great sedition) were interpreted as the most serious crimes, so the principle of enforcing severe punishment for serious crimes was adopted. According to *Tang Lv* (*Tang Code*), those who had committed the crime of "Fan Ni" (treachery) would be all punished by "Zhan" (beheading), with their fathers and sons who were over sixteen years old punished by "Jiao" (hanging) and with other people such as sons under fifteen years old, mothers, daughters, wives, concubines, grandparents, grandchildren, brothers, uncles, nephews, and the disabled exempted from death penalty. However, according to *Ming Lv* (*Ming Code*), not only criminals themselves would be punished by "Ling Chi" (the punishment of dismemberment and lingering death), but their male relatives over sixteen, such as grandfathers, fathers, sons, grandsons, brothers, uncles, and nephews, as well as those with different family names who lived together with them, such as maternal grandfathers, fathers-in-law, sons-in-law, and servants, would also be all punished by "Zhan" (beheading), whether they were from the same places or whether they were "Fei Ji" (the disabled) and "Du Ji" (the incapacitated). Meanwhile, in *Tang Lv* (*Tang Code*), the punishment for those who committed the same crime under different circumstances was also different. For example, "the criminals who were not eloquent enough to instigate the others or who were not powerful enough to lead the others" would be punished by "Zhan" (beheading), with his father and son exempted from death penalty, without his grandfather and grandsons being implicated. As another example, if the criminal only "talked about treason but had not put it into practice," he would only be punished by "Liu" (exile) to places 2000 *li* away. But according to *Ming Lv* (*Ming Code*), the circumstantial differences were totally ignored, so the criminals were brutally punished. For those who knew the details of a case but who concealed or refused to report them to the government, they would be punished by "Jiao" (hanging) according to *Tang Lv* (*Tang Code*) but would be punished by "Zhan" (beheading) according to *Ming Lv* (*Ming Code*). Generally, if a criminal act was committed by one person or if many people were involved in the act, usually dozens of people or even three, nine, or ten of the generations of the clans would be punished, which sometimes might lead to the ruin of the whole village. At the time of intensifying the punishment, in order to disintegrate the forces of the rebels, it was stipulated in *Ming Lv* (*Ming Code*) that "for those who can catch the criminals of 'Mou Fan' (plotting

---

[175]"Xing Fa Zhi" (The Record of the Criminal Law) (Part 1) in *Ming Shi* (*The History of Ming Dynasty*).

rebellion or plotting to endanger the country) and 'Mou Da Ni' (great sedition), if they were ordinary people, they would be appointed government officials; if they were soldiers, they would be appointed army officers, with all the property of the criminals confiscated and awarded to them; for those who knew the details of a case and who reported them to the government, if the criminals were arrested by the government officials, they would only be awarded the property which was confiscated."[176]

Besides, the scope of "Shi E" (The Ten Abominations) was also expanded in *Ming Lv* (*Ming Code*). So if a person killed "Zhi Xian" (magistrate of a county) of the local county or "Zhi Zhou" (subprefectural magistrates) or "Zhi Fu" (magistrate of a prefecture) or if a soldier killed "Bai Hu" (official in charge of 100 families), "Qian Hu" (official in charge of 1000 families), or "Zhi Hui" (general), then he would be accused of the crime of "Bu Yi" (injustice) in "Shi E" (Ten Abominations) and be sentenced to death penalty.

10.3.1.2 Enforcing Severe Punishment on Subordinate Officials Forming Cliques and Officials Inside and Outside the Capital Colluding with Each Other

Considering that officials of the previous dynasties often formed different cliques, which had weakened the power of the emperor and had led to riots and the downfall of a nation in the end, the formation of cliques was strictly prohibited by Zhu Yuanzhang, so it was the first time for the crime of "Jian Dang" (treacherous cliques) to be included in *Da Ming Lv* (*The Great Ming Code*), which was not a feature of the criminal laws of the previous dynasties, including the Han, Tang, Song and Yuan dynasties. It was stipulated that "if officials bring disorder to the affairs of the state by forming treacherous cliques, they shall be punished by 'Zhan' (beheading) with their wives degraded to slaves and with all their properties confiscated"; "if the criminals are punishable by death penalty in accordance with law, but if the officials tried to help him by persuading other officials to have him exempted from death penalty or to secretly win others support, they shall also be punished by 'Zhan' (beheading)"; "if the officials at all levels in 'Xing Bu' (The Department of Punishment) or 'Ya Men' (the government offices) have settled the case by "Gu Chu Ru Ren Zui" (to deliberately increase or reduce the punishment when making sentences) instead of abiding by law by blindly following their superiors' orders, they shall be punished for the same crime." Moreover, "those who instigate the emperor to make false charges against or kill someone" would be regarded as a member of "Jian Dang" (treacherous cliques), so they would be punished by "Zhan" (beheading). Moreover, the emperor had the exclusive power to appoint state officials in order to prevent them from forming cliques by recommending someone else privately; "if the

---

[176]"Zei Dao" (Stealing and Robbery) in "Xing Lv" (The Penal Code) in *Da Ming Lv* (*The Great Ming Code*).

ministers had appointed officials without authorization, they shall be punished by 'Zhan' (beheading)." In addition, "the relatives of ministers are not allowed to be granted official positions unless they have got special permission," and those who violated this rule would also be punished by "Zhan" (beheading). Even the officials of "Ya Men" (the government offices) and the common people "who have praised the excellent governance and virtues of the ministers are regarded as members of 'Jian Dang' (treacherous cliques), so thorough inquiry should be made about the cause and effect; thereafter, those whose behaviors have constituted crimes shall be punished by 'Zhan' (beheading) with their wives degraded to slaves and their property confiscated"; "if the minister of 'Zai Zhi' (the prime minister and the head of Privy Council) knows very well of it, he shall be punished for the same crime." In order to prevent officials from forming cliques, the appointment and promotion of officials could be done solely by the emperor. "If an official has randomly proposed the promotion of civil officials in the office without permission, they shall both be punished by 'Zhan' (beheading)"; if the relatives of officials are appointed officials without the approval of the emperor, they shall also both be punished by 'Zhan' (beheading)." Besides, "if the officials of 'Ya Men' (the government offices) and the civilians have submitted memorials to the emperor and flatteringly praised the minister of 'Zai Zhi' (the prime minister and the head of Privy Council) as virtuous and moral people, they would be regarded as 'Jian Dang' (treacherous cliques), and their acts would be thoroughly investigated, with the criminals punished by 'Zhan' (beheading), with their wives degraded to slaves and with their property confiscated"; "if the minister of 'Zai Zhi' (the prime minister and the head of Privy Council) knows of it, he shall be punished the same crime"; "if the civil officials conceal the fact and require that titles of marquis be conferred upon the civil officials who have not made great contribution to the country, those involved shall be punished by 'Zhan' (beheading)." In the early years of the Ming Dynasty, over 30,000 civil and military officials were killed for the crime of 'Jian Dang' (treacherous cliques) after the two cases of Hu Weiyong and Lan Yu occurred. So in the end, "the veteran generals such as the dukes or marquis who had committed the crime of 'Jian Dang' (treacherous cliques) were sentenced to death one after another, and few of them had escaped."[177] Sun Xingyan, a contemporary of the Qing Dynasty, wrote in *Chong Ke Gu Tang Lv Shu Yi Xu* (*Preface of the Re-engraved Old Comments on Tang Code*):

> After *Yong Hui Ding Lv* (*Yong Hui Code*) is issued, it is followed as a model by both the rulers of Song and Ming dynasties. But only in Ming Dynasty, some provisions are changed and the provision of "Jian Dang" (treacherous cliques) is added, by which men of virtue are often treated unjustly, with the punishment for minor crimes mitigated and the punishment for serious crimes aggravated. So it is said that people tend to commit minor crimes if the punishments are mitigated, but more people will be wronged if the punishments for serious crimes are aggravated, which will never lead to good governance.

---

[177]"Tang He Zhuan" (The Biography of Tang He) in *Ming Shi* (*The History of Ming Dynasty*).

10.3 Criminal Law Reflecting the Thoughts of Ruling the Country with Severe Penalties

Xue Yunsheng, the jurist and minister of "Xing Bu" (The Department of Punishment) in the late Qing Dynasty had pointed out that "on the basis of *Tang Lv* (*Tang Code*) and *Ming Lv* (*Ming Code*), the provisions like "Jian Dang" (treacherous cliques) had been added during the reign of Zhu Yuanzhang, the first emperor of Ming Dynasty. Because Zhu Yuanzhang was doubtful of his officials, strict provisions were obviously made in *Ming Lv* (*Ming code*) to prevent the officials from committing crimes, which was completely different from *Tang Lv* (*Tang Code*)."[178] Therefore, "(the provisions) only showed the honorable status of the emperor without showing any respect to officials."[179] Obviously, they had tried all means "to prevent officials from arrogating power to themselves and exercising dictatorship by forming cliques."[180]

In feudal times, cliques were frequently formed by officials in power; however, in the Ming Dynasty, those involved were slaughtered recklessly, which not only showed the great harm that the cliques had posed to the absolute monarchy but also showed the extreme development of imperial power. At the same time, the growing prevalence of the crime of "Jian Dang" (treacherous cliques) had led to undeniable negative results, so officials tried their best to keep themselves out of trouble, which had often led to a neglect of state affairs. Xue Yunsheng said: "If the emperor is doubtful of his officials, then there will be very few strong-minded officials in imperial court or independent officials in the local places, because they are afraid of expressing their different opinions. In the event of emergency, they would just repeat what the others say or agree to everything, but they seldom put forward their suggestions, which is not beneficial to state affairs."[181]

Besides "Jian Dang" (treacherous cliques), the collusion of palace attendants and outside officials was strictly forbidden in the Ming Dynasty. In the 1st year of Hongwu (1368), "the emperor said to his attendants: I have read some history books, so I feel very sorry for Han and Tang dynasties, because the power is usurped by eunuchs at the end ... The eunuchs worked in the imperial palace, and they should only be allowed to do some cleaning and to deliver some messages instead of intervening in state affairs. So although the perish of Han and Tang dynasties is caused by the dictatorship of eunuchs, but their masters also should be responsible for their indulging of the eunuchs. If eunuchs are not allowed to interfere with civil and military affairs, even if they want to to so, they can not succeed."[182] Therefore, it was ordered that "it is forbidden for the palace attendants are to meddle in state

---

[178] Xue Yunsheng (Qing Dynasty), *Tang Ming Lv He Bian* (*A Collection of Laws in Tang and Ming Dynasties*), Vol. 9.

[179] Xue Yunsheng (Qing Dynasty), *Tang Ming Lv He Bian* (*A Collection of Laws in Tang and Ming Dynasties*), Vol. 30.

[180] Xue Yunsheng (Qing Dynasty), *Tang Ming Lv He Bian* (*A Collection of Laws in Tang and Ming Dynasties*), Vol. 9.

[181] Xue Yunsheng (Qing Dynasty), *Tang Ming Lv He Bian* (*A Collection of Laws in Tang and Ming Dynasties*), Vol. 9.

[182] "Kai Guo Gui Mo" (The Plan for the Founding the State) in *Ming Shi Ji Shi Ben Mo* (*The Ins and Outs of the Records in the History of Ming Dynasty*), Vol. 14.

affairs."[183] In the 2nd year of Hongwu (1369), the emperor "ordered that the official system of palace attendants be made by 'Li Bu' (The Department of Personnel)," "and at the same time, he said to his attendants: It is hard to select one or two kindhearted and honest palace attendants from one hundred. if the palace attendants are used as eyes and ears, then one's eyes will be blind and ears will be deaf; if they are used as 'Fu Xin' (stomach and heart, here it means bosom friend), then one will have heart disease. So the right way to manage them is to let them show respect to law rather than give them opportunities to perform meritorious services, because once they have made achievements, they would become arrogant and willful. Whereas, if they are fearful of law, they would be self-disciplined."[184] In the 5th year of Hongwu (1372), injunctions were especially made for palace attendants by the emperor: "If the eunuchs have committed the crime of 'E Ni' (abusing or murdering the elders) or spoken words of 'Bu Dao' (depravity), they shall be put to death by 'Ling Chi' (the punishment of dismemberment and the lingering death); if they know of the fact, but still help to conceal it, they shall be punished the same; while if they know of the fact but do not report it to the superiors, they shall be punished by 'Zhan' (beheading)."[185] In the 10th year of Hongwu (1377), it was stipulated that "if a palace attendant has discussed state affairs privately because of his rich experience in palace, he will immediately be denounced, and be sent back home. In the meantime, the attendant will be deprived of his qualification to be a palace attendant for all his life. The emperor tells all the officials: 'If the eunuchs have kept company with you for a long time and show loyalty to you, then they will be trusted by you, so they will gradually interfere in the state affairs and give orders in your name so that the situation will become incontrollable in the end. Therefore, the law is made to prohibit palace attendants from intervening in state affairs to avoid future trouble.'"[186] In the 17th year of Hongwu (1384), it was stipulated that "it is forbidden for the palace attendants to deal with the affairs outside the palace, and officials are not allowed to collude with them by writing letters or transmitting documents."[187] At the same time, the emperor "put an iron notice board outside the palace gate with the following words written on it: 'Those who interfere in the state affairs will be punished by 'Zhan' (beheading)."[188] Moreover, it was particularly provided in "Li Lv" (Statutes on Officials) in *Ming Lv* (*Ming Code*) that "the government officials who get in touch with eunuchs or attendants to obtain confidential information to

---

[183] *Ming Tong Jian* (*The History of Ming Dynasty as A Mirror*), Vol. 6.

[184] "Kai Guo Gui Mo" (The Plan for the Founding the State) in *Ming Shi Ji Shi Ben Mo* (*The Ins and Outs of the Records in the History of Ming Dynasty*), Vol. 14.

[185] Shen Jiaben, "Huan Guan Jin Ling" (Injunctions for Eunuchs) in "Lv Ling" (The Laws and Decrees) (Part 9) in *Li Dai Xing Fa Kao* (*A Textual Research of the Criminal Laws in the Past Dynasties*).

[186] "Kai Guo Gui Mo" (The Plan for the Founding the State) in *Ming Shi Ji Shi Ben Mo* (*The Ins and Outs of the Records in the History of Ming Dynasty*), Vol. 14.

[187] "Kai Guo Gui Mo" (The Plan for the Founding the State) in *Ming Shi Ji Shi Ben Mo* (*The Ins and Outs of the Records in the History of Ming Dynasty*), Vol. 14.

[188] "Huan Guan Zhuan" (The Biography of Eunuchs) in *Ming Shi* (*The History of Ming Dynasty*).

take it for illegal purpose shall be punished by 'Zhan' (beheading) with their wives punished by 'Liu' (exile) to some places 2,000 *li* away, so will the compliance be punished." However, this injunction, which was ordered to be followed by the later generations permanently, was not carried out in practice. Moreover, because of the corruption of the authoritarian political regime, the problem of eunuchs' usurping of state power was more serious than that of the previous dynasties.

In Chinese history, state power was often usurped by eunuchs, which was not unexpected as it is an inevitable consequence of an autocratic monarchy. Although the emperor had supreme power, he normally lived alone in the imperial palace and was divorced from the common people all his life. He would often worry that his power would be usurped by the senior ministers, so he would tend to rely more on the eunuchs who surrounded him. Especially in the Ming Dynasty, for decades, many emperors, especially the fatuous and corrupt ones, had never had any contact with their officials out of the palace, which had created an advantageous condition for the usurpation of power by the eunuchs.

Even Zhu Yuanzhang, who had repeatedly issued prohibitions to forbid eunuchs to interfere in state affairs, had often sent Qing Tong, a eunuch, to Hezhou (a place) to supervise the trade of tea and horses on behalf of the emperor in the 25th year of Hongwu (1392). Since then, eunuchs began to engage in state affairs.

Since Emperor Chengzu, namely, Zhudi, had succeeded in seizing power with the help of eunuchs, after ascending the throne, he "entrusted eunuchs with many matters," such as "going abroad for diplomatic missions, collecting special tax, supervising the army, and spying on officials and the common people."[189] When Emperor Yingzong ascended the throne at the age of nine, Wang Zhen, a eunuch, controlled the military and political power and became a substitute of the emperor. Since then, other eunuchs, such as Wang Zhi during the reign of Emperor Xianzong, Liu Jin during the reign of Emperor Wuzong, Feng Bao during the reign of Emperor Shenzong, and Wei Zongxian during the reign of Emperor Xizong, had all organized powerful groups that dominated the country and abroad. For example, when Liu Jin, a favored eunuch of Emperor Wuzong, was interrogated in prison, Liu Jin, who was "Xing Bu Shang Shu" (the minister of the department of punishment), "even dared not speak a word." Instead, Liu Jin, as a prisoner, screamed: "since all officials are my followers, who dare question me."[190] Meanwhile, during the reign of Emperor Xizong, many officials of the imperial court saluted Wei Zhongxian by calling him "Jiu Qian Sui" (9000-year-old, a flattery title for officials), and they were willing to be his juniors, falcons, and hounds. The chief officials of many local provinces even built temples for him, which showed that the prohibitions that were issued to prevent collusion between officials inside and outside the palaces were no longer effective, so the power of the eunuchs was still fairly great.

---

[189]"Huan Guan Zhuan" (The Biography of Eunuchs) in *Ming Shi* (*The History of Ming Dynasty*).
[190]"Liu Jin Yong Shi" (Liu Jin in Power) in *Ming Shi Ji Shi Ben Mo* (*The Ins and Outs of the Records in the History of Ming Dynasty*), Vol. 43.

10.3.1.3 Controlling People's Thoughts and Speeches by Severe Punishments

In *Ming Lv* (*Ming Code*), many provisions were stipulated for the punishment of people's thoughts and speeches. For example, "those who instigate others to commit murder shall be punished by 'Zhan' (beheading)"[191]; "those who spread fallacies or write books to deceive people, or spread rumors to bewitch people shall also be punished by 'Zhan' (beheading)"[192]; those who collect officially banned books or study the knowledge of astronomy privately "shall be punished by 'Zhang' (flogging with heavy sticks) for one hundred strokes"[193]; and "those who attempt to be promoted by using flattery words in written statements to the emperor shall be punished by 'Zhang' (flogging with heavy sticks) for one hundred strokes."[194] Apart from these offenses, countless officials were severely punished or were even punished by "Zhan" (beheading) because the words they used in their memorials were believed to be offensive. For instance, in the memorials, some of the officials praised Emperor Taizu by using expressions like "Zuo Ze Chui Xian" (a person should behave in accordance with law), "Yao Zhan Di Fei" (watching palace gate in the distance), "Rui Xing Sheng Zhi" (born wise), "Ti Qian Fa Kun" (to rule according to the mandate of heaven), "Tian Sheng Sheng Ren" (born saints) and so on, which were all regarded as acts offending the emperor because some of the words had the same pronunciation as "Zuo Zei" (to be a thief in Chinese), "Fa Kun" (to cut the hair in Chinese), "Di Fei" (an emperor being erroneous). Thus, many officials were killed for fabricated crimes because of "Wen Zi Yu" (literary inquisition). Some officials were also punished just because the submitted memorials involved some taboos of the emperor. In the 15th year of Hongwu (1382), "Wang Yundao, an official of Guangping (a place) had submitted a written memorial about the rich iron mine in Linshui town in Cizhou county, and advised the emperor to establish the department of 'Tie Ye Du Ti Ju Si' (ancient government office in charge of metallurgy) to have a better management of the iron mines by following the example of Yuan Dynasty. He pointed out that more than several million *jin* of iron could be produced each year; however, he was punished by 'Zhang' (flogging with heavy sticks) and was exiled according to the emperor's order."[195] In the 6th year of Xuande (1431), Chen Zuo, a "Yu Shi" (the censor) of Jiangxi, submitted a memorial

---

[191]"Jian Dang" (Treacherous Cliques) in "Zhi Zhi" (The State Office System) in "Li Lv" (Statutes on Personnel) in *Ming Lv* (*Ming Code*).

[192]"Zao Yao Shu Yao Yan" (Spreading Harmful Speeches or Books) in "Zei Dao" (Stealing and Robbery) in "Xing Lv" (The Penal Code) in *Ming Lv* (*Ming Code*).

[193]"Shou Cang Jin Shu Ji Si Xi Tian Wen" (Collecting Officially Banned Books or Acquiring the Knowledge of Astronomy Illegally) in "Yi Zhi" (Ceremonial Regulations) in "Li Lv" (Statutes on Rites) in *Ming Lv* (*Ming Code*).

[194]"Shang Shu Chen Yan" (To Express One's Opinions by Memorials) in "Yi Zhi" (Ceremonial Regulations) in "Li Lv" (Statutes on Rites) in *Ming Lv* (*Ming Code*).

[195]"Kai Guo Gui Mo" (The Plan for the Founding the State) in *Ming Shi Ji Shi Ben Mo* (*The Ins and Outs of the Records in the History of Ming Dynasty*), Vol. 14.

to the emperor and persuaded him to read *Da Xue Yan Yi* (*The Deductive Meaning of the Great Learning*) and to learn something useful. The emperor got angry immediately after reading it and said: "I have never read any book and don't know about *Da Xue Yan Yi* (*The Deductive Meaning of the Great Learning*), so I am not suitable to be the emperor?" Then, he ordered him to be sent back to Jingcheng (the capital of Ming Dynasty) by "Ti Qi" (soldiers specializing in seizing criminals) "with his family members imprisoned by 'Jin Yi Wei' (secret service of the Ming Dynasty) for five years."[196] During the reign of Shizong, Li Mo, "Xing Bu Shang Shu" (the minister of the department of punishment), and Ye Jing, "Yu Shi" (the censor), were both sentenced to death for slandering because the questions in "Ke Ju" (the imperial examination) were inappropriate. In order to prevent students from discussing state affairs, in the 12th year of Hongwu (1379), an order was issued by the emperor to all schools, and the students "are forbidden to the government offices" without "important affairs"; meanwhile, "they are forbidden to talk about military and civil affairs."[197] The order was in effect until the end of the Ming Dynasty.

Since the Qin Dynasty, various measures had been taken by rulers to control people's thoughts and speeches, and sometimes public opinion was even controlled by brutal punishments in order to carry out despotism in politics, so we can see that the control of people's behaviors and thoughts were closely related. Under such circumstances, state violence was employed not only to crack down upon illegal acts but also to restrain people's thoughts and speeches, which was nothing more than accepting the illegal acts overtly. However, in the Ming Dynasty, the punishment was further aggravated, which showed that the emperors in the late period of feudal society had no other way of maintaining their dictatorship.

10.3.1.4 Strengthening the Management of Officials and Enforcing Severe Punishments on Corrupt Officials

According to the ideology of "wise rulers administering their officials, rather than their people" put forward by "Fa Jia" (legalists), the functions of the state were exercised by the entities like administrative officials, judges and military forces, so the emperors in history were all devoted to the strengthening of the official management in order to guarantee the operation of state apparatus and functions.

In the early period of the Ming Dynasty, in order to reconstruct the state ruling of absolute monarchy, many decisive measures were taken to strengthen the management of officials. The officials were strictly ordered to obey the law and to be devoted to their duties. It was particularly stipulated in *Ming Lv* (*Ming Code*) that

---

[196]"Ren Xuan Zhi Zhi" (The Governance of Emperor Renxuan) in *Ming Shi Ji Shi Ben Mo* (*The Ins and Outs of the Records in the History of Ming Dynasty*), Vol. 28.

[197]"Li Bu" (The Department of Rites) (Part 36) in *Ming Hui Dian* (*The Collected Statutes of Ming Dynasty*), Vol. 78.

"laws should be read and studied carefully by all officials so as to handle the daily affairs accordingly," which was also used as one of the standards to evaluate officials. "If any official could not explain or understand the meaning of the provision, he shall be imposed with a fine of the suspension of one month's salary for the first time; he shall be punished by 'Chi' (flogging with light sticks) for forty strokes for the second time, and he shall be demoted for the third time"; "if any official is unscrupulous and fraudulent, or defamed the law and changed the contents without authorization, he shall be punished by 'Zhan' (beheading)."[198] On the other hand, in accordance with *Tang Lv* (*Tang Code*), officials who changed the provisions without the permission of "Shang Shu Sheng" (The Department of Secretary) would be put in prison, which clearly showed that the provisions in *Ming Lv* (*Ming Code*) were much stricter than those in the law of the previous dynasties.

To further strengthen the management of officials, corrupt officials should first be severely punished. So Emperor Taizu had once gathered the officials of "Zhou" (subprefecture) and "Fu" (prefecture) nationwide and said:

> Now the country has just been established, so the national financial resources are insufficient. It is like a newborn bird or a newly-planted tree, so we should not pluck the feathers of the newborn bird or break the roots of the newly-planted tree. What we should do is to provide a stable and harmonious environment for people to live. Only a upright and honest people can be self-disciplined and be helpful to other people; ... therefore, you must remember what I have just said and put it into practice.[199]

According to "Xing Fa Zhi" (The Record of the Criminal Law) in *Ming Shi* (*The History of Ming Dynasty*), "at the beginning of Ming Dynasty, a warning list of malfeasants was posted in 'Shen Ming Pavilion' (a court built by Zhu Yuanzhang) by Taizu and the officials of late Yuan Dynasty were severely punished." Meanwhile, it was ordered that "the misconducts of those who were exempted from punishments and who had resumed their posts should be posted on their doors by 'Xing Bu' (The Department of Punishment) so that they could have self-examinations to repent themselves; otherwise, they shall be punished." In addition, in "Xing Lv" (The Penal Code) in *Ming Lv* (*Ming Code*), the punishment for the crime of "Shou Zang" (accepting booty) was especially provided, and in some other codes such as *Hu Lv* (*Statutes on Households*), *Ke Cheng* (*Tax*), and *Yan Fa* (*Regulations of Salt*), similar stipulations, which were much severer than those in *Tang Lv* (*Tang Code*), were included.

According to *Ming Lv* (*Ming Code*), "Shou Zang" (accepting booty) was divided into three different types, namely, "Wang Fa" (taking bribes by bending the law), "Bu Wang Fa" (taking bribes without bending the law), and "Zuo Zang" (embezzlement). They all belonged to the crime of "Shou Zang" (accepting booty), but they were also different from each other. Criminals who were involved in "Wang Fa" (taking bribes by bending the law) would be punished according to the total amount

---

[198]"Jiang Du Lv Ling" (Teaching and Reading the Laws and Decrees) in "Gong Shi" (Formula) in "Li Lv" (Statutes on Personnel) in *Ming Lv* (*Ming Code*).

[199]Ming Tai Zhu Shi Lv (The Record of Taizu of Ming Dynasty), Vol. 29.

of bribes: the criminals would be punished by "Zhang" (flogging with heavy sticks) for eighty strokes for less than five *guan* of money, punished by "Liu" (exile) for 3000 *li* for fifty *guan* of money, and punished by "Jiao" (hanging) for eighty *guan* of money (the punishment includes a fine of fifteen pieces of cloth in *Tang Code*). The punishment for "Bu Wang Fa" (taking bribes without bending the law) was reduced by half, and the criminals would be punished by "Zhang" (flogging with heavy sticks) for seventy strokes for seventy *guan* of money and punished by "Liu" (exile) or 3000 *li* for one hundred and twenty *guan* of money. "Zuo Zang" (embezzlement) referred to a crime where "the officials and staff accept other's property or bribes without making use of their job convenience," which was punished the same way as "Bu Wang Fa" (taking bribes without bending the law), with the penalties reduced by half. So officials were usually punished by "Chi" (flogging with light sticks) for thirty strokes for less than three *guan* of money, punished by "Zhang" (flogging with heavy sticks) for one hundred strokes for eighty *guan* of money, punished by "Tu" (imprisonment) for one year for one hundred *guan* of money, and punished by "Tu" (imprisonment) for three years for more than five hundred *guan* of money. Apart from the punishment for the officials involved in "Zuo Zang" (embezzlement), other participators would be punished with five levels reduced. During the reign of Emperor Hongwu, a special provision was made, and it was declared that "all the officials and the common people, whether in the north or south, if they have committed the crime by 'Wang Fa' (taking bribes by bending the law), they shall be banished to the northern frontier to serve in the army."[200]

Provisions on the punishment of corrupt officials in *Ming Lv* (*Ming Code*) were much more concrete than those in *Tang Lv* (*Tang Code*) and *Song Lv* (*Song Code*). For example, there were respective provisions for the following cases: officials accepting money, officials accepting money after helping others, officials asking for bribes for a favor, claiming bribes, officials asking for bribes for lending and loaning money, officials' family members asking for bribes, "Feng Xian Guan" (official who monitors the enforcement of the law) getting involved in "Zuo Zang" (embezzlement), collecting tax on the pretext of public services, accepting the gifts of marquises, withholding the bribed money, failing to register one's residence after receiving bribes, hiring people to work for themselves without sound reasons, borrowing state vessels for private use, borrowing money and grain for private use, misappropriating state foodstuff without permission, misappropriating materials and supplies, and so on.

In addition, it was stipulated that officials who were removed from their posts because of corruption would not be employed again, which was different from the rules in *Tang Lv* (*Tang Code*), in which it was stipulated that officials could be employed with reduced ranks after some years. If an official accepted bribe after settling a case or if the case was wrongly judged, he would be punished by "Wang Fa" (taking bribes by bending the law); if the case was not wrongly judged, he would

---

[200]"Xing Fa Zhi" (The Record of the Criminal Law) (Part 1) in *Ming Shi* (The History of Ming Dynasty).

be punished by "Bu Wang Fa" (taking bribes without bending the law), which was much severer than the rules in *Tang Lv* (*Tang Code*), in which it was stipulated that the officials should be punished only according to the property they accepted. In law, there were different regulations for taking bribes by "Guan" (official) and "Li" (petty official), which showed that great importance was attached by the emperor to the corruption of "Li" (petty official) in legal practice. If "Yu Shi" (the censor), who was "Feng Xian Guan" (official who monitors the enforcement of the law), who was responsible for supervising all officials, had accepted bribes, he would be severely punished for "Zuo Zang" (embezzlement). If their families had asked for bribes for lending and loaning money, their punishments would be two levels lighter than the punishment for the officials themselves, but they would still be punished the same way as other supervisory officials. If the families had asked for bribes by taking advantage of their duties, punishment reduction would not be allowed.

The punishment for corrupt officials in the Ming Dynasty was much severer than before but was much lenient than the later times. During the reign of Emperor Taizu, corrupt officials were particularly severely penalized. For instance, in the 18th year of Hongwu (1385), someone reported that Guo Huan, "Hu Bu Shi Lang" (Vice Director of Secretariat), and officials from two departments in Beiping had collaborated to misappropriate foodstuff of the state by playing favoritism. Learning about this, Emperor Taizu immediately ordered all the concerned officials to be interrogated by the judicial bureau, so that several hundred officials below "Liu Bu Shi Lang" (vice director of the six department) were punished by "Si" (death penalty); over 7,000,000 *dan* of stolen money and goods were recovered; and many officials in the local province throughout the country were involved, and tens of thousands of them were sentenced to imprisonment. Emperor Taizu even allowed the ordinary people to go to the capital to make direct complaints against the local officials or even to escort the corrupt officials to go to capital. The cases that were recorded in *Da Gao* (*The Great Imperial Mandate*) mostly involved the punishment for corrupt officials, so they were nothing but special criminal laws and regulations, except that the punishments were much severer. For example, according to *Ming Lv* (*Ming Code*), those involved in "Bu Wang Fa" (taking bribes without bending the law) could be exempted from death penalty, but according to *Da Gao* (*The Great Imperial Mandate*), "those officials would be punished by 'Ling Chi' (the punishment of dismemberment and the lingering death) or 'Xiao Shou' (the penalty of hanging the head of the criminal on top of a piece of wood)." Generally speaking, not only the corrupt officials but also their coordinators and families involved would be severely punished. In the 4th year of Hongwu (1371), an imperial order was issued to "Xing Bu" (The Department of Punishment), and it was ordered that "if officials have committed the crime of 'Zuo Zang' (embezzlement), the coordinators shall also be punished with their families exiled to border areas. So the decree shall be abided by everyone."[201] In the 5th year of Hongwu (1372), *Tie Bang* (*Iron Announcement*)

---

[201]"Xing Fa Zhi" (The Record of the Criminal Law) (Part 1) in *Ming Shi* (*The History of Ming Dynasty*).

10.3 Criminal Law Reflecting the Thoughts of Ruling the Country with Severe Penalties

was made by the government to enforce punishment upon the corrupt dukes and princes, which was unprecedented in the history of criminal law of ancient China. According to the law, "if dukes and princes have forcibly occupied mountains, lakes, tea gardens, marshes, and other precious metal of the government and people, such as gold and silver...., they would be exempted from death penalty once for three times," and "the dukes and princes should truthfully record 'Yi Zhang Hu' (guardian in the families of dukes) and tenant peasants in the local official documents. If they have already been registered, but they have privately asked the officials in charge to help them to evade army service and corvee, they shall be punished by 'Zhan' (beheading)."[202] Marquis of Yongjia, Zhu Liangzu, was recalled from Guangdong and was even flogged to death in the imperial court because he had taken bribes by bending the law in Guangdong.

The severe punishment for corruption and malpractice had exerted a positive influence on the management of officials by the government, so that "'Shou Ling' (prefects or magistrates) in the local places show respect to law, discipline themselves and take good care of their people, which has brought about an entirely new look to the official management of government."[203] However, in feudal China, the corruption of officials was rooted in the soil of the feudal system itself, so that severe laws and brutal punishments could only provide a temporary solution rather than address the root cause and could only produce momentary effects rather than prevent the problems in advance. Even Emperor Taizu had to admit during the period of Hongwu: "I want to eliminate the corrupted officials; however, some of them are killed in the morning, but others commit crimes again in the evening."[204] After *Wen Xing Tiao Li* (*The Ordinance for Inquisition*) was made during the reign of Emperor Hongzhi, the punishment for the ordinary crime of corruption was mitigated, except for the misconduct of breaching of duty. After the reign of Emperor Xuande, officials who had committed the crimes of corruption were allowed to atone for their crimes or were sent to defend the border or were removed from office instead of being punished by death penalty, so that only a few of them were sentenced to death but none of them "were allowed to resume their posts."[205] In the 4th year of Xuande (1427), "Yu Shi" (the censor), Shen Run, "was accused of taking bribes, but he was banished to a frontier post instead of being sentenced to death penalty."[206] In the 4th year of Tianqi (1624), "Yu Shi" (the censor), Cui Chengxiu, was accused of

---

[202] Shen Jiaben (Qing Dynasty), "Tie Bang" (Iron Announcement) in "Lv Ling Kao" (A Textual Research on Laws and Orders) in *Li Dai Xing Fa Kao* (*A Textual Research of the Criminal Laws in the Past Dynasties*), Vol. 9.

[203] "Xun Li Zhuan" (The Biography of Excellent Officials) in *Ming Shi* (*The History of Ming Dynasty*).

[204] Liu Chen, *Guo Chu Shi Ji* (*A Chronicle of Events at the Beginning of Ming Dynasty*).

[205] "Wang Ao Zhuan" (The Biography of Wang Ao) in *Ming Shi* (*The History of Ming Dynasty*).

[206] "Ren Xuan Zhi Zhi" (The Governance of Emperor Renxuan) in *Ming Ji Shi Ben Mo* (*The Ins and Outs of the Records in the History of Ming Dynasty*), Vol. 28.

corruption, but he was only "removed from his post."[207] But no doubt lenient punishments had further encouraged corrupt officials, so that it was difficult to contain the trend of corruption. During the reign of Emperor Shizong, Yan Song and his son were accused of corruption, so 30,000 *liang* of gold, more than two million *liang* of silver, as well as thousands of other precious treasures were discovered when their houses were searched by the government.

Officials' dereliction of duties were also very severely punished. For example, "if any official has failed to report the important events to the central government," he would be punished by "Zhang" (flogging with heavy sticks) for eighty strokes in accordance with *Tang Lv* (*Tang Code*), but according to *Ming Lv* (*Ming Code*), different punishments were provided for military and civil officials. According to *Ming Lv* (*Ming Code*), "if a military officer fails to report such matters as criminal activities and the promotion of officials for their merits, he shall be punished by 'Jiao' (hanging); but if a civil official fails to report the matters mentioned above, he shall be punished by 'Zhang' (flogging with heavy sticks) for one hundred strokes; if the official has committed the crimes intentionally, then the punishment will be aggravated...; if the officials have taken measures by themselves before submitting memorials to the emperor, they shall be punished by 'Zhang' (flogging with heavy sticks) for one hundred strokes."[208] In the Qing Dynasty, Xue Yunsheng once commented on this provision: "The penalty for corrupted officials in *Ming Lv* (*Ming Code*) is generally more lenient than that in *Tang Lv* (*Tang Code*), but this provision in *Ming Lv* (*Ming Code*) is an exception because precautions have been taken against the subordinate officials for their usurping of the power no matter what degree it is."[209] If a general failed to report to the emperor or maneuvered armies before submitting memorials to the emperor, "he shall either be punished by 'Zhang' (flogging with heavy sticks) for eighty strokes, or be removed from his post, or be punished by 'Liu' (exile) to the border areas."[210]

Among the various provisions for crimes of dereliction of one's duty, the punishments for crimes such as falling of cities and losing of territories, conniving at stealing, and stealing what was entrusted to their care were the severest. "If the administrative officials are negligent of their duties by misconduct, which has infuriated the common people to gather together to make trouble or to capture the cities, they shall all be punished by 'Zhan' (beheading)."[211] In the 18th year of

---

[207]"Dong Lin Dang Yi" (Comments on Donglin Party) in *Ming Shi Ji Shi Ben Mo* (*The Ins and Outs of the Records in the History of Ming Dynasty*), Vol. 66.

[208]"Shi Ying Zou Bu Zou" (Failing to Report What Should Be Reported) in "Gong Shi" (Formula) in "Li Lv" (Statutes on Personnel) in *Ming Lv* (*Ming Code*).

[209]Xue Yunsheng (Qing Dynasty), "Shi Ying Zou Bu Zou An Yu" (Comments on Failing to Report What Should Be Reported) in *Tang Ming Lv He Bian* (*A Collection of Laws in Tang and Ming Dynasties*), Vol. 10.

[210]"Shan Diao Guan Min" (Manoeuvring Army without Authority) in "Jun Zheng" (Military Administration), "Bing Lv" (Statutes on Military Affairs) in *Ming Lv* (*Ming Code*).

[211]"Ji Bian Liang Min" (Infuriating the Common People) in "Jun Zheng" (Military Administration) in "Bing Lv" (Statutes on Military Affairs) in *Ming Lv* (*Ming Code*).

10.3 Criminal Law Reflecting the Thoughts of Ruling the Country with Severe Penalties

Yongle during the reign of Chengzu (1420), "Chu Yan and Zhang Hai, both 'Bu Zheng Shi' (local administrative officer) of Shandong, and Liu Ben, 'An Cha Shi' (head of judicial commission) of Shandong had connived at stealing, so they were sentenced to death penalty."[212] In the same year, "in Shandong ... Tang Saier rebelled ... so the officials of 'San Fa Si' (Three Judicial Departments), 'Jun' (shire) and 'Xian' (county) were all sentenced to death for conniving at the bandits."[213]

As for those who stole what was entrusted to their care, whether the principal or accessory, they would all be punished according to the total amount of property. Those who had stolen property whose value was over forty *guan* of money would be punished by "Zhan" (beheading).

In the early Ming Dynasty, officials were required to get to know the sufferings of the common people and to be familiar with the agricultural production, natural disaster, and famine within their administrative regions to maintain a stable social environment, and officials who knew nothing about what is mentioned above would be punished. In the 25th year of Hongwu (1392), Wu Congquan, an official of "Xue Zheng" (departmental director of school) in Kelan, and Zhang Heng, a school instructor of Shanyin county, were summoned to the capital. So "the emperor asked about the suffering of the common people. They all answered that they knew nothing since it was beyond their responsibility. The emperor said: '...what could you do for the people if you have no idea of their conditions?' Finally they were punished by demoting to remote places. And then the emperor ordered that it be issued nationwide by 'Xing Bu' (The Department of Punishment) as a warning to everyone."[214] In the 11th year of Yongle (1413), "the emperor told 'Tong Zheng Shi' (The Transmission Officer) and 'Ji Shi Zhong' (the senior assistant of the emperor and the supervisor of officials) of 'Li Bu' (The Department of Rites) that if the natural disaster and famine within one's jurisdiction was not reported by the official in charge but by other officials, the official in charge of this region shall be punished."[215]

10.3.1.5 Aggravating Penalties for Robbers, Thieves, and Vagrants

According to *Tang Lv* (*Tang Code*), the robbers who failed to obtain property should be punished by "Tu" (imprisonment) for two years, while those who obtained over ten *pi* of cloth should be punished by "Jiao" (hanging); however, according to *Ming*

---

[212]"Cheng Zu Ji" (The Record of Emperor Chengzu) (Part 3) in *Ming Shi* (*The History of Ming Dynasty*) (Book 3).
[213]"Ping Shan Dong Dao" (Stealing in the East of Pingshan) in *Ming Shi Ji Shi Ben Mo* (*The Ins and Outs of the Records in the History of Ming Dynasty*).
[214]"Kai Guo Gui Mo" (The Plan for the Founding the State) in *Ming Shi Ji Shi Ben Mo* (*The Ins and Outs of the Records in the History of Ming Dynasty*), Vol. 14.
[215]"Cheng Zu Ji" (The Record of Emperor Chengzu) (Part 2) in *Ming Shi* (*The History of Ming Dynasty*).

Lv (*Ming Code*), "the robbers shall be punished by 'Zhang' (flogging with heavy sticks) for one hundred strokes even if they have failed to obtain any property, and they shall be punished by 'Zhan' (beheading) if they have obtained property, regardless of the principal or accessory"[216] and regardless of how much they had obtained the property or whether they had brought weapons with them or whether they had killed anyone. During the reign of Emperor Shenzong, provisions about defending the cities and the responsibilities of the relevant officials were added in *Wen Xing Tiao Li* (*The Ordinance for Inquisition*) under the circumstance of frequent uprising of the common people. It was stipulated that "in 'Fu' (ancient administrative district between province and county), 'Zhou' (subprefecture) and 'Xian' (county) in the coastal, boarder and inland areas where 'Wei Suo' (border guarding posts) is stationed, or the regions where 'Wei Suo' (border guarding posts) is stationed alone, if it is attacked by the invaders or villains, or if the officials in charge flee away without taking protective measures so that the cities are captured with the common people robbed and killed and the property burned by the invaders and villains, then the chief officials and the officials who are in charge of capturing robbers shall be punished by 'Zhan' (beheading) according to the punishment for the generals' failing to protect the city."[217]

The punishment for "Qie Dao" (robbing and theft) in *Ming Lv* (*Ming Code*) was much severer than that in *Tang Lv* (*Tang Code*). According to *Ming Lv* (*Ming Code*), "the thief who fails to steal any property shall be punished by 'Zhang' (flogging with heavy sticks) for fifty strokes without being tattooed on the face; but if he has stolen some money, he shall be punished according to the amount of property which he has obtained. ... the thief who has committed theft for three times shall be punished by 'Jiao' (hanging)"[218] (the severest punishment in *Tang Lv* (*Tang Code*) was "Liu" (exile) to a remote area). But if a thief stole the property of the government, his punishment would be aggravated. It was stipulated in *Wen Xing Tiao Li* (*The Ordinance for Inquisition*), which was made during the reign of Emperor Jiajing, that "the punishment for those who attempt to get inside a government office and steal money are allowed to be atoned for by serving a life sentence, but those who attempt to steal official suits, imperial edicts and seals, official seals of governments, copper medal for night watching, and official writings for military plan as well as money and grain shall all be regarded as accomplished offenders and be punished by 'Si' (death penalty) according to law."[219] However, when *Wen Xing Tiao Li* (*The*

---

[216] "Qiang Dao" (Robbery) in "Zei Dao" (Stealing and Robbery) in "Xing Lv" (The Penal Code) in *Ming Lv* (*Ming Code*).

[217] "Zhu Jiang Bu Yin Shou" (Chief Commanders' Violation of Law) in "Jun Zheng" (Military Administration) in "Bing Lv" (Statutes on Military Affairs) (Part 2) in *Wen Xing Tiao Li* (*The Ordinance for Inquisition*).

[218] "Qie Dao" (Robbing and Theft) in "Zei Dao" (Stealing and Robbery) in "Xing Lv" (The Penal Code) in *Ming Lv* (*Ming Code*).

[219] "Dao Nei Fu Cai Wu" (Stealing Property from a Royal Place) in "Zei Dao" (Stealing and Robbery) in "Xing Lv" (The Penal Code) (Part 1) in *Wen Xing Tiao Li* (*The Ordinance for Inquisition*).

Ordinance for Inquisition) was revised during the reign of Emperor Wanli, this article was changed: "The thief who attempt to steal official uniforms shall be regarded as accomplished offenders and be sentenced to the punishment of 'Si' (death penalty); the officials who attempt to embezzle more than thirty *liang* of silver or sixty *liang* of cloth which are put under their care, and the common people who attempt to steal sixty *liang* of silver or sixty *liang* of cloth shall be punished by 'Liu' (exile) to border regions or by 'Chong Jun' (to be forced to join the army)."[220] Even those who ate others' fruits in the garden without permission would be punished for the crime of stealing. If it was the state garden, the punishment would be aggravated by two levels. Besides, according to *Jia Jing Xue Cuan Tiao Li* (*Amendment to the Regulations of Jia Jing*), "those who have stolen the property of their father, brothers, uncles whom they live with or shared the booty at the same time shall be punished according to this article with two levels reduced," so the punishment that was made according to "Wu Fu" (relatives within the five degrees of mourning) was no longer applied.

In *Ming Lv* (*Ming Code*), a special article of "Dao Zei Wo Zhu" (a person who harbors criminals of robbery and theft) was added, so it was stipulated that the people who harbored criminals or coordinated in stealing or sharing the booty would be punished by "Zhan" (beheading).

The problem of vagrants had been a very difficult issue, which had had an important influence on social stability since the Tang Dynasty. The large number of bankrupt peasants who were refugees had been the main driving force for fighting against the Yuan Dynasty, but after the establishment of the Ming dynasty, they became a potential threat to the stability of the newly founded state. So in order to prevent them from disturbing social order, the policy of attracting immigrants to reclaim wasteland was carried out; the refugees who refused to do so were severely punished. On the basis of the principle of "registering households according to the permanent residence" in *Da Ming Lv* (*The Great Ming Code*),[221] special provisions were also made on refugees in *Da Gao* (*The Great Imperial Mandate*): "The vagrants are forbidden to live in cities and villages." If they planned to escape into the mountains and marshes and refused to be summoned by the government, the principal offenders should be punished by "Jiao" (hanging), and the others should be punished by "Zhan" (beheading). Moreover, the neighbors and relatives of the "vagrants" were allowed to capture them to be tried in the capital; if the neighbors refused to, "the vagrants shall be punished by 'Zhan' (beheading) and 'Li Jia' (social organizations at the grass-roots level) and the neighbors shall be driven out of villages."[222] If there were still some vagrants or other layabouts after the issuing

---

[220]"Dao Nei Fu Cai Wu" (Stealing Property from a Royal Place) in "Zei Dao" (Stealing and Robbery) in "Xing Lv" (The Penal Code) (Part 1) in *Wen Xing Tiao Li* (*The Ordinance for Inquisition*).

[221]"Ren Hu Yi Ji Wei Ding" (Registering Households according to the Permanent Residence) in "Hu Yi" (Household Corvee) in "Hu Lv" (Statutes on Households) in *Ming Lv* (*Ming Code*).

[222]"Ren Hu Yi Ji Wei Ding" (Registering Households according to the Permanent Residence) in "Hu Yi" (Household Corvee) in "Hu Lv" (Statutes on Households) in *Ming Lv* (*Ming Code*).

of *Da Gao* (*The Great Imperial Mandate*) but "Li Jia" (social organizations at the grassroots level) had turned a blind eye and the vagrants' neighbors failed to capture and send them to the government, "Li Jia" (social organizations at the grassroots level) and the neighbors would be punished by "Liu" (exile) to remote areas and the vagrants would be sentenced to death. The vagrants who dared to gather together to fight against the government would be suppressed resolutely. In March of the 5th year of Hongwu (1372), the vagrants in Xuanhua region rebelled because the government had forced them to serve in the army; consequently, more than one hundred vagrants were killed.

In the early Ming Dynasty, to a certain extent, the problem concerning vagrants was much alleviated because of the enforcement of severe penalties and relevant policies; however, the increasing of tax by the government and the cruel exploitation by landlords had compelled many peasants to leave their home and become refugees. By the middle of the Ming Dynasty, there were so many vagrants that it was impossible to stop them. Under such circumstances, according to *Jia Jing Xue Cuan Tiao Li* (*Amendment to the Regulations of Jiajing*), during the reign of Emperor Jiajing, rigorous sanctions were employed for the punishment of vagrants who fled to remote mountains: "If soldiers and common people in border areas flee to or hide themselves in Yidongzhai to evade corvee, they shall be investigated and punished by 'Liu' (exile) to remote borders to serve in the army for lifetime. 'Li Zheng' (head of 'Li') of this region as well as the other neighbors who know of the fact but who refuse to report it to the government shall be punished."[223]

Apart from the punishments, the registered permanent residence was also controlled strictly during the Ming Dynasty. It was required that every vagrant should be registered in a region and live there permanently; otherwise, he would be punished as an abscondee. In the 2nd year of Zhengtong (1437), because of the increase of vagrants, the government decided to register all of them in a particular region. So ten households formed one "Jia," where they guaranteed each other and were supervised by "Li Zhang" (head of "Li": the basic resident organization in ancient China). If anyone went against the government, he would be sentenced to death.[224] In the early years of Chenghua, Xiang Zhong and Yang Rui were ordered to forcefully carry out the registration of the vagrants in Jingxiang mountainous areas, which had led to a large-scale peasant uprising in which hundreds and thousands of people were killed or wounded. After Chengzu ascended the throne, in order to consolidate his reign and to prevent the local vassals from becoming too powerful to threaten the central government, the policy of weakening the military and political power of local kings and princes was carried out and more precautions were taken to guard against their activities. Such policy was continued after the death of Chengzu, and it was guaranteed in many ways by legislation. For example, it was stipulated particularly

---

[223]"Tao Bi Chai Yi" (Evading Corvee) in "Hu Yi" (Household Corvee) in "Hu Lv" (Statutes on Households) in *Wen Xing Tiao Li* (*The Ordinance for Inquisition*).

[224]"Hu Kou" (Registered Permanent Residence) in "Hu Bu" (The Department of Revenue) in *Ming Hui Dian* (*The Collected Statutes of Ming Dynasty*), Vol. 19.

in *Wen Xing Tiao Li* (*The Ordinance for Inquisition*), which was made during the reign of Hongzhi, that "in the palaces of princes, it is not allowed to employ servants from outside without authorization, because it is considered as an insulting act ... and any events happening in palaces should be reported to the emperor immediately and no further action is allowed to be taken before emperor's permission." Moreover, the princes were forbidden to leave their manors with no reason, and for those who were removed from their posts, their descendants "can be interrogated directly by the relevant officials." In *Wen Xing Tiao Li* (*The Ordinance for Inquisition*) made in Jiajing period, it was further stipulated that "if princes accept food stuff or other property illegally or have land disputes which involved the common people or soldiers, they would be settled by 'Ya Men' (the government offices) in accordance with the fact. It is forbidden for 'Zhang Shi Si' (The Bureau of Aids and Staff) to intervene in, or to accept complaints randomly by abusing his power." If any influential official was accused of "taking advantage of other influential officials and nobilities" or "trying to establish relationship with the emperor's attendants and families or making use of their reputations" or indulging in blackmail, extorting money, defrauding, destroying post roads, or interfering with the affairs of "Ya Men" (the government offices), he would be reported to the emperor to be punished by "Liu" (exile) to remote areas or to be punished by "Chong Jun" (to be forced to join the army). Emperor Yingzong added that "the senior officials of the palaces of princes can get salary increase if they have served for a long time, but they are not allowed to be moved out of the palace for their life time,"[225] which had been carried out since that time. Even the relatives of those officials were not allowed to move out of the palace after the reign of Jiajing in order to restrict the power of the royal families and enfeoffments. Therefore, it can be seen from history that in the early Han Dynasty, during the reign of emperors Wen, Jing, and Wu, the power of dukes and princes was strictly restricted by criminal law in order to maintain the centralization of authority. So in fact, in the Ming Dynasty, the original policy of the Han Dynasty was followed, although it was not so thoroughly and resolutely carried out as in the Han Dynasty.

10.3.2 The Penal System Focusing on the Punishment of Treacherous People and the Applicable Principles of Criminal Law

Under the influence of the ideology of enforcing severe penalties on treacherous people and guiding people according to "Li" (rites), the penal system of the Ming Dynasty was changed in the following aspects.

---

[225] Shen Defu (Ming Dynasty), *Wan Li Ye Huo Bian* (*A Privately Compiled History of the Reign of Wanli*), Vol. 4.

Firstly, the legal penalties were combined with extralegal ones. As for the legal penalty, "Wu Xing" (Five Penalties), namely, "Chi" (flogging with light sticks), "Zhang" (flogging with heavy sticks), "Tu" (imprisonment), "Liu" (exile), and "Si" (death penalty) (be punished by "Jiao" (hanging) or be punished by "Zhan" (beheading)), which had been applied in the Tang and Song dynasties, was carried out in the Ming Dynasty. Besides legal penalties, the penalty of "Chong Jun" (to be forced to join the army), which was passed down from the Song and Yuan dynasties, was also improved in the Ming Dynasty. In the early Ming Dynasty, the penalty of "Chong Jun" (to be forced to join the army) only referred to being punished by "Liu" (exile) to border areas with no particular regulations made on distance. But later, different distances of *li* were gradually specified, and it was further divided into six categories based on different distances, including "Ji Bian" (extreme remote areas), "Yan Zhang" (jungles), "Bian Yuan" (outlying areas), "Bian Wei" (border guarding post), "Yan Hai" (coastal areas), and "Fu Jin" (nearby), among which the farthest was 4000 *li* and the nearest was 1000 *li*. The criminals could do servitude or do military service in the border areas according to their identities. The time of "Chong Jun" (to be forced to join the army) was divided into "Zhong Shen" (lifelong), which meant that the criminal would serve the sentence until his death, and "Yong Yuan" (forever), which meant that after the death of the criminals, their descendants must continue the servitude until no offspring was left. So it was obvious that "Chong Jun" (to be forced to join the army) was much severer than the punishment of "Liu" (exile).

In the 1st year of Hongwu (1368), there were just a few provisions about the penalty of "Chong Jun" (to be forced to join the army) in *Ming Lv* (*Ming Code*), but later they added up to forty six. Until the time of Jiajing, there were already more than two hundred and thirteen provisions, and they were increased to two hundred and forty three during the reign of Wanli because of the influence of the ideology of enforcing severe penalties in the Ming Dynasty and reformation of the army. The basic units of the army in the Ming Dynasty consisted of "Wei" and "Suo." After the nation was unified by Taizu, "'Wei' and 'Suo' were established in all cities from the capital to little counties."[226] "'Suo' was established in the strategic places where there was just one 'Jun' (shire), and 'Wei' was established if there were several 'Jun' (shire) connecting with each other."[227] Generally, 5600 people formed one "Wei," and one "Wei" was made up of 1000 households or 100 households of "Suo." The military unit and garrison system established by "Wei Suo" (border guarding posts) not only strengthened the centralized authority but also provided the basis for the penalty of "Chong Jun" (to be forced to join the army). In addition, the penalty of "Chong Jun" (to be forced to join the army) was an important way to supplement the armed forces. Some particular provisions on "Zheng Bu" (recruitment by arresting) and "Gou Bu" (supplement of troops by catching criminals) were

---

[226]"Bing Zhi" (The Record of Army) in *Ming Shi* (*The History of Ming Dynasty*).
[227]"Bing Zhi" (The Record of Army) in *Ming Shi* (*The History of Ming Dynasty*).

10.3 Criminal Law Reflecting the Thoughts of Ruling the Country with Severe Penalties

made aiming at the penalty of "Chong Jun" (to be forced to join the army) in *Ming Hui Dian (The Collected Statutes of Ming Dynasty)*.[228]

Besides, "Ting Zhang" (being flogged in imperial court) and some extremely cruel extralegal penalties were created in Ming Dynasty.

"Ting Zhang" (being flogged in imperial court) referred to flogging the senior officials in front of Meridian Gate to force them to be obedient to the emperor, which had shown unprecedentedly the despotic power of the emperor. Early in the 8th year of Hongwu (1375), Ru Taisu, who was responsible for "Xing Bu" (The Department of Punishment), was punished by "Ting Zhang" (being flogged in imperial court) for the offensive words in his memorial. In the 14th year of Hongwu, Xue Xiang, "Gong Bu Shang Shu" (the minister of the department of works), was flogged to death. So "Ting Zhang" (being flogged in imperial court) became a common punishment in the years of Zhengde during the reign of Emperor Wuzong when Liu Jin was in power. "Ting Zhang" was enforced by "Jin Yi Wei" (secret service of the Ming Dynasty) and supervised by "Si Li Jian" (in charge of the inner eunuch and intrauterine affairs within the court), by which countless senior officials were killed in the Ming Dynasty. In the years of Zhengde during the reign of Emperor Wuzong, one hundred and sixty eight senior officials were punished by "Ting Zhang" (being flogged in imperial court), and fifteen of them were killed because they had advised the emperor to conduct an inspection tour to the south. In the years of Jiajing during the reign of Emperor Shizong, one hundred and forty three senior officials were punished by "Ting Zhang" (being flogged in imperial court), and sixteen of them were killed because they had debated about the ritual affairs with the emperor. "Ting Zhang" (being flogged in imperial court) had been frequently applied in the Sui, Tang, Song, and Yuan dynasties; however, it was in the Ming Dynasty that it was finally developed into a usual method to intimidate senior officials, to show the tyrannic power of the emperor, and to humiliate the senior officials, which had in fact gone beyond the scope of the policy of "managing officials" with harsh penalties.

There were many extralegal penalties in *Da Gao (The Great Imperial Mandate)*, including "Xiao Ling" (hanging someone's head on the city gate), "Yi Zu" (implicating the nine generations of a family), and "Ci Zi" (to make humiliating tattoo on one's body, especially on one's face). Moreover, the cruelest penalty of "Ling Chi" (the punishment of dismemberment and lingering death) was also formally written into *Ming Lv (Ming Code)* and became a common way of punishment. Shen Jiaben described many such important cases during the 1st year of Hongwu in his book *Li Dai Xing Fa Zhi (The Record of the Criminal Law in each Dynasty)*, and he cried with alarm: "'Ling Chi' (the punishment of dismemberment and the lingering death) is an extremely brutal punishment," so "'Ling Chi' has brought about many injustices."

During the reign of Emperor Yingzong, Li Shimian, "Ji Jiu" (official in charge of teaching and examinations) of "Guo Zi Jian" (the highest educational body in

---

[228]"Jun Zheng" (Military Administration) (Part 1) in *Ming Hui Dian (The Collected Statutes of Ming Dynasty)*, Vol. 154.

ancient China) was persecuted by eunuch Wang Zhi by wearing a shackle weighing over one hundred *jin*; since then, the punishment of "Jia Hao" (cangue: a large wooden collar worn by petty criminals as a punishment) was created. During the reign of Emperor Wuzong, when eunuch Liu Jin was in charge of "Xi Chang" (the imperial spy agency), the penalty of "Da Jia Xing" was created. So the cangue was over one hundred and fifty *jin*, and the criminals who wore such big cangues would die of tiredness in several days, which was therefore similar to death penalty. When Emperor Xizong ascended the throne, the penalty of wearing heavy cangues was abolished; however, other cruel penalties were created by eunuch Wei Zhongxian, such as chopping off one's back or fingers and stabbing one's heart. The cruel criminal penalty and the restoration of corporal punishments in the Ming Dynasty had reflected the extremely sharp class contradiction and the attempt of the ruling class to strengthen the absolute monarchy.

Secondly, the criminal punishment was further closely connected with "Fu Zhi" (mourning apparel system). The tradition of enforcing criminal punishment according to "Fu Zhi" (mourning apparel system) began in the Jin Dynasty, and it was adopted by the later dynasties without any changes. In the Yuan Dynasty, Gong Duanli pointed out in his book *Wu Fu Tu Jie* (*The Diagram of "Wu Fu"*): "If any official has expected to enforce penalties impartially, he must first get familiar with 'Fu Zhi' (mourning apparel system). Where 'Fu Zhi' (mourning apparel system) is fairly implemented, the relevant penalties are justified; where "Fu Zhi" (mourning apparel system) is unfairly implemented, the relevant penalties are inappropriate." So it is obvious that there is a close relationship between "Fu Zhi" (mourning apparel system) and penalty system.

"Sang Fu Tu" (The Diagram of Mourning Apparel) was included in the first page of *Ming Lv* (*Ming Code*) to show the importance that was attached to "Fu Zhi" (mourning apparel system). As regards this point, Zhu Yuanzhang had stated clearly: "In this book (referring to *Ming Code*), 'Sang Fu Tu' (The Diagram of Mourning Apparel) is included in the first page, and then the diagram of 'Ba Li' (eight rites) was included next to show that great importance is attached to 'Li' (rites)."[229] The inclusion of "Fu Zhi" (mourning apparel system) in law had eloquently shown the combination of "Li" (rites) and "Fa" (law) and the actual influence of the family ethic relationship on legislation. Moreover, "Fu Zhi" (mourning apparel system) was an important rule for making convictions and sentences in criminal cases. Wang Kentang from the Ming Dynasty had written in "Jian Shi" (Notes) in *Ming Lv* (*Ming Code*): "'Sang Fu Tu' (The Diagram of Mourning Apparel) is firstly included in laws, so it shows that convictions are made in accordance with the discrepancies of mourning apparels, by which proper penalties are executed by the judges." In juridical practice, any case that was related to relatives should be firstly tried by clarifying the relationship and mourning apparels so that the convicts and sentences could be made according to "Fa" (law) and the system of "Li" (rites).

---

[229]"Xing Fa Zhi" (The Record of the Criminal Law) (Part 1) in *Ming Shi* (*The History of Ming Dynasty*).

10.3 Criminal Law Reflecting the Thoughts of Ruling the Country with Severe Penalties

With respect to the aggressive behaviors and harmful acts among relatives, a set of special provisions were made in *Ming Lv* (*Ming Code*) according to the relationships of seniority and juniority. For example, for the punishment of physical injury among relatives, the closer the relationship was, the severer was the punishment, but the punishment for the senior and junior was different. For further clarification, the descendants who beat up the grandparents or parents would be punished by "Zhan" (beheading); if it led to the death of the grandparents or parents, the descendants would be punished by "Ling Chi" (the punishment of dismemberment and lingering death); the junior or the minor who beat up the brothers and sisters with the same surnames or the brothers and sisters-in-law with the relationship of "Sai Ma" (the person wearing the mourning apparel of soft sackcloth in the fifth mourning degree) would be punished by "Zhang" (flogging with heavy sticks) for one hundred strokes; the brothers and sisters of "Xiao Gong" (the person wearing the mourning apparel of soft sackcloth in the fourth mourning degree) would be punished by "Zhang" (flogging with heavy sticks) for sixty strokes with one year of imprisonment; the brothers and sisters of "Da Gong" (the person wearing the mourning apparel of soft sackcloth in the third mourning degree) would be punished by "Zhang" (flogging with heavy sticks) for sixty strokes with one and half years of imprisonment. On the contrary, if the senior killed or injured the junior, the closer the relationship was, the more lenient the punishment would be, except for forcible rape, for which the punishment would be much severer for closer relatives regardless of rules for seniority. With regard to property violation among relatives, the closer the relationship was, the more lenient the punishment would be, and the level of punishment would usually be reduced. For example, if one had stolen property from his relatives who lived together with him but who had not shared the common property, the punishment would be reduced by five levels if the larcener was "Qi Qin" (relatives being in mourn for one year); the punishment would be reduced by one level if the larcener was "Da Gong" (the person wearing the mourning apparel of soft sackcloth in the third mourning degree) or without relationship of the mourning apparel. Those who defrauded their relatives would be punished one level lighter according to the law of "Qin Shu Xiang Dao" (the theft among relatives), whether they lived together or not.

The applicable principles of penal codes were also different from those of the previous dynasties. First, any crime that was committed before the issuing of new laws should be decided in accordance with the new one. In the Han Dynasty, it was stipulated that "anyone who has committed a crime shall be judged in accordance with the laws and decrees issued at the time when the crime was committed."[230] In the Tang Dynasty, it was further specified that "any crime that is discovered after the issuing of the revised 'Ge' (injunction) or that is in trial proceedings at the issuing of the revised 'Ge' (injunction) shall be decided according to the old one except that in

---

[230]"Kong Guang Zhuan" (The Biography of Kongguang) in *Han Shu* (*The History of Han Dynasty*).

the new one lenient penalty is provided for such crime."[231] In *Ming Lv* (*Ming Code*), it was provided that "any crime, no matter when it is committed, shall be decided according to the new law," and it was further explained with notes in order to emphasize that "in this law it is stipulated that any crime that is committed before but is discovered after the issuing of a new law shall be decided according to the terms and conditions of the new one rather than those of the old one."[232] Then obviously that in *Ming Lv* (*Ming Code*) it was stressed that "the cases shall be settled according to the terms and conditions of the new one" without caring about the differences of punishment in the old and new laws, which was obviously different from *Tang Lv* (*Tang Code*), in which it was ruled that lenient punishment should be used. Second, for "Hua Wai Ren" (foreigners) who had committed crimes, the principle of territorial jurisdiction was applied. It was also provided in *Tang Lv* (*Tang Code*) that "if 'Hua Wai Ren' (foreigners) from the same country have any criminal disputes among themselves, they shall be judged according to the laws of their county; if 'Hua Wai Ren' (foreigners) from different countries have any criminal disputes, they shall be judged according to *Tang Lv* (*Tang Code*),"[233] which was an illustration of the combination of the principle of nationality and principle of territoriality in criminal law. However, it was only specified in "Ming Li" (The Categories of Penalties and General Principles) in *Da Ming Lv* (*The Great Ming Code*) that "'Hua Wai Ren' (foreigners) who have committed crimes shall be judged in accordance with law," and the provision that "if 'Hua Wai Ren' (foreigners) from the same country have any criminal disputes among themselves, they shall be judged according to the laws of their county" was deleted. Finally, for "Hua Wai Ren" (foreigners) who escaped by taking advantage of nationality, severer punishment should be executed.

Compared with *Tang Lv* (*Tang Code*), the punishment for the crimes in connection with jeopardizing the national security or offending the emperor in *Ming Lv* (*Ming Code*) was much severer than that in *Tang Lv* (*Tang Code*), while the punishment for the crimes in connection with infringing upon the feudal ethical codes was much lenient than that in *Tang Lv* (*Tang Code*), so that severe punishments were enforced for felonies and lenient punishments were enforced for misdemeanors. To be specific, "as to the crimes violating the feudal ethical codes," the violator should be sentenced to two-year imprisonment according to *Tang Lv* (*Tang Code*); however, the violator should be punished by "Zhang" (flogging with heavy sticks) for one hundred strokes according to *Ming Lv* (*Ming Code*). If the descendants lived separately and possessed their own property when their grandparents or parents were still alive, they should be sentenced to three-year imprisonment according to *Tang Lv* (*Tang Code*), while they would be punished by "Zhang" (flogging with heavy sticks) for one hundred strokes according to *Ming Lv* (*Ming*

---

[231] *Tang Liu Dian* (*The Six Statutes of Tang Dynasty*), Vol. 6.

[232] "Duan Zui Yi Xin Ban Lv Tiao" (The Provision of Making Convictions according to the Newly Issued Law) in "Ming Li Lv" (Statutes and Terms) in *Ming Lv* (*Ming Code*).

[233] "Ming Li Lv" (Statutes and Terms) in *Tang Lv Shu Yi* (*The Comments on Tang Code*).

Code). Anyone who failed to mourn for the death of the parents should be punished by "Liu" (exile) for 2000 *li* away according to *Tang Lv* (*Tang Code*), while they would be punished by "Zhang" (flogging with heavy sticks) for sixty strokes and one-year imprisonment according to *Ming Lv* (*Ming Code*). Those who raised the children of "Za Hu" (families registered as workers) as descendants would be sentenced to one and a half years of fixed-term imprisonment according to *Tang Lv* (*Tang Code*), while they would get no punishment according to *Ming Lv* (*Ming Code*). Xue Yunsheng in the Qing Dynasty once said that "the punishment for the violation of feudal ethical codes in *Tang Lv* (*Tang Code*) is much severer than that in *Ming Lv* (*Ming Code*), while the punishment for 'Zei Dao' (stealing and robbery) in relation to property and foods is much severer in *Ming Lv* (*Ming Code*) than that in *Tang Lv* (*Tang Code*),"[234] which had not only reflected the principle of "enforcing severe punishment for felonies and lenient punishment for misdemeanors," which was formed in the process of creating *Ming Lv* (*Ming Code*), but also shown the tendency to resort to criminal punishment as a method of intimidation and deterrence under the circumstances that the pressure of class resistance was increased and the restriction of "Li" (rites) was weakened in the late feudal society. Xue Yunsheng said: "The ancient people tended to solve the problems first through 'Li Jiao' (feudal ethical code) and then through criminal punishment, but now people attach more importance to criminal punishment instead of 'Li Jiao' (feudal ethical code)."[235]

10.4 Further Development of Civil Law

In the early Ming Dynasty, the agricultural economy was recovered and developed by employing the refugees and vagrants, organizing immigrants to reclaim the wasteland, launching water conservancy projects, and sending garrison troops or peasants to open up the wasteland, which had further promoted the development of the industry and commerce. For example, the silk produced in Nanjing and Hangzhou, the cotton textiles produced in Suzhou and Shanghai, the dyed cloth produced in Songjiang, the casting products produced in Foshan, and the ceramics produced in Jingdezhen were all famous local specialties. Besides, unprecedented achievements were made in the textile, mining, and metallurgy and shipbuilding industries; meanwhile, the economic relationship among different regions were further strengthened, the market was prosperous, and many handicraft products were sold throughout the country or even abroad. As a result, the development of commodity economy also promoted the development of civil law, so the system of civil law in

---

[234] Xue Yunsheng (Qing Dynasty), "Ji Heng An Yu" (Comments on the Provision of Giving Sacrificial Offerings) in *Tang Ming Lv He Bian* (*A Collection of Laws in Tang and Ming Dynasties*), Vol. 9.

[235] Xue Yunsheng (Qing Dynasty), "Ji Heng An Yu" (Comments on the Provision of Giving Sacrificial Offerings) in *Tang Ming Lv He Bian* (*A Collection of Laws in Tang and Ming Dynasties*), Vol. 9.

the Ming Dynasty was more complete than before and its contents were much richer. However, due to the limitation of the specific national condition, no specific civil litigation was made in the Ming Dynasty, and civil laws were scattered in "Lv" (criminal law), "Ling" (decree), "Tiao Li" (regulation), "Bang Wen" (announcement), "Gao Shi" (public notice), habits, customs, and etiquettes, which were characterized by diversity, dispersibility, and complexity.

It is worth mentioning that on the 19th of March in the 31st year of Hongwu (1398), *Jiao Min Bang Wen (A Public Notice to People)* was issued by "Hu Bu" (The Department of Revenue) to provide instructions for civil affairs, which contained forty one articles involving civil laws relevant to the purchase and sale of land, covenants, family, and inheritance and specific provisions of civil actions, so the legal norms of "Hu Hun" (marriage, tax, and household registration), "Tian Tu" (land), and the litigation system of rural societies in *Da Ming Lv (The Great Ming Code)* were further specified. Thus, it had reached a perfect degree. *Jiao Min Bang Wen (A Public Notice to People)* was a special form of law that was issued according to imperial edicts, and it had the double meaning of teaching and punishment.

10.4.1 *"Ren Hu Fen Bian" (Separation of Registered and Actual Residence) and the Subjects of Civil Rights*

According to the scope of rights that civil subjects enjoyed, the social stratification in Ming Dynasty could be roughly divided into landlords, homesteaders, businessmen, handicraftsmen, sharecroppers, hired workers, slaves, etc. Compared with Song and Yuan dynasties, the stratification of individual civil subjects in the Ming Dynasty was made more complicated. In addition, with the development of the commercial economy, stores, "Ya Hang" (broker house), and other civil subjects with organizational functions like imperial clans, families, households, shops, cart-selling shops, and even states emerged one after another. Except the privately operated and managed stores, stores were also managed by aristocrats and bureaucrats to make profit by employing other people, which were in an unequally competitive position compared with the private ones. "Ya Hang" (broker-house) was an intermediator that did business for customers to collect commissions. On the basis of *Ming Lv (Ming Code)*, all "Ya Hang" (broker house) established in accordance with law were eligible to be civil legal subjects.

Aristocrats, bureaucrats, and landlords not only were civil subjects but also enjoyed privileges in certain civil legal relationships.

Due to the small-scale structure of peasant economy, the subjects of individual civil rights were dominated by the homesteaders; at the same time, the tenant peasants' personal attachment to landlords was further weakened. For example, in the 5th year of Hongwu (1732), it was ordered by Taizu to change the relationship of master and servants between landlords and homesteaders into that of "seniority and juniority." Therefore, the tenant peasants were civil subjects enjoying independence

10.4 Further Development of Civil Law

of identity. The legal status of hired servants was decided by the working time in the agreement which was reached by the two parties in the contract. Although a hired servant is different from "Nu Bi" (the slave girls and maidservants), if a hired servant raped the spouses and daughters of his employer, he would be punished by "Zhan" (beheading), which was the same for "Nu Bi" (the slave girls and maidservants) who had committed the same crime. So it can be seen from this example that the hired servants were unequal with their employers because they were incomplete civil subjects and that they were equal civil subjects only when they had civil relationship with other hired servants. Unlike hired servants, short-term hired servants were civil subjects, and their employment relationship with the employer was established by contracts. In the 26th year of Wanli (1553), it was specified in *Xin Ti Li* (*New Cases*) that "henceforth, all those who are hired by either officials or common families with contracts made for working time, must be classified as hired workers. As for those who work for a short time with low salary, they should be classified as common citizens."[236]

Businessmen were not only civil subjects in the field of commodity circulation but also participators in land purchase, tenancy, loan, and other civil activities.

Although handicraft workers were subjects of civil rights, the registration system of "Jiang Ji" (the craftsman household registration) was implemented in the Ming Dynasty so that they were all included into this system with all of their descendants working for the government for generations. Besides, they were not allowed to break away from the system; if they did so, they would be severely punished, which had more or less restricted their freedom to engage in civil activities.

"Nu Bi" (the slave girls and maidservants) were still considered as objects of ownership, yet at the beginning of the Ming Dynasty, rulers learned a lessons from the fact that social conflict was intensified by the slavery system that was carried out in the central plains back in the Yuan Dynasty, so it was stipulated that although aristocrats and the meritorious families could keep slaves, the number of slaves must not exceed twenty. Once common people were found keeping slaves, they would be punished by "Zhang" (flogging with heavy sticks) for one hundred strokes with their slaves released. At the same time, the abduction and trafficking of common citizens were strictly prohibited by law, and those who violated the law would be punished by "Zhang" (flogging with heavy sticks) for one hundred strokes and be exiled to places 3000 *li* away. As a result, the number of "Nu Bi" (the slave girls and maidservants) in the Ming Dynasty was greatly reduced. Moreover, they enjoyed certain rights of marriage, which could be proved by the marriage agreement preserved in the Museum of Chinese History. "Nu Bi" (the slave girls and maidservants) also had the rights of engaging in industrial and commercial affairs in place of their employers. For example, during the reign of Jingtai (1450–1457), "Du Zhi Hui" (the chief military general) Sun Jizong and Sun Shaozong and "Zhi Hui" (general)

---

[236]"Nu Bi Ou Jia Zhang" (The Slave Girls and Maidservants Assaulting their Masters) in "Xing Lv" (The Penal Code) in *Da Ming Lv Ji Jie Fu Li* (*Great Ming Code with Collected Commentaries and Appended Sub-statutes*), Vol. 20.

Sun Xianzong "had built 'Ta Fang' (places for the storage of commodity goods) and ordered their family slaves to attract merchants to do salt business."[237] So "Nu Bi" (the slave girls and maidservants) in the Ming Dynasty enjoyed certain civil rights, which had played a positive role in easing the contradiction, as well as maintaining the labor force, which was necessary for agricultural and handicraft production. However, in the Ming dynasty, there were no restrictions for the wealthy families to keep "Nu Bi" (the slave girls and maidservants), and human trafficking, which was relevant to slave holding, also went beyond the restriction of law.

"Dan Hu" (those who live on water instead of on land) in Guangdong province, "Yue Hu" (people registered as musicians) in Shanxi, "Duo Min" (the good for nothing or loafers) in Shaoxing in Zhejiang province, "Shi Pu" (life maidservants) in Ningguo in Jiangxi province, and "Ban Dang" (the accompanying servants) in Huizhou were all regarded as "Jian Min" (rabbles or people of lower social status), who were completely deprived of any rights according to the law in the Ming Dynasty. This legal classification was a particular product of the autocratic policy in the Ming Dynasty, which did not exist in the Tang, Song, and Yuan dynasties.

In summary, the civil rights of the tenant peasants, hired workers, and "Nu Bi" (the slave girls and maidservants) were relatively expanded in the Ming Dynasty in the later period of feudal society, which was a reflection of the trend of historical development. However, under the historical background of strict hierarchy, the civil rights and duties of different classes were significantly different, and even the capacity for rights and conduct of civil subjects was limited according to their social, political, and family status. In line with the law of the Ming Dynasty, "at the age of sixteen, the people have become 'Ding' (adult), so he must serve in the army, and only those over sixty years old are exempted from army service,"[238] which showed that people over sixteen had the capacity for civil acts. But in the patriarchal clan system, the disposal of domestic affairs and management rights were still controlled by the senior; therefore, the capacity for civil acts was actually restricted.

It is worth pointing out that the inequality of the capacity for rights and conduct were flexible with the change of personal, family, and social status, as well as land ownership.

Moreover, because different people were registered in different households, and enjoyed different civil rights and civil litigation rights, the cancelation of the registration of households was prohibited by law. On the basis of the regulations in the Ming Dynasty, all soldiers, commons, postmen, chefs, doctors, fortunetellers, workers, and musicians were registered in different registration systems corresponding to their social status, and it was forbidden for them to cancel their registration by defrauding. Taking "Jun Hu" (soldiers) as an example, soldiers had been the undertaker of military duties for generations, and every month they were granted a reward of food and money; therefore, those who pretended to be soldiers

---

[237] *Ming Ying Zong Shi Lu* (*The Record of Meritorious Families in Ming Dynasty*), Vol. 193.
[238] "Shi Huo Zhi" (The Record of National Finance and Economy) (Part 2) in *Ming Shi* (*The History of Ming Dynasty*).

would be punished by "Zhang" (flogging with heavy sticks) for eighty strokes. As another example, if handicraft workers who were included in "Jiang Ji" (the craftsman household registration) had canceled their registration, he or she would be severely punished. "Jun Hu" (soldiers), "Jiang Ji" (the craftsman household registration), and "Zao Hu" (chefs) were not allowed to migrate freely, and the people who lost their identities must reregister in their native place. Those who canceled their registration secretly would be severely punished, and officials who illegally changed the identities of those people and those who privately changed their registration would be punished by "Zhang" (flogging with heavy sticks) for eighty strokes.

10.4.2 The Usufruct of Estate Rights and the Expansion of Guarantee

Under the dominance of natural economy preliminarily composed of agriculture, the core and basic form of estate rights is the ownership of land. Based on the usage, benefit, and transfer of land, "Yong Dian Quan" (rights of permanent rent) and "Dian Quan" (pawn rights), which are now called "Yong Yi Wu Quan" (usufructuary rights), came into being; at the same time, "Zhi Quan" (pledge rights) and "Di Ya Quan" (mortgage rights), which is now called "Dan Bao Wu Quan" (real rights for security), also came into being.

In the Ming Dynasty, the traditional policy of land annexation, which was carried out in the Song Dynasty, was followed, and the policy that "the amount of land is completely decided by the peasants themselves" was carried out,[239] which had further improved the feudal land ownership. According to "Shi Huo Zhi" (The Records of National Finance and Economy) in *Ming Shi* (*The History of Ming Dynasty*), "the land system in Ming Dynasty was divided into two classes: 'Guan Tian' (state-owned land) and 'Min Tian' (private land)." "Guan Tian" (state-owned land) belonged to the country, and it was forbidden to be sold or privately owned according to law. Besides, tax should be collected on "Guan Tian" (state-owned land) according to imperial decrees or established patterns. The main source of such land included the original "Guan Tian" (state-owned land) of the Yuan Dynasty and the land deserted in the chaos of war, the amount of which was much fewer than "Min Tian" (private land). During the reign of emperor Hongzhi, the amount of "Guan Tian" (state-owned land) only accounted for about one seventh of "Min Tian" (private land). And later in this period, "Guan Tian" (state-owned land) gradually

---

[239]Xue Yunsheng (Qing Dynasty), "Qi Yin Tian Liang Tiao An Yu" (Comments on the Provision of 'Concealing Land and Grain') in *Tang Ming Lv He Bian* (*A Collection of Laws in Tang and Ming Dynasties*) (Book 1), Vol. 13.

became the private property of aristocrats and bureaucrats, so its proportion was continually reduced.

"Min Tian" (private land) belonged to individuals. And the privatization of land reached an unprecedented degree by awarding the reclaiming of the wasteland, "opening up wasteland as one's own permanent possession," and allowing the free transaction of land. What is more, those aristocrats and bureaucrats occupied a large amount of land for their political privileges. According to statistics, during the reign of Xiaozong, the royals, aristocrats and eunuchs occupied 598,456 *qing* (a unit of area; one 'qing' is about 6.6667 ha) of land, which accounted for more than one seventh of the national land; during the reign of Emperor Wanli, the emperor granted an award of 20,000 *qing* of land to Prince Fu when he was enfeoffed in Henan; during the reign of Tianqi, princes Gui, Hui, and Rui and princesses Suiping and Ningguo respectively occupied 10,000 to 40,000 *qing* of land. Moreover, there were many ordinary landlords scattered nationwide, who also possessed a considerable amount of land. In the 30th year of Hongwu (1397), according to the report of "Hu Bu" (The Department of Revenue), the number of landlords nationwide (apart from Yunnan, Liangguang, and Sichuan), who possessed more than seven *qing* of land, was more than 14,341.[240] In addition, there were many small landlords.

Since the rich businessmen also invested in land, there were also many businessmen landlords. Take the Huguang area as an example: "there are many businessmen and landlords in Jiangxi who occupied as much as 10,000 *mu* of land."[241]

As for the owner peasants who had a few land, they expanded their scope of land ownership by ways of inheritance, land reclamation, collective reclamation, etc. However, since they had heavy burden of tax and corvée and were devoid of capacity to deal with natural disasters, they had a weak economic foundation and were often forced into selling their own land due to force majeure, thereby losing their land ownerships. In the one hundred and forty years from Hongwu to Xiaozong, the amount of land of the owner peasants was reduced by half, and especially in Huguang, Henan, and Guangdong, the majority of land was seized by aristocrats and bureaucrats.

Joint land ownership, like the land inherited by families and community-shared forests, still existed in the Ming Dynasty.

At the beginning of the Ming Dynasty, on account of the chaotic relationship of ownership in the late Yuan Dynasty, *Huang Ce* (*Yellow Book*) and *Yu Lin Tu Ce* (*Scale Graph*) were compiled by the government to confirm the various forms of land ownership. In the meantime, a series of strict laws was issued by the government to enforce punishments for the crimes of stealing, selling, occupying, and illegally claiming "the land and houses of other people," and it was stipulated that the criminal would be punished by "Zhang" (flogging with heavy sticks) for eighty strokes and "Tu" (imprisonment) for two years; "if the criminal is an official, the

---

[240]*Ming Tai Zu Shi Lu* (*The Record of Emperor Taizu of Ming Dynasty*), Vol. 252.
[241]Fu Yiling, *Ming Qing Feng Jian Suo You Zhi Lun Gang* (*An Outline of the Feudal Land Ownership of Ming and Qing Dynasty*), Shanghai People's Publishing House, 1992, p. 28.

punishment would be doubled"; if the land was occupied forcibly, the criminal would be punished by "Zhang" (flogging with heavy sticks) for at most eighty strokes and be exiled to places 3000 *li* away. But no restriction was imposed on those privileged aristocrats and bureaucrats. Since "Jun Tian Zhi" (The System of Land Equalization) was no longer implemented in the Ming Dynasty, the prohibition of "excessive occupation of land," which was included in "Jun Tian Zhi" (The System of Land Equalization), was abolished, and "the amount of land is completely decided by the peasants themselves."

As for real estate, the ownership of houses was monopolized by the owner himself, so the owner's exclusive right of occupying, utilizing, and disposing the real estate was protected by the law.

As for ownership of personal property, or the so-called owner rights, it was also divided into state ownership and private ownership. The former one aimed at government objects, and its range was not restricted, while the latter one aimed at private objects, and its range was restricted. For example, objects obtained by violating the rules or contraband could not be owned by individuals. Apart from general provisions, the protection on personal property in the Ming Dynasty focused on the acknowledgement of the legitimacy of the obtaining method. For example, the traditional principle of preemption was followed in the laws of the Ming Dynasty. So as far as the forests, bushes, grass, and stones in the wild mountains were concerned, if somebody "had spent efforts and chopped down the firewood in mountains," all these things should be recognized as "the preemption of ownerless objects," so he had achieved ownership, but if other people had arbitrarily taken these away, "they should be punished as larceny."[242] As for the picking up of lost property, if it was an official object, it should be completely returned; if it was a private object that someone claimed ownership of, it should be returned by half, with the remaining half awarded to the person who had picked it up; if the owner did not appear within thirty days, the object should belong to the person who had picked it up. Since according to the law of the Ming Dynasty part or full ownership of the lost property was legally acknowledged, it was different from the regulation in *Tang Lv* (*Tang Code*), according to which "the lost property ... should be returned to original owner of the government or individual." Similarly, if someone "has dug out the buried ownerless objects in 'Guan Tian' (state-owned land) or 'Min Tian' (private land)," generally speaking, he could keep it; however, "if they are precious ancient utensils, such as bronze tripods, etc. which should not be possessed by civilians, it should be given to the government within thirty days: otherwise, the offenders shall be punished by 'Zhang' (flogging with heavy sticks) for eighty strokes with the cultural relics confiscated by the government." This regulation was also different from that in *Tang Lv* (*Tang Code*), according to which "the lost property should be equally shared by the land owners." In *Da Ming Ling* (*The Decrees of Great Ming Dynasty*), the principle of prescription for the ownership of "the objects left behind by the dead

---

[242]"Dao Tian Ye Gu Mai" (Stealing Cereal Crops and Wheat in the Fields) in "Dao Zei" (Theft) in "Xing Lv" (The Penal Code) in *Ming Lv* (*Ming Code*).

businessmen" was also provided: "If his father or brothers ... or legal wife have claimed the objects, they will be returned, but if nobody has claimed for ownership, those objects will be confiscated by the government one year later."[243] As far as the legal protection of ownerships in the Ming Dynasty was concerned, on the one hand, real right was acknowledged and offenses and false claims were prohibited; on the other hand, government-owned objects were strictly protected.

Compared with those in *Tang Lv* (*Tang Code*), the abovementioned regulations about the method of obtaining personal property, which were stipulated in the statutes and decrees of the Ming Dynasty, were more suitable to the conditions of society and people to a greater extent, which was a reflection of a much well-developed legal concept of private ownership in the development of commodity economy.

After the middle of the Ming Dynasty, one of the important developments in land ownership relationship was the emergence of "Yong Dian Quan" (rights of permanent rent). The so-called "Yong Dian Quan" (rights of permanent rent) was a kind of usufruct, according to which the tenant could permanently rent and cultivate the land after paying rent. As early as in the Northern Song Dynasty, there were already records of "Yong Dian Quan" (rights of permanent rent). In the middle of the Ming Dynasty, tenants obtained "Yong Dian Quan" (rights of permanent rent) of certain land by paying expensive rent or by investing on the land. "Yong Dian Quan" (rights of permanent rent) was very popular in the places of Jiangzhe, Jiangxi, Anhui, Fujian, etc. So the establishment of "Yong Dian Quan" (rights of permanent rent) had made tenancy relationship more complicated; meanwhile, it had led to the separation of land ownership and land farming rights, so that here might have two or three owners for one piece of land. The tenants not only enjoyed the right of permanent occupation, utilization, and benefits of the land but also had the ownership of the surface of the land (also known as "Tian Pi": land skin), while the landlords had the ownership of the land itself (also known as "Tian Gu": land bone). Therefore, the landlord was called "Gu Zhu" (bone owner) and the tenant "Pi Zhu" (skin owner).

The legal relationship between "Gu Zhu" (bone owner) and "Pi Zhu" (skin owner) is as follows: "Pi Zhu" (skin owner) had "Yong Dian Quan" (rights of permanent rent), which he obtained by the transfer or disposition of the land, and "Gu Zhu" (bone owner) was not allowed to revoke tenancy at liberty or lease it to other tenants; "Pi Zhu" (skin owner) could perform various kinds of rights as far as the surface of the land was concerned, such as inheritance, pledge, sublease, sale, etc. According to a record in "Feng Su" (Customs) in volume seven of *Jiang Ying Xian Zhi* (*Jiangyin County Annals*), in the years of Zhengde, "the land of a tenant is equivalent to his own property, so he can build nurseries, houses or graves at his own will, and the landlord has no rights to intervene. He can even leave the land to his sons after his death or sell it to others when he is in poverty, which is called 'Que'; When he makes money, it is called 'Shang An Qian', which is usually more than the

---

[243]"Hu Ling" (Decrees on Household) in *Ming Lv* (*Ming Code*).

10.4 Further Development of Civil Law

original investment." But "Pi Zhu" (skin owner) had the responsibility of paying rent, and "Gu Zhu" (bone owner) had the right to revoke tenancy and pay back the rent if the rent was delayed.

The emergence of "Yong Dian Quan" (rights of permanent rent) and the separation of the rights of "Tian Mian" (the surface of land) and "Tian Di" (the land itself) were a reflection of the complexity of tenancy relationship in law under the influence of commodity economy. The tenants were encouraged to positively improve the land and to engage in agricultural production and management; thus, the traditional unequal relationship between landlords and tenants was changed. However, it also had a negative influence on the state tax revenue. According to *Tian Xia Jun Guo Li Bin Shu* (*Merits and Drawbacks of all the Provinces and Counties in China*) by Gu Yanwu, "the land which was given to the people was shared by three owners afterwards. ... the people who obtained the land received rents, and he did not need to hand in grain tax to the state, so he was called the junior taxpayer; the people who rented the land had no land and he was known as the principal taxpayer. ... Then the rent and the tax were separated from each other. ... The land was transferred to tenants, so some treacherous people had collected rent but refused to pay tax. There were no ways out. The land was rented to tenants, but some of them had occupied the land compulsively for a long time, so it was said that some of them had become the real owner of the land."

"Yong Dian Quan" (rights of permanent rent) in the Ming Dynasty had laid an important foundation for its further development in the Qing Dynasty.

After its development in the Sui, Tang, Song, and Yuan dynasties, "Dian Quan" (pawn rights) had become well established, so it was begun to be written in law. According to *Da Ming Lv Shi Yi* (*Interpretation to the Great Ming Code Dynasty*) by Ying Jia, "it is called 'Dian' (pawn) to pledge land and houses for money, and it is called 'Mai' (sell) to exchange land and houses for money. Land and houses can be redeemed back if they are pawned, but not if they are sold," by which the line between "Dian" (pawn) and "Mai" (sell) was clearly drawn, which had played a guiding role in solving disputes about "Dian" (pawn) and "Mai" (sell) in legal practice.

More than that, in *Ming Lv* (*Ming Code*), detailed rules were also made for the establishment of "Dian Quan" (pawn rights), the rights and obligations of lienees and proprietors, the elimination of "Dian Quan" (pawn rights), etc. It was provided that "after pawning, the new owner of land and houses should pay tax to the government according to the pawning contract; if not, he shall be punished by 'Zhang' (flogging with heavy sticks) for fifty strokes with half of the profit of the land and houses confiscated. Those who have not completed the transferring procedures shall be punished by 'Chi' (flogging with light sticks) for forty strokes if the amount is one to five *mu*; the punishment shall double for every five *mu* with its maximum punishment of 'Zhang' (flogging with heavy sticks) for one hundred strokes and with the land confiscated. If someone again pawns the land and houses which has already been pledged to others, the money shall be recognized as booty and he shall be punished for the crime of larceny. The criminal can be exempt from being tattooed, but his land will be confiscated. Also under this circumstance, 'Ya Bao' (intermediary agent) of this deal shall also be punished as the accessory criminal if he knows the truth, but he can be exempt from punishment if he knows nothing of it. If time limit of the pledge like land, houses, gardens, mills, etc. is due and the original owner is ready to redeem, but if the mortgagee doesn't allow the objects to be redeemed, he will be punished by 'Chi' (flogging with light sticks) for forty strokes. In addition, the original owner shall be paid profits which he deserves and he can redeem the pledge back according to the original price. But this rule doesn't apply to those who don't have enough money to redeem the pawn back even though the time limit is due."[244] It not only showed that contracts were very important in pawning land and houses but also reflected that "transferring" was also a legitimate procedure, by which the tax and corvee obligations was clarified so that "the negative effect of defraud was eliminated."[245] For the benefit of mortgagees, it was prohibited for one object to be pawned twice; otherwise, the violators would be punished.

Apart from the regulations in *Da Ming Lv* (*The Great Ming Code*), complementary provisions were also made during the reign of emperors Hongzhi and Jiajing. Take the revision of *Wen Xing Tiao Li* (*The Ordinance for Inquisition*), which was carried out in the 29th year of Jiajing (1551), as an example:

> The pawned objects like land and utensils shall not be illegally used to make profits, if the contract is due, the original owner may prepare the money to have the pawned objects redeemed; if the profit earned by the mortgagee through the pawned objects is enough to offset the cost and profit that should be paid by the original owner, the pawned objects shall be returned to the owner and the mortgagee shall compensate for any damages incurred; if the original owner doesn't have enough money to redeem the land back, the mortgagee can farm on the land for another two years.[246]

In addition, according to the provision of "Tian Zhai" (Land and Houses) in "Hu Lv" (Statutes on Households) in *Ming Lv* (*Ming Code*), "if the original owner doesn't have the capacity to redeem the pawn, the government may evaluate the supplementary payment for the land and the owner shall sign a contract for the permanent sale afterwards; if the mortgagee is unwilling to pay the balance, the land shall be sold to others and the money shall be returned to the mortgagee"; if the original owner was ready to redeem, the request should not be refused by the mortgagee with any excuse. It was stated in *Xin Cuan Si Liu He Lv Pan Yu* (*Newly Edited Judgments in Four-Six Style Prose According to the Catalogue of Laws*) written by an anonymous author: "Since Emperor Wen has died, no concessions are not made anymore by the people like Yu and Rui (two vassal states of ancient China); although Su Qiong (an upright official in ancient Chian) is alive, there are still disputes and fighting between brothers, so there are countless disputes

---

[244]"Dian Mai Tian Zhai" (Land and Real Estate Mortgage) in "Tian Zhai" (Land and Houses) in "Hu Lv" (Statutes on Households) in *Ming Lv* (*Ming Code*).

[245]"Dian Mai Tian Zhai" (Land and Real Estate Mortgage) in "Tian Zhai" (Land and Houses) in "Hu Lv" (Statutes on Households) in *Ming Lv* (*Ming Code*).

[246]"Dian Mai Tian Zhai" (Land and Real Estate Mortgage) in "Tian Zhai" (Land and Houses) in "Hu Lv" (Statutes on Households) (Part 2) in *Ming Dai Lv Li Hui Bian* (*Collections of Laws and Precedents in Ming Dynasty*), Vol. 5.

and lawsuits if the pawning of land and houses is not properly handled. Nowadays, some cunning people have not only tried to illegally get the certificates without registration by evading tax on contracts with various deceitful methods, but also attempted to evade grain tax. So those who have violated the law should be punished by 'Chi' (flogging with light sticks) and 'Zhang' (flogging with heavy sticks) with no exception.[247]

In the abovementioned laws about "Dian" (pawn) and "Mai" (sell), the time limit for "Dian Quan" (pawn rights) is not yet clearly regulated. As people said, "a pawn is effective for one thousand years," which reflected the uncertainty of the duration of "Dian Quan" (pawn rights). No doubt, the uncertainty of the duration was disadvantageous for the protection of the interest of the mortgagees and the development of production; at the same time, it also showed the strong hope of peasants to take their land back one day. However, under the circumstances of high centralization of land, fierce feudal exploitation, and ever-increasing national tax in the Ming Dynasty, there was little possibility for the original owner to redeem his property because it had provided a legitimate method for those officials and landlords to plunder the land of peasants.

In the Ming Dynasty, achievements were also made in "Dan Bao Wu Quan" (Real Rights for Security), such as "Zhi Quan" (pledge rights) and "Di Ya Quan (mortgage rights), and they became more complete than those in the previous dynasties.

10.4.3 The New Development of the Law of Obligation

Great progress was made in the law of obligation in the Ming Dynasty based on those in the Tang and Song dynasties. In *Da Ming Lv* (*The Great Ming Code*), the chapter of *Qian Zhai* (*Debts*) was especially drafted, in which further efforts were made to enrich the contents of the original meaning of debt. According to the original explanation, debt referred to "default in borrowing money or things from people," but it was further divided into two parts, namely, *obligatio ex contractu* and obligation of compensation for injury. In particular, the contract system had been developed to a most perfect degree with which no other dynasties in a feudal society could match.

Besides, the contract forms were already standardized in Ming Dynasty and in fact many contract forms were discovered in the existing contracts of the Ming Dynasty, such as the contract for selling fields, houses, and servants; the contract for pawning fields and houses; the contract for renting fields; the contract for debit and credit, mortgage, employment, contract labor, affreight; the contract for renting houses or stores; and the contract for running businesses in partnership. In order to

---

[247]Guo Chengwei, Tian Tao, *Ming Qing Gong Du Mi Ben Wu Zhong* (*Five Private Copies of Official Documents of Ming and Qing Dynasty*), China University of Political Science and Law Press, 1999, p. 85.

guarantee the collection of tax according to contract, to improve the legal effect of the contract, to clarify each party's rights and obligations, and to reduce the civil disputes caused by draft contracts, a mandatory requirement was once made by "Hu Bu" (The Department of Revenue) to ask people to use official printed contracts.

When entering into a contract, it was required that one party, like a seller, debtor, or tenant, sign his name, make a cross, and offer various terms at the same time, while the other party, like a buyer, creditor, or landowner, need not do that. To insure enforcement of the contract, there should be a third party called "Zhong Bao" or "Bao Ren" (middleman or guarantor), who would become jointly and severally liable with the obligor upon signing his name and making a cross. "Zhong Bao" or "Bao Ren" (middleman or guarantor) played the role of the introducer, presentor, or facilitator in a contract, and he must carry out the contract on behalf of the obligor once the latter could not do so.

The contract that was legitimately signed is not only legally effective but also protected by law, so it could not be changed or terminated randomly. An obligor should undertake due civil as well as criminal liability for failing to perform the obligation stipulated in the contract. Taking the debt covenant as an example, if a debtor failed to perform his obligation according to the contract, the creditor could appeal to the local authority to ask for payment of the debt. In *Ming Lv (Ming Code)* it was also allowed for a creditor to detain the debtor's property on the premise that "the lawsuit must be filed to the government"; otherwise, the creditor would be punished by "Zhang" (flogging with heavy sticks) for eighty strokes. "If the estimated value and profit of the property has exceeded that which a debtor should pay, the extra part should be regarded as dishonest possession of other's property, so it should be returned to the debtor by the creditor."[248] In addition, the debtor could also pay his debt by working for the creditor. In a sale contract, the content that "the one who repudiates first will pay a fine" was usually included to stress the responsibilities of the signing parties and to assure the performance of contracts.

In the Ming Dynasty, the varieties of contracts were increased. Take sale and loan contracts as examples.

Sales contract: because of the continuous and rapid development of commodity economy and the ever-increasing frequent trading activities, sales contract became the main form of contract in the Ming Dynasty. According to the law of the Ming Dynasty, the sale of real estate like farmland and houses should be in compliance with the legal procedures of title deed and the transferring of the ownership or property title. Moreover, tax payment receipts should be pasted at the bottom of sales contract, which was called "Qi Wei" (the identification documents issued by government), and a county seal should be stamped on the perforation, which was called "Hong Qi" (contract with an official seal). Furthermore, the seller should transfer the tax that he should pay and register it on the buyer's tax book, also known as "Guo Ge" (the transferring of the ownership of the land and the due tax to the buyer). Apart

---

[248]"Wei Jin Qu Li" (Making Profits Illegally) in "Qian Zhai" (Debts) in "Hu Lv" (Statutes on Households) in *Ming Lv (Ming Code)*.

from the sale of oxen or horses and other block trade, ordinarily written contracts were not needed for other sale of personal property.

According to the laws of the Tang, Song, and Yuan dynasties, when a person wanted to sell his farmland or houses, as a prerequisite, he needed to ask whether his relatives and neighbors wanted to buy first. Although this stipulation was abolished in the laws of Ming Dynasty, it was retained as a folk custom. So in almost all the existing contracts of selling farmland or houses, there is the record that the seller "has asked the relatives and neighbors for their intention of the purchase, while no one wants to buy."

Anyone who manufactured and sold weapons, farm tools, cloth, or silk or weapons in violation of the law should bear criminal responsibility according to the principle of the liability for warranty against defects in the law of the Tang and Song dynasties. If a buyer received sick animals, he could return the animals and get his money back.

Loan contract: in the laws of the Ming Dynasty, the protection of creditors' interests was taken as the key point in the legal regulation of debtor–creditor relationships. For example, generally the deadline for repaying debt should be made clear in a loan contract. "For those who breached the loan contract, if the default amount is over five *liang* and default time is three months, they shall be punished by 'Chi' (flogging with light sticks) for ten strokes, and the punishment will be aggravated one level for the default of every month with the maximum punishment of 'Chi' (flogging with light sticks) for forty strokes; if the default amount is over fifty *liang* and default time is three months, they shall be punished by 'Chi' (flogging with light sticks) for twenty strokes, the punishment will be aggravated one level for the default of every month with the maximum punishment of 'Zhang' (flogging with heavy sticks) for fifty strokes, and the debtor shall return the principal and interest to the creditor." If the debtor failed to repay the creditor on time, besides returning the principal and interest, he should also be punished by "Chi" (flogging with light sticks) according to the days overdue. The system of "Zhong Bao" or "Bao Ren" (middleman or guarantor) was carried out strictly to insure the payment of debt. "Zhong Bao" or "Bao Ren" (middleman or guarantor) needed to sign in the loan contract to promise that he would repay the debtor in case the debtor was unable to repay the money or had fled for his life. According to the law of the Ming Dynasty, usurious interest rates were stipulated because usurious exploitation had become one of causes of civil riots in the late Yuan Dynasty. Whether in private debt or pawning property, the interest should not exceed three percent every month, and no matter how long the loan time was, the principle of "Yi Ben Yi Li" (the profit made should not be more than the principal) should be followed, and the violator would be punished by "Chi" (flogging with light sticks) for forty strokes. Moreover, possessing surplus amount of money would be regarded as dishonest possession of the property of other people. So if the amount of money was large and the case was serious, the creditor would be punished by "Zhang" (flogging with heavy sticks) for one hundred strokes. "If a domineering and powerful man had seized the livestock and other property of the debtor on the excuse of debt without appealing to the local authority, he shall be punished by 'Zhang' (flogging with heavy sticks) for eighty strokes. After calculating the total values of the debt, if the profit had exceeded the original amount, the extra part should be seen as illegal gains, so it should be returned to the debtor; if the creditor sold the wife, concubines or children of the debtor, he shall be punished by 'Zhang' (flogging with heavy sticks) for one hundred strokes; if the creditor is involved in forcible seizure, the punishment shall be doubled; if the creditor rapes the women after forcible seizure because of debtor's breach of contract, he shall be punished by 'Jiao' (hanging)."[249] It was also stipulated in the law of the Ming Dynasty that it was forbidden for government officials who had the responsibility of supervision and inspection to lend money to earn or to allow people to pawn property within their jurisdiction; it was also forbidden by law for the officials of "Ting Xuan" (candidate officials) and "Jian Sheng" (those who were recommended to study in 'Guo Zi Jian': the highest educational body in ancient China) to lend money to earn interest. If people had illegally crossed the border of the ethnic minority areas (like the Miao nationality of Yunnan and the Li nationality of Guangdong) to lend money to earn interest, they should be punished for the crime of having illegal connection with the ethnics of Tu and Miao nationalities.

The legal adjustment of debt relationships, as mentioned above, shows the state's interference in private debt, the purpose of which was to prevent the intensification of class contradiction and to protect the country's long-term stability and security by bringing debt relationships within the scope of statutory regulations, which was a beneficial experience that emperors of the early Ming Dynasty gained by summarizing the lessons learned from the collapse of the Yuan Dynasty.

In addition to the *obligatio ex contractu* mentioned above, the obligation to pay tort damages is also included in the laws of the Ming Dynasty.

Tort referred to the delict of trespassing the property or personal rights of other people. The victim can sue the tortfeasor for damages, and the tortfeasor has the liability to do so accordingly, which is called obligation of tort compensation when an obligation is incurred thereby.

The civil liability that a tortfeasor incurred by encroaching upon others' personal right was mainly undertaken by paying medical costs. It was also stipulated in the law of the Ming Dynasty that "according to 'Bao Gu System' (the system whereby an offender was ordered by law to help the victim recover within a prescribed period, and the punishment for the crime committed by the offender was determined according to the means of injury and the degree of recovery), the tortfeasor shall take the responsibility of taking care of the victim and paying medical costs of the treatment."[250] Meanwhile, the laws of the Yuan Dynasty on manslaughter, injuring or killing a person by horse or horse coach, and injuring or killing a person by a V crossbow were taken as a reference. According to these regulations, the tortfeasors

---

[249]"Wei Jin Qu Li" (Making Profits Illegally) in "Qian Zhai" (Debts) in "Hu Lv" (Statutes on Households) in *Ming Lv* (*Ming Code*).

[250]"Bao Gu Qi Xian" (The Time Limit for the Guarantee of the Recovery of the Victims) in "Dou Ou" (Fighting) in "Xing Lv" (The Penal Code) in *Ming Lv* (*Ming Code*).

10.4 Further Development of Civil Law

should pay for the funeral expenses and offer alimony to the families of the deceased or offer alimony to the victims who were crippled in the fighting.

The civil liability that a tortfeasor caused by encroaching upon others' property was mainly undertaken by compensation, such as reparation in kind. In the 2nd year of Hongzhi (1489), it was stipulated that "(if the creditor) discard or destroy the implements that belong to the victim, inspections should be conducted by judges to have a check of those implements and the tortfeasor's property so as to compensate for the victim's damages."[251] Nevertheless, in reality, the compensation should be paid at an estimated price. For example, according to the provision of "Setting Houses on Fire Deliberately" in "Za Fan" (Miscellaneous Crimes) in "Xing Lv" (The Penal Code) in *Ming Lv* (*Ming Code*), "(the judges) shall calculate the total losses of what is destroyed in the fire, reduce the price of the losses, then make it clear to the tortfeasor that it is an unlimited liability for the tortfeasor to compensate the victims or the officials with his property." As for the tort of destroying the property of the government, the tortfeasor shall pay back the losses with full compensation and take due criminal responsibility at the same time. During the reign of Emperor Jiajing, Wang Junchuan who had once been "Qin Min Guan" (the most basic local officials) in "Zhou" (subprefecture) and "Xian" (county), had kept the following records in *Jun Chuan Gong Yi Bo Gao* (*Collections of Official Documents by Junchuan*):

> (We have) to to deal with the matters like sending the land tax under guard to the government. As to the expenses of materials and land tax of the affiliated "Zhou" (subprefecture) and "Xian" (county) in interior and the border areas, they are collected and distributed every year with some of them each getting as much as one thousand and some of them one hundred. After the money is distributed, some of them discover that the money can be used to make profit, so they either purchase land and house or lend the money to earn interest in autumn, or embezzle it arbitrarily or take the money for their own use. After the plot is exposed, they are supervised in order that the money be taken back; however, the split water cannot be gathered up again. In spite of the measures taken for the recovery of property by selling the estates, it is only possible to return part of the money. Consequently, the father and the son shall be put into prison and the relatives shall compensate for the losses.[252]

Anyone who had acquired and appropriated the property illegally should return both the original object and the profit; if the original object was lost, the owner should be compensated according to the estimated value of the object. In *Xin Cuan Si Liu He Lv Pan Yu* (*Newly Edited Judgments in Four-Six Style Prose According to the Catalogue of Laws*), which was written by an anonymous author, there was a record of an infringement act of illegal cultivation of the land of the government and civilians, and the court verdict is as follows:

> Good farmers are those who are good at cultivating land, so they will not easily give up until they have got a good harvest. However, the large pieces of land for growing field crops

---

[251] "Hu Bu Lei" (The Department of Revenue) in *Huang Ming Tiao Fa Shi Lei Zuan* (*Annals of the Legal Cases in Ming Dynasty*), Vol. 13.

[252] Guo Chengwei, Tian Tao, *Ming Qing Gong Du Mi Ben Wu Zhong* (*Five Private Copies of Official Documents of Ming and Qing Dynasty*), p. 43.

belong to the government and is it possible for them to cultivate the land furtively? Xiao He who has asked for distributing the land to civilians is put into prison by Li Bang and Dou Xian who has bullied the princess and ravished their land is strongly condemned. So if the civilians are accused of violating the law, and the rich people are benefited. There are licentious people in Wenyang who have no idea of concession made between the people like Yu and Rui (two vassal states of ancient China). The farmland nationwide has all had its respective owners, so alas, they want to get the good land near the towns and cities. The common people will follow the example of the rulers. So it is in fact the idea of officials, which has brought them the hope of worshipping and praying for good harvest without calamity. They begin to plow the field with the calf before dawn and begin to sow the seed in the spring. However, they have not tasted the newly collected tea in Yangxian County, still they are required by the princes and aristocrats to serve corvee. People of the Qi state even regret it is their own fault after the land of Yun and Guan are flooded, therefore, they can not be punished for the crime of robbing, but they can only be taxed according to the amount of land.[253]

For the obligations of tort compensation mentioned above, some of them are civil liability; others are criminal with civil liability. So just like the proliferation of *obligatio ex contractu*, obligation of tort compensation was also a common phenomenon in the social life of the Ming Dynasty.

10.4.4 Marriage and Inheritance Law Adapted from That of the Tang and Song Dynasties

The principles of clan hierarchy, monogamy, and the integration of "Li" (rites) and "Fa" (law) were the basic principles of marriage legislation. The marriage of children was arranged by their parents and grandparents, and marriage contracts and bride price were also needed in marriages. People with the same family names or from the same clan or within "Wu Fu" (relatives within the five degrees of mourning) were prohibited from getting married. Marriages between "Liang" (the common people) and "Jian" (people of a lower social status than common people) were also forbidden. Dissolution of marriages was based on conditions like "Qi Chu" (seven reasons to repudiate the wife: "being unfilial to parents-in-law," "failing to bear a male offspring," "being lascivious," "being jealous," "having severe illness," "gossiping," and "committing theft") and "Yi Jue" (a system of forced divorce because of fighting, scolding, killing, and raping of the relatives of both parties). In line with the development of times, some new contents like emphasis on the disciplinary function of etiquette and customs were also added to marriage law. During the reign of Emperor Jiajing, Wang Junchuan, who had served successively as the official of "Zhou" (subprefecture) and "Xian" (county), wrote in the book *Jun Chuan Gong Yi Bo Gao* (*Collections of Official Documents by Junchuan*):

---

[253]Guo Chengwei, Tian Tao, *Ming Qing Gong Du Mi Ben Wu Zhong* (*Five Private Copies of Official Documents of Ming and Qing Dynasty*), p. 86.

10.4 Further Development of Civil Law

"Guan" (the ceremony of crowning of adulthood), wedding, funeral and sacrifice are all included in family etiquette, which are very important principles for stressing customs and cultivating morality. In recent years, the Confucian scholars have made detailed references and analyses. So family etiquette has been followed by most of the official and aristocratic families. From now on, if there are any good or ill luck or any accidents in the families of "Sheng Yuan" (also called "Xiu Cai": those who passed the imperial examination at the county level in ancient China), they should be taught by their teachers to have a detailed study of "Li" (rites). The most important thing is to accomplish "Li" (rites), but not to show off extravagance and frugality. After the ceremony, the names of the people who have accomplished the ceremony of "Guan" (the ceremony of crowning of adulthood), the married, the dead and the scholars who attend the ceremonies should be recorded and reported by "Sheng Yuan" (also called "Xiu Cai": those who passed the imperial examination at the county level in ancient China) to the local "Ya Men" (the government offices) or "Dao" (the administration district below the province) or marquis for examination and awarding. The ceremony of "Guan" (the ceremony of crowning of adulthood) should be held for a man who is twenty years old; otherwise, the marriage is prohibited. During the period of mourning, buddhist shall not be enshrined and worshiped; if a funeral is not held in the case of "Ding You" (filial mourning), the person involved shall not go back to school; if "Li Jiao" (feudal ethical code) is intentionally violated for failing to hold the ceremony on time or the above mentioned rule and regulations are disobeyed, or a false report is delivered by the teacher to concealing the truth, he shall be punished severely once the plot is exposed.[254]

As another example, it was emphasized that "marriage time should be set for both men and women," which meant that marriage was not allowed until men and women reached the legal age. It was stipulated in the 3rd year of Hongwu (1370) that "marriage may be contracted when the man has reached sixteen years old and the woman fourteen years old."[255] Moreover, "marriage that was arranged through 'Zhi Fu Wei Hun' (the boy and the girl had been engaged to each other before they were born) and 'Ge Yi Jing Wei Qin' (to engage to each other by cutting the one or two pieces of the front of a Chinese jacket) which is popular among civilians are prohibited."[256] In the book *Jun Chuan Gong Yi Bo Gao* (*Collections of Official Documents by Junchuan*), Wang Junchaun pointed out:

> Marriage for male and female is the most important practice in human relationship and it is the source of customs and morality. Therefore, cultivating people's moral character, putting people's family affairs in order and pursuing people's studies are all rooted in marriage. The family members of soldiers and civilians are not allowed to get married if the male and female have not reached the legally marriageable age, so it should especially be paid attention to by the families of the scholars. It is the hope of a local place to be familiar with classic books and steeped in propriety. So if everyone feels ashamed of doing bad things, it is hopeful that the customs can soon be changed. If marriage is contracted before the man has reached the legally marriageable age or the old custom is still followed, when the plot is exposed, those involved will be found guilty. Although the property will not be confiscated, the male and the female shall be divorced; if the thing happens in the families of "Sheng Yuan" (also called "Xiu Cai": those who passed the imperial examination at lower

---

[254] Guo Chengwei, Tian Tao, *Ming Qing Gong Du Mi Ben Wu Zhong* (*Five Private Copies of Official Documents of Ming and Qing Dynasty*), p. 54.
[255] Yu Ruji (Ming Dynasty), *Li Bu Zhi Gao* (*Annals of the Department of Rites*), Vol. 20.
[256] "Hu Ling" (Decrees on Household) in *Ming Lv* (*Ming Code*).

level in ancient China) because he could not conduct himself with etiquette and morality or manage the family by "Lun Li" (ethics), he shall be punished by removing from his office.[257]

As marriage is "the alliance of two families," it must be based upon the will of the parents of both parties. The male of the direct relatives of a senior generation has the right to decide the marriages of the younger generation.

"Before marriage, if there is any disability, the old and the young, 'Shu Chu' (the children born of concubines), 'Guo Fang' (brother's son adopted as one's heir) and 'Qi Yang' (adoption by relatives), the families of both parties shall be informed to make a choice." And then both parties should "sign a marriage contract," and "the male and the female should get married in accordance with rituals,"[258] which were regulations summarized from many marital disputes, so they were in accordance with common sense and were helpful to avoid lawsuits.

According to legal procedures, both parties should "sign a marriage contract" and "the male and female should get married in accordance with 'Li' (rites)." A marriage contract (including private contract) had the force of law, so neither of the parties was allowed to break the contract and marry someone else. It was provided in *Da Ming Lv* (*The Great Ming Code*) that "if the male has broken the contract or broken the pledge of marriage, he shall be punished by 'Zhang' (flogging with heavy sticks) for fifty strokes."[259] So obviously, the penalty for the male who broke off an engagement was aggravated. If the male had already pledged the bride price and the female had accepted the gift, their marriage was also legal even without marriage contracts.

The marriage ceremony that was held "in accordance with 'Li' (rites)" in the Ming Dynasty was different from the conventional "Liu Li" (six kinds of etiquette in feudal marriage). According to "Li Ling" (Decree of Rites) in *Da Ming Ling* (*The Decrees of Great Ming Dynasty*), "a civil marriage should be held according to *Zhu Wen Gong Jia Li* (*The Family Etiquette of Zhu Wengong*)," which included proposing marriage, "Na Cai" (men and women giving gifts to each other), bringing dowry to the woman's family, "Qin Ying" (holding the wedding ceremony), visiting the man's parents, worshipping the man's ancestors, and so on.

In terms of marriage prohibition, besides the prohibition of the "marriage with those with the same surnames,"[260] another regulation was issued to prohibit "marrying the cousin of the same clan,"[261] which had fully demonstrated the constraining force of the patriarchal clan system. In addition, marriage between "Liang" (the

---

[257]Guo Chengwei, Tian Tao, *Ming Qing Gong Du Mi Ben Wu Zhong* (*Five Private Copies of Official Documents of Ming and Qing Dynasty*), p. 54.

[258]"Nan Nv Hun Yin" (The Marriage of Men and Women) in "Hun Yin" (Marriage) in "Hu Lv" (Statutes on Households) in *Ming Lv* (*Ming Code*).

[259]"Nan Nv Hun Yin" (The Marriage of Men and Women) in "Hun Yin" (Marriage) in "Hu Lv" (Statutes on Households) in *Ming Lv* (*Ming Code*).

[260]"Tong Xing Wei Hun" (The Marriage between People with the Same Surnames) in "Hun Yin" (Marriage) in "Hu Lv" (Statutes on Households) in *Ming Lv* (*Ming Code*).

[261]"Qu Qin Shu Qi Qie" (Marrying the Wives and Concubines of Relatives) in "Hun Yin" (Marriage) in "Hu Lv" (Statutes on Households) in *Ming Lv* (*Ming Code*).

10.4 Further Development of Civil Law

common people) and "Jian" (people of a lower social status than common people), between relatives, between a man an escaped woman, and between a local official and a woman in his jurisdiction was also forbidden, so marriage prohibitions were almost the same as those in the Tang and Song dynasties.

As to dissolution of marriage, it was still based on the rules of "Qi Chu" (seven reasons to repudiate the wife: "being unfilial to parents-in-law," "failing to bear a male offspring," "being lascivious," "being jealous," "having severe illness," "gossiping," and "committing theft") and "Yi Jue" (a system of forced divorce because of fighting, scolding, killing, and raping of the relatives of both parties). But in the Ming Dynasty a new interpretation was added in "Yi Jue": "'Yi Jue' should be applied in the following circumstances: if the husband is far away, the wife's parents marry her to another person, or drives her away, or let the son-in-law live in their family, or allow her to commit adultery with other people; if the wife is beaten and wounded by the husband, or if the husband prevents the wife from committing adultery, or if the husband falsely claims that he doesn't get married and wants to marry someone else, or if the husband treats his wife as concubine, or if has his wife and concubine pawned, or if sells them as his sisters for money."[262] Obviously, the status of marriage itself was focused on in the affirmation of "Yi Jue" in the laws of Ming Dynasty, which was different from that of the Tang Dynasty, in which family violence, such as murder, rape, and adultery of both parties toward each other or toward the clans or families of both parties, especially the murder of one's husband, was the focused on.

In addition, "if the husband and the wife are in disharmony, they may divorce if both of them agree to, and they are not to be found guilty,"[263] which was known as "He Li" (peaceful dissolution of marriage); "if the marriage is found illegal ... although the husband and the wife are exonerative, they have still to be divorced and correct their misconducts."[264] In February of the 21st year of Chenghua (1485), provisions were specifically made against the repeated occurrence of illegal marriage: "From now on, the case on the aforementioned illegal marriage shall be accepted by the local government, and the case shall be carefully investigated to find out the facts. The violators will be interrogated according to law, and illegal marriage is forbidden by the government in order to maintain the customs and morality of the society."[265]

---

[262]"Gan Ming Fan Yi" (Violating the Feudal Ethics) in "Su Song" (Litigation) in "Xing Lv" (The Penal Code) in *Ming Lv* (*Ming Code*).

[263]"Chu Qi" (Divorcing the Wife) in "Hun Yin" (Marriage) in "Hu Lv" (Statutes on Households) in *Ming Lv* (*Ming Code*).

[264]"Jia Qu Wei Lv Zhu Hun Mou Ren Zui" (The Crime of Matchmakers for their Illegal Arrangement of Marriages) in "Hun Yin" (Marriage) in "Hu Lv" (Statutes on Households) in *Ming Lv* (*Ming Code*).

[265]"Wei Lv Wei Hun Yi Lv Wen Duan Li" (Hearing the Cases of Illegal Marriage according to Law) in "Hu Bu Lei" (The Department of Revenue) in *Huang Ming Tiao Fa Shi Lei Zuan* (*Annals of the Legal Cases* in *Ming Dynasty*), Vol. 13.

In the Ming Dynasty, which was at the later period of feudal society, although monogamy was the legal principle and "bigamous marriage" was prohibited, the wife was still in a subordinate position in the family under the restriction of the feudal order of "Fu Wei Qi Gang" (husband guides wife). For example, the wife should adopt the husband's surname and accept the husband's instruction, punishment, and supervision. The husband also had the right to marry her off or to sell her to others. It was also provided in the laws of the Ming Dynasty that "if the husband beats the wife or if the wife has not got physical injuries, the husband may not be held liable; if the wife has got physical injuries, the husband may still not be held liable unless the wife has sued the husband by herself."[266] "As for the crimes committed by women, except the crime of adultery and the crime punishable by death penalty, the other miscellaneous crimes can all be handled by the husband."[267]

According to *Ming Lv* (*Ming Code*), "if the husband is forty years old and if he had no children, he is allowed to take concubines,"[268] which was often used as an excuse by the husband to take concubines. Besides, aristocrats enjoyed the special legal privilege of taking concubines, but as to the wife, she was only allowed to be faithful to her husband (except that of the death of husband). More than that, if the wife committed adultery or escaped secretly, "the husband was allowed to sell his wife to others" according to law.[269]

The wife also had certain rights in the management of the family and some property rights under certain conditions or with the husband's permission. For example, if the husband died, a widow may exercise her parental rights. But overall, the rights and obligations of a wife and a husband were not equal under the law. The children, the humble, and the young were in a lower social rank, so they had no right in the family. The parents had the right to instruct and punish the children, to arrange the marriages of their children, and to monopolize their property. "If the grandparents and parents are still alive, the children who divide the family property and live apart shall be punished by 'Zhang' (flogging with heavy sticks) for one hundred strokes." "If the humble and the young who live in the same house have used the property without the permission of the grandparents, they shall be punished by 'Chi' (flogging with light sticks) for twenty strokes for misappropriating twenty *guan* of money, and the punishment shall double with each additional 20 *guan* with the maximum punishment of one hundred strokes."[270]

---

[266]"Qi Qie Ou Fu" (The Wife and Concubine Beating up the Husband) in "Dou Ou" (Fighting) in "Xing Lv" (The Penal Code) in *Ming Lv* (*Ming Code*).

[267]"Fu Ren Fan Zui" (Women Committing Crimes) in "Duan Yu" (Trials and Punishments) in "Xing Lv" (The Penal Code) in *Ming Lv* (*Ming Code*).

[268]"Qi Qie Shi Xu" (The Violation of Ethic Order by the Wife and Concubines) in "Hun Yin" (Marriage) in "Hu Lv" (Statutes on Households) in *Ming Lv* (*Ming Code*).

[269]"Fan Jian" (Adultery) in "Xing Lv" (The Penal Code) in *Ming Lv* (*Ming Code*).

[270]"Bie Ji Yi Cai" (Dividing Property and Registering Separately) and "Bei You Si Shan Yong Cai" (Illegal Disposal of Property by the Young and the Humble) in "Hu Yi" (Household Corvee) in "Hu Lv" (Statutes on Households) in *Ming Lv* (*Ming Code*).

10.4 Further Development of Civil Law

Because the feudal patriarchal family was the pillar of the autocratic system, in *Ming Lv* (*Ming Code*), the patriarchal family was maintained by the compulsory forces of state law; meanwhile, it was required to be abided by in the supreme authoritative form of an imperial edict. In the early years of the Ming Dynasty, "Sheng Yu Liu Tiao" (six imperial edicts), namely, "showing filial piety to parents, showing respect to the seniors, being harmonious in villages, instructing and educating children, living peacefully and abiding the law, was issued by Emperor Taizu."[271] In most of the administrative policies in the early Ming Dynasty, education was combined with penalties, which was a new strategy for ruling the state, which was formed in order to avoid the downfall of the country caused by malpractices, just as what had happened in the Yuan Dynasty.

In terms of inheritance, the lineal primogeniture system was regarded as the "law of the state," and "Di Zhang Zi" (the eldest son born of the legal wife) should be the inheritor, whether for the inheritance of official titles or for the inheritance of "Zong Tiao" (the succession to the headship); for families of the common people, "those who break the law shall be punished by 'Zhang' (flogging with heavy sticks) for eighty strokes." If there was no "Di Zhang Zi" (the eldest son born of the legal wife), the title should be inherited by "Di Zhang Sun" (the eldest grandson of the legal wife) or "Shu Zhang Zi" (the eldest son born of a concubine). But the title should not be inherited by "Yi Zi" (adopted son) with different surnames or else they would be considered in breach of inheritance and should be punished by "Zhang" (flogging with heavy sticks) for sixty strokes.[272] Thus, the following was added to the original provisions of "Hu Jue" (No Male Heirs) and "the appointment of heirs from the same clan who are equivalent to 'Zhao Mu' (the patriarchal system of arranged order and order of generation in the temple or cemetery)" in the laws of the Tang and Song dynasties:

> "The appointed heir shall be the nephew from the same clan who is equivalent to 'Zhao Mu' (the patriarchal system of arranged order and order of generation in the temple or cemetery) if there is no offspring in this family. Firstly, all of the relatives on the father's side should be taken into consideration; secondly, 'Da Gong' (the person wearing the mourning apparel of soft sackcloth in the third mourning degree), 'Xiao Gong' (the person wearing the mourning apparel of soft sackcloth in the fourth mourning degree) and 'Si Ma' (the person wearing the mourning apparel of soft sackcloth in the fifth mourning degree) should be taken into consideration; if there are none of them, then the distant relatives or the people with the same family names should be taken into consideration."[273] If the appointed heir was not filial, he might be sued to the government and deprived of the right to inherit.

As for the inheritance of property, "the property should be divided equally according to the number of the sons born either by the wives, or concubines or 'Nu Bi' (the slave girls and maidservants); if they are adulterine sons, they shall

---

[271] Qiu Jun (Ming Dynasty), *Da Xue Yan Yi Bu* (*Supplement to the Deductive Meaning of the Great Learning*), Vol. 18.

[272] "Li Di Zi Wei Fa" (Illegal Inheritance by the Eldest Son of the Legal Wife) in "Hu Yi" (Household Corvee) in "Hu Lv" (Statutes on Households) in *Ming Lv* (*Ming Code*).

[273] "Hu Ling" (Decrees on Household) in *Ming Lv* (*Ming Code*).

share half of property according to the number of the sons; if there is no son, the property shall be divided equally among the brothers, nephews and the adulterine sons; if there are no brothers and nephews, the adulterine sons shall inherit all of the property."[274] Obviously, the legal status of adulterine child and their rights to inherit the property was improved according to the law, which not only was characteristic of the inheritance law in Ming Dynasty, but also reflected some changes of the feudal legal ideology.

As for the inheritance of the property of the families of "Hu Jue" (No Male Heirs), the property should be inherited by all the daughters of the wives, concubines, and 'Nu Bi' (the slave girls and maidservants); if there were no daughters, the property would be taken over by the government. A childless widow who did not remarry should share the property of the deceased husband; if the adopted sons were abandoned children under three years old, they should share the property at discretion. As for those families of "Zhao Xu" (have the groom live in the bride's house), "the people from the same clan shall be appointed to be the inheritor to be responsible for the sacrifice and to share the property equally."[275]

As seen from the large number of relevant writs of will, testamentary succession was a popular way of transferring property through inheritance. Most testamentary succession was made in written form to ensure its authenticity. The will should be made and signed in the presence of the people of the same clan or in the presence of witnesses. Testamentary succession was supported by law.

As to the inheritance law in Ming Dynasty, on the one hand, the ancient tradition, such as the integration of "identity" and "property" inheritance and the coexistence of "Di Zhang Zi" (the eldest son born of the legal wife) and coinheritance, etc. was retained; on the other hand, property the relationship between "Qing" (human relationships) and "Fa" (law) was stressed and improvements were made in adoption system and the inheritance rights of the adulterine child and so on, which was surely a great progress in feudal inheritance law.

10.5 Economic Legislation Adapting to the Economic Development

Economic legislation accounted for a large portion of the legislative acts in the Ming Dynasty so as to replace the more than ninety years outdated and barbaric economic rules; especially, after the great turmoil in the late Yuan Dynasty, society and the economy were devastated and destructed, which led to the waste of land and the decrease of population. Therefore, it became a very urgent problem to find a way to recover the damaged social economy. In order to "recuperate and build up strength,"

---

[274]"Hu Ling" (Decrees on Household) in *Ming Lv* (*Ming Code*).
[275]"Hu Ling" (Decrees on Household) in *Ming Lv* (*Ming Code*).

10.5 Economic Legislation Adapting to the Economic Development 1023

to resume and develop production, and to reconstruct the economic foundation of the authoritarian regime, a series of economic legislation was carried out by the rulers of the Ming Dynasty on the basis of the economic laws of the Tang and Song dynasties, which had not only increased the number and variety of economic legislation but also made it enter a new and much maturer stage.

10.5.1 The Agricultural Legislation Encouraging Land Reclamation

In the early years of the Ming Dynasty, the flood of vagrants and shortage of labor in agricultural production were not only disadvantageous to the recovery of agricultural production but also potentially threatening to the autocratic regime. Therefore, on one hand, it was ordered by Emperor Taizu to strictly prohibit human trafficking and to prohibit selling "Liang Ren" (the decent people) as "Nu Bi" (the slave girls and maidservants) so that a large number of laborers could devote themselves to agricultural production; on the other hand, it was also ordered to recruit exiled people and engage them in production and to promote immigration and land reclamation. In the Shandong, Henan, and Anhui regions, it was permitted for people to reclaim unclaimed wasteland as their own "without land tax obligations."[276]

During the reign of Emperor Hongwu, many laws on immigration and land reclamation were issued successively, which had played a positive role in promoting agricultural production. For example, in the first year of Hongwu (1368), in "Zhou" (subprefecture) and "Xian" (county) of the whole country, the cultivated land accounted for about 770 $qing$,[277] but in the 13th year of Hongwu (1380), "the cultivated waste land in the whole country accounted for about 53,931 $qing$."[278] In the provision of "Qi Yin Tian Liang" (Concealing Land and Grain) and "Huang Wu Tian Tu" (Wasting of Land) in "Hu Lv" (Statutes on Households) in *Da Ming Lv* (*The Great Ming Code*), the penalties for the unclaimed land were stipulated, according to which the officials in charge were generally promoted or demoted.

Except the reclamation of wasteland by immigrants, "Tun Tian" (wasteland opened up by garrison troops or peasants) was implemented at the beginning of the Ming Dynasty to increase agricultural income. "Tun Tian" (wasteland opened up by garrison troops or peasants) included "Jun Tun" (wasteland opened up by garrison troops or peasants), "Min Tun" (wasteland opened up by peasants), "Shang Tun" (wasteland opened up by businessman), "Xu Zui Tun" (wasteland opened up by the criminals pardoned), "Shu Zui Tun" (wasteland opened up by the

---

[276] "Hu Bu" (The Department of Revenue) (Part 6) in *Ming Hui Dian* (*The Collected Statutes of Ming Dynasty*), Vol. 17.

[277] *Ming Tai Zu Shi Lu* (*The Record of Emperor Taizu of Ming Dynasty*), Vol. 37.

[278] *Ming Tai Zu Shi Lu* (*The Record of Emperor Taizu of Ming Dynasty*), Vol. 134.

criminals stoning for their crimes), and so on. According to *Ming Shi Lu* (*The Records of Ming Dynasty*), the opened up wasteland had reached to 903,313 *qing* and 95 *mu*, which accounted for about one tenth of the land of the whole country. In the 21st year of Hongwu (1388), grain production by "Jun Tun" (wasteland opened up by garrison troops or peasants) was more than five million *dan* a year, which was enough to meet the grain demand of the border guarding posts; this had strengthened the frontier by engaging soldiers in farm work. Because reclaimed wasteland was owned by the state and reclamation was the main way of operating wasteland by the state, in order to protect such land, it was stipulated in the laws of Ming Dynasty that "if people who have occupied over fifty *mu* of wasteland refuse to hand in grain" or if the buyers and sellers who mortgage the wasteland refuse to hand in grain, the officials will be assigned to the frontier to work with pay, the soldiers of 'Qi' (banner, equivalent of a county) will be sent to the frontier to be punished by 'Chong Jun' (to be forced to join the army) and the common people will be sent to remote places ... Therefore, careful investigation shall be conducted by the officials who are responsible for the management of wasteland; otherwise, they shall be punished."[279]

After the middle of the Ming Dynasty, the historical task of "Tun Tian" (wasteland opened up by garrison troops or peasants), which was conducted by the state, was completed. With political corruption and the escaping of garrison soldiers, "the law on 'Tun Tian' (wasteland opened up by garrison troops or peasants) was frequently violated,"[280] so "the system of 'Tun Tian' (wasteland opened up by garrison troops or peasants) existed only in name in the country."[281] Thus, it became a trend of historical development to change "Tun Tian" (wasteland opened up by garrison troops or peasants) into "Min Tian" (private land). During the reign of Chongzhen, the suggestion of minister Wang Shiting was adopted: "Whether the land belonged to army or civilian, it will be taxed according to 'Min Tian' (private land)."[282] So reclaimed wasteland was recognized as "Min Tian" (private land) in law, and the landowner had the right to occupy and cultivate the land if he had handed in grain tax to the state. Therefore, the prohibition on the cultivation and illegal occupation of reclaimed wasteland and the regulation on tax payment, which was issued during the reign of Emperor Xiaozhong, had become a mere scrap of paper.

Because of the implementation of the policy that "the amount of land is completely decided by the peasants themselves," stress was laid on the penalties for cheating and concealing of land, grain, and tax in the laws of the Ming Dynasty,

---

[279]"Dao Mai Tian Zhai Tiao Li" (The Regulation on the Stealing and Selling of the Land and Houses) in "Tian Zhai" (Land and Houses) in "Hu Lv" (Statutes on Households) (Part 2) in *Wen Xing Tiao Li* (*The Ordinance for Inquisition*).

[280]*Ming Xian Zong Shi Lu* (*The Record of Xianzong in Ming Dynasty*), Vol. 244.

[281]Zhang Xuan (Ming Dynasty), "Gong Bu" (The Department of Works) (Part 5) in *Xi Yuan Wen Jian Lu* (*Xi Yuan Sketch Book*), Vol. 91.

[282]"Bi Zi Yan Zhuan" (The Biography of Yan Ziyan) in *Ming Shi* (*The History of Ming Dynasty*).

which was totally different from the prohibition of "the excessive occupation of land" in Tang the Dynasty. People who "cheated and concealed the land and grain" would be punished by "Chi" (flogging with light sticks) and "Zhang" (flogging with heavy sticks), "with his land confiscated by the government. Besides, the landowner should pay the tax which he had concealed accordingly"; "if 'Lin Zhang' (head of 'Li': the basic resident organization in ancient China) knew of the case, but did not reported it to the government, he would be punished the same with the criminal"[283]; if the landowner falsely reported his land and grain and hid the grain in the bureaucratic and rich families to evade tax, both parties should be found guilty in order to ensure the collection of grain tax to maintain the operation of the enormous state machinery. In the early years of the Ming Dynasty, *Huang Ce* (*Yellow Book*) and *Yu Lin Tu Ce* (*Scale Graph*) were also compiled and published to conduct a survey of the land nationwide for the landowners to pay tax in accordance with the acreage under cultivation. In addition to land tax, each "Ding" (adult) should pay poll tax and should be on active service for at least one month per year, by which the pressure of the farmers was considerably reduced compared with that of the Ming Dynasty, so it had stimulated the farmers' enthusiasm for production.

As for those big landlords who occupied a large amount of land, owned a lot of "Hu Kou" (registered permanent residence), and concealed the land and grain to evade the tax and corvée, specific stipulations were made in the laws of the Ming Dynasty. Except for public land granted to meritorious statesmen, the rest of the land must be accurately reported to the government for the payment of grain tax and for the rendering of corvee labor in accordance with law; violators thereof would be severely punished. If he had concealed one to three *mu* of land, he would be punished by "Zhang" (flogging with heavy sticks) for sixty strokes, with the maximum punishment of "Zhang" (flogging with heavy sticks) for one hundred strokes, plus three years of imprisonment; if the rich and influential people had instigated their children and relatives to evade the tax and corvee service by following other officials, the parents who concealed the fact would be punished by "Zhang" (flogging with heavy sticks) for one hundred strokes, and the concerned officials would be punished the same way as fraud.

In order to develop agriculture, it was necessary to build irrigation projects, to renovate ponds and embankments, and to dredge rivers; therefore, in the early years of the Ming Dynasty, "Ying Tian Si" (government office in charge of opening up wasteland and agriculture) was set up to be in charge of water conservancy. In the 27th year of Hongwu (1394), the students of "Guo Zi Jian" (the highest educational body in ancient China) were sent to different places to supervise and urge the construction of water conservancy, so the number of ponds being constructed reached to 40,987. In addition, it was provided in "Gong Lv" (Statutes on Handicraft Industry) in *Da Ming Lv* (*The Great Ming Code*) that "people who have destroyed the river banks shall be punished by 'Zhang' (flogging with heavy sticks) for one

---

[283]"Qi Yin Tian Liang" (Concealing Land and Grain) in "Tian Zhai" (Land and Houses) in "Hu Lv" (Statutes on Households) in *Ming Lv* (*Ming Code*).

hundred strokes; people who have destroyed ponds and embankments shall be punished by 'Zhang' (flogging with heavy sticks) for eighty strokes"; "the people who fail to rebuild the dikes and embankments in time shall be punished by 'Chi' (flogging with light sticks) for thirty strokes; if it has led to the inundation of the land and crops, the relevant people shall be punished by 'Zhang' (flogging with heavy sticks) for fifty strokes"; "if people's houses are flooded and their belongings are destroyed and lost, the people who rebuild the embankments shall be punished by 'Zhang' (flogging with heavy sticks) for sixty strokes; if any person gets injured, the people who rebuild the dykes and embankments shall be punished by 'Zhang' (flogging with heavy sticks) for eighty strokes." The legislation on water conservancy was an important part of the agricultural legislation in the Ming Dynasty, which had no doubt enriched the contents of agricultural legislation.

In summary, the agricultural legislation of the Ming Dynasty contributed greatly to the recovery of agricultural production and development. According to the statistics in the 26th year of Hongwu (1393), the cultivated land area in the whole country had reached to 8,507,623 *qing* and the population had reached to 60,544,812. It was stated in "Shi Huo Zhi" (The Records of National Finance and Economy) (Part 2) in *Ming Shi* (*The History of Ming Dynasty*) that "at this time, the whole country was rich and prosperous, the national revenue increased and millions of *dan* of grain was sent to the capital. There was so much grain in the granaries of the government of "Fu" (ancient administrative district between province and county) and "Xian" (county) that the grain was even rotten and no longer edible."

10.5.2 The Government-Run Handicraft Industry with the Promotion of the System of "Jiang Ji" (The Craftsman Household Registration)

The development of agriculture had greatly contributed to the progress of industries and commerce and the development of industrial and commercial legislation. In the early Ming Dynasty, in order to meet the needs of the developing handicraft industry, craftsmen were classified in a specific household registration, namely "Jiang Ji" (the craftsman household registration), following the system of "Jiang Ji" of the Yuan Dynasty. If a craftsman was classified in this specific household registration, then he would lose his freedom to do business and migrate nationwide. Moreover, it was forbidden for him and his offspring to cancel the household registration; if he had done so, he would be severely punished.

In the 19th year of Hongwu (1386), the shift system of craftsmen was established. The so-called shift lasted for no more than three months for every three years. Apart from "shift," the craftsmen also needed to "keep office hours," and they were demanded to work ten days a month with a total of one hundred and twenty days every year. They could receive grain every month for their work, but no grain was given to them if they did not work. If a craftsman failed to keep office hours, he should be imposed with a fine of thirty *qian* of silver, which was called "Shu Ban." From the reign of Hongwu to that of Yingzong, there were more than 230,000 registered current craftsmen who participated in the "shift" system, which was more than the number of craftsmen who kept office hours. Compared with the craftsman system of "Jiang Bu Li Ju" (the craftsmen prohibited from leaving the office randomly) in the Yuan Dynasty, the craftsmen in the Ming Dynasty had more free time apart from their working hours.

Because the system of "Jiang Ji" (the craftsman household registration) was carried out compulsorily with the support of law, it was more completely established. Initially, through the centralized management of handicraft workers, technical advantages were given to a full play, which had promoted the development of the handicraft industry; however, the system was essentially a system that forced labor into the handicraft industry, so gradually it became a heavy burden to handicraft workers, which not only limited their personal freedom but also reduced their enthusiasm. Following the continuing struggle of the craftsmen, the southern artisans were allowed to pay silver money to be exempted from working by "shift" or "keeping office hours" during the reign of Yingzong. In the 41st year of Jiajing (1562), it was provided that "since the beginning of this spring, it is allowed for the craftsmen who work by "shift" and "keep office hours" to be exempted from the system by paying silver money."[284] After the law was enacted, the system characterized by forced labor was abolished, which had become one of the most important reasons for the development of private handicraft industry in the late Ming Dynasty.

As for the requirement on the quality and specification of the handicraft industry that was provided in the laws of the Ming Dynasty, mostly those of the Tang Dynasty were inherited. If the manufactured goods did not meet the requirement, the manufacturer would be punished by "Chi" (flogging with light sticks) for forty strokes; if the manufactured weapons did not meet the requirement or the quality of the woven satin was not satisfactory, the manufacturer would be punished by "Zhang" (flogging with heavy sticks) for fifty strokes; if the objects could no longer be used and must be remade, the loss of property and money to hire people would be estimated respectively; if the circumstances were severe, violators would be sentenced to imprisonment for the offense of corruption; if the objects were made to be dedicated in sacrificial or royal affairs, the craftsmen would be punished two levels severer according to their respective responsibilities. For the officials concerned, compensation should be paid for losses according to their responsibilities.

It is particularly worth mentioning that the provisions and regulations on the management of handicraft production in the Tang and Song dynasties were sorted out and modified in *Ming Lv* (*Ming Code*), so they became very specific. The following are examples.

If something was to be constructed by armymen, civilians, and officials, it should be reported to their superiors for approval. If the construction was carried out

---

[284]"Gong Bu" (The Department of Works) (Part 6) in *Ming Hui Dian* (*The Collected Statutes of Ming Dynasty*), Vol. 189.

illegally, those involved would be punished for the crime of "Zuo Zang" (embezzlement) according to the number of workers involved and their salaries; if the construction materials, property and labor which were reported were false, those involved would be punished by "Zhang" (flogging with heavy sticks) for fifty strokes; if the property and labor had been used in the construction, they should be estimated and reported separately; if the circumstances were serious, those involved would be sentenced to imprisonment for the crime of "Zuo Zang" (embezzlement).

If the head craftsman of the manufacture bureau had taken materials more than necessary and appropriated them privately for his own use, he would be sentenced for the crime of "Zuo Zang" (embezzlement) with the materials returned to the government; if the official in charge did not report the case after learning the truth, he would be punished the same way as the head craftsman; if the official in charge failed to learn of the case, he would be punished three levels lighter.

If a civilian had woven and sold "Sha Luo" (silk products especially used by royal families) with dragon and phoenix patterns illegally, he or she would be punished by "Zhang" (flogging with heavy sticks) for one hundred strokes with the silk and satin products confiscated, and the household that owned machines for production should be punished the same way as the craftsman.

If people would fail to manufacture and hand in satins and weapons on time every year according to law, they would be punished by "Chi" (flogging with light sticks) with the maximum punishment of "Zhang" (flogging with heavy sticks) for fifty strokes; if an official failed to allocate and transfer the materials to the craftsmen, he would also be sentenced to the punishment of "Chi" (flogging with light sticks).

If there was any damage to official premises such as government offices, warehouses, bureau yards, etc., it would be reported to the relevant agencies to be repaired by the officials in charge; if they had failed to do so, they would be punished by "Chi" (flogging with light sticks) for forty strokes; if official stuff and property were damaged, the officials in charge would be punished by "Chi" (flogging with light sticks) for forty strokes, with the damaged stuff and property compensated.

If the building was not safe or had collapsed within three years, the officials and their seniors responsible for the repairing should compensate for the losses; if the supervisor deliberately concealed the fact after being discovered, he would be ordered to have it repaired and, at the same time, would be punished by "Xing Bu" (The Department of Punishment).

If wood and stone materials were used to make bricks and tiles that were useless, those involved in the making should be punished by "Zuo Zang" (embezzlement) with wasted labor cost calculated. If people were killed because of lack of consideration during the time of construction, those involved would be charged with involuntary manslaughter.[285]

In order to protect mineral resources, the exploitation of minerals such as silver, copper, etc. would be managed by the government, so anyone who had exploited

---

[285]For the above provisions, please see "Gong Lv" (Statutes on Handicraft Industry) in *Ming Lv* (*Ming Code*).

minerals without authorization would be charged with the crime of robbery. However, civilians were allowed to apply for mining right in relation to other mineral resources; anyone who had occupied or destroyed mineral resources without authorization would be severely punished.

10.5.3 The Strengthening of "Jin Que Zhi Du" (The System of State Monopoly for Some Important Goods) in Commerce

Based on the traditional policy of "Zhong Nong Yi Mo" (encouraging agriculture and restraining commerce), the government-run monopoly for salt and tea was strengthened by commercial legislation. As early as the 21st year of Emperor Yuanzhi (1361), *Yan Fa* (*Regulations of Salt*) was ordered to be made by Zhu Yuanzhang, and it was stipulated that 20% should be taken out from the profit made by salt sellers to help pay soldiers' salary. In the 1st year of Hongwu (1368), *Yan Yin Tiao Li* (*The Regulation on the Certificates for Transporting Taxed Salts*) was made, wherein it was declared that anyone who had sold salt illegally would be punished by "Jiao" (hanging); if he was equipped with weapons, he would be punished by "Zhan" (beheading). Afterward, more lenient regulations were made in *Da Ming Lv* (*The Great Ming Code*): "Anyone who sells salt illegally shall be sentenced to three years of imprisonment after being punished by 'Zhang' (flogging with heavy sticks) for one hundred strokes; if anyone brings weapons with him, he would be much severely punished; if anyone resists arresting, he would be punished by 'Zhan' (beheading)"[286] In addition, anyone who bought salt illegally would be punished by "Zhang" (flogging with heavy sticks) for one hundred strokes. Gu Yanwu had once criticized the severity of *Yan Fa* (*Regulations of Salt*) in *Ri Zhi Lu* (*The Record of Daily Reading*) and said: "As to the transportation and sale of salt, it is different in distance. People have to walk long distances to buy the salt which is sold by the government, but people can buy the sold privately salt at nearby places; therefore, the civilians had to buy the salt sold privately. Consequently, the number of salt dealers increased, and more and more people were sentenced to imprisonment for the crime of theft."

Anyone who wanted to do salt business had to get "Yan Yin Kan He" (a letter of introduction to sell salt) first from "Li Bu" (The Department of Personnel) and then obtain salt from specific places. If the businessmen did not follow the rules or acted on their own "or raised the price to sell the salt to others, both parties would be punished by 'Zhang' (flogging with heavy sticks) for one hundred strokes and 'Ya Bao' (intermediary agent) would be punished one level lighter with his salt and

---

[286]"Yan Fa" (Salt Law) in "Ke Cheng" (Tax) in "Hu Yi" (Household Corvee) in *Ming Lv* (*Ming Code*).

money confiscated."[287] However, illegal sale of salt persisted even though it had been repeatedly prohibited since the early Ming Dynasty. During the reign of Xuande, the powerful households even transported and sold salt illegally with military escorts. After the reign of Chenghua, this activity became rampant, which had posed a serious threat to the state's monopoly in the sale of salt. In the late years of the Ming Dynasty, after paying the prescribed "Yan Ke" (salt tax), salt producers could sell salt to merchants, who could then transport the salt to different places for sale, so the previous state monopoly of salt was gradually replaced by private one.

The illegal sale of salt was prohibited and in view of the fact that tea was not only the daily necessity of the common people, but also that of the government offices, *Cha Fa* (*Regulations of Tea*) was enacted in the 20th year of Zhizheng (1360). So people should turn over the one 30th of their profit from the sale of tea to the state to increase state revenue. Meanwhile, tea was exchanged for horses in northwest districts. Therefore, the private sale of tea was strictly prohibited and was solely operated by the government. After the reunification of the Ming Dynasty, "Cha Yin Suo" (the managing office of tea inspection) was set up in the Hangzhou and Jiangning areas for merchants to transport and sell tea to different places. In order to prevent tea smuggling, "Cha Ma Si" (the office in charge of tea-horse trading) was set up in the Shanxi and Sichuan areas to check certificates for the trade of tea and horses. In order to ensure the government's monopoly in the sale of tea, it was provided in *Ming Lv* (*Ming Code*) that tea sellers should present "Yan Yin Kan He" (a letter of introduction to sell salt) when transporting and selling tea, and any tea seller who did not have "Yan Yin Kan He" (a letter of introduction to sell salt) or used overdue "Yan Yin Kan He" (a letter of introduction to sell salt) would be convicted of selling tea illegally and be sentenced to three years of imprisonment after being punished by "Zhang" (flogging with heavy sticks) for one hundred strokes. For example, if "anyone has sold tea privately in the border areas, or traded illegally with small minorities," "no matter how much the illegally sold tea is, the seller and 'Ya Bao' (intermediary agent) who know of the truth will be punished by 'Chong Jun' (to be forced to join the army) to 'Yan Zhang' (jungles) in the southwest areas".[288] In addition to *Cha Fa* (*Regulations of Tea*), which was especially listed in *Ming Lv* (*Ming Code*), in *Wen Xing Tiao Li* (*The Ordinance for Inquisition*), issued in the middle period, "Si Cha Tiao Li" (the provisions on illegally selling of tea) was also included, according to which the penalty for persons who sold tea illegally and for officials who breached their duties was reduced compared to that in the early Ming Dynasty.

In *Ming Lv* (*Ming Code*), it was also prohibited to make and sell alums illegally; otherwise, those involved would be found guilty for the crime of selling illegal salt.

---

[287]"Zu Huai Yan Fa" (The Violation of Salt Law) in "Ke Cheng" (Tax) in "Hu Yi" (Household Corvee) in *Ming Lv* (*Ming Code*).

[288]"Si Cha Tiao Li" (Regulations on Illegal Sale of Tea) in "Ke Cheng" (Tax) in "Hu Lv" (Statutes on Households) in *Wen Xing Tiao Li* (*The Ordinance for Inquisition*).

10.5 Economic Legislation Adapting to the Economic Development

Above all, compared with those in the Song and Yuan dynasties, the monopoly laws of the official-run business represented by *Yan Fa* (*Regulations of Salt*) and *Cha Fa* (*Regulations of Tea*) in the Ming Dynasty were more detailed and the penalties were much severer, which had shown the strengthening of the despotic rule in the economic field.

With the development of commodity and market relationship, the laws on market and warehouse management in *Ming Lv* (*Ming Code*) were much more perfect than before.

Firstly, uniform standards were strictly implemented for weights and measures. "If *hu* (a dry measure used in ancient China), *dou* (a measure for grain in ancient China) and scales which are illegally made and used in the market are not accurate, or they are adjusted privately, both the seller and the craftsman will be punished by 'Zhang' (flogging with heavy sticks) for one hundred strokes." Moreover, the weights and measures used in markets should be "checked," "labelled," and "adjusted" by the government, and any official who had neglected his duty would be punished by "Zhang" (flogging with heavy sticks) for forty to seventy strokes.[289]

Secondly, the responsibilities of market management authorities in stabilizing the market commodity prices were strictly stipulated. "Anyone who has made a wrong evaluation of the commodity prices, either too expensive or too cheap, will be punished for the crime of 'Zuo Zang' (embezzlement)"; anyone who has claimed the goods for his own use by taking advantage of the price evaluation "will be punished for the crime of robbery" with exemption from the punishment of "Ci Zi" (to make humiliating tattoo on one's body, especially on one's face). All middlemen of "Ya Hang" (broker house) in the urban and rural areas and shipyards should have "Ya Tie" (business license) issued by "Bu Zheng Si" (the government office in charge of civil affairs at the provincial level), and they should have official seals and document books for them to register the customer's place of birth, name, serial number of certificate, and amount of goods on a daily basis, which should be reported monthly to the government for approval. "If anyone had pretended to be a 'Ya Ren' (middleman), he would be punished by 'Zhang' (flogging with heavy sticks) for one hundred strokes with his income confiscated; if any 'Ya Ren' (middleman) designated by the government had harbored the convicts, he would be punished by 'Zhang' (flogging with heavy sticks) for one hundred strokes and be dismissed from his office at the same time."[290] When making a comparison between the laws of the Tang and Ming dynasties, Xue Yunsheng in the Qing Dynasty stated

---

[289] "Si Zao Hu Dou Cheng Chi" (Illegal Making "Hu", "Dou" and Scales) in "Shi Chan" (Marketplace) in "Hu Lv" (Statutes on Households) in *Ming Lv* (*Ming Code*).

[290] "Si Chong Ya Hang Bu Tou" (Acting as Fraudulent Substitutes for Broken Houses and Shipyards) in "Shi Chan" (Marketplace) in "Hu Lv" (Statutes on Households) in *Ming Lv* (*Ming Code*).

that "the above-mentioned provision is not stipulated in *Tang Lv* (*Tang Code*), yet it is the most perfect in Ming Dynasty."[291]

Finally, the management of warehouses was strengthened. Grain, money, and property stored in warehouses should not be falsely claimed. If the grain, money, and property that were delivered were insufficient or the chief guard and the relevant officials came up with faked evidence, they would be punished for the crime of stealing what was entrusted to their care. Besides, if the official who was responsible for the examination was corrupted or gave false information, he would be punishment harshly for "Wang Fa" (taking bribes by bending the law); if the official in charge did not collect grain and tax according to provisions or had issued a license with the receipt of other discounted property, he would be punished for the crime of stealing what was entrusted to his care. The receipts and disbursements of money and grain by the government agencies should be used for their specific purpose only; if any official had embezzled the money and grain for other purposes, he would be punished for the crime of stealing what was entrusted to his care; if anyone had used the property and grain of the warehouses to make up for the losses of other programs, he would be punished for the crime of stealing what was entrusted to his care; if officials in charge of property and warehouses did not report their encroachment, embezzlement, and loan of official property and grain, they would be punished according to concrete circumstances.

Because the commercial and industrial laws were very strict, it was much easier for them to be violated by businessmen, so that the commodity economy was restricted in a narrow scope and there had lacked an extensive space for its development.

Overseas trade was strengthened in the Ming Dynasty. Overseas trade was an important part of commercial activities in ancient China, and remarkable progress was already made in the Tang and Song dynasties, which had promoted economic prosperity and increased revenue. However, compared with that in Tang and Song dynasties, the development of overseas trade in the Ming Dynasty suffered a serious setback.

In the early Ming Dynasty, it was ordered by Zhu Yuanzhang that "it is forbidden for the civilians in coastal areas to go out to sea without authorization,"[292] so "anyone who dares to do business with the minorities in border regions shall be severely punished."[293] When *Ming Lv* (*Ming Code*) was finally revised, the following was further stipulated:

> Anyone who sells cattle, horses, military goods, iron, copper, satin, silk and cotton to border regions or goes fishing out on the sea shall be punished by "Zhang" (flogging with heavy sticks) for one hundred strokes. Besides, the people who carry the goods on horse back shall

---

[291] Xue Yunsheng (Qing Dynasty), "Si Chong Ya Hang Bu Tou An Yu" (Comments on the Provision of "Acting as Fraudulent Substitutes for Broken Houses and Shipyards") in *Tang Ming Lv He Bian* (*A Collection of Laws in Tang and Ming Dynasties*), Vol. 27.

[292] *Ming Tai Zu Shi Lu* (*The Record of Emperor Taizu of Ming Dynasty*), Vol. 70.

[293] *Ming Tai Zu Shi Lu* (*The Record of Emperor Taizu of Ming Dynasty*), Vol. 231.

be punished one level lighter, with all of the the goods, carts and the boats confiscated, and with 30% of the profit given to the whistleblower as a reward. If anyone abducts and traffics people and weapons to the border areas and the sea, he shall be punished by "Jiao" (hanging); if anyone leaks out secrets, he shall be punished by "Zhan" (beheading); if anyone who is responsible for the case has released the convict intentionally, or leaks out secrets, he shall be found guilty as well. The people who are not aware of the misconduct beforehand shall be punished three levels lighter with the maximum of "Zhang" (flogging with heavy sticks) for one hundred stokes. The soldiers shall be punished another one level lighter.[294]

After the reign of Yongle and Xuande and in the early period of Jiajing, maritime trade underwent rapid development without strict supervision. But in the feudal times, the development of maritime trade had exerted a great influence on the feudal natural economy, as well as the policy of cutting off China from the outside world, which was disadvantageous to the consolidation of the despotic regime. Therefore, from the 3rd year of Jiajing (1524), many laws were issued to prohibit overseas trade, and the three "Shi Bo Si" (the office in charge of the management of foreign trade), which was in charge of foreign trade in Guangzhou, Ningbo, and Quanzhou, were closed. Even the double mast sea boats should be registered and reported to the government to be destroyed; otherwise, those involved should be severely punished. If "the military and civilian personnel in coastal areas dare to do business with foreigners without permission, or their neighbors fail to report it to the government, they shall also be punished."[295] In the 29th year of Jiajing (1550), it was specifically stipulated in *Wen Xing Tiao Li* (*The Ordinance for Inquisition*) that "as to the officials and civilians who make ships with two or more masts without authorization or put out to sea with prohibited goods to do business with ethnic minorities, or instigate others to rob the common people," the principal offender should be severely punished with the whole family sent to remote places for penal servitude. "If anyone lends the ship to those who put out to sea to make profit or if he colludes with those who put out to sea, even if he doesn't build any ships," "he shall be sent to remote places for penal servitude"; "if anyone inquires about those who put out to sea and purchases and traffics imported goods such as logwood and pepper which weigh as much as 1,000 *jin*, he shall be sent to remote places for penal servitude with the imported goods confiscated." Obviously, the punishment of maritime trade in *Wen Xing Tiao Li* (*The Ordinance for Inquisition*) was much severer than that in *Ming Lv* (*Ming Code*). Because "Li" (precedent) was used as the supplement of "Fa" (law), it became a very important legal basis for handling the affairs of overseas trade, which not only hindered the development momentum of private overseas trade but also prevented social and economic development and restricted the growth of capitalism.

In order to control overseas trade, "Shi Bo Ti Ju Si" (the office in charge of foreign trade and tax) was set up to be in charge of the tribute and commercial trade. So foreign trade was incorporated into the tribute trade to allow the foreign envoy to

---

[294]"Si Chu Wai Jing Ji Wei Jin Xia Hai" (Going abroad and Sea Illegally) in "Guan Jin" (Strategic Pass and Ferry) in "Bing Lv" (Statutes on Military Affairs) in *Ming Lv* (*Ming Code*).
[295]*Ming Shi Zong Shi Lu* (*The Record of Ming Tai Zu*), Vol. 154.

bring some goods for official affairs. Besides, foreigners were forbidden to do business in China. In order to prevent foreign businessmen from smuggling in the guise of envoy, in the 16th year of Hongwu (1383), the policy of "Kan He" (a letter of introduction) was issued. So "'Kan He' (a letter of introduction) is sent by 'Li Bu' (The Department of Rites) to all foreign countries, and when foreigners come to China, they must bring the certificates with them to be examined to eliminate the fraudulent malpractice completely."[296] But with the development of Sino–foreign economic exchanges, the policy of "Kan He" (a letter of introduction) and the relevant decrees had lost their effect gradually, so private overseas trade became very active.

In order to prevent foreign businessmen from concealing their goods, "whenever a merchant ship comes to the shore, the goods it carries must be reported to the government. If the ship anchors at the private ports of merchants and the brokers fail to report, those involved will be punished by 'Zhang' (flogging with heavy sticks) for one hundred strokes; if the merchants fail to report the goods carried in the ship to the government, they will be punished by 'Zhang' (flogging with heavy sticks) for one hundred strokes with the goods confiscated. Anyone who conceals the goods shall be punished by 'Zhang' (flogging with heavy sticks) for one hundred strokes and the whistle-blowers will be rewarded twenty *liang* of silver."[297] Although it was actually equal to evading tax to conceal goods, the penalty for concealing goods was much harsher than that for evading tax because "more goods bring more profit." In *Jian Shi* (*Notes*), it was stated that "it may bring little profit to evade tax, so the penalty is reduced by half" but "it may bring more profit to conceal goods, so the penalty is severer." At the same time, it must be pointed out that it is not solely out of economic reason to enforce punishment on concealing goods, but it is also out of the need to safeguard state sovereignty, as was stated in *Jian Shi* (*Notes*) that "it is enforced to strictly make a distinction between China and foreign countries."[298]

As seen from above, as for the guiding ideology of economic legislation in the Ming Dynasty, it still does not go beyond the stereotypes of "Zhong Ben Yi Mo" (promoting fundamental and containing accidental), and its main task was to build a solid material foundation for the system of centralized authority, to adjust the emerging economic relationship, and to promote social and economic development. After the middle of the Ming Dynasty, its economic laws had gradually lost their binding force, so its social economy began to decline.

---

[296]Shen Guoyuan (Ming Dynasty), *Huang Ming Cong Xin Lu* (*The Chronicles of Ming Dynasty*), Vol. 8.

[297]"Xing Bu" (The Department of Punishment) (Part 6) in *Ming Hui Dian* (*The Collected Statutes of Ming Dynasty*), Vol. 164.

[298]Wang Kentang (Qing Dynasty), "Bo Shang Ni Huo" (Ship Merchants Concealing their Goods) in *Wang Yi Bu Xian Sheng Jian Shi* (*Notes by Wang Yibu*), Vol. 8.

10.5.4 The Making of the Laws on Metallic and Paper Money

In *Da Ming Lv* (*The Great Ming Code*), *Qian Fa* (*The Regulation on Metallic Money*) and *Chao Fa* (*The Regulation on Paper Money*) were specifically made on the basis of the tax legislation of the Song Dynasty. In the Ming Dynasty, the paper money was called "Bao Chao," which was printed by "Hu Bu" (The Department of Revenue), and *"guan"* was used as the monetary unit. The paper money was "concurrently used" at the market with copper coins, and they were with the same credit value. So it could be used to "purchase and sell goods among civilians and to pay for tea and salt tax." If anyone had refused to receive "Bao Chao," he would be punished by "Zhang" (flogging with heavy sticks); if the tax collectors had failed to "distinguish the counterfeit money due to his carelessness," he would be punished by "Zhang" (flogging with heavy sticks) for one hundred strokes; if the civilians had used the counterfeit money, they would also be punished by "Zhang" (flogging with heavy sticks) for one hundred strokes, with the losses compensated.[299] If anyone had counterfeited "Bao Chao," he "shall be punished by 'Zhan' (beheading) regardless of principal or accessory offenders, and his property shall be confiscated. The whistle-blower and the person who has arrested the offender shall be rewarded two hundred and fifty *liang* of silver"; "'Li Zhang' (head of 'Li': the basic resident organization in ancient China) who knows of the truth but fails to report it to the government shall be punished by 'Zhang' (flogging with heavy sticks) for one hundred strokes," and "the policeman who knows of the truth of a case but connives with the criminal shall be punished the same."[300] In the early Ming Dynasty, gold and silver were banned to be used as a means of payment in the transaction. But because paper money devalued easily, it was rejected by the local businessmen, so in the later period of Hongwu, the prohibition of the use of gold and silver was stressed once again. During the reign of Yingzong, under the pressure of the current situation then, the banning of silver was lifted, so silver replaced paper money and was gradually used as a currency, which was recognized by the state.[301]

Apart from "Bao Chao" (paper money), the currency used at the time included "Hong Wu Da Zhong Tong Bao" (silver coin made during the reign of Hongwu in the Ming Dynasty) and other ancient copper coins. According to *Qian Fa* (*The Regulation on Metallic Money*) in the Ming Dynasty, the coinage office was responsible for the casting of coin, and *wen* was used as the monetary unit. Anyone who refused to use coins should be punished by "Zhang" (flogging with heavy sticks) for sixty strokes; "anyone who casts copper coins illegally will be punished by 'Jiao' (hanging) (shall be exiled 3000 *li* away according to the laws in Tang

---

[299]"Chao Fa" (Currency Law) in "Cang Ku" (Warehouse) in "Hu Lv" (Statutes on Households) in *Ming Lv* (*Ming Code*).

[300]"Wei Zao Bao Chao" (Counterfeiting Paper Money) in "Zha Wei" (Fraud and Forgery) in "Xing Lv" (The Penal Code) in *Ming Lv* (*Ming Code*).

[301]"Shi Huo Zhi" (The Record of National Finance and Economy) (Part 5) in *Ming Shi* (*The History of Ming Dynasty*).

Dynasty), and the craftsmen should be punished the same. Those who use the illegal copper coins without knowing it shall be punished one level lighter."[302] In order to prevent the illegal usage of copper coins, selling and collecting waste copper were prohibited. Except for mirrors and weapons in military and civilian families and the temple bells which were used in temples, nunneries, and institutions, the remaining waste copper should be sold to the government. So anyone who had breached the rule should be punished by "Chi" (flogging with light sticks) and "Zhang" (flogging with heavy sticks). After the reign of Xiaozong, silver was not only used in "Chao Guan" (checkpoints for tax collection) but also used as the standard to evaluate monetary value, which had led to the use of silver standard, so the crime of counterfeiting gold and silver was frequently committed. "Anyone who counterfeits gold and silver shall be sentenced to three years of imprisonment after being punished by 'Zhang' (flogging with heavy sticks) for one hundred strokes; anyone who connives with or conceal the truth shall be punished one level lighter."[303]

In order to increase state revenue, tax law was especially made in *Ming Lv (Ming Code)*. In the early Ming Dynasty, the measurement of land was carried out nationwide according to the tax law of the Tang Dynasty. *Huang Ce (Yellow Book)* and *Yu Lin Tu Ce (Scale Graph)* were made and used as the basis for land and poll tax collection. Additionally, there was a fixed term for the collection of grain tax. Summer tax was collected from May 15 to the end of July, and the autumn tax from October 1 to the end of December in the lunar calendar. If the grain tax was still not collected one and half months after the deadline, the officials in charge, "Li Zhang" (head of "Li": the basic resident organization in ancient China), as well as the households owing the grain tax, would be punished with the maximum punishment of "Zhang" (flogging with heavy sticks) for one hundred strokes. Anyone who had accepted money during the collection of tax would be severely punished for the crime of "Wang Fa" (taking bribes and bending the law). If the grain tax was still not collected within a year or after the deadline, the household and "Li Zhang" (head of "Li": the basic resident organization in ancient China) would be punished by "Zhang" (flogging with heavy sticks) for one hundred strokes or be punished by "Qian Xi" (the penalty of banishing criminals to do forced labor in remote areas), and the official in charge would be punished by "Jiao" (hanging).

After the middle of the century, due to heavy tax and corvée, farmers were forced to flee from home, so agriculture production was severely damaged. During the reign of Wanli, in order to carry out tax system reform, "Yi Tiao Bian Fa" (one whip method: the combination of all sorts of corvee, land tax, and incidental charge), which was regarded as an important part of political reform, was implemented by Zhang Juzheng, who was "Shou Fu" (the chief grand secretary) of the cabinet. The so-called "Yi Tiao Bian Fa" (one whip method: the combination of all sorts of

---

[302]"Si Zhu Tong Qian" (Counterfeiting Copper Coin) in "Zha Wei" (Fraud and Forgery) in "Xing Lv" (The Penal Code) in *Ming Lv (Ming Code)*.

[303]"Si Zhu Tong Qian" (Counterfeiting Copper Coin) in "Zha Wei" (Fraud and Forgery) in "Xing Lv" (The Penal Code) in *Ming Lv (Ming Code)*.

10.5 Economic Legislation Adapting to the Economic Development

corvee, land tax, and incidental charge) meant that the tax collection and corvee service of all "Zhou" (subprefecture) and "Xian" (county) were combined together, and after the grain tax was collected, it should be handed over to the government. Besides, the government would pay for the one year of corvee service. For those who worked as laborers, they would be provided with salary and food, which would be calculated according to their workload; for those who serve corvee by paying silvery money, the amount of money they paid was calculated with the consumption added. The fees for the organization of the public affairs, for the reservation of the warehouse of the capital, and for paying tribute of special local products were also combined together, and the grain was converted into silver, which was paid according to the area of land.[304] According to the newly-released tax law, all taxes of the past were combined into one, so the collection procedures were greatly simplified; moreover, the quota allocated to each household and each "Ding" (adult) in the past was decided collectively according to the amount of land, and silver was solely used to pay all other taxes with the tax and corvee combined into one; through this, the practice of doing corvee labor every ten years, which was arranged by "Li Jia" (social organizations at the grassroots level) in the past, was changed, and instead silver was collected every year. No doubt, these reforms were significantly effective in rectifying the malpractices at the time.

As for the tax and corvee law in Chinese feudal society, since the Qin and Han dynasties, household and poll tax had been collected in addition to land tax, and "Liang Shui Fa" (two-tax law) was issued in the middle of the Tang Dynasty, so that the land tax and household tax were combined together, and the silver paid for corvee service was also incorporated into the system. But soon, the old measures were restored and silver was again collected for corvee service, apart from "Liang Shui Fa" (two-tax law). The implementation of "Yi Tiao Bian Fa" (one whip method: the combination of all sorts of corvee, land tax, and incidental charge) eventually terminated the system of "San Zheng" (three taxation, namely, corn, corvee, cloth, and silk), which had been carried out for a long time in Chinese history. So the transformation from household tax to property tax and from property tax to currency tax was basically completed, which surely was a major reform in the tax and corvee system.

As to the tax revenue in the Ming Dynasty, apart from land tax, commodity tax was another important source. In the early Ming Dynasty, in order to develop the economy, the policy of light tax was carried out, and it was stipulated that "one thirtieth of the profit should be collected in terms of commodity tax."[305] During the reign of Xuande, tax rate was greatly increased and the temporary apportionment also became the lump sum tax.[306] In "Fu" (ancient administrative district between province and county), "Zhou" (subprefecture), and "Xian" (county), "'Yin Tie'

---

[304]"Shi Huo Zhi" (The Record of National Finance and Economy) (Part 1) in *Ming Shi* (*The History of Ming Dynasty*).

[305]*Ming Tai Zu Shi Lu* (*The Record of Emperor Taizu of Ming Dynasty*), Vol. 14.

[306]*Ming Xuan Zu Shi Lu* (*The Record of Emperor Taizu of Ming Dynasty*), Vol. 50.

(introduction letter) was placed outside the city gate. So if merchants carried goods to the city, they had to use it as a certificate to pay tax first before they were allowed to enter the gate."[307] Moreover, if anyone had evaded tax, he would be punished according to law and the whistle-blowers would be rewarded. According to *Da Ming Lv* (*The Great Ming Code*), "if the merchants or especially if the wine and vinegar dealers fail to pay tax, they shall be punished by 'Zhang' (flogging with heavy sticks) for fifty strokes with half of their goods, wine and vinegar confiscated. The confiscated goods will be divided into ten parts, three of which would be rewarded to the whistleblower."[308] For the merchants of salt and tea, full commodity tax should be paid at the end of the year; if anyone "is unable to pay the full tax," he would be punished by "Chi" (flogging with light sticks) for forty strokes or punished by "Zhang" (flogging with heavy sticks) for eighty strokes according to the amount of tax unpaid. In addition, they would be forced to pay tax to the government.[309]

From the middle period of Wanli, mine supervision tax and "San Xiang Jia Pai" (the additional three kinds of tax, namely, the taxes of Liao, Jiao, and Lian) were added, which had made it more difficult for people to bear the already high tax burden and which had also become one of the important reasons for the rapid downfall of the Ming Dynasty.

10.6 The Change of Jurisdiction and the Joint Trial System

The extreme development of absolutism in the Ming Dynasty had a profound impact on the judicial system, which was clearly reflected in the direct involvement of eunuch organizations and the trusted followers of the emperor in the arrest and trial of criminals, which was not present in the previous dynasties. Eunuch intervention, which was previously considered illegal, became fully legalized, while the legitimate judiciary and trial system of civil lawsuits suffered great setbacks. In this case, there was nothing left for the so-called justice and legal order, and what was illegal in the judicial system became legal because of the extreme expansion of the imperial power. Accordingly, prosecutorial power of "Yu Shi" (the censor), who had acted as the eyes and ears of the emperor, was greatly expanded, compared with that of the Tang and Song dynasties. Judicial inspection became the focus of "Yu Shi" (the censor) in his inspection tour of the local authorities, so he became more powerful and prestigious. But because judicial condition concerned social stability and the

---

[307]"Ni Shui" (Tax Evasion) in "Hu Lv" (Statutes on Households) in *Da Ming Ji Jie Fu Li* (*Great Ming Code with Collected Commentaries and Appended Sub-statutes*), Vol. 8.

[308]"Ni Shui" (Tax Evasion) in "Ke Cheng" (Tax) in "Hu Lv" (Statutes on Households) in *Ming Lv* (*Ming Code*).

[309]"Ru Hu Kui Dui Ke Cheng" (Default in Paying Household Tax) in "Ke Cheng" (Tax) in "Hu Lv" (Statutes on Households) in *Ming Lv* (*Ming Code*).

10.6 The Change of Jurisdiction and the Joint Trial System

ruling of the state, a system of "Hui Shen" (the joint trial) was set up at the beginning of the Ming Dynasty to ensure the reasonable settlement of important cases.

10.6.1 The Change of the Administration of "San Fa Si" (Three Judicial Departments)

The standing central judicial organs of the Ming Dynasty included "Xing Bu" (The Department of Punishment), "Da Li Si" (The Bureau of Judicial Review), and "Du Cha Yuan" (The Court of Censors), which were collectively called "San Fa Si" (Three Judicial Departments).

Although the names and organizations of "Xing Bu" (The Department of Punishment) and "Da Li Si" (The Bureau of Judicial Review) were the same as those in the Tang and Song dynasties, yet the specific power was different. "Da Li Si" (The Bureau of Judicial Review) in the Tang and Song dynasties was a judicial organ, but in the Ming Dynasty, it was no longer in charge of trials and was especially in charge of reviewing, as was described in the saying that "it was in charge of issuing orders and reviewing the trials, penalties and imprisonment." So all the cases that were settled by "Xing Bu" (The Department of Punishment) and "Du Cha Yuan" (The Court of Censors) "will be reported to 'Da Li Si' (The Bureau of Judicial Review), and all the criminals should also be sent there to be tried." If the case was fairly settled and the criminal had pleaded guilty, they should be reported to the emperor for approval; otherwise, the wrong judgments must be rectified, which was called "Zhao Bo"; if the third drafts were still inappropriate, the officials in charge should be interrogated, which was called "Can Bo"; if the criminal did not make a clear confession of his or her crime, the case might be tried again, which was called "Zhui Bo"; if the case was still not rectified after repeated rejections, it should be submitted to the emperor for final decision, which was called "Zhi Jue" (verdict).[310] According to "Da Li Si" (The Bureau of Judicial Review) in *Ming Hui Dian* (*The Collected Statutes of Ming Dynasty*), "for a case which needs to be decided by the emperor, memorials about the causes for the crime and the relevant charges should also be submitted by 'Da Li Si' (The Bureau of Judicial Review)." According to the procedure in the Ming Dynasty, "Xing Bu" (The Department of Punishment) was in charge of interrogating criminals, while "Da Li Si" (The Bureau of Judicial Review) was in charge of judging the case and then the final judgment would be reported to emperor, which had been a routine practice since Emperor Taizu. Since "Xing Bu" (The Department of Punishment) was in charge of the trial of cases, its organization was expanded accordingly. Initially it had four "Si" (office), and later it was expanded to thirteen "Qing Li Si" (office) to accept and hear the local cases on appeal and to review the local major cases and the cases that were related to the

---

[310]"Zhi Guan Zhi" (The Record of State Officials) (Part 2) in *Ming Shi* (*The History of Ming Dynasty*).

officials of the central government. In addition, the cases of "Si Xing" (death penalties) should be reported to the emperor for approval, and if the official from "Xing Bu" (The Department of Punishment) mishandled a case, he would be severely punished. During the reign of Wanli, Wang Yongji, "Da Li Si Qing" (equivalent to president of the Supreme Court) had once said that "if officials of 'Xing Bu' (The Department of Punishment) have failed to hear cases according to law, or mishandled the cases by following the instructions of the senior officials, they should be severely punished."[311] "The trials which were heard by 'Xing Bu' (The Department of Punishment) and the reviewing which was conducted by 'Da Li Si' (The Bureau of Judicial Review) should all be supervised by 'Du Cha Yuan' (The Court of Censors). For the serious crimes and important criminals, they should be tried jointly by 'Du Yu Shi' (the head of the Court of Censors), 'Xing Bu' (The Department of Punishment) and 'Da Li Si' (The Bureau of Judicial Review)."[312]

As for the major cases in the Ming Dynasty, they should be jointly heard and reviewed by "San Fa Si" (Three Judicial Departments). It was stipulated in the 17th year of Hongwu (1384) that "for the major cases, they should be tried by 'Xing Bu' (The Department of Punishment) and 'Du Cha Yuan' (The Court of Censors), reviewed by 'Da Li Si' (The Bureau of Judicial Review) and reported to the emperor for final judgment."[313] So it was obvious that although "San Fa Si" (Three Judicial Departments) were the supreme reviewing organs, they had no right to decide on the cases because the final decision was usually made by the emperor. For the major cases, they should be jointly heard by "Jin Yi Wei" (secret service of the Ming Dynasty), "Zhen Fu Si" (organization of secret police to suppress the people with torture), and other senior officials. For example, in the 5th year of Jiajing (1526), the case of Li Fuda, who had plotted a rebellion by using witchcraft, was jointly heard by the chief and the deputy chief officials of "San Fa Si" (Three Judicial Departments), "Jin Yi Wei" (secret service of the Ming Dynasty), "Zhen Fu Si" (organization of secret police to suppress the people with torture), and other senior officials. Later, the case was reviewed by "'Jiu Qing' (the the nine high-rank officials in ancient times) of the imperial court."[314] Although "Jin Yi Wei" (secret service of the Ming Dynasty) and "Dong Chang Xi Chang" (the imperial spy agencies) were not judicial organs, they were especially ordered by the emperor to be in charge of arresting criminals and supervising the trial of cases.

"Jin Yi Wei" (secret service of the Ming Dynasty) was originally one of the twelve guards of imperial forces, which functioned as the guard of honor during the emperor's tour of inspection. During the reign of Emperor Taizu, "the major

---

[311]"Wang Yong Ji Zhuan" (The Biography of Wang Yongji) in *Ming Shi* (*The History of Ming Dynasty*).

[312]"Zhi Guan Zhi" (The Record of State Officials) (Part 2) in *Ming Shi* (*The History of Ming Dynasty*).

[313]"Tai Zu Ji" (The Record of Emperor Taizu) (Part 3) in *Ming Shi* (*The History of Ming Dynasty*).

[314]"Li Fu Da Zhi Yu" (The Trial of Li Fuda) in *Ming Shi Ji Shi Ben Mo* (*The Ins and Outs of the Records in the History of Ming Dynasty*), Vol. 56.

10.6 The Change of Jurisdiction and the Joint Trial System

criminals were often sent to the capital to be put into prison under its guard."[315] So since then, "Jin Yi Wei" (secret service of the Ming Dynasty) was given the power to try major cases. In the 15th year of Hongwu (1382), "Bei Zhen Fu Si" (organization of secret police to suppress the people with torture) was set up below "Jin Yi Wei" (secret service of the Ming Dynasty) to be responsible for investigating "the illegal acts, the spreading of heresies, the cases of robbery and homicide," as well as the lawsuits of "Zhou" (subprefecture) and "Xian" (county). After the case was settled, it should be reported to the emperor for final decision. With the gradual expansion of the power of "Bei Zhen Fu Si" (organization of secret police to suppress the people with torture), the power of judicial organs was continuously weakened.[316] In the 20th year of Hongwu (1387), the system was abolished; "the instruments of torture of 'Jin Yi Wei' (secret service of the Ming Dynasty) were burned, and the cases were all transferred to and be tried by 'Xing Bu' (The Department of Punishment) instead."[317] However, after Emperor Chengzu ascended the throne, "the prison system was reestablished ... so it became a usual practice for the criminals to be put into prison by 'Jin Yi Wei' (secret service of the Ming Dynasty)."[318] "Consequently, 'Jin Yi Wei' (secret service of the Ming Dynasty) is not only in charge of imperial guarding, the arresting of criminals and the prison matters ... but also the inquisition and conviction of prisoners together with 'San Fa Si' (Three Judicial Departments)."[319]

Apart from the system of "Jin Yi Wei" (secret service of the Ming Dynasty), "Dong Chang" was set up in the 18th year of Yongle (1420), and "Xi Chang" was set up in the 13th year of Chenghua (1477) to be specifically in charge of "arresting the major criminals who plot to overthrow the state by spreading rumors."[320] The staff of "Dong Chang" and "Xi Chang" (the imperial spy agencies) were sent to different places nationwide to pry into the secrets of civilians and to collect information about the major political affairs, the minor affairs, and even the gossip in local places.[321] Thus, sometimes trivial matters in civilian society, such as dogfighting and

---

[315] "Xing Fa Zhi" (The Record of the Criminal Law) (Part 3) in *Ming Shi* (*The History of Ming Dynasty*).

[316] "Xing Fa Zhi" (The Record of the Criminal Law) (Part 3) in *Ming Shi* (*The History of Ming Dynasty*).

[317] "Xing Fa Zhi" (The Record of the Criminal Law) (Part 3) in *Ming Shi* (*The History of Ming Dynasty*).

[318] "Xing Fa Zhi" (The Record of the Criminal Law) (Part 3) in *Ming Shi* (*The History of Ming Dynasty*).

[319] "Zhi Guan Zhi" (The Record of State Officials) (Part 5) in *Ming Shi* (*The History of Ming Dynasty*).

[320] "Xing Fa Zhi" (The Record of the Criminal Law) (Part 3) in *Ming Shi* (*The History of Ming Dynasty*).

[321] "Wang Zhi Yong Shi" (Wang Zhi in Power) in *Ming Shi Ji Shi Ben Mo* (*The Ins and Outs of the Records in the History of Ming Dynasty*), Vol. 37.

cockfighting, were even considered major crimes, which had seriously disrupted the normal social order.[322]

Because "Jin Yi Wei" (secret service of the Ming Dynasty) and "Dong Chang Xi Chang" (the imperial spy agencies) only obeyed the orders of the emperor himself and their status was very special, they even had the right to attend the trial of "San Fa Si" (Three Judicial Departments). Although they were just "hearing a case," in fact they had the actual power to decide the case. According to records, in the 14th year of Yingzong (1499), eunuch Jin Ying had once attended the trial of a criminal who was imprisoned by "Xing Bu" (The Department of Punishment) and "Du Cha Yuan" (The Court of Censors): "Jin Ying and Zhang Huanggai sat in the middle, while the other officials below 'Shang Shu' (the minister) sat respectively on the right and the left. Since then, the system was continued, and the trial was held once every six years."[323] The officials of "Xing Bu" (The Department of Punishment) and "Da Li Si" (The Bureau of Judicial Review) "dare not even change one word of the cases which were settled by 'Chang Wei' (the imperial spy agency, including Jin Yi Wei, Dong Chang and Xi Chang), even though they knew the cases very well."[324] Moreover, "the judicial organs dare not have these cases rehabilitated."[325] "Chang Wei" (the imperial spy agency, including Jin Yi Wei, Dong Chang, and Xi Chang) had not only the right to inform against and to arrest criminals at any time or to "arrest more than ten people for the criminal acts of one person or to arrest dozens of families for the criminal acts of one family"[326] but also the right to torture criminals brutally at will. "Once people were put into prison, they would never be released."[327] Moreover, the members of "Chang Wei" (the imperial spy agency, including Jin Yi Wei, Dong Chang, and Xi Chang) were sent to all parts of the country, so if an imperial order was received in the morning, it would be carried out before the sunset. Although with grudges, no one dared to argue with them because not only the whole family could be arrested, but dozens of people could also be implicated.[328] So it was obviously a reflection of the brutality of autocratic system for the imperial guards and the trusted attendants of the emperor to enforce penalties casually without being restricted by law, which had led to serious judicial confusion. According to history records, "after Emperor Xianzong and Yingzong, prudent judgment was seldom enforced, but the practice of spying upon others was prevalent; the local tyrants were rampant and the unsettled cases were piled up like mountains. Either these cases

---

[322] "Huan Guan Zhuan" (The Biography of Eunuchs) (Part 1) in *Ming Shi* (*The History of Ming Dynasty*).

[323] "Huan Guan Zhuan" (The Biography of Eunuchs) (Part 1) in *Ming Shi* (*The History of Ming Dynasty*).

[324] "Xu Gui Zhuan" (The Biography of Xu Gui) in *Ming Shi* (*The History of Ming Dynasty*).

[325] "Xu Xian Zhuan" (The Biography of Hu Xian) in *Ming Shi* (*The History of Ming Dynasty*).

[326] "An Pan Zhuan" (The Biography of An Pan) in *Ming Shi* (*The History of Ming Dynasty*).

[327] "Tian Ergeng Zhuan" (The Biography of Tian Ergeng) in *Ming Shi* (*The History of Ming Dynasty*).

[328] "Feng Qi Zhuan" (The Biography of Feng Qi) in *Ming Shi* (*The History of Ming Dynasty*).

10.6 The Change of Jurisdiction and the Joint Trial System

were delayed to be tried or the innocent criminals were ordered randomly to be put into prison or put to death according to emperor's orders. So the arbitrarily trial system of 'Zhao Yu' (the prison directly controlled by the emperor) had led to many disasters. So generally speaking, the criminal law of Ming Dynasty was completely destroyed by the system of 'Chang Wei' (the imperial spy agency, including Jin Yi Wei, Dong Chang and Xi Chang)."[329]

As for the local judicial authorities, two levels of "Fu" (ancient administrative district between province and county) (or "Zhou" (subprefecture)) and "Xian" (county) were still combined with the administrative ones. So the judicial affairs were controlled or were taken charge of by chief executives, such as "Zhi Fu" (magistrate of a prefecture) and "Zhi Xian" (magistrate of a county). "An Cha Si" (The Judicial Commission) was set up at the provincial level, and "it is in charge of the judicial and supervisory affairs of a province."[330] At the same time, it also served as the appellate department of the first trial at the level of "Xian" (county), so it was different from "Ti Dian Xing Yu Si" (judicial commission) in the Song Dynasty, which only functioned as a supervisory organ. "An Cha Si" (The Judicial Commission) had the right to execute sentences lighter than the punishment of "Tu" (imprisonment). For the more serious cases, they should be handled by "Xing Bu" (The Department of Punishment). So a complete judicial trial system was set up in "Zhou" (subprefecture), "Xian" (county), "Sheng" (province), "Xing Bu" (The Department of Punishment), and "San Sheng" (The Three Departments).

In order to strengthen the leadership of the local judicial authorities at all levels, like "Fu" (ancient administrative district between province and county), "Zhou" (subprefecture), and "Xian" (county), all matters that related to land, population, tax, and corvee were controlled by "Bu Zheng Si" (the government office in charge of civil affairs at the provincial level), and the judicial affairs were controlled by "An Cha Si" (The Judicial Commission) of the different provinces. Therefore, the relatively centralized and unitary system of leadership, which was established on the basis of the working objects, had reflected the strictness of the organization of local organs and the strengthening of the work efficiency.

Because the system of strict division of military and civilian registration was carried out, judicial jurisdiction was thereby also different. If soldiers had violated the law, they would be handled by the military organs, so the cases of soldiers were handled by "Du Wei Duan Shi Si" (the office in charge of military legal cases), which was set up by "Du Zhi Hui Si" (the local organs of military command) in each province, and "Qian Hu" (official in charge of 1000 families) and "Bai Hu" (official in charge of 100 families), which were set up by "Wei Suo" (border guarding posts). If military officials had committed crimes, the reasons for their crimes should be stated by the relevant local "Ya Men" (the government offices), then be reported to

---

[329]"Xing Fa Zhi" (The Record of the Criminal Law) (Part 3) in *Ming Shi* (*The History of Ming Dynasty*).

[330]"Zhi Guan Zhi" (The Record of State Officials) (Part 4) in *Ming Shi* (*The History of Ming Dynasty*).

"Wu Jun Du Du Fu" (the five top national military institutions) or "Bing Bu" (The Department of Defense), and finally be reported to the emperor for his decision.

The grassroots organization of "Li Jia" (social organizations at the grassroots level) had jurisdiction over civil and minor criminal cases. Besides "Li Zhang" (head of "Li": the basic resident organization in ancient China), "Lao Ren" (the elder), or "the respected elderly," was appointed to "instruct people to do good deeds and to deal with the village disputes."[331]

In April of the 27th year of Hongwu (1394), the emperor ordered that "the respected and impartial older people shall be chosen by 'You Si' (official) to deal with the lawsuits of the villages, while the cases of marriage, household registration and fighting shall be handled by 'Li Xu' (public errand for the management of village affairs); if the cases are serious, they shall be handled by government; if people sue directly to the county magistrate, it will be considered as 'Yue Su' (overstepping indictment),"[332] which had confirmed that "Li Zhang" (head of "Li": the basic resident organization in ancient China) was in charge of first-instance jurisdiction over civil litigation and minor criminal cases. *Jiao Min Bang Wen* (*A Public Notice to People*), which was issued by "Hu Bu" (The Department of Revenue) on the 19th of March of the 31st year of Hongwu (1398), further consolidated and expanded the jurisdiction of "Li Zhang" (head of "Li": the basic resident organization in ancient China), which had made it the veritable organization of first instance to accept and hear criminal and civil cases. It was provided in *Jiao Min Bang Wen* (*A Public Notice to People*) that "it is forbidden for the trivial matters like 'Hu Hun' (marriage, tax and household registration), 'Tian Tu' (land), 'Dou Ou' (fighting) to be sued to government, and they should first be heard and judged by 'Li Jia' (social organizations at the grass-roots level) or 'Lao Ren' (the elder); otherwise, the complainant shall be punished by 'Zhang' (flogging with heavy sticks) for sixty strokes whether the case is true or not, and the case shall be sent back to 'Li Jia' (social organizations at the grass-roots level) and 'Lao Ren' (the elder) for settlement."[333] "So in future, except the cases of 'Shi E' (The Ten Abominations), 'Qiang Dao' (robbing) and 'Sha Ren' (murder), the other cases, including 'Fan Jian' (adultery), 'Dao' (robbery), 'Zha Wei' (fraud and forgery), 'Ren Ming' (homicide), the cases beyond 'Shi E' (The Ten Abominations), the cases beyond 'Qiang Dao' (robbing) and 'Sha Ren' (murder), shall be all be heard and judged by 'Lao Ren' (the elder) if the people involved in the cases would not like to file the lawsuits to government, or if the defendants had admitted their guilt to avoid brutal punishment. So these cases should not be rejected by 'Lao Ren' (the elder) on any pretext."[334] "If the cases involved other 'Li' (basic resident organization consisting of five

---

[331]"Shi Huo" (National Finance and Economy) in *Xu Tong Dian* (*Xu Tong Code*), Vol. 7.

[332]Gu Yanwu (Ming Dynasty), *Ri Zhi Lu* (*The Record of Daily Reading*), Vol. 8.

[333]"Jiao Min Bang Wen" (A Public Notice to People) (Article 1) in *Hu Bu* (*The Department of Revenue*).

[334]"Jiao Min Bang Wen" (A Public Notice to People) (Article 11) in *Hu Bu* (*The Department of Revenue*).

10.6 The Change of Jurisdiction and the Joint Trial System

neighborhoods), they must be determined together by 'Lao Ren' (the elder) and 'Li Jia' (social organizations at the grass-roots level) of the 'Li' (basic resident organization consisting of five neighborhoods)."[335] In regard to doubtful cases or something involving the relatives of "Li Lao" (or Li Zhang), "they must be judged by the neighboring 'Li' (basic resident organization consisting of five neighborhoods), or 'Lao Ren' (the elder) and 'Li Jia' (social organizations at the grass-roots level) within the areas of three to five *li*."[336] Moreover, the qualification of elders who were eligible to attend the litigation procedure was also stipulated: "It does not matter whether 'Lao Ren' (the elder), who attends the litigation, is an official or not, if he is over fifty years old, or is knowledgeable, virtuous and respectable, he can be chosen to deal with the affairs."[337] Since "Li Jia" (social organizations at the grassroots level) and "Li Zhang" (head of "Li": the basic resident organization in ancient China) often changed according to the number of population and amount of grain tax, the so-called respected "Lao Ren" (the elder) and "Li Lao" (or Li Zhang) were mostly local powerful gentries or clan leaders. Therefore, their judgments were de facto the first instance, which had not only conveniently solved the disputes in the neighborhood and reduced the number of litigation of the relevant parties, but also clearly shown the close relationship between political, gentry and the clan power.

In order to ensure fairness in the settlement of cases, strict supervisory contents were provided in *Jiao Min Bang Wen* (*A Public Notice to People*). For example:

> If "Lao Ren" (the elder) and "Li Jia" (social organizations at the grassroots level) could not make decisions on the complaints of people, which had "caused people to file lawsuits to the government, 'Li Jia' (social organizations at the grass-roots level) and 'Lao Ren' (the elder) shall be punished by 'Zhang' (flogging with heavy sticks) for sixty strokes respectively; those who are over seventy years old shall not be punished by 'Zhang' (flogging with heavy sticks), but they can atone for the crime according to the law"; "if 'Lao Ren' (the elder) and 'Li Jia' (social organizations at the grass-roots level) have played favoritism, committed irregularities and confused what was right and wrong, they will be punished the same as that for the crime of 'Gu Chu Ru Ren Zui' (to deliberately increase or reduce the punishment when making sentences)."[338]

> If "Lao Ren" (the elder) has misconducted, or broken the law, or failed to fulfill the elder's responsibility, or intentionally disturbed the judgments of cases, "he shall be arrested and taken to the capital to be punished."[339]

> If "Lao Ren" (the elder), has coerced "Li Zhang" (head of "Li": the basic resident organization in ancient China), controlled the government and refused to serve the corvee

---

[335] "Jiao Min Bang Wen" (A Public Notice to People) (Article 3) in *Hu Bu* (*The Department of Revenue*).

[336] "Jiao Min Bang Wen" (A Public Notice to People) (Article 5) in *Hu Bu* (*The Department of Revenue*).

[337] "Jiao Min Bang Wen" (A Public Notice to People) (Article 4) in *Hu Bu* (*The Department of Revenue*).

[338] "Jiao Min Bang Wen" (A Public Notice to People) (Article 2) in *Hu Bu* (*The Department of Revenue*).

[339] "Jiao Min Bang Wen" (A Public Notice to People) (Article 8) in *Hu Bu* (*The Department of Revenue*).

with an excuse of handling the civil litigation, "he shall be forced to move to foreign countries."[340]

In settling civil cases, it is forbidden for "Lao Ren" (the elder) and "Li Jia" (social organizations at the grassroots level) to detain the parties by establishing prisons; if they did so, they shall be punished for felony.[341]

"Lao Ren" (the elder) and "Li Jia" (social organizations at the grassroots level) should make judgment according to people's complaints. For the lawsuits which people did not want to file to the government, "they should not be accepted or settled by 'Li Jia' (social organizations at the grass-roots level) and 'Lao Ren' (the elder) according to rumors to create disturbance"; otherwise, they will be punished by "Zhang" (flogging with heavy sticks) for one hundred strokes; if "Lao Ren" (the elder) and "Li Jia" (social organizations at the grassroots level) take bribes, they shall be punished for the crime of "Zuo Zang" (embezzlement).[342]

"Lao Ren" (the elder) and "Li Jia" (social organizations at the grassroots level) are in charge of bringing the villains who are involved in robbing, theft, army deserting, escaping from the prisons or making trouble in the local areas to justice; otherwise, they will be punished.[343]

10.6.2 The Judicial Procedures Emphasizing Judicial Jurisdiction

Early in the Ming Dynasty, the method of prosecution was mainly conducted according to the parties' complaints; at the same time, prosecution was made by the government, and restrictions were strictly specified according to the litigants' age, gender, identity, and health status. The lawsuits that should be accepted must be acknowledged very quickly. For example, if the complaint for "Mou Fan" (plotting rebellion or plotting to endanger the country) and "Pan Ni" (treachery) was not accepted immediately or the crime was concealed, those in charge would be sentenced to three years of imprisonment after being punished by "Zhang" (flogging with heavy sticks) for one hundred strokes. If the common cases of "Hu Hun" (marriage, tax, and household registration), "Tian Tu" (land), and "Dou Ou" (fighting) that should be accepted were not acknowledged, those involved would be punished two levels lighter with the maximum punishment of "Zhang" (flogging with heavy sticks) for eighty strokes.

Generally speaking, prosecution should be initiated by written pleadings in which the time, contents, name, address, and native place of plaintiff and his

---

[340]"Jiao Min Bang Wen" (A Public Notice to People) (Article 9) in *Hu Bu* (*The Department of Revenue*).

[341]"Jiao Min Bang Wen" (A Public Notice to People) (Article 13) in *Hu Bu* (*The Department of Revenue*).

[342]"Jiao Min Bang Wen" (A Public Notice to People) (Article 14) in *Hu Bu* (*The Department of Revenue*).

[343]"Jiao Min Bang Wen" (A Public Notice to People) (Article 15) in *Hu Bu* (*The Department of Revenue*).

10.6 The Change of Jurisdiction and the Joint Trial System

representatives, as well as their signatures, should be included. The prosecution should be made according to the jurisdiction of the trials. For military families, lawsuits should be filed in each level of "Wei" and "Suo" (both military units in the Ming Dynasty) and "Du Zhi Hui Si" (the local organs of military command); for ordinary households, lawsuits should be filed in their own "Zhou" (subprefecture) and "Xian" (county). In addition, the system of "Zhi Su" (direct appeal) was established, by which people could file their lawsuits directly to the emperor. In the 1st year of Hongwu (1368), "Deng Wen Gu" (Deng Wen Drum, one of the most important ways of direct appeal in ancient China) was set outside the Meridian Gate, and "the unjustly treated people can beat the drum so that their complaints can be accepted by the senior and junior officials. Every day, a member of 'Ke', 'Dao' (both government offices including the deaconry and the supervisory censor) and 'Jin Yi Wei' (secret service of the Ming Dynasty) was on duty by turns; if the unjustly treated people had any complaints which were rejected by the local officials ... they could be reported to and decided by the emperor."[344] During the reign of Wanli, people were allowed to beat the drum only when they were severely wronged, and it would be punished to beat the drum for no reason or to prevent people from beating the drum. After receiving the indictment, an imperial edict would be directly drafted by the emperor and be then sent to relevant judicial departments to be executed. From the years of Emperor Zhengtong to the early years of Emperor Jiajing, before a condemned convict was put to death, the families could beat the drum to cry out their grievances.[345] The system of "Yao Che Jia Song" (the parties intercept the emperor on the way to file a lawsuit directly to the emperor himself), which was implemented in the Tang and Song dynasties, was continued as before.

In the early Ming Dynasty, people were constantly bullied by officials, so many people appealed directly to the capital by "Yue Su" (overstepping indictment). For this reason, in the 15th year of Hongwu (1382), "Yue Su" (overstepping indictment) was banned: "As for the cases of 'Hu Hun' (marriage, tax and household registration), 'Tian Tu' (land) and 'Fan Jian' (adultery), the military and civilians must appeal step by step, and 'Yue Su' (overstepping indictment) is not forbidden; otherwise...the violators will be punished."[346] Only for the major and urgent cases was "Yue Su" (overstepping indictment) allowed, so a strict trial-level system of the jurisdiction was set up in order to prevent "Yue Su" (overstepping indictment). During the reign of Xuande, those whose overstepping complaints were real were exonerated, while those whose overstepping complaints were false would be punished to garrison the frontiers. During the reign of Jingtai, regardless of the actual situation, all those involved in "Yue Su" (overstepping indictment) were

---

[344] Sun Cheng Ze (Ming Dynasty), "Xing Bu" (The Department of Punishment) in *Chun Ming Meng Yu Lu* (*The Record of the Capital Areas in Ming Dynasty*).

[345] You Shaohua, *Ming Dai Si Fa Chu Kao* (*A Primary Textual Research of the Judiciary in Ming Dynasty*), Xiamen University Press, 1998, p. 79.

[346] "Xing Kao" (A Textual Research of the Criminal Penalties) (Part 2) in *Qing Chao Xu Wen Xian Tong Kao* (*A Sequel of the General Textual Research of the Documents of Qing Dynasty*).

punished to garrison the frontiers. It was also clearly stated in *Jiao Min Bang Wen* (*A Public Notice to People*) that "civil cases should be sued step by step, so those who sued by 'Yue Su' (overstepping indictment) are found guilty; ... if people do not follow the former rules, they will be sentenced for their dereliction of duty."[347] "If there are still stubborn people who go directly to the government or the capital to file lawsuits without following the stipulation or listen to the elders' warning, they shall be arrested and punished by 'Lao Ren' (the elder)."[348] However, if "Lao Ren" (the elder) and "Li Jia" (social organizations at the grassroots level) "cannot make decisions on the statements of the people and cause people to file lawsuits to the government, they shall be punished by 'Zhang' (flogging with heavy sticks) for sixty strokes; but 'Lao Ren' (the elder) over seventy years old shall not be punished by 'Zhang' (flogging with heavy sticks) and they can atone for their crimes according to the law."[349]

The punishment on "Yue Su" (overstepping indictment) in *Ming Lv* (*Ming Code*) mainly aimed to stabilize the order of jurisdiction and to prevent obstinate people from filing vexatious lawsuits by making use of local judiciary functions. In the judicial jurisdiction of criminal proceedings, the principles of "Yi Qing Jiu Zhong" (the case should be judged and punished according to the more serious crimes the criminal committed), "Yi Shao Jiu Duo" (the case should be judged and punished by those who have more evidence), and "Yi Hou Jiu Xian" (the case should be judged and punished by those who first begin the investigation) were followed. If the case involved two "Zhou" (subprefecture) and "Xian" (county), "the case should be judged according to the plaintiff's request in the complaint,"[350] which had reflected the importance attached to the plaintiff's judicial rights; meanwhile, it also brought about the buck-passing of cases between "Zhou" (subprefecture) and "Xian" (county) and resulted in unnecessary delay. Jurisdiction of civil cases was mainly determined by the household registration of the defendant.

The provisions of "Gao Zuang Bu Shou Li" (not accepting the complaint) and "Jiao Suo Ci Song" (instigating lawsuits) in *Ming Lv* (*Ming Code*) were basically the same as those in *Tang Lv* (*Tang Code*). It needs to be pointed out that "Wu Gao" (false accusation) was strictly forbidden in order to stabilize social order. According to *Tang Lv* (*Tang Code*), the offenders of "Wu Gao" (false accusation) would be punished by "Fan Zuo" (sentence the accuser to the punishment that he falsely accused); however, in *Ming Lv* (*Ming Code*), it was provided that if a person had falsely accused other people and caused them to be punished by "Chi" (flogging with light sticks), the punishment for the accuser should be aggravated by two levels; if

---

[347] "Jiao Min Bang Wen" (A Public Notice to People) (Article 38) in *Hu Bu* (*The Department of Revenue*).

[348] "Jiao Min Bang Wen" (A Public Notice to People) (Article 23) in *Hu Bu* (*The Department of Revenue*).

[349] "Jiao Min Bang Wen" (A Public Notice to People) (Article 2) in *Hu Bu* (*The Department of Revenue*).

[350] "Zhuang Gao Bu Shou Li" (No Accepting the Complaint) in "Duan Yu" (Trials and Punishments) in "Xing Lv" (The Penal Code) in *Ming Lv* (*Ming Code*).

10.6 The Change of Jurisdiction and the Joint Trial System

the person had falsely accused others and caused them to be punished by "Liu" (exile), "Tu" (imprisonment), and "Si" (death penalty), the punishment for the accuser should be aggravated by three levels; if the person had falsely accused others and caused them to be punished by "Liu" (exile) or to have their land and houses sold, the accuser should prepare money for redemption, in addition to payments for traveling expenses; if the person had falsely accused others and caused them to be punished by "Si" (death penalty), the accuser should be punished by "Fan Zuo" (sentence the accuser to the punishment that he falsely accused), so he should also be punished by "Si" (death penalty); "if the government officials had falsely accused people when they reported the cases to the emperor, or 'Feng Xian Guan' (official who monitoring the enforcement of the law) reported made-up facts for personal reasons, they would also be punished."[351] In February of the 1st year of Yongle (1403), *Wu Gao Fa* (*Law of False Accusation*) was especially made by the government, according to which "whoever has falsely accused three or four people, he will be punished by 'Zhang' (flogging with heavy sticks) for one hundred strokes with the punishment of 'Tu' (imprisonment) for three years; whoever has falsely accused five or six people, he will be punished by 'Zhang' (flogging with heavy sticks) for one hundred strokes and then be exiled for 3000 *li*; whoever has conducted serious false accusation, he must be severely punished; whoever has falsely accused more than ten people, he will be punished by 'Ling Chi' (the punishment of dismemberment and the lingering death) and 'Xiao Shou' (the penalty of hanging the head of the criminal on top of a pole for public display) with his family members driven to other countries."[352] Meanwhile, "anonymous false accusation" was not allowed to be accepted by the government; otherwise, the officials would be punished by "Zhang" (flogging with heavy sticks) for one hundred strokes.

10.6.3 The Newly Created "Hui Shen Zhi Du" (The Joint Trial System)

The trial system of the Ming Dynasty fully reflected the spirit of strengthening despotism, whether in the control over the judicial power by the imperial court or in the emperor's discretion on the major cases and the death penalty. From the beginning of the Ming Dynasty, Emperor Taizu had reviewed "the major cases" and "interrogated the prisoners by himself" or "presided over the trial in person without

---

[351] "Wu Gao" (False Accusation) in "Su Song" (Litigation) in "Xing Lv" (The Penal Code) in *Ming Lv* (*Ming Code*).

[352] Shen Jiaben (Qing Dynasty), "Wu Gao Fa" (The Law on False Accusation) in "Lv Ling" (The Laws and Decrees) (Part 9) in *Li Dai Xing Fa Zhi* (*A Textual Research of the Criminal Laws in the Past Dynasties*).

entrusting it to be handled by the judicial organs."[353] In the 1st year of Yongle (1403), Emperor Yongle ordered "the judicial departments to make reports on the prisoners every five days."[354] In the 13th year of Yongle (1415), he ordered that "the crimes punishable by 'Si' (death penalty) must be reported to the emperor for five times before being finally sentenced."[355] In the 17th year of Yongle (1419), he again ordered that "the crimes punishable by 'Si' (death penalty) in each provincial must be reported to the emperor to be reviewed for three times before being executed."[356] In the 1st year of Hongxi, an order was issued by Emperor Renzong: "If the crimes punishable by 'Si' (death penalty) are reported to the emperor by the judicial offices for five times but are rejected by the emperor, they shall be reported to the emperor again together with "San Gong" (the three councilors)."[357] He also especially ordered that "serious cases should be jointly heard by 'Nei Ge Xue Shi' (scholar of the cabinet) with the suspicious people interrogated at the same time."[358] During the reign of Zhengtong, emperor Yingzong instructed "San Fa Si" (Three Judicial Departments) that "the crimes punishable by 'Si' (death penalty) must be submitted to the emperor for three times for approval before being executed."[359] In the 17th year of Chenghua during the reign of Xianzong (1481), the emperor ordered that the prisoners be interrogated by one eunuch from "Si Li Jian" (in charge of the inner eunuch and intrauterine affairs within the court), together with the chief officials of "San Fa Si" (Three Judicial Departments) in "Da Li Si" (The Bureau of Judicial Review), which was called "Da Shen" (the emperor regularly sent emissaries to reexamine the prisoner on behalf of the emperor). "Since then, it has become a rule that 'Da Shen' (the emperor regularly sent emissaries to re-examine the prisoner on behalf of the emperor) is held every five years,"[360] by which the prisoners who had constantly claimed to have been falsely accused were mainly dealt with. Moreover, "Jian Cha Yu Shi" (the supervisory censor), who was assigned to "clean up all the unjust lawsuits," was at the same time also the special envoys who was appointed by the emperor to review the trial records in the country, so he also exercised the power to review major and serious cases on behalf of the emperor. Whenever prisoners

---

[353]"Xing Fa Zhi" (The Record of the Criminal Law) (Part 2) in *Ming Shi* (*The History of Ming Dynasty*).

[354]"Cheng Zu Ji" (The Record of Emperor Chengzu) (Part 2) in *Ming Shi* (*The History of Ming Dynasty*).

[355]"Cheng Zu Ji" (The Record of Emperor Chengzu) (Part 3) in *Ming Shi* (*The History of Ming Dynasty*).

[356]"Cheng Zu Ji" (The Record of Emperor Chengzu) (Part 3) in *Ming Shi* (*The History of Ming Dynasty*).

[357]"Ren Zong Ji" (The Record of Emperor Renzong) in *Ming Shi* (*The History of Ming Dynasty*).

[358]"Xing Fa Zhi" (The Record of the Criminal Law) (Part 2) in *Ming Shi* (*The History of Ming Dynasty*).

[359]"Ying Zong Qian Ji" (The Earlier Record of Emperor Yingzong) in *Ming Shi* (*The History of Ming Dynasty*).

[360]"Xing Fa Zhi" (The Record of the Criminal Law) (Part 2) in *Ming Shi* (*The History of Ming Dynasty*).

were reviewed by the provincial government, joint hearing chaired by "Yu Shi" (the censor), who was designated by the emperor, was also held; after the joint hearing, the results would be reported to the emperor by "Yu Shi" (the censor) himself. So "Chang Wei" (the imperial spy agency, including Jin Yi Wei, Dong Chang, and Xi Chang) had the right to attend and "hear the trial" and to "participate in the judgment," which had shown their rights of jurisdiction and supervision on behalf of the emperor. The eunuchs' participation in judicial affairs had compelled some of the judicial officials to retire, but because most officials were afraid of eunuchs' persecution, they often colluded with them in putting the innocent people into prison by perverting the law, which had obviously not only undermined the established legal order but also endangered the feudal legal system, intensified the conflict of interest within the ruling class, and deepened national crisis.

In addition, the provision for the judicial privilege of "Ba Yi" (The Eight Deliberations), which had been carried out since the Tang and Song dynasties, was faithfully followed in *Ming Lv* (*Ming Code*). Those who enjoyed the privilege of "Ba Yi" (The Eight Deliberations) and their relatives could only be questioned and interrogated according to imperial orders, so it was forbidden for them to be randomly interrogated by others. Besides, the result of the trial must also be reported to the emperor for his final decision. This privilege was also enjoyed by the officials in the capital and the local officials above "Wu Pin" (the fifth rank). In the Ming Dynasty, the emperor had a much stricter control of jurisdiction than the previous dynasties, so he could make laws at his own will or enforce extralegal punishment to kill people without being restricted by law. For example, Fan Wen, "Yu Shi" (the censor) in the early Ming Dynasty, was sentenced to death because of his improper petition, but soon after, Emperor Taizu again ordered that he be "given the right to be exempted from death penalty for five times."[361] "Yuan Wai Lang" (deputy head of a subministry department or an honorary title) Zhang Laishuo was punished by being torn to pieces simply because he had suggested that the emperor not choose betrothed maidens to be imperial palace attendants.

In order to achieve the goal of "Ming Xing Bi Jiao" (integrating punishment with moral teachings), Emperor Taizu also paid great attention to the unity of "Fa" (law), "Li" (reason), and "Qing" (human relationships), which could be clearly proven by the documents of the Ming Dynasty:

Example 1: "A father was arrested falsely, so his son sued to 'Xing Bu' (The Department of Punishment), for which he was punished for the crime of 'Yue Su' (overstepping indictment). Emperor Taizu said: 'The son has sued that his father is innocent because of love, so he shall not be punished.'" Example 2: "A son violated the law, so his father bribed the officials to have him freed, for which the father was punished by 'Yu Shi' (the censor). Emperor Taizu said: 'The father has saved his son because of love, so the father shall be forgiven but the son shall be punished instead." Example 3: In the 20th year of Hongwu (1387), Zhan Hui said: "A soldier has committed a crime punishable by 'Zhang' (flogging with heavy sticks), but his previous punishments have been remitted, so he should be

---

[361] Zhao Jishi (Qing Dynasty), "Jing Zhong Ji" (The Message of the Mirror) in *Ji Yuan Ji Suo Ji* (*Ji Yuan's Messages*), Vol. 2.

punished by death for both his current and previous crimes." Emperor Taizu said: "Since his previous punishments have been remitted, it would be dishonest if we mention them again. So he should be punished by 'Zhang' (flogging with heavy sticks) and be dismissed". Example 4: In the 8th year of Emperor Hongwu, "a father of Shanyang should be punished by 'Zhang' (flogging with heavy sticks), but his son requested that he should be punished instead. So both the father and the son were pardoned because of the son's filial piety."

It was obvious that such cases were less threatening to the safety of society and the country, so the policy of lenient punishment, which was taken according to concrete situations, was not only harmless to the security of the state but also helpful for propagating "Gang Chang Ming Jiao" (feudal cardinal guides and constant virtues), which was advocated by the Confucians in order to achieve the objective effect of wise and benevolent emperors.

In the Ming Dynasty, in the case of serious and doubtful cases and the review of death penalty cases, "Hui Shen" (the joint trial), "Yuan Shen" (joint hearing by relevant ministers), and "Chao Shen" (trials held in imperial court) were usually held. "Hui Shen" (the joint trial) was established in the 15th year of Emperor Hongwu (1382), which mainly referred to the joint trial of "San Fa Si" (Three Judicial Departments); "Yuan Shen" (joint hearing by relevant ministers) referred to the joint trial of the cases of death penalty or the reversal of verdicts by "Li Bu Shang Shu" (the minister of the department of personnel), "Da Li Si Qing" (equivalent to president of the Supreme Court), "Zuo Du Yu Shi" (the head of the court of censors), and "Tong Zheng Shi" (The Transmission Officer); "Chao Shen" (trials held in imperial court) was created in the 3rd year of Tianshun (1459). In view of the fact that "human life was the most valueable and the dead people could not be resurrected," an order was issued by Emperor Yingzong: "Since the 3rd year of Tianshun, after Frost's Descent (the 18th solar term) every year, if there are major cases, they shall be reviewed jointly by 'San Fa Si' (Three Judicial Departments) and other officials, which will be established as a rule."[362] In "Xing Fa Zhi" (The Record of the Criminal Law) in *Ming Shi* (*The History of Ming Dynasty*), there are also the following records:

In the 3rd year of Tianshun, after the Frost's Descent (the 18th solar term), the prisoners who have committed felonies are jointly interrogated by "San Fa Si" (Three Judicial Departments) and "Gong" (duke), "Hou" (marquis) and "Bo" (count), which was called "Chao Shen" (trials held in imperial court).

As "Chao Shen" (trials held in imperial court) was held in autumn, it became the origin of the system of "Qiu Shen" (Autumn Assizes) in the Qing Dynasty. The end result of "Hui Shen" (the joint trial), "Yuan Shen" (joint hearing by relevant ministers), and "Chao Shen" (trials held in imperial court) should all be reported to the emperor to decide whether the prisoners should be put to death or the execution should be put off or the sentence should be mitigated. Therefore, the

---

[362]Xue Yunsheng (Qing Dynasty), "You Si Jue Qiu Deng Di Tiao An Yu" (Comments on the Provision of "the Levels of Punishment for the Prisoners Enforced by the Judicial Officials") in *Tang Ming Lv He Bian* (*A Collection of Laws in Tang and Ming Dynasties*), Vol. 30.

system of "Hui Shen" (the joint trial) was not contradictory to the emperor's intention of grabbing the judicial power by himself.

In the 2nd year of Yongle during the reign of Emperor Chengzu (1404), "Re Shen" (Summer Assizes) was also established. About ten days after Grain Full (eighth solar term), "Re Shen" (Summer Assizes) was held by eunuchs and the two judicial offices in the capital to interrogate the prisoners. Generally speaking, if there were no witnesses, the prisoners punishable by "Chi" (flogging with light sticks) would be released; the punishment for the prisoners punishable by "Tu" (imprisonment), "Liu" (exile), or lighter would be mitigated; and the criminals who had committed felonies, who were suspected and who were punishable by wearing "Jia Hao" (cangue: a large wooden collar worn by petty criminals as a punishment) would be decided by the emperor. In the years of Yongle and Xuande, "Re Shen" (Summer Assizes) was occasionally held; after Zhengtong, it was held more frequently; and in the years of Zhengde, "Re Shen" (Summer Assizes) became an established system.[363] Although "Re Shen" (Summer Assizes) was not important in the trial system of the Ming Dynasty, it was proclaimed to be a "benevolent" policy because of the great importance it attached to human life.

Since the system of "Hui Shen" (the joint trial) was not only helpful to the unitary application of law but also beneficial to the supervision of the trial activities of the judiciary, it was continued to be applied in the Qing Dynasty.

During the trial, the stipulations that "judgments must be made according to the complaint filed by the plaintiff" and that "conviction must be made according to laws and decrees" were continued to be carried out, but some amendments were also made. For example, it was ruled that "from the date of the enactment of the law, if the crimes have been previously committed, they should be tried according to the new law,"[364] which showed that the rulers paid more attention to the unitary application of law to avoid any discrepancy, which was caused by differences in the old and the new laws. In addition, it was provided that "if there are things which are not covered by law, or if there are not corresponding regulations in making judgments, proper conviction should be made and relevant penalties should be enforced by citing similar laws or by 'Bi Fu' (legal analogy), then they should be reported to 'Xing Bu' (The Department of Punishment) for decision. If the judgment is made randomly, which has resulted in unfair judgment, the official in charge will be punished for the crime of negligence."[365] This was different from the principle of "Ju Zhong Ming Qing" (where there are no legal provisions to be applied for the judgment of certain illegal conducts, if there are provisions that are much severer on similar conducts, then lighter punishments shall be implemented) and "Ju Qing Ming

---

[363] You Shaohua, *Ming Dai Si Fa Chu Kao* (*A Primary Textual Research of the Judiciary in Ming Dynasty*), Xiamen University Press, 1998, p. 139.

[364] "Duan Zui Yi Xin Ban Lv Tiao" (The Provision of Making Convictions according to the Newly Issued Law) in "Ming Li Lv" (Statutes and Terms) in *Da Ming Lv* (*The Great Ming Code*).

[365] "'Duan Zui Wu Zheng Tiao' Tiao" (The Provision of "There Being No Relevant Provisions in the Statute to Refer to when Making Convictions") in "Ming Li Lv" (Statutes and Terms) in *Da Ming Lv* (*The Great Ming Code*).

Zhong" (where there are no legal provisions to be applied for the judgment of certain illegal conducts, if there are provisions that are much lenient on similar conducts, then severer punishments shall be implemented) in the Tang Dynasty, which had shown the tendency of the centralization of judicial power. In Ming Dynasty, the range of applying laws by 'Bi Fu' (legal analogy) was very wide, which had involved many punishments such as "Chi" (flogging with light sticks), "Zhang" (flogging with heavy sticks), "Tu" (imprisonment), and "Si" (death penalty). For example, the conviction for tearing "Bao Chao" should be executed according to the provision of "destroying official documents," the conviction for abusing officials who were "San Pin" (the third rank) or above should be executed according to the provision of "abusing grandparents," the conviction for arresting people by falsely taking the arrest warrant of "Yu Shi" (the censor) should be executed according to the provision of "false passing the emperor's edicts," the conviction for interfering with legal cases should be executed according to the provision of "instigating the lawsuits," the conviction for framing innocent people and persecuting civilians by fabricating charges should be executed according to the provision of "falsely accusing of decent people," and so forth. In practice, cases punishable by "Tu" (imprisonment), "Liu" (exile), or lighter did not need to be reported to the emperor for approval, except those punishable by "Si" (death penalty). In the late Ming Dynasty, in order to restrict the random application of "Bi Fu" (legal analogy), it was emphasized that in the cases of "Zui Wu Zheng Tiao" (when making a sentence, if there are no direct relevant provisions in the statute to cite for the crimes of some prisoners, similar statutory provisions and past precedents can be used for conviction and sentencing), it should be petitioned to the emperor for approval; otherwise, the officials should be punished for failing to report what should be reported.

In the early years of Emperor Jiajing, in view of the serious problems caused by the malpractice in criminal punishment and the abuse of power by eunuch Liu Jin, Emperor Shizong emphasized that judgment should be made according to law in his imperial edict for ascending the throne in order to win people's support and to rectify the legal order: "In future trials, punishment should be enforced in conformity with the reality. If there are grievances, the trial of cases should either be transferred to other departments or be held jointly by several officials to clarify the facts. If the people really have grievances, they are allowed to state their reasons, and it is forbidden to settle the cases by extorting confessions by torture to meet the needs of previous officials or to obstruct the redressing of the injustice; otherwise, they should be convicted and punished"; "in future, all prisoners should be interrogated according to *Da Ming Lv (The Great Ming Code)*, and it is forbidden to wrong the innocent people by distorting the law or by misinterpreting the legal provisions and references. For the cases which should be settled according to the imperial edicts, they should be tried by 'Da Li Si' (The Bureau of Judicial Review), and it is

10.6 The Change of Jurisdiction and the Joint Trial System

forbidden to submit memorials randomly to the emperor in order to avoid injustice."[366]

The provision of "Ting Song Hui Bi" (avoidance in hearing cases) was also made in the law of the Ming Dynasty by following those of the Tang and Song dynasties. "If the litigants are the relatives within 'Wu Fu' (relatives within the five degrees of mourning), or the relatives with marriage relationship, or the teachers and students, or the enemies, avoidance is needed according to law; otherwise, those involved should be punished by 'Chi' (flogging with light sticks) for forty strokes. If the punishments are aggravated or mitigated randomly, the officials would be punished for the crime of 'Gu Chu Ru Ren Zui' (to deliberately increase or reduce the punishment when making sentences)." It was further explained that "as to the relationship between relatives, 'Qing' (human relationships) is stressed; as to the relationship between teacher and students, 'Yi' (justice) is stressed, so it is reasonable to be tolerant; as to the relationship between enemies, there is surely hatred; as to the relationship between disagreeable people, there is surely suspicion, so avoidance system is necessary to prevent injustice and evilness and to eliminate the private deal."[367] At the same time, the tradition of "Ming Fu Ming Fu Bu Gong Zuo Yu Song" (because it is only possible for both parties with the same social status to check evidence at court, the people with different identities do not argue with each other; besides, the senior and superior will send their agents in the proceedings, and they do not need to appear in court in person) was followed in the law of the Ming Dynasty. "If officials are involved in the affairs of 'Hun Yin' (marriage), 'Qian Zhai' (debts), 'Tian Tu' (land) and other things, lawsuits can only be filed by the officials' family members, and it is not allowed to settle the disputes by issuing official documents; otherwise, they would be punished by 'Chi' (flogging with light sticks) for forty strokes."[368] It was to "maintain the system," namely, to maintain the statutory privilege of officials of allowing their families to file lawsuits in court.

As for "extorting confession by torture," although some restrictions were made, for example, "extorting confession by torture is not allowed for the young and the old," "the prisoners should not be tortured for more than three times during the interrogation," and "sentences should be made according to law," torture was still an important means to extort confession. Hence, it was unavoidable, and what is more, no restrictions were made for its application. It was recorded in "Xing Fa Zhi" (The Record of the Criminal Law) in *Ming Shi* (*The History of Ming Dynasty*) that "as for the criminal law of Ming Dynasty, some systems and measures were newly made without following the ancient ones: 'Ting Zhang' (being flogged in imperial court), 'Dong Chang Xi Chang' (the imperial spy agencies), 'Jin Yi Wei' (secret service of

---

[366]"Ji Wei Zhao" (Imperial Edict for Ascending the Throne) in *Huang Ming Zhao Ling* (*The Imperial Edicts of Ming Dynasty*), Vol. 9.

[367]"Ting Song Hui Bi" (Avoidance in Hearing Cases) in "Ming Li Lv" (Statutes and Terms) in *Da Ming Lv* (*The Great Ming Code*).

[368]"Guan Li Ci Song Jia Ren Su" (Family Members Filing Lawsuits on behalf of the Officials) in "Ming Li Lv" (Statutes and Terms) in *Da Ming Lv* (*The Great Ming Code*).

the Ming Dynasty) and the prisons of 'Zhen Fu Si' (organization of secret police to suppress the people by torture). So consequently, many people were brutally and illegally killed, and it was even carried to extremes at the end of Ming dynasty. It was really a shame because people's life and death were controlled by a few military men and eunuchs." In the 6th year of Hongzhi (1493), a memorial submitted by Li Dongyang, "Shao Qing" (the vice president) of "Tai Chang Si" (The Bureau of Sacrificial Worship), was approved by the emperor: "Those who have tortured over twenty to thirty criminals to death for minor crimes will be demoted and transferred to other positions according to law."[369] So we can see from what was mentioned above the brutality of the extortion of confession by torture. In the 6th year of Jiajing (1527), an order was issued by emperor Shizong: "If some of the officials have imposed harsh laws upon people or have led to people's injury and death in the capital and in the provincial areas, even if they are gifted, they should be reduced to common people without being recommended as officials any more."[370] "Inquisition by torture can only be applied to convicts of death penalties and those who have committed the felony of theft by the officials in charge of interrogation both in and outside of the capital"; the other criminals could only be punished by whipping and other common instruments of torture. However, it produced very little effect. With the end of "Shen Zong Gai Zhi" (Political Reform by Shenzong), the abuse of punishment resurged.

The trials of grassroots organizations should be held in "Shen Ming Pavilion" (a court built by Zhu Yuanzhang). According to *Jiao Min Bang Wen* (*A Public Notice to People*), "if the common people have complaints, trials should be held by 'Lao Ren' (the elder) and 'Li Jia' (social organizations at the grass-roots level) in 'Shen Ming Pavilion' (a court built by Zhu Yuanzhang) in the forms of 'Hui Yi' (meeting), 'Jue Yi' (resolution), 'Gong Tong' (joint decision)," and so on. It was stated in *Jiao Min Bang Wen* (*A Public Notice to People*) that "if lawsuits are filed by people, a conference should be held and the case should be judged in public by 'Li Jia' (social organizations at the grass-roots level) and 'Lao Ren' (the elder)"[371]; "the civil disputes which should be solved by 'Lao Ren' (the elder) and 'Li Jia' (social organizations at the grassroots level) should be discussed in 'Shen Ming Pavilion' (a court built by Zhu Yuanzhang)."[372] "If 'Lao Ren' (the elder) has criminal responsibility, public meetings should be held and judgments should be made by

---

[369]"Xing Fa Zhi" (The Record of the Criminal Law) (Part 1) in *Ming Shi* (*The History of Ming Dynasty*).

[370]"Xing Fa Zhi" (The Record of the Criminal Law) (Part 2) in *Ming Shi* (*The History of Ming Dynasty*).

[371]"Jiao Min Bang Wen" (A Public Notice to People) (Article 2) in *Hu Bu* (*The Department of Revenue*).

[372]"Jiao Min Bang Wen" (A Public Notice to People) (Article 3) in *Hu Bu* (*The Department of Revenue*).

all other 'Lao Ren' (the elder) and 'Li Jia' (social organizations at the grass-roots level)."[373]

As for civil disputes and minor criminal cases, they should be settled according to the principle of peaceful mediation. According to *Jiao Min Bang Wen* (*A Public Notice to People*), "'Lao Ren' (the elder) should warn the people of 'Li' (a basic resident organization consisting of five neighborhoods) that they should exercise forbearance over the trifle affairs of 'Hun Yin' (marriage), 'Tian Tu' (land), 'Dou Ou' (fighting) and so forth."[374] If they cannot solve the disputes between themselves, resolutions should be made by "Lao Ren" (the elder). "People should exercise forbearance over the trifle affairs of 'Hun Yin' (marriage), 'Tian Tu' (land), 'Dou Ou' (fighting) and so forth; if one party is intolerably abused and humiliated, he can also appeal to 'Lao Ren' (the elder) for the proper solution of the disputes."[375] In order to ensure the implementation of the decisions made by "Lao Ren" (the elder), special provisions were stipulated: "If civil litigation has already been settled by 'Lao Ren' (the elder) and 'Li Jia' (social organizations at the grass-roots level), nevertheless, if the unruly villagers disobey the judgment or fabricate false statements and report them to the officials, they will be punished by death penalties with their families driven out of the village."[376]

10.7 The Achievement of "Lv Xue" (The Study of Statutory Laws) and the World Position of *Da Ming Lv* (*The Great Ming Code*)

10.7.1 The Achievement of "Lv Xue" (The Study of Statutory Laws)

After the formulation of *Da Ming Lv* (*The Great Ming Code*), the legal interpretation advocated by Emperor Zhu Yuanzhang had provided a strong driving force for the further development of "Lv Xue" (the study of statutory laws). According to the records of "Xing Fa Zhi" (The Record of the Criminal Law) in *Ming Shi* (*History of the Ming Dynasty*), because the emperor "worried that *Da Ming Lv* (*The Great Ming Code*) might not be generally known by the common people, he ordered 'Da Li Qing' (the president of the supreme court of justice) Zhou Zhen and his colleagues to

---

[373]"Jiao Min Bang Wen" (A Public Notice to People) (Article 7) in *Hu Bu* (*The Department of Revenue*).

[374]"Jiao Min Bang Wen" (A Public Notice to People) (Article 23) in *Hu Bu* (*The Department of Revenue*).

[375]"Jiao Min Bang Wen" (A Public Notice to People) (Article 23) in *Hu Bu* (*The Department of Revenue*).

[376]"Jiao Min Bang Wen" (A Public Notice to People) (Article 12) in *Hu Bu* (*The Department of Revenue*)

collect all the regulations about civil affairs from the issued laws and decrees, to include them into different categories, and to interpret their meanings except those on 'Li' (rites), 'Yue' (music), 'Qian Liang' (money and grain), 'Zhi Du' (system) and 'Xuan Ju' (election)." So the law was called *Lv Ling Zhi Jie (A Literal Interpretation of the Laws and Decrees)*. *Lv Ling Zhi Jie (A Literal Interpretation of the Laws and Decrees)* was the most authoritative official interpretation of the law, which was carried out according to an imperial order, so it not only played an important guiding role in the accurate understanding and application of the law in judicial practice but also took the lead in the academic atmosphere of legal annotation in the Ming Dynasty.

Legislative interpretation in the Ming Dynasty was somewhat different from that of *Tang Lv Shu Yi (The Comments on Tang Code)* because it was more closely related to specific and practical issues, without making any statements of historical evolution or theoretical comments. Firstly, necessary and precise explanations were given on "Liu Zang Tu" (The Diagram of the Six Crimes of Obtaining Private or Public Property Illegally), "Na Shu Li Tu" (The Diagram of the Regulations on the Atonement for the Crime), "Shou Shu Chao Tu" (The Diagram of the Law on the Atonement for the Crime with Money), "Wu Xing Tu" (The Diagram of Five Penalties), "Yu Ju Tu" (The Diagram of Prison Instruments), "Sang Fu Tu" (The Diagram of Mourning Apparel), and so forth, which were listed at the beginning of *Da Ming Lv (The Great Ming Code)* for better understanding and easy practice. Secondly, the literal meaning of the eight words "Yi," "Zhun," "Jie," "Ge," "Qi," "Ji," "Ji," and "Ruo," which were commonly used in law, were also explained, and it was called "the interpretation of eight words." The details are as follows:

> "Yi" refers to that which is the same as the crimes which are really committed. For example, if the official steals the goods of the government which are entrusted to his care, it will be regarded as "Wang Fa" (taking bribes by bending the law), so he will be punished for the crime of theft...
>
> "Zhun" is different from the really committed crimes, so it means "quasi-". For example, "Zhun Wang Fa" (similar to the crime of taking bribes by bending the law) and "Zhun Dao Lun" (similar to the crime of theft). Although their crimes are considered "quasi-crimes", they are not exempted from the punishment of "being dismissed from their offices" or "Ci Zi" (to make humiliated tattoo on one's body, especially one's face).
>
> "Jie" refers to that both the principal and accessories in a crime should be punished. For example, if the official and the staff have stolen the goods of government in their custody, or if the value of the stolen goods are over one *guan*, they shall all be punished by "Zhan" (beheading).
>
> "Ge" refers to "being punished by the same penalty respectively" ... For example, "Ge" (each of them) shall be punished by "Zhang" (flogging with heavy sticks) for one hundred strokes.
>
> "Qi" refers to "changing the previous regulations. For example, if those of "Ba Yi" (The Eight Deliberations) have committed crimes, the punishment shall be reported to the emperor for final decision. However, this rule does not apply to the crime of "Shi E" (The Ten Abominations).
>
> "Ji" refers to "being closely connected". For example, "the stolen goods and the prohibited things should be confiscated".
>
> "Ji" refers to "to clarify". For example, if the escaped criminal is witnessed by the public, the case is settled.

10.7 The Achievement of "Lv Xue" (The Study of Statutory Laws) and the World... 1059

"Ruo" means "if". For example, if a criminal has committed a crime when he is young and healthy, and becomes old and weak when his crime is exposed, then he will be punished according to the regulations which are applied when the crime is exposed, if he becomes old and weak when he is in prison, the above rules will be applied.[377]

After the middle of the Ming Dynasty, a more extensive unitary application of law was needed because of the further development of the autocratic system. With the increase of regulations, "there are sometimes three or four regulations for a single matter; in addition, many of the regulations are changed every year or even changed for each specific matter,"[378] so that the contradiction between different laws and regulations was becoming increasingly prominent, and the work of legal interpretation had lagged far behind the actual needs of legal application. Consequently, the laws were often subjectively applied by the treacherous court officials, and the unified legal order was severely damaged. At this time of the Ming Dynasty, the emperors were fatuous, the power was usurped by eunuchs, and the politics was extremely corrupted; therefore, the rulers had no time or energy to formulate an official interpretation of the law. Consequently, private law interpretation was approved and encouraged to meet the urgent need of unitary application of law. Under this background, private law interpretation was surging forward, and its achievements received more and more attention. To some extent, some of them even had the legal authority of official interpretation.

As far as private interpretation of law was concerned, the legislative intention and the needs and interests of the government were regarded as its premise, and the maintenance of a correct execution and implementation of the current law was regarded as its tenet, which was the precondition for the acceptance of private law interpretation; otherwise, there would be no prospect for private law interpretation; on the contrary, it would be subject to criminal sanctions. Therefore, private law interpretation was carried out under the supervision of the autocratic government.

As for the major books of legal interpretation in the Ming Dynasty, in addition to *Da Ming Lv Fu Li* (*The Great Ming Code Appended with Sub-Laws*) and *Ming Lv Cuan Zhu* (*Commentaries on Ming Code*), which were annotated by Shu Hua according to imperial edicts, the others mainly include the following: *Xing Shu Ju Hui* (*Collections of Criminal Law*) by Peng Yingbi, *Fa Zhui* (*Works on Law*) by Tang Shu, *Du Lv Suo Yan* (*Trivial Words on Reading Law*) by Lei Menglin, *Da Ming Lv Fu Li Zhu Jie* (*The Annotation of the Great Ming Code Appended with Sub-Laws*) by Yao Siren, *Da Ming Long Tou Bian Du Bang Xun Lv Fa Quan Shu* (*The Complete, Key and Concise Commentary of Law in Ming Dynasty*) by Gong Ju, *Da Ming Lv Li Zhu Shi Xiang Xing Bing Jian* (*Insights on the Detailed Annotation of the Laws and Precedents of the Great Ming Code*) by Ming Yun, *Da Ming Lv Li Lin Min Bao Jing* (*Perceptions of Ruling on the Laws and Precedents of the Great Ming*) by Su Maoxiang, *Da Ming Lv Li Tian Shi Pang Zhu* (*The Additional Sidenotes on the*

---

[377] *Da Ming Lv Ji Jie Fu Li* (*Great Ming Code with Collected Commentaries and Appended Sub-statutes*).

[378] *Huang Ming Tiao Fa Shi Lei Zuan* (*Annals of the Legal Cases in Ming Dynasty*) (Book 4).

Laws and Precedents of the Great Ming) by Xu Changzuo, *Du Lv Guan Jian* (*Opinions on Reading Law*) by Lu Jianzhi, *Du Lv Si Jian* (*Private Connotation on Law*) by Wang Qiao, *Lv Li Jian Shi* (*Annotation of Laws and Precedents*) (also known as *Annotation of Laws and Precedents in Ming Code*) by Wang Kentang, *Da Ming Lv Shi Yi* (*Interpretation of the Great Ming Code*) and *Da Ming Lv Jie* (*Explanation of Great Ming Code*) by Zhang Kai, *Lv Jie Bian Yi* (*Arguments About the Law Interpretation*) by He Guang, *Xing Tai Fa Lv* (*Criminal Law*) by Xiao Jinggao, *Da Ming Lv Ji Jie* (*Great Ming Code with Collected Commentaries*) by Wang Nan, *Da Ming Lv Li Zhi Jun Qi Shu* (*Techniques on Laws and Precedents of the Great Ming*) by Zhu Jingdun, *Da Ming Lv Ji Jie Fu Li* (*Great Ming Code with Collected Commentaries and Appended Sub-statutes*) by Gao Ju, *Du Lv Guan Kui* (*Glimpse of Reading Law*) by Ying Tingyu, *Da Ming Lv Du Fa Shu* (*Books on the Reading of Great Ming Code*) by Sun Cun, *Ming Lv Li Zhu* (*Annotation of Laws and Precedents in Ming Code*) by Lin Zhaoke, *Lv Jie Fu Li* (*Annotation of Laws and Precedents with Appended Sub-statutes*) by Wang Zhiyuan, and so on. Among these works, *Lv Li Jian Shi* (*Annotation of Laws and Precedents*) by Wang Kentang, which consisted of thirty volumes and twenty books, was the most authoritative one, so it was regarded as a model for legal interpretation.

Wang Kentang was "Jin Shi" (those who passed the imperial examination at the national level in ancient China) of the 17th year of Wanli (1589). He once served as "Xing Ren Si Fu" (ancient official in charge of imperial edicts) in Nanjing and "Can Zheng" (ancient official in charge of civil affairs at the provincial level) in Fujian. Additionally, he was familiar with Confucian classic studies and law and had especially inherited the family tradition of "Lv Xue" (the study of statutory laws). His father, Wang Qiao, had written the twenty-four volume *Du Lv Si Jian* (*Private Connotation on Law*), which had had a great influence on Wangken Tang's *Lv Li Jian Shi* (*Annotation of Laws and Precedents*). In the preface of this book, he wrote: "No penalties are enforced during the term of imprisonment so that penalties are applied by no one," which meant that the main purpose of his interpreting the law was to prevent crimes. In *Lv Li Jian Shi* (*Annotation of Laws and Precedents*), the essence of legal interpretation at that time was integrated, and legislative intention and legal principles were interpreted on the basis of judicial precedents. For example, at the end of *Yan Fa* (*Regulations of Salt*) in *Ming Lv* (*Ming Code*), the regulation made in the reign of Wanli was included: "If ten or more salt dealers have gathered ... or resisted official army, or if they have killed and wounded over three people, they should be punished by 'Zhan' (beheading) according to the punishment of robbing property with the leaders punished by 'Xiao Shou' (the penalty of hanging the head of the criminal on top of a pole for public display)." Wang Kentang explained that "in the old precedents, the regulation that 'if two or three people are killed' is mentioned, so interpreters are restricted by the words like 'killing of human being'. Accordingly, for those who are wounded but not killed, this precedent should not be applied. However, according to law, even those who have smuggled salt and resisted arrest will be punished by 'Zhan' (beheading), not to mention those who have wounded others. The punishment is never too severe to prevent crimes, so it is suitable to change 'killing three people' to 'killing two

10.7 The Achievement of "Lv Xue" (The Study of Statutory Laws) and the World...

people.'" Although one word had been changed, it had reflected that the punishment for the crime of forcible salt smuggling was aggravated.

Wang Kentang's *Lv Li Jian Shi* (*Annotation of Laws and Precedents*) had not only provided guidance for legislation and the judiciary since the mid-Ming Dynasty but also affected the legal construction of the early Qing Dynasty. So Wang Kentang's interpretations were not only quoted in "Xiao Zhu" (small-character notes between vertical lines of a book, usu. in two lines) in the law that was made in the 3rd year of Emperor Shunzhi but also used in the amendment of many other regulations. In the middle of the reign of Emperor Kangxi, *Lv Li Jian Shi* (*Annotation of Laws and Precedents*) was recompiled by Gu Ding, which had become an important reference material for the legal scholars in the Qing Dynasty in the interpretation of law at the time. Because of its strong realistic pertinence, *Lv Li Jian Shi* (*Annotation of Laws and Precedents*) was applied until the publication of *Da Qing Lv Ji Zhu* (*Collected Commentaries on Great Qing Code*), which was written by Shen Zhiqi.

In addition to *Lv Li Jian Shi* (*Annotation of Laws and Precedents*) by Wang Kentang, *Xing Shu Ju Hui* (*Collections of Criminal Law*) by Peng Yingbi was written by making reference to the judicial cases and the judicial terminology in interpreting law, so its style was often imitated by legal experts in the Qing Dynasty. In *Fa Zhui* (*Works on Law*) by Tang Shu, the official literature on "Lv Xue" (the study of statutory laws) and private legal annotation texts were arranged in chronological order. Moreover, the outline of the legal system of the early Ming Dynasty was described in detail, and the legal changes of different periods were also compared comprehensively.

The emergence of "Lv Xue" (the study of statutory laws) in late Ming Dynasty was decided by the specific historical condition in the late feudal society. Moreover, "it had inherited the work of the pioneers and taken the specific ideological profile as a prerequisite,"[379] and at the same time, it was influenced by the criticism of the old concepts about marriage, property, and inheritance by the utilitarian school in the Southern Song Dynasty, from which it was easy to understand the criticism by Liu Ji in the early Ming Dynasty of "Qi Chu" (seven reasons to repudiate the wife: "being unfilial to parents-in-law," "failing to bear a male offspring," "being lascivious," "being jealous," "having severe illness," "gossiping," and "committing theft") in the traditional law:

> Someone asked Yu Lizi: "in the law, the husband could repudiate one's wife if she violates 'Qi Chu', is it the rule of saints? He answered: 'it is not the intention of saints'. It is easier for the husband to repudiate his wife if she has committed the five sins of 'being lascivious', 'being jealous', 'being unfilial to parents-in-law', 'gossiping' and 'committing theft', because these are universal evil behaviors. But does anyone want to have serious disease and infertility? So it is unfortunate to have disease and infertility because no one wants to. It is a great misfortune for her. How bearable it is to have her abandoned! The relationship between husband and wife is very important for human beings, the wife considers husband

---

[379]"En Ge Si Zhi Kang Shi Mi Te" (Engels to Kang Schmidt) in *Ma Ke Si En Ge Si Xuan Ji* (*The Selected Works of Marx and Engels*), Vol. 4, The People's Publishing House, 1972.

as 'Tian' (heaven), but the husband shows no sympathy to her misfortune, and abandons her instead. Is it in conformity with 'Tian Li' (heavenly principles)? But it has been stipulated in law, which is the same as instructing people to follow non-benevolence instead of humanitarianism. Therefore, Confucianism has been neglected and heretical ideas have prevailed. For fear that people may not believe it, it is instructed in the name of saints, alas, it is a misfortune for saints, so they have been humiliated for a long time."[380]

10.7.2 The World Position of Da Ming Lv (The Great Ming Code)

Da Ming Lv (*The Great Ming Code*), as one of the key achievements of legal construction of the Ming Dynasty, has not only inherited the contents of *Tang Lv* (*Tang Code*) from the previous dynasties but also initiated lawmaking in the Qing Dynasty. Besides, innovation has been made not only in the legal system but also in the standardization of contents and the interpretation of legal texts. So to a certain extent, it has shown the new features of the times. No doubt, it is a legal code that has not only had an important influence on the history of the development of Chinese legal culture but also has had a considerable influence on Southeast Asian countries after *Tang Lv* (*Tang Code*).

Da Ming Lv (*The Great Ming Code*) has also had exerted great influence on Japan. After the establishment of the Ming Dynasty, Sino–Japanese friendship and the cultural exchanges between the two countries were resumed. As to legal cultural exchange, it also reached and even exceeded the level of the Tang Dynasty. Lawbooks of the Ming Dynasty were brought to Japan successively at its request. According to records, in the 1st year of Zhengde (1506 A.D.), *Da Ming Lv Fu Li* (*The Great Ming Code Appended with Sub-Laws*), with sixteen volumes, was introduced to Japan, and in the 2nd year of Zhengde (1507 A.D.), more legal works such as *Da Ming Lv Li Shi Yi* (*The Laws and Precedents of the Great Ming Code Appended with Sub-Laws*), with eight volumes; *Da Ming Lv Li Tian Shi Pang Zhu* (*The Additional Sidenotes on the Laws and Precedents of the Great Ming*); with four volumes; *Da Ming Lv Li Fu Jie* (*The Annotation of the Great Ming Code*), with twelve volumes; and *Xin Li San Tai Ming Lv Zhao Pan Zheng Zong* (*Authentic Judgment of three New Precedents in Ming Code*), with eight volumes, were introduced to Japan; in the 3rd year of Zhengde (1508), *Da Ming Lv Jian Shi* (*Interpretation of the Great Ming Code*), with two volumes, and *Da Ming Lv Si Jian* (*Private Connotation of the Great Ming Code*), with eight volumes, were introduced to Japan.

In the years of Kyoho during the Edo period of Japan, the 18th generation of General Tokugawa Yoshimune of Shogunate was keen on studying the laws of the Ming Dynasty. According to *De Chuan Shi Ji* (*The Records of Tokugawa*), "there

---

[380]Liu Ji (Ming Dynasty), "Qi Chu" (Seven Reasons to Repudiate the Wife) in "Geng Huo" (Coarse Food) (Part 17) in *Yu Li Zi* (*Civilized Government*).

10.7 The Achievement of "Lv Xue" (The Study of Statutory Laws) and the World... 1063

were many law books in Tokugawa Yoshimune's home, and he was fond of reading *Ming Lv* (*Ming Code*). After enthronement, he still occasionally read it." During this period, the representative works on the interpretation of the laws in the Ming Dynasty by Japanese jurists included the following: *Da Ming Lv Li Shi Yi* (*The Laws and Precedents of the Great Ming Code Appended with Sub-Laws*) with fourteen volumes and *Ming Lv Xiang Jie* (*Detailed Explanation of Ming Code*) with twenty one volumes by Takase Tadaatsu, *Ming Lv Yi* (*Translation of Ming Code*) with thirty volumes by Ogyu Kan, *Da Ming Lv Li Shi Yi* (*The Laws and Precedents of the Great Ming Code Appended with Sub-Laws*) with fourteen volumes by Takase Kiboku, *Ming Lv Yi Zhu* (*Translation and Annotation of Ming Code*) with nine volumes by Oka Hakku, *Ming Lv Guo Zi Jie* (*Japanese Interpretation of Ming Code*) with sixteen volumes by Ogyu Sorai, *Ming Lv Yi Jie Tong Bu Yi* (*Supplementary Translation of the Translation and Comments of Ming Code*) and *Ming Lv Yan Jie Da Cheng* (*Collection of Interpretation of Ming Code*) with thirty volumes by Sakakibara Gensuke, *Ming Lv Yi Yi* (*Doubtful Points of Ming Code*) by Ogyu Dousai, *Xiang Shuo Ming Lv Shi Yi* (*Detailed Interpretation of Ming Code*) by Miura Yosikata, *Ming Lv Xiang Yi* (*Detailed Meaning of Ming Code*) by Shibui Takanori, *Ming Lv Hui Zuan* (*Collected Materials of Ming Code*) by Kannou Hirosi, and so on. Among these books, in *Da Ming Lv Li Shi Yi* (*The Laws and Precedents of the Great Ming Code Appended with Sub-Laws*), specific examples were cited for illustration, in addition to the translation of four hundred and sixty provisions of *Ming Lv* (*Ming Code*). However, because the original context of *Ming Lv* (*Ming Code*) was not cited in this work, Ogyu Kan, the civilian official of Shogunate, was appointed to have the original text of *Ming Lv* (*Ming Code*) rectified with punctuations and Katakana added. Later, the book was published with the name *Guan Zhun Kan Xing Ming Lv* (*Officially Authorized Ming Code*), by which *Ming Lv* (*Ming Code*) was extensively known in Japan. Moreover, the main legislative acts after Xiaozong of the Ming Dynasty were introduced in the work *Ming Lv Guo Zi Jie* (*Japanese Interpretation of Ming Code*) on the basis of *Da Ming Lv* (*The Great Ming Code*) and *Wen Xing Tiao Li* (*The Ordinance for Inquisition*).

Da Ming Lv (*The Great Ming Code*) had exerted great influence on Japanese legal civilization, and it was mainly reflected in two aspects: the first one was the approval of the leading legislative guiding ideology, and the second one was the absorption of the form and contents of codification.

In *Da Ming Lv* (*The Great Ming Code*), the Confucian "Gang Chang Ming Jiao" (feudal cardinal guides and constant virtues) was used as its guiding ideology. During the reign of Xiaozong in the Ming Dynasty, *Da Xue Yan Yi Bu* (*Supplement to the Deductive Meaning of the Great Learning*) by Qiu Jun, which was regarded as "a comprehensive collection of the achievements of Ming Dynasty" and "the agglomeration of Confucian doctrine," had a profound impact on the law circles of Japan. For example, *Wu Xing Lu* (*The Record of Non-Penalty*), written by Japanese scholar Ashino Tokurin, was based on it. As to the provisions relevant to the maintenance of the monarchy, patriarchy, and the authority of the husband in *Ming Lv* (*Ming Code*), they were all adopted into the laws of Japan. For example, the relevant provisions on "Shi E" (The Ten Abominations) and "Ba Yi" (The Eight

Deliberations) in *Ming Lv* (*Ming Code*) were directly adopted by Tosa Hansho in his work *Hai Nan Lv Ling* (*Laws and Decrees of Hainan*). Japanese scholar Uda Hisasi had written in his book *Ri Ben Wen Hua Yu Ru Zhi Ying Xiang* (*Japanese Culture and the Confucian Influence*): "Seen from the rules and regulations of the three hundred years of the Tokugawa Age, Confucianism was reflected in all of their moral elements. During the Edo Period, in *Xing Fa Cao Shu* (*Outline of the Criminal Law*), the most representative work written by Kumamoto-han, both the form and content of *Ming Lv* (*Ming Code*) were adopted. Shortly afterward, the book was amended by imitating *Wen Xing Tiao Li* (*The Ordinance for Inquisition*) of the Ming Dynasty and was then published with the name of *Yu Xing Fa Cao Shu Fu Li* (*Imperial Outline of the Criminal Law with Appended Sub-statutes*).

After Meiji Reform, *Xin Lv Gang Ling* (*The Guiding Principle of New Law*) was also made according to the old laws of China. A Japanese doctor, Hozumi Nobushige, pointed out in *Ri Ben Xini Min Fa* (*The New Civil Law of Japan*): "This code was made according to the old laws of Tang, Ming and Qing dynasties in China and was slightly modified from the old laws of Japan. In fact, *Xin Lv Gang Ling* (*The Guiding Principle of New Law*) was mostly based on *Da Ming Lv* (*The Great Ming Code*)."

Thus, it can be seen that *Da Ming Lv* (*The Great Ming Code*) has had great influence on the Japanese legal system both during the Edo period and during the early years of Meiji, just as was pointed out by a law professor of Japan: "The profound influence of Chinese law on Japanese legal consciousness can be dated back to the ancient times, and now it till lasts, and has never stopped. So it is very necessary to study the legal consciousness of China."[381]

Besides Japan, the influence of *Da Ming Lv* (*The Great Ming Code*) on Korea was particularly profound and extensive. In the later years of the Goryeo Dynasty, politics was corrupted and the legal system was disrupted, which had led to a situation where "the prohibitions were not strictly carried out, but amnesties were randomly offered, so that the treacherous and wicked people escape the legal sanctions without being punished, and corruption became prevalent during the final years of the reign."[382] Therefore, some insightful people had proposed that "both *Yi Xing Yi Lan* (*A General Survey of the Measurement of Penalty*) in Yuan Dynasty and *Da Ming Lv* (*The Great Ming Code*) should be introduced and applied."[383] It could therefore be inferred that *Da Ming Lv* (*The Great Ming Code*) had been introduced into the Korean Peninsula in the Goryeo Dynasty, so that a memorial was found in the code in the 6th year of Wuwang (1380), which stated: "The Korean law should be revised by reference to *Da Ming Lv* (*The Great Ming*

---

[381] *Fa Xue Lun Cong* (*Law Review*), No. 6, Vol. 7, quoted in Yang Honglie, *Zhong Guo Fa Lv Dui Dong Nan Ya Zhu Guo Zhi Ying Xiang* (*The Impact of Chinese Law on East Asian Countries*), China University of Political Science and Law Press, 1999, p. 354.

[382] "Xing Fa Zhi" (The Record of the Criminal Law) (Part 1) in *Gao Li Shi* (*Korean History*), Vol. 84.

[383] "Xing Fa Zhi" (The Record of the Criminal Law) (Part 1) in *Gao Li Shi* (*Korean History*), Vol. 84.

Code)."[384] "Shi Zhong" (the assistant official) Zheng Mengzhou also said: "New laws should be made by referring to *Da Ming Lv* (*The Great Ming Code*), *Zhi Zheng Tiao Ge* (*Legal Provisions and Injunctions in the Period of Zhizheng*) and Korean law."[385] But it was after the establishment of the Chosun Dynasty that *Da Ming Lv* (*The Great Ming Code*) was really implemented in Korea.

After the establishment of the Chosun Dynasty, measures were actively taken to promote its relationship with China, and when Emperor Taizu Li Chenggui ascended the throne, an imperial edict was issued: "From now on, the crimes which involved official or private affairs, such as making sentences, offering amnesties, confiscating property, recording demerits, resuming the positions, atoning for crimes, removing from offices and so on, should all be dealt with by the judicial officials both inside and outside the capital according to *Da Ming Lv* (*The Great Ming Code*). Besides, the previous malpractice should all be eliminated."[386] Zheng Daochuan also stated in *Chao Xian Jing Guo Dian* (*Gyeongguk Daejeon* or *Complete Code of Law*): "Today the emperor is virtuous because of his 'Ren' (benevolence), and orderly because of his 'Li' (rites). So it can be said that the essence of ruling has been obtained, this is because *Da Ming Lv* (*The Great Ming Code*) has been used as an auxiliary tool to govern the country,"[387] from which we can see the effect of the application of *Da Ming Lv* (*The Great Ming Code*) in the Chosun Dynasty. In order to carry out *Da Ming Lv* (*The Great Ming Code*), Zheng Daochuan also pointed out the necessity of translating *Da Ming Lv* (*The Great Ming Code*) in *Chao Xian Jing Guo Dian* (*Gyeongguk Daejeon* or *Complete Code of Law*): "In view of the fact that the ignorant people do not know what is prohibited by law, it is ordered that *Da Ming Lv* (*The Great Ming Code*) be translated into dialect by the relevant offices so that it can be made known to the people. Thereafter, all sentences should be made according to this law to show that the ancestors have been followed as examples and the common people's lives have been emphasized."[388] In February of the 4th year of Emperor Taizu (1395), "Zheng Cheng" (minister) Zhao Jun ordered "Jian Xiao Zhong Shu Yuan" (the honorary general governorate) Gao Shijun and Jin Zhi to have the text of *Da Ming Lv* (*The Great Ming Code*) translated into "Li Du Wen" (Korean language created on the basis of Chinese), and it was then that it was revised, modified, and published with the name of *Da Ming Lv Zhi Jie* (*A Literary*

---

[384]"Xing Fa Zhi" (The Record of the Criminal Law) (Part 1) in *Gao Li Shi* (*Korean History*), Vol. 84.

[385]"Zheng Meng Zhou Lie Zhuan" (The Collected Biographies of Zheng Mengzhou) in *Gao Li Shi* (*Korean History*), Vol. 117.

[386]"Ding Wei Tiao" (The Provision of Ding Wei) in "Tai Zu" (Emperor Taizu) in *Chao Xian Wang Chao Shi Lu* (*The Record of Chosun Dynasty*), Vol. 1, in July of the first year.

[387]Zheng Daochuan (Korea), "Xian Dian Zong Xu" (A General Preface to Constitution) in *Chao Xian Jing Guo Dian* (*Gyeongguk Daejeon* or *Complete Code of Law*) in *San Feng Ji* (*Collections of Sanfeng*), Vol. 7.

[388]Zheng Daochuan (Korea), "Xian Dian Zong Xu" (A General Preface to Constitution) in *Chao Xian Jing Guo Dian* (*Gyeongguk Daejeon* or *Complete Code of Law*) in *San Feng Ji* (*Collections of Sanfeng*), Vol. 7.

Interpretation of the Great Ming Code) by Zheng Daochuan and Tang Cheng, which had provided a convenient condition for the implementation of *Da Ming Lv* (*The Great Ming Code*). However, some amendments were made according to the specific conditions of Korea. In this regard, Emperor Taizu of the Ming Dynasty expressed his understanding; he stated in his edict: "Chosun Dynasty is thousands of *li* away, so it has its own special habits and customs." When it was required that *Da Ming Lv* (*The Great Ming Code*) be introduced into the Chosun Dynasty, Emperor Jianwen also pointed out: "Etiquettes should accord with local customs, and the old systems should be followed in making laws."[389] So although *Da Ming Lv* (*The Great Ming Code*) was adopted by Korea, because of the different customs and circumstances, some of the punishments were aggravated, some were mitigated, and some new articles were added in the Korean law. The details are as follows.

The violation of "Li" (rites) was severely punished. The rulers of the Chosun Dynasty were strongly influenced by Zhu Xi's theory of family etiquettes, so great importance was attached to "Gang Chang" (the Chinese ethical tradition) and "Lun Li" (ethics). Taking the crime of "Gan Ming Fan Yi" (violating the feudal ethics) as an example, offenders were punished according to the law of the Tang Dynasty instead of that of the Ming Dynasty. According to the law of the Ming Dynasty, the offenders of "Gan Ming Fan Yi" (violating the feudal ethics) should be punished by "Zhang" (flogging with heavy sticks) for one hundred strokes and "Tu" (imprisonment) for three years, while according to the law of the Tang Dynasty, it should be punished by "Liu" (exile) or "Jiao" (hanging). So the law of the Tang Dynasty was used in enforcing punishments, which had shown that the offense of "Li" (rites) was severely punished. In the 12th year of Shizong, Qi Shanglian sued his stepmother for the crime of adultery, so minister Xu Chen petitioned: "Although there is negligence between mother and child, they conceal the crimes for each other because of 'Yi' (justice). But Shang Lian sued his mother because he wanted to do harm to his mother and brother just for the domestic property and 'Nu Bi' (the slave girls and maidservants). If his wicked behavior is not punished, there will be no justice. So please follow the rules of Tang Dynasty."[390] As another example, as for "Nu Bi" (the slave girls and maidservants) suing their owners, it was stated in *Da Ming Lv* (*The Great Ming Code*) that "if 'Nu Bi' (the slave girls and maidservants) have sued their owners, the people above 'Si Ma' (the person wearing the mourning apparel of soft sackcloth in the fifth mourning degree) will be punished by 'Zhang' (flogging with heavy sticks) for one hundred strokes and 'Tu' (imprisonment) for three years; if they have falsely accused their owners, they will be punished by 'Jiao' (hanging); if the hiring workers have sued their owners and relatives, the accuser will be punished, but the punishment for 'Nu Bi' (the slave girls and maidservants) will be reduced by one level." But according to the laws of the Chosun Dynasty, "'Nu Bi' (the slave

---

[389]"Kui Mou Tiao" (The Provision of Kui Mou) in "Tai Zu" (Emperor Taizu) in *Chao Xian Wang Chao Shi Lu* (*The Record of Chosun Dynasty*), Vol. 112, in June of the 28th year.

[390]"Ren Shen Tiao" (The Provision of Ren Shen) in "Shi Zong" (Emperor Shizong) in *Chao Xian Wang Chao Shi Lu* (*The Record of Chosun Dynasty*), Vol. 51, in March of the 13th year.

10.7 The Achievement of "Lv Xue" (The Study of Statutory Laws) and the World...

girls and maidservants) and their husbands or the wives of servants will all be punished by 'Zhan' (beheading)."[391] Although it was later changed to "Jiao" (hanging) according to the proposal of the judicial officials, the penalty was still severer than those in the laws of the Tang and Ming dynasties.

Civil and military officials would be punished severely for their public or private crimes. According to the records in "Wen Wu Guan Fan Gong Zui" (Civil and Military Officials Committing Public Crimes) in *Da Ming Lv* (*The Great Ming Code*), "for the government officials both inside and outside the capital who have committed public crimes punishable by 'Chi' (flogging with light sticks), their punishment can be redeemed with property in every season; if they have committed crimes punishable by 'Zhang' (flogging with heavy sticks) or above, the corresponding charges shall be recorded each year, and the frequency and seriousness of crimes shall be judged every nine years to decide whether they shall be demoted or removed." But in the Chosun Dynasty, officials, whatever their positions were, were removed from office simply because of their negligence in performing public service. In addition, according to *Da Ming Lv* (*The Great Ming Code*), "the officials will be punished by 'Chi' (flogging with light sticks) for forty strokes for committing private crimes; if they have committed less serious crimes than that punishable by 'Chi' (flogging with light sticks), their demerit should be recorded; if they have resumed their positions, they shall be punished by 'Zhang' (flogging with heavy sticks) for fifty strokes; if they have greeted each other at parting parties when their term of office is over, they shall be punished by 'Zhang' (flogging with heavy sticks) for sixty strokes with their official ranks reduced by one level. Furthermore, if punishable by 'Zhang' (flogging with heavy sticks) for seventy strokes, the official ranks of those involved shall be reduced by two levels; if punishable by 'Zhang' (flogging with heavy sticks) for seventy strokes, the official ranks of those involved shall be reduced by three levels; if punishable by 'Zhang' (flogging with heavy sticks) for eighty strokes, the official ranks of those involved shall be reduced by four levels. If all 'Liu Guan' (centrally-appointed nonhereditary official) and 'Shi Guan' (official in charge of recording and compiling history) have committed miscellaneous crimes punishable by 'Zhang' (flogging with heavy sticks) for one hundred strokes, they will never be appointed again according to their ranks within their official posts." But in the Chosun Dynasty, if the crime was punishable by "Zhang" (flogging with heavy sticks) for sixty strokes, the official ranks of those involved should be reduced by two levels; if punishable by 'Zhang' (flogging with heavy sticks) for ninety strokes, the official ranks of those involved should be reduced by five levels.

The crimes of murder and theft were severely punished. According to "Dou Ou Ji Gu Sha Ren" (fighting and voluntary manslaughter) in *Da Ming Lv* (*The Great Ming Code*), criminals would be punished by "Jiao" (hanging) for fighting with fists or feet or with mental knives. However, in the Chosun Dynasty, it was stipulated that those

---

[391]"Jia Chen Tiao" (The Provision of Jia Shen) in "Shi Zong" (Emperor Shizu) in *Chao Xian Wang Chao Shi Lu* (*The Record of Chosun Dynasty*) in June of the 10th year.

who fought with or murdered others would be punished by "Jiao" (hanging) and the criminals who killed others with knives would be punished by "Zhan" (beheading). As to theft, it was stipulated in *Da Ming Lv* (*The Great Ming Code*) that "the criminals who have committed theft for three times will be sentenced to death," while in the Chosun Dynasty, it was provided that "the people who have committed theft twice will be punished by 'Jiao' (hanging)."

Next, the criminal law on redemption and exile was adjusted. Because copper coin was used as the currency in the Ming Dynasty and "Wu Sheng Bu" was used as the currency in the Chosun Dynasty, the provision of redeeming crimes with money in the law of the Ming Dynasty was changed into redeeming crimes with cloth in the Chosun Dynasty. For example, the crime punishable by "Chi" (flogging with light sticks) for ten strokes could be redeemed with six hundred copper coins according to the law of the Ming Dynasty; while according to *Da Ming Lv Zhi Jie* (*A Literary Interpretation of the Great Ming Code*), the punishment could be redeemed with three *pi* of "Wu Sheng Bu." As for the punishment of "Liu" (exile), according to the territory of the Chosun Dynasty, the penalty of 2000 *li*, 2500 *li*, and 3000 *li* was changed to 600 *li*, 750 *li*, and 900 *li*, respectively. These adjustments were made according to the reality of Chosun Dynasty, so they were absolutely necessary.

The Chinese legal culture was spread to the Korean Peninsula at very early times, so the legal system of the Goryeo Dynasty was strongly influenced by *Tang Lv* (*Tang Code*), while the legal system of the Chosun Dynasty was more influenced by the legal system of the Ming Dynasty, so *Da Ming Lv* (*The Great Ming Code*) was taken as a model for legislation. When *Xing Fa Da Quan* (*A Complete Collection of Criminal Law*) was made in Korea after the Sino–Japanese War, *Da Ming Lv* (*The Great Ming Code*) was still used as a reference, from which we can see the far-reaching influence of *Da Ming Lv* (*The Great Ming Code*). Apart from *Da Ming Lv* (*The Great Ming Code*), *Da Ming Hui Dian* (*The Collected Statutes of Ming Dynasty*) also provided a model for the making of *Chao Xian Jing Guo Dian* (*Gyeongguk Daejeon* or *Complete Code of Law*). It is thus clear that Chinese legal culture has promoted the progress of Korean legal civilization.

To sum up, as far as legal construction in the Ming Dynasty is concerned, great achievements have been made not only in the legal system but also in the code style and layout, the standardized content, the judicial system, and legal interpretation, so that it had shown a striking feature of diversity. Therefore, it not only occupied an important position in inheriting the old laws of Tang, Song and Qing dynasties and initiating the new laws in Qing Dynasty in the development of Chinese legal system, but also exerted a great influence on Southeast Asian countries besides *Tang Lv* (*Tang Code*).

So the legal system of the Ming Dynasty had forcefully mended the disrupted social order; reconstructed the law and discipline, which were needed in a feudal state; and cracked down upon the various corrupt acts of officials. So it had not only made it possible for the majority of people to work and live in a comparatively good legal order but had also led to rapid economic development and the stability and prosperity of the nation and promoted the fast development of culture and technology, all of which had created a new picture of legal civilization in the Ming Dynasty.

10.7 The Achievement of "Lv Xue" (The Study of Statutory Laws) and the World...

However, the abuse of power caused by the extreme development of autocracy had gradually destroyed the innate mechanisms and legal order of the feudal legal system. After the middle of the Ming Dynasty, the whole bureaucracy became a huge corrupt machine. During the reign of Shenzong, eunuch Zhang Jing should have been sentenced to death; however, he "was pardoned because he had donated money and treasures to the emperor."[392] Li Yi, "Ji Shi Zhong" (the senior assistant of the emperor and the supervisor of officials) of "Li Ke" (the department of personnel), pointed out in his memorial to the emperor: "People hear Zhang Jing has presented money and treasures to you ... the subjects home and abroad do not believe it at first, because we believe that you are so rich that you even own the wealth nationwide, then how is it possible that your majesty like gold and treasures. ... however, the government staff are strongly influenced by Zhang Jing's behavior and rumors have been proved to be true, which not only is harmful to your holiness but also has shown your superficiality."[393] Emperor Shenzong was so angry that he scolded Li Yi: "You have not criticized the corrupt officials, but only claimed that I am greedy. So your crime is inexcusable."[394] The emperor had tried to defend his own corrupt behaviors, so it was difficult for him to control other officials. After the last emperor's, Chongzhen's, succession to the throne, "Ji Shi Zhong" (the senior assistant of the emperor and the supervisor of officials) of "Hu Ke" (the department of revenue) Han Yiliang exposed:

> Today, money is used everywhere because all officials like money. They spent money to get the official positions first, so it is natural for them to collect money everywhere to pay for the cost ... as far as the officials are concerned, the officials of "Xian" (county) rank the first in offering bribes, and "Ji Shi Zhong" (the senior assistant of the emperor and the supervisor of officials) ranks the first in accepting bribes ... the senior officials ask for money either on the excuse of public expenses or on the excuse of litigation cost. So gifts and money are often extorted from everyone and it will often need 3,000 to 4,000 gold to see the emperor. But the gold does not fall from heaven, nor is it produced by earth, is it difficult to believe that these officials are not corrupted?[395]

The eunuch dictatorship, which was brought about by the extreme development of despotism, was a major political feature of the Ming Dynasty, which was typically reflected in the destruction of the normal social order and the violation of the law and discipline. In the late Ming Dynasty, in *Ming Yi Dai Fang Lu* (*Waiting for Dawn*), Huang Zongxi had profoundly exposed the darkness of the society:

> "The disasters of eunuchs also existed in Han, Tang and Song dynasties, but it is not as serious as that in Ming Dynasty. In Han, Tang and Song dynasties, eunuchs also intervened in state affairs, but no states were controlled and ruled by eunuchs. Now the government decrees are all issued by the six departments of 'Zai Xiang' (the prime minister); however, as for the memorials submitted, they are first orally replied and instructed (by the eunuchs), and

---

[392]"Li Yi Zhuan" (The Biography of Li Yi) in *Ming Shi* (*The History of Ming Dynasty*).
[393]"Li Yi Zhuan" (The Biography of Li Yi) in *Ming Shi* (*The History of Ming Dynasty*).
[394]"Li Yi Zhuan" (The Biography of Li Yi) in *Ming Shi* (*The History of Ming Dynasty*).
[395]"Chong Zhen Zhi Luan" (Restoring Things to Order by Emperor Chongzhen) in *Ming Shi Ji Shi Ben Mo* (*The Ins and Outs of the Records in the History of Ming Dynasty*), Vol. 72.

then written ones are issued; as for the state revenue, they are firstly put into the imperial treasury instead of the national treasury; as for the penalties and prison affairs, they are firstly heard by 'Dong Chan' (the imperial spy agency) before being handled by the judicial organs, and it is the same with other things. Moreover, the six departments of 'Zai Xiang' (the prime minister) are simply the followers of eunuchs." "In Han, Tang and Song dynasties, the eunuchs were intoxicated by their successful career by taking the advantage of the fatuous emperors, so that they could interfere with state affairs, but in Ming Dynasty, the situation is more complicated and deteriorated..., so the disaster is the most devastating."

Since the power of the government officials was severely infringed upon by the eunuchs, from the middle of Ming Dynasty, the struggle and internal strife for power between the eunuchs and bureaucratic officials had never been stopped. Till the late Ming Dynasty, the upright officials represented by "Dong Lin Party" (the literati and bureaucratic group in Ming Dynasty) were relentlessly attacked and persecuted by eunuchs, so that the disaster brought by eunuchs became the most devastating in history. However, it was the majority of the people who suffered the most from the dark and corrupted ruling in the late Ming Dynasty. With the further development of land annexation and the oppression and exploitation of people by the ruling class, class contradiction was further intensified. By the early seventeenth century, the peasant uprising of "Bai Lian Jiao" (White Lotus Society), led by Xu Hongru, broke out in Shandong province, which was followed by the famine riots in northern Shaanxi province. Thereafter, the peasant uprising led by Li Zicheng developed rapidly. In the occupied territories, political organizations were established, and slogans such as "land equalization of the rich and poor," "exemption of tax and corvee," and "fair dealing" were put forward, which were warmly received and supported by the broad masses. After the occupation of Henan, Hubei, Shaanxi, and other places, Da Shun state was finally established, and Li Zicheng's army drove straight north, captured Beijing, the capital of Ming Dynasty, by which the ruling of the Ming Dynasty was completely overthrown. Meanwhile, the Da Xi regime was established by Zhang Xianzhong's peasant army in Sichuan province. However, although the corrupted ruling of the Ming Dynasty was overthrown by the peasant uprising in the late Ming Dynasty, it was defeated under the joint military attack of the Manchu nobility and the Han landlords. Finally, it was replaced by the Qing Dynasty, which was manipulated by the Manchu nobility.

Chapter 11
The Legal System of the Qing Dynasty: The Final Form of Chinese Legal Civilization

(1644 A.D.–1911 A.D.)

Before Qing rulers entered Shanhaiguan in 1644, a stable Jurchen state of Later Jin Dynasty (Qing) had already been built in the northeastern region of Liaoning and Shenyang and a unique military and political system had already been established, which not only had become a powerful local political and military group with considerable size and strength after half a century of development but also posed a stiff resistance to the regime of the late Ming Dynasty. Consequently, the Ming Dynasty was overthrown and the Qing Dynasty, which ruled China for over 260 years, was finally established.

The Qing Dynasty was the last dynasty of Chinese feudal society. From the time it was set up in Shanhaiguan in 1644, it had experienced historical development from prosperity to decline. During this period, much greater progress in the feudal economy was made than during the previous dynasties, and remarkable achievements were also made in the construction of legal institutions. As for the legal system, a relatively complete legal system that consisted of department laws such as administrative law, criminal law, civil law, economic law, litigation law, as well as other legal and prison laws, was established; as for the legislative contents, they not only covered a much wider range but also were more suitable to the social actualities and the conditions of the people. Besides, the procedure of the judicial system was complete, the rules on the trial were strict, the system of "Hui Shen" (the joint trial) and death penalty review were further institutionalized and civil mediation was more extensively practiced.

In Qing Dynasty, a highly consolidated and unified multi-ethnic country, great attention was attached to the legal adjustment of the nation. In the border areas inhabited by ethnic minorities, the measures that were adaptable to the local conditions and customs were adopted and a series of specialized laws, such as *Meng Gu Lv Li* (*The Laws and Precedents of Mongolia*), *Li Fan Yuan Ze Li* (*The Regulation for the Bureau of National Minority Affairs*), *Hui Jiang Ze Li* (*Regulations of Huijiang*), and *Qin Ding Xi Zang Zhang Cheng* (*The Statutes of Tibet Made by Imperial Order*), was issued, which made the national legislation of feudal China reach an unprecedented height. In terms of judicial jurisdiction, it exerted such a strong influence on the ethnic minority areas that it had effectively safeguarded the unity of administrative order and law as well as the stability of the nation.

Because the policy of secluding itself from the outside world was strictly implemented, cruel punishments were enforced to maintain an authoritarian rule in politics, ideology, and culture so that any heretical thoughts and actions that were against the ancient and established laws were severely suppressed by the Qing rulers, which made the legal systems of the Qing Dynasty quite conservative and the national politics inevitably corrupted that it began to decline from the middle period. When the tentacles of the capitalist invaders gradually stretched to China, the Qing rulers were still intoxicated in the dream of a heavenly kingdom, and it was not until the outbreak of the Opium War in 1840 that they were finally awaken.

The legal system of the Qing Dynasty was not only the final form of Chinese feudal legal system but also the most complete form. Therefore, no doubt, for the understanding and mastering of the essence and development of the feudal legal system, it is helpful to have an analysis of the legal system of the Qing Dynasty. The Qing Dynasty also existed at the early stage of modern Chinese history, so it initiated the Chinese modern legal civilization.

11.1 The Foundation of the Legal System Before Entering Shanhaiguan

Jurchen was an ancient nationality, and its history could be traced back to the Sushen nationality of the Zhou Dynasty in the eleventh century B.C. At the turn of the fifteenth and sixteenth centuries, a new national community, namely Manchu, was formed, which centered on the Jurchen at Jianzhou. In the 11th year of Wanli (1583), Nurhachi, the distinguished leader of Manchu, launched an attack against the Ming Dynasty. In the 1st year of Emperor Shunzhi (1644), they entered Shanhaiguan and made Yanjing the capital, and this was regarded not only as the period of the founding of the Qing Dynasty but also as one of the most important events that laid down the foundation of the nation. Rising in the northeastern part of China, the Manchu nationality unified the northeast region, eliminated the backward mode of production, and completed the transition from slavery to feudalism.

In order to meet the needs of social development and political administration, arduous work of legal construction was carried out according to the principle of "Can Han Zhuo Jin" (making reference not only to the legal thoughts and culture of Han nationality, but also to the national practice and needs of Jin nationality), which not only was regarded as a glorious page in the early period of Qing Dynasty, but also laid an important foundation for the ruling of the whole country and the establishment of imperial system after entering Shanhaiguan.

During this period, national integration entered a new period of development. Cultural communication between and the integration of the Jurchen, Mongolian,

Khitan, and Han nationalities enabled the Manchu nationality to embark on a path toward unprecedented legal civilization.

11.1.1 The Transition from Jurchen Customary Law to Statute Law

The various Jurchen tribes were finally unified by Nurhachi, the distinguished leader of Manchu nationality after thirty years of brutal struggle since 1583. In 1616 (the 44th year of Wanli in the Ming Dynasty), the state of Later Jin was established, the reign over the country was called "Tianming" (the Mandate of Heaven), and Nurhachi proclaimed himself as the "wise Khan." In the establishment of Later Jin Dynasty, it was inevitable for Nurhachi to come across legal and judicial issues, so he gradually realized that law should be highly emphasized. He once warned the princes and generals of "Ba Qi" (the Eight Banners: banner, a division of the Manchu nationality and the emperor's clan): "What is the most important thing for the ruling of a country? It is the honesty in handling state affairs and it is the strictness and completeness in implementing the legal system. So it is disastrous for the country to destroy its law and to give up the well-planned schemes."[1] He emphasized that "the officials should be fair-minded and should instruct the citizens to keep the laws and decrees in their minds."[2] Besides, "citizens should be well educated about the laws to avoid being punished."[3] He took the Ming Dynasty as an example and pointed out that the reason for its decline was that "its law was unjust and was not strictly enforced."[4] Therefore, he believed that "the way for a nation to survive lies in that the law must be obeyed by the prestigious people of the royal clan, and that the weak, the orphan, the widow and the common people should not be bullied and oppressed."[5] In order to achieve justice in law enforcement, Nurhachi emphasized that dignitaries should abide by the law and that anyone who had "violated the law should be punished according to law. Even doro beile (title of nobility), the rulers of the state, should also be equally punished according to the law." So the generals of "Ba Qi" (the Eight Banners: banner, a division of the Manchu nationality and the emperor's clan) were even forced to "make a pledge" to abide by the law. Moreover, he also demonstrated the necessity of law enforcement

---

[1] "Tai Zu" (Emperor Taizu) in *Man Wen Lao Dang* (*The Past Chronicles in Manchu Language*), Vol. 3, in December of the year of Guichou.

[2] "Tai Zu" (Emperor Taizu) in *Man Wen Lao Dang* (*The Past Chronicles in Manchu Language*), Vol. 11, on the 8th of July of the 4th year of Tianming.

[3] *Qing Tai Zu Gao Huang Di Shi Lu* (*The Record of Qing Emperor Gao Taizu*), Vol. 5, in intercalary April of the 3rd year of Tianming.

[4] "Tai Zu" (Emperor Taizu) in *Man Wen Lao Dang* (*The Past Chronicles in Manchu Language*), Vol. 11, on the 8th of July of the 4th year of Tianming).

[5] "Tai Zu" (Emperor Taizu) in *Man Wen Lao Dang* (*The Past Chronicles in Manchu Language*), Vol. 4, in December of the year of Yimao.

and justice from the perspective of "Tian Dao" (The Way of Heaven) by making use of the superstitious psychology of the Manchurian people, and he said that "the orderly change of four seasons, the smooth operation of wind, rain, the sun and the stars and the immortality of natural law are all the result of faithfully abiding by the law." Even if when his brothers and nephews violated the law, he punished them according to law. For example, Nurhachi killed his son-in-law Menggebulu because he wanted to "usurp the throne"[6]; he killed his eldest son, Chu Ying, because he had evil intentions[7]; and he punished his adopted son, Daerhanxia, because he obtained property from other *doro beile* (title of nobility).[8]

In order to maintain social order, Nurhachi suggested that criminals should be severely punished: "Anyone who has killed others will be convicted and punished; anyone who has grabbed the property of others will make compensation, because this was the only way to eliminate criminal activities."[9] At the same time, he ordered that officials below the rank of "Zong Bing" (commander-in-chief), officials above the rank of "Bei Yu" (junior military officer), and hereditary officials should be strictly supervised because "only through strict inspection is it possible to prevent the villains to make trouble . . .; otherwise, the scoundrel will create disturbance and the state would suffer great losses."[10] With regard to enforcement of penalties, he emphasized that the principal and the accomplice should be differentiated. In the 6th year of Tianming (1621), Nurhachi's "Bao Yi" (family servant), Hanchuha, and his three followers killed some people and robbed their property. Nurhachi tried this case in person. Consequently, "the principal Ahadai was punished by death penalty, the other three were flogged for fifty strokes and were punished by 'Guan Er Bi' (pricked in the ear and nose) before being released."[11]

He once advised the *doro beile* (title of nobility) that they should distinguish right from wrong, and he said: "If people have committed crimes, they should be interrogated carefully . . . If discussions are held, the ministers should not just echo what the others say, and they should distinguish the right from the wrong. Besides,

---

[6] *Qing Tai Zu Wu Huang Di Shi Lu* (*The Record of Emperor Wu of Qing Taizu*), Vol. 2.

[7] *Qing Tai Zu Chao Lao Man Wen Yuan Dang* (*The Past Chronicles in Manchu Language during the Reign of Emperor Taizu*) in *Man Wen Lao Dang* (*The Past Chronicles in Manchu Language*), Vol. 1, in August of the 22nd of the year of Yimao, annotated by Li Xue Zhi in the Bureau of Guanglu.

[8] "Tai Zu" (Emperor Taizu) in *Man Wen Lao Dang* (*The Past Chronicles in Manchu Language*), Vol. 28, on the 1st of November of the 6th year of Tianming.

[9] "Tai Zu" (Emperor Taizu) in *Man Wen Lao Dang* (*The Past Chronicles in Manchu Language*), Vol. 53, on the 30th of May of the 8th year of Tianming.

[10] *Qing Tai Zu Gao Huang Di Shi Lu* (*The Record of Emperor Gao of Qing Taizu*), in June of the 8th year of Tianming.

[11] "Tai Zu" (Emperor Taizu) in *Man Wen Lao Dang* (*The Past Chronicles in Manchu Language*), Vol. 22, on the 24th of the May of the 6th year of Tianming.

11.1 The Foundation of the Legal System Before Entering Shanhaiguan

they should have the courage to put forward their proposals to rectify the malpractice."[12]

On the basis of the rulings under the previous dynasties, Nurhachi also stated that neither law nor education should be neglected because "only through educating people by law" is it possible to make the ignorant people "avoid being punished"[13]; "...the ethos of benevolence and tolerance will be promoted only after the social customs are transformed by taking education as the essence."[14]

Thus, it can be seen that the legal thoughts of Nurhachi were based on Jurchen traditional customary law, as well as the mature legal culture of the Han Dynasty. In the process of creating the legal system of Later Jin Dynasty, importance was also attached to the study of the law of the Ming Dynasty. In the 6th year of Tianming (1621), he ordered "Du Tang" (censor) Adun, lieutenant Li Yongfang, Mao Youming, and Ba Youji (from the Han nationality) to "have all laws and regulations of Nikan (Han nationality) reported to him in written documents with the obsolete laws deleted and appropriate ones added."[15] According to the laws of Later Jin Dynasty, the punishment for the crime of violating the authority of Khan should be aggravated, while the punishment for the crime committed by relatives, nobility, and the meritorious ministers should be mitigated, which reflects the influence of the legal culture of the Han Dynasty.

On the other hand, as the second generation of emperors of Later Jin Dynasty, Huang Taiji paid much attention to the country's historical experience because he knew very well that "if everyone has tried his best to make the country prosperous, and if the legal system is complete and explicit, the state will be able to last long; on the contrary, if the political affairs are neglected and the law and discipline are not strictly enforced, the country will perish."[16] Therefore, he paid particular attention to the drafting of laws and the revision of codes and regulations because he believed that they are very crucial to "safeguarding and ruling the country."[17] In order to urge the aristocratic families to observe and respect the law, he practiced self-discipline and was very strict with himself to show that the law must be abided by and imperial orders must be carried out. In February of his 3rd year as Emperor Tiancong (1629), Huang Taiji made an inspection tour to Dongjing, and the local official, Ke Cheni, and his wife welcomed the emperor at the estuary and invited him to their house to

---

[12] *Qing Tai Zu Gao Huang Di Shi Lu* (*The Record of Emperor Gao of Qing Taizu*), Vol. 7, in April of the 6th year of Tianming.

[13] *Qing Tai Zu Gao Huang Di Shi Lu* (*The Record of Emperor Gao of Qing Taizu*), Vol. 5, in intercalary April of the 3rd year of Tianming.

[14] *Qing Tai Zu Gao Huang Di Shi Lu* (*The Record of Emperor Gao of Qing Taizu*), Vol. 6, in June of the 6th year of Tianming).

[15] "Tai Zu" (Emperor Taizu) in *Man Wen Lao Dang* (*The Past Chronicles in Manchu Language*), Vol. 20, in April of the 6th year of Tianming.

[16] *Qing Tai Zu Gao Huang Di Shi Lu* (*The Record of Emperor Gao of Qing Taizu*), Vol. 36, in June of the 2nd year of Chongde.

[17] *Qing Tai Zu Gao Huang Di Shi Lu* (*The Record of Emperor Gao of Qing Taizu*), Vol. 36, in June of the 2nd year of Chongde.

rest. Huang Taiji said: "I've told you ministers that during this inspection tour I have brought my own food to avoid disturbing the local people and increasing their burden. So it has been made known to the public, how can I violate the rules which I have issued?" Throughout his life, Huang Taiji was able to restrain his personal grievances and attached great importance to national law, which was praiseworthy because under the authoritarian system, "the law was not carried out just because it was violated by the top officials of the state." This was integral to his great ambition of unifying the central plains and overthrowing the Ming Dynasty. So it was in the process of unifying the central plains that Huang Taiji had realized the importance of laying a solid social basis by adjusting the ethnic relationship by law.

In order to include the Mongolian tribes south of the desert into the political and legal system of Manchu nationality, many officials were sent to there to propagate the Manchuria law, so that it had sped up transformation of the customary law of Mongolian tribes south of the desert.

What is particularly worth mentioning is that the legislative ideology of "Can Han Zhuo Jin" (making reference not only to the legal thoughts and culture of the Han nationality but also to the national practice and needs of the Jin nationality) was carried out by Huang Taiji with great courage. On the one hand, he said that "when a country is founded, different systems are also set up by the rulers of each dynasty, so none will inherit and follow those of the others ... I have inherited the family estate, how could I change our system and adopt the systems of other countries?"[18] On the other hand, he was very active in reforming the old customs of the Manchu nationality by adapting the legal culture of the Han nationality.

According to the regulation on informing against others, "it is prohibited for the son to accuse his father, for the wife to accuse the husband and for the brothers and sisters to accuse each other, but it is allowed to accuse those rebellious and treacherous people, or those disloyal to the doro beile (title of nobility)," about which Huang Taiji explained in March of the 6th year of his reign (1632): "The regulation is adopted, this is because it is the practice of the ancient nobles and wise monarchs, so we should follow the convention." In June of the 10th year of Emperor Tiancong (1636), "Ding Shang Xia Wen Dui Ying Ge You Qu Bie" (Different "Wen Dui" (questions and answers) for the Superior and Inferior) was issued, in which he again stressed that "before, the citizens of our country are not familiar with codes and etiquette, so there is not detailed analysis about the languages and rhetorics, nor there are any differences between the superior and the inferior and the noble and the humble. I have read of the ancient systems and learned that there are indeed differences between the superior and the inferior. So from now on, the ancient

---

[18] *Qing Tai Zu Gao Huang Di Shi Lu* (*The Record of Emperor Gao of Qing Taizu*), Vol. 18, in April of the 8th year of Tianming.

11.1 The Foundation of the Legal System Before Entering Shanhaiguan   1077

systems shall be followed in our country."[19] Words like "the practice of the ancient nobles and wise monarchs" and "the ancient systems," which were mentioned by Huang Taiji, referred to the feudal hierarchal ethic laws and institutions of the Ming Dynasty.

So, the formation of the legislative idea of "Can Han Zhuo Jin" (making reference not only to the legal thoughts and culture of Han nationality but also to the national practice and needs of Jin nationality) was not accidental. Based on the strategic objective of fighting against Ming Dynasty to seize state power, Huang Taiji was very active not only in absorbing the advanced and mature legal culture of Han nationality, but also in setting about building the nation's legal system and transforming the "old habits" and "bad habits" of clan system immediately in order to improve the legal and ethical standards of Manchu ethnic group by making use of the ethical laws in *Ming Lv* (*Ming Code*).

Particularly, in order to establish a feudal hierarchy system with the emperor as the supreme authority, the so-called democratic influence of "Ba Wang Gong Zhi" (the joint ruling of eight kings) was eliminated. In this process, the various codes translated by Manchu and Han Confucian ministers played an important role, so that the feudal laws and institutions of the Han nationality and the traditional Confucian "Gang Chang Ming Jiao" (feudal cardinal guides and constant virtues) gradually penetrated into Manchu society and the legal system with distinctive characteristics of the Qing Dynasty was finally formed.

11.1.2 Initiation of the Legal System of "Can Han Zhuo Jin"

According to *Qing Tai Zu Wu Huang Di Shi Lu* (*The Record of Emperor Wu of Qing Taizu*), in the 15th year of Wanli in the Ming Dynasty (1587), Nurhachi built Fei Ala city and constructed "three layers of city walls, towers and various buildings." "On June 24th, the national policy was formulated, so rebellion, theft, and cheating were strictly forbidden."[20] In *Qing Tai Zu Gao Huang Di Shi Lu* (*The Record of Emperor Gao of Qing Taizu*), there were similar records: "In June of the year of Renwu ... the national policy of prohibiting rebellion and theft was promulgated by the emperor, so the legal system was established."[21] We can see that the establishment of a legal system is very important for the creation of a state policy because law was made to mainly deal with "the crime of rebellion" and "theft," so its main function was to "prohibit" and "punish." Therefore, the so-called "establishment of legal system" was nothing but the announcement of some "prohibitions" and "regulations".

---

[19] *Qing Tai Zu Gao Huang Di Shi Lu* (*The Record of Emperor Gao of Qing Taizu*), Vol. 30, in June of the 1st year of Tianming.
[20] *Man Zhou Shi Lu* (*The Record of Manchu*), Vol. 2, in the year of Yiyou to the year of Wuxu.
[21] *Qing Tai Zu Gao Huang Di Shi Lu* (*The Record of Emperor Gao of Qing Taizu*), Vol. 2, in June of the year of Dinghai.

After that, the drafting of statute laws was gradually started. It was recorded in "Tai Zu" (Emperor Taizu) in *Man Wen Lao Dang* (*The Past Chronicles in Manchu Language*) that, in December of the year of Yimao (1615), "the wise Khan ... rectified the rules for hunting and military forces and formulated the law"[22]; it was also recorded in *Qing Tai Zu Chao Lao Man Wen Yuan Dang* (*The Old Manchu Archive During the Reign of Emperor Taizu*) that, in December of the year of Yimao, the wise Khan had "successfully governed the conquered people, suppressed the riots, crack down upon the thieves and established the various legal systems."

But generally speaking, the legal system was still very rudimentary, as was described in the saying that "the folk-custom is unsophisticated and politics is simple. Those which are approved by the rulers are issued as imperial decrees which mainly include 'Bian' (whipping), 'Pu' (flogging) and 'Zhan Jue' (the punishment of cutting down the criminal's head)."[23] After Huang Taiji's ascension to the throne, the development of the feudal economy, the formation of an imperial regime dominated by imperial power, and the establishment of a new relationship with Mongolia were urgently needed to be adjusted and confirmed by law. During the reign of Huang Taiji, legislative activities were frequently held, the scope of adjustment was greatly expanded, the forms of law tended to be diversified, and a certain system was begun to be established, so actually it was the greatest achievement of the development of the legal system in the period when they were outside Shanhaiguan; it had also laid the foundation for the legal system construction after they entered Shanhaiguan.

The legislative activities that were carried out during the reign of Huang Taiji mainly focused on administrative, economic, criminal, military, and ethnic aspects. As for administrative legislation, it is mainly concerned with the formulation of administrative laws after the establishment of "Liu Bu" (The Six Departments) and "Er Yuan" (Two Bureaus). Huang Taiji once ordered to have "the management responsibilities of 'Liu Bu' (The Six Departments) recorded and posted outside the gate."[24] Huang Taiji also specially issued an imperial edit concerning the administration of "Du Cha Yuan" (The Court of Censors): "If government affairs are mishandled, or if the ministers and doro beile (title of nobility) are arrogant, they should be reported to the emperor directly."[25] He also personally told the officials of "Du Cha Yuan" (The Court of Censors): "You are the censors, so it is your responsibility to supervise and give admonition. If I have made mistakes, or if I am excessively luxurious, or if I have wronged the meritorious officials or indulged myself in pleasure, or if I have neglected the state affairs and abandoned myself to debauchery, you should admonish me directly. As for the kings, doro beile (title of

---

[22]"Tai Zu" (Emperor Taizu) in *Man Wen Lao Dang* (*The Past Chronicles in Manchu Language*), Vol. 4, in November of the year of Yimao.

[23]"Xing Kao" (A Textual Research of the Criminal Penalties) (Part1) in *Qing Chao Wen Xian Tong Kao* (*A General Textual Research of the Documents of Qing Dynasty*).

[24]*Qing Tai Zong Shi Lu* (*The Record of Qing Emperor Taizong*), Vol. 12.

[25]"Zhi Guan" (State Officials) (Part 2) in *Qing Shi Gao* (*The Draft of the History of Qing Dynasty*).

11.1 The Foundation of the Legal System Before Entering Shanhaiguan

nobility) and the ministers, if they have neglected their duties, or indulged in debauchery, or seek comfort and pleasure, or accept property and money from the people, or seduce girls of other families, or show disrespect in court, or violate the rituals of dresses, or pretend to be ill without going to court, they should all be supervised by 'Li Bu' (The Department of Rites); if the officials in 'Li Bu' (The Department of Rites) have concealed the facts out of favouritism, you should conduct investigations and make reports to the emperor; if wrong judgments are made by 'Liu Bu' (The Six Departments), you should also conduct supervisions and make reports to the emperor."[26] Besides, the main adjustments made in administrative law before they entered Shanhaiguan included the system of "Chao Hui" (imperial court convention) and "Chao Yi" (imperial court consultation), the ranks and style of clothing of aristocratic officials, as well as the selection and examination of officials. In the 1st year of Chongde (1636), *Hui Dian* (*The Collected Statutes*) was created after some discussions were made. The law was based on *Da Ming Hui Dian* (*The Collected Statutes of Ming Dynasty*), which was a collection of the important administrative decrees issued during the reign of Emperor Tiancong. So it can be said that *Hui Dian* (*The Collected Statutes*), which was compiled in the 1st year of Chongde, had set a precedent for the drafting of a statute by the five emperors of the Qing dynasty after they entered Shanhaiguan.

When they were outside Shanhaiguan, the main body of law was criminal law, and one of their most obvious achievements was including "Shi E" (The Ten Abominations) in the law. In March of the 10th year of Emperor Tiancong (the 9th year of Chongzhen, 1636), an imperial edict of amnesty was issued: "The other criminal offenses shall all be forgiven except for 'Shi E' (The Ten Abominations)."[27] In October of the 5th year of Chongde (the 13th year of Chongzhen, 1640), another imperial edict was issued by Huang Taiji on his birthday:

> Since it is the birthday of the emperor, I am showing grace and kindness to all princes and the common people. So the guilty people can enjoy my grace and be forgiven except the offenders of "Shi E" (The Ten Abominations) which mainly includes the following: first, endangering the country; second, intending to destroy the ancestral temples, tombs and palaces; third, betraying the state and absconding abroad; fourth, "Gu Du Yan Mei" (to agitate and mislead people by demagogy); fifth, destroying sacrificial artifacts and imperial utensils; sixth, physically or verbally abusing grandparents or parents; seventh, elder brothers selling their younger brothers; eighth, wife suing her husband; ninth, adultery among clan members; tenth, murdering people and robbing property.[28]

When they were outside Shanhaiguan, the Khan and the emperor had the supreme power, so it was regarded as a felony to challenge their power. During the reign of Tianming, many people were punished by death penalty because they did not follow the orders of Khan. Moreover, crimes like "stealing the emperor's clothes" and "being negligent in keeping the imperial gates" were added, and the offenders would

---

[26] *Qing Tai Zong Shi Lu* (*The Record of Qing Emperor Taizong*), Vol. 29.

[27] *Qing Tai Zong Shi Lu* (*The Record of Qing Emperor Taizong*), Vol. 28.

[28] *Qing Tai Zong Shi Lu* (*The Record of Qing Emperor Taizong*), Vol. 53.

all be sentenced to death. At the time when Huang Taiji ascended the throne, the emperor's authority had dominated the doro beile (title of nobility) of "Ba Qi" (the Eight Banners: banner, a division of the Manchu nationality and the emperor's clan). Among the provisions of "Shi E" (The Ten Abominations) that were issued after revision, the crime of "Fan Shang" (going against one's superiors) was put in the first place. For example, the elder brother of Huang Taiji, the great doro beile (title of nobility) Daishan was almost dismissed from his office because he was "uncourteous to the emperor."[29]

Before Manchu rulers entered Shanhaiguan, the crime of "Tao Ren" (the escapee) and the crime of harboring escapees were added under certain special conditions. "Tao Ren" (the escapee) mainly referred to the people of Han nationality and the Koreans who were captured and forced to work as slaves but later escaped at the risk of their lives because they could not bear the ethnic and class oppression. Because "Tao Ren" (the escapee) endangered the social foundation of Manchu aristocracy, it became one of the main tasks of the soldiers of "Ba Qi" (the Eight Banners: banner, a division of Manchu nationality and the emperor's clan) to have these people arrested and returned to their original owners. In January of the 8th year of Tianming (1623), Nurhachi ordered Li Yongfang and Tong Yangxing to forcefully drive away the people of Han nationality who lived on the southern coast of Liaoning, which was clearly written on "Xin Pai" (a board to deliver messages): "In the general survey, if anyone has concealed the truth, or if his crime is reported by others and is discovered, 'Tao Ren' (the escapee) will be punished for the crime of escaping, the people who have harbored him will be punished for the crime of theft, and they will both be arrested to serve as 'A Ha' (slave)."[30] This criminal charge was continued to be used even after the Manchu rulers entered Shanhaiguan.

Before the Manchu rulers entered Shanhaiguan, criminal laws were made to restrict religious and superstitious activities. In view of the large number of Buddhists among the people of Han nationality and in order to reduce opposition to the Ming Dynasty, the original temples were protected during the Later Jin Dynasty. On November 30 of the sixth year of Tianming (1621), an order was issued by Nurhachi: "No one was allowed to destroy the temples, or to tie horses and cattle in the temple or to go to the bathroom in the temple"; anyone who violates the rule "will be punished." In June of the 5th year of Emperor Tiancong (1632), when the army led by him passed by Guihua City, an imperial edict was specially posted in the Gegenhan temple: "No demolishing the temple"; otherwise, the violators would be punished.[31] However, in order to prevent people from avoiding corvee by becoming

---

[29] *Qing Tai Zong Shi Lu* (*The Record of Qing Emperor Taizong*), Vol. 25, in September of the 9th year of Emperor Tiancong.

[30] "Tai Zu" (Emperor Taizu) in *Man Wen Lao Dang* (*The Past Chronicles in Manchu Language*), Vol. 43, in lunar January of the 8th year of Emperor Tianming.

[31] *Qing Tai Zong Shi Lu* (*The Record of Qing Emperor Taizong*), Vol. 12, in June of the 6th year of Emperor Tiancong.

11.1 The Foundation of the Legal System Before Entering Shanhaiguan

monks, the construction of new temples was prohibited, but the originally constructed ones were retained.

Since Nurhachi and Huang Taiji learned from the history of the Han nationality that in the previous dynasties the oppressed people often revolted by making use of religion, which often led to the decline of the state, they paid more attention to religious control even inside the Manchu nationality. It was also forbidden to spread Shamanism, and the original monks of the Han nationality were also under strict supervision by the government. Moreover, administrative regulations were likewise provided in *Chong De Hui Dian* (*The Collected Statutes of Chongde*): "If spies were harboured in the temples, all monks of the temples would be killed; if 'Tao Ren' (the escapee) were harboured in the temples, all the monks of the temples would be punished by serving as slaves." In addition, "the numbers of temples, the monks in each temple and the full name of each monk must all be recorded clearly; if the monks have died or new monks come, they must be checked accordingly."

In addition, heretical sects, secret organizations, and associations were brutally suppressed, and "if the people like wizards, lamas, monks and Taoist priests had told lies about the good and ill lucks, seduced women, defrauded monty and property, and had engaged activities which were harmful to the social order, they should be immediately prohibited. If they were discovered, they should be arrested and punished."[32] Even the custom of burning paper money to release the souls of the dead people, which had been practiced since ancient times by the Han nationality, was prohibited; if they were discovered and arrested, they would be severely punished; even the ministers of the Han nationality and their families were not exempted from punishment. After his succession to the throne, Huang Taiji included the crime of "Gu Du Yan Mei" (to agitate and mislead people by demagogy), which was stipulated under the feudal code of the Han nationality, in "Shi E" (The Ten Abominations). But because of the need to strengthen political alliance with the Mongolians to fight against the rulers of the Ming Dynasty, a more tolerant policy was taken for the Mongolian Lamaism. One year before the establishment of Later Jin Dynasty, seven temples were built in the capital, and Nurhachi presided over the ceremony to show respect to Lamaism. After Huang Taiji conquered Jachal, according to his order, "Shi Sheng Si" (The Temple of Real Victory) was built; the statue of Buddha, the law protector, was moved to Shenyang; and four lama temples were built outside the four gates of Shenyang city. The Mongolian lamas, who surrendered themselves to the reign of Later Jin Dynasty, were not only exempted from compulsory labor service and corvee but also given courteous receptions. Huang Taiji also sent envoys to Tibet to "preach Buddhism."[33] The bigwigs of lamas also had the chance to meet with the emperor himself, but the lamas who did not comply with the precepts were often handled by Huang Taiji himself.

---

[32] *Qing Tai Zong Shi Lu* (*The Record of Qing Emperor Taizong*), Vol. 10, in intercalary November of the 5th year of Emperor Tiancong.

[33] *Qing Tai Zong Shi Lu* (*The Record of Qing Emperor Taizong*), Vol. 49, in October of the 4th year of Emperor Chongde.

He said, "If I do not have them punished, who can?"[34] This showed that the Manchu rulers had a very clear political approach on religious issues.

Before they entered Shanhaiguan, punishments like "Guan Er Bi" (pricking the ear and nose), shooting with whistling arrows, and slapping the cheeks, which were commonly used during the reign of Nurhachi, were gradually standardized. The death penalty mainly consisted of "Zhan Tou" (beheading), "Xiao Shou" (hanging the head of a criminal on top of a pole for public display), "Zhe Sha" (opening and splitting or breaking apart a criminal's body), "Lu Shi" (chopping up the corpse of a criminal), etc.; as to physical punishment, it chiefly involved "Guan Er Bi" (pricking the ear and nose), "Bian" (whipping), etc.; with regard to punishment against freedom, it generally included imprisonment, starvation, penal servitude in border areas, etc.; property-related punishments, on the other hand, usually consisted of "Ji Jia" (when a criminal is sentenced to punishment, his wife, children, and other family members will become official handmaids), a fine consisting of silver money, a fine consisting of goods, etc.

The punishment system that was carried out during the period that the Manchu rulers were outside Shanhaiguan mainly consisted of mutilation of human bodies, but it was gradually changed to payment of fine (consisting of silver), starvation, and imprisonment, which reflected a transformation from a slavery society into a feudal one in terms of the criminal system. Meanwhile, before they entered Shanhaiguan, their criminal system had a distinctive ethnic characteristic. For example, penalties such as "Guan Er Bi" (pricking the ear and nose), "Tu Hei Le Wei Le" (tuhere weile or a fine consisting of silver money), and so on were not included in the penalties of the feudal dynasties of the Han nationality.

What is noteworthy is the principle of treating "new people" leniently, which was carried out during the reign of Huang Taiji. The so-called new people referred to the Hans and the Mongols, who had newly submitted themselves to the authority of Huang Taiji. The principle of treating the "new people" leniently fully showed Huang Taiji's strategy of expanding the social foundation of the new regime, which had played an important role in practice.

During the reign of Huang Taiji, in order to adapt to social transformation, a series of laws was made to adjust and protect the agricultural economy. At the same time, in order to win the war, military legislation was also actively carried out.

It is particularly worth mentioning that "Sheng Jing Ding Zhi" (Laws and Regulations Made in Shengjing) which was issued by Huang Taiji to the Mongolian Vassal State was a very important achievement in legal construction when they were outside Shanhaiguan and it had provided the experience for the national legislation after they entered Shanhaiguan.

In order to make the Mongolian vassal state follow the provisions of Manchu law, to affirm and safeguard the rights and obligations of the Qing government and Mongolia, and to change the "backward state of the Mongolian legal system,"

---

[34]*Qing Tai Zong Shi Lu* (*The Record of Qing Emperor Taizong*), Vol. 44, in December of the 3rd year of Emperor Chongde.

11.1 The Foundation of the Legal System Before Entering Shanhaiguan

Huang Taiji did his best to introduce the Manchu legal system into the Mongolian vassal state, which was cited as "Sheng Jing Ding Zhi" (Laws and Regulations Made in Shengjing) in the history books of the Qing dynasty and which is of great historical significance. This was surely their main legislative achievement before they entered Shanhaiguan; at the same time, it also showed that great attention was attached to legislation by the rulers.

The details are as follows.

In January of the 3rd year of Emperor Tiancong (1629), "an imperial edict is issued by Huang Taiji: The five tribes, namely, Koerqin, Aohan, Naiman, Khalkha, Harqin shall follow the system of our regime."[35] In March of the same year, "Ashe Dahl, the prince's maternal uncle, and Nikan (Han nationality) were ordered by the Emperor to inform the tribes of Mongolia and doro beile (title of nobility) to observe the military orders."[36]

In April of the 5th year of Emperor Tiancong (1631), "an imperial decree was issued to doro beile (title of nobility) of the Mongolia tribes who had submitted their authority to the emperor to order them to obey the martial laws and the decrees of theft which were made."[37]

In the 6th year of Emperor Tiancong (1632), doro beile (title of nobility) Jierhalang and Sahalian were sent to "the pasture to order the doro beile (title of nobility) of the Mongolia tribes who had submitted their authority to the emperor to obey the relevant laws which were made and implemented."[38]

Although imperial orders to abide by the laws and stipulations were repeatedly issued by Huang Taiji, the Mongolians south of the desert were still hesitant to accept the laws of Later Jin Dynasty. In September of the 6th year of Emperor Tiancong (1632), Minganzi, the doro beile (title of nobility) of Wulute and "E Fu" (a title of nobility) Duoerji "registered fifty families as civilians by violating the order" and "engaged in hunting without permission"; therefore, in August of the 7th year of Emperor Tiancong (1633), "Ashe Dahl, the prince's maternal uncle and others were dispatched to Tuxietujinong in Koerqin to have the laws made by imperial orders implemented."[39]

---

[35] *Qing Tai Zong Shi Lu (The Record of Qing Emperor Taizong)*, Vol. 5, in lunar January of the 3rd year of Emperor Tiancong.

[36] *Qing Tai Zong Shi Lu (The Record of Qing Emperor Taizong)*, Vol. 5, in lunar January of the 3rd year of Emperor Tiancong.

[37] *Qing Tai Zong Shi Lu (The Record of Qing Emperor Taizong)*, Vol. 9, in April of the 5th year of Emperor Tiancong.

[38] *Qing Tai Zong Shi Lu (The Record of Qing Emperor Taizong)*, Vol. 12, in October of the 6th year of Emperor Tiancong.

[39] *Qing Tai Zong Shi Lu (The Record of Qing Emperor Taizong)*, Vol. 12, in September of the 6th year of Emperor Tiancong; Vol. 15, in August of the 7th year of Emperor Tiancong.

In October of the same year (1633), "Ashe Dahl, the prince's maternal uncle and Tabunangdayaqi were dispatch to the Mongolian Vassal States and other regions to have the imperial laws enacted."[40]

In January of the 8th year of Emperor Tiancong (1634), Huang Taiji, addressing Mongol princes who came to Shenyang to celebrate New Year, proclaimed: "Those who violate our systems will be punished." He stressed that the legal system of Jin Dynasty should be followed by Mongolians.[41]

In April of the 1st year of Chongde (1636), "the laws and decrees were declared and enacted in the fifteen cities in the Vassal States."[42]

In October, Xi Fu, "Da Xue Shi" (grand secretary), was sent to Chahar, Khalkha, and Koerqin to "promulgate the imperial laws and instructions in order to have the crime of adultery and theft punished."[43]

In July of the 2nd year of Chongde (1637), Huang Taiji ordered Ashe Dahl, the prince's maternal uncle, and Saileng and Nikan to go to "Gurbanchagan to have the imperial edicts and instructions declared and enacted…"

In June of the following year (1638), "led by Erdenidaerhannangsulama, Duoerjingdaerhannuoyan, Aisonggu and other officials, more than forty people were dispatched to the Tumote tribes of Mongols to have the ordained system established."[44]

The people of Mongolian vassal state who had accepted "Sheng Jing Ding Zhi" (Laws and Regulations Made in Shengjing) had the obligation to follow Manchu military orders, to mobilize and enlist in the army, and "to pay tribute as scheduled."[45] If the tribute was not paid on time, they would be "imposed with a fine of horses according to the days delayed."

It is noteworthy that in the 9th year of Emperor Tiancong (1635), after Huang Taiji conquered the southern desert of Mongolia, he ordered all the young men inside and outside the Kala region to join his own forces. So except the blind and disabled people, all men from eighteen to sixty years old were enrolled in "Ba Qi" (the Eight Banners: banner, a division of the Manchu nationality and the emperor's clan), and a new administrative system of "Meng Qi Zhi Du" (the allied Mongolian banner system in the Mongolia region) was established. In October of the 1st year of Chongde (1636), Bakeshixifu, "Da Xue Shi" (grand secretary) of "Nei Hong Wen

---

[40] *Qing Tai Zong Shi Lu* (*The Record of Qing Emperor Taizong*), Vol. 16, in October of the 7th year of Emperor Tiancong.

[41] *Qing Tai Zong Shi Lu* (*The Record of Qing Emperor Taizong*), Vol. 17, in lunar January of the 8th year of Emperor Tiancong.

[42] "Chong De" (Emperor Chongde) in "Tai Zu" (Emperor Taizu) in *Man Wen Lao Dang* (*The Past Chronicles in Manchu Language*), Vol. 9.

[43] *Qing Tai Zong Shi Lu* (*The Record of Qing Emperor Taizong*), Vol. 31, in October of the 1st year of Emperor Chongde.

[44] *Qing Tai Zong Shi Lu* (*The Record of Qing Emperor Taizong*), Vol. 42, in July of the 3rd year of Emperor Chongde.

[45] *Qing Tai Zong Shi Lu* (*The Record of Qing Emperor Taizong*), Vol. 38, in August of the 2nd year of Emperor Chongde.

11.1 The Foundation of the Legal System Before Entering Shanhaiguan

Yuan" (an advisory organ of the emperor); Nikan, "Cheng Zheng" (minister) of "Ya Men" (the government offices); Ashe Dahl, the prince's maternal uncle, "Cheng Zheng" (minister) of "Du Cha Yuan" (The Court of Censors); and others were sent to Khalkha, Chahar, Koerqin, and other places to "check up the household registration, to compile the catalog of cattle, to meet with representatives of vassal states, to hear the cases of criminals and to enact laws to have the offences of theft and robbery punished"[46]; through this, effective administration of the Mongolia region was ensured by the Qing Dynasty. In June, Mongolia "Ya Men" (the government offices) were ordered to be set up to deal with Mongolian affairs, so in June of the same year, "Meng Gu Ya Men" (the government office of Mongolia) was set up. In the 3rd year of Chongde (1638), "Meng Gu Ya Men" (the government office of Mongolia) was changed to "Li Fan Yuan" (Bureau of National Minority Affairs), which had become the most important agency to deal with Mongolian affairs and the affairs of other ethnic minorities.

In view of the widespread of cases of theft and violations of marriage rules in Mongolian regions, a series of laws was provided in "Sheng Jing Ding Zhi" (Laws and Regulations Made in Shengjing), according to which "if anyone has stolen camels, horses, cattle and sheep, he will be punished by 'Jiao' (hanging) regardless of the principal and accessory; if two people have committed the crime, one of them will be punished by 'Zhan' (beheading); if three people have committed the crime, two of them will be punished by 'Zhan' (beheading); if a group of people have committed the crime, the two principal will be punished by 'Zhan' (beheading) and the rest will be punished by 'Bian' (whipping) for one hundred strokes and 'San Jiu' (the punishment of a fine of a certain number of livestock)." "For the crime of raping the married women or going to live with other doro beile (title of nobility), both the man and woman will be put to death."[47]

As can be seen from above, during the reign of Huang Taiji, the legal construction in the Mongolian region was strengthened, the legal system in the different Mongolian tribes was initially improved and a relatively stable relationship was formed with Mongolian Vassal State by adopting "Sheng Jing Ding Zhi" (Laws and Regulations Made in Shengjing), so that it had exerted a profound influence on the establishment of the unified and multi-ethnic Qing Dynasty centered by Manchu and Mongolian nationality.

In terms of the judiciary, during the reign of Nurhachi, five ministers were appointed to be in charge of hearing cases, and the judgment would be reported to Nurhachi for approval. In order to eliminate the original rights of the Manchu nobility to settle lawsuits and decide on the punishment of their own family members, Nurhachi warned the doro beile (title of nobility) and the ministers: "Things should not be decided by yourselves alone, because it may lead to

---

[46] *Qing Tai Zong Shi Lu* (*The Record of Qing Emperor Taizong*), Vol. 31, in October of the 1st year of Emperor Chongde.

[47] *Qing Tai Zong Shi Lu* (*The Record of Qing Emperor Taizong*), Vol. 17, in lunar January of the 8th year of Emperor Chongde.

disorder"[48]; therefore, "cases should be heard in public and then reported to the senior officials, they should not be settled by oneself."[49] Meanwhile, as to the old custom of private settlement of cases by the Manchu nationality, he declared: "If disputes arise among people, the cases should be heard by the government offices instead of by the officials themselves at their own homes," so "those who have settled the cases privately without official trial will be punished."[50] In order to hold fair trials, Nurhachi ordered the ministers "to be fair in hearing the trial, because only in this way can the truth be clarified and only when the truth is clarified can the law be implemented impartially, the people be ruled effectively and national peace be finally achieved."[51] As to the criminals, "although it is necessary to have them arrested immediately, they should not be put to death at will … they should be dealt with impartially, and the cases must be heard carefully and prudently."[52]

In the 12th year of Tianming (1626), after Huang Taiji's succession to the throne, reforms were carried out either in the organization of the judiciary or in the litigation system based on the systems of the Ming Dynasty.

Moreover, a system of hearing trials by sixteen ministers was set up. In July of the 5th year of Emperor Tiancong (1631), "Xing Bu" (The Department of Punishment), headed by doro beile (title of nobility) Jierhalang, was established, which was similar to that of the Ming Dynasty, with two Manchu "Cheng Zheng" (minister), one Mongolian "Cheng Zheng" (minister), one "Cheng Zheng" (minister) from the Han nationality, as well as eight "Can Zheng" (ancient official in charge of civil affairs at the provincial level) and one "Qi Xin Lang" (translators). In July of the 3rd year of Chongde (1638), the bureaucratic system was changed, and the post of "Cheng Zheng" (minister) was held by one Manchu, below whom "Zuo You Can Zheng" (chief and deputy official in charge of civil affairs at the provincial level), "Li Shi Guan" (chief official working in auxiliary departments), "Fu Li Shi Guan" (deputy official working in auxiliary departments), "Qi Xin Lang" (translators), and other members who were selected from the Manchu, Mongolian, and Han people were appointed.[53] Generally speaking, the cases heard by "Xing Bu" (The Department of Punishment) would be submitted to Huang Taiji for final approval, and the time of reporting was usually scheduled on dates with the number five every month.

---

[48] *Qing Tai Zu Gao Huang Di Shi Lu* (*The Record of Qing Emperor Gao Taizu*), Vol. 5, in July of the 1st year of Emperor Tianming.

[49] "Tai Zu Xing Jun Ji" (The Marching of Emperor Taizu) in *Man Zhou Mi Dang* (*The Secret Files of Manchuria*).

[50] *Qing Tai Zu Gao Huang Di Shi Lu* (*The Record of Qing Emperor Gao Taizu*), Vol. 5, in July of the 1st year of Emperor Tianming.

[51] *Qing Tai Zu Gao Huang Di Shi Lu* (*The Record of Qing Emperor Gao Taizu*), Vol. 8, in July of the 6th year of Emperor Tianming.

[52] *Qing Tai Zu Gao Huang Di Shi Lu* (*The Record of Qing Emperor Gao Taizu*), Vol. 5, in September of the 2nd year of Emperor Tianming.

[53] *Qing Tai Zong Shi Lu* (*The Record of Qing Emperor Taizong*), Vol. 42, in July of the 3rd year of Emperor Chongde.

11.1 The Foundation of the Legal System Before Entering Shanhaiguan

In addition to the judicial organizations mentioned above, the jurisdiction was also executed by the contention of doro beile (title of nobility) and the contention of departments and ministers, but their roles were incomparable to the judicial organizations.

As seen from the records and existing files, the majority of cases were first heard by the various judicial departments and were then submitted to Huang Taiji for final approval and implementation. As to the cases involving princes, doro beile (title of nobility), the sons of doro beile (title of nobility), and royal relatives, however small, they should all be submitted to the emperor for approval after being settled by the relevant judicial departments.

Before the Qing rulers entered Shanhaiguan, the main methods for prosecution included private prosecution, reporting, impeaching, and surrendering oneself. Only "Min" (or the people: "Shen" or "Irgen" in Manchu) had the right to prosecute. According to Jurchen custom, because an adult man usually inherited property from his father and was the master of his own family, he could be called "Min" and "Jia Zhu" (the master of his family); therefore, regardless of age or status, he had the full legal qualification to be a litigant.

In the early time of the ruling of Manchu nationality, due to the low status of women, their right to prosecute was restricted, so they seldom appeared as litigants. As seen from the hundreds of cases that occurred before the period of entering Shanhaiguan, only a few women had prosecuted privately for their grievances unless they were about felonies of "Shi E" (The Ten Abominations) or unless their husband had died.

"Nu Bi" (slave girls and maidservants) and concubines were only special property of the owner, so they did not have independent legal status or the right of private prosecution.

As for the trial system in the period before entering Shanhaiguan, it was a combination of the system of the Ming Dynasty and some of the customs of the Manchu nationality; thus, to a certain extent, it was a reflection of the principle of "Can Han Zhuo Jin" (making reference not only to the legal thoughts and culture of the Han nationality but also to the national practice and needs of the Jin nationality) in the judicial system. In addition, a new trial system was established that was similar to that of the Ming Dynasty. For example, both the plaintiff and the defendant must appear in court, and they were considered equal during trial, whatever the defendants' official position and identity are.

Verbal trial was the most common method of inquisition when the Qing rulers were outside of Shanhaiguan. In order to obtain confession, a case was often repeatedly heard. Mangguertai, who was in charge of "Xing Bu" (The Department of Punishment) said that "for each case, confessions should be obtained for three times and they should be carefully reviewed to determine the right and wrong." Moreover, a case should be settled according to facts, and in the course of the trial, litigants were allowed to debate and defend for themselves. In addition to oral testimony, evidence was taken seriously. When "Xing Bu" (The Department of Punishment) was set up, Huang Taiji specially pointed out that "it is important to be impartial when hearing the cases, and it is necessary to make judgment according to facts. When hearing the civil cases, if both the plaintiff and defendant do not make any statements, the witness should be interrogated to find out evidence on the spot. If you do not ask for evidence, the plaintiff and defendant will take the chance to collude with each other and to conceal their crimes in order to avoid punishment so that it will be difficult to conduct the trial fairly. So from now on, if officials make judgment without obtaining testimony first, it may lead to grievances; so they will be punished in accordance with the circumstances of the affair."[54] Evidence included witnesses and material evidence. In addition to the owner, in some individual cases, servants could also serve as witnesses. The witnesses would be punished if they did not tell the truth. As to material evidence, in the cases recorded in Shengjing (now Shenyang city), we can find records of documentary evidence and evidence of illicit money and booties.

As for the judges, if they made an erroneous judgment, they would be criminally liable for the case. In the 5th year of Emperor Tiancong (1631), when "Xing Bu" (The Department of Punishment) was set up, it clearly stipulated that "if the case is heard by doro beile (title of nobility) erroneously, which had caused innocent people to die, he will be punished by paying a fine of 600 silver money; if he has falsely punished the innocent people by 'Zhang' (flogging with heavy sticks) and 'Shu' (ransom), he will be punished by paying the fine of 200 silver money."[55]

11.1.3 Characteristics of the Legal System in the Early Period

Although the time for the legislative activities in the period outside Shanhaiguan was short and the number was small, it had the distinct ethnic characteristics of the times.

11.1.3.1 With Traces of Jurchen Customary Law

As far as the legal system is concerned, because Manchu society was experiencing drastic changes at the time, it was inevitable to retain some of the traces of Jurchen customary law:

1. There was no separation of national and family law. After its establishment, the Latter Jin Dynasty was still strongly influenced by the family kinship of the clan system of the previous dynasties, so a unique system which was featured by the integration of the family and the nation and the unity of the relatives and the nobilities was formed. Nurhachi was not only the Khan (head) of the country of

---

[54] *Qing Tai Zong Shi Lu* (*The Record of Qing Emperor Taizong*), Vol. 9, in July of the 5th year of Emperor Tiancong.

[55] *Qing Tai Zong Shi Lu* (*The Record of Qing Emperor Taizong*), Vol. 9, in July of the 5th year of Emperor Tiancong.

Latter Jin Dynasty, but also the Shaikh of the most powerful clan of Jurchen tribe, so he was supported by both of the regime and clan power.

Those who assisted Nurhachi in his ruling at the beginning were five ministers who were also concurrently military generals. When his sons grew up, they were granted the title of doro beile (title of nobility) and began to participate in the national affairs and manage the military affairs, so consequently the political system of clan aristocracy which was made up of by a new generation of influential officials was finally formed. Although their influences were weakened with the continuous strengthening of imperial autocracy, yet they did not disappear from the political stage until the late Qing Dynasty. Under the circumstance that structure of the regime and the state activities should be based on double principles of family blood and politics, the laws enacted by Nurhachi were both family disciplines and state laws, which were unified and indivisible. For example, Nurhachi's instructions of prohibiting clan women from intervening in political affairs were primarily family law, but they also had the nature of state laws, which was only possible when the country was not so developed and mature and the clan leaders had huge authority. In the process of the construction of the political power of Latter Jin Dynasty, Nurhachi deeply felt the special role of patriarchal and clan power, so he tried to fulfill the task of consolidating the regime by the family system.

Till the reign of Huang Taiji, the social, economic, political, and cultural development, as well as the victory of the war against the Ming Dynasty, had made it possible to rapidly change "Ba Wang Gong Zhi" (the joint ruling of eight kings) to the exclusive domination of imperial power. The personal courage and strategy of Huang Taiji also provided subjective conditions for this transformation, which was followed by the replacement of aristocratic democracy by totalitarian monarchical centralization and the domination of bureaucratic politics over the aristocratic politics. The changes in the political system had determined that the proportion of family law in the legal system was gradually weakened and that of state law was gradually strengthened. So family law and state law began to show a trend of separation, which was inevitable in the development of a legal civilization.

2. Marital relationship within the clan, regardless of seniority or inferiority, was allowed. According to Jurchen customary law, marriage between people of different generations was allowed, so the nephew could marry the stepmother and the aunt and the brother could marry the brother's or nephew's wife. It was not until the 3rd year of Emperor Tiancong (1629) that the customary law on marriage was abolished because of the "incestuous relationship in marriage," as influenced by "Lun Li" (ethics) of the Han nationality. So it was stipulated that "it is forbidden to marry the stepmother, aunt, brother's wife and nephew's wife ... and those who marry within the same clan will be punished for the crime of adultery."[56] In *Shi Lu* (*Records*), written by Japanese scholar Goisi Ken, we can

---

[56]Zhu Lin (Qing Dynasty), *Ming Ji Ji Lue* (*Collections of Records in Ming Dynasty*), Vol. 14.

find the following statements: "Initially, there was no prohibition on the marriages of the wives of the same clan, such as aunts and sister-in-law. However, Emperor Taizong had tried to prevent people from marrying his brother's wife who was with the same family name, because it was considered incestuous." In July of the 5th year of Emperor Tiancong (1631), he again explained the reason for banning marriages between people with the same family name as it was regarded as a crime of adultery: "In Ming Dynasty and Korea, for the interests of the states, the marriage within the family is not allowed. As human being, if marriage between family members in the same family is permitted, what is the difference with animals? Therefore, marriage between the family members within the same family should be prohibited."[57] In *Chong De Hui Dian* (*The Collected Statutes of Chongde*), the prohibition of marrying women within the same family was reaffirmed: "Every human being is born a person. If men marry women within the same family, what is the difference with animals?"

3. It was allowed for the favorite wife of the dying man to be buried with him. It was a Jurchen tradition that after the head of the household died, his wives should be buried with him. According to *Jue Yu Ji Lue* (*Records in Remote Areas*), "after a man has died, a sacrificial concubine should be buried alive with him. The woman who is buried with him is chosen when he is alive, so it can not be rejected. The sacrificial concubine is not allowed to cry, so she sits on 'kang' (a heatable brick bed in North China) and is beautifully dressed. Then she is led by the housewife to express her thanks, finally she will kill herself by the bowstring. If she refuses to do so, she will be killed by all others." The customary law of being buried alive with the husband was still effective even after the establishment of Later Jin Dynasty, so it was not restricted until after *Chong De Hui Dian* (*The Collected Statutes of Chongde*) was issued: "For the wife who dies with her husband, if she is a favorite wife, she is allowed to do so, so that she will be praised by people. However, if the favorite wife does not want to die but she has forced the concubine to die instead, she will be sentenced to death penalty; it is forbidden for the husband to order his wife or concubines whom he dislikes to die with him; if the wife or concubine are forced to die by violation of the order, the head of those in charge will be fed to dogs, and the violator will still compensate for it according to the number of people killed. If the informant has prevented her from dying, her brother should compensate for it, and the people involved should be punished accordingly."

4. The patriarchal system was retained. According to Jurchen customary law, parents were called "E Zhen." All property within the family, including herds, "Nu Bi" (slave girls and maidservants), silver, imperial edits, etc., belonged to the parents of the family. The parents also had the right to arrange their children's marriage and the disciplinary authority over their children. In patriarchal customary law, the rights of parents were maintained, and the violators would be

---

[57]"Tai Zong" (Emperor Taizu) in *Qing San Chao Shi Lu Cai Yao* (*An Outline of Records in the Reign of the Three Emperors of Qing Dynasty*), Vol. 2, in July of the 5th year of Emperor Tiancong.

punished within the family and be condemned by the public. The authority of Nurhachi depended on the support of the patriarchal system, so the order of Khan and family law became a binary legal system in the early period. Nevertheless, it should be noted that this patriarchal system of authority was not subject to the influence of Confucian etiquette, so it was more because of the primitiveness of the Jurchen nationality.

5. The early marriage system was implemented. According to Jurchen custom, early marriage was very popular. Till the 9th year of Emperor Tiancong (1635), under the influence of the legal culture of the Han nationality, an imperial edict was issued by him: "The women over twelve years old should get marry; otherwise, they will be punished." It should be noted that before the period of entering Shanhaiguan, the "age" usually referred to nominal age, so "twelve years old" actually meant "eleven years old." Although early marriage was prohibited by Huang Taiji, the legal age for marriage was still too young. After the period of entering Shanhaiguan, the legal age of marriage for men was sixteen and women fourteen.

6. Inheritance of property was determined by the master of the family, instead of being equally distributed. Jurchen custom was also evident in inheritance rules, and the family property could be given to the adult sons while the master of the family is still alive. In Jurchen customary law, the property of the dead father was not equally distributed, and the sons who had divided the family property and lived separately had no right to inherit the property. Among those who had not divided the family property, the youngest son enjoyed preferential inheritance. As to inheritance of the titles of nobility and official positions, because political and economic affairs were involved, in the 6th year of Tianming (1621), the order of inheritance was issued by Nurhachi: "The sons of my subordinate ministers who have devoted themselves to the country, or killed in the wars, or died of disease, are ordered to inherit their fathers' official positions."[58] If the meritorious statesman did not have any heirs, his position could be inherited firstly by his brothers and then by his nephews, and the title of nobility could be inherited by his nephews according to their achievements instead of their seniority.

7. The master of the family was allowed to participate in the interrogation of his servants. In January of the 6th year of Emperor Tiancong (1632), a memorial was submitted by Gao Hongzhong, "Cheng Zheng" (minister) of "Xing Bu" (The Department of Punishment):

> If any servant has committed crimes, the case should be handled first by his owner; if his owner is not present, the case is not to be accepted by the judicial officials. It is very common that after the servant has committed crimes, the head of the household or "Niu Lu" (the grassroots official in Qing Dynasty) will hear the trial together with the judicial officials. Sometimes, the servant does not say a word while the head of the household has never stopped talking ... and he has even secretly instructed the colleagues. Even if the criminal is

---

[58]"Tai Zu" (Emperor Taizu) in *Man Wen Lao Dang* (*The Past Chronicles in Manchu Language*), Vol. 31, on the 14th of December of the 6th year of Emperor Tianming.

guilty, yet they all sit together and keep talking, which is not entrustment but intervention with their privileges. So where are the laws and disciplines?[59]

So under such situation, the system of domestic slavery was still retained, because as the property of his owner, the slave would surely be taken care of by his owner.

As can be seen from above, the Jurchen traditional customary law greatly influenced the legal system of Later Jin Dynasty. However, with social development and progress, and especially with the frequent changes in the legal culture of the Han nationality, the influence of Jurchen customary law steadily weakened and some of its customary laws were even ordered to be banned, but obviously some traces were still retained.

11.1.3.2 The Legislation Adaptable to Social Transformation

Before the Qing rulers entered Shanhaiguan, with the rapid transformation of society, the manor slavery system was quickly changed to serfdom, so the laws which were adaptable to the transformation were also changed accordingly. Furthermore, the fast development of the new mode of production promoted the transformation of society, so during the process the legislative activities were also with distinctive characteristics of the times:

1. A series of laws was made to protect agricultural production. After entering the Liaoning and Shenyang regions, with the influence of the advanced mode of production of the Han nationality, the social economy of the Manchu family was rapidly transformed into feudal agricultural economy. The legal system which belonged to a part of the newly appeared superstructure of the feudal society had played an important role in promoting and adjusting the development of society. In the Qing Dynasty, land was begun to be distributed according to law and the system of small-scale land ownership was established. In the time of Huang Taiji, he repeatedly warned the officials that "it is an important national policy to encourage agriculture and to stress military affairs. So you (the officials) should often go to the places under your jurisdiction and conduct careful investigations, and you should not breach your duties."[60] He also often gave verbal instructions or made laws to protect agricultural production. For example, in order to prevent hunters from trampling the crops and to prevent the livestock from going to the farmland, the crime of "indulging horses to destroy crops" was added, and relative punishments were enforced for destroying farmland. If livestock trampled others' farmland, the owner would be imposed with a fine according to the number of their livestock. If the children of nobility and ministers trampled farmland or hurt livestock while practicing falconry, they would be severely

---

[59]*Tian Cong Chao Chen Gong Zou Yi* (*The Memorials Submitted by the Ministers in the Reign of Emperor Tiancong*), Vol. 1.

[60]*Qing Tai Zong Shi Lu* (*The Record of Qing Emperor Taizong*), Vol. 13.

punished. Besides, it was forbidden for people to use cattle, horses, mules, and donkeys in their sacrificial ceremony to protect agricultural productivity, and "it is forbidden to randomly employ peasants in government services to delay the farm season."[61] Meanwhile, free transaction of grain was permitted and relevant rules were issued on atoneming the crime with grain. So the laws mentioned above had typically reflected the legal changes which took place in order to adapt to the social transformation, because it not only showed the features of feudal production, but also the direction of the social transformation.

2. *Li Zhu Tiao Li* (*The Regulation on Freeing from the Personal Subordinate Relations with the Owner*), was created, which ended the practice of domestic slavery. During the reign of Nurhachi, as personal property, slaves could be bought and sold by their owners arbitrarily. At the end of the reign of Tianming, when tax rules were discussed by the doro beile (title of nobility), it was stipulated that "people, horses, cattle, mules, donkeys, sheep and goats will be taxed one *qian* for each *liang*,"[62] which showed that people were classified within the same category as sheep and cattle, so tax should be paid after they were sold. Thus, we can see the legal status of slaves during the reign of Tianming. To the reign of Huang Taiji, the nature of society and class had undergone significant changes, and inevitably this change had been reflected in the legal relationship. In the 7th year of Chongde (1642), an order was issued by Huang Taiji: "The head of family should promise each other that they should not lend grain to or borrow grain from the slaves," which had fully shown that at the time the servant had already owned his own property, such as houses, livestock, grain, wife and even servants. Although they still belonged to the head of the family according to law, slaves enjoyed the actual right of disposal. So, in their daily lives, it was possible for them to participate in the actual activities of lending and borrowing.

Change of class relationship would surely be reflected in law, and *Li Zhu Tiao Li* (*The Regulation on Freeing from the Personal Subordinate Relations with the Owner*), which was made in the 5th year of Emperor Tiancong, is a good example. In *Li Zhu Tiao Li*, it was provided that if a slave reported to the government that his master hunted without authorization or hid booties obtained in war or murdered people randomly or raped subordinate women and so on, and if what he reported was true, it was allowed for him to leave his master. In the 6th year of Tiancong (1632), the following supplementary provision was added concerning the conditions for slaves leaving their masters:

> The informant should make true reports to the government, if the slave has reported more than two offences to the government, the major one should be punished severely while the minor one should be punished leniently; he is exempted from the crime of "Wu Gao" (false accusation) and is still allowed to leave his master; if he has reported many offences, and there are the same number of major and minor ones, one of the major ones should be

---

[61] *Qing Tai Zong Shi Lu* (*The Record of Qing Emperor Taizong*), Vol. 23.
[62] "Tai Zu" (Emperor Taizu) in *Man Wen Lao Dang* (*The Past Chronicles in Manchu Language*), Vol. 72, on the 3rd of August of the 11th year of Emperor Tianming.

punished severely, and he is exempted from the crime of "Wu Gao" (false accusation); if there are same numbers of true and false charges, he is allowed to leave his master; if most of charges he has reported are false, he is not permitted to leave his master; if he has reported more than two offences, the minor one is true but the major one is false ... he will be charged of "Wu Gao" (false accusation) and will not be allowed to leave his master.[63]

Since it was impossible to confirm the right of filing lawsuits against one's masters in slavery society, the promulgating of "Li Zhu Tiao Li" (The Regulation on Freeing from the Personal Subordinate Relations with the Owner) had shown that the social relationship of slavery society did not occupy a dominate position any more in Latter Jin Dynasty.

After the issuance of *Li Zhu Tiao Li* (*The Regulation on Freeing from the Personal Subordinate Relations with the Owner*), a series of cases of slaves suing their masters was documented. If what the slave had reported was true, "it will be handled according to what he hoped" so that he could leave his master or be raised to "Min" (or the people: "Shen" or "Irgen" in Manchu) or be a slave of other people. Ashe Dahl, "Cheng Zheng" (minister) of "Du Cha Yuan" (The Court of Censors), stated in a memorial: "If a servant has sued his master, and is proved to be true, he would be the slave of other people."[64] Because of the historical condition at that time, however, the slave's right to sue his master was subject to many restrictions. Jierhalang, doro beile (title of nobility), once pointed out: "If someone has sued doro beile (title of nobility), but the person he has sued is not punished, or if he still stays in the same 'Qi' (banner, equivalent of a county), then no one dares to make reports any more."[65]

The making of *Li Zhu Tiao Li* (*The Regulation on Freeing from the Personal Subordinate Relations with the Owner*) resulted in a major change of social relationship; meanwhile, it also reflected the political intention of maintaining the power of Khan and strengthening the control of the aristocratic officials of "Ba Qi" (the Eight Banners: banner, a division of the Manchu nationality and the emperor's clan). Moreover, laws and decrees were also issued on the number of slaves that officials can have according to their ranks, and it was forbidden to increase nonproductive slaves without restriction. Besides, some of the manor slaves of the Manchu aristocratic officials were settled in different villages and registered as "Min" (or the people: "Shen" or "Irgen" in Manchu), who were "managed by the honest and upright officials chosen from Han nationality,"[66] so that the mandatory slaves became serfs in the end.

---

[63] *Qing Tai Zong Shi Lu* (*The Record of Qing Emperor Taizong*), Vol. 11, in March of the 6th year of Emperor Tiancong.

[64] *Qing Tai Zong Shi Lu* (*The Record of Qing Emperor Taizong*), Vol. 30, in June of the 1st year of Emperor Chongde.

[65] *Qing Tai Zong Shi Lu* (*The Record of Qing Emperor Taizong*), Vol. 8, in March of the 5th year of Emperor Tianming.

[66] *Qing Tai Zong Shi Lu* (*The Record of Qing Emperor Taizong*), Vol. 1, in August of the 11th year of Emperor Tianming.

11.1.3.3 Integration with the Advanced Legal Culture of the Han Nationality

Before they entered, it was apparent how monarchs Nurhachi and Huang Taiji were not only admirers of the Chinese culture but also imitators and promoters of the advanced legal culture of the Han nationality. In the transformation of the legal system, the adoption and integration of legal culture of Han nationality had become a prominent feature of at that time.

During the reign of Nurhachi, more attention was paid to assimilating the advanced legal culture of the Han nationality, and Huang Taiji even made use of the legal culture of the Han nationality and regarded it as an important legal basis for legislation and the construction of a legal system. The legislative ideology of "Can Han Zhuo Jin" (making reference not only to the legal thoughts and culture of the Han nationality but also to the national practice and needs of the Jin nationality) had fully shown the positive influence of the legal culture of the Han nationality on the legislative activities of the Qing regime, and the affirmation of this legislative principle also showed Huang Taiji's political foresight. The so-called Can Han, which pertains to making reference to the legal thoughts and culture of the Han nationality, while the so-called Zhuo Jin refers to inheriting some of the customary laws of the Manchu nationality.

In March of the 5th year of Tiancong (1631), Huang Taiji ordered doro beile (title of nobility) and the ministers to put forward their views on reform because he had "heard that many people have complained and criticized the trial of cases and the enforcement of punishment." Some people suggested that "the predecessors know very well about law and established regulations have been made, so they should be followed." In the above sentence, the phrase "the predecessors know very well about law" referred to the legal system of the Han people, and "they should be followed" meant giving up the old tradition and customary law of their own nationality and adopting the feudal legal systems and conventions instead. This proposal was appreciated by Huang Taiji.[67] In order to carry out the ideology of "Can Han Zhuo Jin" (making reference not only to the legal thoughts and culture of the Han nationality but also to the national practice and needs of the Jin nationality), the collected statutes and criminal regulations of the Ming Dynasty were translated, which provided a blueprint for the drafting of new laws.

Many achievements were made through the integration of the legal culture of "Can Han Zhuo Jin" (making reference not only to the legal thoughts and culture of the Han nationality but also to the national practice and needs of the Jin nationality), such as the introduction of "Shi E" (The Ten Abominations) into criminal law; enforcing of different types of punishment for the same crimes committed by the superior and the inferior and by the noble and the humble; the handling of issues like rebellion, escaping, "Fan Shang" (going against one's superiors); providing of

---

[67] *Qing Tai Zong Shi Lu* (*The Record of Qing Emperor Taizong*), Vol. 8, on the 8th of March of the 5th year of Emperor Tiancong.

punishment for the crime of the son suing his father, the wife suing her husband, the younger brother suing his elder brother; other changes like giving up the Manchu backward custom, the making of collected statutes and department regulations, and the affirming of the right of supervision and remonstration of procuratorates.

11.1.3.4 Military Laws Accounting for a Large Proportion

Before the Qing rulers entered Shanhaiguan, military laws were frequently made and issued because of the constant wars, and they became not only an integral part of the legal system but also a major feature at the time. Therefore, military laws were constantly issued during the Later Jin Dynasty in order to restrain military troops, to ensure victory in the war, to reward the winner and punish the loser, and to decide the methods for distributing war trophies. So the regulation that "those who obey the orders will be awarded, while those who violate the orders will be punished by 'Zhan' (beheading)" might be considered the earliest military law.[68] With the expansion of the scale of war, the scope of adjustment of the military law was also expanded and standardized gradually.

Military laws were issued in the form of "Han Yu" (the imperial edicts of Khan), which showed that the emperor's will became the basic source of law. After the system of "Bing Min Bu Fen" (there is no distinction between the army and the people) was implemented by "Ba Qi" (the Eight Banners: banner, a division of Manchu nationality and the emperor's clan), military law also became a legal form which was with universal constraining force, so that it was also applied to the attached Mongolian tribes. In many military laws, prisoners were prohibited from being indiscriminately killed, which had shown the attention paid to the value of labor and the need for the development of the feudal agricultural economy. Those in violation of military law, whether members of "Ba Qi" (the Eight Banners: banner, a division of the Manchu nationality and the emperor's clan) or vassal states, would all be punished by "Zhan" (beheading), "Bian" (whipping), "Ji Mo" (the cancellation of a household registration), removal from office, the wives serving as slaves, "Guan Er Bi" (pricking the ear and nose), and so on. In serious cases, the chief officials in charge had joint liability.

To sum up, before entering Shanhaiguan, the legal construction which was carried out during the reign of Emperor Taizong and Taizu not only reflected the traditional legal concepts of Manchu nationality and the characteristics of customary law, but also showed a great integration of the legal cultures of different nationalities, so it was a new development of the national integration and cultural exchange that was carried out since the Northern and Southern Dynasty, Liao, Jin, Western Xia and Yuan dynasties under the new historical conditions. According to records, comparatively speaking the legal thoughts of rulers were profound, the actual process of the

---

[68] *Chao Xian Ben Chao Shi Lu Zhong De Zhong Guo Shi Liao* (*The Historic Materials of Chinese History in the Records of Chosun Dynasty*), Vol. 4, p. 1530.

construction of the legal system was more detailed and authentic, and the contributions made were more distinctive. So the sixty years outside Shanhaiguan was an era of influence and rapid integration of the Manchu, Han, Mongolian, and other nationalities with different cultural backgrounds and different historical traditions. So a special law which was adaptable to the social development was shown in the legal system set up before the rulers of Yuan dynasty entering Shanhaiguan, and it had been developing all the way along this track in the long years after they entered Shanhaiguan.

Because society was experiencing drastic changes in the period outside Shanhaiguan, a complex, interlacing, and fluctuating social relationship was formed, which was clearly reflected through the mirror of legal relationship. Therefore, it was helpful to understand the social and legal relationship in the changing world of the old and the new to have a detailed study of the legal system of this period.

During the period outside Shanhaiguan, a legal system that was basically adjustable to a variety of relationships was formed, which became an important tool for ruling the state. Specially, more attention was paid to the unity and the special customs of different nationalities and regions. For example, in the Mongolian vassal state, on the one hand, it was required that "the system of Latter Jin Dynasty should be followed"; on the other hand, some adjustments were made according to the concrete situation of Mongolia. So from Nen River in the east to Helan Mountain in the west, the part of Mongolia south of the desert was included within the scope of the Manchu legal system, and it was regarded as the guideline for a considerable long period of time after the establishment of the capital in Yanjing. Therefore, it can be seen that the legal system in the early period of Qing Dynasty had laid a solid foundation for the later legal system construction, so it was not only an inseparable part of the overall legal system of Qing dynasty, but also a brilliant page in the history of the development of the legal system of Chinese ethnic minorities.

11.2 The Complete Implementation of the Legislative Principle of "Can Han Zhuo Jin"

In 1644, after entering Shanhaiguan, out of the need of ruling the country, the legislative activity of completely implementating the legislative route of "Can Han Zhuo Jin" (making reference not only to the legal thoughts and culture of Han nationality but also to the national practice and needs of Jin nationality) was quickly launched by Qing Dynasty. Based on a comprehensive survey of the Qing Dynasty, legislative achievements were mainly made in three aspects: firstly, criminal legislation with *Da Qing Lv Li* (*The Laws and Precedents of Great Qing*) as the basic code; secondly, administrative laws mainly consisting of "Hui Dian" (collected statutes) and other departmental laws; thirdly, national legislation mainly represented by rules and regulations made by "Li Fan Yuan" (The Bureau of National Minority Affairs).

11.2.1 Da Qing Lv Li (The Laws and Precedents of Great Qing): *The Main Achievements of "Can Han Zhuo Jin"*

After entering Shanhaiguan, the Manchu nobility deeply felt that it was unable to meet the needs of the ruling country with the original old laws. Therefore, in June of the 1st year of Shunzhi (1644), an order was issued by Prince Regent Dorgon, who first entered Beijing: "From now on, cases are to be settled according to the law of Ming Dynasty,"[69] which started the application of *Ming Lv* (*Ming Code*) after the Manchu nobility entered the central plains. In August of the same year, Sun Xiang, "Ji Shi Zhong" (the senior assistant of the emperor and the supervisor of officials) of "Xing Ke" (The Department of Punishment), proposed that on the basis of "following *Ming Lv* (*Ming Code*)," "legislations should be made to be issued and applied uniformly home and abroad by making reference to the laws in the past, by taking the conditions of the Qing Dynasty into consideration, and by estimating the pros and cons."[70] Dang Chongya, "Zuo Shi Lang" (left vice minister) of "Xing Bu" (The Department of Punishment), petitioned that "permanent laws and decrees should be made and issued after national system is unified, while the previous *Ming Lv* (*Ming Code*) should only be applied temporarily."[71] Thus, an imperial edict was issued by Emperor Shizu: "In the outer regions, *Ming Lv* (*Ming Code*) should still be applied; nevertheless, if there is the malpractice of aggravation and mitigation of the punishment, the aggravated punishment should be referred to."[72] Thereafter, Li Shiyu, "Ji Shi Zhong" (the senior assistant of the emperor and the supervisor of officials) of "Xing Ke" (The Department of Punishment), requested that laws should be made as early as possible because "only two penalties are stipulated in the trial practice, namely, 'Zhang' (flogging with heavy sticks) and 'Jue' (put to death), which has led to the disadvantage that severe punishment is abnormally severe while the lenient punishment is abnormally lenient."[73] Yang Sichong, "Yu Shi" (the censor) of "Jiang Nan Dao" (an administrative region), also required that "legislations should be made and implemented as soon as possible because the prosperity of the generation relys on the construction of legal systems."[74] So they suggested that "both *Ming Lv* (*Ming Code*) and *Qing Lv* (*Qing Code*) should be adopted with their differences and and similarities analyzed, and with the redundant contents deleted ... the useful legal system be inherited and amended."[75] This principle was approved by the supreme

---

[69] *Qing Shi Zu Shi Lu* (*The Record of Emperor Shizu of Qing Dynasty*), Vol. 5.

[70] *Qing Shi Zu Shi Lu* (*The Record of Emperor Shizu of Qing Dynasty*), Vol. 7.

[71] "Xing Fa Zhi" (The Record of the Criminal Law) (Part 1) in *Qing Shi Gao* (*The Draft of the History of Qing Dynasty*).

[72] "Xing Fa Zhi" (The Record of the Criminal Law) (Part 1) in *Qing Shi Gao* (*The Draft of the History of Qing Dynasty*).

[73] *Qing Shi Zong Shi Lu* (*The Record of Emperor Shizong of Qing Dynasty*), Vol. 14.

[74] *Qing Shi Zong Shi Lu* (*The Record of Emperor Shizong of Qing Dynasty*), Vol. 22.

[75] *Qing Shi Zong Shi Lu* (*The Record of Emperor Shizong of Qing Dynasty*), Vol. 16.

ruler of the Qing Dynasty. Dorgon said clearly: "*Ming Lv* (*Ming Code*) should be carefully translated by the judicial officials and the ministers, the actual situation should be appropriately taken into consideration and discussions should be held collectively so that laws be made and issued nationwide."[76] In the 2nd year of Shunzhi (1645), an imperial edict was issued by Emperor Shizu: "Laws should be made and submitted to the emperor for approval by law revision officials by referring to those of Manchu and Han nationality,"[77] "and it should be completed as soon as possible to be issued nationwide."[78] In May of the 2nd year (1646), after "extensive discussion in court" and "repeated revision of the contents," *Da Qing Lv Ji Jie Fu Li* (*Great Qing Code with Collected Commentaries and Appended Sub-statutes*) was completed. "Because some of the laws are difficult to understand and the some of the explanations are not in detail," notes were added. Eventually, the law was enacted in the following year. *Da Qing Lv Ji Jie Fu Li* (*Great Qing Code with Collected Commentaries and Appended Sub-statutes*) was the first complete written code of the Qing Dynasty. In the preface, Emperor Shizu stated: "As for the ruling of 'Zhong Xia' (China) … Since the country has a large population, and there are various malpractices … if laws and regulations are not made, there would be no standards for 'You Si' (official) to refer to"; therefore, *Da Qing Lv Ji Jie Fu Li* (*Great Qing Code with Collected Commentaries and Appended Sub-statutes*) was made. So he required "'You Si' (official) inside and outside the capital to show respect to the written constitution without changing it randomly," and he expected that "the officials and the people can attach importance to their reputation and morality and take the problem seriously" in order to reach "the realm where no punishments are needed to be enforced." Emperor Shizuhad attached great importance to the making of *Da Qing Lv* (*Code of Great Qing*), and he warned that "the law should be followed by the descendants, officials and subjects forever."[79]

Da Qing Lv Ji Jie Fu Li (*Great Qing Code with Collected Commentaries and Appended Sub-statutes*) was made through a "careful translation of *Ming Lv* (*Ming Code*) with a reference to the Manchu system." In fact, it was a reprint of *Ming Lv* (*Ming Code*) so that some of the provisions were obviously divorced from the social reality of the early Qing Dynasty. Tan Qian said in "Ji Wen" (The Record of What One Heard) in *Bei You Lu* (*The Records of Tour to the North*): "*Da Qing Lv* (*Code of Great Qing*) is actually *Ming Lv* (*Ming Code*) with a different name. Although it was submitted and approved by Gang Lin, it was made by the petty officials. For example, the penalties for 'Nei Yun' (subordinate officials of the prince) was mitigated according to *Da Gao* (*The Great Imperial Mandate*) which was made at the beginning of Ming Dynasty. So *Da Gao* (*The Great Imperial Mandate*) was

---

[76] *Qing Shi Zong Shi Lu* (*The Record of Emperor Shizong of Qing Dynasty*), Vol. 7.

[77] *Qing Shi Zong Shi Lu* (*The Record of Emperor Shizong of Qing Dynasty*), Vol. 14.

[78] *Qing Shi Zong Shi Lu* (*The Record of Emperor Shizong of Qing Dynasty*), Vol. 16.

[79] "Da Qing Lv Li Tong Kao" (A Textual Research of the Laws and Precedents of Great Qing) in *Shi Zu Zhang Huang Di Yu Zhi Da Qing Lv Yuan Xu* (*The Original Preface of the Code of Great Qing Drafted by Emperor Shi Zu*).

applied by different offices of 'Bu Zheng Si' (the government office in charge of civil affairs at the provincial level), according to which all offenders should be punished with one level reduced without being retried. But the real intention of *Da Gao* (*The Great Imperial Mandate*) is misinterpretated. In Qing Dynasty, *Da Gao* (*The Great Imperial Mandate*) is not made, but *Da Gao* (*The Great Imperial Mandate*) which was made in Ming dynasty is frequently referred to, so what is the point of making reference to this law?" For this reason, after *Da Qing Lv* (*Code of Great Qing*) was released, many of the regulations were not seriously implemented. In the 8th year of Shunzhi (1651), Zhao Jinmei, "Ji Shi Zhong" (the senior assistant of the emperor and the supervisor of officials) of "Xing Ke" (The Department of Punishment), stated in a memorial: "The law has been enacted for so long, but it has not been followed."[80] Especially, because *Da Qing Lv Ji Jie Fu Li* (*Great Qing Code with Collected Commentaries and Appended Sub-statutes*) was published in Chinese, it did not have any constraining forces to most of the Manchu officials who did not speak Chinese. In order to encourage officials to abide by the law, in the 12th year of Shunzhi (1655), "more concise rules and precedents were drafted by referring to the previous 'Hui Dian' (The Collected Statutes)."[81] In the 13th year of Shunzhi (1656), the Manchu version of *Da Qing Lv* (*Code of Great Qing*) was enacted.

To sum up, from the laws which were made during the reign of Emperor Shunzhi, it can be seen that after entering Shanhaiguan, some appropriate adjustments and reforms had been made by the Qing rulers in order to adapt to the social reality of the vast areas of Han people in the construction of the legal system and political power. As far as the legal system was concerned, on the basis of the achievements made in the early period, after they entered Shanhaiguan, they had not only comprehensively adopted the legal system of Ming Dynasty, but also actively carried out the legislative route of "Can Han Zhuo Jin" (making reference not only to the legal thoughts and culture of Han nationality but also to the national practice and needs of Jin nationality) in the whole country. As was pointed out by Marx in his discussion of the Germanic invasion of Rome, "the formation of social system which was adopted by the settled conquerors should be adaptable to the level of development of productive forces which they faced..."[82]

After the succession of the throne by Shengzu, with the great change of social circumstances, although new cases continued to occur, yet generally speaking the country was becoming prosperous and peaceful. So it was impossible for some of the legal provisions that were made during the reign of Emperor Shunzhi to adapt to the new social conditions. Moreover, because of the mixture of the old and new regulations, the officials of law departments were at a loss as to what to do. So in

---

[80] *Qing Shi Zu Shi Lu* (*The Record of Emperor Shizu of Qing Dynasty*), Vol. 54.

[81] "Wen Yuan Zhuan" (The Biography of Wen Yuan) (Part 1) in *Qing Shi Gao* (*The Draft of the History of Qing Dynasty*).

[82] *Ma Ke Si En Ge Si Xuan Ji* (*The Selected Works of Marx and Engels*), Vol. 1, The People's Publishing House, 1972, p. 81.

11.2 The Complete Implementation of the Legislative Principle of...

August of the 3rd year of Kangxi (1664), "Xing Bu" (The Department of Punishment) petitioned the emperor to have the legal provisions rectified and new regulations added. According to the order of Emperor Kangxi, law revision was undertaken by "Da Xue Shi" (grand secretary) and "Xing Bu Shang Shu" (the minister of the Department of Punishment), and in the 9th year of Emperor Kangxi (1670), the work was completed. With the expansion of the territory of the Qing Dynasty, in the 18th year of Kangxi (1679), the emperor ordered "Xing Bu" (The Department of Punishment) to have all the old and new provisions revised in order to resolve any contradiction between legislation and judicial practice. In the imperial edict issued on September 14th, he explained that the purpose of "building up the legal system in the state" was to "eliminate violence, to prevent evildoing, and to protect the safety of the decent people." So the reason for "making regulations beyond the established statutes" was to let people show reverence to law, encourage them to abide by the law, and help them avoid being punished; on the other hand, he also pointed out the disadvantage of inconsistencies in the laws and regulations as it had led to circumstances where death penalty should not be enforced according to law but should be enforced according to the new regulations or the penalty in the old law was too lenient but that in the new regulation was too severe. Therefore, "adjustments should be made according to the changing situation," and discussions should be held "together with 'Jiu Qing' (the nine high-rank officials in ancient times) and the officials in different offices, bureaus, and associations to decide 'what should be retained and what should be deleted.'" In this edict, Emperor Shengzu stated that it was not enough to rule the country only by law, because he saw that although laws and regulations had been amended before, yet "the crimes have not been reduced and the fraudulency has not been eliminated", which had made him realize that in order to prevent violence by law, flexible policies should be implemented and "more attention should be paid to people's lives"[83] in preventing violence by law and that the complementary policy of the combination of inflexibility and yielding should be implemented. Following Emperor Shengzu's principle, *Xing Bu Xian Xing Ze Li* (*The Current Regulations of the Department of Punishment*) was compiled by "Xing Bu" (The Department of Punishment) in the following year, in which different penalties were stipulated for different crimes, which were not previously included in the law. In the 28th year of Kangxi (1681), a memorial was submitted to the emperor by Sheng Fusheng, the senior official of "Yu Shi Tai" (The Censorate), about the contradiction between laws and regulations that appeared in legal practice in the past decades. He pointed out that "the laws and regulations should be examined and revised to make them consistent to keep the authority of law."[84] For this reason, Emperor Shengzu especially ordered the revisions to be

---

[83]"Juan Shou" (Preface) in "Da Qing Lv Li Tong Kao"(A Textual Research of the Laws and Precedents of Great Qing) in *Sheng Zu Ren Huang Di Shang Yu* (*The Imperial Edict by Emperor Shengzu*).

[84]"Xing Fa Zhi" (The Record of the Criminal Law) (Part 1) in *Qing Shi Gao* (*The Draft of the History of Qing Dynasty*).

discussed and approved by "Jiu Qing" (the nine high-rank officials in ancient times); thus, *Xian Xing Ze Li* (*The Current Regulations*) was finally included in the provisions of *Da Qing Lv* (*Code of Great Qing*)."[85] Emperor Shengzu also appointed "Shang Shu" (ministers) Tu Na and Zhang Yushu as president, to be in charge of major law revisions. "The ministers think that since the law is based on *Tang Lv* (*Tang Code*), the language is so simple that it may often lead to misunderstanding. So after the main body of the law, general notes should be added to give further interpretation." From the 34th year (1695) to the 46th year (1707) of Kangxi, after repeated checking and revision, *Xian Xing Ze Li* (*The Current Regulations*) was finally included in *Da Qing Lv* (*Code of Great Qing*). However, *Xian Xing Ze Li* (*The Current Regulations*) was just "read by Emperor Shengzu" but as not issued; hence, it only paved the way for the perfection of *Da Qing Lv* (*Code of Great Qing*) during the reign of Emperor Yongzheng and Emperor Qianlong.

In his early years, Shi Zong had tried his best to rectify the disciplines and social order. In view of the malpractice that "some serious crimes are punished leniently, while some minor crimes are punished severely" and "some previously implemented laws are abandoned, while the same affairs are handled according to different laws," Zhu Shi, "Da Xue Shi" (grand secretary), was appointed as the president, to be in charge of law revision following the principle that "the similarities and differences should be analyzed with the complex ones deleted and concise ones retained; the order of priority should be arranged appropriately with the severe ones tempered with leniency."[86] In the 3rd year of Yongzheng (1725), the compilation was completed, and in the 5th year of Yongzheng (1727), *Da Ming Lv Ji Jie* (*Great Ming Code with Collected Commentaries*) was issued. The original style of the law was retained, with only some provisions added, deleted, and adjusted and with collections of annotation attached after the main body of the text. Moreover, improvements were made in the "Xiao Zhu" (small-character notes between vertical lines of a book, usu. In two lines) of the text, through which the contents of the law was made much clearer.

Since there were a large number regulations (in the 3rd year of Yongzheng, there were already eight hundred and fifteen regulations) which were made according to the specific circumstances, and their scope of application was very extensive, they had become specific supplements of the law. In judicial practice, the effectiveness of "Li" (precedent) was often greater than that of the law, but in order to prevent any officials from breaking the law by citing "Li" (precedent), on May 27 of the 3rd year of Yongzheng (1725), an imperial edict was issued by the emperor: "Since there are numerous 'Li' (precedent) . . . so it is more harmful for 'You Si' (official) to settle lawsuits randomly by citing 'Li' (precedent)." Therefore, "it is necessary to have them unified . . . you must try your best to make them as perfect as possible in order

---

[85]"Xing Fa Zhi" (The Record of the Criminal Law) (Part 1) in *Qing Shi Gao* (*The Draft of the History of Qing Dynasty*).

[86]"Xing Fa Zhi" (The Record of the Criminal Law) (Part 1) in *Qing Shi Gao* (*The Draft of the History of Qing Dynasty*).

to realize my intention of enforcing punishment prudently."[87] Among the eight hundred and fifteen established "Li" (precedent), there were three hundred and twenty "old 'Li' (precedent) which were made in the previous dynasties," or "the original precedents"; two hundred and ninety "'Li' (precedent) which were made during the reign of Emperor Kangxi," or "the additional precedents"; and two hundred and four "Li" (precedent) "which were adopted during the reign of Emperor Yongzheng." Additionally, general annotations were attached to the main text of the law, and after that, "Tiao Li" (regulation) was added, which was followed by "Yuan Li" (original regulation), "Zeng Li" (additional regulation), and "Qin Ding Lv" (law approved and made by the emperor) successively. Thereby, the problem of "the inconsistency of 'Fa' (law) and 'Li' (precedent)," which had bothered people since the reign of Emperor Shunzhi and Emperor Kangxi, was finally solved.

In addition, great importance was attached by Shi Zong to the propaganda of law in order to make the people understand and obey law. On the September 9 of 3rd year of Yongzheng (1725), in the preface of *Da Ming Lv Ji Jie* (*Great Ming Code with Collected Commentaries*), Emperor Yongzheng quoted an anecdote, which was recorded in *Zhou Li* (*The Rites of Zhou Dynasty*): "The criminal law is made and issued in all states, the pictures of the penalties are hung on 'Xiang Wei' (the tall building outside the palace gate for posting official notice), and the people are gathered to read it." By citing this anecdote, he further demonstrated that "laws have been enacted and shown to the court and the commonalty by the former emperors so that it is possible for the officials to have the cases settled after the have studied them, and it is possible for the people to obey after have got to know them. So criminal laws can help people to settle disputes and to improve customs." To this end, he required that after the publication of *Da Ming Lv Ji Jie* (*Great Ming Code with Collected Commentaries*) nationwide, the officials should "study it carefully and be extremely familiar with it in order to resolve problems appropriately." Moreover, he instructed "Li Bu" (The Department of Personnel) to ask the officials who were in charge of local affairs "to be well-trained so that they can be competent in the administration of the local affairs and the ruling of people without the assistant of petty officials." He especially noted that "either in metropolis or remote and backward places, either in local 'Zhou' (subprefecture) or 'Xian' (county), laws should be explained by following the systems of *Zhou Li* (*The Rites of Zhou Dynasty*) to make the fellow countrymen to read and interpret law so that they could not only be familiar with law but also show respect to law and show love to themselves. Thereby the cases could be justly settled by the government officials, the lawsuits be mediated by the people themselves, the social mores could be rectified and comity could be recovered."[88] In the 13th year of Yongzheng (1735),

---

[87]"Da Qing Lv Li Tong Kao"(A Textual Research of the Laws and Precedents of Great Qing) in *Shi Zong Xian Huang Di Shang Yu* (*The Imperial Edit by Emperor Shizong*).

[88]"Da Qing Lv Li Tong Kao Xu" (A Preface to the Textual Research of the Laws and Precedents of Great Qing) in *Shi Zong Xian Huang Di Yu Zhi Da Qing Lv Yuan Xu* (*The Original Preface of the Code of Great Qing Drafted by Emperor Shizong*).

Shi Zong urged again and again in his testamentary edict that "the penalties and prohibitions are established in a country in order to punish the wicked people, to eliminate the violence, to prevent corruption, to get rid of the evil forces, to rectify the customs, and to regulate the officials."[89] At that time, according to description, "people are indifferent to each other, the officials only engage in malpractice for selfish ends, bad customs are formed by practice and people have turned a deaf ear to their wrong doing without guilty conscience." Although Shi Zong had advocated to have such social malpractices rectified by applying severe punishment, he also paid great attention to the measures taken, as was described: "severe and lenient punishment should be enforced in accordance with the specific time and circumstances, with necessary changes made."[90] At the same time, from his experience in ruling, he also learned that "it is not enough to just make laws" and that "it is impossible for any legislative and administrative regulation to be applied for long without drawbacks"[91]; therefore, "it is the people who are 'Ben' (the essence) in ruling a country, and the other things are just the leaves and branches."[92] He emphasized that "there is the person who can make the country stable, but there is no law that can make the country stable automatically. If we can not get the right person, even if we have 'Ren' (benevolence) of Yao and Shun, we may still have the tyrannies,"[93] which had shown the view of a feudal emperor on the enforcement of law and the appointment of the people.

After Emperor Gaozong's succession to the throne, he appointed San Tai as the president, to be in charge of law revison during the Qing Dynasty. So accordingly, the original laws and precedents were reedited and checked article by article; at the same time, the established precedents were examined in detail, and they were called "Tiao Li" (regulation), with the gains and losses estimated systematically. Later, the general annotation that was attached to the law was abolished and "Xiao Zhu" (small-character notes between vertical lines of a book, usu. In two lines) was added. The law was finally completed in the 5th year of Qianlong (1740) and was issued under the title *Da Qing Lv Li* (*The Laws and Precedents of Great Qing*) after it was approved by the emperor himself. Soon it was "issued home and abroad to be abided by people forever." So after almost one hundred years, from a simple reproduction of *Ming Lv* (*Ming Code*) at the beginning of the Qing Dynasty to repeated revision afterward, *Da Qing Lv Li* (*The Laws and Precedents of Great Qing*) was finally completed, which had shown that the Qing rulers gradually

---

[89]"Xing Fa Zhi" (The Record of the Criminal Law) (Part 1) in *Qing Shi Gao* (*The Draft of the History of Qing Dynasty*).

[90]"Xing Fa Zhi" (The Record of the Criminal Law) (Part 1) in *Qing Shi Gao* (*The Draft of the History of Qing Dynasty*).

[91]Yong Zheng Chao (The Reign of Emperor Yongzheng) in *Dong Hua Lu* (*The Record of Donghua*), Vol. 5.

[92]Yong Zheng Chao (The Reign of Emperor Yongzheng) in *Dong Hua Lu* (*The Record of Donghua*), Vol. 5.

[93]*Qing Shi Zong Shi Lu* (*The Record of Emperor Shizong of Qing Dynasty*).

realized the importance of the establishment of a unified legal system and the strengthening of the judiciary from their actual experiences in ruling China.

Da Qing Lv Li (*The Laws and Precedents of Great Qing*) was an agglomeration of feudal laws, as was described: "it is in accordance with the ancient meaning" with "the previous mistakes corrected"; meanwhile, it reflected the guiding principles of "condemning the wicked people, preventing violence, punishing corruption, eliminating evilness, rectifying the customs and regulating officials." In the preface, Emperor Gaozong further elaborated the function of the law: "it is not simply to terrorize people by issuing prohibitions, but to make people familiar with the law, to integrate punishment with education and to make them moralized." At the same time, he not only strengthened the deterrent forces of criminal punishment in the name of "Tian" (Heaven), but also advocated that "'Wu Xing' (Five Penalties) should be enforced in order to show 'Tian Tao' (Heavenly condemnation) and 'Tian Wei' (Heavenly power)".[94]

Da Qing Lv Li (*The Laws and Precedents of Great Qing*) was similar to *Ming Lv* (*Ming Code*) in structural form, and it consisted of seven statutes: *Ming Li Lv* (*Statutes and Terms*), *Li Lv* (*Statutes on Officials*), *Hu Lv* (*Statutes on Households*), *Li Lv* (*Statutes on Rites*), *Bing Lv* (*Statutes on Military Affairs*), *Xing Lv* (*The Penal Code*), and *Gong Lv* (*Statutes on Handicraft Industry*), with thirty chapters, forty seven volumes, thirty categories, four hundred and thirty six articles, and one thousand and forty nineattached precedents. As the established legal code, *Da Qing Lv Li* (*The Laws and Precedents of Great Qing*) was called "the established law of the forefathers," so its articles had not been changed since the 5th year of Qianlong (1740), with only additional precedents created to make up for its inadequacy. As a result, the number of "Tiao Li" (regulation) kept increasing, and by the 26th year of Qianlong (1761), it had reached to one thousand four hundred and fifty six. Not only was there vast amounts of "Li" (precedent), but its effect was also greater than that of law. According to "Xing Fa Zhi" (The Record of the Criminal Law) in *Qing Shi Gao* (*The Draft of the History of Qing Dynasty*): "the established 'Li' (precedent) in Qing Dynasty was similar to 'Chi' (instruction) of Song Dynasty, so that 'Li' (precedent) was applied and law was neglected, while law had become outdated and obsolete and 'Li' (precedent) became increasingly redundant." Because "Li" (precedent) was a more flexible form of law, compared with the established law, it was more adaptable to the changing situation. Moreover, it was subject to law. But the overextensive application of "Li" (precedent) in the settlement of lawsuits had inevitably led to great confusion because "severe punishments are often enforced beyond law, or the law is often violated for the application of 'Li' (precedent), or one 'Li' (precedent) is made for one specific affair, province and area, or one 'Li' (precedent) has produced another 'Li' (precedent)."[95] During the early period of

---

[94]"Da Qing Lv Li Tong Kao"(A Textual Research of the Laws and Precedents of Great Qing) in *Yu Zhi Da Qing Lv Yuan Xu* (*The Original Preface of Code of Great Qing*).

[95]"Xing Fa Zhi" (The Record of the Criminal Law) (Part 1) in *Qing Shi Gao* (*The Draft of the History of Qing Dynasty*).

Qianlong's reign, people already saw the contradiction between "Lv" (criminal law) and "Li" (precedent). So in the 11th year of Emperor Qianlong (1746), it was stipulated that "Tiao Li" (regulation) should be revised on a small scale every five years and on a large scale every ten years. In the 1st period of reign of Emperor Qianlong, the contents of "Tiao Li" (regulation) were revised ten times, namely, in the 12th, 16th, 21st, 26th, 32nd, 37th, 43rd, 48th, 53rd and 60th year. But every time, "Tiao Li" (regulation) was newly drafted. By the 9th year of Tongzhi (1871), the number of "Li" (precedent) had reached to one thousand eight hundred and ninety two. But after that, national power started to decline; the practice of regular revision of "Li" (precedent) was abandoned because of domestic problems and foreign aggression.

Da Qing Lv Li (*The Laws and Precedents of Great Qing*) was the last feudal code in Chinese history. In terms of its nature, it was a penalty code. Because it adapted the traditional compiling system of "Zhu Fa He Ti" (the integration of various laws), it also contained administrative, civil, and litigation, as well as other provisions. Although it contained some provisions that reflected privileges of the Manchu nationality, generally speaking, it was a feudal code, which was enacted in accordance with *Tang Lv Shu Yi* (*The Comments on Tang Code*), *Song Xing Tong* (*The Penal Code of Song Dynasty*), and *Da Ming Lv* (*The Great Ming Code*).

Da Qing Lv Li (*The Laws and Precedents of Great Qing*) consisted of complete and detailed laws and precedents and it was a code made by concentrated efforts of the rulers of Qing Dynasty after they had entered Shanhaiguan as well as a fruit of the comprehensive implementation of the legislative route of "Can Han Zhuo Jin" (making reference not only to the legal thoughts and culture of Han nationality but also to the national practice and needs of Jin nationality). Therefore, its contents were more suitable to the social reality of Chinese society because they had fully reflected the unity of "Qing" (human relationships) and "Fa" (law). For example, starting from *Tang Lv* (*Tang Code*), it was stipulated in the laws of almost every dynasty that when the ancestral parents or parents were alive, it was forbidden for their children to register separately or to divide the family property. Although this provision was retained in *Da Qing Lv Li* (*The Laws and Precedents of Great Qing*), it was added that "it is allowed for the children to divide the property if it is approved by their parents."[96] In Chinese feudal society, with a vast territory and different customs, it was a common occurrence for children to live separately from their parents and to divide the family property while their parents are still alive despite repeated prohibition. Because it was allowed for the children to divide the property while the parents were still alive according to Manchu customary law, it was obvious that the supplementary regulation was in accordance with the social reality at the time. As another example, it was stipulated in law that "if anyone has married his maternal or paternal cousin, he or she will be punished by 'Zhang' (flogging with heavy sticks) for eighty strokes and will be ordered to divorce."[97] But since this kind

---

[96]"Hu Lv" (Statutes on Households) in *Da Qing Lv Li* (*The Laws and Precedents of Great Qing*).

[97]"Hun Lv" (Statutes on Marriage) in *Da Qing Lv Li* (*The Laws and Precedents of Great Qing*).

of marriage had become a custom among the folks, a special stipulation was added in the article: "If maternal or paternal cousins have got married, they will be handled according to their own will."[98] This amendment was warmly received by the folks because it was able to show the milk of human kindness. Moreover, *Da Qing Lv Li (The Laws and Precedents of Great Qing)* also exerted a certain influence on neighboring countries like Japan and Korea, so it was really another great achievement of the Chinese legal civilization, although it still inherited the backward and barbaric element of *Ming Lv (Ming Code)*.

11.2.2 Da Qing Hui Dian *(The Collected Statutes of Great Qing)* and the Making of Departmental Regulations

When Emperor Shengzu ascended the throne, he devoted himself to the making of administrative laws. In the 23rd year of Kangxi (1684), he ordered that the collected statutes of the Qing Dynasty be drafted by imitating that of the Ming Dynasty in order to make rules for the management of the activities of the state organs. The law was completed after six years, and it was referred to in history as *Kang Xi Hui Dian (The Collected Statutes of Emperor Kangxi)*. In the preface of the law, Emperor Shengzu stated that "legislative activities are the key to ruling the country and safeguarding the state, isn't it so important? So I specially command you ministers to devote yourselves to the drafting of the collected statutes by collecting the legal provisions and articles carefully and comprehensively in order to trace the whole course of events and clarify the doubtful points. I hope that the laws which are made are as splendid and glorious as the sun and stars and can provide a guidance for people to follow ... We have tried our best to make laws according to specific circumstances, so the laws in our times are more detailed and comprehensive than those of the previous dynasties. They are not the decorative instruments of ruling the state but the perfect laws which will be abided by both officials and the people of the future generation to bring everlasting peace and stability to the county. Therefore, the work must be carried out. Isn't it worth thinking about?"

Kang Xi Hui Dian (The Collected Statutes of Emperor Kangxi) was the first code having the nature of administrative law, which was officially issued after Qing rulers entered Shanhaiguan. As for the structure of the code, the relevant matters of the code were arranged according to different official departments and the official titles were used as the framework of the relevant contents, so the code was divided into "Zong Ren Fu" (The Imperial Clan Court); "Nei Ge" (The Cabinet); "Liu Bu" (The Six Departments), "Li Fan Yuan" (The Bureau of National Minority Affairs); "Du Cha Yuan" (The Court of Censors); "Tong Zheng Shi Si" (The Transmission Office); "Nei Wu Fu" (Board of the Imperial Household) and other "Si" (bureau), "Yuan" (institution), "Fu" (ancient administrative district between province and

---

[98] "Hun Lv" (Statutes on Marriage) in *Da Qing Lv Li (The Laws and Precedents of Great Qing)*.

county), "Jian" (ancient supervisory office). Therefore, the code was both systematic and detailed compared with the former ones. "*Kang Xi Hui Dian* (*The Collected Statutes of Emperor Kangxi*) covered almost all important affairs from early Qing Dynasty to the 26th year of Kangxi (1687), such as the responsibilities of officials, the official system, 'Jun' (shire) and 'Xian' (county), military affairs, land reclamation, meeting with the emperor, tributes and tax, currency as well as the affairs which were taken charge by 'Liu Cao' (the six departments) and other offices."[99] Wei Xiangshu, a contemporary of the Qing Dynasty, once commented that "the collected statute is a constitution of the time, which is an inseparable part of the laws and decrees. The collected statute contains almost all the administrative regulations that the officials should follow, the affairs which were taken charge by different departments and the various systems of official rituals."[100]

After the reign of Emperor Shengzu, in the 10th year of Emperor Yongzheng (1732), *Yong Zheng Hui Dian* (*The Collected Statutes of Emperor Yongzheng*) was issued, and in the imperial preface Shi Zong made the following statement:

> After my succession of throne, I have tried to understand the intention of my great-grandfather and ruled the county according to his instruction. What needs to be done is to have the laws revised according to the concrete situation, to continue the cause of our predecessors and to carry forward the good deeds, doctrines and virtues of the forefathers. So requied by Jiang Tingxi, the minister of "Li" (rites), the the cabinet ministers are ordered to start the law revision, to check out the etiquettes and regulations which were made in each "Ya Men" (the government offices) from the 26th year of Kangxi (1687) to the 5th year of Emperor Yongzheng (1727) and to classify them according to the category of each "Ya Men" (the government offices). So it has taken nine years to complete this work. Emperor Shengzu who has ruled the country for more than sixty years, has organized the revison work of the old collected statutes and made the most important rules in appointing officials and running the state, which are as splendid and glorious as the sun and the stars, and as immortal as *Yu Shu* (*The Record of Yao, Shun and ancient people*) and *Zhou Li* (*The Rites of Zhou Dynasty*).

It can be seen that, apart from the revision of the statutes that were undertaken from the 26th year of Kangxi (1687) to the 5th year of Yongzheng (1727), no stylistic innovation was made in *Yong Zheng Hui Dian* (*The Collected Statutes of Emperor Yongzheng*).

In the 12th year of Qianlong (1747), an order was issued by emperor Gaozong to have the collected statutes revised again, which spanned more than one hundred years from the reign of Nurhachi to the 27th year of Qianlong (1762). So its contents were more complete than those of the collected statutes that were made during the reign of Emperor Kangxi and Emperor Yongzheng. Diagrams of the temple, altar, responsibilities of officials, and geography were attached to the contents. At the same time, in view of the fact that "'Li' (precedent) can be concurrently used, but

---

[99]"Yu Zhi Xu" (Imperial Preface) in "Qian Long Chao" (The Reign of Qianlong) in "Juan Shou" (Preface) in *Da Qing Hui Dian* (*The Collected Statutes of Great Qing*).

[100]Wei Xiangshu (Qing Dynasty),"Han Song Tang Ji" (Collected Works Written in Hang Song Hall) in *Sheng Chao Da Li Ji Xing Qi Qing Geng Ding Hui Dian Shi* (*Memorials about the Imperial Rituals and the Revison of Collected Statutes*), Vol. 1.

'Dian' (code) is can not be changed" and for fear that the concurrent application of "Li" (precedent) and "Dian" (code) might "make the posterity confused by making use of them randomly," "Li" (precedent) which was attached to each article, was compiled separately. According to the principle regarding "Dian" (code) as the "Gang" (outline) and "Li" (precedent) as the "Mu" (the contents) and making "Li" (precedent) and "Dian" (code) complementary to each other without mixing them up, *Qian Long Hui Dian* (*The Collected Statutes of Emperor Qianlong*), which consisted of one hundred volumes, and *Qian Long Hui Dian Ze Li* (*The Regulations of Emperor Qianlong*), which consisted of one hundred and eighty volumes, were made respectively, which was different from the collected statutes made during the reign of Emperor Kangxi and Emperor Yongzheng.

Since *Qian Long Hui Dian* (*The Collected Statutes of Emperor Qianlong*), it had already become the established stylistic rules and layout to "regard 'Dian' (code) as the 'Gang' (outline) and 'Li' (precedent) as 'Mu' (the contents) and to list them separately." Because long-standing and commonly used laws were collected into statutes, generally the main body of laws was not changed and only "Li" (precedent) was added or deleted according to concrete situations. Just as what was stated by Emperor Qianlong in *Da Qing Hui Dian Fan Li* (*Guides for the Collected Statutes of Great Qing*): "If it needs to be amended because of the change of the situation in future, adjustments should be made on a small scale with only 'Li' (precedent) added or deleted. Generally speaking, only one or two articles should be amended, so there is no need to change the overall structure. So the law is made once for all for others to follow in future." After the reign of Emperor Qianlong, in the 6th year of Jiaqing (1801), the revision of the collected statutes continued. So the statute, which consisted of eighty volumes of "Hui Dian" (the collected statutes), nine hundred and twenty volumes of "Shi Li" (precedents), and one hundred and thirty two volumes of collected diagrams, was finally completed in the 23rd year of Jiaqing (1818). In *Jia Qing Hui Dian* (*The Collected Statutes of Emperor Jiaqing*), "Ze Li" (regulation), which was included in *Qian Long Hui Dian* (*The Collected Statutes of Emperor Qianlong*), was changed into "Shi Li" (precedents), but the method of compiling it and its scope were the same as those of "Ze Li" (regulation).

In the 12th year of Guangxu (1886), on the basis of *Jia Qing Hui Dian* (*The Collected Statutes of Emperor Jiaqing*), the collected precedents were again revised. In the 25th year of Guangxu (1899), *Guang Xu Hui Dian* (*The Collected Statutes of Emperor Guangxu*) was issued, which consisted of one hundred volumes, one thousand two hundred and twenty chapters of "Shi Li" (precedents), and two hundred and seventy chapters of diagrams. Among the "Hui Dian" (the collected statutes) made in the Qing dynasty, *Guang Xu Hui Dian* (*The Collected Statutes of Emperor Guangxu*) covered the longest period of time and contained the most chapters, so it was regarded as the final form of the collected statutes of the Qing Dynasty.

In *Da Qing Hui Dian* (*The Collected Statutes of Great Qing*), the responsibilities of the administrative authorities at various levels, "Shi Li" (precedents), the principles of activity, and the relevant systems ranging from the founding years of the state to the reign of Kuangxu in the Qing Dynasty were recorded in detail. Moreover,

"Dian" (code) and "Li" (precedent) were used complementarily, and they were illustrated with diagrams. The statute covered a wide range of contents, which included most of the important aspects of "Li" (rites), "Yue" (music), "Xing" (punishment), and "Zheng" (government) and "the long standing systems which were frequently applied." Just as what was written in *Qian Long Hui Dian Fan Li* (*Guides for the Collected Statutes of Emperor Qianlong*): "The great state law is compiled by listing the 'Dian Zhang' (statutes) and 'Hui Yao' (collections of historical records) as the main content, in which the long standing systems which are frequently applied are included. Moreover, the rules for running the country and the regulations which should be followed by the official departments or abided by government and the commonalty are all included in the statute, so to a certain extent the statute is a perfect book." Some contemporaries of the Qing Dynasty once commented that "the statute has almost included all the administrative orders which should be followed by officials and listed the all the responsibilities of different departments."[101] "As far as the constitution and decrees are concerned, 'Hui Dian' (the collected statutes) is made for the country; meanwhile, 'An Du' (official documents) is made for the officials, so the relevant affairs are managed from top to bottom and the way for ruling the country is unified."[102] Although the style of "Zhu Fa He Ti" (the integration of various laws) was followed in compiling the five collections of "Hui Dian" (the collected statutes) during the reign of the five emperors of the Qing dynasty, the collected statutes were basically administrative laws, in which the national administrative system and the responsibilities of various departments and bureaus were confirmed. Because great principles and laws were included in these statutes, they were called the constitution of Qing Empire. The five collections of "Hui Dian" (the collected statutes) made during the reign of the five emperors of the Qing dynasty were another significant legislative achievement made in that period, which surely added splendor to the legal civilization of the Qing Dynasty.

Besides "Hui Dian" (the collected statutes), "Ze Li" (regulation) was another important achievement that was made in the administrative law of the Qing Dynasty.

To standardize the activities of the departments and institutions, it was instructed that "Ze Li" (regulation) should be drafted by each department and institution. "Ze Li" (regulation) referred to the rules and regulations of each department that was approved by the emperor, which not only was the organic law of each "Ya Men" (the government offices) but also the basis for handling government affairs. In as early as the 7th year of Kangxi, Wang Xi, "Zuo Du Yu Shi" (the head of the court of censors) of "Du Cha Yuan" (The Court of Censors), submitted a written statement to the emperor requiring that "'Shi Li' (precedents) be carefully examined and revised by

---

[101] Wei Xiang Shu (Qing Dynasty), "Han Song Tang Ji"(Collected Works Written in Hang Song Hall) in *Sheng Chao Da Li Ji Xing Qi Qing Geng Ding Hui Dian Shi* (*Memorials about the Imperial Rituals and the Revison of Collected Statutes*), Vol. 1.

[102] Zhang Xuecheng (Qing Dynasty), "Da Zhen Xiu Cai Lun Xiu Zhi Di Er Shu" (The Second Reply to Mr. Zhen for the Record Revision) in "Fang Zhi Lue Li" (An Outline of the Local Records) in *Zhang Shi Yi Shu* (*The Posthumous Papers of Mr. Zhang*), Vol. 15.

11.2 The Complete Implementation of the Legislative Principle of...

'You Si' (official) to make them clarified" so that "they can be applied uniformly."[103] Emperor Shengzu paid great attention to the compilation of "Ze Li" (regulation), and he stated that "if laws and precedents are not made, or if one case is handled according to different standards, how can they be dealt with by the officials of different departments and institutions?"[104]

"Ze Li" (regulation) was divided into general and special regulations. The general regulations referred to those made for the general services performed by "Liu Bu" (The Six Departments), such as *Qin Ding Li Bu Ze Li* (*The Regulation of the Department of Personnel Made by Imperial Order*), while the special ones referred to those made for the special affairs of each department, such as *Qin Ding Ba Qi Ze Li* (*The Regulation for the Eight Banners Made by Imperial Order*). Although some were not called special "Ze Li" (regulation), they actually belonged to this type of regulation, such as *Qin Ding Hu Bu Cao Yun Quan Shu* (*The Pandect on Water Transportation for the Department of Revenue Made by Imperial Order*) and *Qin Ding Xue Zheng Quan Shu* (*The Pandect on the Departmental Director of School Made by Imperial Order*). The making of "Ze Li" (regulation) in the Qing Dynasty mainly started during the reign of Emperor Kangxi.

In the 50th year of Emperor Kangxi (1711), *Liu Bu Xian Xing Ze Li* (*The Current Regulations of the Six Departments*), which was also called *Xin Zuan Geng Ding Liu Bu Xian Xing Ze Li* (*The Newly Revised Current Regulations of the Six Departments*), was published, in which the working rules for all levels of the government and the penalty regulations made from the beginning of the Qing Dynasty to the 41st year of Kangxi were all categorized and considered as established regulations. At the end of the reign of Emperor Kangxi, *Qin Ding Bin Bu Ze Li* (*The Regulation of the Department of Defense Made by Imperial Order*), *Qin Ding Li Bu Ze Li* (*The Regulation of the Department of Personnel Made by Imperial Order*), and *Qin Ding Li Bu Quan Xuan Guan Yuan Ze Li* (*The Regulation for Selecting Officials for the Department of Personnel Made by Imperial Order*) were published.

In the 12th year of Emperor Yongzheng (1734), *Qin Ding Li Bu Ze Li* (*The Regulation of the Department of Personnel Made by Imperial Order*), which mainly covered the duties of each department, the official selection and the official ranks, and punishment for the violations of laws by each department, was issued. The law was revised continuously during the reign of Emperor Qianlong, Emperor Jiaqing, and Guangxu. *Liu Bu Chu Fen Ze Li* (*The Regulation of the Six Departments for Punishment*), which was made during the reign of Yongzheng and issued in the 7th year of Emperor Qianlong, was another significant administrative law with substantial content. To the reign of Emperor Qianlong, the activities of drafting of "Ze Li" (regulation) reached climax. For example, the following "Ze Li" (regulations) were made in "Li Bu" (The Department of Personnel) alone: *Qin Ding Li Bu Ze Li* (*The Regulation of the Department of Personnel Made by Imperial Order*), *Qin Ding Li*

---

[103] "Wang Xi Zhuan" (The Biography of Wang Xi) in *Qing Shi Li Zhuan* (*The Collected Biography of the History of Qing Dynasty*), Vol. 8.

[104] *Kang Xi Qi Ju Zhu* (*The Record of Emperor Kangxi's Daily Life*).

Bu Chu Fen Ze Li (*The Regulation of the Department of Personnel for Punishments Made by Imperial Order*), *Qin Ding Li Bu Quan Xuan Guan Yuan Ze Li* (*The Regulation for Selecting Officials for the Department of Personnel Made by Imperial Order*), *Qin Ding Li Bu Quan Xuan Man Guan Ze Li* (*The Regulation for Selecting Manchu Officials for the Department of Personnel Made by Imperial Order*), *Qin Ding Li Bu Quan Xuan Han Guan Ze Li* (*The Regulation for Selecting Han Officials for the Department of Personnel Made by Imperial Order*), *Qin Ding Li BuYan Feng Si Ze Li* (*The Regulation for the Bureau of Official Management of the Department of Personnel Made by Imperial Order*), *Qin Ding Li BuJi Xun Si Ze Li* (*The Regulation for Bureau of Awarding of the Department of Personnel Made by Imperial Order*), etc. Besides, *Qing Ding Gong Bu Ze Li* (*The Regulation of the Department of Works Made by Imperial Order*) was issued in the 14th year of Emperor Qianlong (1749), and *Qing Ding Hu Bu Ze Li* (*The Regulation of the Department of Revenue Made by Imperial Order*) was issued in the 41st year of Emperor Qianlong (1776). The former was divided into "Ying Shan" (preparing meals), "Chuan Zheng" (ship building), "He Fang" (flood prevention), "Shui Li" (water conservancy), "Jun Huo" (military weapons) and so on, and it mainly included the regulations which were made during the reign of Emperor Guangxu on carriage taking, ceremonial rituals and military weapon production. The latter one was similar to the civil and economic laws, so apart from the responsibilities of "Hu Bu" (The Department of Revenue), it mainly contained the regulations on residence registration, land tax, warehouse, granary, water transportation, salt law, impeaching, currency law, tariff, salary, salaries and provisions for soldiers, pension, and miscellaneous expenses and so on, which was similar to the civil and economic laws. The two regulations mentioned above were amended several times after the reign of Emperor Qianlong.

In the 9th year of Emperor Jiaqing (1804), *Qing Ding Li Bu Ze Li* (*The Regulation of the Department of Personnel by Imperial Order*) was made, and it was further revised in the 24th year of Daoguang (1804). The regulation was divided into four categories, namely, ritual system, ancestor worshipping, receiving guests, and preparing meals, and it mainly concerned the administrative regulations of the country.

Regulations which were made in different provinces level were the main form of legislation of the province and they were the local regulations made for the special local services by provincial officials like "Du Fu" (the viceroys and procurators) and the officials of "Bu Zheng Si" (the government office in charge of civil affairs at the provincial level) and "An Cha Si" (The Judicial Commission) through certain forms and procedures. They mainly included *Fu Jian Sheng Li* (*The Regulations of Fujian Province*), *Guang Dong Sheng Li* (*The Regulations of Guangdong Province*), *Yue Dong Sheng Li* (*The Regulations of Eastern Guangdong*), *Hu Nan Sheng Li* (*The Regulations of Hunan Province*), *Yu Sheng Sheng Li* (*The Regulations of Henan Province*), *Xi Jiang Zheng Yao* (*The Essentials of Administration of Xijiang*), *Jin Zheng Ji Yao* (*Collections of Essentials of Administration of Shanxi Province*), and so on. The administrative regulations which were made in each province mainly included "Gong Shi" (Formula), "Jiao Dai" (transferring of the matters), official appointment and appraisal, salary and so on.

For example, according to the regulation concerning the use of official documents in *Fu Jian Sheng Li* (*The Regulations of Fujian Province*), "in future, for the affairs which involve flood damage and the urgent business which are not convenient to be announced by official documents, 'Bing Tie' (documents sent to the government by the people of lower levels) can be used. Besides, it can be used to handle the documents which are submitted to the emperor for approval; however, if the affairs are not urgent, whether it is about the official management, 'Bing Tie' (documents sent to the government by the people of lower levels) should not be used for prevarication."[105]

As for the regulations about official appointment and assessment, it was stipulated in *Yue Dong Sheng Li* (*The Regulations of Eastern Guangdong*) that "for the official position of 'Hou Bu Zhi Xian' (candidate magistrate of a county), 'Jin Shi' (those who passed the imperial examination at the national level in ancient China) and 'Ji Yong Zhi Xian' (the magistrate of a county who can be appointed if there is a vacancy of the post), the vacancy should be filled by those of the selected candidates by turns. If there are vacancies, they should be filled up by those by turns according to the time sequence of their arrival in the province; for 'Jin Shi' (those who passed the imperial examination at the national level in ancient China) and 'Ji Yong Zhi Xian' (the magistrate of a county who can be appointed if there is a vacancy of the post), the vacancy should be filled up by turns according to the sequence of their ranking (those who have made achievements in army should be appointed first), and evidence should be recorded for future checking."[106] "The officials of each 'Ya Men' (the government offices) are examined in July every year by 'Fu Yuan' (procurators and the officials of the Court of Censors). Except following what has been decided, before the probation, 'Fan Si' (or 'Bu Zheng Si') should send the name list of the staff to 'Du Cha Yuan' (The Court of Censors) for examination, and at the same time, should order the county assistant officials to conduct investigations (aide-de-camp and other junior military officials should conduct the investigation with civil officials). Besides, one official from the two counties of Nanfan should be appointed to call the roll, and 'You Si' (official) should submit the name list to the official in charge for verification. Then they will be examined by 'Ya Men' (the government offices) of 'Fu Yuan' (procurators and the officials of Court of Censors) (the examination paper should be prepared and printed by official staff, turned over to the relevant offices, stamped and filed). Besides, the desks and stools needed should be prepared by Guangzhou prefecture."[107]

---

[105]"Yong Xiang Yong Bing Zhang Cheng" (The Regulation on Making Reports to the Superior) in "Gong Shi Li" (Examples of Formula) in *Fu Jian Sheng Li* (*The Regulations of Fujian Province*).

[106]"Hou Bu Yu Ji Yong Zhi Xian Shi Bu Ci Xu" (The Sequence of the Appointment of Candidate and Current Magistrates) in "Li Juan" (The Volume on Official) (Vol. 31) in *Yue Dong Sheng Li Xin Zuan* (*A New Edition of the Provincial Regulations of Eastern Guangdong*).

[107]"Kao Yi Man Li Yi" (The Performance Appraisal of Manchu Officials) in "Li Juan" (The Volume on Official) (Vol. 31) in *Yue Dong Sheng Li* (*The Provincial Regulations of Eastern Guangdong*).

In a word, in Qing Dynasty, a large number of "Ze Li" (regulation) was made in "Bu" (department), "Yuan" (institution), "Jian" (ancient supervisory office) and in the administrative regions of Mongolia and "Huijiang" (south of Tianshan Mountain). So the administrative legal system was formed with "Hui Dian" (the collected statutes) as the key link and "Ze Li" (regulation) as the supplement, which had become the most valuable part in the construction of legal system in Qing Dynasty, and which had played a positive role in improving the governing efficiency, in instructing the officials to "administrate by law" and in containing the arbitrariness in administration.

11.2.3 The National Legislation Made according to Li Fan Yuan Ze Li (The Regulation for the Bureau of National Minority Affairs)

In order to rule over a vast territory, to consolidate the unified multiethnic country, and to strengthen jurisdiction over the ethnic minority areas, legislation for minorities was especially created by the Qing Dynasty. So the legislation in Qing Dynasty was an integral part of the overall legislation of the nation and it had reached the climax of the ancient Chinese national legislation either in quantity or in contents.

Long before the Qing rulers entered Shanhaiguan, "Sheng Jing Ding Zhi" (Laws and Regulations Made in Shengjing) was announced in the southern Mongolia regions by Huang Taiji. After entering Shanhaiguan, Emperor Shunzhi made a very important agenda the adjustment of the relationship between Han and Manchu nationalities. In the 3rd year of Shunzhi (1646), it was ordered that scholars should be selected through imperial examinations, and in the 5th year of Shunzhi (1648), it was ordered that marriage between Han and Manchu nationalities would be permitted. During the reign of Emperor Kangxi, an order was especially issued to show respect to Confucianism, to offer sacrifice to Confucius, to set up "Bo Xue Hong Ci Ke" (one of the imperial examinations given to select talented scholars skilled in writing), and to unify the ranks of Han and Manchu officials. During the reign of Emperor Shunzhi and Emperor Kangxi, concerning the adjustment of relationship with other nationalities, besides the Han nationality, the relationship with the Mongolians was regarded as a priority, so in the 10th year of Shunzhi (1653), provisions on the number of attendants and the color of clothes of Mongolians whose ranks were above the prince and below the duke were especially stipulated. In the 11th year (1654), it was stipulated that chiefs of vassal states, doro beile (title of nobility), "Bei Zi" (title of nobility, subordinate to doro beile), and dukes should come to the imperial court to be awarded on the first day of new year; in the 12th year (1655), "Li" (precedent) was made for the Mongolian vassal state; in the 15th year (1658), "Li Fan Yuan Da Bi Tiao Li" (Regulation of the Bureau of National Minority Affairs for Capital Punishment) was made; in the 18th year (1661), it was declared that "Li Fan Yuan" (The Bureau of National Minority Affairs) and "Liu Bu" (The

11.2 The Complete Implementation of the Legislative Principle of...

Six Departments) were of the same rank, and "Shang Shu" (the minister) of "Li Fan Yuan" (The Bureau of National Minority Affairs) was allowed to participate in the policy making of national affairs.

After Emperor Kangxi ascended the throne, the guiding ideologies of regarding the Mongolia tribe as "Ping Fan" (the neighboring territory), "ruling according to the local custom," and "governing without setting up border defence" were established.[108] In legislation, it was emphasized that the habits and customs of the frontier minorities should be respected, which was worded as "following the religious beliefs of the minorities without forcing them to change their social custom." This national policy exerted great influence on the rulers of the Qing Dynasty. Emperor Shizong said: "China was united in Qin Dynasty; the areas beyond the Great Wall was united in Yuan Dynasty; but none of the dynasties are as prosperous as our times. Since ancient times, China and the foreign countries are like one big family, so it has a vast territory; but they are incomparable with us."[109] Therefore, he not only abandoned the long-held traditional concept of regarding the inlander as part of China and the outlander as barbarians but also regarded all nationalities as an integrated part of China and made it clear that it was fortunate for Chinese people to have all the border areas "included in Chinese territory to make it more expansive and much broader. How can there be the idea about the difference between China and foreign countries?"[110] This thought was also reflected in an official appointment and the management of state affairs. Emperor Qianlong had expressed it more thoroughly:

> Manchu and Han people are all my subjects, and they are all my right-hand men, so they all belong to an organic whole and are closely interrelated. As for the appointment of officials, they shall be chosen according to their talents and ability, and their personality and status will be stressed without showing any prejudice on Manchu and Han nationality. So whether the people of Manchu or Han nationality, they can all be appointed as officials in border areas ... In future, if anyone still insists on treating Manchu and Han nationality differently or holds discriminatory views for "Qi" (banner, the privileged) and the common people, they will be severely punished.[111]

During the reign of Emperor Yongzheng and Emperor Qianlong, a series of laws was made for the minorities in the northeast and Miao nationality in the southwest; meanwhile, necessary legal adjustments were made. Moreover, fruitful legislative adjustments were also made in the regions inhabited by the Hui, Uighur, and Tibetan nationalities.

It was not accidental that national legislation was much stressed and greater achievement was made in the Qing Dynasty than in the previous dynasties. First of all, the reason was that the regime was mainly ruled by the Manchu aristocrats.

---

[108]"Kang Xi Chao" (The Reign of Emperor Kangxi) in *Dong Hua Lu* (*The Record of Donghua*), Vol. 100.

[109]*Qing Shi Zong Shi Lu* (*The Record of Emperor Shizong of Qing Dynasty*), Vol. 8.

[110]"Yong Zheng Chao" (The Reign of Emperor Yongzheng) in *Dong Hua Lu* (*The Record of Donghua*), Vol. 15.

[111]*Qing Shi Zong Shi Lu* (*The Record of Emperor Shizong of Qing Dynasty*), Vol. 8.

The Manchu nationality, as an ethnic minority, had paid much attention to strengthening their alliance with other ethnic minorities through various measures even during the period when they were outside Shanhaiguan in order to increase their national strength, because only in this way could they unite the regions outside Shanhaiguan and conquer the central plains. Therefore, this statecraft was inherited from the central plains after they entered Shanhaiguan and was carried out throughout the entire Qing Dynasty. Secondly, because Qing Dynasty was the last feudal dynasty in China, they could learn from the rich experience which was accumulated in each dynasty. Generally speaking, all of the emperors of the Qing dynasty attached great importance to the ruling experience of the previous dynasties, so they knew very well the importance of maintaining good ethnic relations in consolidating national law. To some extent, their policy of adjusting to local conditions and custom was made on the experience of governing the country of the previous dynasties. Finally, because Qing Dynasty was also the period when Chinese legal culture began to integrate and to develop rapidly, the legal consciousness of Han nationality and its long-lasting legal cultural tradition had gradually achieved a dominate position. At the same time, the legal cultures of Jurchen, Mongolia and other ethnic minorities also developed rapidly; therefore, it was on the basis of the integration of the legal cultures of all nationalities of the Chinese nation that much more mature, systematic and stable national laws were made. So for us to scientifically understand the characteristics of the Chinese legal system, to know its role in consolidating the unified multiethnic country, and to strength the relationship between the central government and the areas inhabited by small minorities, it is helpful to have a detailed research on the national legislation of the Qing Dynasty.

11.2.3.1 Meng Gu Lv Li (*The Laws and Precedents of Mongolia*) and Li Fan Yuan Ze Li (*The Regulation for the Bureau of National Minority Affairs*)

In September of the 9th year of Shunzhi (1658), "Li Fan Yuan Da Bi Tiao Li" (The Regulation of the Bureau of National Minority Affairs for Capital Punishment) was created by "Yi Zheng Wang" (the national policy makers of Manchu nobility), doro beile (title of nobility), and other ministers according to imperial edicts, which was later used as the prototype for *Meng Gu Lv Li* (*The Laws and Precedents of Mongolia*) and *Li Fan Yuan Ze Li* (*The Regulation for the Bureau of National Minority Affairs*). In the 35th year of Kangxi (1658), with the consolidation of the unified nation, one hundred and twenty five laws and decrees on Mongolian affairs which were issued since Emperor Taizong were collected and included in Ze Li (Regulations) by "Li Fan Yuan" (The Bureau of National Minority Affairs), which had provided the legal basis not only for dealing with the Mongolian affairs, but also for adjusting and strengthening the vassal relationship between the feudal rulers of Mongolian and Qing Dynasty and for maintaining the close relationship between different social classes and for keeping the internal order of Mongolian society.

11.2 The Complete Implementation of the Legislative Principle of... 1117

During the reign of Emperor Qianlong, with the expansion of the territory and the strengthening of national power, national legislation also entered an active and flourishing stage, and *Meng Gu Lv Li* (*The Laws and Precedents of Mongolia*), *Li Fan Yuan Ze Li* (*The Regulation for the Bureau of National Minority Affairs*), and *Qin Ding Xi Zang Zhang Cheng* (*The Statutes of Tibet Made by Imperial Order*) are the best examples.

Meng Gu Lv Li (*The Laws and Precedents of Mongolia*), which was made by the Qing government in the 6th year of Qianlong (1741) and was applied in the Mongolian area, consisted of twelve volumes and two hundred and nine articles. Its main contents are as follows: "Guan Xian Men" (category of government office)—it mainly concerned the title of Mongolian princes and dukes, inheritance, official ranks, ritual system and awards, etc.; "Hu Kou Chai Yi Men" (category of household and corvee)—it mainly concerned the management of registered permanent residence, organizations at the grassroots level, corvee and tax, marriage and inheritance, etc.; "Chao Gong Men" (category of tributary)—it mainly concerned the celebration of Mongolian princes and dukes at the end of year, paying tribute to the court, etc.; "Hui Meng Xing Jun Men" (category of alliance and military marching)—it mainly concerned time and discipline of alliance with foreign countries, discipline of marching, management of military weapons, etc.; "Bian Jing Ka Shao Men" (category of border posts)—it mainly concerned foreign invasion, poaching and trade, buying and selling of military weapons, etc.; "Dao Zei Men" (category of robbing and theft)—it mainly concerned robbery, looting, theft, the relevant punishment for these crimes, etc.; "Ren Ming Men" (category of homicide)—it mainly concerned murder, wounding people, etc.; "Shou Gao Men" (category of lawsuits)—it mainly concerned restrictions on litigation and procedures, etc.; "Bu Wang Men" (category of arresting)—it mainly concerned arresting and harboring escaped prisoners, the capture of escaped thieves, exempting prisoners from the punishment of death, etc.; "Za Fan Men" (category of miscellaneous crimes)—it mainly concerned the illegal use of banned objects, and setting fire, digging up tombs and committing adultery, human trafficking, etc.; "La Ma Li Men" (category of lama)—it mainly concerned the clothes and ranks of lama, the management of lama temple, the punishment of crimes committed by lama, etc.; "Duan Yu Men" (category of lawsuit settling)—it mainly concerned the number of livestock that were fined, the penalty for the crimes committed by princes and dukes, the sentence of death penalty, redemption, etc. So it can be seen from the provisions mentioned above that *Meng Gu Lv Li* (*The Laws and Precedents of Mongolia*) was a collection of national laws and regulations, and it concerned many aspects, such as administrative, civil, criminal, and military legislation and judicial processes. *Meng Gu Lv Li* (*The Laws and Precedents of Mongolia*) was a summary of the gradual systematization of the national legislation of Qing Dynasty, and it had laid an important foundation for the making of *Li Fan Yuan Ze Li* (*The Regulation for the Bureau of National Minority Affairs*).

In the 16th year of Emperor Jiaqing (1817), *Li Fan Yuan Ze Li* (*The Regulation for the Bureau of National Minority Affairs*) was created by "Li Fan Yuan" (The Bureau of National Minority Affairs) based on *Meng Gu Lv Li* (*The Laws and*

Precedents of Mongolia), which was revised in the 54th year of Qianlong (1789), and it was issued in the 22nd year of Jiaqing (1817). *Li Fan Yuan Ze Li (The Regulation for the Bureau of National Minority Affairs)* consisted of seven hundred and thirteen articles and was further divided into sixty three categories, such as "Tong Li" (general rules) (part one and part two) and "Qi Fen" (specific rules for the Manchus). The law was very comprehensive and detailed, so to a certain extent it was an agglomeration of the national legislation of the Qing Dynasty since its founding. Apart from other regions, the law was also applicable to the Mongolians and Tibetan Mongolians in Tibetan and Qinghai regions.

So *Li Fan Yuan Ze Li (The Regulation for the Bureau of National Minority Affairs)* was an inheritance and development of *Meng Gu Lv Li (The Laws and Precedents of Mongolia)*, it was an important development of it. The Mongolian precedents and articles that were included in *Li Fan Yuan Ze Li (The Regulation for the Bureau of National Minority Affairs)* were revised successively according to the scope of their application and the changes in the society. Moreover "Juan Shu Men" (category of donation) was added, so the number of articles finally reached to nine hundred and sixty five.

In *Li Fan Yuan Ze Li (The Regulation for the Bureau of National Minority Affairs)*, the number of staff and the duties of "Li Fan Yuan" (The Bureau of National Minority Affairs) and its subordinate and affiliated offices were provided, and the administrative divisions and the official systems in the Mongolian areas were established. Moreover, many more systems were improved and established, including management of registered permanent residence; land, warehouse, tax, salary systems; the supply of food by the government; "Chao Ji" (paying respects to the central government and the emperor), transportation, banquet, squire, ritual systems; seal; wedding ceremony; "Ci Ji" (after the ministers die, orders are issued by the emperor to make the offerings); commendation; "You Xu" (giving financial help); alliance; military affairs; postal service; "Bian Jin" (prohibition of border trade); lama affairs; etc. Especially, evident progress was made in criminal law and the judiciary compared with *Meng Gu Lv Li (The Laws and Precedents of Mongolia)*. For example, with regard to the calculation of penalty, it was stipulated that "those who have 'Fu Zhi' (mourning apparel system) should be judged according to it," which reflected the influence of "Li Zhi" (the system of "Li") of the Han nationality. In the provision on "Dou Sha" (killing during fighting), it was stated that "if the person is injured seriously in the fight and died within fifty days, the killer will be punished by 'Jiao Jian Hou' (the punishment of suspending hanging)," which was apparently based on the "Bao Gu System" (the system whereby an offender is ordered by law to help the victim recover within a prescribed period, and the punishment for the crime committed by the offender is determined according to the cause of the injury and the degree of recovery) in *Da Qing Lv Li (The Laws and Precedents of Great Qing)*. As for the judiciary, when judging cases that involved the Mongolians, if there were no precedents in the articles of Mongolia, the judiciary was allowed to apply the criminal laws or regulations made by "Li Bu" (The Department of Personnel), "Bing Bu" (The Department of Defense), and "Xing Bu" (The Department of Punishment) by analogy. The cases involving Mongolians and the Manchu people could be handled according to the laws in the local places where the cases occurred. If Mongolians committed crimes inland, they should be punished according to Chinese criminal law, but if civilians committed crimes in Mongolia, they should be punished according to Mongolian law, which reflected the characteristics of making judgment according to national conditions and ruling according to popular custom. In addition, detailed provisions were made about the rights and obligations between the Mongolia aristocracy and the Qing government in order to strengthen political alliance.

In the 22nd year of Daoguang (1842), *Xi Zang Tong Li* (*The Tibetan General Regulation*), which consisted of twenty six articles, was added in the 61st and 62nd volume of *Li Fan Yuan Ze Li* (*The Regulation for the Bureau of National Minority Affairs*), so that its scope of application was expanded to the Tibetan and Qinghai regions. So the official system of Tibet was established in the form of law by *Xi Zang Tong Li* (*The Tibetan General Regulation*), at the same time, the rights of the ministers who were assigned to Tibet and who were in charge of the daily affairs of Xi'ning were stipulated in detail, and the military and financial system and the system of the management of lama affairs in Tibetan region were also established, which had surely strengthened the administrative and judicial right of the Qing government in Tibetan and Qinghai areas. Besides provisions for the management of the affairs in Mongolia and Tibet, *Li Fan Yuan Ze Li* (*The Regulation for the Bureau of National Minority Affairs*), as the most significant national legislation of the Qing Dynasty, also contained provisions for the management of Uygur and Kazak nationalities in Xinjiang, Sauron and Oroqen nationalities in Heilongjiang, "Tu Si" (system of appointing national minority hereditary headmen during the Yuan, Ming, and Qing dynasties), "Tu She" (subordinates to Tu Si), "Tou Ren" (tribal chief) in Sichuan, and so on.

11.2.3.2 *Qin Ding Xi Zang Zhang Cheng* (*The Statutes of Tibet Made by Means of an Imperial Order*)

In the Qing Dynasty, six statutes were mainly made for the national legislation in Tibet: *Zhuo Ding Xi Zang Shan Hou Zhang Cheng* (*The Statutes of Tibet for Rehabilitation by Resolution*), which consisted of thirteen articles, was issued in the 16th year of Qianlong (1751); *She Zhan Ding Jie Shi Yi* (*Affairs for the Establishment of Stations and Demarcation*), which consisted of nineteen articles, was issued in the 54th year of Qianlong (1789); *Zhuo Yi Zang Zhong Ge Shi Yi* (*Affairs for Tibet and China by Resolution*), which consisted of ten articles, was made in the 55th year of Qianlong (1790); *Zang Nei Shan Hou Zhang Cheng* (*The Statutes of Rehabilitation for Tibet*), which consisted of twenty nine articles, was made in the 58th year of Qianlong (1793); *Zhuo Ni Cai Jin Shang Shang Ji Bi Zhang Cheng* (*The Statutes for the Prohibition of Long-Existing Malpractice in Business*), which consisted of twenty eight articles, was made in the 24th year of Daoguang (1844); and *Xin Zhi Xi Zang Zheng Ce Da Gang* (*The Outline of New Policy of Ruling Tibet*), which consisted of nineteen articles, was made in the 33rd year of

Guangxu (1907). Because these six statutes were made under different historical background, each of them had its own focal points. For example, the statute which was issued in the 16th year of Qianlong was drafted after the rebellion in Tibet was suppressed, so it was stipulated that no Tibetan king would be appointed in order to avoid the expansion of the local power and that "Si Ga Long" (the four officials in charge of Tibetan affairs) was instituted to handle the local affairs. For important issues, "reports must be made to Dailai Lama by 'Si Ga Long' (the four officials in charge of Tibetan affairs) and discussions must be held with 'Zhu Zang Da Chen' (the minister sent to Tibet by the central government) according to instructions."[112] At the same time, the tradition of "Ga Long" (official in charge of Tibetan affairs) handling official affairs in his private houses was abolished. Especially, a series of management rights of 'Zhu Zang Da Chen' (the minister sent to Tibet by the central government) was provided in detail to strengthen the jurisdiction of the Qing government in the Tibetan area. For another example, the statute issued in the 54th year of Qianlong was made after the military aggression caused by the maltreatment of "Kuo Er Ka" (Gurkha) by Tibetan local government officials in business was defeated, so the duties and tax standard of the officials in charge of Tibetan foreign trade were stipulated, and the garrison system and judicial system of Tibet were also added in the statute. "The affairs which involves Han and Hui nationalities as well as other vassal states should all be reported to the central government by "Lang Zai" (Tibetan local official) and be dealt with by other officials."[113] This fully showed the great attention paid by the Qing government to the exercise of jurisdiction in Tibet.

Among the six statutes of Tibet, *Zang Nei Shan Hou Zhang Cheng* (*The Statutes of Rehabilitation for Tibet*), which was issued in the 58th year of Qianlong after defeating Tibet's aggression, led by "Kuo Er Ka" (Gurkha), was a relatively complete law that is appropriate for the governance of Tibet. The statute was drafted by general Fu Kangan, together with the Dailai Lama and Panchen, according to the order of Emperor Gaozong, and it was later approved by the emperor himself, so it was also called *Qin Ding Xi Zang Zhang Cheng* (*The Statutes of Tibet Made by Imperial Order*). The statute mainly concerned the establishment of the system of choosing the living Buddha of Dailai and Panchen by drawing lots from "Golden Urn", so the heir selection system of living Buddha was finally legalized. But the practice of "drawing lots from golden urn" must be supervised by "Zhu Zang Da Chen" (the minister sent to Tibet by the central government), which further affirmed the unification of the state and church.

No doubt, the power of "Zhu Zang Da Chen" (the minister sent to Tibet by the central government) was strengthened according to *Qin Ding Xi Zang Zhang Cheng* (*The Statutes of Tibet Made by Imperial Order*), so he was granted the absolute power of supervising the daily affairs of Tibet. According to article ten, "'Zhu Zang

---

[112] Zhang Qiqin, *Qing Dai Zang Shi Ji Yao* (*Collections of the Records of Tibetan Affairs in Qing Dynasty*), The Tibetan People's Publishing House, 1983, p. 179.

[113] Zhang Qiqin, *Qing Dai Zang Shi Ji Yao* (*Collections of the Records of Tibetan Affairs in Qing Dynasty*), The Tibetan People's Publishing House, 1983, p. 240.

Da Chen' (the minister sent to Tibet by the central government) has equal rights with Dailai Lama and Panchen in dealing with the political affairs together, and all officials, the staff below 'Ga Long' (official in charge of Tibetan affairs) and even living Buddha have subordinate relationship with him. 'Suo Ben Kan Bu' (Buddhists in charge of dietary of Panchen) is in charge of all the affairs of the Tashilumpo Monastery before Panchen Lama grows up. But for fair and square, all special affairs will be reported to 'Zhu Zang Da Chen' (the minister sent to Tibet by the central government) beforehand, so that he can deal with the affairs when he makes inspection tour to the area."[114] The foreign and the immigration administration affairs were also presided over by "Zhu Zang Da Chen" (the minister sent to Tibet by the central government). Besides, he had the right to directly submit memorials to the emperor. If Dalai Lama had any problems, or if he had requirements, he should make reports to the emperor via "Zhu Zang Da Chen" (the minister sent to Tibet by the central government).

"Zhu Zang Da Chen" (the minister sent to Tibet by the central government) also had the right to appoint government officials in Tibet. The senior officials of "Ga Long" (official in charge of Tibetan affairs) and "Dai Ben" (title of junior military officials) were appointed and approved by the emperor, while the junior and subordinate officials were appointed by "Zhu Zang Da Chen" (the minister sent to Tibet by the central government) and Dalai Lama. Moreover, full credentials were issued in Manchu, Chinese, and Tibetan languages. To prevent the aristocracy from monopolizing official positions, it was especially provided that if ordinary soldiers had special talents and achievements in battles, they could be promoted to "Ding Ben" (title of junior military officials) and "Dai Ben" (title of junior military officials). In addition, the descendants of aristocratic families could also be appointed as minor secretaries and as "Zong Ben" (local official) at the age of eighteen. At the same time, the local fiscal, tax, and monetary systems, as well as "Wu La Chai Yi" (including tax, corvee, land rent, etc.), were unified, and the local forces of Tibet were also set up. Meanwhile, the local jurisdiction of Tibet was strengthened, and the penalties for offenders, including the confiscation of property, were all ordered to be approved by "Zhu Zang Da Chen" (the minister sent to Tibet by the central government), thereby eliminating the malpractice of enforcing random punishments by the local "Ga Long" (official in charge of Tibetan affairs) under false charges.

So to a certain extent, *Qin Ding Xi Zang Zhang Cheng* (*The Statutes of Tibet Made by Imperial Order*) comprehensively strengthened the central government's control of Tibetan local affairs, which stabilized the social order in Tibet and bolstered the relationship between Tibet's local government and the Qing government.

Zang Nei Shan Hou Zhang Cheng Er Shi Jiu Tiao (*The Twenty-Nine Articles of the Statutes of Rehabilitation for Tibet*) was the basic regulation used by the Qing

---

[114] Ya Hanzhang, *Da Lai La Ma Zhuan* (*The Biography of Dalai Lama*), The People's Publishing House, 1984, p. 66.

government to manage the local affairs of Tibet in the mid and late Qing Dynasty. After its issuance, it was completely implemented, and it made a positive and far-reaching influence, just as what was recorded in *Hui Chou Zang Zhong Ying Ban Shi Yi Zhe* (*Memorial to the Emperor About the Tibetan and Chinese Affairs Which Should Be Handled*) by Ding Baozhen, "Zong Du" (viceroy) of Sichuan province, on the 7th of the intercalary March of the 5th year of Guangxu (1879):

> Many laws and regulations were made in Tibet by the forefathers, and garrison posts and soldiers are stationed in the mountain passes from Chamuduo, Zaya to Qianzang and Houzang, Jiangzi and Dingri to have a better control of the regions. All things are handled by "Zhu Zang Da Chen" (the minister sent to Tibet by the central government) who lives in Tibet. So as to the affairs in Tibet, if they are less important and easier to be handled, they will be dealt with by the local officials and then be reported level by level to the regent for settlement; if they are important and difficult to be handled, they will be reported to "Zhu Zang Da Chen" (the minister sent to Tibet by the central government) by the regent for settlement. Besides, the dismissal, appointment, promotion and demotion of officials will also be decided by "Zhu Zang Da Chen" (the minister sent to Tibet by the central government) who is greatly respected and whose rights are not to be infringed upon. Therefore, the detailed regulations were made on the ruling of Tibet. In the recent two hundred years, the local Tibetan officials are strictly controlled and they have shown great respect to those of Han nationality. The Tibetan affairs are handled jointly by both Tibetan and Han officials, so that all decrees and prohibitions are carried out effectively."[115]

By the unremitting efforts of Song Jun and He Ying, *Qin Ding Xi Zang Zhang Cheng* (*The Statutes of Tibet Made by Imperial Order*) was fully implemented, so that the Tibetan people were aided and protected and the social development in Tibet was legally safeguarded.

In December of the 22nd year of Jiaqing (1815), the Chinese version of *Li Fan Yuan Ze Li* (*The Regulation for the Bureau of National Minority Affairs*) was completed, in which *Xi Zang Tong Ze* (*The General Regulation of Tibet*), which consisted of twenty six articles (the first volume consisting of fifteen articles and the second volume consisting of eleven articles), was included. Among these articles, seventeen articles were adopted from *Zang Nei Shan Hou Zhang Cheng Er Shi Jiu Tiao* (*The Twenty-Nine Articles of the Statutes of Rehabilitation for Tibet*) and twelve articles from other parts of *Li Fan Yuan Ze Li* (*The Regulation for the Bureau of National Minority Affairs*). This was because the system of drawing lots from "Golden Urn" and the lama affairs in Tibet were collectively provided both in *Li Fan Yuan Ze Li* (*The Regulation for the Bureau of National Minority Affairs*) and *La Ma Shi Li* (*Precedents for Lama*).

---

[115] *Qing Dai Zang Shi Zou Du* (*The Memorials on Tibetan Affairs in Qing Dynasty*) (original text by Zhang Qiqin and edited additionally by Wu Fengpei), China Tibetology Publishing House, 1994, p. 495.

11.2.3.3 Hui Jiang Ze Li (Regulations of Huijiang)

In the 26th year of Qianlong (1761), "Lai Yuan Si" (the bureau in charge of the administrative affairs of remote areas) was specially established inside "Li Fan Yuan" (The Bureau of National Minority Affairs) for the management of "Huijiang" affairs. At the same time, some administrative rules in *Da Qing Lv Li* (*The Laws and Precedents of Great Qing*) and *Da Qing Hui Dian* (*The Collected Statutes of Great Qing*) were also applied in different degrees, but *Hui Jiang Ze Li* (*Regulations of Huijiang*) was still the most significant legislation. In the 16th year of Jiaqing (1811), *Li Fan Yuan Ze Li* (*The Regulation for the Bureau of National Minority Affairs*) was started to be compiled by "Li Fan Yuan" (The Bureau of National Minority Affairs); meanwhile, *Hui Jiang Ze Li* (*Regulations of Huijiang*) was also begun to be revised. In the 16th year of Daoguang (1826), after the rebellion of Zhang Ge'er was put down, *Hui Jiang Ze Li* (*Regulations of Huijiang*) was once again revised, and it was issued in the 23rd year of Daoguang (1873).

"Bo Ke Zhi Du" (the official system in Huijiang in Qing dyansty), which was confirmed in the legislation of the early period of Huijiang, was inherited in *Hui Jiang Ze Li* (*Regulations of Huijiang*) with some supplementary regulations added according to the development of the situation. For example, the establishment of the official system, the duties, the official ranks, the inheritance, the appointment and dismissal of officials in the Uighur region were all provided in detail. Moreover, the principle of establishing an official position according to local custom and making adjustments according to local conditions was carried out. The color of the clothes and the sitting cushions of the senior officials of Uighur, such as the king, doro beile (title of nobility), "Bei Zi" (title of nobility, subordinate of doro beile) and "Gong Zhe" (title of nobility) were regulated according to the public precedents of Mongolian princes in order to strengthen the alliance between Manchu and Han aristocratic groups. At the same time, the right of the Qing emperor to appoint local officials in the Uighur area was strictly maintained. In addition, special regulations were made for the various systems in the Uighur area, including "Nian Ban" (annual tribute to the Qing emperor by chiefs of small minorities), reward and punishment, weights and measures, currency, tax and corvee, trade, and garrison management. In order to show favor to the upper class of Uighur who had allegiance to Qing imperial court, all those who were awarded for martyrdom in Xinjiang were exempted from handing in grain and paying tax; moreover, the corrupt practices of excessively levying tax and avariciously extorting money and goods were "prohibited" in order to reduce the class contradiction in Huijiang. Specific regulations were also made for the management of religious affairs and for the jurisdiction of criminal cases. For example, "Akhund," who was in charge of religious affairs in Huijiang, was carefully chosen, and religious preachers at the time were prohibited from reading Koran for the purpose of instigating people; "A Qi Mu Bo Ke" (senior Muslim official in Xijiang) only had the right to punish criminals for misdemeanor, while the major cases must be reported any time to officials in charge, to be settled together with other senior officials, instead of being decided on their own.

As a piece of legislation especially applying to Uighurs, *Hui Jiang Ze Li* (*Regulations of Huijiang*) was of great significance to the governance of the Hui people and the stability of the frontier. In the 3rd year of Guangxu (1877), after Mohammad Yaqub Beg, who planned to split China, was suppressed by the military troops of the Qing government, the systems of "Jun" (shire) and "Xian" (county) were set up in order to strengthen the jurisdiction of the Qing government over Xinjiang. In the 9th year of Guangxu (1883), Xinjiang became a province of Qing dynasty, and the different levels of government agencies such as "Dao" (the administration district below the province), "Fu" (ancient administrative district between province and county), "Zhou" (subprefecture) and "Xian" (county) were instituted; moreover, "Bao Jia Zhi Du" (the household registration management system organized on the basis of households was established at grassroots level and the original "Bo Ke Zhi Du" (the official system in Huijiang in Qing dynasty) was abolished, so the government's control over Huijiang region was further strengthened.

11.2.3.4 The Mongolian Legislation in the Local Regions of Qinghai

In the 2nd year of Yongzheng (1724), after suppressing the insurgency in Qinghai, *Qing Hai Shan Hou Shi Yi Shi San Tiao* (*The Thirteen Articles of the Statutes of Rehabilitation for Qinghai*) and *Qing Hai Jin Yue Shi Er Shi* (*The Twelve Prohibitions in Qinghai*) were approved and issued by Emperor Shizong. The former mainly consisted of administrative legislation, while the latter essentially consisted of criminal and civil legislation, and it was stipulated that "if anyone is ungrateful and treacherous, he will be punished; land should be distributed according to law and forced plundering is forbidden; no robbing the officials or businessmen who pass by; no marrying one's stepmother or one's own brother's wife by force after one's father dies; no illegal gathering or discussing political affairs inside the lama temple of "Cha Han Nuo Men Han" (one of the most influential living Buddha reincarnation system in the Tibetan Buddhism)," etc. Some of the regulations were made in order to strengthen the central government's jurisdiction. For example, a time limit was stipulated for the local leaders to pay tribute to the imperial court, and the local leaders were not allowed to call themselves the heads of the alliance. As for Khalkha, Huite, and Turgut tribes, they were not allowed to forcibly occupy the Qinghai region and appropriate it to themselves; orders for the establishment of "Zuo Ling" (local administrator of the basic unit of organization in Eight Banners in the Qing Dynasty) should be faithfully followed; if the imperial envoy had brought with him the imperial edicts from the emperor, regardless of his official rank, he should be received by all the princes and dukes while down on their knees, and other meetings and receptions should be arranged in accordance with the rules for hosts and guests. In the 11th year of Yongzheng (1733), *Xi Ning Qing Hai Fan Yi Cheng Li* (*The Precedents for the Minorities in Xi'ning and Qinghai Areas*) (also called *Fan Li Tiao Kuan* (*Precedents and Provisions for Minorities*)) was issued, and the law mainly concerned the arresting of "Tao Ren" (the escapee); crimes such as rape, framing up others out of hatred, wrongfully accusing and injuring others, killing others while playing, manslaughter, robbery, starting fire out of hatred, repudiating one's wife, and killing of masters by family slaves; other affairs, such as judicial management; etc., and it was mainly applied to the minority groups in Ningxia, Qinghai, and Gansu provinces. It was expected that *Fan Li Tiao Kuan* (*Precedents and Provisions for Minorities*) could be applied for five years and then be replaced by *Da Qing Lv Li* (*The Laws and Precedents of Great Qing*), but because this regulation was in line with the custom of ethnic minorities in Qinghai and was quite effective and well received, its effective time of application was extended many times. In May of the 3rd year of Qianlong (1748), it was announced by "Xing Bu" (The Department of Punishment) that all civil and criminal cases in Qinghai would be dealt with in accordance with *Fan Li Tiao Kuan* (*Precedents and Provisions for Minorities*), and no more extension for its time of application was allowed. By the 14th year of Jiaqing (1809), *Fan Li Tiao Kuan* (*Precedents and Provisions for Minorities*) had been applied for more than seventy years, so "there is no need for it to be revised or modified any more."

Xi Ning Qing Hai Fan Yi Cheng Li (*The Precedents for the Minorities in Xi'ning and Qinghai Areas*), which was mainly made on the basis of *Meng Gu Lv Li* (*The Laws and Precedents of Mongolia*), consisted totally of sixty eight articles, and it was the most representative national legislation in the Qinghai area. For example, explanations were made in *Da Qing Lv Li Tong Kao* (*A Textual Research of the Laws and Precedents of Great Qing*) after the textual research on the provision that "if one's younger brother has cursed his elder brother's wife, he shall be punished one level severer than that for the common people according to the provision on assaulting people": "If the wife of the younger brother has beaten the elder brother's wife, she shall be punished for assaulting people and be punished one level severer than that for the common people, but no regulations were made on the act of for scolding the wife of the elder brother. Nevertheless, some changes were also made in some provisions. For example, according to *Meng Gu Lv Li* (*The Laws and Precedents of Mongolia*), if chiefs were absent from the ceremony for the alliance of princes and dukes or "Ta Bu Nang" (tabunang, or title of nobility for Mongolian princes) had not paid tribute, they would be imposed with a fine of ten horses, but according to *Fan Li Tiao Kuan* (*Precedents and Provisions for Minorities*), the fine of horses was changed to a fine of "pien niu" (offspring of a bull and a female yak) because there were many "pien niu" (offspring of a bull and a female yak) but few horses in the Qinghai region. Moreover, some provisions were especially made according to the concrete situations in Qinghai areas. For example, it was stipulated that "the chieftain who was in charge of ten households will not be established" and "'Tang Gu Te' (tanggute, or the local Tibetans) are forbidden to trade with Hui people in remote areas."

Although some military, civil, and litigation regulations were included in *Fan Li Tiao Kuan* (*Precedents and Provisions for Minorities*), it was basically a criminal penal code, in which contents concerning theft, killing or hurting others, and "Tao Ren" (the escapee) occupied a large portion. According to *Fan Li Tiao Kuan* (*Precedents and Provisions for Minorities*), if a Mongolian committed a crime, first he should be imposed with a fine of one to ten cows or five to one hundred horses, and if the person could not afford it, he would be punished by "Bian" (whipping) for a maximum of one hundred strokes. Moreover, pledges should be made by the leader of "Zuo Ling" (local administrator the basic unit of organization in Eight Banners in the Qing Dynasty) and "Guan Qi Zhang Jing" (junior official in remote areas), and they should have the wrongdoers reprimanded and punished by themselves. If the person intentionally concealed facts without paying the fine, he would be punished all at once for the other crimes. For some unsettled cases, the parties would also be required to "take oath." Therefore, *Fan Li Tiao Kuan* (*Precedents and Provisons for Minorities*) not only showed a kind of predatory nature, but also a strong color of making judgments by gods. Since its publication, *Xi Ning Qing Hai Fan Yi Cheng Li* (*The Precedents for the Minorities in Xi'ning and Qinghai* Areas) had always been used by the Qing government as the main law to govern the Qinghai areas, and it was even still effective until the early years of the Republic of China.

11.2.3.5 Legislation in the Local Regions of Miaojiang

In the Qing Dynasty, the Miaojiang region generally referred to the ethnic group of Miao nationality distributed in Yunnan, Guizhou, Sichuan, Guangdong, and Hunan provinces. The Miao people were also referred to as Miao, Yao, Zhuang, Yi, Li, and some other small minorities. Thus, the national legislation applicable to the Miaojiang region not only included the traditional customary law of Miao, Yao, Zhuang, Yi, and other ethnic minorities, or the so-called Miao Li (the regulations for the Miao people), whose legal effect was recognized by the Qing Dynasty; what is more important is that it also included thirty six articles concerning Miaojiang areas, which were compiled and included in *Da Qing Lv Li* (*The Laws and Precedents of Great Qing*). And its main contents are as follows: it is the duty of the local officials to strictly regulate the Miao people, so if the Miao people committed robbery because of the dereliction of duty of "Tu Si" (chieftain or hereditary headsmen), he would be convicted by the relevant departments; if more than one hundred people were involved, "Tu Si" (chieftain or hereditary headsmen) and the officials in "Fu" (ancient administrative district between province and county) and "Zhou" (subprefecture) would be dismissed; if people had known of the situation but failed to stop it, they would be dismissed and punished by wearing "Jia Hao" (cangue: a large wooden collar worn by petty criminals as a punishment) for one month; whatever is the position of the officials, as long as they had committed crimes severer than that punished by "Tu" (imprisonment) and "Liu" (exile), they would all be punished; if the crimes were lighter than that punished by "Zhang" (flogging with heavy sticks), they would be punished by the relevant departments. As for the Miao people who had committed crimes of robbery or murder or who had violated local orders, they would be severely punished. At the same time, the Miao people were strictly forbidden to conceal contraband, so "the violators will be convicted according to crime of illegal possession of prohibited weapons by civilians; if the officials in charge fail to report when he knows of the fact, they will be punished by

'Zhang' (flogging with heavy sticks) for one hundred strokes, and the local civil and military officials who neglected their duties of supervision will be punished according to the relevant regulations."[116] This rule was made to prevent the Miao people from rebelling by using weapons illegally. In order to prevent disputes between the Miao and the inland people, the inlanders were not allowed to enter the area of the Miao people, while the Miao people were also prohibited from entering the inland areas without permission; if the inlanders sold military weapons to the Miao people, they would be severely punished, together with the Miao people.[117]

Regulations were also made for the judicial system of the Miaojiang region. For example, a certain deadline was provided for the settlement of cases of the Miao people by the government. The case of theft should be settled within one year from the date of reporting to the government; the case of manslaughter and theft, within six months; the case of other miscellaneous crimes, within four months. If the case was not settled within the time limit, it should be reported to the superior government offices.[118] For the cases of murder and theft in the Miaojiang region in Guizhou province, the time limit was even shorter: three months for the case of ordinary manslaughter and two months for the case of murder with no delay. As for the disputes between the Miao people, they should be handled according to "Miao Li" (the regulations for the Miao people); if the crimes were serious, they would all be handled according to *Da Qing Lv Li* (*The Laws and Precedents of Great Qing*); if the Miao people committed the crime of rape, human trafficking, selling women or wives, expelling the son-in-law, etc. together with the inlander, they would be convicted in accordance with *Da Qing Lv Li* (*The Laws and Precedents of Great Qing*).

Qin Ding Li Bu Ze Li (*The Regulation of the Department of Personnel Made by Imperial Order*) also contained provisions about the relevant affairs of the local officials in the areas of small minorities, such as the inheritance, the awarding ceremony for the collateral branches of the families, the official duties, the demotion and punishment of officials, granting official positions to the descendants whose fathers had died in battles, as well as the detailed requirements for the granting of official titles and the filling the vacant official posts, etc. The abovementioned official legislation was applied in the regions where the hereditary system had not been changed or where no complete changes had been made, so its legal effect was even extended up to the end of the Qing Dynasty.

In addition, the legal forms in Miaojiang areas also included the various prohibitions promulgated during the reign of Emperor Kangxi, which mainly focused

---

[116]"Si Cang Ying Jin Jun Qi" (Illegal Possession of Military Weapons) in *Da Qing Lv Li* (*The Laws and Precedents of Great Qing*), Vol. 19.

[117]"Si Yue Mao Du Guan Jin" (Illegal Crossing or Passing through Strategic Passes and Ferries) in *Da Qing Lv Li* (*The Laws and Precedents of Great Qing*), Vol. 20.

[118]"Dao Zei Bu Xian" (Time Limit for Arresting Thieves) in *Da Qing Lv Li* (*The Laws and Precedents of Great Qing*), Vol. 35.

on criminal laws and regulations. For example, in the 42nd year of Kangxi (1703), "Xiao Yu Miao Ren Gao Shi" (Official Notice to Miao People) and "Jie Miao Tiao Yue" (Prohibitions for Miao People) were promulgated by Yu Yimo, "Ti Du" (military commander) of Hubei and Hunan province in order to warn Miao people against lawbreaking, and in the 50th year of Kangxi (1711), prohibitions were issued in Miaojiang by E Hai, "Zong Du" (viceroy) of Hubei and Hunan province. During the reign of Emperor Yongzheng, in order to promote a large-scale reform of "Gai Tu Gui Liu" (to have the hereditary system changed and be administered by government officials) in Miaojiang, forcible enforcement was needed by way of law. Hence, important laws which mainly involved the adjustment of administrative planning, the establishment of the responsibilities of local officials, the management of household registration, land, tax and military supply, the joint trial of serious crimes of robbery and murder committed by Miao people by both civil and military officials, and so on were issued in Miaojiang regions in Yunnan, Guizhou, Hubei, Hunan, Sichuan and Shaanxi province, and they had become a very important part of the legal form carried out in Miaojiang. So it can be said that the legislation made during the reign of Emperor Yongzheng for Miaojiang was the most important achievement of the Qing Dynasty. After Emperor Yongzheng, some more regulations were also made by emperors Qianlong, Jiaqing, and Daoguang.

The national legislation of Qing Dynasty, which was made by inheriting the national legislations of previous dynasties, was not only complete in system, but also normative in content and effective in function, so it was regarded as the climax of the national legislation in the Chinese feudal society. The principle of acting according to local conditions and showing respect to local custom was faithfully carried out in the legislation. Moreover, the laws were made for different ethnic groups in different regions and periods according to the local customs and culture, so they had their specific features, as was described in the saying that because "the border and inland regions are different, the legislation of the border regions should be different from that of the inland".[119] So "Miaojiang people should be governed according to 'Miao Li' (the regulations for Miao people),"[120] "the Tibetans should be governed according to Tibetan law, the people in Huijiang should be governed according to the law Hui nationality, and they should all be governed according to their own custom."[121]

Through national legislation, the centralization of authority and the administrative, military, and judicial jurisdiction were strengthened; meanwhile, central and local rights and obligations were included into the orbit of the legal system, so an unprecedented, consolidated, unified, and multiethnic country was finally established.

---

[119] *Da Qing Hui Dian* (*The Collected Statutes of Great Qing*), Vol. 5.

[120] *Qing Gao Zong Shi Lu* (*The Record of Qing Emperor Gaozong*), Vol. 52.

[121] *Da Qing Hui Dian* (*The Collected Statutes of Great Qing*), Vol. 53.

11.3 The Legalization of the Administrative System and the System of Official Management

The making and promulgation of "Hui Dian" (the collected statutes) and "Ze Li" (regulation) by each department had made the administrative legal system much more rigorous and its laws more substantial, which had provided a more solid legal basis for the national political system and the management of government officials.

11.3.1 The Change of Administrative System

Qing Dynasty was the last feudal dynasty that was mainly controlled by Manchu nobilities, so the extreme absolutism in Ming Dynasty was further strengthened. During the time outside Shanhaiguan, with the change of slavery society, it was no longer able to meet the demand of social development to manage the state affairs jointly with "Ba Qi" (the Eight Banners: banner, a division of Manchu nationality and the emperor's clan) according to the original national political system. Therefore, after ascending the throne, Huang Taiji started to fight for the centralization of the power of the monarchy. According to the old system, four "doro beile" (title of nobility) were ordered to be on duty by turns every month, but this system was abolished in the 3rd year of Tiancong (1629). What is more, the emperor discussed state affairs with the ministers and made decisions "by sitting in the court and facing the south"; consequently, a set of new administrative organizations that were different from the original system of "Ba Qi" (the Eight Banners: banner, a division of the Manchu nationality and the emperor's clan) was set up, namely, "Liu Bu" ((The Six Departments): "Li Bu" (The Department of Personnel), "Hu Bu" (The Department of Revenue), "Li Bu" (The Department of Rites), "Bing Bu" (The Department of Defense), "Xing Bu" (The Department of Punishment), and "Gong Bu" (The Department of Works)) and "San Yuan" ((the three institutions: "Nei Guo Shi Yuan" (in charge of the editing of document records), "Nei Mi Shu Yuan" (in charge of secretarial work), "Nei Hong Wen Yuan" (an advisory organ of the emperor)), by which the power of the leaders of "Ba Qi" (the Eight Banners: banner, a division of the Manchu nationality and the emperor's clan) was greatly weakened. The old systems of "Ba Jia Ping Fen" (equal distribution of property) and "Ba Jia Ping Yang" (equal sharing by the Eight Banners of the responsibility of supporting families) were regarded as bad customs and were criticized because they led to "San Fen Si Lu" (national disruption) and "Shi Yang Jiu Mu" (people being made confused and disoriented because of the lack of unified leadership). Under such conditions, even if it is possible to enter Shanhaiguan and to conquer the central plains with a powerful military for the time being, still it will not last too long. So the country will be in disorder and will be out of control in several years.[122] Then after ten years of reform, in the 10th year of Emperor Tiancong (1636), Huang Taiji changed the title of his reigning into Chongde (1636), changed the title of the country into great Qing, and officially proclaimed himself the emperor, so it had symbolized the gradual consolidation of the feudal autocratic system.

After entering Shanhaiguan, due to the demands of war, the army of "Ba Qi" (the Eight Banners: banner, a division of the Manchu nationality and the emperor's clan) was commanded uniformly by the emperor, who began to have the three armies directly under his control: namely, "Zheng Huang Qi" (the Plain Yellow Banner), "Xiang Huang Qi" (Xianghuang Banner or the Bordered Yellow Banner), and "Zheng Bai Qi" (the Plain White Banner). At the same time, the rest of the five "Qi" (banner, equivalent of a county), namely, "Xiang Bai Qi" (the Bordered White Banner), "Zheng Lan Qi" (the Plain Blue Banner), "Xiang Lan Qi" (the Bordered Blue Banner), "Zheng Hong Qi" (the Plain Red Banner), and "Xiang Hong Qi" (the Bordered Red Banner), were led by other princes respectively. "Where there are armies, there is power," the emperor had finally controlled the armies of "Ba Qi" (the Eight Banners: banner, a division of Manchu nationality and the emperor's clan), which was a great victory in centralizing the imperial power. In order to weaken the power of the governors of "Qi" (banner, equivalent of a county), the number of subordinate officials of the princes and dukes of "Ba Qi" (the Eight Banners: banner, a division of the Manchu nationality and the emperor's clan) was detailed in the 18th year of Kangxi (1679): in each "Qi" (banner, equivalent of a county), one "Du Tong" (ancient military officer or commander-in-chief) and two "Fu Du Tong" (ancient military officer or deputy commander-in-chief) were appointed to be in charge of "making regulations and rules and governing the people of 'Qi' (banner, equivalent of a county),"[123] and "Du Tong" (ancient military officer or commander-in-chief) was directly under the control of the emperor without any interference from the princes and dukes. Later, in order to strengthen its control, it was decided that the official business of "Qi" (banner, equivalent of a county) should be managed by the sons of the emperor. During the reign of Emperor Yongzheng, the emperor spared no effort to restrict the power of the princes and dukes in order to consolidate his status of ruling, so except for the necessary attendants, if the governors of "Qi" (banner, equivalent of a county) would like to dismiss or appoint the officials inside "Qi" (banner, equivalent of a county), they must first list their names and then ask for the emperor's permission. Besides, the governors had no right to punish the people illegally inside "Qi" (banner, equivalent of a county), so they had to report the issue to the relevant departments, so that the affiliation relationship of each "Qi" (banner, equivalent of a county) was abolished and the governors of "Qi" (banner, equivalent of a county) turned out to be mere figureheads. At the same time, it was forbidden for the princes of imperial clans to collude with the ministers outside the capital, and

---

[122]*Tian Cong Chao Chen Gong Zou Yi* (*The Memorials Submitted by the Ministers in the Reign of Emperor Tiancong*), Vol. 1.

[123]*Qian Long Hui Dian* (*The Collected Statutes of Emperor Qianlong*), Vol. 95.

they were forbidden to visit their private residences except for court meetings. Especially, during the reign of Emperor Yongzheng, the bodyguards of the five banners administered by the princes and dukes were withdrawn and were registered in army camps, which deprived the governors of their military power to fight against the imperial power.

After Emperor Qianlong's succession to the throne, he continued to carry out the plan of centralizing the imperial power and weakening the influence of the governors of "Qi" (banner, equivalent of a county). So "the subordinate personnel of banners ... those who live outside the capital and who come to the capital for business" were forbidden to visit the princes and dukes; "the violators will be punished by 'Zhang' (flogging with heavy sticks) for one hundred strokes."[124] Through the constant struggle of Emperor Kangxi, Yongzheng and Qianlong, the forces which endangered the imperial power were completely eliminated, which had to a certain extent guaranteed the power concentration of absolutism.

The emperor in the Qing Dynasty possessed supreme and absolute power, so all military and administrative affairs were decided by the emperor himself. In view of the lessons learned from the downfall of the Ming Dynasty, Emperor Kangxi said with a deep feeling: "I have seen that the emperors of Ming Dynasty had always stayed in the imperial palace and engaged themselves in luxurious life. Moreover, the emperor did not meet with his liegemen but often stayed with the eunuchs instead; they neither read any books nor attended to state affairs in the imperial court. So there was no communication between the high and the low."[125] For this reason, "every day he held discussions with his ministers to consult about the advantages and disadvantages of the state affairs"[126] "and handled each matter carefully."[127] During the time of war, he even read more than three to four hundred memorials every day. Emperor Gaozong once said publicly in a letter: "It has become a domestic discipline since the first emperor of Qing that the affairs like the appointment and removal of officials and the decisions-making are all handled by the emperor himself and never be entrusted to others. Even the closest liegemen and ministers had no right to conduct rewards or punishments, let alone to decide the life and death of others."[128] He also said: "I often read over the memorials carefully, make decisions prudently and write edicts by myself, so that it is impossible for the

---

[124]*Da Qing Lv Li Hui Zuan Da Cheng* (*The Collections of the Laws and Precedents of Great Qing*), Vol. 6.

[125]"Nan Shu Fang Ji Zhu" (The Records Kept by Nan Shu Fang) in *Nei Ge Dang An* (*The Files of the Cabinet*).

[126]"Kang Xi Chao" (The Reign of Emperor Kangxi) in *Dong Hua Lu* (*The Record of Donghua*), Vol. 46.

[127]"Kang Xi Chao" (The Reign of Emperor Kangxi) in *Dong Hua Lu* (*The Record of Donghua*), Vol. 100.

[128]"Qian Long Chao" (The Reign of Emperor Qianlong) in *Dong Hua Lu* (*The Record of Donghua*), Vol. 28.

cabinet ministers to interfere in the business."[129] In *Qing Gao Zong Shi Lu* (*The Record of Qing Emperor Gaozong*), written by Hong Liangji, there were the following testimonies: "One day, I saw that the emperor wrote very carefully with his brush-pen dipped in red ink and then he folded the paper into a small square piece. Sometimes he asked Zhang and E or sometimes he asked Sun and Zhu's opinions about whether someone was virtuous and whether his decisions about some affairs were right, and he usually asked them for more than ten times a day." Moreover, the emperor had the supreme jurisdiction, which meant that all the final sentences of "Qiu Shen" (Autumn Assizes) and "Chao Shen" (trials held in imperial court) should be made by the emperor himself. At the same time, the emperor presided over the final examination of "Ke Ju" (the imperial examination), and the exam papers of the top ten candidates would be submitted to the him to be checked according to relevant regulations.

The rulers of the Qing dynasty learned the lesson that the eunuchs' usurping of power led to the final destruction of the Ming Dynasty, so the eunuchs were forbidden to be involved in politics in the Qing dynasty. In the 10th year of Shunzhi (1653), an imperial edict was issued: "The eunuchs are only in charge of cleaning the imperial palaces and serving the emperors ... so they are not allowed to go out of the imperial palace without emperor's permission. Therefore, any minister who has associated with eunuchs will be punished by death penalty."[130] Another order was issued in the 12th year of Shunzhi (1655):

> The duties of the government offices and officials inside the palace are stipulated in detail, and relevant laws are made explicitly, so that if anyone has broken the law, or has tried to intervene in politics, or has taken bribes by taking the advantage of their rights, or has requested "Ya Men" (the government offices) inside or outside the capital to do things for him, or has colluded with the Manchu and Han officials, or has reported the outside affairs arbitrarily by acting beyond his authority, he will be published by "Ling Chi" (the punishment of dismemberment and the lingering death) immediately without being pardoned. After the "Tie Bang" (Iron Announcement) is issued, it should be abided by everyone in future. Please do as is instructed."[131]

After Emperor Shengzu's succession to the throne, the thirteen "Ya Men" (the government offices) of the eunuchs were immediately abolished; Emperor Shengzu pointed out: "it will lead to chaos to appoint eunuchs as officials."[132] During the reign of Emperor Qianlong, Zhang Ruoying, the inspector of Rehe, once punished the lawless eunuchs by "Zhang" (flogging with heavy sticks), for which he was promoted seven ranks and was appointed as "Tong Zhi" (the deputy magistrate of a

---

[129]"Qian Long Chao" (The Reign of Emperor Qianlong) in *Dong Hua Lu* (*The Record of Donghua*), Vol. 80.

[130]"Shi Zu Ji" (The Record of Emperor Shizu) in *Qing Shi Gao* (*The Draft of the History of Qing Dynasty*).

[131]*Qing Shi Zu Shi Lu* (*The Record of Emperor Shizu of Qing Dynasty*), Vol. 92.

[132]"Kang Xi Chao" (The Reign of Emperor Kangxi) in *Dong Hua Lu* (*The Record of Donghua*), Vol. 1.

prefecture).[133] In the 10th year of Jiaqing (1805), an order was issued by the emperor, where it was provided that "the eunuchs should be strictly supervised by the ministers of 'Nei Wu Fu' (Board of the Imperial Household), with their whereabouts investigated and recorded in palace history books, which is ordered thereof."[134] In the 21st year of Jiaqing (1816), another imperial order was issued, where "the princes and ministers are forbidden to let eunuchs to submitted memorials for them to avoid being suspected of collusion."[135] In late Qing Dynasty, although eunuch Li Lianying was arrogant and domineering, yet generally speaking, it seldom occurred in Qing Dynasty that the state affairs were interfered by eunuchs secretly.

In the Qing Dynasty, all activities, such as the establishment of national institutions and the change of official positions, were done to ensure the strengthening of the imperial power. The emperor himself commanded military affairs through the institutions, which were directly under his control. The appointment and the dismissal of local officials were also decided by him; the emperor's edict could be passed on to local places directly, and he could effectively command the operation of the national machinery. The memorials and petitions by local officials could also be directly presented to the emperor. During the Tang Dynasty, the power of "Feng Bo" (to return and rectify an edict issued by the emperor that was deemed inappropriate) of "Liu Ke Ji Shi Zhong" (the supervisor of the six offices) was removed and was transferred to "Du Cha Yuan" (The Court of Censors), and the system of "Cheng Xiang" (the prime minister) was completely abolished, so that all national affairs were controlled by the emperor himself. In order to firmly control the appointment of senior officials and to prevent the subordinate officials from colluding with or supporting each other, "Hui Tui Zhi" (the system of appointment by recommendation), which was being manipulated by one or two powerful ministers, was abolished during the reign of Emperor Kangxi.[136] As for local affairs, even trivial matters such as growing of mustard seeds and making of silk trifles must be reported to the emperor and the central government. As such, the centralization of authority reached an unprecedented height.

In the later years of Emperor Qianlong, he listed eight political reasons for "the perishing of Ming Dynasty": powerful vassal states, foreign aggression, powerful subordinate officials, "Wai Qi" (relatives of an emperor on the side of his mother or wife), evil women, eunuchs, treacherous court officials, and obsequious people; he also boasted of his successful ruling: "Today all these are eliminated,"[137]

---

[133] "Zhi Guan Zhi" (The Record of State Officials) (Part 5) in *Qing Shi Gao* (*The Draft of the History of Qing Dynasty*).

[134] "Ren Zong Ji" (The Record of Emperor Renzong) in *Qing Shi Gao* (*The Draft of the History of Qing Dynasty*).

[135] "Ren Zong Ji" (The Record of Emperor Renzong) in *Qing Shi Gao* (*The Draft of the History of Qing Dynasty*).

[136] "Xuan Ju Kao" (An Examination of Election) in *Qing Chao Wen Xian Tong Kao* (*A General Textual Research of the Documents of Qing Dynasty*), Vol. 55.

[137] *Qing Gao Zong Shi Lu* (*The Record of Qing Emperor Gaozong*), Vol. 1112.

During the reign of Daoguang, the famous litterateur Mei Zengliang wrote a vivid description of the highly centralized imperial power in the Qing Dynasty:

> The nation has been prosperous and peaceful for more than one hundred and seventy years, and China has been regarded as the leader and followed as an example by all the neighboring countries within 100,000 *li*; all junior and senior officials including "Du Fu" (the viceroys and procurators) of each province have shown their respect and reverence to the emperor; the officials are controlled, enslaved and supervised by "Fu Xi" (official documents); "Shu Li" (scribes) are manipulated like his own children; even trifles are handled by the junior officials perfectly and even every order is faithfully obeyed. So the rights and responsibilities are so centralized and the disciplines are so strict that it is incomparable by any dynasties in history."[138]

1. The concrete historical condition of Qing Dynasty and its policy of strengthening its authority had brought about some changes to the autocratic system, from which traces of the ups and downs of the power structure of the ruling group could be clearly seen.

In the early Qing Dynasty, the council of ministers of "Yi Zheng Wang" (the national policy makers of the Manchu nobility), which was composed of the Manchu nobility, was the decision-making organization below the emperor, so national and military affairs were often discussed by the council of ministers of "Yi Zheng Wang" (the national policy makers of the Manchu nobility), then proposals were reported to "Liu Bu" (The Six Departments), as was stated in reports: "all important military and political affairs which are beyond the authority of the cabinet ministers should be submitted to the council of the ministers of 'Yi Zheng Wang' (the national policy makers of Manchu nobility)."[139] But making comments on government affairs was totally in conflict with the emperor's plan of centralizing all authority to himself. At the same time, with the establishment of a unified political power in the Qing Dynasty, the emperor needed greater support from the landlords and bureaucrats of the Han nationality in order to gain control over the whole country. So consequently, the dictatorship of the Manchu nobilities could not meet the demand of social development any longer. Therefore, in the process of suppressing the three vassal states, Emperor Shengzu seized the opportunity to dismiss ministers like Leerjin, Chani, and other prince regents for reasons of corruption and delaying military plans and gradually deprived "Yi Zheng Wang" (the national policy makers of the Manchu nobility) of their rights to participate in state affairs. The suppression of the three vassal states and the reunification of Taiwan created a favorable condition for the strengthening of the central power. Since then, the council of ministers of "Yi Zheng Wang" (the national policy makers of the Manchu nobility) had become only a puppet of the emperor.

---

[138] Mei Zengliang (Qing Dynasty), "Shang Fang Shang Shu" (The Ministers of the Royal Logistics Department) in *Bo Gui Shan Fang Wen Ji* (*Collected Works of Bogui Mountain Villa*), Vol. 12.

[139] Zhao Lian (Qing Dynasty), "Han Zheng Da Chen" (The Ministers of Han Nationality) in *Xiao Ting Za Lu* (*The Miscellaneous Records of Xiaoting*), Vol, 4.

11.3 The Legalization of the Administrative System and the System of Official...

During the reign of Emperor Yongzheng, the power of the council of ministers of "Yi Zheng Wang" (the national policy makers of the Manchu nobility) was further weakened, and in the 56th year of Qianlong (1791), it was finally abolished because "it has nothing to do and exists merely in name."[140] So the practice of princes and governors of "Qi" (banner, equivalent of a county) of discussing politics had ended since then. So we can see that this process of evolution was also the process of the centralization of the power of the emperor and that the establishment of "Nei Ge" (The Cabinet) and "Nan Shu Fang" (office of literary courtiers of emperor) had provided the foundation for its implementation.

"Nei Ge" (The Cabinet) of the Qing Dynasty originated from "Nei San Yuan" (the interior three institutions), namely, "Nei Guo Shi Yuan" (in charge of the editing of document records), "Nei Mi Shu Yuan" (in charge of secretarial work), and "Nei Hong Wen Yuan" (an advisory organ of the emperor), which were set up in the 10th year of Emperor Tiancong (1636). In the 15th year of Shunzhi (1659) "Nei San Yuan" (the interior three institutions) was changed to "Nei Ge" (The Cabinet), imitating the system of the Ming Dynasty, and it was composed of four "Dian" (hall) and two "Ge" (cabinet), namely, "Zhong He Dian" (The Hall of Central Harmony), "Bao He Dian" (Hall of Perfect Harmony), "Wen Hua Dian" (Hall of Literary Harmony), "Wu Ying Dian" (Hall of Martial Valor), "Wen Yuan Ge" (Pavilion of the Imperial Library), and "Dong Ge" (East Pavilion). In the 13th year of Qianlong (1748), "Zhong He Dian" (The Hall of Central Harmony) was replaced by "Ti Ren Ge" (Pavilion of Practising Benevolence), so a system of three "Dian" (hall) and three "Ge" (cabinet) was established. In order to prevent "Ge" (cabinet) from possessing excessively powerful rights, Emperor Shizu intentionally reduced the ranks of "Da Xue Shi" (grand secretary) from "Er Pin" (the second rank) to "Wu Pin" (the fifth rank). After the death of Emperor Shizu, according to the testamentary edict of "following the ancestry system and recovering the original constitution," "Nei Ge" (The Cabinet) was abolished and the "Nei San Yuan" (the interior three institutions) was restored. In August of the 9th year of Kangxi (1670), "Nei San Yuan" (the interior three institutions) was again changed to "Nei Ge" (The Cabinet), "Da Xue Shi" (grand secretary) was granted the title of "Shang Shu" (the minister), and "Xue Shi" (secretary) was granted the title of "Shi Lang" (vice minister). The constant change of "Nei San Yuan" (the interior three institutions) and "Nei Ge" (The Cabinet) had reflected the struggle between the conservative forces who supported the maintenance of ancestry system and the new forces who tended to inherit the system of Ming Dynasty in the internal ruling group. Because "Nei Ge" (The Cabinet) was favorable to the centralization of authority, it became an established system during the reign of Emperor Kangxi. And it was not abolished until the reform of the bureaucratic system, which was carried out at the end of the Qing Dynasty.

---

[140]Liang Zhangju (Qing Dynasty), "Xun Yu" (Allocution) in *Shu Yuan Ji Lue* (*The Historical Records of Shu Yuan*), Vol. 1.

"Nei Ge" (The Cabinet) was given great power from the period of early Qing Dynasty to the middle of the reign of Emperor Kangxi. On the one hand, the old system of the Ming Dynasty was adapted, and "'Nei Ge' (The Cabinet) had the right to handle affairs like 'Zhang Shu' (the documents sent by officials the emperor) and 'Piao Ni' (drafting replies to the memorials submitted by officials for emperor's reference)"; on the other hand, people who served as "Nei Ge Da Xue Shi" (cabinet grand secretary), like Suoetu, Mingzhu, etc., randomly handled the memorials submitted to the emperor and formed a mighty and powerful group. But after Mingzhu was removed from the post of "Da Xue Shi" (grand secretary), the power of the cabinet was gradually reduced and the system of the early Ming Dynasty was restored, and it began performing its responsibilities under the strict control of the emperor.

"Nei Ge" (The Cabinet) was in charge of "managing the daily affairs and setting examples to the other officials."[141] It was also in charge of drafting and reading over the imperial edicts and submitting the memorials to the emperor. The number of "Nei Ge Da Xue Shi" (cabinet grand secretary) was not fixed. During the reign of Emperor Kangxi, four "Da Xue Shi" (grand secretary) were chosen from Manchu and Han nationalities, but during the reign of Emperor Yongzheng, six "Da Xue Shi" (grand secretary) were appointed. During the reign of Emperor Qianlong, assistant "Da Xue Shi" (grand secretary) were added, so "sometimes one and sometimes two 'Da Xue Shi' (grand secretary) were appointed, and it all depended on the situation."[142] During the reign of Emperor Yongzheng, "Nei Ge Da Xue Shi" (cabinet grand secretary) was granted "Zheng Yi Pin" (the plain first rank), whose rank was above all other officials, so "except the princes, only 'Da Xue Shi' (grand secretary) has the right to be a member of 'Jun Ji Chu' (The Grand Council), which is incomparable even by 'San Gong' (the three councilors) in Tang and Yuan dynasties."[143] Other official positions below "Da Xue Shi" (grand secretary) were also set up, such as "Nei Ge Xue Shi" (cabinet secretary), "Shi Du Xue Shi" (advisory secretary on reading), "Shi Du" (reading attendant), "Dian Ji" (in charge of ancient books and records), "Zhong Shu" (the prime minister), "Zhong Shu She Ren" (the official in charge of drafting imperial edicts in "Zhong Shu Sheng"), and so on. Since "Da Xue Shi" (grand secretary) was mainly in charge of formulating edicts, he must work and live in the cabinet every day. In the 9th year of Kangxi (1670), Li Wei was appointed as "Da Xue Shi" (grand secretary) of "Bao He Dian" (Hall of Perfect Harmony), so "he was responsible for drafting all of the secret imperial edicts and he often left at midnight or stayed in the cabinet all night."[144] Besides, only with the emperor's

---

[141] *Qian Long Hui Dian* (*The Collected Statutes of Emperor Qianlong*), Vol. 2.

[142] Liang Zhangju (Qing Dynasty), "Da Xue Shi Yuan Qi" (The Origin of the Grand Secretary) in *Lang Ji Cong Tan* (*Miscellaneous Notes Written by Liang Zhangju*), Vol. 4.

[143] "Da Xue Shi Nian Biao Xu" (The Preface of the Chronology of the Grand Secretary) in *Qing Shi Gao* (*The Draft of the History of Qing Dynasty*).

[144] "Li Wei Zhuan" (The Biography of Li Wei) in *Qing Shi Gao* (*The Draft of the History of Qing Dynasty*).

special permission could the cabinet ministers be late or absent. In the 14th year of Qianlong (1688), "in consideration of the old age of 'Da Xue Shi' (grand secretary) Zhang Tingyu, he is allowed to go to the cabinet only once every five days as a consultant."[145] "Da Xue Shi" (grand secretary) could be demoted or dismissed if they commit mistakes in formulating imperial edicts. For example, in the 27th year of Kangxi (1688), "Da Xue Shi" (grand secretary) Ming Zhu was dismissed after he was impeached by "Yu Shi" (the censor) Guo Li for leaking secrets and selling official ranks and titles.

Although "Da Xue Shi" (grand secretary) enjoyed "very high reputation and status" in the Qing Dynasty, since the emperor himself often read over and checked the memorials and made decisions by himself, "the cabinet ministers are not allowed to interfere in the decision-making. If the emperor has any questions, he will call in 'Da Xue Shi' (grand secretary), hold face-to-face discussions with them and order them to draw up the documents, and they are not allowed to leave without the permission of the emperor."[146] Gaozong once pointed out that "the official title of 'Zai Xiang' (the prime minister) has been abolished since the reign of Emperor Hongwu in Ming Dynasty, then 'Da Xue Shi' (grand secretary) is established. The system of Ming Dynasty is followed in Qing dynasty, so the title is retained, but 'Da Xue Shi' (grand secretary) in our time is only responsible for formulating imperial edicts, and he is totally different from 'Zai Xiang' (the prime minister) in the former dynasties."[147] However, the establishment of "Nei Ge Da Xue Shi" (cabinet grand secretary) was necessary not only in adjusting the relationship of the internal power structure of the ruling cliques, but also in acting as a measure to weaken the power of some of the powerful officials, so it was not abolished until the end of Qing Dynasty.

In the 16th year of Emperor Kangxi (1677), out of the need of centralizing state power, the officials of "Han Lin Yuan" (The Hanlin Academy) were selected to serve in "Nan Shu Fang" (office of literary courtiers of emperor) in "Qian Qing Gong" (Palace of Heavenly Purity), which was called "Nan Shu Fang Xing Zou" (attendants of the office of literary courtiers of the emperor). And there was no fixed number for its members, so sometimes there were "as many as eight or nine people."[148] Apart from secretarial work, "Nan Shu Fang" (office of literary courtiers of emperor) was also responsible for drafting imperial edicts and issuing administrative orders according to the emperor's instruction, which had made it a central institution of confidential secretary, so what was described by emperor Shengzu was not true: "I just want some literate officials to accompany me so that they could teach

---

[145]"Gao Zong Ji" (The Record of Emperor Gaozong) in *Qing Shi Gao* (*The Draft of the History of Qing Dynasty*).
[146]Ye Fengmao (Qing Dynasty), *Nei Ge Xiao Zhi* (*A Simple Record of the Cabinet*).
[147]*Qing Gao Zong Shi Lu* (*The Record of Qing Emperor Gaozong*), Vol. 1128.
[148]Wu Zhenxie (Qing Dynasty), *Yang Ji Zhai Cong Lu* (*The Collected Notes of Yang Ji Zhai*), Vol. 4.

me history and Confucian classics"[149] "without intervening in other state affairs."[150] In fact, because the members of "Nan Shu Fang" (office of literary courtiers of the emperor) were "close to the emperor" and were in charge of "drafting secret edicts and acting as counselors of the emperor," it was possible for some of the officials like Xu Qianxue and Gao Shiqi to gradually obtain great power and claim to be an equal of the Manchu big wigs. Someone once said that "except those senior officials, the nobilities and those who are trusted by the emperor, it is impossible for the common people to enter 'Nan Shu Fang' (office of literary courtiers of emperor)."[151] Emperor Shengzu had consciously chosen "Shi Da Fu" (literati and officials) such as Zhang Ying, Wang Hongxu, etc. from the Han nationality and nominated them to work for him in "Nan Shu Fang" (office of literary courtiers of the emperor) as a measure to win over the people's support. But since the founding of "Jun Ji Chu" (The Grand Council), "Nan Shu Fang" (office of literary courtiers of emperor) had no longer handled confidential affairs, and it had become responsible only for tasks like calligraphy, painting, etc.

After Emperor Shizong's succession to the throne, he further weakened the power of royal princes because it was in conflict with the imperial power. In addition, he took back the princes' power of commanding the armies of the five banners. At the same time, "Jun Ji Chu" (The Grand Council) was set up, which not only was one of the most important measures for the centralization of the emperor's authority but also a prominent symbol of the central system, which was different from that of the previous dynasties.

During the reign of Emperor Yongzheng, military forces were used to attack the Jungar region in the northwest. "Because 'Nei Ge' (The Cabinet) is located outside 'Tai He Dian' (The Hall of Supreme Harmony) and there are too many people, it is easy to leak out the secret, a military office was set up inside Long Zong Gate."[152] Therefore, reliable executive secretariats were selected from "Nei Ge" (The Cabinet) to deal with confidential issues. In June of the 7th year of Emperor Yongzheng (1729), he formally appointed prince Yi Yunxiang, Jiang Tingxi, and Zhang Tingyu, who were then "Da Xue Shi" (grand secretary), to be in charge of confidential affairs. In the 8th year of Yongzheng (1730), "Jun Ji Zhang Jing" (or "Xiao Jun Ji," the minor brand council) was set up, and in the 10th year of Yongzheng (1732), "Jun Ji Fang" (the office of military affairs) was moved outside of "Qian Qing Gong" (Palace of Heavenly Purity), with its name officially changed to "Jun Ji Chu" (The Grand Council); meanwhile, the seal of "Jun Ji Chu" (The Grand Council) was made and granted. "Jun Ji Chu" (The Grand Council) was set up on the basis of "Nan Shu Fang" (office of literary courtiers of emperor). Because there was neither an office

---

[149]"Bian Xiu Gong Feng Nei Ting" (Editorial Staff and Operor Actors in the Inner Court) in "Jue Zhi Lei" (Personal Profile) in *Qing Bai Lei Chao (A Collection of Anecdotes in Qing Dynasty)*.

[150]*Ka Xi Qi Ju Zhu (The Record of Emperor Kangxi's Daily Life)*.

[151]Xiao Lai (Qing Dynasty), *Yong Xian Lu (The Record of Yong Xian)*, Vol. 1.

[152]Liang Zhangju (Qing Dynasty), "Za Ji" (Miscellaneous Notes) in *Shu Yuan Ji Lue (The Historical Records of Shu Yuan)*, Vol. 27.

11.3 The Legalization of the Administrative System and the System of Official... 1139

nor special officials and it was not considered a formal institution originally, in *Da Qing Hui Dian (The Collected Statutes of Great Qing)*, it was merely called "the grand council for dealing with affairs." But the establishment of "Jun Ji Chu" (The Grand Council) made it more convenient for the emperor himself to handle military and administrative affairs, so it was not abolished even after the military action of the northwest ended; on the contrary, it became a standing institution. Its special position in the national system of the Qing Dynasty and its power showed that "Jun Ji Chu" (The Grand Council) was the product of a highly developed imperial power.

At the beginning, "Jun Ji Chu" (The Grand Council) was established only to deal with military affairs and to assist the emperor in making decisions when needed; however, the power of "Jun Ji Chu" (The Grand Council) was later expanded to deal with important state and military affairs, such as appointing officials, submitting memorials to the emperor, and drafting imperial edicts according to imperial orders, as was described in records: "it was in charge of handling all military and political affairs, managing confidential work,"[153] "issuing imperial edicts, dealing with the daily routines and the state secrets."[154] "Jun Ji Da Chen" (the grand councilor) "was on duty in 'Jun Ji Chu' (The Grand Council) everyday to wait to be summoned by the emperor"[155]; sometimes they also participated in the trial of major cases.

The establishment of "Jun Ji Chu" (The Grand Council) had deprived "Nei Ge" (The Cabinet) of its function of drafting and checking important governmental documents; at the same time, it had the right to change the "Piao Ni" (drafting replies to the memorials submitted by officials for the emperor's reference) of "Nei Ge" (The Cabinet). The imperial edicts drafted by "Jun Ji Chu" (The Grand Council) were "first passed on to 'Nei Ge' (The Cabinet), then to the various departments,"[156] which was called "Ming Fa"; if the edicts were directly sent to "Du Fu" (the viceroys and procurators) by couriers without being sent to "Nei Ge" (The Cabinet), it was called "Ting Ji," which concerned confidential events. Depending on the degree of emergency, "Ting Ji" traveled in groups of 300, 400, 500, 600, and 800 *li* each day. The memorials of "Du Fu" (the viceroys and procurators) were also sent directly to the emperor through "Jun Ji Chu" (The Grand Council). Thus, the establishment of the "Ting Ji" system further strengthened the connection between the local government and the court, which made it possible for the emperors' edicts to be quickly and directly delivered to local places. Consequently, "Nei Ge Da Xue Shi" (cabinet grand secretary) just became "Ban Shi Chen Xiang" (an incompetent official), who had nothing to do but deal with some daily routines. Especially, the commissioner of

---

[153]"Zhi Guan Zhi" (The Record of State Officials) (Part 1) in *Qing Shi Gao (The Draft of the History of Qing Dynasty)*.

[154]"Zhi Guan Kao" (An Examination of State Officials) (Part 4) in *Qing Chao Xu Wen Xian Tong Kao (A Sequel of the General Textual Research of the Documents of Qing Dynasty)*, Vol. 118.

[155]"Zhi Guan Kao" (An Examination of State Officials) (Part 4) in *Qing Chao Xu Wen Xian Tong Kao (A Sequel of the General Textual Research of the Documents of Qing Dynasty)*, Vol. 118.

[156]"Jun Ji Chu" (The Grand Council) in "Jue Zhi Lei" (Personal Profile) in *Qing Bai Lei Chao (A Collection of Anecdotes in Qing Dynasty)*.

"Tong Zheng Shi Si" (The Transmission Office), who was in charge of correcting memorials and imperial edicts, existed in name only.

Even though the status of "Jun Ji Chu" (The Grand Council) was prominent, they had no right to make decisions; as it was said, "they only have the right to deliver and transcribe the imperial orders without adding or deleting any words."[157] Emperor Renzong said in an imperial edict: "'Jun Ji Da Chen' (the grand councilor) just drafts imperial edicts by following the emperors' orders, so they have not fulfilled their responsibilities of giving advice . . . besides, the emperors in our Dynasty have made decisions arbitrarily . . . never allowing the officials to interfere in the national affairs . . . as for the appointment and management of officials, as long as the orders are issued, they will be followed without any changes, so the emperor's authority has never been challenged or passed into others' hands."[158]

"Jun Ji Da Chen" (the grand councilor) were carefully chosen by the emperor from princes, "Nei Ge Da Xue Shi" (cabinet grand secretary), "Shang Shu" (the minister) of "Liu Bu" (The Six Departments), and "Shi Lang" (vice minister), but most of them were Manchu nobility. The chief minister in "Jun Ji Chu" (The Grand Council) was called "Ling Ban" (the leader or the captain), and the rest were respectively ranked according to their seniority, including "Jun Ji Da Chen" (the grand councilor), "Jun Ji Da Chen Shang Xing Zou" (high-rank ministers of the grand councilor), "Jun Ji Da Chen Shang Xue Xi Xing Zou" (low-rank ministers of the grand councilor), etc. The number of ministers in "Jun Ji Chu" (The Grand Council) was not fixed, and there were at most six or seven of them. Below "Jun Ji Chu" (The Grand Council), "Jun Ji Zhang Jing" (or "Xiao Jun Ji," the minor grand council) was set up, and it consisted of two groups: one from the Manchu nationality and the other from the Han nationality, each consisting of eight members who were responsible for specific tasks of copying the emperor's edicts, recording files and documents, checking memorials, and so on. In order to prevent the leaking of confidential information, clerical staff were forbidden to be employed in "Jun Ji Chu" (The Grand Council), so even the staff in charge of miscellaneous affairs such as cleaning "were selected from the children of 'Nei Wu Fu' (Board of the Imperial Household)," and "they would be replaced when they were twenty years old."[159]

In "Jun Ji Chu" (The Grand Council), the confidential nature of their work was emphasized, and in the 12th year of Emperor Qianlong (1747), it was stated in the imperial edict that "'Jun Ji Chu' (The Grand Council) is a secret place, so the submitted memorials should be kept secret."[160] In the 15th year of Emperor Jiaqing (1800), the emperor also pointed out in the imperial edict: "'Jun Ji Chu' (The Grand

---

[157]Zhao Yi (Qing Dynasty), "Jun Ji Chu" (The Grand Council) in *Yan Pu Za Ji* (*The Miscellanies of Yan Pu*).

[158]Liang Zhangju (Qing Dynasty), "Xun Yu" (Allocution) in *Shu Yuan Ji Lue* (*The Historical Records of Shu Yuan*), Vol. 1.

[159]"Jue Zhi Lei" (Personal Profile) in "Qing Bai Lei Chao"(A Collection of Anecdotes in Qing Dynasty) in *Jun Ji Chu* (*The Grand Council*).

[160]Liang Zhangju (Qing Dynasty), "Xun Yu" (Allocution) in *Shu Yuan Ji Lue* (*The Historical Records of Shu Yuan*), Vol. 1.

11.3 The Legalization of the Administrative System and the System of Official...

Council) is a secret place where the important affairs are dealt with and confidential edicts are drafted, so its primary mission is to keep secret. 'Jun Ji Da Chen' (the grand councilor) is in charge of passing on the emperors' orders and ordering 'Jun Ji Zhang Jing' (or 'Xiao Jun Ji', the minor grand council) to copy them down, so no mistakes are to be made."[161] So the subordinate civil and military officials below the prince were not allowed to get close to "Jun Ji Chu" (The Grand Council); otherwise, they would be severely punished without pardon. In addition, every day one "Yu Shi" (the censor) was sent to supervise "Jun Ji Chu" (The Grand Council); if some mistakes were discovered, they would be reported to the emperor immediately, and those involved would be severely punished. Zhao Yi once had the following report:

> It is forbidden for "Jun Ji Da Chen" (the grand councilor) to communicate with "Yu Shi" (the censor) outside, unless some special urgent affairs have happened. Even the officials in the capital are not allowed to meet "Jun Ji Da Chen" (the grand councilor) frequently. The first time when I was there, I saw the senior official Ma Shaojing and Zhao Jing once knelt in front of the steps of "Jun Ji Chu" (The Grand Council), but they were stopped by the officials standing before the steps. They said: "This is the confidential place where it is not proper for your majesty to come in". Some of them wanted to argue with the court officials in "Jun Ji Chu" (The Grand Council), but unfortunately, they were denied and rebuked, so they were too scared to say anything else.[162]

It was featured by quick decision making and high efficiency because the affairs in "Jun Ji Chu" (The Grand Council) were supposed to be handled by "Jun Ji Da Chen" (the grand councilor) and "Jun Ji Zhang Jing" (or "Xiao Jun Ji", the minor grand council) and the intermediate links were eliminated. "There are at most fifty or sixty memorials every day. Since December 25th is the last day of the year, all imperial edicts, including the edicts of the following day and 'Ting Ji' (the edicts directly sent to the viceroys and procurators by the couriers without going through the Cabinet) should be completed by this day with no delay."[163] However, in late Qing Dynasty, because "Jun Ji Chu" (The Grand Council) was responsible for appointing officials, it unexpectedly became a place that was notorious for selling official titles.

The Qing Dynasty followed the central administrative agencies of the Ming Dynasty, so "Liu Bu" (The Six Departments), namely, "Li Bu" (The Department of Personnel), "Hu Bu" (The Department of Revenue), "Li Bu" (The Department of Rites), "Bing Bu" (The Department of Defense), "Xing Bu" (The Department of Punishment), and "Gong Bu" (The Department of Works), was established. In early Qing Dynasty, the power of the prince was great, and ministerial affairs were often presided over by the prince and doro beile (title of nobility), but this was gradually

---

[161] Liang Zhangju (Qing Dynasty), "Gui Zhi" (The Regulations and Systems) in *Shu Yuan Ji Lue* (*The Historical Records of Shu Yuan*), Vol. 14.

[162] Zhao Yi (Qing Dynasty), "Jun Ji Bu Yu Wai Chen Jiao Jie" (No Association between the Grand Council and the other Officials) in *Yan Pu Za Ji* (*The Miscellanies of Yan Pu*), Vol. 1.

[163] Deng Zhijie (Qing Dynasty), "Tan Jun Ji Chu" (Talking about the Grand Council), carried in *Qing Shi Za Kao* (*A Miscellaneous Textual Research of the History in Qing Dynasty*) by Wang Zhonghan, The People's Publishing House, 1957.

changed during the reign of Emperor Kangxi. "Liu Bu" (The Six Departments) was headed by two "Shang Shu" (ministers), chosen from Manchu and Han nationalities, and four "Shi Lang" (vice ministers), with two of them chosen from Manchu and Han nationalities. Below them, subordinate officials like "Lang Zhong" (head of a subministry department), "Yuan Wai Lang" (deputy head of a subministry department), etc. were appointed. The heads of "Liu Bu" (The Six Departments) were responsible to the emperor, and they only had the right to send memorials to the emperor or to wait for necessary imperial edicts, but they had no right to issue orders to the local government. If there were disputes between "Shang Shu" (minister) and "Shi Lang" (vice minister), both of them could submit memorials to the emperor separately and wait for the emperor's adjudication. "Liu Bu" (The Six Departments) was set up to avoid the malpractice that "all power was centralized in one department", but the measures mentioned above had made the power of "Liu Bu" (The Six Departments) more fragmented and the power of different departments more unbalanced. The heads of "Liu Bu" (The Six Departments) were chosen from Manchu and Han nationalities, but the real power was controlled by Manchu officials. It was not until the late Qing Dynasty that the emperor decided to give the officials of the Han nationality in "Liu Bu" (The Six Departments) some real power in order to get the support of the high-ranking bureaucrats of the Han nationality as the nation was threatened by a growing crisis.

Even though "Li Bu" (The Department of Personnel) was put at the primary position in "Liu Bu" (The Six Departments), it only was in charge of going through the personnel formalities like keeping records and registration, because the power of appointing and dismissing officials was controlled by the emperor and "Jun Ji Chu" (The Grand Council). The subsidiary organs of "Hu Bu" (The Department of Revenue) were miscellaneous, and it was subdivided into fourteen "Qing Li Si" (office) according to different regions, which were not only responsible for the affairs in their districts, but also responsible for the affairs of other provinces or other miscellaneous affairs, except "Qing Li Si" (office) in Shanxi province, which was just responsible for the affairs of money and grain in the native place. For example, "Qing Li Si" (office) in Zhejiang province was also responsible for the statistics of the national population and grain collection, "Qing Li Si" (office) in Yunnan province was responsible for the national grain tribute system, and "Qing Li Si" (office) in Guizhou province was responsible for the national tariffs, which had not only caused great disorder but also led to the discrepancy between the name and the system. "Hu Bu" (The Department of Revenue) was also responsible for setting up offices for donation and raising money by selling official ranks and titles. "Bing Bu" (The Department of Defense) was the supreme military authority, but since the establishment of "Jun Ji Chu" (The Grand Council), "it was only in charge of the supervision, registration as well as examination of soldiers."[164] Division of work in "Xing Bu" (The Department of Punishment) was also very disorganized, and among

---

[164]Liang Zhangju (Qing Dynasty), "Za Ji" (Miscellaneous Notes) in *Shu Yuan Ji Lue (The Historical Records of Shu Yuan)*, Vol. 27.

the seventeen "Qing Li Si" (office), some of them were assigned work in two provinces. For example, "Qing Li Si" (office) of "Feng Tian" (now Shenyang) was in charge of the punishment of criminals in Jilin and Heilongjiang provinces. Moreover, some affairs were handled by two "Qing Li Si" (office). For example, penalty reduction was designated to "Qing Li Si" (office) of Jiangsu and "Jian Deng Chu" (the bureau of penalty reduction). "Du Bu Qing Li Si" (Office of Arresting) was also especially set up in order to manage the affairs of "Ba Qi" (the Eight Banners: banner, a division of the Manchu nationality and the emperor's clan) and the affairs of "Tao Ren" (the escapee) and the provincial garrison. This department was set up in order to enforce punishment on "Tao Ren" (the escapee), which previously belonged to "Bing Bu" (The Department of Defense) and which was later transferred to "Xing Bu" (The Department of Punishment). There were no fixed rules to follow for the division of work in each bureau, so it led to low administrative efficiency and various corrupt practices.

Because the northeast of China was the place of "Long Xing" (the birth of dragon or the ruler) of the Qing Dynasty, "Pei Du" (the second capital) was established by following that of the Ming Dynasty. From the 15th year of Shunzhi (1658) to the 30th year of Kangxi (1691), "Sheng Jing Wu Bu" (the five departments in Shengjing) (except the Department of Personnel) was established with "Shi Lang" (vice minister) acting as the chief executive. From the 3rd year of Yongzheng (1725), one "Yu Shi" (the censor) was sent to conduct investigations every year (later it was changed to once in three years). "Sheng Jing Wu Bu" (the five departments in Shengjing) was abolished during an official system reform in the late Qing Dynasty.

Apart from "Liu Bu" (The Six Departments), many of the "Yuan" (institution), "Si" (bureau), "Fu" (ancient administrative district between province and county) and "Jian" (ancient supervisory office) were either abolished or combined together compared with Ming Dynasty. Among "Jiu Si" (nine bureaus), only "Da Li Si" (The Bureau of Judicial Review), which was in charge of hearing cases and managing the prisons; "Tai Chang Si" (The Bureau of Sacrificial Worship), which was in charge of managing the affairs of making sacrifices to gods; "Guang Lu Si" (the bureau in charge of banquets); "Hong Lu Si" (the bureau in charge of state ceremonies), which was in charge of managing ceremonies, banquets, and courts; and "Tai Pu Si" (the bureau in charge of the emperor's carriages and horses) were retained. Among "Wu Jian" (five supervisory offices), only "Guo Zi Jian" (the highest educational body in ancient China), which was responsible for traditional studies and government decrees, was retained, and "Han Lin Yuan" (The Hanlin Academy), which was responsible for the cultivation of leadership talents, was preserved as it was established during the Ming Dynasty. The chief commissioner of "Tong Zheng Shi Si" (The Transmission Office), as one of the officials of "Jiu Qing" (the nine high-rank officials in ancient times), still participated in major political and military decisions.

With regard to the supervisory organs, the system of the Ming Dynasty was basically adapted. The central organ was still "Du Cha Yuan" (The Court of Censors), but its power was weakened. In the 17th year of Qianlong (1748), "Qian

Du Yu Shi" (assistants of the Court of Censors) was abolished and "Zuo Du Yu Shi" (the head of the Court of Censors) and "You Fu Du Yu Shi" (the deputy of the court of censors) were designated to be in charge of "Du Cha Yuan" (The Court of Censors). "You Du Yu Shi" (the deputy of the Court of Censors) and "You Fu Du Yu Shi" (the deputy of the Court of Censors) were concurrently held by "Zong Du" (viceroy), "Xun Fu" (procurators), "He Dao Zong Du" (viceroy in charge of rivers and channels), and "Cao Yun Zong Du" (viceroy in charge of water transportation) in local places. In order to centralize the imperial power, in the 1st year of Yongzheng (1723), the power of "Feng Bo" (power to return and rectify an edict issued by the emperor that is deemed inappropriate) of "Liu Ke Ji Shi Zhong" (the supervisor of the six offices) was removed, and "Liu Ke" (the six offices) was combined with "Du Cha Yuan" (The Court of Censors). "Liu Ke Ji Shi Zhong" (the supervisor of the six offices) and "Jian Cha Yu Shi" (the supervisory censor) of the fifteen "Dao" (the administration district below the province) (in the late Qing Dynasty they were increased to twenty two) were collectively called "Ke" and "Dao" (both government offices including the deaconry and the supervisory censor), which were responsible for monitoring and controlling of the officials inside and outside the capital respectively. The supervisory power was also adjusted to meet the needs of strengthening the imperial power. In order to expand the rights of the officials of "Ke" and "Dao" (both government offices including the deaconry and the supervisory censor) who had acted as the emperor's eyes and ears, in the 29th year of Kangxi (1690), "Zuo Du Yu Shi" (the head of the Court of Censors) was appointed "Yi Zheng Da Chen" (minister for the deliberation of national affairs) to participate in political decision making. During the reign of Emperor Shizong, the system of "Mi Zhe Yan Shi" (putting forward their suggestions by submitting secret memorials) was established in "Ke" and "Dao" (both government offices including the deaconry and the supervisory censor) and it was stipulated that "each official of 'Ke' and 'Dao' (both government offices including the deaconry and the supervisory censor) should at least submit one secret memorial every day, but only one thing should be reported every time. The matters, whether important or trivial, should all be faithfully reported. Even if there was nothing to report, the reasons should be explained in the memorial."[165] During the reign of Emperor Shizong, "'Ti Qi' (soldiers specializing in seizing criminals) and 'Luo Cha' (patrolling and reconnaissance) were appointed as spies and sent across the country"[166] in order to ensure the supervision of officials at all levels.

The chief officials of "Du Cha Yuan" (The Court of Censors) were concurrently the members of "San Fa Si" (Three Judicial Departments), the highest trial organ at the time. According to law, only "Jun Ji Chu" (The Grand Council) was beyond its scope of supervisory authority, so it can be seen that its prosecutorial power was extremely great. But under the ruling of authoritarian regime, "Jian Cha Yu Shi" (the

---

[165] *Qing Shi Zong Shi Lu* (*The Record of Emperor Shizong of Qing Dynasty*), Vol. 4.

[166] Zhao Zhuang (Qing Dynasty), "Cha Xia Qing" (An Investigation of the Conditions at the Lower Levels) in *Xiao Ting Za Lu* (*The Miscellaneous Records of Xiaoting*), Vol. 1.

supervisory censor) was afraid of losing his official position or even life if he had offended the emperor by what he had said; therefore, what he reported was mostly false. In the 36th year of Kangxi (1697), an imperial edict was issued: "Recently very few suggestions have been put forward in the memorials. Sometimes someone has mentioned the current politics; however, few of them have stated the affairs directly."[167] In the 5th year of Qianlong (1740), another imperial edict was issued: "The officials of 'Ke' and 'Dao' (both government offices including the deaconry and the supervisory censor) are like the emperor's eyes and ears ... Even though memorials are submitted regularly in those years, they are either shoddy comments, or copied words. Are there any useful suggestions which are beneficial to the nation if they are implemented? Recently, there are only a few memorials submitted by the officials of 'Ke' and 'Dao' (both government offices including the deaconry and the supervisory censor), and most of them are completely useless."[168] However, some of the "Yu Shi" (the censors) were punished for their frank suggestions. For example, in the 23rd year of Qianlong (1758), "Yu Shi" (the censor) Zhou Zhao stated in a memorial: "If one is anxious to for quick results in administration, many complicated regulations and strict laws and decrees have to be made. However, they are ineffective when carried out by the junior officials." Emperor Gaozong was enraged by this memorial and said: "I just want to ask you that as for the current administration, are the laws and decrees severer than those in the past dynasties? Which law is complicated? Which decree is strict?"[169] Because of this, Zhou Zhao was severely punished.

In order to consolidate and unify the multiethnic country, a set of national policies were made during the Qing Dynasty, and "Li Fan Yuan" (The Bureau of National Minority Affairs) was established so as to manage the affairs of the Mongols, Huis, Tibetans, and other ethnic minorities, which had never been done during the Tang and Song dynasties. Emperor Shengzu once recalled: "During the reign of Emperor Wen in the period of Taizong, all the Mongolian tribes came to submit to our authority, so 'Li Fan Yuan' (The Bureau of National Minority Affairs) was set up to manage the affairs of national minorities."[170] In the 18th year of Shunzhi (1661), it was declared several times that "for 'Li Fan Yuan' (The Bureau of National Minority Affairs) ... the responsibilities are heavy." So "it is allowed for 'Shang Shu' (the minister) of 'Li Fan Yuan' (The Bureau of National Minority Affairs) to participate in the deliberation of national affairs according to 'Liu Bu Shang Shu' (the minister of the six departments)."[171] After the reign of Emperor Yongzheng, the princes,

---

[167] "Du Cha Yuan" (The Court of Censors) in *Da Qing Hui Dian Ze Li* (*Regulations for the Collected Statutes of Great Qing*), Vol. 145.

[168] *Guang Xu Hui Dian Shi Li* (*The Precedents of the Collected Statutes of Emperor Guangxu*).

[169] *Guang Xu Hui Dian Shi Li* (*The Precedents of the Collected Statutes of Emperor Guangxu*).

[170] *Guang Xu Hui Dian Shi Li* (*The Precedents of the Collected Statutes of Emperor Guangxu*), Vol. 25.

[171] *Guang Xu Hui Dian Shi Li* (*The Precedents of the Collected Statutes of Emperor Guangxu*), Vol. 25.

dukes, and "Da Xue Shi" (grand secretary) also took part in the decision-making of "Li Fan Yuan" (The Bureau of National Minority Affairs). The members of "Li Fan Yuan" (The Bureau of National Minority Affairs) were selected from the Manchu or Mongolians, and "they are in charge of issuing decrees, deciding the official titles and salaries, organizing the court meetings and enforcing punishments upon foreign vassal states"[172]; at the same time, they were also in charge of part of the affairs of the foreign vassal states and the diplomatic relationship with Russia.

"Zong Ren Fu" (The Imperial Clan Court) was the organ in charge of the management of royal family affairs in the Qing Dynasty. The chief officials of "Zong Ren Fu" (The Imperial Clan Court) were selected from princes and dukes, and they were offered the official ranks of "Zheng Yi Pin" (the plain first rank) (or the highest official rank). Below them, "Zuo You Zong Zheng" (head and deputy officials in charge of royal affairs), "Zuo You Zong Ren" (head and deputy officials in charge of making sacrifices to god), and other officials were also appointed, all of whom were chosen from Manchu nobility. "Zong Ren Fu" (The Imperial Clan Court) was in charge of the royal family membership and the compilation of "Yu Die" (the imperial pedigree of a clan). It was also in charge of the rewards and punishment of the imperial officials and the settlement of disputes between the royal family members. The position of "Zong Ren Fu" (The Imperial Clan Court) was much higher than that of the cabinet member of "Liu Bu" (The Six Departments) to preserve the dignity of the royal family.

In order to manage the royal affairs and to provide services for the emperor's food, clothing, shelter and traveling, "Nei Wu Fu" (Board of the Imperial Household) was set up. The position of the chief minister was held by those selected from among officials or held by experienced princes and dukes, imperial ministers, "Shang Shu" (the minister), and "Shi Lang" (vice minister). "Nei Wu Fu" (Board of the Imperial Household) "is in charge of issuing government decrees for 'Bao Yi' (family servant) of 'Shang San Qi' (the upper three banners), the administration of palace affairs as well as the affairs relevant to 'Li Bu' (The Department of Personnel), 'Hu Bu' (The Department of Revenue), 'Li Bu' (The Department of Rites), 'Bing Bu' (The Department of Defense), 'Xing Bu' (The Department of Punishment) and 'Gong Bu' (The Department of Works)."[173] Therefore, the institution was huge in terms of membership size, and except the artisans, soldiers, and eunuchs, there were more than 3000 officials, which were tenfold that of "Hu Bu" (The Department of Revenue), the office in charge of matters concerning national territory, land, household registration, money, and grains, so it had reflected the development of autocratic system at the time.

2. The local government organs were divided into four levels: "Sheng" (province), "Dao" (the administration district below the province), "Fu" (ancient administrative district between province and county), and "Xian" (county). "Zong Du"

---

[172] *Guang Xu Hui Dian Shi Li* (*The Precedents of the Collected Statutes of Emperor Guangxu*), Vol. 63.

[173] *Da Qing Hui Dian* (*The Collected Statutes of Great Qing*), Vol. 89.

11.3 The Legalization of the Administrative System and the System of Official...

(viceroy) and "Xun Fu" (procurators), who were temporarily sent by the central government to local places during the Ming Dynasty, became permanent senior provincial officials, who were in charge of local military and political affairs on behalf of the emperor, which had become an important measure for the rulers of the Qing Dynasty in strengthening the centralization of authority. As for "Du Zhi Hui Shi" (the chief military general), it was abolished and replaced by the system of "Wei Suo" (border guarding posts), and its military power was combined with that of "Du Fu" (the viceroys and procurators). "Bu Zheng Shi" (local administrative officer) and "An Cha Shi" (head of judicial commission) lost their political independence, and they were mainly in charge of the management of civil property and prisons assigned to "Du Fu" (the viceroys and procurators) and were called "Liang Si" (two provincial offices). "Du Fu" (the viceroys and procurators) held the real power and were in charge of the administration of the local regions alone, so according to "the primary resolution made during the reign of Emperor Shunzhi, the position of provincial 'Du Fu' (the viceroys and procurators) should be held by Manchus."[174] During the reign of Emperor Kangxi, only the Manchu people were allowed to hold the position of 'Du Fu' (the viceroys and procurators) of Shanxi and Shannxi provinces. As for the "Du Fu" (the viceroys and procurators) who were from the Han people, it was provided that they should be "patrolled and monitored by the Manchu people"[175]; from this we can see the important status of "Du Fu" (the viceroys and procurators) and the strict control of the Qing rulers. Emperor Shengzu once said: "Whether important or trivial affairs, we must plan and prepare in advance, especially comprehensive investigations are absolutely necessary in the appointment of 'Du Fu' (the viceroys and procurators)."[176] He also often summoned "Du Fu" (the viceroys and procurators), "Ti Du" (military commander), and "Zong Bing" (commander-in-chief) to inquire about local customs and sent some trusted officials to conduct investigations on local bureaucracy. During the reign of Emperor Yongzheng, through the system of "Ting Ji" (the edicts directly sent to the viceroys and procurators by the couriers without going through the cabinet), the relationship between the central government and "Du Fu" (the viceroys and procurators) was further strengthened. Moreover, it was stipulated that every single affair should be faithfully reported by "Du Fu" (the viceroys and procurators), and their activities must all be held in accordance with the imperial edicts.

Below "Sheng" (province), "Dao" (the administration district below the province) was established. As per the system of the Ming Dynasty, "Dao" (the

---

[174]"Man Han Du Fu" (The Viceroys and Procurators of Manchu and Han Nationalities) in "Jue Zhi Lei" (Personal Profile) in *Qing Bai Lei Chao* (*A Collection of Anecdotes in Qing Dynasty*).

[175]"Man Han Du Fu" (The Viceroys and Procurators of Manchu and Han Nationalities) in "Jue Zhi Lei" (Personal Profile) in *Qing Bai Lei Chao* (*A Collection of Anecdotes in Qing Dynasty*).

[176]"Kang Xi Chao" (The Reign of Emperor Kangxi) in *Dong Hua Lu* (*The Record of Donghua*), Vol. 34.

administration district below the province) was a supervisory rather than an administrative district; "Dao Yuan" (local chief administrator) was the "messenger" dispatched to send messages, and he did not have any official ranks. During the reign of Emperor Qianlong, "Shou Dao" (local official from a provincial government) and "Xun Dao" (local official from the judicial commission) were especially set up, and the former had a fixed area of jurisdiction and was mainly in charge of the management of matters concerning "Qian Gu" (money and grain), while the latter was in charge of the patrolling of certain areas, as well as the punishment of crimes and the hearing of cases. After "Dao Yuan" (local chief administrator) was put in charge of specific affairs; he gained greater military power and was given more titles and was responsible for the supervision of military officials below "Du Si" (or "Du Zhi Hui Shi Si": the Provincial Military Commission). In addition, "Dao Yuan" (local chief administrator) was made in charge of special affairs, such as those of "Du Liang Dao" (office in charge of grain collection), "Yan Fa Dao" (office in charge of salt matters), "Bing Bei Dao" (military supervisor), and "Hai Guan Dao" (office in charge of customs house).

Below "Dao" (the administration district below the province), "Fu" (ancient administrative district between province and county) was established. "Zhi Fu" (magistrate of a prefecture) was the local chief executive official, who was also the contact person between the upper and lower levels of officials. In those areas where it was not proper to set up "Zhou" (subprefecture) and "Xian" (county) or in areas inhabited by ethnic minorities, "Ting" (a government department at the provincial level), such as "Zhi Li Ting" (now Hebei province) and "San Ting" (in charge of local affairs in certain aspects), was set up. In addition, "Zhou" (subprefecture) was a subordinate administrative unit of "Fu" (ancient administrative district between province and county), and it was further divided into "Zhi Li Zhou" (now Hebei province) and "San Zhou" (in charge of local affairs in certain aspects). "Ting" (a government department at the provincial level) and "Zhou" (subprefecture) were fixed administrative units, but they were not executive organs of first level.

Below "Fu" (ancient administrative district between province and county), "Xian" (county) was established. "Zhi Xian" (the magistrate of a county) was in charge of government decrees, taxes, corvee, lawsuits, and education, so he was always called "Qin Min Guan" (the most basic local officials). Because the situations were different for each "Xian" (county), generally "Xian" (county) was divided into different categories, like "Chong" (important), "Fan" (prosperous), "Pi" (barren), and "Nan" (troublesome). The magistrates of "Xian" (county) were also divided into four levels: "Jian Que" (with only one or none of the situations above), "Zhong Que" (with two of the situations above), "Yao Que" (with three of the situations above), "Zui Yao Que" (with four of the situations above), and the magistrates must be carefully chosen.

In addition, some special administrative regions like "Shun Tian Fu" (The Capital District) and "Ying Tian Fu" (The Auxiliary Capital District) were also established. "Shun Tian Fu" (The Capital District) had jurisdiction over "Zhou" (subprefecture) and "Xian" (county) around the capital, and "Fu Yin" (the chief official of prefecture) was given the official rank of "Zheng San Pin" (the plain third rank), who was

11.3 The Legalization of the Administrative System and the System of Official...

two levels higher than "Zhi Fu" (magistrate of a prefecture) and who could present memorials to the emperor directly without going through "Zong Du" (viceroy). "Ying Tian Fu" (The Auxiliary Capital District) was set up in "Pei Du" (the second capital) and Shengjing (now Shenyang), which had jurisdiction over five "Fu" (ancient administrative districts between province and county), four "Ting" (government departments at the provincial level), six "Zhou" (subprefectures) and twenty six "Xian" (counties). "Fu Yin" (the chief official of prefecture) was given the official rank of "Zheng San Pin" (the plain third rank), and he could be chosen only from the Manchus. Moreover, he could also send memorials to the emperor directly without going through "Zong Du" (viceroy).

"Bao Jia Zhi Du" (the household registration management system organized on the basis of households) was created by following the basic organization system of "Li Jia" (social organizations at the grassroots level) in Ming Dynasty. "Li Jia" (social organizations at the grassroots level) was only responsible for tax collection, but "Bao Jia Zhi Du" (the household registration management system organized on the basis of households) was different because it was only responsible for monitoring the residents' ideological actions to prevent or to suppress the rebellion. The Qing rulers had repeatedly claimed that "even the good laws for criminal punishment are incomparable to 'Bao Jia Zhi Du.'"[177] In *Sheng Yu Shi Liu Tiao* (*The Sixteen Articles of Imperial Edicts*), Emperor Shengzu regarded the policy of "preventing and punishing theft and robbery by 'Bao Jia' (the household registration management system in ancient time)" as one of his administrative programs. In the 47th year of Kangxi (1708), "Bao Jia Zhi Du" (the household registration management system organized on the basis of households) was reformed, and each household "was given a printed card and was ask to write down their names and the number of the male members to indicate where they wanted to go and to record where they had been when they went home. If someone looked strange or seemed suspicious, he was not allowed stay unless carefully searched and interrogated ..., they should ask 'Bao Zhang' (the leader of 'Bao' consisting of about different households) for 'Gan Jie' (written pledge) at the end of the month to prepare for checking up."[178]

In the 4th year of Yongzheng, it was further declared by the emperor that "one 'Pai Tou' (the leader of ten households in Qing Dynasty) should be set up among ten households; one 'Jia Zhang' (the leader of ten 'Pai Tou') should be set up among ten 'Pai'; one 'Bao Zheng' (the leader of ten 'Jia') should be set up among ten 'Jia.'"[179] "Bao Jia Zhi Du" (the household registration management system organized on the basis of households) was generally established in the areas inhabited by Miao and

---

[177]"Zhi Yi Kao" (A Textual Research of the Corvee Service) in *Qing Chao Wen Xian Tong Kao* (*A General Textual Research of the Documents of Qing Dynasty*), Vol. 22.

[178]"Zhi Yi Kao" (A Textual Research of the Corvee Service) in *Qing Chao Wen Xian Tong Kao* (*A General Textual Research of the Documents of Qing Dynasty*), Vol. 22.

[179]*Qing Shi Zong Shi Lu* (*The Record of Emperor Shizong of Qing Dynasty*), Vol. 46.

Zhuang nationalities or in the areas inhabited by "Peng Min" (homeless people living in the mountains), such as in the mountainous areas of Jiangxi, Zhejiang, and Fujian provinces, and the charcoal burners in the mountainous area of Guangdong province. It was also established in the areas of Suzhou and Jiangsu where there were many cotton-dyeing factories. "Bao Zhang" (the leader of "Bao," consisting of about different households) and "Jia Zhang" (the leader of ten "Pai Tou") were selected from people who could read and write and with good family background,[180] so it was known as "ruling the villages by making use of 'Shi Da Fu' (literati and officials)."[181] During the 22nd to 24th year of Qianlong (1755 A.D.–1757 A.D.), "the system of 'Bao Jia' was reformed" by Emperor Gaozong, so "Bao Jia Zhi Du" (the household registration management system organized on the basis of households), which had been carried out for more than a century since their entering Shanhaiguan was improved and its scope of application was further extended, so it was regarded as one of his basic methods to maintain the ruling order. So it was ordered that registry booklets should be set up by all stores, families, and temples in the cities and countryside to have a record of all the traveling guests and businessmen. What's more, the landlords and the kiln and factories owners were required to have their tenants and servants strictly controlled by arranging them in "Pai" (consisting of ten households) and "Jia" (consisting of ten "Pai"), or by attaching them to their owners. In the regions inhabited by minority nationalities, those who were under the administration of the government were required to be organized into "Bao Jia" (the household registration management system in ancient time) according to households, and those who were not under the administration of the government were required to be administrated by "Tu Si" (chieftain or hereditary headsmen), "Tou Ren" (tribal chief), and "Dong Zhang" (chief of small minorities). The Hui people, on the other hand, were required to be administrated by the imams of mosques and the Mongols by "Za Sa Ke" (Zhasake) of every "Qi" (banner, equivalent of a county). "Bao Jia Zhi Du" (the household registration management system organized on the basis of households) was also implemented among the people of "Ba Qi" (the Eight Banners: banner, a division of the Manchu nationality and the emperor's clan). A huge administration net was created by the organization of "Bao Jia" (the household registration management system in ancient time), so it had fully reflected the degree of the autocratic domination in Qing Dynasty.

It is worth noticing that the agencies which took control of the affairs of minority nationalities and royal affairs of Qing Dynasty had played a very important role, so they were inseparable parts of the overall state organ.

---

[180]"Zhi Yi Kao" (A Textual Research of the Corvee Service) in *Qing Chao Wen Xian Tong Kao* (*A General Textual Research of the Documents of Qing Dynasty*), Vol. 24.

[181]"Zhi Yi Kao" (A Textual Research of the Corvee Service) in *Qing Chao Wen Xian Tong Kao* (*A General Textual Research of the Documents of Qing Dynasty*), Vol. 21.

11.3 The Legalization of the Administrative System and the System of Official...

From the abovementioned we can clearly see the expansion of government bureaucracy, and because of it, a large group of bureaucratic officials was formed. According to the official record in the Qing Dynasty, there were more than 30,000 officials at the time.

In order to bring the function of central agencies into full play, all important military actions and all rewards, punishments, and judgments should be discussed and jointly heard first at the meeting held by "Jiu Qing" (the nine high-rank officials in ancient times), then presented to the emperor. This institution not only provided the emperor with important references in making final decisions but also made it convenient for him to crack down political opponents who often interfered in his exercise of imperial power through "Jiu Qing Hui Shen" (joint hearing by nine high-rank officials in ancient times). Take the case of Nian Gengyao as an example: Nian Gengyao was sentenced to death because according to the resolution made by "Jiu Qing" (the nine high-rank officials in ancient times), he "had violated article ninety two." The members of "Jiu Qing Hui Shen" (joint hearing by nine high-rank officials in ancient times) had to "attend the meeting on time," and two "Yu Shi" (censors) from Han or Manchu nationalities were sent by "Du Cha Yuan" (The Court of Censors) to "keep record of those who did not attend the meeting for no reason for future checking." If it was discovered that someone was absent from the meeting without permission, he would be sued and be imposed a fine of one year's salary, according to the "regulations on prevarication."[182] "Every case heard by 'Jiu Qing Hui Shen' (joint hearing by nine high-rank officials in ancient times) should be settled within thirty days with no delay."[183] In addition, the affairs discussed by "Jiu Qing Hui Shen" (joint hearing by nine high-rank officials in ancient times) should be reported to the emperor. In the 23rd year of Emperor Kangxi (1684), it was stated by the emperor that "if a case involved two departments, it should be jointly reported to the emperor for final decision.[184]

During Qing Dynasty, although it was propagated that Manchu and Han people were equal, the real power was controlled by Manchu people to ensure the advantageous position of the Manchu officials, so that the officials of Han nationality only "repeated what Manchu officials had said, and never dared to express their own opinions."[185] Emperor Shizu said in *Shi Chao Xun Sheng* (*The Imperial Edicts in the Reign of 10 Emperors*): "Since my reign, I have only seen Manchu officials in the various 'Ya Men' (the government offices) submit their memorials to me, but never seen any officials of Han nationality." In the 48th year of Kangxi, the emperor also stated in his edict: "If the case is irrelevant to the officials of Han nationality, they

---

[182] *Qin Ding Li Bu Ze Li* (*The Regulation of the Department of Personnel Made by Imperial Order*), Vol. 11.

[183] *Qin Ding Li Bu Ze Li* (*The Regulation of the Department of Personnel Made by Imperial Order*), Vol. 10.

[184] "Sheng Zu Ji" (The Record of Emperor Shengzu) in *Qing Shi Gao* (*The Draft of the History of Qing Dynasty*), Vol. 2.

[185] Zhao Yi (Qing Dynasty), "Jian Guan Bu Wu" (Being Concurrently in Charge of the Departmental Affairs) in *Yan Pu Za Ji* (*The Miscellanies of Yan Pu*), Vol. 2.

often keep silent."[186] "The officials of Han nationality, no matter what position they hold, always shuffled their responsibilities to Manchu officials; if the affair is beneficial to them, they would claim the credit; if there is something wrong, they will shuffle the responsibility to others instead."[187]

In order to guarantee that the key departments were controlled by the Manchu nobility, the system of "Guan Que" (the vacancy of officials), which was a special system of distributing official positions in Qing Dynasty was established in official appointment. The system was divided into four types: vacancies for Manchu officials, vacancies for Mongolian officials, vacancies for military officials of the Han nationality, and vacancies for Han officials, all of which should be filled up according to the fixed number of official vacancies. For example, the official positions in "Li Fan Yuan" (The Bureau of National Minority Affairs), "Zong Ren Fu" (The Imperial Clan Court) and some important departments which were in control of money, grain, government warehouse, arsenal and the general of garrison; the official positions like "Du Tong" (ancient military officer, or commander-in-chief), "Can Zan Da Chen" (counselor), "Shi Lang" (vice minister) of "Sheng Jing Wu Bu" (the five departments in Shengjing) were specially held by Manchu people. Although the positions of local "Du Fu" (the viceroys and procurators), "Si" (bureau), "Dao" (the administration district below the province), "Ti Du" (military commander), and "Zong Bing" (commander-in-chief) could be held by both Manchu and Han officials, these positions were usually held by Manchu officials in the capital areas and strategic passes. During the reign of Emperor Kangxi, fewer than twenty percent of the positions of "Du Fu" (the viceroys and procurators) were held by Han officials, while during the reign of Emperor Qianlong, half of the official positions of "Xun Fu" (procurators) were held by the officials of the Han nationality and half held by the officials of the Manchu nationality; most of the positions of "Zong Du" (viceroy) were held by the officials of the Manchu nationality.[188] During the reign of Emperor Qianlong, some officials of the Han nationality once asked: "Why are the vital positions all held by the Manchu officials?"[189] It was not until the reign of Xianfeng that the majority of vital local positions were held by the officials of the Han nationality; however, most of the so-called Qin Min Guan (the most basic local officials) below "Zhi Fu" (magistrate of a prefecture) were held by the officials of the Han nationality, which fully reflected the policy of "ruling the Han nationality by Han people" of the Qing government. Those vacant positions usually held by Manchu officials were not allowed to be occupied by the Han people, but the vacant positions in or out of the capital that were usually held by Han officials could be

---

[186]"Kang Xi Chao" (The Reign of Emperor Kangxi) in *Dong Hua Lu* (*The Record of Donghua*), Vol. 83.

[187]*Qin Ding Li Bu Ze Li* (*The Regulation of the Department of Personnel Made by Imperial Order*), Vol. 1.

[188]*Qing Gao Zong Shi Lu* (*The Record of Qing Emperor Gaozong*), Vol. 184.

[189]"Qian Long Chao" (The Reign of Emperor Qianlong) in *Dong Hua Xu Lu* (*A Sequel to the Records of Donghua*), Vol. 17.

11.3 The Legalization of the Administrative System and the System of Official...

occupied by Manchus, from which we can see the unfair political positions between the Han and Manchu nationalities. The distribution of official position was determined by the institution of "Guan Que" (the vacancy of officials) so that the state machinery could be tightly controlled by the Manchu nobility. However, the Manchu rulers knew that they must get the support of the landlords and bureaucrats of Han nationality in order to establish the dictatorship of Manchu and Han landlords predominated by Manchu nobility. During the reign of Emperor Kangxi, different ranks of "Da Xue Shi" (grand secretary) and "Shang Shu" (the minister) for Manchu and Han nationalities were eliminated and the policy of granting same official ranks to the officials who held the same positions was put into practice to show the emperor's trust and dependence on the Han officials. Emperor Shengzu always said that "the civilians and the armymen of the Manchu and the Han nationalities are equal"[190] because "the civil and military officials of Manchu and Han nationalities are organic whole."[191] Besides, "both the people of Manchu and Han nationalities are my officials, so I regard them as an organic whole and I never treat them differently."[192] However, Emperor Shengzu never forgot to take precautions against the Han people. In the 23rd year of Kangxi (1684), the emperor said: "Since ancient times, it is very common for the Han people to form different cliques and to deceive their superiors together with their party members."[193] In the 55th year of Kangxi (1716), the emperor earnestly warned his descendants that "the people of Han nationality are not united, but the millions of Manchus or Mongolians are all of one heart, I have been in power for many years, and I think it is difficult to rule the Han people because they are never of one mind, so we should be mindful of possible danger during the peaceful times."[194]

Because the rulers of Qing Dynasty were from minority nationalities, they often worried that the Manchu nobility might be endangered by the cliques formed by the Han officials, so they always kept an eye on them. For example, the official avoidance system was established by the Manchu nobility and the Han officials were not allowed to serve in their hometown to prevent them from forming local forces with their local relations, and they were even forbidden to serve in the areas within 500 *li* of their hometown. Those who failed to obey the official avoidance system should be demoted or dismissed. As for the appointment in places other than the capital, the official avoidance system should also be followed if the candidate was of the same clan or was of affinity or was of teacher–student relationship with

---

[190]"Kang Xi Chao" (The Reign of Emperor Kangxi) in *Dong Hua Lu* (*The Record of Donghua*), Vol. 9.

[191]"Kang Xi Chao" (The Reign of Emperor Kangxi) in *Dong Hua Lu* (*The Record of Donghua*), Vol. 21.

[192]"Kang Xi Chao" (The Reign of Emperor Kangxi) in *Dong Hua Lu* (*The Record of Donghua*), Vol. 90.

[193]"Kang Xi Chao" (The Reign of Emperor Kangxi) in *Dong Hua Lu* (*The Record of Donghua*), Vol. 53.

[194]"Kang Xi Chao" (The Reign of Emperor Kangxi) in *Dong Hua Lu* (*The Record of Donghua*), Vol. 98.

his superior. In addition, "Bao Ju Lian Zuo" (in ancient China, if a person who was appointed after being recommended by an official did something improper or was inconsistent with the letter of recommendation, the person who recommended him or her would jointly be subject to punishment) was established, and *Zhi Fu Bao Ju Lian Zuo Fa* (*The Law on the Recommendation and Implication of the Magistrate of a Prefecture*) was enacted during the Qing Dynasty, according to which "Zhi Fu" (magistrate of a prefecture) should be jointly responsible for the crimes committed by the officials whom they recommended. Even though the officials who were recommended by "Jiu Qing" (the nine high-rank officials in ancient times) had committed personal crimes, like the crime of corruption, the concerned officials would be demoted by two levels and be transferred to other places. Moreover, the officials with superior and inferior relationships also took joint responsibilities even though they did not have the recommendation relationship. For example, Sun Shiyi, "Xun Fu" (procurators) of Yunnan province, was dismissed and sent to garrison Yili because he failed to impeach "Zong Du" (viceroy) for his bribe taking during the reign of Emperor Kangxi. What is more, the system of "Xing Qu" (after being recommended, local officials are transferred to the capital), which was established in the Ming Dynasty, was abolished in the Qing Dynasty. According to the system, if recommended by senior local officials, the local officials of "Zhou" (subprefecture) and "Xian" (county) could come to the capital to take official exams to be appointed officials in "Ke" and "Dao" (both government offices, including the deaconry and the supervisory censor) and "Bu" (department), so that the method for local officials to be promoted to be officials of central government was completely eradicated to prevent the central officials from communicating with the local officials to form cliques harmful to the despotic rule.

The official organs were mutually checked and restricted in order to maintain the balance of power. For example, revenues were managed by both the agencies of "Hu Bu" (The Department of Revenue) and "Gong Bu" (The Department of Works), with members sent by "Nei Wu Fu" (Board of the Imperial Household) and "Shun Tian Fu" (the Capital District). Obvious power balance also existed between "Liu Bu Shang Shu" (the minister of the six departments) and "Shi Lang" (vice minister), so if "Shi Lang" (vice minister) was against the memorials submitted by "Shang Shu" (the minister), it was impossible for these memorials to be presented to the emperor; instead, each of them could deliver memorials separately in order to prevent the officials from monopolizing power.

The system of mutual interaction and balance of power was also set up between local "Zong Du" (viceroy) and "Xun Fu" (procurators); between "Jiang Jun" (the general), "Du Tong" (ancient military officer or commander-in-chief), and "Du Fu" (the viceroys and procurators); between "Du Fu" (the viceroys and procurators) and "Fan Nie Ti Zhen" ("Bu Zheng Si," "An Cha Si," "Ti Du," and "Zong Bing"); etc.

To a certain extent, the mutual balance between different agencies had caused a discrepancy in power and authority, ambiguous responsibility, and low administrative efficiency. In the 32nd year of Guangxu (1906), Yi Kuang made the following statements in the memorial to the emperor about the reform on bureaucracy:

11.3 The Legalization of the Administrative System and the System of Official...

> The long-standing malpractices are brought about by the ambiguous responsibilities, because everyone has shirked his responsibility, for which there are three reasons: the first is that there is no division of power; ... the second is that there is the ambiguity of responsibility; ...and the third is the inconsistency between the title of the agency and its duty. Although it is named by "Li Bu" (The Department of Personnel), it is only in charge of the management of "drawing lots", it does not have the power of the examination of officials; although it is named by "Hu Bu" (The Department of Revenue), it is only in charge of receiving and paying money, it does not have the power of statistics; although it is named by "Li Bu" (The Department of Rites), it is only in charge of the affairs of ritual and ceremony; it had no power of instructing "Li Jiao" (feudal ethical code); although it is named by "Bing Bu" (The Department of Defense), it is only in charge of the affairs of the registration of the soldiers, it has no power of military actions.[195]

But this was not only the demand of the autocratic dictatorship, but also the result of the fast development of the autocratic system itself.

In the establishment of the state organs of the Qing Dynasty, those of the Ming Dynasty was basically followed. However, since the Qing Dynasty was an era consisted mainly of Manchu nobility and since it was also the last feudal dynasty of China, it was possible for the rulers to learn from the experience of previous dynasties when it comes to the construction of state organs; as such, the Qing Dynasty was able to set up new systems like "Jun Ji Chu" (The Grand Council), "Li Fan Yuan" (The Bureau of National Minority Affairs), "Ba Qi Du Tong Ya Men" (The Office of Commanders-in-Chief of the "Eight Banners"), "Zhu Fang Jiang Jun" (The Garrison General), and the various other official positions in charge of the ruling of vassal states of small minorities. At the same time, in the Qing Dynasty, "Zong Du" (viceroy) and "Xun Fu" (procurators), which had supervisory functions in the Ming Dynasty, were given fixed senior official positions in border provinces. The local "San Si" (with three departments) was reduced to "Er Si" (with two departments); "Dao Yuan" (local chief administrator) was changed to actual functionary officials instead of temporary dispatched ones, and the administrative unit of "Ting" (a government department at the provincial level) was newly set up. Particularly, in order to show the emperor's supreme authority, any officials, from "Da Xue Shi" (grand secretary) and "Shang Shu" (the minister) down to local subordinate officials and magistrates, could all be awarded or be promoted by the emperor.

As for the activities of state agencies, basically laws and regulations were made to be followed and abided by. From Emperor Kangxi, "Hui Dian" (the collected statutes) and "Ze Li" (regulation) were successively drafted by the five emperors in Qing Dynasty, and the administrative system, the scope and function of different agencies and their relationship were established by law in order to regulate the administrative activities, to legalize the function and power of the administrative agencies and to institutionalize the power division between central and local government.

---

[195]"Guang Xu Chao" (The Reign of Emperor Guangxu) in *Dong Hua Xu Lu* (*A Sequel to the Records of Donghua*), Vol. 220.

11.3.2 The Legalization of Official Management

Although there were various ways to select officials in the Qing Dynasty, the main way was to take the "Ke Ju" exam (the imperial examination). In the 2nd year of Shunzhi (1645), soon after the period of entering Shanhaiguan, "Ke Ju" (the imperial examination) was held to select officials, so it was announced that "Ju Ren" (those who passed the imperial examination at the provincial level in ancient China) and "Sheng Yuan" (also called "Xiu Cai": those who passed the imperial examination at the county level in ancient China) of the Ming Dynasty could also take the "Ke Ju" exam (the imperial examination) in order to constrain the "Shi Da Fu" (literati and officials) ideology of the Han nationality and to get rid of the anti-Qing consciousness. In the Qing Dynasty, "Ke Ju" (the imperial examination) was held every three years, and it was divided into three levels, namely, "Xiang Shi" (the provincial examination), "Hui Shi" (the metropolitan examination), and "Dian Shi" (the final imperial examination). "Xiang Shi" (the provincial examination) was held in the provincial capital, and it could be attended by those who had qualified for "Xiu Cai" (one of the subjects for selecting officials in ancient China); "Hui Shi" (the metropolitan examination) was held by "Li Bu" (The Department of Rites) in the capital, and it could be attended by those who obtained qualification for "Ju Ren" (those who passed the imperial examination at the provincial level in ancient China). Meanwhile, those who passed the examination of "Hui Shi" (the metropolitan examination) could then attend "Dian Shi" (the final imperial examination), which was being held by the emperor, and the top three candidates would be enrolled following the system of the Ming Dynasty.

"Ba Gu Wen" (stereotyped writing or eight-part essay in ancient China), which was rigid in form and strict in contents, was taken as a subject of "Ke Ju" (the imperial examination) to constrain the ideology of "Shi Da Fu" (literati and officials). Emperor Shengzu once admitted: "I know that 'Ba Gu Wen' (stereotyped writing or the eight-part essay in ancient China) is really useless, but it is the only way to imprison people's ideology." In order to recruit talented people and to consolidate the bases of ruling, apart from formal examination, the examinations of "Te Ke" (special examination), such as "Bo Xue Hong Ci Ke" (one of the imperial examinations to select talented scholars skilled in writing), "Jing Ji Te Ke" (special examination in economy), and "Xian Lian Fang Zheng Ke" (one of the imperial examinations to select talented scholars with moral excellence), were conducted during the reign of Emperor Kangxi. In the 17th year of Emperor Kangxi (1678), "Bo Xue Hong Ci Ke" (one of the imperial examinations to select talented scholars skilled in writing) was conducted, but the candidates, regardless of their official ranks, should firstly be recommended by the officials inside or outside the capital, then be examined in the imperial palace, and those who performed excellently would all be recruited. Among the fifty people who were recruited, some famous ones included Zhu Yizun, Tang Bin, Pan Lei, Mao Qiling, and You Tong, who were all granted official positions in "Han Lin Yuan" (The Hanlin Academy). So "Te Ke" (special examination) was famous because "many highly talented people were selected."[196] According to historical records, in the 17th year of Kangxi (1678), "Bo Xue Hong Ci Ke" (one of the imperial examinations to select talented scholars skilled in writing) was conducted because "it is regarded as Emperor Shengzu's great strategy to stabilize the country." "Whenever a victory is won and troops are withdrawn, it is the time for the emperor to recruit the remaining talented people ... to get rid of people's suspect towards the new dynasty and to select the extraordinary talents among the people to be the leaders."[197] From then on, in the 1st year of Qianlong (1736), "Bo Xue Hong Ci Ke" (one of the imperial examinations to select talented scholars skilled in writing) was conducted, and in the 26th year (1761), "Tai Hou Wan Sui En Ke" (a subject of examination set up temporarily during imperial celebrations) was conducted.

According to a regulation, all officials of Manchu and Han nationalities should pass the "Ke Ju" examination (the imperial examination); however, the Manchu people could become officials even without passing this exam as they could hold official positions based on their privilege. "Ke Ju" (the imperial examination) was just a stepping stone for the officials of the Han nationality to be able to participate in politics, while only few Manchu officials had passed the examination. According to the regulation for selecting Manchu and Han officials, the person who won the first place in "Ke Ju" (the imperial examination) would be granted official position immediately at the palace court, while the others would be granted official positions only after they had taken "Chao Kao" (imperial examination held by the emperor in the Hall of Perfect Harmony), which was conducted to select officials from "Jin Shi" (those who passed the imperial examination at the national level in ancient China). In Qing Dynasty, the system of "Ke Ju" (the imperial examination) was extensively implemented, the talented people who were needed in feudal government were selected and the administration of the regime was greatly improved.

In addition to "Ke Ju" (the imperial examination), direct appointment, called "Te Jian," can be made by the emperor, which was which was not restricted by any law; on the other hand, recommendation by ministers was called "Hui Tui." In the 6th year of Shunzhi (1646), it was stipulated that if there were vacancies for "Zong Du" (viceroy) and "Xun Fu" (procurators), the positions could be filled up according to the recommendation of ministers through "Hui Tui Zhi" (the system of appointment by recommendation). In the 10th year of Shunzhi (1653), "Hui Tui Zhi" (the system of appointment by recommendation) was abolished, and the people who were supposed to be promoted or transferred were registered. In the 2nd year of Kangxi (1663), it was stipulated that if there were vacancies for "Da Xue Shi" (grand secretary) and "Shang Shu" (the minister), the officials could be recommended through "Hui Tui" (the method of recommendation by ministers) after being approved by the emperor. Besides, the descendants of meritorious officials and the

---

[196]"Xuan Ju Zhi" (The Record of Election) in *Qing Shi Gao* (*The Draft of the History of Qing Dynasty*), Vol. 4.

[197]Meng Seng, *Qing Shi Jiang Yi* (*The Lecture Notes of Qing History*), Zhonghua Book Company, 2006, p. 163.

children of officials who died in the line of duty could all be granted official positions according to "Yin Xi" (children inherit their ancestor's positions). At the same time, the systems of "Bao Ju" (recommending someone to a post with personal guarantee) and "Ju Jian" (recommendation) were implemented. In the 13th year of Kangxi (1684), "court officials were dispatched across the country to look for honest and upright officials."[198] In the 4th year of Yongzheng (1726), "imperial orders were issued to every province to select the talented and virtuous officials."[199] Besides, many imperial edicts were issued by Emperor Qianglong to order officials to select and recommend talented people secretly. But sometimes avoidance was needed when recommendation was made. For example, in the 41st year of Kangxi (1702), an edict was issued wherein it was provided that "it is forbidden for 'Jiu Qing' (nine high-rank officials in ancient times) to recommend the officials of the native village or current provincial officials." Sometimes, avoidance was not necessary. For example, according to an imperial edict that was issued in the 2nd year of Yongzheng (1724), "those who have both ability and political integrity can be recommended to hold the official positions above 'Zhu Shi' (junior official) in capital and 'Zhi Xian' (magistrate of a county) outside capital. In addition, they can also recommend their relatives and descendents without being restricted by the rules of avoidance."[200] According to imperial edicts, Guan Xiangkuan, "Zhi Xian" (magistrate of a county) of Huangbei, recommended his son, who then was sent to study in "Xing Bu" (The Department of Punishment) to be promoted to "Xun Fu" (procurators) in the end. However, if recommendation was false or the recommended person committed a crime, the referrer would be punished by virtue of "Lian Zuo" (being punished for being related to somebody who committed an offense), as was described in the saying that "the people who have recommended the talented people will be awarded, while the people who have recommended the wrong person will be severely punished."[201]

In the early years of the Qing Dynasty, the conditions to qualify for an official appointment were quite strict, and "except those whose families are innocent, the other people, such as the servants of the families of 'Ba Qi' (the Eight Banners: banner, a division of Manchu nationality and the emperor's clan) and the family salves of Han nationality were forbidden to register in 'Shi Ji" (a booklet recording the names of officials)."[202] Some official positions, such as the deputy ministers of "Zhan Shi Fu" (agency in charge of the internal affairs of royal families), "Han Lin

---

[198]"Sheng Zu Ji" (The Record of Emperor Shengzu) in *Qing Shi Gao* (*The Draft of the History of Qing Dynasty*).

[199]"Fang Xian Zhuan" (The Biography of Fang Xian) in *Qing Shi Gao* (*The Draft of the History of Qing Dynasty*).

[200]"Wu Shao Shi Zhuan" (The Biography of Wu Shaoshi) in *Qing Shi Gao* (*The Draft of the History of Qing Dynasty*).

[201]"Xuan Ju Zhi" (The Record of Election) in *Qing Shi Gao* (*The Draft of the History of Qing Dynasty*), Vol. 4.

[202]"Xuan Ju Zhi" (The Record of Election) in *Qing Shi Gao* (*The Draft of the History of Qing Dynasty*), Vol. 5.

11.3 The Legalization of the Administrative System and the System of Official... 1159

Yuan" (The Hanlin Academy), "Li Bu" (The Department of Personnel), and "Li Bu" (The Department of Rites), could only be held by those who passed the official examinations of "Ke Ju" (the imperial examination) (except for the people of "Ba Qi") but could not be held by those who were recommended through "Bao Ju" (recommending someone to a post with personal guarantee) and "Juan Na" (donating food or money to buy an official position). Afterward, "Juan Na" (donating food or money to buy an official position) became so popular that as long as people had enough money, they could become officials regardless of their qualifications.

"Juan Na" (donating food or money to buy an official position) was an unusual way of obtaining an official position, and it was a malpractice that contributed to corruption in the government and thus its decline. The law on "Juan Na" (donating food or money to buy an official position) was divided into two kinds: current precedents and provisional precedents. The former mainly refers to obtaining official titles and "Gong Jian" (those recommended to study in "Guo Zi Jian" as "Gong Sheng") by donating money; it also refers to getting promotions, getting good records, or "Feng Dian" (the emperor granting titles to his subordinate officials) by donating money. Since it was frequently used, it was also called "Chang Juan." The latter, on the other hand, was also called "Da Juan," which mainly refers to donating a large sum of money for the construction of river projects, military expenses, and relief in disaster areas. In the early years of the reign of Emperor Shunzhi, it was declared that "Shi Zi" (scholar) could "study in 'Guo Zi Jian' (the highest educational body in ancient China) as 'Gong Sheng' (those who were recommended to study in 'Guo Zi Jian') by donating money or food," but they were not allowed to become officials. Moreover, the officials who were removed from their official posts "are allowed to be reinstated by donating money."[203] In the 13th year of Kangxi (1674), suppression of the rebellion of "San Fan" (the three local regimes) led to financial strain for the government; hence, for "selecting various talented people to make up for the vacancies of the subjects,"[204] the system of "Juan Na" (donating food or money to buy an official position) was established to make up for the shortage of military expenses. In the end, more than 2,000,000 *liang* of silver was collected within three years, and more than 500 people were appointed as "Zhi Xian" (the magistrate of a county) through donation of money. Thus, buying official positions through "Juan Na" (donating food or money to buy an official position) contributed to corruption in the Qing Dynasty.

In order to prevent officials who were appointed through "Juan Na" (donating food or money to buy an official position) from misusing their power, it was declared by the government that "if the officials appointed by 'Juan Na' (donating food or money to buy an official position) have been in their offices for three years, the

---

[203] Ye Mengzhu (Qing Dynasty), "Fu Shui" (Tax) in *Yue Shi Bian* (*A Collection of Worldly Affairs*), Vol. 6. Please See *Shang Hai Zhang Gu Cong Shu* (*A Series of Books of the Anecdotes of Shanghai*), Vol. 1, p. 64.
[204] "Xuan Ju Zhi" (The Record of Election) in *Qing Shi Gao* (*The Draft of the History of Qing Dynasty*), Vol. 7.

competent officials will be promoted while the incompetent ones would be punished"[205]; however, this regulation was not carried out. After the rebellion of "San Fan" (the three local regimes) was suppressed by the government, "Juan Na" (donating food or money to buy an official position) was stopped for a time; but afterward, because of the famine that occurred in Xi'an and the construction of the Yongding River and the military actions that were taken in Qinghai, "Juan Na" (donating food or money to buy an official position) was restored in the 56th year of Kangxi (1717). During the reign of Emperor Yongzheng, official positions below "Dao" (the administration district below the province) and "Fu" (ancient administrative district between province and county) could all be obtained through "Juan Na" (donating food or money to buy an official position). What is worse is that it was even extended to the obtaining of military positions. During the reign of Emperor Qianlong, the highest civil official positions that could be obtained through "Juan Na" (donating food or money to buy an official position) were the magistrates of "Dao" (the administration district below the province), "Fu" (ancient administrative district between province and county), and "Lang Zhong" (head of a subministry department), while the highest military official position was "You Ji" (the third rank military officer). Although "Juan Na" (donating food or money to buy an official position) had temporarily made up for the government revenue, yet since it had opened up the way for landlords and businessman to buy official positions, it had led to the redundancy of the bureaucracy and further corruption of the government. With the decline of the Qing Dynasty, "Juan Na" (donating food or money to buy an official position) was extensively applied and became a common malpractice during the Qing Dynasty, as was said by the people at that time:

> Since it is cheap to obtain the official position of "Zhou" (subprefecture) and "Xian" (county) by "Juan Na" (donating food or money to buy an official position), the descendents of the people who have power and money competed with each other to monopoly the official positions, while the people who do not have enough money have borrowed from others, because it is easy to pay the money back. The officials are not satisfied with their lower ranks, the scholars are not satisfied with their studies, the people are disunited, and each of them only care about their own personal interests. How is it possible to let them have self-respect?"[206]

"There are many ways of donation, which has not only brought about the corruption of official management, but also resulted in people's blind pursuit of profits and the overdraft of finance, which in turn has led to more ways of donation. So the chaos have led to more serious chaos,"[207] and this vicious cycle lasted till the collapse of the Qing Dynasty.

---

[205]"Xuan Ju Zhi" (The Record of Election) in *Qing Shi Gao* (*The Draft of the History of Qing Dynasty*), Vol. 7.

[206]"Xuan Ju Kao" (An Examination of Election) (Part 10) in *Qing Chao Xu Wen Xian Tong Kao* (*A Sequel of the General Textual Research of the Documents of Qing Dynasty*), Vol. 93.

[207]"Xuan Ju Kao" (An Examination of Election) (Part 10) in *Qing Chao Xu Wen Xian Tong Kao*(*A Sequel of the General Textual Research of the Documents of Qing Dynasty*), Vol. 93.

11.3 The Legalization of the Administrative System and the System of Official...

The system of "Yin Sheng" (the appointment of those whose former generations have made great contribution to the state) was another unusual way of obtaining official positions, which included "En Yin" (the appointment of the descendants of those who had made great contribution to the state), "Nan Yin" (the appointment of the descendants of those who died in their posts), and "Te Yin" (special appointments). "En Yin" (the appointment of the descendants of those who had made great contribution to the state) was established even in the early years of the reign of Emperor Shunzhi, according to which every civil official who had been in office for four years in the capital or who had been in office for three years out of the capital or a military officer whose official rank was above "Er Pin" (the second rank) was allowed to send a son to study in "Guo Zi Jian" (the highest educational body in ancient China), who could be granted an official position according to his father's official rank after graduation; "Nan Yin" (the appointment of the descendants of those who died in their posts) means that the people who died for the royal families could send a son to study in "Guo Zi Jian" (the highest educational body in ancient China), who could be granted an official position according to his father's official rank after graduation; "Te Yin" (special appointments) was established in the 3rd year of Qianlong (1738), according to which the descendants of meritorious officials without official positions or with low official positions could be recommended to be officials in "Liu Bu" (The Six Departments) as an award. According to *Yin Sheng Shou Guan Li (The Regulation for the Appointment of Those Whose Former Generations Have Made Great Contribution to the State)*, the officials of "Yi Pin" (the first rank) could recommend people to be officials of "Wu Pin" (the fifth rank) in case of vacancies; the officials of "Er Pin" (the second rank) could recommend people to be officials of "Liu Pin" (the sixth rank) in case of vacancies, the officials of "San Pin" (the third rank) could recommend people to be officials of "Qi Pin" (the seventh rank) in case of vacancies, and the officials of "Si Pin" (the fourth rank) could recommend people to be officials of "Ba Pin" (the eighth rank) in case of vacancies. As for the order of "Xi Yin" (the ancestors' official posts or titles of nobility are inherited by the offspring), it should be arranged in the following way: "Di Zhang Zi" (the eldest son born of one's legal wife), "Di Ci Zi" (the second son born one's legal wife), "Shu Zhang Zi" (the eldest son born of a concubine), "Shu Ci Zi" (the second son born of a concubine), and the brother and nephew. "The people who did not conduct 'Xi Yin' (the ancestors' official posts or titles of nobility are inherited by the offspring) according to this order would be punished by 'Zhang' (flogging with heavy sticks) for one hundred strokes with "Liu" (exile) for three years, so this order must be followed."[208]

As for the official assessment in early Qing Dynasty, the system of "Kao Man" (the general assessment of each official after he had been in office for a certain period of time during the Ming Dynasty) was followed. In the 4th year of Kangxi (1665), the system of "Kao Man" (the general assessment of each official after he had been in

---

[208]"Zhi Zhi" (The State Office System) in "Li Lv" (Statutes on Personnel) in *Da Qing Lv Li (The Laws and Precedents of Great Qing)*.

office for a certain period of time during the Ming Dynasty) was abolished and the systems of "Jing Cha" (the general assessment of officials in the capital) and "Da Ji" (the general examination of officials every three years) were implemented instead. "Jing Cha" refers to the assessment of officials in the capital, which was held once every three years, in the year of "Zi," "Mao," "Wu," and "You" (terrestrial branch used in combination with the Heavenly Stems to designate years, months, days, and hours in ancient China; here it means every three years). For officials above "San Pin" (the third rank) in the capital, local "Zong Du" (viceroy) and "Xun Fu" (procurators), they should report their strong points and shortcomings by themselves and then would be judged by the emperor; for officials below "San Pin" (the third rank) in the capital, they should be examined by "Li Bu" (The Department of Personnel) and "Du Cha Yuan" (The Court of Censors). "Jing Cha" (the general assessment of officials in the capital) is divided into three levels: first, "Chen Zhi" (competent); second, "Qin Zhi" (hard working); third, "Gong Zhi" (holding office), according to which the officials were awarded or punished. "Da Ji" (the general examination of officials every three years) refers to the assessment of the officials outside the capital, which was also held every three years, in the year of "Yin," "Si," "Shen," and "Hai" (the ten Heavenly Stems, used as serial numbers and also in combination with the twelve Earthly Branches to designate years, months, days, and hours in ancient China; here it means every three years). Besides "Du Fu" (the viceroys and procurators), the officials of "Fan" (Bu Zheng Shi: local administrative officer), "Nie" (An Cha Shi": head of judicial commission), "Dao" (the administration district below the province), "Fu" (ancient administrative district between province and county), "Zhou" (subprefecture), and "Xian" (county) were also assessed in "Da Ji" (the general examination of officials every three years). "Da Ji" (the general examination of officials every three years) was conducted in the following way: the officials of "Fan" (Bu Zheng Shi: local administrative officer), "Nie" (An Cha Shi": head of the judicial commission), "Dao" (the administration district below the province), and "Fu" (ancient administrative district between province and county) would submit their reports to "Du Fu" (the viceroys and procurators) to state whether they are competent, then "Du Fu" (the viceroys and procurators) would check what they had reported and record the result of the assessment in booklets and then report to "Li Bu" (The Department of Personnel) for reviewing. "Da Ji" (the general examination of officials every three years) is divided into two levels: "Zhuo Yi" (excellent) and "Chen Zhi" (competent), according to which the officials would be awarded or punished.

The official assessment was carried out through "Jing Cha" (the general assessment of officials in the capital) and "Da Ji" (the general examination of officials every three years). Generally speaking, the official assessment was divided into "Si Ge" and "Liu Fa". "Si Ge" refers to "Cai" (talents: high, average, low), "Shou" (moral integrity: honest, average, greedy), "Zheng" (professional work: hardworking, average, lazy), and "Nian" (age: young, middle aged, old); "Liu Fa" refers to "Bu Jing" (impropriety), "Ba Ruan Wu Wei" (indecisiveness and inaction), "Fu Zao" (fickleness), "Cai Li Bu Zu" (without talent and wisdom), "Nian Lao" (in years), and "You Ji" (illness). Those who were considered as "Bu Jing"

11.3 The Legalization of the Administrative System and the System of Official... 1163

(impropriety) and "Ba Ruan Wu Wei" (indecisiveness and inaction) would be dismissed; those who were considered as "Fu Zao" (fickleness) and "Cai Li Bu Zu" (without talent and wisdom) would be demoted; those who were considered as "Nian Lao" (in years) and "You Ji" (illness) would be forced to retire; those who were considered excellent in the appraisal would be recommended, appointed, promoted, awarded, and granted royal titles; those who were considered inferior in the appraisal would be punished by salary reduction, demotion, or dismissal; and those who were considered as corrupt or cruel would be punished.

"Kao Ji" (performance evaluation) was held by "Kao Gong Si" (Bureau of Performance Evaluation) of "Li Bu" (The Department of Personnel) with the help of "Li Ke Ji Shi Zhong" (the supervisor of the Department of Personnel) and "Yu Shi" (the censor) of "He Nan Dao" (Henan administrative region). Overall, the evaluation system and elaboration of regulations in the Qing Dynasty were more complete and detailed than those in the Ming Dynasty. Especially, during the reign of emperors Kangxi, Yongzheng, and Qianlong, "Jing Cha" (the general assessment of officials in the capital) and "Da Ji" (the general examination of officials every three years) were more strictly carried out. From the 22nd year to the 61st year of Kangxi (1675 A.D. to 1722 A.D.), "Da Ji" (the general examination of officials every three years) was held fourteen times, in which five hundred and eighty excellent officials were selected and five thousand one hundred and thirty seven officials were demoted and dismissed.[209] Emperor Shizong paid great attention to the management of officials, and he often said that "priority should be given to the selection of talents in administration"[210] because "it is the 'Ben' (the essence) of ruling the country to choose the talents, while the other things are all trivial matters so they the like the leaves and branches of trees."[211] He emphasized that "there is the person who can make the country stable, but there is no law that can make the country stable automatically" "As for the legislation and administration, how is it possible for them to remain flawless for ever? It has always been a fact that there is the person who can make the country stable, but there is no law that can make the country stable automatically, so it is the key to handle the civil and military affairs to make good strategies, because only when the right person is selected can his political views be implemented. In a word, I think that if there is the right person who could make the country stable, then it is possible to make the proper laws to make the country stable automatically."[212] If there are no talented people, "even if we have the benevolence of Yao and Shun, we would still become tyrants." In the 1st year of Yongzheng, "only one or two officials in each department can really perform their

---

[209] Guo Song Yi, *Zhong Guo Zheng Zhi Zhi Du Tong Shi* (*A Comprehensive History of the Chinese Political System*), Vol. 10, The People's Publishing House, 1996, p. 575.

[210] *Shang Yu Nei Ge* (*An Imperial Edict to Cabinet*), Vol. 1, on the 29th of November of the 61st year of Emperor Kangxi.

[211] "Yong Zheng Chao" (The Reign of Emperor Yongzheng) in *Dong Hua Lu* (*The Record of Donghua*), Vol. 9.

[212] *Shang Yu Nei Ge* (*An Imperial Edict to Cabinet*), Vol. 22, on the 2nd of July of the 2nd year of Emperor Yongzheng.

duties seriously, while there are many redundant official who are lazy, incompetent and indolent in their work."[213] This incident indicated that the official assessment system was not carried out effectively, which made Emperor Shizong very anxious as he was afraid that "the promotion and dismissal of officials are not faithfully conducted, the cases are unfairly settled ... So how can the people live peacefully and how can the officials be managed strictly?"[214] Thus, he paid great attention to the assessment and inspection of officials, so the system of "Kao Ji" (performance evaluation) was greatly strengthened.

In the 60th year of Qianlong, "Da Ji" (the general examination of officials every three years) and "Jing Cha" (the general assessment of officials in the capital) were held thirty three times, with eight hundred and seventy six excellent officials selected. Because the problem of aged officials was serious in this period, according to the record in "Da Ji" (the general examination of officials every three years) and "Jing Cha" (the general assessment of officials in the capital), the number of the aged officials was up to one thousand seven hundred and ninety.[215] Emperor Gaozong was quite concerned about this, so he clearly pointed out that "the officials who are old and in poor health should be prohibited from holding official positions to make up the number without active work."[216]

After the middle of the Qing Dynasty, although the system of "Kao Ji" (performance evaluation) was still carried out and it was boasted that "the dismissal or promotion officials was decided by ability and competency to give a warning to others,"[217] gradually both "Jing Cha" (the general assessment of officials in the capital) and "Da Ji" (the general examination of officials every three years) became a mere formality in practice. Take "Da Ji" (the general examination of officials every three years) for example; it was held eight times during the reign of Daoguang, with 1357 excellent officials selected, which was equal to the total number of excellent officials selected during the reign of emperors Kangxi, Yongzheng, and Qianlong and which outnumbered the officials punishable by 'Liu Fa.'"[218]

In addition to the system of "Kao Ji" (performance evaluation), the supervisory organs were in charge of the supervision of government officials. Compared with that of the Ming Dynasty, the supervisory law of the Qing Dynasty was more detailed. As early as the later years of Emperor Shunzhi, *Xun Fang Shi Yi Shi Kuan* (*Ten Articles of the Inspection Tour*) was issued, and the range of application of the law, the mutual supervision of "Du Fu" (the viceroys and procurators) and

---

[213]"Xuan Ju Kao" (An Examination of Election) in *Qing Chao Wen Xian Tong Kao* (*A General Textual Research of the Documents of Qing Dynasty*), Vol. 60.

[214]*Qing Shi Zong Shi Lu* (*The Record of Emperor Shizong of Qing Dynasty*), Vol. 49.

[215]Guo Song Yi, *Zhong Guo Zheng Zhi Zhi Du Tong Shi* (*A Comprehensive History of the Chinese Political System*), Vol. 10, The People's Publishing House, 1996, p. 576.

[216]*Qing Gao Zong Shi Lu* (*The Record of Qing Emperor Gaozong*), Vol. 1159.

[217]"Xuan Ju Kao" (An Examination of Election) in *Qing Chao Wen Xian Tong Kao* (*A General Textual Research of the Documents of Qing Dynasty*), Vol. 59.

[218]Guo Song Yi, *Zhong Guo Zheng Zhi Zhi Du Tong Shi* (*A Comprehensive History of Chinese Political System*), Vol. 10, p. 577.

11.3 The Legalization of the Administrative System and the System of Official...

"Yu Shi" (the censor), the supervision of "Yu Shi" (the censor), etc. were described in detail. In the 8th year of Qianlong (1743), *Tai Gui* (*Regulations*) was made by the Qing government on the basis of *Xian Gang Tiao Li* (*Legal Regulations*), which was created during the Ming Dynasty. After the reign of Emperor Qianlong, through successive revisions conducted during the reign of emperors Jiaqing, Daoguan, and Guangxu, *Tai Gui* (*Regulations*), which consisted of forty two volumes, was issued. *Tai Gui* (*Regulations*) was divided into eight categories, in which "Sheng Zhi" (the imperial institution), "Sheng Yu" (the imperial decree), and "Yu Zhi" (the imperial edict), which were relevant to supervision, were mainly collected and compiled. Moreover, the scope of official duty of "Du Cha Yuan" (The Court of Censors), "Ke" and "Dao" (both government offices, including the deaconry and the supervisory censor), and "Wu Cheng" (the censors of five districts of the capital) were stipulated; rules such as "Tiao Li" (regulation) and "Shi Li" (precedents), which were relevant to "Dian Li" (ceremony), "Kao Ji" (performance evaluation), "Hui Yan" (the review procedure of cases of death penalty), "Bian Su" (the defense of defendants for themselves), "Ji Cha" (checking), "Xun Cha" (a tour of inspection), and so on, were collected; and the assessment, selection, promotion, transfer, and etiquette of "Yu Shi" (the censor) were also stipulated in detail. So *Tai Gui* (*Regulations*) was not only the most detailed supervisory law made in the Qing Dynasty; it was also the basis for the activities of the supervisory organs. Moreover, *Du Cha Yuan Ze Li* (*The Regulation of the Court of Censors*) was implemented in the later years of Emperor Qianlong.

The official positions in the Qing Dynasty were divided into nine ranks and eighteen levels, and the officials who were below "Jiu Pin" (the ninth rank) were regarded as "Wei Ru Liu." The officials' salaries were paid according to their official ranks, and the officials in the capital had "Feng Yin" (money as salary), "Lu Mi" (rice as salary), and "En Feng" (pension), while the officials of "Zheng Yi Pin" (the plain first rank) in the capital were paid one hundred and eighty *liang* of "Feng Yin" (money as salary); "Lu Mi" (rice as salary), which was converted to ninety *liang* of silver; and two hundred and seventy *liang* of "En Feng" (pension). Officials outside of the capital were paid "Feng Yin" (money as salary) and "Yang Lian Yin" (money used to encourage officials to be honest), but they did not have "Lu Mi" (rice as salary) and "En Feng" (pension); the officials of "Yi Pin" (the first rank) outside of the capital were paid one hundred and eighty *liang* of "Feng Yin" (money as salary) and fifteen thousand *liang* of "Yang Lian Yin" (money used to encourage officials to be honest). It can be seen that the officials outside of the capital could earn a much higher salary than those in the capital. In the 1st year of Qianlong (1736), the government especially granted officials in the capital double salary because their salary was not enough for their daily expenses. "Yang Lian Yin" (money used to encourage officials to be honest) for officials outside of the capital was paid to prevent officials from taking bribes by bending the law. Nevertheless, it never achieved the goal of preventing corruption; instead, it only added an item to the official expenses, as was described in the following: "'Zhi Fu' (magistrate of a prefecture) who served one term of office in Qing Dynasty can earn as much as 100,000 *liang* of silver." Thus, it was a true description of the corruption in the Qing

Dynasty. Since the salary of the officials outside of the capital was higher than that of the officials in capital, the officials in the capital usually tried their best to be appointed as local officials of other places.

In the last years of the Qing Dynasty, apart from "Guan Feng" (official salary), "Gong Fei Yin" (money for official business) was paid by the government to officials, and different amounts of "Gong Fei Yin" (money for official business) were paid to officials depending on their ranks. For example, "Jun Ji Da Chen" (the grand councilor) was paid 24,000 *liang* of silver, but the junior department officials were only paid 180 *liang*.

The age of "Zhi Shi" (retirement) was sixty in the Qing Dynasty. Even if an official did not reach sixty years old, he may be allowed to retire to take care of his parents, and this was called "Zhong Yang." After the officials retired, if they still held inherited positions, they could get their salaries according to their official ranks; if not, they could only get half of their salaries. But the officials could not get their salaries if they retired due to sickness. Moreover, important officials would be paid their whole salaries when they retire. In early Qing Dynasty, if important officials retired, they would be paid higher salaries or be granted official titles or be given magnificent robes and clothes or be presented poems by the emperor himself. Sometimes their children would be granted official positions to reward them for their contribution to the state.

11.4 The Criminal Law Made to Strengthen the Autocratic Ruling

The criminal law of Qing Dynasty was the most comprehensive criminal law in the Chinese feudal society; moreover, it had reached to a very high level either in ideology or in principle, content and penal system.

11.4.1 The Main Crimes in Da Qing Xing Lv *(The Criminal Law of Great Qing)*

11.4.1.1 The Crime of "Fan Ni" (Treachery)

"Mou Fan" (plotting rebellion or plotting to endanger the country) refers to planning to endanger the security of "She Ji" (the country), and it was the most serious crime of "Shi E" (The Ten Abominations). During the reign of Emperor Kangxi, Shen Zhiqi, a scholar of "Lv Xue" (the study of statutory laws), explained in his annotation of law that "'Mou Fan' (plotting rebellion or plotting to endanger the country) means that a person does not show respect to the emperor or his families and violates the rules of ethics and morality, so that he is rejected by the whole society and resented by both gods and people. So this crime is listed separately to warn the other people."

"Mou Da Ni" (great sedition) refers to planning to destroy imperial temples, tombs, and palaces. According to *Tang Lv* (*Tang Code*), the crime of "Mou Da Ni" (great sedition) is divided into accomplished and unaccomplished ones, so that different rules were provided for "Lian Zuo Jia Shu" (the family members punished for being related to somebody who committed an offense). However, according to the laws of the Qing Dynasty, "Mou Fan" (plotting rebellion or plotting to endanger the country) and "Mou Da Ni" (great sedition) were considered as crimes "which are intolerable by law" and "which are extremely evil and serious," so the conspirators, both the chief and accessory criminals, should be punished by "Ling Chi" (the punishment of dismemberment and lingering death). At the same time, their father, children, grandfather and grandsons, brothers, and the people who lived with them (regardless of their different family names), as well as uncles and nephews who were older than sixteen three years old, should all be sentenced to death, regardless of whether they were "Du Ji" (incapacitated) or "Fei Ji" (disabled) and regardless of their birth place. In addition, his boys who are under the age of fifteen, his mother, daughters, wife, concubines, sisters, and nephew's wives and concubines would all serve as slaves in the families of the meritorious officials with his property confiscated by the state. Even if his children were really innocent, if they are older than eleven years old, they would be castrated and sent to Xinjiang to become servants of the government. What is more, the scope of application of "Fan Ni" (treachery) was expanded in the Qing Dynasty, so that "those who have violated the taboos in their memorials" or "who have submitted memorials inappropriately" would all be punished for the crime of "insanity" and "discussing state affairs recklessly" according to the law of "Da Ni" (great sedition).

"Mou Pan" (treason) refers to betraying the government or having secret communication with and surrendering to foreign countries. "Anyone who has committed the crime of 'Mou Pan' (treason), whether the chief or the accessory criminal, would be punished by 'Zhan' (beheading) with his wife, concubines and children serving as slaves in the families of the meritorious officials." "The families of the criminals who have escaped and hidden in mountains or refused to obey the rulings of the courts would be regarded as the unaccomplished crime of 'Mou Pan' (treason), so the principal and accessory criminals would be punished differently. The families of criminals who had fought with or resisted against the government troops would be punished as 'Mou Pan' (treason), regardless of the principal or accessory criminals."[219] During the reign of Emperor Kangxi, the scope of application of "Mou Pan" (treason) was expanded, and all of the officials "who have helped to conceal the families of the criminals or their property" would be punished by "Mou Pan"

---

[219]"Dao Zei" (Theft) in "Xing Lv" (The Penal Code) in *Da Qing Lv Ji Jie Fu Li* (*Great Qing Code with Collected Commentaries and Appended Sub-statutes*), Vol. 18.

(treason) if the circumstances were serious.[220] During the reign of Emperor Qianlong, in order to prevent the Han people from gathering a crowd to rebel against the Qing government by taking advantage of religion or by way of becoming sworn brothers, a regulation was provided:

> As to those with different family names, if they have smeared the blood as a sigh of the oath or become sworn brothers, they will be punished for the unaccomplished crime of "Mou Pan" (treason) with the principal criminals punished by "Jiao Jian Hou" (the punishment of suspending hanging) and the accessory criminals punished one level lighter. If more than twenty people have gathered a crowd, the principal criminals will be punished by "Jiao Jue" (the punishment of hanging to death with an immediate execution), and the accessory criminals will be punished by "Chong Jun" (to be forced to join the army) in Guangdong and Guangxi province or in the border areas; if more than forty people have gathered a crowd, the principal criminals will be punished by "Jiao Jian Hou" (the punishment of suspending hanging); if more than twenty to forty people have gathered a crowd, the principal criminals will be punished by "Zhang" (flogging with heavy sticks) for one hundred strokes and then be punished by "Liu" (exile) to places 3000 *li* away; if fewer than twenty people have gathered a crowd, the principal criminals will be punished by wearing "Jia Hao" (cangue: a large wooden collar worn by petty criminals as a punishment) for two months and the accessory criminals will be punished by one level lighter.[221]

What is more, during the reign of Emperor Shunzhi, severe punishments were enforced to prevent "Meng She" (forming an association), and in the 17th year of Shunzhi (1660), it was announced that "it is forbidden for officials to form parties or associations by gathering people"; otherwise, they would be punished.[222]

As for the perpetrators of "Mou Fan" (plotting rebellion or plotting to endanger the country), "Mou Da Ni" (great sedition), and "Mou Pan" (treason), "if people know their whereabouts but have concealed or helped them, they will be punished by 'Zhan' (beheading); if people have arrested them, the civilians will be appointed as civil officials while the soldiers will be appointed as military officers, with all the property confiscated and rewarded to the arresters. If the criminals are arrested by the government, money will be rewarded to the people who learn of the crimes and report first to the government, but the people who do not make reports will be punished by 'Zhang' (flogging with heavy sticks) for one hundred strokes and then be punished by 'Liu' (exile) to places 3000 *li* away."[223]

In addition, if people had refused to turn over grain to the state by gathering a crowd of more than forty people or had boycotted examinations and businesses, the chief criminals would be punished by "Zhan" (beheading) immediately; the accessories of the crime would be punished by "Jiao Jian Hou" (punishment of

---

[220]"Dao Zei" (Theft) in "Xing Lv" (The Penal Code) in *Da Qing Lv Li* (*The Laws and Precedents of Great Qing*), Vol. 22.

[221]"Dao Zei" (Theft) in "Xing Lv" (The Penal Code) in *Da Qing Lv Li* (*The Laws and Precedents of Great Qing*), Vol. 22.

[222]"Xue Xiao Kao" (An Examination of Schools) in *Qing Chao Wen Xiao Tong Kao* (*A General Textual Research of the Documents of Qing Dynasty*), Vol. 69..

[223]"Dao Zei" (Theft) in "Xing Lv" (The Penal Code) in *Qing Chao Lv Jie Fu Li* (*Great Qing Code with Collected Commentaries and Appended Sub-statutes*), Vol. 18.

11.4 The Criminal Law Made to Strengthen the Autocratic Ruling

suspending hanging), and criminals who were threatened by others to participate in the crimes would be punished by "Zhang" (flogging with heavy sticks) for one hundred strokes. If people had interfered in public business or attacked officials by gathering a crowd, the chief criminals would be punished by "Zhan Jue" (the punishment of cutting down the criminal's head) and "Xiao Shou" (the penalty of hanging the head of a criminal on top of a pole for public display), the accessory criminals would be punished by "Jiao Jian Hou" (the punishment of suspending hanging), and the criminals who were threatened by others to participate in the crimes would be punished by "Zhang" (flogging with heavy sticks) for one hundred strokes. "Those who have made up strange tales or published books to confuse other people will be punished by 'Zhan' (beheading); the people who have purchased and hidden such books instead of handing them over to the government will be punished by 'Zhang' (flogging with heavy sticks) for one hundred strokes and then be punished by 'Tu' (imprisonment) for three years."[224]

11.4.1.2 The Crime of Heretical Ideology

The so-called heretical ideology mainly refers to the anti-Qing dynasty ideology. In order to crack down heretical ideology, "Wen Zi Yu" (literary inquisition) was implemented many times. During the reign of Emperors Shunzhi and Kangxi, Zhuang Tinglong in Zhejiang province compiled a book called *Ming Shu (The History of Ming Dynasty)* with other scholars, and it was described in the book that in order to set up "Du Du" (military viceroys and procurators) in "Zhou" (subprefecture), Nurhachi used the titles of the reign of the Southern Ming Dynasty, such as "Long Wu" and "Yong Li," instead of those of the Qing Dynasty, for which he was accused by others. At that time, Zhuang Tinglong had already died, but he was punished by "Lu Shi" (the punishment of chopping up the corpse of a criminal). Consequently, altogether more than seventy people were put to death, including his brothers; children; nephews; the people who participated in the editing, proofreading, or storage of this book; and the local officials who failed to discover it beforehand. Gui Zhuang, a contemporary of the Qing Dynasty said that "in the early period of Emperor Kangxi, many people were killed by the government for discussing state affairs and compiling history books, so since then, the control for literary creation became much stricter."[225] During the reign of Emperor Qianlong, although many times the emperor said in his imperial edits, "I have never punished people for what they say,"[226] actually during his reign, "Wen Zi Yu" (literary

---

[224]"Dao Zei" (Theft) in "Xing Lv" (The Penal Code) in *Da Qing Lv Li (The Laws and Precedents of Great Qing)*, Vol. 23.
[225]*Gui Zhuang Ji (An Anthology of Gui Zhuang)*, Vol. 10.
[226]"Zhe Sun Jia Jin Cha Ming Xie Ji Shi Zhu Shu Ju Zou Yu" (A Memorial Submitted by Sun Jiajin about Checking out Xie Jishi's Annotation) in *Qing Dai Wen Zi Yu Dang (Files of Literary Inquisition in Qing Dynasty)*, Vol. 1.

inquisition) had reached its climax in the Qing Dynasty, so sometimes even one word or one sentence would lead to imprisonment. Since no legal regulations were made on "Wen Zi Yu" (literary inquisition) in the Qing Dynasty and punishments were often enforced according to the regulations on "Da Ni" (great sedition), once a case of "Wen Zi Yu" (literary inquisition) was discovered, it meant a disaster for the whole family, and even the unborn children would become slaves. In the 4th year of Yongzheng (1726), Cha Siting and Yu Hongtu were responsible for the examination of "Ke Ju" (the imperial examination) in Jiangxi, and the examination topics were as follows: "'Jun Zi' (gentlemen) never recommend or promote people for what they say" and "pathway among the mountain streams," but they were imprisoned and killed because they were accused of harboring evil intentions toward the emperor. Later they were even punished by "Lu Shi" (the punishment of chopping up the corpse of a criminal) and "Xiao Shou" (the penalty of hanging the head of the criminal on top of a pole for public display) with their sons put to death and their families punished by "Liu" (exile). During the reign of Emperor Qianlong, cabinet minister Hu Zhongzao wrote a line in his poetry: "Yi Ba Xin Chang Lun Zhuo Qing" (I can tell the filthiness from the purity), but he was killed by the emperor. In the examination of "Ke Ju" (the imperial examination) in Guangxi province, the topic "Qian San Yao Bu Xiang Long" (It is not like a dragon according to the trigram) was made the question of the examination, but he was charged for insulting the emperor and the government and was executed at the market. Xu Shukui in Jiangsu province once wrote in his poetry: "If I can meet the emperors of the great Ming again, I would put the wine pot aside," and "I hope tomorrow morning I can fly high, then I can fly to the capital of Qing dynasty," but he was punished by death penalty and "Lu Shi" (the punishment of chopping up the corpse of a criminal), with all his children and grandchildren and the collators put to death because he was accused of intending to restore the Ming Dynasty. What's more, during the reign of Emperor Shunzhi, severe punishments were enforced to prevent "Meng She" (to form an association); in addition, it was announced in the 17th year of Shunzhi (1660) that "it is forbidden for officials to organize parties or associations"; otherwise, they would be punished. In the process of codifying *Si Ku Quan Shu (Complete Library in the Four Branches of Literature)*, taboo words were deleted, forged, distorted, misrepresented, and even destroyed on a large scale. From the 39th to the 47th year of Emperor Qianlong (1774–1782), twenty four orders were sucessively issued to destroy books, and about 538 kinds of books and 13,862 copies were destroyed in order to strengthen the autocratic control in the ideological and cultural fields.

In order to control people's ideology, "all those who fabricated and spread rumors around, or made up songs to sing in streets or published and spread vulgar and obscure words would be put to death according to the regulations of spreading fallacies to deceive people."[227] In the 53rd year of Kangxi (1714), it was ordered that all sculptors and writers of pornographic novels be punished by "Zhang" (flogging

---

[227]*Da Qing Lv Li Tong Kao (A Textual Research of the Laws and Precedents of Great Qing)*, Vol. 23.

with heavy sticks) for one hundred strokes and "Liu" (exile) for 3000 *li* if they were civilians and military personnel and would be dismissed if they were officials. The people who sold these books would be punished by "Zhang" (flogging with heavy sticks) for one hundred strokes and "Tu" (imprisonment) for three years, and the people who bought or read these books would be punished by "Zhang" (flogging with heavy sticks) for one hundred strokes.[228]

To conclude, there were hundreds of cases of "Wen Zi Yu" (literary inquisition) during the reign of Emperor Kangxi, Yongzheng and Qianlong and many people were punished for "fabricated charges", so it was notorious for its unprecedented severe punishments and extensiveness scope of the implicated crimes, which had not only led to the discrepancy between imperial edicts and the codes and between accusation and judicial trials, but also to the inconsistency of imperial edicts which were issued at different times. No doubt, it had obviously reflected the ideological and cultural control of extreme despotism.

11.4.1.3 The Crime of "Da Bu Jing" (Great Irreverence)

Under the historical condition of extreme development of despotism, the provision of "Da Bu Jing" (great irreverence), which was provided in the laws of Tang and Ming dynasties was adapted in the Qing Dynasty; what is more, its punishment was aggravated. Accordingly, all those who offended the emperor in their memorials or violated the temple taboos would be punished by "Zhang" (flogging with heavy sticks) for eighty strokes; if the emperor's name was offended, those involved would be punished by "Zhang" (flogging with heavy sticks) for one hundred strokes. Moreover, those who did not follow doctors' prescriptions when preparing medicine for the emperor or violated any food prohibition when preparing food for the emperor or did not take good care of the goods and clothes used by the emperor or made imperial ships that did not meet the standards would all be punished by "Zhang" (flogging with heavy sticks) for one hundred strokes and "Tu" (imprisonment) for three years for the crime of endangering the security of the emperor. If people had broken imperial carriages, they would be punished by "Jiao" (hanging), and if officials, soldiers, and the common people had walked straight on the imperial roads or bridges with no reason, they would be punished according to law for showing disrespect to the imperial power.

11.4.1.4 The Crime of "Jian Dang" (Treacherous Cliques)

In the 17th year of Emperor Shunzhi (1660), in order to "permanently eliminate the root of forming cliques", orders were issued to prohibit people from forming alliances

---

[228]*Da Qing Lv Li Tong Kao (A Textual Research of the Laws and Precedents of Great Qing)*, Vol. 23.

at the suggestion of Yang Yongjian, the "Li Ke Ji Shi Zhong" (the supervisor of the department of personnel) at the time was adopted, and orders were issued to strictly prohibit people from forming alliances in order to "permanently eliminate the root of cliques."[229] Before that, Chen Mingxia, "Da Xue Shi" (grand secretary), was punished by death penalty for concealing his evil intention and for ganging up for selfish interests.

In the middle of the reign of Emperor Kangxi, disputes often arose between the officials of Manchu and Han nationalities, and the parties in the south and north took revenge on each other. In order to solve this problem, Emperor Shengzu warned his ministers: "If you refuse to come to your senses and persis in your old ways, you will be severely punished for forming cliques after I have investigated the root reasons."[230] Moreover, dissidents were severely attacked by Emperor Shizong for the crime of forming cliques, and many people were killed in a short span of time. During the reign of Emperor Qianlong, an imperial edict was issued by Emperor Gaozong even before the case of Hu Zhongzao, and it was stated that "cliques are often formed to bend the law for the benefit of party members, which have been noticed in the past by the previous emperors, so strict measures have been taken to prevent such activities." "Nevertheless, if these measures have not been strictly implemented, the old bad habits and evil practice will resurge, and the illegal cases like Cha Siting and Lv Liuliang will occur again in future. So the state constitution should be carried out strictly to warn the diehards, I'd like that you ministers be on alert."[231]

In *Da Qing Lv Li* (*The Laws and Precedents of Great Qing*), the provisions on the crime of "Jian Dang" (treacherous cliques), which were provided in *Da Qing Lv Ji Jie Fu Li* (*Great Qing Code with Collected Commentaries and Appended Sub-statutes*), were all adopted, and the officials inside and outside of the capital were strictly forbidden to collude with each other. So "the officials inside and outside of the capital were not allowed to have contact with other people except their best friends, close relatives and fellow-townsmen. If the officials out of the capital come to work or visit the officials in the capital or send people to visit them, they would be dismissed. In addition, if the officials in the capital had met with those who come from outside of the capital or sent people to visit them, they would be dismissed, too."[232] Especially, it was forbidden for subordinates of princes and dukes in each "Qi" (banner, equivalent of a county) who were outside the capital to visit the princes and dukes who were in charge of their districts when they dealt with official businesses in the capital; otherwise, they would be punished by "Zhang" (flogging with heavy sticks) for one hundred strokes, and the princes and dukes who were in charge of their districts would be sent to "Zong Ren Fu" (The Imperial Clan Court) to

---

[229]"Shun Zhi Chao" (The Reign of Emperor Shunzhi) in *Dong Hua Lu* (*The Record of Donghua*), Vol. 28.

[230]*Qing Shi Zu Shi Lu* (*The Record of Emperor Shizu of Qing Dynasty*), Vol. 153.

[231]*Qing Gao Zong Shi Lu* (*The Record of Qing Emperor Gaozong*), Vol. 153.

[232]*Qin Ding Li Bu Ze Li* (*The Regulation of the Department of Personnel Made by Imperial Order*).

be punished according to law. If the officials had exchanged letters secretly with each other to ask for information or to borrow money, they would be sent to "Zong Ren Fu" (The Imperial Clan Court) to be punished for the crime of "Zuo Zang" (embezzlement).[233] Thus, it can be seen that the prohibition on the collusion of officials inside and outside the capital was made especially for the heads of "Ba Qi" (the Eight Banners: banner, a division of the Manchu nationality and the emperor's clan) because they had imposed great threat to the imperial power at the time, from which we can see that some new contents were added to the crime of "Jian Dang" (treacherous cliques) but also reflected the characteristics of the times.

What is more, if the ministers had contacted the eunuchs or the officials in the capital had contacted the wealthy people, they would be punished by "Zhan" (beheading) or "Chong Jun" (being forced to join the army); if the "officials of 'Ya Men' (the government offices) have contacted the eunuchs and the close servants of nobilities or have leaked secret information, or have practiced fraud by submitting memorials with other people, they will be punished by 'Zhan' (beheading) with their wives punished by 'Liu' (exile) for 2000 *li*"; "if the retired and dismissed officials who live in the capital have entered forbidden palace gates to contact other people without authorization, they will be sent to 'Fa Si' (The Judicial Office) to be investigated and punished by 'Chong Jun' (being forced to join the army) in the areas of 'Yan Zhang' (jungles)."[234] In the annotation to the provision of "getting in touch with the close attendents of nobilities" in the 9th volume of *Tang Ming Lv He Bian* (*A Collection of Laws in Tang and Ming Dynasties*), Xue Yunsheng, who was a contemporary of the Qing Dynasty, said:

> The emperor has spared no efforts to prevent his ministers from forming cliques to usurp the imperial power and authority. However, he is so suspicious and jealous that there are very few upright and outspoken officials in the government. So most of the officials are lazy and indolent, and they only knew how to enjoy themselves; if some great event happen, they always agree with what the superior say and never express their own opinions. Alas, is it beneficial to the state affairs!

But this was necessary to eliminate the threats to the imperial power and to ensure the autocratic centralization of state power.

11.4.1.5 The Crime of "Jiang Yang Da Dao" (Infamous Robbery)

According to the subsidiary rule of "Qiang Dao" (robbery) in "Zei Dao" (theft and robbery) in "Xing Lv" (The Penal Code) in *Huang Chao Zheng Dian Lei Zuan* (*A Collection of the Administrative Laws of the Dynasty*), in the 26th year of Qianlong

---

[233]"Zhi Zhi" (The State Office System) in "Li Lv" (Statutes on Personnel) in *Huang Chao Zheng Dian Lei Zuan* (*A Collection of the Administrative Laws of the Dynasty*), Vol. 377.

[234]"Fu Li" (The Subsidiary Precedent) in "Jiao Jie Jin Shi Guan Yuan" (Associating with Attendant Officials) in "Li Lv" (Statutes on Personnel) in *Da Qing Lv Li Tong Zuan* (*A General Compilation of the Laws and Precedents of Great Qing*).

(1761), the crime of "Jiang Yang Da Dao" (infamous robbery) was provided for the first time, and it mainly referred to the criminals "who rob passenger ships by the sea or along the rivers." All those "who have obtained money," no matter where they come from, "shall be tried according to the regulations on 'Jiang Yang Da Dao' (infamous robbery) and the principal and accessory criminals will be punished by 'Zhan Jue' (the punishment of cutting down the criminal's head) without being forgiven even if they are excusable according to circumstances." It can be seen that after the reign of Emperor Qianlong, "Jiang Yang Da Dao" (infamous robbery) became the focus of criminal crackdown.

After Emperor Renzong's succession to the throne, since "Jiang Yang Da Dao" (infamous robbery) not only threatened coast and river defense but also influenced national water transportation, new regulations were made in the 6th year of Jiaqing (1801), and it was declared that "all 'Jiang Yang Da Dao' (infamous robbery) will be punished by 'Zhan' (beheading) and 'Xiao Shi' (hanging the head of the criminal on top of a piece of wood) according to law."[235] Then a supplementary regulation was added: "If the criminal refuses to be arrested and have killed other people, he will be punished by 'Ling Chi' (the punishment of dismemberment and the lingering death) if the circumstances are serious"[236]; "if people have privately transported vegetables to help the criminals, they will be punished according to the precedent on helping the robbers with rice and grain"[237]; "if the ship owner has colluded with bandits in robbing the goods and passengers, even if he does not participate in the robbery himself, he will be punished according to the precedent of 'Qing You Ke Yuan' (being forgivable)."[238] During the reign of Daoguang, great changes had taken place home and abroad, so the punishment for "Jiang Yang Da Dao" (infamous robbery) became much stricter. In the 16th year of Daoguang (1836), it was ordered by Emperor Xuanzong that the coastal villages and ports be carefully checked and "investigations shall be conducted frequently to get rid of the 'Wo Xian' (a person who spies on the situation and acts as a guide when necessary) and the sources of

---

[235] "Qiang Dao" (Robbery) (revised in the 6th year) in "Dao Zei" (Theft) in "Xing Lv" (The Penal Code) in *Da Qing Lv Li Tong Zuan* (*A General Compilation of the Laws and Precedents of Great Qing*).

[236] "Dao Zei" (Theft) in "Xing Lv" (The Penal Code) in *Huang Chao Zheng Dian Lei Zuan* (*A Collection of the Administrative Laws of the Dynasty*).

[237] "Fu Zou Zhun Jia Qin Shi Jiu Nian Guang Dong An Li" (An Attached Memorial on Approving the Cases of Guangdong in the 19th year of Emperor Jiaqing) and "Fu Zou Zhun Guang Dong Si Jia Qin Shi Wu Nian Shuo Tie"(An Attached Memorial on Approving the Proposal Made in Guangdong Bureau in the 15th year of Emperor Jiaqing) in "Dao Zei" (Theft) in "Xing Lv" (The Penal Code) in *Huang Chao Zheng Dian Lei Zuan* (*A Collection of the Administrative Laws of the Dynasty*).

[238] "Fu Zou Zhun Jia Qin Shi Jiu Nian Guang Dong An Li" (An Attached Memorial on Approving the Cases of Guangdong in the 19th year of Emperor Jiaqing) and "Fu Zou Zhun Guang Dong Si Jia Qin Shi Wu Nian Shuo Tie" (An Attached Memorial on Approving the Proposal Made in Guangdong Bureau in the 15th year of Emperor Jiaqing) in "Dao Zei" (Theft) in "Xing Lv" (The Penal Code) in *Huang Chao Zheng Dian Lei Zuan* (*A Collection of the Administrative Laws of the Dynasty*).

robbers." And it was also ordered that the "civil and military officials in coastal provinces should strictly check up the rogues and evil people to prevent them from colluding with each other to wipe out the robbers and to restore social order."[239]

11.4.1.6 The Crime of Spreading Heresy

In order to prevent people from organizing themselves in order to revolt against the Qing Dynasty by making use of religion, the rulers of the Qing Dynasty always attached great importance to fighting against heresy through criminal legislation. In the provision of "Jin Zhi Shi Wu Xie Shu" (No Teaching of Sorcerer and Witchcraft) in *Da Qing Lv Li* (*The Laws and Precedents of Great Qing*), the following is provided:

> If any sorcerer has pretended to be evil gods and made spells, taken oaths, consulted spirits through the planchette, claimed himself or herself to be "Duan Gong" (man with magical powers), "Tai Bao" (wizard) or "Shi Po" (witch), or disguised himself or herself to be "Maitreya" (a Buddha), a member of "Bai Lian Jiao" (White Lotus Society), "Ming Zun Jiao" (Manichean), "Bai Xue Zong" (White Snow Society) and so on, or employed heretic techniques, concealed pictures, burnt incense and organized gatherings, or gathered at night and scattered in the dawn or pretended to do good things to stir up the people under the disguise of overcoming evil spirits, the principal shall be punished by "Jiao Jian Hou" (the punishment of suspending hanging) and the accessory shall be punished by both "Zhang" (flogging with heavy sticks) for one hundred strokes and "Liu" (exile) for 3000 *li*; if any civilian and armyman have dressed themselves up to play supernatural beings, or beat gongs and drums to greet gods or held illegal celebrations, he shall be punished by "Zhang" (flogging with heavy sticks) for one hundred strokes and the principal criminal shall also be punished; if "Li Zhang" (head of "Li": the basic resident organization in ancient China) has learned of the activities but failed to report, he shall be punished by "Chi" (flogging with light sticks) for forty strokes.

After one hundred years of prosperity, the Qing Dynasty declined rapidly from the reign of emperors Kangxi and Qianlong to the reign of Emperor Renzong. In the early period of Emperor Jiaqing, in view of the fact that peasant uprising was often organized under the guise of religion, the regulations on the prohibition of "Bai Yang Jiao" (White Sun Society, one of the sects of White Lotus Society) and other rebellious religions were revised. The following was provided in the rule issued in the 6th year of Jiaqing (1801), which was attached to the provision of "Jin Zhi Shi Wu Xie Shu" (No Teaching of Sorcerer and Witchcraft) in "Ji Si" (sacrifice) in "Li Lv" (Code of Rites) in *Huang Chao Zheng Dian Lei Zuan* (*A Collection of the Administrative Laws of the Dynasty*):

> Those who have spread or studied heresies like "Bai Yang Jiao" (White Sun Society, one of the sects of White Lotus Society), "Bai Lian Jiao" (White Lotus Society), "Ba Gua" (eight diagrams) and other cults, or have studied ridiculous spells to bewitch the people, or have

---

[239]"Qiang Dao" (Robbery) (attached to the edict issued in the 16th year of Daoguang) in "Dao Zei" (Theft) in "Xing Lv" (The Penal Code) in *Huang Chao Zheng Dian Lei Zuan* (*A Collection of the Administrative Laws of the Dynasty*).

instigated people by following masters and receiving apprentices, the principal criminals will be punished by "Jiao" (hanging) immediately and the accessories who are younger than sixty years old or who are older than sixty years but who still preach the heresy by teaching the students will be sent back to their home town to be punished by the senior or junior "Bo Ke" (the officials of the Hui ethnic group) or be sent to other Hui People to have them supervised and educated to serve as their slaves; those who are induced to follow but who have never preached a cult will be punished by "Chong Jun" (to be forced to join the army) to uncivilized places of "Yan Zhang" (jungles) in Yunnan, Guizhou, Guangdong and Guangxi province if they are older than sixty years old; if they are "Qi Ren" (members of the Manchu ethnic group), they will be punished according to the same law applicable to the common people with their names removed from the files of registration; those who are registered with "Hong Yang Jiao" (Red Sun Society, one of the sects of White Lotus Society) and other religions shall be banished to Urumchi to serve as slaves with Manchu and Han people separately treated, if they have not studied or spread spells, but have just paid sacrifice to "Piao Gao Lao Zu" (the founder of Red Sun Society) by following masters or receiving apprentices in that religion; those who have not preached the religion, but who have paid sacrifice to "Piao Gao Lao Zu" (the founder of Red Sun Society) or collected religious books will be punished by "Chong Jun" (to be forced to join the army) in remote areas; if anyone has taught the methods of mediation and "Qi Gong" (a self-designed system of deep breathing exercises), he will be punished by "Zhang" (flogging with heavy sticks) for eighty strokes; if anyone has repented and surrendered himself to the government, he will be exempted from punishment with his name and files recorded in "Nie Si Ya Men" (the governmental office in charge of the administration of justice) by the local officials; if anyone has believed or preached heresy again, he will be punished one level severer according to law; ... if anyone has repented after being arrested, he will not be subject to penalty reduction but will be punished accordingly; if it is proved after investigation that one really has burnt incense, recited Buddhist texts or worshipped Buddha for the purpose of inviting good fortune rather than preaching, or if he never follows any master or involves in preaching, or if he knows nothing about the heresy, he will be exempted from punishment; if anyone has claimed to be a good friend and offered or asked for donation from more than ten people, or has claimed to be an alchemist and visited the families of the officials in and outside the capital, or entered royal palace without permission to offer bribes, he will be punished by "Chong Jun" (to be forced to join the army) in nearby frontiers; if the hosts of Buddhist or Taoist temples have harbored or sheltered any soldier and civilian or accepted more than ten believers without checking their background, they shall also be punished by "Chong Jun" (to be forced to join the army) in nearby frontiers; if fewer than ten believers have been accepted, the persons who have harbored, hidden, recommended or hired the aforesaid persons, or any neighbors thereof who have knowingly failed to report the aforesaid persons, or any soldiers guarding the royal palace gateways who have failed to perform the duty to catch the aforesaid persons, they shall be punished for violating the regulations respectively; if the circumstances are extremely serious, discretion shall be exercised by the government officials.[240]

As can be seen from above, according to the regulation issued in the 6th year of Jiaqing, the punishment for the leaders of "Bai Yan Jiao" (White Sun Society, one of the sects of White Lotus Society) and "Bai Lian Jiao" (White Lotus Society) was aggravated, and their penalties were changed from "Jiao Jian Hou" (the punishment of suspending hanging) to "Jiao Li Jue" (immediate execution by hanging); at the

---

[240]"Jin Zhi Shi Wu Xie Shu" (No Teaching of Sorcerer and Witchcraft) (attached to the 6th revised precedents in the reign of Emperor Jiaqing) in "Ji Si" (Sacrifice) in "Li Lv" (Statutes on Rites) in *Huang Chao Zheng Dian Lei Zuan* (*A Collection of the Administrative Laws of the Dynasty*).

same time, those who surrendered themselves and showed repentance were exempted from punishment, which was favorable for the disintegration of such religious groups. Also, the officials were granted expedient power to exercise discretion. However, if any officials had failed to conduct thorough investigations or performed their duties of checking at customs or had caused serious losses, they would be punished according to law. During the reign of Emperor Daoguang, it was further provided that "if any convict who has been sent back to his homeland has failed to comply with the law, he shall be punished by 'Qian Xing' (the penalty of banishing the criminals to do forced labor in remote areas) and by wearing 'Jia Hao' (cangue: a large wooden collar worn by petty criminals as punishment) for all his life[241]; if any convict who has been sent back to his homeland but has stayed on the way instead, he would still be punished by 'Qian Xing' (the penalty of banishing the criminals to do forced labor in remote areas)[242] and none of the principals will be pardoned whatever their convictions are."[243] Because heresy had a strong a strong and harmful influence upon the people and had posed a great threat to the ruling of Qing Dynasty, it was strictly prevented and severely punished.

11.4.1.7 The Crime of Opium Trade and Smoking

In the 7th year of Yongzheng (1729), the order on banning opium smoking and opium trade was first issued by the Qing government, and it was provided that opium traders and smokers should be punished by wearing "Jia Hao" (cangue: a large wooden collar worn by petty criminals as punishment) for one month and be punished by "Liu" (exile) to a nearby frontier according to applicable precedents on trading prohibited goods. If anyone had instigated the children of decent families to smoke by opening opium houses, he should be punished by "Jiao Jian Hou" (the punishment of suspending hanging) according to the same regulation on heresy, and the accessories would be punished by "Zhang" (flogging with heavy sticks) for one hundred strokes and "Liu" (exile) for 3000 *li*. Moreover, the boatmen, "Di Bao" (those who take charge of local missions in the Qing Dynasty and the early years of the Republic of China), and their neighbors would all be punished by "Zhang"

---

[241]"Jin Zhi Shi Wu Xie Shu" (No Teaching of Sorcerer and Witchcraft) (attached to the cases in Sichuan in the 7th year of Emperor Daoguang and the additional precedent issued in the 12th year of Daoguang) in "Ji Si" (Sacrifice) in "Li Lv" (Statutes on Rites) in *Huang Chao Zheng Dian Lei Zuan* (*A Collection of the Administrative Laws of the Dynasty*).

[242]"Jin Zhi Shi Wu Xie Shu" (No Teaching of Sorcerer and Witchcraft) (attached to the cases in Sichuan in the 7th year of Emperor Daoguang and the additional precedent issued in the 12th year of Daoguang) in "Ji Si" (Sacrifice) in "Li Lv" (Statutes on Rites) in *Huang Chao Zheng Dian Lei Zuan* (*A Collection of the Administrative Laws of the Dynasty*).

[243]"Jin Zhi Shi Wu Xie Shu" (No Teaching of Sorcerer and Witchcraft) (attached to the cases in Sichuan in the 7th year of Emperor Daoguang and the additional precedent issued in the 12th year of Daoguang) in "Ji Si" (Sacrifice) in "Li Lv" (Statutes on Rites) in *Huang Chao Zheng Dian Lei Zuan* (*A Collection of the Administrative Laws of the Dynasty*).

(flogging with heavy sticks) for one hundred strokes and "Tu" (imprisonment) for two years; if any soldiers or officers in the army had asked for opium to smoke, they would be convicted for bending the law; if any civilian or military officials had worked at port cities or the customs houses but had neglected their duties, they would be sent to relevant departments and be severely punished. So it can be seen from abovementioned that the focus of the punishment was to regulate opium trades and to enhance a sense of responsibility on the part of the officials. During the reign of Emperor Renzong, more than ten orders on banning opium trade and smoking were issued to regulate the conviction and punishment of opium smoking, and it was provided that opium smokers would be punished by "Zhang" (flogging with heavy sticks) for one hundred strokes and by wearing "Jia Hao" (cangue: a large wooden collar worn by petty criminals as punishment) for two months. It was also stated that "foreign ships docking in Macao must be checked one by one so as to eliminate the sources of opium. Since opium trade in Guangzhou had always been a serious problem for a long time, all the local officials would be punished for failing to fully perform their duties." In the 1st year of Daoguang (1821), in order to stop opium smuggling, it was provided that "for all the foreign ships docking in Guangdong, the itinerant traders must first submit a 'Gan Jie' (written pledge) to guarantee that there is no opium on board before they are allowed to unload their cargo; if any itinerant traders have concealed the facts, they will be severely punished if discovered."[244]

The crime of opium trade and smoking was newly emerged and it was a crime which was mainly targeted at by the criminal laws made from the last years of Jiaqing to the 20th year of Daoguang (1840). However, the severer the punishment was, the more smokers and traders there were, and it seemed that all government officials and civilians were indulged in smoking opium. In the meantime, international drug dealers supported by western capital countries began to smuggle opium into China on a considerably large scale, so the number increased rapidly, which made it difficult for the Qing government to prevent the opium business, let alone eliminate the sources.

In May of the 19th year of Daoguang (1839), *Yan Jin Ya Pian Yan Zhang Cheng* (*Regulation on the Prohibition of Opium*), which consisted of thirty nine articles, was enacted according to the advice of "Da Xue Shi" (grand secretary), "Jun Ji Da Chen" (the grand councilor), and the officials of "Zong Ren Fu" (The Imperial Clan Court) and other departments upon the approval of Emperor Xuanzong. Firstly, opium smuggling activities in the coastal areas were regarded as the focus of the struggle, and in the first provision of the regulation, it was stated that "if anyone in coastal areas has communicated with foreign countries, set up kilns and stored opium, he shall be punished by 'Zhan' (beheading) and 'Xiao Shou' (the penalty of hanging the head of the criminal on top of a pole for public display); if anyone has conspired with or protected the opium smugglers, or if the boatmen employed by

---

[244]Xia Jie (Qing Dynasty), *Zhong Xi Ji Shi* (*The Chronicle of China and Western Countries*), Vol. 4.

11.4 The Criminal Law Made to Strengthen the Autocratic Ruling 1179

them knows about the fact, they shall be sentenced to 'Jiao Jian Hou' (the punishment of suspending hanging); if any official in charge is aware of the case, but has connived with those criminals, he shall be dismissed from his official post, and the other officials who have neglected their duties shall be punished separately." It was stated in the second provision that "if any official in the coastal areas has taken bribes or connived with criminals, he shall be punished by 'Jiao Li Jue' (immediate execution by hanging)." Secondly, opium trade and opium houses were listed as the targets and were to be severely punished. It was provided that "the principal who opens opium houses shall be punished by 'Jiao Li Jue' (immediate execution by hanging), while the accessories and those who have rented drug houses shall be exiled to Xinjiang to become the servants of soldiers; if anyone has planted poppy, manufactured and sold opium which is worth more than 500 or 600 *liang* of silver, or engaged in opium trade repeatedly, the principal shall be sentenced to 'Jiao Jian Hou' (the punishment of suspending hanging), and the accessories shall be punished by 'Chong Jun' (to be forced to join the army) to 'Yan Zhang' (jungles); if any dealer has only conducted opium transactions for once or twice, or sold opium which is worth no more than 500 *liang* of silver, they shall be exiled to Xinjiang to become the servants of soldiers." Finally, the advice of "imposing harsh punishments on opium smokers," which was put forward by Huang Juezi, was adopted, and it was stated that "if any smoker has failed to give up opium smoking within one and a half years, he shall be sentenced to 'Jiao Jian Hou' (the punishment of suspending hanging) regardless of his identity; if any civilian has smoked during such period, he shall be punished by 'Zhang' (flogging with heavy sticks) and 'Liu' (exile), while the current officials and staff or their relatives or friends will be punished one level severer than the common people, the officials will be exiled to Xinjiang to serve as laborers, the soldiers will be punished by 'Chong Jun' (to be forced to join the army) to nearby frontier and the members of 'Zong Shi Jue Luo' (royal families and the emperor's near relatives) will be exiled to Shengjing (now Shenyang) and be strictly supervised."

Yan Jin Ya Pian Yan Zhang Cheng (*Regulation on the Prohibition of Opium*) was enacted right on the eve of Opium War, so it had become a very important weapon in fighting against opium trade and smoking. However, with the failure Opium War and the gradual loss of Chinese sovereignty, this statute on opium trade and smoking prohibition became a piece of waste paper.

11.4.1.8 The Crime of Corruption and Extorting Bribes

After Emperor Shunzhi ascended the throne, regulations were much strictly enforced to punish corruption. According to *Da Qing Lv Li Tong Zuan* (*A General Collection of the Laws and Precedents of Great Qing*), except for the punishment enforced according to the amount of bribes, the crime of accepting bribes was punished depending on whether the offender was an official or a member of staff, whether they were paid salaries, and whether they were "Wang Fa" (taking bribes by bending the law) or "Bu Wang Fa" (taking bribes without bending the law). For example, if one accepted bribes of more than eighty *liang* of silver by "Wang Fa" (taking bribes by bending the law), he would be punished by "Jiao" (hanging); if one accepted bribes that were no more than one hundred and twenty *liang* of silver by "Bu Wang Fa" (taking bribes without bending the law), he would be punished with a maximum penalty of "Zhang" (flogging with heavy sticks) for one hundred strokes and "Liu" (exile) for 3000 *li*; if an official had asked for bribery during his office term or "if he has obtained bribery forcefully, he shall be punished; otherwise, he is not liable, but the property should be returned to the original owner."[245] If "Feng Xian Guan" (official monitoring the enforcement of the law) had taken bribes, he should be subject to punishment two levels severer.

During the reign of Emperor Shunzhi, Tan Tai, "Li Bu Shang Shu" (the minister of the department of personnel), was executed with his family property confiscated because he had accepted a lot of bribes. Chen Mingxia, "Da Xue Shi" (grand secretary), and his son had taken bribes and had asked for favor on behalf of others, so Chen Mingxia was punished by "Zhan" (beheading), his son Chen Yechen was punished by "Liu" (exile) to the frontier, and his families were punished to work as servants. According to historical records, "after Emperor Shizu began to rule the country, laws were enforced much more strictly and many imperious ministers such as Chen Mingxia, Tan Tai, Chen Zhilin, and Liu Zhengzong were executed so that the officials were very scared and the malpractice was completely eradicated, which had led to the so called 'excellent ruling of Emperor Yongzheng and Qianlong.'"[246]

After Emperor Shengzu ascended the throne, management of officials was regarded as the key to rectifying malpractice and restoring order in the country, so he demanded that "as an official, what is the most important is to abide by law and to get rid of the misconducts."[247] If evil officials had "accepted bribes from civilians by making false excuses" or "obtained personal gains by taking the advantage of their power," they "shall be subject to harsher penalty."[248] So in the 25th year of Kangxi (1686), Cai Yurong, who was "Zong Du" (viceroy) at the time, was punished by death penalty for misappropriating the property and servants of Wu Sangui, which were confiscated by the government. Later, his punishment was mitigated, and he was punished by "Liu" (exile) to the frontier. In the 28th year of Kangxi (1689), Yi Chang, "Shi Lang" (vice minister), and Jin Jun, "Xun Fu" (procurators), embezzled military funds and public money, which totaled more than 890,000 *liang* of silver, so they were punished by "Jiao Li Jue" (immediate execution by hanging). In the same year, Zhang Qianqian, "Xun Fu" (procurators) of Hubei province, forced his subordinates to compensate for the loss of public money, so he was severely punished.

---

[245]"Fu Li" (The Subsidiary Precedent) in "Shou Zang" (Accepting Booty) in *Da Qing Lv Li Tong Zuan* (*A General Compilation of the Laws and Precedents of Great Qing*).

[246]*Shi Zu Chuan Zan* (*A Laudatory Biography of Emperor Shizu*), quoted from Xiao Yishan, *Qing Dai Tong Shi* (*A General History of Qing Dynasty*) (Book 1), Zhonghua Book Company, 1986, p. 386.

[247]*Qing Sheng Zu Shi Lu* (*The Record of Emperor Shengzu of Qing Dynasty*), Vol. 90.

[248]*Qing Sheng Zu Shi Lu* (*The Record of Emperor Shengzu of Qing Dynasty*), Vol. 73.

11.4 The Criminal Law Made to Strengthen the Autocratic Ruling

In the 3rd year of Yongzheng (1725), a regulation was made: "As to the officials who have embezzled money or food for their own use, if the amount is less than 1,000 *liang*, they shall be sentenced to death penalty for the crime of stealing public property in their custody but they can be imprisoned for five years instead; if the amount is more than 1000 *liang*, they shall be sentenced to 'Jiao Jian Hou' (the punishment of suspending hanging), and be executed after autumn without remission."[249] On the other hand, "the regulation for penalty reduction after the returning of the booty" was made, and it was provided that "for the criminals who have been sentenced to death penalty, if they have returned the money which are embezzled or stolen within the year, they shall be subject to penalty reduction with the punishment mitigated by one level according to the regulation on the exemption of death penalty; for the criminals who have been sentenced to the punishment of 'Chong Jun' (to be forced to join the army), 'Liu' (exile) or 'Tu' (imprisonment), they shall be exempted from punishment." If one failed to return the booties within one year, the period could be extended to two years.[250] So, some officials who had embezzled more than 1000 *liang* of silver were exempted from punishment by taking advantage of the law. In view of the fact that corrupted officials were not effectively suppressed due to the lenient enforcement of the law, in the 23rd year of Qianlong (1758), "the precedents for penalty reduction after the returning of the booty" was abolished. "Except for the cases concerning officials who embezzled money for public usage, or the cases concerning the moldy grain in the warehouses, or the crimes which were excusable, the other cases of embezzlement should not be settled according to the original precedent. So 'the precedents for penalty reduction after the returning of the booty' is abolished for ever."[251] Therefore, this regulation was finally deleted from *Da Qing Lv Li* (*The Laws and Precedents of Great Qing*).

Seen from the entire period of rule of Emperor Qianlong, very strict law was imposed for the crime of corruption. According to *Qing Shi Gao* (*The Draft of the History of Qing Dynasty*), "the corrupt officials are condemned by Emperor Gaozong and punished by 'Da Bi' (capital punishment) with their household registration canceled. Moreover, their children and all those involved in the cases of corruption are punished without remission, so corruption is severely punished."[252] Xue Fucheng, an ideologist in late Qing Dynasty confirmed that "during the reign of Emperor Gaozong, such severe laws are enforced that they are unprecedented in the

---

[249]"Zei Dao" (Stealing and Robbery) in "Xing Lv" (The Penal Code) in "Xing Bu Wu Jiu" (Article 59 of the Department of Punishment) in *Da Qing Hui Dian Shi Li* (*The Precedents of the Collected Statutes of Great Qing*), Vol. 781.

[250]"Zei Dao" (Stealing and Robbery) in "Xing Lv" (The Penal Code) in *Xing Bu Wu Jiu* (Article 59 of the Department of Punishment) in *Da Qing Hui Dian Shi Li* (*The Precedents of the Collected Statutes of Great Qing*), Vol. 781.

[251]*Qing Gao Zong Shi Lu* (*The Record of Qing Emperor Gaozong*), Vol. 570.

[252]Heng Wen Deng Zhuan (The Biography of Heng Wen and Others) in *Qing Shi Gao* (*The Draft of the History of Qing Dynasty*).

previous dynasties."[253] However, in his later years, Emperor Gaozong sheltered He Shen, one of the most notoriously corrupt officials.

At the beginning of the reign of Emperor Jiaqing, because of fiscal deficit, Emperor Jiaqing reinstated "the precedents for penalty reduction after the returning of the booty." and it was further declared that "if officials do not return all the public money within three years, they shall be subject to lifelong imprisonment instead of death penalty,"[254] which rendered the regulation on imposing death penalty upon criminals stealing and embezzling property a piece of waste paper, so it was mocked by Xu Yunsheng: "This rule is the most crucial one in the criminal law."[255]

Apart from being punished for the commission of bribery and corruption, officials who committed other duty-related crimes, such as "recommending the wrong person to the government, failing to recommend the right person whom should be recommended, failing to submit memorials to the Emperor when he is supposed to, failing to ask for his supervisor's opinions when he is supposed to," recommending a dismissed official who was forbidden to serve in court, being fraudulent in examinations, delaying in going to one's post, and delaying in passing imperial edicts, etc. were also punished according to the regulations in *Tang Lv* (*Tang Code*) and *Ming Lv* (*Ming Code*).

As for the crimes of endangering social order and encroaching upon personal safety and property, they were punished separately, with some of the punishments aggravated or mitigated following those of Tang and Ming dynasties.

11.4.2 The Penalty System and the Principle for the Application of Criminal Law

The penalty system of "Chi" (flogging with light sticks), "Zhang" (flogging with heavy sticks), "Tu" (imprisonment), "Liu" (exile), and "Si" (death penalty) was inherited by the Qing Dynasty. "Chi" (flogging with light sticks) was divided into five levels, ranging from ten to fifty strokes; "Zhang" (flogging with heavy sticks) was also divided into five levels, ranging from sixty to one hundred strokes; "Tu" (imprisonment) was divided into different levels with half a year as one level ranging from one to three years, and it is often enforced together with the punishment of "Zhang" (flogging with heavy sticks). As for the punishment of "Tu" (imprisonment), "the criminals will often be sent to some provincial postal stations to serve their sentences; nevertheless, if there are no postal stations in 'Xian' (county), the

---

[253]Xue Fucheng (Qing Dynasty), *Ren Xiang Qi Yuan* (*The Magical Destinity of People*) in *Yong An Bi Ji* (*The Notes of Yong An*), Vol. 3.

[254]"Zei Dao" (Stealing and Robbery) in "Xing Lv" (The Penal Code) in "Xing Bu Wu Jiu" (Article 59 of the Department of Punishment) in *Da Qing Hui Dian Shi Li* (*The Precedents of the Collected Statutes of Great Qing*), Vol. 781.

[255]Xue Yunsheng (Qing Dynasty), *Du Li Cun Yi* (Questions in Reading the Precedents), Vol. 25.

criminals will be sent to serve in 'Ya Men' (the government offices)"[256]; "Liu" (exile) was divided into three levels, ranging from 2000 to 3000 *li*, with each level 500 *li* farther than the previous one, and it was one of the severest punishments, which was just lighter than "Si" (death penalty). Usually it was enforced together with one hundred strokes of "Zhang" (flogging with heavy sticks) and one year of forced labor. "Si" (death penalty) was divided into "Jiao" (hanging) and "Zhan" (beheading), which were further divided into two categories, namely, "Jue Bu Dai Shi" (executed immediately) and "Jian Hou" (to be imprisoned). In addition to the abovementioned two death penalties, other forms of cruel penalties such as "Ling Chi" (the punishment of dismemberment and lingering death), "Xiao Shou" (the penalty of hanging the head of the criminal on top of a pole for public display), and "Lu Shi" (the punishment of chopping up the corpse of a criminal) were set up. According to the explanation in *Da Qing Lv Li Ji Cheng* (*Collections of Laws and Precedents of Great Qing*), "Ling Chi" (the punishment of dismemberment and lingering death) refers to "ending a person's life by dismembering his body, cutting off all his flesh and removing the genitals if the criminal is a male. As for the female, she would be killed by cutting off her vagina and pulling out her internal organs." In the Qing Dynasty, the scope of application of "Ling Chi" (the punishment of dismemberment and lingering death) was significantly expanded compared with that in the Ming Dynasty. The thirteen provisions on "Ling Chi" (the punishment of dismemberment and lingering death), which were provided in the laws of the Ming Dynasty, were all adopted in the Qing Dynasty. Moreover, nine more articles that concerned thirteen crimes, such as rescuing prisoners, digging tombs, murdering, killing three people of a family, killing people by threatening, injuring one's teacher, beating one's grandparents and parents, escaping from prison, and murdering one's husband, were included in the laws of the Qing Dynasty. If those who should be punished by "Ling Chi" (the punishment of dismemberment and lingering death) died before the execution, they should be punished by "Lu Shi" (the punishment of chopping up the corpse of a criminal) instead.

"Xiao Shou" (the penalty of hanging the head of a criminal on top of a pole for public display) refers to hanging the head of a criminal on a pole to give warning to the public after he was killed by "Zhan" (beheading). All the crimes subject to this punishment were clearly provided under the law. At the beginning, it was only applied to criminals who committed extremely serious felonies, but its scope of application was expanded gradually later. In the 6th year of Emperor Jiaqing (1801), it was begun to be applied to the so-called crime of "Jiang Yang Da Dao" (infamous robbery); in the 1st year of Daoguang (1821), it was applied to mobsters who committed robbery by climbing over city walls; in the 25th year of Daoguang (1845), it was applied to sailors who killed others in order to rob them of their money while on boats transporting grain; in the 9th year of Tongzhi (1870), it was applied to robbers in the capital city and the two counties of Daxing and Wanping. In

---

[256]"Xing Fa Zhi" (The Record of the Criminal Law) (Part 2) in *Qing Shi Gao* (*The Draft of the History of Qing Dynasty*).

the 9th year of Tongzhi (1870), it was clearly stated in forty eight of the two hundred and two regulations about "Zhan Li Jue" (immediate execution by beheading) that the criminal should be punished by "Xiao Shou" (the penalty of hanging the head of the criminal on top of a pole for public display) after they were punished by "Zhan" (beheading), which showed that with the intensification of class struggle, much severer measures were taken to suppress the people, so that only the female criminals were exempted from the punishment of "Xiao Shou" (the penalty of hanging the head of the criminal on top of a pole for public display).

The so-called Lu Shi (the punishment of chopping up the corpse of a criminal) refers to cutting off the head of a criminal's dead body in order to punish him for what he had done when he was alive. During the reign of Yongzheng, Lv Liuliang was punished by having his coffin opened up and having his head cut off after his death because he was involved in a case of "Wen Zi Yu" (literary inquisition).

The scope of application of "Zhan" (beheading) and "Jiao" (hanging) was also expanded, and in the final draft of *Da Qing Lv Li* (*The Laws and Precedents of Great Qing*), which was issued in the 9th year of Tongzhi (1870), altogether seven hundred and twenty three precedents and provisions were made on these crimes, and more than one thousand crimes were punished accordingly.

Apart from all the abovementioned penalties, "Qian Xi" (the penalty of banishing criminals to do forced labor in remote areas), which refers to sending criminals to places 1000 *li* away without allowing them to go back home, was also included. Moreover, the punishment of "Chong Jun" (to be forced to join the army), a punishment between "Liu" (exile) and "Si" (death penalty), which was enforced during the Ming Dynasty, was inherited. "Chong Jun" (to be forced to join the army) was divided into five levels: "Fu Ji" (nearby) (2000 *li*), "Jin Bian" (the frontier nearby) (2500 *li*), "Bian Yuan" (outlying areas) (3000 *li*), "Ji Bian" (extreme remote areas) (4000 *li*), and "Yan Zhang" (jungles) (4000 *li*). The punishment of "Fa Qian," which was much severer than "Chong Jun" (to be forced to join the army), was also introduced. Usually, criminals would be punished by serving in the army or serving as laborers in the frontier regions.

In addition, the traditional penalties of "Ci Zi" (the punishment of putting a humiliating tattoo on the criminal's body, especially on the face) and "Jia Hao" (cangue: a large wooden collar worn by petty criminals as a punishment), which were applied during the Ming Dynasty, were also adopted in the Qing Dynasty. The punishment of "Ci Zi" (the punishment of putting a humiliating tattoo on the criminal's body, especially on the face) was originally applied to the crime of "Qie Dao" (robbery and theft) and "Tao Ren" (the escapee) only[257] but was gradually applied more extensively later. The main types of punishment included "Ci Yuan Zuo" (the penalty of tattooing somebody for being related to or friendly with someone who has committed a crime), "Ci Xiong Fan" (the penalty of tattooing a murderer), "Ci Tao Jun Tao Liu" (the penalty of tattooing army deserters), "Ci Wai

---

[257] Shen Jiaben (Qing Dynasty), "Shan Chu Lv Li Nei Zhong Fa Zhe" (A Memorial to the Emperor about Abolishing the Severe Penalties in Law) in *Ji Yi Wen Cun* (The Classics of Ji Yi), Vol, 1.

11.4 The Criminal Law Made to Strengthen the Autocratic Ruling

Qian Gai Qian Gai Fa" (the penalty of branding those who were involved in arbitrarily changing the time and route of banishment), "Ci You Shi Zhe" (the penalty of tattooing offenders), "Ci Di Fang Zhe" (the penalty of tattooing different parts), "Fen Ci Man Han Wen Zi Zhe" (the penalty of tattooing using Manchu and Chinese characters), and so on.[258] Moreover, the part of body that was tattooed varied. Usually, "for the first time, the right arm would be tattooed; for the second time, the left arm would be tattooed; and for the third time right arm would be tattooed, and vise versa."[259] This punishment was deemed harmful to social stability because criminals were deprived of the chance to become normal people.

The penalty of "Jia Hao" (cangue: a large wooden collar worn by petty criminals as a punishment) was a substitute penalty enforced for the purpose of giving preferential treatment to the criminals of "Qi Ren" (members of the Manchu ethnic group), and it was provided that "the criminals of 'Qi Ren' (members of the Manchu ethnic group) who are punishable by 'Chong Jun' (to be forced to join the army), 'Liu' (exile) and 'Tu' (imprisonment) ... can be punished by 'Jia Hao' (cangue: a large wooden collar worn by petty criminals as a punishment) instead. If the criminal is punishable by 'Liu' (exile) for one year, he can be punished by wearing 'Jia Hao' (cangue: a large wooden collar worn by petty criminals as a punishment) for twenty days instead, with five days added for each one level of punishment; if punishable by 'Liu' (exile) for 2,000 *li*, the criminal can be punished by wearing 'Jia Hao' (cangue: a large wooden collar worn by petty criminals as a punishment) for fifty days, with five days added for each one level of punishment; if punishable by 'Liu' (exile) by 'Fu Ji' (nearby), the criminal can be punished by wearing 'Jia Hao' (cangue: a large wooden collar worn by petty criminals as a punishment) for seventy days; if punished by 'Liu' (exile) by 'Jin Bian' (the frontier nearby), by 'Yan Hai' (coastal areas), and 'Bian Wai' (outlying areas), the criminal can be punished by wearing 'Jia Hao' (cangue: a large wooden collar worn by petty criminals as a punishment) for eighty days, if punished by 'Liu' (exile) by 'Ji Bian' (extreme remote areas) and 'Yan Zhang' (jungles), the criminal can be punished by wearing 'Jia Hao' (cangue: a large wooden collar worn by petty criminals as a punishment) for ninety days."[260] However, if "Qi Ren" (members of the Manchu ethnic group) became a shameless recidivist, he would be "deprived of his identity and be punished according to the original punishment."[261] Later, the application of "Jia Hao" (cangue: a large wooden collar worn by petty criminals as a punishment) was expanded so that the dividing line between "Qi Ren" (members of the Manchu ethnic group) and the Han people was broken. "So the thief who has committed theft repeatedly ... and the rapists and

---

[258]"Xing Fa Zhi" (The Record of the Criminal Law) (Part 2) in *Qing Shi Gao* (*The Draft of the History of Qing Dynasty*).

[259]"Xing Fa Zhi" (The Record of the Criminal Law) (Part 2) in *Qing Shi Gao* (*The Draft of the History of Qing Dynasty*).

[260]"Xing Fa Zhi" (The Record of the Criminal Law) (Part 2) in *Qing Shi Gao* (*The Draft of the History of Qing Dynasty*).

[261]"Xing Fa Zhi" (The Record of the Criminal Law) (Part 2) in *Qing Shi Gao* (*The Draft of the History of Qing Dynasty*).

criminals who have escaped from the punishment of 'Liu' (exile) or military service shall all be punished by wearing 'Jia Hao' (cangue: a large wooden collar worn by petty criminals as a punishment)." Later, "all criminals can be punished by 'Jia Hao' (cangue: a large wooden collar worn by petty criminals as a punishment) accordingly."[262] In the 8th year of Kangxi (1669), it was stipulated that "thin iron chains should be used for the imprisonment of prisoners instead of long cangues," "so that cangues were only specially applied to the punishment of criminals."[263] Moreover, the time for the punishment of "Jia Hao" (cangue: a large wooden collar worn by petty criminals as a punishment) was also changed, and it was divided into two kinds: several years of punishment and "life punishment." Also, the weight of the cangue varied, and it was divided into thirty *jin* and thirty five *jin*, respectively.

As for "Shu Xing" (atonement), no exact amount of money was listed for redemption in the twenty levels of "Wu Xing" (Five Penalties), which were made in the 1st year of Shunzhi; hence, it brought many difficulties in the trial of cases and the enforcement of penalty. In the 18th year of Shunzhi (1661), "'Li' (precedent) was made for the atonement of the crimes of 'Liu' (exile), 'Tu' (imprisonment) and 'Ji Mo' (the cancellation of a household registration),"[264] which was the first regulation made in the Qing Dynasty, according to which guilty officials were allowed to get redemption by donating money to the state. In the 18th year of Kangxi (1679), another criminal law was made, and it was provided that "if the regulation of redemption is misused by the judicial officials, they shall be punished by the relevant departments,"[265] which showed that during the reign of Emperor Kangxi, it was very popular for criminals "to atone for their crimes according to 'Li' (precedent)." In addition, the system of "atoning for one's crime according to law" (also called "Lv Shu"), which was once implemented in the Ming Dynasty, was adopted,[266] and the system was applicable to "'Lao' (elder), 'You' (young), 'Fei Ji' (the disabled), 'Tian Wen Sheng' (those engaged in astrology, divination, astronomy and geomantic theory, etc.), women and those punishable by 'Zhe Zhang' (criminal law system, the punishment of imprisonment or exile is converted into the number of flogging in accordance with the provisions to determine the amount of the redemption money),"[267] unless they had committed felonies that were included in "Shi E" (The Ten Abominations). Because the ordinary crimes committed by officials,

---

[262]"Xing Fa Zhi" (The Record of the Criminal Law) (Part 2) in *Qing Shi Gao* (*The Draft of the History of Qing Dynasty*).

[263]"Xing Fa Zhi" (The Record of the Criminal Law) (Part 2) in *Qing Shi Gao* (*The Draft of the History of Qing Dynasty*).

[264]"Xing Fa Zhi" (The Record of the Criminal Law) (Part 2) in *Qing Shi Gao* (*The Draft of the History of Qing Dynasty*).

[265]"Xing Fa Zhi" (The Record of the Criminal Law) (Part 2) in *Qing Shi Gao* (*The Draft of the History of Qing Dynasty*).

[266]"Xing Fa Zhi" (The Record of the Criminal Law) (Part 2) in *Qing Shi Gao* (*The Draft of the History of Qing Dynasty*).

[267]"Xing Fa Zhi" (The Record of the Criminal Law) (Part 2) in *Qing Shi Gao* (*The Draft of the History of Qing Dynasty*).

gentry, nobility, and the wealthy could be atoned through different forms of redemption, it turned out that the powerful and influential were able to atone for their crimes according to "Li" (precedent), but the poor and the helpless were mostly punished according to law.

Except for the penalty system set up by the state, lynching was generally applied in the families of nobility and bureaucrats, following the tradition of the Manchu nationality. It was stipulated in *Da Qing Lv Li* (*The Laws and Precedents of Great Qing*) that "as for the punishment of servants or hired men who have violated 'Jiao Ling' (Doctrines and Instructions), if they are killed accidentally or negligently, those involved are considered innocent." The so called misbehavior of "negligently violating 'Jiao Ling' (Doctrines and Instructions)" in this rule could be arbitrarily explained by the family masters. Even Emperor Shizong had admitted the brutality of lynching, and he said that "the officials and soldiers of 'Ba Qi' (the Eight Banners: banner, a division of Manchu nationality and the emperor's clan) are so strict with their family members that they (the family members) are often beaten to death just because of some trivial matters." But at the same time, he affirmed that "if the slaves have violated 'Jiao Ling' (Doctrines and Instructions), it is lawful for the master to beat the slaves to death or to commit negligent homicide according to law,"[268] which no doubt had provided the most authoritative evidence for the misuse of the practice, so that lynching became a very important way to discipline the young, the inferior, and the servants.

As to the principle of application of the criminal law in Qing Dynasty, those of Tang and Ming dynasties were basically followed. What was different was that the privileges of the Manchu nationality, and especially the legal status of "Zong Shi Jue Luo" (royal families and the emperor's near relatives), were particularly protected. If "Zong Shi Jue Luo" (royal families and the emperor's near relatives) had committed crimes, they should be handled by "Zong Ren Fu" (The Imperial Clan Court). As for the major death penalty cases, they should be judged jointly by "Zong Ren Fu" (The Imperial Clan Court) and "Xing Bu" (The Department of Punishment). According to *Lv Li* (*Laws and Precedents*) on the punishment of "Zong Shi Jue Luo" (royal families and the emperor's near relatives), which was made by "Zong Ren Fu" (The Imperial Clan Court), if the members of royal families below princes and dukes had committed crimes, they should neither be punished by death penalty nor be put to prison by "Xing Bu" (The Department of Punishment) unless they had committed the crime of "Pan Ni" (treachery). In *Da Qing Lv Li* (*The Laws and Precedents of Great Qing*), the privileges of "Qi Ren" (members of the Manchu ethnic group) were also clearly stated. For example, "if Manchus have committed crimes punishable by 'Chi' (flogging with light sticks) and 'Zhang' (flogging with heavy sticks), they should be punished accordingly; however, if they have committed crimes punishable by 'Chong Jun' (to be forced to join the army), 'Liu' (exile) and 'Tu' (imprisonment), they should be exempted from punishment and be punished by wearing 'Jia

---

[268]"Xing Kao" (A Textual Research of the Criminal Penalties) in *Qing Chao Wen Xian Tong Kao* (*A General Textual Research of the Documents of Qing Dynasty*), Vol. 197.

Hao' (cangue: a large wooden collar worn by petty criminals as a punishment) instead." For the Manchu criminals, if they are punishable by "Tu" (imprisonment) for one year, they can be punished by "Jia Hao" (cangue: a large wooden collar worn by petty criminals as a punishment) for twenty days instead; if they are punishable by "Liu" (exile) for 2000 *li*, they could be punished by "Jia Hao" (cangue: a large wooden collar worn by petty criminals as a punishment) for fifty days, with five days added for each level. Moreover, penalty for other miscellaneous crimes or even the death penalty could also be converted into "Jia Hao" (cangue: a large wooden collar worn by petty criminals as a punishment). During the reign of Emperor Qianlong, it was still declared that "if 'Qi Ren' (members of the Manchu ethnic group) have beaten their servants, slaves and the children within 'Wu Fu' (relatives within the five degrees of mourning) to death or if their punishment of 'Zhang' (flogging with heavy sticks) and 'Liu' (exile) can be converted into 'Jia Hao' (cangue: a large wooden collar worn by petty criminals as a punishment) according to law, they should be convicted according to specific situations after the approval of the emperor without being collected in the general reports."[269] But if the criminals had really committed crimes punishable by death penalty or if they had given up their status as a Manchu nationality, it was forbidden for their punishments to be converted into the punishment of "Jia Hao" (cangue: a large wooden collar worn by petty criminals as a punishment). During the late Qing Dynasty, the legal privileges of the Manchu group gradually became "Ju Wen" (rules and regulations that are just in form but have no an actual effect).

Punishments were applied differently between males and females. For female criminals punishable by "Zhang" (flogging with heavy sticks), except those who committed the crime of adultery, those who committed other crimes would be punished while wearing their underwear. Female offenders were all exempted from the punishment of "Ci Zi" (the punishment of putting a humiliating tattoo on the criminal's body, especially on the face), and their crimes could be atoned except for crimes punishable by "Tu" (imprisonment) and "Liu" (exile), for which they would be punished by "Zhang" (flogging with heavy sticks) for one hundred strokes instead. In addition, it was forbidden for them to be imprisoned except those who had committed the crime of adultery and crimes punishable by death penalty. Meanwhile, pregnant women should be tried one hundred days after their babies were born. In the 16th year of Shunzhi (1659), it was declared that except for the crime of murder and the felony, it was allowed for the sons, nephews, and brothers of the female criminal to be tried in their place; in the 3rd year of Kangxi (1664), it was also declared that female criminals from other provinces who were sent for conviction should be held in custody by the constable but should not be imprisoned; as for imprisoned pregnant women, except for the crimes of "Fan Ni" (treachery), "Pan" (treason), and other felonies, they should be sent back to their homes until after their babies were born; women who were implicated in crimes should be placed in the

---

[269]"Ming Li" (The Categories of Penalties and General Principles) in *Da Qing Lv Li* (*The Laws and Precedents of Great Qing*), Vol. 4.

custody of their husbands or relatives, or they should be tried after "Ju Jie" (written guarantee) was written by their neighbors. In the 37th year of Kangxi (1698), it was ordered that if women, whether wives of officials or civilians, were implicated and needed to appear in court, they should be interrogated by officials, clerks sent to their homes, instead of being brought to trial. In the 3rd year of Yongzheng, a memorial was presented by Li Tingyi, "Xing Bu Shang Shu" (the minister of the Department of Punishment), and it was stated that female criminals should be especially kept in separate cells, which was approved by the emperor. In the 9th year of Qianlong (1744), it was declared that if women had not committed crimes punishable by death penalty, they should be bailed out by their relatives after being interrogated by judicial officials. In the 23rd year of Kangxi (1758), it was ordered that for pregnant female criminals punishable by "Ling Chi" (the punishment of dismemberment and lingering death) and "Zhan Jue" (the punishment of cutting down the criminal's head), they should be interrogated and executed one month after the birth of their babies, provided that evidence was clear for the first trial. In the 14th year of Jiaqing (1809), it was declared that for female criminals punishable by "Zhan" (beheading) and "Xiao Shou" (the penalty of hanging the head of a criminal on top of a pole for public display), they should be punished by "Zhan Li Jue" (immediate execution by beheading) instead, without publicly hanging their heads on the top of a pole.

In the 23rd year of Jiaqing (1818), a memorial was submitted by Wu Jietiao, "Jian Cha Yu Shi" (the supervisory censor) of Guizhou Dao (ancient organization, mainly in charge of affairs of the now Guizhou province), according to which if women, "Lao" (elders), and "Fei Ji" (the disabled) in every province had reversed convictions and practiced fraud in trials, they would be punished by a maximum penalty of "Chong Jun" (to be forced to join the army) and "Liu" (exile) without being allowed to atone for their crimes. The memorial was compiled into "Li" (precedent) according to an imperial edict.

11.5 Codification of Civil Law

The civil law of Qing Dynasty was the final form of civil law in ancient China; meanwhile, it was also a transitional form of the modern civil law, so it had played an important role in inheriting the cause of the predecessors and carrying it forward in the history of Chinese civil law. The development of the commodity economy and the weakening of the compulsory affiliated personal relationship of super economic exploitation resulting from it had extended the scope of civilians' participation of civil activities. Moreover, the successive revision of *Hu Bu Ze Li* (*The Regulation of the Department of Revenue*) and the enrichment of the contents of civil law made by "Li Bu" (The Department of Rites) and "Gong Bu" (The Department of Works) had fostered the centralization of civil law. Although a separate civil code was not made, multilevel and diversified civil legal sources were formed, among which were both statutory law and customary law, both central legislation and local regulation. Especially, the customary law, which was popular across the country was endowed with both individual and regional characteristics, which had reflected the historical continuity and a strong family affection and provincialism. Therefore, they were not only more pertinent to certain issues in application than the state legislation, but also much easier to be accepted by the public and more effectively to be adjusted.

But the diversity and dispersibility of civil legal sources also raised a question of how they could be used by judicial officials. In civil trials, judicial officials could make court decisions according to their own choices, namely, according to law, according to "Li" (rites), or according to local customs, which was one of the characteristics of civil trials in the Qing Dynasty, but at the same time, it made it convenient for judges to favor a party and commit irregularities.

11.5.1 Social Structure and Identity

11.5.1.1 The Nobility

Among the privileged nobility of the Qing Dynasty, both "Zong Shi" (royal families) and "Jue Luo" (the emperor's near relatives) were the special privileged class; they were formed on the basis of blood lineage, so their identity was hereditary. Due to the emperor's reward and the system of "En Yin" (the appointment of the descendants of those who had made great contribution to the state), they not only owned lands, houses, and "Nu Bi" (slave girls and maidservants) but also enjoyed all privileges and the special protection of the law.

Below the aristocratic groups and "Zong Shi" (royal families) is a bureaucratic group composed of the government officials of Manchu and Han nationalities, who also enjoyed all kinds of legal privileges. Take civil privileges for example: "for the issues of 'Hu Hun' (marriage), 'Qian Zhai' (debts), 'Tian Tu' (land) and other things, it is allowed for the families to lodge lawsuits to government offices, so if anyone has interfered in the issuing of official documents, he will be punished by 'Chi' (flogging with light sticks) for forty strokes."[270] In addition to the incumbent officials, former officials who were "dismissed for other reasons," retired officials, candidate officials for various departments, and officials appointed by the emperor all belonged to this bureaucratic group, and they enjoyed the same legal privileges as the incumbent officials.

The aristocrats and bureaucrats mentioned above are subjects of civil rights with full civil capacity.

---

[270]*Da Qing Lv Li Tong Kao* (*A Textual Research of the Laws and Precedents of Great Qing*), Vol. 30.

11.5 Codification of Civil Law

Among the landlord class, the bureaucrats, the gentry, and landlords occupied large amounts of land. For example, Gao Shiqi, "Shi Lang" (vice minister) of "Li Bu" (The Department of Rites), had "bought more than 1000 *qing* of land in Pinghu County in Zhejiang province"[271]; Xu Qianxue, "Xing Bu Shang Shu" (the minister of the Department of Punishment), had "purchased 10,000 *qing* of land in Mutianyan in Wuxi county"[272]; and "Kong Fu" (Confucian mansion), had owned 38,000 *mu* of land only in Wuqing, Xianghe, Dong'an, and Baodi in "Zhi Li" (now Hebei province).

There were many ordinary landlords who were regarded as ordinary people according to law and who enjoyed full civil capacity.

Apart from the landlord class mentioned above, there were some landlords and gentry who achieved scholarly honor ("Ju Ren" (those who passed the imperial examination at the provincial level in ancient China), "Gong Sheng" (those who were recommended to study in "Guo Zi Jian"), "Sheng Yuan" (also called "Xiu Cai": those who passed the imperial examination at the county level in ancient China), and "Jian Sheng" (the students in "Guo Zi Jian")) or who enjoyed nominal official titles but who did not hold any official positions. They not only controlled the monetary, tax and judicial affairs, but also treated the people ferociously by abusing their power and by "colluding with the local officials and their old friends", so they were in fact the accomplices of the local officials. Li Zhou, a contemporary of the Qing Dynasty, wrote in the second volume of *Mu Mian Ji Lue* (*Records of Mumian*): "The gentry showed contempt to officials, because the power of local government affairs was controlled in their hands, and the other officials were just keeping official seals for them."

So all the landlord classes mentioned above enjoyed civil rights and the capability of civil conduct.

11.5.1.2 The Peasants

Peasants, mainly referring to owner-peasants and tenant-peasants, were ranked at the top of "Min" (mainly referring to the Hui people), "Jun" (the military), "Shang" (the businessmen), and "Zao" (the chefs) in the Qing dynasty and belonged to the people of "Fan Ren" (ordinary people) or "Liang Ren" (decent people), so they were likewise subjects of civil legal rights. After the period of entering Shanhaiguan, in order to maintain the privileged position of the Manchu nobility and to ensure the supply of daily necessities of the soldiers of "Ba Qi" (the Eight Banners: banner, a division of the Manchu nationality and the emperor's clan), the policies of land enclosure and "Tou Chong" (seeking refuge with and working as slave for the

---

[271] "Kang Xi Chao" (The Reign of Emperor Kangxi) in *Dong Hua Lu* (*The Record of Donghua*), Vol. 44.

[272] "Kang Xi Chao" (The Reign of Emperor Kangxi) in *Dong Hua Lu* (*The Record of Donghua*), Vol. 44.

powerful and influential people) were carried out. At the same time, in order to ensure the supply of laborers who were engaged in plowing the fields and doing odd jobs, *Tou Chong Fa* (*The Law of Tou Chong*) was enacted to encourage landowners and landless farmers and those who were unable to make a living to seek refuge with "Qi Ren" (members of the Manchu ethnic group) and to become laborers or servants of their manors. They had neither personal freedom nor independent economy, so their social status was equivalent to that of serfdom. In the 6th year of Shunzhi (1649), Wang Fulong and others in Qimen decided to seek refuge from the powerful and influential people with their land, so a document is drafted as follows:

> The signer of the document, Wang Fulong, and Helong, now voluntarily seek refuge in the ancestral hall of Xie Zongcheng in Sansidu which is made up of three-room building, doors and other objects, kitchen, pigsty, cowshed, toilets, garden, mountain farm and farm tools. My wife and I now come to live with our master and shall take residence in the future, helping our master with removing graves, constructing houses, paying new year calls, celebrating holidays, preparing wedding, funeral and sacrificial ceremonies and cleaning. Our promise will be kept by our descendants forever without making any trouble or conducting any wrong behaviors. If we have broken our promise, we shall follow the order of our master to be judged by officials. Now in case of no guarantee, this document is drafted, we shall forever...
> March 10th of the 6th year of Emperor Shunzhi
> Signer: Wang Fulong and Wang Helong
> Writer on behalf: Wang Wulong
> Witness: Wang Guilong[273]

After Emperor Shengzu was in power, in view of the serious situation, the enclosure activities were stopped because it had led to great social upheaval. So it was declared that "it is forbidden from now on to occupy the houses of civilians" and "to enclose the land of the peasants." At the same time, in the 8th year of Kangxi (1669), "Geng Ming Tian" (Land of Renamed Owner) was enacted, according to which about 200,000 *qing* of land of the seigniors of the Ming Dynasty were given to "the original residents of the land as permanent family property with the names of the owners of the land changed."[274] So occupation of the land of the former vassal states by these farmers was legalized, and they became owner-peasants.

In addition, during the reign of Emperor Kangxi and Shunzhi, reclamation orders were repeatedly issued. After decades of preferential policies and painstaking efforts during the reign of Emperor Kangxi, the land of the four provinces of Sichuan, Guangxi, Yunnan, and Guizhou were changed from "barren fields which were intolerable to the eye" to "cultivated fields with booming population."[275] Since the newly reclaimed fields were owned by the farmers themselves, the number of owner-peasants increased considerably. According to the second volume of "Feng Su" (natural conditions and social customs) in *Huo Shan Xian Zhi* (*The Annals of Huoshan County*), during the reign of Emperor Qianlong, "the people of lower

---

[273]The official documents returned by Wang Fulong and others in Qimen in the 6th year of Shunzhi.
[274]"Shi Huo" (National Finance and Economy) in *Xu Tong Dian* (*Xu Tong Code*), Vol. 1.
[275]*Qing Shi Zu Shi Lu* (*The Record of Emperor Shizu of Qing Dynasty*), Vol. 249.

11.5 Codification of Civil Law

classes were all self-reliant, and each of them had several *mu* of land which was passed on to their descendants, so that only two or three out of ten were tenant peasants."

The increasing number of owner-peasants had enlarged the range of subjects of civil activities.

As to the identity of the tenant-peasants, in the 17th year of Shunzhi (1660), it was stipulated that "the tenant-peasants are just poor people, so they should not be treated as servants."[276] During the reign of Yongzheng, it was also forbidden for tenant-peasants to be "oppressed as slaves" or "to be sold with the land." So generally speaking, the tenant-peasants were free to withdraw from the tenant relationship and enjoyed freedom of migration. Moreover, it was forbidden for landlords to dominate the bodies of tenant-peasants. Especially in the 5th year of Yongzheng (1727), it was stated in *Qin Ding Li (The Precedents Made by the Imperial Order)* that "from now on, if any gentry has illegally bought and used planks and sticks to punish the tenant-peasants randomly, he will be punished by the local officials, and the relevant supervising officials will be removed from their offices and deprived of their titles; if any gentry has tried to restrict the freedom of or tortured the tenant-peasants at his home, whether there are any injuries, he shall be punished by 'Zhang' (flogging with heavy sticks) for eighty strokes. If the magistrates have not performed their duties, they shall be punished according to the precedent on officials harboring criminals once they are discovered by their supervisors; if women from tenant-peasants families are taken to be servants or concubines, the gentry shall be punished by 'Jiao Jian Hou' (the punishment of suspending hanging). Besides, the local officials who have failed to discover the cases or have sheltered the gentry shall be removed from their posts according to the precedent on the punishment of the dereliction of duty; if the superior officials have failed to report the malpractice of the local officials, they shall be punished according to the precedent on failing to make reports on the incompetent staff."[277] "The cunning and dishonest tenant-peasants who have delayed in paying the rent and tax deliberately, or bullied landowners, shall be punished by 'Zhang' (flogging with heavy sticks) for eighty strokes, with all the rent which they owed the landowner paid back."[278] Generally speaking, landlords and tenant-peasants were not in a relationship of masters and servants, so they usually had meals together, treated each other equally, and neither of them had the right to order the other to serve him. The standard of relationship between landlords and tenants, which was provided in the regulation issued during the reign of Yongzheng, fully showed the equal legal relationship between tenant-peasants and landlords and improved the social status of the tenants.

---

[276] Kangxi, *Jiang Nan Tong Zhi (General Annals of the Regions South of Yangtze River)*, Vol. 65.

[277] Quoted from *Li Yuan Shi Shu (The Historical Record of the Office of Personnel)*, by Chalangati, the minister of the department of personnel, on the 19th of September of the 5th year of Yongzheng, held by the First Historical Archive of China.

[278] *Da Qing Lv Li Tong Kao (A Textual Research of the Laws and Precedents of Great Qing)*, Vol. 27.

11.5.1.3 "Gu Gong Ren" (The Hired Men or Servants in the Families of Common People)

To a certain extent, the status of "Gu Gong Ren" (the hired men or servants in the families of common people) was also improved. In the Ming Dynasty, "Gu Gong Ren" (the hired man or servants in the families of common people) included hired laborers who were with written documents and years of service and the adopted child in the common families who was bought recently. Although the statutes related to "Gu Gong Ren" (the hired men or servants in the families of common people) were not changed in *Da Qing Lv Li* (*The Laws and Precedents of Great Qing*), the subsidiary legislation was constantly revised according to the many cases occurring in practice between "Gu Gong Ren" (the hired men or servants in the families of common people) and their masters. For example, in the 24th year of Qianlong (1759), it was stipulated that "as for the hired men, if they have signed contracts about the years of service or if they only have the relevant agreements about the years of service but have not signed relevant contracts, or if they have worked for more than five years, they shall be punished the same as 'Gu Gong Ren' (the hired men or servants in the families of common people) if they have offended their masters; but the temporary hired men who does not earn much shall be punished the same as civilians."[279] In the 32rd, 51st and 53rd year of Qianlong (1767, 1786, and 1788), *Gu Gong Ren Fa* (*Law for Hired Men*) was again revised, respectively. According to the amendment made in the 53rd year of Qianlong (1788), "as for the servants of official and civilian families, the long-term servants of pawnshops shall be punished according to the established rules, but the people like cart drivers, cooks, the other servants and bearers, and all other handy men who do not dare to live together with nor share the same diet with their masters, or who are not allowed to greet their masters by name, or whose relationship with their master are that of masters and servants, shall be deemed as 'Gu Gong Ren' (the hired men or servants in the families of common people) regardless of the contracts of the terms. As for the hired tenant-peasants who help with farming and the salesmen in small stores who live and eat together, who are equal to each other, who are not ordered about in the official and civilian families and who shared no relationship of master and servant, they shall all be regarded as civilians regardless of working terms or contracts."[280] According to the statute issued in the 53rd year of Qianlong, "Gu Gong Ren'" (the hired men or servants in the families of common people) only referred to hired laborers of officials or civilians, who shared the relationship of servants and masters, such as cart drivers, cooks, other servants and bearers, and all other handy men, and the long-term servants in the families of pawnshops, etc. The employees engaged in agricultural production and commercial service, whether they had contracts or years

---

[279]"Dou Ou" (Fighting) in "Xing Lv" (The Penal Code) in *Da Qing Hui Dian Shi Li* (*The Precedents of the Collected Statutes of Great Qing*), Vol. 810.

[280]"Dou Ou" (Fighting) in "Xing Lv" (The Penal Code) in *Da Qing Hui Dian Shi Li* (*The Precedents of the Collected Statutes of Great Qing*), Vol. 810.

of service, all belonged to civilians, who shared equal legal status with the employers.

As can be seen from the amendments of *Gu Gong Ren Fa* (*Law for Hired Men*) made in Qing Dynasty, it had become the trend of social development to narrow down the scope of "Gu Gong Ren" (the hired men or servants in the families of common people) and to improve the legal status of some hired laborers by distinguishing them from "Gu Gong Ren" (the hired men or servants in the families of common people). During the reign of Emperor Qianlong, with the social and economic development, it was necessary for the workers to be liberated more completely from the feudal relationship of personal dependence, which had not only led to the repeated revision of *Gu Gong Ren Fa* (*Law for Hired Men*) but also changed and replaced the standard of deciding the status of "Gu Gong Ren" (the hired men or servants in the families of common people) according to contracts and years of service by the standard of deciding their status according to the types of work which they had been employed. So it was not only a progress of legislation but also a reflection of the changes of social relationship.

The relationship between "Gu Gong Ren" (the hired men or servants in the families of common people) and their employers was a "contractual relationship" based on agreement. According to contracts, "Gu Gong Ren" (the hired men or servants in the families of common people) were only hired by their employers, but they had not lost their personal freedom and independence. When disputes arose between them and other "Liang Ren" (decent people), they were judged as "Fan Ren" (ordinary people), and once the contract was terminated, the master-servant relationship also ended so that they were "treated as 'Fan Ren' (the ordinary people) when term was over." But during the contract period, the master and servant relationship still existed, and "Gu Gong Ren" (the hired men or servants in the families of common people) still called their employers masters. They also had a relationship of servants and masters with their masters' relatives of "Wu Fu" (relatives within the five degrees of mourning), so that they had an unequal status in law. For example, if "Fan Ren" (ordinary people) assaulted each other without leading to any injuries, they would be punished by "Chi" (flogging with light sticks) for twenty strokes, but if "Gu Gong Ren" (the hired men or servants in the families of common people) fought with their masters or the relatives of their masters without leading to any injuries, they would be punished by "Zhang" (flogging with heavy sticks) for one hundred strokes and "Tu" (imprisonment) for three years, which was thirteen levels severer than that for "Fan Ren" (ordinary people). On the other hand, if the masters had beaten and injured "Gu Gong Ren" (the hired men or servants in the families of common people), they would be punished three levels lighter than "Fan Ren" (ordinary people); if they had not injured "Gu Gong Ren" (the hired men or servants in the families of common people), they would be exempted from any punishment. Especially, "if 'Gu Gong Ren' (the hired men or servants in the families of common people) had violated their masters' instructions, they would be punished according to law, but if the masters had committed negligent homicide or manslaughter for first time, they would not be found guilty."[281]

Because employment relationship was included in the feudal patriarchal relationship in the law of the Qing Dynasty, the employers were actually the masters of "Gu Gong Ren" (the hired men or servants in the families of common people) and "Gu Gong Ren" (the hired men or servants in the families of common people) were the subjects who were supported and raised by the masters, so they also belonged to the whole family. Even the inferior, the young, and the relatives of the employer enjoyed a more privileged legal status than "Gu Gong Ren" (the hired men or servants in the families of common people), which was described as "Fen Yan Qing Shu" (the social status is strict while the family relationship is distant). It was clear that according to the statutes of the Qing Dynasty, "Gu Gong Ren" (the hired men or servants in the families of common people) did not mean free-employed workers. Because of social progress and the struggle of the oppressed, the legal rights of employers were also limited by law. For example, if the employers killed "Gu Gong Ren" (the hired men or servants in the families of common people) who had been hired to work for fewer than five years without contract, they wound be punished for the crime of killing "Fan Ren" (ordinary people).

11.5.1.4 The Artisans

In the Qing Dynasty, because "Jiang Ji" (the craftsman household registration) was abolished, the personal control and super-economic exploitation of artisans by the government were greatly reduced, so the artisans obtained complete freedom of personal identity. Moreover, they were classified as "Fan Ren" (ordinary people) and enjoyed equal rights to participate in civil activities. During the reign of Emperor Yongzheng and Qianlong, the employment system was implemented for the artisans recruited by the government, which meant that the rations of grain and silver (silver paid as wages) were paid according to the category and nature of the work, and it was forbidden to employ laborers without payment. This reform was also extended in local places and to civilians, which was recorded in detail in *Feng Ge Xian Yong Jin Ji Jiang Jiao Xie Bei Ji* (*Tablet Inscription for the Permanent Prohibition of the Strikes by Artisans*): "Many people were employed by 'Ji Hu' (the households specializing in the manual silk industry or cotton industry) in Suzhou city, and they managed and financed the factories, while the artisans were paid according to their work ... As to the salaries, it was paid according to the pieces of the work and the quality and delicacy of the goods."[282] The employment relationship between

---

[281]"Dou Ou" (Fighting) in "Xing Lv" (The Penal Code) (Part 2) in *Da Qing Lv Li* (*The Laws and Precedents of Great Qing*), Vol. 28.

[282]*Feng Ge Xian Yong Jin Ji Jiang Jiao Xie Bei Ji* (*Tablet Inscription for the Permanent Prohibition of the Strikes Staged by Artisans*). Please see *Jiang Su Sheng Ming Qing Yi Lai Bei Ke Zi Liao Xuan Ji* (*Selected Materials of Tablet Inscriptions since Ming and Qing Dynasties in Jiangsu Province*).

owners and employees was equal, and "money wages were paid daily to the workers."

Because handicraft workers were individual laborers with very little economic power, they often went bankrupt because of natural disaster or man-made calamities, so in the end they would either be employed as "Gu Gong Ren" (the hired men or servants in the families of common people) or become "Jian Min" (rabbles or people of lower social status). Accordingly, their civil legal status was also changed.

Merchants in the Qing Dynasty were also regarded as "Fan Ren" (ordinary people), and they were subjects in civil legal relations. Although it did not, though it was also impossible to, change the traditional policy of "Zhong Nong Yi Shang" (encouraging agriculture and restraining commerce) in the Qing Dynasty, many changes had taken place in practice.

Among the merchants in the Qing Dynasty, some belonged to the privileged official merchants who had close connection with the feudal bureaucrats or who themselves were the bureaucrats who purchased goods for royal households, armies, or feudal officials. They not only had the monopoly of money in the national treasury and some merchandise but also enjoyed special policies of tax exemption. Meanwhile, they could compete advantageously by making use of their privileges and plunder various kinds of manual products and merchandise unscrupulously, as such becoming the wealthiest and most powerful merchants.

Apart from official merchants, the folk merchants also became very active along with the unprecedented flourishing of commerce during the reign of emperors Yongzheng and Qianlong, so that their social status was significantly improved. The most prominent evidence was the emergence of various guild halls and clubs that represented the interests of businessmen and the rapid increase of the power of trade associations. These guild halls and clubs were the autonomous organizations of industrialists and businessmen, and commercial guild halls were usually founded by the funds raised and shared by the members. They would provide storage service and accommodation for the members who traveled around, and they were also responsible for making guild regulations and for standardizing the system of weights and measures. As to the industrial and commercial clubs, they were highly strict professional associations, and their main function was to eliminate competition and mediate disputes inside the industry, to protect the interests of merchants in the same trade, to seek common development, and to meet the challenges of other industries.

As far as "Hang" (firm) is concerned, it refers to a group of merchants organized according to the category of goods that they dealt with, such as "Mi Hang" (rice firm) and "Yao Hang" (medicine firm). "Bang" (gang) was either a townsfolk organization of merchants from certain areas or an association of the same trade, such as "Shanxi Bang" (Gang of Shanxi Province) and "Hua Bu Bang" (Gang of Printed Cotton). As the organizations for mutual help and self-service, "Hang" (firm) and "Bang" (gang) usually bought land to be used for common purpose. "Hang" (firm) and "Bang" (gang) could also participate in civil activities as independent civil subjects.

In addition, there were also petty dealers who were converted from farmers or craftsmen and who also belonged to "Fan Ren" (ordinary people) with personal freedom.

11.5.1.5 Servants

According to *Da Qing Hui Dian* (*The Collected Statutes of Great Qing*), "servants, court jesters, and yamen runners belonged to 'Jian Min' (rabbles or people of lower social status)," and "all of those working for the government offices ... 'Zao Li' (Yamen runners: a government-employed laborer, messenger, etc. in ancient times), 'Ma Kuai'(errand boy), 'Bu Kuai' (office errands), 'Jin Zu' (prison guards), 'Men Zi' (doorman), 'Gong Bing' (archer), "Wu Zuo" (legal medical expert), 'Liang Chai' (grain deliver), 'Fan Yi' (staff for arresting criminals) in police battalion were people of lower social status. And 'Chang Sui' (servants of officials) hired by feudal officials had the same social status as servants."[283] People in some areas like "Duo Min" (the good for nothing or loafers), "Gai Hu" (beggars), "Jiu Xing Yu Hu" (fishermen in areas near rivers, men living on fishing, and women living on prostituting), "Dan Hu" (those who live on water instead of on land), and "Shi Pu" (life maidservants) also all belonged to "Jian Min" (rabbles or people of lower social status), and they were all registered as "Jian Ji" (people of inferior household registration). The people who were listed as "Jian Min" (rabbles or people of lower social status) and registered as "Jian Ji" (people of inferior household registration) had no personal freedom, and their legal status was extremely low. "Nu Bi" (slave girls and maidservants) were at the bottom of the list, and their legal status was the same as that of domestic animals and other property, which meant that they were the objects of ownership and were at the discretion of their masters. As early as the period before entering Shanhaiguan, slavery prevailed in Manchu society, so "there were countless servants in the families of officials."[284] After the period of entering Shanhaiguan, many kinds of people, such as prisoners of war, the people of "Tou Chong" (seeking refuge with and working as slave for the powerful and influential people), and criminals banished to frontiers to serve in the military units, were forced to be "Nu Bi" (slave girls and maidservants). Besides, "Nu Bi" (slave girls and maidservants) could also be bought at markets. On each market day, people could buy "Nu Bi" (slave girls and maidservants) and domestic animals at the market, and "contracts of purchasing servants and slaves must be reported to the chief magistrates and be officially sealed when servants were bought,"[285] so if the contract was

---

[283]*Guang Xu Da Qing Hui Dian* (*Collected Statutes of Great Qing in the Reign of Emperor Guangxu*), Vol. 17.

[284]*Qian Long Guan Shan Xian Zhi* (*Annals of Guangshan County during the Reign of Emperor Qianlong*), Vol. 19.

[285]"Dou Ou" (Fighting) in "Xing Lv" (The Penal Code) (Part 2) in *Da Qing Lv Li* (*The Laws and Precedents of Great Qing*), Vol. 28.

11.5 Codification of Civil Law

violated, it would be checked and rectified by the magistrates. The offspring of "Nu Bi" (slave girls and maidservants) must be on active service from generation to generation, even if they were redeemed later, and "their children or grandchildren who are born and brought up at the master's home shall continue to serve the master and shall never be regarded as 'Liang Min' (the decent people)."[286]

It was forbidden by law to buy, sell, or send Manchu and Mongolian people to work as servants in the armies and families of the Han people in order to maintain the ruling status of the Manchu people, so "if any officials have violated the law, they shall be removed from their official positions and for the civilians, they shall be punished by wearing 'Jia Hao' (cangue: a large wooden collar worn by petty criminals as a punishment)."[287]

In the Qing Dynasty, it was legal to own slaves, but it was illegal to turn "Liang Min" (decent people) into slaves. According to *Da Qing Lv Li* (*The Laws and Precedents of Great Qing*), "if 'Liang Min' (the decent people) are enslaved as 'Nu Bi' (slave girls and maidservants) in the families of common people, he or she shall be punished by 'Zhang' (flogging with heavy sticks) for one hundred strokes, and 'Nu Bi' (slave girls and maidservants) shall be released to regain their freedom."[288] "Anyone who has planned to trick 'Liang Min' (the decent people) into slavery or to sell 'Liang Min' (the decent people) to other people as 'Nu Bi' (slave girls and maidservants), even if the transaction has not been completed, he shall still be punished by 'Liu' (exile) for 1,500 *li* after being punished by 'Zhang' (flogging with heavy sticks) for one hundred strokes regardless of his role in the plan."[289] Even those who had sold their own offspring, their relatives, an inferior, their children, their wives, and their concubines to become "Nu Bi" (slave girls and maidservants) would be punished accordingly. This law was applied not only to common people but also to officials. For example, it was forbidden for officials who worked directly under the emperor and officials like "Du Fu" (the viceroys and procurators), "Ti Du" (military commander), and "Zong Bing" (commander-in-chief) "to buy 'Liang Min' (the decent people) as servants or maids or to give them to others as gifts; if anyone has violated the rule, he shall be punished according to 'Li' (precedent) on buying 'Liang Min' (the decent people) as slaves."[290]

In a civil legal relationship, "Nu Bi" (slave girls and maidservants), as the private property of their masters, were at the discretion of their masters. The masters also

---

[286]"Hu Kou" (Registered Permanent Residence) (Part 3) in *Hu Bu Ze Li* (*The Regulation of the Department of Revenue*), Vol. 6.

[287]"Qi Ren Mai Mai Nu Li" (Buying and Selling of Slaves among Manchus) in "Hu Kou" (Registered Permanent Residence) in "Ba Qi Du Tong" (The Military Officer of Eight Banners) in *Da Qing Hui Dian Shi Li* (*The Precedents of the Collected Statutes of Great Qing*), Vol. 1116.

[288]"Hu Yi" (Household Corvee) in "Hu Lv" (Statutes on Households) in *Da Qing Lv Li* (*The Laws and Precedents of Great Qing*), Vol. 8.

[289]"Hu Kou" (Registered Permanent Residence) (Part 3) in *Hu Bu Ze Li* (*The Regulation of the Department of Revenue*), Vol. 3.

[290]"Hu Kou" (Registered Permanent Residence) (Part 3) in *Hu Bu Ze Li* (*The Regulation of the Department of Revenue*).

had the right to arrange for their marriage, so "if 'Nu Bi' (slave girls and maidservants) have disobeyed the arrangement made by their masters or their parents and grandparents, they shall be flogged on buttocks or legs; if they are killed unintentionally during or after the flogging, their masters or parents and grandparents shall not be held liable."[291] In this way, the authority of masters was established, so that "Nu Bi" (slave girls and maidservants) had to do whatever their masters ordered them.

With economic development and the struggle of large numbers of "Nu Bi" (slave girls and maidservants), the slavery system became less and less profitable, so that in the 21st year of Kangxi (1682), by following historical trend, an order was issued for servants to redeem themselves, and it was stipulated that "as for the people who are bought by 'Qi Ren' (members of the Manchu ethnic group) according to contracts, if those who are old or ill among the former servants are allowed to be redeemed by their masters, they can be redeemed as common people after reporting to 'Qi' (banner, equivalent of a county); if the servants in good health are redeemed, the parties involved in the transaction shall be punished according to 'Li' (precedent) on buying and selling the common people."[292] In the 53rd year of Kangxi (1714), another order was issued: "As for the people who are bought according to 'Bai Qi' (contract without an official seal) before the 43rd year of Kangxi (1704), it is up to the masters to decide whether the servants can be redeemed or not; as for the people who are bought according to 'Bai Qi' (contract without an official seal) after the date, they can be redeemed with the same amount of money as their masters have paid for buying them,"[293] regardless of their age or health condition. In the 1st year of Yongzheng (1723), *Bai Qi Mai Ren Li* (*The Regulation on Buying People According to "Bai Qi"*) was issued, and it was stipulated that "the people bought according to 'Bai Qi' (contract without an official seal) from the 43rd year (1704) to the 61st year of Kangxi (1722) are not allowed to be redeemed. However, redeeming was allowed after the 1st year of Yongzheng (1723) if the original money has been paid, and his wife bought according to 'Bai Qi' (contract without an official seal) can also be redeemed; nevertheless, they shall not be redeemed if the masters have arranged marriages for the people whom they have bought."[294] After the 1st year of Qianlong (1736), it was stipulated again that "the people as well as their wives and children bought according to 'Bai Qi' (contract without an official seal) are all redeemable,

---

[291]"Dou Ou" (Fighting) in "Xing Lv" (The Penal Code) (Part 2) in *Da Qing Lv Li* (*The Laws and Precedents of Great Qing*), Vol. 28.

[292]"Nu Bi" (The Slave Girls and Maidservants) in "Hu Kou Kao" (An Examination of the Registered Permanent Residence) (Part 2) in *Qing Chao Wen Xian Tong Kao* (*A General Textual Research of the Documents of Qing Dynasty*), Vol. 20.

[293]"Hu Kou" (Registered Permanent Residence) (Part 3) in *Hu Bu Ze Li* (*The Regulation of the Department of Revenue*), Vol. 3.

[294]"Hu Kou" (Registered Permanent Residence) (Part 3) in *Hu Bu Ze Li* (*The Regulation of the Department of Revenue*), Vol. 3.

but if the masters have arranged marriages for them, they shall not be redeemed."[295] In the 3rd year of Qianlong (1738), it was further stipulated that "the people bought according to 'Bai Qi' (contract without an official seal) before the 1st year of Qianlong (1736) shall not be redeemed as common people."[296] Therefore, as can be seen from above, the regulations on the redemption of slaves were very strict in many aspects, such as the years of the contract and the marital condition. Even if one was redeemed and became a common person, he was "only allowed to work as a farmer but was forbidden to sit the examination of 'Ke Ju' (the imperial examination)."[297] Moreover, though their civil rights were relatively extensive, their political rights were also limited. In the 24th year of Qianlong (1759), *Ba Qi Jia Ren Shu She Li* (*The Regulation on Redemption of People in the Families of the Eight Banners*) was issued, so the redemption system became more standardized and legalized. As long as the masters of the families of "Ba Qi" (the Eight Banners: banner, a division of the Manchu nationality and the emperor's clan) were willing to give their servants or slaves freedom, they could become common people after a report submitted to "Qi" (banner, equivalent of a county) and approved by the government. According to the law, the restrictions such as the contract time and marital condition were abolished and the masters were allowed to decide what to do. "The servants or slaves are forbidden to be redeemed if their master is not willing to."[298] In the meantime, it was strictly forbidden by law for servants to bully their masters or to force their masters to allow them to be redeemed.

In addition, servants were allowed to "Kai Hu"; that is, servants working for the families of "Ba Qi" (the Eight Banners: banner, a division of the Manchu nationality and the emperor's clan) were allowed to acquire semi-independent status via registering in "Qi" (banner, equivalent of a county) where they lived. However, they were not allowed to register in the other "Qi" (banner, equivalent of a county), and they must maintain a subordinate status to their masters. In the 3rd year of Qianlong (1736), *Qi Ren Kai Hu Li* (*The Regulation on the Registering of Manchus*) was issued, and it was stipulated that "as for all the servants of 'Ba Qi' (the Eight Banners: banner, a division of Manchu nationality and the emperor's clan) from Manchu and Mongolia without native places or the people of "Tou Chong" (seeking refuge with and working as slave for the powerful and influential people) who have land but whose native places are difficult to confirm because of the long lapse of time, they are allowed to "Kai Hu" (to acquire semi-independent status via registering in "Qi" where they lived), but are not allowed to be released as the common

---

[295]"Hu Kou" (Registered Permanent Residence) (Part 3) in *Hu Bu Ze Li* (*The Regulation of the Department of Revenue*), Vol. 3.

[296]"Hu Kou" (Registered Permanent Residence) (Part 3) in *Hu Bu Ze Li* (*The Regulation of the Department of Revenue*), Vol. 3.

[297]"Hu Kou" (Registered Permanent Residence) in *Da Qing Hui Dian Shi Li* (*The Precedents of the Collected Statutes of Great Qing*), Vol. 155.

[298]"Hu Yi" (Household Corvee) in "Hu Lv" (Statutes on Households) in *Da Qing Lv Li* (*The Laws and Precedents of Great Qing*), Vol. 8.

people."[299] In the 4th and 6th year of Qianlong (1739 and 1741), the coverage of the regulation of "Kai Hu" (to acquire semi-independent status via registering in the banner where they lived) was extended after being discussed and approved by the emperor, so "it is allowed for all the servants who are brought from Shengjing (now Shenyang), or those people of 'Tou Chong' (seeking refuge with and working as slave for the powerful and influential people) with land, or those who are kidnapped from other places to register in 'Qi' (banner, equivalent of a county) where they live, but not allowed to be released as the common people. It is allowed for the servants bought under stamped contract or who have been brought from Shengjing (now Shenyang), or those people of 'Tou Chong' (seeking refuge with and working as slave for the powerful and influential people) with land to register in the 'Qi' (banner, equivalent of a county) where they lived, but they not allowed to be released as the common people."[300] As can be seen from the abovementioned, the system of "Kai Hu" (to acquire semi-independent status via registering in "Qi" where they lived) at the time was changed to adapt to the needs of transitioning from the system of serfdom to the tenancy system, and servants had become dependent tenants.

The term "to be released as the common people" meant that "Nu Bi" (slave girls and maidservants) were released by their masters and their subordinate relationship was terminated, so that the former servants became common people with relatively lower social status. However, the condition for servants to become common people was strict. First, they must be allowed by the masters to leave the house and to become common people; at the same time, "Gan Jie" (written pledge) was needed for their registration. Second, "if the servant has been hard-working or has served his master for several generations, or the master thinks that the servant is aging and cannot do his job any longer, it is allowed for him to become a common person when he is allowed to be redeemed by his master."[301] Third, for those able-bodied men bought according to "Bai Qi" (contract without an official seal) before the 1st year of Qianlong (1734), "if they are common people sold to 'Qi Ren' (members of the Manchu ethnic group) and if the places of origin can be checked in the contract,[302] they are allowed to be redeemed to become common people after three generations." Because of these regulations, the scope of "Nu Bi" (slave girls and maidservants) who could leave the Manchu families and become common people was merely limited. Later, in the 9th, 21st, and 48th year of Qianlong (1744, 1756, and 1783), the regulations were amended several times, so that its scope was broadened with their rights and treatment improved, and it became possible for the servants who

---

[299]"Hu Kou Kao" (An Examination of the Registered Permanent Residence) in *Qing Chao Wen Xian Tong Kao* (*A General Textual Research of the Documents of Qing Dynasty*), Vol. 20.

[300]"Jia Ren Kai Hu Wei Min" (Family Members of Eight Banner Becoming Common People) in *Qin Ding Ba Qi Ze Li* (*The Regulation for the Eight Banners Made by Imperial Order*), Vol. 3.

[301]"Hu Yi" (Household Corvee) in "Hu Lv" (Statutes on Households) in *Da Qing Lv Li* (*The Laws and Precedents of Great Qing*).

[302]"Fen Xi Hu Ding" (Separate Registration) in "Hu Kou" (Registered Permanent Residence) in "Hu Bu" (The Department of Revenue) in *Da Qing Hui Dian Shi Li* (*The Precedents of the Collected Statutes of Great Qing*), Vol. 155.

11.5 Codification of Civil Law

were released to enjoy basic rights provided by law. After three generations, their offspring could be regarded as common people and take "Ke Ju" (the imperial examination); however, they "are not allowed to be promoted to the officials of 'Jing Tang' (the head of government offices) if they are working in the capital and they are not allowed to be promoted to the officials of 'San Pin' (the third rank) if they are working outside the capital."[303]

In conclusion, "Nu Bi" (slave girls and maidservants) became less dependent on their masters and they conditionally obtained the social status of common people during the reign of emperors Yongzheng and Qianlong.

As far as "Jian Min" (rabbles or people of lower social status) are concerned, except for "Nu Pu" (servants), "Chang You" (court jesters), "Li Zu" (errand person), and "Zao Li" (Yamen runners: a government-employed laborer, messenger, etc. in ancient times), in some areas, those engaged in certain professions were also deemed "Jian Min" (rabbles or people of lower social status) and registered as "Jian Ji" (people of inferior household registration) due to some political, historical, and economic reasons that can be traced back to the Ming Dynasty; these people are "Yue Hu" (those specializing in playing music, singing, and dancing) from Shanxi and Shaanxi provinces, "Duo Min" (the good for nothing or loafers) from Shaoxing in Zhejiang province, "Ban Dang" (accompanying servants) and "Shi Pu" (life maidservants) from southern Anhui province, "Gai Hu" (beggars) from Changshu and Zhaowen counties in Jiangsu province, and "Dan Hu" (those who live on water instead of on land) from Guangdong province. All of these people belonged to "Jian Ji" (the people of inferior household registration) for generations and were at the bottom of the society. For example, "Yue Hu" (those specializing in playing music, singing, and dancing) from Shanxi and Shaanxi provinces were in fact prostitutes, and "they will come the moment summoned by the gentry and local ruffian,"[304] so they were regarded as "the lowliest of those at the bottom of society and were never the equals of the common people." During the reign of Emperor Kangxi, there were several hundreds of "Yue Hu" (those specializing in playing music, singing, and dancing) from Shanxi province. In Zhejiang province, the males of "Duo Min" (the good for nothing or loafers) were only allowed to be engaged in professions like catching frogs, selling tins, and driving out evil spirits, while "the females were only allowed to take jobs such as match making, dressing for brides, making strings of floriation for hair dressing, wandering in streets to inquire about others' privacy ... so they were looked down upon wherever they went."[305] "Ban Dang" (accompanying servants) in Huizhou prefecture and "Shi Pu" (life maidservants) in Xuanzhou prefecture were addressed as "Xi Min," which almost had the same meaning as "Yue Hu" (those specializing in playing music, singing, and dancing) and "Duo Min" (the

---

[303]"Nu Bi" (the Slave Girls and Maidservants) in "Hu Kou Kao" (An Examination of the Registered Permanent Residence) (Part 2) in *Qing Chao Wen Xian Tong Kao* (*A General Textual Research of the Documents of Qing Dynasty*), Vol. 20.

[304]Ruan Kuisheng (Qing Dynasty), *Cha Yu Ke Hua* (*Chatting at Leisure Time*), Vol. 2.

[305]*Yong Zheng Zhu Pi Yu Zhi* (*Imperial Edicts Approved by Emperor Yongzheng*), Vol. 39.

good for nothing or loafers).[306] "Dan Hu" (those who live on water instead of on land) from Guangdong province had "lived on boats and made a living by fishing ... so that they were regarded as inferiors and were not allowed to live on mainland." Moreover, they "did not dare to fight with the common people, so that they had no choice but to hide in boats with no hope of living happily in a comfortable home throughout their lives."[307]

"Jian Min" (rabbles or people of lower social status) who were registered as "Jian Ji" (people of inferior household registration) had no independent personality, so naturally they were not civil subjects. However, with the development of society, gradually there were no reasons for the existence of this group of people who were forced to register in "Jian Ji" (the people of inferior household registration) because of the specific historical background at the beginning of Ming Dynasty. By the middle of the Qing Dynasty, in order to stabilize social order, measures were taken to improve the conditions of "Jian Min" (rabbles or people of lower social status). Thus, in March of the 1st year of Yongzheng (1723), it was ordered that "'Yue Hu' (those specializing in playing music, singing and dancing) from Shanxi and Shaanxi province should changed to 'Liang Ren' (the decent people)."[308] Then in September, another order was issued, and it was stated that "'Duo Min' (the Good-for-Nothing or loafers) and 'Gai Hu' (beggars) from Shaoxing in Zhejiang province should be changed to 'Liang Ren' (the decent people)." In April of the 5th year of Yongzheng (1727), another edict was issued, and it was provided that as for "Ban Dang" (accompanying servants) and "Shi Pu" (life maidservants), "if the contract has been lost because long time has passed and because they have not been supported by their masters, they are not to be called by 'Shi Pu' (life maidservants) any longer."[309] In the 7th year of Yongzheng (1729), according to a new edict, "Dan Hu" (those who live on water instead of on land) from Guangdong province were allowed to live on land, so they were "allowed to live in villages near rivers and to be registered together with the common people."[310] Later, in May of the 8th year of Yongzheng (1730), "Gai Hu" (beggars) from Changshu and Zhaowen counties in Jiangsu province were registered as common people.[311]

In the 36th year of Qianlong (1771), it was declared that for all the people of "Yue Hu" (those specializing in playing music, singing, and dancing), "Gai Hu" (beggars), "Duo Min" (the good for nothing or loafers), and "Dan Hu" (those who live on water instead of on land), if their "Jian Ji" (people of inferior household registration) status

---

[306]"Yong Zheng Chao" (The Reign of Emperor Yongzheng) in *Dong Hua Lu* (*The Record of Donghua*), Vol. 10.

[307]*Qing Shi Zong Shi Lu* (*The Record of Emperor Shizong of Qing Dynasty*), Vol. 81.

[308]"Yong Zheng Chao" (The Reign of Emperor Yongzheng) in *Dong Hua Lu* (*The Record of Donghua*), Vol. 2.

[309]"Yong Zheng Chao" (The Reign of Emperor Yongzheng) in *Dong Hua Lu* (*The Record of Donghua*), Vol. 25.

[310]"Yong Zheng Chao" (The Reign of Emperor Yongzheng) in *Dong Hua Lu* (*The Record of Donghua*), Vol. 10.

[311]*Qing Shi Zong Shi Lu* (*The Record of Emperor Shizong of Qing Dynasty*), Vol. 81.

had been eliminated or if they had changed their professions and reported to the government or if "their relatives have been proved to be honest and self-abiding," they were already granted certifications to take "Ke Ju" (the imperial examination) after four generations. Those people of "Shi Pu" (life maidservants) from Anhui province were allowed to register as common people after two generations, so their descendants were allowed to take "Ke Ju" (the imperial examination). If the local villains still bullied or insulted "Jian Ji" (people of inferior household registration) who had already changed their profession and become "Liang Min" (decent people), they would be punished according to law. Moreover, if former slaves were still willing to stay humble, they should be penalized too; if any local officials had failed to fully carry out these laws, they would be investigated by "Du Fu" (the viceroys and procurators) and be punished accordingly.[312]

In Chinese feudal society, "Jian Min" (rabbles or people of lower social status) and "Jian Ji" (people of inferior household registration) had existed for a long time; this was because they were the product of a system of social hierarchy. Though the policy of changing "Jian Min" (rabbles or people of lower social status) into "Liang Ren" (decent people), carried out during the reign of Emperor Yongzheng, was of great historical and positive significance, it had failed to touch the very basis of social hierarchy, so it was impossible to be thoroughly and completely implemented. This problem of "Jian Min" (rabbles or people of lower social status) and "Jian Ji" (people of inferior household registration), which was left over by history, was not solved until the decrees abolishing "Jian Min" (rabbles or people of lower social status) and "Jian Ji" (people of inferior household registration) were issued by the Nanjing Provisional Government after the Xin Hai Revolution (or Revolution of 1911) upon the advice of provisional president Sun Yat-sen.

11.5.2 The Further Enrichment of Property Rights

The tradition of the Tang and Song dynasties was followed in the civil law of the Qing Dynasty, so personal property was called "Wu" (object), "Cai" (wealth), or "Cai Wu" (belongings); real estate was called "Chan" (estate), "Ye" (property), or "Chan Ye" (estate and property); the owner of personal property was called "Wu Zhu" (owner) or "Cai Zhu" (rich man), and the owner of real estate was called "Ye Zhu" (proprietor), "Tian Zhu" (landowner), "Di Zhu" (landlord), or "Fang Zhu" (house owner). "Chan Ye Quan" refers to the current real rights. In the Qing Dynasty, the concept of real rights was already formed to a certain extent. For example, for the provision of "eating fruits in an orchard without permission" in *Da Qing Lv Li Hui Tong Xin Zuan* (*New Collections of the Laws and Precedents of Great Qing*), an annotation was added, and it was stated that "all things have their owners, so it has not only exceeded one's own rights, but also harmed others to eat

---

[312] *Qing Shi Zong Shi Lu* (*The Record of Emperor Shizong of Qing Dynasty*), Vol. 94.

the fruits in other people's orchards without permission. Thus, one shall be punished according to the value of fruit which he has eaten."[313] In the annotation, the words that "all things have their owners" and "exceeded one's own rights" contained the connotation of property owners. So according to the laws of the Qing Dynasty, the violation of real rights was punished differently according to different situations, and those involved would have either criminal or civil legal liabilities. For example, in the provision of "destroying farm implements and giving up farm work" in "Tian Zhai" (Land and Houses) in "Hu Lv" (Statutes on Households) in *Da Qing Lv Li Hui Tong Xin Zuan* (*New Collections of the Laws and Precedents of Great Qing*), it was stipulated that "anyone who has intentionally discarded and destroyed farm implements and cut down trees of others, or devastated other people's crops, shall be punished according to the regulation on theft with the destroyed property calculated and he is exempted from the punishment of 'Ci Zi' (the punishment of making humiliated tattoo on one's body, especially on the face); if the government property is destroyed, the punishment will be two levels severer"; "if one has lost or destroyed government property unintentionally, his punishment will be three levels lighter, with the destroyed property checked and the losses compensated; if one has destroyed property privately owned, he needs only to recover the damage without being punished; ... if one has destroyed other's houses or walls, the cost of rebuilding the houses and employment of laborers will be estimated and he will be punished according to the regulation on theft with the destroyed houses repaired; if one has destroyed government houses, his penalty will be two levels severer; if one has destroyed the houses unintentionally, he needs only to rebuild the building without being punished." As can be seen from the abovementioned, as for the laws in the Qing Dynasty, real rights were protected and different liabilities were also held according to different circumstances.

With regard to real rights, land and houses were not only the most fundamental subject matter but also the most important private property, as well as the main subject of taxation. The sale, pawn, or mortgage of real estate usually required the making of contract, particularly the preparation of necessary papers such as legal documents. However, as for the sale, pawn, or mortgage of ordinary personal property, usually there was no need to make any legal document except when dealing with important personal property, such as "Nu Bi" (slave girls and maidservants), horses, and oxen and the pawning of personal property at pawnshops.

Because the right of using or the usufruct of real estate concerned the ownership of interest, it was greatly stressed by both the owners and the government. In *Da Qing Lv Li* (*The Laws and Precedents of Great Qing*), a variety of real rights related to real estate was laid down, including "Suo You Quan" (ownership), "Zu Quan" (tenancy rights), "Di Ji Quan" (the rights of homestead), "Dian Quan" (pawn rights), "Ya Quan (mortgage right), "Yong Dian Quan" (rights of permanent rent), and so on. As for personal property, because people only paid attention to the rights of using

---

[313]"Tian Zhai" (Land and Houses) in "Hu Lv" (Statutes on Households) in *Da Qing Lv Li Hui Tong Xin Zuan* (*New Collections of the Laws and Precedents of Great Qing*), Vol. 8.

11.5 Codification of Civil Law

and usufruct, there were very few kinds of personal rights, such as "Zhu Quan" (sovereign rights), "Zhi Quan" (pledge rights), "Di Ya Quan" (mortgage rights), and so on. Unless the subject matter was a contraband article, the owner had unrestricted rights to own, use, make profit, and dispose of his property, and he would not be deprived of ownership even if the object was lost.

With regard to the traditional means of obtaining ownership, the rule of preemption was highlighted in the laws of the Qing Dynasty. For example, it was admitted that those who opened up wasteland had the ownership of the land reclaimed; however, if they had left the land unattended or uncultivated later, they would be deprived of ownership. Besides, "if there are no owners for the things like grass, woods and stones on hills, it is allowed for everyone to cut them down and to make use of them; however, if someone has made some efforts to chop down the woods or cleared them up first, the things all belong to him."[314]

In general, the rules for the picking up of objects left by others, the discovery of buried objects, the obtaining of interests from the property, and the ownership of floating objects were similar to those in the laws of the Tang and Ming dynasties.

11.5.2.1 The Protection of "Suo You Quan" (Ownership)

"Suo You Quan" (ownership) is the most important real right. Since the state was founded on agriculture in ancient China, ownership of land was the core of real right. In the Qing Dynasty, ownership of land was divided into two kinds, namely, state ownership and individual ownership, and the various legal relationships of land ownership were protected and adjusted by law.

At the beginning of the Qing Dynasty, state ownership of land was established by way of enclosure, reclamation, inheritance, confiscation, forfeiture, and "Tou Chong" (seeking refuge with and working as slave for the powerful and influential people), and lands were allocated to "Zong Shi" (royal families), nobility, and officers and soldiers of "Ba Qi" (the Eight Banners: banner, a division of the Manchu nationality and the emperor's clan) to be cultivated or rented; which brought about the manors of "Zong Shi" (royal families) and "Ba Qi" (the Eight Banners: banner, a division of the Manchu nationality and the emperor's clan). The lands could be rented or mortgaged, but they were not allowed to be sold because the owner was the state. However, after the middle period of the Qing Dynasty, the central government's control over these lands was weakened, so the lands gradually became privately owned, which forced the government to change the requirement for granting ownership from tacit consent to recognition of the legality of ownership. Apart from the official manors, there were also other kinds of state-owned land, such as confiscated and forfeited land obtained by "Ji Mo" (the cancellation of a household registration), the abolishment of manors, illegal selling and mortgaging, official redemption, and mortgaging for tax. Besides, the land also included that which

---

[314]Shen Zhiqi (Qing Dynasty), *Da Qing Lv Ji Zhu* (*Collected Commentaries on Great Qing Code*).

belonged to the families with no male inheritors and which was confiscated by the government and "Sui Que Di" which was granted to the officials and soldiers of "Ba Qi" (the Eight Banners: banner, a division of Manchu nationality and the emperor's clan). Usually soldiers could lease "Sui Que Di" to tenants to collect rents, but after the tenants had worked for a long time on a piece of land, they would begin to regard themselves as the owners of the land, so the soldiers were only given the right to collect rents. Other kinds of state-owned land included stud farm, extra rent land, school land, and "Ji Tian" (land used for ancestor worship and sacrifice).

In addition, the state also owned saltmarshes, mines, rivers, lakes, and forests.

As for the land relationship of Qing Dynasty, "Qi Di" referred to the land which was occupied by "Qi Ren" (members of the Manchu ethnic group) by abusing their political power. In order to protect their ownership of land and to maintain their means of livelihood, "Qi Ren" (members of the Manchu ethnic group) were forbidden by law to sell their land, and it was also forbidden for the Han people to buy the houses and land from "Qi Ren" (members of the Manchu ethnic group). However, because "Qi Ren" (members of the Manchu ethnic group) were not good at farming and because their population increased rapidly, they began to sell land to the Han people in the late Kangxi period. So in the 7th year of Yongzheng (1729), it was reiterated that "the land of 'Ba Qi' (the Eight Banners: banner, a division of Manchu nationality and the emperor's clan) is originally the property of 'Qi Ren' (members of the Manchu ethnic group), so their land shall not be sold to Han people according to law."[315] In the meantime, with regard to land that was sold, it could be redeemed by the government compulsively by paying certain amount of money. So accordingly, "the 'Qi Di' (the land owned by Manchu people) sold according to 'Hong Qi' (contract with an official seal) can be redeemed according to the original price, and the 'Qi Di' (the land owned by Manchu people) sold according to 'Bai Qi' (contract without an official seal) can be redeemed at half of the original price or without paying any money."[316] These regulations were revised many times during the reign of Emperor Qianlong, and the new regulation was based on the number of years instead of "Hong Qi" (contract with an official seal) and "Bai Qi" (contract without an official seal). In the 9th year of Qianlong (1744), it was stipulated that "ten years will be used as the standard. If the land has been sold within ten years, one shall pay full amount to have the land redeemed; if the land has been sold for more than ten years, one shall pay one tenths of the original price; if the land has been sold within fifty years, one shall pay half the original price."[317] In the 34th year of Qianlong (1769), it was provided in the amended regulation that "the amount of money used for redemption shall be based on the current rent, no matter when the land is sold and

---

[315]"Tian Fu Kao" (A Textual Research on Land Tax) (Part 5) in *Qing Chao Wen Xian Tong Kao* (*A General Textual Research of the Documents of Qing Dynasty*), Vol. 5.

[316]*Da Qing Hui Dian Shi Li* (*The Precedents of the Collected Statutes of Great Qing*), Vol. 135.

[317]*Da Qing Hui Dian Shi Li* (*The Precedents of the Collected Statutes of Great Qing*), Vol. 159.

how much it has been sold for."[318] During the reign of Emperor Qianlong, "Qi Di" (the land owned by Manchu people) was taken back by the government four times, with a total of 37,611 *qing* of land recovered. However, some poor "Qi Ren" (members of the Manchu ethnic group) could not afford to redeem the land from the government. Emperor Gaozong once admitted in an imperial order that "the government redemption of land might not be beneficial to the poor 'Qi Ren' (members of the Manchu ethnic group)."[319] So it was quite common for "Qi Ren" (members of the Manchu ethnic group) to sell "Qi Di" (the land owned by Manchu people) at that time, which started the gradual privatization of "Qi Di" (the land owned by Manchu people). After the reign of Emperor Qianlong and during the reign of emperors Jiaqing, Daoguang, and Xianfeng, it was repeatedly reiterated that "it is forbidden to sell Qi Di" (the land owned by Manchu people) obtained through either land enclosure or land deals, so if anyone has sold or pawned land, he will be punished according to the "Li" (precedent) on selling official land. However, the sale of "Qi Di" (the land owned by Manchu people) was still popular in practice, and land was often sold in the disguised form of long-term lease and long-term tenancy. In order to deal with this anomaly, in the 25th year of Qianlong (1759), *Wei Jin Si Xing Chang Zu Zhi Li* (*The Regulation on the Private Long-term Lease*) was issued, and it was declared that "if anyone has involved in long-term lease with the owners and tenants privately, he shall be punished. Besides, the rent paid to the owner of the land shall be confiscated by the government and the land occupied by tenants shall be taken back and returned to the land owner to prevent the land owner and the tenant from making any profit from the transaction and to warn against the others."[320]

As it was difficult to stop such economic transaction between "Qi Ren" (members of the Manchu ethnic group) and the common people, *Qi Di Mai Mai Zhang Cheng* (*The Regulation on the Transaction of the Land Owned by Manchu People*) was issued in the 2nd year of Xianfeng (1852), and it was declared that "'Qi Ren' (members of the Manchu ethnic group) are allowed to sell their land." "From now on, the sale of 'Qi Di' (the land owned by Manchu people) in 'Feng Tian' (now Shenyang) is strictly forbidden according to the original regulations. Nevertheless, the 'Qi Di' (the land owned by Manchu people) in 'Shun Tian' (The Capital District) and 'Zhi Li' (now Hebei province) can all be sold not only to 'Qi Ren' (members of the Manchu ethnic group) but also to the common people, whether it is obtained from land enclosure or land dealing or whether it is inhabited by military troops or other people. But tax should by paid in the land transaction. As to those who have sold their land before, whether the owners or the tenants, they shall no longer be held

---

[318] *Qing Yuan Xian Zhi* (*Annals of Qingyuan County*), Vol. 66.

[319] "Tian Fu Kao" (A Textual Research on Land Tax) (Part 5) in *Qing Chao Wen Xian Tong Kao* (*A General Textual Research of the Documents of Qing Dynasty*), Vol. 5.

[320] "Tian Fu Kao" (A Textual Research on Land Tax) (Part 5) in *Qing Chao Wen Xian Tong Kao* (*A General Textual Research of the Documents of Qing Dynasty*), Vol. 5.

liable."[321] Since then, although the provision of "forbidding 'Qi Ren' (members of the Manchu ethnic group) to sell their land" was retained in *Da Qing Lv Li* (*The Laws and Precedents of Great Qing*), it was not implemented in practice. Similarly, wasteland that was cultivated by peasants and armies was also gradually privatized, so the buyers could obtain ownership of the land after reporting to the government and paying the tax.

In terms of private ownership, the most important one is ownership of real estate. The royal families, nobility, and bureaucrats were the largest class of private landowners in the country. By making advantage of their special social status, they obtained lots of land and houses by way of award from the emperor, "Tou Xian" (lessening tax and corvee by registering the land under the name of officials and gentry), and land transaction. Meanwhile, common people and landlords became the most common private landowners by managing cultivated wasteland, renting land, and acting as the heads of some manors. As to the owner-peasants who occupied small pieces of land, they were in a very unstable situation, so they might become land owners or tenants at any time. Apart from these people, some merchants and industrialists also became landowners by buying land. After the middle of the Qing dynasty, the development of the commodity economy promoted the commercialization of land, so it became popular for merchants to buy and obtain land with the profit they made from doing business. During the reign of emperors Jiaqing and Daoguang, some merchants occupied more than 100,000 *mu* of land, so the price of land increased dramatically. For instance, in the regions of Suzhou and Hangzhou in the south of Yangtze River, the price for per *mu* of land was two to three *liang* of silver during the reign of Emperor Shunzhi, four to five *liang* of silver during the reign of Kangxi, seven to eight *liang* of silver at the beginning of the reign of Emperor Qianlong, and more than fifty *liang* in the later period of Emperor Qianlong. As a way to manage their land, it was common for merchants to lease their land to tenants and to collect rents regularly. But "they had never been to the land themselves for years"[322] and "they might not even know the location of their land,"[323] which made it possible for more tenants to have "Yong Dian Quan" (rights of permanent rent).

Some of the private land was used for special purposes, for example the private land could be used by temples, schools, charitable agencies and sacrificial institutions; while the land shared by a family was owned collectively and run by their own representatives. Moreover, individuals had no rights of land disposal, and usually such land was not subject to taxation.

---

[321]"Ji Fu Guan Bin Zhuang Tian" (The Land of Armymen in Capital Regions) in "Tian Fu" (Land Tax) in "Hu Bu" (The Department of Revenue) in "Guang Xu Chao" (The Reign of Emperor Guangxu) in *Da Qing Hui Dian Shi Li* (*The Precedents of the Collected Statutes of Great Qing*), Vol. 160.

[322]*Wan Zai Xian Zhi* (*Annals of Wanzai County*), Vol. 3.

[323]*Wan Zai Xian Zhi* (*Annals of Wanzai County*), Vol. 3.

11.5 Codification of Civil Law

In order to prevent local officials from encroaching upon private property, regulations were made in *Da Qing Lv Li* (*The Laws and Precedents of Great Qing*) and *Hu Bu Ze Li* (*The Regulation of the Department of Revenue*), and local officials were forbidden to buy real estate in places within their jurisdiction, but compared with *Da Qing Lv Li* (*The Laws and Precedents of Great Qing*), the scope of *Hu Bu Ze Li* (*The Regulation of the Department of Revenue*) was much extended. According to *Da Qing Lv Li* (*The Laws and Precedents of Great Qing*), "the officials below 'Can Jiang' (military officer under Commander in Chief) have to pay tax like the common people for their real estate, land and grain." Although the officials in Shengjing (now Shenyang) were forbidden to buy the real estate in places within their jurisdiction, "they are allowed to buy the real estate in the places out of their jurisdiction." In the Qing Dynasty, the purpose of preventing officials from buying real estate within their jurisdiction was to prevent them from encroaching upon the property of civilians by force and from conducting illegal behaviors by abusing their power. However, due to political corruption, the laws and disciplines for official management were not strictly carried out, so they had lost their restraining power.

Apart from the real estate, the owners of personal property had extensive right of disposal, so they could dispose their personal property at will.

Since the stability of the right of ownership was crucial to social order and national security, ownership was protected in many aspects under the laws of the Qing Dynasty, and its violation was strictly punished. As a result, a series of regulations was issued to affirm the right of ownership. For example, in the 33rd year of Qianlong (1768), it was stated in a new regulation that "any disputes among the common people over the ownership of cemetery hills shall be settled according to contracts if the person has obtained the ownership recently; while the name, the acreage of the hill, *Yu Lin Tu Ce* (*Scale Graph*) and the stamps of taxation shall be provided and checked if the person has obtained the ownership a long time ago. Besides, the magistrate shall check and decide the owner accordingly, if it is proved true, the person is allowed to own the land; but if it is proved that the acreage of land is false or there is no stamp of taxation, or if the words on stone tablets could not be used as evidence because the contracts are made a long time ago, the complaint who has lodged false accusation shall be punished accordingly."[324] Although this regulation was made to settle the disputes on cemetery hills, it could also be applied to all land cases.

In the Qing Dynasty, documents and contracts on land were more detailed, as was described in records: "there were volumes of books on land measurement, reclamation, transferring of ownership and taxation. Besides, copies of reference books were written to check the time of relevant contracts, and many data were recorded in

---

[324]"Dao Mai Tian Zhai" (The Stealing and Selling of the Land and Houses) in "Tian Zhai" (Land and Houses) in "Hu Lv" (Statutes on Households) in *Da Qing Lv Li* (*The Laws and Precedents of Great Qing*), Vol. 9.

books to check up the details."³²⁵ If there was not enough documentary evidence, investigations should be conducted on the spot: "The boundary of the land shall be checked first; if the boundary is similar, the landform shall be checked; if there are problems in landform, investigations of the land shall be conducted on spot."³²⁶ Field investigation of the land was the task of a special official assigned by the magistrates of "Zhou" (subprefecture) and "Xian" (county), and investigation records should be made at the same time. The documentary evidence of the investigation and the record of the on-spot examination could be used as evidence of ownership, and if anyone claimed ownership with no reason, he should be punished for the crime of embezzlement. For example, if anyone had "sold others' real estate," or had "plowed others' land," he should be punished depending on the circumstances, but if the land belonged to the government, he should be punished two levels severer; "if the land is public, the profit made shall be given to the government; if the land is private, the profit made shall be given to its owner." In order to protect the ownership of real estate, it was stipulated that even if an official who had made great contribution to the nation had sold out others' land, he would still be punished, but it should be reported to and decided by the emperor.³²⁷

In order to protect the land ownership of Mongolian noble families and herdsmen, *Meng Gu Tu Di Jin Zhi Si Mai Ling* (*Decrees on Private Sale of Mongolian Land*) was passed during the reign of Emperor Yongzheng. In the 13th year of Qianlong (1748), *Di Mu Shu Hui Ling* (*Decrees on Land Redemption*) was issued to deal with the changes of land ownership in Mongolia. In the meantime, the common people were forbidden to reclaim land outside the state boundaries.³²⁸ As to the Mongolian land mortgaged or sold to the common people, it should be settled according to the "Li" (precedent) on the land withdrawn by Mongolians in Tumote in Guihua City (now Huhhot): "if the land is sold for less than two hundred *liang* of silver, or if it has been pawned to be cultivated for more than five years, it can be withdrawn after the buyer has worked on the land for one more year; if the land has been pawned to be cultivated for less than five years, the buyer is allowed to worked on the land which shall be withdrawn after five years; if the land is sold for less than two hundred *liang* of silver, the buyer can work on the land for another three years before it is

---

³²⁵Wang Zhi, "Ting Duan" (Making Adjudication after Hearing the Statement) in "Xing Ming" (The Names of Punishment) (Book 2) in *Mu Ling Shu* (*Regulations on the Prefectural Officials' Behaviors*), Vol. 18, edited by Xu Dongyi (Qing Dynasty).

³²⁶Wang Zhi, "Ting Duan" (Making Adjudication after Hearing the Statement) in "Xing Ming" (The Names of Punishment) (Part 2) in *Mu Ling Shu* (*Regulations on the Prefectural Officials' Behaviors*), Vol. 18, edited by Xu Dongyi (Qing Dynasty).

³²⁷"Dao Mai Tian Zhai" (The Stealing and Selling of the Land and Houses) in "Tian Zhai" (Land and Houses) in "Hu Lv" (Statutes on Households) in *Da Qing Lv Li* (*The Laws and Precedents of Great Qing*), Vol. 9.

³²⁸"Di Mu" (Land) in *Li Fan Yuan Ze Li* (*The Regulation for the Bureau of National Minority Affairs*), Vol. 10.

11.5 Codification of Civil Law

withdrawn and returned to the original owner."[329] Because of these compulsory protective legal measures, the land ownership in Mongolia became relatively stable.

In Tibetan area, the serf owners, who only accounted for five percent of Tibetan population, occupied almost all the land, forests and other materials in the region. In order to make sure that serf owners could plant crops or raise animals in the designated areas without trespassing others' land, *Fan Li Tiao Kuan* (*Provisions and Precedents of Vassal States*) was issued and according to the law it was strictly forbidden for their animals to cross the boundaries illegally; otherwise, their animals would be confiscated by the government according to the specific circumstances.

In Qing Dynasty, not only the ownership of real estate but also that of personal property was protected by law. So the following regulations were provided in *Da Qing Lv Li* (*The Laws and Precedents of Great Qing*):

> Anyone who has stolen others' horses, cattle, donkeys, mules, pigs, goats, chickens, dogs, geese or ducks shall be punished for the crime of theft with the price of the stolen goods evaluated. If the stolen animals belong to the government, he shall be punished for stealing official property; ... anyone who has intentionally destroyed others' utensils or woods and crops shall be punished for the crime of theft according to the total value of the destroyed property with the exemption of "Ci Zi" (to make humiliated tattoo on one's body, especially one's face); anyone who has destroyed official property shall be punished two levels severer[330]; ... anyone who has stolen or destroyed vegetables or fruits on other people's farms shall be punished for corruption;[331] ... anyone who has stolen crops, fruits, vegetables or things unattended shall be punished for the crime of theft according to the total value of the stolen property with the exemption of "Ci Zi" (the punishment of making humiliated tattoo on one's body, especially on the face); anyone who has stolen grass, woods or stones in forests which are cultivated, gathered or chopped down by someone else shall be punished for the crime of theft according to the total value of the stolen property with the exemption of "Ci Zi" (the punishment of making humiliated tattoo on one's body, especially on the face).[332]

In conclusion, it was a prominent feature of the civil law in the Qing Dynasty to provide protection to the real estate of "Qi Ren" (members of the Manchu ethnic group) and "Suo You Quan" (ownership) of minority groups. Besides, since clan was an important social organization of the regime in Qing Dynasty, legal protection was provided to the shared property of family groups, so that it was forbidden for the

---

[329]"Geng Mu" (Farming and Husbandry) in "Li Fan Yuan" (The Bureau of National Minority Affairs) in *Da Qing Hui Dian Shi Li* (*The Precedents of the Collected Statutes of Great Qing*), Vol. 979.

[330]"Qi Hui Qi Wu Jia Se" (Destroying Implements and Crops) in "Tian Zhai" (Land and Houses) in "Hu Lv" (Statutes on Households) in *Da Qing Lv Li* (*The Laws and Precedents of Great Qing*), Vol. 9.

[331]"Shan Shi Tian Yuan Gua Guo" (Eating Melon and Fruit on others' Farms without Permission) in "Tian Zhai" (Land and Houses) in "Hu Lv" (Statutes on Households) in *Da Qing Lv Li* (*The Laws and Precedents of Great Qing*), Vol. 9.

[332]"Dao Tian Ye Gu Mai" (Stealing Cereal Crops and Wheat in the Fields) in "Dao Zei" (Stealing and Robbery) (Part 2) in "Xing Lv" (The Penal Code) in *Da Qing Lv Li* (*The Laws and Precedents of Great Qing*), Vol. 23.

offspring to sell the property of their ancestors randomly in order to protect the unity of family. In the 21st year of Qianlong (1756), another regulation was issued:

> Any offspring of a family who has sold fifty *mu* of inherited sacrificial land shall be punished by "Chong Jun" (to be forced to join the army) in "Bian Yuan" (outlying areas) according to the "Li" (precedent) on "Tou Xian" (to alleviate the tax and corvee by register the land under the name of the officials and gentry) and the "Li" (precedent) on selling the cemetery hills of ancestors. If anyone has sold land less than the amount mentioned above or, stolen or sold "Yi Tian" (fields leased to others with the rental collected for the profit of one's own clan), he shall be punished according to the "Li" (precedent) on selling official land; if one ancestral hall has been sold, he shall be punished by "Zhang" (flogging with heavy sticks) for seventy strokes; he shall be punished one level severer for selling additional three ancestor halls with the maximum punishment of "Zhang" (flogging with heavy sticks) for no more than one hundred strokes and "Tu" (imprisonment) for no more than three years. Those who know the facts but still collude to buy the land shall be punished the same as the criminal, with the houses taken back and managed by the clan leader and confiscated by the government; those who know nothing of the case will not be held liable.[333]

The punishment for selling family property was much severer than that for selling private and official real estate in order to maintain the social order of "Lun Chang" (feudal order of importance) and the principle of "Xiao" (filial piety), because they were the spiritual basis of autocratic dictatorship. Among the various family rules and clan regulations acknowledged by the Qing government, there were contents forbidding the offspring to sell the family property. For example, it was stated in the record of pedigree of the Wei family from Nanchang that "anyone who has occupied family property to bring benefit to himself shall be taken to the ancestor hall and be punished by 'Chi' (flogging with light sticks) for thirty strokes with the profit confiscated by the family."[334] Even if the property was privately owned, certain restrictions had to be obeyed by the owner when it was sold, as was regulated in *Zhang Shi Zu Pu* (*The Pedigree of Zhang's Family*) in Jingding in Hebei province: "The ancestors have experienced great difficulties in their pioneering work, so if any of the younger generation dares to give up the regular duties and destroy the family property, he would be persuaded by the people from the family to take a proper occupation or be stopped from selling the land and houses." Clearly, the main purpose of restricting private property disposition was to maintain economic strength of the whole clan community. That was why the people from the same clan had the right of preemption when the property was sold. Similar regulation was made in *Tong Cheng Zhao Shi Zong Pu* (*The Genealogy of Zhao's Family in Tongcheng*) in Anhui province: "Anyone who has proposed to sell his land and houses shall ask his family first and then his relatives, and only when neither of the family members nor relatives intend to buy them is he allowed to sell them to people outside the family; if

---

[333]"Dao Mai Tian Zhai Tiao Li" (The Regulation on the Stealing and Selling of the Land and Houses) in "Tian Zhai" (Land and Houses) in "Hu Lv" (Statutes on Households) in *Da Qing Lv Li* (*The Laws and Precedents of Great Qing*), Vol. 9.

[334]*Yu Zhang Huang Cheng Wei Shi Zong Pu* (*The Genealogy of Wei Family in Huangcheng in Yuzhang*).

anyone has sold them secretly to people outside the family without the permission of his own family members, he shall be punished."

11.5.2.2 The Development of "Yong Dian Quan" (Rights of Permanent Rent)

"Yong Dian Quan" (rights of permanent rent) continued to be developed in the areas south of Yangtze River during the Qing Dynasty. "Yong Dian Quan" (rights of permanent rent) focused mainly on the rights to use and profit from the land, and it was a kind of surface right obtained by paying rent. In as early as the Song Dynasty, it had already been recorded that "it may help to make a living to be a tenant permanently."[335] Later in the middle of the Ming Dynasty, "Yong Dian Quan" (rights of permanent rent) became popular in the provinces of southeast China. The special historical background of the Qing Dynasty facilitated the expansion of "Yong Dian Quan" (rights of permanent rent). In "Yong Dian Quan" (rights of permanent rent), though a tenant had the obligation to pay rent, he could acquire the right to farm the land from generation to generation, so as long as the landlord took the rent, he could not re-rent the land at will.

There are several ways to acquire "Yong Dian Quan" (rights of permanent rent): (1) if one had reclaimed a publicly or privately owned wasteland and made long-term investment on the land to change the barren land into a fertile one, one could have "Yong Dian Quan" (rights of permanent rent); (2) if one had prepaid considerable rent, one could become a permanent tenant on the condition that every year he would continue to make small payment to the landlord; (3) if a former landowner returned and found that his land had been cultivated by a tenant for a long time, he had to accept the arrangement of "Yong Dian Quan" (rights of permanent rent) with the current tenant; (4) in the areas of Jiangsu, Zhejiang, Anhui, and others that were severely destroyed by "Tai Ping Tian Guo" (Taiping Heavenly Kingdom) and where the population decreased, the land was wasted, and the economy receded, "Yong Dian Quan" (rights of permanent rent) could be granted to some peasants in order to encourage farming and recover production; (5) some small landowners could donate their land or their temples to imperial clans, the wealthy, and the powerful in exchange for land tax exemption; (6) landowners could sell their land at a low price in exchange for "Yong Dian Quan" (rights of permanent rent), to be promised to them by the new owners, or pay their debt by giving their land to a creditor on the condition that they could get "Yong Dian Quan" (rights of permanent rent); (7) a tenant could rent a land permanently to get recognition and approval of the landlord for "Yong Dian Quan" (rights of permanent rent).

The right of a permanent tenant was not lost in the selling of the land by the landlord, as was stated in the saying: "selling the land without selling 'Yong Dian Quan' (rights of permanent rent)" and "changing the landlord without changing the

---

[335]Wei Tai (Song Dynasty), *Dong Xuan Bi Lu* (*The Record of Dongxuan*), Vol. 8.

tenants." In a contract transferring land made by Zhang Dexing on the 15th of October of the 9th year of Emperor Qianlong (1744), the following contents are recorded:

> I would like to transfer my land (a part of my land granted as a clerk) to Li Tai and make him my permanent tenant, but Li Tai is not allowed to rent the land from others. ... I shall not lease the land to anyone else, while Li Tai has the right to stop renting. After signing this contract, if there are any disputes over the land, I myself shall deal with it and there is nothing to do with Li Tai.[336]

Besides cultivating the land, a permanent tenant could perform others acts of ownership over it, such as construction of houses and building of tombs, and also claim ownership over its yield, such as the right to harvest the fruits naturally grown on the land.

It was the duty of the permanent tenant to pay rent. If he intentionally refused to pay it, the government would be forced to interfere; if he defaulted in his payments or performed other illegal actions, the landlord would have the right to cancel "Yong Dian Quan" (rights of permanent rent). However, permanent tenants often refused to move out of the land or asked the landlord to return their rent deposit guarantee.

In accordance with the imperial edict included in volume one hundred and seventy five of *Qing Gao Zong Shi Lu* (*The Record of Qing Emperor Gaozong*), "if the landlord is very poor and he has sold his land to another man," "it is forbidden for the landlord to change the tenant" and the tenant's offspring could "still cultivate the land as before." As a result, "it is very common that more than ten generations or at least five to six, or three to four generations of the tenants have cultivated the land of the same owner."[337] With the development of "Yong Dian Quan" (rights of permanent rent), arrangements such as "one piece of land is regarded as the property of both the landlord and the tenant" and "Yi Tian Er Zhu" (two owners for one piece of land) happened in some areas.

In the so-called Yi Tian Er Zhu (two owners for one piece of land), the upper layer of the land, called "Tian Pi" or "Tian Mian" (the surface of the land or land skin), was occupied by the tenant, called "Pi Zhu" (land skin owner), who had the right to make a profit out of it, while the lower layer of the land, called "Tian Gu" or "Tian Gen" (the land itself or land bone), was owned by the landlord. That was why a landlord was also called a "Gu Zhu" or "Tian Zhu" (the land bone owner). Since both "Pi Zhu" (land skin owner) and "Gu Zhu" (the land bone owner) could dispose of their respective rights of ownership, it was called "Yi Tian Er Zhu" (two owners for one piece of land). "Yi Tian Er Zhu" (two owners for one piece of land) was a product of the Qing government, so it was widely applied in Jiangsu, Zhejiang, Jiangxi, Anhui, and Fujian provinces only but was expanded throughout the whole country later. "Yi Tian Er Zhu" (two owners for one piece of land) not only showed

---

[336]Fu Yiling, *Ming Qing Nong Cun She Hui Jing Ji* (*TheSociety and Economy in the Rural Areas of Ming and Qing Dynasty*), SDX Joint Publishing Company, 1961.

[337]Wei Li (Qing Dynasty), "Yu Li Yi Hou Shu" (Letters to Li Yihou) in *Wei Ji Zi Wen Ji* (*The Collected Works of Wei Jizi*), Vol. 8.

11.5 Codification of Civil Law

the change of traditional tenant-landlord relationship, but also reflected the adjustment of the power of different classes in rural areas. The rulers of the Qing Dynasty knew very well that in order to establish a stable ruling regime over the whole country, they had to restore agricultural production and make the homeless peasants settled again. Thus, the policy of "permanent rent" or "permanent property" was carried out to encourage the reclamation of wasteland. The shift from "permanent rent" to "Yi Tian Er Zhu" (two owners for one piece of land) was a process full of complicated struggles. The tenant's right of "Tian Mian" (the surface of the land or land skin) was limited because "Tian Zhu" or "Gu Zhu" (the land bone owner) should firstly admit that the right was obtained by the profits which they made. However, because of the struggle of tenants to protect themselves, the prohibition on freely disposing "Tian Mian" (the surface of the land or land skin) was changed, so it became possible for "Pi Zhu" (land skin owner) to exercise his rights completely without any restrictions, which was not only the hope of tenants but also the result of their struggle against landlords, which they obtained by making use of the advantages of permanent tenancy. As a folk custom, "Yi Tian Er Zhu" (two owners for one piece of land) was mainly practiced in the economically developed areas south of Yangtze River, which had reflected its close relationship with economic development. Moreover, its continuous expansion nationwide had fully shown the influence of the new renting relationship.

According to custom, "Yong Dian Quan" (rights of permanent rent) would not be canceled even if "Pi Zhu" (land skin owner) delayed the payment of rent for a short period of time. "Pi Zhu" (land skin owner), moreover, also had the rights to re-rent, pawn, and mortgage "Tian Pi" or "Tian Mian" (the surface of the land or land skin). In such case, "Pi Zhu" (land skin owner) could get eight to nine percent of the total profit of the land, while "Tian Zhu" (the land bone owner) could get one or two percent. Consequently, the price of "Tian Pi" (the surface of the land or land skin) would turn out higher than that of "Tian Gu" (the land itself, or land bone), hence the saying "golden skin and silver bone" among the folks.

The emergence and growing practice of "Yi Tian Er Zhu" (two owners for one piece of land) made the feudal landlord–tenant relationship complicated. So the original ownership of "Tian Zhu" (the land bone owner) continued to be weakened, which made the transference of land ownership unprecedentedly complicated. In addition, the tenants changed from a land cultivator a land manager, which had led to the change of class relationship. Because it was difficult for "Tian Zhu" (the land bone owner) to exercise his rights of rent collection, it naturally affected his obligation to pay tax to the government, which forced the government to intervene in this custom. In accordance with *Fu Jian Sheng Li* (*The Regulations of Fujian Province*), during the reign of Emperor Qianlong, it was forbidden to sell and buy "Tian Pi" (the surface of the land or land skin), so the tenants needed only to pay rent to "Tian Zhu" (the land bone owner) without paying it to "Pi Zhu" (land skin owner). If "Pi Zhu" (land skin owner) owed rent, "Tian Zhu" (the land bone owner) could terminate the contract and take back his rights over "Tian Pi" (the surface of the land or land skin). Moreover, the squire was not allowed to delay the payment of rent; if he violates this, he would be severely punished. At the same time, it was required that this rule be inscribed in a stone tablet to make it known to all people in every village. Except for *Fu Jian Sheng Li* (*The Regulations of Fujian Province*), similar regulations were made in *Xi Jiang Zheng Yao* (*The Essentials of Administration of Xijiang*) and *Jiang Su Shan Yin Shou Zu Quan An* (*Cases of Rent Collection in Shanyin of Jiangsu Province*). Later, during the reign of Emperor Daoguang, it was ruled that if "Pi Zhu" (land skin owner) in south of Yangtze River had owed more than one year's rent, it was allowed for "Tian Zhu" (the land bone owner) to take back "Tian Pi" (the surface of the land or land skin) and rent it to others. On the other hand, "Pi Zhu" (land skin owner) was not allowed to sell or rent the land at will. From the regulations in *Fu Jian Sheng Li* (*The Regulations of Fujian Province*), it can be clearly seen that permanent renting in "Qi Di" (the land owned by Manchu people) was strictly forbidden by the Qing government after drawing lessons from the changes from permanent rent to "Yi Tian Er Zhu" (two owners for one piece of land) in order to protect the state interest and the ownership of landlords and to maintain the traditional landlord-tenant relationship.

11.5.2.3 "Dian Quan" (Pawn Rights)

According to the laws of the Ming Dynasty, "pawning should be conducted according to whether the property can be redeemed"; this concept was adapted in *Da Qing Lv Li* (*The Laws and Precedents of Great Qing*), and it was stipulated that "'Dian' (pawn) refers to the property mortgaged which can be redeemed at an agreed term." In the 18th year of Qianlong (1753), it was declared that "from now on, in all pawn contracts, it should be expressively stated that the property can be redeemed, while in all sale contracts, it should be expressively stated that the property is sold for good and can never be redeemed."[338] Thus, it was made clear that "Dian" (pawn) was different from "Mai" (sell). Another difference was that no tax was needed to be paid in "Dian" (pawn), which was contrary in the case of "Mai" (sell). It was provided in *Da Qing Lv Li* (*The Laws and Precedents of Great Qing*) that "tax was exempted for the contracts of pawning of land and houses, but it was not exempted for the contracts of sale."[339]

During the early Qing Dynasty, pawn term was not clarified in some pawn contracts, and most pawnees gave back the pawnage as soon as the pawners paid back the money, which apparently was unfavorable to pawnees in their management of the pawned property, for example, land or houses. If the pawn term was not specified, the pawn could be redeemed at any time, which was described to be "pawning being the work of life time." Because most of the pawn contracts often

---

[338] "Dian Mai Tian Zhai" (Land and Real Estate Mortgage) in "Tian Zhai" (Land and Houses) in "Hu Lv" (Statutes on Households) in *Da Qing Lv Li* (*The Laws and Precedents of Great Qing*), Vol. 9.

[339] "Dian Mai Tian Zhai" (Land and Real Estate Mortgage) in "Tian Zhai" (Land and Houses) in "Hu Lv" (Statutes on Households) in *Da Qing Lv Li* (*The Laws and Precedents of Great Qing*), Vol. 9.

covered a considerably long period of time and their contents were sometimes very confusing, it often led to lawsuits. Therefore, in the 18th year of Qianlong (1753), a regulation was issued: "For the contract which has no fixed term and which is signed before the 18th year of Qianlong, if it is signed within thirty years and if there are no such words as "sale for good" in the contract, the pawners can still get their property back; nevertheless, if it was signed thirty years ago, or if there are no clear records of 'allowing to be redeemed', even if there are no such words as "sale for good" in the contract, the pawnage shall be regarded as property without rightful heirs, so the pawners shall not get their property back.[340] In the 6th year of Jiaqing (1801), the term of redemption was precisely formulated when *Hu Bu Ze Li* (*The Regulation of the Department of Revenue*) was amended:

> The term of redemption in pawn contracts shall not exceed ten years; otherwise, both parties shall be punished. Generally, the term of redemption specified in the pawn contracts of land and houses among citizens shall be fewer than ten years. After ten years, the pawnage can be redeemed. If the original owner is unable to pay for redemption, the pawnee can decide whether to obtain its ownership after paying tax; if the term specified in a contract is over ten years, the tax shall be retrieved and those involved will be punished according to precedents once discovered.[341]

To protect the ownership over land and houses of "Qi Ren" (members of the Manchu ethnic group) and to prevent it from being lost because of failure to redeem in due time, it was provided in *Hu Bu Ze Li* (*The Regulation of the Department of Revenue*) that "the term of redemption specified in the pawn contracts of land which belonged to 'Qi Ren' (members of the Manchu ethnic group) shall not exceed twenty years." If twenty years had passed, the land would be regarded as "Sheng Ke Di" (land taxed according to the common land tax regulations), so it would be reported to the government and be taxed three *fen* of silver money, just like a common land. In such case, the land could no longer be redeemed. "In cases where the pawner is unable to pay for the redemption, the contract for permanent sale can be signed and an supplemental payment for the land shall be estimated by the government. If the pawnee is unwilling to pay the balance (or 'Zhao Tie': pay the balance in buying and selling), it shall be sold to others with the money returned to the pawnee."[342]

To avoid disputes arising after "Zhao Tie" (payment of the balance in buying and selling), it was common among citizens to sign contracts forbidding the raising of the prices. For example, in the 31st year of Qianlong (1766), a contract entitled *Shan Yin Xian Wang Sheng Ji Mai Tian Du Jue Zhao Jia Bai Qi* ("*Bai Qi*" on Forbidding to

---

[340] "Dian Mai Tian Zhai" (Land and Real Estate Mortgage) in "Tian Zhai" (Land and Houses) in "Hu Lv" (Statutes on Households) in *Da Qing Lv Li* (*The Laws and Precedents of Great Qing*), Vol. 9.

[341] "Zhi Chan Tou Shui Bu" (The Section of Real Estate Transaction Taxation) in "Tian Fu" (Land Tax) in *Hu Bu Ze Li* (*The Regulation of the Department of Revenue*), Vol. 10.

[342] "Zhi Chan Tou Shui Bu" (The Section of Real Estate Transaction Taxation) in "Tian Fu" (Land Tax) in *Hu Bu Ze Li* (*The Regulation of the Department of Revenue*), Vol. 10.

Raise the Price of Pawned Land of Wang Shenji from Shanyinging County) was signed, and the contents are as follows[343]:

> Contractor Wang Shenji has a piece of land No. 144.5 on Danzi, with a total of four *mu* three *fen* two *li*, which is pawned for exactly eighty *liang* of silver. Now I'm unable to pay for the redemption and the owner has paid the balance of thirty nine *liang* of silver. After the payment, the ownership and management of the land is hereby transferred permanently, and it is sold for good. This is the certificate written as proof.
> August of the 31st year of Emperor Qianlong,
> Contractor: Wang Shenji (signature)
> Wang Yousheng (signature)
> Middleman: Shen Rubing (signature)

Once the pawn was established, according to the pawn contract, both parties, the pawnee the and pawner, then obtained legal rights and obligations. The pawnee obtained the rights to possess, to use, and to make profit out of the property. The pawnee also had preemptive right over the property. When it comes to obligation, the pawnee was obligated to keep and repair the property and pay tax to the government. In addition, he was obligated to compensate for damages and losses resulting from his intentional or negligent actions, except when they occurred due to force majeure. For instance, in cases where a pawnshop was burned down by fire, based on whether the term of pawn had expired and based on the detailed conditions of the original owners and the owners of the pawnshop, the following are provided under the laws of the Qing Dynasty:

> When it happens that the house for pawnage is burnt down, if the term is expired then, both the pawner and pawnee shall pay half of the expanses for the reconstruction of the house, and the period of mortgage shall be extended for another three years. When it is due, the pawner can redeem the ownership according to the original price. Otherwise, if the pawner has no ability to pay for the reconstruction, the pawner shall redeem ownership with additional four percent of the original price. If the pawnee is unable to rebuild the house, the pawner can redeem ownership with a reduction of four percent of the original price; if the term has expired, then the pawner can redeem ownership according to half of the original price. However, if the pawner cannot pay the price, and the pawnee has rebuilt the house on his own, the period of mortgage shall be extended for another three years; when the term has expired, the pawner can redeem with additional four percent of the original price.[344]

The pawner had the right to redeem ownership of his property for a proper price, though he was not obligated to do so, which means that he could not to be forced by the pawnee to exercise his right of redemption. It was necessary to redeem the ownership according to a proper price, but it was invalid to merely declare the intention of redeeming the ownership. When due time came but the pawner was unable to redeem the property, ownership over the pawnage transferred to the

---

[343]Zhang Chuanxi, *Zhong Guo Li Dai Qi Yue Hui Bian Kao Shi* (*A Textual Research and Interpretation of the Collected Contracts of the Past Dynasties of China*) (Book 2).

[344]"Hu Lv" (Statutes on Households) in "Tian Zhai" (Land and Houses) in *Da Qing Lv Li Xing An Hui Zuan Ji Cheng* (*Collections of the Criminal Cases and the Laws and Precedents of Great Qing*), Vol. 9.

pawnee; if the pawner did not want to obtain the ownership, the pawnee could sell it to someone else, but it was forbidden to sell one property twice in order to protect the right of use and usufruct of the pawner. It was specifically stated in *Qing Jia Qing Shi Yi Nian Beijing Zheng Huang Qi Ping De Dian Fang Bai Qi* ("*Bai Qi*"*Made by Ping De Pawnshop of Plain Yellow Banner in Beijing in the 11th Year of Emperor Jiaqing*) that "after the house is pawned, if the house has been pawned repeatedly with no reason, the pawnee shall bear the sole obligation."[345] As for those who had pawned their property for several times, in addition to being punished according to the rules as were regulated in this law, they should return the money to other pawnee. Besides, the real estate should be returned to the original buyer. If the pawnee and If the pawnee and "Ya Bao" (intermediary agent) had known the truth of the transaction, they would also be punished and the money would be confiscated by the government; nevertheless, the party would be exempted from punishment if they had conducted the transaction without knowing the facts.

To protect the legitimate right and interest of pawnees, the principle of default guarantee was also applied in pawn contracts. In *Wan Ping Xian Guo Shen Yan Chu Ding Fang Cao Qi* (*The Contract of the Transference of the Ownership of Houses by Guo Shenyan from Wanping County*), signed in the 20th year of Kangxi (1681), and *Da Xing Xian Li Rong Fa Xiong Di Dian Fang Cao Qi* (*The Contract of Pawning Houses by Liu Rongfa Brothers from Daxing County*), signed in the 34th year of Kangxi (1695), the following contents are included:

> Both parties are willing to sign the contract without going back on their words, and those who go back on their words first shall be punished and are willing to give half of the silver money mentioned in the contract to the government for public use.[346]

Though the second contract was made fourteen years later, its contents and words were the same as those in the first one, which indicates that there had already been an established format for this kind of default guarantee. Furthermore, the function of "Ya Bao" (intermediary agent) was also stressed in the pawn contracts of Qing Dynasty. In the 56th year of Qianlong (1791), it was stated in *Da Xing Xian Yang Yu Quan Zhuan Dian Fang Bai Qi* ("*Bai Qi*"*Made by Pawning Houses by Yang Yuquan from Daxing County*) that "after the pawning, if any disputes regarding the real estate arise among the members of the owner's family, 'Ya Bao' (intermediary agent) shall be held liable."[347] However, in some contracts, it was specified that both the owner and "Ya Bao" (intermediary agent) would be held liable.

In summary, pawn was very popular in Qing Dynasty, which was inseparable from the Chinese national condition at the time, because it was not only accepted by the public but also confirmed by law. Under the influence of patriarchal system and conception, it was regarded as unfilial to sell the inherited property of the ancestors.

---

[345]Zhang Chuanxi, *Zhong Guo Li Dai Qi Yue Hui Bian Kao Shi* (*A Textual Research and Interpretation of the Collected Contracts of the Past Dynasties of China*) (Book 2).

[346]Zhang Chuanxi, *Zhong Guo Li Dai Qi Yue Hui Bian Kao Shi* (*I A Textual Research and Interpretation of the Collected Contracts of the Past Dynasties of China*) (Book 2).

[347]Zhang Chuanxi, *Zhong Guo Li Dai Qi Yue Hui Bian Kao Shi* (*A Textual Research and Interpretation of the Collected Contracts of the Past Dynasties of China*) (Book 2).

Therefore, their property would rather be pawned than sold so as to ease the pressure from inside the clan and to relive the spiritual burden. More importantly, the owner-peasants or citizens could only sell off their estate to save their lives when facing natural calamities and man-made misfortunes. The reason why they preferred to pawn rather than sell their property was that they hoped to redeem the ownership one day in future. The pawn right in ancient China had experienced more than 1000 years of historical development, and it still occupied a very important place in modern civil law.

11.5.2.4 "Zhi Quan" (Pledge Rights)

There were already records of "Zhi Quan" (pledge rights) in as early as the Han Dynasty. In the Tang Dynasty, pawnshops were already established in temples to make money, which was known as "Chang Sheng Ku" or "Wu Jing Cang." "Dang Pu" and "Dian Pu" (both meaning pawnshop), which appeared after the Song Dynasty, are shops that engaged in the business of "Zhi" (pledge). In the Qing Dynasty, the development of the commodity economy and the prevalence of usury led to the popularity of pawn businesses. According to records, in the 9th year of Qianlong (1744), "there are all together 600 to 700 public and personal pawnshops in and outside the capital,"[348] and the nobility was also involved in pawn business in order to obtain high interest. He Shen, the powerful minister, personally owned seventy five pawnshops.[349] However, illegal profit making was prohibited to prevent causing bankruptcy among the citizens and instability in the society. According to the laws of the Qing Dynasty, for pawnshops, the monthly interest should not exceed three *fen* of silver, and the rule of "Yi Ben Yi Li" (the profit made should not be more than the principal) was practiced. Anyone who broke the rule would be punished by "Chi" (flogging with light sticks) for forty strokes. Nevertheless, many people still made profits via illegal methods. Take the pawnshop in Hunan province for example; interests were collected monthly, but for every five days of overdue, it would be regarded as a month. So if the money was still not returned at the end of the year, "the property will be sold immediately."[350]

The pawn contract or "Tie Zi" (pawn ticket) should be prepared by the pawnshop after receiving the pledge. A pawn ticket was considered as an uninscribed bond, so the holder thereof should inform the pawnshop once his ticket was lost, and his property could be redeemed only when it was testified by a guarantor. Once the

---

[348]"Qian Long Chao" (The Reign of Emperor Qianlong) in *Dong Hua Xu Lu* (*A Sequel to the Records of Donghua*), Vol. 20.

[349]Xue Fucheng (Qing Dynasty), "Cha Chao He Shen Zhu Zhai Hua Yuan Qing Dan" (A List of the Confiscated Properties from the Houses and Flower Gardens of He Shen) in *Yong An Bi Ji* (*The Notes of Yong An*).

[350]Zhao Shenqiao (Qing Dynasty), "Jin Dang Pu Wei Li Qu Xi Shi" (A Notice for Forbidding Pawnshops to Earn Interest Illegally) in *Zhao Gong Yi Gong Zi Zhi Guan Shu Lei Ji* (*Collections of the Official Papers of Zhao Gongyi*), Vol. 9.

"pawn right" was set up, one should give the possession of pawned goods to the owner of the pawnshop, thus making it a real contract. The amortization period of pawnshops varied from place to place, and the longest one was three years. The owner of the pledged property could pay back the money as he liked to regain possession thereof within the period of the pledge, but once the owner paid up the money, his pawn right was terminated. The owner of the pawnshop should not conduct compulsory liquidation or detain the debtors' assets or apply for attachment by the government. Although he had the right of ownership, the right of lien and the right of custody, he had no right of usufruct without special agreement.

In the Qing Dynasty, apart from goods, human beings could also be used as pledges, so contracts of this nature were also often made. In the 49th year of Kangxi (1710), the contract of *Xiu Ning Xian Xiang Fu Sheng Dang Nv Qi* (*A Contract on Pawning of His Daughter by Xiang Fusheng from Xiuning County*) was signed, and the full text is as follows[351]:

> Contractor Xiang Fusheng, who is in short of money, now is willing to pawn one daughter of mine to Wang, for five *liang* of silver. The eight-year-old daughter Xidi, who was born on the 21st of June, shall be given to the buyer once the payment is made.
> In consideration of oral promise being no guarantee, a written statement is hereby made.
> There are two pages for this contract, worth five *liang* of silver.
> The 6th August of the 49th year of Emperor Kangxi.
> Name: Xiang Fusheng (signature)

During the period when pledge right existed, besides holding pledged property in possession, the pledgee could collect an interest monthly. If the debtor failed to pay his debt, the pledgee could exercise his right and sell the pledged property or accept discharge as a matter of priority. However, the pledgee was under obligation to keep the pledged property safe, If the pledged property was lost during the period when the pledge right existed, then the pledgee should compensate accordingly or deduct the monthly interest, depending on the actual situation.

"Di Ya Quan" (mortgage rights) was also one of real rights for security, which required the debtor or the third party to provide real estate property as a warranty of the liquidation of the debt for the debtee without transferring the real rights in order to guarantee the ownership of that property.. The mortgagor should pay interest in accordance with the contract. Hence, "Di Ya Quan (mortgage rights) was different from both "Zhi Quan" (pledge rights) and "Dian Quan" (pawn rights).

There were also contracts for mortgage, in which the price, interest, and term of payment were stipulated. In such cases, a land contract and a real estate contract should be provided; hence, it was called "Qi Ya" (deeds mortgage). One of the most crucial terms in "Qi Ya" (deeds mortgage) is that a mortgage would be changed into a pawn if it was not returned in due time. In December of the 4th year of Xianfeng

---

[351] Zhang Chuanxi, *Zhong Guo Li Dai Qi Yue Hui Bian Kao Shi* (*A Textual Research and Interpretation of the Collected Contracts of the Past Dynasties of China*) (Book 2), Peking University Press, 1995.

(1854), a contract titled *Pan Wei Shi Suo Li Di Ya Qi Wen* (*Mortgage Contract Made by Pan Weishi*) was signed, and the content is as follows[352]:

> Additionally, the deeds for the house numbered Fu-NO. 1080 on Xizhong Street, Tumingtun village are mortgaged. It shall be returned at the end of January; however, if it is not returned in due time, the contract shall be treated as a pawn contract. In consideration of oral promise being no guarantee, a written statement is hereby made.

"Dian Quan" (pawn rights) and "Zhi Quan" (pledge rights) were comparatively more developed in the Qing Dynasty, while "Di Ya Quan" (mortgage rights) was much less developed. It was recorded in *Qing Bi Lei Chao* (*Collections of Anecdotes in Qing Dynasty*) that "for the mortgage business, it is a place where people can mortgage property for money. The one most frequently used is 'Dian' (pawn), the second is 'Zhi' (pledge) and the third is 'Ya' (mortgage)." Because of the lack of the theories of civil law in Oing Dynasty, the three kinds of real rights for security, namely, "Dian" (pawn), "Zhi" (pledge) and "Ya" (mortgage) was not clearly divided at the time, so there lacked due legal interpretation.

11.5.3 The Perfection of "Zhai Fa" (Law of Obligation)

11.5.3.1 Obligations Attached to Contracts

After the constant economic recovery and development during the reign of Emperor Shunzhi and Kangxi, the agricultural production and economic exchanges had reached the climax in the period of the ruling of Emperor Yongzheng and Qianlong, so the contract system also got a rapid development. Contracts were used as certification for land purchase, house renting, labor employment, partnership, marriage, and loan so as to confirm the rights and obligations of both parties. It was said that "contracts were used as the certification in every professional activities among the folks ... So generally speaking, almost no business could be conducted without contracts."[353]

The contract was printed uniformly by the government of the Qing Dynasty, and it was stipulated in *Xie Qi Tou Shui Zhang Cheng* (*The Regulation on Contract Writing and Tax Payment*) that "from now on, in the buying and selling of land and houses, contracts must be written in sealed official paper; otherwise, they shall be regarded as private contracts which will not be accepted as evidence by government"; "from now on, in the buying and selling of land and houses, if contracts are not written on sealed official paper in dealing with the old proprietors, relatives and so on ... the private contracts shall be written off and canceled, a contract written on

---

[352]*Ming Qing Hui Zhou She Hui Jing Ji Zi Liao Cong Bian* (*A Series of Collections of the Materials on Society and Economy in Huizhou during Ming and Qing Dynasties*), Vol. 1.

[353]"Yan Jin Yan Qi Tui Shou Ji Da Shou Zhu Bi Yi Chu Min Lei" (Prohibiting the Malpractice in Checking Contracts and Conducting the Transference of Ownership to Reduce Family Burden) in *Zhi Zhe Cheng Gui* (*The Established Practices and Set Rules in the Governance of Zhejiang*), Vol. 1.

sealed official paper shall be used instead, and half of money shall be confiscated by government as a penalty according to the original price."[354] It was stressed by the government that an official contract paper should be used in writing contracts to ensure consistency of format and to prevent the occurrence of disputes caused by falsified contracts. However, in the contracts made during the reign of emperors Yongzheng and Qianlong that remained to date, there were those written on pieces of paper prepared by the contractors themselves following the official format. The contents of contracts of the common people must be in accordance with law; otherwise, they would be considered invalid.

In the Qing Dynasty, it was illegal to sell and buy land, houses, and "Nu Bi" (slave girls and maidservants) unless approved by the government or the legal procedures for the taxation of the contract were performed. Contracts in the Qing Dynasty were different from those in the past, and it was required that the tax should be paid by the buyer instead of by both the buyer and the seller. The unified form of contract sealed by the government was also changed to other more complicated forms, including "Guan Yin" (the contracts sealed by the government) and "Qi Wei" (the identification documents issued by government), which fully reflected the development of the contract system. Usually, the buyer must pay tax within one year from the date when the contract was signed; otherwise, he would be severely punished. In the meantime, ownership of the land and the due tax must be transferred to the buyer so that "every piece of land has its owner and the grain tax can be collected accordingly," which was called "Guo Ge" (the transferring of the ownership of the land and the due tax to the buyer). "Guan Yin" (the contracts sealed by the government) and "Qi Wei" (the identification documents issued by government) were called "Hong Qi" or "Zhu Qi" (contract with an official seal); otherwise, they were called "Bai Qi" (contract without an official seal). "Bai Qi" (contract without an official seal) was also legally binding, but in lawsuits, its evidentiary value was not as effective as that of "Hong Qi" (contract with an official seal). Moreover, when the subject matter involved human beings, the legal effects of the two types of contracts were different: for "Bai Qi" (contract without an official seal), a person was regarded as an employee who could be redeemed, except for one who had served the employer for a very long time, while for "Hong Qi" (contract with an official seal), a person was regarded as "Nu Bi" (slave girl and maidservant), so her offspring should also be slaves. Although at that time severe punishments were enforced on those who did not go through the procedures of contract taxation, "Bai Qi" (contract without an official seal) was quite common in practice, so it was difficult to enforce any punishment upon those who were not paying contract tax.

Generally speaking, in Qing dynasty contracts were not only very commonly used, but also were very precise and comprehensive. So to a certain extent, they were most representative of the civil legal documents of the Chinese feudal society because they were legal certifications which were with legal restrictions confirmed

---

[354]Zhang Chuanxi, *Zhong Guo Li Dai Qi Yue Hui Bian Kao Shi* (*A Textual Research and Interpretation of the Collected Contracts of the Past Dynasties of China*) (Book 2).

by the government. Therefore, they had played an important role in adjusting the civil legal relationship in practice.

11.5.3.2 The Types of Contract

From the large number of materials on contracts in the Qing Dynasty that remained to date, it can be seen that the most popular types of contract at that time were those concerning sale, mortgage, loan, employment, lease, tenancy, and partnership, as well as the contract of "Zhao Tie" (payment of the balance in buying and selling). According to the records in "Si Fa Bian" (The Volume of Private Law) in *Tai Wan Wen Xian Cong Kan* (*Series of Collections of Documents in Taiwan*), the following are the types of contracts that were very popular in the local place: contract on dividing family property and living separately, mortgage contract, contract on the prohibition of sale, contract on pledging allegiance, contract on bestowal, contract on entrusting, contract on adoption and inheritance, contract on "Tai Jie" (a way of borrowing or lending money by using real estate as the pledge in Taiwan), contract on the exchange of houses, contract on "Shu Tian" (providing subsidy for the children of the clan by using the rent from the public fields), contract on co-ownership, etc. The complexity of the contract form had reflected the characteristics of the development of civil legal relationship of Qing Dynasty. Take the sale, tenancy, lease, and loan contracts for example:

With the development of commodity economy, rapid development was also witnessed in sale contracts which were signed in the transaction of commodities, so to a certain extent it had reflected the characteristics of the times. For instance, in the contract of sale of real estate like land and houses, words like "Jue Mai" (refers to the transfer of ownership of the subject matter due to some reason after the expiry of the housing code period) must be written to show the transference of ownership and to distinguish it from "Huo Mai" (refers to retaining the right to redeem ownership of the subject matter in the sale of land and houses) and pawning. For the conclusion of the contract, mutual agreement of the two parties was required, and forced, fraudulent, and repeated transactions were forbidden. Besides, it was also forbidden for the members of debtee's family to sell his real estate to the debtor if the debtee had failed to pay the debt. After contracts of real estate were made, the parties must go through the legal procedures of paying the contract tax. The evidentiary value of "Hong Qi" (contract with an official seal) was different from that of "Bai Qi" (contract without an official seal). When the subject matter was real estate, the relatives of the owner enjoyed the right of preemption. In areas where "Yi Tian Er Zhu" (two owners for one piece of land) was practiced, if the tenant agreed to sell the land, the buyer can acquire ownership of the land without asking for the landlord's permission. Moreover, it was forbidden to sell or mortgage state-owned land, the land granted by the government for sacrificial activities, wasteland opened up by the army, the land of temples, and the land for sacrifice inherited from ancestors, and it was also forbidden for "Qi Ren" (members of the Manchu ethnic group) to sell their land. Apart from real estate contracts, a contract also needed to be concluded by the

11.5 Codification of Civil Law   1227

buyer and the seller for personal property transactions when the subject matter was human beings. It was legal to buy and sell human beings during the Qing Dynasty, so according to "Hu Kou" (Registered Permanent Residence) (Part Four) in *Hu Bu Ze Li* (*The Regulation of the Department of Revenue*), "if natural disasters occur in the province, it is allowed for the poor people to sell their sons and daughters in order to survive, and it is also allowed for the local residents, merchants and officials to buy them. If the person is employed to work for the government, the price shall be set by the government offices. For those older than ten and younger than sixty years old, the price is ten *liang* of silver for each person; for those older than sixty years old, the price is five *liang* of silver for each person; for those children younger than ten years old, one *liang* of silver will be added for each extra year; for those younger than one year old, no price needs to be made."

The obligation of contract was more developed in Qing Dynasty than those of the previous dynasties due to the development of tenancy relationship. Usually, the subject matter of a tenancy contract was land, in which the quantity, location, term, amount of rent, time and ways to pay rent, prohibition on violation of the contract, and delay of payment by tenants were specified. From the tenancy contracts of the Qing Dynasty that existed to date, it can be seen that the rent was very high, and regardless of whether the harvest of that year was good or bad, the tenant had to pay half or two thirds or sometimes even more than four fifths of the yield to the landowner as rent. The following important contents are usually included in the contract: "The tenant shall not delay the payment or pay less than the amount he is supposed to pay"; "payments must be made according to rules whether the harvest of that year was good or bad." If the tenant failed to pay the rent, it could be used as an excuse by the landowner to lease the land to another tenant. It was clearly stated in *Hui Zhou Bao Ri Huai Zu Tian Pi* (*Agreement to Rent the Land by Bao Rihuai in Huizhou*) that "if the tenant fails to pay the full amount of rent, the land owner is free to find another tenant." According to the principle of equality in a contract relationship, although both of the two parties had the right to withdraw the rent, only landowners had such right in a feudal relationship of production, so it was impossible for tenants to do so. Considering that an increase of rent and withdrawal of the right of tenancy would lead to fierce resistance from the tenants, during the reign of emperor Kangxi and Qianlong, orders were issued to prohibit rent increase and tenancy withdrawal by landowners to ease the tense relationship between landowners and tenants. In the meantime, it was forbidden for tenants to delay the payment of land and house rent; otherwise, they would be punished.

Because the tenancy relationship between Mongolian and Han nationalities was quite special, a regulation was made in *Li Fan Yuan Ze Li* (*The Regulation for the Bureau of National Minority Affairs*):

> If Han people living in Mongolia have rented a piece of land or a house, they shall pay as is agreed. If they delay the payment on account of their authority and power, it will be reported by "Za Sa Ke" (the head of eight banners) or prosecuted by the proprietors and house owners and handled by the government officials like "Tong Zhi" (the deputy magistrate of a prefecture) and "Tong Pan" (official in charge of agriculture, water conservancy and litigation under prefecture and subprefecture). If it is delayed for more than three years or

if it is discovered that they have made deposits in Mongolia, the deposits shall be paid to the Mongolian; if there is no such deposit, the land or house shall be withdrawn to rent to another tenant, but the Han people still owes payment to the land owner or house owner; if the Han people have failed to pay the rent within a certain period of time, they will be punished by wearing "Jia Hao" (cangue: a large wooden collar worn by petty criminals as a punishment) for a month and be reprimanded after the punishment is conducted. Then the Han people shall be sent back to his birth place and be punished.[355] If the tenant who had rented and cultivated the land of Mongolian had gone back to his birth place or refused to plow the land, "the rent that he owes the land owner or house owner should be offset by the deposit. If the deposit is less than the amount of rent that he owes, it should be reported to "Li Shi" (ancient official working in auxiliary departments), "Si Yuan" (subordinate officials) and the local officials to be handled impartially according to the amount he owes.[356]

In lease contracts, the subject matter was mostly about house renting, but there were also other contracts on store and livestock renting.

In the contract of house renting, certain terms, such as the location of the house, the rent, the methods of payment, "Ya Bao" (intermediary agent), and the guarantee for performance should be made clear. Below is a contract titled *Xiu Ning Xian Wang Fou You Zu Fang Pi* (*House Lease Contract of Wang Foyou in Xiuning County*), which was signed in the 58th year of Kangxi (1719)[357]:

> Wang Foyou, on behalf of the house owner, decides to lease part of the house to Mei Zhong. The house is located in Tuming Bamboo Forest. The part leased to Mei Zhong stretches from the front gate to the back gate, including both the ground and the façade rooms above. The rent is one *liang* of silver each year, which is negotiated by three parties and shall be paid in every season. The rent should be paid in full without delay; otherwise the house owner can lease the house to others, regardless of the disagreement of the tenant. As a certificate, the written lease contract is made.
> November of the 58th year of Kangxi.
> Representative of house owner: Wang Foyou.
> Families of Mei Zhong: Wang Yugong.

Because the object of the contract of store renting was complicated, the content of the contract was also more complicated than that of house renting. Below is a contract titled *Wan Ping Xian Shen Jian Tang (Tang Xing) Zu Pu Di Zi Ju* [*A Store Lease Contract Made by Shen Jiantang (with the Family Name of Tan) from Wanping County*] made in the 30th year of Guangxu (1904)[358]:

> Contractor Shen Jiantang, a businessman whose family name is Tan, now rents a one-room store in a three-storey house with a part of the backyard located in the east side of Wudinghouwai Road, Jinshifang Street owned by Yang Jianming himself. The owner cannot run a store by himself, so he turned to an "Ya Bao" (intermediary agent) to lease

---

[355]"Di Mu" (Land) in *Qin Ding Li Fan Yuan Ze Li* (*The Regulation for the Bureau of National Minority Affairs Made by Imperial Order*), Vol. 10.

[356]"Di Mu" (Land) in *Qin Ding Li Fan Yuan Ze Li* (*The Regulation for the Bureau of National Minority Affairs Made by Imperial Order*), Vol. 10.

[357]Zhang Chuanxi, *Zhong Guo Li Dai Qi Yue Hui Bian Kao Shi* (*A Textual Research and Interpretation of the Collected Contracts of the Past Dynasties of China*) (Book 2).

[358]Zhang Chuanxi, *Zhong Guo Li Dai Qi Yue Hui Bian Kao Shi* (*A Textual Research and Interpretation of the Collected Contracts of the Past Dynasties of China*) (Book 2).

the store to Mr. Tan. So Mr. Tan shall pay a deposit of thirty *liang* of silver without delay and shall pay one *liang* and four *qian* of silver per month for the furniture. The period for the lease is ten years, and the store can be redeemed if the money is paid in full. It should be made clear that if Mr. Tan gives back the store to the owner before the contract is due, the deposit shall be confiscated. If the owner asks Mr. Tan to give back the store before the contract is due, the owner shall pay sixty *liang* of silver as a penalty. Mr. Tan shall pay one *liang* and four *qian* of silver for other kitchen utensils in the store. If Mr. Tan fails to pay the rent for three months, the owner can take the store back. All the furniture in the store shall be listed on another paper. Words of mouth being no guarantee, a written statement is hereby given

> Be honest and keeping our words.
> Tenant: Shen Jiantang, Mr. Tan (signature)
> "Ya Bao" (intermediary agent):
> Cao Lianxi (signature), Liu Wanghong (signature)

There were also lease contracts in the Qing Dynasty where the subject matter is livestock, and in those contracts, ownership over the livestock's offspring that was birthed during the period of the contract would usually be clarified. Below is a lease contract on a cow in Xingxian county, Shanxi province[359]:

> Contractor A makes the lease contract to rent a yellow cattle owned by B. A will pay certain amount of money to B. If the cattle gives birth to calves during the period of the contract, each party shall have half of the interest. A shall pay certain *dou* of crop to B annually. When the contract is due, A shall give back the cattle to B with no delay. Words of mouth being no guarantee, a written statement is hereby given.
>
> Tenant: A (signature)
> "Ya Bao" (intermediary agent): so-and-so (signature)

In the Qing Dynasty, loan contracts were the most common form of contract. During the reign of Emperor Shizu, several orders were issued to regulate loan contracts: "For loan contracts, for one *liang* of silver, the monthly interest shall not exceed three *fen* and the interest of the previous month shall not be calculated for the interest of the next month. ... Anyone who violates the regulation by giving or taking the extra interest shall all be severely punished."[360] Later, after *Da Qing Lv Li (The Laws and Precedents of Great Qing)* was made, it was stipulated in "Qian Zhai" (Debts) in "Hu Lv" (Statutes on Households) that "for any private individual who loans money to others, the monthly interest shall not exceed three *fen*. For each year, although the amount of loan is large, the rule of "Yi Ben Yi Li" (the profit made should not be more than the principal) should be followed, so anyone who violates the law shall be punished by 'Chi' (flogging with light sticks) for forty strokes. Moreover, the extra part of the interest shall be deemed as illegal gains, so if the situation is worse, the person shall be punished for the crime of 'Zuo Zang' (embezzlement) with the maximum punishment of 'Zhang' (flogging with heavy sticks) for one hundred strokes."

---

[359] *Min Shang Shi Xi Guan Diao Cha Bao Gao Lu (Collections of Reports on the Research of Civil and Commercial Conventions)*, Jinmin Press, 1969.

[360] *Qing Shi Zu Shi Lu (The Record of Emperor Shizu of Qing Dynasty)*, Vol. 38.

The debtor should pay the interest in time every month and pay back the principal when due. In order to protect the interest of the debtee, the debtor who did not pay the interest or principal would be punished based on the amount they failed to pay and the overdue time of the payment. "If the debtor fails to pay the debt above five *liang* of silver for three months, he shall be punished by 'Chi' (flogging with light sticks) for ten strokes. For every one more month, he shall be subject to the punishment of one level severer with the maximum punishment of 'Chi' (flogging with light sticks) for forty strokes. If the debtor fails to pay the debt above fifty *liang* of silver for three months, he shall be punished by 'Chi' (flogging with light sticks) for twenty strokes; ... if the debtor fails to pay the debt above one hundred *liang* of silver for three months, he shall be punished by 'Zhang' (flogging with heavy sticks) for fifty strokes ... and the interest and principal should be paid to the debtee." However, it was forbidden for the debtee to plunder the property of the debtor, and those who violated the law would be punished by "Zhang" (flogging with heavy sticks) for eighty strokes. "If the amount of money the debtee forcefully extracted from the debtor did not exceed the amount of money that the debtor owed the debtee, the debtee can atone for his crime without being punished. However, "if the estimated price (of the livestock) has exceeded the total amount of principal and interest, the extra amount of money shall be deemed as illegal gains, so the debtee shall be punished for the crime of 'Zuo Zang' (embezzlement) with the maximum punishment of 'Zhang' (flogging with heavy sticks) for one hundred strokes and 'Tu' (imprisonment) for three years."[361] In addition, the livestock should be ordered to be given back to the debtor.

It was written in state law that private debt must be paid, but it was also widely observed by individuals as a popular custom. Even if the debtor had died, his debt should still be paid by his heirs; if the debtor went bankrupt, "Ya Bao" (the intermediary agent) should shoulder the collateral responsibility and pay the debt. Only under the condition that the debtee had committed a crime of "allowing the debtor to pay the debt by mortgaging his wife or daughter(s)" could the debt be extinguished. If the debtor who had borrowed crops or plowed instruments or seeds from the government died with no property left, debt relief might be applied.

Based on the criminal case book of the Qing Dynasty, during the reign of Emperor Qianlong (twenty six years), Emperor Jiaqing (twenty five years), and Emperor Daoguang (twenty two years), among the five hundred and forty nine records of debt cases in eighteen provinces in the northeast area, there were two hundred andn seventy four cases in which the annual or monthly interest rate was three *fen*; in one hundred and twenty eight cases, two *fen*; in fifty two cases, five *fen*; and ninety five cases with double annual or monthly interest rate. Statistics showed that the cases with two *fen* or three *fen* of interest rate accounted for three fourths of all cases.[362] As far as the overall trend is concerned, it showed that loan rate was

---

[361] *Qing Shi Zu Shi Lu* (*The Record of Emperor Shizu of Qing Dynasty*), Vol. 38.
[362] Huang Miantang, *Qing Shi Zhi Yao* (*The Essentials of Ruling the Country in the History of Qing Dynasty*), Qilu Press, 1990, p. 510.

11.5 Codification of Civil Law

reduced, which was caused by the development of production and the commodity economy, as well as the stability of the life of the labor class. In the meantime, to some extent, legal restrictions and punishment on loaning activities were also effective. For example, in the 22nd year of Qianlong (1758), a regulation was made wherein it was stressed that "anyone who has loaned to others for a short term or has illegally required exceedingly high interest shall be severely punished with the money confiscated. But the victim who has surrendered himself to the government shall not be held liable and shall be exempted from paying the interest."[363] "If a powerful debtee (with illegal debtor) has forcefully taken the livestock or other property of the debtor who fails to pay the debt without filing a lawsuit to the government, he shall be punished by 'Zhang' (flogging with heavy sticks) for eighty strokes."[364] "If the debtee allowed the debtor to pay the debt by mortgaging his wife, mistress(es) or daughter(s) to the debtee, he shall be punished by 'Zhang' (flogging with heavy sticks) for one hundred strokes (if the debtee has raped the aforesaid female(s), the punishment shall be one level severer); if the debtee has taken the aforesaid female(s) by force against the debtor's will, the punishment shall be two levels severer [punished by 'Zhang' (flogging with heavy sticks) for seventy strokes and punished by 'Tu' (imprisonment) for one and a half years]; if the debtee has raped the aforesaid female(s), he shall be punished by 'Jiao Jian Hou' (the punishment of suspending hanging), the forcefully taken female(s) shall be sent back to the debtor and the debt shall be acquitted."[365]

Moreover, in order to prevent supervising officials from loaning to people within their jurisdiction to make profit, it was provided in *Da Qing Lv Li* (*The Laws and Precedents of Great Qing*) that "any supervising official who has loaned to or taken mortgages of money and property from the people within their jurisdiction, whether the interest is obtained legally or not, the monthly interest will be evaluated by the extra gains loaned to the civilians and they will be punished according to the relevant rules on 'Bu Wang Fa' (taking bribes without bending the law); however if the situation is serious, those involved will be punished according to the relevant rules on 'Wang Fa' (taking bribes by bending the law)." Apart from punishment, the profit should all be confiscated by the government. For example, "if a supervising official has made profit by violating the regulation, all the profit shall be confiscated by the government, and those involved will be punished according to the relevant rules on 'Bu Wang Fa' (taking bribes without bending the law); however if the situation is serious, those involved will be punished according to the relevant rules on 'Wang Fa' (taking bribes by bending the law) with all the profit confiscated by the

---

[363]"Wei Jin Qu Li" (Making Profits Illegally) in "Qian Zhai" (Debts) in "Hu Lv" (Statutes on Households) in *Da Qing Lv Li* (*The Laws and Precedents of Great Qing*), Vol. 14.

[364]"Wei Jin Qu Li" (Making Profits Illegally) in "Qian Zhai" (Debts) in "Hu Lv" (Statutes on Households) in *Da Qing Lv Li* (*The Laws and Precedents of Great Qing*), Vol. 14.

[365]"Wei Jin Qu Li" (Making Profits Illegally) in "Qian Zhai" (Debts) in "Hu Lv" (Statutes on Households) in *Da Qing Lv Li* (*The Laws and Precedents of Great Qing*), Vol. 14.

government. The interest shall be given to the debtor and the rest shall be confiscated by the government."[366]

For the laws and regulations on illegally obtained profit in the Qing Dynasty, the focus was on maintaining social stability and protecting the normal debt relationship, so they had served as a protection for the debtor. However, the nature of feudal law on loaning had determined that these laws and regulations tended to show favor to the interest of the debtee in the protection of the legal debt relationship. For example, although "Yi Shen Zhe Chou" (paying debt by working without salaries) was abolished by law, such occurrence was still quite common in practice.

11.5.3.3 The Obligation Caused by Torts and Compensation of Damages

The obligation caused by torts and compensation of damages were divided into torts of person and torts of property according to the different objects violated, so civil responsibility should be undertaken by the violators accordingly.

The first was that according to the laws of the Qing Dynasty, the obligation caused by the compensation of torts and damages was established either because one's behavior was clearly prohibited by law or because one's behavior was against reason, although not prohibited by law. As to the first circumstance, it was often termed "forbidden" or "not allowed" in the law of the Qing Dynasty. For example, "it is forbidden for any 'Tu Mu' (the subordinates of "Tu Si") in charge of land administration and any ordinary person to sell or mortgage land without permission. If one has violated the law, the money shall be confiscated by the government and the land shall be given back to the original owner."[367] As to the second circumstance, it was often termed "Bu Ying Wei" (things that should not be done).[368] Illegal behaviors also included negative crimes or nonfeasance, which means failing to perform one's duty as provided by law. For example, "if any person who is in charge of warehouses or the stored property has caused losses and damages because he fails to take good care of the things or fails to air the things timely, he shall be punished for the crime of 'Zuo Zang' (embezzlement), so he shall be held liable for all the losses and damages."[369]

---

[366]"Wei Jin Qu Li" (Making Profits Illegally) in "Qian Zhai" (Debts) in "Hu Lv" (Statutes on Households) in *Da Qing Lv Li* (*The Laws and Precedents of Great Qing*), Vol. 14.

[367]"Dao Mai Tian Zhai" (The Stealing and Selling of the Land and Houses) in "Tian Zhai" (Land and Houses) in "Hu Lv" (Statutes on Households) in *Da Qing Lv Li* (*The Laws and Precedents of Great Qing*), Vol. 9.

[368]"Bu Ying Wei" (Things Forbidden to Do) in "Za Fan" (Miscellaneous Crimes) in "Xing Lv" (The Penal Code) in *Da Qing Lv Li* (*The Laws and Precedents of Great Qing*), Vol. 34.

[369]"Sun Huai Cang Ku Cai Wu" (Damaging the Property in Warehouses) in "Cang Ku" (Warehouse) (Part 2) in "Hu Lv" (Statutes on Households) in *Da Qing Lv Li* (*The Laws and Precedents of Great Qing*), Vol. 12.

11.5 Codification of Civil Law

The second was whether the illegal behavior was caused intentionally or by negligence. According to the annotation to the provision of "'Xi Sha' (killing during playing), 'Wu Sha' (manslaughter) and 'Guo Shi Sha Ren' (involuntary killing)" in "Ren Ming" (Homicide) in "Xing Lv" (The Penal Code) in *Da Qing Lv Li* (*The Laws and Precedents of Great Qing*), "'Guo Shi Sha Ren' (involuntary killing) not only referred to the subjective element of the actor, sometimes, it also referred to the accidents." A regulation was stipulated in the provision of "killing and injuring people by carriages and horses" in "Ren Ming" (Homicide) in "Xing Lv" (The Penal Code) in *Da Qing Lv Li* (*The Laws and Precedents of Great Qing*): "If a carriage or horse is driven fast in scarcely-populated areas in the countryside with no reason, or has injuried or killed people, the person in charge of the carriage or horse shall be punished by 'Zhang' (flogging with heavy sticks) for one hundred strokes. Besides, he should pay ten *liang* of silver for the funeral arrangements." Even if it was an accident or the person had done nothing wrong subjectively, it was still deemed as "negligence." If one had intentionally caused damage to others, he should take both criminal and civil responsibility. However, for negligence, it was a little different because some acts may lead to both criminal and civil responsibilities, while some may not. So in such circumstances, the violator needed "only to pay for the damages without being punished."

The third was that there was a causal relationship between the illegal behavior and the damage done. The result of the analysis of subjective psychological state showed that the illegal behaviors were divided into intentional and negligent ones and that there was also a causal relationship between the damage and result.

Under certain special circumstances, the actor of the tort shall not be held liable for civil responsibility. According to the laws of the Qing Dynasty, if the damage was caused by force majeure or accident, civil responsibility should be remitted. According to "Cang Ku" (Warehouse) in "Hu Lv" (Statutes on Households) in *Da Qing Lv Li* (*The Laws and Precedents of Great Qing*), "if the property stored in the warehouses is damaged due to force majeure such as rain, fire or robbery, the person in charge shall not be held liable if relevant evidence is confirmed by the official"; "if a ship is damaged due to force majeure such wind, waves, fire or robbery, the person in charge shall not be held liable upon report if relevant evidence was confirmed by the official"; if the damage was incurred by avoiding imminent danger, the person involved should not be held liable. In addition, it was provided in "Jiu Mu" (Farming and Husbandry) in "Bing Lv" (Statutes on Military Affairs) in *Da Qing Lv Li* (*The Laws and Precedents of Great Qing*) that "if the livestock (either raised by soldiers or civilians) have hurt people by their horns, or kicked or bitten others, which has led to injury or death, the owner shall not be held liable, so no compensation shall be made." If the party had acted in self-defense, he should not be held liable either. It was provided in *Da Qing Lv Li* (*The Laws and Precedents of Great Qing*) that "if the grandparents or parents have been beaten by others, the sons and grandsons have fought back without delay (otherwise their behavior shall be deemed as fighting) to help their grandparents or parents, which has led to slight injury (to the perpetrators), they shall not be held liable."[370] Moreover, if the two parties had certain family or kindred relationship, they may not be held liable. According to the provision of "Qin Shu Xiang Dao" (Theft Among Relatives) in "Dao Zei" (Theft) in "Xing Lv" (The Penal Code) in *Da Qing Lv Li* (*The Laws and Precedents of Great Qing*), "if one has stolen property from other family members, for 'Qi Qin' (relatives being in mourn for one year), the punishment shall be alleviated by five levels; for 'Da Gong' (the person wearing the mourning apparel of soft sackcloth in the third mourning degree), the punishment shall be alleviated by four levels; for 'Xiao Gong' (the person wearing the mourning apparel of soft sackcloth in the fourth mourning degree), the punishment shall be alleviated by three levels; for "Si Ma" (the person wearing the mourning apparel of soft sackcloth in the fifth mourning degree), the punishment shall be alleviated by two levels; for the relatives outside 'Wu Fu' (relatives within the five degrees of mourning), the punishment shall be alleviated by one level with the exemption of 'Ci Zi' (the punishment of making humiliated tattoo on one's body, especially on the face)." In the subsidiary regulation of this article, it was stipulated that "as for the crime of 'Qin Shu Xiang Dao' (the theft among relatives), except the relatives of 'Wu Fu' (relatives within the five degrees of mourning) of the same clan, the others should all be regarded as relatives without mourning relations. The punishment for the crime of theft committed among the elders of the relatives with marital relationship shall not be alleviated unless clearly stipulated in law; otherwise, the law shall not be misused."

Different kinds of regulations were made on law on torts of person, including but not limited to "death or injury caused 'Xi Sha' (killing during playing), 'Wu Sha' (manslaughter), and 'Guo Shi Sha Ren' (involuntary killing)"; "death or injury caused by carriages or horses"; "death or injury caused by quacks"; "death or injury caused by cross bows and arrows" and "kicking or biting by livestock"; and other infringement acts such as "fighting," "servants assaulting masters," "fighting between family members with the same family names," "assaulting the senior family members below 'Da Gong' (the person wearing the mourning apparel of soft sackcloth in the third mourning degree)," "assaulting the senior family members of 'Qi Qin' (relatives being in mourn for one year)," "scolding," "false accusation," etc. Anyone who committed any of the aforementioned crimes would be subject to both criminal punishment and civil liability, such as payment of medical and funeral expenses and alimony. Usually, medical expenses should be compensated to those who were injured by negligence and assaults, funeral expenses should be compensated to those killed by negligence and assaults, while alimony should be paid to the family of dead people or the disabled people caused by fighting and assaults.

As to torts of property, there were two kinds, namely, torts of personal property and torts of real estate. Torts of real estate mostly referred to stealing, selling or plowing others' land without permission, irrigating one's own land by stealing stored water, making obstruction to others' use of land, setting others' houses on

---

[370]"Fu Zu Bei Ou" (Parents and Grandparents Being Assaulted) in "Dou Ou" (Fighting) (Part 1) in "Xing Lv" (The Penal Code) in *Da Qing Lv Li* (*The Laws and Precedents of Great Qing*), Vol. 28.

fire intentionally or by accident, destroying the walls of others' houses, etc. Torts of personal property mostly referred to stealing, destroying instruments or crops, setting things on fire, killing or injurying livestock, illegally obtaining profit, refusing to pay debt by breaking promises, etc. The obligation caused by torts of personal property and real estate should be fulfilled.

11.5.4 Marriage, Family, and Inheritance Mixed with the Custom of the Jurchen Nationality

11.5.4.1 The series of regulations on marriage in the Qing Dynasty was basically the same with those of the Tang Dynasty, with some new regulations added due to changes in historical conditions. For example, the right to arrange marriage was enjoyed by one's grandparents, parents and other senior family members, but the right to arrange marriage for widows was dealt with separately. According to *Da Qing Lv Li* (*The Laws and Precedents of Great Qing*), "if a widow's grandparents, parents or grandparents and parents-in-law force her to marry another man against her will after the mourning period, he or she shall be punished by 'Zhang' (flogging with heavy sticks) for eighty strokes."[371] So it can be seen that it was totally up to the widow herself to decide whether to marry another man after the death of her husband, which was different from the regulation in *Tang Lv* (*Tang Code*), in which it was stated that "it is allowed for a widow's grandparents and parent to force her to marry another man against her will or to stay loyal to her former husband."[372] As seen from the custom that was popular in various areas, the marriage of the widow was usually arranged by her parents-in-law (or brother-in-law) through her own grandparents or parents, so it was similar to jointly arranged marriages. If the aforementioned senior members of the family were all dead, the widow could arrange her own marriage.

The marriage of "Nu Bi" (slave girls and maidservants) was solely controlled by the master. According to a record in volume seven hundred and fifty six of *Da Qing Hui Dian Shi Li* (*The Precedents of the Collected Statutes of Great Qing*), "it is newly stipulated by the state that if any servant has married a woman off to others without the approval of her master, he or she shall be punished by 'Zhang' (flogging with heavy sticks) for one hundred strokes. The married woman shall divorce her husband and be sent back to the original master regardless of when the marriage is concluded and whether the women has given birth to babies." It was further provided in *Da Qing Lv Li* (*The Laws and Precedents of Great Qing*) that "any servant born in a house of an ordinary master, or bought by a stamped contract, or bought by a 'Bai

---

[371]"Ju Sang Jia Qu" (Marriage in the Period of Mourning) in "Hun Yin" (Marriage) in "Hu Lv" (Statutes on Households) in *Da Qing Lv Li* (*The Laws and Precedents of Great Qing*), Vol. 10.

[372]"Hu Hun" (Marriage, Tax and Household Registration) in *Tang Lv Shu Yi* (*The Comments on Tang Code*), Vol. 14.

Qi' (contract without an official seal) before the 13th year of Yongzheng and raised for a long time in a house of an ordinary master or 'Bei Nv' (a girl enslaved by the rich), as well as their offspring thereof shall all be family servants of the master with their descendants serving the master for generations. The marriage of the aforementioned persons shall be arranged by the master and be registered and reported to the government with records made accordingly."[373] In order to enforce punishment upon servants who arranged the marriage of their daughters without the approval of their masters, in the 6th year of Jiaqing (1801), it was stipulated that "if any servant who has been bought according to a contract or who has served his master for a long time has engaged his daughter to a man, the daughter shall be returned to the master if the marriage is not concluded; if the marriage is concluded, the person who has married the daughter shall pay his master forty *liang* of silver; if the person cannot afford to pay the full amount, at least half should be paid to the master. Those who have engaged in arranging the marriage shall be punished by 'Zhang' (flogging with heavy sticks) for one hundred strokes and 'Tu' (imprisonment) for three years. After the term of the punishment, they shall be returned to the master to be disciplined. If the man who takes the wife knows about the circumstances, he shall be punished the same as the servant, but if he does not know, he shall not be held liable."[374]

As to the marriageable age, a woman was marriageable at the age of twelve because early marriage was practiced by the Manchus before they entered Shanhaiguan. But after entering Shanhaiguan, they were influenced by the culture of the Han nationality and inherited the legal marriageable age of the Ming Dynasty, so the legal marriageable age was sixteen for men and fourteen for women. However, due to different levels of social and economic development of different areas, different customs of marriageable age were formed. In general, the marriageable age in the areas south of Yangtze River where the economy was more developed was later than that in the north, and it was much later than that of the Manchus. According to "Tiao Gui" (Rules) in *Ji Shi Zong Pu* (*The Genealogy of Ji's Family*) which was recorded in Gui'an in Zheijiang province, "marriage is allowed for the male older than twenty years old and the female older than sixteen years." Based on the research of the annual records of Li Guangdi and other twelve bureaucratic scholars, people did not get married until after eighteen three years old.[375] In some remote areas such as Enshi county, males and females usually got married between twelve and fifteen years old, and quite often, the wife was five years or six years older than the husband, and sometimes the wife would be more than ten years older than the husband.

---

[373]"Nu Bi Ou Jia Zhang" (The Slave Girls and Maidservants Assaulting their Masters) in "Dou Ou" (Fighting) (Part 2) in "Xing Lv" (The Penal Code) in *Da Qing Lv Li* (*The Laws and Precedents of Great Qing*), Vol. 28.

[374]Xue Yunsheng (Qing Dynasty), *Du Li Cun Yi* (Questions in Reading *the Precedents*), Vol. 36.

[375]Zhang Yan, "Qing Dai Jia Ting Jie Gou Yu Ji Ben Gong Neng" (The Family Structure and its Basic Function in Qing Dynasty) in *Qing Shi Yan Jiu* (*A Research of the History of Qing Dynasty*), Vol. 3, 1996.

11.5 Codification of Civil Law

As to the marriage taboo, the laws in the previous dynasties were inherited. So according to the laws of the Qing Dynasty, marriages between males and females with the same family names, between the noble and the humble, and between the superior and the inferior were also prohibited. However, in the late Qing Dynasty, the prohibition of marriage between people with the same family names was no longer strictly carried out. In *Da Qing Lv Li Hui Ji Bian Lan* (*A Brief Guide to the Collections of the Laws and Precedents of Great Qing*), it was stated that "the purpose of prohibiting the marriage between the people with the same family names is to prevent the people from the same ancestors from marrying each other. If the two people with the same family names but different ancestors get married, punishments will be enforced by taking all circumstances into consideration instead of just following the law." Moreover, the punishment for the marriage between the noble and the humble was also more lenient than that in the Tang Dynasty. According to law in the Tang Dynasty, any servant who married "Liang Ren" (decent people) should be punished by "Tu" (imprisonment) for one and a half year, but according to the law of the Qing Dynasty, he would only be punished by "Zhang" (flogging with heavy sticks) for eighty strokes, and usually his parents would be blamed for the fault. After the middle period of the Qing Dynasty, with the change of social relationship and the gradual liberation of "Jian Min" (rabbles or people of lower social status), the prohibition on marriage between people from different classes became less strict.

Moreover, according the laws of the Qing Dynasty, marriage between cousins was prohibited; however, since it was a custom in practice, it was more flexibly stipulated in law: "The marriage between maternal or paternal cousins will be decided by themselves and those involved shall not be held liable."[376]

It is worth noting that specific marriage taboos were established among certain ethical groups in the Qing Dynasty.

First, the marriage between Manchu and Han nationalities was prohibited under certain circumstances. After the period of entering Shanhaiguan, in order to curb the rebellious trend of the Han people, an order was issued in August of the 5th year of Shunzhi (1648) wherein it was allowed for the Manchu people to marry the Han people, but the regulation was soon abolished. So the violators of the new regulation should be punished. Later, the following regulation was stipulated in *Hu Bu Ze Li* (*The Regulation of the Department of Revenue*):

> It is forbidden for the daughters of "Qi Ren" (members of the Manchu ethnic group) residing in the capital area to marry the people of Han nationality. If a female of "Qi Ren" (members of the Manchu ethnic group) is engaged with the people of Han nationality without being selected, those who have arranged the marriage shall be punished for violating the law; if the female has gone through the selection procedure but is not selected, those who have arranged the marriage shall also be punished for violating the law. Besides, the people of Han nationality shall be subject to the same punishment as "Qi Ren" (members of the Manchu

---

[376]"Zun Bei Wei Hun" (The Marriage of the Superior and the Inferior) in "Hun Yin" (Marriage) in "Hu Lv" (Statutes on Households) in *Da Qing Lv Li* (*The Laws and Precedents of Great Qing*), Vol. 10.

ethnic group). So although the couple is allowed to conclude their marriage, the household registration of the female shall be canceled. If the female of Han nationality has married "Qi Ren" (members of the Manchu ethnic group), it will be investigated and reported by "Zuo Ling" (local administrator of the basic unit of organization in eight banners in the Qing dynasty) and "Qi Zhang" (head of "Qi") to the government and they shall be awarded by the government at the same time. If one has accepted the award by telling lies, he shall be severely punished. Moreover, it is strictly forbidden for "Qi Ren" (members of the Manchu ethnic group) to marry the daughters of his servants.[377]

But the marriage between "Zong Shi Jue Luo" (royal families and the emperor's near relatives) and the people of Han nationality was especially banned in order to maintain the purity of the royal kinship.

Moreover, it was also forbidden for the people of Han nationality to marry Mongolians. The following regulation was stipulated in *Li Fan Yuan Ze Li* (*The Regulation for the Bureau of National Minority Affairs*):

> It is prohibited for the people of Han nationality to marry Mongolian females inside or outside Zasake. If anyone has arranged for the marriage without permission, once it is discovered and reported to the government, they shall be sentenced to be divorced and the female will be sent back to her family. Moreover, the Mongolians who have arranged for the marriage and the people of Han nationality who have violated the law shall all be punished by wearing "Jia Hao" (cangue: a large wooden collar worn by petty criminals as a punishment) for three months and be punished by "Chi" (flogging with light sticks) for thirty strokes. After three months, and the people of Han nationality shall be sent back to their birth places, the local supervising officials shall be imposed with a fine of thirty nine livestock and the "Za Sa Ke" (the head of eight banners) shall be imposed with a fine of six months' salary for his negligence. However, if the local supervising officials or 'Za Sa Ke' (the head of eight banners) have discovered the illegal marriage by themselves, they shall not be held liable.[378]

In addition, even the Mongolians who had escaped to inland [China] were not allowed to marry the females there. In volume five of *Ji Yi Wen Cun* (*The Classics of Ji Yi*) written by Shen Jiaben, *Du Bu Ze Li* (*Regulation on Supervision and Arrest*) was cited: "If a Mongolian escapes to inland and marries a female there, they shall get divorced and the female shall be sent back to her family." However, the marriage between the Manchu and Han people had already been implemented for a long time; hence, it was not prohibited by law.

Besides, "it is forbidden for people from Fujian and Taiwan to marry the people from the vassal states. So anyone who has violated the law shall get divorced, while the Han people shall be punished by 'Zhang' (flogging with heavy sticks) for one hundred strokes, and the supervising officials for ninety strokes. If the local officials have failed to perform their duties after learning of the marriage, they shall be reported to the senior officials for punishment; if the Han people have married the people from the vassal states and have given birth to babies, it is allowed for the people from the vassal states to reside in that place, but it not allowed for them to go

---

[377]"Hu Kou" (Registered Permanent Residence) (Part 1) in *Hu Bu Ze Li* (*The Regulation of the Department of Revenue*), Vol. 1.

[378]"Hun Li" (Marriage Ceremony) in *Qin Ding Li Fan Yuan Ze Li* (*The Regulation for the Bureau of National Minority Affairs Made by Imperial Order*), Vol. 25.

11.5 Codification of Civil Law

back to the vassal states; if anyone has violated the law, he shall be punished by 'Zhang' (flogging with heavy sticks) for one hundred strokes according to the 'Li' (precedent) of 'Bu Ying Wei' (Things Forbidden to Do)."[379] This provision was first included in a regulation issued in the 2nd year of Qianlong (1737) and later was written into law, which was issued in the 5th year of Qianlong (1740), in order to maintain national security and to prevent the formation of anti-Qing cliques. In the 1st year of Guangxu (1875), because of great social changes, the provision was deleted from the law, according to the memorial submitted by Shen Baozhen, a senior judicial official.

As to divorce law, several principles of previous dynasties were inherited, such as "Qi Chu" (seven reasons to repudiate the wife: "being unfilial to parents-in-law," "failing to bear a male offspring," "being lascivious," "being jealous," "having severe illness," "gossiping," and "committing theft"), "San Bu Qu" (the three conditions under which women should not be divorced), and "Yi Jue" (a system of forced divorce because of fighting, scolding, killing, and raping of the relatives of both parties); however, the regulation on "Yi Jue" in the Qing Dynasty was different from that in Tang Dynasty. According to the law of the Tang Dynasty, "if the principle of 'Yi Jue' is offended in marriage, the couple must divorce; otherwise, they shall be punished by 'Tu' (imprisonment) for one year." According to the explanation in *Tang Lv Shu Yi* (*The Comments on Tang Code*), "the couples should live in harmony, but if the principle of 'Yi Jue' is offended, they should divorce. If they refuse to do so, they both shall be punished by 'Tu' (imprisonment) for one year." Moreover, "if the principle of 'Yi Jue' is offended, the supervising officials shall urge the parties involved to divorce; if they refuse to do so, they shall be punished by 'Tu' (imprisonment) and then get divorced."[380] According to different circumstances, the provisions about whether the couples should get divorced and whether the couples were allowed to be divorced were added in the laws of the Qing Dynasty. So in *Da Qing Lv Li Zeng Xiu Tong Zuan Ji Cheng* (*The Collections of the Laws and Precedents of Great Qing*), *Da Qing Lv Ji Zhu* (*Collected Commentaries on Great Qing Code*) was cited, and it was interpreted that "in the cases of 'Yi Jue' (a system of forced divorce because of fighting, scolding, killing, and raping of the relatives of both parties), if the husband and the wife have beaten each other, which has caused bone fracture, the couples can decide whether to divorce, but if one allows his or her spouse to have an affair with another person or sells his or her spouse to others, they must divorce." So it was obvious that the interpretations in the Qing Dynasty were more reasonable. In the meantime, according to the laws of the Qing Dynasty, "He Li" (peaceful dissolution of marriage) was also accepted, and it was stipulated that "if a couple agree to divorce because they cannot live in harmony,

---

[379] "Jia Qu Wei Lv Zhu Hun Mou Ren Zui" (The Crime of Matchmakers for their Illegal Arrangement of Marriages) in "Hu Lv" (Statutes on Households) in *Da Qing Lv Li* (*The Laws and Precedents of Great Qing*), Vol. 10.

[380] "Yi Jue Li Zhi" (Compulsory Divorce) in "Hu Hun Lv" (Statutes on Marriage, Tax and Household Registration) in *Tang Lv Shu Yi* (*The Comments on Tang Code*), Vol. 14.

they shall not be punished for doing so (since they are on bad terms with each other, there is no need to force them to stay together)."[381] In Mongolia, both the husband and the wife could ask for divorce, but they must notify their parents first. According to "Hu Kou Chai Yao" (The Household Revenue and Corvee) in *Meng Gu Lv Li* (*The Laws and Precedents of Mongolia*), "anyone who has divorced his wife is not liable for the compensation of what they have used up when they are on good terms, and what the wife has brought from her family when they get married shall be returned to her family." If the wife had asked for divorce, she had to return part of the gifts that her husband sent her. In the Tibetan area, if the husband and wife fell out, their relatives and friends should try to mediate first, but if it did not work, they could file an application for divorce to the head of the tribe. If the husband filed the application, he should give half of his property to the wife, but if the wife filed the application, she should give nothing to the husband; if both parties filed the application, the first person to file the application should be imposed with a fine of one horse or a certain amount of money. As to the problem of rearing children after the divorce, girls should be raised by the woman, while boys the man. If there was only one child, the child should be sent to the temple to be a lama. According to *Xi Ning Qing Hai Fan Yi Cheng Li* (*The Precedents for the Minorities in Xi'ning and Qinghai Areas*), "if the wife is divorced by her husband, the husband shall return all the property that the wife has brought from her family when they get married, and all the property shall be given to the wife except those which they have used up when they are on good terms."

The regulations of the marriage system of "Zong Shi Jue Luo" (royal families and the emperor's near relatives) of the Manchu nationality were quite comprehensive.

Before the period of entering Shanhaiguan, the system of polygamy was practiced by the noble families of "Zong Shi" (royal families) of the Manchu nationality. Nurhachi once married fifteen women, his brothers Muerhachi and Shuerhachi both married five women, and Bayala married four. During the time of Huang Taiji, men from noble families began to marry more women, which led to a considerable increase of royal population. After the period of entering Shanhaiguan, as the regime became more stable, it was further regulated that it was allowed for the brothers of the emperor, their sons, and the dukes to take one legal wife, as well as many concubines. According to the set rules, the brothers of the emperor could marry four concubines; their sons and dukes, three; the elder son and doro beile (title of nobility), two; "Bei Zi" (title of nobility, subordinate to doro beile) and lords, one. The above quota was the number of wives and concubines whom one could ask for from the emperor to confer titles by imperial mandate. Besides, the number of mistresses was also stipulated in the law. For example, the brothers of the emperor could have ten mistresses; their sons and dukes, six; the elder son and doro beile (title of nobility) and "Bei Zi" (title of nobility, subordinate to doro beile), five; "Zheng Guo Gong" (title of nobility, subordinate to "Bei Zi") and "Fu Guo Gong" (title of

---

[381]"Chu Qi" (Divorcing the Wife) in "Hu Lv" (Statutes on Households) in *Da Qing Lv Ji Jie Fu Li* (*Great Qing Code with Collected Commentaries and Appended Sub-statutes*), Vol. 6.

nobility, subordinate to "Zheng Guo Gong"), four. Nevertheless, there were in fact no restrictions for the mistresses whom they took secretly or bought from the ordinary people because "it is not necessary to investigate or prohibit such behaviors."[382]

Since the beginning of the Qing Dynasty, it had been stipulated that the marriage of "Zong Shi" (royal families) and dukes must be approved by the emperor. As a result, their marriage usually took a long time that the couple were usually much older when they got married. It was not until the 3rd year of Qianlong (1738) that the rule was changed: those who were close to the emperor had to marry females selected from "Ba Qi" (the Eight Banners: banner, a division of the Manchu nationality and the emperor's clan) and approved by the emperor, while the others could "decide whom to marry by themselves."[383] The system of selecting females from "Ba Qi" (the Eight Banners: banner, a division of Manchu nationality and the emperor's clan) was first established in the Qing Dynasty, and the selection was conducted every three years by "Hu Bu" (The Department of Revenue) and "Nei Wu Fu" (Board of the Imperial Household). Every girl from "Ba Qi" (the Eight Banners: banner, a division of Manchu nationality and the emperor's clan) between thirteen and fourteen years old must be sent to the capital to be selected by "Hu Bu" (The Department of Revenue) and "Nei Wu Fu" (Board of the Imperial Household), so if any "Qi Ren" (member of the Manchu ethnic group) had deliberately hidden his beautiful daughter to avoid being selected, he would be punished; if he was an official, he would be removed from his office; if he was an ordinary person, he would be sent to "Xing Bu" (The Department of Punishment) to be punished. If the head of the clan knew about the circumstance, he would be demoted two ranks lower if he was an official; he would be punished by "Zhang" (flogging with heavy sticks) for seventy strokes if he was a soldier. If the head of the clan knew nothing about the circumstance but had guaranteed for "Qi Ren" (members of the Manchu ethnic group) and written "Ju Jie" (written guarantee), his salary would be suspended for one year if he was an official; he would be punished by "Zhang" (flogging with heavy sticks) for fifty strokes if he was a soldier.[384] In order to maintain the purity of the royal family, it was forbidden for beautiful girls of the Han people who were adopted by "Qi Ren" (members of the Manchu ethnic group) to be selected together with them.

During the time of Nurhachi, it had already become an established system for the daughters of "Zong Shi" (royal families) and dukes to marry the children of the royal families of Mongolia. Therefore, the royal families of Mongolia must submit reports of their single young girls to the emperor by way of "Li Fan Yuan" (The Bureau of

---

[382] *Qin Ding Zong Ren Fu Ze Li* (*The Regulation of the Imperial Clan Court by Imperial Order*) (Part 3) in *Da Qing Hui Dian Shi Li* (*The Precedents of the Collected Statutes of Great Qing*), Vol. 9.

[383] "Hu Kou" (Registered Permanent Residence) in *Hu Bu Ze Li* (*The Regulation of the Department of Revenue*), Vol. 1.

[384] *Da Qing Hui Dian Shi Li* (*The Precedents of the Collected Statutes of Great Qing*), Vol. 99.

National Minority Affairs). Because of the intermarriage between Manchus and Mongolians, many Mongolian girls were married to the Manchu families of "Zong Shi" (royal families) and dukes, so did the girls of the Manchu nationality. However, the economic structure of Mongolia was quite simple and outdated, so the population growth was very slow. At the beginning of the nineteenth century, it was no longer possible for the Mongolian royal families to select beautiful young girls for the central government. So during the reign of Jiaqing, in order to maintain the intermarriage system between Manchu and Mongolia, the central government decided that "it is not necessary for them to have the same age" in selecting young males for the females of Manchu royal families. Therefore, it was allowed for Mongolian nobility to make reports to the central government about the young males who were "five years younger or older than the Manchu females," and "anyone who has deliberately hidden the young males who have met the age requirement shall be punished once they are discovered."[385] The intermarriage system between the Manchu and Mongolian people was carried out until the end of the Qing Dynasty.

11.5.4.2 The feudal patriarchal system was continued to be recognized and protected by the laws of the Qing Dynasty. According to "Hu Lv Ji Zhu" (*Collected Commentaries on Statute on Households*) in *Da Qing Lv Li Hui Ji Bian Lan* (*A Brief Guide to the Collections of the Laws and Precedents of Great Qing*), "the head of a family was in charge of the whole family." The head of a family referred to the senior male in the family, who was given the power of both father and husband, as was illustrated in *Ju Jia Za Yi* (*Miscellaneous Discussions on Family*): "any domestic affairs, whether minor or major, must be approved by the head of the family ... so the order shall be issued by the only person so that the family affairs shall be managed."

The head of the family enjoyed the right of disposing and managing the family property, so it was forbidden for the inferior and the young of the family members to dispose or use the family property without permission, and they would be punished by "Chi" (flogging with light sticks) for twenty strokes for spending twenty *guan* of money, with one level added for each additional twenty *guan* of money and with the maximum punishment of one hundred strokes. The head of the family also enjoyed the right of punishing his children, and he could punish "anyone who disobey his orders. Even if he has accidentally killed someone during punishment ... he shall not be held liable."[386] Besides, the head of the family also enjoyed the right of "Song Cheng," namely, the right of asking the government to punish the members of his family. If the head of the family sent his son to the government and accused him of certain offenses, his son would be punished by the government as was required by the father without being investigated. In the meantime, the head of the family was also regarded as the guardian of the whole family because it was not only the right

---

[385] *Da Qing Hui Dian Shi Li* (*The Precedents of the Collected Statutes of Great Qing*), Vol. 1.
[386] "Ou Zu Fu Mu Fu Mu" (Assaulting Grandparents and Parents) in "Dou Ou" (Fighting) (Part 2) in "Xing Lv" (The Penal Code) in *Da Qing Lv Li* (*The Laws and Precedents of Great Qing*), Vol. 28.

11.5 Codification of Civil Law

given to him by the state but also a duty that he had undertaken for the state. So if a family member had violated the law, the head of the family would be punished as well. In the 28th year of Kangxi (1679), it was ordered that "if the head of a family has failed to discipline his family members, he shall be punished by 'Jiao' (hanging)."[387] During the reign of Yongzheng, the provisions about the head of a clan were written into law, so the legal responsibilities thereof were further clarified and the legal force of family disciplines was recognized. It was stipulated that "if one has committed a crime which is not punishable by death penalty according to law ... but which is punishable by death penalty according to the family discipline, those involved will be exempted from punishment." Based on this imperial edict, "regulations were made by 'Xing Bu' (The Department of Punishment)"[388] in that year.

In a family, the rights and duties of the husband and wife were not equal. It was a traditional belief that "husband and wife should be regarded as an organic whole"; therefore, the domestic affairs should be dominated solely by the husband, and the property of the wife should also be owned and controlled by the husband. In addition, the husband had the right of supervising his wife. If a couple had assaulted each other or if they had committed the same crime, the punishment for each of them was different. The husband could even sell his wife to another man when he had serious economic problems; however, the wife must always be loyal to her husband unilaterally.

As can be seen from above, the principle of feudal family relationship was fully protected and the dominant position of the head of the family was fully established by the laws of the Qing Dynasty.

11.5.4.3 The inheritance laws and precedents and the popular customary laws had reached a perfect degree in the Qing Dynasty. Inheritance was divided into identity inheritance and property inheritance; the former included the inheritance of "Zong Tiao" (the succession to the headship) and the inheritance of knighthood. "Zong" referred to the temple of close ancestors and "Tiao" that of remote ancestors. Usually, "Di Zhang Zi" (the eldest son born of the legal wife) would be the first to inherit "Zong Tiao" (the succession to the headship) in the legal order of inheritance; if there was no "Di Zhang Zi" (eldest son born of the legal wife), it should be inherited by "Di Zhang Sun" (the eldest grandson of the legal wife) and the others in the following order: "Di Shu Zi" (the sons born of the legal wife and a concubine), "Di Ci Zi" (the second son born of the legal wife), "Shu Zhang Zi" (the eldest son born of a concubine), "Shu Zhang Sun" (the eldest grandson born of a concubine), "Shu Ci Zi" (the second son born of a concubine), and "Shu Ci Sun" (the second grandson born of a concubine). So "Zong Tiao" (succession to the headship) was inherited in a proper order, and if the legal order was not strictly followed, one would be punished by "Zhang" (flogging with heavy sticks) for eighty strokes so as to warn

---

[387] *Qing Shi Zi Liao* (*The Historical Materials of Qing Dynasty*), Vol. 1, Zhonghua Book Company, 1981, p. 114.
[388] "Xing Kao" (A Textual Research of the Criminal Penalties) (Part 3) in *Qing Chao Wen Xian Tong Kao* (*A General Textual Research of the Documents of Qing Dynasty*), Vol. 197.

people of the seriousness of inheritance. Inheritance of titles refers to the transferring of political power and privileged status. Therefore, the inheritance of "Zong Tiao" (the succession to the headship) and the inheritance of knighthood were inseparable, and in fact they were not allowed to be separated. But property inheritance was separable, and in fact it was allowed to be separated because it involved the transference of economic rights.

Dominated by the spirit and principle of the patriarchal system, identity was valued over property in inheritance law, so the specific conditions for "Cheng Ji" (being adopted as heir to one's uncle or adopting one's brother's son as one's heir) and "Li Ji" (adopting a male of next generation from the same branch of family or same clan as one's heir) were stipulated in detail, but the disposal of family property was not mentioned even in the article of "Li Di Zi Wei Fa" (Illegal Inheritance by the Eldest Son of the Legal Wife). Instead, the division and inheritance of family property were only stipulated in the supplementary precedents.

"Li Ji" refers to the inheritance of a family by adopting a male of next generation from the same branch of family or same clan as one's heir so as to guarantee the continuance of the branch of a family and sacrificial offerings for its ancestors when there were no descendants either from the legal wife or concubines, or "Hu Jue" (no male heirs). It was stipulated in the first supplementary regulation of "Li Di Zi Wei Fa" (Illegal Inheritance by the Eldest Son of the Legal Wife) in *Da Qing Lv Li* (*The Laws and Precedents of Great Qing*) that "if one does not have a son, he is allowed to adopt a nephew to be his heir according to the rules of 'Zhao Mu' (the patriarchal system of arranged order and order of generation in the temple or cemetery). He shall first choose from the males born of the same father with him, then those from 'Da Gong' (the person wearing the mourning apparel of soft sackcloth in the third mourning degree), 'Xiao Gong' (the person wearing the mourning apparel of soft sackcloth in the fourth mourning degree) and 'Si Ma' (the person wearing the mourning apparel of soft sackcloth in the fifth mourning degree). Only when there were no such people mentioned above can he choose the males from remote relatives with the same family names with him." Therefore, in the inheritance of "Zong Tiao" (the succession to the headship), besides the elements concerning the same ancestors, the appropriateness of 'Zhao Mu' (the patriarchal system of arranged order and order of generation in the temple or cemetery) was also stressed, which of course was also the requirement of the patriarchal system. "Although belonging to the same clan, if the order of superiority and inferiority was not strictly followed, those involved shall still be punished by 'Zhang' (flogging with heavy sticks) for eighty strokes for illegally appointing 'Di Zi' (the son born of the legal wife), even if the heir he has chosen is of the same ancestors with him. So the heir shall be sent back to his own family and another lawful heir shall be chosen."[389] The so-called choosing the person who was equivalent to "Zhao Mu"

---

[389]"Li Di Zi Wei Fa" (Illegal Inheritance by the Eldest Son of the Legal Wife) in "Hu Yi" (Household Corvee) in "Hu Lv" (Statutes on Households) in *Da Qing Lv Li* (*The Laws and Precedents of Great Qing*), Vol. 8.

(the patriarchal system of arranged order and order of generation in the temple or cemetery) referred to choosing one's nephew as the successor according to law.

Because blood ties was stressed in inheritance law, it was prohibited to choose an adopted son with a different family name as an heir to avoid disordering of the clan; anyone violating the law would be punished by "Zhang" (flogging with heavy sticks) for eighty strokes. Anyone from "Ba Qi" (the Eight Banners: banner, a division of the Manchu nationality and the emperor's clan) who did not have any descendants could adopt an heir with a different family name, but 'Gan Jie' (written pledge) should be issued to them by the fathers of both parties, the head of the clan, and the relevant officials and "Zuo Ling" (local administrator of the basic unit of organization in Eight Banners in the Qing Dynasty) and recorded in "Hu Bu" (The Department of Revenue). After the adoptive relationship was established, it was not allowed to be revoked at will, and only when the heir was not filial or had failed to live in harmony with other members of the family could such relationship be revoked and a new heir be chosen. It was stipulated in the laws in the Qing Dynasty that "if an adopted heir cannot live in harmony with other family members, the head of the family can lodge a complaint to the government and choose a new heir. He can choose anyone who is virtuous and capable or anyone he likes. But it is forbidden for others to accuse him of violating the order of generations of that family so long as the new heir was in the order of 'Zhao Mu' (the patriarchal system of arranged order and order of generation in the temple or cemetery). So such cases should not be accepted."[390]

In early Qing Dynasty, it was forbidden by law for the only child to inherit "Zong Tiao" (the succession to the headship) of the two families; however, the situation began to change since the reign of Emperor Qianlong. Yu Yue stated in *Yu Lou Za Cuan* (*Miscellaneous Articles Written in Yulou*) that "it is a special regulation made during the reign of Qinglong that one heir can inherit the 'Zong Tiao' (the succession to the headship) of two families." In the intercalary October of the 40th year of Qianlong (1775), based on the principle of the patriarchal system that "it is not allowed for 'Xiao Zong' (the other sons by concubines except the sons of a legal wife) to be heirless but not 'Da Zong' (the eldest son or sons of of legal wife) to be heirless," an imperial edict was issued:

> From now on, if a widow plans to adopt a son as the heir of the family by "Li Ji" (to adopt a male of next generation from the same branch of family or same clan as one's heir), she is free to choose the one she likes as long as the rule of "Zhao Mu" (the patriarchal system of arranged order and order of generation in the temple or cemetery) is followed. Nevertheless, the opinions of the person's parents must be taken into consideration. If "Gan Jie" (written pledge) has been written by the relevant relatives, the person can be adopted even if he is the only child of his own family. The law is made to protect the peaceful relationship between the heir and his parents, so it should not be disrupted by the statutory "Li" (precedent). The

---

[390]"Li Di Zi Wei Fa" (Illegal Inheritance by the Eldest Son of the Legal Wife) in "Hu Yi" (Household Corvee) in "Hu Lv" (Statutes on Households) in *Da Qing Lv Li* (*The Laws and Precedents of Great Qing*), Vol. 8.

affairs should be handled by the relevant departments according to the edict, so the order is issued.[391]

Based on the imperial edict, *Du Zi Cheng Tiao Li* (*Regulation of Inheritance of the Succession of the Headship by the Only Child*) was completed in the 44th year of Qianlong (1779), in which the specific conditions for such inheritance were clearly regulated. If there was no heir in a family or "if the person chosen to be adopted as the heir is the only child of his family, or if the person's father and the head of that family are born of the same father and the two families both agreed with the adoption, the person is allowed to inherit the 'Zong Tiao' (the succession to the headship) of both families."

It was not only a legal provision but also a popular custom in practice for the only child of a family to inherit "Zong Tiao" (the succession to the headship) of the two families. As the heir of "Zong Tiao" (the succession to the headship) of the two families, he would marry two wives and have sons for the two families, respectively. So the status of the two wives was equal, and their sons should inherit the "Zong Tiao" (succession to the headship) and the property of the two families, respectively. Except in certain areas and under special circumstances, it was forbidden for the oldest son of the superior branch of a family to be adopted as the heir of another family. However, for the inheritance of the families of "Ba Qi" (the Eight Banners: banner, a division of the Manchu nationality and the emperor's clan) and the garrison in other provinces, if there were no heirs in a family, "even the oldest son of the superior branch of a family can be adopted according to the precedents of inheritance of the succession of the headship by the only child."[392]

Since "Li Ji" (adopting a male of next generation from the same branch of family or same clan as one's heir) and the inheritance of "Zong Tiao" (the succession to the headship) were both important affairs concerning inheritance in a family, sometimes documents should be drafted to show their serious nature. According to what was recorded in volume one of *Ming Qing Hui Zhou She Hui Jing Ji Zi Liao Cong Bian* (*Series of Collections of Materials on Society and Economy in Huizhou During Ming and Qing Dynasties*), Hu Changren from Shexian county in Huizhou agreed to let his own son be adopted as an heir, and the document reads as follows:

> This document of adoption for heir is made by Changren. Changfu, my brother, suddenly died because of disease and there is no heir in his family. After discussing with relatives about the adoption of a son as the heir for the succession of family line, I find it is my duty to help him. Now I am willing to let my oldest son, named Zaojin, be adopted to my sister in-law as an heir. He shall follow her orders and be raised by her, and his marriage shall also be arranged by her. Currently my sister in-law is out in Han and has not returned ... After the inheritance of "Zong Tiao" (the succession to the headship), I hope he will bring prosperity to his family. No matter what happens, he shall be a member of that family and this adoption shall not be revoked. Oral words being no guarantee, a written statement is hereby given and it shall be in effect forever.

---

[391] *Qing Gao Zong Shi Lu* (*The Record of Qing Emperor Gaozong*), Vol. 995.

[392] "Hu Kou" (Registered Permanent Residence) (Part 1) in *Hu Bu Ze Li* (*The Regulation of the Department of Revenue*), Vol. 1.

11.5 Codification of Civil Law

September of the 9th year of Emperor Guangxu,
The person making this document: ×××
Heads of the clan and family and other relevant persons: ×××

It was allowed to adopt a child with a different family name if he was not appointed as "Si Zi" (adopted son) of the family. However, if the adopted son had violated the rules of the clan, he would be forcibly sent back to his own family. According to *Da Qing Lv Li* (*The Laws and Precedents of Great Qing*), "if the adopted 'Yi Zi' (adopted son) with a different family name has violated the order of the family, the adopter will be punished by 'Zhang' (flogging with heavy sticks) for sixty strokes; if the adopted 'Yi Zi' (adopted son) with a different family name is appointed as 'Si Zi' (adopted son) of the family, the adopter will be punished the same and the child will be sent back to his family."[393] Only in certain areas and under some special circumstances could an adopted child acquire the identity of "Di Zi" (the son born of the legal wife) and inherit "Zong Tiao" (the succession to the headship) and the property of that family. Of the customs that were very popular in different areas, it was very common to choose an heir with a different family name from the nephews or grandsons who were able and virtuous. In Jiangxi and Zhejiang provinces, "Ying Li" (adopting those who are supposed to be adopted), "Ying Ji" (inheriting that which are supposed to be inherited), "Ai Li" (adopting those whom they prefer to adopt), and "Ze Ji" (selecting those who they prefer to inherit) were carried out simultaneously, and one of those who were equivalent to "Zhao Mu" (the patriarchal system of arranged order and order of generation in the temple or cemetery) was chosen from close relatives as an heir of "Ying Li" (adopting those who are supposed to be adopted). Moreover, it was allowed to choose another child with a different family name as an heir of "Ai Li" (adopting those who they prefer to adopt).[394]

In addition to the adopted child, it was also popular to appoint the son-in-law as the heir to succeed the family line. If a man's family was very poor and he could not afford to pay the betrothal presents to his fiancee, usually he had to become a "Zhui Xu" (son-in-law who lives in the home of his parents-in-law), so that his family name would be changed to that of his wife. Meanwhile, he had to sign a document to state that he would be "Si Zi" (adopted son) of his wife's family and then he was allowed to inherit the "Tiao" (being or becoming heir) and the property of his wife's family upon the approval of the clan members. In most cases, the family members of his wife would regard the son-in-law as one of the members of their family, which was described as "having a son with a different family name but having a grandson with the same family name" or "having an adopted son but not an adopted grandson." Usually, their eldest son should be named after the female's family and their

---

[393] "Li Di Zi Wei Fa" (Illegal Inheritance by the Eldest Son of the Legal Wife) in "Hu Yi" (Household Corvee) in "Hu Lv" (Statutes on Households) in *Da Qing Lv Li* (*The Laws and Precedents of Great Qing*), Vol. 8.
[394] *Min Shang Shi Xi Guan Diao Cha Bao Gao Lu* (*Collections of Reports on the Research of Civil and Commercial Conventions*), Jinmin Press, 1969.

second son after the male's family so that both families should have heirs to carry on their family lineage.

To conclude, the inheritance of "Zong Tiao" (the succession to the headship), which served as an important guarantee for the continuation of the family lineage, not only involved the overall and long-term interest of a family but also was protected by state law, so it had become the core of the system of inheritance of the Qing Dynasty.

As to the inheritance of knighthood, the principle of the priority of "Di Zi" (the son born of the legal wife) was carried out, and the order of inheritance was the same as that of the inheritance of "Zong Tiao" (the succession to the headship). Since the knighthood was a symbol of power and interest, as well as the achievement of the ancestors of the family, the selection of the heir thereof was very strict, and anyone who had inherited the knighthood by illegal means would be severely punished. "Except adopting a person with a different family name as heir, any 'Qi Ren' (members of the Manchu ethnic group) who have fraudulently inherited the titles of their family, or inherited the official positions by 'Yin Xi' (children inherit their ancestor's positions) ... shall be punished by 'Chong Jun' (to be forced to join the army); ... if any 'Qi Ren' (members of the Manchu ethnic group) have fraudulently or falsely claimed grain and money, they shall be punished severely according to the laws of theft and shall return the money and grain which they have obtained."[395] However, if "an official has committed murder, or misconducted, or involved in robbery or any other crimes punishable by death penalty, or is punished by 'Chong Jun' (to be forced to join the army) because he is exempted from death penalty, whether he has been executed, exiled, imprisoned, escapted or committed suicide, his knighthood shall not be inherited by his offspring."[396]

As to property inheritance, since the head of a family had the right to allocate the family property, he had the right to arrange the distribution of family property immediately before dying. So the will of the head of a family was an important evidence for the inheritance of family property, and his offspring could do nothing but follow his will. If the head of a family did not make such arrangement before his death, the distribution of family property should be made according to law. Similar to the laws of the previous dynasties, the rule of "distributing family property equally among the sons" was also adopted in the Qing Dynasty, and it was stipulated that "apart from the property which is inherited by 'Di Zi' (the son born of the legal wife) out of 'Yin Xi' (children inherit their ancestor's positions), the other family property and real estate shall be inherited equally by all the sons, whether they are born by the

---

[395]"Li Di Zi Wei Fa" (Illegal Inheritance by the Eldest Son of the Legal Wife) in "Hu Yi" (Household Corvee) in "Hu Lv" (Statutes on Households) in *Da Qing Lv Li* (*The Laws and Precedents of Great Qing*), Vol. 8.

[396]"Guan Yuan Yin Xi" (The Official's Inheriting of his Ancestor's Titles) in "Zhi Zhi" (The State Office System) in "Li Lv" (Statutes on Personnel) in *Da Qing Lv Li* (*The Laws and Precedents of Great Qing*), Vol. 6.

legal wife, concubines, mistresses or maidservants"[397] to show that "great achievements should be inherited by everyone." If "a senior member of a family fail to distribute family property equally," "he will be punished by 'Chi' (flogging with light sticks) for twenty strokes and be imposed with a fine of ten *liang* of silver, and the punishment shall be one level severer for each additional ten *liang* of silver with the maximum punishment of 'Zhang' (flogging with heavy sticks) for one hundred strokes."[398] However, it was a conventional practice that different amounts of property was distributed to "Di Zi" (the son born of the legal wife) and "Shu Zi" (the son born of a concubine), so that "Di Zi" (the son born of the legal wife) usually inherited more family property than "Shu Zi" (the son born of a concubine). Moreover, and the eldest son and eldest grandson were allowed to inherit more of the family property to be used at sacrificial ceremonies.

In order to make sure that the heir chosen was from the same family, the legal status of the illegitimate child was recognized by law, and the share that was legally inherited by the illegitimate child was also increased. It was stipulated in *Da Qing Lv Li* (*The Laws and Precedents of Great Qing*) that "an illegitimate son shall inherit half of the amount of property that a legitimate son can inherit. If the dead person has no sons, the son of 'Ying Ji' (to inherit that which are supposed to be inherited) shall be the heir, so that the property shall be shared with the illegitimate child equally. But if there are no people of 'Ying Ji' (to inherit that which are supposed to be inherited), he shall inherit all the family property."[399]

As to the daughter's right of inheritance, it was stipulated in *Da Qing Lv Li* (*The Laws and Precedents of Great Qing*) that "if there are no sons in a family and there are no persons of 'Ying Ji' (to inherit that which are supposed to be inherited), the family property shall be inherited by the daughter; however, if there are no daughters in the family, the property shall be confiscated by the government upon reporting to the superior officials in detail."[400] Therefore, it can be seen that usually daughters did not have the right to inherit; nevertheless, if a will was made by the head of the family, it should be followed. In some areas, it was conventional that if a person had no sons, apart from the land for her marriage and the land inherited from the ancestors, it was not allowed for the daughters to inherit all the family property. In some areas, such as Dongle county, if there were no sons in the family, it was

---

[397]"Bei You Si Shan Yong Cai" (Illegal Disposal of Property by the Young and the Humble) in "Hu Yi" (Household Corvee), in "Hu Lv" (Statutes on Households) in *Da Qing Lv Li* (*The Laws and Precedents of Great Qing*), Vol. 8.

[398]"Bei You Si Shan Yong Cai" (Illegal Disposal of Property by the Young and the Humble) in "Hu Yi" (Household Corvee) in "Hu Lv" (Statutes on Households) in *Da Qing Lv Li* (*The Laws and Precedents of Great Qing*), Vol. 8.

[399]"Bei You Si Shan Yong Cai" (Illegal Disposal of Property by the Young and the Humble) in "Hu Yi" (Household Corvee) in "Hu Lv" (Statutes on Households) in *Da Qing Lv Li* (*The Laws and Precedents of Great Qing*), Vol. 8.

[400]"Bei You Si Shan Yong Cai" (Illegal Disposal of Property by the Young and the Humble) in "Hu Yi" (Household Corvee) in "Hu Lv" (Statutes on Households) in *Da Qing Lv Li* (*The Laws and Precedents of Great Qing*), Vol. 8.

allowed for the daughters or the granddaughters to inherit all the property except the land used for sacrificial activities. In the areas of Gansu province, if there were no sons in the family, the sons of the daughters of the family (or nephew) also enjoyed the right to inherit the family property.

As to families where there were no sons or daughters (or "Jue Hu"), "the property thereof shall be confiscated by the government" according to law. However, in order to protect the privilege of "Qi Ren" (members of the Manchu ethnic group), if there was no one to inherit the property in the family of "Qi Ren" (members of the Manchu ethnic group), they should be handled differently. For example, in the 3rd year of Xianfeng (1853), "Dekui, 'Shi Du Xue Shi' (advisory secretary on reading), has submitted a memorial to the emperor about confiscating the property of the families of 'Qi Ren' (members of the Manchu ethnic group) who have no heirs," but he was severely reprimanded by the Emperor.

In *Da Qing Lv Li* (*The Laws and Precedents of Great Qing*), the principle of property inheritance under different circumstances were also stipulated. For example, if a son was born after an adopted heir had been chosen, each of the two should inherit half of the property. If a widow married another man after the husband died, the property of her former husband and her jewelry should be at the disposal of the former family. Any adopted son and son-in-law who were "loved by and lived in harmony with the parents, are allowed to live with the family, and it is forbidden for the step-son and his parents to force them to move out. Besides, he is entitled to inherit part of the family property."[401] "As for those families of 'Zhao Xu' (have the groom live in the bride's house), if 'Zhui Xu' (a son-in-law who lives in the home of his parents-in-law) has changed his family name to that of his wife's and waited upon his wife's parents when they are old, he shall inherit the same amount of family property as the heirs of 'Ying Ji' (to inherit that which are supposed to be inherited)."[402] If one had adopted an abandoned child who was younger than three years old, the adopted child would not be allowed to be appointed as the heir for the succession of family line even if there was no one else to inherit, but he would be allowed to inherit part of the family property and would not to be sent back to his former family. "If someone is killed in the fighting for inheritance, those who have colluded in the plot shall not be chosen as the heir, and the heir shall be chosen by other family members after discussion."[403] If the husband died, his property could be inherited by the wife if there were no sons or if she did not remarry, which was called "He Cheng Fu Fen" (inheriting the husband's share by the wife). However, once an heir was chosen, the property should be inherited by the heir.

---

[401]"Li Di Zi Wei Fa" (Illegal Inheritance by the Eldest Son of the Legal Wife) in "Hu Yi" (Household Corvee) in "Hu Lv" (Statutes on Households) in *Da Qing Lv Li* (*The Laws and Precedents of Great Qing*), Vol. 8.

[402]"Nan Nv Hun Yin" (The Marriage of Men and Women) in "Hun Yin" (Marriage) in *Da Qing Lv Li* (*The Laws and Precedents of Great Qing*), Vol. 10.

[403]"Li Di Zi Wei Fa" (Illegal Inheritance by the Eldest Son of the Legal Wife) in "Hu Yi" (Household Corvee) in "Hu Lv" (Statutes on Households) in *Da Qing Lv Li* (*The Laws and Precedents of Great Qing*), Vol. 8.

11.6 Enriching of the System of Economic Law

In the economic legislation of the Qing Dynasty, some outdated malpractices and systems of the Ming Dynasty were abandoned, and some innovative measures were taken. Besides, both the scope and contents were adjusted and expanded and a primary system of economic law was finally established.

11.6.1 The New Development of Tax Legislation

After the period of entering Shanhaiguan, considering that the burden of tax in the late Ming Dynasty was too heavy, the three kinds of taxes, namely, "Liao Xiang" (the tax collected for the military operation in east of Liaoning), "Jiao Xiang" (the tax collected for the suppressing of peasant uprising), and "Lian Xiang" (the tax collected for the training of troops), which had led to the peasant uprising in the late Ming Dynasty, were abolished. "Since the 1st year of Shunzhi, except those stipulated in the law, such as the aforementioned three kinds of taxes and the compulsory selling of rice and bean, all other taxes are abolished. ... so that if any officials have secretly imposed any tax on people illegally, they shall be subject to death penalty once enough evidence is discovered; if any supervising officials have helped to connive at this kind of behavior, they shall be subject to the same kind of punishment."[404] In order to establish the tax system of the Qing Dynasty, *Fu Yi Quan Shu* (*The Complete Books of Tax and Corvee*) was completed in the 14th year of Emperor Shunzhi (1657) by imitating that of the Ming Dynasty, according to which the amount of tax was to be stipulated on the basis of registered information such as the degree of land and the number of people in a household. So the amount of tax was almost entirely decided according to *Fu Yi Quan Shu* (*The Complete Books of Tax and Corvee*), which was made during the reign of Wanli in the Ming Dynasty. Moreover, the principle of distribution and the use of tax collected by the local government were clearly provided, and the tax collection by the local government must be approved by the central government and the tributes that the local government paid to the royal family and the court must be recorded in detail. As can be seen from above, *Fu Yi Quan Shu* (*The Complete Books of Tax and Corvee*), which was issued in the early Qing Dynasty, had served as a uniform legal basis for local tax collection, the allocation of corvee, and financial revenues and expenditures. Later, after repeated revision during the reign of emperors Kangxi and Yongzheng, *Fu Yi Quan Shu* (*The Complete Books of Tax and Corvee*) was more in line with the actual social and state conditions of the Qing Dynasty. Meanwhile, it was decided that *Fu*

---

[404]"She Zheng Wang Yu Guan Li Jun Min Ren Deng Ling Zhi" (The Orders of Prince Regent to Officials, Armymen and the Common People) in *Ming Qing Shi Liao* (*The Historical Materials of Ming and Qing Dynasties*) (Book 1), Vol. 3.

Yi Quan Shu (*The Complete Books of Tax and Corvee*) would be amended every ten years.

What was most significant of the tax reform in the Qing Dynasty was that tax was decided according to the land owned by every household rather than the number of people therein.

According to the tax law in feudal China, double tax was collected both on the land and people; however, during the reign of Emperor Kangxi, the development of the commodity economy, the increase of land sale, and the weakening of super-economic exploitation contributed to the migration of peasants, so it became very difficult for the government to collect tax according to each individual; therefore, changes needed be made in the tax system. In the 52nd year of Kangxi (1713), it was ordered that "during the time of tax registration in each province, the increase of people in each household shall be investigated, recorded and reported to the emperor by memorials. The tax which should be paid by each household shall be decided according to the number of people registered in the 50th year of Kangxi, while the people increased in each household later shall not be taxed."[405] However, in order to maintain the quota of people registered in the 50th year of Kangxi (1711) and to ensure tax revenue, another order was issued in the 55th year of (1716), and it was stipulated that "the newly increased people shall pay tax to make up for the deficit of the previous years."[406]

Although the policy of "exempting the newly born babies from taxation" had reduced the peasants' burden caused by the increase of family members, yet it had failed to solve the problem of unfair tax payment. Therefore, the tax reform carried out in the late period of Emperor Kangxi mainly focused on collecting tax according to the amount of land that each peasant owned. That is to say, the tax that used to be collected according to each person was included in the tax collected according to land. In the first years of Yongzheng, this policy was implemented in all provinces except Shanxi and Guizhou, but it was not until after about one hundred and fifty years that the new system was finally established. The new policy was historically significant, not just because it simplified the standard of taxation and reduced the burden of peasants but also because it actually abolished the tax that was levied according to each individual and that had been practiced for a long time in the form of law, loosened the personal restriction on peasants, and supplied free labor force for the development of the industry and commerce.

In late Ming Dynasty, money and grain were all monopolized by the gentry, but they were exempted from tax, which led to extremely unfair tax and corvee and greatly weakened the basis of governance. So the rulers of early Qing Dynasty had learned from the lesson and adopted the policy of "the equalization of tax." In the 14th year of Shunzhi (1657), the policy of tax and corvee exemption for the gentry class that had once been applied was changed, and according to the new regulation, "the officials whose official ranks are from 'Yi Pin' (the first-rank) to 'Sheng Yuan'

---

[405]"Dang An" (Files) in *Qian San Chao Ti Ben* (*Memorials of the First Three Periods of Reigning*).

[406]"Dang An" (Files) in *Qian San Chao Ti Ben* (*Memorials of the First Three Periods of Reigning*).

(also called 'Xiu Cai': those who passed the imperial examination at lower level in ancient China) are exempted from corvee, but they still have to pay money or grain to the government." In the 1st year of Kangxi (1662), it was stipulated that "all the gentry and officials of the bureaucratic group shall be registered in 'Li Jia' (social organizations at the grass-roots level) with other ordinary people to pay tax and serve corvee." In the 29th year of Kangxi (1690), it was further stipulated that "if any gentry and landlord have concealed the amount of the land, or failed to pay the full amount of tax and to serve corvee, or embezzled the land rent of other people, they shall be punished according to the 'Li' (precedent) on 'concealing the amount of land.'" In the 5th year of Yongzheng (1727), it was stipulated that any bureaucratic officials like "Gong Jian" (those recommended to study in "Guo Zi Jian" as "Gong Sheng") and "Sheng Yuan" (also called "Xiu Cai": those who passed the imperial examination at the county level in ancient China) who had monopolized the grain and money and delayed the payment of tax should be punished by "removing from their office." Although the policy of "the equalization of tax" was never completely implemented, it had great significance in restraining the bureaucratic gentry from bullying and oppressing the ordinary people and reducing the burden of the ordinary people at that time.

11.6.2 The Industrial and Commercial Legislation of Secluding the Country from the Outside World

At the beginning of the Qing Dynasty, the system of "Jiang Ji" (the craftsman household registration) was abolished. According to an imperial order issued in the 3rd year of Shunzhi (1645), "'Jiang Ji' (the craftsman household registration) is abolished and all craftsmen are regarded as ordinary people,"[407] so that the craftsmen not only were registered as ordinary people but also acquired the same legal status as other ordinary people and began to pay taxes and serve corvee. In the meantime, the government loosened the state monopoly of the handicraft industry and allowed the ordinary craftsmen to do business independently on a much larger scale, so the ordinary craftsmen were allowed to engage in the management of all other businesses except the manufacture of weapons, coins, cloth for the use of royal court, and porcelain, as well as the management of other workshops run by "Nei Wu Fu" (Board of the Imperial Household). But the ordinary people were forbidden to engage in mining without the permission of the government. In the 43rd year of Kangxi (1704), an imperial order was issued: "Mining does no good to the local people, so from now on the application for mining is not to be approved."[408] In the

---

[407] *Qing Shi Zong Shi Lu* (*The Record of Emperor Shizong of Qing Dynasty*), Vol. 16.
[408] Yu Zhengxie (Qing Dynasty), *Gui Si Cun Gao* (*The Manuscripts of the Year of Guisi*), Vol. 9.

50th year of Kangxi (1711), Hunan province, where there were abundant reserves of lead, was "banned from mining forever"[409] because "it is inconvenient to mine there due to the high mountains and deep valleys and because it is also the interchange to Qianyue, Miao and Yao nationalities." In fact, the reason for the banning of mining by legislation was that the rulers were afraid that "it is easy for the miners to gang together but it is difficult for them to be controlled. Moreover, it may also lead to disputes, robbery or uprising."[410] Emperor Shizong once clearly stated that "as for mining ... it is very harmful because of the assembly of the large number of people and because the miners are usually a mob of gangsters." So it was forbidden for the bandits to gather in the remote and barren mountains for "the meager profits."[411] According to reports, merchants and the local people from Nanshan Iron Factory had raised funds, hired people and opened up mines in Shaanxi province, so strict regulations were made in *Hu Bu Ze Li* (*The Regulation of the Department of Revenue*) under the influence of this ideology: "The name and birthplace of the merchants shall be checked up and 'Gan Jie' (written pledge) shall be taken by the local officials. Besides, no one is allowed to open up mines unless certificates are obtained from 'Fan Si' (the government office in charge of civil affairs at the provincial level)."

With regard to commerce, in view of the fact that it was urgently needed to recover and develop economy at the beginning of a new country, the policy of "supporting business" and "showing solicitude for commerce" was adopted by the government in early Qing Dynasty; "therefore, all newly added taxes in late Ming Dynasty are abolished."[412] Besides, "grain purchasing is conducted by the government at the convenience of people according to concrete situations, the amount of goods is calculated, the market price is stabilized, people are encouraged to do business and civilians are persuaded to be economical, the despotic people are suppressed, and arbitrary charges and 'denotions' are prohibited."[413] At the same time, the social status of merchants was raised to "one of the four categories of ordinary people."[414] In order to protect lawful business transaction, "it is forbidden for aristocrats and bureaucrats to plunder and bully businessmen." In the 6th year of Kangxi (1667), the following regulation was made:

> From now on, any family members of officials below princes and dukes who have prevented merchants from doing business by occupying the strategic passes and ferries shall be

---

[409] *Yong Zheng Da Qing Hui Dian* (*Collected Statutes of Great Qing in the Reign of Emperor Yongzheng*), Vol. 53.

[410] *Fen Zhou Fu Zhi* (*Annals of Fenzhou Prefecture*), Vol. 31.

[411] *Qing Shi Zong Shi Lu* (*The Record of Emperor Shizong of Qing Dynasty*), Vol. 24.

[412] "Zheng Que Kao" (An Examination of National Commodity Tax and Government Monopoly) in *Qing Chao Wen Xian Tong Kao* (*A General Textual Research of the Documents of Qing Dynasty*), Vol. 26.

[413] "Shi Di Kao" (An Examination of Grain Collection by the Government) in *Qing Chao Wen Xian Tong Kao* (*A General Textual Research of the Documents of Qing Dynasty*), Vol. 32.

[414] "Kang Xi Chao" (The Reign of Emperor Kangxi) in *Dong Hua Lu* (*The Record of Donghua*), Vol. 28.

11.6 Enriching of the System of Economic Law

punished by wearing "Jia Hao" (cangue: a large wooden collar worn by petty criminals as a punishment) for three months at the place where he has committed the crime. If an ordinary person has committed the aforementioned crime, he shall be punished by "Chi" (flogging with light sticks) for forty strokes; if "Qi Ren" (members of the Manchu ethnic group) have committed the aforementioned crime, they will be punished by "Zhang" (flogging with heavy sticks) for one hundred strokes; if any seignior has failed to stop his family from committing such crimes, he shall be imposed with a fine of 10,000 *liang* of silver; if any duke has failed to do so, he shall be imposed with a fine of 1000 *liang* of silver; if the official in charge of the domestic affairs has failed to do so, he shall be removed from his office; if the military and civilian officials below "Jiang Jun" (the general) and "Du Fu" (the viceroys and procurators) have failed to do so, they will also be dismissed.[415]

Since the family members of the aristocrats and bureaucrats often oppressed the businessmen by making use of their privileges, they were severely punished during the reign of Emperor Yongzheng to give warning to their masters.

Moreover, if the officials who were in charge of "Guan Jin" (Strategic Pass and Ferry) had blackmailed the businessmen illegally, they would also be severely punished. Moreover, in the 25th year of Kangxi (1686), it was ordered that the license for "Ya Hang" (broker house) should be compiled and renewed for every five years to regulate the market order.

The aforementioned legislation of fostering and encouraging the development of commerce had played a positive role in boosting the economy; however, the traditional policy of "Zhong Nong Yi Shang" (encouraging agriculture and restraining commerce) was not fundamentally changed. At the beginning of the Qing Dynasty, the ideological trend of "Gong Shang Jie Ben" (both industry and commerce being the essence) and "Nong Shang Jie Ben" (both agriculture and commerce being the essence) was criticized. In the 5th year of Yongzheng (1727), an imperial edict was issued: "I have examined the profession of 'Si Min' (The four kinds of citizens in ancient China, e.g. scholars, farmers, manufacturers and merchants), besides 'Shi' (scholar) working for the government, the most important profession is 'Nong' (peasant), because both 'Shi' (scholar) and 'Shang' (businessmen) have to live on what 'Nong' (peasant) has produced. Therefore agriculture is the basis of all other trades, and commerce is the least important."[416] Emperor Gaozong once even stated: "how I wish all my people could work hard in the fields."[417] So encouraging and supervising agriculture became a very important criterion in the evaluation of officials that was conducted by "Hu Bu" (The Department of Revenue).

Since customs duties were very important for state finance, whether the businessmen or the local officials, if anyone had tried to pass through customs secretly or to avoid paying duties, he would be punished severely according to law. It was stipulated in *Hu Bu Ze Li* (*The Regulation of the Department of Revenue*) that "the

---

[415] *Qing Shi Zu Shi Lu* (*The Record of Emperor Shizu of Qing Dynasty*), Vol. 14.

[416] *Qing Shi Zu Shi Lu* (*The Record of Emperor Shizu of Qing Dynasty*), Vol. 57.

[417] "Shi Huo" (National Finance and Economy) in *Qing Tong Dian* (*The General Codes of Qing Dynasty*), Vol. 1.

shortage of the customs duties shall be compensated by the officials in charge," so the officials at passes were encouraged to try every means to collect as many tariffs as possible. Apart from customs duties, many kinds of commercial taxes, such as transaction, loading, salt, tea, and wine taxes, were collected. If a businessman had illegally evaded tax, he would "be punished by 'Zhang' (flogging with heavy sticks) for fifty strokes with half of his goods confiscated by the government according to the law."[418] As a result, the businessmen often regarded customs passes as formidable places, and they had to withdraw some of the commercial capital and profit and invest them in land. However, the combination of commercial capital and land rent had made it difficult for commercial capital to be changed into industrial capital, and it was impossible to bring about a massive accumulation of monetary capital, which had become one of the reasons for the long-time stagnation of Chinese feudal society.

As to "Jin Que" (the state monopoly for some important goods), the monopoly of the sale of salt and tea was continued to be strictly enforced by law; meanwhile, the production of the articles that were especially used by the royal family was also monopolized, so that they were neither circulated on the market nor challenged by competition. All these measures had inevitably hindered the development of private industry and commerce and prevented the expanding of markets, as well as the accumulation of capital. Although in some small towns some people who engaged in commerce and industry had become rich, the social forces that were like the citizens in Western Europe who were powerful enough to compete with the landlord class were not formed, and laws and orders were issued by the Qing government just to maintain the traditional economic structure. As was pointed out by Max, "in China, (with regard to the emergence of capitalism, noted by the author), it is even slower, because the direct political power has provided no help in its growth."[419] So it is worth noting that the banning of sea trade, which was carried out for a long time to restrict trade with foreign countries, had severely shackled the development of social economy of the Qing Dynasty.

As early as the 12th year of Shunzhi (1655), an order on banning sea trade with foreign countries had been issued for the first time to suppress the anti-Qing forces. According to the order, no single boat was allowed to go to sea, and those who violated the law would be punished for colluding with the enemies. Later, in the 18th year of Shunzhi (1661), in the 1st year of Kangxi (1662) and in the 17th year of Kangxi (1678), three orders were successively issued to order people to move away from the coastal areas, so that the coastal residents in the provinces of Min (Fujian), Guang (Guangdong), Su (Jiangsu), and Zhe (Zhejiang) were forced to move fifty *li* inland, and those who resisted the orders were punished by death penalty immediately, which had rendered the 4000-*li* coastal line desolate and uninhabited, and

---

[418]"Ni Shui" (Tax Evasion) in "Ke Cheng" (Tax) in "Hu Lv" (Statutes on Households) in *Da Qing Lv Li* (*The Laws and Precedents of Great Qing*), Vol. 13.

[419]*Ma Ke Si En Ge Si Quan Ji* (*The Complete Works of Marx and Engels*), Vol. 25, The People's Publishing House, 1972, p. 373.

completely cut off overseas trade. In the 22nd year of Kangxi (1683), after Taiwan was reunited, in view of the fact that the country was united, the ban was finally lifted in the next year, so that "people are allowed to trade overseas." "At the ports of Shandong, Jiangnan, Zhejiang and Guangdong, it was allowed for the ordinary people and businessmen to trade overseas after they had report to and examined by the local officials at the ports with their names registered, 'Bao Jie' (guarantee of innocence) taken, licenses issued, the ship's name branded on its body. But those who carried illegal articles with them would be punished."[420] In the 24th year of Kangxi (1685), it was further declared that Susong, Ningbo, Quanzhou, and Guangzhou were open to overseas trade, and the customs of Jianghai, Zhehai, and Minhai were set up to be in charge of the affairs of overseas trading. The lifting of the banning of overseas trade had dramatically fostered the development of the handicraft and shipbuilding industries, as well as the overseas trade in the coastal areas. Emperor Shengzu once pointed out: "When I was in Suzhou during the inspection tour in the south, I had talked with people from shipbuilding factories whenever I saw one and they told me that they had built more than 1,000 ships for oversea trade per year."[421] It was recorded in *Cheng Hai Xian Zhi* (*Annals of Chenghai County*) in Guangdong province that "since the banning is lifted, the sea has been peaceful ... thousands of ships loaded with goods have arrived at the coast, so everywhere oversea trade has been prosperous. Besides, the standards are set, plans are drawn up, and goods are stored up to make good bargains, so it has become a metropolis by the sea." Had such trend been maintained, capitalism would have developed rapidly. But although people were allowed to go overseas, the exportation of grains, weapons, woods, iron, gunpowder, saltpeter, and sulfur was banned, and individuals were also not allowed to build ships unless approved by the government. Meanwhile, the food that one could bring when going to sea was strictly restricted because one person was only allowed to bring one *sheng* of rice to eat and another one *sheng* in case of bad weather. If one had brought more food than was allowed by law, both the shipowner and the businessman would be punished.[422]

In the 56th year of Kangxi (1717), considering that the price of rice in the inner land rose because many people had secretly exported rice abroad, the banning was restored in force, so the sea trade in South China Sea was stopped, and it was forbidden to sell ships and to export rice to any foreign countries. If one had sold ships to foreigners, "he and the shipbuilders shall be punished by 'Zhan' (beheading) immediately"[423]; if the person had gone abroad and stayed there (about four tenths to half of the people doing business via the South China Sea did so),[424] those "who know of the transaction or have gone together with that person will be punished by

---

[420] *Guang Xu Da Qing Hui Dian* (*Collected Statutes of Great Qing in the Reign of Emperor Guangxu*), Vol. 120.
[421] *Qing Shi Zu Shi Lu* (*The Record of Emperor Shizu of Qing Dynasty*), Vol. 270.
[422] *Qing Shi Zu Shi Lu* (*The Record of Emperor Shizu of Qing Dynasty*), Vol. 271.
[423] *Qing Shi Zu Shi Lu* (*The Record of Emperor Shizu of Qing Dynasty*), Vol. 271.
[424] *Kang Xi Qi Ju Zhu* (*The Record of Emperor Kangxi's Daily Life*), Vol. 3.

wearing 'Jia Hao' (cangue: a large wooden collar worn by petty criminals as a punishment) for three months. Besides, the supervising officials shall send official documents to the relevant foreign governments to ask them to extradite the person back and to have him punished by 'Zhan' (beheading) immediately."[425] Foreign commercial ships were also under strict government supervision, which had not only severely hindered the growing overseas trade and the coastal commerce and industry at the time but also caused serious consequences. As was commented by people like Fang Bao and Lan Dingyuan: "Since oversea trade has been banned now, there are no markets for the local goods, so half of the fishermen are out of work."[426] "Before the banning of the trade with Nanyang (now Southeast Asia countries), the families in Min (Fujian) and Guang (Guangdong) areas were very wealthy ... but now transactions of general merchandise are no longer active, so their lives are so hard that those who used to be rich have become poor and those who used to be poor have become even poorer; the businessmen engaging in industry and commerce are driven like vagrants, and the vagrants are driven like robbers."[427] In the 22nd year of Qianlong (1757), Emperor Gaozong decided to close the other three customs houses except Guangzhou, to carry out overseas trade. In the meantime, an order was issued to Ke'erjishan, "Zong Du" (viceroy) of Min (Fujian) and Zhe (Zhejiang): "Regulations must be made much stricter according to the current rules of Guangdong customs so that less profit can be made from overseas trading in Zhejiang. As to the commercial ships owned by individuals, they can only harbor at Macao to prevent villains engaged in this business from colluding with each other and from conducting any illegal behaviors and and to make it easier for supervising officials to conduct examination."[428] Later, another order was issued: "From now on, the trading port is set up only in Guangdong and no overseas trade is allowed to be carried on in Zhejiang province."[429] As a result, Guangzhou became the only open port for overseas trade. As seen from the development of the history of western capitalism, it is essential for the development of capitalism to encourage foreign trade and to open up the world market. However, in the Qing Dynasty, the policy of banning overseas trade was carried out for a long time to restrict overseas trade, which not only prevented the exchange of goods home and abroad but also dealt a heavy blow to the development of capitalism.

---

[425]"Kang Xi Chao" (The Reign of Emperor Kangxi) in *Dong Hua Lu* (*The Record of Donghua*), Vol. 99.

[426]Fang Bao (Qing Dynasty), *Fang Wang Xi Xian Sheng Quan Ji* (*The Complete Works of Mr. Fang Wangxi*), Vol. 70.

[427]Lan Dingyuan (Qing Dynasty), *Lun Nan Yang Shi Yi Shu* (*A Memorial about the Affairs of Nanyang*).

[428]*Qing Gao Zong Shi Lu* (*The Record of Qing Emperor Gaozong*), Vol. 522.

[429]*Qing Gao Zong Shi Lu* (*The Record of Qing Emperor Gaozong*), Vol. 550.

11.6.3 The Legislation Ensuring Water Transportation

The law of water transportation, which was made to ensure water transportation, was a very important part of economic legislation in the Qing Dynasty. In the early years of Emperor Kangxi, the complicated and numerous articles on water transportation were edited and collected into *Cao Yun Yi Dan* (*Contracts of Water Transportation*) for the reference of relevant officials. In the 12th year of Yongzheng (1736), according to the memorial presented by Xia Zhifang, "Yu Shi" (the censor) at the time, *Cao Yun Quan Shu* (*The Pandect on Water Transportation*) was approved by the emperor for issuance, which was regarded as the greatest achievement on water transportation in the Qing Dynasty. Moreover, it was ordered that the law be amended every ten years.

In the Qing Dynasty, "Cao Yun Zong Du" (viceroy in charge of water transportation) was appointed to manage water transportation nationwide, with his office located in Huai'an. "Cao Yun Zong Du" (viceroy in charge of water transportation) was in charge of nine provinces, namely, "Zhi Li" (now Hebei province), Shandong, Henan, Anhui, Jiangsu, Jiangxi, Zhejiang, Hubei, and Hunan. Below him, some special subordinate official posts such as "Du Liang Dao" (the official in charge of grain transportation), "Guan Liang Tong Zhi" (the deputy magistrate of a prefecture in charge of grain), and "Tong Pan" (official in charge of agriculture, water conservancy, and litigation under subprefecture) were set up. "He Dao Zong Du" (viceroy in charge of rivers and channels) was especially set up to supervise the dredging of river channels, as well as the building and maintenance of river dams. This complete bureaucratic system of water transportation had shown that great attention was attached to water transportation by the government.

Every year, "Cao Liang" (the grain transported to the capital via water transportation from southeast areas) was collected from October to December. "Cao Liang" (the grain transported to the capital via water transportation from southeast areas) must be collected completely with no delay or default, and "the crime of delaying grain transportation are not to be pardoned," which had reflected its important value in maintaining the ruling of Qing Dynasty. However, no blackmail or overcharge was allowed in the collection of "Cao Liang" (the grain transported to the capital via water transportation from southeast areas); "if any foolish government staff have dared to bully the ordinary and innocent people, they shall be notified to the local officials of 'Zhou' (subprefecture) and 'Xian' (county) by 'Du Fu' (the viceroys and procurators)."[430] As to the collection of defaulted "Cao Liang" (the grain transported to the capital via water transportation from southeast areas) by "Zhou" (subprefecture) and "Xian" (county), "the people should be urged and informed by letters without being forced to, blackmailed or threatened by government staff, any

---

[430]Yang Xiba (Qing Dynasty), "Zheng Na Dui Yun" (Taxation and Water Transportation) in *Cao Yun Ze Li Zuan* (*Collections of Regulation on Water Transportation*), Vol. 8.

officials who have violated the law shall be impeached by 'Du Fu' (the viceroys and procurators)."[431]

In the Ming Dynasty, "Cao Liang" (the grain transported to the capital via water transportation from southeast areas) was collected by carriers, but this was changed in the Qing Dynasty, wherein it was "collected and exchanged by the government" to prevent fraudulent behaviors.[432] To ensure that "Cao Liang" (the grain transported to the capital via water transportation from southeast areas) was transported, the ships that were used to transport the grain were made uniformly and the time for its transportation was also strictly specified. Because it was approximately 2350 *li* from Huangpu, Shanyang County in Huai'an prefecture, to Tianjin, the time for transportation was specified according to mileage. In order to ensure that the ships could sail safely, it was forbidden for military ships and ships owned by noble families to break through the lock or to block the channel. If a ship was overturned or was on fire or the grain was destroyed on the way, "the officials along the channel or in the flooded areas shall make a careful investigation of the accident. Besides, 'Bao Jie' (guarantee of innocence) should be written by each party, 'Jie Zhuang' (certificate for the settlement of the incident) should be claimed from the officials in charge of the transportation, and memorials should be submitted to the emperor by 'Du Fu' (the viceroys and procurators) to ask for exemption."[433] Any carrier who had stolen the transported grain would be severely punished "without pardoning," and the seller would also be punished. As early as the 13th year of Shunzi (1656), it was stipulated that "if anyone has stolen and sold the grain, both the buyer and seller shall be severely punished according to the regulations on the crime of stealing 'Cao Liang' (the grain transported to the capital via water transportation from southeast areas) once caught by the government."[434] If anyone had tried to steal the grain by fraudulently reporting the shipwreck to the government, he would be punished by "Zhan" (beheading) if the amount of grain was more than six hundred *dan*; he would be punished by "Chong Jun" (to be forced to join the army) to "Bian Yuan" (outlying areas) if the amount of grain was less than that.

In order to collect and store grain, "Cang Ku Ya Men" (The Office of Warehouse) was established by the government to handle the relevant affairs of water transportation in the early years of Emperor Shunzhi. Moreover, "Zuo Liang Ting" (office in charge of affairs like land and water transportation, canals, and inspection and receiving of the grains transported to the capital) was established in the new town of Tongzhou to supervise the unloading, reception, and distribution of grains in warehouses and to check the mileage of the voyage. Besides, quota was set for grain

---

[431] Yang Xiba (Qing Dynasty), "Zheng Na Dui Yun" (Taxation and Water Transportation) in *Cao Yun Ze Li Zuan* (*Collections of Regulation on Water Transportation*), Vol. 8.

[432] "Shi Huo Lue" (Food and Commerce) in *Qing Chao Tong Zhi* (*The General Annals of Qing Dynasty*), Vol. 94.

[433] Yang Xiba (Qing Dynasty), "Feng Huo Gua Qian" (Emergency Purchasing on Credit) in *Cao Yun Ze Li Zuan* (*Collections of Regulation on Water Transportation*), Vol. 14.

[434] Yang Xiba (Qing Dynasty), "Tong Cao Jin Ling" (Prohibition of Water Transportation) in *Cao Yun Ze Li Zuan* (*Collections of Regulation on Water Transportation*), Vol. 16.

reception in each warehouse in the capital and Tianjin. In the 13th year of Shunzhi (1648), it was stipulated that "the drying, winnowing, and storing of grain should be completed within ten days from the day when the red receipt (receipt of taxation) was received. If it is not completed on time, or if those involved have blackmailed or deliberately made things difficult for others, the relevant warehouse officials and staff shall be investigated, with their illegal actions ascertained and impeached by the supervising officials."[435] Since "Cao Liang" (the grain transported to the capital via water transportation from southeast areas) was very important to the country, if anyone had stolen the grain stored, whether warehouse officials and staff or ordinary people, they would all be severely punished according to law. "If the amount of grain which one has stolen is worth more than three hundred *liang*, the principal will be punished by 'Zhan' (beheading), while the accessories will be punished by 'Jiao Jian Hou' (the punishment of suspending hanging) and be executed after autumn; if the amount grain which one has stolen is less than three hundred *liang*, the principal will be punished by 'Jiao Jian Hou' (the punishment of suspending hanging) and be executed after autumn, while the accessories will be punished by wearing 'Jia Hao' (cangue: a large wooden collar worn by petty criminals as a punishment) for three months at the gate of the warehouse."[436]

To conclude, the economic laws of the Qing Dynasty were rich in content. A feudal economic legal system was basically formed, and it played an important role in economic recovery and development in early Qing Dynasty and the maintenance of the one hundred years of prosperity during the reign of emperors Kangxi and Qianlong.

11.7 The More Complete Judicial System

Since Qing Dynasty was the last dynasty of feudal ruling, its judicial system, including the judicial structure, litigation procedure, trial system and prison management system, has reached a very advanced level.

11.7.1 Reform of the Judicial System

Due to the change of local administrative system and the expansion of jurisdiction in areas inhabited by ethnic minority groups, a complete judicial system was formed from central to local government.

---

[435] Yang Xiba (Qing Dynasty), "Jing Tong Liang Chu" (The Grain Storage in Jingtong) in *Cao Yun Ze Li Zuan* (*Collections of Regulation on Water Transportation*), Vol. 20.

[436] Yang Xiba (Qing Dynasty), "Jing Tong Liang Chu" (The Grain Storage in Jingtong) in *Cao Yun Ze Li Zuan* (*Collections of Regulation on Water Transportation*), Vol. 20.

The supreme judicial organization was "San Fa Si" (Three Judicial Departments), consisting of "Xing Bu" (The Department of Punishment), "Da Li Si" (The Bureau of Judicial Review), and "Du Cha Yuan" (The Court of Censors); among the three "Xing Bu" (The Department of Punishment), played the leading role in judicial trials. According to *Da Qing Hui Dian* (*The Collected Statutes of Great Qing*), "Xing Bu" (The Department of Punishment) "is in charge of carrying out the administrative orders of the criminal punishment and assisting the Emperor in governing the people nationwide. So, the appropriate application of laws and precedents, the fair settlement of cases, the proper enforcement of judgments and the recovering of illegally obtained money shall all be reported to and discussed by the officials in 'Xing Bu' (The Department of Punishment) headed by 'Shang Shu' (the minister) and 'Shi Lang' (vice minister), with the important issues submitted to the Emperor and the minor ones directly handled by themselves in order to is strictly carry out the fundamental laws of the state."[437] Specifically speaking, "Xing Bu" (The Department of Punishment) was responsible for reviewing serious cases reported by the local places and submitting memorials to the emperor; for hearing "field-trial cases" in the capital that were more serious than those punishable by "Chi" (flogging with light sticks) and "Zhang" (flogging with heavy sticks); for dealing with the appeals from the local places and the affairs of "Qiu Shen" (Autumn Assizes); for presiding in judicial administration; for revising laws and regulations; and for hearing illegal cases of court officials and "special cases involving each 'Ya Men' (the government offices)" assigned by the emperor. That was why it was called "the most powerful department."[438] However, it only had the power to settle cases that were punishable by "Liu" (exile), so its power was balanced by "Da Li Si" (The Bureau of Judicial Review) and "Du Cha Yuan" (The Court of Censors). For example, the judgment made by "Xing Bu" (The Department of Punishment) should be reviewed by "Da Li Si" (The Bureau of Judicial Review) and supervised by "Du Cha Yuan" (The Court of Censors). If the judgment was inappropriate, it could be overruled by "Da Li Si" (The Bureau of Judicial Review) and be reheard; if the judgment was mishandled, "Du Cha Yuan" (The Court of Censors) had the right to start the impeachment proceedings. So the cases that were accepted by "Xing Bu" (The Department of Punishment), whether settled or not, should all be reported to the emperor every month, while the settled cases that involved the penalty of "Tu" (imprisonment), "Liu" (exile), or "Chong Jun" (being forced to join the army) should all "be summarized in every season" or "be reported specifically to the Emperor,"[439] which in fact was a very important method of supervision.

"Xing Bu" (The Department of Punishment) was in charge of judicial affairs and criminal punishment nationwide, and its affiliated agencies included "Qing Li Si"

---

[437] *Da Qing Hui Dian* (*The Collected Statutes of Great Qing*), Vol. 35.

[438] "Xing Fa Zhi" (The Record of the Criminal Law) in *Qing Shi Gao* (*The Draft of the History of Qing Dynasty*), Vol. 3.

[439] "Xing Fa Zhi" (The Record of the Criminal Law) in *Qing Shi Gao* (*The Draft of the History of Qing Dynasty*), Vol. 3.

11.7 The More Complete Judicial System

(office) in the seventeen provinces; "Du Bu Si" (Bureau of Arresting), which was responsible for searching for "Tao Ren" (the escapee); "Qiu Shen Chu" (Office of Autumn Assizes), which was responsible for "Qiu Shen" (Autumn Assizes) and "Lv Li Guan" (an official institution established in the second year of Shunzhi period), which was responsible for law revision. "Qing Li Si" (office) in each province was specifically responsible for the management of criminal cases, files, and notes, which were reported to "Xing Bu" (The Department of Punishment) to "check up the evidence to review the settlements according to the laws and regulations." It was also responsible for putting forward opinions of approval or disapproval to be reported to "Shang Shu" (the minister) and "Shi Lang" (vice minister) for final decision.[440]

"Da Li Si" (The Bureau of Judicial Review) was "in charge of criminal law. So it is not only responsible for discussing and reviewing the severe punishments such as death penalty with its affiliated agencies, but also responsible for discussing the important state affairs together with 'Jiu Qing' (nine high-rank officials in ancient times). At the same time, it is also responsible for 'Qiu Shen' (Autumn Assizes) and 'Chao Shen' (trials held in imperial court)."[441] Moreover, "Da Li Si" (The Bureau of Judicial Review) was mainly responsible for reviewing cases of death penalty and rectifying miscarriage of justice. It had the right to overrule judgments made by "Xing Bu" (The Department of Punishment) if there were misconducts in the application of law and the calculation of punishment. Moreover, it had the right to preside over the trials of "Re Shen" (Summer Assizes).

"Du Cha Yuan" (The Court of Censors) "is not only responsible for disciplining the behaviors of the officials, supervising the officials of the government offices, and evaluating the gains and losses of their governance and the advantages and disadvantages of their performance, but also responsible for urging its affiliated officials to fully perform their duties and maintaining the disciplines of officials and the order of the state. Meanwhile ... it is also responsible for discussing the serious cases together with 'Xing Bu' (The Department of Punishment) and 'Da Li Si' (The Bureau of Judicial Review), ... and responsible for participating in 'Qiu Shen'(Autumn Assizes) and 'Chao Shen' (trials held in imperial court)."[442] The fifteen affiliated "Dao" (the administration district below the province) under the supervision of "Du Cha Yuan" (The Court of Censors) were responsible for the judicial affairs in different provinces. "Ji Shi Zhong" (the senior assistant of the emperor and the supervisor of officials) in "Xing Ke" (the department of punishment) was also "responsible for reviewing the criminal cases." In addition, "it is responsible for handling the unjust cases which were rejected by other government offices or the cases which were mishandled by the local officials. The important cases would be reported to the Emperor and the minor ones should be rehabilitated at once."[443]

---

[440] *Da Qing Hui Dian* (*The Collected Statutes of Great Qing*), Vol. 57.

[441] *Da Qing Hui Dian* (*The Collected Statutes of Great Qing*), Vol. 69.

[442] *Da Qing Hui Dian* (*The Collected Statutes of Great Qing*), Vol. 69.

[443] *Da Qing Hui Dian* (*The Collected Statutes of Great Qing*), Vol. 81.

"Wu Cheng Cha Yuan" (local agency of public security in five districts of the capital city) was responsible for lawsuits in the five districts of the capital area. It had the right to settle cases that were punishable by a penalty lighter than "Zhang" (flogging with heavy sticks), while cases that were punishable by a penalty severer than "Tu" (imprisonment) should be reported to "Xing Bu" (The Department of Punishment) for final decision.

For the local judicial organs, the lowest level was "Xian" (county) ("Ting" (a government department at the provincial level) or "Zhou" (subprefecture)), which had the power to settle cases punishable by "Chi" (flogging with light sticks), "Zhang" (flogging with heavy sticks), and "Tu" (imprisonment). Nevertheless, for cases that were punishable by "Liu" (exile) or cases that were punishable by a penalty severer than "Liu" (exile), they must be reported to superior officials. In *Qin Ding Tai Gui* (*The Regulations Made by the Imperial Order*), an imperial order that was issued in the 8th year of Shunzhi (1651) was cited:

> From now on, anyone who wants to file lawsuits must lodge the complaints to "Ya Men" (the government offices) of "Si" (bureau), "Dao" (the administration district below the province), "Fu" (ancient administrative district between province and county), "Zhou" (subprefecture) and "Xian" (county) first, and only when the complaint is denied is one allowed to file the law suits to "Zong Du" (viceroy), "Xun Fu" (procurators) and the supervising officials.

According to *Da Qing Lv Li* (*The Laws and Precedents of Great Qing*), "any civilian or military personnel who wants to lodge a complaint shall first do so to the county government. If the judgment is unfair, one can state the truth to the supervising officials of higher levels; only when the complaint is handled unfairly by the higher officials is one allowed to lodge the complaint to the capital."[444] If one directly went to the capital without the permission of the relevant officials, even if his case was true, he would be punished by "Chi" (flogging with light sticks) for fifty strokes, or he and the one who had drafted the complaint for him would be punished according to the "Li" (precedent) on ruffians. As to cases of appeal, it was stipulated that "the cases will all be directly denied and will not be accepted for retrial unless the facts are proved to be consistent with original cases, or it is irrelevant to the punishment except for some minor changes of the wording of the judgment."[445] Therefore, it can be seen that appeals were usually just formalities. "The cases about the disputes over land, marriage or fighting" that occurred in "Xian" (county) were all handled by judicial institutes at the county level, so they were called "Zi Li An Jian" (self-heard cases). For the cases of murder and stealing, after primary trial at county level, they should be regularly reported to and reviewed by the offices of higher levels with the criminals escorted by prison staff.

---

[444]"Yue Su" (Overstepping Indictment) in "Su Song" (Litigation) in "Xing Lv" (The Penal Code) in *Da Qing Lv Li* (*The Laws and Precedents of Great Qing*), Vol. 30.

[445]*Dao Guang Yuan Nian Xu Zuan Tiao Li* (*The Laws and Regulations Amended in the First Year of Daoguang*).

"Fu" (ancient administrative district between province and county) was the second-level judicial organ, which was not only in charge of reviewing criminal cases reported by officials of county level but also in charge of putting forward opinions of punishment and submitting them to officials of provincial level. Xue Yunsheng once pointed out that "all the cases and criminals of 'Zhou' (subprefecture) and 'Xian' (county) are later transferred to 'Fu' (ancient administrative district between province and county) and then to 'An Cha Si' (The Judicial Commission), while all the cases and criminals in 'Zhi Li' (now Hebei province) area are transferred to 'Dao' (the administration district below the province) and then to 'An Cha Si' (The Judicial Commission), which is a conventional practice although without stipulated in criminal law."[446]

"An Cha Si" (The Judicial Commission) in the province was the third-level judicial organ, which was responsible for reviewing cases reported by "Fu" (ancient administrative district between province and county) and trying cases punishable by "Chong Jun" (being forced to join the army), "Liu" (exile), and "Si" (death penalty). If "the confession are consistent with the judgment," the case should be reported to "Du Fu" (the viceroys and procurators); however, if the case was misjudged, it might be overruled, reheard, or be assigned to be heard by officials in other "Zhou" (subprefecture) and "Xian" (county). As was described by Emperor Yongzheng: "I know that the settlement of the cases affects people's life and death, so 'An Cha Si' (The Judicial Commission) is established and is entrusted with very great tasks because it has the right to handle all the cases of 'Zhou' (subprefecture) and 'Xian' (county) and the affairs reported by 'Du Fu' (the viceroys and procurators)."

"Zong Du" (viceroy) and "Xun Fu" (procurators) were the fourth-level judicial organs, and they had the right to give official replies to cases punishable by "Tu" (imprisonment) and to review cases punishable by "Liu" (exile); if they had no objection, these cases would be reported to "Xing Bu" (The Department of Punishment). They also had the right to review cases of death penalty, to present memorials to the emperor, and to send copies of the documents to "San Fa Si" (Three Judicial Departments).

Since the 5th year of Yongzheng (1727), "Xun Dao" (local official from judicial commission) also had the right to hear civil cases within his jurisdiction.

As can be seen from above, the higher-level judicial organs had the right to handle cases on appeal and to review judgments made by lower-level ones. The officials of "An Cha Si" (The Judicial Commission) and "Du Fu" (the viceroys and procurators) in each province had the right to convict local officials who had committed crimes, but "Du Fu" (the viceroys and procurators) only had the right to handle cases punishable by "Tu" (imprisonment) or those that were less serious than "Tu" (imprisonment). As to criminal cases that were punishable by "Liu" (exile) or those that were much severer than "Liu" (exile), "Du Fu" (the viceroys and procurators) only had the right to put forward their opinions and then to report them to the emperor for final decision. So it was the emperor who had the real power to decide

---

[446]Xue Yunsheng (Qing Dynasty), *Du Li Cun Yi (Questions in Reading the Precedents)*.

cases of death penalty, to make judgments of special or serious cases, and to supervise all judicial activities, which had reduced "San Fa Si Hui Shen" (joint hearing by three judicial departments in ancient times) and "Jiu Qing Hui Shen" (joint hearing by nine high-rank officials in ancient times) to mere formalities. The centralization of judicial power in the Qing Dynasty had surpassed that of all previous dynasties. Besides, because the judicial organs of each level did not have independent power, it had often led to many malpractices. For example, "it is impossible for some judicial organs in charge of the cases to make decisions, and it is also impossible for some judicial organs in charge of hearing the cases to make the judgments"; "some of the lawsuits filed are not dealt with seriously, some of the cases are not carefully heard, some of the documents are not replied, and some of the inquisition is not ascertained"[447]; "some cases are settled according to the instructions of the judicial organs of higher levels rather than facts, and some of cases are delayed to be settled without following the law."[448] As to the review conducted by judicial organs of different levels, sometimes the organs of lower levels were only responsible for those of higher levels rather than for the parties involved.

In the area of "Jing Shi" (the capital city), apart from "Wu Cheng Cha Yuan" (local agency of public security in five districts of the capital city), which was in charge of the cases of "Hu Hun" (marriage, tax, and household registration), "Tian Tu" (land), "Qian Zhai" (debts), and "Dou Ou" (fighting) in the area, special officials were also appointed in "Bu Jun Tong Ya Men" (The Office of Land Force Commanders), which was responsible for maintaining the security of the capital. These special officials were responsible for settling cases that were punishable by "Zhang" (flogging with heavy sticks) or less serious cases, but cases that were punishable by "Tu" (imprisonment) or severer cases would be reported to "Xing Bu" (The Department of Punishment) for final decision. They were also responsible for handling the lawsuits of "Di Mu" (land) that were filed by "Qi Ren" (members of the Manchu ethnic group).

Since the Qing Dynasty was a regime that was mainly made up of the Manchu nationality, special agencies were set up to be in charge of handling cases involving "Qi Ren" (members of the Manchu ethnic group) in the judicial administrative system. For example, "Nei Wu Fu" (Board of the Imperial Household) had the jurisdiction over lawsuits concerning the Manchu people, so they were specifically in the charge of "Shen Xing Si" (Office of Criminal Affairs); nevertheless, if the punishment was severer than "Tu" (imprisonment), the cases would be transferred to "Xing Bu" (The Department of Punishment). Sometimes it was also in charge of handing cases assigned by the emperor. For cases involving the Manchu people in other provinces, they were handled by "Man Zhou Jiang Jun" (the Manchu general) and "Fu Du Tong" (ancient military officer or deputy commander-in-chief), but if the

---

[447]"Nei Zheng Zhi Guan" (The Officials of Domestic Affairs) in *Zhu Pi Zou Zhe* (*Memorials Approved by the Emperor*), No. 419.

[448]"Nei Zheng Zhi Guan" (The Officials of Domestic Affairs) in *Zhu Pi Zou Zhe* (*Memorials Approved by the Emperor*), No. 419.

punishment was severer than "Liu" (exile), they must be reported to the central government. Lawsuits involving the Manchu people in Shengjing (now Shenyang) district were jointly judged by "Sheng Jing Jiang Jun" (the senior military and civil official in charge of "Feng Tian": now Shenyang) and "Fu Yin" (the chief official of prefecture) of each department. For civil cases and cases of "Di Mu" (land) involving "Ba Qi" (the Eight Banners: banner, a division of the Manchu nationality and the emperor's clan), if the parties thought that the judgment made by "Ba Qi Du Tong Ya Men" (The Office of Commanders-in-Chief of the "Eight Banners"), "Zuo Ling" (local administrator of the basic unit of organization in Eight Banners in the Qing Dynasty), or the officials of "Zhou" (subprefecture) and "Xian" (county) were unfair, they could appeal to "Hu Bu" (The Department of Revenue) for the case to be retried by "Xian Shen Chu" (the subsidiary organ of the department of revenue) of "Hu Bu" (The Department of Revenue). If inquisition needed to be conducted, it must be done together with "Xing Bu" (The Department of Punishment). For serious cases involving "Qi Ren" (members of the Manchu ethnic group) such as murder or stealing, they should be jointly judged by "Li Shi Ting" (the office in charge of mediating the relations between garrison and local places) and the officials of "Zhou" (subprefecture) and "Xian" (county) because the officials of "Zhou" (subprefecture) and "Xian" (county) had no right to settle the cases of "Qi Ren" (members of the Manchu ethnic group). Therefore, judicial organs were especially established to handle cases involving "Qi Ren" (members of the Manchu ethnic group), which was the product of the ethnic policy of the Qing government. Besides, lawsuits involving the nobility and "Zong Shi" (royal families) were all decided by "Zong Ren Fu" (The Imperial Clan Court).

During the ruling of the Qing Dynasty, its judicial jurisdiction within the areas where the ethnic minority groups lived was so broad that it was incomparable to the other dynasties. According to "Hua Wai Ren You Fan" (the invasion by foreigners) in *Da Qing Lv Li (The Laws and Precedents of Great Qing)*, the laws of the Qing dynasty should be applied to all minority groups within the borders of the state to show unity of state laws. However, for the tribes in inner and outer Mongolia and Qinghai and the areas of Tibet, Miao and "Huijiang" (south of Tianshan Mountain) which were subject to the jurisdiction of "Li Fan Yuan" (The Bureau of National Minority Affairs), regulations were especially made according to concrete situations and customs due to the special tradition in these specific areas.

"Li Fan Yuan" (The Bureau of National Minority Affairs) was not only the supreme administrative organ in charge of Mongolian, Tibetan, and Hui areas where the minority groups lived but also the level of trial for the appeals from inner and outer Mongolia, Qinghai, and "Huijiang" (south of Tianshan Mountain). It was provided in *Da Qing Hui Dian (The Collected Statutes of Great Qing)* that "Li Fan Yuan" (The Bureau of National Minority Affairs) "is in charge of handling the executive affairs of the minority groups, deciding the salaries of local officials, organizing 'Chao Hui' (Imperial Court Convention) regularly and rectifying the criminal punishment. Besides, different issues are discussed and decided by the affiliated officials headed by 'Shang Shu' (the minister) and 'Shi Lang' (vice minister), with the important issues reported to the high level officials and the minor ones carried out by themselves to show the power and virtue of the state." In "Li Fan Yuan" (The Bureau of National Minority Affairs), "Li Xing Si" (The Bureau of Criminal Punishment) was especially set up to handle the cases of minority groups. If the crime was punishable by "Fa Qian" (sending criminals to frontiers to serve in the military units or become laborers), it must be handled jointly with "Xing Bu" (The Department of Punishment); however, if the crime was punishable by death penalty, it must be jointly decided by "San Fa Si" (Three Judicial Departments).

The civil disputes and minor criminal cases in inner and outer Mongolia, Qinghai, and Elute Mongolia of the Xinjiang area were all decided by "Za Sa Ke" (the head of Eight Banners) and the head of "Qi" (banner, equivalent of a county) or clan. But if a case was mishandled, "it could be appealed to 'Li Fan Yua' (The Bureau of National Minority Affairs) by the parties involved."[449] Apart from handling the cases on its own, "Li Fan Yuan" (The Bureau of National Minority Affairs) also had the right to assign officials to hear a case together with "Za Sa Ke" (the head of Eight Banners), but if there was no "Za Sa Ke" (head of Eight Banners), the cases should be handled by the garrison generals, "Du Tong" (ancient military officer or commander-in-chief), or the relevant officials at the nearest local office. If the cases were serious, they should be reported to and be checked by "Li Fan Yuan" (The Bureau of National Minority Affairs).

For legal disputes among the Han people and Mongolians, they should be settled by the local officials together with the officials assigned by "Za Sa Ke" (the head of Eight Banners) and "Li Fan Yuan" (The Bureau of National Minority Affairs). Any Mongolians who had committed crimes in inland areas would be punished according to criminal law, while any Han people who had committed crimes in Mongolian areas would be punished according to the laws of Mongolia. For robbery cases that occurred in the Mongolian area, if all the defendants were Mongolians, they should be decided in accordance with the laws of Mongolia; if all the defendants were Han people, then they should be decided in accordance with criminal law. If people from both groups were involved in robbery, the charges should be checked; if punishment in Mongolian law was severer than that in criminal law, Mongolian law should be applied; if punishment in criminal law was severer than that of Mongolian law, criminal law should be applied.

Lawsuits among the Miao people in Miaojiang (the southwest regions of China) were settled according to the regulations of the Miao nationality. After "Gai Tu Gui Liu" (having the hereditary system changed to be administered by government officials), criminal cases and lawsuits between the Miao and Han people were all settled, reviewed, and checked by the senior officials of different levels according to *Da Qing Lv Li* (*The Laws and Precedents of Great Qing*). Then they were reviewed by different levels and finally reported to "Xing Bu" (The Department of Punishment) and "San Fa Si" (Three Judicial Departments).

---

[449]*Da Qing Hui Dian* (*The Collected Statutes of Great Qing*), Vol. 68.

11.7 The More Complete Judicial System

After the Tibetan affairs were jointly managed by Lama and "Zhu Zang Da Chen" (the minister sent to Tibet by the central government), a special regulation was made on judicial judgment: "The lawsuits between the people of 'Tang Gu Te' (tanggute, or the local Tibetans) in Tibet shall be settled separately. The relevant amount shall be recorded in booklets and reported to and filed by 'Zhu Zang Da Chen' (the minister sent to Tibet by the central government). For the punishment of criminal cases, it shall be collected and reported to 'Zhu Zang Da Chen' (the minister sent to Tibet by the central government) for final decision. As to the cases involving the confiscation of family property, except that those which involves a large amount of bribes shall be reported to and decided by 'Zhu Zang Da Chen' (the minister sent to Tibet by the central government), all others shall be settled in accordance with law and it was strictly forbidden to confiscate one's family property illegally."[450]

The judicial affairs in Xinjiang were jointly handled by the garrison generals and "Can Zan Da Chen" (counselor).

To conclude, "Li Fan Yuan" (The Bureau of National Minority Affairs) was a special organ in charge of "the administrative and judicial affairs of vassal states and the enforcement of punishment." It was also in charge of reviewing death penalty cases of the minority groups and accepting appeals for trials. Therefore, its establishment had not only reinforced its jurisdiction in the areas where the minority groups lived but also maintained the unified implementation of law and administrative order and consolidated a nation of multinationalities. Also, it should be pointed out that during the reign of Emperor Shunzhi, in view of the fact that "eunuchs had brought about great harm to the regime in Ming Dynasty because of their interfering with the state affairs," the malpractice of interference of the judiciary by "Dong Chang Xi Chang" (the imperial spy agencies), "Jin Yi Wei" (secret service of the Ming Dynasty), and "Zhen Fu Si" (organization of secret police to suppress the people with torture) and the abuse of "Ting Zhang" (being flogged in imperial court) were finally abolished. Therefore, no interference of judicial affairs by eunuchs occurred in the Qing Dynasty.

11.7.2 The More Specific Criminal and Civil Litigation

11.7.2.1 Criminal Litigation

Generally speaking, the criminal procedure of *Tang Lv* (*Tang Code*) was followed in the Qing Dynasty, so most of the criminal lawsuits were filed by the victims themselves with complaints lodged to the local officials of "Zhou" (subprefecture) and "Xian" (county). The lawsuits mainly included private prosecution, "Yue Su"

---

[450]"Xi Zang Tong Zhi" (A General System for Tibet) in *Li Fan Yuan Ze Li* (*The Regulation for the Bureau of National Minority Affairs*), Vol. 61.

(overstepping indictment), direct appeal, and procuratorial appeal by the relatives of the victims. The elderly and "Du Ji" (the incapacitated) were not allowed to lodge complaints to the government by themselves except for cases of "Mou Fan" (plotting rebellion or plotting to endanger the country), "Pan Ni" (treachery), and "Zi Sun Bu Xiao" (offspring being unfilial). However, if the victim was unable to lodge a complaint by himself due to illness, bodily injury, or other serious accidents, he could let the relatives who lived together with him or his neighbors to lodge a complaint for him. However, if the complaint was false, the person who lodged the complaint for him would also be punished. Generally, "Yue Su" (overstepping indictment) was prohibited.

All the complaints lodged to the government should be filed in the form of document, such as "Cheng Ci" (the diction of complaint), "Zhuang Ci" (the diction of complaint), and "Bing Ci" (the diction of the statement to emperor). It was required that the complaint be written in one hundred and forty four words, and as far as the content is concerned, it should include the time of the incident, the summary of the case, the name and address of the defendant, the names of the plaintiff and procurator, and the signature of the plaintiff. It was allowed for the plaintiff to ask "Shu Li" (scribes) to write the complaint for him, but if people had colluded with each other and practiced fraud, they would be severely punished. It was strictly forbidden for "Song Gun" (those who make money by instigating others to file lawsuits or mean lawyers) to practice champerty. Even if "Sheng Yuan" (also called "Xiu Cai": those who passed the imperial examination at the county level in ancient China) had filed the lawsuit on behalf of others, he would be deprived of his titles and be punished according to law.

If a case occurred within the same "Zhou" (subprefecture) and "Xian" (county), the jurisdiction principle of "Yuan Gao Jiu Bei Gao" (the case shall be under the jurisdiction of the court in the place where the defendant lives) should be followed; if a case occurred within different "Zhou" (subprefecture) and "Xian" (county), the principle of "Qing Qiu Jiu Zhong Qiu" (the case shall be under the jurisdiction of the court in the place where the prisoners have committed much severer crimes), "Shao Qiu Jiu Duo Qiu" (the case shall be under the jurisdiction of the court in the place where there are more prisoners), and "Hou Fa Jiu Xian Fa" (the case shall be under the jurisdiction of the court in the place where the first complaint is filed) should be followed accordingly.

It was forbidden for the lawsuits that were filed in the judicial organs by the prosecutors to be settled privately, so that if anyone had done so, he would be punished; if anyone had intentionally lodged a false accusation, he would also be punished.

Apart from prosecution, there were other ways to make an accusation, including impeaching, self-impeaching, and reporting the case to the government. Impeaching refers to impeachment of a guilty official by supervising officials or by his superiors; self-impeaching refers to the impeachment made by the official himself who had committed the crime of misconduct, and reporting the case to the government refers to the obligation of the ordinary people to inform about the commission of certain crimes according to law.

11.7 The More Complete Judicial System

In criminal lawsuits, if the privileged people of "Ba Yi" (The Eight Deliberations) and the relatives thereof were involved in lawsuits, it was forbidden to arrest or interrogate them without submitting memorials to or obtaining the consent of the emperor in the first place. For officials who had committed public or private crimes in or out of the capital, they should first be reported to the emperor before being interrogated by any superior officials or judicial organs. The unfair status of "Liang Min" (decent people) and "Jian Min" (rabbles or people of lower social status) in lawsuits was also provided in detail. For example, if "Nu Bi" (slave girls and maidservants) had accused the master or a junior accused the senior in a family, they would be punished for the crime of "Gan Ming Fan Yi" (violating the feudal ethics). Even if one had accused the relatives above "Si Ma" (the person wearing the mourning apparel of soft sackcloth in the fifth mourning degree), he would be punished by "Zhang" (flogging with heavy sticks) for one hundred strokes and "Tu" (imprisonment) for three years; if the accusation was fraudulent, he would be punished by "Jiao" (hanging). According to the laws of the Qing Dynasty, the scope of "Qin Shu Xiang Rong Yin" (concealment of crimes among relatives or refusing to testify among relatives in court) was expanded to include "Nu Bi" (slave girls and maidservants) and the hired laborers. So if "Nu Bi" (slave girls and maidservants) and the hired laborers had committed crimes other than the crimes of "Mou Fan" (plotting rebellion or plotting to endanger the country), "Mou Da Ni" (great sedition), and "Mou Pan" (treason), the head of family had the obligation to conceal their crimes without reporting to the government; otherwise, they would be punished. It was also stated that if one's master's relatives committed an ordinary crime, the master had the obligation to conceal the crime without reporting it to the government.

11.7.2.2 Civil Litigation

In the Qing Dynasty, civil legal relationship became more complicated, so civil disputes increased greatly, which contributed to the development of a civil litigation and trial system. Consequently, civil litigation was gradually separated from criminal litigation and became independent. In the existing case files of the Qing Dynasty, there were not only a large number of civil cases, but the procedure was also more standardized. The civil cases were heard and decided by the judicial organs at "Zhou" (subprefecture) and "Xian" (county) without needing to be reviewed by the different levels of government, so they were called "Zi Li An Jian" (self-heard cases). Civil litigation was divided into different jurisdictions based on the different subjects and objects of civil procedure. For ordinary civil cases, they were heard by the local "Ya Men" (the government offices) of "Zhou" (subprefecture) and "Xian" (county) where the case occurred. According to the supplementary regulation of "Yue Su" (overstepping indictment) in "Su Song" (Litigation) in "Xing Lv" (The Penal Code) in *Da Qing Lv Li* (*The Laws and Precedents of Great Qing*), "for the disputes over 'Hu Hun' (marriage), 'Tian Tu' (land), 'Qian Zhai' (debts), 'Dou Ou' (fighting), 'Du Bo' (gambling) and other minor disputes, one shall file the lawsuit to the local government of 'Zhou' (subprefecture) and 'Xian' (county) where the dispute arises and it is forbidden to file the lawsuit in the place where the plaintiff lives," which was very different from the principle of "Yuan Gao Jiu Bei Gao" (the case shall be under the jurisdiction of the court in the place where the defendant lives). For civil cases that occurred in different "Zhou" (subprefecture) and "Xian" (county), "they shall be heard and settled in the place where the plaintiff has lodged the complaint."[451]

A special jurisprudence system was set up to handle lawsuits on inheritance, genealogy of families, and marriage among "Zong Shi Jue Luo" (royal families and the emperor's near relatives) and noble families. It was stipulated in *Da Qing Hui Dian* (*The Collected Statutes of Great Qing*) that "for the lawsuits of 'Hu Hun' (marriage) and 'Tian Tu' (land) filed by 'Zong Shi' (royal families), they should be heard by 'Fu' (ancient administrative district between province and county) and 'Hu Bu' (The Department of Revenue); for the lawsuits filed by 'Jue Luo' (the emperor's near relatives), they should be heard by 'Hu Bu' (The Department of Revenue) and 'Fu' (ancient administrative district between province and county); for the cases of murder or fighting, if they are committed by those of 'Zong Shi' (royal families), they should be heard by 'Fu' (ancient administrative district between province and county) and 'Xing Bu' (The Department of Punishment), but if they are committed by those of 'Jue Luo' (the emperor's near relatives), they should be handled by 'Xing Bu' (The Department of Punishment) and 'Fu' (ancient administrative district between province and county)."[452] *Qin Ding Zong Ren Fu Ze Li* (*The Regulation of the Imperial Clan Court Made by Imperial Order*) served as one of the legal bases for the settlement of various disputes among the royal family.

In addition, a special jurisprudence system was set up to handle civil disputes among "Qi Ren" (members of the Manchu ethnic group). According to "Tong Ze" (The General Regulation) (Part 4) in *Hu Bu Ze Li* (*The Regulation of the Department of Revenue*), "for the cases of 'Di Mu' (land) among 'Ba Qi' (the Eight Banners: banner, a division of Manchu nationality and the emperor's clan) in the capital, the plaintiff shall file the lawsuits to his own 'Qi' (banner, equivalent of a county) or 'Bu Jun Tong Ya Men' (The Office of Land Force Commanders)." So it was forbidden for the lawsuits to be filed in "Zhou" (subprefecture) and "Xian" (county) or "Li Shi Ting" (the office in charge of mediating the relations between garrison and local places); otherwise, the plaintiff and the local and supervising officials thereof shall all be punished. "For the cases of 'Di Mu' (land) which involved Manchu garrison soldiers, they can be reported to the nearest government office of 'Jiang Jun' (the general) or 'Du Tong' (ancient military officer, or commander-in-chief), but it is not allowed for them to be reported to the local government."

For disputes over "Hu Kou" (registered permanent residence), land, and real estate between "Qi Ren" (members of the Manchu ethnic group) and the Han people,

---

[451]"Gao Zuang Bu Shou Li" (No Accepting the Complaint) in "Su Song" (Litigation) in "Xing Lv" (The Penal Code) in *Da Qing Lv Li* (*The Laws and Precedents of Great Qing*), Vol. 30.

[452]*Da Qing Hui Dian* (*The Collected Statutes of Great Qing*), Vol. 1.

11.7 The More Complete Judicial System

"'Qi Ren' (members of the Manchu ethnic group) shall file the lawsuit in his own 'Qi' (banner, equivalent of a county) and Han people shall file the lawsuit to the local government. If the case is mishandled or unfairly tried but if it is rejected by the official, it is allowed for one to lodge the complaint to 'Hu Bu' (The Department of Revenue); if it is indeed necessary to report to 'Hu Bu' (The Department of Revenue), or if it is proved that both the confession and evidence are true, the official should give a detailed report of the doubtful part of the case to 'Hu Bu' (The Department of Revenue)."[453] So "Xian Shen Chu" (the subsidiary organ of the department of revenue) was specially set up by "Hu Bu" (The Department of Revenue) to "hear the lawsuits involving 'Qi Ren' (members of the Manchu ethnic group) and Han people."[454] For local civil lawsuits between "Qi Ren" (members of the Manchu ethnic group) and the Han people, "they shall be settled by 'Zhou' (subprefecture) and 'Xian' (county)." For example, "if the Han people are guilty, he will be punished according to law; if 'Qi Ren' (members of the Manchu ethnic group) are guilty, they will be punished by wearing 'Jia Hao' (cangue: a large wooden collar worn by petty criminals as a punishment) after their confessions are recorded. As to the important criminals, they shall be convicted by 'Li Shi Ting' (the office in charge of mediating the relations between garrison and local places)."[455]

For civil lawsuits between soldiers, "they are to be handled by the supervising military offices."[456]

For civil lawsuits between civilians and soldiers, they should be jointly tried by the supervising military officers and the officials of "Zhou" (subprefecture) and "Xian" (county), which was called "Jun Min Yue Hui Ci Song" (joint trial by military and civil personnel). "If a military officer has heard cases involving civilians and soldiers without the permission of the officials of 'Zhou' (subprefecture) and 'Xian' (county)," he would punished by "Zhang" (flogging with heavy sticks) for fifty strokes for violating the system. Moreover, "the lawsuits of 'Hu Hun' (marriage), 'Tian Tu' (land), 'Dou Ou' (fighting) and 'Ren Ming' (homicide) which have involved soldiers and civilians outside the capital shall be filed to the relevant 'Ya Men' (the government offices), but it is forbidden for other guards and 'You Si' (official) who are not in charge of the official seal to deal with the cases."[457]

For civil lawsuits among the minority groups, the regulations therefor were quite simple because their economy and civil legal relations were not well developed. Taking the Mongolian nationality as an example, although Mongolia had the vastest

---

[453] *Da Qing Hui Dian* (*The Collected Statutes of Great Qing*), Vol. 24.
[454] *Da Qing Hui Dian* (*The Collected Statutes of Great Qing*), Vol. 24.
[455] "Tong Ze" (The General Regulation) (Part 4) in *Hu Bu Ze Li* (*The Regulation of the Department of Revenue*).
[456] "Jun Min Yue Hui Ci Song" (Joint Trials by the Military and Civil Personnel) in "Su Song" (Litigation) in "Xing Lv" (The Penal Code) in *Da Qing Lv Li* (*The Laws and Precedents of Great Qing*), Vol. 30.
[457] "Jun Min Yue Hui Ci Song" (Joint Trials by the Military and Civil Personnel) in "Su Song" (Litigation) in "Xing Lv" (The Penal Code) in *Da Qing Lv Li* (The Laws and Precedents of Great Qing), Vol. 30.

land, the largest population, and a relatively well-developed economy among all minority groups, there was only a general rule in *Meng Gu Lv Li* (*The Laws and Precedents of Mongolia*): "All lawsuits shall first be heard by 'Za Sa Ke' (the head of eight banners) with the title of doro beile (title of nobility)"; if "the case is mishandled by 'Za Sa Ke' (the head of eight banners) or the head of 'Qi' (banner, equivalent of a county), it is allowed to report the case to 'Li Fan Yuan' (The Bureau of National Minority Affairs)."[458] So the "lawsuits" mentioned here also included civil lawsuits.

For cases involving two parties who lived in different "Zhou" (subprefecture) and "Xian" (county) (which are quite rare), they should be heard and settled according to the principle of "Yuan Gao Jiu Bei Gao" (the case shall be under the jurisdiction of the court in the place where the defendant lives). "(If the officials of government offices have mutually made excuses or the officials have accepted bribery) or have refused to accept the case, they shall be punished the same as those of the criminal cases. (Under the aforesaid circumstances), if the case is mishandled, or the official has accepted bribery by bending the law, he shall be severely punished."[459]

As can be seen from above, because of the complexity of the backgrounds and personal identity of "Qi Ren" (members of the Manchu ethnic group) and Mongolians, special judicial agencies were established in Qing Dynasty to handle their lawsuits. So for the civil cases, the primary level of judicial agency was usually "Zhou" (subprefecture) and "Xian" (county), so that the government organs in charge of the affairs of "Qi" (banner, equivalent of a county) and the military affairs were forbidden to interfere with the judicial work, which had not only reduced the influence of the administrative organs on judicial institutes, improved the sense of responsibility of judicial officials and their working efficiency, but also reduced the burden of lawsuits of the parties concerned.

As to the prosecution of civil lawsuits, the party must first file the lawsuits to "Zhou" (subprefecture) and "Xian" (county). At the same time, he should also submit other physical evidence such as complaints in the required form, contracts with "Qi Wei" (the identification documents issued by government), drawing, notes and explanation, marriage certificates, contracts for dividing the family property and living separately, receipts, etc. to the government office. For cases of land disputes, the owners of the neighboring land must show up; for cases of debt, there must be a guarantor; for cases of marriage, there must be a matchmaker; for cases involving disputes over "the right of graveyard and hills," the person in charge must write the relevant complaints based on facts. If they dared "to threaten the others by using the abusive expressions of 'destroying tombs' or 'killing someone or secretly digging others' land', the complaint will be rejected. Moreover, the person who writes the

---

[458]"Li Xing Si" (The Bureau of Criminal Punishment) in "Li Fan Yuan" (The Bureau of National Minority Affairs) in *Da Qing Hui Dian* (*The Collected Statutes of Great Qing*) Vol. 68.

[459]"Yue Su" (Overstepping Indictment) in "Su Song" (Litigation) in "Xing Lv" (The Penal Code) in *Da Qing Lv Li* (*The Laws and Precedents of Great Qing*), Vol. 30.

11.7 The More Complete Judicial System

complaint shall be punished."[460] Huang Liuhong in the Qing Dynasty once said: "If one has filed a lawsuit of household registration, the case shall be settled according to the graveyard property of the head of the clan; if one has filed a lawsuit of marriage, matchmakers and marriage contract are needed to be used as the evidence; if one has filed a lawsuit of land, one must provide a contract and the owners of the neighboring land have to provide the evidence; ... if the form of the complaint was inconsistent with the standard one, the complaint shall not be accepted."[461]

A civil complaint must be written by the plaintiff himself. If he was unable to write it by himself, he could tell it to "Shu Li" (scribes) so that "Shu Li" (scribes) could write down exactly what he had said on his behalf. Moreover, "Shu Pu" (stores for legal document writing) and "Guan Dai Shu" (legal document writing by officials) were set up in almost every county. All the complaints written by someone other than the plaintiff himself must be signed by both the plaintiff and the writer to show that the writer was also responsible for the contents of the complaint. If the writer himself had added or deleted something while writing the complaint, he should be punished according to law.[462] In the meantime, it was strictly forbidden for any "Song Gun" (those who make money by instigating others to file lawsuits or mean lawyers) to practice champerty for a party. According to *Da Qing Lv Li* (*The Laws and Precedents of Great Qing*), "if any shyster has instigated lawsuits to disturb people or to bring trouble to the society, the local officials who have failed to discover or arrest him out of negligence shall be punished severely according to law; if he is fully aware of the fact but has failed to report it to the government, or if the criminal has been arrested by others, he shall be punished according to the 'Li' (precedent) on the negligence of ones duty by the malicious people and be punished by 'Xing Bu' (The Department of Punishment)."[463] "As to the private copies of booklets sold by shysters in the streets, such as *Jing Tian Lei* (*World-Shaking Thunder*), *Xiang Jiao* (*Wrestling*), *Fa Jia Xin Shu* (*New Books on Legalists*), and *Xing Tai Qin Jing* (*Mirrors of Criminal Punishment*), they shall all be destroyed upon discovery and forbidden to be sold on markets. Anyone who has written and printed such booklets shall be punished according to 'Li' (precedent) on writing and distributing obscene books and shall be punished by 'Zhang' (flogging with heavy sticks) for one hundred strokes and 'Liu' (exile) for 3000 *li*; anyone who has printed and distributed the old booklets shall be punished by 'Zhang' (flogging with heavy sticks) for one hundred strokes and 'Tu' (imprisonment) for three years; anyone who has bought such booklets shall be punished by 'Zhang' (flogging with heavy sticks) for one hundred strokes; anyone who owns the old booklets or who refuses to

---

[460] *Da Qing Lv Li Hui Tong Xin Zuan* (*New Collections of the Laws and Precedents of Great Qing*).

[461] Huang Liuhong (Qing Dynasty), "Li Zhuang Shi" (The Format of Complaint) in "Kao Dai Shu" (An Examination of the People Writing Complaints for Others) in "Ci Song" (Lawsuits) in *Fu Hui Quan Shu* (*The Completed Works of Fuhui*), Vol. 11.

[462] *Da Qing Hui Dian Shi Li* (*The Precedents of the Collected Statutes of Great Qing*), Vol. 819.

[463] "Jiao Suo Ci Song" (Instigating the Lawsuits) in "Su Song" (Litigation) in "Xing Lv" (The Penal Code) in *Da Qing Lv Li* (*The Laws and Precedents of Great Qing*), Vol. 30.

destroy them shall be subject to punishment one level lighter than that for printing such booklets; anyone who owns or stores such booklets shall be punished for violating the system. Besides, the supervising officials shall be punished by 'Xing Bu' (The Department of Punishment) according to the number of times that these officials have failed to perform their duties."[464]

"Ya Men" (the government offices) of "Zhou" (subprefecture) and "Xian" (county) had the right to decide whether to accept the case according to whether the complaint was reasonable or whether there was enough evidence. The date for accepting cases was different from that in the Song and Yuan dynasties. According to *Da Qing Lv Li* (*The Laws and Precedents of Great Qing*), "from the 1st of April to the 30th of July of the lunar calendar every year ... the cases including but not limited to 'Hu Hun' (marriage), 'Tian Tu' (land) shall not be accepted because it is farming season, so the cases shall not be accepted until after the 1st of August. So any officials who have accepted the minor cases during the farming season shall be impeached by 'Du Fu' (the viceroys and procurators)."[465] However, "if the cases involve the investigation of irrigation or land boundary or if the delay of settlement might exert a negative impact on farming, they shall be settled by the official of 'Zhou' (subprefecture) and 'Xian' (county) immediately..."[466] In addition, disputes such as marriage by capture, denial of marriage, marrying a woman forcefully, land boundary, and doubtful business transaction were not subject to the time limit for the acceptance of cases because "they might cause fighting and disturb social stability if without being handled in time."[467] Also, it was forbidden for officials to refuse to accept cases at the end of a lunar year on the ground of "stopping hearing cases according to the 'Li' (precedent) on farming seasons"; otherwise "they shall be impeached according to law."[468]

11.7.3 The Criminal Trial and "Hui Shen Zhi Du" (The Joint Trial System)

According to *Da Qing Hui Dian* (*The Collected Statutes of Great Qing*), "the following rules should be followed in hearing the cases: ruling should be made in

---

[464]*Da Qing Hui Dian Shi Li* (*The Precedents of the Collected Statutes of Great Qing*), Vol. 819.

[465]"Gao Zuang Bu Shou Li" (No Accepting the Complaint) in "Su Song" (Litigation) in "Xing Lv" (The Penal Code) in *Da Qing Lv Li* (*The Laws and Precedents of Great Qing*), Vol. 30.

[466]"Gao Zuang Bu Shou Li" (No Accepting the Complaint) in "Su Song" (Litigation) in "Xing Lv" (The Penal Code) in *Da Qing Lv Li* (*The Laws and Precedents of Great Qing*), Vol. 30.

[467]Chen Hongmou, "Shen Ming Nong Mang Fen Bie Ting Song Xi" (The Restatement of no Accepting of Complaints during Farming Season) in "Xing Ming" (The Names of Punishment) (Book 2) in *Mu Ling Shu* (*Regulations on the Prefectural Officials' Behaviors*), Vol. 18, edited by Xu Dongyi (Qing Dynasty).

[468]"Gao Zuang Bu Shou Li" (No Accepting the Complaint) in "Su Song" (Litigation) in "Xing Lv" (The Penal Code) in *Da Qing Lv Li* (*The Laws and Precedents of Great Qing*), Vol. 30.

11.7 The More Complete Judicial System

accordance with the pleadings in the complaint (Yi Zhuang Yi Ju Yu), punishment should be enforced in accordance with law (Ru Fa Yi Jue Fa) and verdict should be made in accordance with confession (Ju Gong Yi Ding An)."

"Yi Zhuang Yi Ju Yu" (ruling should be made in accordance with the pleadings in the complaint): according to the provision of "Yi Zhuang Ju Yu" (ruling should be made in accordance with the pleadings in the complaint) in "Xing Lv" (The Penal Code) in *Da Qing Lv Li* (*The Laws and Precedents of Great Qing*), "as for interrogation, ruling should be made in accordance with the pleadings in the complaint," which means that "during a trial, investigations should be only conducted according to what is stated in the complaint. If a defendant is punished for a crime which is not mentioned in the complaint, the official in charge shall be punished for intentionally incriminating a person."[469] The so-called Gu Chu Ru Ren Zui (deliberately increasing or reducing the punishment when making sentences) refers to the crime of negligently executing wrong punishments when hearing cases. If an official had negligently enforced a severer punishment on a criminal who should be punished leniently, or vice versa, or had punished an innocent person or exonerated a criminal, he would be punished according to the law on "Wu Gao" (false accusation). Considering that officials were executors of law, the crime of "Gu Chu Ru Ren Zui" (deliberately increasing or reducing the punishment when making sentences) was even more serious than that of "Wu Gao" (false accusation); therefore, it was included in the article of "the crime even unpardonable by the general amnesty" in "Ming Li" (The Categories of Penalties and General Principles).[470] However, if the circumstance was not very serious, such as sentencing a person who was supposed to be punished by "Jiao" (hanging) to "Zhan" (beheading) or a person who was supposed to be punished by "Pei" (refers to "Liu" (exile) or "Chong Jun" (being forced to join the army)) to "Shou Shu" (atoning for one's crime with money), the official would be punished according to the "Li" (precedent) on "making inappropriate judgment."[471]

"Ru Fa Yi Jue Fa" (punishment should be enforced in accordance with l aw)[472] refers to extracting confession from defendants by launching an inquisition of torture according to law. Since "Zui Cong Gong Ding" (enforcing punishments in accordance with the convicts' confessions), it became necessary to enforce punishment in accordance with law.

---

[469]"Yi Gao Zhuang Ju Yu" (Making Conviction according to Complaints) in "Duan Yu" (Trials and Punishments) (Part 2) in "Xing Lv" (The Penal Code) in *Da Qing Lv Li* (*The Laws and Precedents of Great Qing*), Vol. 36.

[470]Shen Zhiqi (Qing Dynasty), *Da Qing Lv Ji Zhu* (*Collected Commentaries on Great Qing Code*), Vol. 28.

[471]"Duan Zui Bu Dang" (Inappropriate Judgment) in "Duan Yu" (Trials and Punishments) (Book 2) in "Xing Lv" (The Penal Code) in *Da Qing Lv Li* (*The Laws and Precedents of Great Qing*), Vol. 37.

[472]Shen Zhiqi (Qing Dynasty), *Da Qing Lv Ji Zhu* (*Collected Commentaries on Great Qing Code*), Vol. 28.

Xue Yunsheng once commented that "the punishment of 'Chi' (flogging with light sticks) and 'Zhang' (flogging with heavy sticks) are used under two circumstances, one for punishment, the other for interrogation."[473] "Jia Gun" (the old device for torture, made of two sticks) was used to clamp prisoners' legs, while "Zan Zhi" was especially used to clamp female suspects' fingers by using "Zan Zi" (sticks used to clamp a prisoner's fingers). Since "Jia Gun" (the old device for torture, made of two sticks and was used to clamp the prisoner's legs) was a much brutal instrument of torture, it was only used in the cases of murder and robbery, and "it is not allowed to be used in other minor cases."[474] Sometimes, in order to extract confession from those who refused to confess, the prisoners were forced to wear "Jia Hao" (cangue: a large wooden collar worn by petty criminals as a punishment), which weighed around twenty five to thirty five *jin*. "Zhang Ze" (slapping on the face) was another common measure of inquisition by torture. Although it was a common way to extract confession through inquisition by torture, restrictions were provided for these measures in the laws of the Qing Dynasty. For example, it was forbidden for the people who were older than seventy or younger than fifteen years old and those who belonged to "Fei Ji" (the disabled, including the mentally disabled and mute; those with fractured lumbar vertebra, one crippled arm or leg; etc.) to be tortured during inquisition. If a suspect died because of torture, the chief inquisitor would be punished by "Zhang" (flogging with heavy sticks) for one hundred strokes or be punished by "Liu" (exile) for 3000 *li*. Nevertheless, if inquisition by torture was practiced in accordance with law, the official would not be held liable even if the suspect died.

In order to prevent people from deliberately increasing or reducing punishments in making sentences out of social relationship, the avoidance system in trials was further improved. If the chief official in charge of a case was a relative, friend, teacher, student, or foe of the parties concerned or if he had other relationships with the parties concerned, he must withdraw from the case.

Although confession was an important basis for making judgment, other evidence was also important. "For the serious cases of homicide, autopsy must be performed to examine the injuries,"[475] and "the form of body examination" that was issued by "Xing Bu" (The Department of Punishment) must be filled. Moreover, "in the case of robbery, the evidence of stolen goods must be provided," and "if a person has reported the theft cases to the government, he must provide a detailed list of the things lost."[476] Apart from physical evidence, the testimony and statement of the

---

[473]Xue Yunshen (Qing Dynasty), *Du Li Cun Yi* (Questions in Reading *the Precedents*), Vol. 1.

[474]"Gu Jin Gu Kan Ping Ren" (Banning Intentional and Illegal Interrogation and Torture of the Innocent People) in "Duan Yu" (Trials and Punishments) (Part 1) in "Xing Lv" (The Penal Code) in *Da Qing Lv Li* (*The Laws and Precedents of Great Qing*), Vol. 36.

[475]"Jian Yan Shi Shang Bu Yi Shi" (Cheating in Autopsy) in "Duan Yu" (Trials and Punishments) (Part 2) in "Xing Lv" (The Penal Code) in *Da Qing Lv Li* (*The Laws and Precedents of Great Qing*), Vol. 37.

[476]"Qiang Dao" (Robbery) in "Zei Dao" (Stealing and Robbery) (Part 1) in "Xing Lv" (The Penal Code) in *Da Qing Lv Li* (*The Laws and Precedents of Great Qing*), Vol. 23.

11.7 The More Complete Judicial System

victim and the confession of the defendants were all important basis for judgment. According to the regulation in *Da Qing Lv Li* (*The Laws and Precedents of Great Qing*), "for a prisoner or a suspect who might be sentenced to 'Tu' (imprisonment), 'Liu' (exile), and 'Si' (death penalty), the prisoner and his family members shall be summoned to the trial and be told his accusation. Besides, the criminal shall be asked to write a document stating that he agrees with the accusation. If the criminal refuses to do so, he is allowed to defend for himself."[477] The so-called Fu Bian Wen Zhuang (pleading guilty and admitting the confession) also meant "Fu Shu Gong Ci" (the defendant admitting he has lost the case). In a joint crime, if there was enough evidence, the defendants could be convicted even if the principal criminal had escaped.

In criminal trials, emphasis was laid on settling lawsuits according to law. It was stipulated in *Da Qing Lv Li* (*The Laws and Precedents of Great Qing*) that "all judgments should be made according to 'Lv' (criminal law) and 'Li' (precedent); otherwise the official shall be punished by 'Chi' (flogging with light sticks) for thirty strokes."[478]

In addition to settling cases according to "Lv" (criminal law), officials were also allowed to make judgment by "Bi Fu" (legal analogy). "For the matters which are not included in 'Lv' (criminal law) and 'Ling' (decree), if there are no articles to cite when making judgment, the judicial officials could make proper decisions by aggravating and mitigating the punishment according to a relevant article by 'Bi Fu' (legal analogy). In addition, he should present a memorial to the emperor for final decision. If he has made a judgment without permission of the emperor or has made an inappropriate judgment, he will be punished for his negligence." As for this provision, an annotation was made by "Xing Bu" (The Department of Punishment):

> As far as "Wu Xing" (Five Penalties) is concerned, three thousand categories of crimes are included in the law. As to some minor crimes which are not included in the law, they are stipulated in "Li" (precedent); ... if a crime is included both in "Lv" (criminal law) and "Li" (precedent), the latter shall be applied preferably; if an old "Li" (precedent) and a new one co-existed, the latter one shall be applied preferably; when there are no specific articles to cite in both "Lv" (criminal law) and "Li" (precedent), decisions shall be made according to "Bi Fu" (legal analogy), but at the same time reports shall be made to the emperor to wait for his approval.[479]

In the Qing Dynasty, a series of samples of analogy was compiled according to the experiences of the judiciary and was used as basis for judgment. For example, the case of losing the key to the city gate of the capital could be settled according to the "Li" (precedent) on the crime of losing seals; the case of the students of "Gong Jian" (those recommended to study in "Guo Zi Jian" as "Gong Sheng") asking others to

---

[477]"Yu Qiu Qu Fu Bian" (The Prisoner Pleading for Guilty) in "Duan Yu" (Trials and Punishments) in "Xing Lv" (The Penal Code) in *Da Qing Lv Li* (*The Laws and Precedents of Great Qing*), Vol. 37.

[478]"Duan Yu" (Trials and Punishments) in "Xing Lv" (The Penal Code) in *Da Qing Lv Li* (*The Laws and Precedents of Great Qing*), Vol. 37.

[479]*Da Qing Hui Dian* (*The Collected Statutes of Great Qing*), Vol. 54.

take exams for them to get official positions could be settled according to the "Li" (precedent) on the crime of fraudulently obtaining official positions; the case of taking liberties with his sister-in-law could be settled according to the "Li" (precedent) on the crime of attempted raping. So "Bi Fu" (legal analogy) not only served as the basis for making judgments and passing sentences but also was applied when making appropriate decisions on criminal cases. For example, if a couple had sexual relationships before marriage, it could be settled according to the "Li" (precedent) on the crime of offspring disobeying the instruction of seniors; if government staff instigated the suspects of robbery to make up false facts or to bribe the chief official, it could be settled according to the "Li" (precedent) on the crime of taking bribery and exonerating criminals intentionally. Due to the extensive application of "Bi Fu" (legal analogy) in hearing cases, the number of "Li" (precedent) kept increasing. When *Da Qing Lv Li* (*The Laws and Precedents of Great Qing*) was revised during the reign of Emperor Qianlong, there were 436 articles and 1409 additional "Li" (precedents), but in the 9th year of Tongzhi (1870), the number of "Li" (precedents) reached to 1892. Moreover, "Li" (precedent) was not only abundant in number but also more legally effective than "Lv" (criminal law), so sometimes "Lv" (criminal law) could even be replaced by "Li" (precedent), as was described in the following: "'Lv' (criminal law) shall not be applied when there is 'Li' (precedent)." Besides, "Li" (precedent) was more flexible and specific it had made it convenient for the Emperor to impose his will on the law without being restricted by the original legal articles, so that it was preferred by the rulers. However, arbitrary reference to "Li" (precedent) in legal practice had not only brought about arbitrary decisions but also provided judicial officials with more opportunities to extort money from the ordinary people.

For crimes punishable by "Tu" (imprisonment), cases must first be heard by the officials at "Zhou" (subprefecture) and "Xian" (county), then be reviewed by "Fu" (ancient administrative district between province and county), "An Cha Si" (The Judicial Commission), and "Du Fu" (the viceroys and procurators) step by step, with the final judgment made by "Du Fu" (the viceroys and procurators). According to *Da Qing Lv Li* (*The Laws and Precedents of Great Qing*), "for the ordinary crimes punishable by 'Tu' (imprisonment), a detailed report should be made by 'Du Fu' (the viceroys and procurators) to 'Xing Bu' (The Department of Punishment) to be reviewed in every season after the cases are settled"[480]; for cases punishable by "Liu" (exile), "Chong Jun" (being forced to join the army), and "Qian" (the penalty of banishing criminals to do forced labor in remote areas), relevant documents should be sent to "Xing Bu" (The Department of Punishment) by "Du Fu" (the viceroys and procurators) of each province after the cases were settled. In addition, the officials of "Qing Li Si" (office) in each province should collect and report their opinions to the officials in "Xing Bu" (The Department of Punishment). After the

---

[480]"You Si Jue Qiu Deng Di" (The Levels of Punishment for the Prisoners Enforced by the Judicial Officials) in "Duan Yu" (Trials and Punishments) in "Xing Lv" (The Penal Code) in *Da Qing Lv Li* (*The Laws and Precedents of Great Qing*), Vol. 37.

11.7 The More Complete Judicial System

review by "Xing Bu" (The Department of Punishment), final sentences were delivered to each province to be enforced. As to the cases of death penalty, they should first be heard by the officials at "Zhou" (subprefecture) and "Xian" (county), then be reported to the officials of higher ranks to be reviewed step by step, and finally reported to the emperor by "Du Fu" (the viceroys and procurators) for final decision. Besides, copies of "Jie Tie" (notice) should first be sent to "Xing Bu" (The Department of Punishment) and "'San Fa Si' (Three Judicial Departments) to be reviewed, then be presented to the emperor for final decision" according to the imperial edict. As to the cases of death penalty in the capital, they should be handled directly by "Xing Bu" (The Department of Punishment), then be reported to the emperor and reviewed by "San Fa Si" (Three Judicial Departments). After it was reviewed and checked by "San Fa Si" (Three Judicial Departments), it should be presented again to the emperor for his final decision. Thereafter, the criminal would be sentenced to "Li Jue" (immediate execution) or "Jian Hou" (to be imprisoned) accordingly.

Time limits were specified for the trial of criminal cases. Ordinary cases of murder must be settled within six months. But cases of theft; cases of murder that were punishable by "Zhan" (beheading), "Jiao" (hanging), or "Li Jue" (immediate execution); and all other miscellaneous cases of robbery and theft must be settled within four months.

"Qiu Shen" (Autumn Assizes) was the most representative of the system of "Hui Shen" (the joint trial) in the Qing Dynasty. "Qiu Shen" (Autumn Assizes) is a system set up to review cases of death penalty and cases of "Jian Hou" (to be imprisoned) in each province, and it was so named because it was held in the autumn of each year. As early as the 1st year of Shunzhi (1644), Dang Chongya, "Shi Lang" (vice minister) of "Xing Bu" (The Department of Punishment), had made the following proposal:

> According to the traditional system, the criminals who committed the felonies are all sentenced to "Jian Hou" (to be imprisoned) except for the crime of "Da Ni" (great sedition) and robbery. "Re Shen" (Summer Assizes) and "Chao Shen" (trials held in imperial court) are also held in the capital, and after Frost's Descent (the 18th solar term), death penalty is executed after the approval of the emperor. In other provinces, "Qiu Shen" (Autumn Assizes) is also held by "San Fa Si" (Three Judicial Departments), but the criminals are seldom punished by "Qi Shi" (exposing the executed body publicly at markets). Therefore, I sincerely hope the tradition can be followed and the cases can be settled according to the concrete circumstances so that the Emperor's benevolence can be shown to all the people nationwide.[481]

In the 10th year of Shunzhi (1653), "Chao Shen" (trials held in imperial court) was restored in the capital. In the 15th year of Shunzhi (1658), it was decided that before Frost's Descent (the 18th solar term), the criminals who were to be "executed in the autumn" because they had committed felonies should be carefully investigated by the local officials and then memorials should be submitted to the emperor for final

---

[481] "Xing Fa Zhi" (The Record of the Criminal Law) (Part 3) in *Qing Shi Gao* (*The Draft of the History of Qing Dynasty*).

decision. During the reign of Emperor Kangxi, "Chao Shen" (trials held in imperial court) and "Qiu Shen" (Autumn Assizes) tended to be converged. During the reign of Emperor Qianlong, the system of "Qiu Shen" (Autumn Assizes) was more standardized, and it became a special and complete feudal reviewing system for death penalty and probation cases.

According to the law of the Qing Dynasty, if anyone had committed a felony punishable by immediate execution, he would be punished by "Zhan Li Jue" (immediate execution by beheading) or "Jiao Li Jue" (immediate execution by hanging); if the cases were less harmful or if there were doubtful points in the cases, the criminals might be sentenced to "Zhan Jian Hou" (suspended execution) or "Jiao Jian Hou" (the punishment of suspending hanging), so the execution might be suspended or might be stopped from being carried out until after it was reviewed by "Xing Bu" (The Department of Punishment), "San Fa Si" (Three Judicial Departments), or "Jiu Qing" (the nine high-rank officials in ancient times) in the autumn. Therefore, most cases heard during "Qiu Shen" (Autumn Assizes) were local cases involving "Zhan Jian Hou" (suspended execution) and "Jiao Jian Hou" (the punishment of suspending hanging). Every year, the relevant cases or criminals would be reviewed and interrogated by "Du Fu" (the viceroys and procurators) of each province, who would then put forward his opinions, collect them in booklets, and send copies to "Jiu Qing" (the nine high-rank officials in ancient times) for their reference in "Qiu Shen" (Autumn Assizes). In the process of compilation of the copies, the relevant criminals should be sent under guard to "Du Fu" (the viceroys and procurators) for joint interrogation in each province, but it often became merely a formality. Even Emperor Shizong once openly criticized:

> I have heard that during the "Hui Shen" (the joint trial) in other provinces, all the cases, regardless of the number, are all settled in one day, and all the cases are settled by "Du Fu" (the viceroys and procurators) himself because none of the other officials of "Si" (office), "Dao" (the administration district below the province) and "Shou Ling" (prefects or magistrates) dare to make any comments. Sometimes "Du Fu" (the viceroys and procurators) is not sure of the facts himself, so he just includes the written report of his advisors and "Shi Ke" (a person sponging on an aristocrat) into the booklets, that is why they are nothing but decorations.[482]

"As a major event of trial in autumn," "Qiu Shen" (Autumn Assizes) was held at the west of Jinshui Bridge outside Tian'anmen in August each year when the cases of death penalty in different provinces were jointly reviewed by "Jiu Qing" (the nine high-rank officials in ancient times), "Zhan Shi" (official in charge of the internal affairs of royal families), "Ke" and "Dao" (both government offices, including the deaconry and the supervisory censor), "Jun Ji Da Chen" (the grand councilor), and "Nei Ge Da Xue Shi" (cabinet grand secretary). Before "Qiu Shen" (Autumn Assizes), the cases that "needed to be settled by the emperor" should be reported to the imperial court by all the provinces within a definite time, then they were categorized and delivered to the officials in charge in the various departments to be read in advance by "Xing Bu" (The Department of Punishment), which was called

---

[482]*Da Qing Hui Dian Shi Li* (*The Precedents of the Collected Statutes of Great Qing*), Vol. 846.

11.7 The More Complete Judicial System

"Si Yi"; after that, the cases were transferred to "Qiu Shen Chu" (Office of Autumn Assizes) and "Lv Li Guan" (an official institution established in the second year of the Shunzhi period) for "further discussion." After that, the cases were reported to the senior officials of "Xing Bu" (The Department of Punishment) for joint deliberation and settlement. After "Hui Shen" (the joint trial), "Xing Bu" (The Department of Punishment) would then submit memorials to the emperor for final decision.

The cases that were settled in "Qiu Shen" (Autumn Assizes) were divided into four categories: "Qing Shi" (the cases in which the facts are clear and the punishments are appropriate), "Huan Jue" (the cases in which the facts are clear but there is little harmful social effect and shall be left behind for decision during the next Autumn Assizes or trials in imperial court), "Ke Jin" (the cases in which the facts are clear while the circumstances of the crime are not serious, hence being exempted from death penalty), and "Liu Yang Cheng Si" (the cases in which the circumstances of the crime are serious but the old parents or grandparents of the criminal would be unattended if the criminal is executed, hence being exempted from death penalty). For the cases of the first category, execution could be carried out after being approved by the emperor, but for the criminals of the other categories, they might be exempted from death penalty. In fact, the cases reviewed in "Qiu Shen" (Autumn Assizes) and "Chao Shen" (trials held in imperial court) were usually not serious; therefore, the establishment of the system of "Qiu Shen" (Autumn Assizes) and "Chao Shen" (trials held in imperial court) did not show an indulgent attitude to serious crimes; at the same time, it reduced the punishment of some people within the ruling class and enhanced the emperor's control of judicial power institutionally. For example, every year before "Qiu Shen" (Autumn Assizes), "Tie Huang" (the correction and rectifying of edicts or documents) of the original cases, the diction of the judgment of judicial officials, and "Du Fu" (the viceroys and procurators) were all collected and compiled by "Xing Bu" (The Department of Punishment) for the emperor's reference; after "Qiu Shen" (Autumn Assizes), they were all reported to the emperor for his final decision, and only those ticked by the emperor with brush could be executed. On the 27th of the May of the 3rd year of Yongzheng (1725), Emperor Shizong stated in an imperial edict: "Since I ascended the throne, I have shown great sympathy to the criminals, so whenever memorials are submitted by judicial officials, I shall make careful reviewing just for fear that the judgment is inappropriate."[483] In the 14th year of Qianlong (1749), it was ordered that the number of times for submitting memorials to emperor in "Qiu Shen" (Autumn Assizes) was changed from three times to once. The Emperor emphasized:

> During "Qiu Shen" (Autumn Assizes), the cases are all reported to me three times by all the provinces, which has demonstrated that the cases of death penalty are handled prudently by the officials, and the system of "San Ci" (one of the ways for the ancient Chinese court officials to make conviction. In other words, in handling the major and difficult cases, first it should be discussed by a group of ministers, if it can not be decided after that, then it should

---

[483] "Shi Zong Xian Huang Di Shang Yu" (The Imperial Edict of Emperor Shizong) in "Juan Shou" (The Preface) in *Da Qing Lv Li Tong Kao* (*A Textual Research of the Laws and Precedents of Great Qing*).

be handed over to a group of officials to discuss. If it cannot be decided either, it should be discussed by all the people) and "San You" (the three kinds of circumstances for lenient treatment) in ancient times are all inherited, according to which the cases must be carefully reviewed before execution without negligence, but it does not mean that reports have to be made for just three times. Whenever I have to decide who is to be executed, I often put the relevant documents by my side and read them over and over for at least five or six times to make sure that there are no doubtful points any more. Before I tick the names of criminals to be executed, I often think twice before holding discussion with "Da Xue Shi" (grand secretary), so it is far more than three times. If the officials are required to make reports for three times, they shall read the cases in a hurry without going through the details. Besides, if the time limit is given, it is impossible for them to read all the cases. Therefore, from now on, for each province, the memorials should be presented only once by the office of penalty."[484]

In *Qiu Yan Ji Yao* (*Outline of Autumn Assizes*), the written instructions given by the emperors, from the reign of Emperor Qianlong to the reign of Emperor Guangxu, were recorded, and the emperors' comments were so detailed that there were even as many as 1000 words in some of them. In the 22nd year of Kangxi (1683), an order was issued on "Qiu Shen" (Autumn Assizes): "A person's life is so important that as long as he is excusable, he shall not be executed."[485] In the 40th year of Kangxi (1701), he reiterated the importance he had attached to "Qiu Shen" (Autumn Assizes) and expressed his criticism on "Xing Bu" (The Department of Punishment) at the same time: "When I read the files of the serious cases of 'Qiu Shen' (Autumn Assizes), I have found out many wrong words which the officials have failed to discover. The officials of 'Xing Bu' (The Department of Punishment) are so careless that they deserve to be punished."[486] In the 11th year of Yongzheng (1733), an imperial order was issued to "Xing Bu" (The Department of Punishment), and it was stated that "memorials should be presented to the emperor whenever there is a gleam of hope for the survival for the criminal."[487] Moreover, similar orders were issued during the reign of emperors Qianlong and Jiaqing because they also wanted to show that the lives of the people should be valued, the law should be implemented impartially, and the people should be urged to abide by the law to avoid punishment by making use of the event of "Qiu Shen" (Autumn Assizes), as was described as follows: "it is vitally important to carry out 'Ming Xing Bi Jiao' (integrating punishment with moral teachings)."[488] In the existing *Xing Ke Ti Ben* (*Memorials to the Emperor Submitted by the Office of Punishment*), at the end of each memorial,

---

[484] *Qin Ding Tai Gui* (*The Regulations Made by Imperial Order*), Vol. 14.

[485] "Xing Fa Zhi" (The Record of the Criminal Law) (Part 3) in *Qing Shi Gao* (*The Draft of the History of Qing Dynasty*).

[486] "Sheng Zu Ji" (The Record of Emperor Shengzu) (Part 2) in *Qing Shi Gao* (*The Draft of the History of Qing Dynasty*).

[487] "Xing Fa Zhi" (The Record of the Criminal Law) (Part 3) in *Qing Shi Gao* (*The Draft of the History of Qing Dynasty*).

[488] "Shi Zong Xian Huang Di Shang Yu" (The Imperial Edit of Emperor Shizong) in "Juan Shou" (The Preface) in *Da Qing Lv Li Tong Kao* (*A Textual Research of the Laws and Precedents of Great Qing*).

11.7 The More Complete Judicial System

the following words were written: "We dare not decide on our own, because all the justice and mercy are granted by the Emperor, and we are still awaiting his final decision,"[489] which had fully shown the emperor's control over judicial power. Besides, for cases settled according to the emperor's orders, reports should be made to the emperor after being discussed according to law, and judgments would be made only after the emperor's approval.

"Chao Shen" (trials held in imperial court) refers to the trial of the condemned prisoners of "Zhan Jian Hou" (suspended execution) and "Jiao Jian Hou" (the punishment of suspending hanging) in the capital by "Xing Bu" (The Department of Punishment). According to *Da Qing Lv Li* (*The Laws and Precedents of Great Qing*), the important criminals kept in the prison of "Xing Bu" (The Department of Punishment) should be tried by "Chao Shen" (trials held in imperial court) every year. According to its procedure, the relevant cases should first be discussed by the officials of "Xing Bu" (The Department of Punishment) and then be reported to the ministers especially sent by the emperor for reviewing. "If the specially sent ministers decided to report the case to the Emperor after reviewing, the main plot of the case should be summarized, edited and printed in booklets, with the copies sent to 'Jiu Qing' (nine high-rank officials in ancient times), 'Zhan Shi' (official in charge of the internal affairs of royal families) and 'Ke' and 'Dao' (both government offices including the deaconry and the supervisory censor). At the beginning of August [usually 'Chao Shen' (trials held in imperial court) is held one day before 'Qiu Shen' (Autumn Assizes)], officials would meet at the west of Jinshui Bridge and jointly conduct a careful investigation of relevant criminals. They could make decisions on 'Qing Shi' (the cases in which the facts are clear and the punishments are appropriate), 'Huan Jue' (the cases in which the facts are clear but there is little harmful social effect and shall be left behind for decision during the next Autumn Assizes or trials in imperial court) and 'Ke Jin' (the cases in which the facts are clear while the circumstances of the crime are not serious, hence being exempted from death penalty) and then report them to the Emperor for final decision."[490] There were two different points between "Chao Shen" (trials held in imperial court) and "Qiu Shen" (Autumn Assizes): first, the prisoners should be brought before the officials to be tried on the spot during "Chao Shen" (trials held in imperial court); second, for the cases of "Chao Shen" (trials held in imperial court), memorials must be submitted to the emperor three times until the 20th year of Jiaqing (1815) to show that the emperor had paid great attention to the cases in the capital. It was decided in the 20th year of Jiaqing that "the rules of 'Qiu Shen' (Autumn Assizes) shall be followed

---

[489]"Xing Ke Ti Ben" (Memorials to the Emperor Submitted by the Office of Punishment) in *Zhu Pi Zou Zhe* (*Memorials Approved by the Emperor*).

[490]"You Si Jue Qiu Deng Di" (The Levels of Punishment for the Prisoners Enforced by the Judicial Officials) in "Duan Yu" (Trials and Punishments) (Part 2) in "Xing Lv" (The Penal Code) in *Da Qing Lv Li* (*The Laws and Precedents of Great Qing*), Vol. 37.

in 'Chao Shen' (trials held in imperial court), so memorials will be submitted to the emperor only once in future."[491]

As to "Re Shen" (Summer Assizes), it was held from the 10th day after "Xiao Man" (Grain Full (8th solar term)) to the 1st day before "Li Qiu" (the beginning of autumn) by officials from the left and right bureaus of "Da Li Si" (The Bureau of Judicial Review), "Yu Shi" (the censor) of each "Dao" (the administration district below the province), and "Cheng Ban Si" (the bureau in charge of dealing with routine activities) of "Xing Bu" (The Department of Punishment) (the so-called Xiao San Si (Small Three Departments)) to deal with cases punishable by "Chi" (flogging with light sticks) and "Zhang" (flogging with heavy sticks) in the capital area.

In criminal trials, if the parties or the relatives thereof thought that the case was mishandled, they could lodge complaints step by step all the way to "Jing Kong" (when civilians having grievances that could not be resolved by the highest local officials, they could go to the capital to complain to the imperial court) or "Kou Hun" (the people complaining to the imperial court by knocking on the palace gate). In the Qing Dynasty, the system of lodging complaints was relatively well established, so "Jing Kong" (when civilians having grievances that could not be resolved by the highest local officials, they could go to the capital to complain to the imperial court) especially served as an important means for the ordinary people to appeal their complaints. The following is the procedure of "Jing Kong" (when civilians having grievances that could not be resolved by the highest local officials, they could go to the capital to complain to the imperial court): the people could submit complaints to the emperor or strike "Deng Wen Gu" (Deng Wen Drum, one of the most important ways of direct appeal in ancient China) in front of the imperial court to lodge their complaints. Then the cases would be respectively accepted by "Du Cha Yuan" (The Court of Censors), "Tong Zheng Shi Si" (The Transmission Office), "Bu Jun Tong Ya Men" (The Office of Land Force Commanders), "Li Fan Yuan" (The Bureau of National Minority Affairs), and other departments according to the contents thereof. These cases would either be handled by the relevant organs of the royal court or by "Xing Bu" (The Department of Punishment), which had the right of prior interrogation, or be assigned to be handled by the local "Du Fu" (the viceroys and procurators) or "Fa Shen Ju" (provincial specialized agencies in charge of reviewing cases).

As for the cases of "Jing Kong" (when civilians having grievances that could not be resolved by the highest local officials, they could go to the capital to complain to the imperial court), only a few original judgments of the cases were affirmed, while most were changed, so this procedure became the final protection against miscarriage of justice.

Abuse of power by "Mu You" (staff in charge of handling official documents, punishments, and affairs concerning money and grain) was a major feature, as well as a serious malpractice, in judicial trials during the Qing Dynasty.

---

[491]"Liu Ke Fen Zhang" (The Responsibilities of the Six Offices) in *Qin Ding Tai Gui* (*The Regulations Made by Imperial Order*), Vol. 14.

11.7 The More Complete Judicial System

The system of "Mu You" (advisors and assistants in charge of handling official documents, punishments, and affairs concerning money and grain) had existed for a long time. In the Qing Dynasty, because talents were selected through the examination system of "Ba Gu Wen" (stereotyped writing or the eight-part essay in ancient China), officials knew little about the current affairs, so to a larger extent, they mainly relied on "Mu You" (advisors and assistants in charge of handling official documents, punishments, and affairs concerning money and grain) to handle daily affairs, which led to the rapid development and even flourishing of the system of "Mu You." "Mu You" (advisors and assistants in charge of handling official documents, punishments, and affairs concerning money and grain) refers to the consultants hired by masters, so their relationship was that of guests and masters rather than that of junior and senior officials. Besides, "Mu You" received stipends from their masters rather than from the state treasury, so they served the government mainly because they had good knowledge of criminal punishment and law, money and grain, taxation, accounting, administration, and document handling. Although they did not have any official position in the local government, they did have great power. By working as consultants for officials in governance, they had developed into a group who had special power. The people in the Qing Dynasty had made the following comments: "It is 'Mu You' (advisors and assistants in charge of handling the affairs like official documents, punishments, money and grain) who are actually dealing with the administrative affairs on behalf of the local officials of 'Shou Ling' (prefects or magistrates), 'Xian Ling' (county magistrate), 'Si' (bureau), 'Dao' (the administration district below the province) and 'Du Fu' (the viceroys and procurators) of the seventeen provinces."[492]

Because "Mu You" (advisors and assistants in charge of handling official documents, punishments, and affairs concerning money and grain) were from different family backgrounds with different levels of knowledge, morality, and personality, their behaviors also varied. Some honestly carried out the law to redress injustice, some bent the law to benefit themselves, some made use of loopholes in the law to show off their skills in making fuss of the trifles, and some established a network of power by colluding with their teachers, relatives, and friends. Because the restriction on "Mu You" (advisors and assistants in charge of handling official documents, punishments, and affairs concerning money and grain) was merely a formality and there were no effective systems for supervision and punishment, the moral degeneration of the world was getting worse day by day, which became the source of political corruption in the Qing Dynasty.

"Xing Ming Mu You" (the staff or private assistant and advisor in the government office in charge of lawsuits), who had good knowledge of *Lv Li* (*Laws and Precedents*), had become the actual manipulator of local judicial activities. Due to specific geographical, blood, and teacher–student relationships, most of them were

---

[492]Han Zheng, "Mu You Lun" (On Private Advisors) in "Li Zheng" (The Achievements of Officials) (Part 1) in *Huang Chao Jing Shi Wen Bian* (*Collection of Works on Statecraft in Qing Dynasty*), Vol. 25.

from Shaoxing, so they were called "Shao Xing Shi Ye" (private adviser from Shaoxing). What they had learned from serving as "Mu You" and from their experience in law application were all kept as secret and were passed directly from teacher to student without telling outsiders, which made it a profession that was especially monopolized. In judicial trials, "Xing Ming Mu You" (the staff or private assistant and advisor in government office in charge of lawsuits) was mainly responsible for making comments on the files, preparing the relevant materials, putting forward his opinions for the preliminary examination, and replying to official documents. Wang Huizu, a famous "Mu You" (advisors and assistants in charge of handling official documents, punishments, and affairs concerning money and grain) in the Qing Dynasty once said: "To serve a master, a private advisor and assistant must be familiar with *Lv Li (Laws and Precedents)*" because "laws and precedents to a private advisor are what the masterpieces of *Si Shu (The Four Books*: *Da Xue*: *The Great Learning*; *Zhong Yong*: *The Doctrine of the Mean*; *Lun Yu*: *The Analects of Confucius*; *Mencius*: *Mencius*) to 'Xiu Cai' (those who passed the imperial examination at the county level in ancient China)." Gang Yi, an official in the late Qing Dynasty, once pointed out:

> The local officials are indulged in the affairs like "Zhi Ju" (an examination subject set up temporarily) and "Tie Kuo" (a style of formal writing adopted by candidates in civil-service examinations). Besides, they are careless, simple and crude, and seldom talk much about "Lv" (criminal law), "Ling" (decree), "Ge" (injunction) and "Shi" (standard). Sometimes, although some of them are gifted, knowledgeable and learned, yet they are often looked down upon and are regarded as the followers of "Shen Han" (refers to legalists represented by Shen Buhai and Han Fei), so their opinions are often not accepted. As a result, they had no choice but to "depend on their private advisors and junior officials."[493]

Gu Tongjun also pointed out in *Da Qing Lv Jiang Yi* (*Handouts of the Laws of Great Qing*) that local officials in the Qing Dynasty "were often at a loss when they encountered difficult problems, so they would just turn to their private advisors and junior officials for help in getting out of the trouble. How can you not be angry." So it was only under the circumstance of the extreme development of autocracy, the increasing deterioration of legal culture and the complete breakdown of bureaucratic politics that this phenomenon could occur.

However, every coin has two sides. "Mu You" (advisors and assistants in charge of handling the affairs like official documents, punishments, money and grain) had become a serious social problem because they had not only taken control of judicial affairs, but also destroyed judicial order and increased the corruption of official administration; nevertheless, we should not ignore the fact that they were also famous for their rich experience, good command of legal knowledge, excellent skills in hearing and settling the cases and their concise wording of court verdict, some of which had been summarized in theories. Especially, some of the annotations which were made according to their personal experience were very practical and close to

---

[493] Gang Yi (Qing Dynasty), "Zi Xu" (Author's Preface) in *Shen Kan Ni Shi* (*An Examination of the Drafted Format*).

11.7 The More Complete Judicial System

daily life, and their classification of typical cases also prepared the materials for the senior officials and helped them to put forward their suggestions on law revision.

As to "Li" (petty officials), namely, "Xu Li" (petty officials), also known as "Shu Li" (scribes), they had become the sources of evil practice even in Ming Dynasty because they not only controlled "Xing Ming" (criminal law) and "Qian Gu" (money and grain), but also abused their power by playing favoritism and committing irregularities. Gu Yanwu once exposed:

> Nowadays, although there is no enfeoffment for "Guan" (officials), yet there is for "Li" (petty officials). In "Zhou" (subprefecture) and "Xian" (county) where the petty officials reside, their positions are passed on to their sons or brothers. Especially, some of the cunning petty officials have been promoted to "Shu Li" (scribes) of the government bureaus and departments and usurped great power in "Zhou" (subprefecture) and "Xian" (county). Although the senior officials are fully aware of this problem, yet they are unable to solve it.[494]

In Qing Dynasty, the abusing of power by "Xu Li" (petty officials) was even more serious than that in Ming Dynasty, because more "Xu Li" (petty officials) were assigned to different "Si" (bureau), "Yuan" (institution), "Bu" (department) and because organizations of "Xu Li" (petty officials) were set up in the six departments of "Li" (Personnel), "Hu" (Revenue), "Li" (Rites), "Bing" (Defense), "Xing" (Punishment) and "Gong" (Works) in the local "Ya Men" (the government offices) of "Zhou" (subprefecture) and "Xian" (county). The petty officials in local "Ya Men" (the government offices) enjoyed real power, and "Xing Ming Shu Li" (the scribes in charge of lawsuits) were especially notorious for their abuse of power and their exploitation of people. "Xing Ming Shu Li" (the scribes in charge of lawsuits) were responsible for the preparation of the trials, the recording of the confession, the investigation, the checking and processing of documents and, the collection and storage of the files. Although the local officials in the Qing Dynasty were good at "Ba Gu Wen" (stereotyped writing or the eight-part essay in ancient China), they actually knew little about the local customs, the real condition of the people, and the laws and precedents, so that they had to rely on petty officials, who were familiar with legal knowledge. There was a popular saying during the Qing Dynasty: "Even if the official is upright, honest and is as clear as water, it is inevitable for them to become corrupted because the petty officials are crafty and are as slippery as oil." Moreover, both "Guan" (officials) and "Li" (petty officials) had colluded with each other to exploit the people.

Since there were "Xu Li" (petty officials) everywhere and they had seized every opportunity to do evil things, some people even said that the Qing government was ruled by "Xu Li" (petty officials). In fact, the rulers of the Qing Dynasty were fully aware of this problem. As early as the 13th year of Shunzhi (1656), the emperor pointed out in an imperial order that "if any cunning and stubborn 'Xu Li' (petty officials) in the central and local offices have cheated, falsely accused, slandered, threatened and blackmailed their superiors, they shall be severely punished after

---

[494]Gu Yanwu (Ming Dynasty), *Ri Zhi Lu* (*The Record of Daily Reading*), Vol. 8.

careful investigation."[495] During the reign of Emperor Yongzheng, "it is strictly forbidden for 'Shu Li' (scribes) to take bribes," and it was stressed that "the corruption of various departments mostly had something to do with the treacherousness of 'Shu Li' (scribes) ... the cunning petty officials have openly ignored the laws, played tricks and obtained money illegally ... in the future ... the cases handled by the officials below 'Fan Nie' [refers to 'Bu Zheng Shi' (local administrative officer) and 'An Cha Shi' (head of judicial commission)] shall be strictly supervised and carefully reviewed by 'Du Fu' (the viceroys and procurators). If the petty officials have taken bribes as before, they will be reported to the emperor immediately; otherwise the officials in charge shall be punished for the crime of 'Wang Fa' (taking bribes by bending the law)."[496] Since then, preventive measures had been taken regarding their service terms and their scope of power, so anyone who had violated relevant rules would be severely punished. It was especially provided in *Qin Ding Li Bu Ze Li* (*The Regulation of the Department of Personnel Made by Imperial Order*) that "if the case involves 'Gu Chu Ru Ren Zui' (to deliberately increase or reduce the punishment when making sentences), the head of the staff in charge shall be severely punished and the chief officials thereof shall be punished one level lighter." "If a prisoner is illegally detained, or if both 'Guan' (officials) and 'Li' (petty officials) have been involved in the case, 'Li' (petty officials) shall be punished as the prime culprit." In making judgments, "if other articles are applied by analogy without making reference to the formal regulations in the statutes, which has led to unjust punishments at discretion ... 'Shu Li' (scribes) shall be severely punished." Any "Shu Li" (scribes) who were involved in "Jiao Suo Ci Song" (instigating lawsuits) would be carefully investigated and severely punished. "If 'Shu Li' (scribes) have abused their power by playing with literary skills, or have made troubles and disturbed people in handling cases, or have broken laws deliberately, they shall be punished one level heavier." Nonetheless, in the late Qing Dynasty, the usurping of power by "Xu Li" (petty officials) became "a haunt of malpractice," which was incorrigible.[497] During the reign of emperors Qianlong and Jiaqing, Hong Liangji, who was an official and a progressive thinker and who had served as an advisor himself for a long time, exposed the brutality and savage of "Xu Li" (petty officials): "Three tenths of those taking 'Ke Ju' (the imperial examination) shall be enrolled as 'Guan' (officials), while half as 'Xu Li' (petty officials)" who "have passed on their positions to their sons and grandsons and who are especially expert at engaging in malpractices for selfish ends, which has brought great trouble even to the local officials themselves."[498] Zhang Jian, a representative figure of

---

[495]"Xing Kao" (A Textual Research of the Criminal Penalties) in *Qing Chao Wen Xian Tong Kao* (*A General Textual Research of the Documents of Qing Dynasty*), Vol. 195.

[496]"Xing Kao" (A Textual Research of the Criminal Penalties) in *Qing Chao Wen Xian Tong Kao* (*A General Textual Research of the Documents of Qing Dynasty*), Vol. 198.

[497]"Xuan Ju Kao" (An Examination of Election) (Part 6) in *Qing Chao Wen Xian Tong Kao* (*A General Textual Research of the Documents of Qing Dynasty*), Vol. 89.

[498]Hong Liangji (Qing Dynasty), "Li Xu Pian" (The Chapter of Petty Officials) in *Yi Yan* (*Understanding by Heart*).

modern bourgeois constitutionalists, also pointed out: "In the old system, the quota for 'Xu Li' (petty officials) are filled within three years and they have occupied their positions for much longer time than that which was stipulated in law. Nowadays it has become an inheritable career, so they have sold the official positions to others, played with literary skills and colluded with each other, which had become a major reason for the corruption of official administration."[499] However, there was profound social and historical background for the usurping of power by "Xu Li" (petty officials), and it was an obvious manifestation of the corrupted bureaucratic system in the Qing Dynasty. Although the rulers had tried many ways to prevent the problem and many progressive thinkers also had called out with loud voice to overcome the malpractice, it was not changed even after the Qing Dynasty was overturned.

11.7.4 The Civil Trial with the a Combination of Judgment and Mediation

For the civil cases which were acceptable by the court, one citation would be signed by the officials of "Zhou" (subprefecture) and "Xian" (county) to require the defendants, "Di Bao" (those who take charge of local missions in the Qing Dynasty and the early years of the Republic of China), and the witnesses to appear in court; at the same time, the evidence would be examined. "For the cases of marriage, marriage contracts should be used as the evidence; for cases of disputes over graveyard and hills, the original contracts which were made on the day of transaction should be used as the evidence; for the cases of debts, agreements of debt should be used as the evidence."[500] "If there were disputes over the boundaries of land and irrigation canals or the relationship between family members," it was necessary to conduct on-spot investigations. So "it is ordered that investigations should be conducted by 'Xiang Bao' (petty officials in the rural areas) and reports should be made at the same time"; otherwise, the relevant people and witnesses would be summoned to the site by the county magistrates, "Xian Cheng" (assistant of county magistrate), clerks, and inspection officials to conduct on-spot investigations or measurements and to make maps to be attached to the case files later. When summarizing his experience as an assisting official, Wang Huizu said:

> For the cases of land, real estate and graveyard, on-spot investigations must be conducted. However, if the officials are very busy with their work, how can they conduct on-spot investigations of the rivers and mountains everyday? After the investigation, even if one is pressed for the settlement of cases, everything becomes easy to be handled. Therefore, it is

---

[499]"Xuan Ju Kao" (An Examination of Election) (Part 6) in *Qing Chao Wen Xian Tong Kao* (*A General Textual Research of the Documents of Qing Dynasty*), Vol. 89.

[500]"Su Song" (Litigation) in "Xing Lv" (The Penal Code) in *Da Qing Lv Li* (*The Laws and Precedents of Great Qing*), Vol. 30.

much easier to conduct investigations, but if the boundaries are not clear, it may lead to wrong decisions. If the sites of the disputed land are marked on the map, and relevant details are recorded in *Yu Lin Tu Ce* (*Scale Graph*), any decisions and judgments made by the officials are surely convincing. When it is necessary for officials to conduct on-spot investigations, the task must be completed without delay with details comprehensively recorded. When there is a deadline for publicizing the result of investigation, the date shall not be changed at will because many people must be waiting for the result.

As to the disputed property, such as cereals and livestock that were rented, measures were often taken by the government to preserve the property upon the application of a party. "The disputed land should be first sealed up," or "the disputed cereals which were rented should be stored in a warehouse," then the property should be returned to the legal owner after the settlement of the case.[501]

For the trial of civil cases, they should only be heard by the senior officials of "Zhou" (subprefecture) and "Xian" (county) but not by "other officials without official seals."[502] If a civil case was heard by an unauthorized person, the officials of "Zhou" (subprefecture) and "Xian" (county) should take due responsibilities collectively. Even if the affairs reported by "Xiang Bao" (petty officials in the rural areas), clerks, and inspection officials should be "investigated and settled by the officials of 'Zhou' (subprefecture) and 'Xian' (county) themselves, and it is forbidden for the affairs to be handled by the junior officials such as 'Xiang Bao' (petty officials in the rural areas) and 'Di Bao' (those who take charge of local missions in Qing Dynasty and the early years of the republic of China). If the cases are settled by others instead without being approved, investigations shall be conducted by the supervising officials thereof immediately, and those involved shall be punished according to the law."[503] Although disputes over land and marriage were minor issues for the officials, the rulers worried that the minor disputes might become great problems if they were not handled properly, so they were handled quite prudently, which was proved by existing cases and files of the Qing Dynasty.

During the trial of civil cases, investigations must be conducted on the basis of the complaint itself, and it was forbidden for officials to investigate those that were not included in the complaint; otherwise, those involved would be punished for "Gu Chu Ru Ren Zui" (deliberately increasing or reducing punishment when making sentences). Specific regulations were also made for the time limit for the settlement of cases. "The cases of 'Hu Hun' (marriage) and 'Tian Tu' (land) which are handled by the officials of 'Zhou' (subprefecture) and 'Xian' (county), must be settled within twenty days."[504] Cases must be "settled within the time limit" unless "it is necessary to extend the time in order to arrest or interrogate the parties concerned. But detailed

---

[501] Wang Huizu (Qing Dynasty), "Kan An Yi Su Jie" (The Immediate Settlement of Cases) in *Xu Zuo Zhi Yao Yan* (*A Sequel to the Expostulation on Assisting the Administration*).

[502] *Da Qing Hui Dian* (*The Collected Statutes of Great Qing*), Vol. 52.

[503] "Gao Zuang Bu Shou Li" (No Accepting the Complaint) in "Su Song" (Litigation) in "Xing Lv" (The Penal Code) in *Da Qing Lv Li* (*The Laws and Precedents of Great Qing*), Vol. 30.

[504] *Li Bu Chu Fen Ze Li* (*The Disciplinary Rules of the Department of Personnel*).

11.7 The More Complete Judicial System

reports must be submitted to the emperor for approval." Any official who failed to settle a case within the time limit would be punished by "Li Bu" (The Department of Personnel). Thus, the officials of "Zhou" (subprefecture) and "Xian" (county) were encouraged to work hard and to settle cases in time to avoid increasing the burden of litigation due to delay in the settlement of cases.

As to the civil representative system of the Qing Dynasty, the traditional provision was followed, and it was stipulated that "as to the cases of 'Hu Hun' (marriage), 'Qian Zhai' (debts) and 'Tian Tu' (land), it is allowed for the families to file lawsuits to government offices, but it is not allowed for the officials to transfer the official documents to other departments for prevarication; if anyone has violated the rule, the person involved will be punished by 'Chi' (flogging with light sticks) for forty strokes."[505] This provision was also applied to the retired officials. Moreover, "it is forbidden for 'Sheng Yuan' (also called 'Xiu Cai': those who passed the imperial examination at the county level in ancient China) and 'Jian Sheng' (the students in 'Guo Zi Jian'), the females, 'Lao' (elder), 'You' (young), 'Fei Ji' (disabled, including mentally disabled and mute, fractured lumbar vertebra, one crippled arm or leg, etc.) to file lawsuits without 'Bao Gao' (the family members or servants who file complaints for the plaintiff)."[506] According to *Liu Bu Cheng Yu* (*Terms of the Six Departments*), "Bao Gao" referred to "the family members or servants who have lodged complaints for the plaintiff." Since bureaucratic gentries were the social basis of the administration of the officials of "Zhou" (subprefecture) and "Xian" (county), it was forbidden for their names to be mentioned by the officials in court summons in order to show respect to them. Females were forbidden to appear in court by themselves; they must be represented by other people as it was considered one of the ways to instruct people to be "aware of their sense of honor and shame to maintain the feudal ethical code."[507] Nevertheless, the females of both "Qi Ren" (members of the Manchu ethnic group) and the Han nationality were treated equally. The following regulation was especially stipulated in "Tong Li" (the general rules) in *Hu Bu Ze Li* (*The Regulation of the Department of Revenue*):

> For the lawsuits of "Di Mu" (land) which involve the females of "Ba Qi" (the Eight Banners: banner, a division of Manchu nationality and the emperor's clan) who live in the capital, they shall be filed by their brothers who shared the same family names with them, their nephews, or close relatives from their own families to the court by the way of "Bao Gao" (the family members or servants who file complaints for the plaintiff) on their behalf. If they do not have relatives of "Bao Gao" (the family members or servants who file complaints for the plaintiff), their family member's may appear in court in the way of "Bao Gao" (the family members or servants who file complaints for the plaintiff) on their behalf. If there are no aforesaid family members of "Bao Gao" (the family members or servants who file complaints for the

---

[505]"Guan Li Ci Song Jia Ren Su" (Family Members Filing Lawsuits on behalf of the Officials) in "Su Song" (Litigation) in "Xing Lv" (The Penal Code) in *Da Qing Lv Li* (*The Laws and Precedents of Great Qing*), Vol. 30.

[506]"Yue Su Tiao Fu Li" (The Subsidiary Regulation of the Article of Overstepping Indictment) in *Da Qing Lv Li Hui Tong Xin Zuan* (*New Collections of the Laws and Precedents of Great Qing*).

[507]Yuan Shouding (Qing Dynasty), "Wu Ling Fu Nv Shang Tang" (Forbidding Females to File Complaints in Court) in *Tu Min Lu* (*The Record of the Governance of the People*), Vol. 2.

plaintiff), the heads of the clan shall make statements for them. Moreover, "Can Ling" (military officer below "Du Tong"), "Zuo Ling" (local administrator of the basic unit of organization in eight banners in the Qing dynasty) of the clan shall conduct investigations and make detailed report to the department ... If the accusation is false, the persons involved shall take due responsibilities collectively."[508]

Because "Lao" (elder), "You" (young), "Fei Ji" (disabled, including mentally disabled and mute; with fractured lumbar vertebra, one crippled arm or leg; etc.) lost or did not have legal capability, it was allowed for them to file lawsuits by way of "Bao Gao" (family members or servants who file complaints for the plaintiff). If a soldier or an ordinary person was involved in a lawsuit but "he did not file the lawsuit by himself without due reason ... and sent 'Lao' (elder), 'You' (young), 'Fei Ji' (disabled, including mentally disabled and mute, fractured lumbar vertebra, one crippled arm or leg, etc.) or females, or the family members or 'Bao Gao' (the family members or servants who file complaints for the plaintiff) to lodge the complaint for them instead, the complaint shall not be accepted and ... he shall take due responsibilities."[509]

In order to strictly investigate the legal responsibility of "Bao Gao" (family members or servants who file complaints for the plaintiff), the person who lodged complaints for others should undertake due responsibilities in the case of "Wu Gao" (false accusation).

During the trial, apart from the examination of the evidence provided when the complaint was accepted, sometimes on-spot investigations were needed to be conducted to gather new evidence. In the 33rd year of Qianlong (1768), a new regulation was made, and it was stated that "for the disputes over graveyards and hills, if the transaction has been conducted recently, a contract is necessary to be used as evidence; however, if the transaction is conducted long time ago, the names of the hill, the acreage, *Yu Lin Tu Ce* (*Scale Graph*), and the taxation seals must all be provided and checked up by the officials carefully. If the details are consistent with each other, judgments can be made accordingly; if the details are not consistent with each other, or there are no taxation seals, or the contracts are made long time ago, or the records on stones are not clear enough to be used as evidence to support one's pleading, the person who has falsely accused others of illegally occupying his land shall be punished according to law."[510]

In order to distinguish the authenticity and the validity of the evidence, a systematic and regular understanding was formed by the judicial organs of Qing Dynasty according to long-time judicial experience. For example, for disputes over the ownership of land, close examination of registration books should be made.

---

[508]"Tong Li" (The General Rules) (Part 4) in *Hu Bu Ze Li* (*The Regulation of the Department of Revenue*), Vol. 10.

[509]"Yue Su" (Overstepping Indictment) in "Su Song" (Litigation) in "Xing Lv" (The Penal Code) in *Da Qing Lv Li* (*The Laws and Precedents of Great Qing*), Vol. 30.

[510]"Dao Mai Tian Zhai Tiao Li" (The Regulation on the Stealing and Selling of the Land and Houses) in "Tian Zhai" (Land and Houses) in "Hu Lv" (Statutes on Households) in *Da Qing Lv Li* (*The Laws and Precedents of Great Qing*), Vol. 9.

11.7 The More Complete Judicial System

Since "the measurement, farming, transference and taxation of land are all registered, all the registration books should be examined with their dates checked up. In the registration book, all the relevant materials are included and the dates are also truthfully recorded," so a close examination of the time in the registration books could help to solve the problems. As to disputes over land boundary, the official should have "the four sides of the land checked up; if the four sides are consistent, the official shall then have the topography checked up; if the topography is inconsistent, on-spot investigations shall be conducted." On the other hand, with regard to disputes over graveyards and hills, the official should "inquire about the taxation of the government and the individuals and check up the topography to see whether there are discrepancies. Besides, the official shall ask the party about the hills nearby, the time for the burial and the person who is buried; the official shall ask for evidence based on confessions, check up the confessions with the maps, and check up the maps with topography by examining the landscape. If all the persons buried there share the same family name, anyone who is with a different family name shall not make a complaint; if people of different family names are buried together and the boundaries are not clear, the demarcation of boundary of each tomb shall be nine *bu* from the center of the tomb, which has been regarded as a convention. The middle region of Yue (Guangdong province) is with a large population, so such disputes can be solved by using the method." Concerning documentary evidence whose authenticity was difficult to determine, such as receipts, contracts, and account books, the official should not only check "whether the handwriting is new, whether the papers used are made in the past, but also whether there are traces of worm damages thereon or whether the size of the papers are the same. If the contracts are false, they shall all be confiscated; if the old papers are all of exactly the same color, some of them must be false. As to the forged books for debts made long time ago, if the debts are paid differently but the handwriting and the color of the ink are similar, some of the books must be false." Moreover, the official should "testify the parties' handwriting in court so that the false ones can be distinguished." If "a party insisted he had bought something, or made loans or paid the debt contrary to the fact," "interrogations should be conducted as to where the contract was concluded, what kind of silver was paid, where the transaction was conducted, and who were the witnesses thereof." Also, the parties concerned should "be interrogated separately"; if there were discrepancies in the confession, "they shall be brought together to verify the facts." As to cases of marriage, the official should not only examine the documents of the dates of birth and engagement but also inquire about who the matchmaker was and who had presided over the wedding in order to "find out the truth" and to "make judgments" on the basis of physical and verbal evidence.[511]

The witnesses relevant to the cases, such as the head of a clan, "Zuo Ling" (local adminstrator of the basic unit of organization in Eight Banners in the Qing Dynasty),

---

[511]Wang Zhi, "Ting Duan" (Making Adjudication after Hearing the Statement) in "Xing Ming" (The Names of Punishment) (Book 2) in *Mu Ling Shu* (*Regulations on the Prefectural Officials' Behaviors*), Vol. 18, edited by Xu Dongyi (Qing Dynasty).

and the matchmaker all had the obligation to provide their testimony according to law. However, it was forbidden for the people of "Xiang Rong Yin" (prohibiting indictment or testifying each other between relatives) to provide testimony because they were "exempted from the obligation to provide testimony out of family affection." Besides, it was forbidden for the people of "Lao" (elder), "You" (young), and "Du Ji" (incapacitated) to provide testimony because they were "exempted from punishment" according to law. In order to ensure that the witnesses were aware of the legal responsibility to provide testimony, the witnesses and the parties involved in the lawsuits were ordered to write "Ju Jie" (written guarantee), which was called "Ci Nei Gan Zheng" (oral testimony) and "Liang Zao Tong Ju Gan Jie" (both the plaintiff and defendant should make a written pledge); if the witnesses gave false testimony, they would be punished.

According to *Sheng Yu Shi Liu Tiao* (*The Sixteen Articles of Imperial Edicts*) drafted during the reign of Emperor Kangxi, officials were encouraged "to mediate disputes with the villagers". Since the number of lawsuits was one of the criteria to evaluate the achievements of officials, the officials of "Zhou" (subprefecture) and "Xian" (county) would first try to mediate the cases that they were in charge of, and it was only after the mediation had failed that the cases were tried in court. The method of mediation was mostly applied to civil cases, such as "Hu Hun" (marriage, tax, and household registration), "Tian Tu" (land), "Qian Zhai" (debts), as well as minor criminal cases. Generally speaking, mediation was divided into two kinds, namely, mediation by "Zhou" (subprefecture) and "Xian" (county) and mediation by individuals. The former was conducted under the guidance of the officials of "Zhou" (subprefecture) and "Xian" (county) and so it was a kind of compulsory mediation provided inside the litigation. According to existing case files of the Qing Dynasty, in the "Gan Jie" (written pledge) that one of the parties had written to "require" the cancelation of the litigation, both of the parties had stated that "they agree to settle the disputes according to orders"; namely, "they would like to close the case by following the official's guidance." Some officials of "Zhou" (subprefecture) and "Xian" (county) also tried to help the parties to mediate their disputes by "refusing to accept the complaint," as was described in the saying that "those who are expert at settling lawsuits know how to mediate the disputes before it is filed to the government."[512] Sometimes the officials of "Zhou" (subprefecture) and "Xian" (county) would ask the leaders of "Bao Jia" (the household registration management system in ancient time), namely, the officials of grassroots level, to conduct mediation. Although it was stipulated in the laws of the Qing Dynasty that "the leaders of 'Bao Jia' (the household registration management system in ancient time) shall not be bothered about mediating the cases of 'Hu Hun' (marriage), 'Qian Zhai' (debts) or 'Tian Tu' (land)," many of them had participated in mediation in defiance of orders and prohibitions.

---

[512]Bai Ruzhen, "Lun Pi Cheng Ci" (On the Diction of Complaints) in "Xing Ming" (The Names of Punishment) (Book 2) in *Mu Ling Shu* (*Regulations on the Prefectural Officials' Behaviors*), Vol. 18, edited by Xu Dongyi (Qing Dynasty).

11.7 The More Complete Judicial System

Mediation by individuals was carried out outside of litigation, so it mainly consisted of clan mediation and neighborhood mediation; the first kind of mediation was the most commonly used one. The so-called clan refers to an organization inside the family based on blood relationship, so the disputes among the clan were usually decided by the head of clan, and they were not allowed to be filed to the government randomly. According to *Zhu Shi Zong Pu* (*The Genealogy of Zhu's Family*) in Tongcheng city in Anhui province, "any disputes among the members of the clan shall be handled by the elder and the head of the family first without being filed to the government." The clan members were different in social status not only because of their seniority, but also because of their family relationship. Especially, the wealth and power of family members were different, and the legal wives and concubines in the family enjoyed different legal rights, so the members of a clan might be treated differently in mediation due to their different status in the clan. If one insisted on his own opinion, he would be criticized as disrespecting the seniors in the clan; therefore, clan mediation was to a certain degree coercive.

As to neighborhood mediation, it had profound social basis in China. The enclosed economic and political environment had promoted the formation of the concept of "An Tu Zhong Qian" (living in the native land rather than migrating to other places), which had consequently led to the emergence of the more stable geographical relationship, so that different generations all lived nearby in the same village, with each one of them making up for what the others had lacked and everyone helping each other to get rid of the difficulties. Therefore, whenever there were disputes, neighborhood mediation was very effective to some extent.

It needs to be pointed out that for mediation, whether government or individual, the following rules must be followed.

Mediation was only applied to civil cases and the minor criminal cases because it was ruled in law that cases beyond this scope were not allowed to be mediated.

The litigation mediation was carried out under the restriction of the magistrates of "Zhou" (subprefecture) and "Xian" (county). The neighbors or clan members participated in the mediation in order to settle the disputes, to stop the litigation, and to benefit the country and the people, and they were not allowed to benefit themselves by instigating people to file lawsuits.

State law was the basis of meditation, and any family law, village regulation, and agreement that were against state law were invalid.

The traditional "Li" (rites) could also serve as the basis for mediation, so the traditional "Li" (rites) and state law were mutually supplementary.

It was not coincidental that mediation was widely applied in civil cases in the Qing Dynasty. First, it was not only out of the need for maintaining the stability of the state but also out of the need for developing agriculture and maintaining the social order of the hierarchical society. Second, it was beneficial for giving full play to the social and political function of the blood and geographical relationship on which the feudal autocratic system was based. Third, it was helpful for reducing the caseload of officials; at the same time, it was also a concrete manifestation of the achievements of the officials of "Zhou" (subprefecture) and "Xian" (county). Finally, it was helpful for reducing the economic burden or "Song Lei" (troubles caused by litigation) of the parties concerned in litigation, which had become one of the main reasons why ordinary people accepted mediation. So appropriate combination of government and individual mediation had helped to settle disputes properly, as was stated in *Mu Ling Shu (Regulations on the Prefectural Officials' Behaviors)*: "The villagers usually know more about the reasons for the disputes, while the officials may not be able to find out the truth by the documents submitted. Therefore, it is much fairer to settle the disputes inside the village than to be tried by the officials of the government."[513]

In the promotion of the system of mediation, court trials were combined with out-of-court mediation, so more social forces were motivated to participate in mediation. The basis for mediation varied in different cases due to different subject matters and the parties involved, so the forms of mediation were also different. No doubt, the system did play an important role in settling disputes and stopping litigation; however, the negative effects of the system should not be ignored either. The purpose of mediation was mainly to patch up the quarrel and to reconcile the parties concerned, which had fully reflected the long-term blood and geographical relationship because it was adaptable to the basis of small-scale peasant economy. Moreover, it was profoundly influenced by the theory of "no-litigation" in Confucianism that the importance of finding out the truth and determining the responsibilities of both parties in civil disputes was ignored. Sometimes one party was bullied by the other party who was more powerful, which had damaged the legal rights of the parties concerned. What is worse, when a party insisted on lodging the complaint to the government after mediation failed, he would often be criticized as an "unruly person who was fond of instigating lawsuits." So he might be reprimanded or even flogged before being tried. As a result, most of the people were not only afraid of but also tired of filing lawsuits, which was very harmful to them because it had prevented them from protecting their lawful rights by legal means.

The civil judgment was called "Tang Duan" or "Tang Yu," most of which were instructions or comments about repentance and admit of defeat, and they were written on complaints, guarantees, and "Gan Jie" (written pledge) that were submitted by the parties or guardians and mediators. Here is an example:

> "Gan Jie" (written pledge). Hu Rui, a party of this "Gan Jie" (written pledge), agrees to close the case. "Gan Jie" (written pledge) is made under the guidance of the government. The verbal disputes with Wu Kuan for his destroying the beans in the yard is settled with the help of the government. I shall go back home and live peacefully, and shall not have quarrels with others and make any trouble. What is written in "Gan Jie" (written pledge) is true.
>
> 24th of June in the 16th year of Emperor Jiaqing
>
> Hu Rui (signature)

---

[513] Yuan Shouding, "Ting Su" (Hearing Cases) in "Xing Ming" (The Names of Punishment) (Book 2) in *Mu Ling Shu (Regulations on the Prefectural Officials' Behaviors)*, Vol. 17, edited by Xu Dongyi (Qing Dynasty).

11.7 The More Complete Judicial System

Reply: The case is approved to be closed.[514]

Most of the brief judgments were announced orally in court, and they were just put on record for the verification of superiors, so it was not necessary to be publicized or delivered to the parties. But it was not rare to have judgments with more than one thousand words. Some of the judgments were written after the conviction and after the parties were notified. The judgments would be posted on "Zhao Bi" (a screen wall facing the gate of a house) to show its seriousness. Since the first instance of a civil case was also the final one, it could be executed immediately after the judgment of "Zhou" (subprefecture) and "Xian" (county) with no need to be reported to superiors. What is more is that no special agencies or procedures were established for execution. For instance, for the disputes over "Tian Zhai" (land and houses) and "Qian Zhai" (debts), the parties would deliver money, documents, and contracts to the officials in court, then each party would hand in, accept, and keep the complaints on file for fear that they would go back on their words in the future. If the delivery could not be made in court, the specific time of the delivery would be explained in "Gan Jie" (written pledge), and the delivery should be made within the time limit. The immediate execution of civil judgment in court was common and effective. For the parties who refused to carry out the judgment, they would be inquired about the cases and be punished by "Chi" (flogging with light sticks) and "Zhang" (flogging with heavy sticks) or be put into prison to show their legal responsibility to obey the law. If the parties refused to accept the judgment of "Zhou" (subprefecture) and "Xian" (county), they could then lodge the complaint to "Fu" (ancient administrative district between province and county), "Dao" (the administration district below the province), and "Sheng" (province) or even to "Jing Kong" (when civilians having grievances that could not be resolved by the highest local officials, they could go to the capital to complain to the imperial court) step by step. Although there was no restriction for the levels of trial, it was strictly forbidden to bypass the immediate level. The civil cases filed to the superior government were generally remanded for retrial by the government of "Zhou" (subprefecture) and "Xian" (county). Besides, for the civil cases of "Jing Kong" (when civilians having grievances that could not be resolved by the highest local officials, they could go to the capital to complain to the imperial court), the party would be punished according to a regulation that was issued in the 34th year of Qianlong (1769): "The complaints for the minor cases of 'Hu Hun' (marriage), 'Qian Zhai' (debts) or 'Tian Tu' (land) shall be rejected and retried by the local governments, but those who have lodged the lawsuit should be punished for 'Yue Su' (overstepping indictment)" because "the people in other provinces who dare to file the minor lawsuits of 'Hu Hun' (marriage) and 'Tian Tu' (land) to the capital must be unruly people. Now it is not enough to just reject the cases, so such people shall be punished for 'Yue Su' (overstepping indictment)."[515] Therefore, only very few cases that were mishandled by the officials of "Zhou" (subprefecture) and "Xian" (county) were accepted by the government of

---

[514]"Dang An" (Files) in *Bao Di Xian Quan Zong (The Complete Files of Baodi County)*.

[515]Xue Yunsheng (Qing Dynasty), *Du Li Cun Yi (Questions in Reading the Precedents)*, Vol. 39.

"Fu" (ancient administrative district between province and county), "Dao" (the administration district below the province), and "Sheng" (province).

As can be seen from above, the civil litigation procedure was simple and convenient, and the trial mode was flexible in the Qing Dynasty, which had made it possible for the officials of "Zhou" (subprefecture) and "Xian" (county) to bring their initiative and flexibility into full play in the trial. For example, for the criminal lawsuits attached to civil lawsuits, the magistrates of "Zhou" (subprefecture) and "Xian" (county) had the right to decide whether to apply criminal penalties and what penalties to apply so that they could enforce more lenient penalties or just pardon the parties involved. It was precisely because the magistrates of "Zhou" (subprefecture) and "Xian" (county) had great power of discretion that a relatively complete supervision mechanism was established in the Qing Dynasty. The following regulation was stipulated in *Da Qing Lv Li* (*The Laws and Precedents of Great Qing*):

> The judgment, the dates of accepting the complaint, the trial and settlement of every case every day should be recorded, edited and sent to the government of "Fu" (ancient administrative district between province and county), "Dao" (the administration district below the province), "Si" (bureau), "Xun Fu" (procurators) and "Du" (viceroy) every month by the magistrates of each "Sheng" (province), "Zhou" (subprefecture) and "Xian" (county) and "Ting" (a government department at the provincial level) to be checked up and examined.... As to the officials who have concealed the fact or made false reports, ... if their crime is not serious, their demerit shall be recorded; if their crime is serious, they shall be impeached. If a magistrate has arbitrarily delayed the judicial proceeding of the cases, or has made the parties waiting for so long that their time is wasted or their jobs are lost or the innocent people are incriminated, or the females are implicated for minor issues, or the wife or children are sold, he shall be impeached by his superior officials immediately; if his superior officials fail to make any impeachment or shield him illegally or are accused by others, or are impeached by the officials of "Ke" and "Dao" (both government offices including the deaconry and the supervisory censor), both the superior officials and the magistrate shall be severely punished by the relevant department.[516]

In conclusion, the litigation and trial system of Qing Dynasty had reached a considerably high level. But because of the nature of the feudal judicial system, it was difficult to get rid of the bad practice of abusing one's power to seek personal gain just by carrying out the "solemn and equitable" law. Therefore, in his testament, Emperor Shizong had lamented: "prohibitions are issued and criminal penalties are established by the state in order to eliminate the outlaws, to punish corruption, to crack down upon the evil deeds, to rectify social customs and to supervise officials"; however "I have seen that people are cold and indifferent to each other and officials only care for their own personal gains, so that it has become a common practice and no one knows how to change it."[517]

---

[516]"Gao Zuang Bu Shou Li" (No Accepting the Complaint) in "Su Song" (Litigation) in "Xing Lv" (The Penal Code) in *Da Qing Lv Li* (*The Laws and Precedents of Great Qing*), Vol. 30.

[517]*Qing Shi Zong Shi Lu* (*The Record of Emperor Shizong of Qing Dynasty*), Vol. 159.

11.8 The New Achievement of "Lv Xue" (The Study of Statutory Laws) and Its Impact on Legislation and the Judiciary

For several times, social changes had taken place in Qing Dynasty, which had left behind abundant historical experience that could be used as a great treasury for the study of Chinese sociology, ethnology, politics, history and law. "Lv Xue" (the study of statutory laws) of Qing Dynasty was the epitome of the traditional Chinese "Lv Xue" (the study of statutory laws), meanwhile, it was also the climax of private legal annotation in Chinese history with diversified branches and numerous experts of annotation. They originated from but was not limited to tradition, so that they not only showed various and colorful contents of annotation, but also diverse styles in their common tendency. Moreover, they not only had their own specialty and focus but also influenced and promoted each other, which was unprecedentedly flourishing, glorious, and gorgeous. Besides, many talented people have emerged and they are like twinkling stars in the sky, so that the legal annotation in Qing Dynasty has surpassed all other dynasties in Chinese history, which is almost unimaginable with the practice of "Wen Zi Yu" (literary inquisition) under the extreme autocratic governance of Qing Dynasty, but it does appear miraculously because it has its profound social and historical origins.

After the establishment of a unified regime, both the officials and individuals were encouraged to interpret laws, and some of the achievements of private legal annotation were even confirmed in the name of the emperor in order to make the ignorant officials learn more legal knowledge to implement law and enforce punishment more effectively, as was said in the saying that people would follow the examples of their superiors. So to a certain extent, the prevalence of private legal annotation in the Qing Dynasty was a result of the calling of the supreme ruler of Qing Dynasty, namely, the emperor. The emperor's recognition of the achievement of private legal annotation had reflected the centralization of the power of legal interpretation and the reinforcement of the macro-control of "Lv Xue" (the study of statutory laws) across the nation. The rising of private legal annotation in the Qing Dynasty was in fact a response to the calling of the state, and its purpose was to serve the legal annotation of the state, so it was only one of the several branches of a great systematic project. Consequently, the freedom of private legal annotation was limited, and the annotators were only allowed to interpret law but were forbidden to make any comments on current politics or to change the imperial law without permission. Even when the dignity of the empire was completely lost in the late Qing Dynasty, the law revision carried out by Shen Jiaben was also sharply criticized by the conservatives because the new revision had gone beyond the limit permissible by tradition. Therefore, it was not difficult to understand that it was forbidden to go beyond certain limits in private legal annotation.

Under the ruling of the Qing Dynasty, all ethnic groups were united unprecedentedly, and a much closer relationship was formed between the central and local government. However, because of the vast territory and the extremely unbalanced political, economic, and cultural development in the capital and coastal areas, and in the vast inland area and the areas where the minority communities lived, it was a difficult job how to correctly understand and carry out the law of the imperial state, which, nevertheless, was an important link to consolidate the unified and multiethnic country. Although *Da Qing Lv Li* (*The Laws and Precedents of Great Qing*) consisted of only four hundred and thirty six articles, it covered so many judicial branches that the simple words used had included both rich and complex contents. Moreover, the contents of the law were very general and the language was very abstruse and professional, so that the simper the language was, the more difficult it was to understand its meaning, and the more ambiguous the diction was, the more difficult it was to deduce the reason. Therefore, it was very hard to understand the specific meaning and connotation, and it was more difficult to carry out the law accurately without annotation. Sometimes, it was even difficult to read it. From *Xing An Hui Lan* (*Collections of Criminal Cases*) and *Bo An Xin Bian* (*New Collection of Remanded Cases*), which were compiled in the Qing Dynasty, we can see that the majority of cases remanded by "Xing Bu" (The Department of Punishment) were those mishandled by the local officials because of their misunderstanding of law. Therefore, it became an urgent task for legists to add detailed comments to law because it was necessary for magistrates to accurately understand and grasp the spirits and principles of the law. So it was just out of the need of unitary application of law, and it was encouraged by the supreme rulers that private legal annotation flourished in the Qing Dynasty.

It should also be pointed out that the development of private legal annotation was "preconditioned by the fact that it has inherited some of the ideological legacy from the pioneers of private legal annotation."[518] Since the middle of the Ming Dynasty, private legal annotation had emerged, and more than twenty to thirty influential works of legal annotation had already been published, among which *Da Ming Lv Fu Li Jia Shi* (*Interpretation of the Sub-Laws of Great Ming Code*), written by Wang Kentang, was regarded as the most influential and authoritative book of legal interpretation. The inherited ideological legacy had provided an important foundation for the development of private legal annotation in the Qing Dynasty. For example, in *Da Qing Lv Li Zhu Zhu Guang Hui Quan Shu* (*Collection of Laws and Precedents of the Great Qing with Notes by Emperors*), edited and proofread by Wu Dahai and others during the reign of Emperor Kangxi, the laws of the Qing Dynasty were analyzed according to the thoughts of the scholars of the Ming Dynasty. However, wider scopes were covered by the annotators in the Qing Dynasty, and more abundant information and more detailed explanations were given in their works, which had enabled them to break away quickly from the tendency of relying on the scholars of the Ming Dynasty in legal annotation. Influenced by social development, further efforts were made to eliminate the unreasonable elements of their thoughts on legal annotation based on pragmatism; so far,

---

[518]*Ma Ke Si En Ge Si Xuan Ji* (*The Complete Works of Marx and Engels*), Vol. 4, The People's Publishing House, 1972.

11.8 The New Achievement of "Lv Xue" (The Study of Statutory Laws)...

greater achievements were made than in the Ming Dynasty. In the 13th year of Kangxi (1674), Wang Mingde, a high-ranking official who had served in "Xing Bu" (The Department of Punishment) for thirty years, had written the book *Du Lv Pei Xi* (*A Handbook of Law*) by collecting some of the difficult problems, discussions, and settlements in judicial trials to meet the needs of judicial practice. The publication of *Du Lv Pei Xi* (*A Handbook of Law*) symbolized that the experts of legal annotation in the Qing Dynasty had finally broken away from the influence of the Ming Dynasty and begun their own way of independent innovation, as Wang Mingde said in his autobiographical notes: "My purpose of compiling this book is just to record the discussions of my comrades and to provide a reference for others; ... so I will not simply copy what has been said in the works of Mr. Wang (Wang Kentang)."[519]

Da Qing Lv Ji Zhu (*Collected Commentaries on Great Qing Code*), written in the 54th year of Kangxi (1715) by Shen Zhiqi, a famous "Mu You" (advisors and assistants in charge of handling official documents, punishments, and affairs concerning money and grain) in Zhejiang, was another breakthrough in legal annotation in the Qing Dynasty. In the preface of this book, Mr. Shen said, "Five tenths of the opinions in this book are adopted from those of different authors, while the others are my humble opinions," which had indicated that he had carefully selected from the works of legal annotation in the Ming Dynasty rather than copy them simply. As for his "humble opinions," they were the embodiment of integrated practical judicial experience. So his method and style of annotation had surely played a pioneering role because for more than one hundred years, it greatly influenced the development of "Lv Xue" (the study of statutory laws) in the Qing Dynasty. After Shen Zhiqi, Wan Weihan, another famous "Mu You" (advisors and assistants in charge of handling official documents, punishments, and affairs concerning money and grain) during the reign of Emperor Qianlong, wrote *Da Qing Lv Li Ji Zhu* (*Collected Commentaries on the Laws and Precedents of Great Qing*), which consisted of twenty volumes. The book was in many ways a continuation of *Da Qing Lv Ji Zhu* (*Collected Commentaries on Great Qing Code*), and many of the opinions on legal annotation in this book were followed by the scholars of later ages.

Some of the experts of legal annotation were judicial officials and magistrates, such as Wang Mingde, Yu Kun, Wu Tan, and Xue Yunsheng, while others were "Xing Ming Mu You" (the staff or private assistant and advisor in the government office in charge of lawsuits), such as Shen Zhiqi, Wan Weihan, Shen Xintian, Cai Songnian, and Wang Youhuai. The people of the former group were the major forces of legal annotation in the Qing Dynasty. Although they were not ordered by the emperor, their interpretations were official to a certain extent due to their special identities and the acknowledgement of the royal court. Great achievements were made in private legal annotation by the group of "Xing Ming Mu You" (the staff or private assistant and advisor in government office in charge of lawsuits) because of the support of their superiors, so that their experience had determined that their legal

---

[519]Wang Mingde (Qing Dynasty), "Fan Li" (The Ordinary Cases) in *Du Lv Pei Xi* (*A Handbook of Law*).

annotation was mainly focused on how to apply law more accurately. In the preface of Wan Weihan's *Da Qing Lv Li Ji Zhu (Collected Commentaries on the Laws and Precedents of Great Qing)*, it was clearly stated that "in (this book), the essence of laws and regulations are elaborated with references provided to the judicial officials." In general, private annotation was not legally binding; however, some of the works that were with greater reference value were either prefaced by superior officials or recommended to be published by the official press. Especially, *Da Qing Lv Li Ji Zhu (Collected Commentaries on Great Qing Code)* by Shen Zhiqi was greatly honored because it was even approved by the emperor. Therefore, it can be seen that private legal annotation was quasi-official in nature. No doubt, their identities were not absolutely private but half-official and half-private.

Because legal annotation of the Qing Dynasty always focused on reality and was often a summary of the practical judicial experience, to some extent it had helped to make the judiciary much more improved. Since the Qing Dynasty was a great power with unbalanced political, economic, and cultural development and court conviction and sentences were mostly made by the private advisors of the officials because the local magistrates often lacked legal attainment, the same crime was often punished according to quite different legal provisions. For example, for the crime of "government staff stealing 'Qian Gu' (money and grain) from official warehouses," some of the judgments were made according to the article of taking bribery by government staff, while other judgments were made according to the article of robbery, which had often resulted in different convictions. Sometimes some local high-ranking officials were also denounced by "Xing Bu" (The Department of Punishment) for their "misunderstanding the law" and "rashly making decisions without considering both the specific circumstances and penalties."[520] As can be seen from above, "Lv Xue" (the study of statutory laws) was very significant in giving guidance to the local judiciary.

In the existing files of cases settled by local judicial authorities, there were many examples of settling lawsuits by referring to *Da Qing Lv Ji Zhu (Collected Commentaries on Great Qing Code)*. For example, in Gansu province, one was accused of kidnapping a woman and intending to force her to marry his son. It was proposed by "Xing Bu" (The Department of Punishment) that the suspect should be punished for the crime of rape because he had kidnapped the woman although marriage had not been concluded; nevertheless, the note of *Da Qing Lv Ji Zhu (Collected Commentaries on Great Qing Code)* was cited by the local officials: "The offenders are mainly punished for their intention; ... if a person has raped the wife or daughter of a decent family, he should be punished for the crime of rape; if he has kidnapped the woman to be his wife or concubine, he should be punished for illegally marrying the wife or daughter of the senior relatives." Finally, the opinion of the local official was accepted by "Xing Bu" (The Department of Punishment).

The achievements of legal annotation were not only applied by local judicial organs but also respected, or even cited, in the replies of "Xing Bu" (The Department

---

[520]"Qian Long Si Shi Nian Shuo Tie" (The Memorials of the 40th year of Qianlong) in *Xing An Hui Lan (Collections of Criminal Cases)*, Vol. 50.

of Punishment). For example, a woman was raped first and then she committed adultery with the rapist. Later the adulteress surrendered herself to the government and was convicted of adultery but was sentenced to a lighter punishment. However, the judgment was changed by "Xing Bu" (The Department of Punishment) according to a connotation in *Jian Shi* (*Notes*): "Any criminal who has committed crimes by violating social customs and ethics shall not be regarded as voluntary surrender even if he has done so." Besides, according to *Ji Zhu* (*Collected Commentaries on Great Qing Code*), "there is no differentiation between the principal and the accessory for the crime of adultery," so the judgment was changed by "Xing Bu" (The Department of Punishment) because "those who have committed adultery are not included in the penalty reduction of voluntary surrender."

Cases were often judged according to *Ji Zhu* (*Collected Commentaries on Great Qing Code*), especially when there were no specific laws to follow. For example, one person put poison in food to kill his son for his unworthiness, but the food was mistakenly eaten by others, which led to their death; the local officials settled the case according to *Ji Zhu* (*Collected Commentaries on Great Qing Code*) because "there are no specific articles for mistakenly killing others when trying to murder one's own offspring." In *Ji Zhu* (*Collected Commentaries on Great Qing Code*), it was stipulated that "if people are mistakenly killed during the fighting, they shall be punished as the common people; if the relatives are mistakenly killed with the common people during the fighting, or if the common people are mistakenly killed with the relatives during the fighting, or if the relatives are mistakenly killed with other relatives during the fighting, those involved shall be punished according to both the circumstances and the relevant articles on the superior and the inferior, the elder and the young after weighing the pros and cons carefully." Meanwhile, *Ji Zhu* (*Collected Commentaries on Great Qing Code*) was also cited: "According to the provision, it shall be deemed as intentional killing to mistakenly kill the bystanders in the process of killing or intentional killing, the provision is made to make up for the circumstances in which there are no provisions about the relatives." However, the case should be properly settled "according to the circumstances and the relevant articles." So he was finally sentenced to intentional homicide, but he was punished by "Liu" (exile) instead of death penalty, which was later approved by "Xing Bu" (The Department of Punishment).

However, in order to uphold the authority of the law, restrictions were imposed on local judicial organs by "Xing Bu" (The Department of Punishment), and they were forbidden to apply private annotations randomly. So it was emphasized that when conflicts arose between a legal provision and a private annotation, the legal provision should be used as the only standard, and it was forbidden to replace law with private annotation.

The direct influence of private annotation on legislation was reflected by the legal annotations that were officially recognized. According to the style and layout of *Da Qing Lv Li* (*The Laws and Precedents of Great Qing*), in order to interpret the meaning of the different articles, "Xiao Zhu" (small-character notes between vertical lines of a book, usu. in two lines) was added in the law and general notes were attached to the main body of the text. However, before the 5th year of Yongzheng

(1727), both "Xiao Zhu" (small-character notes between vertical lines of a book, usu. in two lines) and the general notes that were written by the scholars of the Ming Dynasty were adopted. *Da Ming Lv Ji Jie* (*Great Ming Code with Collected Commentaries*) was issued in the 5th year of Yongzheng (1727), and in its general notes, the achievements of legal annotation in *Da Qing Lv Ji Zhu* (*Collected Commentaries on Great Qing Code*), written by Shen Zhiqi, and *Du Lv Pei Xi* (*A Handbook of Law*), written by Wang Mingde, were adopted as one part of the law.

When *Da Qing Lv Li* (*The Laws and Precedents of Great Qing*) was revised in the 5th year of Qianlong (1740), more than eight annotations and many of the opinions in *Da Qing Lv Ji Zhu* (*Collected Commentaries on Great Qing Code*), written by Shen Zhiqi, were adopted either as legal annotation or as the specified reference interpretations of the legal annotation. For example, as to the provision that "if one's younger brother has cursed his elder brother's wife, he shall be punished one level severer than that for the common people according to the provision on assaulting people," it was explained in *Da Qing Lv Li Tong Kao* (*A Textual Research of the Laws and Precedents of Great Qing*) after the textual research: "If the wife of the younger brother has beaten the elder brother's wife, she shall be punished for assaulting people and be punished one level severer than that for the common people, but there are no regulations for scolding the wife of the elder brother. But it was further explained in *Ji Zhu* (*Collected Commentaries on Great Qing Code*) that the provision that 'the criminal in such cases shall be convicted of assaulting people and be punished one level severer than that for the common people' should be added accordingly."[521] Apart from the annotation made by Shen Zhiqi, the achievements of other jurists were also included in the law as legal annotations. For example, as to the article concerning "the crime of the officiator and matchmaker in illegal marriage," a note was added: "Although the officiator of the illegal marriage is the chief culprit, the crime is not punishable by death penalty, so he shall be punished one level lighter. If both the male and female are convicted of the same crime, they shall be punished by 'Liu' (exile) even if they are exempted from death penalty, so that the punishment for the officiator shall not be severer than 'Liu' (exile)." According to *Da Qing Lv Li Tong Kao* (*A Textual Research of the Laws and Precedents of Great Qing*), "'Xiao Zhu' (small-character notes between vertical lines of a book, usu. in two lines) which is attached to the first section of the provision that 'the officiator should be punished one level lighter' is added to the law by 'Lv Li Guan' (an official institution established in the second year of Shunzhi period) upon the approval of the Emperor by following the notes in *Da Qing Lv Li Zhu Zhu Guang Hui Quan Shu* (*Collection of Laws and Precedents of the Great Qing with Notes by Emperors*) in the 5th year of Emperor Qianlong."[522] Another example: the annotations of "the crime of illegal gains," "reducing the punishment

---

[521]"Ma Li" (Scolding) in "Xing Lv" (The Penal Code) in *Da Qing Lv Li Tong Kao* (*A General Textual Research of the Documents of Qing Dynasty*), Vol. 29.
[522]"Hun Yin" (Marriage) in "Hu Lv" (Statutes on Households) in *Da Qing Lv Li Tong Kao* (*A General Textual Research of the Documents of Qing Dynasty*), Vol. 10.

11.8 The New Achievement of "Lv Xue" (The Study of Statutory Laws)...

by half," and "the crime of 'Zuo Zang' (embezzlement)" by Wang Mingde were attached to "Na Shu Zhu Tu" (The Diagram of the Regulations on the Atonement of the Crime) as interpretations in *Da Qing Lv Li* (*The Laws and Precedents of Great Qing*). In "Fan Li" (Ordinary Cases) in *Da Qing Lv Li* (*The Laws and Precedents of Great Qing*), it was clearly stipulated that the interpretations of *Du Lv Pei Xi* (*A Handbook of Law*) should be referred to in practice to "avoid the malpractice of improper judgments."[523] Besides, the annotation of *Du Lv Pei Xi* (*A Handbook of Law*) was also used as the standard interpretation of the eight characters (or "Lv Mu": the origin of law) that were most frequently used in *Da Qing Lv Li* (*The Laws and Precedents of Great Qing*), namely, "Yi" (according to), "Zhun" (standard), "Jie" (all), "Ge" (each), "Qi" (its), "Ji" (and), "Ji" (namely), "Ruo" (if). Besides, many interpretations in *Da Qing Lv Ji Zhu* (*Collected Commentaries on Great Qing Code*), written by Shen Zhiqi, were adopted in the notes of the legal provisions of the Qing Dynasty. Xue Yunsheng once made the following realistic statement in the introduction of "Li Yan" (Introductory Remarks) in *Da Qing Lv Li* (*The Laws and Precedents of Great Qing*): "What are written in *Du Lv Pei Xi* (*A Handbook of Law*) by Wang Mingde, *Jian Shi* (*Notes*) by Wang Kentang, *Da Qing Lv Ji Zhu* (*Collected Commentaries on Great Qing Code*) by Shen Zhiqi and *Shi Zhang* (*Regulations*) by Xia Jingyi are all very reasonable, so some of their opinions are adopted as the notes of the law ... they are just like *Tang Lv Shu Yi* (*The Comments on Tang Code*) drafted on the basis of *Tang Lv* (*Tang Code*)."

In the Qing Dynasty, the correct understanding of the relationship between "Lv" (criminal law) and "Li" (precedent) had affected the exercise of the initiative of legislators. According to "Xing Fa Zhi" (The Record of the Criminal Law) in *Ming Shi* (*The History of Ming Dynasty*), "'Lv' (criminal law) refers to the eternal constant laws, while 'Li' (precedent) refers to the special articles made according to the temporary orders of the Emperor." Therefore, "Lv" (criminal law) referred to general and stable legal norms, while "Li" (precedent) referred to the changeable and special legal norms that were used to adjust the application of law. After *Da Qing Lv Li* (*The Laws and Precedents of Great Qing*) was completed in the 5th year of Qianlong (1740), the legal provisions were no longer revised, and "Li" (precedent) was added to make up for the insufficiency of the legal provisions. As far as the legal status of law was concerned, "Lv" (criminal law) enjoyed a higher status than "Li" (precedent), and it was the "constant law" that was passed down from generation to generation. However, from the perspective of the function of judicial practice, "Li" (precedent) was more important than "Lv" (criminal law) because "Li" (precedent) was in fact the "Lv" (criminal law) that was revised in order to be adaptable to specific circumstances. With the rapid increase of "Li" (precedent), the stability and authority of "Lv" (criminal law) were increasingly challenged, which had led to the imbalance of the efficacy of, as well as the conflicts between, "Lv" (criminal law) and "Li" (precedent). Therefore, it was necessary to illustrate the relationship between "Lv" (criminal law) and "Li" (precedent) from the perspective of

---

[523]"Fan Li" (The Ordinary Cases) in *Da Qing Lv Li* (*The Laws and Precedents of Great Qing*).

jurisprudence and to clarify their status to provide guidance for legislation and jurisdiction. In this aspect, the experts of "Lv Xue" (the study of statutory laws) had indeed made a great contribution. For example, as to the relationship between "Lv" (criminal law) and "Li" (precedent), they pointed out that "'Lv' (criminal law) refers to 'Fa' (law), while "Li" (precedent) refers to 'Bi' (analogy), so they are different not just because whether they are the main body of the text."[524] "'Lv' (criminal law) is made according to the established 'Fa' (law), but 'Li' (precedent) is made according to the indefinite and changeable circumstances."[525] Xue Yunsheng made a much clearer statement in *Du Li Cun Yi* (Questions in Reading *the Precedents*): "'Lv' (criminal law) is the most basic part of 'Fa' (law) that shall remain unchanged forever, while 'Li' (precedent) is the specific part of 'Fa' (law) that is adaptable to the changes in reality." Since it was ordered in the 5th year of Qianlong (1740) that "Lv" (criminal law) would not be amended any longer, many of the new crimes that emerged in the social development are were not included in "Lv" (criminal law). In this case, it was inevitable to supplement "Lv" (criminal law) with "Li" (precedent) because it was simple, flexible, pertinent, and practical. Nonetheless, the principal and accessory status of "Lv" (criminal law) and "Li" (precedent) must be clarified, and the extreme imbalance of their status must be avoided; otherwise, it might bring damage to the legal system. More importantly, the numerous "Li" (precedent) must be cleared up so as to have the obsolete ones deleted and the new ones added. So in this regard, much was done by the experts of "Lv Xue" (the study of statutory laws). For example, in the book *Da Qing Lv Li Gen Yuan* (*The Origins of Laws and Precedents of the Great Qing*), the numerous regulations that were made during the reign of emperors Shunzhi, Kangxi, Qianlong, and Jiaqing were arranged in time order, researches were made to verify their origins, and explanations were made to show the condition of their addition and deletion. Moreover, extensive references were made to testify for each other, and the gains and losses were compared from the perspective of application. The relationship between "Lv" (criminal law) and "Li" (precedent) that was formed in the legislation of the Qing Dynasty and the extensive application of "Li" (precedent) had required the jurists of "Lv Xue" (the study of statutory laws) to pay more attention to making annotations to both "Lv" (criminal law) and "Li" (precedent) with emphasis on changing the sporadic and special "Li" (precedent) into a more universally applied "Tiao Li" (regulation).

As seen from above, the achievements of legal annotation in the Qing Dynasty had great enlightening significance to the legislators, so they were affirmed necessarily in the form of state legislation. Moreover, they were of great practical significance for the guidance of the judiciary.

---

[524]Xia Jingyi (Qing Dynasty), "Xu" (Preface) in *Da Qing Lv Mu Fu Li Shi Zhang* (*A Guide to the Subsidiary Regulations of the Law of Great Qing*).

[525]"Xu" (Preface) in *Da Qing Lv Quan Zuan* (*A Complete Collection of the Laws of Great Qing*).